EQUATION NUMBER	SIGNIFICANCE TEST	=	SIZE OF EFFECT	×	SIZE OF STUDY
13.4	t	=	d	×	$\dfrac{\sqrt{df}}{2}$
13.25	t^*	=	$\dfrac{M_D}{S_D}$	×	$\sqrt{N}$
13.26	t^*	=	d	×	$\sqrt{df}$
14.1	F	=	$\dfrac{r^2}{1-r^2}$	×	df
14.3	F	=	$\dfrac{\text{eta}^2}{1-\text{eta}^2}$	×	$\dfrac{df_{\text{error}}}{df_{\text{means}}}$
14.5	F	=	$\dfrac{S^2_{\text{means}}}{S^2}$	×	n

*correlated observations

Property of:

Lissa Lim
353 W San Marcos Blvd apt #132
San Marcos, CA 92069

ESSENTIALS OF
BEHAVIORAL RESEARCH

ESSENTIALS OF BEHAVIORAL RESEARCH:
Methods and Data Analysis

THIRD EDITION

Robert Rosenthal

University of California, Riverside

Ralph L. Rosnow

Emeritus, Temple University

Boston   Burr Ridge, IL   Dubuque, IA   Madison, WI   New York
San Francisco   St. Louis   Bangkok   Bogotá   Caracas   Kuala Lumpur
Lisbon   London   Madrid   Mexico City   Milan   Montreal   New Delhi
Santiago   Seoul   Singapore   Sydney   Taipei   Toronto

Higher Education

ESSENTIALS OF BEHAVIORAL RESEARCH: METHODS AND DATA ANALYSIS
Published by McGraw-Hill, a business unit of The McGraw-Hill Companies, Inc., 1221 Avenue of the Americas, New York, NY, 10020. Copyright © 2008, 1991, 1984 by The McGraw-Hill Companies, Inc. All rights reserved. No part of this publication may be reproduced or distributed in any form or by any means, or stored in a database or retrieval system, without the prior written consent of The McGraw-Hill Companies, Inc., including, but not limited to, in any network or other electronic storage or transmission, or broadcast for distance learning.
Some ancillaries, including electronic and print components, may not be available to customers outside the United States.

This book is printed on acid-free paper.

2 3 4 5 6 7 8 9 0 DOC/DOC 0 9 8 7

ISBN: 978-0-07-353196-0
MHID: 0-07-353196-0

Vice President and Editor-in-Chief: *Emily Barrosse*
Publisher: *Beth Mejia*
Sponsoring Editor: *Michael J. Sugarman*
Developmental Editor: *Katherine Russillo*
Managing Editor: *Jean Dal Porto*
Project Manager: *Jean R. Starr*
Art Director: *Jeanne Schreiber*
Art Editor: *Emma C. Ghiselli*
Designer: *Srdjan Savanovic*
Senior Photo Research Coordinator: *Nora Agbayani*
Senior Media Producer: *Stephanie Gregoire*
Production Supervisor: *Jason I. Huls*
Composition: *10/12 Times, by Techbooks*
Printing: *45# New Era Matte, R. R. Donnelley & Sons/Crawfordsville*

Credits: The credits section for this book begins on page C1 and is considered an extension of the copyright page.

Library of Congress Cataloging-in-Publication Data

Rosenthal, Robert, 1933-
      Essentials of behavioral research: methods and data analysis / Robert Rosenthal, Ralph L. Rosnow. – 3rd ed.
      p.cm.
      Includes bibliographical references and indexes.
      ISBN-13: 978-0-07-353196-0 (hardcover : alk. paper)
      ISBN-10: 0-07-353196-0 (hardcover : alk. paper) 1. Psychology–Research–Methodology. I. Rosnow, Ralph L. II. Title.
      BF76.5.R6292008
      300.72–dc22

                                        2006017236

The Internet addresses listed in the text were accurate at the time of publication. The inclusion of a Web site does not indicate an endorsement by the authors or McGraw-Hill, and McGraw-Hill does not guarantee the accuracy of the information presented at these sites.

www.mhhe.com

To our students past, present, and future

ABOUT THE AUTHORS

Robert Rosenthal   **Ralph Rosnow**

Photo by Mimi Rosnow.

Robert Rosenthal is Distinguished Professor at the University of California at Riverside and Edgar Pierce Professor of Psychology, Emeritus, Harvard University. His research has centered for some 50 years on the role of the self-fulfilling prophecy in everyday life and in laboratory situations. Special interests include the effects of teachers' expectations on students' performance, the effects of experimenters' expectations on the results of their research, and the effects of clinicians' expectations on their patients' mental and physical health. He also has strong interests in sources of artifact in behavioral research and in various quantitative procedures. In the realm of data analysis, his special interests are in experimental design and analysis, contrast analysis, and meta-analysis. His most recent books and articles are about these areas of data analysis and about the nature of nonverbal communication in teacher-student, doctor-patient, manager-employee, judge-jury, and psychotherapist-client interaction. He has been Co-Chair of the Task Force on Statistical Inference of the American Psychological Association and has served as Chair of the Research Committee of the Bayer Institute for Health Care Communication. He was a co-recipient of two behavioral science awards of the American Association for the Advancement of Science (1960, 1993) and recipient of the James McKeen Cattell Award of the American Psychological Society, the Distinguished Scientist Award of the Society of Experimental Social Psychology, the Samuel J. Messick Distinguished Scientific Contributions Award of the APA's Division 5—Evaluation, Measurement, and Statistics, and the APA's Distinguished Scientific Award for Applications of Psychology.

Ralph L. Rosnow is Thaddeus Bolton Professor Emeritus at Temple University, where he taught for 34 years and directed the graduate program in social and organizational psychology. He has also taught research methods at Boston University and Harvard University and does consulting on research and data analysis. The overarching theme of his scholarly work concerns how people make sense of, and impose meaning on, their experiential world, called the "will to meaning" by Viktor Frankl. Rosnow has explored aspects of this construct in research and theory within the framework of contextualism, the psychology of rumor and gossip, attitude and social cognition, the structure of interpersonal acumen, artifacts and ethical dilemmas in human research, and the statistical justification of scientific conclusions. He has authored and coauthored many articles and books on these topics and, with Mimi Rosnow, coauthored *Writing Papers in Psychology,* a popular writing manual now in its seventh edition (published by Thomson Wadsworth, 2006). He has served on the editorial boards of journals and encyclopedias, was coeditor (with R. E. Lana) of the Reconstruction of Society Series published by Oxford University Press, and chaired the APA's Committee on Standards in Research. He is a fellow of the American Association for the Advancement of Science, the APA, and the Association for Psychological Science, received the Society of General Psychology's George A. Miller Award, and was recently honored with a Festschrift book edited by D. A. Hantula, *Advances in Social and Organizational Psychology* (Erlbaum, 2006).

Rosenthal and Rosnow have also collaborated on other books on research methods and data analysis, including *Artifact in Behavioral Research* (Academic Press, 1969); *The Volunteer Subject* (Wiley, 1975); *Primer of Methods for the Behavioral Sciences* (Wiley, 1975); *Understanding Behavioral Science: Research Methods for Research Consumers* (McGraw-Hill, 1984); *Contrast Analysis: Focused Comparisons in the Analysis of Variance* (Cambridge University Press, 1985); *People Studying People: Artifacts and Ethics in Behavioral Research* (W. H. Freeman, 1997); (with D. B. Rubin) *Contrasts and Effect Sizes in Behavioral Research: A Correlational Approach* (Cambridge University Press, 2000); and *Beginning Behavioral Research: A Conceptual Primer* (6th ed., Pearson/PrenticeHall, 2008).

CONTENTS

Chapter 6   Questionnaires, Interviews, and Diaries

PART III   THE LOGIC OF RESEARCH DESIGNS

Chapter 7   Randomized Controlled Experiments and Causal Inference

Chapter 8   Nonrandomized Research and Functional Relationships   233

Chapter 9   Randomly and Nonrandomly Selected Sampling Units   260

PART VII ADDITIONAL TOPICS IN DATA ANALYSIS 583

Chapter 19 Significance Testing and Association in Tables of Counts 585

Chapter 20 Multivariate Data Analysis 638

PREFACE

The first edition of *Essentials of Behavioral Research* was published by McGraw-Hill in 1984 and the second edition in 1991. When we were asked about a third edition, our answer was generally, "We're thinking about it." We were working on other related projects, and our conceptual thinking about research methods and data analysis had been continually evolving. Some of that work we had published in journal articles and invited chapters, and for several years we had been writing another book: *Contrasts and Effect Sizes in Behavioral Research: A Correlational Approach* (Rosenthal, Rosnow, & Rubin, 2000). As we had also written an undergraduate text, *Beginning Behavioral Research: A Conceptual Primer,* we thought that the next edition of *Essentials* should be clearly addressed to graduate students, researchers, and occasional advanced undergraduates for whom *Beginning Behavioral Research* was a journey begun rather than a journey completed. We have had occasion for over 30 years to teach methods and data analysis not only to students in clinical, cognitive, developmental, experimental, organizational, personality, and social psychology, but also to some in biology, education, communication research, school psychology, business, statistics, and marketing. Thus, we wanted the third edition of *Essentials* to be useful to a wide variety of graduate students and researchers.

As a consequence, there is a great deal that is new to this edition of *Essentials,* including new and deeper discussions of methodological and philosophical issues, and of data analytic issues that were of only passing interest to behavioral researchers in 1991. Nonetheless, we continue to review elementary topics and basic concepts as a brushup for students who have been away from these areas or have had limited exposure to them. These reviews are conceptually integrated with recent developments. As in the previous editions, our approach to data analysis continues to be intuitive, concrete, and arithmetical rather than rigorously mathematical. When we have a mathematically sophisticated student, we encourage her or him to take additional course work in a department of mathematical statistics. We still advise such a student to read this book, as our approach will prove complementary, not redundant or contradictory. As a pedagogical aid, the statistical examples that we use are in most cases hypothetical, constructed specifically to illustrate the logical bases of computational procedures. The numbers were chosen to be clear and instructive, and therefore they are neater than those found in most actual data sets. Readers who are familiar with the primary literature of the behavioral sciences know that most real-world examples involve more observations than are found in our hypothetical cases, and all readers should keep this fact in mind.

The material on data analysis in this edition of *Essentials* reflects much of the spirit, and much of the substance, of the report of the Task Force on Statistical Inference of the Board of Scientific Affairs of the American Psychological Association (Wilkinson & Task Force on Statistical Inference, 1999). There is, for example, a new emphasis on the reporting and interpretation of confidence intervals. Although previous editions of *Essentials* emphasized effect size estimates, we have added greater differentiation among effect sizes, for example, among the different types of correlational effect sizes such as $r_{alerting}$, $r_{contrast}$, $r_{effect\ size}$, and r_{BESD}. For still another example, we continue to illustrate computations by simple calculators in order to facilitate a deeper understanding of the statistical procedures that in readers' research will typically be computer-based. Such deeper understanding permits the researcher to check very roughly the accuracy of computer output by intelligent "guesstimates" and, if discrepancies are detected, to check the results against those provided by another program. As a final example, our newly added material on the complex issue of drawing causal inference includes not only its conceptual basis, but also a simple illustration of the use of Donald Rubin's propensity scores to draw causal inference when random assignment is not possible. These are only some examples of how this new edition of *Essentials* and its authors have benefited from the work of the APA Task Force. That benefit was increased by the opportunity of the first author to serve as co-chair of the Task Force (along with the late Robert Abelson and the late Jacob Cohen).

In addition to the examples listed above, there are many further changes and additions in this new edition of *Essentials*. Examples include new material on test validity, the reliability of items and judgments, the construction of composite variables, strategies for dealing with missing data, the use of bootstrapping and jackknifing, the design and analysis of hierarchically nested designs, and a recently developed effect size estimate for multiple-choice-type data. There is also a new discussion of epistemological issues in human subjects research, focusing on three current perspectives and their limitations. The discussion of ethical guidelines emphasizes the delicate balancing act involved in dealing with moral and methodological imperatives. We also discuss ideas and methods that, although frequently cited or used by behavioral researchers, are limited in ways that appear to be unfamiliar to many users. We hope the tone and writing style of these critical discussions will be perceived as respectful, clear, and explanatory, and that readers will find this edition of *Essentials* a more integrated synthesis of research methods and data analysis than the previous two editions.

The American Psychological Association's (2001) publication manual is generally acknowledged to be the arbiter of style for many journals in our field, so we assume that researchers will usually consult the most recent edition of the APA manual. For students who are not writing for publication but are writing a research proposal or report for a course assignment or creating a poster or a brief summary of research findings to serve as a handout, there are guidelines and tips in Rosnow and Rosnow's *Writing Papers in Psychology: A Student Guide to Research Reports, Literature Reviews, Proposals, Posters, and Handouts.*

Certain tables (noted in the text) have by permission been reproduced in part or in their entirety, for which we thank the authors, representatives, and publishers cited as sources in footnotes.

The authors thank Margaret Ritchie for her outstanding copy editing and we thank Mike Sugarman, our McGraw-Hill Sponsoring Editor, Katherine Russillo, our Editorial Coordinator, and Jean Starr, our Project Manager, for making it easier to tackle a project of this size.

We also thank William G. Cochran, Jacob Cohen, Paul W. Holland, Frederick Mosteller, and Donald B. Rubin, who were influential in developing our philosophy of research in general and data analysis in particular.

We are grateful to the following reviewers whose insights and suggestions were so helpful in preparing this edition of *Essentials:* Nicholas DiFonzo, Rochester Institute of Technology; Morton Heller, Eastern Illinois University; Scott King, Loyola University at Chicago; Donna Lavoie, St. Louis University; Pascale Michelon, Washington University at St. Louis; Robert Pavur, University of North Texas; Daniel Read, University of Durham, UK; and Linda Tickle-Degnen, Tufts University.

Thanks to MaryLu Rosenthal for indexing and many other special contributions that made the completion of the project a reality. And finally, we thank MaryLu Rosenthal and Mimi Rosnow for constructive feedback and counseling in ways too numerous to mention.

This is our 16th book together, and we have had terrific fun throughout the course of this 40-year-long collaboration!

Robert Rosenthal
Ralph L. Rosnow

PART

I

CONCEPTUAL AND ETHICAL FOUNDATIONS

CHAPTER

1

THE SPIRIT OF BEHAVIORAL RESEARCH

SCIENCE AND THE SEARCH FOR KNOWLEDGE

An amiable centipede, out for a stroll, was interrupted by a curious grasshopper. "Don't take offense please, but may I ask you something personal?" the grasshopper inquired. "Sure, go ahead," the centipede replied. "I've been watching you all morning, but for the life of me I can't figure out how you are able to walk without getting constantly tangled up in your hundred legs," said the grasshopper. The centipede paused, because he had never before bothered to think about *how* he did what he did. To his dismay, the more he thought about it, the less able he was to walk without stumbling. Biologist Peter B. Medawar (1969), a Nobel Prize laureate, noted how many experienced scientists seem to hesitate when asked to describe their thought processes as they use the scientific method. What you will see, Medawar wrote, is "an expression that is at once solemn and shifty-eyed: solemn, because [the scientist] feels he ought to declare an opinion; shifty-eyed, because he is wondering how to conceal the fact that he has no opinion to declare" (p. 11). As Medawar further explained, working scientists may be too preoccupied with *doing* research to contemplate *how* they do it so well. (Would thinking about it too much interfere with the doing of it?)

Another idea altogether is implicit in philosopher Paul Feyerabend's radical conception of science. Variously characterized by others as the "anything goes argument" and "epistemological anarchy," Feyerabend (1988) believed that the very term *scientific method* was misleading, as it implied that every scientific finding could be

3

accounted for by the same formulaic strategy. Quite to the contrary, he contended, "successful research . . . relies now on one trick, now on another; the moves that advance it and the standards that define what counts as an advance are not always known to the movers" (p. 1). Consistent with that position, sociologists who have observed and interviewed scientists at work have reported that the scientists' conduct seldom conformed to traditional norms and canons that have been defined as "scientific" (Knorr-Cetina, 1981; Mitroff, 1974). Larry Laudan (1982), another prominent philosopher of science, put it this way:

> From time to time, scientists have ignored the evidence, tolerated inconsistencies, and pursued counter-inductive strategies. More to the point, many of the most noteworthy instances of scientific progress seem to have involved scientists who rode roughshod over conventional methodological sensibilities. (p. 263)

Certainly no one would disagree that researchers in different disciplines do indeed rely on a wide variety of methods, or as one writer said, it would take a "mixed metaphor" to embrace the diversity of tools and methods that are commonly used (Koch, 1959). Hence, it is taken as a given that the scientific method is not merely a single, fixed, empirical strategy. Instead it is sometimes described as an "outlook" that is distinctly characterized by the use of logic and empirically-based content. We call that process **empirical reasoning,** though it should not be confused with logical positivism (as explained in this and the following chapter). Karl Popper, who was in the forefront of modern antipositivist philosophers, referred disparagingly to logical positivism as the "bucket theory of the mind." In particular, Popper (1959, 1972) disputed the positivists' claim that "truth" is revealed and conclusively warranted merely by the amassing of factual observations—a claim known as the *verifiability principle* (noted again in the next chapter). The human mind is not simply a "bucket," Popper argued, in which factual observations accumulate like grapes that, when pressed, produce the pure wine of true knowledge or indisputably prove that this knowledge is correct.

We will have more to say in the next chapter about positivism, Popper's beliefs regarding the nature of scientific progress, and some other relevant philosophical ideas. But to anticipate a little, we can note here that Popper's theory was that scientific knowledge evolves by a cyclical process involving the testing and retesting of plausible suppositions that are stated as **falsifiable hypotheses.** Describing his own view as the "searchlight theory," he explained that the resolution of whether a particular theory or hypothesis is justified is an intensely active process in which the outcome is based on the empirical results of critical experiments, or what Isaac Newton called an *Experimentum Crucis*. Popper also believed that such experiments must always be guided by risky conjectures, which are like searchlights piercing the darkness and illuminating the course in which critical observations must proceed. If there is an empirical disconfirmation of a specific logical consequence of a theory or hypothesis, it should be spotted. Popper (1959) cautioned, however, that "the game of science is, in principle, without end" as "once a hypothesis has been proposed and tested, and has proved its mettle, it may not be allowed to drop out without 'good reason'" (pp. 53–54).

The requirement that scientific explanations, inferences, and generalizations be subject to empirical jeopardy distinguishes true science from pseudoscience. Nonetheless, some philosophers argue that, inasmuch as human understanding is relative and incomplete, it is impossible to fathom the depths of our experiential or material world fully or with absolute confidence no matter how big the bucket or how bright the searchlight. Historians of science further point out that science seldom advances as a result of merely adjudicating and replacing risky conjectures in the cyclical fashion that Popper envisioned. Instead, scientific advance seems to involve a kind of intellectual tinkering process, in which extra-empirical factors also play a vital role. Moreover, there are no consensus definitions of *truth* or *knowledge* in the philosophy of science. Philosopher Bertrand Russell (1992) maintained that knowledge is "a term incapable of precision," inasmuch as "all knowledge is in some degree doubtful, and we cannot say what degree of doubtfulness makes it cease to be knowledge, any more than we can say how much loss of hair makes a man bald" (p. 516).

What's more, the popular impression of a smooth, upward trajectory in the triumphs of science and the advance of fundamental knowledge has for decades been mired in controversy (e.g., Laudan, 1977). Thomas S. Kuhn (1962, 1977), a physicist turned scientific historian, said that science moves in fits and starts and that advances occur erratically. The history of science is punctuated by "paradigm shifts" coupled with revolutionary insights that have essentially altered the way the world is perceived, he argued. For example, in the 15th century, after the pope asked Nicolaus Copernicus to help with calendar reform, he advised the pope that the sun, not the earth, was the center of the universe. That idea, being at odds with ecclesiastical doctrine, was rejected by the church. By the 16th and 17th centuries, as a result of Galileo's and Newton's revolutionary empirical and theoretical contributions, there was finally a successful intellectual uprising against the strictures of ecclesiastical authority outside the church, producing a paradigm shift in science and other areas. In contrast to Kuhn's notion of how science advances, Popper (1962, 1972) preferred an evolutionary metaphor, equating progress in science with Darwin's inspiration of a "survival" mechanism, on the assumption that there is a kind of "natural selection" of risky conjectures. We return to this idea shortly, but one point on which all philosophers of science agree is that knowledge and truth (however one chooses to define these terms) are relative and provisional.

In the same way that scientists in other fields use empirical reasoning to try to separate truth from fantasy, behavioral and social researchers do so as well. Behavioral science originally came out of philosophy, but the philosophical idealization of science that was current at the time, and its application to behavioral research, has been repeatedly challenged over the years. During the 1970s, for example, revolutionary empirical and theoretical insights into the "social psychology of the experiment" were used to question traditional assumptions about the objectivity and moral neutrality of research with human participants; the result was what came to be called *crises of confidence* in some areas of psychology (Rosnow, 1981). As a consequence, psychologists who study human behavior have a deeper understanding of the subtleties and complexities of studying a conscious human being in a controlled research setting (Rosnow & Rosenthal, 1997). Beginning in chapter 3, and again in later chapters, we will discuss these insights and how they are reflected in the values and methods of behavioral and social research.

WHAT DO BEHAVIORAL RESEARCHERS REALLY KNOW?

Generally speaking, philosophers of science distinguish between two kinds of questions that investigators attempt to address: *why-questions* and *how-questions* (Bunzl, 1993). The first are questions about "why" things work the way they do. For example, why do people behave one way rather than another, or why do people perceive or believe one thing and not something else, or why do children say or do the things they do? Why-questions are said to call for explanations that take the form of causal inferences or purposive inferences about the reasons (i.e., motives or intentions) for the particular behavior. How-questions can be thought of as "what-is-happening" questions (i.e., about how things work), or what we call a *descriptive research orientation*. Three points of view have recently dominated discussion in psychology about what behavioral and social researchers purport to know of the whys and hows of behavior and human knowledge. There is some overlap in these positions, but they are distinctly different in both their focus and some of the central assumptions they make.

One viewpoint, called *social constructionism,* might be described as panpsychistic, in that it resembles in some ways Oriental spiritualism by arguing that the social world is a construction of the human mind, which is itself a linguistic construction. The panpsychistic idea is more extreme, as it views everything we call "reality" as the sum total of the human mind, whereas the social constructionists view the natural world that is the subject of scientific scrutiny and replication in physics and biology as an exception that exists independent of human experience. Hence, social constructionists might be described as metaphysical realists in regard to natural and biological science, but as antirealists in regard to social and behavioral "truths" generated in our relations with each other. They dispute the value of experimentation in social science, arguing instead that the only useful way of understanding each person's social world is from the stories and narratives that people tell one another, or from discourse generally.

The second viewpoint, variously referred to as *contextualism* and *perspectivism,* typically dismisses metaphysical realism as a pointless debate. Contextualists and perspectivists accept the idea of limits on knowledge representations, perceiving them as grounded in a particular context or perspective. Empirical research is essential, they insist, but not just for the purpose of deciding whether a theory is true or false. As all theories are cryptic in some ways, it follows that different theoretical perspectives are a necessity. In physics, for example, Werner Heisenberg (1974) spoke of how major theories in that field could best be understood as "closed off" in ways that are not exactly specifiable but nevertheless form a constituency of dependable explanations in their own conceptual domains. A similar idea has been used to describe the "closed theories" of psychology, which contain no perfectly certain statements because their conceptual limits can never be exactly known (Rosnow, 1981).

The third viewpoint, known as *evolutionary epistemology* (also called *organic evolution* by the social psychologist Donald Campbell) takes its inspiration from Charles Darwin's theory of evolution through natural selection and adaptation. There are a number of variants, but in general the idea is an analogy between biological progression and adaptation and the advancement of knowledge. It is, however, a loose analogy at best, because hypotheses and theories can hardly be viewed as random events. Like contextualists and perspectivists, evolutionary epistemologists pay lip service to a pluralistic viewpoint in regard to empirical methods, but evolutionists have a definite affinity for the notion that, fundamentally, human nature is biologically determined and selection pressures have shaped behavior and the brain. The enthusiasm with which this position has been received suggested to one leading researcher "that 50 years from now every psychology department will have Darwin's bearded portrait on the wall" (de Waal, 2002, p. 190).

Together, these three viewpoints give us not only a glimpse into what some psychologists view as the metatheoretical underpinnings of knowledge representations in behavioral and social science, but also a glimpse into the controversial and abstract world of epistemology and some of its applications. We now provide a further flavor of each of these three approaches.

SOCIAL CONSTRUCTIONISM

The most controversial of these three views in psychology is that now described as **social constructionism** by its proponents (Gergen, 1985), although its roots are in classical subjective idealism and another modern philosophical position called *constructivism*. As noted above, one major difference between social constructionism and the other two approaches discussed here is that constructionists in psychology generally dismiss certain traditional scientific methods (such as the experiment) and the hypothetico-deductive model of science as irrelevant to studying the reasons for purposive behavior. Social constructionism's method of choice is narrative analysis based on an "interpretive" model. Recently, others have argued that the deductivist model does perfectly well in science (Bunzl, 1993, p. 99), and later in this chapter we describe a very slight modification of that traditional model for scientific explanations that take the form of what we call *probabilistic assertions*.

Among those psychologists in the forefront of the social constructionist movement has been Kenneth Gergen, a social psychologist, who in a series of provocative essays initially laid siege to the empirical basis of reliable knowledge in experimental social psychology (Gergen, 1977, 1978, 1982). Although encouraging a traditional positivistic view of natural science, Gergen (1973b) rejected a similar view of behavioral and social research, arguing that science is identified by precise laws referring to observable events that can be exactly duplicated, whereas human behavior is subject to free will, and purposive behavior can change abruptly and without notice. His view was that what social psychologists believe to be empirically based generalizations are snapshots of ephemeral events that pass into history, or vaporize like a puff of smoke, the moment a picture is taken. Rather than waste our time conducting experiments that can provide only superficial snapshots of passing events and averaged behavior, it would be more productive and illuminating if psychologists explored the drama of individual lives. To do so, we can simply ask people to tell us their own personal experiences and feelings in narrative terms, using ordinary language (Gergen, 1995; Graumann & Gergen, 1996; Sarbin, 1985).

Although subscribing to traditional materialistic assumptions of realism when alluding to what they perceive is the nature of "true" science, social constructionists nevertheless challenge the assumption that there is a "real" social world out there that some psychological theories reflect or match more correctly than others. "Knowledge" and "truth" in the field of social psychology and related areas (such as developmental psychology) are socially constructed realities, developed out of the active contributions of communities of shared intelligibility, social constructionists assert. John Shotter (1984, 1986), another influential social theorist in this movement, argued that there is no social reality apart from our experience of it, that the very idea of objective foundations of psychological truths is a "conceit" rather than an epistemological necessity. Many critics of that position dismiss it as nihilistic. It would imply, they argue, that any interpretation of social behavior is as good as any other; therefore, there is no room for sweeping statements or "ultimate truths" in social psychology. The philosophical constructivists' finessing of a similar criticism was to redefine truth in a pragmatic way. Truth, they countered, is anything that stands up to experience, enables us to make accurate predictions (however vague), or brings about or prevents certain outcomes (Watzlawick, 1984).

Gergen's and Shotter's arguments moved social psychologists and others to contemplate the epistemological limits of their methods and generalizations and led to a flood of criticisms. For one, Gergen's idea of what constituted "real science" was said to be narrow and exclusionary. It would, for instance, rule out geology as a science, because not every geological event can be re-created at will. Gergen's argument that unrepeatability implies unlawfulness has been called an oversimplification of how scientific reasoning works. Suppose we throw a large number of coins in the air. We would never expect to reproduce the identical pattern of heads and tails the next time we threw the coins. Nevertheless, we can state a valid, scientific "law" (e.g., in the form of a probability table) for the relationship or probability distribution (see Rosnow, 1981).

Another charged discussion centered on Gergen's contention that social psychology is not a science because social behavior (the primary unit of analysis) is active, volatile, and, frequently, unpredictable. It is not like a machine with a button we punch, expecting to observe the same response every time, because humans are sentient, active organisms who can reflect on and then alter their behavior. Critics responded that volatility and change not only are characteristic of social behavior but are also qualities of virtually everything under the sun. Over 2,500 years ago, Heraclitis declared that everything is in a state of perpetual flux, a doctrine that is still influential today. In the science of epidemiology, for example, powerful drugs used to combat virulent diseases often lead to hardier strains of the diseases through spontaneous mutations that become immune to the drugs. Clearly no one would claim that viruses are sentient, reflective organisms, but the point here is that change and volatility are not limited just to human activity. Except for axiomatic assumptions that are presumed to be self-evident (this sentence being an example), the fact is that all things are subject to change.

Another source of spirited debate revolved around Gergen's idea that narrative accounts and interpretive analysis be substituted for experimental methods and the deductivist model. As an example of the potential of narrative accounts, William and Claire McGuire (1981, 1982) used that procedure to explore the salience of characteristics and attributes in children's self-concepts, simply by asking schoolchildren of different ages to "tell us about yourself." Asking participants what they think is a time-honored method in the field of social psychology (later on in this book, we will describe techniques designed to help researchers use it most efficiently). Narrative self-report methods should be thought of not as replacements for experimental methods, but as supplements, the critics argued. Like any method of science, the narrative method is also limited in certain ways. In a classic gem, Polanyi (1966) discussed what he called "tacit knowledge" (unvoiceable wisdom), that is, the idea that we "know" more than we can say. Thus, relying only on narrative self-reports would exclude other valuable information. The doctor asks you how you feel or where it hurts but doesn't rely on your answer alone to figure out what ails you.

Ironically, despite Gergen's skepticism about social psychology as a science, social psychologists have produced scientific evidence of how people construct their own social reality (e.g., Johnson, 1945; Mausner & Gezon, 1967; Rosnow & Fine, 1976). In a classic study, Muzafer Sherif (1936) investigated the effects of groups on individual perceptions. The participants observed a point of light in a pitch-dark room. Although the light was stationary, it appeared to move under these conditions, a phenomenon Sherif called the "autokinetic effect." He had the subjects report the distance the light moved while they were alone and also when they were in groups. After making initial individual judgments, and then being placed in a group, a subject's judgments of distance were influenced by the responses of the others in the group. Judgments of group members tended to become more and more alike with each successive trial. Those who made their first judgments in groups reported the same distance of light movement as that reported by the group. Thus, the group had been able to modify the judgments of its individual members. This study shows not only that social construction can be demonstrated empirically, but that it can be manipulated experimentally.

CONTEXTUALISM/PERSPECTIVISM

The second position, called **contextualism** by many psychologists, and **perspectivism** by McGuire (2004), started as a reaction against a mechanistic model of behavior and cognition but now embraces the idea that more than one model or conception is needed to comprehend human nature. The term *contextualism* was taken from Stephen C. Pepper's book *World Hypotheses* (1942), in which he postulated four basic root metaphors of knowledge representations, including the mechanistic view and the contextualist view (the others being formism and organicism). For contextualism, the root metaphor was that it bears the mark of an "event alive in its present . . . in its actuality" (p. 232). That is, knowledge does not exist in a vacuum but is situated in a sociohistorical and cultural context of meanings and relationships. Subsequently, in another book, entitled *Concept and Quality,* Pepper (1966) proposed a fifth world hypothesis, purposivism, that was inspired in part by psychologist E. C. Tolman's (1932) classic work on purposive behavior.

Although a number of research psychologists have described themselves as contextualists (or perspectivists), there is as yet no agreement on what that term actually means in psychology. Some make claims that are counter to others' claims, but all seem to agree that knowledge representations are necessarily grounded in a perspective and a dynamic context (Bhaskar, 1983; Georgoudi & Rosnow, 1985a,

1985b; Hahn, 1942; Hoffman & Nead, 1983; Jaeger & Rosnow, 1988; Jenkins, 1974; Lerner, Hultsch, & Dixon, 1983; Lewis, 1997; McGuire, 1983; Mishler, 1979; Payne, 1996; Rosnow & Georgoudi, 1986; Sarbin, 1977). McGuire (1986) gave as a simple example the dictum that "2 + 2 = 4," explaining that even this seemingly uncomplicated proposition depends on one's perspective. If we were mixing two cups of salt and two cups of water, the result would be less than four cups of salty water. It is not that 2 + 2 = 4 is false (or true), but that the answer always depends upon the particular vantage point and context.

The purpose of research, McGuire (2004) argued, is to discover "which are the crucial perspectives," not whether one hypothesis or theory is true or false, as "all hypotheses and theories are true, as all are false, depending on the perspective from which they are viewed" (p. 173). A case in point might be research on the process by which the human mind consolidates related ideas into categories. For some time there was considerable controversy surrounding the validity of two alternative conceptions, called the *adding* and *averaging models*. According to the adding model, related cognitions combine in a manner corresponding to a mathematical summing formula. The averaging model, on the other hand, asserted that related cognitions combine in a manner that is similar to an averaging formula. As an example, suppose we know that two persons, A and B, each make $200 a day, and that a third person, C, makes $100 a day. Which should we perceive as higher in economic status, a social club consisting of A and B, or a club consisting of all three? People generally adopt the averaging solution in this case, perceiving that A and B make up a wealthier group than A, B, and C (as "social club members" don't usually pool their incomes). Now imagine that A, B, and C are members of the same communal family. In this case, people generally adopt an adding solution, perceiving that A, B, and C together are the wealthier group (i.e., "communal families" do usually pool money). As the context changes, the cognitive clustering process conforms to whichever perspective the mind invokes (Rosnow, 1972; Rosnow & Arms, 1968; Rosnow, Wainer, & Arms, 1970).

As a further illustration of the context of knowledge, consider how the grand theories of the social world seem to depend on the idiosyncratic perspective of the observer. As in the film classic by Akira Kurosawa, *Rashomon,* in which four narrators describe the rape of a woman and the murder of a man from quite different perspectives, social philosophers and sociologists also regard the dynamic nature of societal change in quite different ways. For example, some writers insist that only an evolutionary model can embrace what they see as a constant struggle, in which successful adaptations survive in a series of stages, from simplicity to increasing complexity and interrelatedness (a view represented in the work of Auguste Comte, Herbert Spencer, Wilhelm Wundt, V. Gordon Childe, C. Lloyd Morgan, and Emile Durkheim). Others contend that a cyclical model is appropriate; they perceive a revolving process of genesis and decay, with societies waxing and waning as a result of conflicts and crises (Vico, 1970, 1988, 1990). Still others favor a dialectical model of societal change; they perceive a continuous process of the canceling out or annulling of opposing forces in the direction of a higher synthesis (reflected in the writings of G. W. F. Hegel, Karl Marx, and the Frankfurt School of philosophy). Which is correct? A contextualist would say they are all presumably viable within particular conceptual and ideological contexts.

Given the assumption of a dynamic context, it follows that change must be intrinsic and, therefore, that no single method or theory can ever be expected to encompass the full complexity of human nature. We call this doctrine **methodological pluralism and theoretical ecumenism,** but it is simply a shorthand way of saying that researchers must, by necessity, avail themselves of different methodological operations (different units of analysis and diverse scientific strategies, for example) as well as theoretical explanations representing different levels of analysis. We return to this point in later chapters, but it should be noted that pluralism has its roots not in philosophical contextualism, but in the insights of Garner, Hake, and Erikson (1956) and D. T. Campbell and Fiske (1959), who asserted that all methods are limited in some ways. Therefore, researchers need to employ different operations (called "multiple operationalism" by Campbell and Fiske) in order to converge (or "triangulate") on the phenomena of interest to them. Theoretical ecumenism echoes Campbell and Stanley's (1963) insight that there is usually more than just one right way of viewing and comprehending a given event: "When one finds, for example, that competent observers advocate strongly divergent points of view, it seems likely on a priori grounds that both have observed something valid about the natural situation, and that both represent a part of the truth" (p. 173). Of course, even complete agreement is no certain proof of "truth" because, as Campbell and Stanley added, the selective, cutting edge of truth is often very imprecise.

A criticism leveled against contextualism is that, like constructionism, its idea of change as "intrinsic" flirts with nihilism. Contextualism's response is that, although behavior certainly is subject to sociocultural and historical forces that are in a state of perpetual flux, this change is "constrained by nature" in varying ways and varying degrees—or fettered by human nature, in the case of behavior (Hayes, Hayes, Reese, & Sarbin, 1993; Kazdin, 1998; Rosnow & Georgoudi, 1986). Thus, change is not simply dismissed as "error," or as a "shimmering paradox" concealing an immutable reality, or as a "temporary instability" within the fixed order of things, or as an "aberration" from a normal course of events in a basically stable, static, structured world. To underscore the assumption that behavior is in flux, some contextualists suggest using gerunds (the English -*ing* forms of verbs, e.g., *loving, thinking, seeing, believing*) to imply that it is active and processlike (Hineline, 1980).

The old philosophical puzzle concerning an external reality that exists independent of our perceptions of it—a bugaboo for the social constructionists—is dismissed by contextualizing behavioral and social researchers (and others) as not worth agonizing over. As Richard Rorty (1979) stated in another context, it is pointless to argue over whether knowledge representations put us in touch with reality or the "truth about things," because we would have to see reality "as it really is" to know when some "real truth" has been revealed. In other words, we would have to already know what we are trying to find out, but there is no way "to get out there" and see reality directly without the biases of our own idiosyncratic and social baggage (Kaplan, 1964). As another writer put it, the reason most scientists do not worry about the philosophical conundrum of an a priori reality is that "we're all wearing rose-colored glasses, meaning that our previous experience, our culture, language, preconceived world views, and so on, all these things get in the way of our seeing the world as it is in itself" (Regis, 1987, p. 212). Thus, instead of exhausting ourselves by arguing for or against "real truth," contextualists set the debate aside as pointless and settle for a less exalted idea of "truth" as *dependable explanation.*

EVOLUTIONARY EPISTEMOLOGY

The core idea of the third position, **evolutionary epistemology,** is that successful theories and knowledge in science evolve in a competition for survival, similar to the way that evolution and adaptation drive the transformation of organisms. For example, Popper (1958, 1962, 1972) perceived a parallel with Darwinian survival when arguing that scientists ultimately choose the theory "which, by natural selection, proves itself the fittest to survive" (1958, p. 108). Donald Campbell (1959, 1988a, 1988b) also viewed the Darwinian analogy as a potentially unifying philosophy of knowledge in psychology (Brewer & Collins, 1981; Campbell, 1988b; Houts, Cook, & Shadish, 1986). Campbell believed all valid knowledge to be what he described as the "social product" of a "self-perpetuating social vehicle," by which he simply meant *science* (quoted in Brewer & Collins, p. 15). However, whereas Darwinian evolutionary mutations are the result of chance, for Popper (1958) the choice of one theory over another was "an act, a practical matter" (p. 109). Contextualists believe that theories survive because they still make sense within the current milieu, whereas evolutionary epistemologists argue that theories survive because of their usefulness (e.g., in predicting some real outcome) in a game of empirical jeopardy.

Campbell had an enviable knack for making lists of things, and in a later chapter we will examine work in which he and others have developed comprehensive lists of potential threats to the validity of standard research designs. Campbell also envisioned a nested hierarchy of what he perceived as "mechanisms" that people use to make sense of the real world, including procedures, rules, and social and personal factors that govern the use of the scientific method. As Campbell described that process, there is a constant sifting and winnowing of hypotheses and theories, as a consequence of which some false explanations drop out and the leftovers become the scientists' "best guesses" at that moment, which later selection may eliminate in turn. Evolutionists, like contextualists, assume that knowledge is in constant flux as scientists use their "best guesses" as points of departure to promote new "guesses" (hypotheses and theories) to advance knowledge. Ultimately there is an a priori reality waiting to be discovered and described by a process of elimination, evolutionary epistemologists assume. As mentioned previously, a problem with the Darwinian analogy is that, as Ruse (1995) noted, the raw variants of biology are random, but the raw ingredients of science (new hypotheses) are seldom random.

Beyond the philosophical domain, the evolutionary idea has taken on a life of its own in behavioral and social science as a basis of fascinating hypotheses regarding the evolutionary aim of behavior (e.g., Buss, Haselton, Shackelford, Bleske, & Wakefield, 1998; Conway & Schaller, 2002; Kenrick & Keefe, 1992; Martindale, 1978). Some critics, however, have questioned what they see as a "loose application of adaptationist thinking" (de Waal, 2002, p. 187). Nevertheless, they also regard the evolutionary approach as having "the potential to introduce a conceptual framework that will accommodate or replace the current proliferation of disconnected theories in the study of human behavior" (p. 190). However, as de Waal (2002) cautioned, not everything can be understood as necessarily purposeful in a survivalist way, such as diseases that have a genetic basis, but those genes must be only part of the story since "no one would argue that they contribute to fitness" (p. 188).

Philosopher Jason Scott Robert (2004) cautioned that, at least in developmental biology, researchers typically design their studies in ways that preclude the possibility of observing the role of environmental factors and then conclude that such factors do not play a role in the processes they are studying. Conceding that point, biologist Günter P. Wagner (2004) added:

> The real difficulty we face in understanding organisms is that they are not simply formed by a combination of well-defined factors and effects—unlike a cannonball's trajectory, which can be understood as resulting from the combined effects of gravity, air friction, propulsive forces, and inertia. The only proper word we have for what is going on in biology is interaction. Interaction means that the effect of a factor depends on many other so-called factors, and this dependency on context ensures that the explanatory currency drawn from measuring the effects of causal factors is very limited. (p. 1404)

That epiphany of insights notwithstanding, in every generation there is some explanation or analogy that strikes a resonant chord but, in retrospect, seems deceivingly simple in addressing questions of profound complexity. For example, Einstein and Infeld (1938) mentioned how, in an industrial civilization wedded to the machine, the mechanical model of physics was applied to all manner of things, including "problems apparently different and non-mechanical in character" (pp. 57–58). As a case in point, the most complex current machine has frequently served as a metaphor for cognitive functioning, from a simple engine in the 18th century, to the telephone switchboard and then the digital computer in the 20th century. Scientists are inquisitive, restless, and intellectually competitive, forever creating and discovering things, but also refurbishing old ideas with a new veneer. As de Waal (2002) counseled psychological scientists, "My hope is that this generation will turn evolutionary psychology into a serious and rigorous science by being critical of its premises without abandoning the core idea that important aspects of human behavior have been naturally selected" (p. 187).

PEIRCE'S FOUR WAYS OF KNOWING

We began by characterizing "the scientific method" as an eclectic, pragmatic intellectual outlook (or orientation), but there are, of course, other orientations used to make sense of the experiential world. Charles Sanders Peirce, a leading American philosopher, who established the doctrine of pragmatism (an emphasis on practical consequences and values as the standards used to evaluate the caliber of "truth"), spoke about the scientific method and also described three other traditional foundations of knowledge: the method of tenacity, the method of authority, and the a priori method. He asserted that it was by the use of one or more of these "methods" that people's beliefs about what they feel they really know tend to become fixed in their minds as convictions—a process he called the "fixation of belief" (Reilly, 1970; Thayer, 1982; Wiener, 1966).

Peirce thought the **method of tenacity** to be the most primitive orientation of all: People cling to certain assumptions and beliefs mainly for the reason that they have been around for some time. A classic case was the ecclesiastical insistence for centuries that the earth was fixed, immobile, and at the center of the universe. That conviction may have provided peace of mind to those who accepted it, but like an ostrich with its head in the sand, they refused to see anything disturbing that might upset the status quo. A more contemporary variation is the finding in several areas of psychology that being subjected to the same message over and over (e.g., hearing malicious gossip or a scurrilous rumor again and again, or seeing the same grating TV commercial day after day) will make it seem more palatable and credible (cf. F. H. Allport & Lepkin, 1945; Fine & Turner, 2001; Hasher, Goldstein, & Toppino, 1977; Zajonc, 1968). Another factor that might account for the tenaciousness of beliefs is the false consensus phenomenon, which takes its name from the observation that people often overestimate the extent to which others hold the same beliefs; this feeling of "consensus" seems to bring closure to the mind (Ross, Green, & House, 1977). Tenacious beliefs are hard to shake loose by reason or demonstration, Peirce concluded.

Peirce thought the **method of authority** somewhat better than the method of tenacity, but also limited in some ways. The defining characteristic of this way of knowing is that people often consult an expert to tell them what to believe. On the positive side, cutting back on fatty foods because the doctor told you to do so is a beneficial effect resulting from the method of authority. On the negative side, however, are unscrupulous "authorities" who claim oracular wisdom but merely use fakery and showy schemes to prey on human weaknesses, such as medical quacks, food faddists, faith healers, TV psychics, cult leaders, and eccentric sexual theorists (M. Gardner, 1957; Shermer, 1997). As another classic example, Peirce noted the false accusations of witchcraft that at one time resulted in atrocities of the most horrible kind, as some people obeyed the word of authority to carry out their cruelties. Unless we live like hermits, all of us are subject to the ubiquitous influence of authority simply because we choose to live in a society requiring that we abide not only by institutionalized rules of various kinds but also by a "social contract" that takes different forms. An example, to be discussed in chapter 3, is certain ethical guidelines, rules, and regulations defining and circumscribing the conduct of behavioral and social researchers, as well as other scientists who work with human or animal subjects.

In a third way of knowing, the **a priori method,** we use our individual powers of reason and logic to think for ourselves in a way that is ostensibly unimpeded by any external authority. Reasoning that $12 \times 100 = 120 \times 10 = 1 \times 1,200$ is an example of the use of the a priori method. Interestingly, Bertrand Russell (1945) mentioned that mathematical reasoning may be the chief source of the belief in "exact truth," that is, the idea of truth as "static, final, perfect, and eternal" (pp. 37, 820). Thus, Russell added, "the perfect model of truth is the multiplication table, which is precise and certain and free from all temporal dross" (p. 820). Some traditional academic fields in which the a priori method is used are art history, literary criticism, philosophy, and theology, although the traditional notion of "truth" in many fields regards predilection as temporal rather than static and final. Reason can also be a defense against hucksters who prey on human gullibility. By approaching their dubious claims with questioning minds, we are using the a priori method to resist becoming overly impressed and victimized (Gilovich, 1991).

However, Peirce recognized that the a priori method is not infallible, because it is subject to one's own biases and tastes. If I conclude one thing is true and you conclude the opposite, how can we hope to resolve our disagreement? Peirce argued that dilemmas of this kind are a reason why people need a fourth way of knowing, one by which they can base their beliefs on something reliable and tangible. This, he said, was the role of the "scientific method"—but he conceded that scientists are generally cautious and tentative. Nonetheless, if we slavishly follow the method of tenacity, we ask no questions. Alternatively, the method of authority requires that we look to others for the answers to our questions. The a priori method, because it is based on pure reason and logic, also seems to rule out turning to an external world for tangible substantiation. The scientific method, Peirce believed, surpasses those other three because it encourages us to *investigate* the world as well as to use reason and logic. For example, if we conclude that the earth is round because we have circled the globe by foot, boat, and vehicle and not fallen off, we are using empirical reasoning as our grounds for belief, thus the scientific way of knowing.

RHETORIC, PERCEPTIBILITY, AND AESTHETICS

Earlier, we alluded to the idea that scientists' convictions are also predicated on a number of extraempirical factors, such as rhetoric, perceptibility, and aesthetics. Each of these factors, as is also true of empirical content, is limited and imperfect in some ways. As a metaphor, we might think of a chair. Conviction is the seat. Supporting the seat are the four legs of empirical content, rhetoric, perceptibility, and aesthetics. Because each factor is imperfect in some way, we need all four factors in science to form a structure for conviction that will, even tentatively, bear weight.

The Rhetoric of Justification

By *rhetoric,* we mean the persuasive language that people use—technically referred to as the **rhetoric of justification** because it implies the use of prose to warrant, defend, or excuse certain beliefs (Gross, 1996; Pera & Shea, 1991). Communications in science are intended not only to describe what the researchers found, but to inform and persuade in a compelling way (Ziman, 1978). As in learning a new language, the neophyte researcher must absorb the linguistic rules and grammatical conventions in the chosen field in order to encode information in acceptable ways. Without this fluency, it would be impossible to make one's way through the thicket of difficult concepts and assumptions, to communicate ideas, or to persuade skeptics and, ultimately, to gain acceptance as an authority in one's own right. As a consequence, students learn to mimic the speech patterns and written forms of authorities, with the result that scientists in the same field frequently seem to sound alike—in the same way that lawyers sound like lawyers, philosophers like philosophers, ministers like ministers, doctors like doctors, police like police, and so on.

One conventional medium for communicating information in science takes the form of written reports. But although each of the sciences has a privileged rhetoric of its own, we live in a world in which scientists think and communicate in the vernacular as well. Possibly because they represent our earliest ways of thinking and communicating, the vernacular may come closer to the intuitions and hunches, the rational and emotional ideas, that each of us uses in the formative stage of thinking about and trying to explain things. The pressure to conform to the style of the science, however, produces tensions to communicate efficiently rather than in a way that reveals the full underlying pattern of reasoning. With this notion in mind, we once described the pattern of reasoning and argument in modern science as "think Yiddish, write British." The focused, yet intuitive ways in which scientists think and reason often seem to resemble the creative arguments of a wise Talmudic scholar, but the tightly logical outcome of this "thinking Yiddish" is written up in the traditions of British empirical philosophy (Rosnow & Rosenthal, 1989).

Further, according to the classical Whorfian hypothesis, the language that each of us uses is our window into the world; it also expresses how we experience the world (e.g., Gumperz & Levinson, 1996). For example, people use different languages to communicate a word by a hand sign, but no language has a sign for every spoken word. In written and spoken English, we make a distinction between *rumor* and *gossip,* but in American Sign Language the same sign is used to denote both terms: Both hands are held before the face, the index fingers and thumbs are extended, and the fingers are opened and closed rapidly several times; sometimes the hands also move back and forth (M. L. A. Sternberg, 1981). In the same way that signing and speaking English appear to divide up our experiential world differently, the vocabulary of each researcher's discipline divides up the experiential world in ways that can influence nonlinguistic aspects of beliefs. To figure out whether the hand sign refers to rumor or gossip, we would have to get the meaning from the context. If we have no appropriate context, or if concepts are foreign to our experience, we may end up not only talking past one another but perceiving matters of material substance quite differently, thus reaching different conclusions and believing different things to be true.

Visualizations and Perceptibility

The philosopher W. V. Quine (1987) called rhetoric the "literary technology of persuasion" (p. 183). Often, however, we also need a pithy image in order to shake the stubborn preconceptions that people harbor. Thus, another way in which humans carve up the world is by means of imagery, or what some philosophers refer to as "visualizations" and we refer to more broadly as **perceptibility.** The use of images seems to have a hand in virtually all reasoning and thinking (e.g., Bauer & Johnson-Laird, 1993; Johnson-Laird, 1983; Johnson-Laird & Byrne, 1991; Taylor, Pham, Rivkin, & Armor, 1998). The more pungent the image, the more it seems to reverberate in the mind's eye as a justification for some relevant conclusion or belief. Images are also like maps (another image!), because maps provide a direction for our activity. Newton presumably had an image in mind when he created his laws of motion, just as Michelangelo had an image that he said he "released" when sculpting figures out of stone. Presumably, behavioral and social scientists also begin with perceptible images as they carve out their middle-range theories and hypotheses and then figure out ways to test them (R. Nisbet, 1976). As Einstein (1934) observed, "It seems that the human mind has first to construct forms independently before we can find them in things" (p. 27).

Images are not limited only to science, of course. Our social world contains a remarkable assortment of analogical images in the form of metaphors and proverbs that create pictures in our minds, enabling us to perceive novel situations and problems in terms of familiar ones (Gentner, Holyoak, & Kokinov, 2001; Honeck, 1997; Lakoff & Johnson, 1980; Miller, 1986, 1996; Oppenheimer, 1956; Randhawa & Coffman, 1978). Some images, for example, encapsulate the idea of a biological function, such as explaining that the cat's running after the ball is like "chasing a mouse" or the baby's sucking its thumb is like "nursing at the mother's breast" (Gombrich, 1963). As Peirce explained, some pithy metaphors ultimately become "habits of mind" that can govern our actions as well as our beliefs (H. Margolis, 1993). Lakoff and Johnson (1980) called them "metaphors we live by" and described how communicating or reasoning by the use of analogies may play a central role in cognitive systems (see also Honeck, 1997). For example, the image of "time as money" is reflected in phrases such as *EX'* "You're *wasting* my time" or "How do you *spend* your time?" or "I *lost* a lot of time when I was sick" (Lakoff & Johnson, 1980, pp. 7–8). Other examples are *ontological metaphors* (i.e., ideas that are simply taken for granted); they enable us to treat experiences as entities or substances, such as thinking of the mind as a "machine": "My mind just isn't *operating* today" or "Boy, the *wheels are turning* today!" or "We've been working on this problem all day and now we're *running out of steam*" (p. 27). Lakoff and Johnson argued that linguistic regularities, beliefs, and communication strategies that cannot be easily explained in formal terms can often be explained (and sustained) in a conceptual framework of perceptible representations.

Aesthetics

In science, as in daily life, the reaction to failures in perceptibility is often "I just don't see it!" But sometimes this is a response not to misperceiving the idea, but to rejecting it on aesthetic grounds. That is, perceptible images are evaluated on their "beauty" or **aesthetics,** a faculty that is presumably a basic psychological component of every human being (Averill, Stanat, & More, 1998; Dissanayake, 1995) and, we would argue, every conviction. A notable scientific dispute involved Albert Einstein and the leading quantum theorists, who found it hard to convince Einstein and other physical determinists that, given a very great many atoms, all capable of certain definite changes, it is possible to predict the overall pattern but not possible to tell what particular change any given atom will undergo. God "does not play dice with the world" was Einstein's famous riposte (Jammer, 1966, p. 358). It was not that he was unable to "see" the implications of the idea that, at the level of simple atomic processes, activity is ruled by blind chance (Clark, 1971; Jammer, 1966), but that he found it viscerally objectionable.

Philosophers and scientists have written extensively about the similarity of the creative act in the arts and poetry to that in the sciences (Chandrasekhar, 1987; Garfield, 1989a, 1989b; R. Nisbet, 1976; Wechsler, 1978), using words like *beautiful* and *elegant* to express the precision and accuracy of great scientific insights (scientific laws, equations, theories, and so on). Indeed, there may be no greater praise of a colleague's work than to say of it that it is "just beautiful." A classic scientific example was Mendeleyev's periodic table in the field of chemistry. The beauty of Mendeleyev's insight was not only that he saw a way to organize all the chemical elements, but that he "was bold enough to leave gaps where no known elements fit into the pattern and to suggest that the atomic weights of some elements had been calculated incorrectly" (Uppenbrink, 2000, p. 1696). The chemist Primo Levi (1984) told how, as a young student, he was struck by the beauty of Mendeleyev's periodic table, which he experienced as "poetry, loftier and more solemn than all the poetry we had swallowed" (p. 1).

LIMITATIONS OF THE FOUR SUPPORTS OF CONVICTION

Previously, we said that the factors of perceptibility, rhetoric, aesthetics, and empirical content are imperfect supports of convictions. For example, thinking in terms of visual images (perceptibility) is limited by each person's experience and imagination, and by whatever visual metaphors are salient at that moment in historical time. The rhetoric of justification is limited by the human capacity to express experiences in prose. To borrow an analogy suggested by Robert E. Lana (1991), we can bend our arms forward at the elbow, but not backward, because nature has imposed a limit on how far the human forearm can be bent. Similarly, language enables us to bend our experiences in prose, but nature has imposed a limit on our cognitive capacity to process the world's richness of information. As regards aesthetics, what people perceive as "beautiful" is conditioned in part by culture and training. Thus, although it is true that beauty can be fashioned and twisted, it is biased because it is ultimately in the eye (and sensibility) of the beholder, or as the great film director Josef von Sternberg (1965) wrote, "Though beauty can be created, it cannot be put to a test or arbitrated; it consists only of its appeal to the senses" (p. 319).

Scientists do not simply rely on armchair theorizing, political persuasiveness, or personal position to settle opinions; they use empirical methods that are made available to other competent scientists. Traditionally, the way this process works was compared by one scientist to someone who is trying to unlock a door with a set of previously untried keys (Conant, 1957). The person says, "If this key fits the lock, then the lock will open when I turn the key." Similarly, the scientist has a choice of methods, decides on one, and then says in essence, "Let's try it and see if it works" (Conant, 1957, p. xii). This analogy is another idealization and oversimplification, however, because there are powerful generalizations that cannot be restricted to the available empirical facts alone. For example, Newton's first law of motion asserts that a body not acted on by any force will continue in a state of rest or uniform motion in a straight line forever. Of course, no scientist has ever seen a body not acted on by any force (e.g., friction or gravity), much less observed or measured any physical entity traveling in a straight line forever. Recognizing limitations like these is important so that we do not credit empiricism with properties it does not have (M. R. Cohen, 1931/1978).

BEHAVIORAL RESEARCH DEFINED

The expression **behavioral research** in the title of this book is another huge umbrella term, as it covers a vast area. The "behavior" of early primitive humans, humans as political animals, economic animals, social animals, talking animals, humans as logicians—these are of interest to behavioral and social scientists in fields as diverse

TABLE 1.1
Illustrative fields and explanatory focus on behavior

Field	Focus	Explanatory emphasis
Neuroscience	Most micro	Biological and biochemical factors
Cognition	More micro	Thinking and reasoning
Social psychology	More macro	Interpersonal and group factors
Sociology	Most macro	Societal systems

as psychology (clinical, cognitive, counseling, developmental, educational, experimental, industrial and organizational, social, etc.), sociology, economics, education and communication research, psycholinguistics, neuroscience, behavioral biology, and many other disciplines. For most purposes it probably makes little difference whether we can distinguish among those disciplines. There are differences nonetheless. Table 1.1 implies two basic differences, which are that the explanatory emphasis as well as the units of analysis used are often quite dissimilar in different disciplines, as well as in different areas of the same discipline. Imagine a continuum anchored on one end by the smallest and most concrete, or most diminutive (i.e., *most micro*) units of analysis and at the other end, by the largest and most abstract (*most macro*) units. If we open any basic text in psychology, we will see that explanations of behavior range from the nervous system (most micro) to society and culture (most macro), with the factors of personality, cognition, and development somewhere in between.

Staying with this idea, suppose we were walking along a beach and a small object on the sand aroused our curiosity because it suddenly moved or made a noise. We might stop to look at it more closely. If we happened to notice certain regularities in its behavior, we might try to get it to respond by poking it or pushing it to see how it will react. Neuroscientists who are interested in the biology or biochemistry of behavior might want to look inside the object to see what makes it tick. Determining how it is constructed, they might be able to predict its responses. This is the "most micro" level of explanation, because the units of analysis are so small. The neuroscientists interested in behavior might experiment with how a motivational state can be controlled by the stimulation of a portion of the brain, or how brain waves in a particular area are correlated with a particular emotional sensation, or how testosterone is related to sexual activity or aggressiveness, or how low levels of progesterone are related to premenstrual tension.

Illustrative of a "relatively micro" focus (where the units of analysis are not as diminutive as in neuroscience) would be some areas of cognitive and personality psychology. A cognitive researcher interested in intelligence, for example, might give the research participants letters with blank spaces between some of them and ask them to fill in the blanks to make words. Using that procedure the researcher attempts to delve into a certain cognitive dimension of intelligence. A personality researcher might approach the topic quite differently, creating a test to pick out people who are high and low in "social intelligence." Such a test might, for example, consist of a series of scenarios visually depicting or verbally describing certain interpersonal roles that people play. The subject's task is to identify the actor's actions and intentions in each particular scenario. The personality researcher examined the traits of people who are good (or bad) at reading other's actions and intentions, whereas the cognitive researcher was interested in the reasoning process used by intelligent people to form words. The similarity between those two approaches is that they are not as micro as the explanatory focus of interest to the neuroscientist, but somewhat more micro than in some other areas of behavioral research, such as social psychology.

At the next level, experimental social psychologists who investigate how social behavior is influenced by interpersonal and group factors are interested in "more macro" explanations than are neuroscientists or cognitive psychologists. Studies of how judgments and perceptions might be influenced by subtle group processes are an illustration. In a classic study by Solomon Asch (1951), a subject arrived at the research laboratory along with several others who, unbeknownst to the subject, were really confederates of the investigator. All participants, once they were seated together at the same table, were told by the experimenter that they would be asked to make judgments about the length of several lines. Each participant was to judge which of three lines was closest in length to a standard line. The confederates always stated their judgments first, after which the real subject gave his opinion. The confederates, acting in collusion with the experimenter, sometimes gave obviously incorrect judgments. To Asch's surprise, one third of the real subjects gave the same opinion as the confederates in the experiment; only 29% of the real subjects remained completely independent. Interviews with the real subjects revealed that they were deeply disturbed by the discrepancy between what they saw and what they believed others saw. Asch interpreted this result as evidence that our sense of reality is partly social (Gleitman, Rozin, & Sabini, 1997).

At the "most macro" level, other social psychologists, anthropologists, and sociologists study how behavior is acted out in particular societal systems, that is, the "roles" people play, which are theorized to be related to the person's "position" in the societal system (e.g., Alexander & Knight, 1971; Biddle & Thomas, 1966; J. A. Jackson, 1972; Rosnow & Aiken, 1973; Sarbin & Allen, 1968). For example, someone who is in the position of "professor" is expected to be scholarly and inquisitive, and to have primarily intellectual interests. Of course, a person can occupy a number of different positions, playing a number of different roles at the same time—that of student, wife or husband, daughter or son, part-time waiter, filmmaker, and so on. It has been observed that each of us enacts many different roles with varying degrees of intensity. There is disagreement, however, about whether multiple role taking produces distress or implies that we are better prepared to face the complexities of modern life (cf. Barnett & Rivers, 1996; Hochschild, 1989). One researcher, who took the latter position, compared the multiple role taker with the skilled motorist who can withstand unusual stress and long-term strain on the highway (Cameron, 1950).

Realizing the importance of studying things from different perspectives, researchers often borrow methodological strategies from one another in order to explore more than one dimension of a phenomenon. An analogy proposed by the existentialist philosopher Jean-Paul Sartre (1956) is relevant. Sartre described how, when we look at someone who is looking back at us, it is hard to see the "watcher" behind the "look" at the same time that we focus on the person's appearance. The more we concentrate on one dimension, the less we notice other things about the individual. Other dimensions of the person are neutralized, put out of play. To try to catch a glimpse of the whole person, we need to shift our concentration back and forth, attending first to one thing and then to another. In behavioral research, multiple methods and theories allow us to expand our grasp and understanding, one reason why interdisciplinary fields are constantly being created—so we can share methods and ideas and ultimately to benefit from the insights that can come from shifting our concentration back and forth. Researchers in the new boundary-melting disciplines hope that they will show the same vigor and potential for breakthrough that has been evident when other sciences have combined to form a new discipline.

THREE BROAD RESEARCH ORIENTATIONS

Although the methods used by behavioral researchers are often diverse, the objective in psychological science is the same: to describe and explain how and why people behave the way they do, including how and why they feel and think about things as they do. William James, who founded the first psychology laboratory in the United States, called psychology the science of mental life, by which he meant that it examines how people feel, think, and behave. The job of the behavioral researcher in psychology is, as James said, to describe and explain consciousness in the context of behavior and processes in the body. Other questions of equal importance in psychology deal with the nature of language, planning, problem solving, and imagination in the context of reasoning, thinking, intentions, and mental representations (Kimble, 1989). The scientific methods used to address these aspects of behavior include a variety of laboratory and nonlaboratory procedures. To simplify this picture, we lump together the various methods and orientations of researchers into three broad types: descriptive, relational, and experimental.

By **descriptive research orientation,** we mean an *observational focus* whose goal is carefully mapping out a situation to describe what is happening behaviorally (or what philosophers call how-questions). This focus does not, by definition, directly concern itself with causal explanations (i.e., why-questions), except perhaps speculatively. For example, the educational psychologist who is interested in the study of children's failure in school may spend a good deal of time observing the classroom behavior of children who are doing poorly. The researcher can then describe as carefully as possible what was observed. Careful observation of failing pupils might lead to some revision of the concepts of classroom failure, to factors that may have contributed to the development of failure, and even perhaps to speculative ideas for reversing failure.

That type of orientation is frequently considered a necessary first step in the development of a research program, but it is rarely regarded as sufficient, because the study cannot tell us *why* something happens or how what happens is related to other events. If our interest is in children's failure, we are not likely to be satisfied for very long with even the most careful description of that behavior. We still want to know the antecedents of failure and the outcomes of various procedures designed to reduce classroom failure. Even if we were not motivated directly by the practical

[handwritten margin note: We need multiple disciplines B/c that way we have more diverse research methods to pool from. (✗)]

implications of the causes and cures of failure, we would believe our understanding of failure to be considerably improved if we knew the conditions that increase and decrease its likelihood.

For us to learn about the increase or decrease of failure, or any other behavior, our observations must focus on at least two variables at the same time, that is, two or more sets of observations that can be related to one another in what is called a **relational research orientation,** whose focus is the description of how what happens changes when some other set of events changes. Research is relational when two or more variables or conditions are measured and related to one another. Continuing with the classroom example, let us suppose the researcher notes that many of the scholastically failing students are rarely looked at or addressed by their teachers and are seldom exposed to new academically relevant information. At that stage the researcher may have only an impression about the relation between learning failure and teaching behavior. Such impressions are a frequent, and often valuable, by-product of descriptive research. But if they are to be taken seriously as a relational principle, they cannot be left at the impressionistic level for very long.

To examine those impressions, one might arrange a series of coordinated observations on a sample of pupils in classrooms that adequately represents the population of pupils about whom some conclusion is to be drawn. For each pupil it could be noted (a) whether the student is learning anything or the degree to which the student had been learning and (b) the degree to which the teacher has been exposing the student to material to be learned. From the coordinated observations it should then be possible to make a quantitative statement concerning the degree of correlation between the amount of pupils' exposure to the material to be learned and the amount of material they did in fact learn. The scientist would indicate not just (a) whether "X and Y are significantly related" (i.e., whether, over the long run, this nonzero relationship is likely to emerge consistently when the research is repeated) but also (b) the form of the relationship (e.g., linear or nonlinear, positive or negative) and (c) the strength of the relationship, or *effect size* (a concept defined in the next chapter).

To carry the illustration one step further, suppose that the pupils exposed to less information were also those who tended to learn less. On discovering that relationship, there might be a temptation to conclude that children learn less because they are taught less. Such an **ad hoc hypothesis** (i.e., one developed "for this" special result), although plausible, would not be warranted by the relationship reported. It might be that teachers teach less to those they know to be less able to learn. Differences in teaching behavior might be as much a result of the pupils' learning as a determinant of that learning. To pursue that **working hypothesis** (i.e., the supposition we are using, or working with), we could make further observations that would allow us to infer whether differences in information presented to pupils, apart from any individual differences among them, affected the pupils' learning. Such questions are best answered by manipulation of the conditions believed to be responsible for the effect. That is, we might introduce some change into the situation, or we might interrupt or terminate it in order to identify certain causes.

What has just been described is an **experimental research orientation,** whose focus is the identification of causes (i.e., *what* leads to what). Relational research can only rarely provide such insights, and then only under very special conditions (discussed later in this book). The difference between the degree of focus on causal explanation of relational and experimental research can be expressed in the difference between the two statements "*X* is related to *Y*" (relational research) and "*X* is responsible for *Y*" (experimental research). In our example, teaching is *X* and learning is *Y*. Our experiment is designed to reveal the effects of teaching on pupil learning. We might select a sample of youngsters and, by tossing a coin or by means of some other random method of selection, divide them into two equivalent groups. One of these groups (the **experimental group**) would have more information given them by their teachers than would the other group (the **control group**). We could then assess whether the experimental group surpasses the control group in learning achievement. If we find this result, we could say that giving the experimental group more information was *responsible* for this outcome.

There might still be a question of what it was about the better procedure that led to the improvement. In the case of increased teaching, we might wonder whether the improvement was due to (a) the amount and nature of the additional material; (b) the increased attention from the teacher while presenting the additional material; (c) any increases in eye contact, smiles, or warmth; or (d) other possible correlates of increased teaching behavior. In fact, those various hypotheses have already been investigated by behavioral and social researchers. The results indicate that the amount of new material that teachers present to their pupils is sometimes predicated not so much on the children's learning ability, as on the teachers' beliefs or expectations about their pupils' learning ability. The teachers' expectations about their pupils' abilities become a self-fulfilling prophecy, in which the expectations are essentially responsible for the outcome in behavior (Babad, 1993; Raudenbush, 1984; Rosenthal, 1966, 1976, 1985; Rosenthal & Jacobson, 1968; Rosenthal & Rubin, 1978).

We have described a series of hypothetical studies, and we now turn to a series of actual studies that are considered classics in psychological science. These examples illustrate the way in which sound research is *programmatic;* that is, it follows a plan of attack involving more than a single study or a single set of observations. The first project illustrates a program of research used to develop innovative assessment techniques in a famous applied setting during World War II. The second program of research was designed to develop a tool to measure social desirability bias in virtually any measurement setting. Whereas the subjects in the first two programs of research were human participants, those in the final set of studies were animal subjects in experimental studies in the area of comparative psychology. These three cases (a) flesh out the descriptive, relational, and experimental orientations; (b) introduce additional key concepts (to which we return in later chapters); (c) underscore how vast the territory covered by behavioral and social research is in psychology; and (d) allow us to follow the step-by-step thinking of researchers as they proceeded toward a specific objective.

THE DESCRIPTIVE RESEARCH ORIENTATION

Our first illustration involves the development of assessment techniques by psychologists during World War II, under the auspices of the Office of Strategic Services (OSS)—this nation's first organized nonmilitary espionage and sabotage agency, which

We need all three orientations: descriptive, relational & experimental for good psychological research.

came into being in 1942 under the directorship of William J. "Wild Bill" Donovan. The OSS was charged with tasks such as intelligence gathering, sabotage behind enemy lines, the mobilization of guerilla groups to resist the Nazi occupation of Europe, and the preparation and dissemination of propaganda (OSS Assessment Staff, 1948). The OSS was "disestablished" in October 1945 by a directive issued by President Harry S Truman, who in another Presidential Directive then "established" something called the Central Intelligence Group and the National Intelligence Authority, a forerunner of the Central Intelligence Agency, which was created by Congress in 1947 (Griffin, 2002). The program of assessment studies conducted by the OSS investigators illustrates what we characterized as the descriptive research orientation.

Thousands of men, drawn from both military and civilian life, were recruited to carry out the often hazardous missions of the OSS. Initially, it was not known what type of personnel to select for each of the various missions, and a group of psychologists and psychiatrists was assembled to aid in the assessment of the special agents. The chief contribution of these researchers was to set up a series of situations that would permit more useful and relevant descriptions of the personalities of the candidates, although the original intent of the assessment staff had been more ambitious. It had been hoped that in the long run it would be possible to increase the likelihood of assignment of agents to those missions they could best perform. Unfortunately, several factors made impossible the development of a screening and placement system that could be fairly and properly evaluated. Chief among these factors were the assessment staff's not knowing what particular mission would finally be assigned to a recruit and, most important, several weaknesses in the final appraisal of how good a job an agent had actually done.

From December 1943 to August 1945, more than 5,000 recruits were studied by the assessment staff. The primary station was located about an hour's ride from Washington, DC, in a rustic setting of rolling meadows and stately trees. It was there that the recruits were sent for a 3- to 5-day period, during which they were given identical clothes to wear and assigned pseudonyms so that colonels and privates and college professors would be indistinguishable to the assessment researchers. Besides a false name, each recruit had to invent a cover story giving himself a new occupation, a new residence, a new place of birth, and a new educational background. Candidates were warned that the assessment researchers would try to trick them into breaking cover and giving away their true identities.

Virtually everything that a recruit did from the moment he arrived at the station was observed and assessed: how he got off the truck that brought his group of recruits, how he asked questions of the staff members who explained procedures to the candidates, what he said during the first dinner, and what he chose to do after dinner when he was free to read or talk or withdraw. The first evening, the candidates filled out a great many paper-and-pencil tests of personality and ability and also answered questions concerning their personal background. The next days were filled with many situational tests, in which the staff had the opportunity to evaluate each man's level of initiative, leadership, functioning intelligence, social relationships, and physical ability. For example, a group of four to seven men had to move a log and a rock across an 8-foot-wide brook. The situation was rigged so that either a bridge or an overhead cable system could be constructed to solve the problem. The achievement of a solution was not the main purpose of the exercise, however. Instead, it was to give the researchers an opportunity to observe the different roles the men assumed in the team effort required to solve the problem.

One of the most trying, and probably most revealing, situations was a task in which the candidates were to direct the efforts of two helpers in building a 5-foot cube out of a giant Tinkertoy set. To the candidates the task seemed to be another assessment of their leadership abilities, but it was actually a test of stress tolerance. "Kippy" and "Buster," the two helpers, were really two members of the research staff. Kippy was a passive sort who did nothing unless ordered to, except occasionally to get in the way. Buster offered useless suggestions, griped repeatedly, and harped on the candidates' weaknesses. Kippy and Buster were sufficiently obstructive that, in the whole history of the OSS assessment program, no recruit was ever able to complete the task in the allotted 10 minutes.

Some of the candidates perceived immediately that the two "helpers" were confederates of the researchers. That insight sometimes, but not always, helped the candidates to contain their tempers and persist in trying to get the job done. Other candidates wondered why the OSS could not afford better farmhands around the estate and admitted that the obstreperousness and insolence of the helpers tempted them more than once to lay an uncharitable hand upon one or the other of them. On more than one occasion a fight did erupt. Some candidates learned enough about themselves from that experience that they asked to be excused from the program, realizing that the kind of stress involved would be too much for them.

As this project unfolded, its primary objective was descriptive, but it should be noted again that description had not been the only goal of the research staff. They had hoped to correlate the assessments made of the men with their performance in the field, thus using a relational strategy as well as a descriptive one. Such correlations would define the adequacy of the selection procedures. If those correlations were high, they would tell the researchers that the assessment (the **predictor variable**) had done its job of predicting actual task performance (the **criterion variable,** or outcome). Because the researchers had only vague (and probably many erroneous) ideas about the nature of the jobs for which the candidates were being selected, there was no satisfactory evaluation of just how good a job had been done by agents in the field. It would be impractical to think that one could select people for the performance of unspecified functions. However, it seems unlikely that, either before or since, have so many people been observed and described so carefully by so many behavioral researchers.

THE RELATIONAL RESEARCH
ORIENTATION

The OSS assessment researchers were in a position to make many detailed observations relevant to many of the candidates' motives. However, there was no organized attempt to relate the scores or ratings on any one of these variables to the scores or ratings on some subsequently measured variable that, on the basis of theory, should show a strong correlation with the predictor variable. In this next illustration, we examine how relational research was used in another classic set of studies to develop a personality construct and then to validate a psychological scale to measure this construct, called the *need for social approval*. This series of studies also illustrates the value of replications that vary slightly from one another (**varied replications**), which can help to pinpoint the relationships of interest. (We will have more to say about this issue in chapter 4 when we discuss the relationship between reliability and replication.)

The term **construct** refers to an abstract idea that is used as an explanatory concept (we will also have more to say about this later). The construct *need for social approval* (also called *social desirability*) was investigated by Douglas P. Crowne and David Marlowe, who performed this research at Ohio State University in the late 1950s. *Social desirability* refers to the idea that people differ in their need for approval and affection from respected others. Crowne and Marlowe were interested in developing a scale to measure the degree to which people vary on this personality dimension. They wanted their scale to measure the respondent's social desirability independent of his or her level of psychopathology and began by considering hundreds of personality test items that could be answered in a true-false format. To be included, an item had to be one that would reflect socially approved behavior and yet be almost certain to be untrue (i.e., behavior too good to be true). In addition, answers to the items could not have any implications of psychological abnormality or psychopathology. By having a group of psychology graduate students and faculty judge the social desirability of each item, the researchers developed a set of items reflecting behavior too virtuous to be probable but not primarily reflecting personal maladjustment.

The final form of the Marlowe-Crowne Social Desirability (MCSD) scale contained 33 items (Crowne, 1979; Crowne & Marlowe, 1964). In approximately half the items a "true" answer reflected the socially desirable (i.e., the higher need for approval) response, and in the remainder a "false" answer reflected this type of response. An example of the former type of item is "I have never intensely disliked anyone," whereas the latter is exemplified by "I sometimes feel resentful when I don't get my way." Interested readers will find the MCSD scale and some related social desirability (SD) scales that are used to measure "good impression" responding in Robinson, Shaver, and Wrightsman's *Measures of Personality and Social Psychological Attitudes* (1991), which includes a discussion of the background of this topic (Paulhus, 1991). For a brief overview of the ideas and research that ultimately led to the creation of the MCSD scale, described by one of the authors of this test, see Crowne (2000).

The MCSD scale showed high correlations with those measures with which it was expected to show high correlations. For example, it correlated well with itself, which is to say an impressive statistical relation was obtained between the two testings of a group of subjects who were tested in a **reliable** (i.e., consistent) manner. In addition, although the MCSD scale did show moderate correlations with measures of psychopathology, there were fewer of these and they were smaller in magnitude than was the case for an earlier developed SD scale (Edwards, 1957a). Those were promising beginnings for the MCSD scale, but it remained to be shown that the concept of need for social approval (and the test developed to measure it) was useful beyond predicting responses to other paper-and-pencil measures. As part of their program of further validating their new scale and the construct that was its basis, Crowne and Marlowe undertook an ingenious series of varied replications relating scores on their scale to subjects' behavior in a number of non-paper-and-pencil test situations.

In the first of those studies the subjects began by completing various tests, including the MCSD scale and were then asked to get down to the serious business of the experiment. That "serious business" required them to pack a dozen spools of thread into a small box, unpack the box, repack it, reunpack it, and so on for 25 minutes while the experimenter appeared to be timing the performance and making notes about them. After these dull 25 minutes had elapsed, the subjects were asked to rate how "interesting" the task had been, how "instructive," and how "important to science," and they were also asked how much they wished to participate in similar experiments in the future. The results showed quite clearly that those subjects who scored on the MSCD scale above the mean on desire for social approval said that they found the task more interesting, more instructive, and more important to science, and that they were more eager to participate again in similar studies than those subjects who had scored below the mean. In other words, just as we would have predicted, subjects scoring higher in the need for social approval were more ingratiating and said nicer things to the experimenter about the task.

Next, Crowne and Marlowe conducted a series of studies using the method of verbal conditioning. In one variant of that method, the subject is asked to make up sentences and state them aloud. In the positive reinforcement condition, every time the subject utters a plural noun the experimenter responds affirmatively by saying "mm-hmm." In the negative reinforcement condition, every time the subject utters a plural noun the experimenter responds negatively by saying "uh-uh." Researchers who use this procedure define the magnitude of verbal conditioning by the amount of change in the production of plural nouns from before the reinforcement to some subsequent time block after the subject has received the positive or negative reinforcement. Magnitude of verbal conditioning is theorized to be a good indicator of susceptibility to social influence. Subjects who are more susceptible to the experimenter's reinforcements are hypothesized to be more susceptible to other forms of elementary social influence.

In the first of their verbal conditioning studies, the investigators found that subjects higher in the need for social approval responded with far more plural nouns when "rewarded" with positive reinforcement than did subjects lower in this need. Subjects higher in the need for social approval also responded with fewer plural nouns when "punished" with negative reinforcement than did subjects lower in this personality characteristic. Those subjects who saw the connection between their utterances and the experimenter's reinforcement were dropped from the analysis of the results. In this way the relation obtained was between subjects' need for social approval as measured by the MCSD scale and their responsivity to the approval of their experimenter, but only when they were not explicitly aware (or said they were unaware) of the role of the experimenter's reinforcements.

In the second of their verbal conditioning studies, the investigators wanted to use a task that would be more lifelike and engaging than producing random words. They asked subjects to describe their own personality, and every positive self-reference was positively reinforced by the experimenter's saying "mm-hmm" in a flat monotone. A positive self-reference was defined **operationally** (i.e., defined in an empirical way) as any statement that reflected favorably on the subject, and two judges working independently showed a very high degree of consistency in identifying positive self-references. Results of that study indicated that subjects above the mean in need for social approval made significantly more positive self-references when reinforced for doing so than did subjects scoring lower in the need for social approval. Regardless of whether the subjects' responses were as trivial as the production of random words or as meaningful as talking about themselves, that behavior could be increased much more by subtle social reinforcement in people who were higher rather than lower in their measured need for social approval.

In their third verbal conditioning study, the investigators used a *vicarious* (substitute) reward method. The subject was not rewarded for a given type of response but instead watched someone else receive a reward. The real subjects of the study observed a **pseudosubject** (i.e., a confederate of the experimenter) make up a series of sentences using one of six pronouns (*I, you, we, he, she, they*) and a verb given by the experimenter. When the pseudosubject began a sentence with the pronoun *I* or *we,* the experimenter responded with the word *good.* Before and after the observation interval, the subjects themselves made up sentences using one of the same six pronouns. The results were that subjects higher in the need for social approval showed a greater increase in their use of the reinforced pronouns (*I, we*) from their preobservational to their postobservational sentence-construction session than did subjects lower in the need for social approval. Once again, Crowne and Marlowe had demonstrated that subjects, on the average, can be successfully predicted to be more responsive to the approving behavior of an experimenter when they have scored higher on the MCSD scale.

Another set of studies used a derivative of Asch's conformity procedure in which each judgment is stated aloud, because the purpose of Asch's procedure is to permit an assessment of the effects of earlier subjects' judgments on the judgments of subsequent subjects. In order to control the judgments made earlier, accomplices of the experimenters serve as pseudosubjects. All the pseudosubjects make the same uniform judgment, one that is quite clearly in error. Conformity is defined as the real subject's "going along with" (conforming to) the majority in his or her own judgment rather than giving the objectively correct response. In one of Crowne and Marlowe's variations on that procedure, the subjects heard a tape recording of knocks on a table and then reported their judgment of the number of knocks they had heard. Each subject was led to believe that he or she was the fourth participant and heard the tape-recorded responses of the "three prior subjects" to each series of knocks that was to be judged. The earlier three subjects were the pseudosubjects, and they all agreed with one another by consistently giving an incorrect response on 12 of 18 trials. Therefore, the researchers could count the number of times out of 12 that each subject yielded to the wrong but unanimous majority. The subjects who had scored higher in the need for social approval conformed more to the majority judgment than did the subjects who had scored lower in the need for social approval.

In these studies, the real subjects heard the taped response of the "majority." In follow-up studies, the researchers investigated whether the same effect would result if the accomplices were actually present. This time the task was a discrimination problem in which the subjects had to judge which of two clusters of dots was larger. Pseudosubjects were again used to give responses that were clearly wrong but unanimous, and as before, the subjects who had scored above the mean on social desirability yielded more often to the unanimous but erring majority than did the subjects who had scored below the mean.

We have described here a number of studies that supported the validity of the MCSD scale and the construct of the need for social approval. As with almost any other well-researched problem in behavioral and social science, many additional, relevant studies (not described here) support or do not support the findings. An exhaustive literature search would turn up these additional results, but our purpose here is not to be exhaustive but to illustrate the use of a series of varied replications in relational research. Other measures of social desirability have also been developed, and the factor analysis of these scales has revealed that they can be described by two factors: self-deception and impression management (Paulhus, 1991). Later in this book we turn to techniques that are often used to minimize or eliminate the influence of social desirability bias in personality and attitude measurement. As Crowne (2000) noted, although we know a great deal about social desirability and its measurement, dimensions, and correlations with other measures, there is still much that we do not know about when people are motivated to respond in a biased way in evaluative situations.

THE EXPERIMENTAL RESEARCH ORIENTATION

Our final illustration is a series of experimental studies characterized by the controlled arrangement and manipulation of one or more conditions calculated to identify the causes of resulting variations in one or more outcome variables or measures. In the research by Crowne and Marlowe there were instances in which some condition was controlled and manipulated by the investigators. Even though we used the terms *experiment* and *experimenter* to describe some aspects of this research, we still do not regard it as "experimental research" in its broad purpose. It was not experimental because its goal was not to identify the causes of the need for social approval, nor was need for approval a manipulated variable in these studies. Instead, the purpose of that research was to measure the variable and then relate it to other behavior in order to decide whether the MCSD scale measured the construct the researchers had in mind when creating it. We now turn to a highly publicized series of studies in the annals of comparative psychology to illustrate the nature of varied replications in the work of Harry and Margaret Harlow dealing with affection in primates.

There are few personality theories that do not consider early life experiences especially important in the development of personality. Among the early life experiences often given special attention are those involving mother-child relationships. A generally posed proposition might be "loving mother-child relationships are more likely to lead to healthy adult personalities than hostile, rejecting mother-child relationships." A simple way to investigate that hypothesis experimentally would be to assign half a sample of young children to loving mothers and half to rejecting mothers, and then to follow the development of each child's adult personality. Such an experimental plan is an ethical absurdity in our culture's value matrix, although there are no special problems of experimental logic involved. Does this mean that behavioral researchers can never do experimental work on important questions of human development and human personality? Another approach to the problem has capitalized on the biological continuities between nonhuman organisms and human beings. Primates especially have been shown to share some attributes with humans sufficiently to make primates valuable, if far from exact or even very accurate, models for human behavior. We cannot, for the sake of furthering our knowledge of personality development, separate a human baby from its mother, but the important lessons we might learn from separation make it seem rational, if not easily (or readily) justifiable, to separate a nonhuman primate from its mother. (In chapter 3 we discuss ethical issues of research that have implications for nonhuman as well as human subjects.)

In their extensive research program at the University of Wisconsin at Madison, the Harlows and their coworkers used arrays of procedures and approaches of both the psychologist and the biologist, a typical technique in the field of comparative psychology. Much of the Harlows' research on the affectional system of monkeys was of the descriptive type (e.g., young monkeys become attached to other young monkeys) and of the relational type (e.g., male monkeys become more forceful with age, and female monkeys become more passive). However, our interest here is on their experimental research, although we will be able to describe only a fraction of it in this limited space.

As part of the research program, infant monkeys were separated from their mothers just a few hours after birth and were then raised by bottle with great success. The Harlows had been advised by another researcher, Gertrude van Wagenen, to have available for their infant monkeys some soft pliant surfaces, and folded gauze diapers were consequently made available to all the baby monkeys. The babies became very much attached to these diapers, so much so that the diapers could be removed for laundering only with great difficulty. These observations led to an experiment designed to show more systematically the shorter and longer term effects of access to a soft material. Also the research was planned to shed light on the relative importance to the development of the infant's attachment to its mother of being fed by her as opposed to being in close and cuddly contact with her (Harlow, 1959; Harlow & Harlow, 1966).

Accordingly, two "pseudomothers" were built: one, a bare welded-wire cylindrical form with a crude wooden head and face attached, and the other, a similar apparatus covered with soft terry cloth. Eight newborn monkeys were given equal access to the wire and the cloth mother figures, but four were fed at the breast of the wire mother and four were fed at the breast of the cloth mother. When the measures were of the amount of milk consumed or the amount of weight gained, the two pseudomothers made no difference. The monkeys fed by both drank about the same amount of milk and gained about the same amount of weight. But regardless of which mother had fed them, the baby monkeys spent much more time climbing on the cloth mother and clinging to her than they did the wire mother. That finding demonstrated the importance of what the researchers called "contact comfort"; it also appeared to imply that an earlier formulation of love for mother was really much too simple. That earlier theory held that mothers become prized because they are associated with the reduction of hunger and thirst. The Harlow results showed quite clearly that being the source of food is not nearly so good a predictor of a baby's subsequent preference as is being a soft and cuddly mother. When the monkeys were about 100 days old, they spent an average of approximately 15 hours a day on the cloth mother but only about 1.5 hours on the wire mother, regardless of whether it had been the cloth or the wire mother that had fed them.

Later experiments showed that when the infant monkey was placed into a fear-arousing situation, it sought out the cloth mother for comfort and reassurance. A frightened monkey, confronted by a mechanical bear that advanced while beating a drum, would flee to the cloth mother, secure a dose of reassurance, and then gradually explore the frightening object and turn it into a toy. When the cloth mother was not in the room, the infant monkeys hurled themselves to the floor, clutched their heads and bodies, and screamed in distress. The wire mother provided the infants no greater security or reassurance than no mother at all.

Robert A. Butler, a coworker of the Harlows, had discovered that monkeys enclosed in a dimly lit box would spend hour after hour pressing a lever that opened a window in the box and gave them a chance to see something outside. Monkeys barely able to walk pressed the lever for a brief peek at the world outside. One of the variables that determined how hard the monkey would work to look out the window was what there was to be seen. When the monkey infants we have been discussing were tested in the "Butler box," it turned out that they worked as hard to see their cloth mothers as to see another real monkey. However, they worked no harder to see the wire mother than to see nothing at all outside the box. Not only in that experiment, but to a surprising degree in general, a wire mother is not much better than no mother at all, but a cloth mother comes close to being as good as the real thing.

A number of the female monkeys became mothers themselves, although they had not had any monkey mothers of their own and no physical contact with agemates during the first year of their life (Harlow & Harlow, 1965). Compared to normal monkey mothers, those unmothered mothers were usually brutal to their firstborn offspring, hitting, kicking, and crushing them. Motherless mothers who were not brutal were indifferent. The most cheerful result of this experiment was that those motherless monkeys who went on to become mothers for a second time treated their second babies normally or even overprotectively.

A series of studies called for infant monkeys to be raised in social isolation (Harlow & Harlow, 1970). When the isolation was total, the young monkey was exposed to no other living human or nonhuman animal. All the monkey's physical needs were met in automated fashion. A major influencing factor was the length of isolation from birth: 0, 3, 6, or 12 months. All the monkeys raised in isolation were physically healthy, but when placed in a new environment, they appeared to crouch in terror. Those monkeys that had been isolated only 3 months recovered from their neurotic fear within a month or so. Those monkeys that had been isolated for 6 months never did quite recover. Their play behavior, even after 6 months, was minimal and isolated. Their social identity, when it did occur, was directed only toward other monkeys that had been raised in isolation.

Those monkeys that had been isolated for 12 months showed the most severe retardation of play and of the development of aggression. Apathetic and terrified, these monkeys were defenseless against the attacks of the healthy control group monkeys.

Longer term effects of early social isolation were also uncovered. Several years later, the monkeys that had been isolated for 6 months showed a dramatic change in their orientation to other monkeys. Whereas earlier they had been attacked by other monkeys and had not defended themselves, they had by now developed into patho-logical aggressors, attacking other monkeys large and small, acts virtually never occurring among normal monkeys of their age. Another long-term effect of early social isolation could be seen in the inadequacy of the sexual behavior of these mon-keys. Even females who had been only partially isolated in infancy avoided contact with breeding males; did not groom themselves; engaged in threats, in aggression, in clutching themselves and biting themselves; and often failed to support the male when mounting did occur. Normal females rarely engaged in any of these behaviors. Male monkeys who had been isolated showed even more serious sexual inadequacy than did the isolated females. When contrasted with normal males, they groomed less, threatened more, were more aggressive, initiated little sexual contact, engaged in unusual sex behavior, and almost never achieved intromission.

EMPIRICAL PRINCIPLES AS
PROBABILISTIC ASSERTIONS

From the results of the investigations we have described (and follow-up studies that were conducted), have emerged a number of empirically-based generalizations, or what we term **empirical principles.** We call them *empirical* because they are based on controlled empirical investigations, and we call them *principles* because we think of them not as universal laws, but rather as generally accepted scientific truths about how behavior is *likely* to manifest itself in the situations specified. Table 1.2 lists several other empirically based statements at the descriptive, relational, and experimental levels in three different areas of research. Notice that descriptive and relational statements are answers to how-questions, either "how things are" (descriptive) or "how things are in relation to other things" (relational). Experimental statements provide answers to why-questions, that is, "why things are the way they are." Each of these statements is presumed to have a reasonable likelihood of being *applicable, valid,* or *true* in a given set of circumstances. The term we will use for this likelihood, coined by philosopher Hans Reichenbach (1938), is an "implicit probability value," where *implicit* connotes that the probability value is usually unstated but is understood as implying that the statement is likely to be applicable, or valid, or true. Thus, we think of the empirical principles of the behavioral sciences as **probabilistic assertions,** on the assumption that, based on empirical evidence or probable reasons, each is reasonably likely to be applicable in the circumstances specified.

To take these ideas a step further, we borrow another distinction defined by Carl Hempel, which is called the *Hempel model* or the *Hempel-Oppenheim model* (Hempel & Oppenheim, 1965) or the *covering law model*. Hempel's view was that scientific principles can be cast as deductive arguments that contain at least one prem-ise that is universally true. The traditional form of an argument affirming that a

TABLE 1.2
Further examples of descriptive, relational, and experimental statements

Research area	Descriptive	Relational	Experimental
Primate behavior	Baboon groups vary in size from 9 to 185 (DeVore & Hall, 1965)	Baboon groups found at higher elevations tend to have fewer members (DeVore & Hall, 1965)	Monkeys separated from their mothers prefer cloth-covered mother surrogates to wire-mesh-type surrogates (Harlow, 1959)
Behavioral study of obedience	A majority of research subjects were willing to administer an allegedly dangerous level of electric shock to another person when requested to do so by a person in authority (Milgram, 1963)	Research subjects who are more willing to administer electric shocks to other persons report themselves as somewhat more tense during their research participation than do subjects who are less willing to apply shocks to others (Milgram, 1965)	Research subjects are less obedient to orders to administer electric shocks to other persons when they are in close rather than remote contact with these persons (Milgram, 1965)
Speech behavior	When people are being interviewed for civil service positions, the length of their utterances tends to be short in duration, with only a few lasting as long as a full minute (Matarazzo, Wiens, & Saslow, 1965)	In interviews with both normal subjects and mental patients, it was found that average speech duration was longer with normals and shortest with the most disturbed patients (Matarazzo et al., 1965)	In interviews with applicants for civil service positions, the length of the applicants' utterances could be approximately doubled simply by the interviewers' approximately doubling the length of their utterances (Matarazzo et al., 1965)

particular conclusion is true if its premises are true can be represented by the following syllogism: "All A is B; all B is C; therefore all A is C." A case in which both premises (i.e., a *and* b) are universally true would be (a) only mammals feed their young with milk from the female mammary glands; (b) whales feed their young from the female mammary glands; (c) therefore whales must be mammals. Since (a) and (b) are true, then (c) must be true; and given that (a) and (b) are universally true, (c) must be universally true as well. In other words, the conclusion is unequivocal. That form of reasoning has been termed **deductive-statistical explanation;** the word *statistical,* as used here, means that the deduced conclusion has an implicit likelihood associated with it. In this instance the implicit likelihood of being true is 100%.

Here is another example, but instead of stating the premises and conclusion as definitive assertions, we will express the premises more tentatively and the final statement in the form of a question: "If it is true that (a) all the coins in William's piggy bank are pennies and also true that (b) William draws a coin from his piggy bank, then (c) what is the likelihood that the coin is a penny?" The answer, of course, is 100%. Simply by restating one of the two premises (not both) as a percentage, we can also raise a question that implies a probabilistic conclusion: "If it is true that (a) 95% of the coins in Jane's piggy bank are pennies and also true that (b) Jane draws a coin from her piggy bank, then (c) what is the likelihood that the coin is a penny?" The answer is 95% and implies a probabilistic conclusion (i.e., "the coin is *probably* a penny"). The name of that kind of syllogistic argument, in which the conclusion is probabilistic, is **inductive-statistical explanation.** A hypothetical example in survey research might be (a) 80% of Maine residents are Republicans; (b) John Smith is a resident of Maine; (c) John Smith is *probably* a Republican (cf. Capaldi, 1969; Kourany, 1987). Although these are simplified examples, you can see how deductive-statistical explanation and inductive-statistical explanation might be used to justify an assertion that is either absolutely true (i.e., a "universal truth") or probably true (a probabilistic assertion).

Inductive-statistical reasoning, in turn, implies two fundamental ideas about probabilistic assertions: (a) They deal with relative uncertainty, and (b) they are not absolute, or what is called a *universal* (Landesman, 1971). Statements about behavior (such as the how and why-question statements in Table 1.2) are thus qualified and probabilistic. But even universals may be qualified statements, like Newton's previously discussed first law of motion. Another example in physics is the principle explaining changes that individual atoms undergo from one energy level to another. Given a very great many atoms, all capable of certain definite changes, physicists can predict what proportion will undergo each change but cannot predict with certainty what changes any given atom will undergo. As Einstein said, the changes are like "throwing dice." There are several reasons why empirical principles in the behavioral and social sciences are not able to specify *exactly* how an individual or a group will act at a given moment. Human behavior can be affected, for example, by (a) personal values and the individual's state of mind, (b) the nature of the situation at that historical moment, and (c) sociocultural conditions (which may not be very predictable). Social and idiosyncratic factors like these can, in turn, introduce variability and relative uncertainty (into premises) and are why we think of empirical principles in behavioral and social research not as universal truths, but as probabilistic assertions.

ORIENTING HABITS OF GOOD SCIENTIFIC PRACTICE

Social psychologist Judith Hall (1984a) observed that many methods texts are filled with guidelines for what results in good research, but not what results in a good researcher. She listed the following nine traits:

1. *Enthusiasm.* For Hall, enthusiasm meant a passion for the topic of inquiry as well as the actual activity of research. Another wise researcher, Edward C. Tolman (1959), once stated, "In the end, the only sure criterion is to have fun" (p. 152). He did not mean that good research is merely fun and games, but that the activity of research should be as engrossing as any game requiring skill that fills a person with enthusiasm. We would add that, like any game requiring skill, good

research also requires concentration. The good researcher enjoys the opportunity to concentrate on the research and to approach the written reporting of results with eagerness.

2. *Open-mindedness.* The good researcher sees the world with a keen, attentive, inquisitive, and open mind, because sometimes a great discovery is made by sheer luck (i.e., serendipity). The Harlows began to study the influence of different pseudomothers only after discovering that their baby monkeys became very much attached to some soft diapers. Open-mindedness allows us not only to learn from our mistakes, but to listen carefully to others' insights and criticisms.

3. *Common sense.* As Hall (1984a) noted, "All the book learning in the world cannot replace good sense in the planning and conduct of research" (p. v). The good researcher asks not only whether a plan is technically sound, but also whether it makes sense to look at a problem that particular way. There is an old axiom of science called the *principle of the drunkard's search:* A drunkard lost his house key and began searching for it under a street lamp even though he had dropped the key some distance away. Asked why he wasn't looking where he had dropped it, he replied, "There's more light here!" Much effort is lost or vitiated when the researcher fails to use good sense and frames a problem in a convenient way rather than in a way that is likely to lead to the right answers.

4. *Role-taking ability.* The good researcher thinks of herself or himself as the user of the research, not just as the person who has generated it. As Hall (1984a) noted, role-taking ability implies asking oneself questions like "Are my demand characteristics obvious?" "Are my questionnaire items ambiguous?" "Is the study so boring that my research subjects will stop functioning in a normal or intelligent way?" Role-taking ability also means being able to cast oneself in the role of critic in order to anticipate and address people who are determined to find fault with one's research.

5. *Inventiveness.* The good researcher is not only clever but also practices principled inventiveness, which means developing sound hypotheses and technical designs that are also ethically sound. Being inventive also means finding solutions to problems of financial resources, laboratory space, equipment, and the recruitment and scheduling of research participants. The good researcher responds to emergencies during the conduct of research, finds new ways to analyze data if called for, and comes up with honest, convincing interpretations of the results.

6. *Confidence in one's own judgment.* Tolman (1959) also said that great insights come when the scientist "has been shaken out of his up-until-then approved scientific rules" (p. 93), and that, given the intrinsic relative uncertainty of behavioral research, "the best that any individual scientist, especially any psychologist, can do seems to be to follow his own gleam and his own bent, however inadequate they may be" (p. 152). As another author said, "You have to believe that by the simple application of your own mind to the facts of experience, you can discover the truth—a little part of it anyway" (Regis, 1987, p. 209).

7. *Consistency and care about details.* The good researcher takes pride in his or her work, which implies a constructive attitude toward the relentless detail work involved in doing good research. The good researcher understands and accepts

that there is no substitute for accuracy and the hours of care needed to keep complete records, organize and analyze data accurately, state facts precisely, and proofread carefully.

8. *Ability to communicate.* Somebody (a procrastinator, no doubt) once described writing as an "unnatural act," but it is a skill that is basic to the practice of good research. It has been stated, "The literature of science, a permanent record of the communication between scientists, is also the history of science: a record of truth, of observations and opinions, of hypotheses that have been ignored or have been found wanting or have withstood the test of further observation and experiment" (Barrass, 1978, p. 25). Thus, the good researcher understands that "*scientists must write,* therefore, so that their discoveries may be known to others" (p. 25). Science is not an appropriate career for someone who finds it hard to sit down and write, or for someone who is undisciplined.

9. *Honesty.* Finally, the good researcher respects integrity and honest scholarship and abhors dishonesty and sloppiness. However, there is evidence that fraud in science is not uncommon and exists in many parts of the scientific community (e.g., rigged experiments, the presentation of faked results). Fraud is devastating to science because it undermines the basic respect for the literature on which the advancement of science depends (Koshland, 1988). The good researcher under- stands that safeguarding against dishonesty is the responsibility of each and every scientist, and it is a duty that must be taken very seriously (e.g., American Association for the Advancement of Science, 1988; American Psychological Association, 1973, 1982, 1998; Bridgstock, 1982; Sales & Folkman, 2000).

We will have more to say about ethical responsibility in chapter 3. Virtually all aspects of the research process are subject to ethical guidelines, and as a consequence, researchers are sometimes caught between conflicting scientific and societal demands. The Greek poet Archilochus once wrote, "The fox knows many things, but the hedge- hog knows one big thing" (Berlin, 1953). Throughout the formative years of behav- ioral research, successful researchers were like "hedgehogs," with a single, central vision of science as an "endless frontier" unencumbered by tough moral dilemmas (Holton, 1978). The situation now faced by researchers is far more complex because of the constantly evolving ethical rules to which all researchers are held. The develop- ment of behavioral research took root in the imagination and hard work of scientific hedgehogs, but the future belongs to the "foxes," that is, researchers who know and can deal with many things. The good researcher must be able to work effectively on ethical, substantive, and methodological levels simultaneously (Rosnow, 1997).

2

CONTEXTS OF DISCOVERY AND JUSTIFICATION

INSPIRATION AND EXPLANATION

The title of this chapter borrows from a traditional distinction made by the 20th-century German philosopher Hans Reichenbach (1938). Reichenbach used the term **discovery** to refer to the origin of ideas or the genesis of theories and hypotheses. As we will show, the circumstances conducive to stimulating new insights are as "nonspecific" as the energy used to excite a neuron. That is to say, a nerve impulse will occur whether your finger is hit with a hammer, slammed in a car door, or bitten by a dog. As long as the excitation is there, the result will be the same: ignition. In the same way, there is no single source of exciting ideas and hypotheses for research. Instead, many different circumstances can light the fuse of creative inspiration. We describe some of those circumstances in this chapter.

Justification, as the term is used here, refers to the processes by which hypotheses and theories are empirically adjudicated and logical conclusions are reached. Popper (1959, p. 109) recommended that *decision* be substituted for *justification,* on the grounds that a decision implies an active process in which a tentative conclusion is submitted to a "jury" for deliberation and a "verdict" on its acceptability. He added, however, that a jury of scientific peers' decision that a conclusion is justified does not mean that the decision cannot be overturned by some future argument. Verdicts tend to be reached in accordance with specific procedures, which, in turn, are governed by rules and conventions. Rules and conventions can change, particularly in the face of technological innovations, empirical observations, revolutionary theoretical insights, and historical events.

Later chapters focus on other aspects of the context of justification. In this chapter we review the logic and the limitations of a traditional "dichotomous decision-making paradigm" known as *null hypothesis significance testing* (NHST). This discussion is intended to serve as an introduction to our more detailed discussion (later in this book) of statistical power, effect size indicators, and the relationship between these concepts and the *p* value. In recent years there has been a spirited discussion in psychology of the limitations of NHST and how our science can be improved by adopting an alternative strategy (e.g., Bakan, 1967; Cohen, 1990, 1994; Danziger, 1985; Hagan, 1997; Harlow, Mulaik, & Steiger, 1997; Kirk, 1996; Loftus, 1996; Meehl, 1978; Morrison & Henkel, 1970; Nelson, Rosenthal, & Rosnow, 1986; Oakes, 1986; Pollard & Richardson, 1987; Rosenthal, 1968; Rosenthal & Rubin, 1985; Rosnow & Rosenthal, 1989; Rozeboom, 1960; Schmidt, 1996; Thompson, 1993, 1996; Zuckerman, Hodgins, Zuckerman, & Rosenthal, 1993). A task force sponsored by the American Psychological Association (Wilkinson & Task Force on Statistical Inference, 1999) proposed, among other things, that (a) the relationship between the independent and dependent variables (i.e., the *effect size*) becomes the primary coin of the realm when researchers speak of "the results of a study," and (b) there be an indication of the accuracy or reliability of the estimated effect size (e.g., a confidence interval placed around the effect size estimate).

THEORIES AND HYPOTHESES

Before proceeding, we want to distinguish between **theories** and **hypotheses,** and also to note that these terms are frequently used interchangeably. Hypotheses are sometimes referred to as *theoretical statements* or *theoretical propositions,* and theories are frequently described as *conjectural* (i.e., hypothetical formulations). Generally speaking, theories can be understood as aggregates of hypotheses (and other things, of course, like assumptions and facts). Popper (1959) called theories in the sciences "nets cast to catch what we call 'the world': to rationalize, to explain, and to master it" (p. 59). In psychology, another writer called theories "blueprints" designed to provide investigators with an overall conceptual plan (Overton, 1998). A further distinction is made between theories that are far-reaching (macrolevel theories) and those (microlevel) that focus on a specific phenomenon or activity (Kaplan, 1964). But whatever their particular level of abstraction or reach, theories are essentially explanatory shells for relationships, whereas hypotheses are conjectural instances that are typically derived from the theoretical assumptions of knowledge representations.

Broadly speaking, thinking inductively is thinking "theoretically." One of us lives near a dog park. The remarkable thing about the park is that dogs of all shapes, sizes, and kinds amiably interact. If any one of them should suddenly spot a squirrel or a cat that happens to wander in, virtually all the dogs seem to go berserk. They bark and chase the interloper until it climbs a tree or finds a hiding place. The dogs behave as if they recognize one another as a pack of "dogs" (even the tiniest ones that are no bigger than squirrels or cats) and have an inductive idea of what constitutes a "dog" and how dogs differ from squirrels and cats. Are dogs capable of theorizing in a way that might be analogous to humans' abstract concepts of classes of things, such as those entities we call "houses" (ranch, Cape Cod, bungalow, townhouse, and so on)? Feyerabend (the "anything-goes" theorist) believed that all human observations are theory-laden to some degree, inasmuch as human perceptions are colored by linguistic and cultural experiences. Dogs don't have a universal language or a culture (we presume), but is it plausible to think their observations are "theory-laden"? It is hard to imagine a world without theory-laden observations. Without the benefit of abstract concepts, how would we ever generalize beyond our immediate experience?

By tradition in science, theories and hypotheses are also presumed to be "testable." Testability in contemporary science means not that researchers simply try to "confirm" theories and hypotheses, but rather, according to Popper, that theories and hypotheses are stated in a way that should allow disconfirmation (falsification). We return to this idea shortly, but it further implies that theories and hypotheses give direction to researchers' observations. Popper illustrated this process by telling his students to "take pencil and paper; carefully observe, and write down what you have observed." They, in turn, invariably asked *what* it was he wanted them to observe, as observation needs a chosen object, a definite task, an interest, a point of view, and a problem (Popper, 1934, 1962). Popper answered, that the role of theories and hypotheses is to chart a direction for our observations and measurements. Of course, a theory cannot be sustained from top to bottom by those observations and measurements or (we might add) be decisively falsified by the results of a single experiment (though exceptions have been claimed in natural science).

SOURCES OF INSPIRATION AND INSIGHT

Discovery implies a bold new insight, or a creative inspiration, or a dramatic finding or application, like those of the legendary explorers Columbus, Balboa, and Magellan, or brilliant scientists like Newton and Einstein, or inventive geniuses like Edison and Bell. In the case of scientists, it is hard to imagine how momentous accomplishments can be achieved without singular brilliance. However, philosopher Peter Caws argued that scientific discovery is inevitable, not just due to one particular genius's inspiration. Caws (1969) recalled in Proustian detail the exact setting in which, as a schoolboy, he suddenly grasped the principle of linear simultaneous equations. He "saw, in a flash of intuition, why two equations were needed for two unknowns, and how the substitution from one equation in the other proceeded" (p. 1375). Many years later, he came to understand that the "Eureka feeling" he had experienced (as if he had invented simultaneous equations himself) was "a very poor index of success in the enterprise at hand" (p. 1375). The development of science, he argued, is "a stepwise process" that "starts from a large set of premises already demonstrated to be true" and that inevitably leads to a particular insight (pp. 1377, 1380). Presumably, that is also what Newton meant when he remarked about "standing on the shoulders of giants." According to Caws's argument, had Newton never lived, a similar theoretical insight would have emerged quite naturally once all the relevant evidence was in, because "scientific discovery is no less logical than deduction" (p. 1375).

In fact, there are many mundane examples of researchers coming up with hypotheses and research questions simply from knowing the relevant evidence or being familiar with a particular phenomenon. As Klahr and Simon (2001) noted, quite often "the discovery of a phenomenon led to a hypothesis, rather than a hypothesis leading to an experimental phenomenon" (p. 77). Simply observing something surprising is frequently enough to get a scientist "to ascertain the scope and import of the surprising phenomenon and its mechanisms" (p. 77). Although it is also true that many research questions are handed to investigators—for example, by advisers or by funding institutes and companies that seek information regarding matters of particular concern to them—more often than not researchers get ideas from reading narrowly within the explosion of millions of scientific abstracts that are published annually (Adair & Vohra, 2003) and by attending paper presentations and poster sessions. They read or listen with an open mind that is seeking exciting opportunities for research. William McGuire (1973, 1997), whose work we mentioned in the previous chapter, has listed a multitude of situations and creative heuristics for generating promising research ideas and hypotheses, and we have selected a few of them to illustrate.

Modifying a Classic Relationship

One useful strategy used to stimulate the imagination is to reverse a common relationship and to think about how to account for the reversal in a plausible way. As an illustration, Daryl Bem (1965, 1972) reversed the classic principle stating that attitudes shape behavior. Bem raised the possibility that behavior might also shape attitudes. A plausible example is a politician who takes a stand on an issue for the sake of expediency but, after defending it repeatedly, starts to think, "I really believe this stuff." Reflecting on your behavior may encourage you to shift your attitude, because you infer that your attitude resembles your behavior, Bem argued. Another example of the reversal strategy was described in detail by the sociologist Robert K. Merton (1968), who coined the term *self-fulfilling prophecy* to refer to his own variation on another classic principle called the *suicidal prophecy* by the logician John Venn. Venn's idea was that people's negative beliefs about certain outcomes can sometimes *inhibit* the occurrence of those outcomes, and Merton's twist on that theme was that beliefs can sometimes *facilitate* the occurrence of predicted events.

Using a Case Study for Inspiration

Another strategy that is used by behavioral and social scientists to come up with research-able ideas is to exploit a qualitative case study as a point of reference. The term *case study* refers to an in-depth analysis of an individual (as in a clinical case study) or a group of people with shared characteristics. There are numerous examples of case studies in clinical and educational psychology, as well as in other applied fields (Allport, 1937; Davison & Lazarus, 1995; Lazarus & Davison, 1971; McGuire, 1973, 1976; Merriam, 1988; Ragin & Becker, 1992). Davison (2000) mentioned how psychoanalytic case studies stressing developmental factors were exploited by psychoanalytically oriented authors to cast doubt on behaviorally oriented theories, whereas behaviorally oriented authors used their own case studies and reinforcement explanations to cast doubt on psychoanalytic interpretations. In one famous case study, psychologist Leo Kanner was engaged in clinical casework with disturbed children when he happened to notice certain striking similarities. To describe those similarities, Kanner (1943) proposed a new syndrome that he called "early infantile autism." Characterized by "impaired development in social interaction and communication and a markedly restricted repertoire of activity and interests," it is also referred to psychiatrically as *Kanner's autism* (American Psychiatric Association, 1994, p. 66).

Making Sense of a Paradoxical Situation

A situation that seems to cry out for new ideas can inspire clever researchers suddenly confronted with a paradoxical set of circumstances. An example in the field of social psychology involved Bibb Latané and John M. Darley (1970), who were confronted with a puzzling situation involving a lurid murder in the Queens section of New York City. A nurse named Kitty Genovese was coming home from work at 3 A.M. when she was set upon by a man who stabbed her repeatedly. More than three dozen of her neighbors came to their windows to see what was happening, but not one of them went to her aid or phoned for help when they heard her cries of terror (though it took the stalker over a half hour to murder her). Latané and Darley were struck by the paradox that, even though there were so many opportunities to assist Kitty Genovese, no one bothered to phone the police. The psychologists wondered whether the large number of onlookers might be the key to explaining the failures of intervention. The reason why *so many* people failed to intervene, Latané and Darley theorized, was that each onlooker believed that someone else would phone for help, and the result was a "diffusion of responsibility."

Metaphorical Thinking

Still another strategy is to use a metaphor or an analogy as a way to describe something (Holyoak & Thagard, 1995; Kolodner, 1993). McGuire (1964) employed a biological immunization analogy to come up with a strategy for "inoculating" people against the harmful effects of propaganda. He started with the idea that cultural truisms (e.g., the saying that eating healthy makes you live longer, or the maxim that brushing your teeth after you eat prevents tooth decay) exist in something analogous to a "germ-free" environment, inasmuch as truisms are hardly ever subject to attack. Therefore, he reasoned, they should be vulnerable to reversals when people who believe them are unexpectedly inundated by a massive amount of counterpropaganda. The situation reminded him of the person brought up in a germ-free environment who appears to be vigorously healthy but is highly vulnerable to a massive viral attack if he or she has not been vaccinated. From that analogy, McGuire logically developed specific hypotheses regarding ways to "vaccinate" people with weakened doses of counterpropaganda to help them build their defense against future massive attacks of the same counterpropaganda, without giving them the "disease."

In situations like these, the creative scientist is using a metaphor not as an aesthetic tool, as it is used by poets, but as an explanatory tool for conceptual comprehension and insight (Pepper, 1973). Another example is Stanley Milgram's (1970) use of a systems analogy to explain how people living in overcrowded urban areas, such as Manhattan, cope with sensory overload. Systems are designed to deal with overload, for instance, by disregarding unimportant input; Milgram's example was residing in a city that is so teeming with people that a person feels overloaded and ignores a sick drunk on the street. Another way that systems deal with overload is to allot less time to each stimulus; Milgram used the example of people who are consumed with making upward strides in their careers and end up spending less and less time with family members. Sharing the overload with an alternative system is also a coping mechanism; the human analogy is shifting change making from the harried bus driver to the passengers by requiring them to have exact bus fare. Systems can also block off certain stimuli before they can gain entry, as in using an answering machine to screen calls, or having an unlisted telephone number, or, when out for a walk, projecting an unfriendly appearance (uncivil behavior) in order to prevent any new contacts. Milgram postulated that one result of sensory overload is what earlier researchers called "deindividuation" (Festinger, Pepitone, & Newcomb, 1952), meaning that overloaded people feel they are no longer respected as individuals.

SERENDIPITY IN BEHAVIORAL RESEARCH

The examples we have described barely tap the wide range and variety of circumstances in which promising ideas are stimulated in science (McGuire, 1973, 1976). What all these cases seemed to have in common is the important element of keeping one's eyes and ears open to the world, because one never knows when a chance encounter will excite the creative mind. The term for lucky findings is **serendipity,** which was inspired by a 16th-century tale told of three princes of Serendip (now called Sri Lanka) who, through sagacity and luck, had fortuitous insights. The term *serendipity* was coined by Horace Walpole, an 18th-century English novelist. In current usage, serendipity usually implies a combination of accident and sagacity (Dean, 1977; Evans, 1993; Roberts, 1989).

For example, James Watson (1993), who was a codiscoverer of the DNA double helix, observed, "To have success in science, you need some luck" (p. 1812); he went on to illustrate that, had it not been for serendipity, he might never have gotten interested in genetics in the first place:

> I was 17, almost 3 years into college, and after a summer in the North Woods, I came back to the University of Chicago and spotted the tiny book *What Is Life* by the theoretical physicist Erwin Schrödinger. In that little gem, Schrödinger said the essence of life was the gene. Up until then, I was interested in birds. But then I thought, well, if the gene is the essence of life, I want to know more about it. And that was fateful because, otherwise, I would have spent my life studying birds and no one would have heard of me. (p. 1812)

In fact, as Watson (1969) recounted in his lively autobiographical description of the adventure of discovering the structure of the DNA molecule, his encounters with serendipity were not limited to that single incident.

The history of science is replete with examples of lucky encounters and great insights that were unanticipated (e.g., Dean, 1977; Roberts, 1989). A case in the area of behavioral psychology was recalled by Murray Sidman (1960), who described the behind-the-scenes details of a program of experiments by Joseph V. Brady in what came to be known as the *ulcer project*. Brady, who was then working at Walter Reed Army Hospital in Bethesda, Maryland, was conducting a series of experiments on

There are many, many ways scientists & researchers are inspired in their research ideas.

monkeys, using long-term conditioning, electric shocks, food reinforcements, and brain stimulation. There was an unusually high mortality rate among the monkeys, which Brady might have continued to treat simply as an unavoidable problem were it not for a remark made to him. A pathologist, R. W. Porter, who had heard about the large number of deaths, asked Brady for permission to do postmortems on the next five monkeys that died. During the following few months, Porter would occasionally appear in Brady's office holding a piece of freshly excised monkey gut. Somewhere in the tissue would invariably be a clear hole, which (Porter explained to Brady) was a perforated ulcer. One day, Porter remarked that, of several hundred monkeys he had examined before coming to Walter Reed, not one had shown any sign of an ulcer.

Hearing Porter's remark changed the course of Brady's thinking and research. He thought to himself: Could ulcers have something to do with the "executive" role the monkeys had been forced to play in the stress situation? He designed a new series of experiments in which monkeys were subjected to training in the avoidance of electric shock and were paired with other monkeys who received the same shocks but without the opportunity to avoid them. When the monkeys were examined, those forced to make "executive" types of decisions in the stress situation showed stomach ulcers, but the "subordinate" monkeys exhibited no unusual pathology (Brady, 1958; Brady, Porter, Conrad, & Mason, 1958). Porter's remark had inspired Brady to design a program of research to pinpoint the role enactments leading to stomach ulcers. Interestingly, later work revealed that rats that lacked "executive" control over stressful events suffered weight lost and ulcers from *not* being made the "executive" animal (Weiss, 1968).

This example shows not only that serendipity can sometimes start a researcher on a new path, but also that when a profound observation leads to further investigation, new observations may lead to dramatic new insights. "What marks the profound observer from the casual one is the ability to see a pattern or implication that has gone unnoticed and, having exposed it, to find it in other social settings," Fine and Deegan (1996, p. 439) wrote.

MOLDING IDEAS INTO WORKING HYPOTHESES

Once the scientist has an idea for an investigation, the next step is to weigh its credibility and value and, assuming it passes muster, to mold the idea into a working hypothesis. Questions that researchers ask themselves at this juncture generally pertain to (a) the novelty, utility, and consistency of the idea; (b) its testability and refutability; and (c) the clarity and conciseness of the statement of the idea in the form of a testable (and empirically refutable) working hypothesis.

Novelty, Utility, and Consistency

One question is whether others are likely to perceive the idea as novel (not merely as a minor variation on an older idea). Research findings from an idea regarded as merely a trivial departure or a minor contribution would be difficult to publish in a journal that other scientists were likely to read. Each month, there is a flood of journal articles in psychology and related fields. Publishing a paper that few people are apt to notice may add a line or two to one's résumé but is unlikely to have any significant impact on the field. According to popular wisdom, the bimodal citation rate for journal articles is 0 and 1, which, if correct, implies that the vast majority of articles sink without a ripple. Since it generally seems to take the same effort and preparation to conduct research on a novel hypothesis and on an old hypothesis, why bother with the latter? One good answer is that, in a systematic program of research, it is often valuable to perform experiments that are relatively exact replications or that contain only minor variations on previous studies. It is by means of those and of less exact attempted replications that researchers clarify and expand the meaning and generalizability of reported relationships (McGuire, 1986; Sidman, 1960).

By *utility* and *consistency,* we mean that researchers think about whether the idea seems useful in regard to some valued end (McGuire, 1986) and whether it seems consistent with what is generally known in their field. The question of utility does not *have* to pertain to a practical application, however, although many accomplished scientists certainly get their fulfillment from engaging in research with "purely utilitarian purposes" (Einstein, 1934, p. 1). However, *utility* might refer just as well to a theoretical incentive as to a practical end. Indeed, as Kurt Lewin, the father of modern experimental social psychology, asked: What is more useful than a good theory? Consistency with scientific truth implies that ideas that correspond closely with all the available evidence are likely to have a higher payoff potential. Caws (1969) suggested that there is then a "powerful Gestalt phenomenon," in which the researcher gets closure "by the addition of a premise which is the obviously missing one, the only one which fits in with the rest of the pattern" (p. 1377). That closure, he argued, is precisely what occurred in the case of evolutionary theory: "*All* the premises for the hypothesis of the origin of species through natural selection were present both for Darwin and for Wallace, and, once they had them all (including the indispensable contribution from Malthus), they both got the point at once" (p. 1377).

To ensure that ideas are novel, useful, and consistent, scientists review the literature and solicit the opinions of respected colleagues with common interests and sound critical judgment. However, as Medawar (1969) cautioned, there is no foolproof way of guaranteeing that one will not spend weary and scientifically profitless years pursuing some pet idea that, although it may have seemed plausible and exciting at the time, later proves groundless. Another potential risk is that accepted wisdom is not infallible. A famous case involved a young physicist, Michael Polanyi (1963), who in 1914 had recently published a formulation of the adsorption (adhesion) of gases on solids and, within a few years, had gotten what he believed was convincing empirical evidence to support his theory. Albert Einstein happened to be present for a conference at which Polanyi was a featured speaker, and Einstein soundly criticized Polanyi's "total disregard" of what was then "known" about the structure of matter. As it turned out, Polanyi's insight was in fact correct, and he was later awarded the Nobel Prize for his work. The lesson? Resist being blinded by what passes for "accepted wisdom" if your empirical data truly suggest an alternative. Science is certainly not lacking in cases in which leading scientists were unreceptive to bold new insights that, while they eventually proved correct, were ignored at the time because they seemed counter to popular understanding (Barber, 1961; Beveridge, 1957; Hurvich, 1969; Mahoney, 1976).

Testability and Refutability

Once one has decided an idea is worth pursuing, traditionally the next question is whether it is "testable" and can be stated in a hypothesis that can be empirically refuted. The reason why scientific hypotheses must be falsifiable is that, in a complex world, it is possible for someone with a fertile imagination to find "support" (e.g., in the form of "examples" and testimonials) to prop up any claim, even the most absurd fads, fallacies, cults, and ridiculous panaceas (M. Gardner, 1957). Suppose we said humans are direct descendants of extraterrestrials who, thousands of years ago, arrived in flying saucers to colonize Earth. Though that argument is not refutable by any conceivable observation, it would not be impossible for an active intellect to "find" or manufacture support for a prior existence on this planet of intelligent creatures from outer space. For this reason, astrology has been called the "prophecy that never fails." Those people who believe in it interpret all astrological prophecies only in ways that support their biases and gratify their superstitions (Bunge, 1982; Shermer, 1997; Weimann, 1982). Popper's idea was that it is not *verifiability,* but *falsifiability,* that is the essential difference between science and nonscience (or pseudoscience).

Although in physics, and perhaps some other areas, it might be possible to subject certain falsifiable consequences of theoretical conjectures to crucial experimental tests (and it is certainly true that Popper's idea of falsifiability is accepted by most scientists as essential), philosophers of science have often expressed skepticism about the idea of *crucial experimental tests* of theories or hypotheses. In a later chapter we describe Isaac Newton's famous *Experimentum Crucis* to prove that white light is a heterogeneous mixture. However, the idea of the "crucial instance" originated in English philosopher Francis Bacon's *Novum Organum* (*instantia crucis,* Bacon called it), originally published in 1620 (Bacon, 1994, p. 210). Modern philosophers have noted that the testing of theoretical conjectures or hypotheses in science often seems to take the form of looking for authentication. Some argue that it would be counter to human nature to expect scientists who have invested substantial intellectual and financial resources in their research to try to "prove that they are wrong." (It is not uncommon, of course, for scientists to attempt to show that some rival theory or hypothesis is wrong.) It is true that even when scientists find that their hypotheses or theories failed to stand up in some isolated test, they are usually loathe to concede the possibility that pet theoretical ideas could be wrong. Rather than abandon a favorite theory or hypothesis when faced with "crucial" unfriendly evidence, they think about what might have gone wrong in the testing process, or they think about how to adjust the theory or hypothesis so that it implies a higher order interaction, or they argue that the particular prediction did not accurately represent their theory, or that the results were analyzed incorrectly, or that some vital contextual boundaries were unexplored or left unspecified (McGuire, 1986).

Clarity and Conciseness

Let us assume the ideas the scientist has can be expressed in the form of falsifiable hypotheses. It is important that the terms used are clearly understood; that is, they must be properly defined. Traditionally, scientific terms in behavioral research are defined empirically and theoretically. The technical name for an empirically based definition is **operational definition;** an example is the definition of "need for social approval" by scores earned on the Marlowe-Crowne Social Desirability scale (chapter 1). In contrast to such operational definitions, **theoretical definitions** do not attempt to force our thinking into a rigidly empirical mold (Cronbach & Meehl, 1955; Cronbach & Quirk, 1971). In practice, the distinction between these two kinds of definitions is often blurred, however, and indeed, some philosophers and behavioral researchers have recommended abolishing the distinction as merely an outmoded remnant of positivism (e.g., Campbell & Fiske, 1959; Feyerabend, 1988).

The term *operational definition* was first proposed by the physicist Percy W. Bridgman (1927), who contended that in science the "concept [the term requiring definition] is synonymous with the corresponding set of operations" (p. 5). Another name for this thesis is **operationalism,** that is, the idea that scientific concepts can be defined on empirical grounds by certain specifiable observational procedures. Subsequently, Bridgman (1945) modified his view, once he realized that it is not always possible (or even necessary) to define every theoretical concept in observational terms. For example, physicists speak meaningfully of the "weight of an object while it is falling," although the only instruments for observing its weight would require that its motion be stopped (Easley, 1971; Easley & Tatsuoka, 1968). Thus, it is said that operational definitions generally "underdetermine" (i.e., only partly define) perfectly valid concepts, and therefore it is necessary to measure a given concept by many different operations—Campbell and Fiske's (1959) strategy of multiple operationalism.

The difficulty in trying to define a theoretical concept by a single method is illustrated by the concept of aggression. Many world bodies—from the 1915 Congress of Vienna, and the Hague and Versailles peace conferences, to the United Nations—have struggled with the definition of aggression. One French law expert who had been asked to define aggression concluded, after exhaustive review, that he was like the person asked to define an elephant: He did not know how to do it, but he knew it was something big (Shenker, 1971). Rosenzweig (1977) mentioned that the United Nations held more than 25 years of off-and-on discussions by various committees before anything like an adequate definition of aggression was accepted. Like any other aspect of behavior, aggression does not occur in a social vacuum but takes its meaning from the total context in which it occurs, and simply varying the perspective context can alter perceptions of the "aggressiveness" of behavior (e.g, Crabb & Rosnow, 1988). Indeed, the very same behavior may be called aggressive or defensive depending on which side of the fence one is viewing it from. Nonetheless, there have been valiant attempts to develop unambiguous definitions of aggression.

For example, one researcher (Rosenzweig, 1977, 1981) defined aggression in theoretical terms as "generic assertiveness which includes both constructive and destructive behaviors" of various kinds, and he operationalized it by using scores on a "picture-frustration test" he had developed. Table 2.1 lists additional definitions of aggression, which, like Rosenzweig's, also imply motive or intent as a necessary defining feature ("intended to inflict pain," "goal of harming or injuring," "drives toward change"). But how shall we objectively measure motive or intent empirically? We cannot intrude into people's "intentions" to perceive them directly. We might ask them to confess their motives and feelings, but there is never a guarantee they will be forthcoming, or that they will not fabricate an answer to trick or try to impress us. Some people define aggression in quite general terms, for example, "the delivery of

TABLE 2.1
Some definitions of aggression

"A response intended to inflict pain or discomfort" (Averill, 1982, p. 30)

"Any form of behavior directed toward the goal of harming or injuring another living being who is motivated to avoid such treatment" (R. A. Baron, 1977, p. 7)

"Drives toward change, even against the will of others" (Galtung, 1972, p. 85)

"The fighting instinct in beast and man which is directed *against* members of the same species" (Lorenz, 1971, p. ix)

"The use or threat of force, in territory not clearly one's own, without clear evidence that a majority of the emotionally involved people in that territory want such intervention" (R. K. White, 1984, p. 14)

"Any and every activity of an animal that is directed toward another animal and that inflicts partial or complete destruction upon that animal or that is associated with a high probability of so doing" (Zillman, 1979, p. 16)

some measurable injury to another organism" (Baenninger, 1980)—but, it could be argued, this definition would include surgeons and dentists and leave out aggressive threat displays of the kind that some comparative psychologists study (e.g., threat displays in Siamese fighting fish). Another definition states that aggression is an "actual or threatened delivery of either physical or psychological intent to injure" (Baenninger, 1988). By that definition, an aggressor need not actually do anything physically, and the victim need not show any actual effect of the interaction (or even be aware of the implied aggression).

Another alternative to trying to condense the definition of a psychological concept into a single sentence (or into a single measuring operation) is to formulate a *typology* (i.e., a systematic classification of types). Table 2.2 illustrates this alternative approach by showing one researcher's typology of various kinds of aggression, which

TABLE 2.2
A typology of aggression showing all possible classes of aggressive behaviors in humans

		Physical aggression	Verbal aggression
Active aggression	Direct aggression	Punching someone	Insulting someone
	Indirect aggression	Playing a practical joke on someone	Maliciously gossiping about someone
Passive aggression	Direct aggression	Blocking someone's passage	Refusing to talk to someone
	Indirect aggression	Refusing to do some necessary task	Refusing to give one's consent

Note: Adapted from "Aggression Pays," by A. H. Buss. In J. L. Singer (Ed.), 1971, *The Control of Aggression and Violence*, New York: Academic Press. Adapted by permission of the author and Academic Press.

avoids the problem associated with boiling a quite complex concept down to a single measuring operation (Buss, 1971). That researcher's typology was developed intuitively, but it is possible to use a logical technique known as **facet analysis** to formulate a classification system based on assumed structural patterns; the facets are thought of as dimensions of the construct of interest (Foa, 1963, 1965, 1968, 1971). Another approach is to use descriptive quantitative procedures, such as factor analysis or a multidimensional scaling procedure, to identify the dimensions of interest and then the locations of classes of variables along the dimensions. Thus, the idea behind formulating a typology is to try to step beyond the assumption that it is possible to identify a concept with just a single measuring operation.

Assuming the researcher has properly defined everything, the last question is whether the precise statement of the hypothesis "sticks together" logically (called *coherence*) and whether it is as simple as necessary (called *parsimony*). To that end, scientists are said to use an intellectual ruminative and winnowing process called **Occam's razor** to "cut away" what is superfluous. The use of this sculpting process takes its name from William of Ockham, a 14th-century English scholastic philosopher and Franciscan, who was known to his fellow friars as *doctor invincibilis*. Occam's razor requires us to "cut away" what is unnecessary or unwieldy, because what can be explained on fewer principles or with fewer entities is explained needlessly by more. Occam's razor may not apply to nature, however, because nature can be quite complicated (Battig, 1962; Kazdin & Kagan, 1994; Luchins & Luchins,1965). It is simply the principle that we ought to state our hypotheses as succinctly as we can, but not to go too far, or to cut off too much—or, as is sometimes said, not to cut off "chins" but only "beards."

POSITIVISM, FALSIFICATIONISM, AND CONVENTIONALISM

Before moving on, we will pick up a thread from this and the previous chapter, in which we alluded to the distinction between positivism and falsificationism. We will briefly describe the development of these two positions, still another position called *conventionalism,* and summarize what seems to be the currently accepted, hybrid position of most working scientists.

Positivism

The term *positivism* (or *positivisme*) was coined by the French philosopher and sociologist Auguste Comte in the 19th century. He envisioned that sociology (another term he coined) could, by embracing the "positive observational" approach that had served chemistry and physics so well, develop into a natural science, which he called "social physics" (Andreski, 1974, p. 27). Those who rejected this visionary methodology he dismissed with the derogatory label of *negativiste* (i.e., the opposite of a positivist). Over time, Comte became so enthralled and hypnotized by his own ideas that he began to apply them to virtually everything, calling one of his books *Positivist Catechism* and suggesting that positivism was like a new religion; he formulated detailed prescriptions for daily worship that included a substitute for the sign of the cross (Andreski, 1974, p. 9).

Logical positivism, simply called *positivism* by many writers, evolved in the 1920s and reigned supreme in philosophy for another two decades. In Austria, where the logical positivist movement first took hold, it was inspired both by seminal work in philosophy (W. M. Simon, 1972) and by observational scientific work. Led by Moritz Schlick, an eminent professor of philosophy at the University of Vienna, a group of celebrated intellectuals in philosophy, economics, mathematics, and social science (such as Rudolf Carnap, Gustav Bergmann, and Kurt Gödel) met for seminar discussions, calling themselves the Vienna Circle. The idea was proposed that, just as there was a sound verifiable basis of knowledge in natural science, there could be a similar objective foundation for philosophical propositions. Not all propositions, of course, are predicated on empirically based assumptions (e.g., ethical and metaphysical assertions), but the idea was that statements authenticated by sensory experience are more likely to be true. Logical positivism was said to provide a foundation for knowledge similar in spirit to Cartesian skepticism (*cogito ergo sum*: "I think, therefore I am"—the philosophical principle of René Descartes), although with the stipulation that it is our ability to experience the material world (not just our ability to ruminate on sense experiences) that might serve as a positive basis of knowledge that "cannot be doubted." Among the guests from abroad who visited the Vienna Circle were the American philosopher W. V. Quine and the British philosopher A. J. Ayer. In 1936, Ayer expounded on logical positivism in a book, *Language, Truth and Logic,* that made him into an instant celebrity in academic circles (Edmonds & Eidinow, 2001). Until it was overturned by a series of developments, the positivist position ruled the academic roost in European and British philosophy in the mid-20th century.

However, one crack in the positivist foundation had been anticipated by the 18th-century Scottish philosopher David Hume, who wrestled with induction well before the idea of positivism was even a gleam in Comte's eye. In what was similar to what we called probabilistic assertions in chapter 1, Hume argued that "all knowledge resolves itself in probability" (Hume, 1978, p. 181), and thus it is impossible to prove beyond doubt that a generalization is incontrovertibly true. The possibility always remains that an exception is lurking in the shadows somewhere. Furthermore, it is human nature to explain away exceptions. A classic illustration is the generalization that "all swans are white": If I say, "Look, there's a black swan," you might say, "Yes, I see it is black, but I wouldn't call it a swan." Popper recognized the slippery slope of this dilemma, but he perceived a way of phrasing conjectures that seemed to avoid the problem. In chapter 1 we mentioned Popper's derogatory appellation of positivism as the "bucket theory of the mind" because it assumed that knowledge proceeds from observation to generalizable knowledge. His "searchlight" metaphor implied that risky conjectural propositions (i.e., those that are falsifiable) can be adjudicated by critical observations and debate. For some time, in fact, it was true that doubt and skepticism had been growing even among members of the Vienna Circle, and Popper's insights reinforced those misgivings. The final demoralizing blow occurred in June 1936, when Schlick, while on his way to deliver a lecture at the University of Vienna, was shot to death by a crazed student. This was during a period of increasingly pro-Nazi sentiment in Austria, and passions and hatred had been inflamed against intellectuals, whose views were said to be a threat to the "new world order." These events conspired to lead to the demise of the Vienna Circle and also signaled the beginning of the end of logical positivism. In an absorbing account of that period, Edmonds and Eidinow (2001) noted that Ayer, when later asked about the failings of logical positivism, replied, "Well I suppose that the most important of the defects was that nearly all of it was false" (p. 157).

Falsificationism

In 1934, Popper had published the German edition of his seminal book, *Logik der Forschung (The Logic of Scientific Discovery)*. In 1936, he left Austria to accept a permanent lectureship at Canterbury University College in Christchurch, New Zealand. After World War II, he emigrated to England and spent the remainder of his academic career at the London School of Economics. As he later described his own thinking, it was quite early in his career that he began to harbor doubts about the verification principle that was the foundation of positivism. In 1919–1920, while he was still a student, he was led to what he later described as certain "inescapable conclusions," on the basis of which he formulated his own antipositivist view, *falsificationism*. As he recollected, he had originally dismissed his own ideas as "almost trivial" and did not recognize their full scientific importance or their philosophical significance until a fellow student suggested they be published. In the 1940s, Popper presented the lecture in which he first invoked the "bucket theory" metaphor to disparage the positivist strategy of verification.

Like the logical positivists, Popper was not only an empiricist but also a scientific realist (i.e., he believed in universal truths and assumed the existence of an objective reality quite apart from our perceptions or experience of it). Where he took issue with them, however, was in their faith in the verifiability principle. Popper's favorite examples of the absurdity of the positivist strategy were Marxist theory, Freudian psychoanalysis, and Alfred Adler's individual psychology:

> A Marxist could not open a newspaper without finding on every page confirming evidence for his interpretation of history; not only in the news, but also in its presentation—which revealed the class bias of the paper—and especially of course in what the paper did *not* say. The Freudian analysts emphasized that their theories were constantly verified by their "clinical observations." As for Adler, I was much impressed by a personal experience. Once, in 1919, I reported to him a case which to me did not seem particularly Adlerian, but which he found no difficulty in analyzing in terms of his theory of inferiority feelings, although he had not even seen the child. Slightly shocked, I asked him how he could be so sure. "Because of my thousandfold experience," he replied; whereupon I could not help saying, "And with this new case, I suppose your experience has become thousand-and-one-fold." (Popper, 1963, p. 35)

The falsifiability criterion has for some years been the standard in science to which other views of the justification of knowledge are compared (W. M. Simon, 1972). In philosophy of science, however, it is only one of a number of views that have superseded the logical positivist position (Stockman, 1983). To be considered scientific, according to the "fallibilists" (Popper's name for people who embraced falsificationism), the proposition in question (a certain theoretical prediction, for example) must be stated in such a way that it can, if incorrect, be rejected by some finite set of observations. That viewpoint does not simply mean, however, that because certain predictions fail a test, the theory is automatically wrong. But if one theory (call it T_1) is more falsifiable than another theory (T_2), and if T_1 has survived more severe empirical testing than T_2, it is presumed that T_1 must be a better theory than T_2. Popper's quarrel with Marxism, Freudian psychoanalysis, and Adlerian psychology was that there "seemed to be an incessant stream of confirmations, of observations which 'verified' the theories in question; and this point was constantly emphasized by their adherents" (Popper, 1963, p. 35).

In theory, that all sounds very reasonable, but in practice, there were several problems with Popper's conceptualization. First, unless a theory is restricted to a single statement, it is hard to imagine how the entire theory might be falsified by even the most reliable observation. Theories, at least in the behavioral and social sciences, are usually so amorphous and cryptic that substantial portions may extend beyond the range of empirical observations, or beyond a single set of observations. The elimination of part of a theory may be possible, but it would hardly constitute rejection as required by falsificationism. Second, social and behavioral scientists do not always agree on what constitutes an adequate test of a theory, or even on how to analyze and interpret the results in order to falsify the theory. Third, it could be argued that finding circumstances in which a theory does not hold may be tacit evidence of the circumscribed nature of all knowledge. In the previous chapter we mentioned Heisenberg's idea that grand theories in physics are "closed off" in ways that cannot be precisely specified. As humans are neither prescient nor omniscient, it is impossible to foresee the exact boundaries of any given theory (Heisenberg, 1971). Similarly, it has been argued that theories in psychology are constrained by boundaries that may forever wait to be discovered (Rosnow, 1981; Rosnow & Georgoudi, 1986).

Conventionalism

If scientific theories do not develop in the way that falsificationism described, then how do they grow and evolve? Still another view, called **conventionalism,** plays on the role of language. This position, known as the *Duhem-Quine thesis,* originating in the work of French physicist, philosopher, and historian of science Pierre Duhem (who has frequently been identified with the positivist tradition), was later refined by American philosopher W. V. Quine (whose name was mentioned earlier in this discussion). One of its implications is that scientific theories can never be logically refuted by any body of evidence (Laudan, 1982; Nye, 1985). The reason generally offered is that theories evolve ostensibly on the basis of certain linguistic conventions (like "simplicity"), not merely on the basis of their ability to withstand empirical disconfirmation. Thus, if there are no such things as completely decisive falsifying tests, the possibility of a crucial experiment (*experimentum crucis*) must be a myth. What happens when a "refutation" occurs? According to Duhem (1954), it is usually taken as a signal that the theory needs tinkering or adjustment, not that it must be discarded. Thus, whereas Popper argued that new theories replace outmoded theories in a scientific game of empirical jeopardy, the Duhem-Quine thesis implies that scientific theories are fluid, and that new ideas or findings may become appendages of older theories. Sometimes, however, the modifications are so fundamental that it is difficult to recognize the old theory, or impossible to use the new theory to explain phenomena accounted for by the old theory.

A prominent example of such a metamorphosis is the evolution of cognitive dissonance theory (Festinger, 1957). Leon Festinger got his initial inspiration in the 1950s, after reading an article by the noted Indian psychologist Jamuna Prasad (1950) that described the aftermath of terrible earthquakes in India. Festinger was puzzled by Prasad's report that villagers several miles away from one earthquake had been swamped in rumors of impending disasters. That finding did not seem to make sense, because the rumors predicting a further calamity were being spread by those who had not been harmed by the earthquake. Festinger cleverly reasoned that, having no concrete grounds for their anxiety, the earthquake survivors had unconsciously manufactured a rationale that was consistent in their thinking and reduced their cognitive dissonance. This drive, *dissonance reduction,* then became the basis of one of the most influential theories in social psychology and, in the 1960s, stimulated an enormous amount of research to test various claims and assumptions of how dissonance arose, affected cognition and behavior, and could be reduced. According to Festinger's theory, the dissonance produced by discrepant cognitions functions in the same way as a biological drive: If we are hungry, we do something to reduce our feeling of hunger; if we experience cognitive dissonance, we do something to reduce our discomfort. Countless studies followed, resulting in a series of emendations of Festinger's theory. As a result of all the additions and modifications, cognitive dissonance theory now asserts that being responsible for one's own actions is essential for dissonance reduction to occur. But how could the earthquake survivors have possibly felt responsible for their own survival? The disaster must have come as a complete surprise to them, and their personal survival was beyond their own control (although some may have rationalized that it was the responsibility of a divine will). Ironically, the old theory of cognitive dissonance is no longer serviceable, and the new theory cannot explain the results that inspired Festinger in the first place (Greenwald & Ronis, 1978).

An Amalgamation of Ideas

The views of most pragmatic behavioral researchers about the requirements of scientific theories and hypotheses now seem a mixture of falsificationism, conventionalism, and practicality. As is consistent with Popper's argument, most would agree (a) that a theory or hypothesis, to be considered scientific, must be stated in a form so that, if it is false, aspects can be disconfirmed by a finite set of observations (called "finite testability" by H. A. Simon, 1983, p. 355), and (b) that a scientific theory or hypothesis can only be falsified and can never be proved correct. Consistent with the Duhem-Quine thesis, most behavioral researchers would also probably agree (c) that (in actuality) scientific theories can evolve as additions to, as well as replacements of, outmoded models of behavior. However, they would perhaps add (d) that if a conjectural proposition does not receive support, the theoretical model on which it is based *might* not be right. But (e) if a formulation of behavior is repeatedly not supported, despite every attempt by scientists to produce rigorously designed tests, then it may be discarded or revised. However, (f) if a working hypothesis derived from a theory *is* supported, the model on which the hypothesis is based is not immediately proved to be correct, as it is impossible to rule out the prospect that a theory still waiting to be created might better account for all the existing results. Nonetheless, (g) as no experiment is entirely free of all alternative explanations, those known and those waiting to be discovered, both findings consistent and findings inconsistent with a theory's predictions can have probative value (Brinberg, Lynch, & Sawyer, 1992). Of course, for all these criteria to be applicable, the theory must also be precisely articulated so there will be no confusion or disagreement about what is asserted or predicted (H. A. Simon, 1979; Simon & Groen, 1973).

TYPE I AND TYPE II DECISION ERRORS

We turn now to null hypothesis significance testing (NHST), the dichotomous decision-making process in which a hypothesis to be nullified (called the **null hypothesis,** symbolized as H_0) is contrasted with a specific working hypothesis (called the **alternative hypothesis, H_1**). In most cases in behavioral research, the H_0 implies that no relationship between two variables is present in the population from which the sample data were drawn, or that there is no difference in the responses of treated and untreated subjects to an experimental manipulation, whereas H_1 does imply a relationship or real difference. Table 2.3 is a traditional way of representing four possible outcomes of NHST. The mistake of rejecting H_0 when it is true and should not have been rejected is called **Type I error,** and the mistake of not rejecting H_0 when it is false and should have been rejected is called **Type II error.** The ***p* value** (or **significance level**) indicates the probability of Type I error and is denoted as **alpha (α)** when *p* has been stipulated in advance (as a threshold or cutoff point). The probability of Type II error is symbolized as **beta (β). Confidence,** defined as $1 - \alpha$, is the probability of not making a Type I error. The **power of a test,** or $1 - \beta$, indicates the probability of not making a Type II error (i.e., the sensitivity of the significance test in providing an adequate opportunity to reject H_0 when it warrants rejection). As NHST is now construed, it is a hybrid

TABLE 2.3
Four outcomes involving the decision to reject or not to reject the null hypothesis (H_0)

Scientist's decision	Actual state of affairs	
	Null hypothesis is true	Null hypothesis is false
Reject null hypothesis	Type I error refers to a decision to reject H_0 when it is true and should not be rejected. Alpha (α) is the probability of Type I error.	No error. Statistical power ($1 - \beta$) refers to the probability of not making a Type II error.
Do not reject null hypothesis	No error. The confidence level ($1 - \alpha$) refers to the probability of not making a Type I error.	Type II error refers to a failure to reject H_0 when it is false and should be rejected. Beta (β) is the probability of Type II error.

endeavor that evolved out of the work (and arguments) of several different statisticians (for historical accounts, see Gigerenzer, Swijtink, Porter, Daston, Beatty, & Krüger, 1989; Stigler, 1986).

It has been well documented that behavioral researchers (as well as many other scientists who use NHST) have gotten into the habit of worrying more about Type I errors than about Type II errors. Some philosophers have suggested that this greater concern over Type I errors reflects the "healthy skepticism" of the scientific method (Axinn, 1966; Kaplan, 1964), the idea being that Type I error is an error of "gullibility," and Type II error is an error of "blindness." An analogy of Wainer's (1972) helps illustrate what is implied by this use of the terms *gullibility* and *blindness*. Suppose you were walking along the street and a shady character approached and said he had a quarter to sell you "for only five dollars." You might say to yourself, "He must think I'm stupid to ask me to hand over five dollars for an ordinary quarter." As if reading your mind, he says, "Don't think it's an ordinary quarter, pal, but one with special properties that make it worth five dollars. This quarter doesn't just come up heads and tails equally often; it is a biased coin. If you're as shrewd as you look, you're going to win fame and fortune by simply betting on which outcome is the more likely."

In this illustration we will think of the alternative hypothesis (H_1) as predicting that the probability of heads is not equal to the probability of tails in the long run. And since the null (H_0) hypothesis and the alternative hypothesis are mutually exclusive, we think of H_0 as predicting that the probability of heads *is* equal to the probability of tails in the long run. Thus, if H_0 is true, H_1 cannot be true. In Table 2.4 we have recast this situation into the framework of Table 2.3. The implication of Table 2.4 is that "Type I error" is analogous to being "taken in" by a false claim that the coin is biased when it is merely an ordinary coin (i.e., an error of gullibility), whereas "Type II error" is analogous to failing to see that the coin is biased as claimed (i.e., an error of blindness). We could subject H_1 to an empirical test by flipping the coin a large number of times and recording each time whether it landed heads or tails. We could state a particular probability (p value) as our alpha rejection criterion and be as stringent as we like in setting such a rejection criterion. However, we may eventually pay for this decision by failing to reject what we perhaps should reject.

TABLE 2.4
Example illustrating definitions of type I and type II errors

	Actual state of affairs	
Your decision	**The coin is fair**	**The coin is not fair**
The coin is not fair (i.e., it can win you fame and fortune, since it will not come up heads and tails equally).	Error of "gullibility"	No error
The coin is fair (i.e., it cannot win you fame and fortune, since it is just an ordinary coin).	No error	Error of "blindness"

STATISTICAL SIGNIFICANCE AND THE EFFECT SIZE

Because a complete account of "the results of a study" requires that the researcher report not just the p value but also the effect size, it is important to understand the relationship between these two quantities. The general relationship, which we will refer to again in the second half of this book, is given by

Significance test = Size of effect × Size of study.

In other words, the larger the study in terms of the total number (N) of observations or sampling units, or the larger the effect size, the larger the value of the significance test (e.g., t, F, χ^2) and, therefore, the smaller (and usually more coveted) the p value. This is true unless the size of the effect is truly zero, in which case a larger study (i.e., a larger N) will not produce a result that is any more significant than a smaller study (although effect sizes of exactly zero are rarely seen in behavioral research). A further implication of this general relationship is that if we are able to specify any two of these three factors, the third can be determined. Thus, if we know the level of risk of drawing a spuriously positive conclusion (i.e., the p value) and can estimate what the size of the effect will be, we can readily determine how large a total sample we will need to achieve a desired level of statistical power. (We show how in chapter 12.)

In fact, any particular test of significance can be obtained by one or more definitions of the effect size multiplied by one or more definitions of the study size. For example, if we were interested in chi-square (discussed in detail in chapter 19), we could write

$$\chi^2_{(1)} = \phi^2 \times N, \tag{2.1}$$

where $\chi^2_{(1)}$ is a chi-square on 1 degree of freedom (e.g., from a 2 × 2 table of counts), ϕ^2 is the squared Pearson product-moment correlation between membership in the row category (scored 1 or 0) and membership in the column category (scored 1 or 0), and N (the study size) is the total number of sampling units (e.g., found in the cells of the 2 × 2 table). (We will see Equation 2.1 again later in this book.)

Were we interested in t as a test of significance (discussed in chapter 12), we would have a choice of many equations (Rosenthal, 1991a, 1994b), of which two are

$$t = \frac{r}{\sqrt{1 - r^2}} \times \sqrt{df} \tag{2.2}$$

and

$$t = \frac{M_1 - M_2}{\sigma_{\text{pooled}}} \times \frac{\sqrt{df}}{2}, \tag{2.3}$$

where, in Equation 2.2, r is the point-biserial Pearson r between group membership (scored 1 or 0) and obtained score. In Equation 2.3, the effect size indicator is represented as Cohen's d (i.e., the difference between means, M_1 and M_2, divided by the pooled standard deviation, σ). In both equations, df is the degrees of freedom (usually $N - 2$). (We will see Equations 2.2 and 2.3 later in this book as well.)

When the relationship between statistical significance and the effect size is understood, it is less likely that researchers who employ NHST will do significance testing with low power. In the 1960s and later, Jacob Cohen hammered this point home in articles and a handy reference text on the analysis of statistical power (e.g., Cohen, 1962, 1965, 1988). To illustrate, suppose Smith conducts an experiment (with $N = 80$) to show the effects of leadership style on productivity and finds that Style A is better than Style B. Jones, however, is skeptical (because he invented Style B) and repeats Smith's study with $N = 20$. Although Jones's results are clearly in the same direction as Smith's, Jones nevertheless reports a "failure to replicate" because his t was only 1.06 ($df = 18$, $p > .30$), whereas Smith's t was 2.21 ($df = 78$, $p < .05$). Although it is certainly true that Jones has not replicated Smith's t test result or p value, the magnitude of the effect obtained by Jones (as measured by the Pearson correlation statistic) is $r = .24$, which is exactly the size of the effect in Smith's study! In other words, Jones has found exactly the same relationship that Smith found even though the obtained t and p values of the two studies are not very close. Because Jones's total sample size (N) was so much smaller than Smith's total sample size, Jones's *power* to reject at $p = .05$ is substantially less than Smith's power. In this case the power (i.e., $1 - \beta$) of Jones's t test is .18, whereas the power of Smith's t test is .57.

TWO FAMILIES OF EFFECT SIZES

Two of the most important families of effect sizes in behavioral and social science are the *correlation family* and the *difference family,* and we will discuss in more detail examples of each of these classes later in this book. There is also a third family, which we call the *ratio family,* and within these three families there are subtypes as well (Rosnow & Rosenthal, 2003). Three primary members of the difference family are Cohen's *d* (i.e., the effect size component of Equation 2.3), Hedges's *g,* and Glass's Δ. All three of these effect size indices employ the same numerator (the difference between the means of the two groups that are being compared), but each uses a slightly different denominator:

$$\text{Cohen's } d = \frac{M_1 - M_2}{\sigma_{pooled}} \tag{2.4}$$

$$\text{Hedges's } g = \frac{M_1 - M_2}{S_{pooled}} \tag{2.5}$$

$$\text{Glass's } \Delta = \frac{M_1 - M_2}{S_{control}}, \tag{2.6}$$

with terms in Cohen's *d* as indicated previously (Equation 2.3). In Equation 2.5, S is the square root of the pooled unbiased estimate of the population variance. In Equation 2.6, the $S_{control}$ is like the S in the denominator of Hedges's *g*, but it is computed only for the control group. Computing S only from the control group is a useful procedure when we know or suspect that the treatment may affect not only the mean but also the variance of the scores in the treatment condition.

The second important family of effect sizes is the *correlation family*. In Equation 2.1 we noted a popular incarnation of this family, the phi coefficient (ϕ), which is a special case of the Pearson product-moment r when both variables are dichotomous. In Equation 2.2 we noted another special case, the point-biserial correlation (r_{pb}), which is the Pearson product-moment correlation between a dichotomous variable and a continuous variable. Also included in the correlation family is z_r (the Fisher transformation of r) and various squared indices of r and r-like quantities such as r^2 (called the *coefficient of determination*), Ω^2 (omega squared), ε^2 (epsilon squared), and η^2 (eta squared). Because squared correlational indices lose their directionality (Is the treatment helping or hurting, is the correlation positive or negative?), they are of little use as effect size indices in scientific work in which information on directionality is essential. There are several other reasons that we prefer the product-moment r rather than squared indices, and we explain those reasons in chapters 11 and 12. To anticipate a little, another reason is that squared indices can be misleading in terms of the practical value of small effect sizes.

To illustrate, at a specially called meeting held in December 1987, it was decided to end, prematurely, a randomized double-blind experiment on the effects of aspirin in reducing heart attacks (Steering Committee of the Physicians' Health Study Research Group, 1988). The reason for this unusual termination was that it had become abundantly clear that aspirin prevented heart attacks (and deaths from heart attacks), and thus it would have been unethical to continue to give the control subjects a placebo. The subjects in that study were 22,071 male physicians, roughly half of whom (11,037) had been given an ordinary aspirin tablet (325 mg) every other day, and the remainder of whom (11,034) had been given a placebo. A portion of the results of the study are shown in Table 2.5. Part A shows the number of participants in each condition who did or did not suffer a heart attack, and Part B shows the survival rates in the heart attack group. And what was the magnitude of the experimental effects that were so dramatic as to call for the termination of that research? To find the answer, we compute the phi coefficient on the raw data in this table. In Part A, we find the effect size $r = .034$, and thus the corresponding $r^2 = .00$ or, to four decimal places, .0012.

TABLE 2.5
Aspirin's effect on heart attack

A. Myocardial infarctions in aspirin and placebo conditions

Condition	No heart attack	Heart attack
Aspirin	10,933	104
Placebo	10,845	189

B. Fatal and nonfatal myocardial infarctions

Condition	Lived	Died
Aspirin	99	5
Placebo	171	18

In Part B, the effect size $r = .084$, with a corresponding $r^2 = .0071$. Using a simple method described in more detail in chapter 11 (the binomial effect size display, or BESD), we would find that these r values imply a 3.4% greater success rate for aspirin than for placebo in preventing a heart attack and an 8.4% greater success rate for preventing death when a heart attack has occurred. The point is that, had we considered only the squared rs, we might have concluded there were *no benefits* of taking aspirin, a costly mistake to make in terms of human lives saved.

It is sometimes necessary to decide how to convert effect size indices to one particular index (e.g., in meta-analytic work, discussed in chapter 21). In that situation, there are several reasons to view the family of correlational indices as a more generally useful group of effect size measures. Suppose the data came to us as rs. We would not ordinarily want to convert rs to ds, gs, or Δs, because the concept of a mean difference index makes little sense in describing a linear relationship over a great many values of the independent variable of interest. On the other hand, if we were working with effect sizes reported as ds, gs, or Δs, the r index (as we show in chapter 11) makes perfectly good sense in its point-biserial form (two levels of the independent variable of interest). If the data were structured in a 2×2 table of counts, the phi form of the effect size index would be suitable. However, suppose the design involved more than two conditions. For example, suppose a hypothesis called for five levels of arousal, and the scientist predicted better performance on the outcome measure at the middle levels of arousal than at the more extreme levels, and the very best performance in the midmost level of arousal. The magnitude of an effect associated with a curvilinear trend is quite naturally indexed by r (discussed in chapter 15), but not so naturally by d, g, or Δ.

INTERVAL ESTIMATES AROUND EFFECT SIZES

Earlier we also mentioned the importance of reporting interval estimates along with effect size estimates. For example, the confidence interval of the effect size is the margin of error that surrounds the obtained value of the effect size index. For example, a 95% confidence interval around the obtained effect size r of .16 might range from a lower limit r of .10 to an upper limit r of .22. Our interpretation of this 95% confidence interval would be that there is a 95% chance the population value of the r that our obtained effect size r of .16 was trying to estimate falls between the lower and upper limits of .10 and .22. Of course, researchers need not restrict themselves to only 95% confidence intervals if they prefer working with more (or less) stringent levels of confidence. Decreasing the confidence level from 95% to 90% will shrink the interval, and vice versa. Increasing the size of the study (i.e., working with a larger total sample size) will also shrink the confidence interval.

Another type of interval estimate (described in chapter 11) is called the **null-counternull interval** (Rosenthal & Rubin, 1994). This interval estimate is based on the actual p value rather than on a previously specified alpha. The "null" anchoring one end of the interval is the effect size that is associated with the null hypothesis (and is typically zero); *counternull* refers to the non-null magnitude of the effect size that is larger than the obtained effect size and is supported by the same amount of evidence as the null value of the effect size. This interval (null value to counternull value) can alert a researcher to whether a conclusion of "no effect" might be in error. In this way it provides some protection against mistaken interpretations of failure to reject the null hypothesis (Rosenthal & Rubin, 1994; Rosnow & Rosenthal, 1996a).

SUMMING UP

We will have more to say about all these topics later on. The vital point here is that, if the results of a study always include both an estimate of the effect size and an interval estimate, the researchers better protect themselves against Type I and Type II errors. In behavioral and social research, there is little doubt that Type II error is far more likely than Type I error (e.g., Brewer, 1972; Chase & Chase, 1976; Cohen, 1962, 1988; Haase, Waechter, & Solomon, 1982; Sedlmeier & Gigerenzer, 1989). The frequency of Type II error can be reduced drastically by our attention to the magnitude of the estimated effect size. If the estimate is large and the researcher finds a nonsignificant result, the researcher would do well to avoid concluding that variables X and Y are not related (i.e., that "nothing happened"). Only if the pooled results of a good many replications point to a very small effect (on the average), and to a combined test of significance that does not reach the researcher's preferred alpha level, would a researcher be justified in concluding that no nontrivial relationship exists between X and Y.

Table 2.6 summarizes decision errors and possible consequences as a joint function of the results of significance testing and the population effect size (Rosenthal, 1983, 1991a). Suppose a nonsignificant effect. What should it tell the researcher? Low power may have led to failure to detect the true effect, and this line of investigation should probably be continued with a larger sample size before the researcher concludes that "nothing happened." Had the medical researchers in the aspirin study worked with a much smaller total sample, they would not have gotten statistical significance: It would

TABLE 2.6
Population effect sizes and results of significance testing as determinants of inferential errors

Population effect size	Results of significance testing	
	Not significant	Significant
Zero	No error	Type I error
Small	Type II error[a]	No error[b]
Large	Type II error[c]	No error

[a]Low power may lead to failure to detect the true effect; however, if the true effect is quite small, the costs of this error may not be very great.

[b]Although this is not an inferential error, if the effect size is very small and N is very large, we may mistake a result that is merely very significant for one that is of practical importance.

[c]Low power may lead to failure to detect the true effect, and with a substantial true effect the costs may be very great.

have been like trying to read small print in a very dim light and finding it harder to make out the information. On the other hand, suppose a significant but small effect. What should it tell the researcher? The answer depends on what the researcher considers the practical importance of the small estimated population effect. In the aspirin study, even a "quite small" effect was considered important, because the criterion was "who lives and who dies." The lesson is that a test of significance without an effect size estimate fails to tell the whole story. Fortunately, as we shall see later, just from the basic information that many journals require scientists to report, effect sizes (and interval estimates) can usually be directly derived even from the barest of raw ingredients (e.g., Rosenthal & Rubin, 2003; Rosnow & Rosenthal, 1996a).

Finally, we also want to mention a new statistic proposed by Peter Killeen (2005) that increases the utility of p values. This statistic, called p_{rep}, gives the probability that a same size replication (e.g., of a treatment vs. control group study) will obtain an effect in the same direction as did the original study.

Killeen's equation for estimating p_{rep} is:

$$p_{rep} = \frac{1}{1 + \left(\dfrac{p}{1-p}\right)^{2/3}} \tag{2.7}$$

where p is the obtained significance level. Table 2.7 shows for 15 p values the corresponding estimates of p_{rep}. It should be noted that p_{rep} is not an effect size index, nor is it intended to be. But it does give us far more useful information to learn that there is an 88%, 96%, or 99% chance of obtaining the same direction of result on replication (assuming the context and the experimental circumstances are relatively unchanged) than that our p values are .05, .01, or .001. In the end, of course, significance tests and their associated p values alone are not nearly as informative as estimates of effect sizes along with their corresponding interval estimates (e.g., 95% confidence intervals), but p_{rep} is a useful advance as well.

TABLE 2.7
Probabilities of replicating the direction of treatment effects (p_{rep}) from obtained p values

p value	p_{rep}	p value	p_{rep}
.50	.500	.01	.955
.40	.567	.005	.971
.30	.638	.001	.990
.20	.716	.0005	.994
.15	.761	.0001	.998
.10	.812	.00005	.999
.05	.877	.00001	.9995
.025	.920		

ETHICAL
CONSIDERATIONS,
DILEMMAS,
AND
GUIDELINES

PUZZLES AND PROBLEMS

As mentioned in chapter 2, shortly after World War II, Karl Popper settled in England and took a position at the London School of Economics. On October 25, 1946, he gave an invited talk at Cambridge University before the Moral Science Club. Chairing the club was a renowned professor of philosophy at Cambridge, Ludwig Wittgenstein, whose views dominated British philosophy at the time (Monk, 1990). Also present was another eminent Cambridge professor of philosophy, Bertrand Russell, whose seminal work had been an early inspiration for Wittgenstein and Popper (though Wittgenstein came to regard Russell as having lost his edge and regarded his work as antediluvian). Usually at these meetings a visiting lecturer would present preliminary remarks, and Wittgenstein would then dominate the discussion. Popper and Wittgenstein harbored a deep cynicism concerning each other's views, and Russell had taken on the role of a kind of umpire at this meeting. Central heating was still virtually unknown in Britain, and the room was warmed by a coal hearth. Every so often, someone would poke the coals and clear out some of the ash in order to stir up a little more heat.

What ensued that day became the stuff of legend in philosophy. In their book entitled *Wittgenstein's Poker,* Edmonds and Eidinow (2001) recounted the controversial incident that occurred. Popper was expounding on moral philosophy when Wittgenstein, who had grabbed a red hot poker and was gesticulating with it, shouted that Popper was confusing the issues, and challenged him to name one valid moral principle. The sequence of events is murky, but apparently Russell told Wittgenstein to put the poker down, saying to him that it was he who was confusing the issues. Popper, in response to Wittgenstein's challenge to state a valid moral principle, responded with something like, "One ought not to threaten visiting lecturers with pokers." Witnesses to the incident have never agreed on whether Wittgenstein threatened Popper (as Popper claimed), or even whether Wittgenstein was still present in the room when Popper took up the challenge. In one version of the story (which Popper repeated in his memoirs), it was Popper's pungent retort that aggravated Wittgenstein so much that he stormed out of the room, slamming the door behind him.

The controversy between Wittgenstein and Popper revolved around their different views of the proper role of philosophy. In an influential book entitled *Tractatus Logico-Philosophicus,* which first appeared in German in 1921 and was published in an English translation the following year (with an introduction by Russell), Wittgenstein had deconstructed philosophy to an atomistic level. Consisting of a series of numbered, tightly condensed, precisely articulated statements, the book begins, "The world is all that is the case," and ends with the oracular statement: "What we cannot speak about we must pass over in silence" (Wittgenstein, 1978, pp. 5, 74). Going back to the ancient Greeks, the orientation of philosophy had been the elucidation of problems—moral principles, metaphysical and epistemological issues, and so on. Wittgenstein dismissed that work as futile wordplay, contending instead that philosophers' imprecise use of ordinary language had trapped them in a bottomless pit of ambiguity. There simply are no valid *problems* in philosophy, he argued, but only linguistic *puzzles* to be resolved by revealing the misuse of language. Popper, who was as irascible as Wittgenstein, thought this argument was nonsense, and Russell had come to think that Wittgenstein's dismissal of the problem-oriented approach jeopardized the existence of philosophy as an academic discipline. Nonetheless, Wittgenstein's view dominated the British scene, and those who dared to disagree with it (like Popper) were relegated to the role of disgruntled outsiders.

Wittgenstein's and Popper's philosophical views notwithstanding, the distinction between puzzles and problems offers a convenient way to conceptualize ethical issues in science. The usual dictionary definition of a *problem* implies a dubious matter that is proposed for discussion and a solution. The problem of moral accountability in science has provoked considerable discussion and has led to a number of proposed solutions in the form of rules, regulations, and ethical guidelines. Their interpretation and implementation, however, can often be mystifying for researchers, who are obliged to *puzzle* out ways of adhering to ethical and scientific values simultaneously. We begin by giving a sense of this delicate balancing act, and throughout this chapter we mention examples of how scientists need to be attentive to societal and scientific imperatives. We also refer to the term **ethics** (derived from the Greek *ethos,* meaning "character" or "disposition"), which has to do with the values by which the conduct of individuals is morally evaluated.

Although there are a number of ethical codes in the United States and abroad, we will focus on the most prominent set of guidelines in the field of psychology, that promulgated by the American Psychological Association (APA). We review the societal context in which these guidelines were originally inspired, and we then give a flavor of the most recent guidelines. Federal and state legal dictates imposing restrictions on the use of human subjects take precedence over the APA guidelines, but the APA ethics code (American Psychological Association, 1998) is far more focused and restrictive in many respects. Because many behavioral researchers belong not to the APA, but to the Association for Psychological Science (APS) or to other, more specialized societies (some with their own ethical guidelines, such as the Society for Research in Child Development, 1993), there is no consensus in behavioral research. Nonetheless, we will use the framework of the APA code as a way of organizing our discussion of ethical issues, including conflicts between ethical accountability and the technical demands of scientific practices. Although the primary emphasis of this discussion is on research with human subjects, we end with a brief discussion of the ethical implications of using animals in behavioral research.

A DELICATE BALANCING ACT

As Wittgenstein implied, the very language we use is loaded with traps for the unwary. For example, when clinically oriented researchers say that certain behavior is "normative" (i.e., usual or typical), the implication to the layperson is that such behavior is to be expected and is therefore desirable. When social researchers study prejudice or mental illness, they touch on highly charged societal problems. Even when researchers study topics that may seem to them to be neutral (learning behavior, for example), they must realize that to others these topics may be supercharged with values and conflicts. Thus, it seems that virtually every aspect of the research process may be viewed as value-laden to some degree, from the statement of a topic, through the conceptualization and implementation of the investigation, to the data analysis, interpretation, and reporting of findings. When research involves a societally sensitive issue (Lee, 1993), concerns about values and ethics are further heightened. To address such concerns, various national codes of ethics have been formulated by psychological associations in the United States, Canada, France, Germany, Great Britain, the Netherlands, Poland, and other countries (Kimmel, 1996; Schuler, 1982). The purpose of those codes is to provide guidelines to enable researchers to assess the morality of their scientific conduct. However, researchers must also make their way through a maze of cumbersome rules and regulations that are overseen by an independent group of evaluators, called an **institutional review board (IRB).**

As if this situation were not puzzling enough, a further problem is that ethical guidelines cannot possibly anticipate every eventual case. At best, they can provide an evolving framework for evaluating (and trying to prevent) ethical transgressions. The interpretation of the guidelines is left to IRBs, researchers, and any others who feel the need to express an opinion. Collectively, these guidelines constitute what might be described as an idealized "social contract" of do's and don'ts, to which behavioral researchers are expected to subscribe as a prerequisite of conducting any empirical studies. Broadly speaking, the agreement to which social and behavioral scientists are generally held accountable can be summed up as the responsibility (a) not to do psychological or physical harm to the subjects and (b) to do beneficent research in a way that is likely to produce valid results (Rosnow, 1997).

A further problem, however, is that, even when acting with the most noble intentions, investigators can inadvertently transgress. As philosopher John Atwell (1981) noted, research with human subjects always "treads on thin moral ice" because investigators "are constantly in danger of violating someone's basic rights, if only the right of privacy" (p. 89). Moreover, because scientists are also ethically bound to use their abilities to advance knowledge, it has been argued that the scientific validity of the research design can also be viewed as an ethical issue, because poorly designed research cannot yield benefits and may actually be harmful (Rosenthal, 1994c, 1995a; Rosenthal & Blanck, 1993). Thus, research that is of higher scientific quality is presumed to be more ethically defensible, because of its better investment of the time of the research subjects, the funds of the granting agency, the space of the journals, and, not least, of the general investment that society has made in supporting science and its practitioners.

As we shall see in this chapter, even very experienced researchers often find themselves caught between the Scylla of scientific and theoretical requirements and the Charybdis of ethical dictates and moral sensitivities. Ironically, many seminal studies in social and behavioral science (including some of those mentioned in the previous chapter) can no longer be replicated because of obstacles imposed by daunting arrays of ethical guidelines, bureaucracies, formalities, and legalities that simply did not exist in their present form a generation or more ago (Bersoff, 1995; Fisher & Tryon, 1990; Kimmel, 1988; 1996; Koocher & Keith-Spiegel, 1990, 1998; Rosnow, Rotheram-Borus, Ceci, Blanck, & Koocher, 1993; Scott-Jones & Rosnow, 1998; Sieber, 1982a, 1982b). And yet, society and science have benefited from the accrued wisdom of those findings. A further irony is that researchers are usually held to a higher standard of accountability than are many designated and self-appointed guardians of human rights. For example, although ethical guidelines circumscribe the use of deceptive practices and the invasion of privacy, the violation of privacy as well as deception by omission (called a **passive deception**) and commission (an **active deception**) are far from rare: Lawyers routinely manipulate the truth in court on behalf of clients; prosecutors surreptitiously record private conversations; journalists often get away with using hidden cameras and other undercover practices to get stories; and police investigators use sting operations and entrapment procedures to gain the information they seek (Bok, 1978, 1984; Kimmel, 1998; Saxe, 1991; Starobin, 1997).

HISTORICAL CONTEXT OF THE AMERICAN PSYCHOLOGICAL ASSOCIATION CODE

To put the original set of APA guidelines into context, we go back to the 1960s. During that period the American public had been whipped into a frenzy of anxiety by published reports of domestic wiretapping and other clandestine activities by the federal government. Caught up in the temper of the times, leading psychologists voiced concerns about the status of human values in research with human participants, in particular expressing disillusionment over the use of deception in social psychology (Kelman, 1967, 1968) and calling for more humanistic research methodology (Jourard, 1967, 1968). Deception was used rarely in social psychology until the 1930s, then gradually increased until the 1950s, and sharply increased in the 1950s and 1960s—and more recently there has apparently been a decline in its use (Nicks, Korn, & Mainieri, 1997). Going back to Asch's seminal studies of conformity in the 1950s, confederates had been required to deceive participants by keeping a straight face while making ridiculous perceptual judgments. A decade later, obedience experiments done by Stanley Milgram (mentioned in Table 1.2) became the lightning rod for a heated debate about the morality of deception. Some critics argued that *any* deception in research was morally reprehensible because of its presumed adverse effects on the participants and the profession's reputation (see Kimmel, 1998, 2004, for citations and an updated discussion of this issue).

Interestingly, a subsequent survey implied that psychologists might be more concerned about ethical issues in research than were their typical participants (Sullivan & Deiker, 1973). Adding fuel to the debate were more shocking events elsewhere. In bio-medical research, flagrant abuses—some resulting in the death of the human participants—were uncovered (Beecher, 1966, 1970). A notorious case, not made public until 1972, involved a U.S. Public Health Service study, conducted from 1932 to 1972, of the course of syphilis in more than 400 low-income African American men in Tuskegee, Alabama (Jones, 1993). The participants, who had been recruited from churches and clinics, were not told they had syphilis but were only told they had "bad blood." Nor were they given penicillin when it was discovered in 1943. They were given free health care and a free annual medical examination but were told they would be dropped from the study if they sought treatment elsewhere. The Public Health Service officials went so far as to have local physicians promise not to give antibiotics to subjects in the study (Stryker, 1997). As the disease progressed in its predictable course without treatment, the subjects experienced damage to the skeletal, cardiovascular, and central nervous systems and, in some cases, death. The Tuskegee study was not halted until 1972, when details were made public by a lawyer who had once been an epidemiologist for the Public Health Service. Among the horrendous abuses in this study were that subjects were not informed of the nature of the inquiry or the fact that their disease was treatable by medical care readily available at that time (Fairchild & Bayer, 1999).

Already in the 1960s, however, there were demands for reforms, with issues of research abuses and misconduct raised in newspapers, magazines, and congressional hearings (Kelman, 1968). For some time the APA (in its code of professional ethics) had addressed issues such as the confidentiality of research data. Spurred on by eloquent spokespersons who called for the codification of the research methods used in psychological research (e.g., M. B. Smith, 1967, 1969), the APA in 1966 created a task force—called the Cook Commission, after Stuart W. Cook, its chair—that was assigned to write a code of ethics for research with human participants. Out of those deliberations came a 1971 draft report (Cook et al., 1971) and a revised report in 1972 (Cook et al., 1972). The complete code was formally adopted by the APA in 1972, reissued a decade later (American Psychological Association, 1982), and in the late 1990s rewritten by a task force, which for a time was cosponsored by the APA and the APS. After a disagreement about the spirit and content of the draft report (American Psychological Association, 1998), the APS withdrew its collaboration; a draft report was then circulated by the APA alone (American Psychological Association, 1998).

Table 3.1 lists the ten ethical guidelines representing the core of the requirements that appeared in the 1982 version of the APA code. Drawing from philosophy, law, and the American experience, European psychologists had by the early 1980s formulated their own codes of ethical principles to help them meet their responsibilities to subjects (Schuler, 1981). Three principles that appeared without

TABLE 3.1

Ethical principles for research with human participants

The decision to undertake research rests on a considered judgment by the individual psychologist about how best to contribute to psychological science and human welfare. Having made the decision to conduct research, the psychologist considers alternative directions in which research energies and resources might be invested. On the basis of this consideration, the psychologist carries out the investigation with respect and concern for the dignity and welfare of the people who participate and with cognizance of federal and state regulations and professional standards governing the conduct of research with human participants.

A. In planning a study, the investigator has the responsibility to make a careful evaluation of its ethical responsibility. To the extent that the weighing of scientific and human values suggests a compromise of any principle, the investigator incurs a correspondingly serious obligation to seek ethical advice and to observe stringent safeguards to protect the rights of human participants.

B. Considering whether a participant in a planned study will be a "subject at risk" or a "subject at minimal risk," according to recognized standards, is of primary ethical concern to the investigator.

C. The investigator always retains the responsibility for ensuring ethical practice in research. The investigator is also responsible for the ethical treatment of research participants by collaborators, assistants, students, and employees, all of whom, however, incur similar obligations.

D. Except in minimal-risk research, the investigator establishes a clear and fair agreement with research participants, prior to their participation, that clarifies the obligations and responsibilities of each. The investigator has the obligation to honor all promises and commitments included in that agreement. The investigator informs the participants of all aspects of the research that might reasonably be expected to influence willingness to participate and explains all other aspects of the research about which the participants inquire. Failure to make full disclosure prior to obtaining informed consent requires additional safeguards to protect the welfare and dignity of the research participants. Research with children or with participants who have impairments that would limit understanding and/or communication requires special safeguarding procedures.

E. Methodological requirements of a study may make the use of concealment or deception necessary. Before conducting such a study, the investigator has a special responsibility to (1) determine whether the use of such techniques is justified by the study's prospective scientific, educational, or applied value; (2) determine whether alternative procedures are available that do not use concealment or deception; and (3) ensure that the participants are provided with sufficient explanation as soon as possible.

F. The investigator respects the individual's freedom to decline to participate in or to withdraw from the research at any time. The obligation to protect this freedom requires careful thought and consideration when the investigator is in a position of authority or influence over the participant. Such positions of authority include, but are not limited to, situations in which research participation is required as part of employment or in which the participant is a student, client, or employee of the investigator.

G. The investigator protects the participant from physical and mental discomfort, harm, and danger that may arise from research procedures. If risks of such consequences exist, the investigator informs the participant of that fact. Research procedures likely to cause serious or lasting harm to a participant are not used unless the failure to use these procedures might expose the participant to risk of greater harm or unless the research has great potential benefit and fully informed and voluntary consent is obtained from each participant. The participant should be informed of procedures for contacting the investigator within a reasonable time period following participation should stress, potential harm, or related questions or concerns arise.

H. After the data are collected, the investigator provides the participant with information about the nature of the study and attempts to remove any misconceptions that may have arisen. Where scientific or humane values justify delaying or withholding this information, the investigator incurs a special responsibility to monitor the research and to ensure that there are no damaging consequences for the participant.

I. Where research procedures result in undesirable consequences for the individual participant, the investigator has the responsibility to detect and remove or correct these consequences, including long-term effects.

J. Information obtained about a research participant during the course of an investigation is confidential unless otherwise agreed upon in advance. When the possibility exists that others may obtain access to such information, this possibility, together with the plans for protecting confidentiality, is explained to the participant as part of the procedure for obtaining informed consent.

Note: From *Ethical Principles in the Conduct of Research with Human Participants,* 1982, Washington, DC, pp. 5–7. Used by permission of the American Psychological Association.

exception in all of the European and American codes were (a) to avoid physical harm, (b) to avoid psychological harm, and (c) to keep the data confidential (Schuler, 1982). The third principle, which evolved to safeguard the information divulged by clients in clinical situations, was commonly justified on the basis of three claims: (a) that fairness required respect for the research participants' privacy, (b) that scientists had the professional right to keep such disclosures secret, and (c) that more honest responding by subjects should result when the investigator promised to keep the subjects' personal disclosures confidential (Blanck, Bellack, Rosnow, Rotheram-Borus, & Schooler, 1992; Bok, 1978). Despite the value of those guidelines, professional codes had not incorporated much in the way of penalties for noncompliance. The negative sanction for violating the APA ethical code was censure or expulsion from the APA—by no means considered a severe penalty, as many psychologists engaged in productive, rewarding research careers do not belong to the APA.

The 10 guidelines in Table 3.1 were formulated with the aim of instructing psychological researchers about what their moral responsibilities are, how to decide what aspects of a proposed study might pose ethical risks, and how to choose an ethical strategy for addressing such problems. Notice, for example, that Principle E does not prohibit deception; instead, it implies when a deception may be permissible and also the attendant ethical responsibilities of researchers who want to use a deception. In fact, by the time of the first adoption of the APA research code, an assortment of deceptions had slipped into many researchers' methodological arsenals (Arellano-Galdames, 1972; Gross & Fleming, 1982). Active deceptions included misrepresenting the purpose of the study or the identity of the investigators, falsely promising something to subjects, misrepresenting the equipment or procedures, and using placebos, pseudosubjects, and secret treatments. Passive deceptions included disguising experiments in natural settings, observing people in a public setting without telling them they were being studied, secretly recording potentially embarrassing behavior, and using projective tests and other instruments without disclosing their purpose to the participants.

THE BELMONT REPORT, FEDERAL REGULATIONS, AND THE INSTITUTIONAL REVIEW BOARD

A moment ago we alluded to a survey that showed psychologists to be more concerned about ethical sensitivities than were their typical participants (Sullivan & Deiker, 1973). Not every person felt the urgent need to codify such sensitivities, however. For example, Kenneth Gergen (1973a) expressed another popular sentiment among researchers when he warned of the possibility of a precarious trade-off of scientific advances for excessive constraints:

> Most of us have encountered studies that arouse moral indignation. We do not wish to see such research carried out in the profession. However, the important question is whether the principles we establish to prevent these few experiments from being conducted may not obviate the vast majority of contemporary research. We may be mounting a very dangerous cannon to shoot a mouse. (p. 908)

A few years later, however, what Gergen characterized as a "dangerous cannon" seemed more like a popgun in light of dramatic changes that occurred when the review process was set in motion in 1974 by the National Research Act (Pub. L. No. 93-348). That statute also created the National Commission for the Protection of Human Subjects of Biomedical and Behavioral Research.

The National Commission conducted hearings over a 3-year period, which culminated in the **Belmont Report,** named from the discussions that were held at the Smithsonian Institution's Belmont Conference Center in Washington, DC (National Commission for the Protection of Human Subjects of Biomedical and Behavioral Research, 1979). Ethical guidelines, the report concluded, should emphasize (a) showing respect for individuals as autonomous agents and the protection of those with diminished autonomy, (b) maximizing plausible benefits and minimizing possible harms, and (c) using fairness or justice in distributing risks and benefits. In addition, federal directives now ordered institutions applying for grant support to create review boards to evaluate grant submissions (e.g., Department of Health, Education, and Welfare, 1978). If participation in a research study is classified by the IRB as involving more than "minimal risk," that study requires the use of specific safeguards. The safeguards include providing the participants with an adequate explanation of the purposes of the research, the procedures to be used, the potential discomforts and risks to subjects, the benefits that subjects or others may receive, the extent of anonymity in any records that are kept, and the identity of an individual that subjects can contact about the research (Delgado & Leskovac, 1986). Most important perhaps is the investigator's responsibility to make sure that participants understand their prerogative to withdraw from the study at any time without penalty. The spirit of the federal dictates is the same as that of the APA guidelines (Table 3.1), except that the government's rules are legally enforceable in a significant way.

Only a few years after they were created, IRBs had become a source of consternation to many researchers, who felt their research "had been impeded in a way that was not balanced by the benefits of the review process" (Gray & Cook, 1980, p. 40). In recent years, particularly with the development of research on AIDS (acquired immune deficiency syndrome), the sphere of responsibility of IRBs has been expanded as a result of a proliferation of self-imposed safeguards, legally mandated constraints, pressures by advocacy groups, and methodological innovations. The responsibility of IRBs is no longer limited to the evaluation of grant submissions or funded research and may encompass any proposed study in an institution. **Minimal risk research** (i.e., studies in which the likelihood and extent of harm to the subjects is perceived to be no greater than that typically experienced in everyday life or in routine physical or psychological examinations or tests) is authorized to get an expedited review, but even the most innocent study can touch a nerve in some designated regulatory body. Not many years ago, IRBs were seen as the guardians of informed consent, confidentiality, and the safety and autonomy of the research participants. Today, some IRBs, particularly in medical schools, evaluate technical and statistical aspects of research.

As if the pursuit of behavioral research were not already complicated, there are also state laws that limit the type of information requested of participants and the degree of acceptable risk to them, implying that some IRBs are legally bound to impose stricter standards. It is not uncommon that a research proposal approved without alterations at one institution will be substantially modified or even rejected by an IRB at another participating institution (Ceci, Peters, & Plotkin, 1985; P. C. Williams, 1984). The problem of variability in decision making about research on sensitive issues is compounded by the subjectivity of an ethical review and the individual biases of IRB members (Kimmel, 1991). As Ceci et al. (1985) noted, getting a socially sensitive proposal approved is sometimes a matter of the luck of drawing a particular group of IRB members whose values just happen to be congruent with the values of the researchers. In light of these developments, the latest version of the APA research code is self-described as more "aspirational" than "prescriptive," although there are, of course, certain behaviors that cannot be condoned under any circumstances (e.g., fraud). The emphasis of the current APA code is on five broad principles (reflecting the spirit of both the Belmont Report and various federal statutes and directives), which we explore next: (a) respect for persons and their autonomy, (b) beneficence and nonmaleficence, (c) justice, (d) trust, and (e) fidelity and scientific integrity (American Psychological Association, 1998).

PRINCIPLE I: RESPECT FOR PERSONS AND THEIR AUTONOMY

The first principle of the current APA document is a reflection of the earlier Principle D (see Table 3.1) and implies that our ethical (and legal) responsibility is to ensure that people's privacy is adequately protected, that potential participants know what they will be getting into, that they will not be humiliated, and that they are free to decide whether or not to participate. The heart of this principle is **informed consent,** which refers to the procedure in which prospective subjects (or their legally authorized representatives or guardians) voluntarily agree to participate in the research after being told about its purpose, including the nature of the instruments to be used and any anticipated risks and benefits (Scott-Jones & Rosnow, 1998). To the extent they are capable, prospective participants must be given the opportunity to choose what shall or shall not happen to them. If they have diminished autonomy (e.g., because of immaturity, incapacitation, or other circumstances that limit or restrict their ability or opportunity for autonomous choice), or if they have difficulty understanding the nature of the research because they are young or feeling anxious (Dorn, Susman, & Fletcher, 1995; Susman, Dorn, & Fletcher, 1992), then they must be appropriately represented and protected. The responsibility for obtaining legally effective informed consent is the obligation of the principal investigator (Delgado & Leskovac, 1986).

For example, whenever children or adolescents are proposed as subjects, researchers are required to obtain legally effective parental consent before proceeding and are not permitted to make appeals to children to participate before parental consent is obtained. If the children do not live with their parents (e.g., are wards of some agency), the researcher can speak with an advocate who is appointed to act in the best interests of the child in the consent process. Once informed consent of the parent or advocate has been obtained, the researcher asks the child on the day of the study whether he or she wishes to participate—assuming the child is mature enough to be asked about participation (Scott-Jones & Rosnow, 1998). It has been noted, however, that an unfortunate consequence of increased scrutiny by IRBs is that the disclosure procedure has become so detailed and cumbersome in many institutions that it may actually defeat the purpose for which informed consent was intended (Imber et al., 1986). One psychologist reported that many of his adult subjects mistakenly thought they had relinquished their legal protection by signing an informed consent agreement (Mann, 1994), although the right to sue for negligence is protected by federal regulations on the use of human participants (Department of Health and Human Services, 1983).

A further concern is that, sometimes, informing subjects of some pertinent aspect of the investigation may impair the validity of the research. For example, Gerald T. Gardner (1978) performed a series of studies of the effects of noise on task performance. The aim of the research was to replicate a phenomenon first reported by Glass and Singer (1972), indicating that exposure to uncontrollable, unpredictable noise can negatively affect task performance. Although Gardner's initial experiments duplicated Glass and Singer's findings, two subsequent experiments did not. Bewildered by that outcome, Gardner sought to puzzle out a reason for the discrepancy. The only difference in procedure between the early and later studies in the series was that the first studies had been performed before the implementation of federal guidelines requiring informed consent, and the later studies had been carried out using informed consent. This difference inspired Gardner to hypothesize that informed consent might actually have been responsible for the discrepant results.

Acting on this hypothesis, Gardner conducted a final study in which two groups were exposed to uncontrollable noise; one group had given informed consent, whereas the other group had not. The results of this study were that the group that had given informed consent did not show the emergence of negative effects of the noise, but the other group did. Gardner reasoned that negative effects did not emerge because the informed consent had created a perception in the subjects of control over the noise. As Gardner (1978) explained, perceived control "could result from references . . . in the consent form to subjects' ability to withdraw from the study without penalty, to their freedom to choose an alternative to [subject] pool participation" (p. 633). Apparently, conforming to the new ethical guidelines in this instance seriously impaired the emergence of the negative effects of laboratory stressors. Had federal guidelines been instituted when Glass and Singer initiated their research in the late 1960s, is it possible that important facts about environmental noise would never have come to light?

Another early study was performed by clinical researchers Jerome H. Resnick and Thomas Schwartz (1973), who suspected that, in some circumstances, informed consent might trigger "paranoid ideation in otherwise nonsuspicious subjects" (p. 137). Using the traditional verbal conditioning procedure described in chapter 1 (used by Crowne and Marlowe), Resnick and Schwartz experimentally manipulated the ethical standard of informed consent. The subjects were presented with a sequence of cards, each of which showed a specific verb and six pronouns (*I, you, we, he, she, they*) and were told to make up a sentence using the verb and any of the six pronouns. They were then verbally reinforced by the experimenter, who said "good" or "ok" each time the subject chose either *I* or *we*. Before the study began, half the prospective subjects were told the nature of the conditioning procedure in strict adherence with informed consent guidelines; the control subjects were not given that information, but were run just as the study would have been conducted before the era of informed consent.

The principal finding was that the control group conditioned as expected, but the fully informed subjects exhibited an unexpected reversal in the pattern of their conditioning behavior. Using postexperimental questionnaires, Resnick and Schwartz discovered that many of the fully informed subjects, after having been told so much about the study, questioned in their own minds the experimenter's "true" hypothesis. One subject stated that he "had wanted to play it cool; and to give the impression that the experimenter's reinforcements were having no effect" (p. 138). When told that his use of the two reinforced pronouns had decreased by more than half from the first 20 trials to the last 20, this person laughed and said, "I was afraid I would overdo it" (p. 138). Not only was it distressing to Resnick and Schwartz that their fully informed subjects were distrustful, but it was unclear what was happening in, as these researchers put it, "a room full of mirrors where objective reality and its perception blend, and thereby become metaphysical" (p. 138). The results seemed to imply that standard textbook principles of verbal learning would turn backward if all previous studies in this area had strictly adhered to fully informed consent. This study raised a red flag signaling that full disclosure may sometimes be an impediment to the pursuit of knowledge.

Thus, we see that, as Gergen (1973a) and others anticipated, there are scientific puzzles associated with strict compliance with informed consent. In a later chapter we allude to another potential concern, which is the "delicate balance" between *experimenter and subject artifacts* (i.e., specific threats to validity that can be attributed to uncontrolled researcher- or participant-related variables) and ethics in behavioral research (Rosnow & Rosenthal, 1997; Suls & Rosnow, 1981). In chapter 9 we will describe how using volunteer subjects could introduce biases that then make the research results more difficult to generalize to populations consisting in part of potential nonvolunteers (Rosenthal & Rosnow, 1969b, 1975; Rosnow & Rosenthal, 1970, 1976).

PRINCIPLE II: BENEFICENCE AND NONMALEFICENCE

Beneficence means the "doing of good," which implies that the research is expected to have some conceivable benefit, and **nonmaleficence** implies that, as in the Hippocratic oath that physicians take, behavioral and social researchers are also expected to "do no harm." The avoidance of harm as a standard for ethical research originally emanated from the Nuremberg Code of 1946–1949, developed in conjunction with expert testimony against Nazi physicians at the Nuremberg Military Tribunal after World War II. The risks of behavioral and social research pale by comparison with the appalling "experiments" done by Nazi physicians in the name of science, but federal regulations nevertheless insist that assessment of risk be part of the ethical evaluation of all proposed research with human subjects. Generally speaking, the most significant risks in traditional psychological research are associated with privacy invasion or the use of some active or passive deception. When deception is used, the assumption is that (a) the research has genuine scientific value, (b) providing the subjects with full details of the research would seriously impair its validity, (c) no undisclosed "risks" to the subjects are more than minimal, and (d) the subjects will be adequately debriefed at some appropriate time.

Prior to the Belmont Report, a classic example of behavioral research that became the focus of concerns about the use of deception was social psychologist Stanley Milgram's research on how far a person would go in subjecting another person to pain by the order of an authority figure (Milgram, 1963, 1965). Volunteer subjects, placed in the role of the "teacher," were deceived into believing that they would be giving varying degrees of painful electric shocks to another person (the "learner") each time he made a mistake in a learning task. Milgram varied the physical proximity between the teacher and the learner, to see whether the teacher would be less ruthless in administering the electric shocks as he or she got closer to the learner. The results were that a great many subjects (the teachers) unhesitatingly obeyed the researcher's command as they continued to increase the level of shock administered to the learner. Even when there was feedback from the learner, who pretended to cry out in pain, many subjects obeyed the researcher's order to "please continue" or "you have no choice, you must go on." The subjects were not told at the outset that the shock apparatus was fake but were extensively debriefed once the experiment was over. Even though the learner was a confederate of Milgram's and there were no actual shocks transmitted, concerns about ethics and values have dogged these studies since they were first reported (Milgram, 1963, 1965, 1975, 1977).

For instance, psychologist Diana Baumrind (1964) quoted Milgram's own descriptions of the reactions of some of the subjects:

> I observed a mature and initially poised businessman enter the laboratory smiling and confident. Within 20 minutes he was reduced to a twitching, stuttering wreck, who was rapidly approaching a point of nervous collapse. He constantly pulled on his earlobe, and twisted his hands. At one point he pushed his fist into his forehead and muttered: "Oh God, let's stop it." And yet he continued to respond to every word of the experimenter and obeyed to the end. (Milgram, 1963, p. 377)

Baumrind posed the question of why Milgram had not terminated the deception when he saw that it was so stressful to his subjects. She concluded that there could be no rational basis for doing this kind of research, unless the subjects were forewarned of the psychological risks. Another criticism was that Milgram's deception had instilled in his subjects a general distrust of authority, and thus the study was unethical no matter whether the subjects were debriefed afterward.

Milgram (1964) responded that it was not his intention to create stress, and, further, that the extreme tension induced in some subjects had not been expected. He noted that, before carrying out the research, he had asked professional colleagues for their opinions, and none of the experts anticipated the behavior that subsequently resulted. He stated that he also thought the subjects would refuse to follow orders. In spite of the dramatic appearance of stress, he believed there were no injurious effects to the subjects. Each subject was shown that the learner had not received dangerous electric shocks but had only pretended to receive them. Milgram also sent questionnaires to the subjects to elicit their reactions after they had been given a full report of his investigation. Less than 1 percent said they regretted having participated, 15 percent were neutral or ambivalent, and over 80 percent responded that they were glad to have participated. As for the criticism that his use of deception had instilled a general distrust of authority, he replied that the experimenter in his research was not just *any* authority, but someone who ordered the subjects to act harshly and inhumanely toward another person. Milgram added that he would consider the result of the highest value if participation in the research did indeed inculcate a skepticism of that kind of authority.

Duping subjects into believing they were administering painful electric shocks to another person is inherently disquieting, but it is hard to imagine how forewarning them about the use of deception would not have destroyed the validity of the investigation. Furthermore, Milgram's follow-up treatments were unusually extensive. During the postexperimental debriefing session, he made sure that each subject was shown the reality of the experimental situation and had a friendly reconciliation with the learner and an extended discussion with the experimenter about the purpose of the study and why it was thought necessary to use deception. Subjects who had obeyed the experimenter when ordered to keep administering the electric shocks were told that their behavior was not abnormal, and that the feelings of conflict or tension they had experienced were shared by other subjects. The subjects were told that they would receive a comprehensive written report at the conclusion of the study. The report they received detailed the experimental procedures and findings, and the subject's own part in the research was treated with dignity. Subjects also received a questionnaire that asked them once again to express their thoughts and feelings about their behavior. One year after the experiment was completed there was an additional follow-up of 40 of the experimental subjects, who were intensively interviewed by a psychiatrist in order to rule out any delayed injurious effects resulting from the experiment.

Milgram's follow-up treatments were more comprehensive than is characteristic of most studies. Subsequent ethical guidelines call for **debriefing** if deception is used in research (also referred to as *dehoaxing*) in order to remove any misconceptions the subjects may have about the research, allay any negative emotions or thoughts, and leave them with a sense of dignity, knowledge, and a perception of time not wasted. That debriefing can also provide researchers with information that subjects may be either reluctant or unable to disclose at any other point in the study (Rotheram-Borus, Koopman, & Bradley, 1989). For example, in experimental trials with persons infected by HIV, it has been a common practice for many participants to share medication with each other, gain access to drugs or treatments available outside the study, and take multiple drugs simultaneously, thereby making it almost impossible to conduct an evaluation of a single drug uncontaminated by auxiliary treatments (Blanck et al., 1992). Debriefing in this situation includes monitoring the degree and type of multiple drug use among subjects in the trials. Jones and Gerard (1967) suggested that debriefing also include discovery about what each subject thought of the research situation, providing the investigator with an experiential context in which to interpret the results.

As mentioned, if the research involves any sort of deception, debriefing is usually expected to be used to reveal the truth about the study and the careful consideration that has been given to the use of the deception. For example, it might be explained to subjects that science is the search for truth, and that sometimes it is necessary to resort to withholding information in order to uncover the truth. In some cases, however, the revelation that a deception was part of the study spawns skepticism and leaves the subjects feeling gullible, as if they have been "had" by a fraudulent procedure. Thus, it is also important to weigh the welfare and rights of the participants against the possibility that dehoaxing might itself lead to psychological discomfort (Fisher & Fyrberg, 1994). Assuming that debriefing can be done, the researcher might explain that being "taken in" does not reflect in any way on the subject's intelligence or character but simply shows the effectiveness or validity of the research design. Presumably, the researcher took some pains to achieve an effective design so as not to waste the subjects' time and effort. Most important, the debriefing should proceed gradually and patiently, with the chief aim of gently unfolding the details of any deceptions used and reducing any negative feelings. Instead of thinking of themselves as "victims," the subjects should then more correctly realize that they are "coinvestigators" in the search for truth (Aronson & Carlsmith, 1968; Mills, 1976; Rosnow & Rosenthal, 1997).

PRINCIPLE III: JUSTICE

The third principle, simply called **justice,** implies "fairness" and, in behavioral research, refers to the ideal that the burdens as well as the benefits of the scientific investigation should be distributed equitably. The men who participated in the Tuskegee study could not have benefited in any significant way, and they alone bore the awful burdens as well. However, suppose it had been an experiment to test the effectiveness of a new drug in curing syphilis, the strategy being to give half the men at random the new drug and the other half a fake "pill" masquerading as the real thing (i.e., a **placebo**). Would that approach have made the study any more acceptable? Research on AIDS has made investigators sensitive to such ethical questions, and one response is to include potential participants or surrogates for them in the decision-making process—although this inclusion does not absolve investigators themselves of their own responsibilities to protect the safety and rights of their subjects (Melton, Levine, Koocher, Rosenthal, & Thompson, 1988). If an effective treatment is available, use of the effective treatment can be the control condition, so that the experimental comparison is now between the new therapy and the effective alternative. The Declaration of Helsinki, adopted by the general assembly of the World Medical Association in 2000, stipulated that a placebo be used only when there is no other effective drug or therapy available for comparison with the therapeutic being tested. In the case of the Tuskegee study, there was an effective treatment available (penicillin), and depriving men of that treatment made the study profoundly unjust. Another design alternative (discussed in chapter 7), which is useful in certain randomized experiments (the Tuskegee study was not a randomized experiment), is to use a **wait-list control group;** in such a design the alternative therapy is given to the control group after it has been administered in the experimental group and the results have been documented.

As daily life constantly reminds us, however, social, political, and legal justice are ideals that are unlikely to be achieved in a world that is never fully just. Is fairness or justice, then, merely in the eyes of the beholder? Philosophers make a distinction between two orientations, the consequentialist and the deontological, and argue that how people view ethical questions depends on their orientation. The **consequentialist view** refers to the argument that whether an action is right or wrong depends on its consequences. The **deontological view** is that some actions may be presumed to be categorically wrong no matter what their consequences (e.g., threatening a visiting lecturer with a red hot poker). In fact, there is empirical support for the idea that people tend to judge the world from one of these two perspectives, or from a pluralistic orientation that encompasses aspects of both (Forsyth, 1980; Forsyth & Pope, 1984). Milgram lied to his subjects, and that lying was immoral if we believe that lying in *any* form is wrong (a deontological argument). On the other hand, it would appear that Baumrind's views of Milgram's research were influenced by her awareness of his results (the consequentialist view), just as Milgram's ideas may have been colored by his own pluralistic approach (i.e., containing elements of both the consequentialist and the deontological views, but not a blanket condemnation of deception). But some have also argued that deception was not all that was at stake. The studies were "unjust" because Milgram exposed his subjects to a possibility of unwanted and unasked-for self-knowledge (Cassell, 1982). How we ourselves perceive those issues may be a window into the nature of our personal orientation as consequentialist, deontological, or pluralistic (Forsyth & Pope, 1984; C. P. Smith, 1983; Waterman, 1988).

Another early study helped to underscore the problem that injustice is not always easily anticipated. It involved a 1973 field experiment designed in part to improve the quality of work life at the Rushton Mining Company in Pennsylvania (Blumberg, 1980; Susman, 1976). Developed on the basis of previous research in the United Kingdom (Trist & Bamforth, 1951; Trist, Higgin, Murray, & Pollock, 1963), the Rushton project had as its specific aims to improve employee skills, safety, and job satisfaction while raising the level of performance and company earnings (Blumberg & Pringle, 1983). After months of preparation by the researchers and the mining company, a call was issued for volunteers for a work group that would have direct responsibility for the production in one section of the mining operations. The volunteers were instructed to abandon their traditional roles and, after extensive training in safety laws, good mining practices, and job safety analysis, were left to coordinate their own activities. Paid at the top rate, that of the highest skilled job classification in that section, they became enthusiastic proponents of "our way of working."

All was not so rosy in the rest of the mine, however. Other workers, those in the control condition, expressed resentment and anger at the "haughtiness" of the volunteers and the injustice of the reward system. The volunteers had even been treated to a steak and lobster dinner by the president of the company, the others complained. Why should these "inexperienced" workers receive special treatment and higher pay than other miners with many more years on the job? Rumors circulated through the mine that the volunteers were "riding the gravy train" and being "spoon-fed," and that autonomy was a "communist plot" because all the volunteers received the same rate and the company was "making out" at their expense. The researchers were rumored to be politically motivated to "bust the union" (Blumberg & Pringle, 1983). No matter what the important theoretical and applied benefits of the research would have been, the seeds of conflict were planted, and the experiment had to be prematurely concluded.

In this case we see that applied research can have its own problems and puzzles, quite apart from those encountered by Milgram. There was no deception or invasion of privacy in the Rushton study, but there was the problem of "injustice" because a sizable number of workers (nonvolunteers, to be sure) did not receive the benefits enjoyed by those in the experimental group. Still other risks may occur in applied research. For example, a moral cost may be involved simply in the publication of the results. That is, the report might (a) upset some persons who are able to identify themselves in the publication, (b) subject the community to possible embarrassment or to unwanted publicity, (c) make those who are identifiable vulnerable to others who have power over them, or (d) weaken the scientific enterprise by communicating to people that science is exploitive (Johnson, 1982). On the other hand, what would be the social and scientific costs of *not* disseminating research findings? In chapter 1 we listed the ability to communicate—and by extension, the written record—as one of the essentials of sound scientific practice. The written record of the search for truth is the official archive that tells us about the observations that were made, the hypotheses that were examined (and those that were ignored), the ideas that were found wanting, and those that withstood the test of further observations. One author was quoted in chapter 1: "Scientists must write . . . so that their discoveries may be known to others" (Barrass, 1978, p. 25).

Furthermore, "unfairness" and "injustice" are hardly limited to research situations. For example, Broome (1984) discussed the ethical issue of fairness in selecting people for chronic hemodialysis—a medical procedure that can save the life of a person whose kidneys have failed. It is expensive, and in many countries there are just not enough facilities available to treat everyone who could benefit. Because without treatment a patient quickly dies, how should a candidate for hemodialysis be selected? First come, first served was one way that some hospitals chose candidates. The inventor of hemodialysis, B. H. Scribner, is said to have selected people on the basis of their being under 40 years old, free of cardiovascular disease, pillars of the community, and contributors to the community's economics. He is also said to have taken into account whether they were married and whether they went to church. Still another approach uses randomness. Broome (1984) pointed out that selecting people randomly—such as by using a lottery to choose conscripts to fight in a war—is often justified as the "fairest" procedure because everyone has an equal shot at being selected for life or death. But suppose conscripts for the military were instead selected not randomly, but on the grounds of who was the biggest and strongest? Which approach is fairer: randomness or selection on the grounds of who is more likely to survive? Some hospitals chose candidates for hemodialysis on the basis of a lottery among those patients who were judged to be most medically suitable.

PRINCIPLE IV: TRUST

This principle refers to the establishment of a relationship of trust with the participants in the study. It is based on the assumption that subjects are fully informed about what they will be getting into, that nothing is done to jeopardize this trust, and that their disclosures are protected against unwarranted access. This last requirement is what is meant by **confidentiality,** which is intended to ensure the subjects' privacy by setting in place procedures for protecting the data. For example, the investigator might use a coding system in which the names of the participants are represented by a sequence of numbers that are impossible for anyone else to identify. In cases in which participants respond anonymously and are never asked to give any information that would identify them, their privacy is obviously protected. In certain government-funded biomedical and behavioral research, it is sometimes possible for researchers to obtain from the funding agency a **certificate of confidentiality,** which is a formal agreement that requires the researcher to keep the data confidential and thus exempts the data from subpoena. However, the extent to which such a certificate can actually provide legal protection has not yet been established in the courts, and it is further complicated by the existence of laws that require the reporting of certain sensitive information.

For example, as stipulated by the Child Abuse Prevention and Treatment and Adoption Reform Act (1992) and its revisions and amendments (Pub. L. No. 102-295), each state must pass laws to require the reporting of child abuse and neglect. The nature and wording of the statutes is left to the discretion of the states, which have increasingly expanded the lists of individuals who are obligated to report suspected cases (Liss, 1994). As a result, developmental psychologists working in the area of intervention research are often pressed to report child abuse. Researchers who are investigating abuse may be torn between reporting a suspected culprit (jeopardizing the relationship of trust?) and losing a valuable participant in the study (jeopardizing the validity or generalizability of the study?), or they may feel they do not have the moral right to report a parent on the basis of their limited training and the evidence they have. It may be that charges of abuse will not be proven, but this possibility does not excuse researchers from their legal responsibilities (Liss, 1994). Researchers who lack the training and clinical acumen to recognize abuse may overreport suspected cases (Scott-Jones, 1994). These are obviously knotty problems, and they have led to suggestions about the need for specialized training opportunities for some researchers, new reporting methods in research protocols, the restructuring of ethical guidelines in populations at risk, and further research on the predictive power and diagnostic validity of the relevant assessment tools (e.g., C. B. Fisher, 1994; Scarr, 1994; Scott-Jones, 1994).

PRINCIPLE V: FIDELITY AND SCIENTIFIC INTEGRITY

The relationship between scientific quality and ethical quality is the essence of the fifth principle, which includes a wide range of issues (Rosenthal, 1994c, 1995a; Rosenthal & Blanck, 1993). One issue involves telling prospective participants, granting agencies, colleagues, administrators, and ourselves that the research is likely to achieve goals that it is, in fact, unlikely to achieve, that is, *hyperclaiming* (Rosenthal, 1994c). It is true that colleagues can often figure out for themselves whether research claims are exaggerated, but prospective subjects are not usually equipped to question "hyperclaims," such as the idea that an investigation will yield a cure for panic disorder, depression, schizophrenia, or cancer. Closely related to this problem is **causism,** which means implying a causal relationship where none has been established by the available data. Characteristics of this problem include (a) the absence of an appropriate evidential base; (b) the use of language implying cause (e.g., "the effect of," "the impact of," "the consequence of," "as a result of") where the appropriate language would actually be "was related to," "was predictable from," or "could be inferred from"; and (c) self-serving benefits, because it makes the causist's result appear more important or fundamental than it really is (Rosenthal, 1994c). A perpetrator of causism who is unaware of the hyperclaim shows poor scientific training or lazy writing. The perpetrator who is aware of the hyperclaim shows blatant unethical misrepresentation and deception.

To illustrate how a poorly trained investigator might stumble into causism, imagine that a research protocol that comes before an IRB proposes the hypothesis that private schools improve children's intellectual functioning more than public schools do. Children from randomly selected private and public schools are to be tested extensively, and the research hypothesis is to be tested by a comparison of the scores earned by students from private and public schools. The safety of the children to be tested is certainly not an issue; yet it can be argued that this research violates the principle of scientific integrity because of the inadequacy of the research design. The purported goal of the study is to learn about the "causal impact on performance of private versus public schooling," but the design of the research does not permit sound causal inference because of the absence of random assignment to conditions or of a reasonable attempt to consider plausible rival hypotheses (Cook & Campbell, 1979). The design provokes ethical objections to the proposed research because (a) students', teachers', and administrators' time will be taken from potentially more beneficial educational experiences; (b) the study is likely to lead to unwarranted and inaccurate conclusions that may be damaging to the society that directly or indirectly pays for the research; and (c) the allocation of time and money to this poor-quality science will serve to keep those finite resources of time and money from better quality science. However, had the research question addressed been appropriate to the research design, these ethical issues would have been less acute. If the investigator had set out only to learn whether there were "performance differences between students in private versus public schools," the design would have avoided the causism problem and been appropriate to the question.

The analysis of research data is another area that raises ethical issues involving fidelity and scientific integrity. The most obvious and most serious transgression is the fabrication of data. Perhaps more frequent, however, is the omission of data contradicting the investigator's theory, prediction, or commitment. There is a venerable tradition in data analysis of dealing with outliers (extreme scores), a tradition going back over 200 years (Barnett & Lewis, 1978). Both technical and ethical issues are involved. The technical issues have to do with the best statistical ways of dealing with outliers without reference to the implications for the data analyst's theory (discussed in chapter 10). The ethical issues have to do with the relationship between the data analyst's theory and the choice of method for dealing with outliers. For example, there is some evidence that outliers are more likely to be rejected if they are bad for the data analyst's theory and are treated less harshly if they are good for the data analyst's theory (Rosenthal, 1978b; Rosenthal & Rubin, 1971). At the very least, when outliers are rejected, that fact should be reported. In addition, it would be useful to report in a footnote the results that would have been obtained had the outliers not been rejected.

Many researchers have been traditionally taught that it is technically improper (perhaps even immoral) to analyze and reanalyze their data in multiple ways (i.e., to "snoop around" in the data). We ourselves were taught to test the prediction with one particular preplanned analysis and take a result significant at the .05 level as our reward for a life well lived. Should the result not be significant at the .05 level, we were taught, we should bite our lips bravely, take our medicine, and definitely not look further at the data. Such a further look might turn up results significant at the .05 level, results to which we were not entitled. All this makes for a lovely morality play, and it reminds us of Robert Frost's poem about losing forever the road not taken, but it makes for bad science and for bad ethics. It makes for bad science because, although exploratory data analysis does affect p values, it is likely to turn up something new, interesting, and important (Tukey, 1977). It makes for bad ethics because scientific data are expensive in terms of time, effort, money, and other resources, and because the antisnooping dogma is wasteful of time, effort, money, and other resources. If the research is worth doing, the data are worth a thorough analysis and being held up to the light in many different ways so that the research participants, funding agencies, science, and society will get their time and money's worth. We have more to say on this topic in chapter 10, but before leaving this issue, we should repeat that exploratory data analysis can indeed affect the p value obtained, depending on how the analysis was done. In chapter 14 we will show how statistical adjustments can be helpful here. Most important, replications will be needed no matter whether the data were snooped or not.

Although all misrepresentations of findings are damaging to the progress of science, some are more obviously unethical than others. The most blatant deliberate misrepresentation is the reporting of data that never were, which constitutes fraud (Broad & Wade, 1982). That behavior, if detected, ends (or ought to end) the scientific career of the perpetrator. **Plagiarism** (which comes from a Latin word meaning "kidnapper") is another breach of the fidelity principle; it refers to stealing another's ideas or work and passing it off as one's own—or as one author characterized it, "stealing into print" (LaFollette, 1992). A further distinction is sometimes made between "intentional" and "accidental" plagiarism (Rosnow & Rosnow, 2006). By *intentional plagiarism,* we mean the deliberate copying or taking of someone else's ideas or work and then knowingly failing to give credit or failing to place the quoted passage in quotation marks with a specific citation (Mallon, 1991). By *accidental plagiarism,* we mean the use of someone else's work but then innocently forgetting (not *neglecting*) to credit it (i.e., lazy writing). Intentional plagiarism is illegal, but this warning does not mean that researchers cannot use other people's ideas or work in their writing; it does mean that the writer must give the author of the material full credit for originality and not misrepresent (intentionally or accidentally) the material as one's own original work.

COSTS, UTILITIES, AND INSTITUTIONAL REVIEW BOARDS

We previously mentioned that, as required by federal law, institutions in which research with human subjects is conducted are required to maintain a review board (IRB) for the purpose of evaluating proposed investigations and monitoring ongoing research. The researcher provides the IRB with a detailed description (or "protocol") of the proposed investigation, and the IRB is then required (a) to evaluate whether the study complies with the standards for the ethical treatment of research participants and (b) to ensure that the potential benefits to individual participants (and society) will be greater than any risks the participants may encounter in the research (Stanley & Sieber, 1992). Some categories of studies may be exempt from IRB review, such as those in normal educational settings on normal educational processes; those involving educational tests, surveys, interviews, or observations of public behavior, as long as the individual participants cannot be identified; and research involving existing public data (e.g., archival material) in which the individuals cannot be identified. In practice, however, universities often require that the protocol of any proposed study be submitted for review, so that the IRB can decide whether the study falls into a category that is exempt from review (Scott-Jones & Rosnow, 1998).

How can researchers forearm themselves against a capricious or overly zealous ethical review? There is no easy answer to this question, except to say that prudent researchers must sharpen their understanding of how risks and benefits are assessed in the review process (e.g., Brooks-Gunn & Rotheram-Borus, 1994; Ceci, Peters, & Plotkin, 1985; Diener & Crandall, 1978; Kimmel, 1996; Rosenthal, 1994c, 1995a; Rosnow, Rotheram-Borus, Ceci, Blanck, & Koocher, 1993; Wilcox & Gardner, 1993). When IRBs are confronted with a problematic or questionable protocol, they are expected to adopt a cost-utility approach in which the costs (or risks) of doing a study are evaluated simultaneously against such utilities (or benefits) as those accruing to the research participants, to society at large, and to science. Presumably, the potential benefits of higher quality studies and studies addressing more important topics are greater than the potential benefits of lower quality studies and studies addressing less important topics. Figure 3.1 shows a two-dimensional plane representing this type of analysis, in which the costs are one dimension and the utilities are the other (Rosenthal & Rosnow, 1984; Rosnow, 1990). In theory, any study with high utility and low cost should be carried out forthwith, and any study with low utility and high cost should not be carried out. Studies in which costs equal utilities are very difficult to decide on (B–C axis). In the case of low-cost, low-utility research, an IRB might be reluctant to approve a study that is harmless but is likely to yield little benefit.

As many researchers know from personal experience, however, the review process often ignores utilities and merely uses the A–C axis value for the criterion. Moreover, we have become convinced that, even when utilities are considered, this cost-utility model is insufficient because it ignores the costs of research not done. By concentrating only on the act of doing research and ignoring the act of not doing research, the review process uses a less rigorous standard of accountability than that aspired to by most researchers (Haywood, 1976; Rosenthal & Rosnow, 1984).

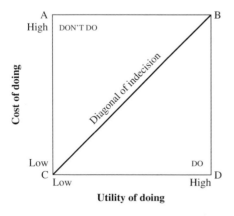

FIGURE 3.1
A decision-plane model of the costs and utilities of doing research. Studies falling at Point A are *not* carried out. Studies falling at Point D *are* carried out. Studies falling along the diagonal of indecision, B–C, are too hard to decide on.

Researchers often complain of their frustration at having research with possible societal benefits impeded by the review process or by political interference (Brooks-Gunn & Rotheram-Borus, 1994). In the 1990s, a prominent case involved a sexual survey of adolescents. The study was terminated prematurely on the grounds that it had violated community norms, but this decision simply deprived the community of data essential to addressing health problems of general concern (Wilcox & Gardner, 1993). If an IRB sent back a proposal for research that could conceivably find a way of preventing AIDS, on the grounds that its methodology did not ensure the privacy of the participants, the cost in human terms of the research not done could be high. Similarly, rejecting a sociopsychological investigation that might help to reduce violence or prejudice, but that involved a disguised experiment in a natural setting (i.e., a deception), would not solve the ethical problem, essentially trading one ethical issue for another.

It has been argued that it is incumbent upon researchers and their scientific organizations to educate IRBs about the costs of research not done, and about the costs to science and to society of not being able to replicate classic experiments that have generated important findings (Rosnow, Rotheram-Borus, Ceci, Blanck, & Koocher, 1993). A more complete analysis is represented by the two decision planes shown in Figure 3.2 or by the more complex model shown in Figure 3.3 (Rosenthal & Rosnow, 1984). Figure 3.2 is self-explanatory. Suppose, however, we added a new diagonal A–D (not shown) to these two planes and called it the "decision diagonal" (in contrast to B–C and B′–C′, the diagonals of indecision). For any point in the plane of *doing,* there would be a location on the cost axis and on the utility axis. Any such point could then be translated to an equivalent position on the decision diagonal. For example, if a point were twice as far from A as from D, we would see the translated point as located two thirds of the way on the decision diagonal A–D (i.e., closer to D than to A). The same reasoning would apply to *not doing,* except that closeness to A would mean "do" rather than "not do."

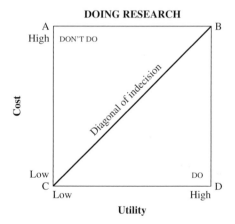 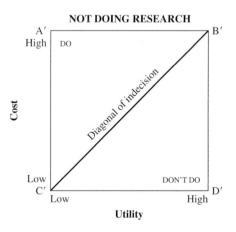

FIGURE 3.2

Decision planes representing the costs and utilities of doing (left plane) and not doing (right plane) research.

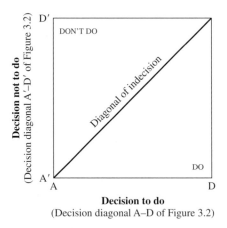

Decision to do
(Decision diagonal A–D of Figure 3.2)

FIGURE 3.3
Composite plane representing both cases in Figure 3.2.

Putting these decision diagonals together gives Figure 3.3, and we are now back to two dimensions. In this composite plane, points near D tell us to do the study. Points near D′ tell us not to do the study. Points on the indecision diagonal leave us unsure. Points on the D′–D decision diagonal (not shown) tell us whether we are closer to "don't do" or "do." The purpose of this figure is to get us all to think about issues of cost and utility in terms of a more complete analysis. For example, the Tuskegee study reminds us that there have been shocking instances in which the safety of human subjects has been ignored or endangered (see also Beecher, 1970; Bok, 1978; Katz, 1972), but bureaucratic imperialism can also have serious consequences. As West and Gunn (1978) pointed out, if ethical guidelines are imposed absolutely, then "researchers may simply turn their attention to other topic areas that ethics committees and review boards find less objectionable" (p. 36). The result could be that research that needs to be done, to address vital scientific and societal questions, would cease. Considerations such as those indicated by Figures 3.2 and 3.3, if adopted by an IRB, would make it harder to give absolute answers to questions of whether or not particular studies should be carried out. Those who argue that a given study is unethical and should be prohibited would have to answer in ethical and moral terms for the consequences of *their* decision no less than the researchers proposing the study.

SCIENTIFIC AND SOCIETAL RESPONSIBILITIES

We have examined the kinds of questions concerning ethics and values that constantly confront behavioral researchers in studies with human participants. The ethical propriety of using animals in behavioral research has also attracted considerable attention, as research on animals has played a central role in our science since its beginning (e.g., studies by Ivan Pavlov and E. L. Thorndike). Attitudes toward the use of animals in behavioral research vary greatly among psychologists, most of whom nevertheless seem to approve of standard observational studies in which animals were confined in some way but apparently disapprove of studies involving pain or death (Plous, 1996).

Although the usual justification of animal research in psychology has been that it has clinical applications in humans and animals, questions have been raised about how often clinicians or clinical investigators actually draw on the results of animal research (Giannelli,1986; Kelly, 1986). On the other hand, a strong case has been made by many scientists that research on animals has been the foundation for numerous significant advances, including the rehabilitation of persons suffering from spinal cord injuries, the treatment of diseases and eating disorders, improvement in communication with the severely retarded, and a better understanding of alcoholism (Domjan & Purdy, 1995; N. E. Miller, 1985). For example, animal experiments by Roger Sperry, who won a Nobel Prize for his work, revealed that severing the fibers connecting the right and left hemispheres of the brain (resulting in a so-called split brain) did not impair a variety of functions, including learning and memory. That important discovery led to a treatment for severe epilepsy and made it possible for people who would have been confined to hospitals to lead normal lives (Gazzaniga & LeDoux, 1978; Sperry, 1968).

Just as the scientific community recognizes both an ethical and a scientific responsibility for the general welfare of human subjects, it also assumes responsibility for the humane care and treatment of animals used in research. There is an elaborate regulatory system to protect animals in scientific research, including professional and scientific guidelines (American Psychological Association, 1996), federal regulations, Public Health Service specifications, and state and local laws (see, e.g., Plous, 1996). Some years ago, the British zoologist William M. S. Russell and microbiologist Rex L. Burch made the argument that, given scientists' own interest in the humane treatment of the animals used in research, it would be prudent to search for ways to (a) *reduce* the number of animals used in research, (b) *refine* the experiments so that there is less suffering, and (c) *replace* animals with other procedures whenever possible. Called the "three Rs principle" by Russell and Burch (1959), this principle defines part of the moral contract to which researchers who use animal subjects subscribe.

Each researcher must weigh his or her responsibilities to science and to society very carefully. Even when the research is not directly funded by some agency of society, it is at least countenanced and indirectly supported, because our society places a high value on science and gives scientists a relatively free hand to study whatever they want to study. There are, to be sure, limits on how far scientists can go in the quest for knowledge, and we discussed some of those limits earlier. Society provides the circumstances and a psychological environment that are conducive to the practice of science. Because no scientist can guarantee that the outcome of his or her work will actually benefit society, what then does the scientist owe society in return for that privilege? As we have tried to show in this chapter, the researchers' ethical responsibilities are twofold: On the one hand, researchers must protect the integrity of their work in order to ensure that it measures up to the technical standards of sound scientific practice. On the other hand, researchers must also respect the dignity of those they study and the values that allow the pursuit of scientific knowledge in a free society.

PART
II

OPERATIONALIZATION AND MEASUREMENT OF DEPENDENT VARIABLES

RELIABILITY AND VALIDITY OF MEASUREMENTS

RANDOM AND SYSTEMATIC ERROR

In this chapter, and in the following two chapters, we turn to the operationalization and measurement of the variables of interest. Generally speaking, **reliability** implies the degree to which it is possible to repeat or corroborate these measurements (i.e., Do the measures give results that are consistent, dependable, or stable?), and **validity** implies the degree to which the measures are appropriate or meaningful in the way they claim to be. Whatever the measuring instruments employed (e.g., paper-and-pencil or computerized tests or questionnaires, devices like magnetic resonance imaging, or a group of judges who make ratings), researchers are usually interested in their reliability and validity. As we will illustrate, although particular kinds of reliability and validity have quite specific meanings, these concepts are generally related to each other in ways that are often misunderstood. Later in this chapter we examine the widespread (but incorrect) belief that having "acceptable validity" invariably depends on having some minimum level of reliability.

We will show how to improve reliability by increasing the number of individual components (e.g., the number of test items or the number of judges) that define the particular instrument. However, a measure can be very reliable without being at all valid. For example, it is possible to imagine that people blink their eyes the same number of times a minute under a variety of circumstances (i.e., the eye-blink measure has high reliability), but under no conditions could one predict their running speed from their eye-blink rate (i.e., the eye-blink measure has low validity as a predictor of running speed).

It is commonly assumed that measurements made in the behavioral and social sciences (the so-called soft sciences) are less replicable than measurements made in the "hard sciences" (e.g., physics, astronomy, and chemistry). However, Hedges (1987) observed that measurements reported in the hard sciences, although they were usually more precise than in behavioral research (e.g., physical science measurements may be quoted in which the uncertainties are billionths of a second), are not necessarily more replicable than precise experimental measures in psychology. Hedges collected a number of cases in astronomy and thermochemistry where there were substantial differences between the reported values of experimental results. In the experimental field of thermodynamics, he noted that of 64 values reported for 64 elements in 1961, 25 of them (as of 1975) were later found to be in error by over 10%, 16 by over 30%, 8 by over 50%, 2 by over 100%, and 1 by over 245%. Hedges added that "in other areas (such as X-ray crystallography and certain protein assays), the folklore of the research community is that between-laboratory differences are so large that numerical data should only be compared within laboratories" (p. 453). In analytic chemistry, scientists working in different laboratories often arrange for "cooperative experiments" in the expectation that there will be differences in their quantitative analyses.

The fact is that all measurements are subject to fluctuations (called **error**) that can affect reliability and validity, and this is true no matter how precise the measurements. To illustrate, the scales at your local supermarket or corner grocery are based on a set of standard weights. Those and other standard measurements, which are housed at the National Bureau of Standards (NBS) in Washington, DC, are periodically checked by the NBS in a rigorously controlled setting. The purpose of this repeated checking is to ensure that we get what we pay for when, say, we ask for a pound of string beans. One such standard weight is called NB10 because its nominal value is 10 grams (the weight of two nickels). NBS technicians have weighed NB10 weekly ever since it was acquired around 1940, while keeping all factors known to affect such measurements (like air pressure and temperature) as constant as possible. Listed below are five values borrowed from a longer list noted by Freedman et al. (1991). These values represent the estimated weight of NB10 calibrated in micrograms to 6 decimal places:

9.999591 grams
9.999600 grams
9.999594 grams
9.999601 grams
9.999598 grams.

Notice that although the first four digits are consistent (at 9.999), the last three digits are, as Freedman et al. called them, "shaky" (p. 92). They vary from one measurement to another because of chance error (also frequently described as *noise*).

No matter whether the obtained measurements are of a pound of string beans, a 10-gram weight, or a psychological attribute, they can be understood as a combination of two components: (a) the presumed actual value (or "true value") of the thing measured (i.e., an ideal that would be obtained with a perfect measuring instrument) and (b) chance error (or noise). Traditionally, this general relationship is expressed as follows:

Observed value = Actual ("true") value + Chance (random) error.

In psychological testing, for example, because the reliability of a test reflects both real individual differences and error fluctuations, if everyone were alike the only measurable differences among them would be due to chance error (Graham & Lilly, 1984). The technical name for this type of error is **random error,** and it is presumed to be uncorrelated with the actual value.

A further distinction is made between random error and **systematic error** (also called **bias**). The basic difference is that random errors are thought to push measurements up and down around an exact value, so that the average of all observed values over many random trials should be very close to the actual value. Systematic error, on the other hand, is understood to push measurements in the same direction and thus to cause the mean value to be either too big or too small. Another way of thinking about this distinction is that random errors, on the average over many repeated measurements, are expected to cancel out, but systematic errors are not expected to cancel out. Suppose the grocer always weighs string beans with a thumb on the scale; he will inflate the price by tacking extra ounces onto the obtained measurement (a systematic error). Or suppose we want to estimate the weight of a child, and we weigh the child several times in a row but still get small variations in the measurements. Assuming the fluctuations are a function of random errors (which cancel out over the long run), we can estimate the child's true weight by averaging all the observed values. But suppose the scale has never been calibrated properly and is always 3 pounds too high. To cancel this known systematic error, we simply subtract 3 pounds from the mean of the observed values.

In chapter 7 we will describe how systematic errors in experimental research are the main concern of *internal validity*—which refers to the degree of validity of statements about whether changes in one variable result in changes in another variable. In some situations, a little systematic error may actually be better than a lot of random error, particularly when the direction and magnitude of the systematic error are known and can be compensated for (Stanley, 1971). We will also discuss how certain fluctuations in experimental responses due to the behavior or expectations of experimenters and research participants constitute systematic errors and what can be done to control for these biases, and in the next chapter we will discuss systematic rating errors made by judges and observers and the ways in which they are usually handled. The remainder of the present chapter is primarily concerned with methods that can be used by researchers to assess reliability and validity in different situations. We also explore the relationship between the concept of reliability and the role and limitations of replication in science.

ASSESSING STABILITY AND EQUIVALENCE

One situation in which reliability is a major concern is in the use of a psychological test to measure some attribute or behavior. If the researchers are to understand the functioning of the test, they must understand its reliability. Three traditional types of reliability in this situation are test-retest reliability, alternate-form reliability, and internal-consistency reliability. Each in turn is quantified by a particular **reliability coefficient,** which tells researchers what they might expect in repeated samples or replications with similar mean values. We start by explaining test-retest and alternate-form reliability, and then we will have much to say about internal-consistency reliability in separate sections.

Test-retest reliability (also called **retest reliability**) refers to the stability of a measure or particular instrument from one measurement session to another. The procedure for estimating the test-retest coefficient involves administering the instrument to a group of subjects and then administering it to the same group again later. The Pearson correlation (r) between these two sets of scores indicates the test's retest reliability. Most researchers believe that it is important to know this type of reliability if they plan to use a psychological test to predict or to measure *trait characteristics* (which are, by definition, individual attributes that are expected to have high temporal stability, such as someone's usual reaction time). On the other hand, if researchers are interested in something that is understood to be changeable or volatile under specifiable conditions (called a *state characteristic,* such as mood), much lower retest reliability would be expected.

In practice, many useful measuring instruments in the social and behavioral sciences have test-retest reliabilities substantially lower than $r = 1.0$. For instance, Parker, Hanson, and Hunsley (1988) estimated an average retest reliability for the Wechsler Adult Intelligence Scale (WAIS) of $r = .82$, for the Minnesota Multiphasic Personality Inventory (MMPI) of $r = .74$, and for the Rorschach inkblot test of $r = .85$. Braun and Wainer (1989) noted that typical retest reliabilities obtained by the Educational Testing Service (the company in Princeton, NJ, which developed, revises, and administers the Scholastic Assessment Test, or SAT) included correlations between .3 and .6 for SAT essay scores in the humanities, and between .6 and .8 for chemistry. To give us a feeling for what these numbers mean, Braun and Wainer mentioned that if we ranked a group of boys by height at age 6 and then again at age 10, the expected retest correlation would be greater than .8. If we ranked the boys by performance on an objectively scored intelligence test at two different ages, the expected correlation would be greater than .6. By way of comparison, if the boys were ranked once by height and again by performance on the intelligence test at the same age, the expected correlation would be only about .2 or .3 for these relatively unrelated variables.

Alternate-form reliability refers to the degree of equivalence of different versions of an instrument with different components (e.g., test items) that are all intended to measure the same thing (e.g., an attribute of some kind). Because alternate forms of a test must, by definition, be interrelated, we expect them to be highly correlated with one another when they are administered to the same individuals in the same session. Thus, the correlation between them at a particular time is one indication of how equivalent the measurement content of one form of the instrument is to the content of another form (also called **equivalent-forms reliability** by Guilford, 1954). To be equivalent in a statistical sense, however, the instruments are also expected to have similar variances, as well as similar intercorrelations with other theoretically relevant criteria (Gulliksen, 1950; Nunnally & Bernstein, 1994). Why should a researcher want more than one form of a measuring instrument? Suppose the research participants were administered the same test twice. The retest reliability might be artificially inflated because of the subjects' familiarity with the

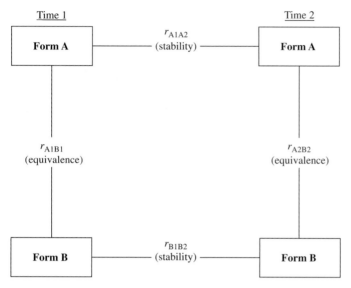

FIGURE 4.1
Correlational indices of stability and equivalence of a test administered in two forms (A and B) to the same participants at Time 1 and Time 2.

items, but we can avoid this problem by using two or more equivalent forms of the same instrument. Not all measuring instruments have equivalent forms, but many of the most popular psychological tests do.

Figure 4.1 illustrates the reliability coefficients for stability and equivalence in the case of alternate forms A and B of a test administered to the same participants at Times 1 and 2. Some of the correlations can be more precisely characterized as **stability coefficients** (i.e., correlations between scores on the same form administered to the same people at different times) and others, as **coefficients of equivalence** (i.e., correlations between scores on different forms administered to the same people at approximately the same time). Stability coefficients include the correlation between repeated administrations of Form A at Times 1 and 2 (r_{A1A2}) and the correlation between repeated administrations of Form B at Times 1 and 2 (r_{B1B2}). Coefficients of equivalence include the correlation between Forms A and B at Time 1 (r_{A1B1}) and the correlation between Forms A and B at Time 2 (r_{A2B2}). Not shown in this figure are the correlation between Form A at Time 1 and Form B at Time 2 (r_{A1B2}), or the correlation between Form B at Time 1 and Form A at Time 2 (r_{B1A2}); they are sometimes referred to as **cross-lagged correlations** because one of the two variables (*A* or *B*) is treated as a time-lagged value of the other variable. In chapter 8 we will illustrate how cross-lagged correlations have been used to try to tease out hypothesized causal chains in relational research designs.

We repeat that there can be difficulties in interpreting test-retest correlations. For example, one difficulty is distinguishing between the effect of memory and the effect of real changes (Remmers, 1963). If the interval between the two testing sessions is too short, the test-retest correlation may be inflated by the effect of memory in increasing the consistency of responses. On the other hand, if the interval is too long, there may be some real change in the characteristic being measured, which in turn could lower the retest correlation. Practice might also lead to varying amounts of improvement in the retest scores of some individuals on certain reasoning tests, because a person who has figured out a general solution will find it easier to solve similar problems more quickly on the retest (Anastasi & Urbina, 1997). If many respondents are inattentive because they do not feel the research is very important, their attitude could be reflected in noticeably diminished retest reliability (Rosnow, Skleder, Jaeger, & Rind, 1994). Furthermore, there really is no *single* retest reliability for a test, as the stability coefficient depends in part on the time interval between the two measurements (Thorndike, 1933).

Professional standards for educational and psychological testing nevertheless insist that test manuals attempt to specify an optimum interval between the test and the retest as well as any real changes (e.g., the effects of counseling, career moves, psychotherapy) that may affect measurement stability (American Psychological Association, 1985). If we know (through some independent observations, for example) that real changes in behavior have occurred, we can infer whether an instrument used to measure that behavior was **sensitive** enough to detect the changes (Martin & Bateson, 1986). Knowing that the behavior changed, resulting in changes in persons' relative standings, but finding a retest correlation near $r = 1.0$ would be a red flag that the instrument is insensitive to the behavioral change (Lindzey & Borgatta, 1954).

INTERNAL-CONSISTENCY RELIABILITY AND SPEARMAN-BROWN

The third type of reliability is **internal-consistency reliability;** it tells us the degree of relatedness of the individual items or components of the instrument in question when we want to use those items or components to obtain a single score. Because it indicates how well the separate items or components "hang together," it is also called the **reliability of components.** To distinguish it from other indices of reliability, we use the symbol R (and a superscript to denote the approach used to calculate this reliability). We focus this and the following section on three popular, classic approaches: (a) the Spearman-Brown equation, (b) Kuder and Richardson's Formula 20, and (c) Cronbach's alpha coefficient. If we judge the internal-consistency reliability of a test to be too low, we can increase the value of R by increasing the number of items, as long as the items remain reasonably homogeneous (i.e., the new items are similarly correlated with the old items and with each other, and all items, old and new, have the same variance). What constitutes an acceptable level of internal-consistency reliability? There is no specific criterion of acceptability; it would depend on the situation, but Parker et al. (1988) estimated the average internal-consistency reliability of the WAIS to be .87, which they compared with their estimate of the average internal-consistency reliability of the MMPI (.84) and the Rorschach inkblot test (.86). Generally speaking, values of this magnitude are considered very substantial by psychometric standards, but tests with much lower levels of reliability have still been found very useful.

We begin with R^{SB} and the **Spearman-Brown equation** that is used to calculate it. This approach is particularly convenient to use in predicting how changing the length of a test should affect the total reliability of the test. The Spearman-Brown equation, which takes its name from the fact that Charles Spearman (1910) and William Brown (1910) independently reported it in the same issue of the *British Journal of Psychology,* is represented in the following expression:

$$R^{SB} = \frac{nr_{ii}}{1 + (n-1)r_{ii}} \tag{4.1}$$

where R^{SB} is the reliability of the sum of n item scores, and r_{ii} is the mean intercorrelation among all the items (i.e., the item-to-item correlation, or the reliability of a single item).

To illustrate, suppose we administer a three-item test to a group of people and calculate the following correlations among the items: $r_{12} = .45$ (i.e., the correlation between scores on Item 1 and Item 2), $r_{13} = .50$, and $r_{23} = .55$. The mean of these correlations is $r_{ii} = .50$ (i.e., the average item reliability), and substituting in Equation 4.1, with $n = 3$ items, gives us

$$R^{SB} = \frac{3(.50)}{1 + (3-1).50} = .75,$$

which is the overall (or composite) reliability of the test as a whole, when it is also assumed that all items have the same variance. This reliability will increase monotonically with increased test length as long as the items being added are relevant and are not less reliable than the items already in the test (Li, Rosenthal, & Rubin, 1996). To give an extreme case, suppose the items being added were pure noise. Because their addition would increase the error variance, the reliability of the total of all items would decrease (unless the new items were given zero weight when the test is scored). The point is that the Spearman-Brown equation formally assumes that the items in the composite test, whose score is the simple total of all items, measure the same trait and have the same variance, and that all pairs have the same correlation. To the extent that those assumptions are more and more violated, the Spearman-Brown equation and its implications are less and less accurate.

However, let us assume those assumptions are not violated by the addition of three new items we have created that will double the test length. We now want to estimate the reliability of the six-item test as a whole. Assuming no change in the item-to-item (i.e., mean) correlation with the addition of our three new items (i.e., r_{ii} remains at .50), using Equation 4.1 gives us

$$R^{SB} = \frac{6(.50)}{1 + (6-1).50} = .86.$$

What if we want to further increase the length of the test, going to nine items? Assuming the new items meet the aforementioned assumptions, using Equation 4.1 gives us

$$R^{SB} = \frac{9(.50)}{1 + (9-1).50} = .90.$$

In all, if we double the test length, we expect to increase its internal-consistency reliability from .75 to .86. Tripling the test length, we expect to increase its internal-consistency reliability to .90. We find that, by adding similar new items, we can keep improving the internal-consistency reliability. However, there is a psychological limit to how many items we should add, because the larger the number of items, the more likely it is that fatigue and boredom will result in inattention and careless (or inaccurate) responding.

To find out quite directly how many items (n) we will need to reach any particular level of internal-consistency reliability, we rearrange Equation 4.1 as follows:

$$n = \frac{R^{SB}(1 - r_{ii})}{r_{ii}(1 - R^{SB})}, \tag{4.2}$$

with all symbols defined as before. Continuing with our three-item test, where we had mean item-to-item reliability of $r_{ii} = .50$, we want to know how many items, all averaging $r_{ii} = .50$, we need to achieve a Spearman-Brown internal-consistency reliability of .90. Substituting in Equation 4.2, we find

$$n = \frac{.90(1 - .50)}{.50(1 - .90)} = 9.$$

Thus, the value of the Spearman-Brown procedure is not only that it allows us to estimate the expected increase in internal-consistency reliability (Equation 4.1), but that it can also tell us quite directly the number of items we need to reach a desired level of reliability (Equation 4.2).

Table 4.1 is a useful summary table (Rosenthal, 1987a). It gives the internal-consistency reliability (R^{SB}) of values ranging from one to 100 items. Thus, given the obtained or estimated mean reliability (r_{ii}) and the number of items (n) in a test, we can look up the internal-consistency reliability (R^{SB}) of the test. Alternatively, given the obtained or estimated mean reliability (r_{ii}) and the desired internal-consistency reliability (R^{SB}), we can look up the number of items (n) we will need. As we illustrate shortly, Table 4.1 is also useful when, instead of a test made up of a number of items, we have a group of judges or raters and want to estimate values similar to those above.

KR20 AND CRONBACH'S ALPHA

The reliability literature is immense, and the Spearman-Brown method is one of several classic approaches to internal-consistency reliability. Another method was created by Kuder and Richardson (1937). For a long time, the standard method for estimating the reliability of components was to correlate one half of the test with the other half, a correlation yielding **split-half reliability** (e.g., correlating the odd- and even-numbered items). The problem is that we can get different split-half correlations, depending on how a test is divided in half. Kuder and Richardson created a number of equations, of which the 20th has become the most famous and has come to be called **KR20** (symbolized here as R^{KR20}). It implies the split-half reliability based on all possible splits, and it is used when test items are scored dichotomously. In a true-false achievement test, for example, correct answers would be scored 1 and incorrect answers 0. In a psychological test in which there are no right or wrong answers, the score of the answers would be 1 or 0 based on the scoring key and the objective of the test.

TABLE 4.1

Internal consistency reliability (R^{SB}) of the sum or mean of a sample of n items or judges

n	.01	.03	.05	.10	.15	.20	.25	.30	.35	.40	.45	.50	.55	.60	.65	.70	.75	.80	.85	.90	.95
									Mean reliability (r_{ii} or r_{jj})												
1	.01	.03	.05	.10	.15	.20	.25	.30	.35	.40	.45	.50	.55	.60	.65	.70	.75	.80	.85	.90	.95
2	.02	.06	.10	.18	.26	.33	.40	.46	.52	.57	.62	.67	.71	.75	.79	.82	.86	.89	.92	.95	.97
3	.03	.08	.14	.25	.35	.43	.50	.56	.62	.67	.71	.75	.79	.82	.85	.88	.90	.92	.94	.96	.98
4	.04	.11	.17	.31	.41	.50	.57	.63	.68	.73	.77	.80	.83	.86	.88	.90	.92	.94	.96	.97	*
5	.05	.13	.21	.36	.47	.56	.62	.68	.73	.77	.80	.83	.86	.88	.90	.92	.94	.95	.97	.98	*
6	.06	.16	.24	.40	.51	.60	.67	.72	.76	.80	.83	.86	.88	.90	.92	.93	.95	.96	.97	.98	*
7	.07	.18	.27	.44	.55	.64	.70	.75	.79	.82	.85	.88	.90	.91	.93	.94	.95	.97	.98	.98	*
8	.08	.20	.30	.47	.59	.67	.73	.77	.81	.84	.87	.89	.91	.92	.94	.95	.96	.97	.98	.98	*
9	.09	.22	.32	.50	.61	.69	.75	.79	.83	.86	.88	.90	.92	.93	.94	.95	.96	.97	.98	*	*
10	.10	.24	.34	.53	.64	.71	.77	.81	.84	.87	.89	.91	.92	.94	.95	.96	.97	.98	.98	*	*
12	.11	.27	.39	.57	.68	.75	.80	.84	.87	.89	.91	.92	.94	.95	.96	.97	.97	.98	*	*	**
14	.12	.30	.42	.61	.71	.78	.82	.86	.88	.90	.92	.93	.94	.95	.96	.97	.98	.98	*	*	**
16	.14	.33	.46	.64	.74	.80	.84	.87	.90	.91	.93	.94	.95	.96	.97	.97	.98	.98	*	*	**
18	.15	.36	.49	.67	.76	.82	.86	.89	.91	.92	.94	.95	.96	.96	.97	.97	.98	.98	*	*	**
20	.17	.38	.51	.69	.78	.83	.87	.90	.92	.93	.94	.95	.96	.97	.97	.98	.98	*	*	*	**
24	.20	.43	.56	.73	.81	.86	.89	.91	.93	.94	.95	.96	.97	.97	.98	.98	*	*	*	*	**
28	.22	.46	.60	.76	.83	.88	.90	.92	.94	.95	.96	.97	.97	.98	.98	.98	*	*	*	**	**
32	.24	.50	.63	.78	.85	.89	.91	.93	.95	.96	.96	.97	.98	.98	.98	*	*	*	*	**	**
36	.27	.53	.65	.80	.86	.90	.92	.94	.95	.96	.97	.97	.98	.98	*	*	*	*	**	**	**
40	.29	.55	.68	.82	.88	.91	.93	.94	.96	.96	.97	.98	.98	*	*	*	*	*	**	**	**
50	.34	.61	.72	.85	.90	.93	.94	.96	.96	.97	.98	.98	.98	*	*	*	*	**	**	**	**
60	.38	.65	.76	.87	.91	.94	.95	.96	.97	.98	.98	.98	*	*	*	*	*	**	**	**	**
80	.45	.71	.81	.90	.93	.95	.96	.97	.98	.98	.98	*	*	*	*	**	**	**	**	**	**
100	.50	.76	.84	.92	.95	.96	.97	.98	.98	*	*	*	*	*	*	**	**	**	**	**	**

Note: * = approximately .99; ** = approximately 1.00.

To illustrate the application of KR20, we refer to Table 4.2, in which 8 people responded to three dichotomous items. The formula for computing KR20 is

$$R^{KR20} = \left(\frac{n}{n-1}\right)\left(\frac{\sigma_t^2 - \Sigma PQ}{\sigma_t^2}\right), \tag{4.3}$$

in which n = number of items in the test; σ_t^2 = variance of the total test score; P = proportion of responses scored 1 for each item in turn; $Q = 1 - P$ (i.e., the proportion of responses scored 0 for each item); and ΣPQ instructs us to sum the products of P and Q over all items. The variance of the total test score (σ_t^2) is obtained from the total scores (t) of the persons (p) tested:

$$\sigma_t^2 = \frac{\Sigma(t_p - \bar{t}_p)^2}{p}, \tag{4.4}$$

where $\bar{t}_p$ is the mean of all the t_p scores. For our three-item test, we would compute the variance of the total test score as follows:

$$\sigma_t^2 = \frac{\left[(3-2.25)^2 + (3-2.25)^2 + (2-2.25)^2 + (3-2.25)^2 + (1-2.25)^2 + (0-2.25)^2 + (3-2.25)^2 + (3-2.25)^2\right]}{8}$$
$$= 1.1875$$

We obtain the value of ΣPQ from Table 4.2 as follows:
$$\Sigma PQ = .234 + .188 + .109 = .531$$

TABLE 4.2
Responses of eight participants to three dichotomous items

	Items			
Participants	1	2	3	Total (t)
Person 1	1	1	1	3
Person 2	1	1	1	3
Person 3	0	1	1	2
Person 4	1	1	1	3
Person 5	0	0	1	1
Person 6	0	0	0	0
Person 7	1	1	1	3
Person 8	1	1	1	3
P	.625	.750	.875	
Q	.375	.250	.125	
[a]$PQ = \sigma_i^2$	.234	.188	.109	$\sigma_t^2 = 1.188$
[b]S^2	.268	.214	.125	$S_t^2 = 1.357$

$r_{12} = .745$ [a]$\Sigma PQ = .531$

$r_{13} = .488$ [b]$\Sigma S^2 = .607$

$r_{23} = .655$

$r_{ii} = .629$

Substitution in Equation 4.3 yields

$$R^{KR20} = \left(\frac{3}{3-1}\right)\left(\frac{1.188 - 0.531}{1.188}\right) = .830$$

The Kuder-Richardson equation is also understood to be a special case of a more general expression called **Cronbach's alpha,** or the **alpha coefficient**—which we symbolize as $\boldsymbol{R^{Cronbach}}$ to emphasize that it was Lee J. Cronbach (1951) who developed this approach. The σ_t^2 value of Equation 4.3 is replaced by S_t^2, the variance of the total test scores of the p persons tested:

$$S_t^2 = \frac{\sum(t_p - \bar{t}_p)^2}{p-1} \tag{4.5}$$

The ΣPQ value of Equation 4.3 is replaced by $\Sigma(S_i^2)$, the sum of the variances of the individual items, that is,

$$R^{Cronbach} = \left(\frac{n}{n-1}\right)\left(\frac{S_t^2 - \sum(S_i^2)}{S_t^2}\right), \tag{4.6}$$

or alternatively,

$$R^{Cronbach} = \left(\frac{n}{n-1}\right)\left(1 - \frac{\sum(S_i^2)}{S_t^2}\right). \tag{4.7}$$

For the data of Table 4.2, we find

$$R^{Cronbach} = \left(\frac{3}{2}\right)\left(\frac{1.357 - .607}{1.357}\right) = .829,$$

within rounding error of the value we obtained for KR20.

Cronbach's alpha coefficient can also be estimated from the analysis of variance, which makes the alpha coefficient convenient when there are large numbers of items and it becomes cumbersome to calculate the intercorrelations by hand. To illustrate we refer to Table 4.3, which summarizes the analysis of variance obtained on the data in Table 4.2. The estimation of coefficient alpha from those results is as follows:

$$R^{Cronbach} = \left(\frac{n}{n-1}\right)\left(1 - \frac{MS_{persons} + (n-1)MS_{residual}}{(n)MS_{persons}}\right), \tag{4.8}$$

TABLE 4.3
Repeated-measures analysis of variance on results in Table 4.2

Source	Sum of squares	df	Mean squares
Between persons	3.167	7	.452
Within persons			
Items	.250	2	.125
Items × Persons	1.083	14	.077

where n is the number of items, and the other symbols are defined in Table 4.3 (Li & Wainer, 1998). Substitution in Equation 4.8 gives us

$$R^{Cronbach} = \left(\frac{3}{2}\right)\left(1 - \frac{.452 + (2).077}{(3).452}\right) = .830$$

To bring the discussion full circle, we now use the Spearman-Brown formula (Equation 4.1) to compute the reliability of the data in Table 4.2:

$$R^{SB} = \frac{3(.629)}{1 + (3 - 1).629} = .836.$$

In this illustration, all the obtained estimates of internal-consistency reliability are quite similar. Li and Wainer (1997) showed that when all item variances are equal, the estimates obtained from these methods should be identical, as the methods are mathematically equivalent.

EFFECTIVE RELIABILITY OF JUDGES

The same reliability procedures are applicable when researchers use judges to classify or rate things and want to estimate the reliability of the judges as a group, or what we call **effective reliability.** Suppose there are three judges who rate five clients who have been administered a counseling or clinical treatment, with the results shown in Table 4.4. We approach this question the same way we approached that of "How many items?" in the previous discussion. Using the Spearman-Brown formula (Equation 4.1), with notation redefined, we can estimate the effective reliability of the 3 judges (assuming the reliability of the individual judges is similar; Li et al., 1996; Tinsley & Weiss, 1975; Overall, 1965) by using the following formula:

$$R^{SB} = \frac{nr_{jj}}{1 + (n - 1)r_{jj}},\qquad(4.9)$$

TABLE 4.4
Ratings and intercorrelations for three judges

Clients	Judges		
	A	B	C
Person 1	5	6	7
Person 2	3	6	4
Person 3	3	4	6
Person 4	2	2	3
Person 5	1	4	4

$r_{AB} = .645$
$r_{AC} = .800$
$r_{BC} = .582$
$r_{jj} = .676$

where R^{SB} is the effective reliability (i.e., reliability of the total set of judges), n is the number of judges, and r_{jj} is the mean correlation among all the judges (i.e., our estimate of the reliability of an individual judge). Applying Equation 4.9 to the results in Table 4.4, we find

$$R^{SB} = \frac{3(.676)}{1 + (3 - 1).676} = .862.$$

We again consult Table 4.1, in which case we can estimate any one of the three values once we know the other two. For example, given an obtained or estimated mean reliability of $r_{jj} = .40$, and assuming we want to achieve an effective reliability of $R^{SB} = .85$ or higher, we will need at least $n = 9$ judges.

Alternatively, using Equation 4.8, we can compute Cronbach's alpha coefficient from the information in Table 4.5, with results as follows:

$$R^{Cronbach} = \left(\frac{3}{2}\right)\left(1 - \frac{6.00 + (2)0.85}{(3)6.00}\right) = .858.$$

Another classic analysis of variance (ANOVA) procedure, introduced by C. Hoyt (1941), allows us to estimate the effective reliability by

$$R^{Hoyt} = \frac{MS_{persons} - MS_{residual}}{MS_{persons}}, \qquad (4.10)$$

from which we obtain

$$R^{Hoyt} = \frac{6.00 - 0.85}{6.00} = .858.$$

It turns out that R^{Hoyt} is identical to Equation 4.8, the ANOVA-based procedure for estimating $R^{Cronbach}$.

To obtain an estimate of the judge-to-judge reliability, we use the following formula to calculate the **intraclass correlation:**

$$r_{intraclass} = r_{jj} = \frac{MS_{persons} - MS_{residual}}{MS_{persons} + (n - 1)MS_{residual}}, \qquad (4.11)$$

which, applied to the results in Table 4.5, yields

$$r_{jj} = \frac{6.00 - 0.85}{6.00 + (3 - 1)0.85} = .669.$$

TABLE 4.5

Repeated-measures analysis of variance on results in Table 4.4

Source	Sum of squares	df	Mean squares
Between persons	24.0	4	6.00
Within persons			
Judges	11.2	2	5.60
Judges × Persons	6.8	8	0.85

The estimate of effective reliability that we obtained by the Spearman-Brown procedure (R^{SB} = .862) differs by only .004 from the estimate obtained by Cronbach's approach ($R^{Cronbach}$ = .858) or by Hoyt's method (R^{Hoyt} = .858). Furthermore, the mean correlation shown in Table 4.4 (r_{jj} = .676) differs by only .007 from the estimate (.669) obtained by the analysis of variance. In general, the differences obtained between those approaches are quite small. In this simple example, the Spearman-Brown procedure was also not an onerous one to use, with only three correlations to compute. However, as the number of judges (or number of items) increases, it becomes increasingly more convenient to use the analysis of variance approach. (We will see the results in Tables 4.4 and 4.5 again in a later chapter, when we discuss repeated-measures designs and the intraclass correlation, which is another name for the average judge-to-judge or item-to-item reliability.)

EFFECTIVE COST OF JUDGES

In our discussion of judges, we have assumed that they were of a "single type." That is, they are more-or-less interchangeable, in that different judges showed similar variance in ratings and the intercorrelations among pairs of judges were also very similar. In many research situations that employ judges or raters, the interchangeability criterion applies pretty well. The judges may be undergraduate students enrolled in introductory psychology courses, or they may be graduate students in psychology, or they may be highly specialized mental health professionals (e.g., psychiatrists, clinical or counseling psychologists, or psychiatric social workers). But suppose *all* those types were available for use as judges. Without special care, it does not work well to select judges with such different backgrounds, who would very likely differ considerably in their reliabilities, or in their cost to the researcher. Procedures are available that allow us to select the type of judge we ought to employ to maximize effective reliability for fixed cost (Li et al., 1996). The selection rule requires the computation of a simple quantity, called **effective cost** (EC_j for judge type *j*, i.e., the effective reliability cost of a judge of this type):

$$EC_j = C_j \left(\frac{1 - r_{jj}}{r_{jj}} \right), \tag{4.12}$$

where C_j is the cost per judge of type *j*, and r_{jj} is the average intercorrelation of judges of type *j* with one another. Table 4.6 provides a feel for the quantity EC_j at various levels of reliability and cost.

Once we have computed the effective reliability cost of each type of judge, the selection rule requires us to rank the judge types by their effective reliability cost from smallest (best) to greatest (worst) and to select judges starting from the best until either the number of judges or the funds available are exhausted. By way of illustration, suppose we want to rate the degree of anxiety shown by a series of clients undergoing psychotherapy. Hiring college students to do the ratings would cost us $20 per rater, and the average intercorrelation among these college students (their

TABLE 4.6
Table of effective reliability cost (*EC*)

Cost ($)	Reliability (r_{jj} or r_{ii})									
	.05	.10	.20	.30	.40	.50	.60	.70	.80	.90
1	19	9	4	2.33	1.50	1	0.67	0.43	0.25	0.11
5	95	45	20	11.67	7.50	5	3.33	2.14	1.25	0.56
10	190	90	40	23.33	15.00	10	6.67	4.29	2.50	1.11
15	285	135	60	35.00	22.50	15	10.00	6.43	3.75	1.67
20	380	180	80	46.67	30.00	20	13.33	8.57	5.00	2.22
30	570	270	120	70.00	45.00	30	20.00	12.86	7.50	3.33
40	760	360	160	93.33	60.00	40	26.67	17.14	10.00	4.44
50	950	450	200	116.67	75.00	50	33.33	21.43	12.50	5.56
60	1140	540	240	140.00	90.00	60	40.00	25.71	15.00	6.67
70	1330	630	280	163.33	105.00	70	46.67	30.00	17.50	7.78
80	1520	720	320	186.67	120.00	80	53.33	34.29	20.00	8.89
90	1710	810	360	210.00	135.00	90	60.00	38.57	22.50	10.00
100	1900	900	400	233.33	150.00	100	66.67	42.86	25.00	11.11
200	3800	1800	800	466.67	300.00	200	133.33	85.71	50.00	22.22
300	5700	2700	1200	700.00	450.00	300	200.00	128.57	75.00	33.33
400	7600	3600	1600	933.33	600.00	400	266.67	171.43	100.00	44.44

Note: The effective cost values can be obtained from the following equation:

$EC = \text{Cost}\left(\dfrac{1-r}{r}\right)$, where r can refer either to the average judge-to-judge reliability (r_{jj}) or the average item-to-item reliability (r_{ii}).

reliability) is .40. Thus, from Equation 4.12, the effective reliability cost for each college student is

$$EC_{\text{student}} = C_{\text{student}}\left(\frac{1 - r_{\text{student}}}{r_{\text{student}}}\right)$$

$$= \$20\left(\frac{1-.40}{.40}\right) = \$30$$

Hiring experienced clinicians would cost $400 per clinician rater, and the average intercorrelation among these clinicians is .60. The effective reliability cost for each clinician is

$$EC_{\text{clinician}} = C_{\text{clinician}}\left(\frac{1 - r_{\text{clinician}}}{r_{\text{clinician}}}\right)$$

$$= \$400\left(\frac{1-.60}{.60}\right) = \$266.77$$

In this example, our best strategy to maximize the effective reliability for a fixed cost would be to choose only college students as raters. Table 4.1, based on the

Spearman-Brown procedure, indicates that it would take 6 college student raters (with a mean reliability of .40) to produce an effective reliability of .80. The total cost is the effective cost multiplied by the number (n) of judges, and so the total cost = $30 × 6 = $180. To achieve an effective reliability of .90 would require that we employ 14 college student raters with total cost of $30 × 14 = $420. If we used experienced clinicians (with a mean reliability of .60), Table 4.1 shows that we would require only 3 raters to reach an effective reliability of about .80 and 6 raters to reach an effective reliability of .90. We would need fewer raters, but the cost would be a good deal more than that of choosing college students, that is, $266.67 × 3 = $800 to reach an effective reliability of about .80 (compared to $180 for college students). Employing clinicians to reach an effective reliability of .90 would cost $266.67 × 6 = $1,600 (compared to only $420 for college student raters).

Suppose that, in our thinking about the selection of raters to maximize reliability for a fixed cost, we add a third type of rater, for example, graduate students in clinical psychology. Further, assume that hiring a graduate student rater would cost $35, and that the average intercorrelation among graduate student raters is .55. Then, from Equation 4.12, the effective reliability cost is

$$EC = \$35\left(\frac{1 - .55}{.55}\right) = \$28.64$$

Because the effective reliability cost of $28.64 per graduate student is lower than the effective cost of $30 per undergraduate student, our best strategy to maximize effective reliability would be to choose only graduate students. If not enough graduate students are available (e.g., we want seven to achieve an effective reliability of .90, but only four are available), we can employ all that are available and add raters of the type with the next lowest effective reliability cost (college students in this example).

When two or more different types of judges (i.e., those differing in their average judge-to-judge intercorrelations, as in the present example) are employed, the Spearman-Brown formula does not apply, nor does Equation 4.1, which is based on the Spearman-Brown. Instead, we can use slightly more specialized equations, which are described elsewhere (Li, 1994; Li et al., 1996). These equations allow us to compute an overall reliability when two or more different types of judges are employed and we want to estimate a single effective reliability as opposed to computing reliabilities for each different type of judge or rater.

EFFECTIVE COST OF ITEMS

We have discussed the effective reliability of judges in two conditions: (a) when judges are of a single type and (b) when they are of two or more types. Everything we have said about judges or raters applies equally to the items of a test. Thus, the selection rules for choosing the type of judges to maximize effective reliability (for fixed cost) also apply to the selection of items to maximize the internal-consistency reliability of a test (for fixed cost).

For example, suppose we want to construct a test of content mastery with both essay questions and multiple-choice items available. The essay items cost $1.00 to score, and their average intercorrelation (i.e., item-to-item reliability) is $r_{ii} = .60$. Multiple-choice items cost only \$.01 to score, but their average intercorrelation is only $r_{ii} = .10$. Using Equation 4.12, we find that the effective cost (EC) for an essay item is

$$EC_{\text{essay}} = C_i\left(\frac{1 - r_{ii}}{r_{ii}}\right)$$

$$= \$1.00\left(\frac{1 - .60}{0.60}\right) = \$0.67,$$

and the effective cost for a multiple-choice item is

$$EC_{\text{multiple-choice}} = \$0.01\left(\frac{1 - .10}{.10}\right) = \$0.09.$$

To maximize internal-consistency reliability—say, for a fixed cost of \$7—we would choose 700 multiple-choice items (mean reliability of .10), yielding an internal-consistency reliability of $R^{SB} = .99$. If we had spent \$7 on 7 essay items (mean reliability of .60), our internal-consistency reliability would have been lower ($R^{SB} = .91$). Had there been only 200 multiple-choice items available, we would have used these at a cost of \$2 and added 5 essay items at a cost of \$5. Using equations that are available elsewhere (Li et al., 1996), we could compute the internal-consistency reliability of this hybrid test as $R^{SB} = .97$, which is lower than the test composed of 700 multiple-choice items but higher than the test composed exclusively of 7 essay items.

INTERRATER AGREEMENT AND RELIABILITY

An unfortunate practice among many researchers is to confuse the percentage of agreement of judges or raters with their interrater reliability. *Interrater agreement* and *interrater reliability* are not merely synonyms. As we will now show, percentage agreement is often ambiguous and can be quite misleading (even in the case of just two judges). To calculate the percentage of agreement of the judges, we need to know the number of agreements (A) and the number of disagreements (D) among them. Then we simply substitute this information in the following formula:

$$\text{Percentage agreement} = \left(\frac{A}{A + D}\right)100, \qquad (4.13)$$

or we can compute the net agreement of the judges by

$$\text{Net agreement} = \left(\frac{A - D}{A + D}\right)100. \qquad (4.14)$$

The specific failing of both these indices is that they do not differentiate between accuracy and variability (Cohen, 1960; Robinson, 1957; Rosenthal, 1987a; Tinsley & Weiss, 1975).

Table 4.7 shows that percentage agreement can be a very misleading indicator of interjudge reliability. In Part A of this table, Smith and Jones independently have two judges evaluate the same 100 film clips of children for the presence or absence

TABLE 4.7
Examples of percentage agreement

A. Two cases of 98% agreement						
Smith's results				Jones's results		
	Judge A				Judge C	
Judge B	Frown	No frown		Judge D	Frown	No frown
Frown	98	1		Frown	49	1
No frown	1	0		No frown	1	49
Agreement = 98%				Agreement = 98%		
r_{AB} (phi) = −.01, and $\chi^2_{(1)}$ = 0.01				r_{CD} (phi) = +.96, and $\chi^2_{(1)}$ = 92.16		

B. Two cases of 50% agreement						
Hill's results				Reed's results		
	Judge E				Judge G	
Judge F	Frown	No frown		Judge H	Frown	No frown
Frown	50	25		Frown	25	50
No frown	25	0		No frown	0	25
Agreement = 50%				Agreement = 50%		
r_{EF} (phi) = −.33, and $\chi^2_{(1)}$ = 11.11				r_{GH} (phi) = +.33, and $\chi^2_{(1)}$ = 11.11		

of frowning behavior, with the results as shown. Based on Equation 4.13, Smith finds that the percentage agreement between Judges A and B is

$$\text{Percentage agreement} = \left(\frac{98}{98+2}\right)100 = 98\%$$

and Jones finds that the percentage agreement between Judges C and D is

$$\text{Percentage agreement} = \left(\frac{98}{98+2}\right)100 = 98\%$$

The percentages are identical, yet in Table 4.7 we can clearly see that the original data collected by Smith and Jones are very different. Judges A and B in Smith's study may have shared the same bias, each judge showing a variance (S^2) of only .01. Judges C and D in Jones's study were consistently unbiased, each judge showing a variance (S^2) of .25.

A better procedure would be to report the product-moment correlation (r). In this case, it is natural to report the phi (ϕ) coefficient, which is the product-moment r for a 2 × 2 table of counts. Rearranging Equation 2.1 in Chapter 2, we obtain

$$\phi = \sqrt{\frac{\chi^2_{(1)}}{N}}, \tag{4.15}$$

For Smith's results, solving Equation 4.15 yields

$$r = \sqrt{\frac{.01}{100}} = -0.01,$$

whereas for Jones's results, we find

$$r = \sqrt{\frac{92.16}{100}} = .96.$$

Clearly the effect size correlation is more sensitive than percentage agreement to the quite noticeable difference between Smith's and Jones's results in Table 4.7.

Part B of Table 4.7 shows two additional cases of percentage agreement obtained by Hill and Reed. This time, the two investigators both obtained an apparently chance level of agreement (i.e., 50%). Both results, however, are very far from reflecting chance agreement, both with $p = .0009$. Most surprising, perhaps, is that Hill obtained a substantial negative reliability ($r = -.33$), whereas Reed obtained a substantial positive reliability ($r = +.33$). This is another illustration of why percentage agreement is not a very informative index of reliability.

COHEN'S KAPPA

Jacob Cohen (1960) developed a popular index called **kappa** (κ), which successfully addresses some of the problems of percentage agreement. In particular, kappa is adjusted for agreement based on simple lack of variability, as illustrated in Table 4.7, where in Smith's study both judges reported 99% of the expressions they saw as frowning behavior. Table 4.8 gives an example of the type of situation in which kappa is often employed. Suppose that two clinical diagnosticians have examined 100 people and assigned them to one of four classifications (schizophrenic, neurotic, normal, and brain damaged). The three quantities needed to compute kappa are symbolized as O, E, and N.

TABLE 4.8
Results of two diagnosticians' classification of 100 persons into one of four categories

Judge 2	Judge 1				
	A Schizophrenic	B Neurotic	C Normal	D Brain-damaged	Sum
A Schizophrenic	13	0	0	12	25
B Neurotic	0	12	13	0	25
C Normal	0	13	12	0	25
D Brain-damaged	12	0	0	13	25
Sum	25	25	25	25	100

$$\kappa(df = 9) = \frac{O - E}{N - E} = \frac{50 - 25}{100 - 25} = .333$$

The value designated as O refers to the *observed* number on which the two judges have agreed (i.e., numbers on the diagonal of agreement), which in this example is $O = 13 + 12 + 12 + 13 = 50$. The value designated as E refers to the *expected* number under the hypothesis of only chance agreement for the cells on the diagonal of agreement. For each cell, the expected number is the product of the row total and the column total divided by the total number of cases, which in this example gives us $E = (25 \times 25)/100 + (25 \times 25)/100 + (25 \times 25)/100 + (25 \times 25)/100 = 6.25 + 6.25 + 6.25 + 6.25 = 25$. And N is the *total number* of cases classified, or in this example $N = 100$. The equation for Cohen's kappa is

$$\kappa = \frac{O - E}{N - E},$$ (4.16)

and substitution in this equation yields $(50 - 25)/(100 - 25) = .333$.

Although Cohen's kappa is clearly an improvement over percentage agreement, as an index of interrater reliability it does raise some serious questions. When we are working with tables larger than 2×2 (e.g., the 4×4 example in Table 4.8), kappa suffers from the same problem as does any statistic with $df > 1$ (which we call **omnibus statistical procedures,** distinguishing them from 1-df tests, called **focused statistical procedures**). The problem with most omnibus kappas is that we cannot tell which focused or specific judgments are made reliably and which are made unreliably. Only when kappa approaches unity is its interpretation straightforward; that is, all judgments are made reliably (Rosenthal, 1991b).

We illustrate the difficulty in interpreting kappa by returning to Table 4.8. The 4×4 table we see, based on 9 df (i.e., the number of rows minus 1 times the number of columns minus 1), can be decomposed into a series of six pairwise 2×2 tables, each based on a single df, and each addressing a focused (very specific) question about the reliability of dichotomous judgments. These six focused questions pertain to the reliability of

Variable A versus Variable B,

Variable A versus Variable C,

Variable A versus Variable D,

Variable B versus Variable C,

Variable B versus Variable D, and

Variable C versus Variable D

Table 4.9 shows the results of computing kappa separately for each of these six pairwise 2×2 tables. Of the six focused or specific reliabilities that were computed, the subheadings note that four are kappas of 1.00, and two are kappas near zero (.04 and $-.04$). The mean of all six of these 1-df kappas is .667, and the median is 1.00; neither value is predictable from the omnibus 9-df kappa value of .333.

To demonstrate even more clearly how little relation there is between the omnibus values of kappa and the associated 1-df kappas (i.e., the focused reliability kappas), we refer to Tables 4.10 and 4.11. Table 4.10 shows an omnibus 9-df kappa value of .333, exactly the same value as that shown in Table 4.8. Table 4.11 shows the six focused reliabilities of $df = 1$ associated with the omnibus value of kappa

TABLE 4.9

Breakdown of the 9-*df* omnibus table of counts of Table 4.8 into six specific (focused) reliabilities of *df* = 1 each

A. Schizophrenic versus neurotic (kappa = 1.00)

Categories	A Schizophrenic	B Neurotic	Sum
A Schizophrenic	13	0	13
B Neurotic	0	12	12
Sum	13	12	25

B. Schizophrenic versus normal (kappa = 1.00)

Categories	A Schizophrenic	C Normal	Sum
A Schizophrenic	13	0	13
C Normal	0	12	12
Sum	13	12	25

C. Schizophrenic versus brain-damaged (kappa = .04)

Categories	A Schizophrenic	D Brain-damaged	Sum
A Schizophrenic	13	12	25
D Brain-damaged	12	13	25
Sum	25	25	50

D. Neurotic versus normal (kappa = −.04)

Categories	B Neurotic	C Normal	Sum
B Neurotic	12	13	25
C Normal	13	12	25
Sum	25	25	50

E. Neurotic versus brain-damaged (kappa = 1.00)

Categories	B Neurotic	D Brain-damaged	Sum
B Neurotic	12	0	12
D Brain-damaged	0	13	13
Sum	12	13	25

F. Normal versus brain-damaged (kappa = 1.00)

Categories	C Normal	D Brain-damaged	Sum
C Normal	12	0	12
D Brain-damaged	0	13	13
Sum	12	13	25

TABLE 4.10

Alternative results of two diagnosticians' classification of 100 persons into one of four categories

Judge 2	Judge 1				
	A	B	C	D	Sum
A	25	0	0	0	25
B	0	0	25	0	25
C	0	25	0	0	25
D	0	0	0	25	25
Sum	25	25	25	25	100

$$\kappa\left(df=9\right)=\frac{O-E}{N-E}=\frac{50-25}{100-25}=.333$$

(.333). We see that of those six focused kappas, four are kappas of .00, one is a kappa of +1.00, and one is a kappa of −1.00. The mean and median focused kappas both have a value of .00. Table 4.12 summarizes the two omnibus kappas of Tables 4.8 and 4.10 and their associated focused kappas of Tables 4.9 and 4.11. Thus, we have two identical kappas, one made up primarily of perfect reliabilities, and the other made up primarily of zero reliabilities.

Although the greatest limitations on kappa occur when it is based on $df > 1$, there are some problems with kappa even when it is based on a 2 × 2 table of counts with $df = 1$. The basic problem under these conditions is that very often kappa is not equivalent to the product-moment correlation computed from exactly the same 2 × 2 table of counts. This is certainly not a criticism of kappa, since it was never intended to be a product-moment correlation. The limitation, however, is that we cannot apply various interpretive procedures or displays to kappa that we can apply to product-moment correlations (such as the binomial effect size display, or BESD, which is described in chapter 11).

Here, we need indicate only the conditions under which a 1-df kappa would, or would not, be equivalent to a product-moment correlation (referred to as a **Pearson r** in the general case or, as noted previously, the phi coefficient in the case of a 2 × 2 table of counts). Simply stated, κ and r are equivalent when the row totals for levels A and B are identical to the column totals for levels A and B, respectively. Consider the examples in Table 4.13. Computing kappa on the data in the 2 × 2 table in Part A, where the marginal totals for level A are identical for Judges 1 and 2 (i.e., both sums = 80), from Equation 4.16 we obtain

$$\kappa(df=1)=\frac{80-68}{100-68}=.375,$$

and r (or equivalently, ϕ) yields the identical value of .375 by computations fully described in chapter 11, or simply by computation of the 1-df chi-square and then substituting in Equation 4.15. In chapter 11 we also describe the binomial effect size

TABLE 4.11
Breakdown of the 9-*df* omnibus table of counts of Table 4.10 into six specific (focused) reliabilities of *df* = 1 each

A. Variable A versus Variable B (kappa = .00)

Variables	A	B	Sum
A	25	0	25
B	0	0	0
Sum	25	0	25

B. Variable A versus Variable C (kappa = .00)

Variables	A	C	Sum
A	25	0	25
C	0	0	0
Sum	25	0	25

C. Variable A versus Variable D (kappa = 1.00)

Variables	A	D	Sum
A	25	0	25
D	0	25	25
Sum	25	25	50

D. Variable B versus Variable C (kappa = −1.00)

Variables	B	C	Sum
B	0	25	25
C	25	0	25
Sum	25	25	50

E. Variable B versus Variable D (kappa = .00)

Variables	B	D	Sum
B	0	0	0
D	0	25	25
Sum	0	25	25

F. Variable C versus Variable D (kappa = .00)

Variables	C	D	Sum
C	0	0	0
D	0	25	25
Sum	0	25	25

TABLE 4.12
Summary of omnibus and focused examples

	Location of example	
Summary of results	Tables 4.8 and 4.9	Tables 4.10 and 4.11
Omnibus kappa	.33	.33
Mean focused kappa	.67	.00
Median focused kappa	1.00	.00

display (BESD), which can be used to interpret this particular kappa because it is equivalent to a Pearson r.

Now consider the example in Part B of Table 4.13, in which we have the same four cell entries and the same marginal totals as in the preceding example. The only thing that has changed is the location of the cell with the largest count (70) so that the marginal totals for level A differ for Judges 1 and 2 (i.e., 20 versus 80). In this example, using Equation 4.16, we find

$$\kappa(df = 1) = \frac{20 - 32}{100 - 32} = -.176,$$

but r (ϕ) yields a markedly different value of $-.375$. We can, therefore, use the BESD (chapter 11) for the r, but not for the kappa. Therefore, we generally recommend using

TABLE 4.13
Comparison of kappa and the product-moment correlation

A. Kappa equivalent to phi (kappa = .375; phi = .375)

	Judge 1		
Judge 2	A	B	Sum
A	70	10	80
B	10	10	20
Sum	80	20	100

B. Kappa not equivalent to phi (kappa = $-.176$; phi = $-.375$)

	Judge 1		
Judge 2	A	B	Sum
A	10	70	80
B	10	10	20
Sum	20	80	100

the other procedures discussed in this chapter rather than using kappa as an index of reliability.

REPLICATION IN RESEARCH

Before we turn to the concept of validity, we must say something about the relationship between reliability and **replication** (or *repeatability*). The undetected equipment failure, the possible random human errors of procedure, observation, recording, computation, or report are well enough known to make scientists wary of unreplicated research results. Generalizability is sought in the replication of research results across time (a generalizability similar to test-retest reliability) and across different measurements, observers, or manipulations (a generalizability similar to the reliability of components). However, whereas replicability is universally accepted as one of the most important criteria of the establishment of true constants (e.g., the speed of light), even in the natural sciences it is not possible to repeat and authenticate every observation at will or with exactitude. In research with human participants, we should not think of replication as analogous to an exact photographic reproduction from a negative.

Clearly, the *same* experiment in behavioral research can never be repeated by a different worker. Indeed, it can never be repeated by even the same experimenter, because at the very least the participants and the experimenter are older. But to avoid the not very helpful conclusion that there can be no replication, we can speak of *relative replications*. We might, for example, rank experiments on how close they are to each other in terms of participants, experimenters, tasks, and situations, and perhaps agree that *this* experiment, more than *that* one, is like a given standard experiment. When researchers speak of replication, then, they are referring to a *relatively* exact repetition of a research result. Three factors affecting the utility of any particular replication as an indicator of reliability are (a) *when* the replication is conducted, (b) *how* the replication is conducted, and (c) *by whom* the replication is conducted (Rosenthal, 1990b).

The first factor—*when* the replication is conducted—is important because replicated studies conducted early in the history of a particular research question are usually more useful than replications conducted later in the history of that question. The first replication doubles our information about the research issue; the fifth replication adds 20% to our information level; and the fiftieth replication adds only 2% to our information level. Once the number of replications grows to be substantial, our need for further replication is likely to be due not to a real need for repetition of results but to a desire for the more adequate evaluation and summary of the replications already available (described in chapter 21).

How the replication is conducted is another important factor to keep in mind, as shown in Table 4.14. It has already been noted that replications are possible only in a relative sense. Still, there is a distribution of possible replications in which the variance is generated by the degree of similarity to the standard (i.e., the original study) that characterizes each possible replication. Let us assume the original study and the replication were correctly derived from a theory and that the original study and the replication addressed the same prediction or theoretical claim. A *precise*

TABLE 4.14
Theoretical implications of precision and success of replication

	Nature of the replication	
Result of replication	Precise replication	Varied replication
Successful	Supports the theory	Extends the theory
Unsuccessful	Damages the theory	Limits the theory

replication would be one that was intended to be as close to the original design as possible, and a *varied replication* would be one in which some aspect of the original design was intentionally varied in some way. A precise replication, if successful, would increase our confidence in the stability of the original finding and, in turn, in the theory that had predicted it, whereas a precise replication, if unsuccessful, would damage the theory by making us question the original result. A varied replication, if successful, would extend the generalizability of the theory, whereas a varied replication, if unsuccessful, would imply either specifiable limits (or boundaries) of the theory or make us question the original result. Thus, if we design replications to be as exactly like the original as possible, we may be more true to the standard, but we pay a price in terms of generalizability. However, if all we know is that the results of a replication did not support the original result, we cannot say (without further details) whether the lack of support stems from the instability of the original result, an unknown problem in the original study, or the imprecision of the replication.

The third factor—*by whom* the replicated research is conducted—is important because of the problem of **correlated replicators** (Rosenthal, 1990b). So far, we have assumed that the replications are independent of one another, but what does "independence" mean in this situation? The usual minimum requirement for independence is that the participants be different persons. What about the independence of the replicators? Are 10 replications conducted by a single investigator as independent of one another as a series of 10 replications each conducted by a different investigator? A scientist who has devoted her life's work to the study of vision is less likely to carry out a study of verbal conditioning than is an investigator whose interests have always been in the area of verbal learning. To the extent that researchers with different interests are different kinds of people—and as such are likely to obtain different data from their participants—we are forced to the conclusion that, within any given area of science, researchers come "precorrelated" by virtue of their common interests and any associated characteristics (i.e., they are correlated replicators). Thus, there is a limit on the degree of independence we may expect from workers or replicators in a common field. In different fields, however, the degree of correlation or similarity among the workers may be quite different. We all know of researchers in a common field who obtain data quite dissimilar from those obtained by others in that field. The actual degree of reliability, then, may not be very high and may even be represented by a negative correlation.

Behavioral research is commonly conducted nowadays by a team of researchers. Sometimes these teams consist entirely of colleagues; often they consist of one or more faculty members, one or more postdoctoral students, and one or more students at various stages of progress toward the Ph.D. degree. Researchers within a single research group may reasonably be assumed to be even more highly intercorrelated than any group of workers in the same area of interest who are not within the same research group. Students in a research group are perhaps more correlated with their major professor than would be true of another faculty member of the research group. There are two reasons for this likelihood: *selection* and *training*. First, students may elect to work in a given area with a given investigator because of their perceived or actual similarity of interest and associated characteristics. Colleagues are less likely to select a university, area of interest, and specific project because of a faculty member at that institution. Second, students may have had a larger proportion of their research training under the direction of a single professor. Other professors, although collaborating with their colleagues, have more often been trained in research elsewhere by other persons. Although there may be exceptions, it seems reasonable, on the whole, to assume that student researchers are more correlated with their adviser than another professor might be.

The correlation of replicators that we have been discussing refers directly to a correlation of *attributes* and indirectly to a correlation of the *data* the investigators will obtain from their participants. The issue of correlated replicators is by no means a new one; Karl Pearson (1902) spoke of the "high correlation of judgments [suggesting] an influence of the immediate atmosphere, which may work upon two observers for a time in the same manner" (p. 261). He believed the problem of correlated observers to be as critical for the physical sciences as for the behavioral sciences. Out of this discussion a simple principle emerges, which is that, generally speaking, replications yielding consistent results tend to be maximally informative and maximally convincing when they are maximally separated from the first study and from each other along such dimensions as time, physical distance, personal attributes of the researchers, expectancies on the part of the researchers and participants, and the degree of personal contact between the researchers.

VALIDITY CRITERIA IN ASSESSMENT

We turn now to the major approaches used by researchers to assess validity. Determining the validity of a test or questionnaire for use in behavioral research generally means finding out the degree to which it measures what it is supposed to measure, considered the most important concern in test evaluation. Determining validity typically involves accumulating evidence in three categories: (a) content-related validity, (b) criterion-related validity, and (c) construct-related validity (American Psychological Association, 1985). King and King (1990) described a number of interrelated activities specifically in relation to the assessment of construct validity, including the assessment of content- and criterion-related validity, but also defining the construct both theoretically and operationally (discussed in chapter 2) as well as weighing and justifying its position and role in some larger conceptual scheme.

Content validity requires that the test or questionnaire items represent the basic kinds of material (or content areas) they are supposed to represent. In the creation of standardized educational and psychological tests, the subjective evaluations of expert judges are usually required to assess this factor. Haynes, Richard, and Kubany (1995), among others, recommended that a multimethod approach be used, particularly in clinical test development, in which not only the experts would be consulted, but also a sample of patients from the target population. In the spirit of that recommendation, Vogt, King, and King (2004) described a focus group and interview procedure for use early in the item selection process. Less formal methods are used as well. For example, if we were creating a final exam in a particular course, we might start by asking ourselves, "What kinds of material should students be able to master after studying the textbooks and taking this course?" We would make a list of the material the exam would be expected to sample and then write questions to represent that material. Tests and questionnaires are regarded as more content-valid the more they cover all the relevant material. This type of validity is traditionally expressed either as a global, nonquantitative judgment or in terms of the adequacy of the sampling of the content to be covered.

Criterion validity refers to the degree to which the test or questionnaire correlates with one or more relevant criteria. If we were developing a test of college aptitude, we might select as our criterion the successful completion of the first year of college, or perhaps grade point average after each year of college. If we were developing a test to measure anxiety, we might use as our criterion the pooled judgments of a group of highly trained clinicians who rate (e.g., on a scale of anxiety) each person to whom we have administered the test. In testing for criterion validity, we try to select the most sensitive and meaningful criterion in the past, present, or future.

When a criterion is in the immediate present, we speak of **concurrent validity.** Clinical diagnostic tests are ordinarily assessed for criterion validity by this procedure, because the criterion of the patients' "real" diagnostic status is in the present with respect to the test being validated. Shorter forms of longer tests are also often evaluated for their concurrent validity; the longer test is used as the criterion. It could be reasonably argued in such cases that it is not validity but reliability that is being assessed. Thus, although reliability and validity are conceptually distinguishable, it is sometimes difficult to separate them in practice.

Another type of criterion-related evidence is relevant when researchers attempt to predict the future. Tests of college aptitude are normally assessed for **predictive validity,** inasmuch as the criteria of graduation and grade point average will occur in the future. The aptitude test scores are saved until the future-criterion data become available and are then correlated with them. The resulting correlation coefficient serves as another statement of criterion validity. Grade point average tends to be a fairly reliable criterion; clinicians' judgments (e.g., about complex behavior) may be a less reliable criterion. Previously, we showed how the reliability of pooled judgments can be increased by the addition of more judges. We can increase the reliability of pooled clinical judgments by adding more clinicians to the group whose pooled judgments will serve as our criterion (Rosenthal, 1987).

It is also sometimes necessary to be concerned about the validity of the criteria chosen by researchers. Suppose a researcher wants to develop a short test of anxiety that will predict the scores on a longer test of anxiety. The longer test serves as the criterion, and the new short test may be relatively quite valid with respect to the longer test. But the longer test may be of dubious validity with respect to some other criterion (e.g., clinicians' judgments). Sometimes, therefore, criteria must be evaluated with respect to other criteria. However, there are no firm rules (beyond the consensus of the researchers in the particular area) about what would constitute the "ultimate" criterion.

More sophisticated views of the validation of tests, or of observations generally, require that researchers be sensitive not only to the correlation between their measures and some appropriate criterion, but also to the correlation between their measures and some inappropriate criterion. Suppose we develop a measure of adjustment and find that it correlates positively and substantially with our criterion of clinicians' judgments. Imagine, however, that we administer a test of intelligence to all our participants and find that the correlation between our adjustment scores and intelligence is also positive and substantial. Is our new test a reasonably valid test of adjustment, of intelligence, of both, or of neither? That question is difficult to answer, but we could not claim on the basis of our results to understand our new test very well. It was not intended, after all, to be a measure of intelligence. In short, our test has good concurrent validity but fails to discriminate: It does not correlate differentially with criteria for different types of observation.

CONVERGENT AND DISCRIMINANT VALIDITY

The ability to discriminate is a characteristic of construct validation evidence. The term **construct validity** refers to the degree to which the test or questionnaire score is a measure of the psychological characteristic of interest. However, it is possible for an instrument to have good construct validity and yet not predict very well in a given situation because of the problem of range restriction (Nunnally & Bernstein, 1994). For example, scores on the Graduate Record Examination (GRE) are required of applicants to many selective graduate schools, but the GRE is often criticized for relating poorly to grades in graduate school. The problem is that students enrolled in graduate programs usually are fairly homogeneous in their cognitive ability, which is what the GRE is intended to measure. Thus, graduate admissions committees routinely use other selection criteria as well (including recommendations, grades in college, statements of career objectives, and relevant experience).

As Popper's falsificationist approach implies, constructs (just like theories) can never be verified or proved, as one can never expect to complete every possible check on a construct (Cronbach & Quirk, 1971). Furthermore, it is impossible to rule out an undiscovered disconfirmation (like Hume's black swan, noted in chapter 2). In a classic paper, Campbell and Fiske (1959) sought to formalize the construct validation procedure by proposing two kinds of construct validation evidence: (a) the testing for "convergence" across different methods or measures of the same trait or behavior and (b) the testing for "divergence" between methods or measures of related but conceptually distinct behaviors or traits. To illustrate, suppose we are developing a new test to assess people's ability to read other people's emotions from still photographs. We would want the test to correlate highly with other tests of sensitivity to nonverbal cues; if it does so, we have achieved **convergent validity.** But we would not want our new test to correlate very highly with ordinary intelligence as measured by some standard IQ test. If it does correlate highly, it could be argued that what we have developed is simply one more test of general intelligence. The lack of divergence would argue for poor **discriminant validity.**

In other words, researchers want their measures to correlate highly with the measures that their constructs imply they should correlate highly with (convergent validity), but to correlate less with measures that the constructs imply they should not correlate so highly with (discriminant validity). Campbell and Fiske proposed that a **multitrait-multimethod matrix** of intercorrelations be constructed to help researchers triangulate (zero in on) the convergent and discriminant validity of a construct. Thus, the researcher could pair different methods (A, B, C, etc.) with different trait variables (1, 2, 3, etc.), as illustrated by the following design:

	Method A	Method B	Method C	Method D	Method E
Traits	1 2 3 4 5	1 2 3 4 5	1 2 3 4 5	1 2 3 4 5	1 2 3 4 5

The idea behind using multiple methods to measure the same and differing traits is that it avoids the problem that high or low correlations may be due not to convergent or discriminant validity, but to their common basis in the same method of measurement. Later in this book, we will turn to statistical procedures that can be used to quantify the degree to which a particular test shows a desirable combination of convergent and discriminant validity (Rosenthal & Rubin, 1986; Westen & Rosenthal, 2003). Called *contrasts,* these procedures operate on the assumption that the test developer is able to describe the desired pattern of (a) correlations between the new test and other measures that are predicted to be highly correlated and (b) correlations between the new test and other measures that are predicted to be correlated much less.

Campbell (1998b) also advocated the use of multiple independent perspectives and triangulation in research in general, on the assumption that multiple independent vantage points permit fixing on a real effect in a way that is impossible to achieve from a single perspective (see Brewer & Collins, 1981). However, some have argued that multiple independence is an ideal that may not exist (Alwin, 1974; Jackson, 1969), and that the "hidden hand of common influence" makes it uncertain whether scientists can ever arrive at conclusions completely independently (Skagestad, 1981). Philosophers and methodologists have wrestled with this problem (Brewer & Collins, 1981; Browne, 1984; Campbell & O'Connell, 1967, 1982; Fiske, 1982; Kalleberg & Kluegel, 1975), but all seem to agree on one point: Given fallible measurements, our recourse as scientists is always to use multiple operations even if they are not completely independent (Houts, Cook, & Shadish, Jr., 1986; Rosnow & Georgoudi, 1986).

Earlier, we mentioned estimates of the average retest and internal-consistency reliability of the Rorschach and the MMPI tests, and we can also say something about the criterion-related validity evidence for these same tests. Only limited claims can be made about multidimensional instruments, such as these two, but in general the typical level of criterion-related validity of the Rorschach has been estimated as $r = .29$, and of the MMPI as $r = .30$, based on a comparative meta-analysis (Hiller, Rosenthal, Bornstein, Berry, & Brunell-Neuleib, 1999). These values contradict earlier claims of higher mean validity coefficients for the same instruments (Atkinson, 1986; Parker et al., 1988). However, as noted by Jacob Cohen (1988), "when one looks at near-maximum correlation coefficients of personality measures with . . . real-life criteria, the values one encounters fall at the order of $r = .30$" (p. 81). Thus, the validity estimates reported by Hiller et al. may actually be about as high as can be expected of personality tests, overall.

TEST VALIDITY, PRACTICAL UTILITY, AND THE TAYLOR-RUSSELL TABLES

The Rorschach and the MMPI are classic test instruments. In reporting their typical levels of validity, we are not implying that validity coefficients (rs) must reach these levels to be useful either for purposes of research or for purposes of practical application. In a classic paper, H. C. Taylor and J. T. Russell (1939) demonstrated that the practical utility of tests used in personnel selection increased not only as the validity coefficient increased, but also as the employers could afford to become more and more selective. The "selection ratio" is the proportion of applicants to be selected by a test. If that ratio is very high (e.g., .95 or higher, where nearly all applicants must be employed—perhaps because there is a severe shortage of this occupational group at this place, at this time), then even a test with very high validity would be of little value. If that ratio becomes very low (e.g., .05 or lower, so that only the very best applicants—the top 5% or so—are employed), then even a quite modest validity coefficient could be of great practical value.

Taylor and Russell gave a large number of examples in the form of tables. To illustrate, we turn to Table 4.15, which shows the percentage of employees selected by a given test who are successful for 5 levels of validity coefficients and 11 levels of selection ratios. This table is also predicated on an employment situation in which, before the test, about half of all employees are successful and half are not. Thus, if no test were used, or if the test had a validity coefficient of $r_{xy} = .00$, it follows that 50% of the employees would be successful. As this table illustrates, if the employing organization could not be very choosy and had to employ 95% of those applying (i.e., selection ratio = .95), even a validity coefficient as high as .75 would improve the number of selected employees who succeeded only from 50% (i.e., validity coefficient of .00) to 53%. But if the employing organization could be very choosy and selected only the top 5% (i.e., selection ratio = .05) of the applicants, that same validity coefficient of .75 would improve the number of selected employees who succeeded from 50% to 99%! Even with a much lower validity of $r_{xy} = .25$, the number of selected employees who succeeded would improve from 50% to 70% with a .05 selection ratio (very few are hired), whereas with a .95 selection ratio (almost all are hired), the improvement would be only from 50% to 51%. Overall, this table shows that selection accuracy increases as (a) validity coefficients increase, (b) selection ratios decrease, and (c) the benefits of increasing validity coefficients are usually greater and greater as selection ratios decrease.

TABLE 4.15
Selection accuracy (percentage of those selected who are successful) as a function of validity coefficient (r_{xy}) and selection ratio for an employment context in which 50% of the employees are successful before the test is introduced

Selection ratio	Validity coefficient (r_{xy})				
	.00	**.25**	**.50**	**.75**	**1.00**
.95	50	51	52	53	53
.90	50	52	54	55	56
.80	50	54	57	61	63
.70	50	55	60	66	71
.60	50	56	63	72	83
.50	50	58	67	77	100
.40	50	60	70	82	100
.30	50	62	74	87	100
.20	50	64	78	92	100
.10	50	67	84	97	100
.05	50	70	88	99	100

TABLE 4.16
Selection accuracy (percentage of those selected who are successful) as a function of validity coefficient (r_{xy}) and selection ratio for an employment context in which 10% of the employees are successful before the test is introduced

Selection ratio	Validity coefficient (r_{xy})				
	.00	**.25**	**.50**	**.75**	**1.00**
.95	10	10	11	11	11
.90	10	11	11	11	11
.80	10	11	12	12	13
.70	10	12	13	14	14
.60	10	13	15	16	17
.50	10	13	17	19	20
.40	10	14	19	23	25
.30	10	16	22	29	33
.20	10	17	26	37	50
.10	10	19	32	51	100
.05	10	22	39	64	100

The effects would be even more dramatic for employment situations in which smaller and smaller percentages of employees are successful before the test is introduced. To illustrate, Table 4.16 is predicated on an employment context in which only 10% of the employees are successful before the test is introduced. Just as in Table 4.15, Table 4.16 shows that selection accuracy increases as (a) validity coefficients increase, (b) selection ratios decrease, and (c) the benefits of increasing validity coefficients are usually greater and greater as selection ratios decrease. Because the employment context of Table 4.16 is such that only 10% of employees are successful before the test is introduced, the practical benefits of greatly increasing validity coefficients as selection ratios decrease are even greater in this table than in Table 4.15. At a selection ratio of .95, increasing the validity from .00 to 1.00 results in an increase of only 1% (from 10% to 11%). However, at a selection ratio of only .05, increasing the validity from .00 to 1.00 results in an increase of 90% (from 10% to 100%).

RELATIONSHIP OF VALIDITY TO RELIABILITY

In the evaluation of the measuring instruments of behavioral research, be they based on test items or on judges' ratings, researchers usually prefer their validity coefficients to be as high as possible and their reliability coefficients to be as high as possible as well. The bottom line characteristic, however, is validity. It rarely serves the researcher's scientific or applied goals to have a highly reliable test or group of judges whose items or ratings correlate with nothing of consequence.

It is a widespread belief that an acceptable level of validity depends on some minimum level of internal-consistency reliability, but that is not the case. Table 4.17 shows that both the predictor variable (made up of items or judges) and the criterion variable can both show internal-consistency reliability of .00 with a predictor-criterion validity of 1.00. In this illustration, the predictor variable is the sum (but it could also be the mean) of two peer raters (A and B) of students' current adjustment. The criterion variable is the sum (or mean) of two experts' (C and D) subsequent ratings of mental health. In practice, such low reliabilities associated with high validity are not common, but they can occur. For example, "different aspects of the truth" may be captured in the ratings of both the two predictor raters (A and B) and the two criterion raters (C and D). The combination of the two predictor peers (A + B) provides a good predictor, and the combination of the two criterion experts (C + D) provides a useful criterion.

In general, the validity of a composite instrument ($r_{nx.y}$), made up of a set of items, subtests, or judges, depends on three factors, which are all incorporated in the following equation suggested by J. P. Guilford (1954, p. 407):

$$r_{nx.y} = \frac{r_{xy}}{\sqrt{\left(\dfrac{1 - r_{xx}}{n}\right) + r_{xx}}} \qquad (4.17)$$

The three factors are (a) the average validity of each individual item, subtest, or judge (r_{xy}); (b) the number of items, subtests, or judges (n); and (c) the average intercorrelation (reliability) with each other of the items, subtests, or judges (r_{xx}). First, the

TABLE 4.17
Example of perfect validity with zero reliability of both predictor and criterion

	Peer raters of current adjustment		Expert raters of subsequent mental health	
	A	B	C	D
Student 1	3	1	2	4
Student 2	5	2	3	6
Student 3	2	3	4	3
Student 4	4	4	5	5
	Reliability = .00		Reliability = .00	

Predictor variable (A + B)	Outcome variable (C + D)
4	6
7	9
5	7
8	10

Predictive Validity = 1.00

	Peers		Experts		Predictor	Criterion	
	A	B	C	D	(A + B)	(C + D)	
A	—	.00	.00	1.00	.71	.71	Validity of A
B		—	1.00	.00	.71	.71	Validity of B
C			—	.00	.71	.71	
D				—	.71	.71	
(A + B)						1.00	Validity of (A + B)

larger the average validity (r_{xy}), the greater the validity of the composite. Second, the larger the number (n) of items, subtests, or judges, the greater generally the validity of the composite. Third, the larger the average intercorrelation (r_{xx}), the *less* the benefit that will accrue from increases in n. This third relationship, though not widely known, is quite intuitive. If two items or judges are perfectly correlated with each other, having two of them adds nothing new to having either one of them alone.

Equation 4.17 can be rewritten as follows to show more clearly these three factors:

$$r_{nx.y} = r_{xy} \times \sqrt{n} \times \frac{1}{\sqrt{1 + (n-1)r_{xx}}} \tag{4.18}$$

TABLE 4.18

Validity coefficients of a composite predictor ($r_{nx.y}$) as a function of the reliability (r_{xx}), validity (r_{xy}), and number (n) of its elements

Validity (r_{xy})	n	Reliability (r_{xx})					
		.00	.10	.20	.30	.40	.50
	1	.02	.02	.02	.02	.02	.02
	4	.04	.04	.03	.03	.03	.03
	9	.06	.04	.04	.03	.03	.03
.02	16	.08	.05	.04	.03	.03	.03
	25	.10	.05	.04	.03	.03	.03
	100	.20	.06	.04	.04	.03	.03
	225	.30	.06	.04	.04	.03	.03
	1	.05	.05	.05	.05	.05	.05
	4	.10	.09	.08	.07	.07	.06
	9	.15	.11	.09	.08	.07	.07
.05	16	.20	.13	.10	.09	.08	.07
	25	.25	.14	.10	.09	.08	.07
	100	.50	.15	.11	.09	.08	.07
	225	.75	.16	.11	.09	.08	.07
	1	.10	.10	.10	.10	.10	.10
	4	.20	.18	.16	.15	.13	.13
	9	.30	.22	.19	.16	.15	.13
.10	16	.40	.25	.20	.17	.15	.14
	25	.50	.27	.21	.17	.15	.14
	100	1.00	.30	.22	.18	.16	.14
	225	1.00	.31	.22	.18	.16	.14
	1	.20	.20	.20	.20	.20	.20
	4	.40	.35	.32	.29	.27	.25
	9	.60	.45	.37	.33	.29	.27
.20	16	.80	.51	.40	.34	.30	.27
	25	1.00	.54	.42	.35	.31	.28
	100	1.00	.61	.44	.36	.31	.28
	225	1.00	.62	.44	.36	.32	.28
	1	.30	.30	.30	.30	.30	.30
	4	.60	.53	.47	.44	.40	.38
	9	.90	.67	.56	.49	.44	.40
.30	16	1.00	.76	.60	.51	.45	.41
	25	1.00	.81	.62	.52	.46	.42
	100	1.00	.91	.66	.54	.47	.42
	225	1.00	.93	.66	.54	.47	.42

Note: The composite validities shown in this table ($r_{nx.y}$) can be obtained by Equation 4.18.

Applying Equation 4.18 to the data of Table 4.17 yields the correlations indicated in the matrix at the bottom of that table (i.e., $r_{xy} = .71$, $n = 2$ judges, and $r_{xx} = 00$), so that

$$r_{nx.y} = .71 \times \sqrt{2} \times \frac{1}{\sqrt{1 + (2 - 1).00}} = 1.00$$

Table 4.18 shows the validity coefficients of composite predictors ($r_{nx.y}$) as a function of (a) five levels of average item or judge validity ($r_{xy} = 02$, .05, .10, .20, .30); (b) seven levels of n (1, 4, 9, 16, 25, 100, 225); and (c) six levels of item or individual judge reliability ($r_{xx} = .00$, .10, .20, .30, .40, .50). Examination of this table shows that the validity of the composite predictor increases as the average validity of its items or judges increases, a result that is hardly surprising. More interesting is the observation that as the number of items or judges increases, so does the validity of the composite predictor. Most interesting, however, and most surprising to many researchers, is the observation that this benefit to composite validity of adding items or judges increases dramatically as the reliability of items or judges *decreases*. For example, for the validity of an average item or judge of $r_{xy} = .10$, when we go from one item or judge to 100 items or judges, the composite validity increases from .10 to 1.00 if the item-to-item or judge-to-judge reliability (r_{xx}) is .00, but it increases only from .10 to .14 if the reliability is .50!

CHAPTER
5

OBSERVATIONS, JUDGMENTS, AND COMPOSITE VARIABLES

OBSERVING, CLASSIFYING, AND EVALUATING

"You see, but you do not observe," Sherlock Holmes says to Dr. Watson in *A Scandal in Bohemia* (Baring-Gould, 1967, p. 349). Holmes was not only a keen observer, but extraordinarily intuitive and a remarkably astute logician; he was constantly astounding Watson by deducing solutions to the most baffling mysteries. Earlier, we described situations in which behavioral researchers used intuition and logic to formulate working hypotheses for scientific inquiry and empirical observations. In this chapter we describe strategies and procedures for categorizing and interpreting the variables measured or observed. We begin by describing an approach called *participant observation*. We will explain how ethnographic researchers and others who use this approach impose meaning (called **sense-making**) on qualitative data. By the term **qualitative,** as used in this context, we simply mean that the data do not exist in some numerical (or **quantitative**) form, but instead consist of people's spoken words, recorded conversations, narrative responses in nondirective or unstructured (also called *open-ended*) interviews, and observable behavior (Denzin & Lincoln, 2000; Taylor & Bogdan, 1998).

The qualitative-quantitative distinction, although frequently invoked by sociologists and other social scientists, is not unambiguous (cf. Wolcott, 1994); nor are the two classes mutually exclusive. The same investigation may integrate both qualitative and quantitative methods. For example, when human subjects in lab experiments are debriefed, it might be informative to interview a selected sample to find out what they thought about their participation. It may also be enlightening to observe the demeanor of subjects in the experimental setting. Were they paying attention, or bored and distracted? Were they calm and composed, or anxious to know how they would be evaluated? Sometimes it is possible to observe or measure behavior in inconspicuous ways or to use archival data to test hypotheses, and we will give examples. We can also quantify qualitative data, for example, by having judges rate well-defined variables (e.g., rate the intensity of expressions of feelings) or categorize archival data based on precisely described dimensions. In developmental psychology, researchers have long used scaling methods to test hypothesized qualitative models of developmental processes (e.g., review by Henning & Rudinger, 1985).

In the previous chapter we illustrated a procedure for estimating the effective cost reliability of judges; in this chapter we describe how to select the most accurate judges. The procedures used to identify accurate judges can be used in other situations as well. For example, they might also be used in signal detection experiments where researchers are interested in the accuracy of each subject's responses, or in organizations where the most accurate job applicants are chosen. We will explain the relationship between category and rating judgments, and how to decide on the number of response alternatives to use. We will also discuss the effects of guessing and of omitted items on the accuracy of judgments. In the previous chapter we mentioned that another name for systematic error is *bias;* we will examine some sources of response bias and how they are usually controlled. Finally, we will describe procedures for forming and assessing composite variables when the dependent variables are interrelated and there is no theoretical or practical advantage in treating them separately.

OBSERVING WHILE PARTICIPATING

Social scientists who identify themselves as **ethnographers** are usually interested in "cultures" (a term that is broadly defined), and their preferred strategy of investigation is **participant observation** (i.e., interacting while participating as observers in a culture). Indigenous members of the culture studied who provide these researchers with information are known as *informants*. In feminist ethnographic research, for instance, a popular area of investigation is cultures that are defined as "living in oppression." Some ethnographers have studied their own social scientific culture, calling such studies *autoethnography* (Tedlock, 2000). In the late 1800s and early 1900s, the culture of interest to many sociologists who wanted to promote social change (called *action research*) was made up of immigrants living in urban areas, which at the time were considered exotic settings (Hallett & Fine, 2000). Other classical examples of qualitative ethnographic research conducted in a wide variety of cultural settings include the work of Howard Becker, Ruth Benedict, Franz Boas, Raymond Firth, Margaret Mead, Bronislaw Malinowski, William Whyte, and other prolific sociologists and anthropologists. These social scientists spent many months, sometimes years, observing behavior, collecting narrative accounts, and recording personal impressions and reflections based on fieldwork in particular societies. In all societies, humans relate to one another by role and by affect (emotion). In employing participant-observer methods to explore the social context of human behavior, ethnographers believe they are able to discern the frustrations and enthusiasms of people in ways that are beyond the reach of other methodological strategies.

The term *participant observation* is used liberally to embrace diverse strategies, flexible research designs, and different levels of involvement. The participant observer might be an interested outsider, an unobtrusive observer who tries to "blend into the woodwork" (Taylor, Bogdan, & Walker, 2000), an active member of the culture or group, or in some cases, a skilled investigative reporter (Levine, 1980). In one fascinating case, psychologist David Rosenhan (1973) was interested in how people who are labeled "mentally ill" become stigmatized and what determines the way they are treated. A number of volunteers, including Rosenhan himself, feigned psychiatric symptoms in order to be admitted to mental hospitals. During their hospitalizations, they then behaved quite normally. They kept detailed records of their interactions with the psychiatrists, psychologists, and resident physicians. Research like this involves making judgments about the actions and conversations of individuals, trying to apprehend their experiential world (cf. Fine & Elsbach, 2000; Heritage, 1984; Spradley, 1980). Rosenhan and his volunteer participants observed how the staff members avoided interacting with patients. This finding, Rosenhan concluded, explained the "depersonalization" that he and the other participants felt, similar to the powerlessness felt by mental patients.

In this study the psychiatrists, psychologists, and others working in the hospitals were not told that their behavior was being investigated by Rosenhan and his team of participant observers. It is more typically true of participant-observer research that the members of the "culture" being studied are aware that they are being observed for research purposes. Sensitive to their loss of privacy, they may become increasingly selective in cooperating with the researchers. In one case, 40 researchers visited a single Indian settlement in the Northwest Territories of Canada one summer; another who then showed up to observe these same Indians nearly ended up being thrown into the river (Lotz, 1968). Each person has an individual sense of the loss of privacy and the invasion of his or her personal life, and participant observers (as well as any other researchers) must be attuned to such psychological limitations and mindful of their ethical responsibility to respect people's privacy.

MAXIMIZING CREDIBILITY
AND SERENDIPITY

In the early development of ethnographic research, there was not yet a tradition of how to ensure the most credible qualitative data. In recent years, ethnographic researchers have been sensitive to ways of trying to maximize credibility and not sacrifice flexibility. In the earlier era it was not uncommon for the researchers not even to describe how their data had been collected, leaving it to readers to figure out what was done (Hallett & Fine, 2000). That is no longer the case; journal editors require detailed descriptions of the procedures used—although, as Taylor et al. (2000) noted, qualitative researchers pride themselves in being free spirits. Participant observers also frequently work in teams and use checks and balances to try to control for biases in observations and interpretations. Nevertheless, the sense-making process, in which meaning is imposed on qualitative observations, depends a great deal on intuition and serendipity, such as stumbling on an unpredicted but poignant event or quote (Glaser & Strauss, 1967). Fine and Deegan (1996) reminded researchers, however, that there are often ways to "maximize the chances of obtaining memorable data" by anticipating "just the right time and just the right place" to court serendipity (p. 439). Suppose a researcher wanted to observe barroom brawls. Clearly, the researcher is more likely to witness such behavior on weekend nights than during afternoons in the middle of the week. Thus, as Fine and Deegan (p. 435) advised, "Courting serendipity involves planned insight married to unplanned events."

Animal behaviorists who engage in field research often adopt this common-sense strategy when investigating the social life and customs of wild animals in their natural habitats. A hypothesis-testing observational study conducted in Africa by comparative psychologist Ronald Baenninger and coworkers is illustrative (Baenninger, Estes, & Baldwin, 1977). These researchers unobtrusively watched the course of actions taken by a troop of baboons that suddenly encountered a cheetah drinking in the river. Other researchers had claimed that adult male baboons will actively defend their troops against predators, but there were few accepted observations of this kind of behavior at the time of this particular study (DeVore & Washburn, 1963). The results of Baenninger et al.'s observational research dispelled any doubts as to baboons' defensive behavior. As the researchers watched and recorded what they saw, they observed two male baboons harass the cheetah until they had successfully chased the cheetah far away from the main body of the troop. For these researchers, being in the right place was planned, although they were fortunate to be there at the most opportune time.

The animal behaviorists who engage in this kind of field research make distinctions that have been borrowed by, and from, social scientists who do participant-observer studies of human cultures (Altmann, 1974). One distinction is made between the observation of *events* (relatively brief occurrences that are observed at their onset or at some single defining moment) and *states* (occurrences of more appreciable duration). The researchers in the investigation above observed and recorded the course of actions of a troop of baboons chasing a cheetah from the very onset of that event; they might also have appraised the organizational structure of the troop (a state). As Altmann (1974) noted, questions about frequencies of behavior (i.e., the number of occurrences) usually entail considering the behavior as a set of events. Several types of data sampling for behavior events have been used. One popular type, *time sampling,* involves sampling specified periods and recording everything of interest during each period. For example, in other field research conducted by Baenninger (1987), the objective was to document the yawning response in different species (humans, Siamese fighting fish, lions, and mandrills), and he observed the subjects over sampled periods and counted the number of times yawning occurred. Another popular type of data sampling, *behavioral sampling,* is used when a particular ongoing behavior is of interest; the researcher samples the behavior periodically, typically using tally sheets and field notes to keep records of a multitude of occurrences. For a detailed discussion of sampling methods employed by animal behaviorists, see Altmann (1974).

Several conventions and guidelines have been adopted by ethnographers when they take field notes. One rule of thumb is to indicate for every written note referring to a conversation whether it is based on a verbatim quote or is instead the researcher's paraphrase. Where there are paraphrases, the risk is that the researcher may have unwittingly distorted what the informants reported. For that reason, audio and video recordings are routinely made, but only with the permission of the informants. In the case of written notes, one type is called the *condensed account* because it consists of phrases, single words, and unconnected sentences quoted on the spot. The shortened version of what was observed is amplified in the *expanded account,* which fills in details from recall of things that were not recorded earlier. The *fieldwork journal* is the ethnographer's written diary of particular experiences, ideas, fears, mistakes, confusions, and problems; like any diary, it represents the researcher's personal reactions to the events of the day (Spradley, 1980).

ORGANIZING AND SENSE-MAKING IN ETHNOGRAPHIC RESEARCH

After all this qualitative information has been gathered, it must be organized and interpreted. To help researchers put their thoughts in order, Goodenough (1980) listed several questions they might ask themselves. First, assuming the observations were of a well-defined group or culture and that specific activities or events were observed, what was the occasion or purpose of each activity? Second, what procedures or operations were involved, and were any raw materials used or particular skills required of the participants? Third, what were the time and space requirements of each activity (e.g., how much time was needed, what areas or facilities were required, and were any obstacles in the way of these activities)? Fourth, how many people participated, who were they, and were there specialized roles? Fifth, regarding the state of the social organization, what were the particular categories of all the various actors, including their rights, duties, privileges, and powers and the types of sanctions used? Assuming any of these questions are pertinent, they would still need to be tailored to each situation.

Wolcott (1994) listed other traditional ways to organize qualitative information. For example, if the data are related to events, a simple fallback way to present this information is in chronological sequence. Alternatively, it may be illuminating to specify a problem of interest and then to build the data around this problem, that is, "slowly zooming from broad context to the particulars of the case, or starting with a close-in view and gradually backing away to include more context" (p. 18). Another strategy is the day-in-the-life approach, where a real or fictionalized account of an entire day (or a customary sequence of events) is described. Still other ways of relating qualitative information are to focus on critical or key events, or on plots and the sociological roles of the characters involved, or on groups in interaction. One other approach is to present the events as if one were writing a mystery story, that is, not giving away the ending in advance, but gradually leading to an exciting discovery or insight.

Fine and Deegan (1996) provided tips and cautionary advice on how best to go about the process of trying to make theoretical sense of the data, a process they characterized as "analytical serendipity" (p. 442). First, it is important to know the published literature, especially what respected researchers believe is true about the culture or activities under study. In Fine and Deegan's words, "Theory never develops out of thin air, but is responsive to those intellectual currents that are in circulation and to which the researcher has been exposed" (p. 442). A cautionary note, however, is that the researcher must rely on well-documented conclusions rather than stereotypes. A second piece of advice is to keep one's eyes and ears open to the unexpected (i.e., things that elicit "Ah-ha!" experiences), because there are almost always exceptions to conventional wisdom. This advice, of course, applies to other research situations as well. Third is to ask oneself the reporter's question: "What is it like?" Thinking of dramatic metaphors is the way that ethnographers try to conceptualize activities in a new light. Fourth, however, is our own cautionary note to beware of interpreter and observer biases.

INTERPRETER AND OBSERVER BIASES

 Interpreter and observer biases illustrate what Rosenthal (1966) generally categorized as **noninteractional artifacts,** meaning that they are systematic errors that operate, so to speak, in the mind, in the eye, or in the hand of the scientist but are not due to uncontrolled variables that might interact with the subjects' behavior. The first type, **interpreter biases,** refers to systematic errors that occur during the interpretation-of-data phase of the research process (cf. MacCoun, 1998). A glance at any of the research journals will suggest that, although behavioral and social researchers only rarely question the observations made by one another, they often question the interpretation of those observations. It is as difficult to state rules for the accurate interpretation of data as it is to state rules for the accurate observation of data, but the variety of interpretations offered to explain the same data implies that many researchers must turn out to be wrong, or at least partly wrong. The history of science generally, and of behavioral and social research more specifically, suggests that more of us are wrong longer than we need to be because we hold our theories not quite lightly enough. Clinging to a theory does have its advantages, however. It keeps researchers motivated to make crucial observations. The usual way to control for interpreter bias is to make the results available to other researchers, who are then free to agree or disagree with the interpretation.

An illustration of interpreter biases was described by John J. Sherwood and Mark Nataupsky (1968). They were interested in whether biographical characteristics of individual researchers might predict how the researchers interpreted certain data pertaining to racial differences in IQ research. Questionnaire data were gathered from 82 investigators who had published comparative studies of the IQs of blacks and whites. The information (the age of the investigator when the research was published, birth order, whether the researcher's grandparents were American or foreign-born, father's and mother's educational level, childhood in rural or urban community, and undergraduate scholastic standing) was then analyzed for its possible relationship to the nature-versus-nurture conclusions reached by the 82 investigators. These were among the alternatives considered: (a) Differences in IQ between blacks and whites are due to the innate inferiority of blacks; (b) racial differences in IQ are due to environmental factors; and (c) no reliable racial differences in IQ exist. Based on their analysis of the relationship between the biographical data and the published conclusions of the investigators studied, Sherwood and Nataupsky concluded that it was possible statistically to discriminate particular conclusions reached by the investigators studied.

The second type of noninteractional artifact noted above, **observer biases,** refers to systematic errors in the observation or recording phase of research. The problem, as one writer put it, is the tendency of many people to "equate what they *think* they see, with what actually happens" (Lane, 1960). For example, biologist M. L. Johnson (1953), in an article entitled "Seeing's Believing," told about a radiologist who mistook a button caught in a patient's throat for a button "on the vest"—where a button *ought* to be present. Johnson concluded:

> Our assumptions define and limit what we see, i.e., we tend to see things in such a way that they will fit in with our assumptions even if this involves distortions or omissions. We therefore may invert our title and say 'Believing is Seeing.' (p. 79)

In another case, one of us (Rosenthal, 1969, 1978b) counted the recording errors in a small set of experiments that just happened to be available for another purpose (viz., an analysis of the unintended effects of researchers). The studies, all of which were designed (at least in part) to permit the quantitative assessment of error rates, ranged widely in terms of research areas and locus of data collection (e.g., studies of reaction time, person perception, human and animal learning, task ability, psycho-physical judgments, questionnaire responses, and even mental telepathy). Because this was not a random sample of experiments, we make no claims beyond the data in this set. However, when there were recording errors, they generally favored the experimenter's hypotheses about two thirds of the time, which was more frequently than would be expected by chance. There appeared to be no clear relationship between the area of research and either the rate of errors or the likelihood of errors being biased when they did occur.

A notorious case of observer bias in science involved the "discovery" of so-called N rays by the physicist André Blondlot in the early part of the 20th century. N rays, he contended, made reflected light more intense and were bent by aluminum; anyone could see this effect with the naked eye under the proper condi-tions. Many scientists claimed to have observed Blondlot's N rays, though others reported difficulty trying to replicate his experiments. How this episode unfolded was recounted in an entertaining book by Richard P. Feynman (1989), who told how the physicist R. W. Wood "put an end to the N-ray." Blondlot gave a lecture and demonstration to show how N rays were bent by aluminum. He told the audience that he had constructed a sandwich of different kinds of lenses, with an aluminum prism in the middle. He then manipulated an apparatus that was supposed to turn the prism slowly to reveal how N rays "came up this way and bent that way" (Feynman, 1989, p. 147). All the while, Blondlot's assistant kept announcing the intensity of his readings for different angles. Blondlot told the audience that it was necessary to darken the room because N rays were affected by light, and turning the light off would make the assistant's readings more sensitive. When the lights came back on at the end of the demonstration, there was Wood in the front row. Previously unbeknownst to anyone, he had surreptitiously removed the prism from Blondlot's apparatus and was holding it high in the air, balanced on the tips of his fingers, for all to see! Here, for all *really* to see, was incontrovertible proof that N rays were nothing more than a figment of imagination.

UNOBTRUSIVE OBSERVATIONS AND NONREACTIVE MEASUREMENTS

In contrast to noninteractional artifacts, there are also **interactional artifacts,** which are uncontrolled variables that *do* have a direct impact on the reactions of research participants (Rosenthal, 1976). We will have more to say about interactional artifacts in Chapter 7, but another relevant distinction in this context is made between **reactive measures** and **nonreactive measures** (Campbell & Stanley, 1963; Webb, Campbell, Schwartz, & Sechrest, 1966). The two terms are used to differentiate measurements that do (reactive) from those that do not (nonreactive) affect the behavior that is being measured. For example, in a study on therapy for weight control, the initial weigh-in may be a reactive stimulus to weight reduction, even without the therapeutic intervention (Campbell & Stanley, 1963). Or suppose we wanted to measure blood pressure while subjects were presented a list of stimulus words or pictures; merely applying the cuff of the sphygmomanometer would introduce changes in the subjects' blood pressure (Sarbin, 1944). Eugene J. Webb and his coauthors (Webb et al., 1966, 1981) collected a miniencyclopedia's worth of nonreactive strategies, procedures, and measurements, including numerous illustrations of the use of archives, physical traces, and unobtrusive observations. We will give a flavor of each, as well as describe how the method of content analysis is sometimes used to categorize and evaluate such data.

Archives

As Webb et al. (1981) noted, the quantity of information that is recorded and stored in various archives is staggering. All that is required of researchers is to "know where to look and what to do with what they find" (p. 139). Elder, Pavalko, and Clipp (1993) discussed methods of implementing this kind of search and then working with the recovered data. Webb et al. described two subcategories of archives as *running records* (many of which can be accessed from Web sites) and *personal documents and episodic records.* Running records include things like actuarial data (birth, marriage, and death records), political and judicial information (voting records of legislators or speeches printed in the *Congressional Record*), other records in federal depositories (records of inventions, crime reports), mass media information (news reports, advertisements, editorials), records of sales (sales at airport bars, sales of trip insurance policies), and industrial and institutional information (sicknesses and absences from the job, complaints, unsolicited communications from the public, accident reports). Personal documents and episodic records include things like diaries and letters (e.g., from captured soldiers in wartime or letters of protest sent to large corporations), rumors that people phoned in to rumor control centers, photographs and picture postcards, and visual presentations in picture books (e.g., Allport, 1942). A classic study by Thomas and Znaniecki (1927) of Polish immigrants in America and their families in Europe was based largely on letters written to relatives overseas, which the researchers obtained by placing ads in newspapers and newsletters.

A study by cognitive psychologist Robert W. Weisberg (1994), who has written extensively about human creativity (e.g., Weisberg, 1986, 1993), illustrates the use of archival data. Fascinated by an old theory asserting that genius and madness are intimately related (cf. Martindale, 1997), Weisberg decided to test that theory by means of a case study of the great 19th-century German composer Robert Schumann, who suffered from manic-depression and eventually committed suicide. By searching library archives, Weisberg was able to compile a comprehensive list of Schumann's musical compositions, identify those that experts considered either ordinary or works of genius, and document the specific years in which Schumann was reported to have suffered from depression or hypomania (a mild form of mania, characterized by elation and quickness of thought). Weisberg found no convincing support for the general prediction that madness fostered brilliance in Schumann's work (i.e., the *quality* of his work was not significantly related to his mental health). Weisberg did find, however, that the state of Schumann's mental health was associated with the *quantity* of compositions that he wrote: Schumann created more musical compositions when he was in a hypomanic than when he was in a depressive state. In other work, by Arnold M. Ludwig (1995), in which 20th-century biographical data on more than 1,000 eminent people were collated, creativity appeared to be linked to moderate (as opposed to very low or very high) levels of alcohol abuse, neurosis, or somatic dysfunction.

Archival Data and Content Analysis

Another example of archival data, as well as an illustration of the method of content analysis, was a study done by Crabb and Bielawski (1994). These investigators were interested in how visual presentations in influential books written for children portrayed female and male roles. **Content analysis** is the name given to a set of procedures that are used to categorize and evaluate pictorial, verbal, or textual material. In fact, many different procedures have been developed for this purpose; for example, leading researchers in group dynamics and communication networks have developed their own content categories and procedures for analyzing verbal data in human interactions (Gersick, 1989, 1991; Wheelan, 1994). Crabb and Bielawski chose for their study all the picture books that had received a particular prestigious award (the Caldecott Medal) over 53 years, with the idea that those books would have a high profile in libraries and bookstores. The books identified contained 416 illustrations showing female characters and 1,197 showing male characters. Because the coding was done by hand, Crabb and Bielawski wanted to pare down the number of illustrations, so they randomly sampled 300 representative pictures of gender and decade for the judges to analyze.

When designing a content analysis, the idea is to use commonsense logic, theory, or a question or hypothesis as a basis of the categorical judgments to be made. It is certainly possible to use a computer to do the itemizing and counting, though the researcher still must decide what is to be analyzed and how it is to be categorized (Stone, 2000). In Crabb and Bielawski's study, the 300 sampled pictures were given to two independent judges for coding after the judges had been rehearsed in how to use a simple coding sheet. They were instructed to record the sex of each character depicted and then to record whether that individual appeared to be using household tools (e.g., those used in food preparation, cleaning, repair, or family care), nonhousehold tools (e.g., construction, agricultural, or transportation tools), or other utensils or paraphernalia not falling in the above two categories. Also coded were various features of the characters and the nature of the situation depicted in each scene. The judges' results were in strong agreement with one another. Regarding the question that inspired

Crabb and Bielawski, they concluded that household tools were more often used by female characters and that nonhousehold tools were more often used by male characters. Another finding was that the proportion of male characters depicted with household tools had increased over time, but the proportion of female characters with nonhousehold tools had not changed very much over time.

There was, in fact, a long history of doing content analyses by hand, even before this strategy got its name (McCormack, 1982; Woodrum, 1984). Many years before computers existed, priests burrowed through texts and sermons for evidence of heresy, philosophers through ancient books and documents for their hidden meaning, and censors through books and documents for taboo matter. The model of content analysis for coding thematic characteristics of textual data was introduced by the political theorist Harold Lasswell in the 1920s, but it was not until 1952 that the first definitive published text appeared (Bernard Berelson's *Content Analysis in Communication Research*). Another important early contribution (with detailed procedures, later adapted for computers) was Stone, Dunphy, Smith, and Ogilvie's (1966) text on a method and a computer program they called the General Inquirer. Researchers who are interested in doing a content analysis will find a number of helpful resources, including Holsti's (1968) and Stone's (1997) incisive reviews, Boyatzis's (1998) instructions for thematic coding based on an approach created by David McClelland, and various handbooks and texts (e.g., Krippendorff, 1980; Rosengren, 1981; Weber, 1985). The three essentials of any content analysis are (a) that the sorting of the data be consistent among judges; (b) that the specific categories and units chosen be relevant to the question of interest; and (c) that if not all the material available is to be analyzed, an appropriate sampling procedure be used (Berelson, 1954; see also Woodrum, 1984).

Physical Traces

In writing about physical traces, Webb et al. (1966, 1981) took as their point of departure the brilliant way that Sherlock Holmes depended on physical evidence for clues. An example of a behavioral trace was discovered by a committee that had been formed to set up a psychological exhibit for children in a science museum. The committee learned that the vinyl tiles around one particular exhibit (which showed live, hatching chicks) needed to be replaced every six weeks, whereas tiles around other exhibits in the museum lasted for years without being replaced. A problem, however, was that it was not clear exactly what this nonreactive measure implied (a puzzle that Webb et al. mentioned was common when physical traces are used). That is, without actually observing what was happening in front of each exhibit, it was impossible to say whether the erosion was due to the children's standing around and shuffling their feet, or to a constant flow of large numbers of people viewing certain exhibits. Another interesting physical trace appeared on the exhibits' glass fronts; it was learned that each evening they had to be dusted for noseprints. Webb et al. raised the possibility that counting the noseprints might provide a crude, nonreactive measure of which exhibits were more frequently or more closely scrutinized. The distance of the noseprints from the floor might even provide a rough measure of the ages of the children.

As another example of physical traces, Webb et al. described a statistician's measure of the wear and tear on separate sections of an encyclopedia as a nonreactive indicator of which parts were actually being consulted a lot; he simply recorded the pages on which there were dirty edges, dirt smudges, finger marks, and underlining. One more example of a physical trace involved an automobile dealer who had his mechanics record the radio dial settings in cars brought in for service. The dealer used these data to select the radio stations to carry his ads. This case also illustrates what Webb et al. described as *simple unobtrusive observation,* which means that the mechanics' observations were inconspicuous to the car owners and there was nothing contrived or manipulated in the situation. In a comprehensive literature review of unobtrusive studies of racial discrimination and prejudice, Crosby, Bromley, and Saxe (1980) concluded that discriminatory behavior was "more prevalent in the body of unobtrusive studies than we might expect on the basis of survey data" in which respondents were asked directly to express their racial attitudes (p. 557).

Unobtrusive Observation

Another illustration of simple unobtrusive observation (and another example of content analysis) was some research conducted by University of South Australia psychologist Prashant Bordia (1996; Bordia & Rosnow, 1995), who was interested in Internet chat group discussions of rumors. Because many group discussions on the Internet are in a public forum, Bordia reasoned that the participants were aware that their communications were open and visible to all. He concluded, therefore, that there could be no ethical problem of invasion of privacy (which would be a concern had he decided to snoop into people's private e-mail correspondence). However, to ensure people's privacy, Bordia did not publish any lengthy segments of the communications that could in any way possibly identify people as individuals. Bordia's interest in this area was piqued by studies reported by Allport and Postman (1947) employing a "telephone game" simulation of the process of rumor transmission. The simulation procedure consisted of showing a picture of a complex social scene to a subject and asking the subject to describe the scene to a second subject. The first subject then left the room, and the second subject described what he or she had been told to a third subject, who told it to a fourth subject, and so on. The descriptions, as they were passed from person to person, became noticeably shorter in certain systematic ways—a characteristic that Allport and Postman believed was typical of all rumors. That finding has been successfully replicated, but other researchers have raised a criticism that the one-way transmission process studied by Allport and Postman did not reflect how rumors are usually transmitted in everyday life, where there are often give-and-take discussions (Buckner, 1965; Shibutani, 1966). It was also observed that not all rumors shrink in everyday life; some have been known to expand to mammoth proportions (e.g., Rosnow & Fine, 1974, 1976). Bordia was intrigued by the opportunity to observe a give-and-take discussion of a rumor in vivo, although he realized that an Internet chat group is also a special situation with its own limitations.

For his content analysis study, Bordia developed categories into which the various statements and responses could be sorted. For instance, one category was called "apprehensive statements," identified by a detectable level of anxiety. Another category consisted of "interrogatory statements," either questions or statements seeking information. Still another category consisted of "belief or disbelief statements" because credulity or a lack of credulity was apparent. There were other categories as well. A general finding was that the frequency of "prudent statements" (i.e., those with qualifiers) was particularly high in the beginning of the chat group discussion;

the participants were cautious (writing things like "This may or may not be true"). As the discussion progressed, the cautiousness seemed to diminish as the participants realized that others had similar ideas and concerns. By tracking individual responses, Bordia was able to identify "communicative postures" that the people adopted, including such transient roles as "skeptical disbelievers," "apprehensive believers," "the curious," and "prudent initiators." Sometimes the same person was a prudent initiator early on, sought more information along the way (becoming one of the "curious"), and ended as a skeptical disbeliever (Bordia & DiFonzo, 2002). In Allport and Postman's (1947) classic studies, it would have been impossible to identify roles like these because of the one-way transmission paradigm that was used.

In Crosby et al.'s (1980) literature review of unobtrusive studies of racial discrimination, some of the studies used simple unobtrusive measures, whereas others used unobtrusive measures in manipulated situations (called *contrived unobtrusive observation* by Webb et al., 1981). Experiments by social psychologist Roy E. Feldman (1968) illustrate contrived unobtrusive observations in a field study. Feldman was interested in identifying certain national differences in helping behavior. For many kinds of behavior, the cultural context is presumed to be an important factor. Feldman repeated several standard experiments in Athens, Paris, and Boston using foreigners and locals as confederates. In one experiment, he had confederates ask directions from passersby. In another, the confederates asked strangers to mail a letter for them, explaining that they were waiting for someone and could not leave the spot right then. In a third experiment, the confederates overpaid merchants and taxi drivers and then observed whether those people were honest and returned the money. From his cross-tabulations of the reactions of more than 3,000 individuals, Feldman concluded that when a difference in helping behavior occurred in these experiments, the Parisians and Bostonians treated their compatriots better than they treated foreigners, whereas Athenians were more helpful to foreigners than to compatriots. The reason we also consider this study an example of nonreactive measurement is not that the confederates were concealed or inconspicuous (which they were not), but that their *role* as experimental accomplices was unknown to the people observed and the dependent variables were measured unobtrusively.

SELECTING THE MOST APPROPRIATE JUDGES

In the observational studies we have discussed so far in this chapter, observations and judgments were directly made by the researchers or by the researchers' associates or accomplices. In other studies, however—generally known as **judgment studies**—judges are used to evaluate or categorize the variables of interest. In most judgment studies, the researchers have no special interest in any individual differences among the judges when considering interjudge reliability. The researcher simply decides on the type of judges to be used (e.g., college students, industrial psychologists, linguists, mothers) and then regards each judge as more-or-less equivalent to, or interchangeable with, any other judge in the sample. The choice of the most appropriate judges is pretty much left to the researcher's intuitions. If a sample of educated judges were needed for a content analysis, the researcher might conveniently select graduate or advanced undergraduate students.

To rate nonverbal cues to psychoses, the researcher would probably want to recruit experts, such as clinical psychologists or psychiatrists. For judgments of nonverbal cues to discomfort in infants, mothers, child psychologists, or pediatricians might be recruited. If judgments of nonverbal cues of persuasiveness were required, the judges chosen might be trial lawyers, fundamentalist ministers, or salespersons.

However, suppose we wanted judges with the highest possible levels of general accuracy. In this case, we might do even better by making a nonrandom selection of judges. We could search the literature to find out whether anyone has identified specific characteristics of those who are more sensitive to what is being judged, and then we could recruit those particular kinds of judges. In the case of those sensitive to nonverbal cues, for example, the research literature suggests that judges who are female, college-aged, cognitively complex, and psychiatrically unimpaired will give us the most accurate judgments (Rosenthal, Hall, DiMatteo, Rogers, & Archer, 1979). Another way to select judges for accuracy is to compare those in a pool of potential judges in terms of their accuracy of judgments on some relevant criterion. Say we want to select judges who are likely to be the most accurate in categorizing or rating nonverbal behavior. We can test a number of potential judges in a pilot study in which we give them certain known nonverbal stimuli to identify, and then we can simply pick the most accurate judges for our research.

To illustrate, suppose we begin by generating photographs of skilled actors who are instructed to exhibit six different facial emotions: anger, disgust, fear, happiness, sadness, and surprise. We select 60 of these photos to serve as the stimuli in our pilot study, 10 to represent each of the emotions. We show the 60 photos in random order to participants, instructing them to circle the one of the six emotions that is most like the one in the photo. In analyzing these data we want to assess how biased or accurate each participant is, and afterward we will recruit those who were the most accurate. Table 5.1 shows a full data matrix indicating one participant's responses to all 60 photos (Rosenthal, 1987). For each of the correct categories of emotion as listed in the column headings, we see the distribution of responses according to the category chosen by this

TABLE 5.1
Full data matrix for one hypothetical participant

Chosen category	Correct category						Sum
	Anger	Disgust	Fear	Happiness	Sadness	Surprise	
Anger	8[a]	4	3	1	2	2	20
Disgust	1	4[a]	2	1	3	1	12
Fear	1	1	3[a]	2	1	2	10
Happiness	0	0	0	3[a]	0	1	4
Sadness	0	1	2	1	4[a]	2	10
Surprise	0	0	0	2	0	2[a]	4
Sum	10	10	10	10	10	10	60

[a]Items scored as accurate; total accuracy = 24.

individual. This person correctly identified 8 of 10 anger stimuli but missed 2 others; one missed stimulus was mistakenly identified as disgust and the other as fear. The column totals of a full data matrix are fixed by the design of the study. In this case, each column sums to 10 because we balanced the set of stimuli for the frequency with which each emotion was the correct alternative. The row totals in the far right column define the participant's bias. A fully unbiased judge, regardless of his or her total level of accuracy, would show no differences in the row totals. If we want to test statistically whether the illustrative participant of Table 5.1 is significantly biased, we can compute a one-sample chi-square test (Siegel, 1956). We will have more to say about the chi-square statistic in chapter 19, but to anticipate a little, the basic data and calculations are illustrated in Table 5.2. For this person, the bias—based primarily on choosing the category of anger too often, and the categories of happiness and surprise not often enough—was statistically significant at $p = .0035$.

As Table 5.1 implies, the bias of seeing "too much" of one category (e.g., anger) tends to inflate accuracy for the biased category. If there were perfect bias for one category (e.g., anger), all categories would be identified as *that* category, and all items for which that particular category is the correct answer would be scored correct. Therefore, there is generally a positive correlation between bias toward a category and accuracy in that category. For the illustrative data of Table 5.1, the correlation between bias (the sums in the far right column) and accuracy (the entry with the superscript a in each column) is $r = .93$. Inasmuch as the accuracy score is one component of the row total (or bias), we expect to see a positive correlation between accuracy and bias. It often happens that even when we correct the row total for accuracy by subtracting the accurately categorized items from the row total, the correlation between accuracy and bias remains positive. For example, for the data of Table 5.1, the row totals of 20, 12, 10, 4, 10, 4 become 12, 8, 7, 1, 6, 2 when corrected by accuracy scores of 8, 4, 3, 3, 4, 2 (i.e., when this last set is subtracted from the first). Still, the correlation between these accuracy scores and the accuracy-corrected bias scores remains positive and substantial: $r = .85$. As before, we could also compute a one-sample chi-square test for bias on the accuracy-corrected row totals, that is, if we should want an estimate of bias omitting the items categorized accurately. In this case, when we use the accuracy-corrected observed row totals, the test for bias is $\chi^2 = 13.67$, $df = 5$, $N = 60 - 24 = 36$, $p = .018$.

TABLE 5.2
Contingency table and one-sample χ^2 for single judge's bias in Table 5.1

	Anger	Disgust	Fear	Happiness	Sadness	Surprise	Total
			Category of emotion				
Expected	10	10	10	10	10	10	60
Observed	20	12	10	4	10	4	60

$$\chi^2 = \sum \frac{(O-E)^2}{E} = \frac{(20-10)^2}{10} + \frac{(12-10)^2}{10} + \frac{(10-10)^2}{10} + \frac{(4-10)^2}{10} + \frac{(10-10)^2}{10} + \frac{(4-10)^2}{10} = 17.6,$$

where E = expected frequency, O = obtained frequency, and for one-sample χ^2 tests, the degrees of freedom (df) are computed as the total number of categories (k) minus 1 (i.e., $df = k - 1 = 5$).

CHOOSING THE NUMBER OF
RESPONSE ALTERNATIVES

Another concern of researchers who are using category judgments is to decide on the optimal number of response alternatives in a given situation. In the case we have been discussing, we chose a category format of six response alternatives. However, suppose, for certain theoretical reasons, the design of the research required only two or three response categories. When the needs of the research speak clearly on the number of categories to use, it pays to listen. Often, however, there is no compelling reason to prefer any particular number of categories, and choosing the number becomes a matter of intuition. Multiple-choice achievement tests, for example, everything else being equal, tend to be more reliable when the number of response alternatives is increased (Nunnally, 1978). In fact, when more alternatives (or judgment categories) can be used without the sacrifice of other desirable features of the test or task, the increase in alternatives yields other practical benefits as well. For example, it is easier to estimate the probability that any *particular* judge has shown accuracy greater than chance. Typically, when samples of judges are used, this may not be a great advantage, however. The reason is that the number of judges gives us the statistical power to establish that all of the judges, in the aggregate, can do better than chance, whatever the task. In clinical contexts or in selection contexts, where the clinicians or researchers are interested in evaluating the performance of a single patient or a job applicant, having a larger number of response alternatives is quite useful, however, especially when it is necessary to keep the total number of items or judgments fairly low.

Table 5.3 lists for each of several numbers of response alternatives the minimum number of items (or judgments) required to show that a single judge is

TABLE 5.3

Minimum number of items required to establish individual judge's accuracy at various levels of statistical significance

Number of alternatives	Chance level	Significance levels (one-tailed)				
		.10	.05	.01	.005	.001
2	.50	4	5	7	9	10
3	.33	3	3	5	5	7
4	.25	2	3	4	4	5
5	.20	2	2	3	4	5
6	.17	2	2	3	3	4
7	.14	2	2	3	3	4
8	.12	2	2	3	3	4
9	.11	2	2	3	3	4
10	.10	1	2	2	3	3
11	.09	1	2	2	3	3
12	.08	1	2	2	3	3

significantly accurate (Rosenthal, 1987). Suppose the chosen criterion of "real" accuracy is accuracy at $p = .005$ one-tailed. Table 5.3 indicates that reaching this criterion will require 9 items (or judgments) having 2 response alternatives, but only 3 items (or judgments) having 6 response alternatives. This table is also of use in clinical applications in which the accuracy of individual clinicians is of interest, or in small-N judgment studies in which the accuracy of individual participants is of interest. This usefulness assumes, of course, that the researchers are interested in the statistical significance of the accuracy of individual clinicians or research subjects. As Table 5.3 also implies, should the researchers need to keep the number of items (or judgments) to a minimum, they can improve the statistical efficiency of the instrument or task by increasing the number of response alternatives for each item (or judgment).

EFFECTS OF GUESSING AND OMISSIONS ON ACCURACY

Another question that is frequently of interest is the effect of a judge's (or a research participant's) guessing on estimates of the person's accuracy. We again consult Table 5.3, which shows the probability of obtaining a correct response by random selection of a response alternative (guessing) as a function of the number of alternatives. With only 2 response alternatives, there is a probability of .50 of guessing the correct category; with 10 response alternatives, the probability is .10. Thus, if we had an instrument with 100 items, we would regard a score of 50 correct quite differently if the number of response alternatives (A) were 2 as opposed to 10. For example, if $A = 2$, the performance is no better than chance, but with $A = 10$, the performance is substantially better than chance ($\chi^2 = 178$, $df = 1$, $N = 100$, $p = 1.32^{-40}$). Our evaluation of the effects of guessing on the level of a judge's accuracy therefore depends heavily on the number of response alternatives.

Under many conditions, however, researchers are not concerned about the estimation of the judges' levels of accuracy. In studies of individual differences, for example, the researchers may be concerned only about the judges' relative positions on a distribution of accuracy scores. In such cases, the number of response alternatives per item are of no importance. However, in experiments in which the researchers do require some estimate of how well a subject, a judge, or a group of subjects or judges has done, it is necessary to take into account the effect of successful guessing as a function of the number of response alternatives. The standard estimate, given by Nunnally (1978), states that the number of items that are correct after adjustment for guessing (R-adjusted) is a function of the number of correct or right (R) responses, the number of incorrect or wrong (W) responses, and the number of alternative (A) responses for each item or judgment. The adjusted number correct is given by

$$R\text{-adjusted} = R - \frac{W}{A-1}. \tag{5.1}$$

For example, on a true-false achievement test (i.e., two response alternatives per item), if a person got 50 of 100 items correct, the adjusted score we obtain from Equation 5.1 is

$$R\text{-adjusted} = 50 - \frac{50}{2 - 1} = 0,$$

no better than randomly choosing, or guessing, one alternative. Or suppose a person got 50 of 100 items correct on a multiple-choice achievement test with 4 response alternatives per item; the adjusted score becomes

$$R\text{-adjusted} = 50 - \frac{50}{4 - 1} = 33.3.$$

In a judgment study with 10 categories to choose among, if 50 of 100 stimuli were categorized correctly, the adjusted score is

$$R\text{-adjusted} = 50 - \frac{50}{10 - 1} = 44.4$$

Table 5.4 shows the adjusted accuracy scores on a sample 100-item test for varying numbers of response alternatives (Rosenthal, 1987). The first column lists the number of correctly answered items (R) in steps of five. The second column lists the number of incorrectly answered items (W), which is simply $100 - R$ for this table. In each column of the body of the table, a perfectly chance level of performance is given by an adjusted accuracy score of zero. Because Table 5.4 shows steps of five items correct, a nearly exact score of zero is not found in each column. Interpolation can be used to find the level of approximate zero or any other value located between adjacent entries. Alternatively, a more precise location for zero values of adjusted accuracy scores is given by

$$R\text{-adjusted} = \frac{K}{A} \tag{5.2}$$

where K = total number of items ($R + W$), and $K = 100$ in the case of Table 5.4.

Although we have defined the total number of items (K) as the sum of the right (R) and wrong (W) answers, this relationship holds only if we score as wrong any items that are omitted. However, scoring omitted items as zero gives them too little credit in computing R. It seems preferable to credit omitted items with the score that would be obtained by purely random guessing, that is, the reciprocal of the number of alternatives ($1/A$). Thus, if there were two categories of response, we would credit omitted items with .5 points. Similarly, if there were four response alternatives, we would credit omitted items with .25 points, and so forth (Nunnally, 1978, p. 650; Rosenthal, Hall, DiMatteo, Rogers, & Archer, 1979). Because judges often know more than they think they do, it seems best to do all one can to avoid omitted items. Judges can usually be successfully urged to "leave no blanks." If blanks *are* left and we do not credit them with ($1/A$) points, we run the risk of having individuals who do not like to guess scoring significantly below chance.

TABLE 5.4
Estimated accuracy adjusted for guessing (100-item test)

Number right (R)	Number wrong (W)	Number of alternatives								
		2	3	4	5	6	7	8	9	10
100	0	100	100.0	100.0	100.0	100	100.0	100.0	100.0	100.0
95	5	90	92.5	93.3	93.8	94	94.2	94.3	94.4	94.4
90	10	80	85.0	86.7	87.5	88	88.3	88.6	88.8	88.9
85	15	70	77.5	80.0	81.2	82	82.5	82.9	83.1	83.3
80	20	60	70.0	73.3	75.0	76	76.7	77.1	77.5	77.8
75	25	50	62.5	66.7	68.8	70	70.8	71.4	71.9	72.2
70	30	40	55.0	60.0	62.5	64	65.0	65.7	66.2	66.7
65	35	30	47.5	53.3	56.2	58	59.2	60.0	60.6	61.1
60	40	20	40.0	46.7	50.0	52	53.3	54.3	55.0	55.6
55	45	10	32.5	40.0	43.8	46	47.5	48.6	49.4	50.0
50	50	00	25.0	33.3	37.5	40	41.7	42.9	43.8	44.4
45	55	−10	17.5	26.7	31.2	34	35.8	37.1	38.1	38.9
40	60	−20	10.0	20.0	25.0	28	30.0	31.4	32.5	33.3
35	65	−30	2.5	13.3	18.8	22	24.2	25.7	26.9	27.8
30	70	−40	−5.0	6.7	12.5	16	18.3	20.0	21.2	22.2
25	75	−50	−12.5	0.0	6.2	10	12.5	14.3	15.6	16.7
20	80	−60	−20.0	−6.7	0.0	4	6.7	8.6	10.0	11.1
15	85	−70	−27.5	−13.3	−6.2	−2	0.8	2.9	4.4	5.6
10	90	−80	−35.0	−20.0	−12.5	−8	−5.0	−2.9	−1.2	0.0
5	95	−90	−42.5	−26.7	−18.8	−14	−10.8	−8.6	−6.9	−5.6
0	100	−100	−50.0	−33.3	−25.0	−20	−16.7	−14.3	−12.5	−11.1

INTRINSIC FACTORS AND THE LEVEL OF ACCURACY

So far, we have discussed only the effect on item difficulty (or lack of "guessability") of an extrinsic factor of format: the number of response alternatives. Intrinsic factors also contribute to item or judgment difficulty, such as length of stimulus exposure time or quality of stimulus materials. From the point of view of developing psychometrically sound stimulus materials, what should be the level of accuracy of the items or judgments? Suppose there were two response alternatives, in which case an average accuracy rate of 50% would clearly be undesirable because it would imply that the judges were unable to categorize the material better than chance. Similarly, with only two response alternatives, an average accuracy rate of 100% would be undesirable because no individual differences in accuracy can be assessed. Moreover, we would have no idea of how much more difficult the task might have been made without the average level of accuracy dropping noticeably.

There is no uniformly appropriate answer to the question of a desirable level of average accuracy for stimulus materials of varying numbers of response alternatives. As an approximation, we might expect reasonably good performance (e.g., discrimination power) from items with an adjusted accuracy of R-adjusted = .7. Table 5.4 can be used to obtain raw score accuracies (R) equivalent to the adjusted accuracies for each column (number of categories). For most practical applications, the raw score accuracies (R) equivalent to the adjusted accuracy of .7 range between .7 and .85. The latter value (.85) applies to the situation of only two response alternatives, and the former value (.7), to a larger number of response alternatives (Guilford, 1954, p. 391; Nunnally, 1978, p. 273). To illustrate a range of categorical judgment studies, we describe three further applications: trait checklists, forced-choice judgments, and scaling for cumulative judgments.

APPLICATIONS OF CATEGORICAL JUDGMENTS

Word Checklists

The popular word checklist has a long history in the psychological assessment field (Guilford, 1954) and was used in classic research on personality impression formation (Asch, 1946). Those making judgments of others are shown a list of words that describe personality traits, and the instructions are to indicate (e.g., by circling, checking, or underlining) the traits that, in each judge's opinion, describe the person being judged. Thus, the categorical judgment is a simple yes (circle the trait) or no (don't circle it). Table 5.5 shows a list of "likable" and "unlikable" traits that Rosnow, Wainer, and Arms (1969) pared down from a much longer list (developed by N. H. Anderson, 1968). The likable traits are those indicated by a positive rating, and the unlikable traits, by a negative rating. Suppose all we needed was a crude index of relative likability; we can subtract the number of negative traits checked from the number of positive traits checked. Assuming that the ratings in Table 5.5 remain current, a more precise score is the median or mean of the ratings of traits selected by the judge. For example, if a judge circled "respectable" (+29), "wordy" (−5), and "ungrateful" (−38), the median score would be −5 and the mean score would be −4.7.

In obtaining the ratings in Table 5.5, Rosnow et al. used a dimensional rating procedure to trim the longer list. Half the raters were asked to think of a young man their own age and educational level who possessed traits they found *extremely favorable,* and to assign a score of 100 to this individual. Next, they were asked to imagine another young man with traits they perceived as *extremely unfavorable,* and to assign a score of 0 to that person. They were then given the full list and instructed to assign a score from 0 to 100 to each trait, depending on how likable a young man possessing that trait would be perceived as by them. Other raters were given similar instructions, except that "young woman" was substituted for "young man." The traits that are listed in Table 5.5 are those for which no significant disagreement was found between the male and female raters regarding male and female traits (Rosnow et al., 1969). The positive and negative ratings listed are average overall ratings minus the constant value of 50. The higher the positive rating, the more likable was the trait ("good-natured" being the most likable

TABLE 5.5
Likableness ratings of personality traits

Rating	Adjective	Rating	Adjective	Rating	Adjective
+37	good-natured	+19	brilliant	−19	moody
+37	trustworthy	+19	inoffensive	−19	unpopular
+36	honorable	+18	high-spirited	−22	downhearted
+35	good-tempered	+17	upright	−23	egotistical
+35	loyal	+16	idealistic	−24	childish
+35	trustful	+14	religious	−24	inconsistent
+34	kind	+13	untiring	−24	self-possessed
+33	alert	+12	humble	−25	boisterous
+33	kindhearted	+11	opinionated	−26	scheming
+33	reasonable	+10	excitable	−26	unenterprising
+33	unselfish	+10	nonconforming	−26	unindustrious
+32	admirable	+9	lucky	−27	careless
+32	adventurous	+9	outspoken	−27	fickle
+31	conscientious	+9	philosophical	−27	irrational
+31	good	+9	sophisticated	−27	resentful
+31	helpful	+8	deliberate	−27	touchy
+31	kind	+8	dignified	−28	disturbed
+30	amusing	+7	excited	−28	gloomy
+30	calm	+7	middle-class	−29	cowardly
+30	cool-headed	+6	opportunist	−29	jumpy
+30	tolerant	+6	prudent	−30	short-tempered
+29	grateful	+4	daring	−30	unentertaining
+29	respectable	+3	righteous	−30	unsocial
+29	well-spoken	+2	argumentative	−31	nosey
+28	efficient	+2	self-contented	−31	wasteful
+28	hopeful	+1	impressionable	−32	antisocial
+27	confident	0	theatrical	−32	petty
+27	curious	−1	discriminating	−32	ungracious
+27	realistic	−2	critical	−32	unsociable
+26	ambitious	−2	bashful	−33	scornful
+26	frank	−2	shy	−34	disrespectful
+26	logical	−3	shrewd	−34	irritable
+26	sensitive	−4	cunning	−34	quarrelsome
+25	generous	−4	daydreamer	−35	belligerent
+25	neat	−4	painstaking	−35	bossy
+25	observant	−5	extravagant	−35	ill-mannered
+25	prompt	−5	meticulous	−35	impolite
+25	punctual	−5	wordy	−35	loudmouthed
+25	rational	−7	daredevil	−37	boastful
+24	modest	−8	irreligious	−37	greedy
+23	outstanding	−8	self-righteous	−38	unfriendly
+23	wholesome	−9	crafty	−38	ungrateful
+22	agreeable	−11	eccentric	−39	irritating
+22	orderly	−11	unmethodical	−40	bragging
+21	decent	−16	dissatisfied	−41	insulting
+21	gracious	−17	impractical	−41	untrustworthy
+20	literary	−17	unsystematic	−42	dishonorable
+20	positive	−19	angry		

trait); the higher the absolute value of the negative rating, the less likable was the trait ("dishonorable" is the least likable).

To illustrate the use of these stimuli, social psychologist Marianne Jaeger and her colleagues (1994) showed the list of words in Table 5.5 to members of a service sorority at a large university. They were then instructed to indicate next to the name of each sorority sister the traits that best described that person (no minimum or maximum number of traits was suggested by the researchers). Jaeger et al. were interested in identifying various characteristics of people who gossip and those they gossip about. One finding in this research was that those identified as "low gossip-ers" (i.e., they gossiped only a little, or not at all) were judged as more likable than those who were identified as "moderate gossipers" or "high gossipers." It was also found that those who were most frequently perceived as targets of gossip (i.e., high-frequency gossipees) were judged to be less likable than those who were less frequently perceived as gossipees.

Forced-Choice Judgments

Another traditional use of categorical judgments is in forced-choice ratings, a procedure that was developed to overcome what was believed to be a ubiquitous response bias called the "halo error" by Thorndike (1920). More commonly known today as the **halo effect,** it refers to a type of response set in which the person being evaluated is judged not impartially, but in terms of a general impression (i.e., a "halo") surrounding him or her, resulting in high intercategory correlations or low intercategory variance. For example, a person who is athletic and good-looking might be judged as more popular than is actually the case. From the results of an early study by Symonds (1925), it was traditionally believed that halo effects were most prevalent when the traits being judged were not easily observed, not clearly defined, involved relations with other people, and possessed some moral importance.

Suppose a judge is dominated by the desire to make the person being evaluated "look good" and to avoid making him or her "look bad." Instead of allowing the judges to pile up favorable traits, the forced-choice method requires them to make difficult choices, such as choosing between two equally favorable characteristics. An example would be having to choose between "X is good-natured" and "X is trustworthy." The judge is *forced* to say whether Person X has more of one favorable trait than of another. From a comparison of several different forced-choice formats (Highland & Berkshire, 1951), the most preferable format was believed to be one in which judges are presented with four favorable traits and required to choose only the two most descriptive characteristics. Various ways of detecting and reducing halo effects have been described (see, e.g., W. H. Cooper, 1981; Lance & Woehr, 1986), although recently it has been argued that halo effects may not be as ubiquitous as earlier researchers believed (Murphy, Jako, & Anhalt, 1993).

Categorical Responses and Hierarchical Effects

A recent application of categorical judgments is in research on the ability to discriminate actions and intentions, called "interpersonal acumen" by Rosnow,

Skleder, Jaeger, and Rind (1994). This research was initially inspired by some earlier theoretical work of Howard Gardner (1985), who postulated that the process of discriminating actions and intentions begins with the bond established between an infant and its caregiver, usually the child's mother. The infant has a range of feelings but does not have the social savvy or insight to interpret them or to infer how or why she or he is feeling this way. As the infant seeks to maintain a positive feeling of well-being, the caregiver provides a clue concerning the relationship between certain actions and intentions. The mother responds affectionately, so the infant has the opportunity to learn that positive actions are often consonant with feelings of affection. The infant also has opportunities to respond to the cries of other infants or of others in pain and thereby begins to associate negative feelings and intentions with negative actions (e.g., crying). As children step beyond the family circle to forge friendships and peer relationships, they have opportunities to develop a keener sense of the often complex relationship between actions and intentions. For example, through talk, pretend play, gestures, and so on, they may encounter sequences in which the neutral action is a guise to mask the actor's positive or negative intent. In this way, people learn how not to fall prey to menacing action-intention patterns and also how to manipulate situations for their own hidden purposes.

In the research of Rosnow et al. (1994), it was theorized that generic combinations of actions and intentions also vary in their cognitive complexity to adult subjects, resulting in a hierarchy of action-intention combinations from least to most cognitively taxing. The least cognitively taxing were presumed to be actions and intentions that shared the same valence (e.g., a sincerely benevolent action), whereas the most taxing were theorized to be positive or negative actions that were coincidental. As an illustration of the latter, something favorable happens, but the favorable event was not created to benefit a particular recipient. Thus, it is important not to read more causal relations into situations than really exist. Rosnow et al., created stimuli to represent generic combinations of actions and intentions, ranging on theoretical grounds from least to most cognitively taxing. Adult subjects were then tested on their ability to differentiate the actions and intentions in those stimuli; the test used a number of procedures to ensure that the observed findings were generalizable across different judgment methods. The premise of the research was that the more interpersonal acumen a person has, the better able that person is to differentiate complex combinations of actions and intentions. If there is indeed a hierarchy of such combinations, then we should find that people who demonstrate mastery of one generic combination will show mastery of other generic combinations that are presumably less cognitively taxing. Similarly, a person who fails to display mastery of a particular generic combination is expected to fail to differentiate combinations that are presumably higher in the hierarchy.

The results were analyzed by means of contrasts (discussed in chapter 15) and a traditional scaling procedure developed by L. Guttman (1994). The way the scaling procedure works is illustrated with the aid of Table 5.6. Suppose we have sets of generic action-intention stimuli in five categories (A, B, C, D, E), which in turn are theorized to vary in complexity from least to most cognitively taxing in the following sequence: A < B < C < D < E. Each time a subject displays

TABLE 5.6

Hypothesized response profiles and cumulative scores for five levels of interpersonal acumen (IA)

Level of IA	Action-intention stimuli					Score
	A	B	C	D	E	
1	+	0	0	0	0	1
2	+	+	0	0	0	2
3	+	+	+	0	0	3
4	+	+	+	+	0	4
5	+	+	+	+	+	5

Note: A plus weight indicates a correct response, and a zero weight indicates an incorrect response; the score is the total number of plus weights. Underlying these idealized response profiles is the assumption that the stimuli vary from least to most cognitively taxing as follows: A < B < C < D < E.

mastery of one generic category, the subject receives a weight of 1; failure to differentiate a category is assigned a weight of 0. Thus, if all subjects respond as shown in Table 5.6, knowing only a subject's total score allows us to state exactly how the subject responded. If there are discrepancies in the way that subjects responded, then the total score is not a perfect indicator of individual results. There are virtually always going to be discrepancies; alternative procedures for scoring such discrepancies have been developed, as well as criteria for deciding whether the data support the idea of a cumulative scale (Edwards, 1957b; Torgerson, 1958). In the research by Rosnow et al., the results supported the idea of a hierarchy of combinations of actions and intentions that ranged from least to most complex. Similar results (from another set of stimuli) were reported by Aditya (1997; Aditya & Rosnow, 2002), who found that levels of interpersonal acumen scores were correlated positively with managers' upward mobility in organizations. That is, the more successful managers scored higher in interpersonal acumen.

CATEGORY SCALES AND RATING SCALES

In contrast to categorical judgments, **dimensional judgments** require that the judges make their responses on some form of more-or-less continuous rating scale. For example, they may be asked to rate the tone of voice of physicians talking about alcoholic patients (Milmoe, Rosenthal, Blane, Chafetz, & Wolf, 1967). The judges might be given between 2 and 20 scale points to indicate the particular degree of affective state (e.g., warmth or hostility) that they perceive in the physician's voice. Shortly, we will describe two popular types of rating scales, the *numerical* and the *graphic,* and another interesting type in which the number of total points is decided by the judges rather than preset by the researcher, called a *magnitude scale.* Before we turn to these three, however, we want to mention a relationship between category scales and rating scales that is not generally recognized.

Traditionally, the distinction between category scales and rating scales was based on the notion that people who worked with category scales were "classifiers" as opposed to "evaluators." That is, people who worked with category scales merely read, listened to, or watched some behavior and then simply classified it as accurately as possible, but no evaluation was made of whether one behavior was more appropriate or effective than another. Those who worked with ratings were said to be evaluators, who not only classified or counted but also assigned a numerical value to certain judgments or assessments. Our view, however, is that classifying and evaluating are characteristic of all judgments. A categorical format with A alternatives to choose from is analogous to a set of A ratings that each offer only two scale points.

To illustrate, suppose the categorical response format offered the following alternatives, and the judge was instructed to check the traits that applied to Person X:

_____ good-natured
_____ conscientious
_____ scornful
_____ boisterous
_____ tolerant
_____ wasteful

That instruction to select one or more traits to describe Person X is analogous to the dimensional response format:

0____1 good-natured
0____1 conscientious
0____1 scornful
0____1 boisterous
0____1 tolerant
0____1 wasteful

with the instruction to rate Person X on each of the six rating scales offered. The end points (0 and 1) of the rating scales might be labeled "*absent* = 0 and *present* = 1" or "*low* = 0 and *high* = 1" or "*does not apply* = 0 and *does apply* = 1," and so forth. Thus, however one may choose to label the end points, both formats will yield one of two possible scores for each category or each dimension. That is, 0 for the dimensional rating is the same as "unselected" for the categorical, and 1 for the dimensional is the same as "selected" for the categorical.

NUMERICAL, GRAPHIC, AND MAGNITUDE RATINGS

Numerical Formats

There are several alternative **numerical scale** formats, but what they all have in common is that judges or raters work with a sequence of defined numbers.

The numbers may be quite explicit, as illustrated by the following item, which was taken from a behavior rating scale for adolescents (Baughman & Dahlstrom, 1968):

How popular is each of your classmates?

(1) extremely popular

(2) above average

(3) about average

(4) below average

(5) not at all popular

In the example above, there are 5 scale points. Another example of a 5-point numerical scale, but one in which the numbers are implicit rather than explicit, would be:

Do you feel that a large-scale homeland security program will incite an enemy to prematurely attack this country, or do you feel that such a program will lessen the chances of an enemy attack? (Check one.)

_____ It would considerably increase the chance of an enemy attack.

_____ It would somewhat increase the chance of an enemy attack.

_____ It would neither increase nor decrease the chance of an enemy attack.

_____ It would somewhat decrease the chance of an enemy attack.

_____ It would considerably decrease the chance of an enemy attack.

In both examples above, the items are written in simple, straightforward language. It is important that the statements not be ambiguous or complexly worded, for such statements ask the respondent to provide a one-dimensional response to a two-dimensional (or multidimensional) question—quite impossible! In the second item, note that the middle alternative ("neither increase nor decrease") represents something like indifference. Many researchers prefer to omit middle categories, so as to push their respondents to one or the other side (Bradburn, 1982).

Graphic Formats

The **graphic scale** format is simply a straight line resembling a thermometer, presented either horizontally or vertically:

Unpopular _____	Popular
Shy _____	Outgoing
Solitary _____	Gregarious

The judge or subject responds with a check mark, and the researcher then uses a ruler to read the position of the check mark on the scale.

A variation on this format is to divide the line into segments, to create a numerical scale or segmented rating scale. For example, a bipolar 10-point scale would look like this:

Unpopular ____:____:____:____:____:____:____:____:____:____ Popular

Shy ____:____:____:____:____:____:____:____:____:____ Outgoing

Solitary ____:____:____:____:____:____:____:____:____:____ Gregarious

Because this scale is divided into an equal number of segments, there is no obvious neutral point, unless we think of the two middle segments as representing "neutrality" (e.g., neither unpopular nor popular). If we divided the scale into an uneven number of segments, there would be a clear-cut middle point for neutrality.

For example, Osgood, Suci, and Tannenbaum (1957) used 7-point bipolar segmented scales to measure what they described as the "meaning of meaning." Calling their scaling and association method the *semantic differential,* they had respondents judge the meaning of concepts (such as the concept of *father*) on certain relevant dimensions. We will have more to say about this procedure in the following chapter, but in particular, Osgood et al. used the semantic differential method to operationalize and tap into three primary dimensions of meaning, which they named *evaluation* (bad-good, unpleasant-pleasant, negative-positive, ugly-beautiful, cruel-kind, unfair-fair, worthless-valuable), *potency* (weak-strong, light-heavy, small-large, soft-hard, thin-heavy), and *activity* (slow-fast, passive-active, dull-sharp). In a classic application of this procedure, Osgood and Luria (1954) constructed three-dimensional graphs of semantic differential results to represent Thigpen and Cleckley's (1954) famous case of multiple personalities, which was later depicted in the film *The Three Faces of Eve.* Interestingly, in the 1968 U.S. presidential campaign, one of Richard M. Nixon's first moves was the appointment of advertising researchers who traveled through the United States asking people to judge the candidates on semantic differential scales, based on which it was possible to compare Nixon's semantic differential profile with the plotted curves for Hubert Humphrey and George Wallace (McGinniss, 1969).

Scale Points and Labels

The advantage of the dimensional format begins to appear as the number of scale points or segments increases. In a computer simulation study of interrater reliability, a team of researchers found that the greatest benefits to reliability accrued as they went from 2 to 7 points, with only trivial improvements between a 7-, 8-, 9-, or 10-category ordinal scale and a 100-point continuous scale (Cicchetti, Showalter, & Tyrer, 1985). However, there are circumstances in which it may still be beneficial to reliability to use up to 11 scale points (Nunnally, 1978), and as many as 20 scale points may prove useful in some circumstances (Guilford, 1954; Rosenthal, 1966, 1976). From a practical point of view, there are some advantages to using 9 or 10 scale points. This number is usually enough to reap most of the benefits of added reliability, but it keeps each judge's response at a single digit, which can effect some economies of data processing (i.e., 1–9 or 0–9, the former if a neutral midpoint is desired, the latter if not).

There is no clear agreement on the optimum number of labels for rating scales. At a minimum, we would label the end points (e.g., not warm-warm, cold-warm, not cold-cold). In choosing the end labels (or anchor words), it is important to select terms or short statements (e.g., extremely unpopular-extremely popular) that are simple, straightforward, and unambiguous. The anchors also need to be clearly relevant to the behavior or variable being rated, and consistent with other cues. For example, in a 9-point or 10-point rating scale of "warmth of interpersonal manner," we might label the end points "not at all warm" and "very warm" and distribute the three interior labels ("somewhat warm," "moderately warm," "quite warm") so that all five labels are approximately equidistant. This is an example of a **unipolar scale.** An example of a **bipolar scale** might run from "very cold" on one end to "very warm" on the other end, with interior labels like "somewhat cold," "neither cold nor warm," and "somewhat warm" spaced along the rating scale. (Some special problems of bipolar scales will be discussed shortly.)

It is easier to find nonredundant labels for bipolar scales, and some researchers may want to use more than five labels. For the scale we have been discussing, we might use nine labels: "very cold," "quite cold," "moderately cold," "somewhat cold," "neither cold nor warm," "somewhat warm," "moderately warm," "quite warm, "very warm." Experience suggests that judges who make ratings (e.g., college students, college graduates, most high school students) can do about as well with just a few labels on a rating scale as with many labels. Different judges tend to use different sections of the rating scales more often, but these biases do not ordinarily affect the judges' reliability.

When designing rating scales for judgment studies, it is less confusing to judges and data processors always to place the higher numbers on the right, as most people learn in elementary school that numbers increase to the right. In addition, the tradition is to place the "good end" of bipolar rating scales (e.g., warm, friendly, empathic) on the right (as illustrated in the graphic and segmented scales shown previously). Although there *may* be a tendency for the grand mean ratings to increase somewhat, it is likely that, on average, errors of judging, of coding, and of interpretation will be reduced by this practice (Guilford, 1954). Numbers on the rating scales should be equidistant, and the overall format of the entire instrument should be designed to make it unlikely that any items will be overlooked or "skipped." If the scale is administered on a computer, it can be programmed to ensure that each item is rated before the judge can respond to the next one.

Magnitude Scaling

In the dimensional formats described above, the lower and upper range of scores is defined by the researchers. In what has come to be known as **magnitude scaling**—a method developed by experimental psychologist S. S. Stevens (1936, 1966)—the upper range is left to the judges. For example, Sellin and Wolfgang (1964) had juvenile court judges, parole officers, and college students weight the seriousness of such crimes as trespassing, stealing and abandoning a vehicle, arson, rape, and murder.

Each of the stimuli was presented to the subjects in a number of contexts, from verbal threats to gunpoint with different degrees of injury resulting. In one variant of this procedure, the subjects were told to assign a score of 10 to a person who steals a bicycle parked on the street, and then to score other situations in terms of their relative seriousness as crimes (Figlio, 1978; cited in Lodge, 1981). For example, if they thought of a particular situation as 20 times more serious than the bicycle theft, they would score it 200; if they thought a situation was half as serious as the bicycle theft, they would score it 5; a situation not perceived as a crime would be scored 0. In analyzing these results, the researchers took the common log (base 10) of each person's score, calculated the arithmetic mean of the logs for each stimulus, and then worked with these values (Lodge, 1981). Magnitude scaling involving the estimation of ratios and magnitudes was effectively used by Stevens and Galanter (1957) to study a wide variety of sensory and perceptual continua.

RATING BIASES AND THEIR CONTROL

The use of all rating scales proceeds on the assumption that the person doing the rating is capable of an acceptable degree of precision and objectivity. However, there are potential rating biases that need to be considered by researchers who use these procedures. Earlier, we mentioned the halo effect; another type of rating bias that is similar, in a way, to the halo effect is an **error of leniency** (Kneeland, 1929). This type of bias takes its name from the idea that some observers or judges (i.e., lenient judges) tend to rate someone who is very familiar (or someone with whom they are socially involved) more positively than they should. Judges who are made aware of this potential bias may, however, "lean over backward" and rate the person more negatively than they should, producing the opposite type of error **(severity error).** In numerical and graphic scales, the traditional way to control for errors of leniency is to arrange the rating scale a little differently by simply stretching one end. For instance, we might give one unfavorable cue word ("poor") and have most of the range given to degrees of favorable responses ("poor," "fairly good," "good," "very good, "excellent"). Another solution is to ask judges to rate positive and negative qualities on two separate unipolar scales (as we will describe shortly). For a more detailed overview of leniency and halo biases, and of formulas for correcting the effects of such errors on estimates of means and variances, see Hoyt (2000).

Another type of rating bias is called an **error of central tendency;** it occurs when judges hesitate to give extreme ratings and instead tend to rate in the direction of the mean of the total group. In the case of numerical and graphic scales, this problem is traditionally controlled in the way that the positive range was expanded in the example noted above. Thus, in a numerical or a segmented graphic scale, it is often a good idea to allow for 1 or 2 more points than are absolutely essential for the research. If we feel it is essential to have at least 5-point scales, it would be prudent to use 7-point rather than 5-point scales, on the assumption that some raters may be reluctant to use the extreme categories.

Still another type of error is called a **logical error in rating;** it refers to the problem that many raters are likely to give similar ratings to variables or traits that seem logically related in their own minds (but may not be similar in the person who is being evaluated or rated). This type of error is also similar to the halo effect, in that both types increase the intercorrelation of the variables or traits being rated. The difference is that the halo effect results from the observer's or judge's favorable attitude toward one person, whereas the logical error results from the rater's perception of the relatedness of certain variables or traits irrespective of individuals. One way to address this problem is to construct precise definitions and to make sure that the instructions are also clear, precise, and explicit (characteristics that can be tested in a pilot study). Practice sessions followed by a discussion of each possible error are also used to teach judges what to watch for and how to be objective in their evaluations.

BIPOLAR VERSUS UNIPOLAR SCALES

Previously, we gave an example of a *bipolar* segmented scale, which is simply a scale that ranges from a great amount of a characteristic to a great amount of its opposite (e.g., cold-warm); *unipolar scales* run from a great amount of a characteristic to the absence of that characteristic (e.g., not warm to warm; not cold to cold). For many practical purposes, it seems not to matter much whether bipolar or unipolar scales are used. The correlation between judges' ratings of warmth on a scale of "cold-warm" and a scale of "not warm-warm" is likely to be substantial, perhaps as high as the retest reliability of either rating. Experience also suggests, however, that the negative correlation between ratings of "not warm-warm" and "not cold-cold" will not necessarily be as high as we would expect it to be. This potentially low correlation between unipolar rating scales that would appear to be opposites has been superbly documented in work on masculinity-femininity (e.g., S. L. Bem, 1974; Spence & Helmreich, 1978). This research has shown that the ratings obtained on the unipolar scales of masculine and feminine are correlated sufficiently poorly that it is possible to identify a generous proportion of people who score high on both or low on both (as well as people we would expect to predominate, those who score high on one and low on the other).

In their research on nonverbal communication, DePaulo and Rosenthal (1979a, 1979b, 1982) used unipolar scales of liking and disliking. Despite substantial negative correlations between ratings on these unipolar scales, the researchers found it possible to identify encodings of nonverbal behavior in which a person being described was both liked and disliked considerably. This result has, in fact, served as an operational definition of an "ambivalent interpersonal affect." It was also possible to identify encodings in which a person being described was neither liked nor disliked, and this result was used as an operational definition of an "indifferent interpersonal affect." The lesson of these examples is that it may often be worth the effort to use more unipolar scales in hopes of turning up some surprises.

FORMING COMPOSITE VARIABLES

In many situations it is advisable to treat each variable measured individually, but it may also be beneficial in many situations to form composites and other redescriptions of variables. We have more to say in the second half of this book about the statistical tools described in this section (including a basic review, beginning in chapter 10).

However, on the assumption that the reader is familiar with standard scores (Z scores), correlation matrices, and so on, we will describe some procedures for recasting a set of dependent variables as a composite variable. To illustrate, suppose a group of judges have rated the nonverbal behavior of a set of psychotherapists on three dimensions: warmth, empathy, and positiveness of regard. Suppose further that the retest reliabilities and the internal consistency reliabilities of all three variables are .70, and that the mean intercorrelation of each variable with the others is .70. Under these conditions, when the variables are so highly correlated with each other—as highly correlated as they are with themselves—we may find no advantage to analyzing the data separately for the three variables.

To form a composite variable of all three, we might begin by standard scoring (Z-scoring) each of the three variables and replace each therapist's three scores by the mean of the three Z scores the therapist earned from the judges. A mean Z score of zero would tell us that the particular therapist scored as average on the new composite variable of warmth, empathy, and positiveness of regard. A very large positive Z score would tell us the therapist scored very high on the new composite variable, and a large negative Z score would tell us the therapist scored very low on the new composite variable. As we will illustrate in chapter 10, the means of Z-scores are not themselves distributed as Z scores. Thus, if our composite variables are to be used in the construction of further composites, we will need to Z-score each composite variable before we take the next step in this process.

Benefits of Forming Composite Variables

In the example given above, and in many more complex cases as well, there are conceptual and practical reasons for forming composite variables. Conceptually, if variables cannot be discriminated from one another (because they are as highly correlated with each other as they are with themselves), it is hard to defend treating them as separate variables. Practically, we are able to obtain more accurate (and usually larger) estimates of the relationships of composites with other variables of interest than if we are working with the individual variables before they are combined into composites. Furthermore, reducing a larger number of variables to a small number of composites makes it easier to interpret appropriately any significance levels we may want to work with.

Suppose we are interested in the effects of therapists' training on patients' behaviors on some dimension of interest (e.g., their nonverbal behaviors). We might use 5, or 10, or 20 variables on which patients are to be rated by judges. If we find the relationship between therapists' training and patients' behavior significant at .05 for only 1 of 10 of the behaviors, it will be very difficult to interpret what the "true" level of significance of that result is, because 10 tests of significance have been performed. If our 10 patient behaviors were combined into a single meaningful composite, we would be able to interpret the obtained level of significance more appropriately. (We return to this problem of interpreting the results of numerous tests of significance in chapter 14, when we discuss the Bonferroni adjustment for multiple tests of significance.)

Forming Composites and Increasing Effect Sizes

When each of the separate variables shows approximately the same magnitude of correlation with some other variable, and when the correlations among the various separate variables are also fairly homogeneous in magnitude, we can estimate the effects of forming composites on the magnitude of the effect size of interest. For reasons discussed in chapter 2, we prefer the family of correlational (r) indices as a generally useful group of effect size measures. Thus, suppose we had examined the effects of therapists' training on 10 dependent variables, and say we found the correlation between therapist training and each of those 10 individual dependent variables (symbolized as $r_{individual}$) was roughly .30, and that the average intercorrelation among the 10 dependent variables was $r_{yy} = .50$. We want to estimate the new correlation ($r_{composite}$) of a composite variable with the independent variable of therapist training.

To obtain this estimate, we first need to calculate what we term the multiplier (m) factor, or the factor by which we will have to multiply the average individual r (i.e., $r_{individual}$) in order to obtain the composite r (i.e., $r_{composite}$, the effect size correlation based on the composite variable). The multiplier m is defined as

$$m = \sqrt{\frac{n}{1 + r_{yy}(n-1)}},\tag{5.3}$$

where n = number of variables entering into the composite, and r_{yy} = mean intercorrelation among the variables entering into the composite. To obtain our estimate of the new r, we use the following equation (based on rearrangement of terms of an equation given by Guilford, 1954):

$$r_{composite} = r_{individual} \times m,\tag{5.4}$$

which states simply that the effect size correlation based on the composite variable is the product of the typical effect size based on the individual variable multiplied by a factor m. Substitution in Equation 5.3 gives us

$$m = \sqrt{\frac{10}{1 + .50(9)}} = 1.35,$$

and thus, Equation 5.4 yields:

$$r_{composite} = .30 \times 1.35 = .40.$$

Table 5.7 shows the values of m for varying levels of n and r_{yy}. Only when individual variables are perfectly correlated with each other is there no benefit from forming composites. In general, the larger the number of separate variables (n) that are combined into a composite, the greater will be the increase in the effect size r obtained (i.e., $r_{composite}$). Further, the *lower* the mean intercorrelation among the individual variables (i.e., r_{yy}), the greater will be the increase in $r_{composite}$. It should be noted, however, that as r_{yy} decreases, the effect sizes for the individual variables will be homogeneous more rarely. Finding that they are homogeneous means that all the individual variables are equivalently related to the external or criterion variable, but each is "predicting" an independent portion of that criterion. The values of the

TABLE 5.7

Factors (m) by which effect sizes (r) increase as a function of the number of variables in a composite, and the mean intercorrelation among variables

	Number of individual variables (n)			
Mean intercorrelation r_{yy}	2	5	10	20
1.00	1.00	1.00	1.00	1.00
.90	1.03	1.04	1.05	1.05
.75	1.07	1.12	1.14	1.15
.50	1.15	1.29	1.35	1.38
.25	1.26	1.58	1.75	1.87
.10	1.35	1.89	2.29	2.63
.00	1.41	2.24	3.16	4.47

factor m shown in the body of Table 5.7 need only be multiplied by the typical effect size for individual variables ($r_{individual}$) to yield the effect size based on the composite variable ($r_{composite}$).

There are also situations, however, where $r_{composite}$ is known and we would like to find $r_{individual}$, the likely value of the typical effect size for individual variables. We readily find this result from the following relationship:

$$r_{individual} = \frac{r_{composite}}{m}, \tag{5.5}$$

which would be useful in the following type of situation. Investigator A reported a correlation of .70 between therapists' gender and perceived nonverbal warmth. Investigator B feels the r must be too high and tries to replicate, obtaining an r of .40. Because both investigators used large samples, the two rs of .70 and .40 differ very significantly. Investigator B wonders where A went wrong until B recalls that her own operational definition of warmth was based on a single item (i.e., one variable), whereas Investigator A used a composite variable made up of 10 variables with an average intercorrelation of .25. Using Table 5.7, Investigator B finds $m = 1.75$, and from Equation 5.5 she finds that

$$r_{individual} = \frac{.70}{1.75} = .40,$$

a result suggesting that the data of Investigators A and B were not discrepant after all. In both cases, the "per single variable effect size" was $r_{individual} = .40$.

Forming Multiple Composites

So far, our discussion of forming composites has focused on the simple case in which the variables are homogeneously related to each other. In such situations, it is reasonable to form only a single composite. There are many situations, however, in which the intercorrelations among the dependent variables are not homogeneous, so we would want to form two or more composite variables. Consider the intercorrelations among the five variables *A, B, C, D,* and *E* of Table 5.8. Variables *A, B,* and *C* are ratings of health care providers' warmth, friendliness, and likability, and variables *D* and *E* are ratings of the health care providers' self-confidence and professional demeanor. The mean intercorrelation of the five variables is $r_{yy} = .36$ (median $= .15$), with a standard deviation (S) of .37. Closer inspection of the correlation matrix of Part A of Table 5.8, however, suggests that combining all five variables would make a poor composite, given the large variability of the intercorrelations. Part B of Table 5.8 shows the decomposition of the lower left triangle of the correlation matrix into three groupings. The first grouping shows that the three intercorrelations among variables *A, B,* and *C* range between .70 and .90. The third grouping shows that the correlation between *D* and *E* is similarly high (.70). The second grouping in Part B shows that the six correlations among the three variables *A, B,* and *C* and the two variables *D* and *E* range only from .00 to .20. These correlations suggest strongly that a composite formed of variables *A, B,* and *C* would be relatively independent of a composite formed of variables *D* and *E*.

TABLE 5.8
Illustration of the formation of multiple composite variables

A. The correlation matrix

	Variables				
Variables	*A*	*B*	*C*	*D*	*E*
A	1.00	.80	.70	.10	.00
B	.80	1.00	.90	.20	.10
C	.70	.90	1.00	.10	.00
D	.10	.20	.10	1.00	.70
E	.00	.10	.00	.70	1.00

B. Decomposition of the lower left triangle

	A	*B*			*A*	*B*	*C*			*D*
B	.80			*D*	.10	.20	.10		*E*	.70
C	.70	.90		*E*	.00	.10	.00			

C. The intra/intermatrix of mean intercorrelations

	Composites	
Composites	I	II
I	.80	.08
II	.08	.70

The Intra/Intermatrix

In Table 5.8, Part C represents the intra/intermatrix of mean intercorrelations. The mean r of .80 in the upper left cell of the matrix is the *intra*composite average for Composite I. The r of .70 in the lower right cell of the matrix is the *intra*composite average for Composite II. The off-diagonal value of .08 is the *inter*composite average characterizing the level of relationship between the ingredient variables of composites with the ingredient variables of other composites.

The value of an intra/intermatrix of mean (or median) intercorrelations is that it tells us at a glance how justified we are in claiming that we have formed clear, defensible composites (Rosenthal, 1966). For example, if our intra/intermatrix were as follows:

	I	II
I	.75	.60
II	.60	.50

we would not have a strong case for two composites (rather than one). The reason is simply that the typical (mean or median) correlation between composites (.60) is noticeably higher than the typical correlation within one of the composites (.50).

In Table 5.9, Part A shows a much larger correlation matrix, namely, the intercorrelations among 14 variables, which have been reduced to a set of four composite variables (I, II, III, IV). Part B of this table shows the intra/intermatrix. The mean correlations within composites (intra) appear on the principal diagonal, and the mean correlations between composites (inter) appear off the principal diagonal. For simplicity, we have omitted the mean correlations below the diagonal, because they would simply be relistings of mean correlations shown above the diagonal. As the number of variables increases, we can get help in the construction of composites by using such procedures as clustering, principal components analysis, factor analysis, and dimensional analysis (Rosenthal, 1987).

QUANTIFYING THE CLARITY OF COMPOSITES

Two of the most valuable strategies for quantifying the degree of success in constructing clear composite variables are what we term the **r method** and the **g method.** We will also describe a third alternative (the **range-to-midrange-ratio method**), which is useful when the other methods cannot be used because certain basic ingredients required by those methods are unavailable.

The r Method

In this method, we compute the point-biserial correlation (i.e., the Pearson r, where one of the variables is continuous and the other is dichotomous) between the mean (or median) correlations of the intra/intermatrix (this is the continuous variable) with their (dichotomously coded) location *on* the principal diagonal (coded as 1) versus *off* the diagonal (coded as 0) of the intra/intermatrix. The more positive the correlation is, the higher (on average) are the *intra* mean correlations (i.e., those on the diagonal) than the *inter* mean correlations (those off the diagonal).

TABLE 5.9
Illustration of the formation of four composite variables

A. The correlation matrix

		Composite I				Composite II			Composite III				Composite IV		
								Variables							
Composites		*a*	*b*	*c*	*d*	*e*	*f*	*g*	*h*	*i*	*j*	*k*	*l*	*m*	*n*
I	*a*		.40	.60	.50	.30	.25	.20	.15	.20	.20	.25	.25	.30	.25
	b			.50	.40	.25	.20	.15	.20	.25	.15	.10	.30	.25	.30
	c				.60	.10	.15	.20	.30	.15	.15	.10	.20	.30	.25
	d					.30	.20	.25	.25	.10	.15	.20	.30	.20	.20
II	*e*						.70	.60	.30	.30	.25	.35	.10	.20	.25
	f							.50	.30	.25	.25	.30	.30	.10	.15
	g								.35	.25	.30	.35	.20	.10	.15
III	*h*									.30	.40	.50	.15	.30	.25
	i										.50	.40	.15	.20	.30
	j											.30	.10	.25	.10
	k												.25	.10	.15
IV	*l*													.35	.45
	m														.55
	n														

B. The intra/intermatrix

	Composites			
	I	II	III	IV
I	.50	.21	.18	.26
II		.60	.30	.17
III			.40	.19
IV				.45

Table 5.10 shows the 10 mean correlations of the intra/intermatrix of Table 5.9 (Part B), now listed as "within-composite" (intra) or "between-composite" (inter) values. The correlation between the mean correlation and location on the diagonal (rather than off the diagonal) is .92. This tells us that the average internal consistency of the four composite variables is much greater than the average correlation between the ingredient variables of different composites with one another.

The *g* Method

In chapter 2, we described the difference family of effect sizes. We gave as one popular example of this family the index known as Hedges's *g*, which in Equation 2.5 was

TABLE 5.10

Example of r and g methods of quantifying the clarity of composite variables from the intra/intermatrix of Table 5.9 (Part B)

	Intracomposite mean (r_{intra})	Intercomposite mean (r_{inter})
	On-diagonal coded as 1[a]	Off-diagonal coded as 0[a]
	.50	.21
	.60	.18
	.40	.26
	.45	.30
		.17
		.19
Mean	.49	.22
S^2	.0073[b]	.0026[b]

[a]The correlation between magnitude of mean correlations and their location on (rather than off) the diagonal is .92.

[b]Weighted value of $S = .066$, $g = 4.1$.

defined as the difference between two means ($M_1 - M_2$) divided by the square root (S) of the pooled unbiased estimate of the population variance (S^2). The g method for quantifying the clarity of composites takes its name from that index (Hedges, 1981), but in this case we define g as

$$g = \frac{r_{intra} - r_{inter}}{S_{aggregated}}, \tag{5.6}$$

that is, the difference between the mean of the mean rs on the diagonal (r_{intra}) and the mean of the mean rs off the diagonal (r_{inter}) divided by the weighted S combined from the on-diagonal (intra) and off-diagonal (inter) values of r.

Applying Equation 5.6 to the data of Table 5.10, we find

$$g = \frac{.49 - .22}{.066} = 4.1,$$

indicating that the average relationship of variables within a composite to one another is just over 4 standard deviations larger than the average relationship of variables between composites to one another. There is no firm rule to help us decide when the r and g indices are large enough to suggest that our composites show clarity of differentiation from one another. Certainly, however, rs of .25 and gs of .50 provide suggestive evidence of such clarity (Cohen, 1988).

The Range-to-Midrange Ratio

When we have access to an intra/intermatrix, both the r method and the g method are extremely informative. If it should happen, however, that we know only the mean of the intracomposite (on-diagonal) mean rs (i.e., the r_{intra}) and the mean of the intercomposite (off-diagonal) mean rs (the r_{inter}), we cannot use either the r method or the g method. An index that can be used in such cases is the range-to-midrange ratio (rmr), defined as

$$rmr = \frac{r_{intra} - r_{inter}}{\left[\frac{r_{intra} + r_{inter}}{2}\right]}, \tag{5.7}$$

which divides the difference between the mean of the intracomposite means (r_{intra}) and the mean of the intercomposite means (r_{inter}) by the mean of these mean rs. Dividing by the mean of these mean rs makes a particular raw difference between r_{intra} and r_{inter} relatively more meaningful when the mean of these rs is smaller rather than larger.

Table 5.11 lists rmr values obtained for various values of r_{intra} and r_{inter}. Note that when $r_{intra} = .90$ and $r_{inter} = .70$, so that $r_{intra} - r_{inter} = .20$, the value of $rmr = .25$. When $r_{intra} = .50$ and $r_{inter} = .30$, the difference between them is still .20, but the value of $rmr = .50$. For $r_{intra} = .30$ and $r_{inter} = .10$, $rmr = 1.00$, though the absolute difference (or range) between r_{intra} and r_{inter} is still .20. No firm guidelines are available for what value of rmr should be regarded as strong evidence for the clarity of differentiation of composite variables. Perhaps any value of .33 or larger (i.e., the difference between the intra- and intermeans of mean intercorrelations is at least one third of the value of the mean of the intra- and intermean intercorrelations) can be regarded as providing fairly good evidence for the clarity of differentiation of the composite variables.

TABLE 5.11

Range-to-midrange ratios (rmr) for values of mean intracomposite average correlations (r_{intra}) and mean intercomposite average correlations (r_{inter})

		Values of r_{intra}										
		.00	.10	.20	.30	.40	.50	.60	.70	.80	.90	1.00
Values of r_{inter}	.00	.00	2.00	2.00	2.00	2.00	2.00	2.00	2.00	2.00	2.00	2.00
	.10		.00	.67	1.00	1.20	1.33	1.43	1.50	1.56	1.60	1.64
	.20			.00	.40	.67	.86	1.00	1.11	1.20	1.27	1.33
	.30				.00	.29	.50	.67	.80	.91	1.00	1.08
	.40					.00	.22	.40	.55	.67	.77	.86
	.50						.00	.18	.33	.46	.57	.67
	.60							.00	.15	.29	.40	.50
	.70								.00	.13	.25	.35
	.80									.00	.12	.22
	.90										.00	.11
	1.00											.00

Note: Values below the diagonal of .00 values are negative, indicating no support for the clarity of differentiation of the composite variables considered as a set.

CHAPTER 6

QUESTIONNAIRES, INTERVIEWS, AND DIARIES

CONCERNS ABOUT SELF-REPORT DATA

When investigators believe that research participants have the language and experience to describe their own feelings, attitudes, thinking, and behavior, then interviews, questionnaires, and self-recorded diaries are frequently used to obtain **self-report data.** One case in which such data are typically encountered is where other relevant data exist but are too difficult or costly to obtain (Baldwin, 2000). Suppose we wanted to know how many children a woman has, and whether she was single, married, or divorced when she had each of the children. We should be able to find the information in an assiduous search of institutional records, assuming we know where to look and have permission (and the resources) to do so. It would be a lot easier to ask her directly. Another situation calling for self-report data is where there is no other way to find out something except by asking people to tell us about themselves (Baldwin, 2000). If you go to a doctor to be treated for pain, you will be asked where it hurts and what the pain feels like. In research on pain, there are questionnaires we can use to gather specific information about symptoms, such as the duration of pain (momentary, periodic, or constant) and whether it is dull and aching, pulsing and throbbing, sharp and stabbing, and so on (Melzack, 1975; Melzack & Katz,1992). If we want to know how the subjects in a psychological experiment perceived their role, or what they perceived as the cues about what the study was "really" about and what they thought we "really" wanted to find out, we might ask them detailed questions about their experience (Orne, 1962, 1969).

One problem, however, is that respondents in interview and questionnaire studies may simply not know the right answers to some of the questions they are asked, so they can only guess the answers. Baldwin (2000) noted that most mothers can probably tell us exactly, or a close approximation of, the birth weight of each of their children but cannot tell us the length of their newborn infants with the same degree of accuracy. If we need precise information, we would be better advised to search the official records that were made at the time of each child's birth. But what if we cannot access those original records, or if we suspect the data we have are inaccurate? Particularly suspect are data that depend on recalling events that were not especially momentous when they occurred, because subjects usually find it difficult to reconstruct such events. In a study in which parents were interviewed as they were leaving an HMO immediately after their children had received one or more vaccinations, the parents' reports of what had occurred only a few minutes earlier were riddled with errors of recall (Willis, Brittingham, Lee, Tourangeau, & Ching, 1999). Furthermore, both adults and children can be easily *led* to "recollect" events that never happened, and to describe their "recollections" in persuasive detail (cf. Ceci & Bruck, 1995; E. F. Loftus, 2004).

Another concern is that people are not always open and forthcoming when asked personal questions. In chapter 1 we mentioned the construct of need for social approval and Crowne and Marlowe's (1964) scale for detecting social desirability biases. We will have more to say about social desirability and its control later in this chapter. In a study by Esposito et al. (1984), college students were given the Marlowe-Crowne Social Desirability Scale (SDS) along with a popular self-report measure of trait and state anxiety, curiosity, and anger. Before responding, some of the students (at random) were told that their responses would be kept strictly confidential, but other students (those in the control group) were not told this. All the respondents were essentially "captive subjects" because the questionnaires were administered to entire classes, and the treatments were randomly assigned in each class. The results were that the magnitude of the positive and negative correlations between the SDS and the self-report subscales (positive correlations for curiosity and negative correlations for anxiety and anger) were noticeably lower in the confidentiality condition than in the control condition. Esposito et al. raised the question of whether strict confidentiality might sometimes "pay off" not only ethically but also methodologically, by reducing the biasing effects of distortions due to socially desirable responding. Interestingly, Ceci and Peters (1984) found that faculty advisers' letters of recommendation were more critical (i.e., presumably more honest and forthcoming) when the cover forms showed that the students had waived their right to inspect the letters.

Other researchers have found subtle differences in how subjects respond when told that data are confidential. Singer, Hippler, and Schwarz (1992) studied the effects of confidentiality assurances in stimulating people's willingness to participate in survey studies. In two studies, both of which used convenience samples of students, the findings were that the more elaborate the assurance of confidentiality was, the *less* willing the students were to agree to take part in later survey interviews. Singer et al. speculated that perhaps the more elaborate assurances of confidentiality may have raised expectations that the later survey interviews would touch on sensitive, highly personal information. Frey (1986) used a confidentiality reminder in a telephone survey

("Now, I need to know some information about you for statistical purposes only. *Remember, your responses are confidential.*") Half the people contacted were given both sentences above, and the others were given the first sentence but not the confidentiality reminder. The confidentiality reminder was associated with higher item nonresponse rates, as in Singer et al.'s (1992) finding.

A third concern was raised by R. E. Nisbett and Wilson (1977), who argued that people cannot dispassionately or realistically look within themselves or have a clear sense of themselves apart from the immediate situation. This interesting argument is reminiscent of an old criticism of the method of introspection, which goes back to the earliest days of psychology as an empirical science (Bakan, 1967; Danziger, 1988). As David Bakan (1967) cautioned, "A characteristic of good science is that it is ever alert to the possibility of the commission of systematic types of errors" (p. 101). Bakan added that, although one of the major criticisms of introspection (and, by implication, the method of self-report) is that such data are untrustworthy, it is possible for introspective observations to be more trustworthy than sensory observations. Sensory data are subject to illusion (recall the example of "N rays" in the previous chapter), and sense organs may also be defective. With introspection, Bakan concluded, researchers are at least aware of the possible error tendencies and can take the precaution of using more than one method of data collection. More recently, Dunning, Heath, and Suls (2004) reviewed an extensive body of research on the validity of self-assessment, and concluded that people's self-ratings of skill and actual performance, their impressions about their own health, and so on are often quite flawed.

Still another old concern about self-report data, particularly when they are based on the use of rating scales, has been discussed prominently by Bartoshuk (2000, 2002; Bartoshuk, Duffy, Fast, Green, & Prutkin, 2001). Her thesis is that one individual's self-reported rating of the intensity of a sensation or experience may not be equivalent to another person's rating even if they both give the same numerical response. Suppose that on a 10-point scale of appetite level, you rate yourself as 1 ("not at all hungry"). Is your 1 really equivalent to someone else's rating of 1 on the same scale? Defending the use of self-report data, Norwick et al. (2002) responded that when large numbers of subjects are randomly assigned to groups, it does not matter in the overall picture that one subject's rating of 1 may be different from another subject's rating of 1, because these random differences should cancel out. Second, as Bartoshuk stated in an interview (Goode, 2001), if we use the same scale to find out how the person may have changed over time, we have a baseline of the person's original rating in a repeated-measures design. Third, Bartoshuk (2000) emphasized that using multiple methods to converge on conclusions is another way of tempering doubts. In her own research, she has often used a scaling method we described in the previous chapter, magnitude scaling, as a way of quantifying participants' perceptions of sensory stimuli and identifying the special sensibilities of different individuals.

We will return to some of these issues and concerns as we describe the use of interviews, questionnaires, and self-recorded diaries. Only the interview is characterized by a continuing oral exchange between the researcher and the subject, though a questionnaire is sometimes used in an interview and there is an exchange as the researcher explains the purpose of the questionnaire and how the subjects are to respond. We will also discuss variants of these popular methods. Many researchers frequently combine interviews and questionnaires in the same study. For example, it may be useful to present some items outside an interview so that the subjects can read them several times. It can also be informative to use interviewing to supplement a questionnaire when the nature of the questions is sensitive and personal contact is needed to elicit a full, frank response (Gorden, 1969). On the other hand, Tourangeau and Smith (1998) found that women reported higher numbers of sex partners when self-administered questionnaires were used. Schaeffer (2002) interpreted this and other relevant findings as implying that it is the *privacy* of responding that encourages people to be frank and forthcoming when asked to report sensitive information.

OPEN-ENDED VERSUS STRUCTURED ITEMS

In the previous chapter we mentioned the use of open-ended interviews as an example of a qualitative research method. Whether to use open-ended or structured items is a basic concern in interview and questionnaire work. Generally, open-ended items offer the respondents a chance to expand on their answers and spontaneously express feelings, motives, or behavior (Campbell, 1950). An example of an open-ended item is "Tell me, in your own words, how you felt the day you graduated from high school." In contrast to open-ended items, **structured items** (also described as **fixed-response** or **closed items**) give clear-cut response options, like the following:

> How would you describe your study habits when you were a senior in high school and getting ready to graduate?
> _____ I studied very hard.
> _____ I studied more than the average student.
> _____ I studied about like the average student.
> _____ I studied somewhat less than the average student.
> _____ I didn't study at all.

In the view of most experienced researchers, structured questions produce more relevant and comparable responses, whereas open-ended questions produce fuller and "deeper" responses (Bradburn, 1983). The researcher who uses a structured format is looking for responses in which subjects select a particular choice. The researcher who uses an open-ended format is looking for the nuances of meaning that may not be revealed when the response options are more limited. In a review of methodological studies, it was concluded that, for nonthreatening topics, one format has no overall superiority over another; for threatening topics, however, open-ended items tend to elicit higher levels of reporting by subjects (Sudman & Bradburn, 1974). That is, open-ended questions generally produce more self-revelations (Dohrenwend, 1965). But we still need some degree of standardization if we want to collect comparable data across all the respondents. We can accomplish that goal by using a *semistructured* interview, that is, a kind of hybrid instrument that is often used in professional survey research and the so-called "guided conversation of the ethnographer" (Massey, 2000, p. 148).

Researchers who use open-ended interviews generally rely on tape- or digital-recording devices to capture the entire reply verbatim, so the interviewer is free to attend to the direction of specific questions and to visual details and impressions that can be filled in later. If this procedure is used, permission should be asked of the subject to record his or her replies. Recording devices have some drawbacks, however: They can break, make noise, and interrupt the interview, and they make some subjects anxious. A further problem is that the qualitative responses obtained may be long and rambling, providing little information of interest to the researcher. Because it is often necessary to fragment the responses into thematic (codable) categories, having complete records of entire responses lends itself to computer-assisted analytic strategies (Seale, 2002). But even if the analysis of qualitative information is done by hand, there are strategies and procedures for thematic analyses of personal narratives, oral history interviews, and so on (e.g., Czarniawska, 1997, 1998, 1999; DeVault, 1999; Gubrium & Holstein, 2002; Riessman, 1993).

For some purposes the researcher may have no choice but to use a structured format. In large-scale interview studies that are not well funded, it would be too costly to employ highly experienced interviewers, but the personal prejudices of neophyte interviewers may bias the results (Pareek & Rao, 1980). Summarizing a number of studies of interviewer competence and bias, Hyman et al. (1954) concluded that more experienced interviewers were somewhat more competent and less likely to bias their results, but these authors then tempered that conclusion by noting that the interviewers' selective retention might also have been operating. That is, the better interviewers may have had greater longevity with the research organization, so experience may have been the dependent rather than the independent variable. Other experts disagree with even the modest conclusion drawn by Hyman et al. For example, Cantril (1944) contended that training does not make much difference in the quality of the data obtained, and Eckler and Hurwitz (1958) reported that census interviewers showed no decrease in net errors, for at least certain types of questions, when additional training was provided.

The interview is an oral exchange, and as in any two-way communication, the process can be improved or inhibited by human complexities. Communications are often guarded when the topics touch on sensitive issues, the most apprehensive research subjects preferring to "look good" rather than to give more revealing answers (Rosenberg, 1969). One study found that white respondents interviewed over the phone by a black interviewer gave more pro-black responses than did white respondents interviewed by a white interviewer (Cotter, Cohen, & Coulter, 1982). Other early studies also imply the interactive nature of the skin color of the investigator and of the subjects. In an interview study during World War II, Hyman et al. (1954), found that white interviewers received more guarded responses from their black respondents than did black interviewers. Generally, subjects provide only the information they want to share (Downs, Smeyak, & Martin, 1980), and neophyte interviewers may depart from the instructions and volunteer their own feedback to draw the sensitive material out.

Also characteristic of an oral exchange of questions and answers is that certain cognitive and linguistic processes may affect the degree to which the respondents can figure out how some questions specifically apply to their particular situations (Graesser & Franklin, 1990). It is like shaking hands, Schober and Conrad (2001) suggested, in that one person cannot begin the handshake until the other person has extended a hand, and the process continues only as long as each person is engaged in just the right manner. In other words, the handshake is a coordinated action in the same way that a successful interview requires a collaborative interaction. With this idea in mind, these investigators have experimented with a conversational interviewing method in which the language of certain questions is not rigidly standardized, and the interviewer is given some flexibility in rephrasing questions to ensure that they make sense to the respondent (Conrad & Schober, 2000; Schober, 1999). The downside is that much more time is required to complete flexible interviews, and the interviewers must be well trained and perspicacious. But the payoff is that this type of interviewing seems to improve the quality of the information obtained when the questions involve cognitive or linguistic complexities.

CRITICAL INCIDENT TECHNIQUE

To avoid vague, rambling, irrelevant responses in open-ended interviews, John Flanagan (1954) developed a general approach to focusing questions that he called the **critical incident technique.** The idea for this approach grew out of research to identify the reasons that a thousand pilot candidates washed out of flight training schools in 1941. Information from the proceedings of a number of elimination boards revealed only clichés and stereotypes such as "poor judgment" or "insufficient progress." Other research was designed to identify specific incidents by using open-ended interviews, but asking very focused questions. Out of all this research, Flanagan's critical incident technique took root. Basically, it involves having the respondent describe an observable action, the purpose of which is fairly clear to the respondent, and the consequences sufficiently definite to leave little doubt about its effects. Nonetheless, the critical incident technique is considered open-ended because it allows a range of answers not specifically limited by a given range of responses.

As described by Flanagan (1954), a typical interview begins with the interviewer explaining to the respondent the purpose of the study (e.g., "We are making a study of [specific activity] and we believe you are especially well qualified to tell us about this activity") and then explaining what kind of data are desired by the interviewer ("What would you say is the primary purpose of [specific activity]?" and "How would you summarize the general aim of this activity?"). Having thus established the nature and objective of the activity, the critical incident technique begins in earnest by having the respondent focus on a specific happening. Suppose we want critical incidents about workplace situations involving subordinates whose helpful actions have increased production. A series of questions used to collect effective critical incidents might look like this:

> Think of the last time you saw one of your subordinates do something that was very helpful to your group in meeting their production schedule. *(The interviewer then pauses until the respondent indicates that he or she has such an incident in mind.)* Did this person's action result in an increase in production of as much as one percent for that day?—or some similar period. *(If the respondent answers "no," then the interviewer coaxes the respondent again by saying "I wonder if you could think of the last time that someone did something that did have this much of an effect in increasing production." When the respondent indicates he or she has such a situation in mind, the interviewer continues, patiently allowing the respondent to give a complete response to each question.)*

What circumstances led up to this incident? What exactly did this person do that was so helpful at that time? Why was this so helpful in getting your group's job done? When did this incident occur? What was the person's job? How long had he (she) been on this job? How old is he (she)? (Flanagan, 1954, p. 342)

The critical incident technique was developed to serve not as a hypothesis-testing method, but as an exploratory tool to identify actual incidents that could then be incorporated into questionnaires. For example, researchers interested in developing questionnaires to study power tactics began in some cases by collecting actual tactics that were reportedly used by people to get their way (Falbo, 1977; Kipnis, 1976, 1984). As an illustration, Fung et al. (1987) used the critical incident technique in a study to identify specific instances in which people attempted to influence or persuade someone by acting negatively or pretending to act negatively as a cover for the actor's true feelings (called a "synthetically malevolent action"). They also collected actual incidents in which people attempted to influence or persuade someone by acting positively (or pretending to act positively) but not according to their true feeling (called a "synthetically benevolent action"). Other data were also collected concerning the nature of the person who was the target of the action, and the incidents were then content-analyzed for the particular tactics used by these subjects (threat, refusal to help, denial, flattery and support, modeling, reasoning, etc.). The general finding was that synthetically benevolent power tactics tended to be targeted on higher status, more powerful others, whereas synthetically malevolent power tactics were targeted on lower status, less powerful others. Synthetically benevolent tactics involved flattery, modeling, and pretending; synthetically malevolent tactics involved threat, refusal, and denial.

More recently, Ewart and his associates have employed a variant of the critical incident technique in their development of a brief interview to measure stress-coping capabilities and vulnerabilities to stress-related illnesses (e.g., Ewart, Jorgensen, Suchday, Chen, & Matthews, 2002; Ewart & Kolodner, 1991). In other research in organizational psychology, the critical incident technique was used with company managers in the United States and India who were interviewed as part of an investigation of how organizations dealt with harmful or potentially harmful rumors (DiFonzo, Bordia, & Rosnow, 1994). After emphasizing the confidentiality of the taped interviews, the respondents were asked a long list of probing questions, some of which were:

Describe the rumor and the situation in which it occurred. *(Instructions to the interviewer were to probe for when the rumor occurred.)*

What effects did the rumor have? *(Instructions were to probe for measurable effects such as product sales, number of phone calls.)*

What actions precisely did you take in responding to the rumor?

Could this rumor have been anticipated and/or prevented. If so, how? If not, why not?

How would you deal with a similar rumor in the future?

The results were used to identify the circumstances in which specific rumor-control strategies had worked or failed. DiFonzo et al. inferred that success in dealing with these particular rumors was generally consistent with recent theorizing on this question.

In still other work in organizational psychology, Hollander and his associates used the critical incident technique to sketch profiles of poor management (Elgie, Hollander, & Rice, 1988; Hollander, 1992; Kelly, Julian, & Hollander, 1992).

STAGES IN DEVELOPING INTERVIEW PROTOCOLS

The overall plan, specific design, and structure of an interview are sometimes referred to as its *protocol;* the set of questions and instructions is called the **interview schedule.** There are usually four steps in developing protocols and interview schedules: (a) deciding on the objective, (b) outlining a plan or a design for acquiring the data, (c) structuring the interview schedule, and (d) testing and revising the specific questions. We will examine each of these in turn.

The first step is to spell out the objectives of the interview. Are we interested in specific hypotheses or research questions? What kind of data will we need to address these hypotheses or questions? What kinds of participants should produce the most relevant responses? Suppose the researcher is operating on the assumption that certain information tends to flow from the mass media to local opinion leaders, and from them to the population at large, or to rank-and-file members of specified groups or organizations. This traditional idea, called the *two-step flow process* in classic research in the field of communication (Katz & Lazarsfeld, 1955; Lazarsfeld, Berelson, & Gaudet, 1944), implies that we need to identify the opinion leaders in question. We must have patience, because it might not be immediately evident who the opinion leaders are; we may need a long series of trial interviews to find the type of persons we want to interview in depth.

One pilot strategy for developing relevant items is to interview people in a **focus group** (Morgan, 1996, 1997). This is a loosely defined procedure that takes on many different forms, but the general idea is to lead a group discussion that concentrates on particular issues or a basic question or problem. The focus group procedure got its impetus in marketing research, where it was used to figure out ways to brand and market products in highly competitive situations. Thus, instead of interviewing individuals, the focus group strategy takes a set of questions to a group as a whole so they can explore and dissect some general issues. The questions are posed by a skilled moderator, who guides the discussion, shifting interactions back and forth among the discussants. Depending on the composition of the focus group, the verbal abilities and talent of the moderator to keep the discussion on the topic, and the general question of interest, creative leads for items may be churned up. Because focus groups can be costly, and the results may not be generalizable beyond the groups interviewed, most researchers prefer to develop their ideas in traditional ways, that is, by simply thinking about the problem, reading the relevant literature, paying attention to everyday behavior, and consulting with colleagues or advisers.

The second step in developing interview protocols is to devise a strategy for acquiring the data to address the hypotheses or research questions. This plan includes drafting relevant items, specifying how the responses will be coded or analyzed, and deciding how the interviewers will be recruited. There are ethical issues to be considered as well, for example, the respondents' right not to disclose information they would feel is too personal or private (Bersoff & Bersoff, 2000). If the interviewers are undergraduate students or untrained graduate students, the clinical nature of the information (e.g., information about sexuality or traumatic life events) raises ethical concerns about the potential for abuse and misinterpretation; there is also the issue of competence and what such an interviewer "will do if faced with the disclosure of conduct or a frame of mind that is potentially injurious to the participant, injurious to others, and/or illegal" (Bersoff & Bersoff, 2000, p. 15). If there are distinctive respondents—for example, children and adolescents, older people, or the ill—special issues must be considered (see, e.g., Gubrium & Holstein, 2002). For instance, because of the limited vocabulary and verbal facility of children, care must be taken to ensure that the questions and answers are within their cognitive and intellectual grasp. The use of simple, conversational language is imperative. Furthermore, children may think of the interview as a "test" and want to please the interviewer by responding in ways they feel that adults want or expect (Blair, 2000).

There are ways of trying to improve the accuracy of self-reported information, which we will turn to shortly. But there is, of course, no guaranteed method of interviewing children or any other special population that will ensure perfectly valid data. Blair (2000) described how this problem was addressed by the use of not one strategy, but three different interview protocols in a study of foods eaten by children. One might think that, instead of asking the children, we could ask their parents what the children ate. For example, if we wanted to know what the children ate for lunch, we could ask their parents what they packed for the children. The problem is that some children may not eat what their parents gave them, and unbeknownst to their parents, children frequently discover other tempting delights. Blair called his three protocols Open, Meals, and Locations. In the Open protocol, the questions were completely unstructured; the child was asked to report all of the foods eaten or drank on the previous day. In the Meals protocol, the questions were more structured, asking things like "What was the first meal that you had?" and "Did you eat anything prior to that meal?" and "What was the next meal you had?" In the Locations phase, the questions were structured similarly to the second phase but were asked in chronological order about locations and activities from the previous days. The accuracy of the responses was increased by convergence on the information from these different vantage points, and interviews with parents were a further means of triangulating the data. The overall design required patience to implement, but the advantage was that it provided checks on the reliability of the information obtained.

The third step in developing an interview protocol is structuring the interview schedule, which, in turn, involves several further considerations. One of these is to check that each item is relevant to the working hypotheses, exploratory aims, or key topics of the investigation. Early in this process it may be informative to meet with small groups of participants and go over some of the preliminary questions with the objective of having these people tell us their perceptions and reactions (Singleton & Straits, 2002, p. 63). We want to make certain that the items address our theoretical objectives and also that they meet quality standards. Thus, the interview schedule may require an Occam's razor that cuts away superfluous or redundant items, a reworking of ambiguously worded questions, and assurance that the interviews will not be unnecessarily time-consuming. Interviews that are too long produce boredom, as concentration begins to wane and the quality of the data is diminished. Pareek and Rao (1980) suggested that 90 minutes is the outermost limit before boredom usually sets in, but in some distinct populations (children, for example), the interviews may need to be considerably shorter, and the format may need to be varied to maintain the interest of the respondents.

One way to vary the format—which will also encourage more relevant replies and make it easier to code the data and analyze the results—is to provide the participants with specified ranges of responses. Suppose we are interested in having college students tell us the satisfaction they receive from some activities of interest to them. Instead of reading them a list of activities (so they must remember the list), or having them free-associate (a likely source of irrelevant data), we could say something like "I'm now going to show you a list of activities, and I'd like you to tell me in which *single* area you find your greatest satisfaction. Remember, I want the one area *most satisfying* to you as a college student." The subject is then shown a list including, for example, course work, self-discovery, "bull sessions," social life, organized extracurricular activities, getting acquainted, and close friendships. Or suppose we are interested in salary information; instead of asking for an exact amount (which most people will be reluctant to tell us), we can show a list of ranges of income levels and ask the person to identify the range that is relevant. Even when given a range of responses, however, some individuals may end up making *false negative reports* (a failure to report information) because of true memory lapses or because of carelessness or unwillingness to tell us certain things, or because they do not want to make the effort to cooperate (Cannell, Miller, & Oksenberg, 1981).

We also need to decide on the best sequence of items. The research literature does not provide any clear-cut or consistent answers about where to put particular items, but there may sometimes be a *logical error* (noted in the previous chapter) in that respondents are apt to give similar answers to related items when they are contiguous (Bishop, Oldendick, & Tuchfarber, 1982). Separating them by interposing neutral items may help a little but may still not eliminate that effect, because the answers *should* be relatively similar (Schuman, Kalton, & Ludwig, 1983). Broadly speaking, it appears that specific questions are affected less than general questions by what preceded them (Bradburn, 1982). One point on which there is some agreement is that, when sensitive topics are to be discussed, they are usually better placed at the end of the interview. Questions about an adult's age, education, and income may seem like an invasion of privacy to some interviewees and, when asked at the beginning of an interview, may hamper the establishment of trust. But even when they are asked at the end of the interview, it may be beneficial to preface such items with a reassuring statement. In one study, the interviewer prefaced them by informing the subjects that the information was needed to find out how accurately the interview sample represented census estimates of the area population (which was true). As an unusually blunt afterthought, he added, "Some of the questions may seem like an invasion of your privacy, so if you'd rather not answer any of the questions, just tell me it's none of my business" (C. Smith, 1980).

Another consideration at this stage is to establish the best wording of items to ensure that all questions will be readily understood in equivalent ways by all the interviewees. During the pilot stage (the next step), there will be an opportunity to find out what jargon and expressions are inhibitors or facilitators of communication in the circumstances. Of special importance is the phrasing of the opening item, because variations in wording can affect how the respondents will interpret later questions (Bradburn, 1982). The opening item should be clearly connected with the explanation of the interview, so that the interviewee knows immediately that the researcher is pursuing the stated purpose. Incidentally, research evidence suggests that disclosing very little about the interview in the introduction has no methodological benefits in reducing refusals or bias, or in improving rapport or communication (Sobal, 1982). This issue is probably irrelevant in many research interviews because of the requirements of informed consent. But the golden rule here is that we want to be open and honest with the subjects, just as we want them to be forthcoming in their responses. Interestingly, disclosing the length of the interview may have a cost in terms of refusals. In one study, it was found that telling the potential respondents that the interview would last 20 minutes resulted in more refusals than telling them it would last "a few minutes" (Sobal, 1982).

The final step in this process is to pilot the interview schedule and make modifications wherever necessary. Esposito et al. (1992) suggested using a focus group or a questionnaire in a debriefing session when pretesting survey items. Assuming that pilot interviews are conducted face-to-face, it is important that the interviewers listen analytically to the subjects' responses (Downs, Smeyak, & Martin, 1980). Skilled interviewers do not jump in and interrupt before an idea is sufficiently developed by the respondent; they are patient, get the main ideas, hear the facts, make valid inferences, hear details, and demonstrate other good listening skills (Weaver, 1972). Having pretested and polished the interview schedule, selected the potential interviewees, and trained the interviewers, the researcher can begin the actual interviews. One related point, however, is whether the training should consist of teaching the interviewers to be neutral (also called *nondirective*) or teaching them to attempt to motivate the respondents. Motivational procedures (e.g., in the form of selective feedback by a skilled interviewer) are thought by some experienced interviewers to be an effective means of promoting good respondent behavior. Both positive and negative feedback, if properly used, can facilitate good performance. Examples of positive feedback would be statements such as "Uh-huh. I see. This is the kind of information we want"; "Thank you. You've mentioned _____ things"; "Thank you. We appreciate your frankness"; and "Uh-huh. We are interested in details like these." Examples of negative feedback are "You answered that quickly"; "Sometimes it's easy to forget all the things you felt you noticed here. Could you think about it again?"; and "That's only _____ things" (Cannell, Miller, & Oksenberg, 1981).

Recently, other innovative ideas have been put forward about some ways to coax out the most accurate responses when the interview questions touch on highly sensitive, possibly illegal, behaviors (e.g., drug using). Often, these interviews are conducted in the respondents' homes, and others may be present. In research by Turner et al. (1998), a new way to address this problem was successfully used. Instead of having to express their answers to sensitive questions out loud, the respondents were allowed to essentially interview themselves and answer by using audioenhanced computer methodology. The interviewer sets up a laptop computer on which all or part of the interview questions are presented (e.g., just the most sensitive questions); the audio part is useful because of some subjects' limited literacy, so questions can be read to them as well as shown on the screen. This method is a way of preserving the privacy of the subjects' answers by depersonalizing and standardizing the interview, reducing the effects of an interviewer's race, gender, sex, body language, intonation, speed of delivery, and so on (Bloom, 1998).

RESEARCH INTERVIEWS BY TELEPHONE

Beginning in the 1960s, various changes in society led many survey researchers to turn to telephone interviews and mail questionnaires. Among the changes contributing to that shift were (a) the increased costs of labor-intensive face-to-face interviews; (b) a decrease in the pool of married women seeking part-time employment (a large source of interviewers); (c) rising urban crime rates and fewer people being at home during the daytime; (d) the development of random-digit dialing, allowing the representative sampling of telephone households; and (e) the invention of computer-assisted methods in which questions are flashed to the interviewer on a screen and the interviewer then keys in the responses for computer scoring (Rossi, Wright, & Anderson, 1983). As a consequence, telephone interviewing has swept the survey industry in recent years and is now the dominant approach (Shuy, 2002; Singleton & Straits, 2002).

There is considerable speculation about the relative merits and restrictions of face-to-face and telephone interviewing, but few data have been collected comparing these two strategies. Based on the available data and conjecture, Shuy (2002) concluded that among the relative advantages of the telephone interview are, generally speaking, that it is less expensive to implement; that the situational variables may be easier to control; and that the data are easier to code and quantify (particularly when computerized methodology is used). Typically, the methodology of telephone interviews is more uniform and standardized than that of face-to-face interviews because the telephone interviewers are merely reading questions from a computer screen. What telephone interviews lack are the advantages of physical presence, including an opportunity for the interviewer to perceive and react to facial expressions, gestures, and other clues to the respondent's state of mind (confusion, reluctance to answer, discomfort, etc.), which enable the interviewer to reframe a question in order to avoid a no-answer response (Shuy, 2002). Other limitations of telephone interviews are that they are restricted to households in which people answer their telephones (i.e., instead of having an answering machine constantly on duty), and that visual aids cannot be used as supplements unless they are mailed out in advance of the call.

Generally speaking, the same procedures are followed in developing interview schedules and training interviewers whether telephone or face-to-face interviewing is used. One difference, however, is that telephone interviewers have less time to establish rapport: The person on the other end can always hang up without listening to the introduction. If the interviewer fails to enunciate clearly or conveys an annoying attitude, the interview is bound to be counterproductive. Various strategies have been used to impress the respondents with the seriousness of the telephone interview and to motivate them to cooperate. Assuming the respondent is willing to listen (and busy people may not want to do so), the interviewer can explain the important goal of the research and allude to it again at some other juncture in the interview. We will have more to say about response rates when we turn to survey sampling procedures in chapter 9, but simply getting people to respond to survey interviews is a knotty problem for researchers. Particularly as levels of responding and cooperation have declined in our society (e.g., T. W. Smith, 1995; Steeh, 1981), the threat to the generalizability of vital data looms ever larger (Dillman, Singer, Clark, & Treat, 1996).

DEVELOPING RESEARCH QUESTIONNAIRES

Questionnaires are among the most widely used self-report methods of data collection and may be incorporated into an interview schedule either as noted previously (i.e., presented on a laptop computer) or by giving the respondents a subset of questions in written form or a list of items to be read or checked off. As in the writing of an interview schedule, the initial steps in the development of a written or computer-administered questionnaire are exploratory, such as consulting with key informants (Oppenheim, 1966). Pilot work is also needed in devising the final wording of items, which can take several forms to elicit specific responses, for example, yes-no items or acceptable-unacceptable items. Fill-in-the-blank is another form, useful when specific responses are sought. Of course, these structured forms are effective only if the material to be covered can be simplified to this extent.

Piloting enables the researcher to determine whether the items are worded properly, for example, whether terms like *approve* and *like* (or *disapprove* and *dislike*) are being used as synonyms or whether there are differences in implication. Suppose we want to study workers' perceptions of the quality of a manager's performance, but we phrase the item in the following way: "How do you feel about the manager? Do you like him _____, or do you dislike him _____ (Check one only)?" The item is quite useless because it does not distinguish between liking and approving. It is possible, for example, for people to like someone personally without approving of the person's managerial ability (Bradburn, 1982). Thus, we need to have more than one item to zero in on these different variables, and we need to articulate the items in such a way that the respondents are not confused by questions that are double-edged or imprecise or too vague to elicit the information we seek.

However, we must also be sure that the way we word and present the items does not lead the respondent to give an unrealistically narrow answer. A poor question produces a very narrow range of responses or is misunderstood by the respondents. Take the following hypothetical item from a political survey: "Do you approve of the way the mayor is handling his duties? _____ Yes; _____ No." One may approve of the way the mayor handled the "school crisis" but not the "snow removal crisis" or may disapprove of the way the mayor handled the "threat by sanitation workers to strike" but not the "impending tax increase." Once again, several different items are needed to get at the various issues on which we want an opinion, and all those issues need to be spelled out to prevent any misunderstanding on the part of respondents. Suppose the "school crisis" and the "sanitation workers' threat" both involved union negotiations and confrontations, but the former situation was resolved without a strike and the latter involved a protracted strike. We need a separate question, or set of questions, regarding each situation and whether the respondent approved or disapproved of the mayor's handling of it.

We must also avoid a leading question that produces a biased answer (known as *push polling*). Take the question "Do you agree that the mayor has an annoying, confrontational style? _____ Yes; _____ No." The way the question is phrased pushes the respondents to be overly negative or critical of the mayor. In coming up with an alternative way to phrase the question, we want to be sure that the new item is not worded so as to produce another meaningless answer: "Do you agree with the mayor's philosophy of government? _____ Yes; _____ No." If someone replied "yes" (or answered "no"), what would that answer really tell us? We need to do some probing to get the kind of information we consider meaningful. Problems like these can usually be identified when the questionnaire is piloted and can be easily corrected by a rewording of the items or by the use of a set of probing questions instead of a single item.

The issue of whether to use open-ended or more structured items, or a combination of both, can also be explored in pilot work. Converse and Presser (1986, p. 52) suggested using the following exploratory questions to help identify trouble areas when pretesting the items: "What did the whole question mean to you?" "What was it you had in mind when you said _____?" "Consider the same question this way, and tell what you think of it: _____" "You said _____, but would you feel differently if I said _____?" Frank, insightful replies to exploratory questions will help the researcher rewrite items.

As noted, the chief advantage of open-ended items is the flexibility they provide for the respondents to let their thoughts roam freely and spontaneously. However, although free-response questionnaires are relatively easy to construct, many subjects find them difficult or too time-consuming to respond to in writing (Oppenheim, 1966). One strategy is to use fixed-response (i.e., structured) items but add one or two open-ended questions at the end. Not only do structured items require less time to answer, but the answers are also easier to code and analyze statistically. On the other hand, they leave no room for spontaneity and expressiveness. The respondents may feel that the fixed-response format forces them to choose between alternatives, none of which are exactly the best ones. Converse and Presser (1986) suggested that open-ended questions be used to measure the salience of certain behavior and to capture modes of expression. In the previous chapter, we mentioned the use of content analysis; software is available for the analysis of open-ended questionnaire and interview content (Seale, 2002).

Another interesting strategy is the use of a **funnel sequence of questions,** in which very general questions ultimately narrow down to more specific ones. Some researchers like to use many open-ended questions at the start or exploratory stage of a research project and then, once there is a clear direction to the research and specific issues to be addressed, to use more focused, fixed-response items. Whatever strategy is adopted, it is usually prudent to ask several questions on a topic, not only for statistical reasons, but because we want to converge on the required information. Each item may be cause for specific concern, but the overall results should converge on a specific conclusion. And, of course, the instrument should be tested before it is used in the research.

It is also important that the information elicited be a reflection of what the respondents really feel or think, not just an expedient or impromptu response. As a rule, however, people have not thought very much about most issues that do not affect them directly, and their replies may reflect only a superficial feeling or understanding. In survey research, investigators often ask the respondents how they feel about such and such (e.g., "How deeply do you feel about it?" or "How strongly do you feel about the opinion you've expressed?") and, in this way, attempt to determine whether the respondents truly believe what they have articulated or indicated in some other way (Labaw, 1980). There is another side to this issue, which is related to the idea of response sets (discussed in the previous chapter), particularly to the control of social desirability and acquiescent response sets.

DEFENSIVENESS, INCONSISTENCY, AND YEA-SAYING

Faking and Inconsistency

Earlier in this chapter we referred again to the classic research of Crowne and Marlowe (1964) on social desirability bias, discussed in detail in chapter 1. Other researchers have also investigated the influence of the social desirability set on the responses to self-report personality inventories. When appreciable correlations are obtained between scores on a social desirability scale and responses on another self-report inventory, this result is often interpreted as implying a tendency on the part of respondents to present themselves in a more favorable light on the latter instrument. We mentioned Esposito et al.'s (1984) study using this paradigm, and in an earlier study by Rozynko (1959), it was found that psychiatric patients who scored high on a measure of social desirability produced sentence completions that were also high in socially desirable content. In fact, it has long been assumed that scores on self-report personality tests are often influenced by factors other than the manifest content of the items. Just because a person responds "no" to the statement "Once in a while I think of things too bad to talk about" does not mean that the person's thoughts are indeed pure.

Previously, we mentioned the use of audioenhanced computer technology to encourage frank responding (Bloom 1998; Turner et al., 1998). An earlier method employed successfully in survey research is the **randomized response technique** (S. L. Warner, 1965). In this approach, an attempt is made to reduce the likelihood of evasive or dishonest responding by guaranteeing the confidentiality of the responses. The technique works this way: The subject uses a randomizing method (such as flipping a coin) to select how to respond to a sensitive item. Suppose the item asks, "Have you ever used cocaine?" The subject is told to flip the coin out of the researcher's sight and to respond "yes" if it lands heads and to respond truthfully (i.e., to answer the question "yes" or "no") if it lands tails. There is no possible way for the researcher to know how each particular subject answered. However, by knowing that 50 percent of the subjects are expected to get heads to respond "yes," the researcher can estimate the proportion who actually said they had sampled cocaine. There is some evidence that the randomized response technique promotes the truthful reporting of sensitive information (Boruch & Cecil, 1979; Fidler & Kleinknecht, 1977).

Beginning some years ago, researchers in psychology began to develop keys for scoring standardized questionnaires and "lie scales," which are used to detect faking by the respondents (Ruch, 1942). One traditional way to construct a "fake key" is simply to compare the responses of subjects who are instructed to fake their answers with those of subjects who are instructed to respond truthfully. The differences in responding are analyzed, and a scoring key is developed from that information (cf. Gordon & Gross, 1978; Lautenschlager, 1986). The Minnesota Multiphasic Personality Inventory (MMPI) provides another illustration of how "faking" is analyzed. The MMPI contains a "lie scale" (the L Scale) of 15 items to reveal the degree to which the respondent is projecting a falsely perfectionist impression. Respondents' replies to these items are interpreted as indicators of conscious deception, naive responding, or a highly introspective personality, the interpretation depending on the particular score (Groth-Marnat, 1984).

Other scales identify responses that are made without regard to item content, also called a **random response set** (Graham, 1993). However, the reasons for the "random" responding may include deliberate faking, poor reading ability, a limited facility with English, carelessness, lack of attention, indecisiveness and vacillation, and so on. The MMPI-2 (the latest version of the MMPI scale) uses a matched-pair scaling procedure to determine whether the items have been answered consistently (Graham, 1993). Another significant clinical inventory used with adolescents has a built-in "index" of two bizarre items that should not be endorsed even by the most disturbed subjects (McCann, 1999). Scoring keys for the detection of response inconsistency have been developed for a number of clinical inventories (Pinsoneault, 1998, 2002).

Acquiescent Response Set

Another variation on this problem is an **acquiescent response set,** in which the subjects tend to respond "yes" or "true"—also called *yea-saying*—regardless of what the items or questions state. In this case, the inconsistency is clear because not all the items endorsed should be automatically agreed with. The opposite error would be responding "no" or "false" regardless of the items or questions—called *nay-saying* (Couch & Keniston, 1960). Scoring keys have been designed to detect these sets (see, e.g., citations noted by Pinsoneault, 2002). However, in a famous case of the acquiescent response set, all that was apparently required to suppress the yea-saying (or nay-saying) bias was to vary the direction of the response alternatives, i.e., to have scores (on the characteristic being measured) increase half the time by saying "yes" and half the time by saying "no." It still serves as an object lesson for researchers to pay careful attention to the direction of how statements are worded.

This classic case goes back to the 1920s, when a group of leading social scientists at the University of Frankfurt were engaged in interview research with hundreds of German citizens. The results convinced these investigators that anti-Semitic prejudices were rife in Germany and that the explosion of fascism was imminent. When Adolf Hitler came to power, the researchers left Germany and immigrated to the United States. Their investigation continued, but with the emphasis now on the authoritarian personality of the fascist mentality. At the University of California at Berkeley, the researchers developed a personality inventory called the F Scale, which included 38 statements such as the following:

> One should avoid doing things in public that appear wrong to others, even though one knows that these things are really all right.

> No insult to our honor should ever go unpunished.

> It is essential for learning or effective work that our teachers or bosses outline in detail what is to be done and exactly how to go about it.

Such statements were thought to go together to form a syndrome of behavior that renders a person receptive to antidemocratic propaganda (Adorno, Frenkel-Brunswik, Levinson, & Sanford, 1950). The authoritarian personality was also viewed as having a strong sense of nationalism, a rigid morality, definiteness, a strong tendency to perceive things in absolutes, and a strong need to align himself or herself with authority figures and protective in-groups. Other instruments, including the Rorschach, were brought in to flesh out the authoritarian personality.

Although this is regarded as one of the most influential studies done in psychology, it was later recognized that there was a significant problem in the wording of the items making up the F Scale. They had been written in such a way that only by disagreeing with a statement could a respondent obtain a completely nonauthoritarian score. However, some amiable, obliging souls, who had no fascist tendencies, had a penchant for responding "yes" to virtually every statement. In other words, the F Scale was confounded because it was measuring not only authoritarianism but also the acquiescent response set (Couch & Keniston, 1960). The obvious remedy was simply to vary the direction of the statements and then have positive and negative statements interspersed in random order. To obtain a nonauthoritarian score now required the subject to agree with some statements and disagree with others.

CROSS-CULTURAL QUESTIONNAIRE AND INTERVIEW RESEARCH

When self-report measures are used in cross-cultural research, a usual concern is that the language may mean something different in each culture. As an illustration, LeVine and Campbell (1972) faced such a problem when they were conducting fieldwork among the Gusii people of western Kenya to try out a preliminary version of a field manual for the cross-cultural study of ethnocentrism. Many Gusii terms for aggression and hostility did not have any exact equivalents in English. Furthermore, English terms carry their own connotations, which were not present in their Gusii equivalents. One way to deal with this problem is to minimize the verbal content by using pictorial items whenever possible (Shea & Jones, 1982). Of course, even pictorial items carry their own implications, and not all verbal items can be readily recast in a pictorial form. Thus, a more conventional strategy in a verbal measure is to use a procedure called **back-translation.**

Suppose we want to use a questionnaire or an interview originally written in English (the *source language*) in another society in which another language (the *target language*) is other than English. In back-translation, the researcher looks beyond the constraints of the source language to find a middle ground in which the distinctive meanings and blind spots of the source language and the target language are absent. To achieve this, the researcher has one bilingual person translate the text from the source language to the target language, and afterward another bilingual person independently translates it back into the source language. In this way, the researcher can compare the original with the twice-translated version (i.e., the back-translation) to see whether anything important has been lost in the translation. A number of back-translations may be needed to find a middle ground without significant discrepancies.

ONE-DIMENSIONAL AND MULTIDIMENSIONAL ATTITUDE SCALES

The methods we discuss in the following sections are in the traditional vein of using verbal items in attitude questionnaires. In the previous chapter we briefly mentioned the method known as the *semantic differential,* and we will begin by examining its use as a multidimensional measure. We then turn to three other traditional procedures in attitude and personality research: the Q-sort for self-reports, the Likert method of item analysis, and Thurstone's equal-appearing intervals method. There are, in fact, other useful strategies for the development of questionnaires and inventories, including a popular procedure and theoretical rationale for the item analysis of one-dimensional scales (called item response theory, or IRT), which was developed by Georg Rasch (1960, 1966), a Danish researcher. Although primarily of use in achievement testing, in which cumulative responses are expected to be associated with difficulty levels, Rasch scales have been the focus of work and much interest in psychology, sociology, and education (for example, see de Jong-Gierveld & Kamphuis, 1985, for a type of Rasch scale they developed to measure loneliness). The technical details of this procedure go beyond the scope of this text, but researchers interested in learning about IRT and the nature of Rasch scales will find informative monographs and books on this method, particularly Nunnally and Bernstein's (1994) text, which includes a detailed overview of technical aspects, issues, and the relationship of IRT to other psychometric developments. The procedures discussed in the following sections are far simpler than IRT, have fewer assumptions, and thus are convenient to use in a wide range of situations of interest to most students and many professional researchers.

A word of caution, however, is that using an explicit attitude or personality questionnaire to predict behavior has long been known to be fraught with problems (cf. Eagly & Chaiken, 1993; Lana, 2002; McGuire, 1985; Mischel, 1968; Triandis, 1971). Some critics have even questioned whether it is reasonable to expect that explicit responses on a questionnaire *should* be correlated with important behaviors. On the other hand, some social psychologists have shown that certain behavior can be predicted from explicit, recently expressed intentions of respondents on attitude questionnaires (Fishbein, 1963; Fishbein & Azjen, 1974, 1975). More recently, an approach to measuring "implicit attitudes" was developed by Greenwald, Banaji, and associates (Greenwald & Banaji, 1995; Greenwald, Banaji, Rudman, Farnham, Nosek, & Rosier, 2000).

In a computer-administered test (the Implicit Association Test), these researchers measured people's automatic associations with certain target concepts and the time it took them to make these associations. Although this research has exposed various prejudiced attitudes and stereotypes that the subjects would presumably be reluctant to reveal explicitly, it is not yet entirely clear whether implicit attitudes predict behavior better than explicit attitudes can (Karpinski & Hilton, 2001). Other researchers have argued that using a multimethod, multidimensional strategy to measure social attitudes can be useful in many cases, because what a person says or does is determined not only by what the person would *like* to do, but also by what the person believes is *required* as well as by the *expected consequences* of behaving in a certain way (Triandis, 1971). Or as Eagly and Chaiken (1998) explained, "Because people express their likes and dislikes in many ways, all aspects of responding, including emotions, cognitions, and overt behavior, are infused with evaluative meaning that attitudes impart" (p. 269).

SEMANTIC DIFFERENTIALS FOR ATTITUDINAL MEANING

As conceptualized by Osgood et al. (1957), an important assumption of the semantic differential method was that the "meaning" of everyday stimuli can be represented by a spatial configuration consisting of more than one dimension. In their research, these investigators often found that *evaluation, potency,* and *activity* were the dominant dimensions in many cultures and societies. In statistical terms, the evaluation dimension was found to account for approximately half the extractable variance, whereas the potency and activity dimensions (together referred to as *dynamism*) each accounted for approximately half as much variance as the evaluation dimension. Osgood et al. identified other factors that accounted for increasingly less variance, including stability, tautness, novelty, and receptivity. Nonetheless, it is the dimensions of evaluation, potency, and activity that are used most often in semantic differential research (cf. Brinton, 1961; Oskamp, 1977; Snider & Osgood, 1969; Triandis, 1964).

As noted in the previous chapter, in appearance a semantic differential resembles the segmented graphic scale. It usually consists of a set of 7-point rating scales anchored at each end by bipolar pairs of adjectives, such as

bad ____ : ____ : ____ : ____ : ____ : ____ : ____ good

tense ____ : ____ : ____ : ____ : ____ : ____ : ____ relaxed

stingy ____ : ____ : ____ : ____ : ____ : ____ : ____ generous

The particular bipolar pairs are selected from a list made by Osgood et al. on the basis of the underlying dimensions of attitudinal meaning. For example, if we were interested in subjects' evaluative responses, any of the following bipolar pairs could be chosen: bad-good, unpleasant-pleasant, negative-positive, ugly-beautiful, cruel-kind, unfair-fair, and worthless-valuable. If it were the potency dimension we were interested in, any of the following pairs would suffice: weak-strong, light-heavy, small-large, soft-hard, and thin-heavy. For the activity dimension, we could choose from the following: slow-fast, passive-active, and dull-sharp. For the lesser dimensions, still other bipolar pairs would be considered: stability dimension (changeable-stable, intuitive-rational, and rash-cautious), tautness dimension (rounded-angular, curved-straight, and blunt-sharp), novelty dimension (old-new, usual-unusual, and mature-youthful), and receptivity dimension (tasteless-savory, boring-interesting, and insensitive-sensitive).

In a given study, the scales do not always load on the same dimensions, and thus, many researchers check to see whether their scales do cluster in the expected way. We have been told by some researchers that potency and activity are often conflated; all they obtained was one factor (evaluation) or two factors (evaluation and a kind of conflated factor). In practice, however, most researchers stick with evaluation, potency, and activity. The instructions to the subjects are to put check marks in the appropriate positions. In scoring these responses, the researcher then assigns numbers to the subjects' ratings, for example, +3 extremely good, +2 quite good, +1 slightly good, 0 equally good and bad or neither, −1 slightly bad, −2 quite bad, and −3 extremely bad.

Previously, we mentioned some of the ways in which the semantic differential procedure has been used. As a further illustration, Figure 6.1 shows a three-dimensional representation of eight role concepts (self, father, mother, adult, college student, juvenile delinquent, adolescent, and child) that were rated by male and female college students using the semantic differential procedure (Friedman & Gladden, 1964). The instructions to the subjects were first to evaluate the concepts "as you *actually* think they are, in terms of the meanings they have to you" (the two diagrams at the top of Figure 6.1), and then to rate each concept "on the basis of how it should *ideally* be, the way it is supposed to be as opposed to how it actually is" (the two diagrams at the bottom). The subjects were told that there were no right or wrong answers, as this was not a test. The various diagrams reveal differences in the three-dimensional spatial relationships and also show certain similarities. For instance, we see (a) the general clustering on the left side, with the lone role number 6 ("juvenile delinquent") on the right; (b) the roles "self" and "college students" perceived as somewhat weaker in actuality by men than by women; and (c) the role of "father" perceived to be stronger, ideally, by men than by women. The researchers theorized that these differences were due to the influence of learned expectancies regarding role attitudes.

Q-SORTS FOR SUBJECTIVITY RATINGS

Another traditional method is the Q-sort, which was developed by William Stephenson (1953), a British physicist and psychologist, to study a single individual or a few persons at a time. It takes its name from so-called Q-methodology (a classical procedure in factor analysis), and some researchers now use the terms *Q-sort* and *Q-methodology* as synonyms. The Q-sort has been particularly useful in personality assessment research, for example, to arrive at an overall picture of a person's attitudes, strengths, and weaknesses. Although developed before the days of personal computers, Q-sorts can now be readily scored by computers. Researchers interested in this method will find a large number of references to it on the Internet, including Web sites with actual items used in certain Q-sorts.

Traditionally, the Q-sort calls for the preparation of a set of stimuli (phrases, pictures, or statements) covering some aspect of behavior or personality. Typically, these stimuli differ from one study to the next, because the purpose of the studies is different and the stimuli are chosen according to the aspect of behavior of interest to

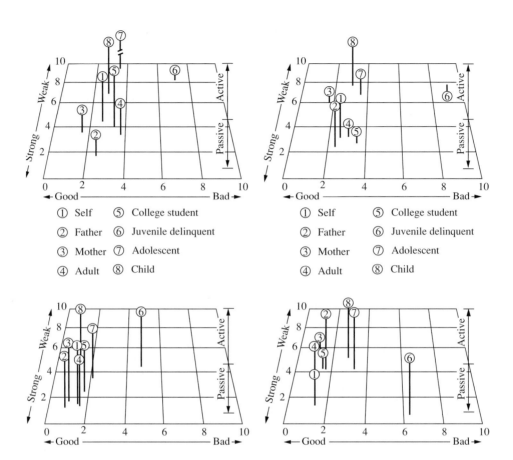

FIGURE 6.1

Actual (*top*) and ideal (*bottom*) locations of eight role concepts on three semantic dimensions for males (*left*) and females (*right*). The three dimensions are the evaluative (bad-good), the potency (weak-strong), and the activity (passive-active). (From "Objective Measurement of Social Role Concept Via the Semantic Differential," by C. J. Friedman and J. W. Gladden, *Psychological Reports,* 1964, *14,* pp. 239–247.)

the researcher. Each stimulus appears on a separate card, and the respondent's job is to sort through the cards and place them in one of a number of piles to resemble a bell-shaped curve. Depending on the number of piles used by the researcher, the number of cards allowed in each pile is determined by a formula for the normal distribution. For instance, if there were 80 cards, they would be sorted into 11 piles as follows:

Pile number	11	10	9	8	7	6	5	4	3	2	1
Number of cards	2	4	6	9	12	14	12	9	6	4	2

If there were 98 cards, they would be sorted into 13 piles as follows:

Pile number	13	12	11	10	9	8	7	6	5	4	3	2	1
Number of cards	2	4	6	8	10	12	14	12	10	8	6	4	2

In a representative study, Stephenson (1980) had children sort through 48 photographs of different faces. They were told to decide which *two* photos they liked *most* and to put them in the extreme favorable pile, and then to decide which *two* they liked *least* and to put them in the extreme unfavorable pile. They then had to decide which *four* photos they liked *next most* and put them in the corresponding pile, and which *four* they liked *next least,* and so forth. In this case there were 9 piles, which were scored from -4 to $+4$:

Pile number	9	8	7	6	5	4	3	2	1
Number of photos	2	4	5	8	10	8	5	4	2
Score	-4	-3	-2	-1	0	$+1$	$+2$	$+3$	$+4$

Several different statistical analyses are possible. For instance, the average position of a specific subset of pictures (e.g., pictures of ethnic females) can be calculated and compared with the average positions of other subsets (e.g., pictures of nonethnic females). Still another method is simply to correlate Q-sorts (for example, an idealized Q-sort portrait correlated with the Q-sort portrait of a particular subject), and in this way to assess the degree of similarity between them (e.g., D. J. Bem and Funder, 1978). There are also standardized Q-sorts consisting of descriptive statements about personality for use in clinical and social psychological situations, such as Block's (1978) California Q-Sort and Funder et al.'s (2000) Riverside Behavioral Q-sort. Funder et al.'s Q-sort contains 100 statements, including things like "Acts irritated," "Speaks fluently and expresses ideas well," "Offers advice," "Is unusual or unconventional in appearance," and "Appears to be relaxed and comfortable." Instead of using the Q-sort as a self-report method, Funder and his colleagues have used it in judgment studies in which observers are asked to watch a videotaped social interaction and then to rate one of the individuals. The items are distributed into nine categories that range from (1) "negatively characteristic" to (9) "highly characteristic," with irrelevant items placed in the middle categories. Funder and Dobroth (1987) found that the most perceptible personality traits are those implying behaviors that would confirm or disconfirm the traits, and that are easy to imagine, occur often, and are subjectively easy to discern.

LIKERT METHOD OF ITEM ANALYSIS

The term **Likert scale** is among the most misused in the behavioral and social sciences. Many researchers call any rating instrument a Likert scale if it instructs subjects to indicate the degree of their agreement or disagreement on a five-step numerical scale. To constitute a true Likert scale, a particular method of item analysis (called the *method of summated ratings*) must be used to construct the instrument. Created by Rensis Likert (1932), the method results in an instrument that resembles a numerical rating scale in that numbers can be understood as being implicitly associated with the response alternatives (e.g., strongly agree, agree, undecided, disagree, strongly disagree) to statements that are easily classifiable as favorable or unfavorable.

The first step in constructing a Likert questionnaire to measure people's attitudes is to gather a large number of statements on the topic of interest. These are given to a sample of subjects from the target population, who indicate their evaluations, usually by means of a 5-point numerical rating scale. The technique of item analysis used to sort through the data consists of calculating the extent to which the responses to individual statements are correlated with the total score (the sum of all the items). Statements that correlate well with the total score are then chosen for the final scale. The rationale is that statements that have low correlations with the total score will not be as good at discriminating between those respondents with positive attitudes and those with negative attitudes.

As an older illustration of a questionnaire developed by the Likert procedure, a 20-item scale on a topic that is still current is shown in Figure 6.2 (Mahler, 1953). This particular attitude scale was shown to have high internal-consistency reliability, and to predict the responses of a convenience sample of Stanford University students with positive and negative attitudes about socialized medicine (as established by independent interviews). In scoring the answers, the pro-socialized-medicine statements would be weighted from 4 ("strongly agree") to 0 ("strongly disagree"). For the anti-socialized-medicine statements (marked by an asterisk), the weighting is reversed. A person's score is the sum of the weighted responses, with a high score indicating an accepting attitude toward socialized medicine.

THURSTONE EQUAL-APPEARING INTERVALS METHOD

Another traditional approach is based on the **method of equal-appearing intervals,** which was proposed by L. L. Thurstone (1929), a pioneer in the early development of attitude research. The name of the procedure derives from the assumption that judges, who are asked to sort items into different piles, are presumed to be able to keep the piles psychologically equidistant. Other useful methods of scaling were also developed by Thurstone, and many of his ideas have been picked up by contemporary researchers and psychometricians. However, this particular method, also frequently called the *Thurstone scale,* is the one most closely associated with him.

The procedure begins with a large number of statements, but this time each statement is typed on a separate card. Judges (not the subjects to be tested later) then sort the statements into 11 piles numbered from 1 ("most favorable statements") to 11 ("most unfavorable statements"). In this respect, the equal-appearing intervals method resembles the Q-sort method. Unlike in the Q-sort, the judges in Thurstone's approach are allowed to place as many statements as they wish in any pile. A scale value is calculated for each statement, and by tradition it is the median of the responses of all judges to that particular item. In selecting items for the final Thurstone scale, we would choose those that are most consistently rated by the judges (i.e., have the smallest variabilities) and that are spread relatively evenly along the entire attitude range. The former criterion (consistency) refers to any particular items, and the latter criterion (range) refers to the whole set of items.

Please indicate your reaction to the following statements, using these alternatives:

Strongly Agree = SA   Disagree = D

Agree = A   Strongly Disagree = SD

Undecided = U

*1 The quality of medical care under the system of private practice is superior to that under a system of compulsory health insurance.

SA   A   U   D   SD

2 A compulsory health program will produce a healthier and more productive population.

*3 Under a compulsory health program there would be less incentive for young people to become doctors.

4 A compulsory health program is necessary because it brings the greatest good to the greatest number of people.

*5 Treatment under a compulsory health program would be mechanical and superficial.

6 A compulsory health program would be a realization of one of the true aims of a democracy.

*7 Compulsory medical care would upset the traditional relationship between the family doctor and the patient.

*8 I feel that I would get better care from a doctor whom I am paying than from a doctor who is being paid by the government.

9 Despite many practical objections, I feel that compulsory health insurance is a real need of the American people.

10 A compulsory health program could be administered quite efficiently if the doctors would cooperate.

11 There is no reason why the traditional relationship between doctors and patient cannot be continued under a compulsory health program.

*12 If a compulsory health program were enacted, politicians would have control over doctors.

*13 The present system of private medical practice is the one best adapted to the liberal philosophy of democracy.

14 There is no reason why doctors should not be able to work just as well under a compulsory health program as they do now.

15 More and better care will be obtained under a compulsory health program.

*16 The atmosphere of a compulsory health program would destroy the initiative and the ambition of young doctors.

*17 Politicians are trying to force a compulsory health program upon the people without giving them the true facts.

*18 Administrative costs under a compulsory health program would be exorbitant.

*19 Red tape and bureaucratic problems would make a compulsory health program grossly inefficient.

*20 Any system of compulsory health insurance would invade the privacy of the individual.

FIGURE 6.2
Example of a Likert scale that was developed to measure attitudes toward socialized medicine. The response alternatives (SA, A, U, D, SD) would be repeated for each item. The asterisks (*) indicate negative items, whose weights must be reversed for purposes of scoring. (From "Attitudes Toward Socialized Medicine," by I. Mahler, *Journal of Social Psychology,* 1953, *38,* pp. 273–282.)

The following statements express opinions about divorce. Please indicate your agreement or disagreement with each of the statements by marking them as follows:

(✓) Mark with a check if you agree with the statement.

(✗) Mark with a cross if you disagree with the statement.

Scale
Value

3.7	1	Divorce is justifiable only after all efforts to mend the union have failed.
6.6	2	Present divorce conditions are not as discreditable as they appear.
8.5	3	If marriage is to be based on mutual affection, divorce must be easy to obtain.
1.6	4	Divorce lowers the standards of morality.
.5	5	Divorce is disgraceful.
8.4	6	Divorce is desirable for adjusting errors in marriage.
4.8	7	Divorce is a necessary evil.
9.8	8	Divorce should be granted for the asking.
6.2	9	A divorce is justifiable or not, depending on the wants of the persons involved.
10.1	10	A person should have the right to marry and divorce as often as he or she chooses.
.5	11	Divorce is never justifiable.
8.8	12	Easy divorce leads to a more intelligent understanding of marriage.
3.3	13	Divorce should be discouraged in order to stabilize society.
5.8	14	The evils of divorce should not prevent us from seeing its benefits.
9.4	15	The marriage contract should be as easily broken as made.
.8	16	The best solution of the divorce problem is never to grant divorce.
1.2	17	Lenient divorce is equivalent to polygamy.
7.1	18	Divorce should be permitted so long as the rights of all parties are insured.
4.2	19	Divorce should be discouraged but not forbidden.
.8	20	Divorce is legalized adultery.
3.8	21	Long and careful investigation should precede the granting of every divorce.
8.1	22	Permanence in marriage is unnecessary for social stability.

FIGURE 6.3
Example of a questionnaire, based on Thurstone's equal-appearing interval scaling, to measure attitudes toward divorce. In actual practice the scale values noted would not be shown on the questionnaire administered to the subjects. (After Shaw & Wright, 1967; *The Measurement of Social Attitudes,* by L. L. Thurstone, Chicago: University of Chicago Press, © 1931.)

Illustrative of an attitude scale developed by this procedure, Figure 6.3 shows a 22-item questionnaire with reportedly high test-retest reliability. Although this early scale of attitudes toward divorce contains items relevant to the issue today, with the passage of time the original scale values might be expected to change (Thurstone, 1929–1934). Thus, the scale values noted in this figure were subsequently obtained from a small sample of graduate students (Shaw & Wright, 1967). These values may need to be updated if used currently, in which case the same procedures could be used (see Edwards, 1957b).

Incidentally, a classic variant on Thurstone's equal-appearing intervals method is called the **method of successive intervals.** It was developed by Edwards (1952) to provide a check on the assumption of equal intervals. The data collection is similar to that used in the equal-appearing intervals scaling of items, but the scaling is a little more complex, although it can be done easily by hand. Edwards's gem of a book, *Techniques of Attitude Scale Construction* (1957b), contains easy-to-follow, detailed illustrations of the Likert, Thurstone, Edwards, and some other traditional scaling procedures.

MEMORY AND THE USE OF SELF-RECORDED DIARIES

Whatever interview or questionnaire procedures are used, autobiographical items can run into problems when the respondents must rely on memory (e.g., how often they have done something or how much of something they bought or consumed). Some examples would be "How many weeks have you been looking for work?" and "How much did you pay for car repair expenses over the previous year?" As mentioned before, there may even be memory errors about the nature of events that have just occurred. Among the sources of forgetting are problems in encoding, storage, retrieval, and reconstruction errors (Schacter, 1999; Tourangeau, 2000; Tourangeau, Rips, & Rasinski, 2000). For example, aspects of the event may never have been noticed in the first place or, if noticed, then only casually observed (an encoding problem). Assuming the event was encoded, it still might not stand out in memory. On the other hand, cognitive researchers (Brown & Kulik, 1977) speak of "flashbulb memories" that appear to be immediately and forever imprinted in our minds, such as viewing the destruction of the World Trade Center in New York City when terrorists crashed two hijacked airplanes into the Twin Towers on September 11, 2001. Retrieval errors occur because of forgetting, or because a question is phrased differently from the way the answer is stored in our minds (Norman, 1973). Reconstruction errors happen when people mistakenly associate events that were not connected when they occurred, or when they make faulty assumptions based on the wording of items, or when there are too many facts and people fill in the gaps of what they cannot retrieve (Bernard & Killworth,1970, 1980; Bradburn, Rips, & Shevell, 1987; Cicourel, 1982; S. K. Reed, 1988; Webber, 1970; Zechmeister & Nyberg, 1982).

For example, it is often especially difficult to remember names and exact dates, whereas most people recognize faces easily (Tourangeau, 2000). Bradburn (2000) summarized a number of empirically supported generalizations. First, the better an event is remembered, the easier it is to date. Second, when dating errors occur, they are usually off by some calendar-related factor, such as a week, a month, or a year. Third, the longer the time that has elapsed, the more numbers tend to be rounded, so 9 days might become a week, and 3 weeks a month. Fourth, there is a tendency to remember events as having occurred more recently than they really did occur. Fifth, important events that occurred only once are generally easier to date than recurring events on different dates. Sixth, pleasant events are frequently easier to date than unpleasant ones, but there are obvious exceptions (e.g., the 9/11 tragedy or the death of a loved one). Seventh, women remember dates better than men do. Eighth, events at the beginning or end of a meaningful period, cycle, or term are generally easier to date than events in the middle. For a more detailed discussion of the fallibility of human memory, and how and why memory errors can get people into trouble, see Schacter's (1999) fascinating article, and for a comprehensive discussion of every aspect of memory, see his absorbing book *Searching for Memory* (Schacter, 1996).

An alternative that is less dependent on recall for collecting autobiographical data is the **self-recorded diary** (e.g., Conrath, 1973; Wickesberg, 1968). For example, Csikszentmihalyi and Larson (1984) used this approach in their investigation of teenagers' day-to-day lives. The 75 teenagers who participated in this study were given beepers and were then signaled at random by the researchers. When the beeper went off, the teenager recorded his or her thoughts and feelings at that moment, and this information was collated with what the teenager was doing (e.g., viewing TV, eating dinner, being in class). As another illustration, DePaulo, Kashy, and their coworkers used self-recorded diaries in studies in which college students were asked to keep records of their lying behavior (DePaulo & Kashy, 1998; DePaulo, Kashy, Kirkendol, Wyer, & Epstein, 1996; Kashy & DePaulo, 1996). Among the findings were that students who indicated they told more lies were also more manipulative and more concerned with self-presentation and, not surprisingly, told more self-serving lies.

Investigations of autobiographical data obtained in this way have supported the accuracy of the information (Tourangeau, Rips, & Rasinski, 2000). For example, Mingay et al. (1994) found that diary reports about the frequencies of everyday events were more accurate than the retrospective memories of the diary keepers' partners, who had experienced the same events. A. F. Smith et al. (1991) observed that diary reports about the foods that diary keepers had consumed were more accurate than information obtained in survey reports. In another study, Conrath et al. (1983) collected data from managers and staff personnel in three organizations. Each participant was instructed to keep a diary of 100 consecutive interactions, commencing on a specific date and at a specific time. The instructions were to indicate the other party, the initiator of the activity, the mode of interaction, the elapsed time, and the process involved. The diary was constructed in such a way that the participant could record all this information with no more than four to eight check marks next to a particular item. At a later time, each participant answered a questionnaire in which similar estimates had to be made. For all the participants the data from the self-recorded diary and the standard questionnaire were compared afterward. If a person noted talking to particular others, the responses of those others were investigated by the researchers to see whether they had also reported that activity. In this way, a measure of reliability was obtained for the self-recorded diary and the questionnaire data separately (i.e., concerning the reporting of specific events at the time of the events as opposed to a later time). The results were that the questionnaire data (the recalls from autobiographical memory) were less reliable than the diary data. Thus, given ample preparation, and assuming the willingness of people to keep precise records, the self-recorded diary can be an informative and reliable source of autobiographical information.

PART

III

THE
LOGIC
OF
RESEARCH
DESIGNS

CHAPTER
7

RANDOMIZED CONTROLLED EXPERIMENTS AND CAUSAL INFERENCE

EXPERIMENTATION IN SCIENCE

In chapter 1 we said that the orientation of experimental research is the search for causes, and in this chapter we begin by describing typical experimental designs that use the principle of randomization to assign the sampling units to groups or conditions. Next, after noting several features and limitations of randomization, we turn to the philosophical puzzle of causality. As one author commented, "Though it is basic to human thought, causality is a notion shrouded in mystery, controversy, and caution, because scientists and philosophers have had difficulties defining when one event *truly causes* another" (Pearl, 2000, p. 331). We review the justification for the use of control groups in randomized experiments, and after a brief discussion of a historically significant contribution to control group design by Richard L. Solomon, we turn to the work of Donald Campbell and his associates that has focused on an assortment of threats to the validity of causal inferences. We conclude this chapter with a discussion of subject-related and experimenter-related artifacts and the strategies used to control for them.

Although the primary emphasis of this chapter is on randomized controlled experiments, we generally use the term *experimentation* in a broad sense rather than restricting it only to randomized experiments; this broad usage is also frequent in science. Shadish, Cook, and Campbell (2002) recommended that *experimentation* be understood as referring "to a systematic study design to examine the consequences of deliberately varying a potential causal agent" (p. xvii). Four features that Shadish et al. thought representative of all experiments are "(1) variation in the treatment, (2) posttreatment measures of outcomes, (3) at least one unit on which observation is made, and (4) a mechanism for inferring what the outcome would have been without treatment" (p. xvii). As an illustration of this broad conception, students who have taken a course in chemistry know that the typical experiment consists of mixing reagents in test tubes. How does this process fit in with Shadish et al.'s four features of experiments? The variation in treatment is analogous to an implicit comparison with other combinations of reagents; the posttreatment measure is the resulting compound; the observations typically require calibrated measurements; and the outcome without treatment is analogous to the status of the reagents before they were combined. As another illustration of nonrandomized experiments, an article in *Physics World* invited readers to nominate the "most beautiful experiments of all time" (G. Johnson, 2002). None of the top ten involved randomization. The experiment ranked first was not even an empirical demonstration, but a classic thought experiment (by Thomas Young) to demonstrate that light consists of particles that act like waves. The second-ranked experiment was Galileo's revelation, in the late 1500s, that because all bodies necessarily fall with the same velocity in the same medium, it follows that objects of different weights dropped from the Leaning Tower of Pisa would land at the same time.

It is not hard to find many fascinating examples of nonrandomized experiments in psychology as well. For instance, Jose M. R. Delgado (1963) showed that the electrical stimulation of various brain regions resulted in decreased aggressive behavior. In one study, the boss monkey (named Ali) in a colony of monkeys that lived together had an electrode inserted in his caudate nucleus. The switch that turned on the current to Ali's electrode (via a tiny radio transmitter) was available to the other monkeys. They learned to approach and press the switch whenever Ali began to get nasty, causing him to become less aggressive immediately. In a more dramatic demonstration, Delgado got into a ring with a fierce bull whose brain had been implanted with electrodes. Just as the bull was charging toward him, Delgado turned on radio-controlled brain stimulation, causing the bull to stop in midcharge and become passive. Few experimenters have opportunities to demonstrate such confidence in their causal generalizations. In the next chapter we will have more to say about experiments that focus on only one unit (called a *case*), or on only a few units, and in which randomization is seldom used (called *single-case experiments*).

RANDOMIZED EXPERIMENTAL DESIGNS

By far the most common randomized controlled experiments are those in which the sampling units are assigned to receive one condition each, called a **between-subjects design** (or a **nested design,** as the units are "nested" within their own groups or conditions). In biomedical research, these experiments are regarded as the "gold standard," such as randomly assigning the subjects to receive an experimental drug or a **placebo** (a substance without any pharmacological benefit that is given as a pseudomedicine to subjects in a control group). This particular design is shown in Table 7.1, in which the

TABLE 7.1
Simplest between-subjects design

New drug	Placebo
Subject 1	Subject 2
Subject 3	Subject 4
Subject 5	Subject 6
Subject 7	Subject 8
Subject 9	Subject 10

randomly assigned subjects of the experimental group are arbitrarily labeled 1, 3, 5, 7, 9, and the randomly assigned subjects of the control group are arbitrarily labeled 2, 4, 6, 8, 10. Suppose, however, that the drug in question is intended to treat a terminal illness. Assigning some of the subjects to receive only a placebo would deny them access to a potentially life-extending treatment. According to an international declaration adopted in Helsinki in October 2000 by the general assembly of the World Medical Association, placebos may be used only when there are no other drugs or therapies available for comparison with a test procedure. Thus, one option is to give control subjects not a placebo, but the best currently available treatment, so that the comparison is between the experimental drug and the best available option. Another declaration, issued in 2002 by the Council of International Organizations of Medical Sciences (CIOMS), stated that the only ethical exception to *not* using an effective treatment as the control condition is if there is no such treatment available and it is unlikely to become available in the foreseeable future (Levine, Carpenter, & Appelbaum, 2003).

Our earlier discussion of the ethics of placebo control groups (chapter 3) noted that another possibility in some situations is to use a **wait-list control group**— assuming, of course, that the design has been approved by an ethical review committee. For example, there might be an alternative treatment, that is unavailable for logistic or cost reasons, thus leaving the placebo condition as our *only* viable option. The simplest randomized wait-list design using a placebo control consists of two conditions:

Group 1	R	O	X	O		O
Group 2	R	O		O	X	O

where R denotes random assignment, O denotes observation (i.e., measurement or testing), and X denotes the experimental treatment. In this example, the participants randomly assigned to Group 1 are given the drug (X) over a specified period, during which the participants assigned to Group 2 (the wait-list control group) receive not the drug or any alternative medicine, but a placebo. Once it becomes clear that the new drug is effective, the trial is terminated, and the wait-list group is given the new drug.

If there are a sufficient number of participants in the wait-list control condition, and if it would not violate the international declarations or be hazardous to the subjects' health to wait to receive the new beneficial drug, another possibility is to introduce different periods of delay before the new drug is administered to these subjects:

Group 1	R	O_1	X	O_2		O_3		O_4		O_5
Group 2	R	O_1		O_2	X	O_3		O_4		O_5
Group 3	R	O_1		O_2		O_3	X	O_4		O_5
Group 4	R	O_1		O_2		O_3		O_4	X	O_5

Groups 2, 3, and 4 are subgroups of the wait-list control condition. Once it is clear that the experimental drug (X) is effective, Groups 2, 3, and 4 receive the drug at different intervals. Repeated measurements (O) allow us to gain further information about the temporal effects of the drug by comparing O_2, O_3, O_4, and O_5 in Group 1 with the same set of observations in the wait-listed controls.

In between-subjects studies in which the participants are asked to make subjective judgments, their implicit ranges may be different if they are not operating from the same emotional, psychological, or experiential adaptation levels or baselines (Helson, 1959; cf. Birnbaum, 1999). Consequently, we might wish to have the subjects make repeated judgments based on different conditions, called a **within-subjects design** because each participant receives more than one condition (also called a **crossed design** because the subjects are thought of as "crossed" by conditions). A problem with within-subjects designs, however, is that the order in which the conditions are administered to the subjects may be confounded with the condition effect. Suppose there are four conditions (A, B, C, and D) to be administered to young children who are to be measured following each condition. The children may be nervous when first measured, and they may respond poorly. Later, they may be less nervous, and they may respond better. To address the problem of systematic differences between successive conditions, the experimenter can use **counterbalancing,** that is, rotating the sequences of the conditions (as illustrated in Table 7.2) in what is called a **Latin square.** Notice that it is a square array of letters (representing the conditions) in which each letter appears once and only once in each row and in each column. In this illustration, all four

TABLE 7.2
Latin square design

	Order of administration			
	1	2	3	4
Sequence 1	A	B	C	D
Sequence 2	B	C	D	A
Sequence 3	C	D	A	B
Sequence 4	D	A	B	C

TABLE 7.3
2 × 2 Factorial design

A1. Experimental treatment		A2. Placebo control	
B1. Women	**B2. Men**	**B1. Women**	**B2. Men**
Subject 1	Subject 11	Subject 2	Subject 12
Subject 3	Subject 13	Subject 4	Subject 14
Subject 5	Subject 15	Subject 6	Subject 16
Subject 7	Subject 17	Subject 8	Subject 18
Subject 9	Subject 19	Subject 10	Subject 20

conditions are administered to the children in a counterbalanced pattern, so that the children randomly assigned to Sequence 1 receive conditions in the sequence A, then B, then C, and finally D. In Sequences 2 through 4, the conditions are administered in different sequences, BCDA, CDAB, and DABC, respectively.

Another popular arrangement of conditions in experimental research is called a **factorial design** because there is more than one variable (or factor) and more than one level of each factor. Suppose that women and men are randomly assigned to a drug or a placebo group. We have a two-factor design with two levels of the factor of gender (women vs. men) and two levels of the manipulated variable (drug vs. placebo), with the assignment of the subjects illustrated in Table 7.3. This arrangement is described as a 2 × 2 factorial design (2 × 2 is read as "two by two") or 2^2 factorial design. Of course, factorial designs are not limited to only two factors or to only two levels of each factor. We will have much more to say about the analysis of factorial designs in chapters 16–18, but one common procedure in the case of the design shown in Table 7.3 is to compute a 2 × 2 analysis of variance in which we analyze the between-group variation of the drug versus the placebo condition (A1 vs. A2), the between-group variation of women versus men (B1 vs. B2), and the interaction of factors A and B. However, if we are primarily interested in some predicted pattern of all four condition means, we might prefer to address this prediction by means of a 1 × 4 contrast, as described in chapter 15.

Other variations include **fractional factorial designs,** also called *fractional replications* (Winer, et al., 1991), which use only some combinations of factor levels (rather than using all combinations of all factor levels, also known as **full factorials**), and **mixed factorial designs,** consisting of both between- *and* within-subjects factors. An experiment in which women and men (a between-subjects factor) both received a sequence of treatments (and were measured after each one, so that "treatments" is now operationalized as a within-subjects factor) is an example of a mixed factorial design.

CHARACTERISTICS OF RANDOMIZATION

In their classic statistics text, George W. Snedecor and William G. Cochran (1989) made the point that "randomization gives each treatment an equal chance of being allotted to any subject that happens to give an unusually good or unusually poor response, exactly as assumed in the theory of probability on which the statistical analysis, tests of significance, and confidence intervals are based" (p. 95). Earlier, in another classic text, R. A. Fisher (1971) had noted that by the use of "the full procedure of randomisation . . . the validity of the test of significance may be guaranteed against corruption by the causes of disturbance which have not been eliminated" (p. 19). That is, randomization is a way of dealing with unsuspected sources of bias, though, of course, it cannot guarantee that all important natural differences among the subjects will be *exactly* balanced out. Suppose we were working with pairs of subjects, one of whom in each pair is to be randomly assigned to the experimental condition by the flip of a coin. Snedecor and Cochran (1989, p. 95) noted that, with n pairs, the probability that any one treatment will be assigned to the superior member in every one of the n pairs was $1/2^{n-1}$. Thus, with 5 pairs, the probability is .06, with 10 pairs it is .002, and with 15 pairs it is .00006. In other words, as sample sizes increase, it becomes less and less likely that the treatment condition subjects will be very different from the control condition subjects even before the subjects receive the treatment condition. Those relatively rare instances in which very large differences between conditions existed even before the treatments were administered are sometimes referred to as *failures of randomization.*

Instead of flipping a coin, most researchers prefer using a computer, a scientific calculator, or a table of random digits to generate the random numbers they need. To use Table B.9 (in Appendix B), we start by blindly choosing a place in the table and then simply reading across the row or down the column. We must decide in advance which numbers will determine the units to be assigned to different conditions. Suppose we decide that odd numbers will determine the units to be assigned to the experimental group and that even numbers (including zero) will determine those to be assigned to the control group. Say we want to assign 20 subjects, and the 20 digits that we randomly select are 10097, 32533, 76520, and 13586. We number our subjects from 1 to 20 and align all subjects with their random digits, for example:

Random digit   1 0 0 9 7   3 2 5 3 3   7 6 5 2 0   1 3 5 8 6
Subject number 1 2 3 4 5   6 7 8 9 10   11 12 13 14 15   16 17 18 19 20

Then, because we want to assign 10 subjects to the treatment and 10 to the control, Subjects 1, 4, 5, 6, 8, 9, 10, 11, 13, and 16 are assigned to the treatment condition (their associated random digits are odd), and the remaining subjects are assigned to the control condition. If there are fewer than 10 odd numbers in our series of 20 random digits, we simply select the first 10 even-numbered subjects to be our control sample, and the remaining subjects become the treatment sample. Another procedure for the random assignment of subjects, or other sampling units, is simply to number the units from 1 to 20, write the numbers on slips of paper, put them in a bag, shake the bag well, and then blindly draw a slip for each participant.

In chapter 15 we will discuss the allocation of different numbers of units to the samples, usually because of cost factors and because only one or two specific patterns of effects are of primary interest. This approach is traditionally known as *optimal design* in statistics, and the goal of the differential allocation of sample sizes is to increase statistical precision (Kuhfield, Tobias, & Garratt, 1994; McClelland, 1997).

Although we may sometimes want to use this procedure, it may also limit our options to discover something new and interesting from a "nonoptimal" design. We will illustrate all these ideas in the later chapter.

Although randomization is also intended to avoid the problem that experimenters might, even if unconsciously, let their feelings influence their decisions about which subjects will be placed in different conditions (Gigerenzer, Swijtink, Porter, Daston, Beatty, & Krüger, 1989), perfect experimental control is an ideal that can be elusive. Suppose the problem is not that experimenters' feelings are suspected of having gotten in the way, but that the sample sizes are small and it simply happens that the experimental and control groups are not comparable to begin with. Say that the mean pretest scores in the experimental and control groups are 50 and 40, respectively, and the mean posttest scores in these same groups are 52 and 48. Concentrating our attention only on the posttest scores, we would conclude that the experimental group showed a positive effect. However, when we take into account the mean baseline differences, we see that the positive effect was an illusion; the mean pre-to-post gain in the experimental group was one quarter the size of that in the control group. Thus, another variation on the randomized designs noted before is to use pretest measurements to establish baseline scores for all subjects. For example, in a drug trial of a pharmaceutical that treats high blood pressure, the researchers would want to know what the subjects' blood pressures were before they received the drug. For a detailed discussion of pretest-posttest designs (particularly those used in pharmaceutical trials), including many of the advantages and limitations of the common statistical procedures that are used to analyze these designs, see Bonate (2000). Incidentally, in randomized drug trials, one concern is that the participants, fearing that they have been placed in the placebo group, may surreptitiously arrange to split and then share with other participants the pills they've received; the result may be an underestimation of the true effectiveness of the pharmaceutical treatment. Another issue is that potential subjects may be reluctant to volunteer in the first place because they are concerned about being assigned to the group that will not receive the experimental drug; their reluctance reduces the pool of available subjects and thus could seriously jeopardize the generalizability of the observed results (Kramer & Shapiro, 1984).

Before leaving this section we should also mention that, although we have used the term *random* we have not actually defined it. Dictionaries frequently propose "aimlessness" or the "lack of purpose" as synonyms of *randomness,* or they note that the "equal probability of being chosen" is a statistical characteristic of *randomness.* We will have more to say about probability and randomness in chapter 9, but it is important not to confuse randomness with aimlessness, or "hit-or-miss" sampling, which can seldom be accurately described as random in the scientific sense. We can illustrate by asking someone to write down "at random" several hundred one-digit numbers from 0 to 9. When we tabulate the 0s, 1s, 2s, and so on, we will see obvious sequences and that some numbers clearly occur more often than others; these patterns would not occur if each digit had an equal probability (10%) of being listed (Wallis & Roberts, 1956). Interestingly, psychologist Allen Neuringer (1992), using a single-case experimental strategy, was able to reinforce the behavior of pigeons to make left-right choices that looked pretty random, and he then used feedback to reinforce some individual Reed College students to generate sequences of numbers that also looked like random sequences (Neuringer, 1996; Neuringer & Voss, 1993). As Kolata (1986) mentioned in *Science* magazine, randomness is a difficult concept even for statisticians and philosophers to define, one reason that "books on probability do not even attempt to define it" (p. 231). The problem, as one leading scholar, Persi Diaconis, observed, is that "if you look hard, things aren't as random as everyone assumes" (Kolata, p. 1069). However, Diaconis noted that some outcomes at least turn out to be "almost random," such as flipping an ordinary coin millions of times to discover any bias.

THE PHILOSOPHICAL PUZZLE OF CAUSALITY

Turning the key in a car's ignition gets the motor going; taking an aspirin when you are running a fever will usually lower your temperature; studying for an exam is better than not studying for it; pulling a sleeping dog's tail usually evokes an aggressive response; smoking cigarettes over a long period of time can cause emphysema, lung cancer, and heart disease; aesthetically applying paint to a canvas produces a painting. All these are examples of **causal relations.** That is to say, they imply a relation between a *cause,* which may be a responsible human or physical agent or force, and an *effect,* which may be an event, a state, or an object. They also emphasize what Aristotle called "efficient causation" (more about this below), which developmental psychologists now believe is perceptible even in infants (Schlottmann, 2001). Interestingly, some historians and others have argued that, for thousands of years, well before the Golden Age of Greece, the idea of effects caused by objects or physical forces was hardly of much interest. The reason, they say, is that events and personal ordeals were presumed to be either under the control of a divine will (physical catastrophes were expressions of angry gods, and felicitous events were expressions of benevolent gods) or attributed to human or animal agents (e.g., a hunter or a forager gathering food, or an animal trampling a person to death).

By the fifth century B.C., Greek philosophers (such as Parmenides, Anaxagoras, and Empedocles) had begun to explore the problem of causality more deeply, particularly with reference to the elemental origin of the universe and the nature of change, on the assumption that change requires a cause of some kind. A century later, a major conceptual advance occurred when Aristotle differentiated four types of causation: material, formal, efficient, and final (Wheelwright, 1951). The *material cause* refers to the elementary composition of things. The *formal cause* is the outline, conception, or vision of the perfected thing. The *efficient cause* is the agent or moving force that brings about the change. The *final cause* (or *teleological explanation*) refers to the purpose, goal, or ultimate function of the completed thing. For Aristotle, the ultimate teleological explanation for everything that undergoes change was divine will and, thus, God's final plan. To recast the four causes in a modern context, we might ask, "What causes a skyscraper to be built?" The material cause would be the concrete, bricks, and steel; the formal cause, the architect's blueprint; the efficient cause, the physical work of the architect, the contractor, and the laborers and their tools; and the final cause (i.e., the ultimate objective), a building for people to occupy.

By the 13th and 14th centuries A.D., we find a symbiosis of the emerging idea of causal inference and the empirical method of "experimentation," that is, in its broadest interpretation (Rosnow, 1981). It is during this period that we see a further emphasis on efficient causation. For example, Robert Grosseteste, at Oxford University, proposed that the forces or agents (the efficient causes) accountable for the nature of light are subject to manipulability and critical observation, thereby establishing optics as both an empirical and an experimental science (Wallace, 1972). Grosseteste's vision- ary idea was subsequently embraced by his student, Roger Bacon, who stressed the "very necessity" of empirical experimentation and the essential role of quantification. In his *Opus Maius,* published in 1267, Bacon stated that "if . . . we are to arrive at certainty without doubt and at truth without error, we must set foundations of knowledge on mathematics, insofar as disposed through it we can attain to certainty in the other sciences, and to truth through the exclusion of error" (Sambursky, 1975, p. 155). Of two ways of acquiring knowledge of efficient causation, by reason and by experimen- tation (or *experience* in Bacon's words), he argued that it was only by experimentation that we can demonstrate what reason teaches us. For example, a person who has never seen fire may be persuaded by a well-reasoned argument that fire burns and injures things and destroys them, but until he has witnessed an experimental demonstration of combustion, he cannot accept what he learned as an indisputable fact, for "reasoning does not suffice, but experience does" (W. S. Fowler, 1962, p. 36).

Although medieval science seemed to explain everything, it was nonetheless a tangle of unwieldy, interlaced, cumbersome theories. Revolutionary developments occurred from the 16th to the 17th century that changed all this by undermining ancient intellectual foundations and replacing them with a theoretical foundation of mechanics that explained the action of forces on bodies. In his biography of Isaac Newton, James Gleick (2003) likened the scientific revolution that began in the 16th century with Nicolaus Copernicus, the Polish astronomer, and "staggered under the assaults of Galileo and Descartes and finally expired in 1687, when Newton pub- lished a book" (p. 49) to an "epidemic spreading across the continent of Europe during two centuries" (p. 48). Galileo Galilei, by virtue not only of his empirical methodology but also of his mathematical formulations of causal experimental effects, was a seminal figure in the development of the experimental method of science. In 1609, he made his first observations with the use of a telescope, constructed by "inserting spectacle makers' lenses into a hollow tube" (Gleick, p. 49), providing powerful evidence to support Copernicus's heliocentric theory of the universe (which in the 17th century was still at odds with ecclesiastical doctrine on the incorruptibil- ity of the heavens). Galileo's mathematical definitions of velocity and acceleration and their dependence on time, his kinematic laws, and his laws concerning the oscil- lation of the pendulum—all these and other insights inspired the development of an experimental science of mechanics, emphasizing efficient causation. In particular, Galileo's *Dialogo* of 1632 and his *Discorsi* of 1638 were a reservoir of ideas that were tested experimentally by himself and others.

Nearly coinciding with Galileo's work were the contributions of the French philosopher René Descartes and his profoundly mechanistic view of nature, which, he argued, provided logical proof of the existence of God. In his *Principia Philoso- phia,* published in 1644, Descartes argued that everything that exists requires a cause, and thus, the physical world can be likened to a complex machine and its parts. "As regards the general cause," he argued, "it seems clear to me that it can be none other than God himself. He created matter along with motion and rest in the beginning; and now, merely by his ordinary co-operation, he preserves just the quantity of motion and rest in the material world that he put there in the beginning" (Sambursky, 1975, p. 246). Thus, Descartes reasoned, in the same way that the complexity inherent in the design and working parts of a complicated machine confronts us with wonder about the nature of its human creator, the machinery that constitutes the universe demands that we consider the majesty of its divine creator, God.

Isaac Newton, born in the year of Galileo's death, extended the mechanistic conception by his own powerful theories on the mechanics of motion while passionately championing the experimental method of science. Like Galileo and Descartes, Newton believed in the uniformity of nature, an idea he developed in detail in *Philosophiae Naturalis Principia Mathematica* (cited as *Principia*), published by the Royal Society in 1687. Proceeding on the premise that "space is absolute," his three axiomatic laws of motion replaced the clutter of Aristotelian and medieval science with a compact mechanical theory that stood unchallenged for over 200 years. His love of the experimental method of science was no less intense than Galileo's, and in *Principia,* Newton wrote,

> For since the qualities of bodies are only known to us by experiments, we are to hold for universal all such as universally agree with experiments; and such as are not liable to diminution can never be quite taken away. We are certainly not to relinquish the evidence of experiments for the sake of dreams and vain fictions of our own devising; nor are we to recede from the analogy of Nature, which is wont to be simple, and always consonant to itself. (longer passage in Sambursky, 1975, p. 303)

In his second great work, *Opticks—or, a Treatise on the Reflections, Refractions, Inflexions and Colours of Light,* published in 1706, Newton described his famous *Experimentum Crucis* on light and color. He directed a sunbeam of white light through a triangular prism to produce a rainbow of colors (an old, but inexplicable, phenomenon) and then sent a single colored beam through another prism to show unequivocally that "white light is a mixture, but the colored beams are pure" (quoted in Gleick, 2003, p. 80).

CONTIGUITY, PRIORITY, AND CONSTANT CONJUNCTION

As word of the *Principia* spread, Newton's monumental formulation was embraced by philosophers who contended that the "new philosophy of mechanism" was also quite adequate to comprehend purposive human behavior (cf. Lowry, 1971; Wilkes, 1978). Inspired by bold extrapolations, arguments began to be made that almost everything in the panoply of natural and human phenomena could be understood by means of "Newtonianism" and the laws of motion. Humans, after all, are merely the product of biological and social engineering, a complex piece of machinery that efficiently modifies force or energy (cf. Aleksander, 1971). However, it was David Hume, the great 18th-century Scottish philosopher, who, in the words of Judea Pearl (2000), "shook up causation so thoroughly that it has not recovered to this day," for, according to Hume, the sensation of causation was "almost as fictional as optical illusions and as transitory as Pavlov's conditioning" (p. 336). Hume reasoned that, because it is intrinsic in human nature to expect the future to be like the past, the mind is essentially programmed to perceive causal links even though they are mere illusions "deriv'd from nothing but custom" (Hume, 1978, p. 183). Motion is lawful, but causality is in the mind's eye, conditioned by sensory repetitions and the mechanics of the association of ideas.

In his *Treatise of Human Nature* (subtitled *An Attempt to Introduce the Experimental Method of Reasoning Into Moral Subjects*), Hume listed a set of "rules" for defining causality. Eight years later, in his *Inquiry Concerning Human Understanding,* he argued that the appropriate method of adducing causality was Newton's, because it is by the experimental method that we "discover, at least in some degree, the secret springs and principles by which the human mind is actuated in its operation" (Hume, 1955, p. 24). Hume's eight "rules by which to judge of causes and effects" (Hume, 1978, pp. 173–175) could be boiled down to three essentials: First, "the cause and effect must be contiguous in space and time" (called *contiguity*). Second, "the cause must be prior to the effect" (called *priority*). Third, "there must be a constant union betwixt the cause and effect" so that "the same causes always produce the same effect, and the same effect never arises but from the same cause" (called a *constant conjunction*).

To illustrate, Hume (1978, p. 148) gave the example of a man who is hung from a high tower in a cage of iron. Even though he is aware that he is secure from falling, he nevertheless trembles from fear. The reason he trembles has to do with his "custom" of associating contiguous events in a causal sequence (the ideas of "fall and descent" and "harm and death")—which modern psychologists would call an *illusory correlation* of events (Fiedler, 2000). Another favorite example of Hume's was of a billiard ball lying on a table with another ball rapidly moving toward it; they strike, and the ball that was previously at rest is set in motion. This, he stated, "is as perfect an instance of the relation of cause and effect as any which we know, either by sensation or reflection" (Hume, 1978, p. 649). And yet, all that can be confidently said, he argued, is that

> the two balls touched one another before the motion was communicated, and that there was no interval betwixt the shock and the motion. . . . Beyond these three circumstances of contiguity, priority, and constant conjunction, I can discover nothing in this cause. . . . In whatever shape I turn this matter, and however I examine it, I can find nothing farther. (pp. 649–650).

Of course, merely because a physically or temporally contiguous event invariably precedes another event—and thus predicts the event well—does not automatically implicate one as the cause of the other. The barometer falls before it rains, but a falling barometer does not *cause* the rain (Pearl, 2000, p. 42). Another example (discussed by Edmonds & Eidinow, 2001) that consumed Cambridge University philosophers in the 1940s involved the idea of two factories in two towns in England, one in the south and the other in the north, but both in the same time zone. Each factory has a hooter that signals the end of the morning shift at exactly twelve noon, and every time the northern hooter sounds, the southern workers lay down their tools and exit. Although we see, as Hume might have said, *contiguity, priority,* and a *constant conjunction* of events, the northern hooter is obviously not the *cause* of the southern workers' stopping work. It appears that what baffled the Cambridge philosophers was how to clarify, unequivocally, the essential difference between *coincidentally* and *causally* linked events. Monday precedes Tuesday, just as night precedes day; these are not *coincidental* linkages, but it would be equally absurd to say that Monday *causes* Tuesday or that night *causes* day. Some psychologists say the missing ingredient that explains the perception of causality is simply the ability to connect events by some plausible mechanism, whereas others argue that mere prediction is the necessary mechanism. Neither is a particularly satisfying answer, however. As Schlottmann (2001) observed, "Even infants have perceptual sensitivity to the causal structure of the world" and "if we always relied on mechanisms we would be locked into prejudice, having no way to go beyond what we already know" (pp. 111, 115). Edmonds and Eidinow (2001) concluded by asking: What is causality, then, merely "a furtive, cloak-and-dagger agent, never seen or touched?" or is it "a chimera, a trick played on us by our imagination" (p. 65)?

FOUR TYPES OF EXPERIMENTAL CONTROL

To make this long story a little shorter, we skip to the 19th century and British philosopher John Stuart Mill. Like Hume, Mill was skeptical about ever removing all possibility of doubt when speaking of causality. However, he reasoned that demonstrating empirically that there are both necessary *and* sufficient conditions of a presumed causal relation would produce by far the most convincing evidence of efficient causation. Mill's methods for demonstrating these necessary and sufficient conditions became the basis of an important empirical strategy of causal explanation in science, the use of *control conditions*. Before we explore this particular application, we pause briefly to note three other uses of the term *control* in experimental research. In this discussion we draw on the writing of Edwin G. Boring (1954, 1969), who was well known for his classic texts on the history of experimental psychology (Boring, 1942, 1957).

Boring (1954) noted that the original meaning of *control* was "check," because the word *control* was the diminutive of *counterroll (contre-rolle),* the term for a "duplicate register or account made to verify an official or first-made account and thus a check by a later roll upon the earlier" (p. 573). Apparently, the idea of a check (or test observation) to verify something first came into scientific parlance during the last half of the 19th century, and by 1893, *control* also was used to refer to "a standard of comparison" (p. 574). A variation on the idea of a check or restraint is implicit in the idea of control referring to the "constancy of conditions" in an experimental research situation. For example, unless a scientist wants to study the effect of extreme temperature variation, it would not be advisable to allow the temperature in a laboratory to vary capriciously from very chilly to very hot. If such variation occurs, the scientist will be unable to claim the constancy of conditions that allows certain statements of cause-and-effect relations to be made. To avoid this problem, the scientist *controls* (i.e., holds in check) the laboratory temperature by keeping it constant, removing the possibility of systematic error variability leading to spurious correlations and errant conclusions.

Two other contemporary uses of the term *control* can be found in psychophysical research and in single-case research on behavioral learning principles. In psychophysical research, experimenters use the term *control series.* To illustrate, suppose that blindfolded subjects are asked to judge whether their skin is being touched by one or two fine compass points. When two points are very close to one another, they should be perceived as only one point. A control series of psycho-physical trials would consist of varying the distance between the two points and presenting one point on a certain percentage of trials. In this way, it is possible to identify the smallest detectable distance between two points while controlling for suggestibility. That is, if the subjects believe they are *always* being touched by two points, they might never report being stimulated by only one point. In single-case experimental research (discussed in the next chapter), the term *behavior control* is often used; it refers to the shaping of learned behavior based on a particular schedule of reinforcement designed to elicit the behavior in question.

As Boring (1954) noted, although the use of the term *control* to refer to "a standard of comparison" is of relatively recent origin in the history of science, the idea can be deduced from John Stuart Mill's work and is also implicit in much earlier work (e.g., F. P. Jones, 1964; Ramul, 1963). For example, F. P. Jones (1964) mentioned an example going back to the Greek philosopher Athenaeus in the second century A.D., in which he described how a magistrate in ancient Egypt had discovered citron to be an antidote for poison. According to the story, the magistrate had sentenced a group of criminals to be executed by being exposed to poisonous snakes. Although the sentence was carried out with due diligence, it was reported back to him that none of the prisoners had died. What apparently had happened was that, while they were on their way to the place where they were to be executed, a market woman took pity on them and gave them some citron to eat. The next day, on the hypothesis that it must have been the citron that had saved their lives, the magistrate had citron fed to one of each pair of criminals and nothing to the others. Exposed to poisonous snakes a second time, those prisoners who had eaten the citron survived and those not given it died instantly. This story not only illustrates the early use of a control group but also provides another example of serendipity as well as the early use of replication, for Athenaeus noted that the experiment was repeated many times to firmly establish that citron was indeed an antidote for poison.

MILL'S METHODS OF AGREEMENT
AND DIFFERENCE

John Stuart Mill proposed four methods of experimental inquiry in his 1843 classic, *A System of Logic, Ratiocinative and Inductive,* but it was his methods of agreement and difference that best provide the logical basis of the use of a control group or comparison condition in simple randomized controlled experiments. The **method of agreement** states, "If *X,* then *Y,*" *X* symbolizing the presumed cause and *Y* the pre-sumed effect. The statement means that if we find two or more instances in which *Y* occurs, and if only *X* is present on each occasion, *X* is implied as a **sufficient condition** of *Y.* In other words, *X* is *adequate* (i.e., capable or competent enough) to bring about the effect (*Y*). In baseball, for example, we would say there are several sufficient conditions for scoring runs, such as hitting a home run (X_1), stealing home (X_2), a wild pitch with the bases loaded (X_3), a hit that moves a runner home (X_4), and so forth. Another example would be sufficient conditions for starting a fire (Y), which include striking a match (X_1), using a flint to create a spark that ignites dry leaves (X_2), turning on a gas stove (X_3), or just waiting in a storm for lightning to strike (X_4). In social psychology, an example of sufficient conditions might be those that are adequate to cause a person to pass a rumor, for example, seeking confirmation of information (X_1), manipulating a situation by sending up a trial balloon (X_2), impressing someone with one's privileged position (X_3), trying to convince people to conform to a set of group or societal norms (X_4), or trying to manipulate stock prices (X_5).

The **method of difference** states, "If not-X, then not-Y." It means that, if the presumed effect (Y) does not occur when X is absent, then we suspect X is not just a sufficient condition of Y, but a **necessary condition** for Y to occur In other words, X is *indispensable*, or absolutely essential in order for Y to occur. For example, to win in baseball (Y), it is *necessary* to score more runs (X) than the other team. Though we noted that there were several (sufficient) ways of scoring runs, the fact is that not scoring any runs (not-X) will inevitably result in not winning (not-Y). Similarly, we all know that oxygen is a necessary condition of fire, for without oxygen (not-X) the fire goes out (not-Y). The necessary condition for rumor generation appears to involve an optimum combination of uncertainty and anxiety, as rumors are essentially suppositions intended to make sense of ambiguous events or situations that make us feel apprehensive or nervous about what to believe and how to behave appropriately (Rosnow, 2001).

Table 7.4 illustrates the idea of necessary and sufficient conditions in still another situation. Suppose we are told that five people have been diagnosed with food poisoning. After some probing, we discover that all five people reported

TABLE 7.4
Illustration of agreement and difference methods

Persons	Ate burger	Ate tuna sandwich	Ate fries	Ate salad	Drank shake	Got food poisoning
Mimi	Yes	No	Yes	No	No	Yes
Gail	No	No	No	Yes	Yes	No
Connie	No	No	Yes	No	No	No
Jerry	No	Yes	No	Yes	No	No
Greg	No	Yes	No	No	Yes	No
Dwight	No	No	No	Yes	No	No
Nancy	Yes	No	Yes	Yes	No	Yes
Richard	No	Yes	Yes	Yes	No	No
Kerry	No	No	No	Yes	No	No
Michele	Yes	No	Yes	Yes	Yes	Yes
John	Yes	No	Yes	Yes	No	Yes
Sheila	Yes	No	No	No	No	Yes

Note: Based on a similar example in *Logic and Philosophy: A Modern Introduction* (6th ed.), by H. Kahane, 1989, Belmont, CA: Wadsworth. Used by permission of Howard Kahane and Wadsworth Publishing Co.

having eaten in a fast-food restaurant; seven others, who also ate at the same place around the same time, did not get sick. This table lists the foods consumed by each of them. Notice that the burger appears in each case of food poisoning, but no other food was consistently present in each case of food poisoning. This evidence suggests that the burger was the necessary and sufficient causal agent. However, the manager tells us that one of the waiters left early on the day in question, after complaining of dizziness and nausea. Thus, we have an alternative hypothesis to the burger hypothesis, which is that the waiter was the necessary condition and the foods he touched were the sufficient conditions. Going through the checks given to customers that day, the manager thinks that some of those identified as having food poisoning were probably not served by this waiter, and others who did not become ill *were* probably served by him. If correct, this assessment rules out the waiter hypothesis and leaves us with only the burger hypothesis. Because the burger was present (X) in every case in which food poisoning (Y) occurred, and the burger was absent (not-X) in every case in which food poisoning did not occur (not-Y), we conclude that the burger was necessary and sufficient to produce the outbreak of food poisoning.

BETWEEN-GROUP DESIGNS AND MILL'S JOINT METHOD

To understand the application of Mill's two methods to the logic of causal inference in a randomized controlled experiment, imagine that X represents a tranquilizer that can be obtained without prescription, and Y represents a reduction in measured tension. Say we give a group of people who complain of tension a certain dosage of the drug, and they show a reduction in measured tension. Can we now conclude from this observation that it was the tranquilizer that led to the reduction in tension? Not yet, because what we require is a control condition (a not-X condition) with which to compare the reaction in the drug group. In other words, we need a group of similar subjects to whom we do not give drug X. On the assumption that these subjects are, in fact, similar to those in the drug group in all respects except for the absence of X, then finding no reduction of tension (i.e., not-Y) in the control condition would lead us to conclude that taking drug X is an effective tension reducer and that not taking it (or an equivalent drug) will result in no observable reduction in tension.

Notice that the group given the drug, the *experimental condition,* resembles Mill's "If X, then Y" method of agreement, whereas the group not given the drug (the *control condition*) resembles his "If not-X, then not-Y" method of difference. When viewed together in this way, Mill's two methods are collectively referred to as the **joint method of agreement and difference.** Mill believed the joint method could be generalized to many different situations in which we use empirical observation and reason to rule out some hypotheses and argue for others. He realized, however, that other logical stipulations may be required to make the most solid case for causation. In the example we have been discussing, although we are on safer grounds to conclude that taking the drug (X) is what led to tension reduction (Y), it is necessary to stipulate that "taking the drug" means something different from just getting a chemical into people's bloodstreams. "Taking the drug" means, among other things, (a) having someone give people a pill,

(b) having someone give them the attention that goes with pill giving, (c) having them believe that a relevant medication has been administered, and (d) having the ingredients of the drug find their way to the subjects' bloodstreams.

Usually, when testing a new medication, the researcher is interested only in the subjects' physical reactions to the active ingredients of the medication. The researcher does not care to learn that the subjects will get to feel better if they *believe* they are being helped, because this fact (i.e., the power of suggestion) is already established. But if the researcher knows this, then how is she or he to separate the effects of the chemical ingredients of the drug from the effects of pill giving, subjects' expectations of help, and other psychological variables that may also be sufficient conditions of Y? The answer is by the choice of a different (or an additional) control condition. For example, in Table 7.1 we showed a between-groups design in which the control group was given a placebo rather than given nothing. If there were an appropriate drug already on the market, then the Helsinki declaration (mentioned earlier in this chapter) stipulates that the controls must receive the appropriate alternative treatment. Nonetheless, it has long been a convention in drug research that biomedical experimenters routinely use placebo control conditions. The general finding, incidentally, is that placebos are often effective, and sometimes even as effective as the far more expensive drugs for which they serve as the controls. Of course, in order to tease out the effect of the placebo, we would also need to control for the power of suggestion implicit in being given a placebo and thinking it is an active pharmaceutical. For example, when an individual has received the therapeutic drug in the past, the person may be conditioned to make "drug-anticipatory responses" to the placebo (Ramsay & Woods, 2001, p. 785). Thus, a model randomized drug experiment might have more than one control group (Dennenberg, 2002; Ross, Krugman, Lyerly, & Clyde, 1962) as well as stipulations concerning the prior treatment status of the participants.

INDEPENDENT, DEPENDENT, AND MODERATOR VARIABLES

Frequently it is clear what kind of control condition is needed, but sometimes it is not immediately apparent what kind of control group (or groups) to use. Thus, researchers rely on the wisdom of experience to decide how to frame the control condition. In the research described above, we first used a no-pill control group and then a placebo control. When there is a choice of control groups, how can the researcher decide on the most appropriate variables to control for? Two important considerations are what the particular question (or questions) of interest are and what is already known about the research area. However, even an experienced experimenter may go astray in choosing control groups when he or she makes a major shift of research areas or draws analogies that lead to faulty inferences or spurious assumptions (cf. Lieberman & Dunlap, 1979; Peek, 1977; Rosenthal, 1985a; Shapiro & Morris, 1978; Wilkins, 1984). We will have more to say shortly about teasing out causal connections in an experimental design where there is more than one control condition, but there are other considerations as well.

Hume's idea was of a "constant conjunction" between causes and effects. In actuality, there is hardly ever a perfect (or even a near-perfect) association between the presence and absence of causes and effects. We return to this idea in chapter 11 when we give a number of examples of quite meaningful, but very small, effect size correlations in drug trials (similar to the small effect sizes in the aspirin study noted in Table 2.5 of chapter 2). Indeed, effect size correlations smaller than .10 are quite common in this area, but effect size correlations in any area may vary considerably even when similar cause-and-effect variables are observed over a period of time or in different situations. One reason for all this variability is that other factors (called **moderator variables**) may alter the relationships between cause-and-effect variables. For example, rewarding a child while she or he is in the presence of a group of other children may influence the child's attitude toward the group (A. J. Lott & B. E. Lott, 1968; B. E. Lott & A. J. Lott, 1960), but it is conceivable that variables such as the child's state of mind, personality, and degree of familiarity with the group may moderate (alter) that relationship. Similarly, it is also generally true that attributing a persuasive communication to a highly respected (as opposed to a less respected) source will improve its effectiveness in influencing attitudes, but it is also true that respectability is in the eye of the beholder. Moderator variables in this situation include idiosyncratic factors related to how each individual perceives the trustworthiness of the particular source of the communication. As another case in point, there is research that shows that the positive or negative mood people are in when subjected to persuasive communications may moderate their receptivity or resistance to those communications (Rosnow, 1968). Incidentally, it is important not to confuse moderator variables with **mediator variables;** the latter are defined as conditions, states, or other factors that intervene between the independent variable and the outcome variable in a causal chain (R. M. Baron and Kenny, 1986).

Although we have used the terms *cause* and *effect,* the terms *independent variable* and *dependent variable* are perhaps more commonly used by behavioral and social researchers. With the rise of positivism, it became unfashionable for a time to speak of causal relations. Instead, terms like *functional relations* (discussed in the next chapter) and *functional correlations* became fashionable (Gigerenzer, 1987; Wallace, 1972). Researchers might refer to the "effects of X on Y," but not to *causal effects.* By X and Y, they generally meant whatever were conceived to be the stimulus (X) and outcome (Y) conditions in a study. The term **variable** became popular because it implied that the factors of interest were subject to variation. However, as psychologist David Bakan (1967) commented, "Variables, whatever they may be *in re,* do not exist there as variables. For variables are, by definition, sets of categories; and categories are the result of someone's delineation, abstraction, and identification" (p. 54). Though the idea of a variable is further qualified by means of a distinction between the dependent variable (Y) and the independent variable (X), it should be understood that any condition or factor can be conceived of as either an independent or a dependent variable, depending on how we frame the situation or conceptualize the particular context of defined antecedents and consequences. Operationally, the **dependent variable** is the status of a measurable consequence (e.g., its presence or absence, or an increase or a decrease in a measured outcome) that presumably depends on the status of an antecedent condition, or **independent variable.**

Another reason for the use of the terms *independent variable* and *dependent variable* is that they are broad enough to encompass suspected causal agents or conditions that are not subject to manipulation. Suppose we found a relationship between gender and height and wanted to call one an independent variable and the other a dependent variable. Common sense leads us to conclude that gender is more likely to determine height than that height is likely to determine gender, because we know that a person's gender is biologically established at conception. By changing the context, however, we can view gender as a dependent variable; for example, we can say that gender is determined by genetic factors, so the independent variable now is "genetic factors." To provide another illustration, we can also conceive of rumors as independent or dependent variables, depending on the context. For example, we know that rumors can trigger needs that instigate new rumors, which can then trigger new needs, and so on (Rosnow, 1980). Without getting drawn into murky metaphysics, suffice it to say that, as Bakan implied, all definitions of independent and dependent variables are always influenced by someone's "delineation, abstraction, and identification."

SOLOMON'S EXTENDED CONTROL GROUP DESIGN

We turn shortly to the influential ideas of Campbell and Stanley, but first, we want to mention some earlier work of experimental psychologist Richard L. Solomon. As Campbell and Stanley (1966) reminded readers, it was psychological and educational researchers between 1900 and 1920 who created the orthodox control-group design in which a pretested experimental group was compared with a control group. Designs like these were used with some frequency, usually "without need of explanation," Campbell and Stanley noted (p. 13; see also Dehue, 2000). Solomon's work represents a cutting-edge transition in thinking about control group designs in behavioral and social experimentation. In an article published in 1949, he raised the question of whether pretesting subjects in pre-post designs might have a sensitizing effect on their reactions to the experimental treatment, and he argued that orthodox two-group designs were unable to address this problem. Solomon also anticipated some ideas that were later developed in more depth by Campbell and Stanley, and though we would not endorse the specific details of all of his recommendations, we nevertheless want to recognize the historical sequence of Solomon's forward-looking work.

To put the pretest sensitization problem in context, Solomon described a popular design strategy in the field of attitude change research. The participants received a pretest that, if not identical to the posttest, was similar in terms of the scale units on the posttest. Typically there was an experimental group and a control group, and either the groups were matched on some criterion or the subjects were randomly assigned to the groups. Solomon's position was that the two-group design was deficient because of its failure to control for the possibility that merely taking the pretest could affect how the subjects responded to the experimental treatment. For example, the pretest might change their attitudinal "set" or influence some other attentional factor so that they perceived the experimental treatment differently than if they had not been pretested, and their responses to the treatment were affected accordingly. To control for this problem, Solomon cautioned researchers to use either a three-group or, preferably, a four-group design.

TABLE 7.5
Solomon's (1949) three-group design

A. Basic three-group design			
Conditions	**Experimental group**	**Control Group I**	**Control Group II**
Pretest	Yes	Yes	No
Treatment	Yes	No	Yes
Posttest	Yes	Yes	Yes

B. Results of an experiment in spelling ($n = 10$)			
Results	**Experimental group**	**Control Group I**	**Control Group II**
Pretest means	3.2	2.8	3.0 (est.)[a]
Posttest means	9.9	3.5	11.2
Improvement means	6.7	0.7	8.2

[a]Estimated from $(3.2 + 2.8)/2$, the average of the two available pretest means.

Note: Control Group I is easily recognized as a control for the treatment in the experimental group, but Control Group II receives the treatment and yet is called a "control group" because it controls for the presence of the pretest in the experimental group.

The three-group design that Solomon proposed appears in Part A of Table 7.5, and Part B shows the results of a spelling experiment in which 30 students in two grammar school classes were assigned to the three groups ($n = 10$). Pupils in the experimental group and in Control Group I were pretested on a list of words of equal difficulty (Control Group II was out of the room at the time). Then the experimental group and Control Group II were given a standard spelling lesson covering some general rules of spelling (Control Group I was out of the room), and afterward all the children were posttested on the same words as in the pretest. The (unobserved) pretest mean of Control Group II was estimated from an average of the pretest means of the experimental group and Control Group I. Solomon believed that, in order to tease out pretest sensitization, it was necessary simply to remove the combined improvement effects of Control Groups I and II from the experimental condition improvement effect, so that what remained would be either a positive or a negative effect of pretest sensitization. Solomon concentrated on the posttest means in his later work, but in this early paper (Solomon, 1949), he focused on the improvement means in Table 7.5. Then he computed $6.7 - (0.7 + 8.2) = -2.2$ and concluded that, in light of this "interaction," the "taking of the pre-test somehow diminished the effectiveness of the training in spelling" (p. 145). It was not clear why the negative effect occurred, but one possibility that he raised was that taking the pretest might have been emotionally disturbing to the children. What was clear, he concluded, was that if he had used only the experimental group and Control Group I, he would have erroneously underrated the teaching procedure, as the pretest apparently "vitiated some of the effectiveness of the teaching method" (p. 145).

TABLE 7.6
Solomon's (1949) four-group design

A. Basic four-group design

Conditions	Experimental group	Control Group I	Control Group II	Control Group III
Pretest	Yes	Yes	No	No
Treatment	Yes	No	Yes	No
Posttest	Yes	Yes	Yes	Yes

B. Numerical values needed

Results	Experimental group	Control Group I	Control Group II	Control Group III
Pretest means	A_1	A_2	A_3 (est.)[a]	A_4 (est.)[a]
Posttest means	B_1	B_2	B_3	B_4
Change means	$D_1 = B_1 - A_1$	$D_2 = B_2 - A_2$	$D_3 = B_3 - A_3$	$D_4 = B_4 - A_4$

Value of I $D_1 - (D_2 + D_3 - D_4)$ or equivalently, $(D_1 + D_4) - (D_2 + D_3)$

[a]Estimated from $(A_1 + A_2)/2$.

Continuing to follow the train of Solomon's thinking, Table 7.6 shows his four-group design. The additional group (Control Group III) is a control for what Campbell and Stanley subsequently called "history," or the effects of uncontrolled events that may be associated with the passage of time. Solomon (1949) mentioned certain field studies on attitude change that had been conducted during World War II; some of that research had experimented with propaganda effects. It was possible, he argued, that uncontrolled events taking place in the time between the pretest and the posttest might have impinged on all the subjects. Notice that there are two estimated pretest means (Control Groups II and III); Solomon gave them identical values based on averaging the pretest means of the experimental group and Control Group I. The value noted as D_4 is the change from the estimated pretest to the observed posttest for Control Group III that can be attributed to outside, uncontrolled events (i.e., history), he reasoned. The value of I is the difference between differences. Because there is no within-error term for the difference scores in Control Groups II and III, the ANOVA option would be to compute a 2×2 analysis on the posttest scores (with treatment vs. no treatment as one factor, and pretest vs. no pretest as the other factor), or simply to impute an error term for difference scores from error terms of the experimental group and Control Group I. Interestingly, Solomon's definition of I anticipated the most frugal way of operationalizing the 2×2 interaction, but calling the difference score of -2.2 for the results in Table 7.5 an "interaction" was simply wrong (cf. Rosnow & Rosenthal, 1989a, 1995)—we have much more to say in chapter 17 about statistical interactions in the context of analysis of variance.

Before leaving this discussion, we should note that other research has uncovered both positive and negative effects of pretesting. Solomon (1949) mentioned in a footnote that he had "preliminary evidence that the pre-test may operate to reduce post-test variance in studies of attitude change" (p. 148). In another investigation, Lessac and

Solomon (1969) used a four-group Solomon design to study the effects of sensory isolation on beagle pups. In this way they were able to estimate pretest mean scores of unpretested animals before they were placed in isolation and pretest means of their corresponding unpretested controls. Lessac and Solomon concluded that "the behavioral deficiencies found in the isolated subjects . . . must represent an active, destructive, atrophic process produced by the isolation experience" (p. 23; see Solomon & Lessac, 1968, for implications of the extended control-group design in developmental research). Using the Solomon design in an investigation of children's ability to learn state locations of large U.S. cities, Entwisle (1961), found that pretesting aided recall for the high-IQ subjects and was "mildly hindering" for the average-IQ subjects. In an attitude change study, Rosnow and Suls (1970) found that pretesting enhanced the volunteer subjects' receptivity to the experimental treatment (which involved a persuasive communication) and reduced receptivity in nonvolunteer subjects. Thus, it would appear that when a pre-post design is used in some fields (such as educational training, inducing changes in attitudes, transfer of training, performance skills) it might be prudent, as Solomon (1949) recommended, to control for the possibility of moderating effects of the pretest measurements.

THREATS TO INTERNAL VALIDITY

In chapter 4 we examined uses and definitions of the term *validity* in the context of measurement, and we now describe some additional, specialized uses of the term in the context of experimental and other research designs. In a 1963 chapter that, after the authors were inundated with hundreds of reprint requests, was published in a slightly revised version as a separate little book, *Experimental and Quasi-Experimental Designs for Research,* Campbell and Stanley introduced the terms *internal validity* and *external validity* (Campbell & Stanley, 1963, 1966). The book also stimulated considerable debate, and specific issues that Campbell and Stanley labeled one way were perceived and labeled differently by some others (Albright & Malloy, 2000). The next version of the book was greatly expanded (Cook and Campbell, 1979), in which these authors expounded on two further validity distinctions, termed *statistical conclusion validity* and *construct validity.* The most recent version of this seminal work appeared in a book coauthored by William R. Shadish, Cook, and Campbell (2002), which has continued the tradition begun by Campbell and Stanley by specifying variables and circumstances that may threaten the four types of validity not only in experimental studies but in other research as well. In this section and the two that follow, we will try to communicate a sense of this work. We should note, however, that the Shadish et al. book is encyclopedic in its coverage, reaching well beyond our abilty to summarize it in this brief discussion.

We alluded to the concept of **internal validity** in chapter 4 when we spoke of the idea of trying to rule out plausible rival hypotheses that undermine causal interpretations. That strategy is understood to be as elemental to causal inference in science as are evidence of temporal precedence and covariation. Causal inference, in other words, depends (a) not only on operationalizing a reliable relationship between an event and its presumed cause (*covariation*), as well as (b) providing some proof that the cause preceded the effect (*temporal precedence*), but also on (c) ruling out plausible rival explanations (*internal validity*). Stated still another way, the concept of internal validity is now said to imply "the validity of inferences about whether observed covariation between A (the presumed treatment) and B (the presumed outcome) reflects a causal relationship from A to B as those variables were manipulated or measured" (Shadish et al., 2002, p. 38). Among several threats to internal invalidity are what Campbell and Stanley (1966) referred to as *history, maturation, instrumentation,* and *selection.* We will describe each of these in turn, but we begin with another threat to internal validity, called *regression* (a shorthand expression for "regression toward the mean"), a subject on which Campbell and Kenny (1999) wrote an entire volume.

Regression toward the mean has to do not with the actual (or raw) scores of a measure, but with the standard (or predicted) scores (Campbell & Kenny, 1999; Cohen & Cohen, 1983; Cohen, Cohen, West, & Aiken, 2003). We review standard scores (Z scores) in chapter 10, but they are raw scores from which the sample mean has been subtracted and the difference is then divided by the standard deviation. The regression equation, stated in standard score units, is $Z_y = r_{xy}Z_x$, where the standard score of Y is predicted from the product of the XY correlation (r_{xy}) times the standard score of X. Given a perfect correlation between X and Y (i.e., $r_{xy} = 1$), it follows that Z_y is equivalent to Z_x. However, if $r_{xy} < 1$, then Z_y cannot be equivalent to Z_x. For example, if $r_{xy} = .4$, then Z_y can be only 0.4 as large as Z_x. Regression toward the mean occurs when pre and post variables (X and Y) consist of the same measure taken at two points in time, and $r_{xy} < 1$. Therefore, it can be understood as a mathematical necessity whenever two variables are correlated less than perfectly. For example, finding that overweight people appear to lose weight, or that low-IQ children seem to become brighter, or that rich people appear to become poorer is a common observation in longitudinal research, but the findings might be evidence of a regression toward the mean.

Table 7.7 helps to explain how history, maturation, instrumentation, and selection affect internal validity. The table lists two of what Campbell and Stanley (1966) called "preexperimental designs" because of their relatively primitive nature. One is described in the table as a "one-shot case study" and the other, as a "one-group pre-post." One-shot case studies can be symbolized as X-O, where X denotes the exposure of a group to a variable, and O is an observation or measurement. An example of an X-O study would be introducing an educational intervention to improve reading skills and then testing the students exposed to the intervention on their reading skills. One-group pre-post studies can be symbolized as O-X-O, which means the subjects

TABLE 7.7

Four threats to internal validity in two preexperimental designs and the Solomon design of Table 7.6

Design	Threats to internal validity			
	History	**Maturation**	**Instrumentation**	**Selection**
One-shot case study	−	−	Not relevant	−
One-group pre-post	−	−	−	−
Solomon design	+	+	+	+

Note: A minus (−) indicates a definite weakness; a plus (+) that the source of invalidity is controlled for.

would be measured both before and after exposure to the teaching intervention. In neither preexperimental design, however, is an allowance made for a comparison with the reactions of subjects not exposed to the intervention. The minus signs in Table 7.7 imply that both preexperimental designs are totally deficient in terms of history, maturation, and selection. Only the one-group pre-post is deficient in terms of instrumentation, which is not relevant to the one-shot case study because there is no premeasurement instrument with which the postmeasurement can be compared. Also implied in Table 7.7 is that the Solomon design of Table 7.6 controls for all four threats to internal validity, as would any other randomized experiment. Now let us see how history, maturation, instrumentation, and selection are defined.

First, the term **history** implies a plausible source of error attributable to an uncontrolled event that occurs between the premeasurement (the pretest) and the postmeasurement (the posttest) and can bias the postmeasurement. History becomes a threat to internal validity when the inferred causal relationship is confounded by the irrelevant, uncontrolled event. Suppose a sudden snowstorm results in an unexpected cancellation of classes. Neither preexperimental design allows us to isolate the effects on motivation of a school closing, or to assess that variable apart from the effects of the new educational intervention designed to improve concentration. In the case of the Solomon design, there are two pretested and posttested groups, one with and the other without a treatment, so we can assess the factor of history in the treated groups apart from the untreated groups.

Second, **maturation** refers to intrinsic changes in the subjects, such as their growing older, wiser, stronger, or more experienced between the premeasurement and the postmeasurement. Maturation is a threat to internal validity when it is not the variable of interest and the causal relationship is confounded by the presence of these changes. Imagine a study in which the posttest is given 1 year after the pretest. If the students' concentration improved as a result of getting older, so they have became better at the task, neither preexperimental design could tell us whether those gains were due to students' maturing or to their being subjected to the educational innovation. The use of the Solomon design gives us an opportunity to find out how the subjects improved as a function of growing older (i.e., during the period of the experiment), as we have pre-post data on a group that did not receive the experimental treatment.

Third, **instrumentation** refers to intrinsic changes in the measuring instruments. Instrumentation is a threat to internal validity when an effect might be due to unsuspected changes in the instruments over time. In the case of the new educational innovation, we might ask whether the observed effect was due to instability (i.e., deterioration) in the achievement test or to changes in the students that were caused by the treatment. Or suppose the "instruments" were actually judges who were asked to rate the subjects. Over time, the judges might have become better raters of student concentration, so that the confounding is due not to instrument deterioration but to instrument improvement. Instrumentation bias is not a relevant issue in the one-shot case study design because the instrument is administered only once. However, it is both relevant and uncontrolled in the one-group pre-post design. It is also relevant, but specifically controlled for (i.e., identifiable), in the Solomon design, because there are two pretested groups with which we can compare the groups that were not pretested.

Finally, **selection** is a potential threat to internal validity when there are unsuspected differences between the participants in each condition. In the one-shot case study, we simply do not know beforehand anything about the state of the subjects because they are observed or measured only after the treatment has been administered. The addition of an observation before the treatment in the one-group pre-post design is a slight improvement in that it enables us to assess the prior state of the participants. The Solomon design and all other randomized experiments control for selection bias by randomly allocating participants to the groups. However, as noted earlier, random allocation is not a guarantee of comparability between groups, particularly in small-sample experiments.

THREATS TO EXTERNAL VALIDITY

The concept of **external validity,** which some argue was originally confounded with other types of validity, is currently defined as the "validity of inferences about whether the cause-effect relationship holds over variation in persons, settings, treatment variables, and measurement variables" (Shadish et al., 2002, p. 38). Nonetheless, external validity is often used by researchers as a synonym for generalizability or representativeness. Lynch (1982) identified three issues that are frequently conflated in this broader use of the term. First, there is *statistical generalizability,* which refers to the representativeness of the results to a wider population of interest. Second is *conceptual replicability or robustness,* which Lynch believed to be closest to Campbell and Stanley's (1966) conception of external validity. Third is *realism,* which is also similar to what Aronson and Carlsmith (1968) referred to as **mundane realism,** or the extent to which an experimental treatment is apt to be encountered in an analogous form in a natural setting. Incidentally, Aronson and Carlsmith made a further distinction between mundane and **experimental realism,** the latter referring to the psychological impact of the experimental manipulation on the participants. As if external validity were not already elusive enough, Lynch (1982) also argued that it "cannot be evaluated either a priori or a posteriori (e.g., on the basis of sampling practices or realism) in the absence of a fairly deep understanding of the structural determinants of the behavior under study" (p. 239). Lynch's position is that we must have an implicit or explicit model of the behavior we are investigating, or else we leave judgments of the external validity of experiments to experts in the substantive area who have a sense of the behavior under investigation (i.e., as opposed to mere specialists in methodology).

If external validity seems a mercurial concept and not easy to pin down, another issue is that a number of psychological experimenters have questioned the importance of external validity as a criterion of a sound experimental design. Douglas Mook (1983) contended that the insistence on external validity is often misguided. The point of many laboratory simulations, he argued, is not to generalize to the real world, but instead to try to make predictions about the real world from the laboratory. Mook noted the monkey love studies of Harlow (discussed in chapter 1) as an example of experiments that are lacking in external validity (because using baby monkeys, and wire mesh or cloth-covered mother surrogates, to study human babies falls far short of the ideal) but that nevertheless tell us something theoretically valuable about personality development. Mook cautioned that, before condemning any experiment as lacking in external validity, it would be far more instructive to ask: (a) Is the investigator really trying to estimate from sample characteristics the characteristics of a population, or is the purpose of the study instead to draw conclusions about a theory that predicts what *these* subjects will do? And (b) Is the purpose of the study to predict what would happen in a real-life situation, or is its purpose to test under very controlled conditions a predicted causal relationship that is purported to be a universal principle of behavior (and that should therefore operate in the laboratory as well as in real life)? More recently, Anderson, Lindsay, and Bushman (1999) reexamined the issue addressed by Mook, this time by asking whether there is actually a correspondence between lab and field experimental findings that have addressed similar questions. They inspected the effect sizes in a range of studies (including studies of aggression, helping, leadership style, social loafing, self-efficacy, depression, and memory) and concluded that there was considerable similarity in the pooled effect sizes of laboratory and field studies using conceptually similar independent and dependent variables.

Some years before the terms *external validity* and *internal validity* were coined by Campbell and Stanley, another noted experimentalist, Egon Brunswik (1947), had addressed the issue of representativeness in a way that now seems conceptually related to both external and internal validity. If we want to generalize the results of a psychological experiment to a population of subjects and a population of stimuli, then we must sample from both populations, Brunswik argued (see also discussion by Maher, 1978). Brunswik used the expression **representative research design** to describe an idealized experimental model in which both the subjects and the experimental stimuli are representative of specified populations. Experiments that satisfy this criterion were called **ecologically valid.** Suppose we wanted to test the hypothesis that male and female patients respond quite differently to a certain psychotherapeutic treatment when the clinician is male or female. A convenient experimental design would consist of randomly assigning patients of both genders to either a male or a female clinician. Though it might be claimed that the design is representative in terms of the selection of patients (assuming they were properly sampled), it could *not* be claimed that the design is representative as regards the stimulus (i.e., the clinicians presenting the treatments). Because the experimenter did not sample from among populations of male and female clinicians, we would be hard-pressed to conclude that there is a generalizable relationship of the type hypothesized. Thus, Brunswik might say that, inasmuch as the use of other male or female clinicians might produce quite different results, the design of the study is deficient in ecological validity (Hammond, 1954)—and by implication, we might add, deficient in external validity as well.

What does this also have to do with internal validity? The argument is that our use of only one clinician of each sex as a stimulus does not preclude the possibility that some other characteristics of this person may have stimulus values that are unknown and uncontrolled for. In other words, there are two major limitations in this so-called "single stimulus design" (Maher, 1978). First, it is possible that differences among the patients who are exposed to the male clinician and those exposed to the female clinician may be due to the effects of uncontrolled stimulus variables. On the basis only of the information available from our data, we cannot conclude whether the obtained differences are due to the validity of the tested hypothesis or to the effects of another uncontrolled variable (i.e., clearly a threat to internal validity). Second, the failure to find differences between those subjects exposed to the male clinician and those exposed to the female clinician might also be due to the presence of an uncontrolled stimulus variable operating either (a) to counteract the effect of the intended independent variable or (b) to increase that effect artificially to a ceiling value (i.e., a top limit) in the different groups. We have no way of distinguishing between this explanation and the possibility that the lack of difference is due to the invalidity of the tested hypothesis.

Earlier we mentioned the idea of moderator variables that affect relationships between independent and dependent variables. Presumably, given an adequate theory, we can formulate a model on which to predicate the carving out of moderator variables. For example, Alice H. Eagly (1978) was intrigued by the claim that, generally speaking, women are more conforming and more easily influenced than men. The explanation proposed for this idea was that socialization processes taught men to be independent thinkers, a cultural value not as frequently thought to be suitable for women. The empirical findings, however, were inconsistent. Some failed to find gender differences in influenceability. Using a historical model in which she reasoned that the era in which the empirical data were collected was a plausible moderator of the association between gender and influenceability, Eagly meta-analyzed all the relevant studies she could find. Just as her model predicted, there was a pronounced difference in the correlation between gender and influenceability in studies published before 1970 and those published during the era of the women's movement in the 1970s. In contrast to the older research studies, which had found greater influenceability among females than among males, the later studies identified few gender differences in influenceability.

Brinberg et al. (1992) cautioned that when researchers know little about the moderator variables lurking beneath the surface of their aggregated variables, they may unwittingly misrepresent the external validity of their causal inferences and recommendations based on those inferences. It is quite possible, for example, that critical patterns that hold true in the aggregate may not hold for only a small number of individuals (Hutchinson, Kamakura, & Lynch, 2000; Yule, 1903), and thus, it is always prudent to explore the individual data. In biomedical research, standard moderator variables include demographic descriptors like age, sex, ethnic group, and prior pathology. Suppose that research shows a particular treatment of flu is effective. Still, we want to break down the aggregate scores so that we can state with more precision when the treatment can be expected to be *most* (and *least*) effective. We might find that Caucasian men do better on certain dosages of the treatment than non-Caucasian men, or that both men and women with prior pathology do the poorest, or that younger people do better than older people in some ethnic groups. In the field of experimental psychology it is quite common for researchers to rely on what are called *convenience samples,* which simply means samples made up of people who are readily accessible, usually sophomores in introductory psychology courses. As a way of exploring for possible moderator variables, it is standard practice in many psychology departments to request that students in introductory psychology classes complete a battery of psychological instruments (typically including some measure of major factors of individual personality; cf. Goldberg, 1993; McCrae & Costa, 1997; Wiggins, 1996), as well as provide demographic information that can then be correlated with the students' total scores or with residuals about the mean in the research in which they participate.

Frequently, the problem with convenience samples is that researchers seem oblivious even to the possibility that their subject samples may not be representative of the population they are presumed to be theorizing about, as if all humans were the same, or all rats were the same. We return to this issue in chapter 9, but the latter problem was illustrated some years ago by Marshall B. Jones and Robert S. Fennell, III (1965). In the 1940s, there was a controversy between two leading psychological researchers, Clark L. Hull and Edward C. Tolman, over the nature of learning. Hull, inspired by Pavlov's research on conditioned reflexes, developed a systematic behavior theory that asserted that animals learned stimulus-response connections and that the strength of these connections accumulated in small increments from trial to trial. In contrast, Tolman's model (known as *purposive behaviorism, sign gestalt theory,* or *expectancy theory*) emphasized the cognitive nature of learning, arguing that animals learned "what leads to what" by acquiring expectations and forming "cognitive maps." Learning is not an automatic, mechanical process, but a discontinuous process that largely depends on exploratory behaviors, the Tolmanians argued.

Not only were there distinct theoretical and methodological differences between those two camps, but they also used different strains of rats. The Tolmanians, centered at the University of California, used rats that had been selectively descended from crossed matings of wild males and laboratory albino females. The Hullians, at Yale University under Hull's direction and a second camp at Iowa University under Kenneth W. Spence, used descendents of a "nonemotional" strain of rats that had descended from very different crossed matings. That the two strains of rats had been separated for over thirty years, during which time they had been differently and selectively bred, raised the question of whether genetic differences were involved in the clearly different results of the Hullians and the Tolmanians. So Jones and Fennell (1965) obtained a sample of rats from each strain, placed them on a 23-hour food or water deprivation schedule and, beginning on the fourth day, subjected them to three learning trials daily in a U-maze for ten consecutive days. There were noticeable differences in the performance of the two strains, differences that were also entirely consistent with the nature of the theoretical differences that separated the two schools of learning. The Tolman rats "spent long periods of time in exploratory behaviors, sniffing along the walls, in the air, along the runway" (p. 294). In contrast, the Hull-Spence rats "popped out of the start box, ambled down the runway, around the turn, and into the goal box" (p. 294). Findings like these would not necessarily lead us to question either the logic or the internal consistency of Hull's or Tolman's theory of learning, but they do raise a serious question about the external validity of the empirically based causal generalizations that "were involved in the great debate over the nature of learning" (p. 295).

STATISTICAL CONCLUSION AND CONSTRUCT VALIDITY

Besides internal and external validity, there is statistical conclusion validity and construct validity. As defined by Shadish et al. (2002), **statistical conclusion validity** is concerned with "inferences about the correlation (covariation) between treatment and outcome" (p. 38), in other words, Hume's "contiguity of events." If we are interested in effect sizes, for example, the question of interest is whether a statement about the association between membership in the treatment or control group and the dependent variable can be made with a reasonable degree of confidence. If we are using a significance test, was there enough statistical power to detect a likely relation between the treatment and outcome and to rule out the possibility that the observed association was due to chance? In the second half of this book we have more to say about statistical power, assumptions of particular tests of statistical significance, and related issues. Among the threats to statistical conclusion validity discussed by Shadish et al. are low statistical power (in which case we are apt to make Type II errors), violations of assumptions of statistical tests (which lead to spurious estimates of p values), "fishing" for statistically significant effects without making proper adjustments of p values, unreliable tests and measurements, and spurious or uninterpretable or ambiguous estimates of effect sizes.

Turning finally to construct validity, recall our discussion in chapter 4, where we defined *construct validity* as referring to the degree to which a test or questionnaire measures the characteristic that it is presumed to measure. We also noted that, as Popper's falsificationist view implies, constructs can never be completely verified or proved, because it is impossible to complete every conceivable check on the construct (Cronbach & Quirk, 1971). Shadish et al. (2002) define **construct validity** as referring to "higher order constructs that represent sampling particulars" (p. 38). In research in which causal generalizations are the prime objective, *construct validity* is the soundness or logical tenability of the hypothetical idea linking the independent (X) and dependent (Y) variables, but it also refers to the conceptualization of X and Y. One way to distinguish between construct validity and internal validity is to recall that internal validity is the ability to logically rule out competing explanations for the observed covariation between the presumed independent variable (X) and its effect on the dependent variable (Y). Construct validity, on the other hand, is the validity of the theoretical concepts we use in our measurements and causal explanations. Thus, whenever we ask what is *really* being measured (e.g., "What does this test really measure?"), we are asking about construct validity rather than internal validity.

Put another way, construct validity is based on the proper identification of the concepts being measured or manipulated (i.e., "Do we have a clear conception of what we are measuring or manipulating?"), and internal validity is based on whether a variable other than X (the causal variable we *think* we are studying) may have caused Y to occur. Hall (1984a) proposed a further distinction among the four kinds of validity in experimental research. Poor construct or internal validity has the potential to actively mislead researchers because they are apt to make causal inferences that are plain "wrong." Poor statistical-conclusion or external validity puts the researchers in a "weak position" to make *any* causal inferences or broad generalizations, because it limits what can be learned or what can be generalized to other situations. Thus, according to Hall's argument, the distinction comes down to being wide of the mark (i.e., poor construct or internal invalidity) or being in a vulnerable position on statistical or sampling grounds (statistical-conclusion and external validity).

SUBJECT AND EXPERIMENTER ARTIFACTS

We turn now to a class of threats to the construct, internal, and external validity of experiments (as well as threats to the valid interpretation and generalization of nonexperimental results) that we have studied and written about for many years (e.g., Rosenthal, 1966, 1976; Rosenthal & Rosnow, 1969a; Rosnow & Rosenthal, 1997). The term **artifacts** is used, generally, to refer to research findings that result from factors other than the ones intended by the researchers, usually factors that are quite extraneous to the purpose of their investigations (e.g., Orne, 1959; Rosenthal & Rosnow, 1969a; Rosnow, Strohmetz, & Aditya, 2002). By **subject and experimenter artifacts,** we mean that systematic errors are attributed to uncontrolled subject- or experimenter-related variables (Rosnow, 2002). The term *experimenter* is understood to embrace not only researchers who perform laboratory or field experiments, but those working in any area of empirical research, including human and animal experimental and observational studies. The sociologist Herbert H. Hyman and his colleagues (1954) wisely cautioned researchers not to equate ignorance of error with lack of error, because all scientific investigation is subject to both random and systematic error. It is particularly important, they advised, not only to expose the sources of systematic error in order to control for them, but also to estimate the direction (and, if possible, the magnitude) of this error when it occurs. The more researchers know about the nature of subject and experimenter artifacts, the better able they should be to isolate and quantify these errors, take them into account when interpreting their results, and eliminate them when possible.

Though the term *artifact* (used in this way) is of modern vintage, the suspicion that uncontrolled sources of subject and experimenter artifacts might be lurking in investigative procedures goes back almost to the very beginning of modern psychology (Suls & Rosnow, 1988). A famous case around the turn of the twentieth century involved not human subjects, but a horse called Clever Hans, which was reputed to perform remarkable "intellectual" feats. There were earlier reports of learned animals, going all the way back to the Byzantine Empire when it was ruled by Justinian (A.D. 483–565), but no animal intelligence captured the imagination of the European public and scholars alike as that attributed to Hans (Rosenthal, in Pfungst, 1965). Hans gave every evidence that he could tap out the answers to mathematical problems or the date of any day mentioned, aided ostensibly by a code table in front of him based on a code taught to him by his owner. It seemed unlikely that his owner had any fraudulent intent because he allowed visitors (even in his absence) to question Hans, and he did not profit financially from the horse's talents. Thus, it was possible to rule out intentional cues as the reason for the horse's cleverness. One visitor, the German psychologist Oskar Pfungst, discovered in an elegant series of experiments that Hans's accuracy diminished when he was fitted with blinders so he could not see his questioners, when the distance between Hans and his questioners was increased, or when the questioner did not know the answer. These results implied that the horse's apparent talents were due to something other than his capacity to reason. Pfungst found that Hans was responding to subtle cues given by his questioners, not just intentional cues, but unwitting movements and mannerisms (Pfungst, 1911). For instance, someone who asked Hans a question that required a long tapping response would lean forward as if settling in for a long wait. The horse responded to the questioner's forward movement, not to the actual question, and kept tapping away until the questioner unconsciously communicated the expectancy that Hans would stop tapping. This the questioner might do by beginning to straighten up in anticipation that Hans was about to reach the correct number of taps.

Pfungst's unraveling of the mystery of Clever Hans provided an object lesson in the susceptibility of behavior (even animal behavior) to unconscious suggestion. Given the influence on animal subjects, might not the same phenomenon hold for human subjects who are interacting with researchers oriented by their own hypotheses, theories, hunches, and expectations? Although Pfungst's discovery was duly cited and circulated, its wider methodological implications did not strike a resonant chord in behavioral science during that period. To be sure, a number of leading experimenters, including Hermann Ebbinghaus (1885, 1913), voiced their suspicions that researchers might unwittingly influence their subjects. However, their concerns, along with the wider methodological implications of Pfungst's discovery, went largely unheeded until, several decades later, another influential development fostered the idea that human subjects behave in special ways *because* they know they are "subjects" of an investigation. This principle, which came to be known as the **Hawthorne effect,** grew out of a series of human factors experiments between 1924 and 1932 by a group of industrial researchers at the Hawthorne works of the Western Electric Company in Cicero, Illinois (Roethlisberger & Dickson, 1939). One set of studies examined the impact of higher levels of electric lighting, increased rest periods, and other conditions on the work productivity of young women who inspected parts, assembled relays, or wound coils (Gillespie, 1988). According to news reports and a Western Electric memorandum, one study revealed that any improvement in working conditions resulted in greater worker satisfaction and increased productivity. When the improvements were removed, however, the productivity did not decline; the efficiency actually continued to increase, according to the reports. On interviewing the team of six workers who had participated in that study, the researchers concluded that the workers' productivity increases had derived from their feeling flattered by being subjects of investigation. That is, they had been motivated to increase their output because of their special status as research participants. Not only had their opinions been solicited by management, but they had been singled out for free morning tea, rest periods, and shorter hours of work.

The term *Hawthorne effect* was coined by the contributor of a chapter to a popular textbook in the 1950s (French, 1953). Subsequently, however, the original reports and secondary accounts of this study were subjected to critical analysis by other investigators (cf. Adair, 1984; Bramel & Friend, 1981; Franke & Kaul, 1978; Gillespie, 1988; Schlaifer, 1980), who argued, among other things, that the historical record was tainted by sweeping generalizations embroidered by overzealous, and possibly biased, authors. In another fascinating piece of detective work, H. McIlvaine Parsons, a specialist in human factors research, described his discovery of a long-ignored confounding variable that also explained the Hawthorne effect (Parsons, 1978, 1992). The assembly-line workers in the Hawthorne studies had been told their output rates, and the higher the rates, the more they were paid, Parsons learned. Putting those facts together, he theorized that the increased productivity had been reinforced by the feedback the workers had received about their output rates. Like some projective test into which people read their own meanings, the Hawthorne effect was a mixture of fantasy and reality into which textbook authors had read their own meaning, Parsons argued. Nevertheless, the principle of the Hawthorne effect entered into the vocabulary of behavioral research as implying a kind of "placebo effect" in psychological research with human subjects (Sommer, 1968). That is, it implies that subjects responded not just to the experimental treatment, but also to uncontrolled factors, including the belief that they were being administered a treatment designed to have a particular effect. A generation of researchers was warned to be wary of unleashing a Hawthorne effect by their manipulations, observations, or measurements.

In 1933, another important development (which went largely unnoticed for many years) involved a conceptual advance. Saul Rosenzweig, a clinical psychologist fresh out of graduate school, published an insightful critique in a leading psychology journal, in which he examined various aspects of the psychology experiment and identified three distinct sources of artifacts. For example, he described how artifacts might result from, first, the "observational attitude" of the experimenter. Using chemistry as his prototype of scientific experimentation, he noted how chemists take into account the ambient temperature, possibly even their own body heat, when running certain lab experiments. Experimenting psychologists, Rosenzweig said, needed to consider their own attitudes toward their research subjects and the subjects' beliefs about and attitudes toward the experiment. His second point was that, of course, "chemicals have no power of self-determination" (p. 338), whereas experimenting psychologists usually work with people who may try to outguess the experimenter and to figure out how their behavior will be evaluated. Rosenzweig called this the "motivational attitude" problem, and he claimed that it could creep into any experiment and bias the results. Third were what he called "errors of personality influence," for example, the warmth or coolness of the experimenter, his or her unguarded gestures or words, and the experimenter's sex and race—all possible confounding factors that might affect the attitudes and reactions of the research subjects, quite apart from the experimental treatment. Rosenzweig sketched some procedures that he thought would prevent some of these problems, including the use of deceptions to prevent errors of motivational attitude. Nonetheless, he also cautioned that it was frequently unclear whether the experimenter or the subject was the "true deceiver"—a concern voiced again by other writers in the 1960s (e.g., Stricker, 1967).

Beginning in the 1960s and throughout the 1970s, increased attention was paid to concerns about subject and experimenter artifacts. There are several possible reasons for that development, one of which has to do with the rise of cognitive psychology. First, many earlier behavioral psychologists had been fixed on a dustbowl-empiricist view that emphasized only observable responses as acceptable data in science, but renewed interest in the cognitive dimension and the neobehaviorist reshaping of the empiricist view made it respectable to talk about cognition as a variable of scientific relevance (Toulmin & Leary, 1985). A second reason was that scientific psychology was coming into its own; its identity crisis seemed virtually over (Silverman, 1977, pp. 18–19). Following World War II, there had been a tremendous growth in psychology departments and an increased role for research psychologists in the government, the military, and industry as a result of optimism about the likely benefits of psychological science. Those who voiced concern over artifacts were seen as undermining the empirical foundations of the scientific facts and theories that were proliferating in psychological science. By the 1960s and 1970s, increasing numbers of researchers felt secure enough to, as Hyman (1954, quoted earlier) put it, accept that ignorance of error was not synonymous with lack of error, but that it merely signaled a primitive understanding and thus a less advanced stage of scientific development. For these, and probably other good reasons, the stage was set for programmatic investigations of subject and experimenter artifacts by researchers working independently in different institutions.

DEMAND CHARACTERISTICS AND THEIR CONTROL

Among those in the first wave of contemporary artifact researchers was Martin T. Orne, an eminent psychiatrist, social psychologist, and clinical psychologist at the University of Pennsylvania. Starting in the late 1950s, Orne had begun to explore the role of uncontrolled task-orienting cues in experimental research. He was primarily interested in the complex nature of hypnosis when he began this program of investigation and had observed that, at the conclusion of many of his hypnosis experiments, the subjects asked questions such as "Did I ruin the study?" By the use of sensitive postexperimental interviewing, he learned that what the subjects were asking was "Did I perform well in my role as experimental subject?" or "Did my behavior demonstrate what the study was designed to show?" That is, it appeared that the subjects were responding, at least in part, to what they interpreted as cues about what the experiment was "really" about and what the experimenter "wanted" to find out. Borrowing a concept from the theoretical work of Kurt Lewin (1935)—*Aufforderungscharakter* (or "demand value")— Orne (1959) coined the term **demand characteristics** to denote the subtle, uncontrolled task-orienting cues in an experimental situation. In an earlier paper, Sarbin (1944) had drawn an analogy with the Heisenberg effect in atomic physics to argue that the observation or measurement of behavior could alter the behavior observed. In fact, a similar idea had been anticipated by Rosenzweig (1933), whose work we discussed above, particularly his "motivational attitude" idea. Orne and his associates advanced this idea a giant step by demonstrating, in a series of ingenious studies, how demand characteristics could produce artifacts in the research.

In one early study, using college students in an introductory psychology course as the participants, Orne (1959) conducted a demonstration of hypnosis on several subjects. The demonstration subjects in one section of students were given the suggestion that upon entering a hypnotic trance, they would manifest "catalepsy of the dominant hand." All the students in this section were told that catalepsy of the dominant hand was a standard reaction of the hypnotized person, and the group's attention was called to the fact that the right-handed subject had catalepsy of the right hand and the left-handed subject had catalepsy of the left hand. In another section (the control group), the demonstration of hypnosis was carried out, but without a display of Orne's concocted "catalepsy" reaction. In the next phase of the study, Orne asked for volunteers for hypnosis from each section and, after they had been hypnotized, had them tested in such a way that the experimenter could not tell which lecture they had attended until after the completion of the experiment. Of the nine volunteers from the first section (the one in which catalepsy of the dominant hand had been demonstrated), five of them showed catalepsy of the dominant hand, two showed catalepsy of both hands, and two showed no catalepsy. None of the nine control subjects showed catalepsy of the dominant hand, but three of them showed catalepsy of both hands. Because catalepsy of the dominant hand (the reaction that Orne had invented) was known not to occur spontaneously, its occurrence in the first group but not in the second was interpreted by Orne as support for his demand characteristics theory. That three of the nine subjects in the control group spontaneously displayed catalepsy of both hands was explained by him in terms of the experimenters' repeated testing for this reaction, which Orne thought may have introduced its own set of implicit demand cues.

Orne referred to this cooperative behavior as the **good subject effect,** and he argued that subjects would often go to remarkable lengths to comply with demand characteristics. For example, at one point in his research on hypnosis he tried to devise a set of dull, meaningless tasks that participants who were not hypnotized would refuse to do or would try for only a short time and then abandon. One task consisted of adding hundreds of thousands of two-digit numbers. Five and a half hours after the subjects began, Orne gave up! Even when the subjects were told to tear each worksheet into a minimum of 32 pieces before going on to the next, they persisted in adding up the digits. Orne explained this behavior as the role enactment of volunteer subjects who reason that, no matter how trivial and inane the experimental task seems to them, it must surely have some important scientific purpose or they would not have been asked to participate in the first place. Thus, he theorized, they complied with the demand characteristics of the experiment in order to "further the cause of science" (Orne, 1962).

Orne gained another insight into the good subject effect when he asked a number of casual acquaintances to do an experimenter a favor and, on their acquiescence, asked them to do five push-ups. They seemed amazed and incredulous, and all responded "Why?" When he asked a similar group of individuals whether they would take part in an experiment and, on their acquiescence, asked them to do five push-ups, their typical response was "Where?" (Orne, 1962). What could account for the dramatic difference in responses? Orne theorized that people who agree to participate in an experiment implicitly agree to comply with whatever demand cues seem implicit in the experimental situation. Subjects are concerned about the outcome of the experiment in which they have agreed to participate. Consequently, they are motivated to play the role of the good subject who responds to overt and implicit cues in ways designed to validate the experimenter's hypothesis. Other researchers obtained similar kinds of effects, all suggesting compliance with demand characteristics. The phenomenon also seemed wide-ranging, as it was demonstrated in attitude change research, prisoners' dilemma games, verbal operant conditioning, testing, and on and on (for further discussion and citations, see Rosnow & Rosenthal, 1997, p. 68). Furthermore, Orne surmised, it is not possible to control for the good subject effect in the classic sense; what is needed is a means of ferreting out the demand characteristics in each experimental situation. In theory, he thought, having this information should allow researchers to interpret their data more accurately and, sometimes, even to circumvent the demand artifact in question.

Guided by this vision, Orne proposed that researchers use the subjects themselves to assist in the detection and interpretation of demand characteristics. It is important, he argued, not to attribute to demand characteristics even more potency than they possess, for that will surely lead to "a nihilistic view at least as naïve as that which denies the potential importance of these factors" (Orne, 1970, p. 260). In science, the proof of the pudding is in confronting a problem empirically, and thus, Orne showed that it was no longer necessary merely to speculate on the role of "errors of motivational attitude." In what he called a **quasi-control strategy,** his idea was to have some of the research subjects step out of the good subject role and act as "coinvestigators" in the search for truth. Orne proposed several techniques for having quasi-control subjects reflect on the experiment and tell how their behavior might be compromised or influenced by uncontrolled factors rather than by the controlled independent variable. One technique was to have subjects serve as their own quasi controls in postexperimental interviews. In these interviews, they were asked to disclose the factors that were important in determining their reactions in the experiment and to reveal their beliefs about, and perceptions of, the experiment and the experimenter. These subjects must be convinced that the study is over and that they are now playing the role of coinvestigators (or aides), or the data they provide should also be suspect as biased by demand characteristics.

In another use of quasi controls, called *preinquiry* by Orne, some of the prospective subjects are sampled and afterward are separated from the subject pool. The experimental procedures are then carefully described to these quasi controls, and they are asked to speculate on how they would be likely to behave in the experiment. Comparisons are later made between their projected role responses and the actual responses of the participating subjects. In this way, Orne theorized, it should be possible to get an insight into how the experimental outcome might be affected by the real subjects' guesses and role responses to how they *should* behave. Still another alternative used what Orne called a "sacrifice group" of quasi controls. These are people who are pulled out of the experiment at different points and questioned about their perceptions of the experiment up to that point. Another option discussed by others is to have the preinquiry individuals tell how they think they would react to different deception treatments. The idea here is that, if no differences are apparent between different intensities of deception, the least intense deception should be as effective as the most intense deception (Fisher & Fyrberg, 1994; Suls & Rosnow, 1981).

Orne noted the volunteer status of his research subjects, as well as the fact that they seemed to be remarkably cooperative. Insights like these inspired other researchers to compare volunteer subjects and nonvolunteer subjects (e.g., coerced participants or captive participants) on a range of tasks (Rosenthal & Rosnow, 1975), using volunteer status as a proxy for the "good subject." Horowitz (1969) observed that volunteers responded differently from nonvolunteers to fear-arousing communications in an attitude change experiment. In our earlier discussion of the Solomon design, we mentioned the finding that the volunteer status of subjects was also associated with reversals in pretest-treatment interactions in an attitude change experiment, the volunteers again being the more compliant participants (Rosnow & Suls, 1970). Kotses, Glaus, and Fisher (1974) reported volunteer biases in a study of physiological responses to random bursts of white noise, and Black, Schumpert, and Welch (1972) observed that perceptual-motor responses were also associated with subjects' volunteer status. In another study, the volunteer status of the participants in a verbal operant-conditioning study was associated with a greater degree of compliance with demand cues (Goldstein,

Rosnow, Goodstadt, & Suls, 1972). Volunteer bias has also been found in clinical and counseling studies (King & King, 1991; Strohmetz, Alterman, & Walter, 1990). We will have more to say about volunteer subjects and strategies for predicting the direction of the response bias in chapter 9, but it appears that volunteers for research participation tend to be more sensitive and accommodating to demand cues than are coerced subjects or captive nonvolunteers.

Interestingly, not all artifact researchers agreed with Orne's conception of the good subject effect. For example, Milton J. Rosenberg got into a spat with some leading cognitive dissonance theorists when he argued that an experimental design used in an important cognitive dissonance study had produced spurious effects resulting from the participants' anxieties about how they would be evaluated—which Rosenberg (1965) called **evaluation apprehension.** Based on a series of other experiments of his own, he found that when subjects worry that the experimenter plans to evaluate an aspect of their performance, they behave in ways designed to win the experimenter's approval or to avoid disapproval. Experiments in which some evaluation apprehension appeared likely were those containing an element of surprise or having an aura of mystery to them. The more explicit the cues, the more control the experimenter has in granting positive evaluation, and the less effortful the subjects' responses, the greater may be the resulting response bias due to the subjects' feelings of evaluation apprehension. One solution to this problem may be to ensure the confidentiality of the subjects' responses, on the assumption that individual subjects will then be less apprehensive and more forthcoming in their responses (e.g., Esposito, Agard, & Rosnow, 1984). However, in some research—for example, research on sensitive topics (such as sexual behavior and AIDS)—it may be exceedingly difficult to control for evaluation apprehension and related problems (e.g., Catania, Gibson, Chitwood, & Coates, 1990). It is also conceivable that in some (probably rare) experimental situations some subjects may feel a conflict between evaluation apprehension and the good subject effect (e.g., Rosnow, Goodstadt, Suls, & Gitter, 1973; Sigall, Aronson, & Van Hoose, 1970), in which case the evidence suggests that "looking good" may emerge as the predominant motivation of many subjects, as opposed to helping the cause of science (i.e., "doing good").

INTERACTIONAL EXPERIMENTER EFFECTS

In chapter 5 we spoke of noninteractional artifacts, that is, artifacts that are not directly associated with the interaction between the experimenter and the research subjects. Two general classes discussed in that chapter were interpreter and observer biases. The other side of this coin comprises five general classes of artifacts called **interactional experimenter effects** (Rosenthal, 1966, 1976). These artifacts are recognized by being attributable to some aspect of the interaction between experimenters and their subjects. We first briefly describe all five of these classes (i.e., biosocial attributes, psychosocial attributes, situational factors, modeling effects, and expectancy effects) and then discuss the fifth type and its control in greater detail. Researchers interested in learning more about the nature and control of subject and experimenter artifacts will find a fully detailed discussion of experimenter effects in Rosenthal's (1966, 1976) *Experimenter Effects in Behavioral Research* and a more recent theoretical and ethical overview in our book entitled *People Studying People* (Rosnow & Rosenthal, 1997).

First, *biosocial attributes* include the biological and social characteristics of experimenters, such as gender, age, and race. For example, a good deal of research has been reported showing that male and female experimenters sometimes obtain significantly different data from their subjects. It is not always possible to predict for any given type of experiment just how subjects' responses will be affected by the experimenter's gender, if indeed there is any effect at all. However, when such effects have occurred, it seems that the male and female experimenters behaved differently toward their subjects, thereby eliciting different responses because the experimenters had altered the experimental situation for the subjects (e.g., Barnes & Rosenthal, 1985). In one study, the male experimenters were found to be friendlier than the female experimenters. It was also found that 12% of the experimenters, overall, smiled at their male subjects, whereas 70% smiled at their female subjects (Rosenthal, 1967, 1976). A further finding was that smiling by the experimenters predicted the results. The lesson is that before we claim a gender difference in the results of behavioral research, we must make sure that male and female subjects were treated identically. If they were not, then gender differences in the results might be due not to constitutional or socialization variables, but to the fact that male and female subjects did not participate in the "same" experiment (i.e., they were treated differently).

Whereas biosocial attributes are usually readily accessible by inspection, the second class, termed *psychosocial attributes,* are readily accessible but not simply by inspection. These attributes include factors such as personality and temperament, which are often assessed more indirectly, frequently by the use of standard psychological tests or trained observers' judgments. For example, experimenters who differ in anxiety, approval need, hostility, authoritarianism, status, or warmth also tend to obtain different responses from their subjects. Experimenters higher in status generally have a tendency to elicit more conforming but less pleasant responses from their subjects, and experimenters who are warmer in their interactions with the subjects often obtain more competent and more pleasant responses. Examiners who act more warmly to people being administered a test of intelligence are apt to elicit better intellectual performance than are cooler examiners or examiners who are perceived as threatening. In simple tasks with ostensibly little meaning, the subjects' expectations may assume increasingly greater importance. The subjects who view experimenters more favorably may view the tasks more favorably, thus transforming a compellingly inane procedure into one that simply "must" have more value. An experimenter perceived as threatening might arouse feelings of evaluation apprehension, leading to a more defensive posture or simply distracting the subjects from the task and thus eliciting less-than-ideal performance.

Third are *situational effects*. More than experimenters' scores on a psychological test of anxiety or approval need, their status and warmth are defined and determined in part by the nature of the experimental situation and the particular subject being contacted. Experimenters who are acquainted with their subjects may behave differently toward them than toward unfamiliar subjects. Experimenters who are more experienced in conducting a given experiment often obtain different responses from subjects than do less experienced experimenters. Things that happen to experimenters during the course of their experiments, including the responses they obtain from their first few subjects, may also influence the experimenters' behavior, and in turn, those changes may lead to further changes in subjects' responses. When the first few subjects respond as they are expected to respond, the behavior of the experimenter may change in such a way as to influence the subsequent subjects to respond too often in the direction of the experimenter's hypothesis (Rosenthal, 1976). Thus, when subjects are run one at a time, we may want to block on (subdivide by) time periods, to see whether the results are similar at the beginning, middle, and end of the experimental trials.

A fourth type of interactional experimenter artifact is a **modeling effect.** It sometimes happens that before the experimenters conduct their studies, they try out the tasks that they will later have their subjects engage in. Although the evidence on this point is not all that clear, it would seem that, at least sometimes, the investigator's own performance becomes a factor in the subjects' performance. When the experimental stimuli are ambiguous, subjects' interpretations of their meaning may too often agree with the investigator's interpretations of the stimuli. The problem is that the experimenter's behavior, rather than the hypothesized psychological processes, may have produced the results (Rosenthal, 1976). In survey research, there is evidence that the interviewer's own opinion, attitude, or ideology may affect the responses obtained from the respondents. If a modeling effect occurs, it is most likely to be patterned on the interviewer's opinion or attitude, but in a minority of cases the subjects may respond in a direction opposite to that favored by the interviewer (Rosenthal, 1976). In laboratory studies, it appears there is a tendency for happier, affable, less tense experimenters to model their subjects negatively, and for less pleasant, more tense experimenters to model their subjects positively. Why this should be so is unclear, but one methodological implication may be to use more naturally "neutral" experimenters in order to reduce the possibility of modeling effects.

Generally speaking, the most critical control for all four classes of interactional artifacts above is woven into the fabric of science by the tradition of replication. This is also true of a fifth type of artifact, experimenter expectancy, but there are other ways of addressing this particular problem (which we discuss in the next section). The term *experimenter expectancy* takes its name from the idea that some expectation of how the research will turn out is virtually a constant in science. In the same way that the questioners of Clever Hans unintentionally altered their own behavior and that in turn affected the horse's responses, so can hypotheses, theories, or expectations that are held by experimenters lead them unintentionally to alter their behavior toward their subjects. We are speaking, then, of the investigator's hypothesis or expectancy as a **self-fulfilling prophecy,** but not exactly in the way this term was conceived of by its originator, Robert Merton (1948), who defined it as a "*false* definition of the situation evoking a new behavior which makes the originally false conception come *true*" (p. 195). By **experimenter expectancy effect,** we mean that the experimenter's expectation (true *or* false) may come to serve as a self-fulfilling prophecy, which can be conceived of as a type of interpersonal expectancy effect. That is, someone acting in accordance with a personal set of expectations treats another individual in such a manner as to increase the likelihood of eliciting behavior that conforms to the first person's expectations (e.g., Blanck, 1993). An example would be a teacher who believes certain pupils are especially bright and then acts toward these pupils more warmly, teaches them more material, and spends more time with them, behavior that, over time, results in greater gains in achievement for these students than would have occurred in the absence of the interpersonal expectation (Rosenthal & Jacobson, 1968).

EXPERIMENTER EXPECTANCY EFFECTS AND THEIR CONTROL

In one early study designed to demonstrate the effects of experimenters' expectancies on the results of their research, the experimenters were given rats that were to be taught to run a maze with the aid of visual cues (Rosenthal & Fode, 1963). Half the experimenters were told their rats had been specifically bred for maze brightness, and the remaining experimenters were told their rats had been bred for maze dullness. Actually, there were no differences between the rats assigned at random to each of the two groups. At the end of the experiment the results were clear. The rats run by the experimenters expecting brighter behavior showed learning significantly superior to that of the rats run by the experimenters expecting dull behavior. The study was later repeated, this time using a series of learning trials, each conducted in Skinner boxes (Rosenthal & Lawson, 1964). Half the experimenters were led to believe their rats were "Skinner box bright"; the other experimenters were led to believe their animals were "Skinner box dull." Once again, there were not really any differences in the two groups of rats, at least not until the results were analyzed at the end of the study. Then, the allegedly brighter rats really did perform better, and the alleged dullards really did perform more poorly. Neither of the animal studies showed any evidence that the student experimenters might have been falsifying their results. Thus, it could be concluded that the experimenters' expectations had acted not on the experimenters' evaluation of the animals' performance, but on the actual performance of the rats.

In the period since those two studies were conducted, literally hundreds of additional studies have examined the possible occurrence of expectancy effects both inside and outside the experimental lab (e.g., Harris & Rosenthal, 1985; Rosenthal & Rubin, 1978). By the beginning of the 1990s, there were over 450 studies. In a meta-analysis of 345 studies in the 1970s (Rosenthal & Rubin, 1978), the probability of no relation between experimenters' expectations and their subjects' subsequent behavior was smaller than .00000001. One analysis was designed to determine how many of the predicted results were significant at p equal to or less than .05 within each of eight different research areas. The results are shown in Table 7.8. The assumption was that, if the 345 had been a randomly selected sample of studies from a population of all possible studies for which the null hypothesis were true, we would expect 5% of the studies to achieve .05 significance by chance alone. The first column of numbers in Table 7.8 shows that all the proportions exceeded the expected value and that the median proportion of .39 is almost eight times larger than the expected value. Still, some unknown factors might have kept any negative results out of sight so that only these 345 studies were accessible. However, from a file-drawer analysis (the procedure is described in chapter 21), it was calculated that

TABLE 7.8
Expectancy effects in eight areas

Research area	Proportion of results that reached $p < .05$ in the predicted direction	Mean effect size in Cohen's d	Mean effect size in Pearson r
Lab interviews	.38	0.14	.07
Reaction time	.22	0.17	.08
Learning and ability	.29	0.54	.26
Person perception	.27	0.55	.27
Inkblot tests	.44	0.84	.39
Everyday situations	.40	0.88	.40
Psychophysical judgments	.43	1.05	.46
Animal learning	.73	1.73	.65
Median	.39	0.70	.33

it would take over 65,000 studies with null results to move the overall associated p to a barely acceptable .05. Other analyses concentrated on the size of the expectancy effect in each area, and those results are also listed in Table 7.8 as Cohen's d (Equation 2.4) and the Pearson r (described in detail in chapter 11).

Table 7.9 lists several strategies for controlling the effects of experimenters' expectancies and also notes one or more consequences of adopting these strategies (Rosenthal, 1979b; Rosenthal, Hall, DiMatteo, Rogers, & Archer, 1979). First, assume

TABLE 7.9
Strategies for the reduction of experimenter expectancy effects

1. Increasing the number of experimenters
   - Decreases learning of influence techniques
   - Helps to maintain "blindness"
   - Randomizes expectancies
   - Increases generality of results
2. Monitoring the behavior of experimenters
   - Sometimes reduces expectancy effects
   - Permits correction for unprogrammed behavior
   - Facilitates greater standardization of experimenter behavior
3. Analyzing experiments for order effects
   - Permits inference about changes in experimenter behavior
   - Permits correction for expectancy effects
4. Maintaining "blind" contact
   - Minimizes expectancy effects
5. Minimizing experimenter-subject contact
   - Minimizes expectancy effects
6. Employing expectancy control groups
   - Permits assessment of expectancy effects

that the experimenter unwittingly learns from the participants' responses how to influence them unintentionally. This learning takes time, and with fewer participants from whom to learn the unintentional communication system, the experimenter may learn less of the system. Therefore, by increasing the number of experimenters so that each experimenter works with fewer subjects, it may be possible to reduce the likelihood of expectancy effects. Having more experimenters also helps to maintain blind contact between the experimenters and the subjects (i.e., the experimenters are unaware of which of the subjects are receiving the experimental and control treatments). The fewer the participants contacted by an experimenter, the less the chance of an unwitting breakdown in the blind procedure. A further advantage of increasing the number of experimenters is that the positive and negative expectancies may act like random errors that cancel one another. And finally, even beyond expectancy bias, we can be more confident of a result obtained by a larger number of experimenters than of a result obtained by only one experimenter.

Second, monitoring the behavior of experimenters may not by itself eliminate expectancy biases, but it may help in identifying unprogrammed expectancy behaviors. If we make our observations during a preexperimental phase, we may be able to use this information to select good experimenters. The problem is that this selection procedure may be unintentionally biased, and therefore, it may be preferable simply to assign experimenters to experiments randomly. Nevertheless, monitoring may alleviate some of the other biasing effects of experimenters noted previously, and it should facilitate greater standardization among the experimenters.

Third, analyzing experiments for order effects enables us to compare early results with later results. We can do a median split of the participants seen by each experimenter and compare the behavior of the participants in each half. Are the means of the groups the same? Is the amount of variability in the performance of the participants the same in both halves? We may also be able to correct for expectancy effects. In some cases, for example, we will find expectancies distributed only dichotomously; either a result is expected or it is not. At other times, we will have an ordering of expectancies in terms of ranks or absolute values. In any of these cases, we can correlate the results obtained by the experimenters with their expectancies. If the correlation is trivial in size, we are reassured that expectancy effects were probably not operating. If the correlation is substantial, we conclude that expectancy effects did occur. These can be "corrected for" or at least analyzed by such statistical methods as partial correlation (chapter 11) or blocking strategies (chapter 16).

The fourth strategy is based on the idea that, if the experimenter does not know whether the subject is in the experimental or the control group, the experimenter can have no validly based expectancy about how the person *should* respond. In drug trials, for example, in a **single-blind study** the participants do not know the group or condition (e.g., drug vs. placebo) to which they have been randomly assigned. In a **double-blind study,** both the experimenters and the subjects are kept from knowing what drug has been administered. Psychologists have been slow to adopt the double-blind method for other than drug trials, but when it is feasible, it is more than warranted to minimize the possibility of expectancy effects. A problem, however, is that single-blind and double-blind methods are not very easy to implement. Imagine a study in which anxiety

TABLE 7.10
Basic expectancy control design

Treatment conditions	Expectancy conditions	
	Experimental treatment	Control treatment
Experimental	Group A	Group B
Control	Group C	Group D

is the independent variable. People who have just been through an anxiety-arousing event, or who have scored high on a test of anxiety, may behave in an identifiable way in an experiment. The "blind" experimenters may then covertly "diagnose" the level of anxiety. If they know the hypothesis, they may unwittingly bias the results of the experiment in the expected direction or, by bending over backward to avoid bias, "spoil" the study. A score of subtle signs (the subject's arrival time, fidgeting behavior, and so on) may break down the most carefully arranged double-blind study.

A fifth strategy is to minimize the experimenter-subject contact, perhaps easier than trying to maintain blind contact. The day may come when the elimination of the experimenter, in person, will be a widespread, well-accepted practice. By computer, we can generate hypotheses, sample hypotheses, sample the experimental treatment conditions from a population of potential manipulations, select our participants randomly, invite their participation, schedule them, instruct them, record and analyze their responses, and even partially interpret and report the results. In experiments that require human interaction, it may still be possible to minimize the contact. For example, we might use an ordinary tape recorder and have a screen interposed between the experimenter and the participants.

The final strategy is the use of **expectancy control groups.** Although expensive to implement if many experimenters are randomly assigned to conditions, the advantage of this method is that we can compare the effects of experimenter expectancies with the effects of some other behavioral variable. Table 7.10 shows the most basic expectancy control design, in which there are two row levels of the behavioral research variable and two column levels of the experimenter expectancy variable. Group A is the condition in which the experimental treatment is administered to the subjects by a data collector who expects the occurrence of the treatment effect. In Group D, the absence of the experimental treatment is associated with a data collector who expects the nonoccurrence of the treatment effect. Group B is the condition in which subjects receiving the experimental treatment are contacted by an experimenter who does not expect a treatment effect. Subjects in Group C do not receive the experimental treatment and are contacted by an experimenter who expects a treatment effect.

Table 7.11 shows the results of a study by J. R. Burnham (1966) that used the expectancy design in Table 7.10. Burnham had 23 experimenters each run one rat in a T-maze discrimination problem. About half the rats had been lesioned by the removal of portions of the brain; the remaining animals had received only sham surgery, which involved cutting through the skull but no damage to the brain tissue. The purpose of the study was explained to the experimenters as an attempt to learn the effects of

TABLE 7.11
Expectancy control design used by Burnham (1966) to study discrimination learning in rats

	Expectancy conditions		
Treatment conditions	"Lesioned"	"Nonlesioned"	Sum
Lesioning of brain	46.5	49.0	95.5
No lesioning of brain	48.2	58.3	106.5
Sum	94.7	107.3	

Note: Cell values in this table are transformations of ranks to normal deviates, using a procedure described by Walker and Lev (1953, pp. 424–425), on the assumption that the underlying metric is normally distributed. The reason the cell values do not resemble Z scores (discussed in chapter 10) is that the transformation of ranks is based on a mean of 50 and standard deviation of 10. The range will vary, depending on the number of ranked scores. In Burnham's study, the sample size was 23; the top-ranked rat having a standard score of 70 and the bottom ranked rat, a standard score of 30. Thus, higher cell values in this table imply better performance in the T-maze discrimination problem.

lesions on discrimination learning. The design manipulated the expectancies by labeling each rat as lesioned or nonlesioned. Some of the really lesioned rats were labeled accurately as "lesioned" (the upper-left cell), and some were falsely labeled as "nonlesioned" (the upper-right cell). Some nonlesioned rats were labeled accurately (the lower-right cell), and some were falsely labeled as "lesioned" (the lower-left cell). Table 7.11 shows the standard scores of the ranks of performance in each of the four conditions (higher scores denote superior performance). Animals that had been lesioned did not perform as well as those that had not been lesioned, and animals that were believed to be lesioned did not perform as well as those that were thought to be nonlesioned. What makes this experiment of special interest is that the effects of expectancy were similar to those of the actual removal of brain tissue. Thus, it emphasizes the value of separating expectancy effects from the effects of the independent variable of interest, to avoid misrepresenting the causal impact of either variable.

CONCLUDING COMMENTARY

We do not want to end this chapter by leaving readers with a princess-and-the-pea image of human subjects as overly sensitive and overly responsive to the slightest experimental variations. It is possible for even the most outrageous manipulation to have no effect, and it is not easy to foresee when biasing effects will actually emerge (Sommer, 1968). In 1928, H. B. Hovey described administering an intelligence test to 171 people divided into two groups. One group took the test in a quiet room, and the other group took it in a second room with seven bells, five buzzers, a 550-watt spotlight, a 90,000-volt rotary-spark gap, a phonograph, two organ pipes of varying pitch, three metal whistles, a 55-pound circular saw mounted on a wooden frame, a photographer taking pictures, and four students doing acrobatics! Events in the second room were choreographed so that a number of distractions sometimes occurred concurrently and at other times the room was quiet. The remarkable result reported by

Hovey was that the group in the second room scored as well as the group in the first. Although we do not know whether anyone ever replicated Hovey's finding, we assume that it was accurately reported. Nonetheless, one major purpose of this chapter was to sensitize researchers to the kinds of threats to validity of the causal inferences discussed here. When we act as though we are oblivious to those threats, our science and the society that supports it both suffer.

As another poignant illustration, the physicist Richard Feynman (1999) described an incident in a psychology department in which an experimenter was running rats through mazes consisting of a long corridor with doors along one side where the rat entered, and doors along the other side in which the food was placed. The experimenter was trying to condition rats to enter the third door down from wherever they started, but try as he might, the rats invariably went immediately to the door where the food had been on the previous trial. The experimenter suspected that an uncontrolled variable of some kind was cueing the rats, so he painted the doors, making sure they appeared exactly alike. That did not work, so he then used chemicals to change the smell after each trial, and when that still did not work, he tried altering the lighting and the arrangement in the laboratory. It was maddening, until he finally figured out that the rats could tell which door they had previously entered by the way the floor sounded to them. The way he was finally able to fool them was to cover the corridor in sand, so the rats had to go in the third door if they wanted the food. Feynman told how, years later, he looked into the history of this research and learned that the control criteria developed by that experimenter were never absorbed by colleagues of the experimenter. They just went right on running rats in the same old way, oblivious to the methodological insights because the experimenter had not seemed to discover anything about rats. However, as Feynman (p. 215) noted, the experimenter had discovered things you have to do to find out something about rats.

In the 1970s, many psychological researchers expressed being overwhelmed by all the plausible sources of subject- and experimenter-related artifacts. We once compared this situation with a juggler's trying to balance dozens of spinning plates on the ends of sticks. The juggler has to keep running back and forth to keep them all balanced, just as the researchers in the 1970s felt they had to concentrate on one source of artifacts after another in order to keep everything properly balanced. What was needed, it seemed, was a conceptual pulling together of what was known about demand cues and artifacts within the framework of a workable, comprehensive model. Such a model has evolved in a collaboration by Rosnow successively with Leona Aiken, Daniel J. Davis, and David Strohmetz (Rosnow & Aiken, 1973; Rosnow & Davis, 1977; Strohmetz & Rosnow, 1994). Instead of focusing on specific artifact-producing variables, this "mediational model" concentrates on intervening (or mediational) steps in a theorized causal chain from the sources of uncontrolled task-orienting cues to their resulting artifacts. Readers interested in learning about the model will find a general description in Rosnow and Rosenthal (1997, ch. 4) and an operationalization and elegant series of studies in C. T. Allen (2004).

Another intriguing aspect of the artifact work was mentioned by McGuire (1969), who described the three stages in the life of an artifact as ignorance, coping, and exploitation. At first, most researchers seem unaware of the artifact and deny its existence even when it is pointed out. Next, they view it as a nuisance variable and look for ways to isolate, eliminate, or control it. Finally, they realize that it can also be exploited as an independent variable of substantive interest. For example, we mentioned how the role of demand characteristics has evolved, so that what were once regarded as mere nuisance variables are now perceived as powerful substantive agents with practical implications in their own right. Demand characteristics are now conceived of as a potent source of behavioral change and accommodation in a wide variety of circumstances, including not only the experimenter-subject interaction in psychological research but also therapeutic change in the clinical situation (Orne & Bauer-Manley, 1991; Orne & Whitehouse, 2000). As Orne wisely noted many years ago, to understand the meaning of any social interaction, it is vital to take into consideration the role of demand characteristics in each and every situation. The same lesson applies to empirical research on the role of interpersonal expectations, which took root in the work on experimenter expectancy effects and has stimulated the burgeoning growth of interpersonal insights. In fact, the awareness of sources of artifacts has enhanced our understanding not only of the experimental setting but also of the nature of behavior and of the limitations of understanding.

Finally, we want to return to a point made in chapter 2: Most researchers would agree that it is simply impossible to design an experiment that will forever be free of plausible rival explanations. Probative experiments are designed to test hypotheses, theories, and models anchored in the experimenter's experiential world; their conceptual limits can never be exactly known because it is only by the discovery of experiences outside their jurisdiction that their boundaries are revealed. In spite of this uncertainty, our hypotheses, theories, and models form a constituency of intellectual assumptions about the world in which we live. Furthermore, our hypotheses, theories, and models are idealizations of reality, which restrict or stylize reality by forgoing all those features that cannot be entirely captured by the formulation. If there is no such thing as an experiment that can be confidently regarded as entirely free of alternative explanations, then the falsificationist view is an oversimplification of the way that scientific knowledge evolves. A paper by Brinberg, Lynch, and Sawyer (1992) makes the further point that "both findings consistent and findings inconsistent with a theory's predictions can be informative" (p. 140), and using a Bayesian analysis of hypothesis testing, they showed that both a priori and post hoc explanations may have equal merit in certain circumstances. Though internal validity may be viewed by most behavioral and social researchers as the sine qua non of valid causal inference, the reality may be that it is an ideal that is forever beyond our grasp. There is always the possibility that some theory or observation awaiting discovery will threaten the internal validity of even the most brilliantly designed experiment.

CHAPTER 8

NONRANDOMIZED RESEARCH AND FUNCTIONAL RELATIONSHIPS

NONRANDOMIZED AND QUASI-EXPERIMENTAL STUDIES

Randomization is not always possible in human subject research, and researchers have used a number of alternative strategies that sometimes (under ideal conditions of implementation) serve as an approximation of randomized controlled experiments. Campbell and Stanley (1966) introduced the term **quasi-experimental** to refer to research designs for data collection that are "something like" randomized experiments but lack "the full control over the scheduling of experimental stimuli (the *when* and to *whom* of exposure and the ability to randomize exposures)" that make randomized experiments possible (p. 34). Their seminal chapter (Campbell & Stanley, 1963), which became the basis of their influential monograph (Campbell & Stanley, 1966), appeared in a handbook on teaching and educational practices. Campbell and Stanley (1966) insisted that randomized experiments (they called them "true experiments") were

> the only means for settling disputes regarding educational practice, . . . the only way of verifying educational improvements, and . . . the only way of establishing a cumulative tradition in which improvements can be introduced without the danger of a faddish discard of old wisdom in favor of inferior novelties. (p. 2)

Campbell and Stanley were not alone in eschewing studies that did not use active interventions and randomized controls to establish causal relationships, but they conceded that it remained an ideal that was impossible to implement in many situations.

For example, it would be ethically absurd to think that we could randomly assign nonsmokers to an experimental condition that required them to smoke for many years. Instead, we might plan an observational study in which we would measure the association of heart attack and lung cancer with smoking. *Association* implies covariation, but it is not the same thing as causation. It is possible that some hidden variable might induce people to smoke, and that that variable might also give them heart attacks and lung cancer. Using sophisticated statistical procedures (noted at the end of this chapter), we may be able to adjust the results of large sample studies by matching the nonsmokers and the smokers. Then we might compare the results of our observations with those of animal experiments using single-case designs, and also with the results of other quasi-experimental and survey studies, to see whether there is a convergence of evidence. This is the spirit of *methodological pluralism* that we alluded to in chapter 1, that is, the assumption that, because all research designs are limited in some ways, we need to draw on multiple methods of empirical investigation.

In this chapter we describe several general types of nonrandomized studies, all of which are, by implication, concerned with causal effects. We say "by implication" because the tradition in some areas is not to speak of "causal effects," but to finesse the metaphysical conundrum regarding the nature of *causation* by referring to *functional relationships between independent and dependent variables*. For example, in single-case behavioral research on learning and conditioning, researchers refer to *stimuli* and the *responses* to them (Skinner, 1938, p. 41); they seldom mention "causal effects" but quite often mention "functions of stimuli," following in the tradition of Skinner (1938, p. 232). In Sidman's (1960) incisive text in this area, he stated that "a sufficient number of experiments have demonstrated that the behavior of the individual subject is an orderly function of a large number of so-called independent variables" (p. 49). Sidman provided a detailed rationale for single-case experiments—which are reminiscent in many ways of lab experiments in chemistry, biology, and physics. That they are called *experiments* implies that they are focused on the operation of causal relationships (what is *responsible* for what, or what *causes* what), but many methodologists, adopting Campbell and Stanley's (1966) labeling convention, refer to them as "quasi-experimental" on the assumption that they are similar to, but not exactly like, randomized experiments.

In particular, we will discuss four types of nonrandomized strategies. The first type, *nonequivalent groups designs,* resemble between-groups experiments except that the researcher has no control over how the subjects (or other sampling units) are assigned to different groups. In clinical trials, a popular (but potentially perilous) variation on this strategy is *historical control trials,* in which the control group is based on the nonrandomly selected archival records of patients diagnosed with a disease similar to the disease of those in the experimental treatment group. A second nonrandomized approach, *interrupted time-series designs,* uses large numbers of consecutive outcome measures that are interrupted by a critical intervention, the objective being to assess the causal impact of the intervention by comparing before and after measurements. A third approach, *single-case studies,* has (as noted above) played a prominent role in the exploration of behavioral learning and conditioning. Single-case designs are also used as detection experiments in biological and medical areas. This approach, similar in some ways to the interrupted time-series study, is characterized by the repeated observation of only one or a few units while one or more behavioral manipulations are introduced and withdrawn. A fourth approach, which is really a kind of "catchall category," is generally described as consisting of *correlational designs.* It is characterized by the simultaneous observation of interventions (or X treatments) and their possible Y outcomes, so that *correlation* in this case refers to the retrospective covariation of X and Y.

Some of the procedures used involve between-groups observations and others, within-subject observations. The tracking of the variable of interest over successive periods of time is sometimes referred to as **diachronic research.** An example would be longitudinal research on child and adult development, in which the same people are observed repeatedly over the life span. The name for studies that take a slice of time and examine behavior only at one point is **synchronic research.** Most experimental studies are illustrative of synchronic research. As noted above, the chapter concludes with a discussion of a statistical matching procedure for controlling extraneous variation in studies in which causal effects are of interest, but in which the researcher has no control over the assignment of subjects to conditions. In this procedure, so-called *propensity scores* take into account all of the information that is available, and we "match" the nonrandomized groups on all these variables (Rosenbaum & Rubin, 1983a; Rubin, 1988). Of course, there may be variables that we do not know about, but that might have produced relevant observed causal effects. Once again, what we mean by a *causal effect* is that something happens (Y) because of something else that happened (X), so that X was not only prior to Y but was also presumably responsible for Y.

NONEQUIVALENT GROUPS AND HISTORICAL CONTROLS

Another defining characteristic of **nonequivalent-groups designs,** in addition to their resemblance to nonrandomized between-groups experiments, is that there is usually a pre and post observation or measurement. Suppose that, in a traffic safety project designed to reduce drinking and driving, a court-ordered treatment program is to be evaluated by researchers (Vaught, 1977). The objective of the project is to compare four conditions: (a) drug therapy using Antabuse (which causes an unpleasant reaction when alcohol is consumed); (b) group psychotherapy administered by clinical psychologists; (c) a volunteer program along the lines of Alcoholics Anonymous; and (d) a zero-control condition (no treatment of any kind). A number of complications make it impossible to use a randomizing procedure to assign the individuals to groups. One problem is that those who operate the volunteer program will accept only participants who attend of their own accord; they refuse to accept randomly assigned nonvolunteers. A second problem is that the judge feels a legal and moral obligation to assign the worst offenders to either a drug or a group psychotherapy condition and is adamant about not assigning the worst offenders to the zero-control group. A third problem is that the administrator at the institution conducting the research is concerned about risks inherent in the use of random assignment. Her fear is that the institution may be sued by repeat offenders who find themselves assigned to a condition not to their liking, or by future victims of participants assigned to the zero-control condition.

Difficulties like these are not uncommon in field experiments. The problem is that, in employing a nonequivalent-groups design, researchers can expect participants in different conditions to differ because of self-selection or assignment biases because the assignment to groups is uncontrolled. Researchers use alternative methods to increase the likelihood that the groups will be comparable, but these methods are not without problems of their own in many cases. For example, one alternative is to try to overcome the objections to random assignment by proposing randomization *after* assignment (Vaught, 1977). In our example, the assignment might be made to each of the three treatment groups on the basis of a group decision process involving the judge, the institutional administrator, the volunteer program coordinator, and the researchers. Afterward, each group of participants might be randomly divided into experimental and control subgroups. The experimental subgroups would receive the experimental treatment, and the controls would receive nothing. Within these groups, the experimental and control subgroups should be roughly comparable because each experimental subgroup is naturally paired with its own control subjects. Once the experimental treatments have ended, the control subjects would receive them (i.e., in a wait-list control design). One nagging problem, however, is that the treatment of those in the wait-list control group is delayed for a significant period of time. The ethical and legal reasons that were raised for why we should not randomize to begin with may also prevent us from using randomization to determine which subjects will have to wait for their treatment to begin. Moreover, using no-treatment controls is usually ethically questionable when some standard treatment is known to be better than no treatment at all. There are situations, however, in which wait-list controls may be ethically quite defensible. Those are the situations in which the resources to administer the treatment to all the subjects/patients are simply unavailable. Wait-list controls have been used, for example, in psychotherapy research where there were too few psychotherapists available to treat all the subjects/patients. Under those conditions, randomization to treatment now versus treatment later seemed to be a fair and realistic way to cope with the lack of resources.

Ethical and legal objections to depriving some people of the benefits of the experimental treatment, or concerns that the experimental treatment might be ineffective or counterproductive, have led to the use of historical controls in many clinical studies with nonequivalent-groups designs. **Historical controls** (also described as *literature controls* because they are retrieved from file records) are recently treated patients all of whom suffered from the same disorder. Proponents of the use of historical controls argue that it is advantageous on logistic and ethical grounds, in that not only is it less costly than a fully randomized design, but it also provides results more rapidly without exposing patients to possibly ineffective treatments. However, in an important paper, Sacks, Chalmers, and Smith (1982) compared randomized control trials (RCT) with historical control trials (HCT) in six areas of medical research and found the HCT dangerously flawed. The HCT typically reported clinical treatments to be effective, whereas the RCT usually reported no statistically significant beneficial effects of the treatments. Sacks et al. noted that the RCT were generally low-power studies (i.e., using not enough units) and thus subject to *false-negative conclusions,* in which real differences presumably went undetected. Although the treated patients seemed to respond similarly in both HCT and RCT, the historical controls tended to be worse off than the control groups in RCT. Thus, the HCT had a tendency to imply beneficial effects of the treatment procedures. Furthermore, poor-risk patients in HCT were often excluded from treatment or, if selected for treatment, might "not be selected for the report of the treatment" (p. 237). An example of this mystifying reporting procedure was documented in an earlier paper noting that in uncontrolled trials of cancer therapy, there were frequently higher proportions of patients listed as "nonevaluable" than in RCT (Block, Schneiderman, Chalmers, & Lee, 1975). As a consequence, Sacks et al. concluded, the HCT were often uninterpretable and dangerously misleading. Moreover, the accuracy of HCT left little room for improvement, as "the data presented suggest that such biases in patient selection may irretrievably bias the outcome of the HCT" (Sacks et al., 1982, p. 237).

Before we leave this discussion of clinical trials, we want to repeat one more point, and that is the problem that pooled effects (also called *net effects*) may often mask true individual effects (we made a similar point in the previous chapter). It is standard practice in randomized drug and clinical trials for the research to be conducted in more than one medical center or hospital. Because the sample sizes are often relatively small in each setting, the principal investigators may simply cumulate the results as a way of improving the overall statistical power and then report only the net effects. Though this practice has a long history (Turner, 1997), it can lead to spurious conclusions because of a statistical irony now known as **Simpson's paradox**—which, according to Pearl (2000), was recognized by Karl Pearson in the late 19th century. In general, the paradox is that bivariate statistical relationships may be reversed by the inclusion of other factors in the analysis. Pearl's interesting example was the hypothetical finding that students who smoked got higher grades than nonsmokers, but when the data were adjusted for age, the smokers actually got lower grades in every age group (p. 78). Here is a quite different illustration of ours: Suppose we have the results of three studies, each with three subjects, and with the X and Y scores listed in Table 8.1. The correlation of these X and Y scores in each of the studies is $r_{xy} = -1.0$, but when we combine the nine scores, we find $r_{xy} = +1.0$, which is the opposite result. The lesson is that raw data should not be pooled before the individual results are first examined to ensure that there is good justification for looking at the net effects. Unfortunately, it is a lesson that has not been fully absorbed by many biomedical researchers, as

TABLE 8.1
Hypothetical results of three studies

Study A			Study B			Study C		
Subject	X	Y	Subject	X	Y	Subject	X	Y
1	10	12	1	100	102	1	1000	1002
2	11	11	2	101	101	2	1001	1001
3	12	10	3	102	100	3	1002	1000
r_{xy}	-1.00			-1.00			-1.00	

reporting only the pooled results and not reporting the individual center data is still a common practice in the leading medical journals.

INTERRUPTED TIME SERIES AND THE AUTOREGRESSIVE INTEGRATED MOVING AVERAGE

In **interrupted time-series designs** the effects of an intervention are inferred from sampled measurements obtained at different time intervals before and after the intervention is introduced. The data structure is called a *time series* because there is a single data point for each point in time, and it is called an *interrupted* time series because, presumably, there is a clear-cut dividing line at the beginning of the intervention (Judd & Kenny, 1981). In order to describe these data the researcher tries to choose a sampling interval that will capture the effects of interest, although when there is a finite number of data points and the data are not very costly to collect and store, it is possible to work with all the relevant data points. If not, the researcher must balance the risks of too-frequent and too-infrequent sampling, that is, between being potentially wasteful and losing some of the essential features (Diggle, 1990, p. 2). Time-series analysis is a branch of statistics, and the methodology for analyzing data and using the results for modeling and forecasting causal effects is specialized beyond the focus of this text. However, we will summarize an example of an interrupted time-series study in order to give a sense of how the data were analyzed. This study was conducted by Diana DiNitto, a social welfare professor who was interested in the effects of government-mandated changes in the food stamp purchase requirement of 1977 (DiNitto, 1983). One of the effects of the mandated changes was to increase the number of qualified participants by awarding them a bonus equivalent to the monthly value of the stamps for which they were eligible. DiNitto studied the food stamp program participation in one state, Florida, in order to evaluate the impact of the 1977 law.

The first step in DiNitto's analysis was to define the period of observations in this interrupted time-series design. She selected for her analysis the period from March 1972 to December 1981, a period that enabled her to examine food stamp participation before, during, and following the 1977 law's initiation. The next step was to obtain the data to be analyzed, but there were four important considerations. First, there had to be a sufficient number of observations and time points—usually 100, but no fewer than 50—in order to use the data-analytic method she chose (the Box-Jenkins procedure, described below). Second, she had to observe the same units throughout the analysis to ensure that the observations and the time points were equally spaced. She could not, for example, take monthly observations one year and then quarterly observations another year. Third, the time points had to be sensitive to the particular effects being studied. If there were a drop in food stamp recipients one week each month, the time points should reflect such variations. Fourth, the measurements should not fluctuate very much as a result of instrumentation changes (i.e., the observations would have to be reliable). The final step was to use a procedure called ARIMA (for autoregressive integrated moving average) to assess change (Box & Jenkins, 1970).

ARIMA proceeds in three steps: identification of an underlying model of serial effects; estimation of the model parameters; and checking the fitted model (cf. Diggle,

1990, pp. 165–187). DiNitto began by considering three possible underlying models. One model implied a sharp increase in participation in the program followed by maintenance of the new level. Given a hypothetical mean of 3 for the pretreatment series, we might visualize this model as 3, 3, 3, 5, 5, 5, 5, 5. The second possibility she considered was that there might be gradual, constant improvements in participation. This model might be visualized as 3, 3, 3, 4.5, 4.5, 5, 5, 5.5, in which the series after the intervention shows a drift upward. The third model implied what is called a **pulse function**—an abrupt change lasting only a short time, for example, 3, 3, 3, 5, 4, 3, 3, 3, in which the effect pulses upward but then reverts to the preintervention level.

The third step was to evaluate the efficacy of each of the three models. There were some technical considerations to deal with first. In later chapters we refer to the "IID normal" assumptions that underlie the use of certain statistical tests, and there are similar kinds of assumptions underlying the use of ARIMA. We will note two considerations as a way of acquainting readers with the terminology of this procedure. One important assumption is that a series of observations must be **stationary.** That is, it is assumed that the integer values of the observations fluctuate normally about the mean, as opposed to systematically drifting upward or downward. Most time-series observations, however, do show systematic increases or decreases in the level of the series, referred to as a **secular trend.** For statistical purposes, a secular trend can be made stationary by **differencing,** which consists of subtracting the first observation from the second, the second from the third, and so forth. In the series 2, 3, 4, 5, 6, for example, differencing would give us: $3 - 2 = 1; 4 - 3 = 1; 5 - 4 = 1; 6 - 5 = 1$ (which has no secular trend). Mathematically, differencing does not affect the actual pattern of the results, only how the data are entered into the time-series analysis. A problem, however, is that we forfeit an observation in this series; that is, differencing results in a loss of some data.

Another consideration concerns what is termed **autocorrelation,** which refers to whether the data points or observations are dependent on one another (*autocorrelated*) or instead can be assumed to be independent. In time-series analysis, a distinction is made between two kinds of autocorrelations: *regular,* which describes the dependency of adjacent observations or data points on one another, and *seasonal,* which describes the dependency of observations separated by one period or cycle (e.g., biannual separation; Cook & Campbell, 1979). If food stamp recipients one month received them the previous month and the month before, the data points are regularly autocorrelated. We must allow for (or "correct for") this autocorrelation so as not to increase the risk of Type I error. After doing all this, DiNitto concluded that her first model provided the best fit for the interrupted time-series data. The actual results in this study were that the new law was associated with a sharp increase of 5 percent (12,117 households) to Florida's food stamp program.

SINGLE-CASE EXPERIMENTAL DESIGNS

Single-case experimental studies also involve repeated observations, but on a single unit (a *case*) in most diagnostic studies or a few units in exploratory and hypothesis-testing studies. The treatment or intervention (characterized by some behavioral or cognitive control manipulation) is generally under the control of the experimenter.

Many different designs have been used in this kind of research, but the simplest ones are reminiscent of the causal reasoning one experiences in everyday life. As an illustration, suppose your hand has been bitten by a dog. You go to a doctor, who prescribes a tetanus shot and an oral antibiotic. You ask the doctor to give the tetanus shot in your bad arm so that you have your good arm to use. But the doctor points out that if she did so and you had a reaction to the tetanus, she would not be able to separate it from the possible continued reaction to the dog bite—which could, in the worst case, also cause the arm, not the hand, to swell. For this reason, she gives the shot in your good arm, so that any swelling caused by an allergy to the tetanus will not be confounded with a possible reaction to the dog bite. Her causal reasoning will be based on a comparison of her before and after observations, so her strategy is similar to an interrupted time-series design (cf. Campbell & Stanley, 1966). One big difference is that interrupted time-series studies call for much larger numbers of repeated observations so that statistical analyses like ARIMA can be used. Traditionally, single-case researchers have been more interested in inspecting graphs of individual behavioral trends (or in neuroscience, trends in brain imaging responses, for example), or even possibly pooled curves based on averaged results, rather than computing significance tests. As one leading researcher argued, "If the effect of treatment is not sufficiently substantial to be detected by visual inspection . . . then the treatment applied is not clinically potent and its controlling effects have not been clearly documented (Hersen, 1982, p. 196). Nonetheless, it is also common to see p values reported for within-subjects analyses in some fields in which these designs are used.

There are many papers, chapters, books, and standard references that provide a rationale for single-case research on learning and conditioning of behavior and the special nomenclature associated with this strategy of investigation, beginning with the seminal work of B. F. Skinner (1938, 1953, 1957). The idea of experimenting with a single organism by scheduling and removing different conditions has been traced back to the 19th century and the work of the French physiologist Claude Bernard (1865/1957), who argued that medical practice could be based on diagnostic reasoning by means of a kind of single-case experimental strategy (Hineline & Lattal, 2000). To illustrate, he described how he had diagnosed that a starving rabbit had survived on its own stored nutrients; he then demonstrated by manipulating the physiological state of the animal. As a more contemporary illustration of the diagnostic use of single-case methodology, Terry L. Rose (1978) was interested in the "functional relationship" between a child's ingestion of artificial food colors and subsequent hyperactive behavior. Earlier studies had provided mixed results and had been criticized on methodological grounds. Rose decided to use a double-blind design to diagnose the effects of a particular artificial food color ingested by two 8-year-old children who had previously been on a restricted diet. The independent variable was an oatmeal-type cookie containing either the questionable food color or no additive, and the dependent variables were duration of attention, out-of-seat frequency (a measure of fidgetiness), and physical aggression. Each child's behavior was recorded by two independent observers, and the children's parents were asked to fill in a daily checklist and to keep a log of informal observations. The parents (but not the independent observers) knew the intent of the study but (like the observers) were blind to the sequencing of the two types of cookies, which looked identical. Unfortunately, the results were confounded because of dietary infractions during the course of the study, though the graphic results did suggest a functional relationship between food color and hyperactivity as hypothesized. More recently, Morgan and Morgan (2001) proposed the applicability of single-case designs in managed-care programs.

The use of single-case designs in clinical, counseling, organizational, and educational settings is a subject of considerable scholarly discourse (e.g., Barlow, 1984; Hersen & Barlow, 1976; Hineline, 2000; Johnston & Pennypacker, 1993; Kazdin & Tuma, 1982). Whether they are used as a diagnostic or a hypothesis-testing strategy, the hallmark of all single-case designs is that the individual subject's behavior is first assessed under certain baseline conditions against which any subsequent changes in behavior can be evaluated after an environmental treatment is manipulated (Hersen, 1982). For example, in learning and conditioning research, one popular design is the A-B-A (also called a **reversal design**), where A is the no-treatment (baseline) phase and B is the treatment phase. If the treatment is observed to have a beneficial effect, the sequence may be extended to end on the B phase rather than the A phase (i.e., A-B-A-B). A more complex design with two treatments would be A-B-BC-B, where B and C might refer to two different clinical or educational treatments, so that there are repeated observations before B or C are introduced, then during treatment B, next during the combination of B and C, and finally when only B is operating. The purpose of this design is to tease out the effect of B both in combination with C and apart from C.

In choosing the baseline the researcher looks for an orderly, relatively stable pattern of behavior during the initial period of observation. Experience has taught researchers to look for different baseline patterns, however. For example, one person's baseline might consist of steadily worsening behavior, and another's might consist of steadily improving behavior, or even a consistently variable pattern. Suppose a child is increasingly belligerent and the purpose of the experiment is to see whether a particular treatment might reverse this baseline trend, or a child periodically engages in disruptive antics (i.e., high baseline variability) and the treatment procedure is intended to eliminate the negative behavior and stabilize positive behavior. The A phase, in which the baseline pattern is first identified, thus requires a sufficient number of data points to establish the pattern of negative and positive behavior. In some cases multiple baselines might even be established for different behaviors that are to be targeted and evaluated (Hersen, 1982). For example, both disruptive antics and tic behavior might be targeted in the same child. Although intersubject variability is usually of less interest than intrasubject variability (because the treatment is focused on a particular subject), if the objective of the investigation is to generalize to other individuals and other settings, then replications across persons and settings would be essential. Nonetheless, the philosophy of most single-case research is that the statistical averaging of people washes out individual differences, so it is important to establish baseline characteristics and not be blind to the vicissitudes and idiosyncrasies of individuals.

Among the advantages of single-case studies is that they are processual, which means that they are focused not just on effects measured at one point in time, but instead on effects monitored during the entire course of treatment and observation. If the treatment is counterproductive or ineffective, the researcher can terminate the environmental manipulation or alter the scheduling of events. Another advantage is that these studies are cost-effective in terms of the number of subjects needed to test functional hypotheses. The rule of thumb when using animal subjects appears to be that no fewer than two, and usually no more than six, are used, on the assumption that one or two animals may have to be eliminated from the study because of some odd problem beyond the experimenter's control (P. H. Hineline, personal communication, 2000). Although cost-effective in terms of the number of human or animal subjects, these studies are nevertheless time-consuming because of their processual nature. An early criticism was that, because they focused on only one or a few organisms, the results might not be generalizable beyond the limited circumstances of the observations. In the case of diagnostic studies, of course, the objective is to learn about a particular human subject. In the case of exploratory and hypothesis-testing studies, Sidman (1960) responded to the criticism by elaborating on two kinds of replications, one involving repetition of the same study (**direct replication**) and the other, varying an aspect, or the scheduling, of the stimulus conditions or treatments (**systematic replication**). Direct replication on the same subjects (intrasubject replications) presumably identifies the reliability of functional relationships over time, whereas systematic replications on other subjects would identify the generality of the functional relationships across variations of independent and dependent variables, and over other subjects (although a tiny sample of the general population). Sidman (1960) concluded that a powerful feature of intrasubject replication was "the ease with which experimental control can be exercised, *at will,* over the course of time" (p. 87), the reason being that it "has the obvious virtue of eliminating intersubject variability as a factor in the evaluation of an experimental finding" (p. 88).

In fact, it is quite common to see single-case replication designs in neuroscience research. For example, a team of researchers at Princeton University and the University of Pittsburgh collaborated on a correlational study of how the brain responds as a person weighs a moral dilemma (Greene, Sommerville, Nystrom, Darley, & Cohen, 2001). The dilemma might be a story about a runaway trolley that is hurtling toward five people, all of whom will be killed unless you throw a switch that routes the trolley onto a spur, where it will kill one person instead of five. In another variation of the trolley dilemma, you are standing next to a large stranger on a footbridge over the tracks, and the only way to save the five people is to push the stranger onto the tracks, where he will die but his heavy body will also stop the trolley, saving the five others. Most people say they would not push the stranger. Sixty dilemmas involving moral and nonmoral issues were presented to two groups of nine subjects, who responded to each dilemma while undergoing brain scanning by functional magnetic resonance imaging (fMRI). The results were that different parts of the brain lit up when these subjects were responding to an "impersonal dilemma" (e.g., throwing a switch) and when they were responding to a "personal dilemma" (e.g., shoving a person off a bridge). The researchers interpreted these results as implying a functional association between how people process information involving moral reasoning and how parts of their brains respond physiologically.

CROSS-LAGGED CORRELATIONAL DESIGNS

We turn now to the third general type of quasi-experimental designs, called **correlational designs** as a catchall name for odds and ends of relational methods. The term *correlational* is really a misnomer, as we know that correlation (i.e., some evidence of covariation between X and Y) is also what one looks for in randomized controlled experiments (e.g., effect size correlations). As our first example we describe an old correlational design that was used with some frequency by sociologists and social psychologists and was subsequently viewed with "skeptical advocacy" by Campbell, who was one of its developers (Cook & Campbell, 1979, p. 309). This design is called a **cross-lagged panel design.** *Cross-lagged* implies that some data points are treated as temporally "lagged" values of the outcome measures; *panel design* comes from sociological survey research, where *panel study* is another name for longitudinal research (Lazarsfeld, 1948). We will have more to say about longitudinal research shortly, but two advantages of such designs are assumed to be that (a) they increase the precision of the defined "treatment" comparisons by the observation of each individual under all the different conditions to be compared, and (b) they identify how people's responses change over time (N. R. Cook & Ware, 1983).

When the cross-lagged panel model was conceived, the assumption was that longitudinal measures of the same two variables, *A* and *B,* should provide information about the (bivariate) causal relationships between them (Lazarsfeld, 1978). Stated another way, the cross-lagged panel model was envisioned as a useful template with which to choose among competing causal hypotheses (cf. Campbell, 1963; Campbell & Stanley, 1966; Lazarsfeld, 1978; Pelz & Andrew, 1964; Rozelle & Campbell, 1969). A problem is that, like any quasi-experimental designs that depend on the time sampling of data points, cross-lagged panel designs may miss a causal relationship that is transient, transitional, elusive, obscured by measurement biases, or just hard to pin down. As Shadish, Cook, and Campbell (2002) wisely cautioned, "Observed bivariate correlations can be too high, too low, spurious, or accurate (as indices of causation) depending on the pattern of relationship among the variables in the structure that actually generated the data" (p. 413). Thus, just as the presence of path coefficient correlation in time-series designs is not proof of causation, the absence of correlation in cross-lagged designs is not proof of the absence of causation.

Figure 8.1 diagrams the simplest model, in which *A* and *B* denote two variables, each of which is measured individually at two successive time periods. Three sets

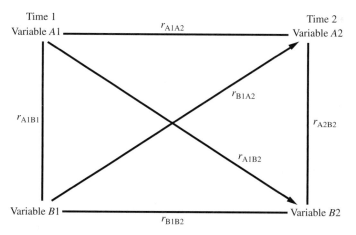

FIGURE 8.1
Design for cross-lagged and other correlations between variables *A* and *B*.

of paired correlations are represented: **test-retest correlations** (r_{A1A2} and r_{B1B2}), **synchronous correlations** (r_{A1B1} and r_{A2B2}), and **cross-lagged correlations** (r_{A1B2} and r_{B1A2}). The test-retest correlations indicate the reliability of A and B over time. The synchronous correlations, when compared with one another, imply the reliability of the relationship between A and B over time. The cross-lagged correlations show the relationships between two sets of data points, in which one is treated as a lagged value of the outcome variable. As originally conceived, the question that was ostensibly addressed by this model was whether A is a stronger cause of B than B is of A. The logic was that, given reliable test-retest and synchronous correlations, comparing the cross-lagged correlations should answer this question. That is, the answer would be "yes" if r_{A1B2} were higher than r_{B1A2}, and it would be "no" if r_{B1A2} were higher than r_{A1B2} (i.e., B is presumed to be a stronger "cause'" of A than A is of B).

Figure 8.2a shows several hypothetical test-retest, synchronous, and cross-lagged correlations at three successive time periods. In this idealized case we see that A and B are highly reliable variables, with a strikingly consistent retest reliability of .85. The synchronous correlation between A and B is consistent as well (i.e., .40 at times 1, 2, and 3). The cross-lagged correlations are also unusually the same within each level throughout the investigation. If these numbers were represented as real data, we would

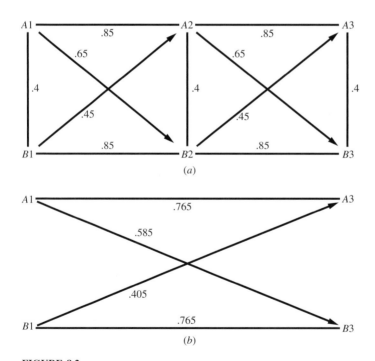

FIGURE 8.2
Hypothetical panel correlations between variables A and B measured at three successive time periods: (a) test-retest, synchronous, and cross-lagged correlations at two successive periods; (b) estimated test-retest and cross-lagged correlations based on a given temporal erosion rate.

be suspicious because they are so remarkably identical. However, putting our suspicion aside (because this is merely a hypothetical case), we might conclude from the fact that $r_{A1B2} > r_{B1A2}$ and $r_{A2B3} > r_{B2A3}$, and the further fact that all of the correlations are far from zero, that the path from A to B contributes more to the (presumed) causal relationship between A and B than the path from B to A. As all the cross-lagged correlations are nonzero, we also conclude that both paths (i.e., $A \rightarrow B$ and $B \rightarrow A$) remain quite tenable. Of course, even if the cross-lagged correlations had been zero, the lack of correlation would not disprove causation because, as one author put it, "It is only when we isolate the cause and effect from all other influences that correlation is a necessary condition of causation" (Bollen, 1989, p. 52).

Interpretability is considered maximum when the correlations remain similar at each period. In fact, relationships are seldom stationary, but instead are usually lower over longer lapses of time–described as **temporal erosion** (Kenny, 1973). Suppose the test-retest correlation of A eroded from .85 between two successive periods (i.e., $A1$ with $A2$, and also $A2$ with $A3$) down to .765 between periods 1 and 3 (i.e., $A1$ with $A3$). That 10% reduction (also called **attenuation**) in test-retest reliability leaves a 90% leftover (or *residual*) effect per unit of time (shown in Figure 8.2b), that is, $(.765/.85) \times 100 = 90$ percent. After making necessary statistical corrections, we might use this figure to estimate the attenuation of the cross-lagged correlations. In this hypothetical case we multiplied the 90% residual times each of the cross-lagged correlations in Figure 8.2a. The results are given as idealized values in Part b of Figure 8.2, for example, $.65 \times .90 = .585$.

INVISIBLE VARIABLES AND
THE MEDIATION PROBLEM

To reiterate, in real life the correlations are rarely, if ever, as reliable or clear-cut as in the example that we just discussed. Thus, there is seldom a firm and clear inference that can be made even in the most simple cross-lagged design (cf. Mayer & Carroll, 1987). We turn next to actual data as a way of illustrating another correlational strategy, now simply called **path analysis,** which has been mired in controversy since it was first proposed (cf. Niles, 1922, 1923; Wright, 1921, 1923). As it is typically used to infer causation from nonexperimental data, a problem is that none of the variables are under the control of the researchers; they are simply observed, and thus all we really know is that they are correlated. By statistically removing some associations between the variables and then appraising the partial correlations, social scientists who use path analysis attempt to rule out alternative pathways of causal influence on the basis of quantitative models, the goal being to settle on the plausible causal pathway that is most viable. Although critics may grant that ingenious theoretical solutions have been proposed, they also argue that the causal claims are illusions based on assumptions that are not only unverifiable but often spurious (Freedman, 1987; Reichardt, 2002; Rogosa, 1987; see McKim & Turner, 1997, for a fascinating range of viewpoints).

Before we turn to path analysis, we also need to mention the **third-variable problem**—which might be characterized as the *invisible variables problem,* because there may be more than one hidden, confounding variable. The third-variable problem is that some variable that is correlated with both A and B may be the cause of both. Mathematician

John Paulos (1990, 1991) discussed a number of fascinating examples. For instance, there is a positive correlation between milk consumption and the incidence of cancer in various societies. Paulos explained this correlation by the fact that people in relatively affluent societies live longer, and increased longevity (the invisible third variable) is associated with an increase in the likelihood of getting cancer. Thus, any health practice (such as milk drinking) that increases longevity will probably correlate positively with cancer incidence. Another example is the small negative correlation observed between death rates and divorce rates (more divorce, less death) in various regions of the United States. The invisible third variable proposed by Paulos to explain this relation is the age distribution of the various regions, because older married couples are less likely to divorce and more likely to die than are younger couples. Another Paulos example was the high positive correlation between the size of children's feet and their spelling ability. Should we, he asked facetiously, use foot stretchers to increase children's spelling scores? The invisible third variable is age, because children with bigger feet are usually older, and older children spell better. (We will return to the third-variable problem in chapter 11.)

More recently, Shrout and Bolger (2002) focused on still another relevant issue in the context of causal modeling in nonexperimental studies, which is the possibility that a causal effect of some variable X on an outcome variable Y is explained by a **mediator variable**—briefly alluded to in the previous chapter and described as a condition, a state, or another factor that is presumed to intervene between X and Y. As Shrout and Bolger noted, mediation is of equal interest to experimenters and social scientists who do non-experimental studies. For example, in the previous chapter we ended by mentioning a mediational model of how subject- and experimenter-related artifacts may occur in experimental and nonexperimental research (Rosnow & Aiken, 1973). Shrout and Bolger described the standard methods for estimating direct and indirect causal paths and the concerns associated with them (a) when there are mediator variables that are measured with error (leading to model misspecification), or (b) when the intervening variable is a partial mediator on average, and (c) other problems. In particular, they recommended the estimation of parameters by the use of a procedure called the *bootstrap* by Efron (1979), a variation on another procedure called the *jackknife* by Tukey (1958). (We will have more to say about the bootstrap and the jackknife in chapter 13.)

PATH ANALYSIS AND CAUSAL INFERENCE

Path analysis is much more widely used than cross-lagged panel analysis, but to continue the thread of the preceding discussion, we will present a path analysis example in the framework of the simple model previously depicted in Figure 8.1. The case we discuss is also another illustration of longitudinal research, and we will have more to say about this kind of research in the following section. In this particular study, the researchers were interested in the increasing prominence of violence in American society, with a special emphasis on the role of media violence viewing as a factor contributing to the development of aggression. Led by Leonard D. Eron and L. Rowell Huesmann, this team of investigators (Eron, Huesmann, Lefkowitz, & Walder, 1972) focused on television programming and its heavy emphasis on violence and lawlessness as one causal contributor to violence in American society. In earlier lab experiments, it had been observed that there was an immediate effect on the extent of aggressive behavior among participants who witnessed aggressive displays in films. The question addressed by Eron, Huesmann, and associates was whether a similar finding might be observed long term, especially in regard to children's exposure to television violence and their subsequent aggressive and violent behavior when they were young adults. There was a body of theory suggesting that long-term aggressive effects were due to a long-term observational learning of beliefs and cognitive biases, whereas short-term (immediate effects) were theorized to be due to other psychological processes such as priming, imitation, and excitation transfer (see Bushman & Huesmann, 2001, for a more detailed discussion). More recently, this same team of researchers reported a follow-up of their earlier longitudinal study, including more detailed analyses that we describe next (Huesmann, Moise-Titus, Podolski, & Eron, 2003), but here we are primarily interested in illustrating the logic of path analysis.

To address the long-term effects of children's exposure to TV violence, the researchers collected archival and interview data in 1970 on several hundred teenagers of an original group of children who had participated in a study of third-grade children growing up in Chicago in 1960 (Eron, 1963; Eron, Walder, & Lefkowitz, 1971). In our discussion (above) of the cross-lagged panel design, we considered the possibility that $A \rightarrow B$ or $B \rightarrow A$. However, a causal relationship can be either positive or negative, and it may also follow a more circuitous path involving, for example, $A1 \rightarrow A2 \rightarrow B2$ or $B1 \rightarrow A1 \rightarrow B2$. Figure 8.3 shows some of the results obtained by these researchers. The information collected in 1960 and 1970 fell into two general categories: (a) measures of aggression (such as asking children, "Who starts a fight over nothing?" and "Who takes other children's things without asking?") and (b) possible predictors of aggression (particularly a child's preference for violent television programs, e.g., learned by asking each mother to identify her child's three favorite television programs). The results in Figure 8.3 represent the correlations between a preference for violent TV, labeled as A, and peer-rated aggression, labeled as B, for boys over the 10-year lag (Eron, Huesmann, Lefkowitz, & Walder, 1972, p. 257). In contrast to the mock data in Figure 8.2, note that these actual data indicate some not very reliable relationships. First, the correlation

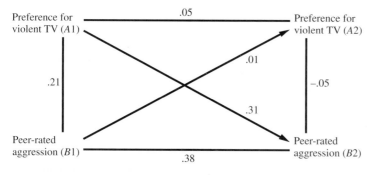

FIGURE 8.3
Correlations between a preference for violent television and peer-rated aggression for 211 boys in 1960 and 1970. (After "Does Television Violence Cause Aggression?" by L. D. Eron, L. R. Huesmann, M. M. Lefkowitz, and L. O. Walder, 1972, *American Psychologist, 27,* pp. 253–263.)

between A and B in the third grade was positive ($r = .21$), but 10 years later it was negative and quite small ($r = -.05$). Second, the test-retest correlation was only .05 for a preference for violent TV, and it was .38 for aggression. Third, there was a statistically significant relationship between children's preference for violent television in the third grade and their aggressive habits 10 years later ($r = .31$), but the correlation between peer-rated aggression in the third grade and a preference for violent TV 10 years later was near zero ($r = .01$).

The challenge in this case was to try to explain how a childhood preference for violent TV might be understood as causally related to teenage aggression in view of all these different correlations. It is not possible to prove that a causal hypothesis is true, but it might be possible to reject untenable hypotheses and, in this way, narrow down the number of plausible hypotheses. In this case the researchers came up with five alternative hypotheses for the results shown in Figure 8.3, which are represented by the five different paths of causal influence in Figure 8.4. For example, labeled as Path 1 in Figure 8.4 is the major hypothesis of this investigation, which was that preferring to watch violent television was a long-term cause of aggressive behavior. The results of both the synchronous correlation between $A1$ and $B1$ (.21) and the cross-lagged correlation between $A1$ and $B2$ (.31) seemed logically consistent with this hypothesis. The low test-retest reliability of variable A might be explained by the notion that some of the children, by the time they were teenagers, had turned to other, more overtly aggressive activities (e.g., stealing and fighting) rather than getting their "kicks" vicariously by watching violent TV. It might also explain the near-zero correlation between $A2$ and $B2$ ($-.05$).

Turning our attention next to Path 2 in Figure 8.4, we find the hypothesis that the preference for violent TV as a young child stimulated the person to be aggressive, and this aggressive behavior carried over into the teenage years. The researchers ruled out this hypothesis on the grounds that the correlation between the end points (indicated in Figure 8.3 as $r = .31$ between $A1$ and $B2$) was much higher than the product of the intermediate correlations. They reasoned that, if the second hypothesis were correct, the relationship between the end points (i.e., $A1$ and $B2$) would have been no stronger than the product of the relations between all adjacent intermediate points (i.e., $.21 \times .38 = .08$). On similar grounds, the hypothesis represented by Path 3 was also ruled out. In this case the hypothesis was that aggressive children preferred aggressive television, and that a preference for aggressive TV then led to their aggressive behavior as teenagers. The researchers eliminated this hypothesis on the grounds that the strength of the relationship between the end points ($B1$ and $B2$, where $r = .38$ in Figure 8.3) was noticeably greater than the product of the relationships between all adjacent intermediate points in Figure 8.4.

Path 4 was not so easily rejected. It hypothesized that aggressive children were both more likely to enjoy watching aggressive television *and* more likely to become aggressive teenagers. The researchers reasoned that if this were the complete explanation of the relation between $A1$ and $B2$, adjusting for third-grade aggression would result in a near-zero correlation between $A1$ and $B2$. They evaluated the idea by examining the correlation between $A1$ and $B2$ while controlling for $B1$; the result was a partial r of .25. Because this correlation was only .06 below the original correlation between $A1$ and $B2$ (.31 in Figure 8.3), they concluded that the fourth hypothesis was implausible as a "complete" causal explanation.

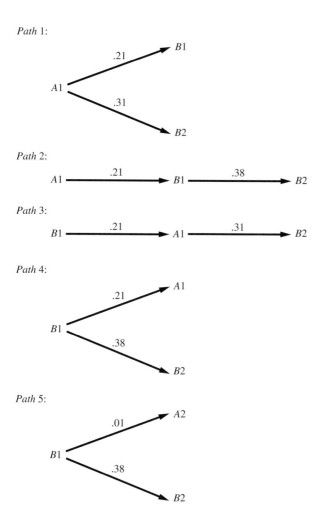

FIGURE 8.4
Five plausible causal paths to explain the correlations presented
in Figure 8.3. (After "Does Television Violence Cause
Aggression?" by L. D. Eron, L. R. Huesmann, M. M. Lefkowitz,
and L. O. Walder, 1972, *American Psychologist, 27,* pp. 253–263.)

Path 5 hypothesized that early aggression caused both a weaker preference
for TV violence as a teenager and a penchant for continuing to be aggressive. To
test this hypothesis the researchers decided they needed a correlation not reduced
by the passage of time as a comparison base to evaluate the $r = .01$ between $B1$
and $A2$. Without going into detail, it will suffice to say that they found that .01
was very close to that comparison base, leading them to reject this fifth hypothesis.
Thus, having ruled out four out of five hypotheses, they concluded that Path 1
could best account for the observed data. That is, they concluded that watching
violent television has a direct causal influence on aggressive behavior in some

children. In a more recent assessment of archival and interview data collected in this important study, the researchers reached a similar conclusion, "that childhood exposure to media violence predicts young adult aggressive behavior" (Huesmann, Moise-Titus, Podolski, & Eron, 2003, p. 201).

In this follow-up analysis, even more fine-tuned than the earlier analyses, the researchers concluded that identification with aggressive TV characters and the perceived realism of TV violence also predicted later aggression in these children (Huesmann, Moise-Titus, Podolski, & Eron, 2003). When the effects of socioeconomic status, intellectual ability, and various parenting factors were statistically controlled for, the relationship between TV violence and aggression remained. Interestingly, a meta-analysis by Paik and Comstock (1994) of the results of 217 different studies of the relation between exposure to media violence and different forms of antisocial behavior reported effect size correlations of .32 for aggressive behavior, .10 for violent criminal behavior, and .28 for nonviolent criminal behavior. Bushman and Huesmann (2001) suggested an analogy between smoking and lung cancer as a way of interpreting the implications of findings like these, because the smoking-cancer literature is largely based on a similar kind of analysis and, according to data reported in their paper, the overall correlation between media violence and aggression was only slightly smaller than that between smoking and lung cancer (see also Bushman & Anderson, 2001). Bushman and Huesmann argued that, just as there is not a perfect one-to-one relationship between smoking and lung cancer, there is not a one-to-one relationship between watching violent TV as a child and growing up to be aggressive or hostile. However, they added, the direction of the relevant data do strongly suggest that watching violent TV is a contributing factor, and the more young children are exposed to violence in the media, the more cumulative will be the negative behavioral effects on some of them. (For a detailed discussion and review of the literature on the influence of media violence on youth, see Anderson, Berkowitz, Donnerstein, Huesmann, Johnson, Linz, Malamuth, & Wartella, 2003.)

THE COHORT IN LONGITUDINAL RESEARCH

The investigation just described is an example of **longitudinal research,** its purpose being to examine people's responses over an extended time span. The advantages of longitudinal research are particularly evident when one is interested in changes that occur over a lengthy period of time, because problems can arise when cross-sectional (i.e., synchronic) research is used to study the life course of some variable but the data are collected during a particular slice of time. We will illustrate this problem shortly, but another term that is commonly used in longitudinal research is **cohort,** denoting a "generation" that has experienced a significant life event (birth, marriage, etc.) at the same period of time (Ryder, 1965). Hence, a group of people born about the same time and having had similar life experiences constitutes a cohort. As we will show, researchers can use longitudinal research to track several different cohorts to find out, for example, whether a generation gap on some variable is observable. In some studies the researchers are not only interested in measuring one or more cohorts repeatedly through time but are also interested in making age comparisons on some variable. They may be interested in the period (calendar date) of measurements as well, but this could complicate the analysis because any combination of two dimensions then determines the third (as we will illustrate).

Longitudinal data are usually collected *prospectively,* which means the participants are tracked and measured over time (as in panel studies, or in the investigation described previously), but the data can also be gotten *retrospectively* from historical records (Rosnow, 2000). For example, another classic prospective study was begun by Lewis Terman and his associates in 1921 (Terman et al., 1925) and was summarized in a volume by Terman and Oden (1947). The study tracked the psychosocial and intellectual development of a cohort of over a thousand gifted California boys and girls from preadolescence through adulthood. Later, other researchers picked up the earlier trail by gathering the death certificates of the people in Terman's study (Friedman, Tucker, Schwartz, Tomlinson-Keasey, Martin, Wingard, & Criqui, 1995). The average IQ of the children was 135, and various follow-up analyses found little difference between those lost from the study and those who remained. Coding their dates and causes of death, these researchers were able to identify a number of psychosocial and behavioral "risk" factors that were correlated with premature death. For example, they found that the trauma of going through a divorce predicted premature mortality, as did particular personality factors. These findings were interpreted as providing confirmation of the current view in psychology and medicine that a cluster of individual and social factors is critical to longevity. More recently, after additional analyses, the team of researchers concluded that childhood cheerfulness (operationalized as a combination of two items measuring a child's "cheerfulness/ optimism" and "sense of humor," as rated by the child's parents or teacher) "should not be assumed to be related to health in a simple manner" (Martin, Friedman, Tucker, Tomlinson-Keasey, Criqui, & Schwartz, 2002, pp. 1155, 1158).

In another prominent longitudinal study, the principal investigator, K. Warner Schaie, began the data collection when he was a graduate student working on his doctoral dissertation; he continued to collect information regarding the intellectual development of several thousand individuals during a series of other testing cycles spanning several decades (see Schaie, 1993, 1994). Among the major findings are that a number of factors account for individual differences that appear to reduce the risk of cognitive decline in old age, including (a) not having a chronic disease; (b) living in favorable environmental circumstances; (c) engaging in complex, intellectually stimulating activities; (d) having a flexible personality style; (e) having a marital partner who is cognitively active; and (f) feeling satisfied about life (Schaie, 1994). Together with Sherry L. Willis, his collaborator, Schaie has also been studying methods of reversing intellectual decline by certain educational interventions (Schaie & Willis, 1986; Willis & Schaie, 1986, 1988).

Not all longitudinal studies track participants over so long a period as the Terman or the Schaie and Willis studies. In another longitudinal study, E. W. Morrison (1993) was interested in the socialization effects of information seeking in accountants during their first six months of employment. Using data reported by workers, she concluded that the newcomers tended to seek out knowledge and take an active role in adjusting to their environment.

As implied above, longitudinal research has come to play a prominent role both in developmental investigations (e.g., Loeber & Stouthamer-Loeber, 1998; Scarr, 1998; McLoyd, 1998) and in medicine. In medical research, for example, an important, and continuing, longitudinal study, known as the Framingham Heart Study, was begun by the

U.S. Public Health Service in 1948. Responding to concerns about the soaring coronary disease rate in the United States, this longitudinal study has followed several thousand residents of Framingham, Massachusetts. The findings have produced insights into the risk factors that predict cardiovascular disease. In 1960, cigarette smoking was first revealed to be a risk factor, and in 1961, high blood pressure was identified as another risk factor. The correlational findings have led to randomized clinical trials, which in turn have confirmed the preventive approach to combating heart disease by exercise (which at one time was considered dangerous for people at risk for heart disease), not smoking, lowering harmful cholesterol, and reducing stress, blood pressure, and obesity.

DIFFERENT FORMS OF COHORT STUDIES

One way to visualize the various forms and combinations of cohort studies is with the help of a **cohort table.** Table 8.2 provides basic data and enables us to see some important differences between cross-sectional and cohort designs. The values in this table, adapted from a more complete cohort table provided by Jacques Hagenaars and Niki P. Cobben (1978), give the percentages of women in the Netherlands who reported having no religious affiliation, according to age and time period. The results are shown for seven different cohorts of respondents. The analysis of any given column would be comparable to the "one-shot case study" design discussed in the previous chapter in Table 7.8. An example is shown with reference to period 4; Figure 8.5 shows the shape of the cross-sectional age curve in 1969. These data seem to support the idea that, with the passing of years and the approach of the end of life, there is an increase in religious observance (i.e., the percentage of nonaffiliation decreases). The analysis of any particular

TABLE 8.2

Percentages of women in the Netherlands with no religious affiliation, according to age and time period

	Period 1 (1909)	Period 2 (1929)	Period 3 (1949)	Period 4 (1969)
Age 20–30	Cohort 4 4.8%	Cohort 5 13.9%	Cohort 6 17.4%	Cohort 7 23.9%
Age 40–50	Cohort 3 3.1%	Cohort 4 11.9%	Cohort 5 17.2%	Cohort 6 22.0%
Age 60–70	Cohort 2 1.9%	Cohort 3 6.7%	Cohort 4 11.9%	Cohort 5 19.4%
Age 80–	Cohort 1 1.2%	Cohort 2 3.8%	Cohort 3 6.6%	Cohort 4 12.2%

Note: An example of a cross-sectional design is shown by the vertical analysis (Period 4), and an example of a longitudinal design is shown by the diagonal analysis (Cohort 4).

Note: From "Age, Cohort and Period: A General Model for the Analysis of Social Change," by A. Hagenaars and N. P. Cobben, 1978, *Netherlands Journal of Sociology, 14,* 59–91. Reprinted by permission of Elsevier Scientific Publishing Co.

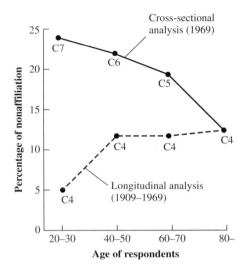

FIGURE 8.5
Percentages of women in the Netherlands not
affiliated with a church, as shown by a
cross-sectional design in 1969 and a longitudinal
design from 1909 to 1969 (after Hagenaars &
Cobben, 1978). Cohorts are symbolized as C7
(Cohort 7), C6 (Cohort 6), and so forth.

cohort would be equivalent to a longitudinal study with data collected periodically
to follow the life course of that generation of individuals. An example is shown
with reference to Cohort 4 (on the diagonal of Table 8.2), and Figure 8.5 shows
the shape of the age curve from 1909 to 1969. We can clearly see that the conclusion
based on the cross-sectional data is wrong.

   When we have an adequate cohort table, such as Table 8.2, other types of
analyses are also possible. For example, we could improve on the one-shot analysis
by plotting all the cross-sectional curves as shown in Figure 8.6a. We see that the
exact percentages of affiliation and the slopes of the age curves are different for different periods. We could also plot the values according to cohort of women, as shown
in Figure 8.6b, to help us avoid assuming that the results of an analysis of one given
time period are generalizable to other periods (called the **fallacy of period centrism**).
This design can also be used with survey data to study age trends by reexamining not
the same persons, but a specific age group (persons aged 21–29 in 1963) several years
later (persons aged 30–38 in 1972). It approximates a pure longitudinal design because
the sampling units are all based on a random selection procedure (discussed in the
next chapter).

   The concepts of age, cohort, and period may not be operationally defined the
same way in different fields. In the literature on counseling and student development,
age is often taken to mean the person's year in school rather than chronological
age (Whiteley, Burkhart, Harway-Herman, & Whiteley, 1975). In research on social
change, *period* is often defined as some environmental effect or cultural change

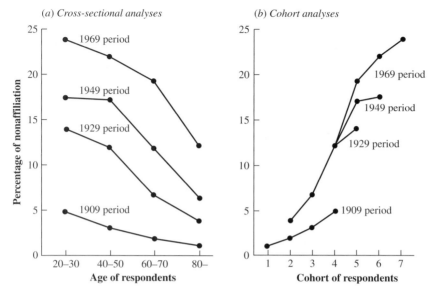

FIGURE 8.6
Percentages of women in the Netherlands not affiliated with a church, according to (a) age of women and (b) cohort of women (after Hagenaars & Cobben, 1978).

resulting from a lengthy historical process such as industrialization or urbanization (Hagenaars & Cobben, 1978). In general, however, (a) an *age effect* implies changes in average responses due to the natural aging process; (b) a *time-of-measurement effect* implies some kind of impact of events in chronological time (occurring at the points of measurement); and (c) a *cohort effect* implies "past history" specific to a particular generation and contributes to all measurements of the generation (N. R. Cook & Ware, 1983).

Table 8.3 provides a comparison of different longitudinal and cross-sectional designs in which age, time of measurement (period), and cohort are the major variables (Schaie, 1965; Wohlwill, 1970). The three effects cannot be estimated simultaneously in any of these designs:

In the **simple cross-sectional design,** subjects at different ages are observed at the same time. The limitation of this design is that it confounds the age of the subject and the cohort. That is, 20-year-olds would be from only one generation.

In the **simple longitudinal design,** subjects of the same cohort are observed over several periods. The deficiency in this case is that the design does not control for the effect of history (or period). That is, different results might have been obtained if people from different time periods had been studied.

In the **cohort-sequential design,** several cohorts are studied, the initial measurements being taken in successive years. The design takes into account cohort and age, but does not take time of measurement (period) fully into account. That is, different results might have been obtained if all the blank spaces representing time of measurement were filled in.

TABLE 8.3

Five sampling designs according to age (grades 1–6), period (history or time of measurement), and cohort (C1–C11)

Simple cross-sectional design (1980)

Age	1975	1976	1977	1978	1979	1980
			Period			
G1	C6	C7	C8	C9	C10	C11
G2	C5	C6	C7	C8	C9	C10
G3	C4	C5	C6	C7	C8	C9
G4	C3	C4	C5	C6	C7	C8
G5	C2	C3	C4	C5	C6	C7
G6	C1	C2	C3	C4	C5	C6

Simple longitudinal design

Age	1975	1976	1977	1978	1979	1980
			Period			
G1	C6					
G2		C6				
G3			C6			
G4				C6		
G5					C6	
G6						C6

Cohort-sequential design

Age	1975	1976	1977	1978	1979	1980
			Period			
G1						
G2						
G3	C4	C5	C6			
G4		C4	C5	C6		
G5			C4	C5	C6	
G6				C4	C5	C6

Time-sequential design

Age	1975	1976	1977	1978	1979	1980
			Period			
G1				C9	C10	C11
G2				C8	C9	C10
G3				C7	C8	C9
G4				C6	C7	C8
G5				C5	C6	C7
G6				C4	C5	C6

Cross-sequential design

Age	1975	1976	1977	1978	1979	1980
			Period			
G1	C6					
G2	C5	C6				
G3	C4	C5	C6			
G4		C4	C5	C6		
G5			C4	C5		
G6				C4		

Note: Each sampling design is accentuated by dotted lines. Only the first subtable is completely labeled to show all possible cohorts; in addition it shows the simple cross-sectional design for the 1980 period (set off by dotted lines).

In the **time-sequential design,** subjects at different ages are observed at different times. This design considers age and time of measurement, but as the blank spaces indicate, it does not take cohort fully into account.

In the **cross-sequential design,** several different cohorts that are observed over several periods are initially measured in the same period. This design takes into account the time of measurement and the cohort but (again as indicated by the blank spaces) does not take age fully into account.

Even though the more complex designs are a distinct improvement over the simple cross-sectional design in the study of maturational processes, we see that each design is limited in some way. This is not a startling revelation, however, for all empirical research has its limitations. Table 8.3 also reminds us that, in order to achieve clarity of understanding, it is best whenever possible to use more than one strategy, in the spirit of methodological pluralism.

SUBCLASSIFICATION ON PROPENSITY SCORES

By now we know that valid causal inferences are hard to come by in the absence of randomized controlled experiments. We have seen a variety of procedures designed to increase the validity of causal inferences in situations where randomized experiments could not be conducted for ethical, monetary, or logistical reasons. But of all the procedures available for drawing causal inferences from nonexperimental data, none has captured the imagination of the social science, biomedical, and statistical communities as much as matching groups by a subclassification on **propensity scores** (Rosenbaum & Rubin, 1983a; Rubin, 1973; Rubin & Thomas, 1996). The procedure involves reducing all the variables on which the "treated" and the "untreated" participants differ into a single composite variable that effectively summarizes all the differences on all the variables (the covariates). The reason for quotes around *treated* and *untreated* is that the "treatment" can be operationalized as an active experimental (or quasi-experimental) manipulation or intervention, or it can be an observed action, behavior, event, or condition.

The basic idea of matching by propensity scores is seen most clearly when we consider just a single covariate, for example, age in a nonexperimental study of the effects of smoking on death rates. Donald B. Rubin (1998) illustrated the propensity score procedure, which he developed, by using data from Cochran (1968) in which an American study found (quite surprisingly) higher death rates for cigar and pipe smokers than for cigarette smokers or nonsmokers, whose death rates did not differ. Table 8.4 lists those death rates per 1,000 person years for three conditions: (a) not smoking, (b) smoking cigars or a pipe, and (c) smoking cigarettes (i.e., death rates of 13.5, 17.4, and 13.5, respectively). In other words, it appears that, compared with cigar and pipe smoking, cigarette smoking is actually quite harmless (i.e., no difference was found between the nonsmokers and the cigarette smokers). Clearly, such a conclusion goes against common wisdom. Further inspection of Table 8.4 reveals that the cigar/pipe smokers in the study were older on average (59.7) than the nonsmokers (57.0) and the cigarette smokers (53.2). The propensity score procedure adjusts for these age differences, which we suspect were confounded with the treatment conditions.

TABLE 8.4

Death rates (per 1,000 person years) for three levels of smoking behavior

Group	Death rate per 1,000	Mean age	Number of subclasses		
			2	3	9+
1. Nonsmoker	13.5	57.0	13.5	13.5	13.5
2. Cigar or pipe smoker	17.4	59.7	14.9	14.2	13.7
3. Cigarette smoker	13.5	53.2	16.4	17.7	21.2
4. Increased risk of cigar or pipe smoking			10%	5%	1%
5. Increased risk of cigarette smoking			21%	31%	57%

Note: In row 4, *increased risk* refers to the excess death (given as a percentage) of cigar or pipe smokers versus nonsmokers divided by the death rate of nonsmokers. In row 5, the increased risk is the excess death rate of cigarette smokers versus nonsmokers divided by the death rate of nonsmokers.

If we consider the nonsmokers as the baseline condition, we will essentially "standardize" the death rates in the other two conditions relative to the age distribution of the nonsmokers. The most crude kind of adjustment would be to divide each entire sample into a younger half and an older half, to compare the three conditions within each of these levels, and finally to average the results for the younger and older halves. These results are shown in Table 8.4 as death rates per 1,000 of 13.5 for nonsmokers, 14.9 for cigar or pipe smokers, and 16.4 for cigarette smokers. Cochran (1968) called this proce-dure "subclassification," and he showed that increasing the number of subclasses increased the precision of the analysis, assuming that there are reasonable numbers of subjects in each subclass and that the subclassifications of the different treatment groups overlap. Thus, if there are $k = 3$ subclasses in one group or condition, we need $k = 3$ subclasses in the other groups or conditions as well. If there were no young people in one group, for example, subclassification would be inappropriate. Table 8.4 shows what happened when Rubin increased the number of subclasses of age to three equal-sized levels. The death rate of cigarette smokers increased to 17.7, and the death rate of cigar or pipe smokers decreased slightly (down to 14.2). Increasing the subclassification on age to nine or more age levels greatly increased the precision of the subclassification, and cigar and pipe smokers showed a death rate only slightly higher than the nonsmokers, but the cigarette smokers showed a far greater increase in death rate. Thus, with an increase in the number of subclasses from two to three to nine or more, the excess risk of cigar and pipe smoking, compared to nonsmoking, decreased from 10% to 5% to 1%, whereas the excess risk of cigarette smoking, compared to nonsmoking, increased from 21% to 31% to 57%. It has been shown that a clearer, more precise picture emerges as the number of subclasses increases, five or six subclasses ordinarily reducing the bias in the raw comparisons by some 90% (Rubin, 1998).

MULTIPLE CONFOUNDING COVARIATES

In the example above, the subclassification on propensity scores was predicated on the assumption of a single confounding covariate. In most practical applications, however, there are multiple confounding covariates. Cigarette smokers might differ from nonsmokers not only in age but in education, ethnicity, income, general health, health care access, personality variables, stress exposure, and the like. The beauty, simplicity, and transparency of the propensity score procedure flow from the combining of all confounding covariates into a single score. This single score—in our example, the propensity to be in the (a) cigarette-smoking group versus the non-smoking group, (b) the cigar/pipe-smoking group versus the nonsmoking group, or (c) the cigarette group versus the cigar/pipe group—becomes our single confounding covariate. (When there are three or more conditions, we apply propensity score methods to two conditions at a time.) In work with multiple confounded covariates, the propensity score is computed from the prediction of group membership scored one or zero (e.g., cigarette smoking vs. nonsmoking) by logistic regression or discriminant analysis. The estimated propensity score is the estimated probability, based on participants' scores on the covariates, of ending up in Group 1 or Group 2 (e.g., cigarette smoking vs. nonsmoking). The logic of the propensity score procedure is that if we have two participants with identical propensity scores, one person in Group 1 and one in Group 2, the differences in outcomes are due to their belonging to Group 1 or to Group 2. They cannot be due to differences in confounding covariates, because the subjects have scored identically on the propensity score that indexes the entire set of covariates. The technical underpinnings of this method and its effectiveness in practice have been well documented (Rosenbaum & Rubin, 1983a, 1983b, 1984, 1985a, 1985b; Rubin, 1979, 1980; Rubin & Thomas, 1992a, 1992b, 1996, 1997).

As a further illustration, suppose we are interested in the effectiveness of a new clinical treatment for improving psychological adjustment. Though the treatment has not yet been evaluated in a randomized controlled trial, we have available the adjustment scores of 250 people who were exposed to stress and also happened to receive the new treatment and another 250 participants who were exposed to stress but did not receive the new treatment. The adjustment index ranges from zero to 9, and the mean adjustment scores of the treated and untreated groups are identical (3.2 in each case). Before concluding that the treatment was not effective, we consider the possibility that the treated and untreated individuals differed on a number of available covariates, making it more or less likely that they would obtain the treatment rather than not obtain it. We create propensity scores for all these people and then subclassify each person into one of five levels of the likelihood of having or not having received the treatment. Table 8.5 shows for each of the five subclasses the mean adjustment score and sample size (n) for the treated (T) and the untreated control (C) members of each subclass. The important result in this hypothetical study is that, although the overall mean adjustment scores of the treated (M_T) and untreated (M_C) groups were identical ($M_T = M_C = 3.2$), our findings after we subclassified the individuals were noticeably different. For every level of our subclassification, the treated individuals scored higher than the untreated individuals. Propensity score procedures greatly clarified what was really going on when we adjusted for our full set of covariates.

More typical at present than the use of propensity scores is the use of regression methods to adjust for covariates. A serious risk of the regression approach, however, is that the conditions being compared may not overlap adequately on the confounding

TABLE 8.5

Mean adjustment scores and sample sizes for treated and untreated participants in five levels of propensity score subclasses

Propensity score subclass[a]	Treatment Mean (M_T)	n	No-treatment control Mean (M_C)	n	$M_T - M_C$
1	6	10	5	90	1
2	5	30	3	70	2
3	4	50	2	50	2
4	3	70	1	30	2
5	2	90	1	10	1
Sum (Σ)	20	250	12	250	8
k	5		5		5
Unweighted M (Σ/k)	4		2.4		1.6[b]
S^2	2.5		2.8		0.30
Weighted M ($\Sigma Mn/\Sigma n$)	3.2		3.2		

[a]Lower numbered subclasses were less likely to have received the treatment.

[b]One-sample $t_{(4)} = 6.53$, $p = .0014$, $r = .96$.

covariates. When nonoverlap occurs in propensity score procedures, it is detectable immediately from the fact that the sample sizes are too small or even zero for some subclasses. Regression procedures do not normally warn us of these serious problems of failure to overlap sufficiently. We are likely to think we have obtained a sensible answer to our causal question even if every member of Condition A scored higher (or lower) on every covariate than did any member of Condition B. If all our smokers were older than any of our nonsmokers, it would be hopeless to attempt to adjust for age as a covariate. A further advantage of the propensity score method is that it does not require a particular kind of relationship (e.g., linear, log-linear) between the covariate and the outcome within each condition, whereas the regression approach does (Rubin, 1973). The major limitation of the propensity score method is that it can adjust only for observed confounding covariates. If we have not measured a confounding covariate or have overlooked one altogether the propensity score method cannot help us, at least not for the hidden confounding covariates. Another limitation of the propensity score method is that it works best with larger sample sizes, but that limitation is not unique to the propensity score method.

CHAPTER
9

RANDOMLY AND NONRANDOMLY SELECTED SAMPLING UNITS

SAMPLING A SMALL PART OF THE WHOLE

Because the world is large and we can study only a small part of it in our research, we use samples to represent the whole. In this chapter we discuss a number of considerations to be weighed in selecting the sampling units randomly or nonrandomly from the larger aggregate (the **population**). The units might be human or animal subjects, cities, groups, classrooms, hospitals, numbers, or any other entities believed to be characteristic of the population. We will explain the method known as **probability sampling,** in which (a) every sampling unit has a known nonzero probability of being selected, (b) the units are randomly drawn, and (c) the probabilities are taken into account in making estimates from the sample (Snedecor & Cochran, 1980, pp. 437–438). Probability sampling is used primarily in survey research; it is seldom used in experimental research, in which it is typical to study the most convenient participants. Thus, we will also explore issues in attempting to generalize from samples that are merely convenient (i.e., rather than from random probability samples) to a wider population.

As we mentioned in chapter 7, many experimenters, after they go to elaborate lengths to design and implement carefully crafted studies, depend only on college students as the research participants. Many. years ago, this practice prompted one critic to assert that "the existing science of human behavior is largely the science of the

of white, middle class, male, sophomores!!
↓

behavior of sophomores" (McNemar, 1946, p. 333). Concerns about the use of students as the model of "persons in general" are based not only on the very obvious differences between college students and more representative persons in age, intelligence, and social class, but also on the suspicion that college students, because of their special relationship with the teacher-investigator, may be especially sensitive and responsive to demand characteristics. Silverman (1977) compared this situation, in which researchers struggle to find out what college-student subjects *really* feel and think about serving in experiments, to the fable of the emperor's new clothes:

> A student and seasoned subject once said to me, with apparent innocence: "If everyone does things in experiments for the same reasons I do, I don't understand how you can find out anything that's true." I liken her to the child in the fable, to whom we may now say: "Yes the Emperor is naked." (p. 19)

Even so, it is also true that college students as experimental subjects have taught us a tremendous amount about cognition, perception, and countless aspects of psychological behavior. Thus, it is important not to exaggerate the problem of using such subjects, but it is also important not to be lulled into overgeneralizing from such findings. The issue becomes further complicated when only volunteer subjects are used but the findings are generalized to a population including nonrespondents or likely nonvolunteers. As social researchers turn increasingly to the Internet for volunteers for questionnaire studies, the concern about generalizability is raised in a whole new context (Gosling, Vazire, Srivastava, & John, 2004). We will discuss nonresponse bias and volunteer subject bias, but without implying that research results are *always* different for volunteers and for nonrespondents or nonvolunteers. We know enough about the characteristics of volunteers for behavioral and social research to be able to predict the direction of volunteer subject bias as well as to suggest recruitment procedures for improving the subject sample by enticing more nonvolunteers to enter the subject pool. A related concern is that the participating subjects—whether they are volunteers or nonvolunteers—may not respond to all the questions put to them by survey researchers, experimenters, or other investigators. At the conclusion of this chapter, we will sketch a number of procedures for dealing with missing data.

Probability sampling, although it is the gold standard of external validity in survey research, is also based partly on a leap of faith, or what Abraham Kaplan (1964) called the "paradox of sampling":

> On the one hand, the sample is of no use if it is not truly representative of its population, if it is not a "fair" sample. On the other hand, to know that it is representative, we must know what the characteristics of the population are, so that we can judge whether the sample reflects them properly; but in that case, we have no need of the sample at all. (p. 239)

Kaplan went on to explain that this predicament was reminiscent of other situations. In fact, all inductive inferences are based on samples, he noted. We make generalizations about a whole class of cases although we have observed only some of them, or we make predictions about certain future outcomes on the basis of nonrandom samples of events from the past. The way this paradox is resolved in survey research is "by the consideration that the representativeness is not a property of the sample but rather of the procedure by which the sample is obtained, the *sampling plan*" (Kaplan, 1964, pp. 239–240).

We begin by defining some basic concepts used in survey research and probability sampling as well as examining the kinds of sampling plans used in surveys. The survey researcher asks questions and looks for the answers in the replies of the respondents. **Sampling plans** specify how the respondents will be selected. In particular, we will discuss *probability sampling plans,* which specify how randomness will enter into the selection process at some stage so that the laws of mathematical probability apply. Data selection plans based on the use of probability sampling enable the researcher to assume—but never for sure (because of the paradox of sampling)—that the selected sample is in fact representative of its population (i.e., without already knowing the population value).

BIAS AND INSTABILITY IN SURVEYS

Frequency distributions, including all sampling distributions in survey research, can be described in terms of their central values **(point estimates)** and variability **(interval estimates).** For example, the point estimate might be the mean, median, or modal cost of housing in a community or the percentage of voters who favor Candidate X over Candidate Y. In survey research, interval estimates are frequently expressed in terms of the *margin of error,* or the confidence limits of the estimated population value based on a specified probability that the value is between those limits. For example, a survey researcher might state "with 95% confidence, that 47% of the registered voters favor Candidate X, given a margin of error of plus-or-minus 2 percentage points." The margin of error is conceptually related to the **standard error,** which indicates the degree of imprecision with which we have estimated, for example, the mean or median of a population. The standard error is usually symbolized as *SE* in psychology (American Psychological Association, 1994), and we illustrate its use shortly. The actual population value is referred to as the **true population value** (i.e., the point value we would obtain based on analyzing all the scores in the population). The difference between the true population value and our estimate of it from a sampling distribution is called **bias,** which (as noted in chapter 7) is simply another name for systematic error. An unbiased sampling plan is one in which the estimated population value is equal in the long run to the true population value. The variability of observations or of samples drawn on the basis of probability sampling is inversely related to the **stability** or **precision** of the observations or measurements.

It is also conceivable that the amount of bias and instability (imprecision) will vary in a number of more subtle ways, such as those illustrated in Figure 9.1, where X denotes the true population value and the Os are the point estimates of X based on biased and nonbiased sampling plans. The differences between the averages of the sample Os and the true population value (X) indicate the amount of bias. Notice that the instability is constant within each row, going from a high amount in row 1 to no instability in row 3. The amount of bias is constant within each column, going from a high amount in column 1 to zero bias in column 3. In all three cases in column 3

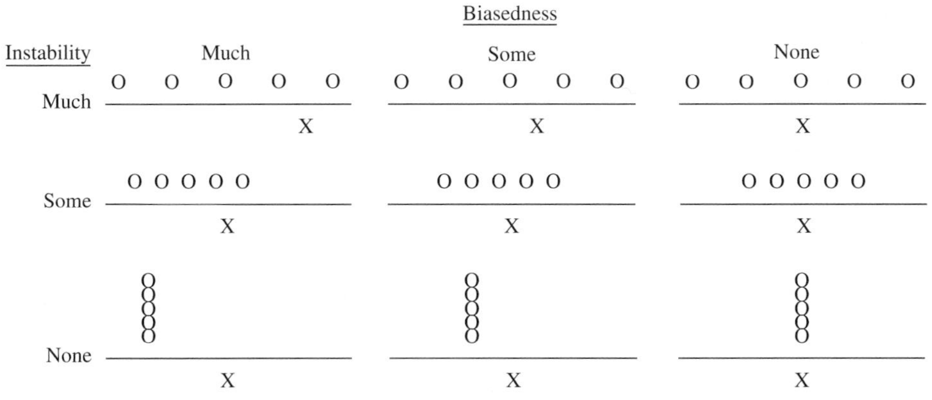

Biasedness

Instability	Much	Some	None
Much	O O O O O ——————————— X	O O O O O ——————————— X	O O O O O ——————————— X
Some	O O O O O ————————— X	O O O O O ————————— X	O O O O O ————————— X
None	(O stacked) ————————— X	(O stacked) ————————— X	(O stacked) ————————— X

FIGURE 9.1

Illustrations of biasedness and instability in sampling. An O denotes a particular sampling unit, X represents the true population mean, and the horizontal line indicates the underlying continuum on which the relevant values are determined. The distance between the true population mean and the midpoint of the sampling units indicates the amount of biasedness. The spreading (variability) among the sampling units indicates their relative degree of instability.

the sample values are balanced around X, but with much instability in row 1, some instability in row 2, and none in row 3. In the three cases in row 3 there is no instability, but there is much bias in column 1, some bias in column 2, and none in column 3. The case at the intersection of row 3 and column 3 is the best of all situations because there is no bias and no instability.

Generally speaking, instability results when the observations within a sample are highly variable and the number of observations is small. Thus, the more alike (homogeneous) the members of the population, the fewer of them that need to be sampled. If all members of the population were exactly alike (as at the intersection of row 3 and column 3), we could choose any observation (O) to provide information about the population (X) as a whole. A variation on this idea is sometimes presumed to be an implicit assumption in experimental research in which convenience samples are used, the notion being that people are people, and that probabilistic assertions derived from any of them will be characteristic (although to varying degrees) of all of them. Of course, within convenience samples there may be specifically designated subgroups (e.g., women vs. men), on the further assumption that moderating variables may be operating (e.g., gender). However, the subgroups are usually selected in a convenient or haphazard way (as if all women were the same, or all men the same). Increasing the size of the samples might reduce the instability or imprecision, but by itself it cannot reduce the bias.

A famous historical case occurred in 1936, when Franklin D. Roosevelt (the Democratic candidate) ran for U.S. president against Governor Alfred Landon of Kansas (the Republican candidate). Most people thought that Roosevelt would win easily, but a nonrandom poll conducted by a current events magazine, the *Literary Digest,* predicted that Landon would win an overwhelming victory. What gave the prediction credence was that the *Digest* had predicted the winner in every presidential election since 1916. Moreover, this time, they announced they had based their prediction on a sample of 2.4 million respondents! They got the 2.4 million by generating a nonrandom sample of 10 million people from telephone directories, automobile registration lists, and club membership lists; they then mailed straw vote ballots to each person in their sample. The lists had actually been compiled for solicitation purposes, and advertising was included with the straw vote ballot (D. Katz & Cantril, 1937).

One problem was that few people in 1936 had a telephone (only one in four households), owned a car, or belonged to a club, so that the final list was biased in favor of wealthy Republican households. Another problem was that there was a large number of nonrespondents, and subsequent analyses suggest that had they responded, the results might have been very different (Squire, 1988). As it turned out, the election voting was split pretty much along economic lines, the more affluent voting for Landon and the less affluent voting for Roosevelt. The *Digest* predicted that Landon would win by 57% to Roosevelt's 43%, but the election results were Roosevelt 62% and Landon 38%. The *Digest* could have used the fact that the sample was top-heavy in upper-income Republicans to correct its estimate, but it deliberately ignored this information. Instead, the *Digest* proudly proclaimed that the "figures had been neither weighted, adjusted, nor interpreted." After making the largest error ever made thus far by political prognosticators in a presidential election, the *Digest* (which had been in financial trouble before the election) declared bankruptcy.

SIMPLE RANDOM-SAMPLING PLANS

In the *Literary Digest* debacle the "polling" was not random, and there were other variables besides party affiliation that would have constituted informative strata. We will have more to say about stratified sampling, but the least complicated method of random sampling is to take a list of people and randomly select names from the list, a procedure called **simple random sampling.** The *simple* means that the sample is selected from an undivided population, and the *random* means that the sample is chosen by a process that gives every unit in the population the same chance of being selected. Simple random sampling can also be done in other ways, although the most common procedure is to use random digits. However, suppose we want to dramatically select numbers at random for a state lottery. We might have ping-pong balls, each with a different number painted on it, and then stir them and use a chance procedure to select one ball at a time. Or we might use a roulette wheel to select the numbers, although the same numbers might turn up more than once.

As another illustration of the use of random digits, suppose we want to select 10 men and 10 women from a population totaling 96 men and 99 women, and we have a list of all of them. We would begin by numbering the men in the population consecutively from 01 to 96 and the women in the population consecutively from 01 to 99. We are now ready to use the 5 × 5 blocks of random digits in Table 9.1, which were extracted from Table B.9 in Appendix B. Table B.9 is a small segment of a mammoth table that was generated by an electronic roulette wheel programmed to produce a random frequency pulse every tiny fraction of a second (RAND Corporation, 1955). A million random digits were generated, and afterward, as a check on the hypothesis

TABLE 9.1
Random digits

Line	Random digits					
000	10097	32533	76520	13586	34673	54876
001	37542	04805	64894	74296	24805	24037
002	08422	68953	19645	09303	23209	02560
003	99019	02529	09376	70715	38311	31165
004	12807	99970	80157	36147	64032	36653
005	66065	74717	34072	76850	36697	36170
006	31060	10805	45571	82406	35303	42614
007	85269	77602	02051	65692	68665	74818
008	63573	32135	05325	47048	90553	57548
009	73796	45753	03529	64778	35808	34282

Note: This abbreviated table is taken from Table B.9 in Appendix B. The left-hand column is for reference only, and the other columns contain random digits in sets of five. (Adapted from *A Million Random Digits With 100,000 Normal Deviates,* by The RAND Corporation, 1955, New York: Free Press.)

of randomness, the computer counted the number of 0s, 1s, 2s, and so on. Each digit from 0 to 9 occurred 10 percent of the time in the overall table of random digits. The reference numbers in the left-hand column of Table 9.1 are there only to help us refer to a particular line. We now do our simple random sampling by putting our finger blindly on some starting position. We can start anywhere in the table and move our finger in any direction, as long as we do not pick some set of numbers because they look right, or avoid some set of numbers because they do not look right.

Suppose we put our finger on the first five-digit number on line 004 (i.e., 12807). We read across the line two digits at a time, then across the next line, and so forth, until we have chosen individually at random the 10 male subjects. We do the same thing, beginning at another blindly chosen point, until we have selected the 10 female subjects. Beginning with the number 12807, we would select men numbered 12, 80, 79, and so on. Suppose we chose the same two-digit number more than once, or chose a two-digit number not represented by any name in the population. We would go on to the next two-digit number in the row. What if we were forced to skip many numbers in the table because they were too large? That would be terribly inefficient. For example, what if there were 450 members in the population and we wanted to select 50 individually at random? Because the population is numbered from 001 to 450 we will have to skip approximately half the three-digit numbers our finger points to. One way to handle this problem (acceptable in terms of random sampling) is mentally to subtract 500 from any number in the range from 501 to 999.

Previously, we alluded to random sampling with or without the replacement of the chosen unit. In **random sampling without replacement,** a selected unit cannot be reselected and must be disregarded on any later draw. Survey researchers usually prefer this procedure because they do not want to question the same individuals twice. If we were randomly choosing winners of door prizes and wanted to spread out the prizes, we would not put the chosen tickets back into the pool, because we do not want to give the same person more than one prize. In the lottery example mentioned above, if there were 100 ping-pong balls, the probability of the first ball drawn is 1/100. When we eliminate the first ball, the probability of the second ball drawn is 1/99, and so on. The population shrinks, but the balls remaining still have an equal chance of being selected on the next occasion. In **random sampling with replacement,** the selected units are placed in the sampling pool again and may be reselected on subsequent draws. Thus, every unit in the population continues to have the same likelihood of being chosen every time a random number is read. Tossing a coin would be sampling with replacement, in this case from a population consisting of two elements, heads and tails (Kish, 1965).

Instead of using a table of random digits, or spinning a roulette wheel, or drawing ping-pong balls, another method was used in World War II, and again in the war in Vietnam, to choose an order in which to draft men into military service. In 1970, while the war in Vietnam was in progress, the U.S. Congress passed a bill allowing the use of a random lottery to select conscripts for the armed forces. To give each man an equal chance of being selected, the 365 days of the year were written on slips of paper and placed inside tiny cylindrical capsules. Once the capsules were inside the urn, it was shaken for several hours, and then the capsules were removed, one by one. However, capsules are very difficult to stir thoroughly, and it turned out that the results were biased: The birth dates in December were more likely to be drawn first, those in November next, then those in October, and so on. The reason was that the January capsules were put in the urn first, the February capsules next, and so forth, and layers were formed with the December capsules on top. Even stirring the urn for several hours did not ensure a thorough mixing of the capsules (Broome, 1984; Kolata, 1986). Something similar occurred during World War II. Instead of birth dates, selective service numbers were put into capsules, and the capsules into a bowl and stirred, but subsequent analysis of the results indicated that they were also biased. As statisticians Mosteller, Rourke, and Thomas (1961) observed, "The moral, as every cook knows, is that thorough mixing is not as easy as it sounds" (p. 102).

IMPROVING ACCURACY IN RANDOM SAMPLING

In contrast to the method of simple random sampling, the method of randomly sampling strata has distinct advantages. To illustrate, we refer to Table 9.2, which is based on a simple random sampling plan in which the raw data were the batting averages of six infielders of the 1980 Philadelphia Phillies baseball team. We chose the 1980 team because one of us is a Phillies fan, and it happened that 1980 was the only time the Phillies ever won a World Series championship (though that year they had been trying for over 97 years). Batting averages are calculated by dividing the number of hits the player made by the number of official times that

TABLE 9.2
Results for all possible simple random samples of size two

Sample	Estimate of population mean	Error of estimate	(Error of estimate)^2
Aviles, Bowa	.272000	+.011167	.000125
Aviles, Rose	.279500	+.018667	.000348
Aviles, Schmidt	.281500	+.020667	.000427
Aviles, Trillo	.284500	+.023667	.000560
Aviles, Vukovich	.219000	−.041833	.001750
Bowa, Rose	.274500	+.013667	.000187
Bowa, Schmidt	.276500	+.015667	.000245
Bowa, Trillo	.279500	+.018667	.000348
Bowa, Vukovich	.214000	−.046833	.002193
Rose, Schmidt	.284000	+.023167	.000537
Rose, Trillo	.287000	+.026167	.000685
Rose, Vukovich	.221500	−.039333	.001547
Schmidt, Trillo	.289000	+.028167	.000793
Schmidt, Vukovich	.223500	−.037333	.001394
Trillo, Vukovich	.226500	−.034333	.001179
Sum	3.912500	.0000	.012319
Mean	.260833	.0000	.000821

the player went to bat. The batting averages at the end of the year for the six infielders were

.277 Ramon Aviles
.267 Larry Bowa
.282 Pete Rose
.286 Mike Schmidt
.292 Manny Trillo
.161 John Vukovich

Taking the sum of these six batting averages (1.565) and dividing by 6 (the size of the population) gives the mean of this population (.260833, ordinarily rounded to .261, although for this illustration we will be working with the more precise estimate). We now ask, "How good an estimate of the precise true population mean do we obtain by simple random sampling?"

To answer this question we must first decide on the size of the sample we will use to estimate the mean of the population. For convenience we will define the sample size as any two infielders selected at random. The sample value is the arithmetic mean of the two batting averages. Hence, a sample consisting of Aviles (.277) and Bowa

(.267) has a mean score of .272000. The first column in Table 9.2 shows all the two-member samples. The second column shows their corresponding estimates of the population value. The overall mean is exactly .260833, which indicates that the random sampling plan is unbiased. The third column lists errors of estimate, obtained by subtracting the true population value from the sample estimate. Although the simple random sampling plan is clearly unbiased, we notice that some samples overestimate the true population value and others underestimate it.

Another way of thinking about the accuracy of the sampling plan is based on the standard deviation of chance fluctuations of the sample estimates of the population value (Snedecor & Cochran, 1980). The last column in Table 9.2 lists the squared errors of estimate, with the sum of all the squared errors shown at the bottom as .012319. Dividing this sum by the number of samples (15) gives the average of the squared errors of estimate, or mean square error (*MSE*). The divisor of the *MSE* is not usually the total N (as we explain in a later chapter), but in this case the error scores were measured from the true population value. The standard error of the population value is $\sqrt{MSE}$, that is, the standard deviation of all the errors of estimate. As $MSE = .012319/15 = .000821$, the standard error is $\sqrt{.000821} = .028658$. Dividing .028658 by the average of the sample means in Table 9.2 (.260833) tells us that the standard error amounts to about 11% of the population value. Now let us see how much more accuracy we would get with a stratified random sampling plan of similar sample size.

In doing stratified random sampling we divide the population into a number of parts and randomly sample in each part independently. Returning to Table 9.2, we notice that every simple random sample that contains Vukovich's name underestimates the true population value, but every sample without Vukovich's name overestimates it. If we had reason to suspect this fact before the sampling, we could make use of the information to divide the population into two strata. Stratum 1 consists of Vukovich alone, and Stratum 2 consists of Aviles, Bowa, Rose, Schmidt, and Trillo. We again draw simple random samples of Size 2, but now each sample will contain Vukovich and one name randomly drawn from Stratum 2. The total score of each sample is Vukovich's batting average plus the Stratum 2 member's batting average after it is multiplied by 5 (because we measured 1 member out of 5). We obtain the estimated population value by dividing this total by 6 (the total N). For example, the first sample listed in Table 9.3 consists of Vukovich (.161) and Aviles (.277 × 5 = 1.385), so that the estimated population value is (.161 + 1.385)/ 6 = .257667. Once again, it is evident that the stratified sampling plan is unbiased because we see that the average of the five sample estimates is exactly .260833. The errors of estimate are again the differences between the sample values and the true population value, and the *MSE* is the mean of the squared errors of estimate, or .000050. The standard error is $\sqrt{MSE} = .007057$, which, divided by the population mean (.007057/.260833 = .0271), indicates an improvement over the standard error obtained with simple random sampling. In this case the standard error of our stratified random sample amounts to only 2.7% of the population value, or one quarter the size of the standard error of the simple random sampling plan. The lesson? As Snedecor and Cochran (1980) noted, although some forethought is needed in deciding how to divide a population into strata, it can pay off handsomely

TABLE 9.3
Results for all possible stratified random samples of size two

Sample	Stratum 1	Stratum 2	Estimate of population mean	Error of estimate	(Error of estimate)^2
1	Vukovich	Aviles	.257667	−.003166	.000010
2	Vukovich	Bowa	.249333	−.011500	.000132
3	Vukovich	Rose	.261833	+.001000	.000001
4	Vukovich	Schmidt	.265167	+.004334	.000019
5	Vukovich	Trillo	.270167	+.009334	.000087
Sum			1.304167	.0000	.000249
Mean			.260833	.0000	.000050

in improved accuracy by enabling us to randomly sample strata that are less variable than the original population. *(*)Stratified random sampling is better than simple random sampling*

CONFIDENCE INTERVALS FOR POPULATION ESTIMATES

When reporting statistical inferences in survey research, it is customary to state that the population value is within a certain interval and to give the level of statistical confidence. The statement is based on the confidence interval (*CI*) around the estimated population value. Suppose we have 10 sampling units with scores of 3, 3, 4, 5, 5, 6, 8, 8, 9, 9, which have a mean (*M*) of 6.0 and a sample standard deviation (*S*) of 2.357. The 95% upper and lower limits for the estimated population value are based on the *t* distribution (discussed in chapter 13), where

$$95\% \ CI = M \pm \frac{(t_{(.05)})(S)}{\sqrt{N}}, \tag{9.1}$$

and *N* is the sample size, and $t_{(.05)}$ is read from Table B.2 (in Appendix B as 2.262) in the column headed .05 and *df* = 9 (the number of degrees of freedom in *S*, or *N* − 1).

Substituting these values in Equation 9.1, we find

$$95\% \ CI = 6.0 \pm \frac{(2.262)(2.357)}{\sqrt{10}} = 6.0 \pm 1.686,$$

which leads us to conclude, with 95% statistical confidence, that the estimated population mean is between 4.314 and 7.686. If we choose some other confidence level, we simply select another column in Table B.2 (e.g., the column labeled .01 for 99% confidence, or the column labeled .1 for 90% confidence). Increasing the confidence level from 90% to 95% to 99% will, of course, also increase the interval between the upper and lower limits. We can also use Table B.3 (which is more detailed), but we need to look in the column that lists a *p* value one half the *p* value we chose to define the confidence level, because the column headings in Table B.3

are one-tailed p values. In our example we would look in the column headed .025 and the row labeled $df = 9$ in Table B.3 to find the value of $t_{(.05)}$.

In many cases the sample estimate of the population value is a binomial proportion. For example, in a random survey of 200 of 3,000 graduating seniors at a large university, each student is asked, "Do you plan to join the alumni association after you graduate from college?" Of the sampled students, 25 reply "yes."

Expressed as a proportion of the sample N of 200 students, this value becomes $25/200 = .125$. The estimate of the population proportion is symbolized as P, and $1 - P$ is symbolized as Q, so $Q = .875$. The 95% upper and lower limits for the binomial population proportion are obtained from the following equation:

$$95\% \ CI = P \pm \left(1.96\sqrt{PQ/N}\right), \tag{9.2}$$

where $\sqrt{PQ/N}$ is the standard deviation of theoretical random samples estimating the binomial P, on the assumption that the binomial sample estimates of P are approximately normally distributed about the true population P (Snedecor & Cochran, 1980). The value of 1.96 is the standard normal deviate of $p = .05$ two-tailed, which we obtain from Table B.1 (in Appendix B). Because Table B.1 shows only the one-tailed p values, we instead locate one-tailed $p = .025$ in the body of Table B.1 and then find the standard normal deviate from the corresponding row and column headings. If we want a 90% confidence level, we substitute 1.645 for 1.96. If we prefer a 99% CI, we substitute 2.576.

Continuing with our original specifications, where $P = .125$, $Q = .875$, and $N = 200$, we find by substituting in Equation 9.2 that

$$95\% \ CI = .125 \pm \left[1.96\sqrt{\frac{(.125)(.875)}{200}}\right] = .125 \pm .0458,$$

which leads us to conclude, with 95% confidence, that the estimated population proportion is between .08 and .17. What if we double the size of the sample, from 200 to 400? The 95% CI becomes .09 to .16, a slight improvement but probably not worth the cost of interviewing another 200 students. And what if we double this sample, from 400 to 800? The 95% CI is .10 to .15, which also is probably not a cost-effective improvement. Given certain statistical assumptions, once a survey researcher has decided on the tolerable confidence limits and confidence level (e.g., 90%, 95%, 99%), the sample size needed to estimate the population value is easily computed. Later in this book we will have more to say about the choice of sample size in the context of significance testing, including the use of power tables to guide our selection of the sample size (chapter 12).

SPEAKING OF CONFIDENCE INTERVALS

In speaking of confidence intervals we have interpreted them to mean: If we find the lower and upper limits of a 95% confidence interval around our obtained estimate, we can be 95% confident, or sure, or certain, that the population value we are trying to estimate falls between those lower and upper limits. This view of the meaning of confidence intervals reflects a particular statistical approach, a so-called *Bayesian approach* (Gelman, Carlin, Stern, & Rubin, 1995; Lewis, 1993; Winkler, 1993).

There are alternative views of confidence intervals, however. These views have been variously labeled as *traditional, classical, sampling theorist,* or *frequentist.* The interpretation of a 95% confidence interval given by a statistician representing these views might be: With repeated samplings, and repeated calculations for each sample of 95% confidence intervals, we will be correct in 95% of our samples when we say that the quantity estimated (e.g., a mean, a median, an effect size) will fall within the 95% confidence interval.

Because both of these meanings of confidence intervals are "correct," we are not inclined to choose for others which view of confidence intervals they should hold. Perhaps because the Bayesian interpretation is the more "commonsense" view, it is the one we are likely to use in our own everyday analyses of data. Later in this book we have occasion to return to a comparison of Bayesian and non-Bayesian approaches to data analysis.

OTHER SELECTION PROCEDURES

There are many variations on the basic procedures we have discussed so far. Another popular variant of stratification is **area probability sampling.** The population is divided into selected units that have the same probablity of being chosen as the unselected units in the population cluster, all done in stages, a procedure described as **multistage cluster sampling.** Suppose we need an area probability sample of dwellings in a city. We would begin by dividing the city into a number of geographic clusters, then subdivide the geographic clusters into wards, then into precincts, then blocks, and finally into households. As a simplified example, suppose we needed an area probability sample of 300 out of 6,000 estimated dwellings. We might divide the area into blocks and then select 1 of every 20 blocks. If we define the sample as the dwellings located within the boundaries of the sample blocks, any dwelling's probability of selection is the selection of its block, set at 1/20 to correspond to the desired sampling rate of 300/6,000 (Kish, 1965).

Another procedure is called **systematic sampling** because it involves the methodical selection of the sampling units in sequences separated on lists by the interval of selection (Kish, 1965). It is often used when only manual procedures are available for sampling and the sample and population are both large. For example, suppose we want to select 1,000 households from the white pages of the telephone directory. Systematic selection starts randomly and is based on the selection of units from the population at particular intervals (Sudman, 1983). Thus, we need two things: (a) the sampling interval and (b) a random start. We can use a table of random digits to select the initial page and the name on that page. We then add to (or subtract from) the page selected a constant number and choose the name in the same place on that page. Afterward, we do the same thing again, and so forth. To illustrate, suppose we chose the number 48 by closing our eyes and pointing our finger to a particular row and column in our random digits table (i.e., a random start). We open the telephone directory to page 48 and find the forty-eighth name on every tenth page (i.e., a sampling interval of 10 pages) from page 48 (pages 8, 18, 28, 38, 58, 68, etc.).

A problem is that the systematic samples may not be exactly random samples. They are, in fact, complex samples with unknown properties (Sudman, 1983). To illustrate, we make a slight modification in our systematic sampling to help us deal more efficiently with refusals and unanswered calls. Whenever we encounter either problem we add 1 to the last digit in the telephone number of the person just called and try that number as an alternative. This approach is economical—and certainly it is systematic—but not all the numbers will be independent. We might be dialing into a bank of numbers from the same exchange, which will introduce a nonrandom element.

The most common strategy of nonrandom selection involves the use of **haphazard** or **fortuitous samples** (Kish, 1965). Archeologists who stumble on specimen bones, or people who draw conclusions from whatever ideas come to their minds, or artists who create sculptures from found objects—all are doing haphazard or fortuitous selection. A famous case of this research strategy involved the interview studies conducted by Alfred Kinsey and his associates (Kinsey, Pomeroy, & Martin, 1948; Kinsey, Pomeroy, Martin, & Gebhard, 1953). The research was conducted before the sexual revolution of the 1960s, and the results were not only surprising to many people but also suspected of being biased. Through a series of intensive interviews of about 8,000 American women and 12,000 American men, Kinsey concluded that as many as 50% of the men and 28% of the women had, by the age of 45, engaged in homosexual behavior, and that 8% of the men and almost 4% of the women had, by the time they were 21, had sexual contact with animals. And 50% of the men and 26% of the women reported having had extramarital relations before they had reached the age of 40.

Kinsey's conclusions became a source of intense discussion and controversy, as statisticians and social scientists questioned the accuracy of his population estimates (e.g., Cochran, Mosteller, & Tukey, 1953; Dollard, 1953; Geddes, 1954). One interesting attempt to address this criticism was based on some empirical studies in which it had been found (a) that people who were high in self-esteem tended to have somewhat unconventional sexual attitudes and behavior and (b) that volunteers for Kinsey interviews had scored higher on the measure of self-esteem than others who were unwilling to participate in a Kinsey interview (Maslow, 1942; Maslow & Sakoda, 1952). From this combination of results it was theorized that Kinsey's subjects probably differed from those who declined to be interviewed on the very dimensions of sexual behavior that the researchers were intent on identifying. In particular, it seemed that the Kinsey estimates might be overestimates of true population values.

A more familiar example of haphazard sampling is the "informal polls" conducted by the media, in which the procedure is to pose a question about some current controversial issue and then ask people to phone in or e-mail their opinions. In one case it was reported that WABC-TV in New York suspected that organized groups had jammed its telephone lines. In another case, Albuquerque's KOB-TV skipped its polling one night and still received about 20 calls voting "yes" and 38 voting "no" (Doan, 1968). Another example is how do-it-yourself pollsters now pose questions online at Web sites without an inkling of an idea of the generalizability of the responses. One reason for the online surveys is that they cost little or nothing to include on Web sites; another reason is that more and more people are reluctant to participate in telephone surveys or mailed questionnaire studies. We will have more to say about nonresponse in the next section, but many years ago, Wallis and Roberts (1956) called it the "Achilles heel" of opinion polling (p. 300).

Another form of subject selection is called **quota sampling** because it involves obtaining specified numbers of respondents to create a sample that is roughly proportional to the population (Kish, 1965). The problem is that, within the quotas, the interviewers are left to their own devices to obtain the respondents, though the characteristics of the desired respondents are spelled out in advance. This method goes back to the 1930s and early political polling, in which the interviewers were given ranges of characteristics and told to identify by sight people who seemed to fit the quota. For example, an interviewer might be told to find so many people of ages 25–35, 36–55, and 56 or over. As noted by Rossi et al. (1983), we do not know how much of the interviewing actually took place on busy corners and trolley stops rather than in house-to-house canvassing, but bias might have been introduced as a consequence of the interviewed individuals being more accessible than others.

NONRESPONSE BIAS AND ITS CONTROL

Even in the most carefully designed and precisely executed survey, not everyone who is contacted automatically agrees to participate. In a nationwide consumer tracking study done over a consecutive 12-month period in 1980–1981, marketing researchers Roger A. Kerin and Robert A. Peterson (1983) attempted to contact a large number of households in the United States. Those called were selected by means of a computerized telephone-numbering system used to generate households with both listed and unlisted numbers within the continental United States. The outcomes were then coded as (1) no answer (after five rings); (2) busy signal; (3) out-of-service number; (4) ineligible respondent (e.g., underage, or the number of a business or similar organization); (5) refusal to be interviewed; and (6) completion of the interview. The independent variables coded were (1) period of the day; (2) geographic location of the household; (3) day of the week; and (4) month. The results of this study, although conducted some years ago, might still serve as a guide to help us anticipate the best and worst times for a telephone interview.

In all, 259,088 dialings were made, but only 8.4% resulted in actual completions of the interview. The remainder, the nonrespondents, included 1.4% who refused to participate even though eligible, 34.7% no answers, 2% busy signals, 20.3% out-of-service numbers, and 33.2% ineligible respondents. The researchers divided the day into two unequal parts for their phone calls and analyses. The refusal rate was slightly lower when the dialing period was 5–9 p.m. (14.0%) as opposed to 8 a.m. to 9 p.m. (15.7%). It was also lower in rural (10.2% refusals) than in urban locations (16.7% refusals), and lowest on Sundays and Tuesdays (13.1% refusals for both days) and highest on Wednesdays (16.0% refusals) and Fridays (16.2% refusals). Potential interviewees were most likely to be at home during the months of December (11.3% at home) and January (12.0% at home) and less likely to be available during the other months of the years (ranging from 9.0% in September to 10.7% in February).

Can high rates of nonresponse impair the validity of survey studies, and if so, what can be done about it? Some answers to both parts of this question were provided by

TABLE 9.4

Example of bias due to nonresponse in survey research (Cochran, 1963)

| Basic data | Response to three mailings | | | | |
	First wave	Second wave	Third wave	Non-respondents	Total population
1. Number of respondents	300	543	434	1,839	3,116
2. Percentage of population	10	17	14	59	100
3. Mean trees per respondent	456	382	340	290	329
Cumulative data					
4. Mean trees per respondent (M_1)	456	408	385		
5. Mean trees per nonrespondent (M_2)	315	300	290		
6. Difference ($M_1 - M_2$)	141	108	95		
7. Percentage of nonrespondents (P)	90	73	59		
8. Bias $= (P)(M_1 - M_2)$	127	79	56		

William Cochran (1963), based on the results summarized in Table 9.4. The data pertain to three waves of questionnaires that were mailed out to fruit growers. One variable in this study was the number of fruit trees owned, and data were available for the entire population of growers for just this variable. As a consequence, it was possible to calculate the degree of bias attributable to nonresponse present after the first, second, and third waves of questionnaires. Rows 1 to 3 provide the basic data in the form of (1) the number of respondents to each wave of questionnaires and the number of nonrespondents, (2) the percentage of the total population represented by each wave of respondents (and nonrespondents), and (3) the mean number of trees owned by the respondents and the nonrespondents in each wave. Examination of row 3 reveals the nature of the nonresponse bias, which is that the earlier respondents owned more trees on the average than did the later responders.

The remaining five rows of data are based on the cumulative number of respondents available after the first, second, and third waves. For each wave, five items of information are provided: (4) the mean number of trees owned by the respondents up to that point in the survey, (5) the mean number of trees owned by the nonrespondents up to that point, (6) the difference between these two means, (7) the percentage of the population that had not yet responded, and (8) the magnitude of the bias up to that point in the study. Examination of this last row shows that, with each successive wave of respondents, there was an appreciable decrease in the magnitude of the bias, a result that appears to be fairly typical of studies of this kind. That is, increasing the effort to recruit the nonrespondents decreases the bias of point estimates in the sample.

Considerable theoretical attention has for some time been paid to sample selection bias in many areas of research (e.g., Berk, 1983; Berk & Ray, 1982; Gniech, 1986; Heckman, 1980; Nederhof, 1981; Rosenthal & Rosnow, 1975; Sudman, Sirken, & Cowan, 1988). In most circumstances of behavioral and social research we can compute the proportion of our population participants (P) and the statistic of interest for these respondents (M_1), but we cannot compute the same statistic for those who do not respond (M_2). Therefore, we are often in a position to suspect bias but unable to give an estimate of its magnitude. In survey research conducted by telephone or questionnaire a further problem is that researchers are frequently unable to differentiate the household refusals from the potential respondent refusals. In the former instance the nonrespondent is not the person who should be interviewed, but a "gatekeeper" within the household (Lavrakas, 1987).

A number of ideas have been suggested for stimulating response rates (Linsky, 1975). In the case of mail surveys these techniques include (a) using one or more follow-ups or reminders, such as telephone calls, postcards, and letters sent to the initial nonresponders; (b) contacting potential respondents before they receive the questionnaire and describing the study and why it is important for them to respond, (c) using "high-powered" mailings such as special delivery, and (d) offering a cash incentive or a desirable premium for responding. Church (1993) concluded that prepaid monetary incentives produce higher response rates than promised incentives or gifts offered with the initial mailing. A related concern is that the increasing use of incentive payments may raise the future expectations of survey respondents (Singer, Van Hoewyk, & Maher, 1998), possibly leading to perceptions of inequity and thus noncooperation in the future, although the latter does not yet seem to be a significant problem (Singer, Groves, & Corning, 1999; Singer, Van Hoewyk, & Maher, 2000).

A meta-analytic review of the literature on the effect of using incentives in telephone surveys concluded that paying an incentive is effective in increasing the response rate; its effectiveness is similar to that in mail surveys (Singer, Van Hoewyk, Gebler, Raghunathan, & McGonagle, 1999). In experiments conducted by Singer, Van Hoewyk, and Maher (2000), the finding was that prepaid incentives enclosed with advance letters reliably increased the response rates in random-digit-dialed telephone surveys by at least 10 percentage points. Another strategy is to train interviewers to handle difficult people and refusals by being politely persuasive without being aggressive, for example, to tell the person who picks up the phone how helpful his or her cooperation will be to the investigators. This procedure may have been more effective some years ago, but we suspect it is likely nowadays to elicit the opposite reaction from busy people, to the point where the interviewer can expect an almost instantaneous negative response.

Wainer (1999) underscored another general strategy for dealing with non-response, which is the creation of a theory-based model for the selection process. The model must describe not only what is to be observed, but also what cannot be observed. Such a model, he noted, was developed by the statistician Abraham Wald in work he did during World War II. Wald was trying to figure out where to place extra armor on military aircraft that had been shot at, and he began by recording on the outline of a plane the patterns of bullet holes in the returning planes. Reasoning that these were not the most vulnerable spots for extra armor, because those planes had returned safely despite being hit, he concluded that the best areas on the planes for extra armor must be every place else. As Wainer noted, Wald's "model for the nonresponse" was thus based on his assumption that military aircraft that did not return must have been hit in more vulnerable areas, and these needed extra protection. Of course, to properly test this model he would also need to find planes that did not return and record the pattern of bullet holes in them as well.

to increase response rates. (*)

Wald's model was correct, but it worked not because of the "magic of statistics," but because of his key insight into the "unsampled population" (Wainer, p. 255).

STUDYING THE VOLUNTEER SUBJECT

The volunteer subject problem can be understood as a variant on, or as encompassing, the problem of nonresponse bias. We have long been interested in the volunteer subject and, some years ago, wrote a book that summarized the results of hundreds of empirical findings regarding the characteristics of these subjects and the situational correlates of volunteering for research participation (Rosenthal & Rosnow, 1975). Our review of the relevant literature took the form of a number of quantitative summaries of research domains. (Such summaries were not common at the time, and a year later Gene Glass, 1976, gave such a summary its current name: *meta-analysis.*) Some of our results were given in terms of effect sizes, and some in terms of directional trends in statistically significant results. In the following discussion we describe some of our main conclusions, but first, we want to address two questions that have frequently been raised about research on the volunteer subject: (a) How does one study people who, by definition, are nonparticipants or nonvolunteers? And (b) how reliable is the act of volunteering for research participation?

In the spirit of methodological pluralism, several different strategies have been used to compare the characteristics of volunteers and nonvolunteers. One approach begins with an archive containing for each person listed all the information desired for a comparison between volunteers and nonvolunteers. Requests for volunteers are then made some time later, sometimes years later, and those who volunteer are compared to those who do not volunteer on all items in the archive in which the researcher is interested. For example, many colleges administer psychological tests and questionnaires to incoming students during an orientation period. Assuming there are safeguards of individuals' privacy, and that the study is approved by the ethics review board, the data may be used to compare students who volunteer with those who do not volunteer for a psychological study. In some cases the researchers have used similar data to compare the respondents and non-respondents to an alumni-organization questionnaire sent out years later.

A second approach calls for the recruitment of volunteers for research, usually in college classes, so that the volunteers and the nonvolunteers can be identified from the class rosters. Shortly thereafter, a test or questionnaire is given to the entire class by someone ostensibly unrelated to the person who recruited the subjects. Volunteers can then be compared to nonvolunteers on any of the variables measured in the classwide testing or surveying.

In a third approach, all the subjects or respondents are volunteers to begin with, and so any required data can be easily obtained from all of them. From this sample of volunteers, new volunteers for additional research are then recruited, and these second-level, or second-stage, volunteers can be compared to second-level non-volunteers on the data available for all. The differences between the second-level volunteers and the second-level nonvolunteers are likely to underestimate the differences between "true nonvolunteers" and "true volunteers," however, because the second-level nonvolunteers had at least been first-level volunteers. Thus, the procedure requires extrapolation on a gradient of volunteering, but it is also based on a leap of faith. For example, it might be hypothesized that, if the repeat volunteers were higher in the need for social approval than one-time volunteers, the nonvolunteers would be lower still in need for social approval.

A fourth approach is similar to the one described in Table 9.4, in which respondents are solicited from some sampling frame or list. After a suitable interval, another request for volunteers is made of those who were identified originally as nonvolunteers, and this process of repeat requesting may be repeated three or four or more times. The characteristics of those volunteering in each wave are plotted as data points from which a tentative extrapolation is made to the characteristics of those who never responded. In some cases the incentive might be periodically increased to show whether those who volunteer with less incentive, or those who volunteer more quickly, are further down the curve from those who volunteer with more incentive or less quickly.

In a fifth approach, only a single request for volunteers is issued, but the latency of volunteering is recorded. The characteristics of those responding at each of the two or more levels of latency are used as data points from which to extrapolate to characteristics of those who did not volunteer at all. This method has been used primarily in survey research, and it appears to have some promise. However, it is probably less effective as a basis for extrapolating to nonvolunteers or nonrespondents than the method of increasing the incentive. Nonetheless, this fifth strategy can be combined with the method of increasing the incentive, and the trends within waves or requests can be compared with the trends between the waves or requests.

With regard to the reliability of volunteering, Table 9.5 shows the results of 10 studies available to us when we addressed this question after we were given an opportunity

TABLE 9.5
Reliability of volunteering behavior

Author	Index	Magnitude	p	Type of study
Barefoot (1969) I	r_{pb}	.45	.001	Various experiments
Barefoot (1969) II	r_{pb}	.42	.001	Various experiments
Dohrenwend & Dohrenwend (1968)	ϕ	.24[a,b]	.02	Interviews
Laming (1967)	ρ	.22[b]	.05	Choice-reaction
Martin & Marcuse (1958) I	r_t	.91[a]	.001	Learning
Martin & Marcuse (1958) II	r_t	.80[a]	.001	Personality
Martin & Marcuse (1958) III	r_t	.67[a]	.001	Sex
Martin & Marcuse (1958) IV	r_t	.97[a]	.001	Hypnosis
Rosen (1951)	ϕ	.34	.05	Personality
Wallace (1954)	C^{c}	.58	.001	Questionnaires
Median		.52	.001	

Note: Different types of correlations listed under Index are described in chapter 11.

[a]In these studies the second request was to volunteer for the same research as the first request.

[b]All subjects had been volunteers at one time, so that the reliabilities were probably lowered by a restriction of range of the volunteering variable.

[c]The symbol C refers here to the contingency coefficient.

to respond to an earlier published critique (cf. Kruglanski, 1973; Rosnow & Rosenthal, 1974). Notice that the median reliability coefficient was .52, with a range from .22 to .97. As a standard with which to compare these values, we examined the subtest intercorrelations for what is perhaps the most widely used and carefully developed test of intelligence, the Wechsler Adult Intelligence Scale, or WAIS (Wechsler, 1958). Repeated factor analyses of the WAIS had suggested that there was a very large first factor, g, that in its magnitude swamped the other factors extracted, typically accounting for 10 times more variance than the other factors. The full-scale WAIS, then, was an excellent measure of this first factor, or g. The WAIS subtest intercorrelations were reported by Wechsler to range from .08 to .85, with a median of .52, which, by coincidence, is the median value of the reliabilities of volunteering shown in Table 9.5. Of the studies listed in this table the median reliability of the laboratory studies was .56, whereas the median for the field studies was .41, but there were too few studies (only two) in the latter group to allow conclusions about this difference.

As indicated in the footnote to Table 9.5, five of the studies requested people to volunteer a second time for the same task. In the remaining studies, the second and subsequent requests were to volunteer for a different study. Assuming there are propensities to volunteer, then surely these propensities should be more stable when people are asked to volunteer for the same, as opposed to a different, type of research experience. The data in the table bear out this plausible inference. The median reliability for studies that requested volunteers for the same task was .80, whereas the median reliability for studies that requested volunteers for different tasks was only .42. Both these median reliabilities are very significantly different from zero (p much less than .001). Although the 10 studies were not very many on which to base such a conclusion, the findings nevertheless suggested to us that volunteering, like IQ, might have both general and specific predictors. That is, some people volunteer reliably more than others for a variety of tasks, and these reliable individual differences might be further stabilized when the task for which volunteering was requested is specifically considered.

It should also be noted that all of the indices of correlation in Table 9.5 underestimate the degree of association relative to the Pearson product-moment correlation (under most conditions), even though most of these indices are product-moment correlations. The contingency coefficient (C), not a member of the r family, shows this underestimation most dramatically. In a 2 × 2 table, C_{max} is equal to .71 when a product-moment correlation would yield $\phi = 1.00$. The median overall index of association noted in Table 9.5, therefore, is likely to be biased in the low direction and should be regarded as a rough estimate.

CHARACTERISTICS OF THE VOLUNTEER SUBJECT

Proceeding attribute by attribute, we considered a large number of empirical studies investigating the question of how volunteer subjects differ from their more reluctant colleagues (Rosenthal & Rosnow, 1975). Our quantitative analysis now seems primitive to us in light of subsequent developments in meta-analysis (discussed in chapter 21). However, on the assumption that all of our major conclusions remain tenable and their implications remain methodologically relevant, Table 9.6 shows an overall tabulation of several hundred

TABLE 9.6

Summary of the results of studies of volunteer characteristics (Rosenthal & Rosnow, 1975)

Volunteer characteristic	Number of studies available	Percentage of total significant studies	Percentage of total studies significantly favoring conclusion	Percentage of significant studies favoring conclusion
Female	63	44	35	79
Firstborn	40	25	18	70
Sociable	19	68	63	92
Extraverted	8	50	25	50
Self-disclosing	3	100	100	100
Altruistic	4	100	100	100
Achievement-motivated	9	67	44	67
Approval-motivated	19	58	58	100
Nonconforming	17	29	29	100
Nonauthoritarian	34	44	35	80
Unconventional	20	75	55	73
Arousal-seeking	26	62	50	81
Anxious	35	46	26	56
Maladjusted	34	71	44	62
Intelligent	37	59	54	91
Educated	26	92	92	100
Higher social class	46	80	70	86
Young	41	56	34	61
Married	11	55	36	67
Jewish > Protestant or Protestant > Catholic	17	41	41	100
Interested in religion	11	45	36	80
From smaller town	10	40	40	100
Median	20	57	42	80

17/23 are me!.

studies, listed in the order in which we discussed these characteristics in more detail in our earlier book (Rosenthal & Rosnow, 1975, p. 85). The first column lists the characteristics more often associated with the volunteer subject (i.e., except for the extraversion variable, which was as often associated significantly with volunteering as introversion). The second column lists the number of studies providing evidence on the relationship between volunteering and the characteristic in question. The minimum requirement for inclusion in this list was that there be at least three statistically significant results, in either direction, bearing on the relationship between any characteristic and volunteering.

The third column of Table 9.6 shows the percentage of the total number of the relevant results that reported a statistically significant relationship between volunteering and the listed characteristic. The range was from 25% to 100%, indicating that for all the characteristics listed, there were clearly more statistically significant results than would be expected if there were actually no relationship between the characteristic listed and volunteering. Although this column indicates that all the listed characteristics are too often associated with volunteering, it does not provide evidence on the direction of the relationship. Thus, in the first row, the characteristic listed is "female" and the corresponding third column indicates that 44% of the 63 relevant studies found some statistically significant relationship between being female and volunteering. Some of these relationships were positive, however, whereas others were negative. The fourth column gives the percentage of all the relevant studies that found volunteers to be more likely to show the characteristics listed in the first column. Thus, in the first row, the fourth column shows that 35% of the 63 relevant studies found females to be significantly more likely than males to volunteer for participation in a study. The range of percentages listed in the fourth column runs from 18% to 100%, indicating that for all the characteristics listed, there were more statistically significant results than we would expect if volunteers were not actually more likely to be characterized by the attribute listed in the first column.

Even this fourth column, however, does not give sufficient information, as it is possible that there was an equally large percentage of the total number of relevant studies that yielded results significant in the opposite direction. That is exactly what occurred in the fourth row, which lists "extraverted" as a volunteer characteristic. Exactly one half of the eight relevant studies revealed a statistically significant relationship between volunteering and extraversion (column 3) and 25% showed that extraverts were significantly more likely to volunteer than introverts (column 4). The difference between column 3 and column 4, however, shows that an equal number of studies (25%) yielded a significantly opposite effect. As a convenient way of showing the net evidence of a specific relationship between volunteering and any characteristic, column 5 was added. This final column lists the percentage of all significant results that favor the conclusion that volunteers are more often characterized by the attribute listed in the first column. The range of percentages runs from 50% to 100%. This range indicates that for some characteristics all significant results favor the conclusion implied by the first column, whereas for others the evidence is equally strong for the conclusion implied by the first column and for the opposite of that conclusion. This latter situation occurred only once, and that was in the case of the attribute we have already noted, extraversion.

Table 9.7 lists all the characteristics by the degree to which we felt confident that they were indeed associated with volunteering for research participation. The table sorts the characteristics into four groups, and within each group the characteristics are listed in approximately descending order of the confidence we expressed in the relationship between volunteering and the particular characteristic. By *confidence* we imply not a statistical confidence level, but an empirically driven, intuitive judgment. The definition of the degree of confidence involved an arbitrary, complex multiple cutoff procedure in which a conclusion was felt to be more warranted when (a) it was based on a larger

TABLE 9.7

Volunteer characteristics grouped by degree of confidence of conclusion

I. Maximum confidence	III. Some confidence
1. Educated	12. From smaller town
2. Higher social class	13. Interested in religion
3. Intelligent	14. Altruistic
4. Approval-motivated	15. Self-disclosing
5. Sociable	16. Maladjusted
II. Considerable confidence	17. Young
6. Arousal-seeking	**IV. Minimum confidence**
7. Unconventional	18. Achievement motivated
8. Female	19. Married
9. Nonauthoritarian	20. Firstborn
10. Jewish > Protestant or Protestant > Catholic	21. Anxious
11. Nonconforming	22. Extraverted

number of studies; (b) a larger percentage of the total number of relevant studies significantly favored the conclusion; and (c) a larger percentage of those studies showing a statistically significant relationship favored the conclusion drawn. If we were to repeat this analysis today, we would use a more informative meta-analytic approach in which the effect sizes were estimated, interval estimates around the pooled effect sizes were calculated, the fail-safe numbers were reported for overall significance levels, and a further effort would be made to uncover more recent studies that explored for moderating variables. That qualification notwithstanding, the three criteria we used were based on the second, fourth, and fifth columns of Table 9.6, with the minimum values of each criterion that we used shown in Table 9.8.

In Table 9.8, to qualify for "maximum confidence" a relationship had to be based on a large number of studies, of which a majority significantly favored the conclusion drawn and of which the vast majority of just the significant outcomes favored the conclusion. To qualify for "considerable confidence" a large number of studies was also required, but the fraction of total studies significantly favoring the conclusion drawn was permitted

TABLE 9.8

Cutoff requirements for each degree of confidence

Degree of confidence	Number of studies available	Percentage of available studies significantly favoring conclusion	Percentage of significant studies favoring conclusion
Maximum	19	54	86
Considerable	17	29	73
Some	3	29	61
Minimum	3	18	50

to drop somewhat below one-third. The percentage of significant results that favored the conclusion, however, was still required to be large (73%). The major difference between the categories of "considerable" and "some" confidence was in the number of studies available on which to base a conclusion, although some characteristics that often had been investigated were placed in the "some confidence" category when the fraction of significant studies favoring the conclusion fell to below two thirds. The final category, "minimum confidence," comprised characteristics that did not so clearly favor one direction of relationship over the other and characteristics that had not been sufficiently investigated to permit a stable conclusion. To put the basis for the grouping shown in Tables 9.7 and 9.8 in a slightly different way, we can say that the degree of confidence in a conclusion was based on the degree to which future studies reporting no significant relationships, or even relationships significantly in the opposite direction, appeared unlikely to alter the overall conclusion drawn. Thus, for example, when 24 of 26 studies showed volunteers to be significantly better educated than nonvolunteers, it would take a good many studies showing no significant relationship and even a fair number of studies showing a significantly opposite relationship before we would decide that volunteers were not, on the whole, better educated than nonvolunteers.

So far in our summary of characteristics associated with volunteering, we have counted all relevant studies, paying no attention to the type of task for which volunteering had been requested, nor to the sex of the sample of subjects, nor to the particular operational definition of the characteristic investigated in each study. Yet each of these variables has been found to affect the relationship between volunteering and some of the characteristics investigated. Hence, we conclude this section with a listing of specific conclusions that also seemed warranted by the evidence, taking into account the effects of various moderator variables. The order of our listing follows that shown in Table 9.7, beginning with conclusions warranting maximum confidence and ending with conclusions warranting minimum confidence. Within each of the four groups, the conclusions are again ranked in the approximate order of the degree of confidence we can have in each.

Conclusions warranting maximum confidence:

1. Volunteers tend to be better educated than nonvolunteers, especially when personal contact between investigator and respondent is not required.
2. Volunteers tend to have higher social-class status than nonvolunteers, especially when social class is defined by the respondents' own status rather than by parental status.
3. Volunteers tend to be more intelligent than nonvolunteers when volunteering is for research in general, but not when volunteering is for somewhat less typical kinds of research (e.g., hypnosis, sensory isolation, and small-group and personality research).
4. Volunteers tend to be higher in the need for social approval than nonvolunteers.
5. Volunteers tend to be more sociable than nonvolunteers.

Conclusions warranting considerable confidence:

6. Volunteers tend to be more arousal-seeking than nonvolunteers, especially when volunteering is for studies of stress, sensory isolation, and hypnosis.

7. Volunteers tend to be more unconventional than nonvolunteers, especially when volunteering is for studies of sexual behavior.

8. Females are more likely than males to volunteer for research in general, but less likely than males to volunteer for physically and emotionally stressful research (e.g., electric shock, high temperature, sensory deprivation, interviews about sexual behavior).

9. Volunteers tend to be less authoritarian than nonvolunteers.

10. Jews are more likely to volunteer than Protestants, and Protestants are more likely to volunteer than Catholics.

11. Volunteers tend to be less conforming than nonvolunteers when volunteering is for research in general, but not when subjects are female and the research task is relatively "clinical" (as in hypnosis, sleep, or counseling research).

Conclusions warranting some confidence:

12. Volunteers tend to be from smaller towns than nonvolunteers, especially when volunteering is for questionnaire studies.

13. Volunteers tend to be more interested in religion than nonvolunteers, especially when volunteering is for questionnaire studies.

14. Volunteers tend to be more altruistic than nonvolunteers.

15. Volunteers tend to be more self-disclosing than nonvolunteers.

16. Volunteers tend to be more maladjusted than nonvolunteers, especially when volunteering is for potentially unusual situations (e.g., studies involving pharmaceuticals, hypnosis, high temperature, or vaguely described experiments) or for medical research using clinical (rather than psychometric) definitions of psychopathology.

17. Volunteers tend to be younger than nonvolunteers, especially when volunteering is for laboratory research and especially if the volunteers are female.

Conclusions warranting minimum confidence:

18. Volunteers tend to be higher in need for achievement than nonvolunteers, especially among American samples.

19. Volunteers are more likely to be married than nonvolunteers, especially when volunteering is for studies requiring contact between investigator and respondent.

20. Firstborns are more likely than laterborns to volunteer, especially when recruitment is personal and when the research requires group interaction and a low level of stress.

21. Volunteers tend to be more anxious than nonvolunteers, particularly when volunteering is for more standard, nonstressful tasks, and especially if the volunteers are college students.

22. Volunteers tend to be more extraverted than nonvolunteers when interaction with others is required by the nature of the research.

IMPLICATIONS FOR THE INTERPRETATION OF RESEARCH FINDINGS

Before we turn to the situational correlates of volunteering, we should mention the implications of the preceding discussion for the validity of inferred causal relation-ships as well as the generalizability of descriptive conclusions. Figure 9.2 illustrates the threat to generalizability from using volunteer subjects to establish test norms, in this case for a hypothetical IQ test. The figure depicts roughly the positive bias that is expected to result from using only volunteer subjects, who (as noted in Conclusion 3) have a tendency to score higher on intelligence tests than nonvolunteers. Similarly, were we to recruit volunteers to provide the norms for a test that correlated with any of the other characteristics of volunteer subjects, we would also predict positive or negative biasing effects. Insofar as any of those characteristics might be conceptualized as a potential threat to generalizability, we should be able to predict the direction of the bias resulting from this threat. Of course, merely increasing the size of the sample of volunteers will not reduce the bias, but an effort to recruit more nonvolunteers or, better still, to use probability sampling as well as attempting to reduce the nonresponse rate, would be expected to address this problem.

We should also be able to predict the direction of the volunteer bias in randomized experimental studies. Suppose we want to evaluate the effect of an experimental treatment on the dependent variable of gregariousness. If we draw a sample of volunteers, any

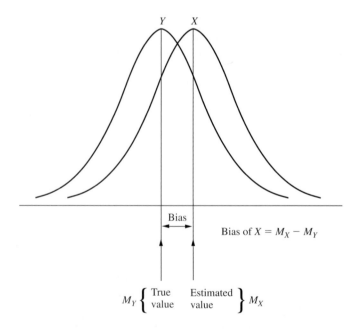

FIGURE 9.2

The curve symbolized by Y represents a theoretical normal distribution of IQs in the general population, and the curve labeled X represents a theoretical normal distribution of IQs among volunteers. To the extent that the mean of the X is different from the mean of the Y (as shown), the resultant bias constitutes a threat to the generalizability of the data.

We are creating norms out of a select group of people who volunteer.

treatment designed to increase gregariousness may be too harshly judged as ineffective because the untreated group is already unusually high in sociability (Characteristic 5). Similarly, suppose we want to assess the validity of a new educational procedure that is purported to make students less rigid in their thinking. If we randomly assign volunteers to an experimental group that receives the procedure or to a control group that does not receive it, we predict that the controls will already be unusually low on the dependent variable (because volunteers tend to be low in authoritarianism, i.e., Characteristic 9). Thus, even though we've designed a randomized controlled experiment, we have again inadvertently minimized the true difference between the two groups by using just volunteer subjects.

The opposite type of error can also be imagined. Suppose we want to find out how persuasive an advertising appeal is by using a sample of volunteers, half of whom will randomly receive the message (the experimental group) and half of whom will not (the control group). Given that volunteers tend to be higher in the need for social approval (Characteristic 4), and that people who are high in the need for social approval tend to be more readily influenced than those low in this need, we predict that volunteers exposed to the advertising appeal will overreact to it. Comparing their reactions with those in the control group will have a tendency to exaggerate the impact of the appeal in the general population.

One lesson, of course, is that randomized experimental designs usually do not control for sampling biases and may therefore yield less generalizable results. A second lesson is that knowing the general characteristics of volunteer subjects in Table 9.7, and also being sufficiently familiar with the literature in one's field to know how certain characteristics may interact with the experimental treatment, allows the investigator to predict the direction of the bias. In studies that involve any sort of stress, for example, the volunteer subjects' sex, arousal-seeking inclinations, and anxiety may be biasing factors. In clinical research, volunteers' nonconformity tendency may be suspect; in medical research, the volunteer subjects' psychological adjustment; and so on.

SITUATIONAL CORRELATES AND THE REDUCTION OF VOLUNTEER BIAS

We turn now to situational correlates of volunteering for research participation. As was the case in our examination of the more stable characteristics of volunteers, our inventory of situational variables was developed intuitively rather than deductively (Rosenthal & Rosnow, 1975). The question that we put to the empirical literature was "What are the variables that tend to increase or decrease the rates of volunteering?" The answers have specific implications for both the theory and the practice of behavioral and social science. First, we can learn something about the social psychology of volunteering, and second, we are in a better position to reduce the bias in our samples that derives from volunteers' being systematically different from nonvolunteers in a variety of characteristics.

Table 9.9 lists the situational correlates of volunteering by the degree of confidence we expressed in each variable. The definition of *confidence* was again based both on the number of studies relevant to the relationship under consideration (although there were fewer in this case than in our investigation of the characteristics of volunteer subjects) and on the proportion of the relevant studies whose results supported

TABLE 9.9
**Situational correlates of volunteering grouped by degree
of confidence of conclusion**

Maximum confidence	Some confidence
1. Subject interest	6. Recruiter characteristics
2. Expectation of favorable evaluation	7. Aversive tasks
Considerable confidence	8. Normative expectations
	Minimum confidence
3. Task importance	
4. Guilt, happiness, and competence	9. Prior acquaintance
5. Material incentives	10. Public versus private commitment

a directional hypothesis. To qualify for "maximum confidence" a relationship had to be based on at least 20 studies, and at least 6 out of 7 studies had to support it. To qualify for "considerable confidence" a relationship had to be based on at least 10 studies, and at least two-thirds had to support the relationship. To qualify for "some confidence" a relationship had to be based either on 3 studies, all of which supported the relationship, or on 9 studies, most of which supported it, with none showing a significant reversal of the relationship. Relationships not meeting these standards are listed in Table 9.9 under the heading of "minimum confidence." We list the following conclusions that also seemed warranted by the evidence, taking into account the effects of moderator variables suggested by the data. The order of our listing follows that shown in Table 9.9, beginning with the conclusions warranting maximum confidence and ending with those warranting minimum confidence. Within each category, the conclusions are again ranked in approximate order of the degree of confidence we expressed in each.

Conclusions warranting maximum confidence:

1. Persons more interested in the topic under investigation are more likely to volunteer.
2. Persons with expectations of being more favorably evaluated by the investigator are more likely to volunteer.

Conclusions warranting considerable confidence:

3. Persons perceiving the investigation as important are more likely to volunteer.
4. Persons' feeling states at the time of the request for volunteers are likely to affect the probability of volunteering. Persons feeling guilt are more likely to volunteer, especially when contact with the unintended victim can be avoided and when the source of guilt is known to others. Persons made to "feel good" or to feel competent are also more likely to volunteer.
5. Persons offered greater material incentives are more likely to volunteer, especially if the incentives are offered as gifts in advance and without being contingent on the person's decision to volunteer. Stable personal characteristics of the potential volunteer may moderate the relationship between volunteering and material incentives.

Conclusions warranting some confidence:

6. Personal characteristics of the recruiter are likely to affect the subject's probability of volunteering. Recruiters higher in status or prestige are likely to obtain higher rates of volunteering, as are female recruiters. This latter relationship is especially modifiable by the sex of the subject and the nature of the research.

7. Persons are less likely to volunteer for tasks that are more aversive in the sense of being painful, stressful, or dangerous biologically or psychologically. Personal characteristics of the potential volunteer and level of incentive may moderate the relationship between volunteering and task aversiveness.

8. Persons are more likely to volunteer when volunteering is viewed as the normative, expected, appropriate thing to do.

Conclusions warranting minimum confidence:

9. Persons are more likely to volunteer when they are acquainted with the recruiter. The addition of a "personal touch" may also increase volunteering.

10. Conditions of public commitment may increase rates of volunteering when it is normatively expected, but they may decrease rates of volunteering when nonvolunteering is normatively expected.

Previously, we mentioned some of the procedures that are used to try to improve response rates in survey research. In a similar vein, there are a number of steps that may prove useful in reducing volunteer bias in experimental and other studies. Here is a list of recommendations, offered in a tentative spirit and subject to further empirical testing:

1. Make the appeal for volunteers as interesting as possible, keeping in mind the nature of the target population.

2. Make the appeal for volunteers as nonthreatening as possible so that potential volunteers will not be put off by unwarranted fears of unfavorable evaluation.

3. Explicitly state the theoretical and practical importance of the research for which volunteering is requested.

4. Explicitly state in what way the target population is particularly relevant to the research being conducted and the responsibility of would-be volunteers to participate in research that has potential for benefiting others.

5. When possible, potential volunteers should be offered not only pay for participation but small courtesy gifts simply for taking time to consider whether they will want to participate.

6. Have the request for volunteering made by a person of status as high as possible, and preferably by a woman.

7. When possible, avoid research tasks that may be psychologically or biologically stressful.

8. When possible, communicate the normative nature of the volunteering response.

9. After a target population has been defined, make an effort to have someone known to that population make the appeal for volunteers. The request for volunteers may be more successful if a personalized appeal is made.

10. In situations where volunteering is regarded by the target population as normative, conditions of public commitment to volunteering may be more successful; where nonvolunteering is regarded as normative, conditions of private commitment may be more successful.

A hasty reading of these recommendations might give the impression that they are designed only to increase rates of volunteering and thus to decrease volunteer bias. A more careful reading, however, should reveal that the recommendations may have other beneficial effects. They should make us more careful and thoughtful not only in how we make our appeals for volunteers, but also in our planning of research. Our relations with our potential participants may become somewhat more reciprocal and more human, and our procedures may become more humane. Finally, if we are to tell our research subjects as much as possible about the significance of our research (as though they were another granting agency, which in fact they are, granting us time instead of money), then we will have to give up trivial research.

THE PROBLEM OF MISSING DATA

At the beginning of this chapter we alluded to the problem of *missing data,* which is a concern of all behavioral and social researchers (West, 2001). The term is most commonly applied to situations in which each research subject has supplied multiple responses to a test, a questionnaire, a longitudinal study, or a set of psychophysiological measures, but one or more responses that were to be collected by the investigator are unavailable. The proportion of data missing per research subject may range from .00 to 1.00. Subjects who provide all the desired data have *no* missing data, and those who never show up for the research have *only* missing data. Analyzing the data from only those who show up and provide all the data desired does not really address the primary problem of missing data, which is that the quantities to be estimated (means, variances, correlations, etc.) are likely to differ systematically from the values that would have been obtained had all the data been available.

In short, the primary problem of missing data is the introduction of bias into our estimates; an additional problem is decreased statistical power. Recent works have discussed the issues involved in the handling of missing data, including the importance of the reasons underlying the "missingness" (its mechanisms) and the older and newer approaches to missing data (Collins, Schafer, & Kam, 2001; Enders, 2001; Sinharay, Stern, & Russell, 2001). Thus, it has been noted how missingness can occur completely at random (MCAR), not quite at random but explainably so (MAR), and not at random but explainably so (MNAR). We will first define each of these expressions in a little more detail and then describe alternative procedures for dealing with missing data.

MCAR *(missing completely at random)* is said to occur when the missingness is unrelated to any variables of substantive interest. In this case the data observed give unbiased estimates of what would have been observed had no data been missing.

MAR *(missing at random)* is said to occur when the missingness is related to variables of interest, but when these relationships can be accounted for by other variables that have been observed. Because missingness is not uncorrelated with variables of interest, MAR has a potential of yielding biased estimates. However, when these correlations can be explained by other variables, bias can be reduced or eliminated.

MNAR *(missing not at random)* is said to occur when the missingness is related to variables of interest but cannot be fully accounted for by other variables that have been observed. To the extent that the correlations between missingness and variables of interest are neither zero nor explainable, MNAR will yield biased estimates.

Mechanisms of missingness have been conceptualized in recent years by Donald B. Rubin and his collaborators and colleagues (Dempster, Laird, & Rubin, 1977; Little & Rubin, 1987; Rubin, 1976, 1978, 1987, 1996; Schafer, 1997). The importance of these conceptualizations is that the procedures used to minimize bias and maximize power depend for their effectiveness on the mechanisms of missingness. These procedures have recently been summarized by Sinharay et al. (2001), and in the following discussion we provide thumbnail sketches of each procedure.

PROCEDURES FOR DEALING WITH MISSING DATA

Table 9.10 lists the two broad types of approaches for dealing with missing data and their various subcategories. **Nonimputational procedures** are those that yield estimates of parameters without "filling in" the missing data. **Imputational procedures** are those that yield their estimates after filling in the missing data. Two quite venerable and simple approaches to nonimputational procedures are listwise and pairwise deletion. In **listwise deletion** the procedure is to drop all subjects who have *any* missing data. If the missing data are known to be MCAR, listwise deletion yields unbiased estimates, but it suffers from loss of power in proportion to the number or percentage of the total number of subjects that were dropped. In **pairwise deletion** the procedure does not drop any subjects but simply computes the parameters of interest (e.g., means, variances, correlations) on all data that are available for that particular computation. This procedure is more powerful than listwise deletion but also requires that missing data be MCAR to yield unbiased estimates. What makes listwise deletion and pairwise deletion problematic, however, is that it is virtually impossible to know whether the missing data are, in fact, MCAR. Thus, two newer, more sophisticated procedures are **maximum likelihood estimation** and **Bayesian estimation.** Both of these procedures can yield unbiased results when missing data are MAR. For both approaches, computations may be very complex, and both approaches are very dependent on the specific statistical model applied to the data set.

TABLE 9.10

Procedures for dealing with missing data

I. Nonimputational procedures	II. Imputational procedures
A. Listwise deletion	A. Single imputation
B. Pairwise deletion	1. Mean substitution
C. Maximum likelihood estimation	2. Regression substitution
D. Bayesian estimation	3. Stochastic regression imputation
	4. Hot deck imputation
	B. Multiple imputation

Imputational procedures can also be divided into two general types, single and multiple, with the single imputational procedures further subdivided into four alternative procedures as noted in Table 9.10. The **single imputation procedures** have in common that each missing value is replaced by a reasonable estimate of what that value might have been had it been observed. The now "complete" data set is then analyzed by the procedures that would have been used had there been no missing data, but with some adjustments, for example, decreasing *df* so that they cannot exceed the *df* available before imputation.

In the **mean substitution procedure** all missing values for any given variable are replaced by the mean value of that variable. Only if the missing data are MCAR does this procedure yield unbiased estimates, and even then estimates of variability are likely to be too low. In the **regression substitution procedure** all missing values are replaced by the predicted value of that variable from a regression analysis using only cases with no missing data. As with mean substitution, the estimates are unbiased only if the missing data are MCAR, but even then estimates of variability are likely to be too low. **Stochastic regression imputation** adds a random residual term to the estimates based on regression substitution and often yields more accurate analyses than does regression substitution. In **hot deck imputation** the procedure finds cases without the missing data that are similar to the cases with the missing data. From several cases that are close matches to each case with missing data, one is chosen at random as the case whose corresponding value is to be imputed for the missing observation. This method, although quite appealing, can be difficult to implement when a good many data points are missing.

In **multiple imputation** each missing observation is replaced not by a single estimate, but by a set of *m* reasonable estimates that will yield *m* pseudocomplete data sets. These multiple data sets are then analyzed as complete data sets to address all questions of scientific interest. The results of the *m* analyses are combined to yield minimally biased results with more accurate estimates of variability than are obtained from single imputation procedures. Compared to maximum likelihood estimation and Bayesian estimation, multiple imputation procedures tend to be much simpler computationally under most circumstances. The mathematical bases for the multiple imputation approach are beyond the scope of this text (and its authors). Currently, multiple imputation procedures seem to be the most useful under most conditions (Collins et al., 2001; Sinharay et al., 2001). The application of multiple imputation procedures requires sophisticated software that is currently available in Jöreskog and Sörbom (2001) and Schafer (1999). Because maximum likelihood approaches give results similar to those of multiple imputation under a good many conditions, we note that software is also available for these approaches in Arbuckle and Wothke (1999).

PART

IV

FUNDAMENTALS
OF DATA
ANALYSIS

CHAPTER
10

DESCRIBING, DISPLAYING, AND EXPLORING DATA

DESCRIPTIONS OF SAMPLING UNITS

As noted at the beginning of the previous chapter, much of the fundamental data-analytic work in behavioral and social research involves the description of a group of sampling units. A number or metric value is assigned to each unit, or to some attribute of that unit, and the task of describing the data is summarizing the numbers representing the units or counting the data in different categories. Summaries of numerical values typically indicate the location of the central value and the spread of the values around it. Those summary values are usually means, medians, modes, variances, standard deviations, and ranges (all of which are reviewed in this chapter).

There are also various options for exhibiting the values. One common way of presenting summary data is in a table, but graphic displays are also widely used. The advantage of tables is that exact values can be provided, whereas when data are reported in graphics, viewers can usually make only an educated guess about the exact values. An important exception, described in this chapter, is the stem-and-leaf chart, which provides the exact values and also gives a picture of the distribution of the values. Whatever the form summary data take, however, it is essential that the information be reported clearly, accurately, precisely, and in enough detail to allow research consumers to reach their own conclusions. Fortunately, for those skilled enough in statistical reasoning and patient enough to explore the data, it is possible to calculate secondary analyses even with the barest of available ingredients.

That idea of "exploring the data" is one of the themes of this chapter—and indeed of this text. It is also a reflection of a seminal book, *Exploratory Data Analysis,* written by one of the most influential statisticians of our time, John W. Tukey. Before its publication, many researchers believed it to be "poor form," or even cheating, to snoop around in the data, looking for interesting findings that had not been predicted. Tukey's (1977) work made it not only acceptable, but even desirable and sophisticated, to explore the data (Wainer & Velleman, 2001). Although such snooping, or data exploration, may complicate the calculation of accurate significance levels, it seems a small price to pay for opportunities to learn something new and important about our disciplines. Of course, it is ethically imperative that researchers not misrepresent ad hoc interpretations of data as a priori predictions.

Traditional kinds of visual representations, going all the way back to R. A. Fisher, Karl Pearson, and other leading statisticians and methodologists, include correlational diagrams, bar graphs, trend charts, pie diagrams, and so forth, all of which can now be easily created with readily accessible software. Intricate aspects of the visual representation of data have been discussed in a number of articles and specialized texts in a detail that is beyond the scope of this chapter (e.g., Basford & Tukey, 1999; Chambers, Cleveland, Kleiner, & Tukey, 1983; Cleveland, 1985, 1993, 1994; Cleveland & McGill, 1985; Gross, 1983; Kosslyn, 1994; Tufte, 1983, 1990, 1997, 2001; Wainer, 1984, 2000). Emphasized in this chapter are two strategies for displaying data, the stem-and-leaf and the box plot, although we begin by reviewing the most common of all graphics, the frequency diagram. We also have more to say about commonly used indices of the precision of estimating population means. And finally, we describe how to deal with outliers that might result in a biased index of central tendency, and we also give a flavor of the exploration of a particular correlational diagram.

FREQUENCY DIAGRAMS AND STEM-AND-LEAF DISPLAYS

The most common graphic displays in the behavioral and social sciences are distributions that indicate the patterning of increasing and decreasing values, called "frequency diagrams" by R. A. Fisher (1973, p. 33). As a simplified example, suppose we have measured nine people on a scale of anxiety and obtained the following values: 5, 8, 7, 6, 4, 6, 7, 5, 6. We might begin by ordering the values from lowest to highest to get a better view of their beginning and end points and how they clump or bunch: 4, 5, 5, 6, 6, 6, 7, 7, 8. The graphic display on the left side of Figure 10.1 is intended to clarify the nature of the nine observations by showing score values increasing from left to right, with the height of the overarching curve reflecting the frequency of occurrence of the values. By tradition, the independent variable is plotted on the X axis (the abscissa) and the dependent variable on the Y axis (the ordinate). But there is no hard-and-fast rule that frequency diagrams must adhere to this tradition; the display on the right side of Figure 10.1 shows the same values plotted sideways.

Tukey's stem-and-leaf display, which has been called "the most important device for the analysis of small batches of numbers to appear since the *t*-test" (Wainer & Thissen, 1981, p. 199), is another example of a graphic in which the values are plotted sideways. As Emerson and Hoaglin (1983) noted, the stem-and-leaf enables us not only

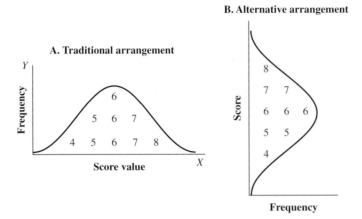

FIGURE 10.1
Distributions of the same metric values, with variables interchanged on the two axes.

to see the batch as a whole, but also to notice such features as (a) what the degree of symmetry is, (b) what the dispersion of individual values is, (c) whether there are outliers, (d) whether the data are concentrated in specific areas, and (e) whether there are gaps in the patterning of the data. The stem-and-leaf also stores the data for present and later usage. It has been said that pictures of numbers are often more instructive than the actual numbers (Tufte, 1983). In short, the beauty of the stem-and-leaf is that, at the same time, it exhibits both the numbers and the picture of the numbers.

To illustrate the use of the stem-and-leaf, we refer again to our discussion in chapter 9 of the research on volunteer characteristics (Rosenthal & Rosnow, 1975). As part of that program of investigation, we were also interested in the nature of the volunteers who become "no-shows" (i.e., who fail to show up for their scheduled appointments to participate as research subjects). In our investigations we uncovered 20 studies that reported the proportion of research participants who failed to show up when scheduled. Those proportions of no-shows were as follows (not in any particular order): .41, .30, .14, .36, .19, .38, .12, .31, .24, .37, .10, .37, .40, .16, .30, .36, .42, .32, .03, .37. To help us make sense of these data, we plotted the values economically by means of a stem-and-leaf. Because these were two-digit numbers, we listed the leading digits (or **stems**) just once and then recorded for each stem the second digits (the **leaves**) attached to it. These results are shown in Part A of Figure 10.2, where the scores are entered in the same sequence as noted above. The first score above, .41, is the first value (1) shown on the leaf corresponding to a stem of .4, and thus is read as ".41." The second score above, .30, appears as the first value (0) shown on the leaf corresponding to a stem of .3, and is read as ".30."

One other fillip, shown in Part B of Figure 10.2, is to arrange the unordered scores of Part A from smallest to largest on each stem. The result of this operation is called the *ordered sample* (perhaps more accurately in this case, the *ordered samples,* as there were 20 sampled studies). Thus, in Part B of Figure 10.2, we read the top row, which has a stem of .4 and the three leaves 0, 1, and 2, as representing the values of .40, .41.,

A. Unordered sample		B. Ordered sample	
Stems	Leaves	Stems	Leaves
.4	1 0 2	.4	0 1 2
.3	0 6 8 1 7 7 0 6 2 7	.3	0 0 1 2 6 6 7 7 7 8
.2	4	.2	4
.1	4 9 2 0 6	.1	0 2 4 6 9
.0	3	.0	3

FIGURE 10.2
Stem-and-leaf displays of no-shows.

and .42. These three values are the 13th, 1st, and 17th entries in the unordered listing of results in the paragraph above. It is informative to provide a summary of the ordered stem-and-leaf with certain key values of the distribution, typically the highest (the maximum) value, the values located at the 75th, 50th (the median), and 25th percentiles, and the lowest (the minimum) value. For the ordered stem-and-leaf display in Figure 10.2, we would report these five summary values as follows:

Maximum	.42
75th percentile	.37
Median (50th percentile)	.32 (.315 rounded to the nearest even digit)
25th percentile	.17
Minimum	.03

What can these results tell us? The 50 percent of the studies that were midmost (25 to 75 percent) had values between .17 and .37, with a median no-show rate of .32. The implication is that if we are counting on 40 volunteer subjects to participate in a research study, we ought to schedule about 60, on the assumption that, on average, only two-thirds may actually show up. Incidentally, findings by Aditya (1996) also seem to support this assumption; in an analysis of more recent studies, he found that the median no-show rate had remained relatively unchanged (still about one-third).

Identifying the maximum and minimum values is simple enough. A convenient way to locate the median is to multiply $N + 1$ (where N is the number of scores in the set) by .50 to get the *location* of the median value. In this example, $N = 20$, so the location of the median value is $(20 + 1).50 = 10.5$, or halfway between the 10th-ordered value of .31 and the 11th of .32, that is, .315 (which we rounded to the nearest even value). The 25th and 75th percentile values can be located, respectively, by $(N + 1).25$ and $(N + 1).75$. For this example, these locate the $(21).25 = 5.25$th values (i.e., adding to the 5th-ordered value 25 percent of the distance between it and the 6th-ordered value) and the $(21).75 = 15.75$th value (i.e., adding to the 15th value 75 percent of the distance between it and the 16th-ordered value). Stem-and-leaf displays and their numerical summaries should be flexibly, not rigidly, used; thus it is not surprising that some investigators prefer using other means of locating the 25th and 75th percentile values (e.g., the nearest whole number).

BOX PLOTS

Particularly when a stem-and-leaf display presents a large amount of data, and espe-cially when there are several stem-and-leaf displays to be compared, it is quite useful to convert the five-value summary into another graphic, called by Tukey (1977), its originator, a "box-and-whisker" plot. Most others now call it a **box plot** or **box graph.** For our five-number summary (Figure 10.3), we plotted the graphic on the left (A) so that the top and bottom dots denote the maximum and the minimum values; the top and bottom of the rectangle denote the 75th and 25th percentiles, and the line dividing the rectangle denotes the median value. This box plot, like the stem-and-leaf chart in Figure 10.2, shows that the values are not symmetrically distributed about the median. Instead, the data are skewed, with the values furthest from the median heavily concentrated below rather than above the median.

Variations of the box plot abound. Some investigators prefer to indicate the 10th and 90th percentile scores instead of the highest and lowest scores, and to record a dot mark for every value more extreme than the 10th or the 90th percentile (Cleveland, 1985), as illustrated in Figure 10.3 on the right (B). Other data analysts add the mean value to the box plot by placing an asterisk or other symbol at the spot on the box plot where the mean would be found. In Figure 10.3 such an asterisk appears below the median on both box plots (Mean = .28). Before leaving the discussion of box plots, we should mention that an early precursor of the box plot was a display created by Francis Galton, which he called a "dot diagram" and used to represent the theoretical distribution of the heights of a million hypothetical men in his work on "hereditary genius" (Galton, 1869, p. 28). Galton's dot diagram, which was based on the standard normal distribution (discussed later in this chapter), was in the shape of a vertical

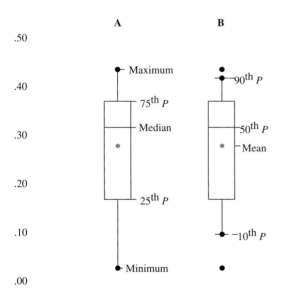

FIGURE 10.3
Box plots. (*P* denotes percentile)

rectangle containing a million dots, each of which was calibrated along a metric scale of feet; it showed horizontal lines intersecting the rectangle at several points: the average male height and the points above and below which there were 100 per million men (Stigler, 1986, p. 269).

COMPARING DISTRIBUTIONS
BACK TO BACK

In chapter 9 we also mentioned the conclusion that volunteers for psychological research were generally more likely to be females, whereas volunteers for studies involving stress were more likely to be males (Rosenthal & Rosnow, 1975). This conclusion was based on the reported results of 63 studies that compared females with males for rates of volunteering for research. For each of those studies we subtracted the percentage of males volunteering from the percentage of females volunteering. We did this separately for general psychological studies and for the studies involving stress. The results are shown in Figure 10.4, in which positive values of the differences in percentages denote that females volunteered more than males did, and negative values denote that females volunteered less than males did. For obvious reasons this comparison is described as a **back-to-back stem-and-leaf.** It reveals immediately that females were much more likely to volunteer than males for general studies, whereas for studies involving stress, males were much more likely to volunteer.

One can also speak of **back-to-back box plots.** The display depicted in Figure 10.5 is based on the same data shown in Figure 10.4. We immediately perceive that both distributions in Figure 10.5 are fairly symmetrical and unremarkable, but the one for

Stress studies ($N = 12$)		General studies ($N = 51$)
Leaves	Stems	Leaves
	+3	5
	+3	
	+2	5 9
	+2	0 1 1 1 1 2 2 2 4
	+1	6 6 7 8 8 8
	+1	0 1 1 1 2 2 2 3 3 3 4
9	+0	5 5 5 6 8 8 9
	+0	1 1 1 2 3 4 4
	0	0
2 1	−0	2 4
8 6	−0	
4 0	−1	1 3
6	−1	
0	−2	0 3
8 5	−2	6
	−3	
	−3	
	−4	
6	−4	

FIGURE 10.4
Back-to-back stem-and-leaf plots.

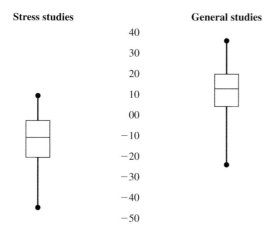

Stress studies   **General studies**

FIGURE 10.5
Back-to-back box plots.

general studies is clearly higher than the one for stress studies. At a glance, these back-to-back box plots inform us in still another way that females were much more likely to volunteer than males for general studies, and that the reverse occurred for studies involving stress. The point of these examples is to show that researchers have alternative ways of grouping data, each option providing a somewhat different perspective on the pattern of results.

MEASURES OF CENTRAL TENDENCY

As the graphics we have discussed would suggest, one characteristic of distributions that researchers almost always want to describe is the location of the bulk of the data, which is to say, the central or typical values. Several measures are available for this purpose, including the mode, the median, and the mean.

The **mode** is the score that occurs with the greatest frequency. In the series of scores 3, 4, 4, 4, 5, 5, 6, 6, 7, the modal score is 4. The series 3, 4, 4, 4, 5, 5, 6, 7, 7, 7, has two modes (at the values 4 and 7) and is called **bimodal.** In the case of a stem-and-leaf display, there might be one or more modal stems, that is, stems with the greatest frequency of values on their corresponding leaves. Thus, there is some flexibility in the use of the term *mode* in describing the bulk of data in a given type of distribution.

The **median (*Mdn*),** already discussed above, is the midmost score in a series of N scores when N is an odd number. When N is an even number, the median is half the distance between the two midmost numbers. In the series 2, 3, 3, 4, 4, 5, 6, 7, 7, 8, 8, the *Mdn* = 5. In the series 2, 3, 3, 4, 4, 7, the *Mdn* = 3.5, halfway between the 3 and 4 at the center of the set of scores. Ties create a problem. In the series 3, 4, 4, 4, 5, 6, 7, there is one score below 4 and three above, four scores below 5 and two above, four scores below 4.5 and three above. What should we regard as the median? One strategy is to view the series as perfectly ranked, so that a series consisting of

1, 2, 3, 3, 3 is viewed as consisting of a 1, a 2, a "small" 3, a "larger" 3, and a "still larger" 3—on the assumption that a more precise measurement procedure would have broken the ties. Thus, in the series 1, 2, 3, 3, 3, we would regard 3, the "smallest" 3, as the median. There are two scores below this particular 3, and two above it. When reporting this median, we would simply specify "the median value is 3."

When the term **mean** is used, it typically refers to the arithmetic average (the arithmetic mean) of the values, written symbolically as

$$M = \frac{\Sigma X}{N} \tag{10.1}$$

and read as "the sum of the scores divided by the number of scores." The mean can be thought of as the "center of gravity" or balance point of a distribution of numbers. If we turned a stem-and-leaf chart on its side and balanced it, the balance point would be the arithmetic mean (Wilkinson & Engelman, 1999). Incidentally, there are other variations on the mean, including the harmonic and geometric mean. The **harmonic mean** is the reciprocal of the arithmetic mean of numbers that have been transformed to their reciprocals. The **geometric mean** is the antilog of the mean of log-transformed values.

We will also discuss another way of dealing with outlying scores, but one traditional way to deal with nettlesome outliers is by **equitable trimming,** which results in a **trimmed mean.** In trimming, the same number of scores is dropped from both ends of the distribution, and then the arithmetic average of the remaining scores is taken. Consider the series of scores −20, 2, 3, 6, 7, 9, 9, 10, 10, 10. The untrimmed mean is 4.6, but after 10% of the scores are trimmed from each end, the trimmed mean is 7.0. Trimming 10 percent from each end eliminated the −20 and the "highest" 10. The median is unaffected by trimming, so the $Mdn = 8$ with or without trimming. The mode, which may be affected by trimming, is 10 before trimming, but is bimodal at 9 and 10 after trimming.

Medians and trimmed means are typically preferred over ordinary arithmetic means when the distribution of values is strongly asymmetrical. The reasoning is that trimming protects against misleading interpretations based on highly unusual scores. For example, suppose 9 of 10 families have zero income, and the remaining family has a $10-million income. Reporting the mean income of $1 million would be highly unrepresentative compared with the trimmed mean, the median, or (in this case) the mode. Medians and trimmed means also provide protection against the intrusion of certain "wild" scores. We say more about this later, but consider the following scores: 4, 5, 5, 6, 6, 6, 7, 7, 8. The mean, median, mode, and trimmed mean are all 6. Suppose we had entered the highest number not as 8, but as 80, so the series is 4, 5, 5, 6, 6, 6, 7, 7, 80. The new (erroneous) mean is 14, but the median and the trimmed mean remain unaffected.

MEASURES OF SPREAD

In addition to knowing the central tendency (or roughly the typical value of a batch of data), researchers almost always also want to know the degree to which the scores deviate from the measures of central tendency (that is, how spread out the scores are). Several measures of spread, dispersion, or variability are available, including the range and its variants (the crude range, the extended range, and the trimmed range), the average deviation, the variance, and the standard deviation.

The **crude range** (*CR*) indicates the distance between the highest (*H*) and the lowest (*L*) score, that is,

$$CR = H - L \qquad (10.2)$$

In the series 2, 3, 4, 4, 6, 7, 9, the crude range is $9 - 2 = 7$.

A refinement is often introduced on the assumption that a score of 9 might, under conditions of more accurate measurement, fall somewhere between 8.5 and 9.5, and that a score of 2 might, under conditions of more accurate measurement, fall somewhere between 1.5 and 2.5. Therefore, we can view the **extended range,** or corrected range, as running from a high of 9.5 to a low of 1.5 (i.e., $9.5 - 1.5 = 8$). The use of the extended, or corrected, range thus adds a half unit at the top of the distribution and a half unit at the bottom of the distribution, or a total of one full unit. Hence, the extended range (*ER*) is computed as

$$ER = (H - L) + 1 \text{ unit} \qquad (10.3)$$

If the units are integers, then $(H - L) + 1$ serves as the definition of the extended range. If the units are tenths of integers, we have $(H - L) + .1$ as the extended range. For example, consider a series consisting of 8.4, 8.7, 8.8, 9.0, 9.1. The crude range, using Equation 10.2, is $9.1 - 8.4 = 0.7$. The extended range, using modified Equation 10.3, runs from 9.15 to 8.35 and thus is $9.15 - 8.35 = 0.8$, or $(H - L) + .1$.

For most practical purposes, reporting either the crude range or the extended range will suffice. When measurements are not very accurate, and when the crude range is small, we obtain a more accurate picture of the actual range when we use the extended range. We illustrate with an extreme example. Suppose we have used a 3-point rating scale in our research and all the judges made ratings at the midpoint value, say, 2 on a scale of 1 to 3. The crude range would be zero $(2 - 2)$, but the extended range would be 1 $(2.5 - 1.5)$, because some of those judges might have rated nearly as high as 2.5 and some nearly as low as 1.5 had such ratings been possible. If an intuitive, but quantitative, index is desired to help researchers decide between the crude and extended range, we suggest dividing the former by the latter. This index (*CR/ER*) is zero in the extreme example just given, and it is .90 if the crude range is 9 and the extended range is 10. With *CR/ER* as high as .90, it seems reasonable to report either of the ranges. With *CR/ER* much lower, it may be more informative to report the extended range.

The range is very convenient to compute and quite informative in describing the spread of certain well-balanced distributions. It suffers badly, however, from being very much affected by even a single very deviant score. These kinds of wild scores are sometimes due to recording errors, such as recording a 10 as 100. **Trimmed ranges** are a type of range designed to make the index of spread less affected by a small number of extreme scores. The guiding rule is again to drop an equal number of cases from both ends of the distribution and then to report the crude range for the data that remain. To illustrate, suppose we decided to drop the extreme 10% of the data from each end; that would leave $X_{.90}$ as the highest remaining score (the score falling at the 90th percentile) and $X_{.10}$ as the lowest remaining score (the score falling at the 10th percentile). The trimmed range of the middle 80% of the scores is $X_{.90} - X_{.10}$.

However, before we can compute this range, we must first identify $X_{.90}$ and $X_{.10}$. We find $X_{.90}$ by computing the location of the $X_{.90}$ score as $(N + 1).90$ and the location of the $X_{.10}$ score as $(N + 1).10$. Suppose we have the following scores: 10, 11, 12, 13, 14, 15, 16, 17, 18, 28, where $N = 10$ scores. Thus, $(N + 1).90 = 11(.90) = 9.9$, and $(N + 1).10 = 1.1$. Keep in mind that 9.9 and 1.1 are not the actual scores, but the *locations* of those scores. The 9.9th score is nine-tenths of the distance between the 9th and 10th scores in the ordered series, which in this case is nine-tenths of the way between 18 and 28, or 27. The 1.1th score is one-tenth of the distance between the 1st and 2nd scores in the ordered series, which for this example is one-tenth of the way between 10 and 11, or 10.1. The trimmed range is $X_{.90} - X_{.10} = 27 - 10.1 = 16.9$.

A particular trimmed range that is frequently reported is the **interquartile range,** defined as $X_{.75} - X_{.25}$, which we encountered earlier in our discussion of box plots and related summaries of stem-and-leaf displays. Recall that we locate the required endpoints by $(N + 1).75$ and $(N + 1).25$, respectively. Thus, for $N = 5$ scores of 4, 6, 9, 11, 15, we find $(N + 1).75 = 6(.75) = 4.5$, and $(N + 1).25 = 6(.25) = 1.5$. The locations we want, therefore, are the 4.5th score and the 1.5th score, or 13 and 5, respectively. The interquartile range is $X_{.75} - X_{.25} = 13 - 5 = 8$. In the normal distribution (discussed below) the interquartile range is roughly equal to one-and-a-third standard deviations. There is a particular point in the normal distribution that we encountered earlier, $X_{.50}$, which is the median, and it is located by $(N + 1).50$.

The **average deviation** $(\overline{D})$ tells us the average distance from the mean of all the scores in the batch. To compute the average deviation, we subtract the arithmetic mean (M) from each score (X) in turn, add these differences (D) disregarding signs, and finally divide by the number of scores (N) in the batch, that is,

$$\overline{D} = \frac{\Sigma |X - M|}{N} = \frac{\Sigma |D|}{N} \tag{10.4}$$

To illustrate, given a series of scores, 4, 5, 5, 6, 10, we find the mean (M) to be $30/5 = 6$. The signed deviations (D) are $-2, -1, -1, 0, +4$ for the values 4, 5, 5, 6, 10, respectively. The sum of the signed deviations **(algebraic values)** about the mean is always zero, but the sum of the unsigned deviations **(absolute values)** is not zero. The latter sum is 8 for the present scores $(2 + 1 + 1 + 0 + 4)$, which, when divided by N, or 5 for this series, yields an average deviation of $8/5 = 1.6$. Notice that $\overline{D}$ uses more information in a series of scores than does the range (which uses only the largest and smallest scores), but $(\overline{D})$ is clearly less convenient to compute or estimate than the range.

The **variance** of a set of scores is the mean of the squared deviations of the scores from their mean. Thus, the variance is also called the **mean square** (MS) because it is the mean of the squared deviations. Symbolically, the variance, or σ^2 (read as sigma-squared), is written as

$$\sigma^2 = \frac{\Sigma (X - M)^2}{N} \tag{10.5}$$

The square root of the variance, $\sqrt{\sigma^2} = \sigma$, is the **standard deviation** (also known as the *root mean square,* or *RMS*), perhaps the most widely reported of all measures of dispersion, spread, or variability. Both the variance (σ^2) and the standard deviation (σ) are frequently computed for populations or circumscribed sets of scores.

However, suppose we wanted to estimate the σ^2 of the population from which a particular sample has been randomly drawn; the most accurate estimate uses a slightly different statistic, S^2, which is defined as

$$S^2 = \frac{\Sigma(X - M)^2}{N - 1}, \qquad (10.6)$$

and N is the sample size. The name for S^2 is the **unbiased estimator of the population value of σ^2.** Unbiased estimators are measures that, under repeated random sampling, give the most accurate estimates of the values in question (where accuracy is defined by estimates that are not too high or too low, in the long run). The reason S^2 is called the unbiased estimator of σ^2 is that if repeated random samples with replacement were drawn from a population of values, the average value of S^2 would be equal to σ^2. In large data sets, the difference between S^2 and σ^2 is usually trivial. Although S is not an unbiased estimator of the population value of σ, that fact rarely imposes a hardship on researchers.

We illustrate the computation of σ^2, σ, S^2, and S for the following set of scores: 2, 4, 4, 5, 7, 8. The mean of these scores, using Equation 10.1, is

$$M = \frac{2 + 4 + 4 + 5 + 7 + 8}{6} = 5.$$

Using Equation 10.5, we calculate

$$\sigma^2 = \frac{(2 - 5)^2 + (4 - 5)^2 + (4 - 5)^2 + (5 - 5)^2 + (7 - 5)^2 + (8 - 5)^2}{6}$$

$$= \frac{24}{6} = 4,$$

and therefore

$$\sigma = \sqrt{\sigma^2} = \sqrt{4} = 2$$

Using Equation 10.6, we find

$$S^2 = \frac{(2 - 5)^2 + (4 - 5)^2 + (4 - 5)^2 + (5 - 5)^2 + (7 - 5)^2 + (8 - 5)^2}{(6 - 1)}$$

$$= \frac{24}{5} = 4.8$$

and

$$S = \sqrt{S^2} = \sqrt{4.8} = 2.19.$$

In most situations in which the objective is to *generalize* to some population, S^2 (or S) is typically used. In most situations in which the objective is only to *describe* a particular set of scores (as in a classroom test), then σ^2 (or σ) is typically used.

THE NORMAL DISTRIBUTION

The **normal distribution** is that special bell-shaped distribution that can be completely described once the mean and the standard deviation are known. It has been called "the most important probability distribution in the whole field of probability and statistics" (Mosteller, Rourke, & Thomas, 1961, p. 230). A traditional reason for its importance is that "the distribution of many statistics tends to the normal form as the size of the sample is increased" (R. A. Fisher, 1973, p. 42), and thus, it is useful in a wide variety of statistical procedures. Descriptively, it is especially useful (as we illustrate shortly) because we can specify what proportion of the area is found in any region of the curve. In addition, many biological, psychological, and sociological attributes are actually distributed in a normal or nearly normal manner, or they can be transformed so they will be distributed normally or nearly normally.

A normal distribution with mean set equal to zero and σ equal to 1 is called a **standard normal distribution** (curve). Figure 10.6 shows such a curve as sloping downward on both sides. Other features of this curve are that it is perfectly symmetrical, its highest point is at the center, and the two tails stretch into infinity. It can also be seen that approximately two thirds of the area of the curve is between -1σ and $+1\sigma$, and that about 95 percent falls between -2σ and $+2\sigma$. Over 99 percent is between -3σ and $+3\sigma$, but the tails never do quite touch down.

Departures from normality generally involve skewness and kurtosis. **Skewness** means that one of the tails is extended more than the other. For example, the lower tail (the tail on the left side of the curve) may be the extended one, in which case the distribution is described as **negatively skewed.** If the upper tail is the extended one, then the distribution is described as **positively skewed.** Highly skewed binomial distributions may take the form of Poisson distributions, named after S. D. Poisson,

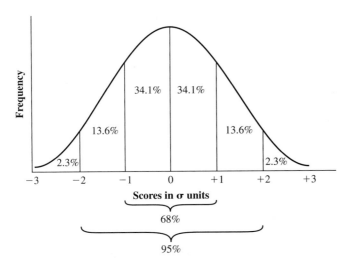

FIGURE 10.6
Standard normal curve showing different percentages of area.

the French statistician who first reported them in 1837. A famous example, noted by Snedecor and Cochran (1980, p. 133), was the number of Prussian soldiers killed during a year by being kicked by horses. Poisson distributions are often used to model the occurrence of rare events in medical research and in particle physics. **Kurtosis** refers to the flatness or peakedness of the curve. A very peaked curve (with values clustering closely around the mean) is described as **leptokurtic;** a relatively flattened curve, as **platykurtic.**

STANDARD SCORES

Assuming a normal curve with mean set equal to 0 and σ equal to 1, any obtained score can be converted into a score corresponding to a location on the abscissa. That is, the obtained score is transformed into a standard deviation score, more commonly referred to as a **standard score,** or **Z score.** This conversion is achieved by a simple calculation:

$$Z \text{ score} = \frac{X - M}{\sigma}, \tag{10.7}$$

in which X = obtained score, M = mean obtained score, and σ = standard deviation of the original distribution. For example, assuming the Scholastic Assessment Test (SAT) is set at $M = 500$ and $\sigma = 100$, an obtained SAT score of 625 is equivalent to a standard score of 1.25, that is,

$$Z \text{ score} = \frac{625 - 500}{100} = 1.25.$$

Referring to the table of standard normal deviates (Z values) in Appendix B (Table B.1), we find that only about 10.6 percent of those people tested should score as high as 625 or higher, and about 89.4 percent should score lower.

   A positive Z score is above the mean; a negative Z score is below the mean. An important use of Z scores is to permit the comparison (and the averaging) of scores from distributions of widely differing means and standard deviations. For example, by computing Z scores for height and weight, we can say whether a person is taller than he or she is heavy, relative to others in the distribution of height and weight. Or suppose we have two measures of course grades, one based on a midterm multiple-choice exam of 100 points with $M = 70$ and $\sigma = 12$, another on a final essay exam of 10 points with $M = 6$ and $\sigma = 1$. It would make no sense to sum or average each person's scores on the two exams. However, converting the exam scores to Z scores would allow us to compare the sums and averages.

   As a further illustration, consider Part A of Table 10.1, which shows the original exam scores of three students earning a total of 76 points. From the total scores, the three students are indistinguishable, but we see that Student 1 scored at the mean both times, Student 2 was slightly above average on the first exam and far below average on the final exam, and Student 3 was slightly below average on the first exam and far above average on the final exam. Using Equation 10.7 to convert each original score to a standard score (Z score), we find the results shown

TABLE 10.1

Original and standard scores of three students on two exams

A. Original scores

Student	Exam I	Exam II	Total	Average
1	70	6	76	38
2	73	3	76	38
3	67	9	76	38

B. Standard scores

Student	Exam I[a]	Exam II[b]	Total	Average
1	0.00	0.00	0.00	0.00
2	0.25	−3.00	−2.75	−1.38
3	−0.25	3.00	2.75	1.38

[a]$M = 70$, $\sigma = 12$ for the class as a whole.
[b]$M = 6$, $\sigma = 1$ for the class as a whole.

in Part B of Table 10.1. Whereas the sums and averages of the raw scores were quite misleading as indices of the students' course performance, the sums and averages of the Z scores take into account all the differences in how the students scored on the two exams.

And finally, Z scores can be weighted if we want them to be. In Table 10.1, we weighted the Z scores for midterm and final equally (Z scores come equally weighted because their σ values are all alike; i.e., unity). Had we wanted to weight the final exams double, we would simply multiply the Z scores on the final exam by 2 before adding. Had we done that, the three students would have sums of weighted Z scores equal to 0.00, −5.75, and +5.75, respectively. Note that the sums of Z scores are not themselves Z scores of the distribution of summed Z scores. If we want these sums Z-scored, we must compute their mean and standard deviation, then convert each sum of Z scores to a new Z by Equation 10.7. For the three students of Table 10.1, this process would produce Z scores of 0.00, −1.22, and +1.22, respectively. As a check on our arithmetic, we can compute the mean and σ of this set of Z scores. As with any distribution of Z scores, these computations should yield a mean of 0 and a σ of 1. Happily, they do.

DATA NOT DISTRIBUTED NORMALLY

Before leaving the topic of Z scores, we should also note that when the Z scores are based on data that are approximately normally distributed, they tell us quite a lot about the proportion of scores likely to be found above and below the level of the Z score, as shown in Figure 10.6 and in Table B.1 (Appendix B). That is a bonus of the Z score. However, Z scores need not be based on a normal distribution to be used to put variables with widely differing metrics onto a common scale (as we did in the example in Table 10.1).

We can illustrate that Z scores of data that are not normally distributed—though the scores are useful—do not tell us what we might expect based on the normal distribution in Figure 10.6 (and Table B.1). Consider the set of raw scores $-3, -3, +1, +1$. Their mean is -1 and $\sigma = 2$, and they become Z scores of $-1, -1, +1, +1$. Whereas Z scores of $+1$ from a normal distribution exceed about 84% of the distribution, these Z scores of $+1$ exceed only 50% of the distribution.

PRECISION OF ESTIMATING POPULATION MEANS

As far back as R. A. Fisher's seminal texts, it has been accepted that properly sampled measures of central tendency are the best estimators of population means (R. A. Fisher, 1990). Reporting the precision with which the population mean was estimated is highly recommended (e.g., Estes, 1997). Two commonly reported indices of the precision of estimates of population means (and other population statistics) are the standard error of the mean (denoted as SE_M) and the confidence interval (CI) of the mean. Both indices are based on the variability around the sample mean and the sample size. For both the SE_M and the CI around the mean, the smaller the standard deviation of the sample, and the larger the sample size, the more precisely the sample mean estimates the population mean. In his enlightening and rigorous comparison of the history and purpose of the SE_M versus the CI of the mean, Estes (1997) noted that the SE_M came to psychology via the physical sciences and engineering and is used to evaluate the replicability of the sample mean. The CI of the mean, on the other hand, came to psychology more recently via statistical theory and is used to evaluate how precisely the population mean has been estimated. The SE_M measures the variability of sample means, whereas the CI of the mean measures the interval that includes the population mean with a specified degree of confidence.

Since around the mid-1980s, confidence intervals have been regularly reported in medical journals, the 95% CI being the most often reported. By contrast, the reporting and interpretation of confidence intervals has not been embraced with the same commitment in the behavioral and social science journals—although it has been recommended often enough by methodologists and statisticians (see, for example, recent discussions and reviews by, among others, Fidler, Thomason, Cumming, Finch, & Leeman, 2004; Loftus, 1996; Masson & Loftus, 2003). In chapter 9 we described the calculation of the 95% CI for population estimates of means (Equation 9.1). To review, three quantities were required: the sample size (N), the value of t significant at .05 two-tailed ($t_{.05}$) when df = sample size minus 1, and the standard deviation (S) of the N scores, calculated directly as

$$S = \sqrt{\frac{\Sigma(X - M)^2}{N - 1}}, \tag{10.8}$$

that is, the square root of Equation 10.6.

As another example, suppose we have scores of 2, 4, 4, 5, 7, 8, with $M = 5$, $S = 2.19$, and $t_{.05} = 2.57$ (where $t_{.05} = 2.57$ is from Table B.2 in Appendix B). Using Equation 9.1 to obtain the lower limit of the 95% CI interval around the estimated

TABLE 10.2
Values of two-tailed α and t_α ($df = 5$) for five different confidence intervals

CI (%)	α	t_α ($df = 5$)
99.9	.001	6.87
99	.01	4.03
95	.05	2.57
90	.10	2.02
80	.20	1.48

population mean of 5, we calculate

$$95\%\ CI\ \text{Lower Limit} = M - \frac{(t_{.05})S}{\sqrt{N}} = 5 - \frac{(2.57)2.19}{\sqrt{6}} = 2.70,$$

and for the upper limit, we find

$$95\%\ CI\ \text{Upper Limit} = M + \frac{(t_{.05})S}{\sqrt{N}} = 5 + \frac{(2.57)2.19}{\sqrt{6}} = 7.30.$$

In sum, there is a 95% probability that the population mean falls between the lower and upper limits of 2.70 and 7.30.

To use other than the 95% CI, we need only replace the quantity $t_{.05}$ with the quantity t_α, where α is the two-tailed probability of Type I error. Table 10.2 shows the values of α and t_α (for $df = 5$) for five different confidence intervals. Values of t_α are larger for the more demanding confidence intervals (99% CI and 99.9% CI), as we would expect in general, but these values of t_α (4.03 and 6.87, respectively) are especially large because of the small sample size in this example (i.e., 6 subjects). Table 10.3 provides the values of t_α required to compute the 95% CI for each of 13 values of df.

TABLE 10.3
Values of two-tailed t_α required for different values of df for 95% CI

df	t_α	df	t_α
1	12.71	30	2.04
2	4.30	40	2.02
3	3.18	60	2.00
4	2.78	100	1.98
5	2.57	1000	1.96
10	2.23	∞	1.96
20	2.09		

DEFINING OUTLIERS

Earlier in this chapter we brought up the issue of outliers. Sometimes it is obvious that an error has occurred when a score seems far too high or far too low for the particular data set. If a score of 35 turns up in a set of test scores in which the highest possible score is 22, it must be an error. However, it is not always so clear whether an outlier is an error or just a far-out score. An error may be dealt with by equitable trimming, but observing far-out scores that are not errors is a signal to look further into the data. One question in dealing with outliers is how to define them. In a monograph on the topic of outliers, Iglewicz and Hoaglin (1993) reviewed a number of definitions and found themselves adopting one offered by Barnett and Lewis (1978) in which outliers are viewed as scores that are "inconsistent with the remainder of that set of data" (p. 4). But a basic question still remained about how to define *inconsistent with the remainder of the data*. For example, screening for outliers has sometimes been done by Z-scoring the data. But Iglewicz and Hoaglin (1993) demonstrated that Z scores do not always work well in defining certain outliers, especially when data sets are small. Thus, they proposed an alternative procedure based on theory and on empirical (simulation) studies.

Iglewicz and Hoaglin's new procedure yields modified Z scores, which we indicate here as $Z_{modified}$. The calculation of $Z_{modified}$ for each score in the data set is achieved by

$$Z_{\text{modified}} = \frac{0.6745(X - Mdn)}{Mdn_{AD}}, \tag{10.9}$$

where 0.6745 is a constant, X is any original score, Mdn is the median value of the original set of scores, and Mdn_{AD} is the median of the *absolute* (unsigned) deviations from Mdn.

As an illustration, suppose we have the following five scores: 10, 12, 14, 16, 26. The $Mdn = 14$, and the absolute (unsigned) differences between each score and the Mdn are 4, 2, 0, 2, 12. The median of these five absolute deviations about the median gives us $Mdn_{AD} = 2$, so the $Z_{modified}$ value for the original score of 10, using Equation 10.9, is

$$Z_{\text{modified}} = \frac{0.6745(10 - 14)}{2} = -1.35.$$

Similarly, for the original score of 12, we calculate

$$Z_{\text{modified}} = \frac{0.6745(12 - 14)}{2} = -0.67,$$

and for the original score of 26, we find

$$Z_{\text{modified}} = \frac{0.6745(26 - 14)}{2} = +4.05.$$

Adopting Iglewicz and Hoaglin's well-documented suggestion that modified Z scores of 3.5 or greater serve as the definition of an outlier, we see that in our array of 5 scores (10, 12, 14, 16, 26), the last score, 26, qualifies as an outlier with $Z_{modified} = 4.05$, a quantity greater than the criterion value of 3.5.

COPING WITH OUTLIERS

Once we have identified all the outliers, the question is what to do next. There are at least three options: dropping outliers, equitable trimming, and reeling in outliers by data transformations.

Dropping Outliers

We might be tempted just to drop the outlier, but this is very likely to result in a biased index of central tendency (e.g., the mean or median) for the remaining data. For example, if we have found scores of 10, 12, 14, 16, 26 and drop the outlier score of 26, the predrop median of 14 becomes a postdrop median of 13. For the same five scores, dropping the outlier (26) changes the mean more noticeably, from a predrop mean of 15.6 to a postdrop mean of 13. The reason that dropping the outlier alone is a biased procedure is that *some* score has to be the largest (or the smallest), and if we drop only that offending score, we always move the mean and median *downward* if the outlier is the highest score, and *upward* if the outlier is the lowest score.

Equitable Trimming

Previously, we described the procedure of equitable trimming in the context of our discussion of measures of central tendency. Equitable trimming is a less biased procedure than dropping the outlier. In this procedure, if the outlier is the highest score, we set aside that score *and* the lowest score. If we had two outliers for the two highest scores, we would set aside those two scores *and* the two lowest scores. The basic principle is simply that we set aside the same number of scores from the lowest and from the highest scores. This method works especially well when the sample sizes are not very small. After all, as Occam's razor teaches, we do not want to trim too much (even if equitably done) if the trimming leaves us too little.

Reeling in Outliers by Data Transformations

An often very effective method of dealing with outliers, even when the samples are quite small, is to find a suitable transformation to pull in the outlying stragglers and make them part of the group. Three very common transformations for pulling in scores that are far out (listed here in order in the degree to which they pull in extreme scores from a little to a lot) are (a) square roots, (b) logarithms, and (c) negative reciprocals (Tukey, 1977).

By way of an example, we return to Iglewicz and Hoaglin's (1993) modified Z procedure for defining the degree to which scores are outliers, with the proposed cutoff value of 3.5 or higher suggesting an outlier. We gave a simple example of a set of five scores (10, 12, 14, 16, 26), in which the score of 26 was an outlier by Iglewicz and Hoaglin's definition, earning a modified Z score of 4.05. Table 10.4 shows the results of that analysis as well as three additional modified Z scores computed for (a) the square roots of the original data, (b) the logs of the original

TABLE 10.4

Reeling in outliers by transformations of the original data $\left(X, \sqrt{X}, \log X, \text{and} -\frac{1}{X}\right)$

	Original data (X)	|deviation|[a]	$\sqrt{X}$	|deviation|[a]	Log X	|deviation|[a]	$-\frac{1}{X}$	|deviation|[a]
					Transformations of X			
	10	(4)	3.16	(.58)	1.00	(.15)	−.100	(.029)
	12	(2)	3.46	(.28)	1.08	(.07)	−.083	(.012)
	14	(0)	3.74	(.00)	1.15	(.00)	−.071	(.000)
	16	(2)	4.00	(.26)	1.20	(.05)	−.062	(.009)
	26	(12)	5.10	(1.36)	1.41	(.26)	−.038	(.033)
Median (Mdn)	14	(2[b])	3.74	(.28[b])	1.15	(.07[b])	−.071	(.012[b])
Possible outlier (O_p)	26		5.10		1.41		−.038	
Mdn_{AD}[b]		2		.28		.07		.012
$Z_{modified}$[c]	4.05		3.28		2.51		1.85	

[a]Absolute deviations of scores from their median.
[b]Median of 5 absolute deviations about the median.
[c]Based on Equation 10.9, and the idea that larger values of $Z_{modified}$, especially greater than 3.5, are defined as more outlying.

data, and (c) the negative reciprocals of the original data. The table shows very clearly how the modified Z score decreases in a linear way ($r = .9993$) as we go from the original data (X), to the square root $\left(\sqrt{X}\right)$, to the logarithm (log X), and, finally, to the negative reciprocal $\left(-\frac{1}{X}\right)$.

If the data were real, and we wanted to eliminate outliers, we would be content to use the negative reciprocal as the appropriate transformation. These same transformations are also useful when our goal is less specifically dealing with outliers, but reshaping our distributions to be more nearly symmetrical and therefore more nearly normal. In addition, these transformations tend to increase the homogeneity of the variability found in two or more groups or conditions we want to compare or combine. The importance of the normality of distributions and the homogeneity of variability will be discussed in chapter 12 when we describe the assumptions underlying the use of t tests to compare two groups or conditions.

EXPLORING THE DATA

We began by mentioning the importance of exploring the data, and we conclude with a brief example of a simple exploration of the data found in a scatter plot, a correlational diagram consisting of scattered dots, each denoting a score on the X axis and the Y axis. In other words, scatter plots show the relation between scores on the X axis and scores on the Y axis. Simple as scatter plots may be, we should not underestimate their value. They have been described as "the single most powerful statistical tool for analyzing the relationship between two variables, X and Y" (Chambers et al., 1983, p .75).

Figure 10.7 shows a scatter plot of the results of a pilot study in which 10 children with reading difficulties were given regular weekly tutoring in reading, each session consisting of 1 hour. To learn the degree to which increasing the number of these hourly tutorial sessions per week would increase reading improvement scores, two children were randomly assigned to one, two, three, four, or five hourly tutorials per week. The hypothesis that more such tutorials would lead to greater reading improvement was supported by an impressive correlation between the number of hourly tutorial sessions and reading improvement ($r = .51$). Concentrating only on the correlation, and not also inspecting the scatter plot, would have led the researchers to miss an important nuance of the data. However, these were patient researchers, and they did explore the data further.

In examining the scatter plot represented in Figure 10.7, the researchers were puzzled by increasing differences between the corresponding data points as the number of weekly sessions increased. The differences between the two scores (1, 1, 2, 5, 11) corresponded with the number of sessions per week (one, two, three, four, and five, respectively). The researchers' initial impression of increasing differences in scores as the sessions per week increased was supported by a large correlation ($r = .89$) between difference in scores and the number of sessions per week. Seeking an explanation, the researchers scrutinized the differences between the children whose scores were furthest apart (five hourly sessions). For the two children who received five hourly tutorials per week, the girl had scored much higher (13) than the boy (2). When the researchers also examined the reading improvement scores for the two children who received four hourly tutorials per week, there was again a much higher score earned by the girl (10) than by the boy (5). The researchers suspected that the benefits of tutoring might be different for girls and boys.

As a way of displaying the different benefits of tutoring for girls and boys, the researchers separated the two sets of results, using a small diamond indicator for each girl and a small square for each boy in the sample. Figure 10.8 shows the five small

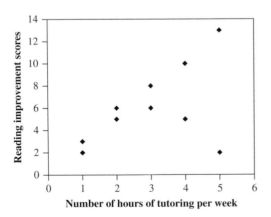

FIGURE 10.7
Reading improvement scores for five levels of tutoring (hours per week).

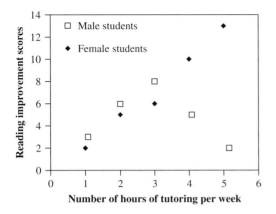

FIGURE 10.8
Reading improvement scores for male and female students for five levels of tutoring.

diamonds as arrayed in a nearly straight line, reflecting a near-perfect positive correlation ($r = .99$) between reading improvement and number of hourly sessions of tutoring per week for the girls. The figure shows that the five small squares representing the boys reflected a *non*linear relation between reading improvement and number of hourly sessions of tutoring (Pearson r for linear association $= -.20$). Specifically, the pattern for boys can be described as ∩-shaped, the greatest benefit in reading scores being associated with the midmost number of sessions and decreasing as the number of sessions became too few (one) or too many (five). Boys' reading gains were correlated very highly ($r = .95$) with the pattern defining a ∩-shaped curve (using a particular statistical procedure described later in this book, which in this case employed contrast weights of $-2, +1, +2, +1, -2$ to represent the ∩-shaped pattern). On the basis of having explored the data in their pilot study, the researchers learned the wisdom of examining the results of their full-scale study separately for girls and boys.

In this example of exploring the data, the researchers found Figure 10.8 to be a valuable picture of their data. As Tukey (1977) put it, "The greatest value of a picture is when it *forces* us to notice what we never expected to see" (p. vi). We conclude this chapter with two of Tukey's (1977) further insights. The first is that "many problems do not have a single 'right answer'. . . it will often be quite reasonable for different analysts to reach somewhat different analyses" (p. viii). The second is that "to unlock the analysis of a body of data, to find the good way or ways to approach it, may require a key, whose finding is a creative act" (p. viii). In short, thoroughness in describing, displaying, and exploring data requires practice, thoughtfulness, open-mindedness, and considerable patience.

CHAPTER
11

CORRELATION

PEARSON *r*

One of the major purposes of all the sciences is to describe relationships among variables, and there is no more widely used index of relationship than the Pearson *r*, short for **Karl Pearson's product-moment correlation coefficient.** The Pearson *r* can take on values between -1.00 and $+1.00$. A value of $r = .00$ means that there is no linear relationship between the two variables we are examining. (A linear relationship is one in which a fixed change in one variable is always associated with a fixed change in the other variable.) A value of $r_{xy} = 1.00$ means that there is a perfect positive linear relationship between variables X and Y, so that as scores on X increase, there are perfectly predictable *increases* in the scores on Y. A value of $r_{xy} = -1.00$ tells us that there is a perfect negative linear relationship, so that as scores on X increase, there are perfectly predictable *decreases* in the scores on Y. Correlations (rs) of $+1.00$, .00, and -1.00 are illustrated in Table 11.1 for three sets of four subjects, each of whom has been measured on two tests of personality, X and Y. (Also see Figure 11.1.).

Illustration A in Table 11.1 shows that X and Y may be perfectly correlated in the sense of Pearson's *r* even though the scores on X and Y never agree. Thus, were we computing the degree of correlation between two judges of classroom behavior (e.g., their ratings of teacher warmth), we could achieve a high degree of correlation even though one judge rates systematically higher than the other. Inspection of Illustration A shows also that the values of Y were chosen to be exactly twice the values of X. Had the values of Y been identical with the corresponding values of X, the Pearson *r* would also have been 1.00. Surprisingly to many students, doubling the values of one of the variables has no effect on the Pearson *r*. Thus, even when Y is chosen to be equal to $2X$, the Pearson *r* is still 1. In general, it is the case that multiplying the values of either or both variables by any (nonzero) constant number, or adding any constant to either or both variables, does not affect the value of the Pearson *r*.

314

TABLE 11.1
Illustration of three correlations

	A $r = 1.00$		B $r = .00$		C $r = -1.00$	
	X	Y	X	Y	X	Y
Subject 1	8	16	8	6	8	−4
Subject 2	6	12	6	4	6	−3
Subject 3	4	8	4	4	4	−2
Subject 4	2	4	2	6	2	−1
Σ	20	40	20	20	20	−10

Note: To allow the computation of any correlation coefficient, each sampling unit (e.g., subject) must have two scores, one on variable X and one on variable Y.

Such behavior is what we might expect if each set of scores (X and Y) were standard-scored (Z-scored) before we computed r. Indeed, that is exactly what is done, because r can be defined as

$$r_{xy} = \frac{\Sigma Z_x Z_y}{N}, \tag{11.1}$$

where the correlation r_{xy} between X and Y is equal to the sum of the products of the Z scores of X and Y, divided by the number (N) of pairs of X and Y scores. Now we can see why the r is called a *product-moment correlation;* the Zs are distances from the mean (also called **moments**) that are multiplied by each other to form **products.**

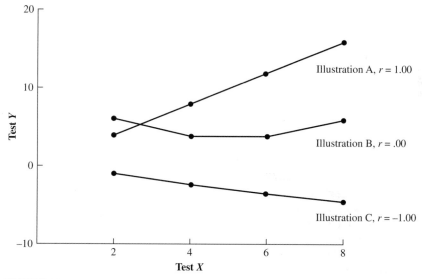

FIGURE 11.1
Plots of illustrations A, B, and C in Table 11.1.

TABLE 11.2
Calculating r on the basis of Equation 11.1

	X	Z_x	Y	Z_y	$Z_x Z_y$
Subject 1	8	1.34	16	1.34	1.80
Subject 2	6	0.45	12	0.45	0.20
Subject 3	4	−0.45	8	−0.45	0.20
Subject 4	2	−1.34	4	−1.34	1.80
Σ	20	0	40	0	4.00
M	5	0	10	0	1.00[a]
σ	2.24	1.00	4.47	1.00	—

[a]This is the value of r.

To use Equation 11.1 for computation, we begin by transforming the X and Y scores to Z scores. Returning to Illustration A in Table 11.1, we find $(X - M_x)/\sigma_x = Z_x$ and $(Y - M_y)/\sigma_y = Z_y$ for each subject and then compute the products $Z_x Z_y$ as shown in Table 11.2. It should be noted that the Z scores for Y (i.e., Z_y) are identical with those for X although $Y = 2X$. The reason is that multiplying a set of scores by a constant also multiplies the standard deviation of that set of scores by the same constant, so that constancy of scale is preserved when Z scores are used. The last column in Table 11.2 shows the products of the Z scores and their mean; that is,

$$\frac{\Sigma Z_x Z_y}{N} = \frac{4}{4} = 1.00,$$

which, as indicated in Equation 11.1, equals r_{xy}. Examining that equation for r shows that larger positive rs are found when Z scores far above the mean of X are found alongside Z scores far above the mean of Y. Larger positive rs are also found when Z scores far below the mean of X are found alongside Z scores far below the mean of Y (a large negative Z score multiplied by a large negative Z score yields an even larger *positive* Z score).

PROPORTION OF VARIANCE INTERPRETATION OF CORRELATION

Although it is very useful to think of r simply as an index number, so that a larger positive r represents a higher degree of linear relationship than does a smaller r, a number of other interpretations are possible. Perhaps the most common interpretation involves the squared correlation (r^2) rather than r. The squared r is interpreted as the proportion of the variance shared by variables X and Y. That is, r^2 is the proportion of the variance among the Y scores that is statistically attributable to variation in the X scores, as well as the proportion of the variance among the X scores that is attributable to variation in the Y scores. This relationship is sometimes expressed as $r^2 + k^2 = 1.00$, where r^2 is called the **coefficient of determination** (the proportion of variance "accounted for"), and k^2 is called the **coefficient of nondetermination** (the proportion of variance "not accounted for"). Although useful in some statistical applications (e.g., multiple regression and analysis of variance), the r^2 interpretation of correlation is only a poor reflection of the practical value of any given effect size correlation coefficient (Rosenthal & Rubin, 1982a).

As an illustration of the r^2 interpretation of r, consider two predictor variables, X_1 and X_2, that have been used to predict or explain the dependent variable Y, as shown in Part A of Table 11.3. The correlation between the two predictor variables is .00, and the correlation (r) between either X_1 or X_2 and Y is .707. Squaring the r of .707 yields .500, the proportion of variance among the Y scores predictable from *either* the X_1 or the X_2 scores. That this .500 proportion of variance should be found seems appropriate, because we actually created variable Y by summing variables X_1 and X_2, and we also saw to it that they would be weighted equally by ensuring

TABLE 11.3
Examples of two predictors of a dependent variable

A. Example with equal variance

	Predictor variables		Dependent variable
	X_1	X_2	Y
Subject 1	3	3	6
Subject 2	3	1	4
Subject 3	1	3	4
Subject 4	1	1	2
Σ	8	8	16
M	2	2	4
σ	1	1	1.41
σ^2	1	1	2

B. Example with unequal variance

	Predictor variables		Dependent variable
	X_1	X_2	$Y(X_1 + X_2)$
Subject 1	3	4	7
Subject 2	3	0	3
Subject 3	1	4	5
Subject 4	1	0	1
Σ	8	8	16
M	2	2	4
σ	1	2	2.24
σ^2	1	4	5

that they had equal variances or standard deviations. If they did not have equal variances, the predictor with larger variance would correlate more highly with their sum, as shown in Part B of Table 11.3, in which we have left the values of X_1 intact but changed the values of X_2 for the sake of illustration.

Notice that Table 11.3 shows the standard deviation (σ) of X_2 increasing from 1 (in Part A) to 2 (in Part B). This change does not affect the correlation between X_1 and X_2 (still zero), but the correlation between X_2 and Y has increased to .894 ($r^2 = .80$), and the correlation between X_1 and Y has decreased to .447 ($r^2 = .20$). This example shows that the ratio of the two values of r^2 (.80/.20) is proportional to the ratio of the variances (σ^2) of the predictor variables (4/1). For either example given in this table (equal or unequal r^2 values), it is useful to note that the proportions of variance in the dependent variable (Y) predictable from X_1 and X_2 are additive and, when added, yield what is called the **multiple R^2.** In this case the multiple $R^2 = 1.00$, because .50 + .50 = 1.00, and .80 + .20 = 1.00. Whenever we are given predictor variables that are uncorrelated ($r = .00$) with each other, the multiple R^2 (which can take any value between .00 and 1.00) between the entire battery of predictor variables and the dependent variable is simply the sum of the individual r^2 values. It is not common in practice, however, for predictor variables to show a zero correlation with each other.

We have more to say about multiple correlation and its close relative, multiple regression, in chapter 20 (on multivariate procedures). We refer to **regression** in those contexts in which we want to relate changes in the level of one or more predictor variables to changes in the level of the outcome variable, and we refer to **correlation** as a more global index of the closeness of relationship.

BINOMIAL EFFECT-SIZE DISPLAY

Earlier in this book we mentioned our preference for r as an effect size indicator in a wide variety of situations, and we turn to this idea again shortly (and also again in the next chapter). A particular reason we prefer r is that it can be easily interpreted by a method of displaying the magnitude and, by implication, the practical significance of an effect size r, a method called the **binomial effect-size display,** or **BESD** (Rosenthal & Rubin, 1979b, 1982a; Rosenthal, Rosnow, & Rubin, 2000). When variables for which the observations or scores can take one of two possible values, they are called *binomial, binary,* or *dichotomous.* In the case of the binomial effect size display, *binomial* refers to the fact that the BESD casts the effect size r into dichotomous outcomes, such as success versus failure, improved versus not improved, or survived versus died. Rosenthal and Rubin (1982a) found that neither experienced psychological researchers nor experienced statisticians had a good intuitive sense of the practical meaning of such indices of effect size as r^2 or such near relatives of r^2 as omega-squared (Hays, 1994) and epsilon-squared (Welkowitz, Ewen, & Cohen, 2000). The BESD was introduced because (a) its interpretation is quite transparent to researchers, students, and policymakers, (b) it is applicable whenever r is used, and (c) it is very conveniently computed.

If we think of "success rate" as a general expression that includes, for example, survival rate, cure rate, improvement rate, or selection rate, the purpose of the BESD can be understood as addressing the question "What is the effect on the success rate of the institution of a specified treatment or intervention?" The BESD specifically preserves the magnitude of the effect size r and demonstrates its practical implications in the framework of a 2×2 display with uniform marginal values of 100 each. The BESD does not, however, require that the raw data be limited to 2×2 tables with uniform margins, and it should not be confused with the empirical or raw data on which the effect size r was originally computed. Although most actual values in the margins of empirical 2×2 tables are not equal, the BESD helps us to conceptualize the practical implications of an effect size r in a standardized context. Some examples will illustrate what we mean.

We begin with a seminal meta-analysis reported by Mary Lee Smith and Gene Glass in 1977 (it was Glass who coined the term *meta-analysis*). That analysis has been extended over the years (e.g., Smith, Glass, & Miller, 1980), but for this illustration, we focus only on the original results. Smith and Glass systematically integrated the results of nearly 400 controlled evaluations of psychotherapy and counseling. On average, they found, the typical psychotherapy client was better off than 75% of untreated "control" individuals, an outcome that would certainly appear to be a pretty convincing argument for the efficacy of psychotherapy. Smith and Glass reported their findings in terms of Glass's Δ index of effect size, an effect size that was equivalent to $r = .32$. However, instead of agreeing with Smith and Glass's conclusion, some critics argued that the results of this meta-analysis sounded the death knell for psychotherapy because of the "modest" size of the effect. Viewing the $r = .32$ in terms of the coefficient of determination (r^2), they said the observed effect accounted for "only 10% of the variance." To help resolve this inconsistency in interpretation, it is instructive to examine the BESD corresponding to an r of .32.

Table 11.4 shows such a BESD, but with the dependent variable defined differently than in Smith and Glass's meta-analysis. We return to their result in a moment, but the purpose of the strikingly dramatic dependent variable in Table 11.4 (Alive vs. Dead) is that it reflects in a most profound way that an r of .32, accounting for "only" 10% of the variance, is hardly something to be dismissed as merely a "modest" effect. First, however, note that all the row and column totals of the display are set at 100. What this table indicates is that the effect size r of .32 amounts to increasing the survival rate from 34% in the nonintervention condition to 66% in the intervention condition, given that half the population received the intervention and half did not, and half the population

TABLE 11.4
BESD for effect size $r = .32$

	Treatment outcome		
	Alive	**Dead**	**Total**
Intervention	66	34	100
No intervention	34	66	100
Total	100	100	200

survived and half did not. To reiterate, these values are not raw percentages in the actual data but "standardized" percentages based on setting all marginal values to 100. Clearly, an r of .32 can hardly be viewed as modest or as sounding the death knell for psychotherapy, because that effect size r would be equivalent to increasing the success rate from 34% in the controls to 66% in the psychotherapy intervention conditions.

A great convenience of the BESD is how easily it can be converted to r (or r^2) and how easy it is to go from the r (or r^2) to the display. Table 11.5 shows systematically the increase in success rates associated with various values of r^2 and r. Thus, an r of .30, accounting for 9% of the variance, is associated with an increase in success rate from .35 to .65 (or 35% to 65%). The last column of Table 11.5 underscores the idea that the difference in success rate proportions is identical to r. Thus, the experimental group success rate proportion is computed as $.50 + r/2$, which we then multiply by 100 to display as a percentage, and the control group success rate percentage is $.50 - r/2$ multiplied by 100. Of course, if the empirical results indicated that the control group performed better than the intervention or experimental group, we would simply reverse the above calculations so that relative relationships are preserved in the BESD. Table 11.5

TABLE 11.5
Increases in success rate corresponding to values of r^2 and r

r^2	r	Success rate increased		Difference in success rates (r)
		From	To	
.00	.02	.49	.51	.02
.00	.04	.48	.52	.04
.00	.06	.47	.53	.06
.01	.08	.46	.54	.08
.01	.10	.45	.55	.10
.01	.12	.44	.56	.12
.03	.16	.42	.58	.16
.04	.20	.40	.60	.20
.06	.24	.38	.62	.24
.09	.30	.35	.65	.30
.16	.40	.30	.70	.40
.25	.50	.25	.75	.50
.36	.60	.20	.80	.60
.49	.70	.15	.85	.70
.64	.80	.10	.90	.80
.81	.90	.05	.95	.90
1.00	1.00	.00	1.00	1.00

also underscores how squaring the r can sometimes make small, but often quite meaningful, effects seem to disappear. We illustrate that idea with some further examples in the next section.

We want to emphasize that the BESD is not limited to dichotomous empirical data. In fact, it can be shown that, for many distributions, there is quite good agreement between (a) the effect size correlation r between the treatment variable and the continuously distributed outcome variable and (b) the correlation (phi) between the treatment variable and the dichotomous outcome variable (Rosenthal & Rubin, 1982a). One further benefit of the routine use of a display procedure such as the 2 × 2 table of the BESD to represent the **practical validity** of the research results is that it provides useful assessments of how well the research is progressing in a given area. The appropriate use of the BESD requires that for any significance test computed, the effect size r estimate associated with the test also be reported. Interpretation of that effect size r is in terms of the improvement in success rates, but we can also represent the confidence level of r by providing BESDs for the upper and lower limits. We show how confidence intervals are obtained for rs in the next section, but we also want to emphasize that the applicability of the BESD is not limited simply to experimental designs. Whatever the nature of the study, the essential point here is that the effect size, and in turn the BESD, must always be interpreted within the context of the variables investigated and the design of the study.

For example, it is possible to use the BESD to represent effects in correlational designs, where we think of the "effects" not in terms of the rhetoric of causal inference, but in relational terms. To illustrate, as part of a massive relational study conducted by the Centers for Disease Control, a total of 4,462 Army veterans of the Vietnamese War era (1965–1971) were examined. Of this group, some 2,490 had served in Vietnam, and 1,972 had served elsewhere. At the time of the study, approximately 13.7% of Vietnam War veterans were identified as having suffered from alcohol abuse or dependence, compared with approximately 9.2% of non-Vietnam veterans (Centers for Disease Control, 1988; Roberts, 1988). Thus, Vietnam War veterans were about half again more likely to suffer from alcohol abuse or dependence than were non-Vietnam veterans (13.7/9.2 = 1.49). Part A of Table 11.6 shows the empirical findings. How do these relational results translate into a correlation coefficient and a BESD?

The correlation between the variable of "being or not being a Vietnam veteran" and the variable of "having or not having an alcohol problem" can be computed in different ways, to be described in the section on the phi coefficient presented later in this chapter. For now we simply note that the correlation r (or equivalently, phi) can be obtained from

$$r = \frac{\text{difference between cross products}}{\sqrt{\text{product of all four marginal totals}}}$$

$$= \frac{(341 \times 1,791) - (181 \times 2,149)}{\sqrt{(2,490)(1,972)(522)(3,940)}}$$

$$= \frac{221,762}{3,177,872.7} = .0698$$

TABLE 11.6
Alcoholism problem in Vietnam veterans study

A. Empirical findings

Veteran status	Alcohol problem	No alcohol problem	Total
Vietnam	341	2,149	2,490
Non-Vietnam	181	1,791	1,972
Total	522	3,940	4,462

B. BESD corresponding to empirical findings

	Problem	No problem	Total
Vietnam	53.5	46.5	100
Non-Vietnam	46.5	53.5	100
Total	100	100	200

Thus, the Pearson r (or phi) associated with the difference between 13.7% and 9.2% is about .07, and this r is preserved in the BESD in Part B of Table 11.6. The upper left cell was calculated as $50 + 100r/2 = 50 + 7/2 = 53.5$, and because rows and columns must add up to 100 in a BESD, the other three cell values were then simply obtained by subtraction. Our reason for mentioning this study is to illustrate another instance in which the BESD is applicable, but in which the term *effect* is used loosely because the study was relational rather than experimental. We cannot conclude that it was serving in Vietnam that *caused* the additional problem of alcohol use. All we can conclude is that having served in Vietnam was associated in this sample with a greater likelihood of developing problems of alcohol use.

CONFIDENCE INTERVALS FOR EFFECT-SIZE CORRELATIONS

In chapter 9 we discussed procedures for evaluating the precision with which population values of means and proportions have been estimated (Equations 9.1 and 9.2). We described how to compute the upper and lower limits within which there is, for example, a 95% probability of finding the mean (or a proportion) of the population from which the sample was obtained. When reporting r, it is generally informative to accompany this information with a confidence interval around the r. Although confidence intervals for rs (and other effect size measurements) are not yet routinely reported in psychological research, when they are reported, the confidence interval used is usually the 95% confidence interval. The interpretation of such an interval is that there is a 95% probability that the population value of r will fall between the upper and lower limits that define the confidence interval placed around the r obtained from the sample.

When the population value of r is not zero (and usually it is not), the distribution of sampled rs becomes skewed, and the more so the further the population value of

r falls from zero. R. A. Fisher devised a transformation of r (known as Fisher's z_r) that is distributed more normally than r and defined as

$$z_r = \tfrac{1}{2} \log_e \left(\frac{1 + r}{1 - r} \right). \tag{11.2}$$

We use the quantity z_r to get the upper and lower limits of a 95% confidence interval around an obtained effect size r by first finding the z_r transformation of the obtained r. Equation 11.2 can be used to obtain z_r, but Table B.7 of Appendix B is a more convenient way of finding the Fisher z_r corresponding to any r. For example, suppose we obtained an effect size r of .77 in a study of 12 subjects. Table B.7 shows that an r of .77 transforms to a Fisher z_r of 1.02 (at the intersection of the row labeled .7 and the column headed .07). The 95% confidence interval (CI) is then found from

$$95\% \, CI = z_r \pm 1.96 / \sqrt{N - 3} \tag{11.3}$$

For the obtained r of .77 and $N = 12$, using Equation 11.3 yields

$$95\% \, CI = 1.02 \pm 1.96 / \sqrt{12 - 3} = 1.02 \pm .65,$$

so the confidence interval ranges from a lower limit of $1.02 - .65 = .37$ to an upper limit of $1.02 + .65 = 1.67$.

These confidence limits are in units of z_r, but we prefer to express the CI in units of r for several reasons. First, most researchers have a good deal more experience in interpreting r than in interpreting Fisher's z_r. Second, squaring r gives the proportion of variance accounted for, and it can sometimes be useful information (e.g., in a context of allocating variance to each of a set of predictor variables). Third, the statistical magnitude, and in turn its implications for practical significance, of the obtained r can be readily shown in a BESD. And fourth, we can also use the BESD for the lower and upper confidence limits.

For the obtained r of .77, we had found the 95% CI to extend from .37 to 1.67 in units of z_r. To transform these lower and upper limits back to units of r, we use the following equation:

$$r = \frac{e^{2z_r} - 1}{e^{2z_r} + 1}, \tag{11.4}$$

or we simply use Table B.8 of Appendix B to find the r transformation of z_r. Using Table B.8, we see that the z_r of .37 is equivalent to an r of .354 (at the intersection of the row labeled .3 and column headed .07). For the upper confidence limit of 1.67 in units of z_r, the equivalent in units of r is .932 in Table B.8 (at the intersection of the row labeled 1.6 and the column headed .07). To summarize, the obtained r of .77 is surrounded by a 95% confidence interval extending from a low r of .35 to a high r of .93. We should note that, although the lower and upper confidence limits in units of z_r are equally far from the obtained z_r (i.e., .65 units of z_r), the lower and upper confidence limits in units of r are *not* equally spaced around the obtained r $(.77 - .35 = .42$ versus $.93 - .77 = .16)$.

The example of computing a confidence interval around an obtained effect size r was for a 95% confidence interval, as shown in Equation 11.3. The quantity 1.96 in that equation is the value that yields a 95% CI. That is, it is the standard normal deviate,

TABLE 11.7
BESDs for obtained result ($r = .77$) and for lower
($r = .35$) and upper limit ($r = .93$) of 95%
confidence interval straddling the obtained result

A. Obtained $r = .77$

	Improved	Not improved	Σ
Treatment	88.5	11.5	100
Control	11.5	88.5	100
Σ	100	100	

B. Lower limit $r = .35$

	Improved	Not improved	Σ
Treatment	67.5	32.5	100
Control	32.5	67.5	100
Σ	100	100	

C. Upper limit $r = .93$

	Improved	Not improved	Σ
Treatment	96.5	3.5	100
Control	3.5	96.5	100
Σ	100	100	

Z, associated with a two-tailed p of .05 or a one-tailed p of .025. Should we want a different CI, such as 80%, 90%, 99%, or 99.9%, we simply replace the Z of 1.96 with a Z of 1.28, 1.64, 2.58, or 3.29, respectively. The BESD for the obtained r of .77 is shown in Part A of Table 11.7, where we have also labeled the columns as "Improved" and "Not improved" to simulate the BESD for the hypothetical effect of a new medical intervention on level of health. When we have computed a confidence interval for the obtained effect size r, it is often useful to show the BESD for both the lower and upper confidence limits. These BESDs give the reader a more concrete picture of a range of likely outcomes for population values of r that may not have been very precisely estimated because of small sample size. Thus, Part B of Table 11.7 shows the BESD for the lower limit ($r = .35$), and Part C shows the BESD for the upper limit ($r = .93$).

SMALL CORRELATIONS, BUT IMPORTANT EFFECTS

These hypothetical effects are actually substantially larger than what one usually finds in calculating rs for observed effects in randomized clinical trials of pharmaceuticals. Table 11.8 gives a flavor of a wide variety of effects that we calculated on the basis of

TABLE 11.8
Effect sizes of various independent variables

Independent variable	Dependent variable	$|r|$	r^2
Breast implants[a]	Connective tissue disease	.00	.00
Salk vaccine[b]	Paralytic poliomyelitis	.01	.00
Tamoxifen[c]	Major vein blood clots	.01	.00
Tamoxifen[c]	Lung blood clots	.02	.00
Pravastatin[d]	Death	.02	.00
Tamoxifen[c]	Uterine cancer	.02	.00
Aspirin[e]	Heart attacks	.03	.00
Beta carotene[f]	Death	.03	.00
Streptokinase[g]	Death	.03	.00
Estrogen + progestin[h]	Dementia	.04	.00
Plavix[i]	Serious cardiac events	.04	.00
Propranolol[j]	Death	.04	.00
Tamoxifen[c]	Breast cancer	.04	.00
Teacher's aide[k]	Achievement scores	.04	.00
Raloxifene[l]	Breast cancer	.05	.00
Male status[m]	Self-esteem	.06	.00
Magnesium[n]	Convulsions	.07	.00
Vietnam veteran status[o]	Alcohol problems	.07	.00
AZT + ddC[p]	Death	.07	.01
Male status[q]	Assertiveness	.08	.01
Male status[r]	Cardiac catheterization referral	.08	.01
White status[s]	Cardiac catheterization referral	.08	.01
Garlic[t]	Death	.09	.01
Vitamin E[u]	Nonfatal heart attacks	.09	.01
Indinavir[v]	Serious AIDS events	.09	.01
AZT + ddl[p]	Death	.10	.01
Intelligence[w]	Popularity	.10	.01
Classroom size[k]	Achievement scores	.11	.01
Social support[x]	Health outcomes	.11	.01
Depression[y]	Death	.12	.01
Testosterone[z]	Adult delinquency	.12	.01
Workshops[aa]	Sexually transmitted disease	.12	.01
Compulsory hospitalization vs. treatment choice[bb]	Alcohol problems	.13	.02
Physical attractiveness[cc]	Intelligence	.14	.02
Cyclosporine[dd]	Death	.15	.02
Low-dose warfarin[ee]	Blood clots	.15	.02

(continued . . .)

TABLE 11.8 (*continued*)

Independent variable	Dependent variable	$|r|$	r^2
Ganzfeld perception[ff]	Accuracy	.16	.03
Fingerprint asymmetry[gg]	Sexual orientation	.18	.03
Cisplatin + Vinblastine[hh]	Death	.18	.03
Education level[ii]	Volunteering for research	.20	.04
AZT for neonates[jj]	HIV infection	.21	.04
Female status[kk]	Decoding nonverbal behavior	.21	.04
Ritonavir[ll]	AIDS: disease or death	.21	.04
Cholesterol-lowering regimen[mm]	Coronary status	.22	.05
AZT[nn]	Death	.23	.05
Female status[oo]	Smiling	.23	.05
Alcohol[pp]	Aggression	.24	.06
Group cohesion[qq]	Productivity	.25	.06
Intelligence[rr]	Leadership role	.25	.06
Treatment choice versus AA[ss]	Alcohol problems	.27	.07
Myelin[tt]	Severity of multiple sclerosis	.31	.09
Interpersonal expectancy effects[uu]	Human and animal behavior	.33	.11
Acupuncture[vv]	Depression	.38	.14
Psychotherapy[ww]	Improvement	.39	.15
Compulsory hospitalization vs. AA[xx]	Alcohol problems	.40	.16
Viral load[ll]	Death	.40	.16
Social support[yy]	Weight loss	.41	.17
Vaccination[zz]	SIV health	.47	.22
Anxiety[aaa]	Rumormonger	.48	.23
AZT[bbb]	SIV health	.48	.23
Thalidomide[ccc]	Severe mouth ulcer	.55	.30
Antibody cA2[ddd]	Rheumatoid arthritis symptoms	.58	.34
Early linguistic ability[eee]	Alzheimer's disease	.65	.42
Progesterone[fff]	SIV infection	.65	.42
PMPA[ggg]	SIV infection	.80	.63

[a] Kong, 1996.   [a] Cromie, 1996.   [b] Meier, 1978; see also Rosnow & Rosenthal, 2003.   [c] Altman, 1998.   [d] Knox, 1995.   [e] Steering Committee of the Physicians Health Study Research Group, 1988.   [f] Alpha-Tocopherol, Beta Carotene Cancer Prevention Study Group, 1994.   [g] GISSI, 1986.   [h] Shumaker et al., 2003.   [i] Haney, 2001.   [j] Kolata, 1981.   [k] Mosteller, 1995.   [l] Altman, 1999.   [m] Feingold, 1994.   [n] Foreman, 1995.   [o] Centers for Disease Control Vietnam Experience Study, 1988.   [p] Holden, 1995b.   [q] Feingold, 1994.   [r] Schulman et al., 1999.   [s] Schulman et al., 1999.   [t] Goldfinger, 1991.   [u] Stephens, N. G. et al., 1996.   [v] Knox, 1997.   [w] Mann, 1959.   [x] Smith, Fernengel et al., 1994.   [y] Frasure-Smith et al., 1999.   [z] Dabbs & Morris, 1990.   [aa] Shain et al., 1999.   [bb] Cromie, 1991.   [cc] Jackson, Hunter, & Hodge, 1995.   [dd] Canadian Multicentre Transplant Study Group, 1983.   [ee] Grady, 2003.   [ff] Chandler, 1993.   [gg] Holden, 1995a.   [hh] Cromie, 1990.   [ii] Rosenthal & Rosnow, 1975.   [jj] Altman, 1994.   [kk] Hall, 1984.   [ll] Cohen, 1996.   [mm] Roberts, 1987.   [nn] Barnes, 1986.   [oo] Hall & Halberstadt, 1986.   [pp] Bushman & Cooper, 1990.   [qq] Mullen & Copper, 1994.   [rr] Mann, 1959.   [ss] Cromie, 1991.   [tt] Weiner et al., 1993.   [uu] Rosenthal & Rubin, 1978.   [vv] Allen, Schnyer, & Hitt, 1998.   [ww] Smith, Glass, & Miller, 1980.   [xx] Cromie, 1991.   [yy] Wing & Jeffery, 1999.   [zz] Cohen, 1993.   [aaa] Rosnow, 1991.   [bbb] Van Rompay & Marthas, 1995.   [ccc] Associated Press, 1995.   [ddd] Sands & Gillyat, 1996.   [eee] Associated Press, 1996 (February).   [fff] Associated Press, 1996 (May).   [ggg] Tsai et al., 1995.

TABLE 11.9

Vaccination status and diagnostic class of 401,974 children in 1954 Salk vaccine trial

Condition	Paralytic polio present	Paralytic polio absent
A. Raw counts in four conditions		
Vaccination	33	200,712
Placebo	115	201,114
B. Percentages in four conditions		
Vaccination	0.016	99.984
Placebo	0.057	99.943
C. Binomial effect size display of $r = .011$		
Vaccination	49.5	50.5
Placebo	50.5	49.5
Total	100.0	100.0

the information in journal articles or newspaper stories, including page-one newspaper articles about breakthrough medical findings. Many researchers are surprised to learn that biomedical and behavioral interventions and outcomes of possibly great public health consequence may be associated with such small correlations as shown in this table. The table shows by no means a random sample of biomedical and behavioral effect sizes, but it is still noteworthy that only about half of these studies accounted for more than 1% of the variance or showed an effect size r greater than .12.

One of the effect size rs is for the aspirin study described in chapter 2 (see again Part A of Table 2.5), where the effect on preventing a heart attack had an associated r of .034, and thus the corresponding $r^2 = .00$, or to four decimal places, .0012. An even smaller r in Table 11.8 is the second one listed, which we calculated from data in the 1954 Salk vaccine trial (Rosnow & Rosenthal, 2003), called "the biggest public health experiment ever" by Meier (1978, p. 3). The purpose of this famous biomedical experiment was to evaluate the effects of inoculating young children with the Salk poliomyelitis vaccine versus a placebo consisting of a simple salt solution (Francis, Korns, Voight, Boisen, Hemphill, Napier, & Tolchinsky, 1955). Brownlee (1955) noted a number of serious problems with the design and implementation of the study but nevertheless concluded that there was "convincing evidence for the effectiveness of the vaccine" (p. 1010). Part A of Table 11.9 shows the specific raw frequencies to which Brownlee was alluding; Part B displays the percentages corresponding to the empirical data in Part A, and Part C shows the BESD.

The effect size r for the results in Part A of Table 11.9 is .011 (rounded to .01 in Table 11.8), and thus the corresponding $r^2 = .000$ or, to four decimal places, .0001. Most people would be surprised to learn that an effective biomedical intervention could be associated with an r and an r^2 this small, but as Table 11.8 shows, rs smaller than .10 are not at all unusual in biomedical research. In Part C of Table 11.9, the BESD helps us to perceive the practical significance of the effect size r corresponding to a vaccination success rate (i.e., paralytic polio absent) of $100(.50 + .005) = 50.5$, and a placebo success rate of $100(.50 - .005) = 49.5$. The difference between these rates, divided by 100 is .01, the effect size indexed by r. When we think of $r = .011$ as reflecting a 1.1% decrease in paralytic polio, the r does not seem quite so "small." This result also makes us more sanguine about the magnitude and importance of effect sizes for research findings in behavioral science. It is, however, important to remember that everything under the sun is defined in part by context, and this is no less true of the interpretation of the practical importance of an effect size measure of any particular magnitude. The point is that, whereas any effect size is mathematically determined by characteristics of the study design and the results, the interpretation of its real-life implications will always depend on the nature of the variables and how they were operationalized.

COUNTERNULL VALUES OF EFFECT SIZES

Many behavioral researchers (particularly those insensitive to the implications of power considerations when doing significance testing) have acquired the unfortunate habit of thinking (a) that failure to reject the null hypothesis implies an effect size of zero, and (b) that finding a statistically significant p value implies an effect size of important magnitude. We have much to say about statistical power in the next chapter, but here we want to pick up another thread from chapter 2. In that chapter we briefly described another type of interval estimate, called the *null-counternull interval* (Rosenthal & Rubin, 1994). As we illustrate now in more detail, this interval (null value to counternull value) can alert researchers to the degree to which their conclusions of "no effect" might be in error, and in this way it provides some protection against mistaken interpretations of the failure to reject the null hypothesis (Rosenthal, Rosnow, & Rubin, 2000; Rosenthal & Rubin, 1994).

The counternull value of an obtained effect size is the nonnull magnitude of effect size that is supported by exactly the same amount of evidence as is the null value of the effect size. That is, if the counternull value is taken as the null hypothesis, the resulting p value will be the same as the obtained p value for the actual null hypothesis. The null-counternull interval can be understood as conceptually related to confidence intervals. But whereas confidence intervals provide lower and upper limits for such intervals as the 95% or 99% CI, they do not involve the null hypothesis or the obtained p value. The counternull, on the other hand, is based directly on the null value of the effect size and the obtained effect size.

The obtained effect size estimate always falls between the null value of the effect size and the counternull value. For effect size estimates that are based on symmetrical distributions, such as the normal or t distributions (e.g., Cohen's d in Equation 2.4, Hedges's g in Equation 2.5, or the Fisher z_r in Equation 11.2), the obtained effect size falls exactly midway between the null value of the effect size and the counternull value. The following equation gives the counternull value for any effect size indicator with a symmetrical distribution (e.g., the normal or t distribution), no matter what the magnitude of the effect size (ES) is under the null:

$$ES_{counternull} = 2ES_{obtained} - ES_{null}. \qquad (11.5)$$

Because the effect size expected under the null is zero in so many applications, the value of the counternull is often simply twice the obtained effect size, or $2ES_{obtained}$.

As the effect size correlation, r, is not symmetrically distributed, we work instead with the symmetrically distributed transformation of r, which is the Fisher z_r. Working with units of z_r we find the counternull value of z_r and transform this back into units of r. Suppose we have an r of .50 between increasing levels of medication and the increasing clinical improvement in a sample of 10 patients. With a sample this small, the very substantial r of .50 has an associated two-tailed p value of .14, and thus, we cannot reject the null hypothesis of $r = .00$ at the .05 level. To avoid concluding that the null value of $r = .00$ is a plausible estimate of the population correlation, we should compute the counternull value of the obtained effect size r of .50. From Table B.7 of Appendix B (or computed directly from Equation 11.2), we find the obtained effect size r is associated with the z_r value of .549. From Equation 11.5, we find $ES_{counternull} = 2(.549) - .00 = 1.098$ (in units of z_r). To find the value of r associated with this counternull z_r, we consult Table B.8 of Appendix B (or compute it directly from Equation 11.4) and find $r_{counternull} = .800$. Thus, if someone were tempted to believe that the population value of r is close to the null value of .00, we would remind that person that the counternull value ($r_{counternull} = .80$) of the obtained effect size ($r = .50$) is exactly as likely as the null value of $r = .00$.

When the Pearson product-moment correlation is a point-biserial correlation (i.e., where one variable is continuous, and the other variable is dichotomous), the following formula can be used to estimate $r_{counternull}$ directly from the obtained r:

$$r_{counternull} = \sqrt{\frac{4r^2}{1 + 3r^2}} . \tag{11.6}$$

For example, suppose we obtained a point-biserial correlation of .50. We could directly use Equation 11.6:

$$r_{counternull} = \sqrt{\frac{4(.50)^2}{1 + 3(.50)^2}} = .756.$$

Obtaining $r_{counternull}$ by way of the z_r transformation for the Pearson r does not necessarily yield the same value as Equation 11.6, but the results tend to be similar.

Having computed the counternull value of the effect size estimate, we can create a null-counternull interval. This interval spans from the null value of the effect size to the counternull value of the effect size. In the example of an obtained effect size $r = .50$ with an associated p value of .14 two-tailed, or .07 one-tailed, the null-counternull interval extends from an r of .00 (the null value in this example) to an r of .80 (the counternull value). We can also express the percentage coverage of the null-counternull interval ($NC\%$) using the following equation:

$$NC\% = 100[1.00 - 2(p \text{ one-tailed})], \tag{11.7}$$

which for this example yields

$$NC\% = 100[1.00 - 2(.07)] = 100(.86) = 86\%.$$

TABLE 11.10

BESDs for null and counternull results straddling the obtained result (86% interval)

Null result (r = .00)			Obtained result (r = .50, p = .14 two-tailed)					Counternull result r = .80		
	MI	LI			MI	LI	Σ		MI	LI
T	50	50		T	75	25	100	T	90	10
C	50	50		C	25	75	100	C	10	90
				Σ	100	100	200			

86% null-counternull interval

↑_____↑

r = .00   r = .80

Note: T, C, MI, and LI refer to Treatment, Control, More Improvement, and Less Improvement, respectively.

Our interpretation is that there is an 86% chance that the population value of r falls between the lower (null) and upper (counternull) limits of this null-counternull interval (i.e., between .00 and .80). Just as is the case for the confidence interval, it is often instructive to show the BESDs for both the null value and the counternull value. Table 11.10 shows these BESDs along with the obtained result they straddle.

SPEARMAN RANK CORRELATION

Most of the useful correlation coefficients are product-moment correlations, and they are typically the special cases of the Pearson r we have been discussing. When data are in ranked form, we apply the **Spearman rho (ρ),** but that is nothing more that a Pearson r computed on numbers that happen to be ranks. Ranked numbers are more predictable than unranked numbers, because knowing only the number of pairs of scores (N) tells us both the mean and the standard deviation of the scores obtained. There is a simpler computational formula than Equation 11.1 for scores that have been ranked:

$$\rho = 1 - \frac{6\Sigma D^2}{N^3 - N},\tag{11.8}$$

and the only new ingredient is D, the difference between the ranks assigned to the two scores representing each of the N sampling units.

In the example shown in Table 11.11, four schools have been ranked by two observers on the warmth of the psychological climate created by the school's principal. The column headed D shows the differences between the ranks assigned by Observers A and B, and the column headed D^2 shows these differences squared. The sum of the D^2 values (ΣD^2) is needed for computation of ρ from Equation 11.8. The columns headed Z_A and Z_B show the Z scores of the ranks assigned by Observers A and B, respectively. The column labeled $Z_A Z_B$ shows the products of the Z-scored ranks

TABLE 11.11
Two observers' rankings of four schools

	Observers						
	A	B	D	D^2	Z_A	Z_B	$Z_A Z_B$
School 1	2	1	1	1	−0.45	−1.34	0.60
School 2	1	2	−1	1	−1.34	−0.45	0.60
School 3	3	3	0	0	0.45	0.45	0.20
School 4	4	4	0	0	1.34	1.34	1.80
Σ	10	10	0	2	0	0	3.20
M	2.5	2.5			0	0	0.80
σ	1.12	1.12			1.00	1.00	

$$\rho = 1 - \frac{6\Sigma D^2}{N^3 - N} = 1 - \frac{6(2)}{4^3 - 4} = 1 - \frac{12}{60} = .800$$

$$r = \frac{\Sigma Z_A Z_B}{N} = \frac{3.20}{4} = .800$$

assigned by Observers A and B. Ordinarily we would need no Z scores to compute ρ, but here we wanted to illustrate that, when there are no ties in the ranking, ρ is equivalent to the Pearson r on the ranks.

The equivalence of the Spearman ρ and the Pearson r computed from ranked data holds only when there are no ties in the ranking. As Table 11.12 shows, when there are only a few ties, ρ tends to be quite similar to r. In Set 1 we see that Observer A has equal ranks of 1.5 and 1.5 for the tied ranks of 1 and 2, and we find $\rho = .950$ and $r = .949$. When a larger proportion of the ranks is involved in ties, the difference between ρ and r tends to be larger, as shown in Set 2, where Observer A has equal ranks of 2, 2, 2 for the tied ranks of 1, 2, and 3, and we find $\rho = .800$ and $r = .775$. Set 3 is a more extreme case of tied ranks, in that Observer A has equal ranks of 2, 2, 2 for the tied ranks of 1, 2, and 3, and Observer B has equal ranks of 3, 3, 3 for the tied ranks of 2, 3, 4, and now we find $\rho = .600$ and $r = .333$.

TABLE 11.12
Further examples of ranked scores

Set 1		Set 2		Set 3	
A	B	A	B	A	B
1.5	1	2	1	2	1
1.5	2	2	2	2	3
3	3	2	3	2	3
4	4	4	4	4	3
$\rho = .950$		$\rho = .800$		$\rho = .600$	
$r = .949$		$r = .775$		$r = .333$	

RANKS AS A TRANSFORMATION

The Spearman rank correlation coefficient is used when the scores to be correlated are already in ranked form, as when raters have been asked to rank a set of sampling units. In addition, however, ρ is sometimes used as a very quick index of correlation when ρ is easy and painless to compute by hand, and r is hard and slow. Consider computing r between the pairs of scores shown in Table 11.13 when no calculator is available. The computation of r would be arduous, whereas computing ρ would be easy because ranks are so convenient to work with. But suppose both ρ and r were computed, and the researcher wondered, "Which is the better estimate of the 'true' correlation, the r of .627 or the ρ of .800?" That question cannot be answered readily.

   If, for some reason, we regarded the obtained scores as being on just the scale of measurement required, we might prefer r to ρ. However, if there were nothing sacrosanct about the particular scale used (and usually there is not), we might choose to transform the scores to achieve greater symmetry (i.e., lack of skewness) of distribution. Such transformations tend to increase the accuracy of statistical analyses, and ranking the scores is one form of transforming the data to reduce skewness. In this instance we might have decided that the data should be transformed to improve the symmetry of our distributions, as symmetrical distributions are generally preferable to skewed distributions for subsequent statistical analyses (Tukey, 1977). We might, for example, have decided to take the square roots of the data obtained. Had we done so, as Table 11.14 shows, the r between the square-root-transformed scores would have become .799 in this case, essentially the same value we obtained from the rank correlation ρ.

   For the data in Table 11.14, transforming to improve symmetry led to a higher r. But sometimes transforming data leads to a lower r. Consider the data in Table 11.15 and the corresponding plots in Figure 11.2. The correlation between X and Y is .9999, but the correlation between the more symmetrical transformed data (logs to the base 10 of X and Y) is only .80; this is precisely the value obtained by use of the rank correlation ρ. In this case we find that ranking the data was a better transformation than the original data. That is, ranking the data was better from the point of view of achieving symmetry. Ranking the data had the same effect as taking the logs of the original data.

TABLE 11.13
Computation of ρ

	X	Y	Rank X	Rank Y	D	D^2
Pair 1	6.8	79.713	2	1	1	1
Pair 2	12.2	47.691	1	2	−1	1
Pair 3	1.7	28.002	3	3	0	0
Pair 4	0.3	11.778	4	4	0	0

$$\rho = 1 - \frac{6(2)}{4^3 - 4} = 1 - \frac{12}{60} = .800$$

TABLE 11.14
Square root transformations

	X	Y	$\sqrt{X}$	$\sqrt{Y}$
Pair 1	6.8	79.713	2.61	8.93
Pair 2	12.2	47.691	3.49	6.91
Pair 3	1.7	28.002	1.30	5.29
Pair 4	0.3	11.778	0.55	3.43

$r_{xy} = .627$ $\qquad r_{\sqrt{x}\sqrt{y}} = .799$
$\rho_{xy} = .800$ $\qquad \rho_{\sqrt{x}\sqrt{y}} = .800$

TABLE 11.15
Logarithmic transformations

	X	Y	Log X	Log Y
Pair 1	100	10	2	1
Pair 2	10	100	1	2
Pair 3	1000	1000	3	3
Pair 4	10000	10000	4	4

OBSERVATIONS OF DISPROPORTIONATE INFLUENCE

In chapter 10 we discussed the value of examining the data quite closely, for example, looking for any anomalies such as outliers in a distribution of scores, or trying to understand an odd pattern of scores such as that of Figure 10.7. In that example we were able to generate a useful hypothesis by considering a third variable (gender), as shown in Figure 10.8. Before leaving the topic of ranks as a transformation of the original data for correlational analyses, we want to note that outliers can sometimes contribute much more than their "fair share" to the magnitude of a correlation. Consider the following pairs of scores on variables X and Y:

Pairs	1	2	3	4	5	6	7	8	9
X	1	2	3	4	5	6	7	8	18
Y	7	6	5	4	3	2	1	0	17

We note for Pair 9 that both values seem far out of line with the rest of the scores on the X and Y variables. As a check on our impression of outlier status for the X and Y scores of the 9th pair, we can use Iglewicz and Hoaglin's (1993) procedure (Equation 10.9) to obtain $Z_{modified}$. For variable X of Pair 9 (score of 18), using Equation 10.9 we find

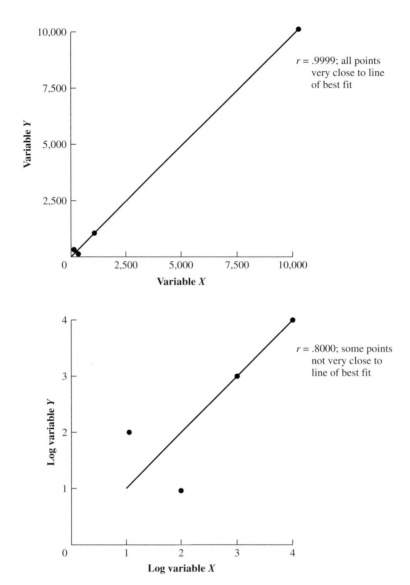

FIGURE 11.2
Plots of the relationship between variables X and Y and variables log X and log Y.

$$Z_{\text{modified}} = \frac{0.6745(X - Mdn)}{Mdn_{\text{AD}}} = \frac{0.6745(18 - 5)}{2} = 4.38,$$

and for variable Y of Pair 9 (score of 17), using the same equation (with Mdn now at 4, instead of 5) we obtain the same value:

$$Z_{\text{modified}} = \frac{0.6745(17 - 4)}{2} = 4.38$$

Figure 11.3 shows these data in a scatter plot where our "doubly outlying" (i.e., on both the X and Y variables) observation pulls our eye (and the Pearson product-moment r) upward to the right. Computing r yields a value of .588. A simple transformation to ranks will bring in the doubly outlying observation close to the bulk of the X and Y observations. Computing rho on the ranked data (using Equation 11.8) yields $\rho = -.400$, the same value we obtain computing r on the rank-transformed data (using Equation 11.1).

When a single observation (or more generally, a small proportion of the total number of observations) can change a correlation's magnitude so radically (e.g., from $r = +.59$ to $r = -.40$), we have found an **observation of disproportionate influence (OODI).** Dealing with an OODI brings up the same issues raised whenever we find outliers, but it is of special concern precisely because such a small number of data points can so radically affect our conclusion about the results in the scatter plot. Simply dropping the OODI of Figure 11.3 would change the overall correlation from an r of $+.59$ to an r of -1.00. Dropping the OODI but trimming more equitably by also dropping the observations showing the *lowest* values on the X and Y variables would also yield an r of -1.00.

In the previous chapter (see again Table 10.4), we described three transformations for reeling in outliers: square roots, logarithms, and negative reciprocals. Of these three, outliers are pulled back to the bulk of the data least by square roots, more by logarithms, and most by negative reciprocals. Applying these same transformations to the data of Figure 11.3 and then computing correlations (r) on the transformed scores,

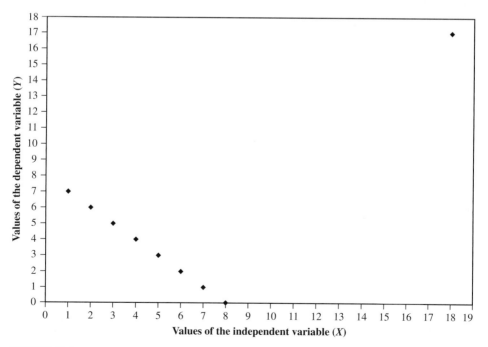

FIGURE 11.3
Observation of disproportionate influence (OODI).

we find (a) $r = +.14$ for the square root transformation; (b) $r = -.09$ for the log transformation; and (c) $r = -.38$ for the negative reciprocal transformation. In this example, the "hardest working" of these three transformations gives an r very close to that obtained by our use of ranks as a fourth transformation ($r = -.40$). Our four transformations have left the data in a more tractable format, and we might well be willing to report the overall results as reflecting, in general, a fairly substantial negative correlation (e.g., $-.38$ or $-.40$) between the two variables.

Now that we have coped with the OODI, should we forget about that doubly outlying observation? Probably not. After ruling out a clerical or other recording error, it will be useful to learn as much about that observation as possible. For all the variables for which information is available about the subjects, we should note the ways in which the outlier differs from the other units.

Suppose the data of Figure 11.3 resulted from a pilot study on the relation between the dosage of an antidepressant intervention (X) and the degree of patient unhappiness (Y). Studying other variables, for which we have data for the patients, may reveal that of those nine patients in the pilot study, eight were being seen in a college counseling center and the ninth, the doubly outlying OODI, was an inpatient on a psychiatric service. Such a serendipitous observation raises the possibility of the patient recruitment site's being an important moderator variable, that is, that the relationship of interest (r_{xy}) might be noticeably different in patients receiving different dosages of antidepressant intervention. Thus, merely suggestive data, garnered from our close scrutiny of an OODI, may provide interesting new leads for future research. In this example these data may suggest that patients with mild levels of depression should be studied separately from patients with more severe levels of depression.

POINT-BISERIAL CORRELATION

Another case of the product-moment correlation r is the point-biserial correlation, r_{pb}. In this case one of the variables is continuous (as are the variables used for the usual case of r), whereas the other variable is dichotomous, with arbitrarily applied numerical values, such as 0 and 1 or -1 and $+1$. (Such quantification of the two levels of a dichotomous variable is often called **dummy coding** when the numerical values 0 and 1 are employed.) A typical illustration might have us compare females with males on some measure (e.g., verbal skill). Suppose the results were as follows:

Males	Females
2	4
3	5
3	5
4	6

Although we see two groups of scores, it does not look like a correlation coefficient situation, in which we would see *pairs* of scores (i.e., X and Y) for each unit or subject, not just one score for each subject as above. In this example, the scores on variable Y (the verbal skill measure) are shown, but X is "hidden." The reason, of course, is that the group identification (i.e., male vs. female) implies the variable X scores. Rewriting the data array into a form that "looks more correlational" is shown in Table 11.16, where the sum of the products in the last column is 6.56, and dividing this value by the N of 8 tells us that the correlation between verbal skill and gender for these eight pairs is .816.

Although we will be reviewing the t test in detail in chapter 13, we may note here, in anticipation, the special relationship between t and the point-biserial correlation r_{pb}. The t statistic enables us to assess the probability that the means of two samples may differ by the obtained amount if in nature (i.e., the population) there is a zero difference between the means, or if the null hypothesis of no relationship between the independent variable and the dependent variable is true. The independent variable in the case of the t test is membership in one of the two groups being compared (usually scored as 0 and 1, or as -1 and $+1$), and the dependent variable is the score earned on the measures we want to compare for the two groups. Based on the data shown in Table 11.17 (which we recognize as a rearrangement of the results in Table 11.16), we use the following formula to compute the t statistic:

$$t = \frac{M_1 - M_2}{\sqrt{\left(\frac{1}{n_1} + \frac{1}{n_2}\right)S^2_{pooled}}} \tag{11.9}$$

and substituting the results in Table 11.16, we find

$$t = \frac{5 - 3}{\sqrt{\left(\frac{1}{4} + \frac{1}{4}\right)0.6667}} = 3.46,$$

which with 6 df is significant at $p < .01$, one-tailed test. The symbol df refers to the degrees of freedom, that is, the number of observations diminished by the number of

TABLE 11.16
Correlation between gender and verbal skill

	Verbal skill (Y)	Gender (X) (0 = male; 1 = female)	Z_y	Z_x	$Z_y Z_x$
Subject 1	2	0	−1.64	−1	1.64
Subject 2	3	0	−0.82	−1	0.82
Subject 3	3	0	−0.82	−1	0.82
Subject 4	4	0	0.00	−1	0.00
Subject 5	4	1	0.00	1	0.00
Subject 6	5	1	0.82	1	0.82
Subject 7	5	1	0.82	1	0.82
Subject 8	6	1	1.64	1	1.64
Σ	32	4	0	0	6.56
N	8	8	8	8	
M	4.0	0.5	0	0	
σ	1.22	0.5	1	1	

TABLE 11.17
Basic data for a *t* test

	Males	Females
	2	4
	3	5
	3	5
	4	6
Σ	12	20
M	3	5
n	4	4
*S*²	0.6667	0.6667

restrictions limiting the observations' freedom to vary. Thus, the *df* for a single sample of size *n* is equal to $n - 1$, as once the mean of the sample has been determined, only $n - 1$ of the observations are still free to vary. Analogously, when two samples are involved, as in the case of the *t* test illustrated here, 1 *df* is lost or "used up" for each of the two samples so $df = (n_1 - 1) + (n_2 - 1) = n_1 + n_2 - 2 = N - 2$. The result above tells us that a *t* this large would be obtained less than 1% of the time if we were drawing random samples from the populations of females and males (from which these subjects were randomly sampled), if those parent populations of females and males showed zero difference between the means or a zero correlation between the obtained scores (Y) and the dichotomously scored (e.g., 0 and 1, or -1 and $+1$) variable (X) of group membership.

For the same data in Tables 11.16 and 11.17, we now have both a correlation r_{pb} of .816 and a *t* value of 3.46. If it is so easy to obtain either *r* or *t* for the same data, it must be possible to obtain *t* directly from *r*, or to obtain *r* directly from *t*, and so it is. Indeed, there is an important relation between *r*s of any form (or any other measure of the size of an effect or a relationship) and a test of significance. We introduced this relationship in chapter 2, and it can be understood as another fundamental equation of data analysis:

$$\text{Significance test} = \text{Size of effect} \times \text{Size of study} \qquad (11.10)$$

Thus, for any given (nonzero) effect size (such as *r*), the *t* test, or any other test of significance, increases as the size of the study (i.e., the number of sampling units) increases.

The particular index of the size of the study (e.g., $N, df, \sqrt{N}, \sqrt{df}$) varies with the particular index of effect size used, which might be $r, r^2,$ or $r/\sqrt{1 - r^2}$, depending on the test of significance involved. In the case of *t* and *r*, the appropriate equation is that listed in chapter 2 as Equation 2.2, that is,

$$t = \frac{r}{\sqrt{1 - r^2}} \times \sqrt{df}.$$

In this equation the size of the effect is defined by $r/\sqrt{1 - r^2}$, and the size of the study is defined as $\sqrt{df}$ (or, in this application, as $N-2$). The quantity $r/\sqrt{1 - r^2}$ may be seen as the square root of $r^2/(1 - r^2)$ which is the ratio of the proportion of variance explained by r to the proportion of variance not explained by r, or a kind of signal-to-noise ratio. For our example, r was .816, so $r/\sqrt{1 - r^2} = 1.41$. The df (the number of pairs of scores minus 2) for r was $8 - 2 = 6$, so $t = 1.41 \times \sqrt{6} = 3.46$.

Equation 11.10 follows the scientific logic of first estimating the size of the relationship and from that, by using an index of the size of the study, computing the test of significance that provides information about the probability that the null hypothesis of no relationship between X and Y is true. In practice, however, researchers have traditionally computed the significance test before they have computed the size of the effect because of the primacy of significance testing (chapter 2). In such cases it is easy to obtain the effect size estimate r from the obtained t by means of the following relationship:

$$ r = \sqrt{\frac{t^2}{t^2 + (n_1 + n_2 - 2)}}, \tag{11.11} $$

where n_1 and n_2 represent the sizes of the samples on which each of the means being compared was based.

The t test for the significance of a correlation coefficient (Equation 2.2) applies not only to the point-biserial correlation (r_{pb}), but to the Pearson r and to the rank-correlation coefficient (ρ) as well. However, in the case of ρ, we would want to have at least seven pairs of scores to obtain a good approximation—a rule of thumb suggested by a comparison of Tables A11[i] and A11[ii] in Snedecor and Cochran (1980).

EXACT TESTS FOR RHO

More exact tests of the significance of ρ, the rank correlation coefficient, are also readily available for sample sizes from 4 to 16 pairs of scores (Nijsse, 1988; Zar, 1984). The logic of these exact tests is illustrated by this small example: Suppose two executives have ranked three managers on their suitability for promotion. Executive 1 has ranked them as A, B, C. What is the exact probability that the correlation between the executives' rankings is 1.00? Executive 2 can rank the managers only six ways (not allowing for ties): ABC, ACB, BAC, BCA, CAB, CBA. Only one of these rankings (ABC) results in a correlation of 1.00, and under the null hypothesis of zero correlation, all six rankings are equally likely. Therefore, the probability of a perfect correlation is 1/6, or .167. The probability of a perfect correlation for four ranked stimuli is 1 divided by the total number of ways in which four stimuli can be ranked, or $1/4! = 1/(4 \times 3 \times 2 \times 1) = 1/24 = .042$. The expression "4!" is read as "four factorial" and interpreted as $4 \times 3 \times 2 \times 1$ or, more generally, as $N(N - 1)(N - 2) \ldots (2)(1)$. Simply listing all possible rankings of N stimuli allows the ready calculation of the probabilities of any outcome or of any set of outcomes (e.g., correlations exceeding any given value). Table B.10 of Appendix B shows, for various sample sizes, the magnitude of ρ required to reach specific levels of significance.

PHI COEFFICIENT

Another special case of the product-moment correlation r is the phi (ϕ) coefficient. In this case both of the variables are dichotomous with arbitrarily applied numerical values such as 0 and 1, or -1 and $+1$. As an example, we compare five Democrats and five Republicans on a yes-no question that each of them answered. The small sample sizes are for pedagogical convenience; we assume that the sample sizes in an actual case would be larger. Our hypothetical results are as follows:

	Democrats	Republicans	Σ
Yes	1	4	5
No	4	1	5
Σ	5	5	10

This 2×2 table of counts, also called a *contingency table*, shows that one Democrat and four Republicans answered "yes" and that four Democrats and one Republican answered "no."

This is another set of results that does not seem to resemble the typical situation for a correlation coefficient, where we would expect to see pairs of scores (i.e., X and Y) for each unit. However, dummy-coding the row and column variables does immediately produce such a typical correlational situation. That is, we dummy-code the dichotomous independent variable of party membership as 0 and 1, and so, too, the yes-no dependent variable. These results are shown in Table 11.18. In our rewriting of the table of counts, Respondent 1 in Table 11.18 was drawn from the upper-left cell of the 2×2 table (the Democrat who answered "yes"), Respondents 2, 3, 4, and 5 are from the upper-right cell (the Republicans who answered "yes"), Respondents 6, 7, 8, and 9 are from the lower-left cell (the Democrats who answered "no"), and Respondent 10 is from the lower-right cell (the Republican who answered "no").

Using Equation 11.1, we obtain the Pearson r between party membership and the yes-no responses by dividing the sum of the standard-score products in the last column of Table 11.18 ($\Sigma Z_x Z_y = 6$) by $N = 10$, which yields $r = .60$, suggesting that Republicans were more likely to say "yes" to this yes-no question. The obtained r is given as phi (ϕ) to denote the dichotomous nature of both variables. If the sample size (N) is not too small (that is, $N > 20$), and if both variables are not too far from a 50:50 split of 0s and 1s (no greater than 75:25), the significance of a phi coefficient can be evaluated by t, once again using Equation 2.2:

$$t = \frac{r}{\sqrt{1 - r^2}} \times \sqrt{df} = \frac{.60}{\sqrt{1 - (.60)^2}} \times \sqrt{8} = 2.12.$$

This application of Equation 2.2 (above) for testing the significance of the phi coefficient is not well known, but it is well documented (Cochran, 1950; Lunney, 1970; Snedecor & Cochran, 1967). The more common test of significance of the phi coefficient is chi-square (χ^2), which is reviewed below (and discussed in more

TABLE 11.18
Correlation between response and party membership

	Party (X) (Rep. = 1; Dem. = 0)	Response (Y) (yes = 1; no = 0)	Standard scores for variables X and Y		
			Z_x	Z_y	$Z_x Z_y$
Respondent 1	0	1	−1	1	−1
Respondent 2	1	1	1	1	1
Respondent 3	1	1	1	1	1
Respondent 4	1	1	1	1	1
Respondent 5	1	1	1	1	1
Respondent 6	0	0	−1	−1	1
Respondent 7	0	0	−1	−1	1
Respondent 8	0	0	−1	−1	1
Respondent 9	0	0	−1	−1	1
Respondent 10	1	0	1	−1	−1
Σ	5	5	0	0	6
N	10	10	10	10	
M	.5	.5	0	0	
σ	.5	.5	1	1	

detail in chapter 19). It comes as a surprise to many to learn that χ^2 does not necessarily yield more accurate tests of the significance of phi than the t test in Equation 2.2 (Cochran, 1950; Lunney, 1970).

So far in our discussion of phi we have treated it no differently from any other product-moment correlation. For two reasons, however, it is useful to adopt an alternative approach to the phi coefficient. One reason is computational convenience; the second, is the availability of other approaches to assessing the significance of ϕ. Our alternative approach takes advantage of the fact that the data come to us in a 2 × 2 contingency table. Part A of Table 11.19 shows again the data on the relation between political party affiliation and response to the yes-no question. This time, however, we have added one of four labels to each of the four cells: A, B, C, D. We now compute phi from

$$\phi = \frac{BC - AD}{\sqrt{(A + B)(C + D)(A + C)(B + D)}},$$ (11.12)

which in this case yields

$$\phi = \frac{(4)(4) - (1)(1)}{\sqrt{(5)(5)(5)(5)}} = \frac{15}{25} = .60,$$

the identical value obtained from Equation 11.1.

TABLE 11.19
Results in 2 × 2 contingency table

A. Table of counts

	Democrats	Republicans	Σ
Yes	A　1	B　4	(A + B) = 5
No	C　4	D　1	(C + D) = 5
Σ	(A + C) = 5	(B + D) = 5	(A + B + C + D) = 10

B. Observed (O) and expected (E) frequencies

	Democrats	Republicans	
Yes	$O = 1$ $E = 2.5$	$O = 4$ $E = 2.5$	$\Sigma O = 5$ $\Sigma E = 5$
No	$O = 4$ $E = 2.5$	$O = 1$ $E = 2.5$	$\Sigma O = 5$ $\Sigma E = 5$
	$\Sigma O = 5$ $\Sigma E = 5$	$\Sigma O = 5$ $\Sigma E = 5$	$\Sigma\Sigma O = 10$ $\Sigma\Sigma E = 10$

Returning to the general relationship in Equation 11.10 (between tests of significance and measures of effect size and size of experiment), another significance test for the phi coefficient is χ^2 with 1 df, written here $\chi^2_{(1)}$. This test of significance, previously noted in chapter 2 as Equation 2.1, can be used whenever the N is not too small (i.e., $N > 20$) and the two variables are not too far from a 50:50 split of 0s and 1s. It can be computed as:

$$\chi^2_{(1)} = \phi^2 \times N,$$

in which ϕ^2 represents the size of the effect, and N represents the size of the study (again within the conceptual framework of Equation 11.10). For the data we have been examining (in Table 11.19), using the above equation (Equation 2.1) gives us

$$\chi^2_{(1)} = (.60)^2 \times 10 = 3.60,$$

which has an associated p value of .058 (obtained from a computer, a hand-held calculator, or, somewhat less precisely, Table B.5 of Appendix B). For χ^2 with $df = 1$ (i.e., based on a 2 × 2, or a 1 × 2, table), these tabled values of χ^2 are two-tailed with respect to the direction of the correlation (plus or minus), so that we divide this tabled p value by 2 if a one-tailed test is desired.

Sometimes, $\chi^2_{(1)}$ is computed before ϕ, in which case two equations are available, one of which is

$$\chi^2_{(1)} = \frac{N(BC - AD)^2}{(A + B)(C + D)(A + C)(B + D)}, \tag{11.13}$$

which, for the data in Table 11.19, yields

$$\chi^2_{(1)} = \frac{10[(4)(4) - (1)(1)]^2}{(5)(5)(5)(5)} = \frac{2250}{625} = 3.60,$$

where $N = A + B + C + D$. Alternatively,

$$\chi^2_{(1)} = \sum \frac{(O - E)^2}{E}, \tag{11.14}$$

which is read as the sum of the squared differences between the observed frequencies (O) and the expected frequencies (E), with each squared difference first divided by the expected frequency. The null hypothesis of zero correlation (i.e., $\phi = 0$) leads to the computation of the expected frequencies. If the observed frequencies are nearly the same as those expected under the null hypothesis of zero correlation, then $O - E$ will be small and $\chi^2_{(1)}$ will be small, and these results will not strongly suggest that the null hypothesis is false.

We obtain the expected frequency (E) for any cell by multiplying the total of the row in which we find the cell by the total of the column in which we find the cell and then dividing this product by the total number of observations (N). For the data in Part A of Table 11.19, we find the expected frequencies are all alike because $(5 \times 5)/10 = 2.5$ for all four cells. Part B of Table 11.19 shows the observed (O) and expected (E) frequencies for all four cells. Then, using Equation 11.14, we find

$$\chi^2_{(1)} = \frac{(1 - 2.5)^2}{2.5} + \frac{(4 - 2.5)^2}{2.5} + \frac{(4 - 2.5)^2}{2.5} + \frac{(1 - 2.5)^2}{2.5} = 3.60.$$

When $\chi^2_{(1)}$ is computed before ϕ, and if the total N is not too small, then ϕ can be conveniently estimated from an equation previously noted in chapter 4 as Equation 4.15, that is,

$$\phi = \sqrt{\frac{\chi^2_{(1)}}{N}}.$$

The sign we give our ϕ depends on how we want to dummy-code the variables. In this example we would indicate a positive correlation between being Republican and saying "yes" if we score being a Republican as 1 and being a Democrat as 0, while scoring a "yes" response as 1 and a "no" response as 0. If the balance of the observed over the expected frequencies favors the cells agreeing in value of the dummy coding (1, 1 or 0, 0), we call phi "positive." If the balance favors the cells disagreeing in value of the dummy coding (0, 1 or 1, 0), we call phi "negative."

Before leaving the topic of $\chi^2_{(1)}$ as a test of significance for ϕ, we should mention that *corrections for continuity* are suggested in many textbooks for χ^2 computed from 2×2 tables. The effect of these corrections is to reduce the size of the $\chi^2_{(1)}$, by diminishing the absolute difference between O and E by .5 (before squaring), in order to adjust for the difference between discrete and continuous distributions. Some evidence suggests, however, that this correction sometimes does more harm than good in terms of yielding accurate p values (Camilli & Hopkins, 1978; Conover, 1974, 1999; Fienberg, 1977). In any case, the correction described should *not* be used if the object is to compute phi as in the above equation (i.e., Equation 4.15), because this equation requires that $\chi^2_{(1)}$ be defined in the standard (not "corrected") manner.

Related to the chi-square approach to the testing of the significance of a phi coefficient is the approach via the standard normal deviate Z. In this case the relationship between the test of significance and the size of the effect and size of the study in Equation 11.10 is given by

$$Z = \phi \times \sqrt{N}. \tag{11.15}$$

For the data we have been using for illustration, with $\phi = .60$ and $N = 10$, Equation 11.15 yields

$$Z = .60 \times \sqrt{10} = 1.90,$$

which is significant at the .029 level, one-tailed test, from a table of p values associated with standard normal deviates (Z), such as Table B.1 of Appendix B. That value agrees perfectly with the one-tailed p value based on the $\chi^2_{(1)}$ approach to testing the significance of phi. It *should*, because $\sqrt{\chi^2_{(1)}}$ is identical to Z.

Because it is sometimes necessary to compute someone else's phi from a reported p value, it is useful to keep in mind the following relationship:

$$\phi = \frac{Z}{\sqrt{N}}. \tag{11.16}$$

For example, suppose a researcher reports $p = .005$ but neglects to give any effect size estimate. As long as we can find N (the total size of the study), it is simple enough to estimate phi by using Equation 11.16 and Table B.1 in Appendix B. In Table B.1 we find the areas in the tails of the normal curve, and we find the Z associated with a one-tailed p level of .005 to be 2.58. If we found N to be 36, we would be able to compute phi from Equation 11.16 as follows:

$$\phi = \frac{2.58}{\sqrt{36}} = .43.$$

In a later chapter on chi-square and tables of counts (chapter 19), we will give more detail on special problems arising from 2×2 tables of counts with small expected frequencies. For now, however, we want to provide a cautionary note about χ^2 tests of significance based on small sample sizes. Our concern is not so much with the errors in obtained p values that we might encounter with small sample sizes. Our concern is more with inaccuracies in the estimation of effect size ϕ that we might compute from our obtained $\chi^2_{(1)}$ (and its square root, Z), for example, from Equations 4.15 and 11.16. Although these equations do provide the accurately computed values of r, it has been shown that these rs may be substantial overestimates of the population values of r (Rosenthal & Rubin, 2003).

CURVILINEAR (QUADRATIC) CORRELATION

So far our discussion has been only of linear correlation, in which the dependent variable (Y) can be seen to increase regularly as a function of regular increases (or regular decreases) in the independent variable (X). Sometimes, however, our predictions are not linear but *curvilinear,* as, for example, if we predicted that

TABLE 11.20
Correlation between performance and arousal

	Arousal level (X)	Performance level (Y)	Z_x	Z_y	$Z_x Z_y$
Subject 1	4	1	−1.24	−1.58	+1.96
Subject 2	5	6	−1.04	0.00	0.00
Subject 3	8	9	−0.41	+0.95	−0.39
Subject 4	11	10	+0.21	+1.27	+0.27
Subject 5	15	7	+1.04	+0.32	+0.33
Subject 6	17	3	+1.45	−0.95	−1.38
Σ	60	36	0.00	0.00	+0.79
N	6	6			
M	10	6			
σ	4.83	3.16			

$$r_{xy} = \frac{\Sigma Z_x Z_y}{N} = \frac{+0.79}{6} = .13$$

performance (Y) will be better for medium levels of arousal (X) than for either high or low levels of arousal. Table 11.20 shows the Pearson r (Equation 11.1) between performance level (Y) and arousal level (X) for six subjects. The correlation is quite modest ($r = .13$), and Figure 11.4 (the plot of the level of performance as a function of arousal level) shows why. The relationship between X and Y is not

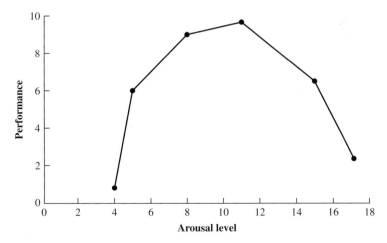

FIGURE 11.4
Curvilinear relationship between arousal level and performance.

TABLE 11.21
Correlation between performance and extremeness of arousal

	Extremeness of arousal level ($|X - M|$)	Performance level (Y)	Z_x	Z_y	$Z_x Z_y$
Subject 1	6	1	+0.78	−1.58	+1.23
Subject 2	5	6	+0.31	0.00	0.00
Subject 3	2	9	−1.09	+0.95	−1.04
Subject 4	1	10	−1.56	+1.27	−1.98
Subject 5	5	7	+0.31	+0.32	+0.10
Subject 6	7	3	+1.25	−0.95	−1.19
Σ	26	36	0.00	0.00	−5.34
N	6	6			
M	4.33	6			
σ	2.13	3.16			

$$r = \frac{\Sigma Z_x Z_y}{N} = \frac{-5.34}{6} = -.89$$

linear, but noticeably curvilinear. More specifically, it seems to be substantially quadratic (the term *quadratic* means that the nonlinear relationship is ∪-shaped or ∩-shaped). How can we compute a coefficient of curvilinear (quadratic) correlation between X and Y?

A number of procedures are available, and one of the simplest requires us only to redefine the variable X from "amount of X" (low to high) to "extremeness of X" (distance from the mean of X). Table 11.21 shows this redefinition. Each value of X is replaced by the absolute (unsigned) value of that score's difference from the mean score. Therefore, a positive correlation between the extremeness of X and the original score of Y means that more extreme levels of arousal are associated with higher levels of performance, whereas a negative correlation means that more extreme levels of arousal are associated with lower levels of performance. In their original form, the scores for arousal level (X) showed little correlation with the performance level (Y). In their redefined form ($|X - M|$) in this table, the scores indicating absolute distance from the mean were very substantially correlated with performance level ($r = -.89$). This substantial correlation is quite consistent with what we can see in Figure 11.4, which is that more extreme levels of arousal are associated with poorer performance. Later chapters will deal with the topic of curvilinear relationships in more detail.

FIVE PRODUCT-MOMENT CORRELATIONS

In this chapter we have described five different product-moment correlations. Table 11.22 summarizes the chief characteristics of each. In the chapter on contrast analysis (chapter 15), we describe additional product-moment correlations.

TABLE 11.22
Product-moment correlations

Correlation	Characteristics of variables	Tests of significance[a]
Pearson r	Both continuous	t
Spearman rho (ρ)	Both ranked	t (or exact probability test if N is small, especially if $N < 7$)
Point biserial (r_{pb})	One continuous, one dichotomous	t
Phi (ϕ)	Both dichotomous	χ^2, Z, t
Curvilinear r	Both continuous	t

[a] Table B.6 of Appendix B shows critical values of p associated with correlations based on varying df, where df = number of pairs of observations minus 2.

COMPARING CORRELATIONS

It often happens in behavioral research that the primary question is not so much about the relationship between two variables, but about the *difference* in such relationships between two groups of subjects or between the same subjects measured under two conditions. For example, the superiority of females over males in the decoding of non-verbal cues is well established (Hall, 1984b). Such superiority can be indexed by the correlation between sex (coded as 0, 1) and skill in decoding nonverbal cues (a continuous measure; see, for example, Rosenthal, Hall, DiMatteo, Rogers, & Archer, 1979). If we are interested in whether this superiority is greater among high school students than among college students, we would compare the sex-skill correlations found in high school and college samples. Because the two correlations being compared are based on different independent subjects, comparisons of this type are called *comparisons of independent correlation coefficients*. If the two correlations being compared are based on the *same* subjects, the procedures are called *comparisons of nonindependent* (or *correlated*) *correlation coefficients*. An example is the comparison of the correlation between sex and sensitivity to nonverbal cues in the video versus the audio channels of nonverbal communication. It turns out, for example, that the correlation between sex and skill is higher, on the average, for decoding facial expressions than it is for decoding tone of voice (Rosenthal & DePaulo, 1979a, 1979b). Procedures for computing tests of significance of the difference between independent or correlated correlation coefficients are given in chapter 21. In that chapter we describe procedures for combining as well as comparing correlation coefficients and other estimates of the magnitude of effects.

CONSIDERING THIRD VARIABLES

We have been concentrating on the degree of association between two variables, X and Y. Much later in this book, we describe procedures in which any number of predictor variables (e.g., X_1, X_2, X_3, ... X_k) may be used to predict scores on a single dependent variable (e.g., Y) or on any *set* of Y variables (e.g., Y_1, Y_2, Y_3, ... Y_k). We turn now to two common situations in which a third variable (Z) is brought into the analysis for one of two different purposes. One purpose is **multiple correlation,** in which we use two independent (or predictor) variables to learn how well the two predictors, used together, do in predicting the dependent variable, especially compared to how well each predictor does working alone. The other quite common purpose is learning how a two-variable correlation changes if we control completely for a third variable. For example, suppose we find a correlation of $r = .70$ between the height and the vocabulary test scores of 6- to 12-year-old girls. Our first reaction to such a high correlation might well be to suspect that it was the older girls who were both taller and more accurate in defining the vocabulary test items, whereas the younger girls were both shorter and less accurate in defining vocabulary test items. That very reasonable hypothesis implicates age as a "third variable," one that we should control for to learn whether there will still be such a high correlation between height and vocabulary test performance after we have controlled for the variable of age by computing a **partial correlation.**

Computing a Partial Correlation

We designate our three variables as (1) vocabulary test scores, (2) height, and (3) age, and suppose we know the correlation for each pair of variables. The correlation r_{12} between (1) vocabulary test scores and (2) height is .70. The correlation r_{13} between (1) vocabulary test scores and (3) age is .80. The correlation (r_{23}) between (2) height and (3) age is .60. To obtain the partial correlation $r_{12.3}$ (i.e., the correlation between variables 1 and 2, with variable 3 partialed out), we use the following equation:

$$r_{12.3} = \frac{r_{12} - r_{13}r_{23}}{\sqrt{(1 - r_{13}^2)(1 - r_{23}^2)}} \quad (11.17)$$

and find

$$r_{12.3} = \frac{.70 - (.80)(.60)}{\sqrt{[1 - (.80)^2][1 - (.60)^2]}} = \frac{.22}{\sqrt{(.36)(.64)}} = \frac{.22}{.48} = .458$$

From this result we see that the correlation between vocabulary performance and height drops from .70 to .46 after we partial out the effect of age.

Computing a Multiple Correlation

Suppose we want to know how well we can predict vocabulary test scores from a knowledge of students' heights *and* ages. We will need the three correlations r_{12}, r_{13}, r_{23} defined above and indicated as .70, .80, and .60, respectively. Using the following equation, we can compute the multiple correlation $r_{1.23}$, that is, the correlation between vocabulary scores (variable 1) and the joint action of our two predictor variables, height (variable 2) and age (variable 3):

$$r_{1.23} = \sqrt{\frac{r_{12}^2 + r_{13}^2 - 2r_{12}r_{13}r_{23}}{1 - r_{23}^2}} \quad (11.18)$$

and we find

$$r_{1.23} = \sqrt{\frac{(.70)^2 + (.80)^2 - 2(.70)(.80)(.60)}{1 - (.60)^2}} = \sqrt{\frac{.458}{.640}} = .846$$

From this result we see that the multiple correlation predicting vocabulary scores from *both* the variables of height *and* age yields a higher correlation (.846) than we find using only the single variable of height ($r_{12} = .70$) or the single variable of age ($r_{13} = .80$).

Although our multiple correlation of $r_{1.23}$ was indeed higher than either of the single predictors' correlations, the single predictors did quite well for themselves (*r*s of .70 and .80) working alone. It is surprising to some to see that adding a second variable as a predictor does not raise the multiple correlation more than was the case here, where a single predictor's correlation of .80 (r_{13}) was raised only to .846 when a second, also very good predictor, was added ($r_{12} = .70$). What kept the multiple *r* from showing a greater improvement was the fact that the predictor variables were mostly doing the same job. We get our largest benefit in going from one to two good predictors when each is predicting different aspects of the dependent variable. As the correlation between two predictors gets lower and lower, the predictive benefits of adding another good predictor grow increasingly larger. In fact, when the correlation between the two predictors is .00, Equation 11.18 simplifies to

$$r_{1.23} = \sqrt{r_{12}^2 + r_{13}^2} \qquad (11.19)$$

In short, when predictor variables are uncorrelated with each other, the multiple correlation is simply the square root of the sum of the squared correlations of each predictor variable with the dependent variable. We gave a simple example of this relationship in Table 11.3 earlier in this chapter.

EFFECTS OF VARIABILITY ON CORRELATIONS

Suppose we are developing a new test to help college admissions committees select the students who will be more successful during their first year of college. Among the various possible criteria of success, we might choose first-year grade point average (GPA). As part of our preliminary validation efforts, we administer our new test to a class of graduating high school seniors and correlate these test scores with the seniors' overall high school GPA. The correlation we find is impressively high, $r = .60$, and the standard deviation of our new test is 100.

In a subsequent validation study, we compute the correlation between (a) first-year college students' scores on our new test and (b) their first year college GPA. We find this correlation to be .35, which is a substantial drop from .60. Should we regard this drop in validity coefficients from .60 to .35 as reflecting a "failure to replicate" our noticeably higher validity correlation? Probably not.

On a test designed for high school seniors as part of their college admissions process, our test takers include, by and large, all the students who may be applying for college admissions. We would expect to find greater variability in those high school students' test scores (e.g., $S = 100$) than we would expect to find for high school seniors who are actually accepted (e.g., $S = 50$) into the selective college of their choice. Correlations usually shrink in magnitude when the samples shrink in variability on either of the variables being correlated. This fact was recognized long ago by Karl Pearson, who proposed a solution to this problem (Guilford, 1950).

Correcting for Restriction of Variability

Pearson's solution was an equation that can be used when the variables being correlated are normally distributed. He showed how to compute the predicted value of a correlation, R_{12}, based on the full unrestricted variability of the correlated variables from a knowledge of three factors: (a) the correlation $r_{12\ restricted}$ obtained between the two variables with shrunken, restricted variabilities ($S_{restricted}$); (b) the standard deviation of the full variability (S_{full}); and (c) the standard deviation of the shrunken or restricted variability ($S_{restricted}$). In our example of a new test for college admission, the correlation between the high school seniors' test scores and their high school GPA is R_{12}. The variability of the new test for these high school seniors is S_{full}, and the correlation between first-year college students' selection test scores and their GPA is $r_{12\ restricted}$. The following equation shows Pearson's solution:

$$R_{12\ full} = \frac{r_{12\ restricted}\left(\frac{S_{full}}{S_{restricted}}\right)}{\sqrt{1 - r_{12\ restricted}^2 + r_{12\ restricted}^2\left(\frac{S_{full}}{S_{restricted}}\right)^2}} \tag{11.20}$$

As an aid to conceptualizing the relationships among the four variables of Equation 11.20, we can display them as a 2×2 table:

	Restricted	Unrestricted
Variability	$S_{restricted}$	S_{full}
Correlation	$r_{12\ restricted}$	$R_{12\ full}$

For our example of a new test for college admission, using Equation 11.20 we find

$$R_{12\ full} = \frac{.35\left(\frac{100}{50}\right)}{\sqrt{1 - (.35)^2 + (.35)^2\left(\frac{100}{50}\right)^2}}$$

$$= \frac{.70}{\sqrt{1 - .1225 + .49}} = \frac{.70}{1.17} = .60,$$

which is the value we had originally found when we correlated high school seniors' selection test scores with their grade point averages.

From this result of our application of Pearson's equation, we learn that the validity coefficient ($r_{12\ restricted}$) of .35 for the college students was not a failure to replicate the validity coefficient ($R_{12\ full}$) of .60, but the simple inexorable consequence of having a more highly selected and therefore a less variable sample of students. In fact, knowing of Pearson's correction for restriction of variability, we could have predicted the magnitude of the validity coefficient for our college sample (i.e., $r_{12\ restricted}$) by rearranging the terms of Equation 11.20 and then solving for $r_{12\ restricted}$, as in the following:

$$r_{12\ restricted} = \frac{R_{12\ full}\left(\frac{S_{restricted}}{S_{full}}\right)}{\sqrt{1 - R_{12\ full}^2 + R_{12\ full}^2\left(\frac{S_{restricted}}{S_{full}}\right)^2}} \tag{11.21}$$

One example of our use of Equation 11.21 is to recall that we had started the validation process for our new test with the high school sample and found for that sample a validity coefficient of $r = .60$. In planning our next study we decide to go to a less heterogeneous sample of college students. Given our more heterogeneous sample r of .60, and variabilities of (a) college students' $S_{restricted} = 50$ and (b) high school students' $S_{full} = 100$, we would find

$$r_{12\ restricted} = \frac{.60\left(\frac{50}{100}\right)}{\sqrt{1 - (.60)^2 + (.60)^2 \left(\frac{50}{100}\right)^2}}$$

$$= \frac{.30}{\sqrt{1 - .36 + (.36)(.25)}} = \frac{.30}{\sqrt{.73}} = .35,$$

the value we found when we correlated college students' test scores with their grade point averages.

Correcting for Expansion of Variability

In the early stages of the development of a new test, it is often wise to begin to establish criterion validity by administering the test to extreme groups that should earn very different average scores on the new test. For example, if a new test of physical fitness cannot differentiate Olympic athletes from patients who have been advised to begin exercising by their concerned physicians, the new test of physical fitness holds little promise. If a new test of anxiety level cannot distinguish patients hospitalized for anxiety disorders from well-functioning college students who have never felt excessive anxiety, the new test of anxiety holds little promise. But what if the new tests do a very good job of discriminating our two extreme groups? What if criterion validity correlations are in the .70s? Can this marked success be problematic? It could be, if our longer term plan is to use the new tests for the entire population, most of whom will have far less extreme scores on the tests.

To get some sense of how well a new test will do (i.e., as an estimate of criterion validity) for the overall population of interest, we can use Equation 11.21 rewritten with changed, more appropriate subscripts as

$$r_{12\ full} = \frac{R_{12\ extreme}\left(\frac{S_{full}}{S_{extreme}}\right)}{\sqrt{1 - R_{12\ extreme}^2 + R_{12\ extreme}^2 \left(\frac{S_{full}}{S_{extreme}}\right)^2}} \tag{11.22}$$

For example, assume a preliminary estimate of criterion validity of $r = .70$ based on extreme groups, with a standard deviation of our measure of $S_{extreme} = 7.0$. As an estimate of the validity coefficient we might expect when we use the full distribution of scores ($S_{full} = 2.0$) on our new measure, we find from Equation 11.22:

$$r_{12\ full} = \frac{(.70)\left(\frac{2.0}{7.0}\right)}{\sqrt{1 - (.70)^2 + (.70)^2 \left(\frac{2.0}{7.0}\right)^2}} = \frac{.20}{\sqrt{.55}} = .27,$$

a remarkable drop in validity levels from $r = .70$ to $r = .27$, but one that we could have expected had we wanted to use our new test with a full range of scorers rather than only with extreme scorers.

Clarifying Correlations by Subgroup Analysis

Suppose we have used two measures of communication skill in a pilot study of the relationship between language ability and sensitivity to nonverbal communication. Scores for the first eight participants are shown in the scatter plot of Figure 11.5. The plot suggests a positive linear relationship between these two variables, and when computed, we find $r = .80$, a very substantial degree of correlation.

While examining this plot to understand it better, we may recall that, in general, females perform better than males on various measures of language ability. Suppose our records show that Participants a, b, c, and d are males, and Participants e, f, g, and h are females. We also note, perhaps as expected, that the females' mean score on variable X (language ability) is 3.5 compared to males' mean score of 1.5. We see a similar degree

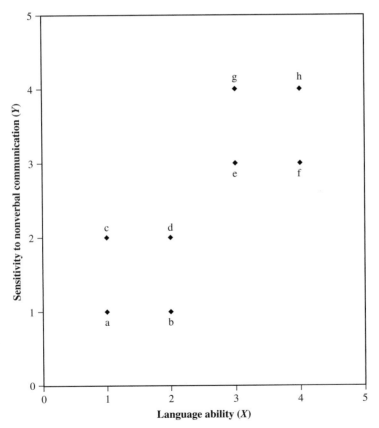

FIGURE 11.5
Scores of eight participants on two measures of communication skill.

of superiority of females over males on variable Y (sensitivity to nonverbal communication), with means of 3.5 and 1.5 for females and males, respectively. That our female participants scored so much higher than the male participants suggests that some of the linearity apparent in Figure 11.5 may be due to female superiority on both X and Y variables. In fact, when we follow up this hunch with separate correlations between variables X and Y, we discover that, for the male participants alone, *and* for the female participants alone, the correlation r_{XY} is exactly zero.

In this example we found that combining subgroups (females and males) created sizable correlations where none were found in the subgroups considered separately. We sometimes find the opposite phenomenon: Sizable correlations found in several subgroups may shrink. They may sometimes shrink to zero, or even reverse their sign, when subgroups are combined. These phenomena often occur because of differences in means (on the X and Y axes) among the various subgroups.

The concepts and computations of correlations, broadly defined, are so central to the data-analytic enterprise that we shall have occasion to refer to those concepts and to those computations repeatedly in the chapters that lie ahead.

CHAPTER 12

STATISTICAL
POWER
AND
EFFECT
SIZE
REVISITED

WHY ASSESS STATISTICAL POWER?

The dual purpose of this chapter is to illustrate how a power analysis is done and to delve further into the concept of an effect size indicator. In chapter 2 we first mentioned that the power of a significance test (defined as $1 - \beta$) is the probability that the test will reject a null hypothesis (H_0) that is false and *should,* therefore, be rejected. We also introduced the conceptual relationship stating that significance test = size of effect $\times$ size of study (discussed again in the previous chapter, Equation 11.10). The implication is that the larger the observed magnitude of effect, or the greater the total number of observations, the larger will be the value of the significance test, and therefore the smaller its associated p value. There are a number of strategies for improving statistical power, but the one that is probably most familiar to behavioral researchers is to increase the sample size. In this chapter we provide simple tables for estimating the number of sampling units needed to detect a particular magnitude of effect at a given p level and a specified level of statistical power. What if the effect size is so small that it may be unreasonable to think that an adequate number of subjects will be available? One possibility is to replicate the study and, assuming the results are similar, to estimate the overall (combined) p of the original study and the replication after pooling the results meta-analytically (illustrated at the end of this chapter).

However, you may be wondering why a detailed discussion of statistical power is needed, as we also stated that the primary coin of the realm when behavioral researchers speak of "the results of a study" should not be whether the p values of their tests of statistical significance are .05 or less. Instead, it should be information about the magnitude of the research finding (i.e., the effect size) and its accuracy or reliability (e.g., a confidence interval around the effect size). Although it is certainly true that "the initial emphasis on power analysis spearheaded by Cohen (1962) has now given way to a more sophisticated emphasis on precision of estimation," it is also true that "there are numerous obstacles to change in behavioral studies practice" (Steiger, 2004, pp. 178–179). For example, funding agencies frequently insist that a power analysis be included in a grant application to ensure that the resources requested will not be wasted in a study that implies the use of significance testing but has little chance of statistically detecting an effect that exists. Furthermore, statistical reforms regarding the use and interpretation of effect sizes and interval estimates (Wilkinson et al., 1999) have not been fully absorbed into the mainstream of behavioral research (Fidler, Thomason, Cumming, Finch, & Leeman, 2004; Thompson, 1999). An unfortunate consequence is that researchers sometimes give up prematurely on promising hypotheses when they mistakenly interpret an underpowered significance test's failure to detect an existing effect as indicating "no effect."

Some years ago, Jacob Cohen, in his seminal book *Statistical Power Analysis for the Behavioral Sciences* (1969, 1988), noted that without a conception of the relative seriousness of Type I to Type II errors (i.e., the risk of false H_0 rejection to the risk of false H_0 acceptance), researchers who do null hypothesis significance testing tend to handicap themselves by working with ridiculously low power. We begin by drawing on Cohen's conception to operationalize the effect of the neglect of power. How much statistical power is needed? We describe Cohen's benchmark recommendation, but the number of units or observations needed depends on the anticipated magnitude of the effect, the preferred p level, and the available resources. You may be thinking; "Isn't the purpose of doing research to *find out* the size of the effect? So how can we realistically anticipate its size?" There are, in fact, several options. One is to do a literature search and, assuming similar circumstances will be operating in the planned study, to base our estimate of the anticipated effect size on the average effect size reported in the literature. A second option is to rely on preliminary data in a pilot study to help us make a plausible estimate of the size of the effect in the full study. A third option is simply to assume that "medium-sized" effects are probably typical in the area of investigation, which often seems to be the case in behavioral and social research (cf. Brewer, 1972; Chase & Chase, 1976; Cohen, 1962, 1973; Haase, Waechter, & Solomon, 1982; Sedlmeier & Gigerenzer, 1989). Cohen's definitions of "medium" effects (and also "small" and "large" effects) are discussed in this chapter.

Nonetheless, we cannot stress too strongly our preference for effect sizes and confidence intervals rather than the counterproductive practice of interpreting as "anti-null" any p that is not greater than .05 and as "pro-null" any p that is greater than .05. It may not be an exaggeration to say that, for many Ph.D. students, the .05 alpha has acquired an ontological mystique. A dissertation p less than .05 means joy, a doctoral degree, and a tenure-track position, but a p greater than .05 means ruin, despair, and the adviser's suddenly thinking of a new control group that should be

(marginal handwritten notes)

Confidence interval → accuracy or reliability / effect size → magnitude of research finding.

of findings.

(*) It is much more useful to report effect size & confidence intervals than the trivial $p > .05$ or $p < .05$.

run. Gigerenzer (1987) and associates (Gigerenzer & Murray, 1987; Gigerenzer et al., 1989), in discussions that examined the development of statistical inference, noted that the idea of dichotomous significance testing was initially developed out of agricultural experimentalists' need to answer questions such as "Is the manure effective?" It may be harder to object to the necessity of an accept-reject approach when the question is phrased in exactly that way, but the composition of behavioral research data, certainly, is substantively different, as is the phraseology of the questions that behavioral researchers attempt to address. R. A. Fisher at one point (largely as a reaction against the criticisms of J. Neyman and E. S. Pearson) objected to the idea of a fixed, dichotomous decision-level approach and instead recommended a cumulative, more provisional conception of statistical data analysis in science (Gigerenzer, 1987, p. 24).

Fisher's objection is not to imply that confidence intervals around effect sizes are unaffected by power. Table 12.1 shows 99%, 95%, and 90% confidence intervals for

TABLE 12.1

99%, 95%, and 90% confidence intervals (*CI*) for $r = .1, .3,$ and $.5$ in samples of 10 to 800

N	$r = .1$	$r = .3$	$r = .5$
10	99%*CI*: −.70 to +.79 95%*CI*: −.57 to +.69 90%*CI*: −.48 to +.62	99%*CI*: −.58 to +.86 95%*CI*: −.41 to +.78 90%*CI*: −.30 to +.73	99%*CI*: −.40 to +.91 95%*CI*: −.19 to +.86 90%*CI*: −.07 to +.82
20	99%*CI*: −.48 to +.62 95%*CI*: −.36 to +.52 90%*CI*: −.29 to +.46	99%*CI*: −.31 to +.73 95%*CI*: −.16 to +.66 90%*CI*: −.09 to +.61	99%*CI*: −.08 to +.83 95%*CI*: +.07 to +.77 90%*CI*: +.15 to +.74
30	99%*CI*: −.38 to +.53 95%*CI*: −.27 to +.44 90%*CI*: −.21 to +.39	99%*CI*: −.18 to +.67 95%*CI*: −.07 to +.60 90%*CI*: −.01 to +.56	99%*CI*: +.05 to +.78 95%*CI*: +.17 to +.73 90%*CI*: +.23 to +.70
40	99%*CI*: −.31 to +.48 95%*CI*: −.22 to +.40 90%*CI*: −.17 to +.35	99%*CI*: −.11 to +.62 95%*CI*: −.01 to +.56 90%*CI*: +.04 to +.52	99%*CI*: +.13 to +.75 95%*CI*: +.22 to +.70 90%*CI*: +.27 to +.67
50	99%*CI*: −.27 to +.44 95%*CI*: −.18 to +.37 90%*CI*: −.14 to +.33	99%*CI*: −.07 to +.59 95%*CI*: +.02 to +.53 90%*CI*: +.07 to +.50	99%*CI*: +.17 to +.73 95%*CI*: +.26 to +.68 90%*CI*: +.30 to +.66
100	99%*CI*: −.16 to +.35 95%*CI*: −.10 to +.29 90%*CI*: −.07 to +.26	99%*CI*: +.05 to +.52 95%*CI*: +.11 to +.47 90%*CI*: +.14 to +.44	99%*CI*: +.28 to +.67 95%*CI*: +.34 to +.63 90%*CI*: +.36 to +.61
200	99%*CI*: −.08 to +.28 95%*CI*: −.04 to +.24 90%*CI*: −.02 to +.21	99%*CI*: +.13 to +.46 95%*CI*: +.17 to +.42 90%*CI*: +.19 to +.40	99%*CI*: +.35 to +.62 95%*CI*: +.39 to +.60 90%*CI*: +.41 to +.58
400	99%*CI*: −.03 to +.23 95%*CI*: .00 to +.20 90%*CI*: +.02 to +.18	99%*CI*: +.18 to +.41 95%*CI*: +.21 to +.39 90%*CI*: +.22 to +.37	99%*CI*: +.40 to +.59 95%*CI*: +.42 to +.57 90%*CI*: +.44 to +.56
800	99%*CI*: +.01 to +.19 95%*CI*: +.03 to +.17 90%*CI*: +.04 to +.16	99%*CI*: +.22 to +.38 95%*CI*: +.24 to +.36 90%*CI*: +.25 to +.35	99%*CI*: +.43 to +.56 95%*CI*: +.45 to +.55 90%*CI*: +.46 to +.54

three levels of effect size rs (.1, .3, and .5), assuming zero effect null hypotheses, with samples ranging from $N = 10$ to $N = 800$. For example, with a total N of 100 and an observed effect size r of .30, we can state with 95% confidence that the true population effect size r is between .11 and .47. Given the same observed effect size r of .3, but quadrupling the size of the sample to an N of 400, we see that the 95% CI is noticeably smaller, from .21 to .39. Within each batch of confidence intervals, it is evident that the interval is wider as the confidence level increases from 90% to 95% to 99%. If we wanted to be 100% confident, we could say the true population effect size r is between -1.0 (the lower limit of r) and 1.0 (the upper limit).

THE NEGLECT OF STATISTICAL POWER

Although leading textbooks on psychological statistics in the 1950s and 1960s routinely mentioned statistical power (e.g., Edwards, 1964; Guilford, 1956; Hays, 1963; McNemar, 1962; Siegel, 1956; Walker & Lev, 1953; Winer, 1962), the design implications of power analysis did not make their way into the consciousness of psychological researchers until quite recently. In the 1960s, in a series of articles and invited chapters, culminating in his seminal book published in 1969, Cohen pioneered in demonstrating that null hypothesis significance testing in behavioral research is conducted with a remarkably high risk of committing Type II errors. In an early meta-analysis, he reported the median power for detecting what he characterized as "medium" effects at $\alpha = .05$ in articles published in the *Journal of Abnormal and Social Psychology* during a single year (1960) was no better than flipping a coin (Cohen, 1962). Indeed, the odds were better than 50:50 that the null hypothesis would *not* be rejected when false. In an article entitled "Do Studies of Statistical Power Have an Effect on the Power of Studies?" which was published nearly three decades later, Sedlmeier and Gigerenzer (1989) reported that the median power of studies in the same journal was slightly worse.

Cohen (1969) proposed a convenient way to operationalize the relative seriousness of the neglect of power in any given situation by simply examining the ratio of β to α. For example, suppose a researcher has set α at .05 and is conducting a test of significance with power $= .40$, in which case β is $1 - .40$ (or .60), and the β/α ratio becomes $.60/.05 = 12$. In other words, the researcher ostensibly believes that mistakenly rejecting the null hypothesis should be regarded as 12 times more serious than mistakenly accepting it. Table 12.2 shows the ratio of β/α for sample sizes from 10 to 1,000 under the conditions of assumed effect size noted in Table 12.1 (rs of .1, .3, and .5) and two levels of statistical significance ($p = .05$ and $p = .10$). The generally greater weight attached to the avoidance of Type I errors relative to Type II errors clearly increases the smaller the effect size r, the smaller the N, and the more stringent the level of significance. Some critics have argued that psychologists working in labs typically have ample power to detect even "small" effects (to be defined shortly), on the assumption that error terms are usually small in lab studies (because of homogeneous samples and highly standardized procedures). However, Table 12.2 shows that at $r = .1$, a small sample (say, $N = 20$, or 10 per group), and a binary decisional $p = .05$, significance testing will be a precarious exercise ($\beta/\alpha = 19$).

TABLE 12.2
**Ratios of Type II to Type I error rates (β/α) for various
sample sizes, effect sizes, and significance levels (two-tailed)**

| | Effect sizes (r) and significance levels (.05 and .10) | | | | | |
| | r = .10 | | r = .30 | | r = .50 | |
N	.05	.10	.05	.10	.05	.10
10	19	9	17	8	13[a]	5[b]
20	19	9	15	6	7[a]	2[b]
30	18	8	13	5	3	1
40	18	8	10	4	2	*
50	18	8	9	3	*	*
60	18	8	7	2	*	*
70	17	8	6	2	*	*
80	17	8	4	1	*	*
90	17	8	4	1	*	*
100	17	7	3	*	*	*
120	16	7	2	*	*	*
140	16	7	1	*	*	*
160	15	6	*	*	*	*
180	15	6	*	*	*	*
200	14	6	*	*	*	*
300	12	5	*	*	*	*
400	10	4	*	*	*	*
500	8	3	*	*	*	*
600	6	2	*	*	*	*
700	5	2	*	*	*	*
800	4	1	*	*	*	
900	3	*	*	*	*	
1000	2	*	*	*	*	

*Values less than 1.
[a] For r = .70 these ratios drop to 6 and <1, respectively.
[b] For r = .70 these ratios drop to 2 and <1, respectively.

Given that alpha is typically set at .05, Cohen (1965) recommended .80 as a baseline of the statistical power usually needed in behavioral research. With power set at .80, it follows that β = .2, and the β/α ratio (.2/.05 = 4) implies that Type I error is regarded as 4 times more serious than Type II error. Setting the power higher than .80 obviously reduces the β/α ratio. With power at .90 and α at .05, Type I error would be regarded as 2 times more serious than Type II error (.1/.05 = 2). If the effect size is small and recruiting subjects is expensive, the cost in terms of the number of sampling units needed may be prohibitive. Nonetheless, it behooves every researcher who does null hypothesis significance testing to be mindful of the potential constraints imposed by the neglect of statistical power.

In the next section we describe the principal effect size indices operationalized in Cohen's (1988) text on power analysis. Before we do so, however, we want to reiterate our suggestion in chapter 1 that, when it is necessary to make a decision to convert all the effect size measures to a particular index (e.g., in meta-analytic work), the correlation family is the most generally useful. If our research calls for a comparison of two groups, we might use Cohen's d (Equation 2.4), or Hedges's g (Equation 2.5), or Glass's Δ (Equation 2.6). In practice, effect sizes are often needed for comparisons that are based on more than two groups, for example, in computing linear trends or any other predicted pattern of three or more means (Rosenthal, Rosnow, & Rubin, 2000). In such cases it is not as natural to use a two-group-based effect size indicator, but it is quite natural to use a member of the r family of effect size indicators (discussed in chapter 15). We will note ways of converting certain effect sizes to r and r-type indices (viz., Fisher's z_r), and we will show how to conceptualize the study design so that an effect size r can be directly estimated. Even when all we have are minimal raw ingredients, we still are able to compute an interpretable effect size r, as illustrated next.

THE $r_{\text{equivalent}}$ STATISTIC

Suppose all we have are the total sample size (N) and an accurate p value, but nothing else. A quite serviceable approach to estimating an interpretable effect size r is the $r_{\text{equivalent}}$ procedure (Rosenthal & Rubin, 2003). It takes its name from the fact that the estimated r is equivalent to a sample point-biserial correlation (r_{pb}) between the treatment indicator and an exactly normally distributed outcome in a two-treatment experiment with $N/2$ units in each group and the obtained p value. All that is needed to compute $r_{\text{equivalent}}$ is to identify the value of t that corresponds to the accurate p (usually with $df = N - 2$) and simply to substitute in the following equation (which is a variation on Equation 11.11):

$$r = \sqrt{\frac{t^2}{t^2 + df}},$$ (12.1)

where r in this case refers to $r_{\text{equivalent}}$, and t can be obtained from a standard table such as Table B.2 or B.3 in Appendix B. This procedure is especially useful when (a) in meta-analytic work, or in other reanalyses of others' studies, neither effect sizes nor significance test statistics (such as an obtained t or F value) are provided, but only p values and sample sizes are given; (b) no effect size index has yet been generally accepted for the data-analytic procedure used (as is true of certain nonparametric statistics, such as the Mann-Whitney U test); or (c) an effect size estimate can be computed directly from the reported data, but because of small sample sizes or severe nonnormality, the estimates may be seriously misleading.

Say that all we have available from a study report is the result of a Mann-Whitney U test, which is commonly used in small sample studies by experimenters who want to avoid the t test's assumptions. Expert judges were used to rank the performance of nine children on a reading-ability measure. Four of the children were randomly assigned to a condition (the treatment) in which they were taught by a new method, and five children were taught by an old (control) method. And let us further assume that all four treated children were ranked higher than any of the five control children. This outcome would yield an exact probability of .008, one-tailed Mann-Whitney U (Siegel, 1956, p. 271). Given $p = .008$ and $N = 9$, $t(df = 7) = 3.16$, and from Equation 12.1 ($df = N - 2$) we find

$$r_{\text{equivalent}} = \sqrt{\frac{(3.16)^2}{(3.16)^2 + 7}} = .77.$$

When reporting this result, we would also want to report an interval estimate, which is typically the 95% confidence interval. In this case we use the procedure described in the previous chapter in connection with Equation 11.3; that is, 95% $CI = z_r \pm 1.96/\sqrt{N - 3}$. For $r_{\text{equivalent}} = .77$, we see in Table B.7 that Fisher $z_r = 1.02$, and so the 95% CI extends from a z_r of .22 to a z_r of 1.82. Using Table B.8 to transform this 95% CI into units of r gives us an interval from $r = .22$ to .95.

The $r_{\text{equivalent}}$ method can be used to estimate an effect size r in any two-group comparison of means of a normally distributed outcome. As we show in chapter 15, a limitation of Equation 12.1 is that with more than two treatment conditions, this formula is an estimate of what we call r_{contrast}. The distinction is that $r_{\text{effect size}}$ is the unpartialed correlation between group (or condition) membership and individual scores on the dependent measure, and r_{contrast} is the partial correlation (with noncontrast variation removed) and therefore tends to overstate what might be viewed as the more natural effect size correlation (i.e., $r_{\text{effect size}}$). In any two-group comparison, however, r_{contrast} is equivalent to $r_{\text{effect size}}$ because there is no noncontrast variation to be partialed out.

COHEN'S MULTIPURPOSE POWER TABLES

The expression *power analysis* is another umbrella term, as it may refer to estimating the number of sampling units needed to detect a particular magnitude of effect at a stipulated α, or to estimating the statistical power of a study already conducted. The way these procedures work involves estimating one of four parameters from our knowledge of the other three. For example, given a p level, an effect size value, and the number of subjects participating in a study, we can estimate the power of an already completed study, which we call the **effective power.** Suppose the study design was based on equal sample sizes, but something unexpected happened and we ended up with more no-shows in one group. In the next chapter we will show how to estimate the loss of power in an unequal-n study relative to an equal-n design. In some situations, however, a study may be specifically designed to allocate the subjects to various conditions unequally, the objective being to "optimize" statistical power by emphasizing some conditions over others. We have more to say about this approach in chapter 15, but by far the most common reason for a power analysis is to estimate the number of sampling units that will be needed in an equal-n study (given an α, the desired level of power, and an anticipated magnitude of effect).

Table 12.3 is a composite based on seven of Cohen's (1988) effect size indicators for use in a power analysis. In the first column, the effect size d is based on the t test

TABLE 12.3
Multipurpose power tables with sample size estimates

			Statistic				
	t	r	$r_1 - r_2$	$P - .50$	$P_1 - P_2$	χ^2	F
Effect size index d		r	q	g	h	w	f
Effect size:							
Small	.20	.10	.10	.05	.20	.10	.10
Medium	.50	.30	.30	.15	.50	.30	.25
Large	.80	.50	.50	.25	.80	.50	.40

A. Sample size (rounded) required to detect "medium" effect at $p = .05$ two-tailed

Power	t	r	$r_1 - r_2$	$P - .50$	$P_1 - P_2$	$\chi^2(df = 1)$	F ($df = 1$ in numerator)
.25	14	20	40	20	13	18	14
.50	32	42	88	44	31	43	32
.60	40	53	112	54	39	54	40
.70	50	67	140	67	49	69	50
.75	57	75	157	75	56	77	57
.80	64	85	177	85	63	87	64
.85	73	97	203	97	72	100	73
.90	85	113	236	113	84	117	85
.95	105	139	292	138	104	144	105
.99	148	195	411	194	147	204	148
Definition of n a (see note below)	b	c	d	c	d	a	

B. Sample size (rounded) required to detect "medium" effect at $p = .01$ two-tailed

Power	t	r	$r_1 - r_2$	$P - .50$	$P_1 - P_2$	$\chi^2(df = 1)$	F ($df = 1$ in numerator)
.25	31	40	83	44	29	40	31
.50	55	72	150	74	53	74	55
.60	66	87	181	88	64	89	66
.70	79	103	217	105	77	107	79
.75	86	113	238	115	85	117	86
.80	95	125	263	127	93	130	95
.85	106	139	293	141	104	145	106
.90	120	158	334	160	119	165	120
.95	144	189	399	191	143	198	144
.99	194	254	537	255	192	267	194

(continued)

TABLE 12.3   (*continued*)

C. Sample size (rounded) required to detect "small" effect at $p = .05$ two-tailed

Power	t	r	$r_1 - r_2$	$P - .50$	$P_1 - P_2$	$\chi^2(df = 1)$	F ($df = 1$ in numerator)
.25	84	168	333	166	83	165	84
.50	193	386	771	384	192	384	193
.60	246	491	983	489	245	490	246
.70	310	617	1,237	616	309	617	310
.75	348	692	1,391	692	347	694	348
.80	393	784	1,573	783	392	785	393
.85	450	896	1,799	895	449	898	450
.90	526	1,048	2,104	1,047	525	1,051	526
.95	651	1,295	2,602	1,294	650	1,300	651
.99	920	1,829	3,677	1,827	919	1,837	920

Note: The definitions of n indicated at the bottom of Section A are symbolized as follows: a = each group or condition; b = n of score pairs; c = n of each sample; and d = total N.

(The sample sizes are based on tables in *Statistical Power Analysis for the Behavioral Sciences* (2nd ed.), by J. Cohen, 1988, Hillsdale, NJ: Lawrence Erlbaum Associates, Publishers, and on Foster's (2003) METASTATS software.)

for independent means (e.g., Equation 11.9), where the null hypothesis is $M_1 - M_2 = 0$. The next effect index is r, the point-biserial correlation discussed in the previous chapter. Cohen's recommended test of the null hypothesis that $r = 0$ is again based on the t distribution (e.g., Equation 2.2). The effect size q (in the third column) refers to the difference between two independent Fisher z_r transformed correlations. The null hypothesis is that $z_{r1} - z_{r2} = 0$, and the significance test might be Z (as we illustrate shortly), from which we get a p value from which we can get the value t that will let us use Equation 12.1 to compute the $r_{equivalent}$ statistic. Next in the table is the effect size index g, which is different from Hedges's g and is instead the difference between an observed proportion (symbolized in Cohen's text by a capital P) and .50. The null hypothesis is $P - .50 = 0$, and Cohen's test of significance is the sign test, which is a nonparametric procedure that uses plus and minus signs rather than quantitative measures as its data (Siegel, 1956). Next is the effect size index h, which measures the difference between independent arcsine-transformed proportions; the null hypothesis is that this difference is zero. The effect size index w is that for the chi-square test (Equation 11.13, discussed in more detail in chapter 19), although the sample sizes in Table 12.3 refer only to 1-df χ^2 tests. Finally, the effect size f is for F tests on means in the analysis of variance, but the sample sizes in Table 12.3 refer only to F tests with numerator $df = 1$ based on a comparison of the means of two samples.

Cohen's quantitative definitions of "small," "medium." and "large" effect sizes are shown in the top panel of Table 12.3, and the values in the body of the table are the rounded sample size estimates. In Section A, the statistical power and sample size equivalences are given for an alpha level of .05 two-tailed and the assumption of "medium" effects. Section B shows equivalences for "medium" effects at $\alpha = .01$ two-tailed, and Section C shows the equivalences for "small" effects at $\alpha = .05$

two-tailed. One other important feature is that the definition of sample size is not the same for all seven statistics. Sample sizes for t and F are for "each group or condition"; those for r are for "n of score pairs"; those for $r_1 - r_2$ and $P_1 - P_2$ are for "n of each sample"; and those for $P - .50$ and χ^2 are for "total N."

Whenever Table 12.3 involves a comparison of two samples (e.g., t, F, $r_1 - r_2$, $P_1 - P_2$), the sample sizes are assumed to be equal. If the sample sizes are unequal, we can use the harmonic mean sample size (n_h) to provide an approximate n. The harmonic mean sample size for two samples of n_1 and n_2 size is obtained by

$$\text{Harmonic mean} \quad n_h = \frac{2n_1 n_2}{n_1 + n_2} \tag{12.2}$$

In an equal-n design, the harmonic mean sample size is equal to the arithmetic mean sample size, but in an unequal-n design, the harmonic mean sample size is always smaller than the arithmetic mean sample size. Suppose we have two groups with sample sizes of 12 and 18. The arithmetic mean sample size is $n = (12 + 18)/2 = 15$, and the harmonic mean sample size is

$$n_h = \frac{2(12 \times 18)}{12 + 18} = 14.4$$

We also want to note that Cohen's benchmark labels of "small," "medium," and "large" are for use solely with his power tables. Cohen (1988) advised that effect sizes should be interpreted "relative not only to each other, but to the area of behavioral science or even more particularly to the specific content and research method being employed in any given investigation" (p. 25). Nonetheless, many researchers cite Cohen's benchmark labels as if they were context-free, though he specifically cautioned that "the *meaning* of any given ES [effect size] is, in the final analysis, a function of the context in which it is embedded" (p. 535). In the previous chapter we showed that even small effects (by Cohen's definition) can sometimes be loaded with profound practical implications (see again Table 11.8).

Table 12.3 reveals a number of fundamental relationships in the subtables in Sections A, B, and C. First, as the statistical power increases from .25 to .99 in these subtables, the sample size needed for each significance test also increases. Second, the more stringent or conservative the p value, the more sampling units needed, so that more units are needed with $p = .01$ two-tailed than with $p = .05$ two-tailed. Third, as a comparison of Sections A and C will reveal, the smaller the effect size, the more sampling units needed at the same significance level. Fourth, different statistics call for different sample sizes to detect the same benchmark levels, so, for example, it will take fewer units for r than for $r_1 - r_2$ (we explain why shortly).

THE t TEST FOR COMPARING TWO MEANS

We have mentioned Cohen's d (Equation 2.4), Hedges's g (Equation 2.5), and Glass's Δ (Equation 2.6) as effect size indices for the difference between two means, but another option in some situations is the raw difference itself. Suppose we choose as the dependent variable the daily number of cigarettes smoked by experimental and

Cohen's small, medium, large are relative. The more strict the cutoff the more subjects we need, as the power increases the # of subjects needed increases too. The smaller diff sample size the effect size the more units needed @ same sig level. Did test need (✗)

control subjects. The raw difference between M_1 and M_2 (where M is the mean number of cigarettes in a group) is intrinsically meaningful. As another example, suppose we want to compare a method of vocational rehabilitation to a control, and we have a record of the days that workers were reported absent in each condition. If we found that workers in the control condition averaged five more absences per month than did workers in the rehabilitation condition, this difference would be fraught with practical meaning. The point is that raw mean differences can, in some instances, be informative and useful as effect size indicators, whether we are analyzing differences in a specific study (Rosnow & Rosenthal, 2003) or making cross-study comparisons in the context of a meta-analysis (Bond, Wiitala, & Richard, 2003).

 Nonetheless, the most popular measure of effect size for comparing two means is Cohen's d, where the effect size is expressed in standard deviation units. Assuming two populations with equal variability and equal sample sizes, Cohen recommended dividing the difference between the sample means ($M_1 - M_2$) by the standard deviation of either group (i.e., σ_1 or σ_2) to obtain d. With σ_1 and σ_2 unequal, he recommended dividing $M_1 - M_2$ by the square root of the mean of the two variances for the denominator, that is,

$$d = \frac{M_1 - M_2}{\sqrt{\dfrac{\sigma_1^2 + \sigma_2^2}{2}}}. \tag{12.3}$$

As an all-purpose expression of Cohen's d in the case of two independent means, we recommend Equation 2.4:

$$d = \frac{M_1 - M_2}{\sigma_{pooled}},$$

where the difference between two independent means is divided by the common within-group σ. For the sample sizes in Table 12.3, we see that when the power level is no better than a coin flip (.50), we need respective samples of 32, 55, and 193 in *each group* for the three combinations of the stipulated effect size d and the α in Sections A, B, and C. Before we examine an extended power table, it is of interest to review how Cohen chose the benchmark values of small, medium, and large ds.

For $d = .2$, Cohen (1988) reasoned that "in new areas of research, the effect sizes are likely to be small (when they are not zero!)" because "the phenomena under study are typically not under good experimental or measurement control or both" (p. 25). Assuming the populations being compared are normal and have equal variability, then if d is zero, the two distributions will perfectly overlap. With $d = .2$, the amount of nonoverlap will be 14.7%, because the two means are separated by one-fifth of a standard deviation difference, a "small" difference. An example was the larger size of the difference in mean IQ of non-twins as opposed to twins. Another example was the magnitude of the difference between the mean height of 16-year-old girls and 15-year-old girls (about one-half inch, where $\sigma = 2.1$, for a rounded d of .2). For $d = .5$, Cohen (1988, p. 26) thought that a difference just "visible to the naked eye" was a good way of thinking about "medium" effects, and he theorized that ds of about .5 (one-half a standard deviation difference) should be visible, because there is 33% nonoverlap of the normal population curves. An

TABLE 12.4

Sample size per group (*n*) needed to detect "small," "medium," and "large" differences between two independent means at various levels of power and statistical significance

	d = .2			d = .5			d = .8			
	.10	.05	.01	.10	.05	.01	.10	.05	.01	two-tailed *p*
Power	.05	.025	.005	.05	.025	.005	.05	.025	.005	one-tailed *p*
.50	136	193	333	22	32	55	9	13	22	
.60	181	246	402	30	40	66	12	16	27	
.70	236	310	482	38	50	79	15	20	32	
.80	310	393	586	50	64	95	20	26	38	
.85	360	450	654	58	73	106	23	29	43	
.90	429	526	746	69	85	120	27	34	48	
.95	542	651	892	87	105	144	35	42	57	
.99	789	920	1203	127	148	194	50	58	77	

Note: The sample size values in this table are based on Foster's (2003) METASTATS program.

example was the higher mean IQ of managers and professionals versus clerical and semiskilled workers (about 8 points, where $\sigma = 15$, rounded to $d = .5$). For $d = .8$, Cohen (1988) thought that 47.4% nonoverlap of normal population curves might be a good indicator of a "large" effect (four-fifths of a standard deviation difference). An example was the mean IQ difference of typical Ph.D.s versus typical college freshmen, which he said was a "grossly perceptible and therefore large" difference (1988, p. 27).

Table 12.4 focuses in on Cohen's three benchmark levels of *d* for two groups of equal size ($n_1 = n_2$). Values indicated in the body of the table refer once again to the sample size needed in each group. Suppose the researcher is interested in working with power of .80, sets α at .05 two-tailed, and predicts that the difference between means will be a half standard deviation (i.e., $d = .5$). Table 12.4 indicates that the researcher will need 64 subjects in each group. Had the researcher predicted the direction of the difference, then with α set at .05 one-tailed and statistical power of .80, the researcher would need 50 subjects in each group.

We will provide conversion formulas for Hedges's *g* and Glass's Δ in the next chapter, but assuming equal-sized samples ($n_1 = n_2$), we can transform Cohen's *d* into *r* as follows:

$$r = \sqrt{\frac{d^2}{d^2 + 4}} \qquad (12.4)$$

Thus, a "medium" Cohen's *d* of .50 is equivalent to $r = .24$, which is interpreted as the correlation between the independent variable of group or condition (e.g., a treatment, usually coded as 1, vs. a control, usually coded as 0) and the score on the dependent or outcome variable for sample sizes found, or assumed on theoretical grounds, to be equal. Notice that, although $d = .5$ is the benchmark level of a "medium" d, the r of .24 is slightly smaller than the benchmark level of a "medium" r (i.e., .3). We will have more to say about this discrepancy shortly.

What if the sample sizes were inherently unequal? In that case we could use the following formula to convert Cohen's d into r:

$$r = \sqrt{\frac{d^2}{d^2 + \left(\frac{1}{PQ}\right)}}, \qquad (12.5)$$

where P denotes the proportion of the overall total sample (N) or population represented by the sample in one group (n_1), and $Q = 1 - P$. Thus, $P = (n_1)/N$, and $Q = (n_2)/N$. As an illustration, say that we compare scores from patients with a rare disorder to scores from patients with common disorders, or to scores obtained from people in general. If the rare disorder occurs in 5% of people, then $P = .05$ and $Q = .95$. (Of course, when $P = Q$, then Equation 12.5 is equivalent to Equation 12.4.) The r obtained from Equation 12.5 is interpreted as the correlation between the independent variable of group or condition (e.g., a treatment, usually coded as 1, vs. control, usually coded as 0) and the score on the dependent or outcome variable for sample sizes that (a) are observed to be unequal and (b) are assumed on theoretical grounds to be inherently unequal.

THE SIGNIFICANCE OF A PRODUCT-MOMENT r

Cohen's effect size associated with the relationship between two variables is the product-moment r (Equation 11.1). Table 12.3 indicates the benchmark levels of small, medium, and large rs as .1, .3, and .5, respectively. As noted before, there is not consistently an exact correspondence between Cohen's benchmark levels for r and d. This fact is illustrated in more detail in Table 12.5, where we see that "small" rs and ds do not run afoul of Cohen's labeling convention. However, an r of .3 (a "medium" r) corresponds to a Cohen's d of .63, and an r of .5 (a "large" r) corresponds to a Cohen's d of 1.15 (a "jumbo" effect). As the third column of Table 12.5 shows, the relationship between Cohen's d and r is not a perfectly straight line. It is another reason not to mindlessly use the labeling convention when reporting effect sizes, but to specify the particular index and its precise value.

Consulting the sample sizes in Table 12.3, we see that to achieve the "flipping-the-coin" power level of .50 requires sample sizes of 42, 72, and 386 score pairs, respectively, for the three combinations of expected effect size and α shown in Sections A, B, and C. Comparing the effect sizes listed for the t statistic (i.e., effect size index d) and r reveal the sample sizes required for r to be uniformly higher. However, the entries under t are the ns for each of the two groups, whereas the entries for r are the total sample size. In fact, for most power levels, and for most effect sizes and α levels, the total sample size required by r is smaller than that required by the t statistic. Part of the reason for this difference is that the standard independent t test comparing two means cannot take advantage of both between-group and within-group linearity of regression. In chapter 15 we will describe a t test that *does* take advantage of this information and

TABLE 12.5
Relation between *r* and Cohen's *d*, assuming two conditions of equal sample size

r	Cohen's *d*	*d/r*	*r*	Cohen's *d*	*d/r*
.01	.02	2.0	.35	.75	2.1
.02	.04	2.0	.40	.87	2.2
.03	.06	2.0	.45	1.01	2.2
.04	.08	2.0	.50	1.15	2.3
.05	.10	2.0	.55	1.32	2.4
.10	.20	2.0	.60	1.50	2.5
.15	.30	2.0	.70	1.96	2.8
.20	.41	2.1	.80	2.67	3.3
.25	.52	2.1	.90	4.13	4.6
.30	.63	2.1	1.00	∞	∞

therefore is more powerful in multiple comparisons when there is a specific prediction about the pattern of the group means. To anticipate a little, the problem is explained by Table 12.6, which shows the scores of two subjects each in a control condition and an experimental condition, where the means are 3.0 and 7.0, respectively.

TABLE 12.6
Comparisons between two sets of scores

A. No specific prediction other than $M_{control} \neq M_{experimental}$

Subject	Condition	Within-condition specific prediction	Score	*M*
1	Control	None	2	3.0
2	Control	None	4	
3	Experimental	None	6	7.0
4	Experimental	None	8	

B. Linear prediction that Subject 1 < Subject 2 < Subject 3 < Subject 4

Subject	Condition	Within-condition specific prediction	Score
1	Control	-3	2
2	Control	-1	4
3	Experimental	$+1$	6
4	Experimental	$+3$	8

Suppose the only prediction is that the means will be different, in which case $t = 2.83$, $df = 2$, and p is approximately .11 two-tailed. In Equation 12.1, the effect size r associated with this t test is $r = .895$. Clearly, it would make no difference to the t test whether the two scores in each condition were in the order that is shown in Part A of Table 12.6, or if the order had been reversed within conditions (Subject 2 and then Subject 1 in the control condition, and Subject 4 and then Subject 3 in the experimental condition). The means remain unchanged, and those are what the standard t test is focused upon. However, suppose we had predicted (based on some theory) that Subject 1 would have the lowest score, Subject 2 would have a higher score, Subject 3 would have an even higher score, and Subject 4 would have the highest score. We can express this linear prediction by weights of -3, -1, $+1$, $+3$. Correlating these four weights with the four individual scores gives $r = 1.00$, which is what it should be, as the prediction of a perfect linear relationship is confirmed by the pattern of the scores. The t test of this r is infinitely large, because there is no "within-group" variability (the "groups" are the subjects, and there is a single subject in each "group"). But if even one of the pairs of numbers of the experimental or control condition is interchanged, the r drops from 1.00 to .80 ($t = 1.89$, $df = 2$, p approximately .20 two-tailed). Therefore, where there really is more nearly perfect linear regression between the predicted and obtained results, r is likely to be more powerful than the standard t test comparing two independent means. The reason is that the t test has lost some information in the independent (or predictor) variable by dichotomizing the predictor values (-3, -1, $+1$, $+3$) into just two levels.

Before leaving this discussion of r, see Table 12.7, which is an extended table for use when alpha is set at .05 two-tailed (or .025 one-tailed). Suppose we had estimated that it was 95% likely that an effect size in the population would be

TABLE 12.7

Sample sizes (rounded) to detect r by t test at $p = .05$ two-tailed or .025 one-tailed

Power						Effect size correlation (r)								
	.05	.10	.15	.20	.25	.30	.35	.40	.45	.50	.55	.60	.65	.70
.25	664	168	76	44	29	21	16	13	10	9	8	7	6	5
.50	1,538	386	172	97	63	44	33	25	20	16	14	11	10	8
.60	1,960	491	218	123	79	55	41	31	25	20	16	14	12	10
.70	2,469	617	274	154	99	68	50	38	30	24	20	16	14	12
.80	3,138	784	348	195	124	86	63	48	37	30	24	20	17	14
.85	3,589	896	397	222	142	98	71	54	42	34	27	22	19	16
.90	4,200	1,048	464	260	165	114	83	62	49	39	31	26	21	18
.95	5,193	1,295	573	320	203	140	101	76	59	47	38	31	25	21
.99	7,341	1,829	808	451	286	196	142	106	82	65	52	42	34	28

Note: Based on Arno Ouwehand's Power Calculator 2, available via UCLA Department of Statistics (http://calculators.stat.ucla.edu).

TABLE 12.8
Planning the sample size

Power	$r = .1$	$r = .2$	$r = .3$
.80	784	195	86
.85	896	222	98
.90	1048	260	114

between $r = .1$ and .3. Using the information in Table 12.7, we might create a summary like that in Table 12.8 to help us plan our study. To work with a power of .80 and $p = .05$ two-tailed, the total number of subjects we need is 784, 195, or 86, depending on whether we want to place our bet on the r of .1, .2, or .3, respectively. If subjects were readily available and not costly to run, we might be more comfortable setting the power higher than .80. With the power set at .85, we need 896, 222, or 98 total subjects, given an r of .1, .2, or .3, respectively. With power set at .90, we will need a total N of 1,048, 260, or 114 subjects, given an r of .1, .2, or .3, respectively.

DIFFERENCES BETWEEN CORRELATION COEFFICIENTS

Cohen operationalized the difference between two independent correlation coefficients by the effect size index q, where

$$\text{Cohen's } q = z_{r_1} - z_{r_2}, \tag{12.6}$$

which is the difference between the Fisher z_r transformations associated with each r. The Fisher z_r (Equation 11.2) makes equal differences between Fisher z_r values equally detectable, because equal differences between rs are not equally detectable. For instance, the difference between .90 and .70 in units of r is much more detectable statistically than is the difference between .40 and .20. Tests of significance among rs are also more accurate when Fisher's z_r transformation is used (Alexander, Scozzaro, & Borodkin, 1989). As Table 12.3 shows, to achieve a power level of .80, we would need, respectively, 177, 263, and 1573 units for *each r* for the combinations of expected effect size and alpha indicated in Sections A, B, and C.

Why should it be so difficult to detect the difference between the value of one r and another r when it is so much easier to detect the difference between the value of one r and zero? The answer lies in the difference between the confidence interval around a second observed r and that around a theoretical value of zero. The latter, of course, has no confidence interval, but the former has a real confidence interval "to be overcome." Consider an r of .30 based on an N of 45. The t associated with this r is 2.06, and $p < .05$ two-tailed. The 95% confidence interval around the obtained r is between .01 and .54. There is no overlap with zero. Suppose we wanted to compare this r with another study with an r of zero based on the same sample size of 45. The confidence interval of the latter r ranges from $-.29$ to $+.29$ and overlaps

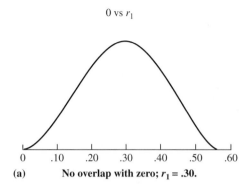

(a)   No overlap with zero; $r_1 = .30$.

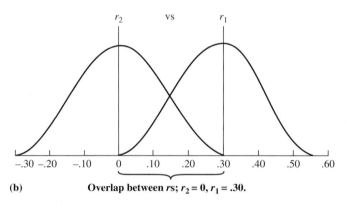

(b)   Overlap between rs; $r_2 = 0, r_1 = .30$.

FIGURE 12.1
Comparison of a correlation coefficient with (a) a theoretical value of zero, and (b) a correlation coefficient of zero.

considerably with the confidence interval of our r of .30, as represented in Figure 12.1. It is this overlap that keeps the rs from being found to differ significantly.

Table 12.9 is an expanded list of sample sizes needed to detect Cohen's q at $p = .05$ two-tailed. Suppose we hypothesize that the correlation between two tests will be higher for younger than for older children, because younger children show less cognitive differentiation (DePaulo & Rosenthal, 1979a). For our study we have available 30 younger children and 50 older children. We know that much larger sample sizes are necessary to obtain significant differences between two rs than to show a single r to differ from zero, but these 80 children are all we have. What we want to know is the level of power at which we will be operating, assuming various differences between our rs (measured in units of Fisher's z_r). To use Table 12.9, we need the harmonic mean of the two sample sizes, which we obtain from Equation 12.2:

$$n_\mathrm{h} = \frac{2n_1 n_2}{n_1 + n_2} = \frac{2(30)(50)}{30 + 50} = 37.5.$$

If we assume a "small" q of .10, then Table 12.9 shows we will clearly be operating at a level of power well below .25. With a "medium" q of .30, we are close to power

TABLE 12.9
Sample sizes (*n* for *each* of two samples) needed to detect Cohen's *q* at *p* = .05 two-tailed

	Values of Cohen's *q*						
Power	.10	.20	.30	.40	.50	.60	.70
.25	333	86	40	24	16	12	10
.50	771	195	88	51	34	24	19
.60	983	248	112	64	42	30	23
.70	1237	312	140	80	52	37	28
.80	1573	395	177	101	66	47	35
.85	1799	452	203	115	75	53	40
.90	2104	528	236	134	87	61	46
.95	2602	653	292	165	107	75	56
.99	3677	922	411	233	150	105	78

Note: Based on *Statistical Power Analysis for the Behavioral Sciences* (2nd ed.), by J. Cohen, 1988, Hillsdale, NJ: Lawrence Erlbaum Associates, Publishers.

of .25, but that is not as good as flipping a coin (50:50). Assuming a "large" *q* of .50, we will be working with power that is only a little better than a coin flip.

Suppose another researcher has also investigated our hypothesis of different correlations for different age groups. By now we know not to take too seriously the finding of "no significant difference" apart from the actual effect size obtained. Therefore, when we learn of the other researcher's study, we go directly to the effect size and assess the power level at which the study was operating, given the obtained effect size as the best guess of the population value of the effect size (or given some other postulated population effect size). For this example, let us again assume sample sizes of 30 and 50 ($n_h = 37.5$), and we now assume the obtained correlations are .60 and .37. Converting each *r* into a Fisher z_r gives .69 and .39. In Table 12.9, with a population or true effect of $q = .69 - .39 = .30$, and n_h rounded to 38, we conclude that the researcher was working with a power level well below .50.

To operationalize an effect size *r*, the one we want in the case of *q* (or r_q) would be the correlation between (a) the magnitude of the relationship between two variables as computed in two different samples or studies and (b) some attribute that distinguishes the samples or studies. One way to conceptualize this idea is in a 2 × 2 analysis of variance design where the treatment is crossed by patient gender. The effect size indicator *q* can be viewed as an index of the magnitude of the interaction effect. For example, if we found a treatment effect of size r_1 for the female patients and a treatment effect of size r_2 for the male patients, the effect size *q* would index the extent to which the treatment effects differ for females and males. As *F* with *df* = 1 in the numerator is equal to t^2, given the value of the 1-*df* interaction *F*, we can use Equation 12.1 to solve for r_q. In this case, however, the *df* in the denominator of Equation 12.1 is defined as $(n_1 - 3) + (n_2 - 3)$.

Another way to estimate r_q is by (a) comparing Fisher z_r values by a Z test, (b) using the p value of the Z test (and the sample sizes) to get an associated t value, and (c) then using Equation 12.1. We can illustrate this procedure with the results above, in which the Fisher z_r values of the obtained correlations of .60 and .37 (ns of 30 and 50) are .69 and .39. To compare independent z_r values, we use a variant of a more general expression described later in this book (chapter 21):

$$Z = \frac{z_{r1} - z_{r2}}{\sqrt{\dfrac{1}{n_1 - 3} + \dfrac{1}{n_2 - 3}}}, \tag{12.7}$$

where Z is the standard normal deviate, and the other symbols are defined as above. Substitution gives us

$$Z = \frac{.69 - .39}{\sqrt{\dfrac{1}{30 - 3} + \dfrac{1}{50 - 3}}} = 1.24,$$

which we see in Table B.1 has an associated p of .1075 one-tailed.

When looking up the critical t value, we use $df = (n_1 - 3) + (n_2 - 3)$. With $df = 74$ and $p = .1075$ one-tailed, we find $t = 1.2507$. Using Equation 12.1, with df now defined as $(n_1 - 3) + (n_2 - 3)$, we find

$$r_q = \sqrt{\frac{t^2}{t^2 + (n_1 - 3) + (n_2 - 3)}}$$

$$= \sqrt{\frac{(1.2507)^2}{(1.2507)^2 + 27 + 47}} = .144,$$

where r_q can be understood as the magnitude of the effect of a moderator variable. That is, we think of it as the effect of a third variable on the magnitude of the difference between the effect sizes in the different samples or studies. For example, think of how a 2×2 analysis of variance embodies three 1-df comparisons (contrasts) that are essentially "wired in" (i.e., they are inherent in the design). One contrast is the 1-df top-versus-bottom-row effect. The second contrast is the 1-df left-versus-right-column effect. The third contrast is the 1-df row-times-column-interaction effect. It is the third contrast that is most relevant in this case, because it helps us conceptualize the moderator effect r_q in terms of individual sampling units. This moderator effect is the correlation between each sampling unit's raw score and the interaction contrast weight ($+1$ or -1) assigned to that unit's condition.

Before we leave this discussion, we want to say a little more about the idea of an effect size r of zero. Suppose that zero is the true population r. With random samples of $N = 5$ units each, the 95% confidence interval would range from $-.88$ to $+.88$. In other words, in 95 out of 100 samples, the observed correlation is expected to fall within this range, and thus an effect as large as $r = .7$ would not be unusual in a sample of five observations. With random samples of $N = 10$ units, the 95% confidence interval would be from $-.63$ to $+.63$, in which case an effect size r of .7 *would* be unusual. The point is that generalizing from one small sample to the population value can be perilously imprecise. This is another argument for the importance

working backwards from z_r

of replications, as well as for meta-analytic summaries and for confidence intervals around the meta-analytically pooled effect sizes (described in chapter 21).

THE TEST THAT A PROPORTION IS .50

The difference between an obtained proportion (P) and .50 is denoted as g, but Cohen's g should not be confused with Hedges's g (Equation 2.5). Cohen's g is simply the distance in units of proportion from .50, that is,

$$\text{Cohen's } g = P - .50, \text{ or } .50 - P \text{ (if directional)}$$
$$= |P - .50| \text{ (if nondirectional)}, \tag{12.8}$$

with small, medium, and large effects defined in Table 12.3 as corresponding to a raw difference of .05, .15, and .25, respectively. As we noted previously, Cohen's significance test of choice in this situation is the sign test (see Siegel, 1956, pp. 68–75; Siegel & Castellan, 1988, pp. 80–87). To achieve a power level of .80, Table 12.3 shows that we would need 85, 127, and 783 total N for the three combinations of expected effect size and alpha in Sections A, B, and C.

It is important not to read too much into the benchmark labels of Cohen's g. Suppose that two candidates received all the votes in a U.S. presidential election, and that 55% of the electorate voted for the winner, so that Cohen's $g = .55 - .50 = .05$. Although it is called a "small" effect, the difference between a high proportion of .55 (for the winner) and a low proportion of .45 (for the loser) would be a landslide victory in a presidential election. A similar magnitude of Cohen's g might be viewed as far less noteworthy if it pertained to an instructional treatment to boost the scores of a class of high school students on a true-false test on American history. The lesson, as Cohen (1988) cautioned, is that the practical interpretation of the effect size depends on the context.

There are often alternative ways of thinking about research situations in which the variables are dichotomous and we want to test certain observed outcomes against a null hypothesis of .50. For example, if we have two classes of events (e.g., vote Democrat vs. vote Republican) with P_1 the proportion of cases in one class and P_2 the proportion in the other class, the null hypothesis is $P_1 = P_2 = .50$. In this case, one possibility is to obtain a p value that we can then use to compute the $r_{equivalent}$ statistic (Equation 12.1). Siegel and Castellan (1988, pp. 38–44) described a binomial test that provides accurate p values. Another possibility, also described by Siegel and Castellan (pp. 45–51), is a 1×2 chi-square (Equation 11.14) goodness-of-fit test. With large sample sizes, we can use Equation 11.16 ($\phi = Z/\sqrt{N}$) to estimate the effect size r (in this case, phi), as $\sqrt{\chi^2_{(1)}}$ is distributed as Z when the sample size is large.

THE DIFFERENCE BETWEEN PROPORTIONS

The difference between two obtained proportions is indexed by the difference h between the arcsin transformations of the two proportions, that is,

$$\text{Cohen's } h = (\arcsin P_1) - (\arcsin P_2) \tag{12.9}$$

Table 12.3 shows that to achieve a power level of .80 requires 63, 93, and 392 units *for each sample* for the three combinations of the expected effect size and alpha shown in Sections A, B, and C. We can use Table B.13 (Appendix B) to find the arcsin equivalent (a) of each proportion (X). The purpose of this transformation is to make the hs comparable, because differences between raw proportions are not all comparable (e.g., with respect to power). Thus, a difference between proportions of .95 and .90 yields a Cohen's h of .19, whereas the difference between proportions of .55 and .50 yields a Cohen's h of only .10 (Cohen, 1988).

As a further illustration of Cohen's h, suppose that subjects are asked to identify four expressions of emotions (joy, anger, disappointment, and fear) in posed photographs, and the instruction is to choose one of four responses (like a multiple-choice test in which one of four answers is correct and its position is assigned at random). Guessing should yield an accuracy rate of .25, and suppose the actual observed performance is .75. In Table B.13, we find the arcsin value of $X = .75$ is $a = 2.0944$, and the arcsin value of $X = .25$ is $a = 1.0472$. Hence, Cohen's $h = 2.0944 - 1.0472 = 1.0472$.

Another effect size index, called Pi (Π), is expressed as the proportion of correct guesses (Rosenthal & Rubin, 1989). It enables us to summarize the overall performance so that we can compare performance on tests made up of varying numbers of alternatives per item. The way it works is that an obtained proportion (P) is compared with a proportion expected under the null hypothesis. Pi gives the proportion of hits on a scale on which .50 is the null value, and it is found from the following:

$$\Pi = \frac{P(k-1)}{1 + P(k-2)}, \qquad (12.10)$$

where P is the raw proportion of hits, and k is the number of alternative choices available. For example, if there are four choices, choosing the correct alternative .60 of the time is equivalent to choosing the correct alternative .82 of the time given only two choices. Power analyses for Π can be carried out on Cohen's h (i.e., $a_1 - a_2$), where one of the values of a is a constant. To use Cohen's (1988) power tables, we first need to multiply h by $\sqrt{2}$ to adjust for the fact that one of our proportions is a constant with no sampling variation. For example, with $\Pi = .60$, the arcsin transformation (Table B.13) is 1.7722. The null constant of .50 has an equivalent arcsin value of 1.5708. Thus, Cohen's $h = 1.7722 - 1.5708 = 0.2014$, which we multiply by $\sqrt{2}$ to obtain $.2014 \times 1.414 = .2848$. This value of Cohen's $h = .2848$ is the one we use in consulting Cohen's (1988) power tables. Further details regarding Π can be found in chapter 19 and in Rosenthal and Rubin (1989, 1991).

FOCUSED CHI-SQUARE TEST

Table 12.3 notes that Cohen's w is the effect size associated with a 1-df χ^2 test, which is a *focused* chi-square. We will have more to say about this distinction in chapter 19, but chi-square tests with 1 df are focused, and chi-squares with $df > 1$ are diffuse or unfocused (and are called *omnibus* tests). Cohen's w is the square root of the sum over all cells (of any size table of frequencies) of the square of the difference between the proportion expected and the proportion obtained in each cell divided by the proportion expected in that cell, or

$$\text{Cohen's } w = \sqrt{\sum \frac{(P_{\text{expected}} - P_{\text{obtained}})^2}{P_{\text{expected}}}}. \tag{12.11}$$

The definition of Cohen's w resembles the square root of the definition of the chi-square test in the previous chapter (Equation 11.13), except that the raw frequencies used to compute Equation 11.13 have been replaced by the proportions of total N found in each cell or expected in each cell. For a 2×2 table, Cohen's w is equivalent to the phi (ϕ) coefficient, so

$$\phi = w = \sqrt{\frac{\chi^2_{(1)}}{N}}, \tag{12.12}$$

where the subscript in $\chi^2_{(1)}$ denotes a 1-df chi-square. To achieve a power level of .80 for Cohen's w for a 1-df chi-square, Table 12.3 shows that we will require a total N of 87, 130, and 785 units, respectively, for the three combinations of effect size and alpha in Sections A, B, and C.

F TESTS FOR FOCUSED COMPARISONS

Cohen's f is his effect size index associated with the F test in the analysis of variance, and is defined as

$$\text{Cohen's } f = \frac{\sigma_{\text{means}}}{\sigma_{\text{within}}}, \tag{12.13}$$

where the standard deviation of the population means to be compared is divided by the pooled standard deviation within conditions. Given our emphasis on focused statistical tests, Table 12.3 shows f only for F with numerator $df = 1$. Achieving a power level of .80 (or for that matter, any other power level) when only two groups are involved requires sample sizes identical to those required for t.

When the F has more than 1 df in the numerator, the power decreases in tests of main effects as the number of df of the between-groups factor increases for a given fixed total N. In addition, the power for an interaction decreases as the number of df of the interaction increases for a given fixed total N. When using Cohen's power tables, we redefine n to n^1 before entering the tables, where

$$n^1 = \frac{df_{\text{error}} + df_{\text{effect}} + 1}{df_{\text{effect}} + 1} \tag{12.14}$$

For example, suppose we were given a 3×4 design with the sample sizes (ns) shown here:

	A_1	A_2	A_3	Σ
B_1	10	10	10	30
B_2	10	10	10	30
B_3	10	10	10	30
B_4	10	10	10	30
Σ	40	40	40	120

In this case we would find the degrees of freedom to be as follows:

$$df_{\text{error}} = 120 - 12 = 12(10 - 1) = 108$$
$$df_{\text{effect}} \text{ for A} = 3 - 1 = 2$$
$$df_{\text{effect}} \text{ for B} = 4 - 1 = 3$$
$$df_{\text{effect}} \text{ for AB} = (3 - 1)(4 - 1) = 6$$

Therefore, based on Equation 12.13, we find

$$n^1 \text{ for A effect} = \frac{108 + 2 + 1}{2 + 1} = 37,$$

and

$$n^1 \text{ for B effect} = \frac{108 + 3 + 1}{3 + 1} = 28,$$

and finally

$$n^1 \text{ for AB effect} = \frac{108 + 6 + 1}{6 + 1} = 16.4.$$

Consulting the power tables in Cohen's (1988) text, we would find the power levels for $\alpha = .05$ and a "medium" effect of $f = .25$ to be .65, .58, and .46 for the A, B, and AB effects, respectively. These results illustrate the loss of power involved when, for a fixed total N, the df for various effects show an increase. Here, then, is a reason to organize our scientific questions into focused questions such as are addressed by t tests, F tests with a single df in the numerator, and chi-square tests with 1 df, and, more generally, by contrasts of any type. The details of the use of contrasts will be given in later chapters, but here we can illustrate one possible contrast among the four means of the B effect.

Suppose our contrast is to compare the mean of Groups B_1 and B_2 with the mean of Groups B_3 and B_4. We can compute such a contrast by the procedures in chapter 15. Then, using Equation 12.14, we calculate

$$n^1 = \frac{108 + 1 + 1}{1 + 1} = 55,$$

because the df for the effect is always 1 for any contrast. The power level for this contrast is .75, noticeably greater than for any of the three effects involving multiple df in the numerator of the F test. For χ^2 tests of $df > 1$, and for F tests with numerator $df > 1$, we suggest doing power calculations on the contrasts that address specific scientific questions whenever possible. If the power calculations must be made on χ^2 tests of $df > 1$, or F tests with numerator $df > 1$, tables in Cohen's (1988) book provide all the information required.

ADDITIONAL STRATEGIES FOR IMPROVING POWER

Among the strategies for improving power mentioned in this chapter, we have discussed increasing the sample sizes and using focused contrasts rather than omnibus tests. In chapter 15 and subsequent chapters, we illustrate contrast procedures and also discuss other procedures that improve power. For example, in the next chapter we will discuss the standard two-sample t test in more detail, and we know that the numerator of such a t test is the difference between two means. Therefore, a treatment that is more likely to drive the means further apart will also improve the statistical power relative to a weaker treatment. Similarly, because the denominator of the t test reflects the variability within the two samples, using a homogeneous population will also improve power.

In discussing Cohen's $q,$ we illustrated the comparison of independent z_r values by a variant of a more general meta-analytic equation to be described in chapter 21. We can also combine significance levels of independent studies in order to get an overall estimate of the probability that the combined effect size (and significance test) value may have been obtained if the null hypothesis of no relationship was true. It is another way of improving power, and we will also have more to say about it in chapter 21. As another preview, suppose Studies A and B predicted the direction of a result, and the observed result was in that direction and the effect sizes were similar in both studies. In Study A the obtained p was .121, and in Study B it was $p = .084.$ We first use Table B.1 to find Z values for these ps: $Z = 1.17$ for the p of .121, and $Z = 1.38$ for the p of .084. Next, we divide the sum of the independent Z values by the square root of the number of Z values:

$$\text{Combined } Z = \frac{Z_{\text{Study A}} + Z_{\text{Study B}}}{\sqrt{\text{Number of } Z \text{ values}}}$$

$$= \frac{1.17 + 1.38}{\sqrt{2}} = 1.81.$$

The final step is to consult Table B.1, where we find that the one-tailed probability of our combined Z of 1.81 is $p = .035.$

When we discuss the factorial analysis of variance, we will show how blocking variables is another way of improving power. In the next chapter we elaborate on how unequal-n designs are often less powerful than their equal-n equivalents. As implied in chapter 11, using reliable measures and instruments also improves power. The lesson is that, although increasing the sample size may be the procedure most closely associated with improving statistical power, it is just one of a number of design and analytic alternatives. If you know the old Tarzan movies, where he swings from tree to tree, you may also know that Tarzan was originally played by Johnny Weissmuller. Asked about his philosophy of life, Weissmuller's response was "The main thing is not to let go of the vine." It is also good advice for researchers who do null hypothesis significance testing: Pay heed to all the various circumstances that are most and least conducive to statistical power, so you don't let go of good hypotheses prematurely.

PART
V

ONE-WAY
DESIGNS

COMPARING
MEANS BY
STANDARD
t TESTS

GOSSET AND THE t TEST

Often in behavioral research we want to compare the means of two groups. We might want to compare an experimental and a control group, or one diagnostic category and another, or one school system and another. The most common statistical procedure for comparing two means is the t test. We draw two samples to test the hypothesis that there is in the populations from which the samples were drawn either (a) no difference between the two means or, equivalently, (b) no relationship between the independent variable of membership in one of the groups and the dependent variable of score on the response measure. Introduced in 1908 by William Sealy Gosset, the t test of significance is predicated on probability curves known as *Student's distribution,* which "revolutionized the statistics of small samples" (Snedecor & Cochran, 1989, p. 54). Trained as a chemist, Gosset worked for Guinness, the Irish brewery. Staff members were prohibited from publishing their research, but Gosset quietly published under the pseudonym Student. The name Gosset may not come readily to mind to many researchers, but "the name 'Student' is one of the most celebrated in the history of statistics" (Wallis & Roberts, 1956, p. 417). (See Salsburg, 2001, for a fascinating account.)

Before Gosset's work on the t test and the t distribution, researchers were in a quandary over the issue of generalizing from treatment procedures in small samples with varying effects to populations whose variability was unknown. For example, researchers who experimented with fertilizers, crop rotation, and different strains of potatoes observed that similar treatments did not produce the same yields. Averaging the yields in the treated plots gave an overall estimate, and it was possible to describe the "probable error" (the 50% confidence interval), but this description still did not resolve the generalizability issue. Gosset's genius was to perceive a way of testing the equality of population means whose variability was unknown, given sample means (Gigerenzer et al., 1989). R. A. Fisher (1973a) wrote of Gosset's contribution that, "important as it was in itself, [it] was of far greater importance in inaugurating the first stage of the process by which statistical methods attained sufficient refinement to be of real assistance in the interpretation of data" (p. 4). Fisher also noted that, as a result of Gosset's insight, "by about 1930 all statistical problems which were thought to deserve careful treatment were being discussed in terms of mathematically exact distributions, and the tests of significance based upon them" (p. 4).

The focus of this chapter is on two major variants of the t test, including their associated effect size indices. In chapter 15 we discuss another use of t when there are more than two groups or conditions and we want to test a predicted trend involving all, or at least more than two, of those groups or conditions. One of the two kinds of t tests discussed in this chapter is the **independent sample** t, so named because the scores in one group are presumed to be unrelated to the scores in the other group. The second kind of t test is called a **paired sample** t, or a **one-sample** t, or a **correlated sample** t, or a **matched pair** t, as it is used when the two samples are not independent, or when we want to compare a single sample of scores against a theoretical mean. We also discuss statistical assumptions underlying t, those underlying nonparametric procedures, and the nature of certain "resampling" procedures called the *bootstrap*, the *jackknife*, and *permutation tests*. We begin, however, by reiterating the relationship between the p value and the effect size, as it has specific implications for maximizing the t and is a constant reminder of the importance of reporting and interpreting effect size indices.

TWO COMPONENTS OF t TESTS

Like any test of statistical significance, the t test consists of two components: the size of the effect and the size of the study. In Equation 11.10 we expressed this general relationship as

$$\text{Significance test} = \text{Size of effect} \times \text{Size of study},$$

a relationship that we also mentioned in chapter 12. In our discussion of correlation in chapter 11, we saw that when the size of the effect of the independent variable is indexed by r, the general relationship above could be rewritten in the form of an equation that was introduced in chapter 2 (Equation 2.2):

$$t = \frac{r}{\sqrt{1 - r^2}} \times \sqrt{df}.$$

Thus, we can compute the point-biserial r between membership in one of the two groups (coded, for example, as 0, 1 or -1, $+1$) and the dependent variable, and we find t for this equation, which requires only that we also know the df for r. For this application, the df equals the number of pairs of scores minus 2 (i.e., $N - 2$).

We also know that an alternative to indexing the size of the effect by r is to index it by the standardized difference between group means, which might be expressed by Cohen's d (Equation 2.4), Hedges's g (Equation 2.5), or Glass's Δ (Equation 2.6). The following equation shows the effect size component expressed as Hedges's g, the difference between two group means divided by the pooled sample estimate of the population standard deviation:

$$t = \frac{M_1 - M_2}{S} \times \frac{1}{\sqrt{\frac{1}{n_1} + \frac{1}{n_2}}}. \tag{13.1}$$

With Hedges's g again used as the effect size index, an alternative equation is

$$t = \frac{M_1 - M_2}{S} \times \sqrt{\frac{n_1 n_2}{n_1 + n_2}}. \tag{13.2}$$

Comparing the three equations above, we note that not only the size-of-effect component is defined differently, but so is the size-of-study index. Just as $(M_1 - M_2)/S$ does not equal $r/\sqrt{1 - r^2}$, neither does $\sqrt{n_1 n_2 / (n_1 + n_2)} = \sqrt{df}$. In general, whenever we change the size-of-effect index, we must also change the size-of-study index in the t-test formula. Suppose we choose Cohen's d for our size-of-effect index, in which case:

$$t = \frac{M_1 - M_2}{\sigma} \times \left[\frac{\sqrt{n_1 n_2}}{(n_1 + n_2)} \times \sqrt{df} \right]. \tag{13.3}$$

When $n_1 = n_2$, the first term in the brackets in Equation 13.3 simplifies to $\frac{1}{2}$, and we can write

$$t = d \times \frac{\sqrt{df}}{2}. \tag{13.4}$$

MAXIMIZING *t*

The equations above also give us an insight into how t is maximized in three ways. One way, clearly implied in the numerator of Hedges's g and Cohen's d, is to drive the means further apart. A second way, implied in the denominator of Hedges's g and Cohen's d, is to decrease the within-group variability. A third way, discussed in the previous chapter, and also implied in the size-of-study components of the equations above, is to increase the total sample size. Not so intuitively apparent, however, is that, given any total N, departures from equal sample sizes can also reduce t. However, there are circumstances in which researchers sometimes choose to allocate the sampling units to different conditions in unequally sized samples so as to "optimize" power (discussed in chapter 15).

In the first instance, strong treatment effects drive the means further apart and, other things being equal, maximize the t. Suppose we hypothesized that longer treatment sessions will be more beneficial than shorter treatment sessions. In testing this prediction, we are more likely to find a statistically significant difference when we compare treatment sessions lasting 15 minutes with those lasting 45 minutes than if we compare treatment sessions lasting 30 minutes with those lasting 35 minutes. Or suppose we hypothesized an age trend in performance but have the resources to compare only two age groups. The more extreme the age groups we select, the further apart the average performance in the two groups should be. Of course, the limitation of this strategy is that we foreclose on the possibility that a more subtle relationship is present. By sampling additional age groups, we at least allow a possibily complex pattern to emerge. Moreover, even if all we predicted was a linear pattern, observing this relationship across three, four, or five different groups (rather than just finding a difference in the predicted direction between the two most extreme age groups) lends further credence to our hypothesis because it is subjected to a riskier empirical confrontation.

In the second instance, the t test is maximized by decreasing S or σ, the variability within the groups. Thus, the more homogeneous the samples in those characteristics that are substantially correlated with the dependent variable, the smaller S or σ will be. The more standardized the procedures used in the study, the better we are able to control the variability of response. Of course, if every experiment designed to investigate the same question uses similar subjects and the same standardized procedure, we may increase our understanding of that procedure for those kinds of subjects, but not our understanding of the generalizability of the findings beyond the circumscribed design and its rigid implementation.

Finally, we know from the discussion in the previous chapter that, when sample sizes (n_1 and n_2) are increased, the size of the t is also increased. We also alluded to the usual advantage of making sample sizes as equal as possible, because t tests are generally more effective when the sample sizes are not very different for any fixed total N. This premise is illustrated in Table 13.1, where the first two columns show various values of n_1 and n_2, with $n_1 + n_2$ fixed at $N = 100$. In the third column we see the arithmetic mean of the two sample sizes, that is, $\bar{n} = (n_1 + n_2)/2$, and the next column shows

TABLE 13.1
Effects of unequal sample sizes on loss of relative efficiency and the effective loss of N

Sample size		Arithmetic mean n	Harmonic mean n	Effective size of study	Loss of relative efficiency	Effective loss of N
n_1	n_2	$(\bar{n})$	(n_h)	$\sqrt{\dfrac{n_1 n_2}{n_1 + n_2}}$		
50	50	50	50.00	5.00	.00	0
55	45	50	49.50	4.98	.01	1
60	40	50	48.00	4.90	.04	4
65	35	50	45.50	4.77	.09	9
70	30	50	42.00	4.58	.16	16
75	25	50	37.50	4.33	.25	25
80	20	50	32.00	4.00	.36	36
85	15	50	25.50	3.57	.49	49
90	10	50	18.00	3.00	.64	64
95	5	50	9.50	2.18	.81	81
99	1	50	1.98	.995	.96	96

harmonic mean sample sizes (defined in Equation 12.2). The fifth column is based on the definition of the size-of-study component in Equation 13.2. Calculations for the values in the last two columns are described shortly, but shown in the next-to-last column is the loss of relative efficiency in *t* as we have increasing inequality of n_1 and n_2, and the last column shows the effective loss of total sample size (N) as we have increasing inequality of n_1 and n_2. Notice that, compared with a study with $n_1 = n_2 = 50$, a study with $n_1 = 99$ and $n_2 = 1$ will show a loss of relative efficiency of .96 (i.e., a 96% decrease in effective sample size), the same effect we would have if we had lost 96 of our 100 subjects! Put another way, for any given value of the effect size index, the *t* is about the same if we have 99 subjects in one group and 1 subject in the other group as if we had 2 subjects in each group.

EFFECT SIZES AND ADJUSTMENTS FOR UNEQUAL SAMPLE SIZES

In the preceding chapter we described a shortcut formula (Equation 12.1) for obtaining an effect size *r* directly from *t* as

$$r = \sqrt{\frac{t^2}{t^2 + df}},$$

where *df* is the degrees of freedom for the *t* statistic, equal to $N - 2$ in the case of two groups that are independent of one another, and $N = n_1 + n_2$.

Similarly, we can estimate Cohen's *d* from *t* and the sample sizes (i.e., n_1 and n_2), because

$$d = \frac{t(n_1 + n_2)}{\sqrt{df}\,\sqrt{n_1 n_2}}. \tag{13.5}$$

When $n_1 = n_2$, Equation 13.5 simplifies to another commonly used formula:

$$d = \frac{2t}{\sqrt{df}}, \tag{13.6}$$

which is useful when the sample sizes are equal, but problematic when they are not. As n_1 and n_2 become increasingly different, Equation 13.6 progressively underestimates Cohen's *d*. This result is indicated in Table 13.2, which shows for eight studies, all with $t = 3.00$ and $df = n_1 + n_2 - 2 = 98$, the increasing underestimation of *d* for increasingly unequal sample sizes when Equation 13.6 is used.

A similar problem is evident when the following (equal-*n*) formula is used to calculate Hedges's *g* from *t*:

$$\text{Hedges's } g = \frac{2t}{\sqrt{N}}, \tag{13.7}$$

as this formula also tends to underestimate the actual *g* as sample sizes grow more and more unequal. Furthermore, even in the presence of a large total *N*, there may be insufficient power to obtain a *p* value at some predetermined level of significance if the sample sizes are unequal. As mentioned in the previous chapter, sample sizes smaller than 30 have frequently been considered acceptable in psychology.

TABLE 13.2
Underestimation of *d* by "equal-*n*" formula

Study	n_1	n_2	Estimated *d*	Accurate *d*	Difference
1	50	50	.61	.61	.00
2	60	40	.61	.62	−.01
3	70	30	.61	.66	−.05
4	80	20	.61	.76	−.15
5	90	10	.61	1.01	−.40
6	95	5	.61	1.39	−.78
7	98	2	.61	2.16	−1.55
8	99	1	.61	3.05	−2.44

Note: For all eight studies, $t = 3.00$ and $df = N - 2 = 98$. The "Estimated *d*" is based on Equation 13.6 (the equal-*n* formula), and the "Accurate *d*" is based on Equation 13.5 (the general formula).

However, it would be difficult (power approximately .12) for effects that are commonly characterized as "small" (Hedges's $g = .20$) or "medium" (Hedges's $g = .50$; power $= .46$) to be found significant at the .05 level when the smaller of the two samples is less than 30.

The ratio of the harmonic mean sample size (n_h) to the arithmetic mean sample size ($\bar{n}$) is a useful index of the retention of power in the unequal-*n* design relative to the equal-*n* design. Subtracting this ratio from unity gives us the proportional loss of relative efficiency (the next-to-last column in Table 13.1), that is,

$$\text{Efficiency loss} = 1 - \left(\frac{n_h}{\bar{n}}\right), \tag{13.8}$$

where the harmonic mean sample size in $k = 2$ samples of n_1 and n_2 size was defined in Equation 12.2 as

$$n_h = \frac{2n_1 n_2}{n_1 + n_2}.$$

Because the harmonic mean sample size equals the arithmetic mean sample size when $n_1 = n_2$, the ratio of n_h to $\bar{n}$ is always 1.0 in equal-*n* designs, and Equation 13.8 therefore yields a value of zero loss in such designs. In samples of unequal sizes, the harmonic mean is less than the arithmetic mean, and so the value given by Equation 13.8 increases with corresponding increases in the inequality of the sample sizes. We obtain the effective loss of total sample size (the last column in Table 13.1) by multiplying Equation 13.8 by the total *N*:

$$\text{Effective loss of } N = N\left[1 - \left(\frac{n_h}{\bar{n}}\right)\right], \tag{13.9}$$

which, as implied before, is relevant to considerations of cost when the cost per sampling unit is constant. For example, as shown in Table 13.1, a 60:40 split of 100 cases is equivalent to losing 4 of 100 total cases, whereas an 85:15 split is equivalent to losing virtually half the total *N*.

Regardless of whether the two samples are equal or unequal in size, the valid estimate of Hedges's g is always given by Equation 2.5:

$$\text{Hedges's } g = \frac{M_1 - M_2}{S_{\text{pooled}}},$$

and the valid estimate of Cohen's d is always given by Equation 2.4:

$$\text{Cohen's } d = \frac{M_1 - M_2}{\sigma_{\text{pooled}}}.$$

Both these indices of effect size can also be transformed back and forth, whether the sample sizes are equal or unequal. We convert Hedges's g into Cohen's d by

$$\text{Cohen's } d = g\sqrt{\frac{N}{df_{\text{within}}}} \qquad (13.10)$$

and Cohen's d into Hedges's g by

$$\text{Hedges's } g = d\sqrt{\frac{df_{\text{within}}}{N}}. \qquad (13.11)$$

Suppose our hypothesis is that treating subjects with a particular clinical intervention (the experimental treatment) will, relative to nonintervention (the control), result in improvement on some psychological criterion. There are 50 subjects in each randomly assigned condition, with resulting mean scores of $M_1 = 6.0$ and $M_2 = 4.8$, respectively, in the experimental and control groups, and we will assume $S_{\text{within}} = 2.0$. The valid Hedges's g is

$$\text{Hedges's } g = \frac{M_1 - M_2}{S} = \frac{6.0 - 4.8}{2.0} = 0.60.$$

And since

$$\sigma_{\text{within}} = S_{\text{within}}\sqrt{\frac{df_{\text{within}}}{N}}, \qquad (13.12)$$

which gives

$$\sigma_{\text{within}} = 2.0\sqrt{\frac{98}{100}} = 1.98,$$

the valid Cohen's d is

$$\text{Cohen's } d = \frac{M_1 - M_2}{\sigma_{\text{pooled}}} = \frac{6.0 - 4.8}{1.98} = 0.61$$

Transforming our Hedges's g of .60 into Cohen's d by Equation 13.10, we find

$$\text{Cohen's } d = 0.60\sqrt{\frac{100}{98}} = 0.61,$$

and transforming our d of 0.61 into Hedges's g by Equation 13.11, we find

$$\text{Hedges's } g = 0.61\sqrt{\frac{98}{100}} = 0.60.$$

However, the expression used to obtain Hedges's g from t (Equation 13.7) needs adjustment for the loss in relative efficiency (Rosenthal, Rosnow, & Rubin, 2000). In an unequal-n design, we obtain Hedges's g from t by

$$\text{Hedges's } g = \left(\frac{2t}{\sqrt{N}} \right) \sqrt{\frac{\bar{n}}{n_h}}. \tag{13.13}$$

Similarly, in an unequal-n design we need an adjustment to obtain Cohen's d from t:

$$\text{Cohen's } d = \left(\frac{2t}{\sqrt{df_{\text{within}}}} \right) \sqrt{\frac{\bar{n}}{n_h}}. \tag{13.14}$$

In an equal-n design, it makes no difference whether we use the equal-n or unequal-n formula. For example, with $t = 3.00$, $df = 98$, $n_1 = n_2 = 50$, and Hedges's $g = .60$ from equal-n Equation 13.7, the value of Hedges's g is unchanged by our use of Equation 13.13, since $\bar{n}/n_h = 1.0$ when sample sizes are equal.

We also require an adjustment when transforming Hedges's g into the point-biserial effect size r in an unequal-n design:

$$r_{\text{pb}} = \frac{g}{\sqrt{g^2 + 4\left(\dfrac{\bar{n}}{n_h} \right) \left(\dfrac{df_{\text{within}}}{N} \right)}}. \tag{13.15}$$

In our example, with means of 6.0 and 4.8, sample sizes of 85 and 15, and valid $g = 0.60$, Equation 13.15 gives

$$r = \frac{0.60}{\sqrt{(0.60)^2 + 4\left(\dfrac{50}{25.5} \right) \left(\dfrac{98}{100} \right)}} = .21.$$

To transform Cohen's d into the point-biserial effect size r in an unequal-n design, we use the following modification:

$$r_{\text{pb}} = \frac{d}{\sqrt{d^2 + 4\left(\dfrac{\bar{n}}{n_h} \right)}}. \tag{13.16}$$

So with means of 6.0 and 4.8, sample sizes of 85 and 15, and valid $d = 0.61$, Equation 13.16 gives

$$r = \frac{0.61}{\sqrt{(0.61)^2 + 4\left(\dfrac{50}{25.5} \right)}} = .21$$

INTERPRETING THE INDEPENDENT SAMPLE t

Researchers ordinarily like to get large t values from their investigations, because larger t values are rarer events (i.e., they are less likely to occur if the null hypothesis is true). As we stated at the beginning of this chapter, two major ways of thinking about the null hypothesis for the t test situation are that (a) the means do not differ in the populations from which we have randomly sampled the subjects, and (b) there is no relationship between the independent variable of group membership and the dependent, or response, variable. As an illustration of these two ways of thinking about the null hypothesis, imagine that we have two populations of patients requiring treatment for some problem. The populations are identical in all ways except that the sampled members of one population have received Procedure A, and sampled members of the other population have received Procedure B. The null hypothesis would be true in our first way of thinking if the mean benefit score of the population receiving A is identical to that of the population receiving B. The null hypothesis would be true in our second way of thinking if the correlation between the treatment condition (coded, e.g., A = 1, B = 0) and the benefit score is exactly zero for the members of Populations A and B combined.

We think of the *t* test as a single test of statistical significance, and so it is in terms of the equations we have described. Gosset's idea, however, was that we should think of the *t* test as a family of tests of significance, a family of infinite size. That is, there is a different distribution of *t* for every possible value of *df*. The two most extreme *t* distributions are those when *df* = 1 and *df* = ∞. When *df* = ∞, the *t* distribution is the normal distribution. When *df* = 1, the *t* distribution is lower in frequency in the center and higher in frequency in the tails, so that it takes a larger *t* to reach the same level of significance than it does when *df* is larger. Figure 13.1 shows the two most extreme *t* distributions.

The vast majority of all *t* distributions look much more like the normal distribution than like the *t* distribution when *df* = 1, and it is only when *df* is quite small that the divergence from normality is marked. All *t* distributions, however, resemble the standard normal distribution in (a) being symmetrical; (b) being centered at zero, so that half the values are positive and the other half are negative; (c) having their greatest frequency near the center of the distribution; and (d) having tails that never quite touch down (the upper and lower limits are ±∞). Table 13.3 illustrates the differences in *t* distributions by giving the areas found in the upper tail (the right-hand tail) of selected *t* distributions. (More extensive tables of *t*

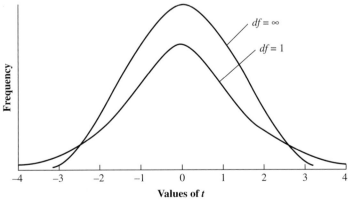

FIGURE 13.1
The two most extreme *t* distributions.

TABLE 13.3

t values required for significance at various p levels

df			One-tailed p			
	.25	.10	.05	.025	.005	.001
1	1.00	3.08	6.31	12.71	63.66	318.31
2	.82	1.89	2.92	4.30	9.92	22.33
3	.76	1.64	2.35	3.18	5.84	10.21
4	.74	1.53	2.13	2.78	4.60	7.17
5	.73	1.48	2.02	2.57	4.03	5.89
6	.72	1.44	1.94	2.45	3.71	5.21
8	.71	1.40	1.86	2.31	3.36	4.50
10	.70	1.37	1.81	2.23	3.17	4.14
15	.69	1.34	1.75	2.13	2.95	3.73
20	.69	1.32	1.72	2.09	2.84	3.55
25	.68	1.32	1.71	2.06	2.79	3.45
30	.68	1.31	1.70	2.04	2.75	3.38
40	.68	1.30	1.68	2.02	2.70	3.31
60	.68	1.30	1.67	2.00	2.66	3.23
80	.68	1.29	1.66	1.99	2.64	3.20
100	.68	1.29	1.66	1.98	2.63	3.17
1000	.68	1.28	1.65	1.96	2.58	3.10
10,000	.68	1.28	1.64	1.96	2.58	3.09
∞	.67	1.28	1.64	1.96	2.58	3.09

values are in Appendix B, i.e., Tables B.2 and B.3.) Studying Table 13.3, we see that for any level of significance (p), the t value that is required to reach that level becomes smaller as the value of df increases. Of course, for any given df, a higher t value is required to reach more extreme (smaller) p levels. Perhaps the most surprising fact about this table is the difference in t values required to reach the .001 level. When the df is quite large, a t of only about 3 is required, but when $df = 1$, a t of about 318 is required!

Another way to think about t is that if the null hypothesis were true (i.e., the means of the populations did not differ, or there were an r of zero between group membership and scores on the dependent variable), the most likely value of t would be zero. But even if the population mean difference were truly zero, we would often find nonzero t values by sheer chance. For example, with $df = 8$, we would obtain a t value of 1.40 or more about 10% of the time, or a t of 1.86 or more about 5% of the time, or a t of 4.50 or more about 0.1% (one-tenth of one percent) of the time.

We must decide for ourselves whether we will regard any given t as an event rare enough to make us doubt that the null hypothesis is true. The larger the t and the smaller the p, the less likely it is that the null hypothesis is true. As discussed earlier, American behavioral researchers have an informal agreement to regard as "statistically significant" t values (and other tests of statistical significance) with associated p levels of .05 or less (i.e., $p \leq .05$). There is evidence that decisions to believe or not to believe (accept or reject) the null hypothesis are made in a binary manner based simply on whether p does or does not reach the .05 level (Minturn, Lansky, & Dember, 1972; Nelson, Rosenthal, & Rosnow, 1986; Rosenthal & Gaito, 1963, 1964; Zuckerman, Hodgins, Zuckerman, & Rosenthal, 1993). As we commented earlier, there is something absurd in regarding as a "real" effect one that is supported by $p = .05$ and as a zero effect one that is supported by $p = .06$, and yet this binary decision process does occur. Thus, it is helpful to keep in mind the general relationship that Significance test = Size of effect × Size of study, as it is also a reminder that we can achieve any level of significance desired by adding to the size of the study so long as the true effect size is not exactly zero.

COMPUTING THE INDEPENDENT SAMPLE t

In this chapter we have already provided a number of formulas for computing t, namely, Equations 13.1, 13.2, 13.3, and 13.4. Each is useful in a particular situation in which we have not the original data, but summary data such as the r, means, S, σ, Cohen's d, Hedges's g, sample sizes, or df. In chapter 11 we gave a more generally useful formula for a t test designed to compare the sample means of two independent populations, with the population variability unknown (but presumed to be equal, or nearly so, in both populations). That formula (Equation 11.9) was as follows:

$$t = \frac{M_1 - M_2}{\sqrt{\left(\frac{1}{n_1} + \frac{1}{n_2}\right)S^2_{pooled}}},$$

where S^2 is the pooled estimate of the population variance, computed as

$$S^2 = \frac{\Sigma(X_1 - M_1)^2 + \Sigma(X_2 - M_2)^2}{n_1 + n_2 - 2}, \tag{13.17}$$

or, given the sums of the squared scores, as

$$S^2 = \frac{\left(\Sigma X_1^2 - \frac{(\Sigma X_1)^2}{n_1}\right) + \left(\Sigma X_2^2 - \frac{(\Sigma X_2)^2}{n_2}\right)}{n_1 + n_2 - 2}. \tag{13.18}$$

Notice that Equation 11.9 is similar to Equation 13.1. However, whereas Equation 13.1 separates the effect size estimate from the index of the size of the study, Equation 11.9 is written more compactly, reducing the t to a kind of "signal-to-noise" ratio, where the *signal* refers to the magnitude of the difference between two independent means, and the *noise* is implied by the standard error of the difference. We will see this compact formula again in the next chapter.

The basic data for these computations appear in Table 13.4, which lists the scores of four subjects in Group 1 under X_1, and the scores of four independent others in Group 2 under X_2. The $(X_1 - M_1)^2$ and $(X_2 - M_2)^2$ columns list, for each subject, the squared

TABLE 13.4
Basic data for computation of independent sample *t*

	Group 1			Group 2		
	X_1	$X_1 - M_1$	$(X_1 - M_1)^2$	X_2	$X_2 - M_2$	$(X_2 - M_2)^2$
	2	−1.5	2.25	1	−0.5	0.25
	3	−0.5	0.25	2	0.5	0.25
	4	0.5	0.25	1	−0.5	0.25
	5	1.5	2.25	2	0.5	0.25
Σ	14	0	5.00	6	0	1.00
M	3.5	0		1.5	0	

deviation of that individual's score from the group mean. In the next to last row we see the sum of squares of the deviations of the scores from the group means: $\Sigma(X_1 - M_1)^2 = 5.00$ for Group 1, and $\Sigma(X_2 - M_2)^2 = 1.00$ for Group 2. From Equation 13.17, we find

$$S^2 = \frac{5.00 + 1.00}{4 + 4 - 2} = 1.00,$$

and from the more compactly written formula for *t* (Equation 11.9), we find

$$t = \frac{3.5 - 1.5}{\sqrt{\left(\frac{1}{4} + \frac{1}{4}\right)1.00}} = \frac{2}{\sqrt{.5}} = 2.83,$$

which, with 6 *df*, has an associated one-tailed *p* of .015.

For the alternative Equation 13.18, we need the sum of scores and the sum of the squared scores in each group. Table 13.4 shows the sum of the scores in Group 1 to be $\Sigma X_1 = 14$, and in Group 2 to be $\Sigma X_2 = 6$. Squaring the raw scores in Group 1 (2, 3, 4, 5) gives us 4, 9, 16, 25, and these sum to $\Sigma X_1^2 = 54$. In Group 2, squaring the individual scores (1, 2, 1, 2) gives us 1, 4, 1, 4, which sum to $\Sigma X_2^2 = 10$. Substitution in Equation 13.18 yields

$$S^2 = \frac{\left[54 - \frac{(14)^2}{4}\right] + \left[10 - \frac{(6)^2}{4}\right]}{4 + 4 - 2} = \frac{5 + 1}{6} = 1.00$$

REPORTING THE RESULTS

When reporting the *t* and related results, we have several options. In all cases, however, we want to provide sufficient information to give a complete picture of our findings. To accomplish this, we should report not only the *t*, but also the group means, the standard deviations, the size of each sample, a confidence interval for each mean, and an effect size index (e.g., *r*, *d*, or *g*) and its confidence interval. To illustrate with another set of results, suppose that $M_1 = 12$ and $M_2 = 10$, the sample estimate of the population standard deviation is $S = 4$ in each group, and $n_1 = n_2 = 36$. In

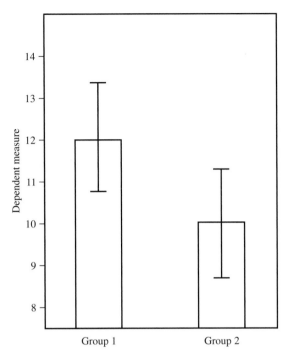

FIGURE 13.2
Bar graph emphasizing group means and 95% confidence intervals.

chapter 9 we described the calculation of a 95% confidence interval of a mean (see Equation 9.1). Repeating that procedure, we conclude there is a 95% probability that the population mean estimated by $M_1 = 12$ is between 10.65 and 13.35, and there is a similar 95% probability that the population mean estimated by $M_2 = 10$ is between 8.65 and 11.35. Figure 13.2 shows what these results might look like in a sample bar graph, where the thin error bars show the 95% confidence limits. The more the overlap in the error bars, the less likely it is that the means are significantly different at the .05 alpha (see also Masson & Loftus, 2003). The ordinate axis is more compact than that generally recommended in the *Publication Manual of the American Psychological Association* (2001), which suggests that the zero point be indicated.

We have several options in our choice of an effect size index, including r, Cohen's d, and Hedges's g, all of which can be directly obtained from t with the formulas given earlier, the t being computed as

$$ t = \frac{M_1 - M_2}{\sqrt{\left(\frac{1}{n_1} + \frac{1}{n_2}\right)S^2}} = \frac{12 - 10}{\sqrt{\left(\frac{1}{36} + \frac{1}{36}\right)16}} = 2.12, $$

and $df = n_1 + n_2 - 2 = 70$, $p = .019$ one-tailed. Thus, we estimate the point-biserial effect size r from t by the shortcut formula (Equation 12.1), where

$$ r = \sqrt{\frac{t^2}{t^2 + df}} = \sqrt{\frac{(2.12)^2}{(2.12)^2 + 70}} = .246. $$

Using the procedure in Equation 11.3 to compute the 95% *CI*, we first find in Table B.7 that $r = .246$ has an equivalent z_r of .25. With $N = 72$ and critical two-tailed $Z_{(.05)} = 1.96$, we calculate that $.25 \pm 1.96/\sqrt{72 - 3} = .25 \pm .24$, indicating that the 95% *CI* in units of z_r ranges from .01 to .49. Using Table B.8 to convert these z_r values back to units of r, we conclude with a 95% probability that the *CI* ranges from $r = .01$ to .45.

Suppose instead we wanted to express the size of effect as Cohen's *d*. We know that $S = 4$ in each group, and we compute σ_{pooled} from Equation 13.12:

$$\sigma_{within} = S_{within} \sqrt{\frac{df_{within}}{N}} = 4\sqrt{\frac{70}{72}} = 3.944,$$

so

$$\text{Cohen's } d = \frac{M_1 - M_2}{\sigma_{pooled}} = \frac{12 - 10}{3.944} = .507.$$

The 95% confidence interval of Cohen's *d* is computed as

$$95\% \ CI = d \pm t_{(.05)} (S_{\text{Cohen's d}}), \tag{13.19}$$

where $t_{(.05)}$ is the critical value of *t* at $p = .05$ two-tailed for our *df* of $n_1 + n_2 - 2 = 70$, which Table B.3 indicates as 1.994 (in the column headed $p = .025$, because this is a one-tailed table). We find the square root of the variance of Cohen's *d* from

$$S^2_{\text{Cohen's d}} = \left[\frac{n_1 + n_2}{n_1 n_2} + \frac{d^2}{2df} \right] \frac{n_1 + n_2}{df}, \tag{13.20}$$

so

$$S^2_{\text{Cohen's d}} = \left[\frac{36 + 36}{(36)(36)} + \frac{.507^2}{2(70)} \right] \frac{36 + 36}{70} = .059,$$

and then we find $S_{\text{Cohen's d}} = \sqrt{S^2_{\text{Cohen's d}}} = \sqrt{.059} = .243$. Fom Equation 13.19, we find

$$95\% \ CI = .507 \pm 1.994(.243) = .507 \pm .485,$$

which tells us there is a 95% probability that the population value of Cohen's *d* is between .022 and .992.

Had we chosen Hedges's *g*, we would obtain it directly from

$$\text{Hedges's } g = \frac{M_1 - M_2}{S} = \frac{12 - 10}{4} = .500,$$

and for the 95% *CI*, we redefine $S_{\text{Cohen's d}}$ in Equation 13.19 to be $S_{\text{Hedges's g}}$. Then, because

$$S^2_{\text{Hedges's g}} = \frac{n_1 + n_2}{n_1 n_2} + \frac{g^2}{2df}, \tag{13.21}$$

we find

$$S^2_{\text{Hedges's g}} = \frac{36 + 36}{(36)(36)} + \frac{.500^2}{140} = .057$$

and $S_{\text{Hedges's g}} = \sqrt{S^2_{\text{Hedges's g}}} = \sqrt{.057} = .239$. Hence, the 95% $CI = .500 \pm 1.994(.239)$ $= .500 \pm .477$, so the lower and upper limits of Hedges's g are .023 and .977.

Notice that not only is the value of Cohen's d slightly larger than the value of Hedges's g, but the confidence interval of d is also larger than that for Hedges's g. The reason is that Cohen's d uses N for the denominator of the estimated variance to obtain the standard deviation, whereas Hedges's g uses $N - 1$. Of course, as the sample sizes grow larger, the difference between d and g becomes smaller. A word of caution: These confidence intervals are based on assumptions about the t distribution, which are discussed later in this chapter. Although the t test is a robust statistic, serious violations of assumptions may jeopardize the accuracy of these estimates. In addition, when the samples are biased in some way (e.g., volunteer subject bias), the problem may be compounded. We know it is often possible to hypothesize the direction of volunteer bias (chapter 9), but we almost never know the magnitude of the actual bias. The good news is that when sampling biases are small, even biased samples may provide tolerable estimates of population parameters (Snedecor & Cochran, 1989).

t TESTS FOR NONINDEPENDENT SAMPLES

So far in our discussion of the t tests used to compare the means of two groups, we have assumed the two groups of scores to be independent. That is, we thought of the scores in one group as having no relationship to the scores in the other group. Suppose, for example, that the members of the two groups are children aged 10 to 11 who have been rated by judges on a 5-point scale of sociability. If Group 1 is girls and Group 2 is boys, might we still not conclude that the children of Groups 1 and 2 are independent of each other? But what if the four boys and the four girls all come from just four families, as indicated in Table 13.5?

When we examine the girls' and boys' scores over the four families, we find that a family member's sociability score is to some degree predictable from family membership. We see, for example, that the Smith children are judged to be most sociable, and the Brown children are judged to be least sociable. For these

TABLE 13.5
Sociability scores

Family	Girls (Group 1)	Boys (Group 2)	M
Brown	2	1	1.5
Clark	3	2	2.5
Jones	4	1	2.5
Smith	5	2	3.5
M	3.5	1.5	2.5

data, then, common family membership has introduced a degree of relatedness between the observations of Group 1 and Group 2. Other ways in which a degree of correlation might have been introduced include membership in the same dyad, as when female and male couple members are to be compared with each other. Perhaps the most common example is a repeated-measures design, in which the same subjects are each measured more than once. Suppose they are measured twice, for example, once before and once after having been exposed to a learning experience, or perhaps once after a treatment condition and once after a control condition.

Whenever pairs of observations *could* have been lined up next to each other because they are from the same family or the same dyad, or are of the same person, but were *not* lined up next to each other, computing an independent t typically results in a t value that is too small. The reason is that in these situations there is usually a positive correlation between scores earned by the two paired observations. In the example in Table 13.5, correlating the scores of 2, 3, 4, 5 (Group 1) with the scores of 1, 2, 1, 2 (Group 2) would give us $r = .45$. Had the correlation been negative rather than positive, computing an independent t would give a t value that was too large (Kenny & Judd, 1986).

When computing t tests for correlated data (or matched pairs, or repeated measurements), we perform our calculations not on the original $n_1 + n_2$ scores, but on the *differences* between the n_1 and n_2 scores. Table 13.6 shows each difference score (D), where $D = X_1 - X_2$ for each pair of lined-up scores. For the Brown siblings, for example, $X_1 = 2$ and $X_2 = 1$, and $D = 2 - 1 = 1$. The mean of the four D scores is $M_D = 2$. The column headed $D - M_D$ shows the differences between the D scores and the M_D of 2. For the Brown children, $D - M_D = 1 - 2 = -1$. The last column has the squared differences between the D scores and M_D, with the sum of these squared differences indicated as $\Sigma(D - M_D)^2 = 4$. We perform the following calculation of t, with $df = N - 1$:

$$t = \frac{M_D}{\sqrt{\left(\frac{1}{N}\right)S_D^2}}, \tag{13.22}$$

TABLE 13.6
Basic data for paired sample t test

Family	X_1 (girls)	X_2 (boys)	D	$D - M_D$	$(D - M_D)^2$
Brown	2	1	1	−1	1
Clark	3	2	1	−1	1
Jones	4	1	3	1	1
Smith	5	2	3	1	1
Sum	14	6	8	0	$\Sigma(D - M_D)^2 = 4$
Mean	3.5	1.5	$M_D = 2$		

where N is the number of D scores, and S_D^2 is the unbiased estimate of the population value of σ_D^2, computed as

$$S_D^2 = \frac{\Sigma(D - M_D)^2}{N - 1}. \tag{13.23}$$

Substituting in Equation 13.23, we find $S_D^2 = 4/(4 - 1) = 1.333$, and then from Equation 13.22 we find

$$t = \frac{2}{\sqrt{\left(\frac{1}{4}\right)1.333}} = 3.46.$$

Notice that the X_1 and X_2 scores in Table 13.6 are identical to those in Table 13.4. The difference is that we assumed the two groups were independent in Table 13.4, and then found $t = 2.83$ for independent means, which with 6 df was significant at about the .02 level, one-tailed test. In the case of the matched-pair t of 3.46 for the same raw scores, our df are not $n_1 + n_2 - 2 = 6$, because we operated on only a single sample of four difference scores, and so $df = N - 1 = 3$. For a t of 3.46 and $df = 3$, our p value is still about .02, because our larger t was offset by the loss of 3 df. Ordinarily, the sample sizes are larger than in this illustration, and when the data of the two groups are highly correlated, we find substantial increases in the value of t accompanied by substantially lower (more "significant") p levels. One other point regarding Equation 13.22: It can also be used when a single set of scores is to be compared with some theoretical mean. Then we can form a D score for each subject by subtracting the specific theoretical mean from each person's obtained score; that is, D would equal the X obtained minus the mean (M) hypothesized by the theory.

If we are interested in the 95% confidence limits of the mean difference (M_D), we use the following procedure in a paired design:

$$95\% \ CI = M_D \pm t_{(0.5)} (S_D)/\sqrt{N}, \tag{13.24}$$

where $t_{(.05)}$ is the critical two-tailed t for $df = N - 1$, and S_D is the square root of S_D^2 in Equation 13.23. For the data above, where $M_D = 2$, $S_D = 1.155$, and $N = 4$, we find in Table B.2 that, with $df = 3$, the critical value of t is 3.182, and thus

$$95\% \ CI = 2 \pm (3.182)(1.155)/2 = 2 \pm 1.84,$$

which gives lower and upper limits of M_D as 0.16 and 3.84.

EFFECT SIZE AND STUDY SIZE COMPONENTS OF NONINDEPENDENT SAMPLE t

Just as the independent t was shown to consist of two components, a similar relationship can be shown for the t test for nonindependent samples. Because Significance test = Size of study $\times$ Size of effect, one way to show this relationship is by

$$t = \frac{M_D}{S_D} \times \sqrt{N}, \tag{13.25}$$

where the size-of-effect component is the mean of the D scores (M_D) divided by S_D, the square root of the value of S_D^2 computed by Equation 13.23, and this quantity is weighted by the square root of the number of difference scores (N). Using the example in the previous section, where $S_D^2 = 1.333$, and thus, $S_D = \sqrt{1.333} = 1.155$, from Equation 13.25 we find

$$t = \frac{2}{1.155} \times \sqrt{4} = 3.46,$$

which, of course, is the same value of t that we obtained using Equation 13.22.

An alternative way of representing the relationship of t for correlated observations to size of effect and size of study is

$$t = d \times \sqrt{df}, \tag{13.26}$$

where the size-of-effect component is Cohen's d, the mean of the difference scores divided by the σ of the difference scores:

$$\text{Cohen's } d = \frac{M_D}{\sigma_D}, \tag{13.27}$$

and because for the data in Table 13.6, $\sigma_D = 1.00$, therefore Cohen's $d = 2/1.00 = 2$. Keeping in mind that for matched pairs there are N pairs to operate on (rather than $n_1 + n_2$ observations), using Equation 13.25 with $df = N - 1$, we find $t = 2 \times \sqrt{3} = 3.46$.

Our own preference (for the various reasons stated earlier) is to express the effect size in units of r, in which case another way of representing the relationship between the size of effect and the size of study for the t for correlated observations is the familiar one first introduced in chapter 2 and discussed earlier in this chapter (i.e., Equation 2.2):

$$t = \frac{r}{\sqrt{1 - r^2}} \times \sqrt{df}.$$

When we use this equation in the context of the nonindependent t, the r is understood as a partial correlation, that is, the correlation between membership in group (girls vs. boys) and observed score *corrected for family membership*. The r does not refer to the correlation between the first and second measurement made within families, dyads, or individuals. It also does not refer to the correlation of the eight scores "uncorrected" for family membership with membership in the groups (girls vs. boys). If we compute this r (scoring, e.g., girls $= 1$, boys $= 0$), we obtain the point-biserial r corresponding to the t test for uncorrelated observations, with $r = .756$ rather than .894, which we simply calculated from Equation 12.1 (with $df = N - 1$) as

$$r = \sqrt{\frac{t^2}{t^2 + df}} = \sqrt{\frac{(3.46)^2}{(3.46)^2 + 3}} = .894$$

As the interpretation of this value is not transparent, it requires some further explanation of where we get an effect size r for the treatment or group effect for matched pairs. One way to understand where we get this r is by "correcting" the original data for the systematic effects of membership in a particular pair (e.g., the family, dyad, or individual that generated the two scores). We accomplish this by subtracting for each member of a pair the mean of the two pair members, a procedure that eliminates any differences between the means of families, dyads, or individuals. Having thus removed statistically (or *partialed out*) the effect of belonging to a particular pair, we compute the point-biserial r between group membership (coded as 0, 1, or as -1, $+1$, for example) and the corrected observed score. In the process of correcting for pair membership, we lose all the df for pairs, however. Because in our example there are four pairs, we lose $4 - 1 = 3$ df in the process of computing r from our pair-corrected, or residual (i.e., leftover), scores. Part A of Table 13.7 shows the calculation of the corrected mean scores for girls (X_1) and boys (X_2). Part B of this table shows the Z-scored dummy-coded values of gender (the predictor variable, designated X) and the Z-scored "corrected" scores of $N = 8$ subjects (the dependent variable, designated as Y), and in the last column we see the products of these Z scores, which sum to 7.16. Then, from Equation 11.1, we find

$$r_{xy} = \frac{\Sigma Z_x Z_y}{N} = \frac{7.16}{8} = .895.$$

TABLE 13.7

Correlation after correction for family membership

A. Means corrected for family membership

Family	Girls (X_1)	Boys (X_2)	M	$M_{corrected}$ $X_1 - M$	$X_2 - M$
Brown	2	1	1.5	+0.5	−0.5
Clark	3	2	2.5	+0.5	−0.5
Jones	4	1	2.5	+1.5	−1.5
Smith	5	2	3.5	+1.5	−1.5
Σ	14	6	10.00	4.0	−4.0
M	3.5	1.5	2.5	1.0	−1.0

B. Z-scored independent and dependent variables

Child	Gender (1 = female; 0 = male) X	Score (corrected) Y	Gender Z_x	Score Z_y	$Z_x Z_y$
1	1	0.5	1	0.45	0.45
2	1	0.5	1	0.45	0.45
3	1	1.5	1	1.34	1.34
4	1	1.5	1	1.34	1.34
5	0	−0.5	−1	−0.45	0.45
6	0	−0.5	−1	−0.45	0.45
7	0	−1.5	−1	−1.34	1.34
8	0	−1.5	−1	−1.34	1.34
Σ	4	0	0	0	7.16

TABLE 13.8

Table of variance

Source	SS	df	MS	F	t	r
Pairs	4	3	1.333			
Gender groups	8	1	8.000	12.00	3.46	.894
Residual or error	2	3	0.667			

In the next chapter and in subsequent chapters, we turn to analysis of variance, which is another way to understand where we get the r for the size of the treatment or group effect for the matched-pairs t test. In this approach we compute the "sums of squares" for the group or condition effect and for the "error term" for the group or condition effect, and then find r as

$$r = \sqrt{\frac{SS_{\text{groups}}}{SS_{\text{groups}} + SS_{\text{error}}}}. \tag{13.28}$$

For the present data, Table 13.8 shows the table of variance, and from Equation 13.28 we find

$$r = \sqrt{\frac{8}{8 + 2}} = \sqrt{.80} = .894.$$

Therefore, our r based on the computation from residuals (i.e., differences between scores and family means) agrees within rounding error with our r based on the analysis of variance. The process of correcting for pair membership will be described further in chapter 16, where we deal with the two-way analysis of variance.

The estimation of confidence intervals for effect sizes in association with nonindependent means is currently a matter of debate, but we can show what the effect size would look like as a binomial effect-size display (BESD). This is shown in Table 13.9, where once again we see that the BESD sets the marginal totals at 100. In the upper left cell, the 95 is calculated as $100(.50 + r/2)$, where r is our effect size of .894 rounded to .90. In the upper right cell, 5 is calculated as $100(.50 - r/2)$. The difference between 95 and 5, divided by 100, is the rounded effect size r.

TABLE 13.9

BESD for results in Table 13.7

	More sociable	Less sociable	Row sum
Girls	95	5	100
Boys	5	95	100
Column sum	100	100	

ASSUMPTIONS UNDERLYING *t* TESTS

Several statistical assumptions are made in the use of *t* tests, and to the extent that these assumptions are not met, we may make incorrect inferences from *t* tests. The basic assumptions are sometimes summarized by the statement that errors are IID normal, where *errors* refers to the deviation of each score from the mean of its group or condition, and *IID normal* is read as "independently and identically distributed in a normal distribution" (Box, Hunter, & Hunter, 1978, p. 78). The shorthand format of *IID normal* translates into three assumptions about the distribution of observations within conditions ("errors"). The same three assumptions underlying the *t* test are also relevant to the *F* test, which we turn to in the next chapter.

1. *The errors are independent (independence).* If the errors are not independent of one another, the *t* we obtain may be spurious. For example, if observations are strongly positively correlated, the obtained *t* may be several times larger than the accurate *t* (Snedecor & Cochran, 1989). Correlations among errors can be introduced in many ways. Suppose that we want to compare two types of group therapy. We assign 30 patients to each of the two types and within each type assign 10 patients to each of three groups. It might turn out that being in the same therapy group has made the patients in each group "too much alike," so that they are no longer independent or uncorrelated. If that is so, thinking that we had 30 independent units in each condition could be quite misleading. In such a situation we may have to regard *groups* rather than persons as our sampling units, and we would then suffer a loss of *df* from $30 + 30 - 2 = 58$ down to $3 + 3 - 2 = 4$. In this case, each person within a group would be seen as a "repeated measurement" of each group. The analysis of such data is considered in chapter 18. A valuable discussion of problems of independence can be found in the work of Charles Judd and David Kenny (1981; Kenny & Judd, 1986).

2. *The errors are identically distributed (homogeneity of variance).* For the *t* test situation in which two groups are being compared, the *t* obtained will be more accurate if the variances of the populations from which the data were drawn are more nearly equal. Only if the population variances are very different *and* if the two sample sizes are very different is the violation of this assumption likely to lead to serious consequences. One approach to this problem is to make the variances in the two samples more nearly equal and then perform the *t* test on the transformed data. The most commonly used transformations involve taking the square roots, logs, reciprocal square root, and reciprocals of the original data. Details are given, for example, in Box, Hunter, and Hunter (1978) and Tukey (1977). Tukey described a "ladder of powers" to which to raise and thus "reexpress" the raw data, ranging from X^3 to X^{-3}, where X is a raw score. We will return to this procedure when we discuss factorial designs in chapter 16, as transformations can also be of value in removing complexities and simplifying relationships, such as interactions in analysis of variance, which can sometimes be simplified to linear relationships by transformations.

   When suitable transformations are unavailable or are ineffective, a serviceable way to make an independent *t* more accurate is to use Satterthwaite's approximate method (Snedecor & Cochran, 1989). This method can be employed either for continuous data or for dichotomous (0, 1) data and involves (a) a modified computational formula for t and (b) an estimate of the adjusted df with which to enter the t table along with the modified t. We first compute t from

$$t = \frac{M_1 - M_2}{\sqrt{\dfrac{S_1^2}{n_1} + \dfrac{S_2^2}{n_2}}}, \qquad (13.29)$$

where S_1^2 and S_2^2 are the within-group sample variances based on $n_1 - 1$ and $n_2 - 1$ degrees of freedom, respectively. We then enter a t table with this value and with the Satterthwaite-adjusted df, obtained as follows:

$$df_{\text{Satterthwaite}} = \frac{\left[\dfrac{S_1^2}{n_1} + \dfrac{S_2^2}{n_2}\right]^2}{\left[\dfrac{\left(S_1^2/n_1\right)^2}{n_1 - 1} + \dfrac{\left(S_2^2/n_2\right)^2}{n_2 - 1}\right]} \qquad (13.30)$$

For an illustration of the use of dichotomous data, consider an experiment in which 10 patients were assigned at random to a treatment condition, and the remaining 20 patients were assigned to a control condition. Patients who improved were scored as 1, and those who did not improve were scored as 0, with the summary results shown in Table 13.10. We first compute t from Equation 13.29:

$$t = \frac{.50 - .05}{\sqrt{\dfrac{.2778}{10} + \dfrac{.0500}{20}}} = 2.59.$$

Before entering a table of t, we must compute the adjusted degrees of freedom from Equation 13.30:

$$df_{\text{Satterthwaite}} = \frac{\left[\dfrac{.2778}{10} + \dfrac{.0500}{20}\right]^2}{\left[\dfrac{\left(.2778/10\right)^2}{10 - 1} + \dfrac{\left(.0500/20\right)^2}{20 - 1}\right]}$$

$$= \frac{.000917}{[.0000857 + .000000329]} = 10.6,$$

TABLE 13.10

Results based on dichotomous data

	Improved	Not improved	Σ	M	S^2
Treated	5	5	10	.50	.2778
Controls	1	19	20	.05	.0500
Σ	6	24	30		

which we truncate to the next lower integer, 10. We now enter our *t* table with $t = 2.59$ and $df = 10$ to find $p = .013$ one tailed. Had we computed *t* from Equation 11.9, we would have found

$$t = \frac{M_1 - M_2}{\sqrt{\left(\frac{1}{n_1} + \frac{1}{n_2}\right)s^2}} = \frac{.50 - .05}{\sqrt{\left(\frac{1}{10} + \frac{1}{20}\right).1232}} = 3.31,$$

which, with $df = n_1 + n_2 - 2 = 28$, has an associated one-tailed p of .0013, a substantially more significant value, but inappropriately so. To compute the effect size r from t, we use the Satterthwaite t of 2.59, the original degrees of freedom $(n_1 + n_2 - 2)$, and Equation 12.1, that is,

$$r = \sqrt{\frac{t^2}{t^2 + df}} = \sqrt{\frac{(2.59)^2}{(2.59)^2 + 28}} = .44$$

3. *The errors are normally distributed (normality).* When there is extreme nonnormality in the distribution of the errors, some inaccuracy may be introduced into the *t* test. However, if the distributions are not *too* skewed, or not *too* bimodal, there seems to be little cause for concern unless the sample sizes are tiny (Hays, 1994).

NONPARAMETRIC PROCEDURES

Many experimenters use **nonparametric statistical tests** to compare treatment and control groups in research with small samples. Also called *distribution-free,* and more generally, *sturdy statistics,* these tests have in common the fact that they make fewer assumptions than do such parametric procedures as *t* and *F* tests (Mosteller & Rourke, 1973). Although more rigorous distinctions can be made between the terms *nonparametric* and *distribution-free* (e.g., Huber, 1981; Marascuilo & McSweeney, 1977), those fine distinctions are not necessary for the purpose of this discussion. The assumptions that are made by nonparametric procedures have to do with the shape of the underlying distributions from which the samples were drawn, and so they refer to Assumptions 2 and 3 in the preceding section. Most nonparametric procedures make the independence assumption (Assumption 1), and some make assumptions of identity of shapes of distributions or of the symmetry of the population distribution (Siegel, 1956; Siegel & Castellan, 1988). Nonparametric procedures, therefore, are not at all "assumption-free," but they can be useful adjunct procedures when, for example, homogeneity of variance (Assumption 2) or crude normality (e.g., absence of serious skewness, Assumption 3) cannot be achieved with appropriate transformation. Ordinarily, nonparametric procedures are equivalent to parametric procedures applied to appropriately transformed data (Judd & McClelland, 1989).

Shapes and Variances of Distributions

As an example in which differences in the variances and shapes of distributions can lead to erroneous conclusions when nonparametric procedures are used, suppose we have a sample of 20 patients with severe psychological symptoms. A new, but expensive, intervention has been developed to treat such patients. If we could do so, we would prefer to randomly assign half our sample to an experimental group that would receive the new intervention and half to a control group that would receive the usual treatment procedure. However, because of the expense of the intervention, only a single patient can receive it. Thus, at random, we select 1 of the 20 patients to receive the intervention. After the results of this experiment become available, and we have ranked all 20 patients on the degree of improvement shown, we find that our solitary intervention patient has made the greatest gain of any of the 20 patients.

Applying one of the most powerful of the nonparametric procedures, the Mann-Whitney U test (for ranked data), we find the one-tailed $p = .05$ that our lone intervention patient would show the greatest benefit of any of our 20 patients (Siegel, 1956, p. 277). If we treat the 20 rank values of outcomes as scores, we find the t test on the ranks is also significant at $p = .05$ one-tailed. These results are quite transparent, and even if we use no formal test of significance (e.g., U or t), we can readily see that our lone treated patient could occupy any one of 20 ranks and that only 1 of 20 ranks yields the most favorable outcome for the intervention (i.e., $p = 1/20 = .05$).

All these procedures, nonparametric as well as parametric, depend on the assumption that the intervention will not dramatically affect the shape and variance of the distribution of the outcome measures for the intervention condition. Suppose that the effect of the intervention is such as to greatly benefit about half the treated patients but to actually harm the other half. And suppose also that half the treated patients show greater benefit than any of the control patients, but the other half of the treated patients show less benefit than any of the control patients. If we find our lone intervention patient to benefit more than any of our control patients, the p value for that outcome is not .05, but .50, as there is now a 50:50 chance that our lone intervention patient would benefit more (or benefit *less*) than any of our control patients.

If, in our original sample of 20 patients, we could have administered the treatment to 3 of the patients (instead of only 1), and if all 3 of those patients had shown greater benefits than any of our 17 control patients, the Mann-Whitney U test for ranked data would be significant at $p = .001$ (Siegel, 1956, p. 274). Normally that p value would be accurate, but if the effects of treatment were such as to drive half the treated patients above all the controls in degree of benefit, while driving the remaining half below the controls in degree of benefit, the accurate one-tailed p value would be .125 rather than .001. The lesson of this example is that even the more robust nonparametric procedures can yield inaccurate p values, given certain underlying distributions of treatment and control groups. We can protect ourselves to some degree against these inaccuracies by routinely examining the distribution of ranks or other scores of all the treatment and control conditions of our research.

Sometimes, when sample sizes are very small, there is no alternative to some form of nonparametric test. That was the situation we encountered in our discussion of Spearman's rank-correlation coefficient (chapter 11). When the number of pairs of scores being correlated is very small, we are forced to go to nonparametric procedures to compute the exact probabilities of various outcomes of rankings. Later in this book, we encounter an analogous situation when we discuss tables of counts in which the expected frequencies in a 2×2 table fall critically low (chapter 19).

There is now such a rich profusion of nonparametric procedures that even a brief discussion of the major ones would require at least a small textbook of its own. Fortunately, a growing list of texts can be recommended, beginning with the classic by Sidney Siegel (1956) and its revision (Siegel & Castellan, 1988), and including Bradley (1968), Conover (1999), Fraser (1957), Gibbons (1985), Gibbons and Chakraborti (2004), Hollander and Wolfe (1999), Lehmann and Dabrera (1998), Marascuilo and McSweeney (1977), Mosteller and Rourke (1973), Noether (1967), and Pratt and Gibbons (1981).

THE BOOTSTRAP, THE JACKKNIFE, AND PERMUTATION TESTS

With the ready availability of high-capacity personal computers, it is now possible to obtain accurate estimates not only of significance levels, but of measures of central tendency, variability, confidence intervals, simple and complex indices of correlation, regression, and more, even when the data are not normally distributed. The estimation methods, known as the **bootstrap,** the **jackknife,** and **permutation tests,** all use certain **resampling procedures.** The underlying rationale for these estimation methods is not new.

Jackknifes and Bootstraps

Histories of the computer-intensive methods of resampling credit the work of Quenouille (1949, 1956) as having introduced the idea of estimating the bias of a statistic by deleting one observation at a time and recalculating the estimated statistic (Barbe & Bertail, 1995; Davison & Hinkley, 1999; Dudewicz, 1992; Efron, 1982; Gray & Schucany, 1972; Shao & Tu, 1995). Whereas Quenouille introduced the concept of the jackknife, it was Tukey (1958) who named it the jackknife and applied it to estimating standard errors and confidence intervals (Efron & Tibshirani, 1993; Gray & Schucany, 1972; Mosteller & Tukey, 1977). Although much of the literature on resampling procedures is directed at other statisticians, resampling techniques are finding their way into the literature directed at behavioral researchers (e.g., Hildebrand, 1986; Myers & Well, 2003; Wilcox, 1996).

  Although the jackknife introduced the idea of resampling from an obtained sample to create "replications," it was Efron (1979) who broadened the idea of resampling with his introduction of the bootstrap. The bootstrap can be applied to more problems than the jackknife but ordinarily requires more computation than does the jackknife (Shao & Tu, 1995). Neither the jackknife nor the bootstrap requires that the assumption of normality be met, but both procedures work better if the data are at least independent and identically distributed. However, with some complications, they can be used with data not meeting even those assumptions. In any case, both the jackknife and the bootstrap are more robust than more traditional methods. The more the assumptions of IID normal are violated, the more we benefit from the resampling procedures of the jackknife and the bootstrap (Shao & Tu, 1995).

  Although we speak of "the" jackknife and "the" bootstrap, there are many versions of each, and those different versions serve different purposes, with varying degrees of cost in computer time. For example, we may be able to compute some standard errors more efficiently using the jackknife, whereas for other computations the bootstrap may be more accurate though requiring more computations (Shao & Tu, 1995). The actual computation of jackknifes and bootstraps may require heavy-duty computational resources. To give readers an intuitive feel for resampling, we provide a very small example. Created to illustrate bootstrap procedures, this example benefited greatly from our reading of the very clear exposition of Efron and Tibshirani (1993).

The Bootstrap: An Example

For a sample of size N for which we want an estimate of, say, the standard error of the median (or of some other statistic), we repeatedly draw samples of size $N - S$, where S refers to the number of elements of the sample to be set aside. Suppose we have a sample of the following $N = 10$ scores: 1, 2, 3, 4, 6, 7, 13, 14, 15, 27. We decide to draw samples of size 7 (i.e., $N - S = 10 - 3 = 7$). We would then draw a large number of samples of size 7 from our $N = 10$ scores, perhaps several hundred or more such samples. Our sampling would be with *replacement,* meaning that after every score selected by the computer, that score is put back into the pool from which we are sampling. Thus, it could easily happen (e.g., 10% of the time) that we will draw the replaced score as our second draw. In this example, if the first random draw is a sample score of 27, our second draw is as likely to be another 27 as any other of our N of 10 scores.

Tables 13.11 and 13.12 illustrate bootstrapping from a tiny sample of just 3 observations. Table 13.11 shows our 3 scores, their median, mean, S, S^2, and the standard error $[(S^2/N)^{1/2}]$ of the mean. Table 13.12 shows 27 possible subsamples based on the data in Table 13.11. The first listed subsample (1, 1, 1) implies that in one of our 27 random samplings with replacement, the first drawn, the second drawn, and the third drawn values were all scores of 1. Subsamples can take on such values only because we replace each drawn score before we draw the next score. Of our 27 possible samples, only 6 contain our original sample scores of 1, 2, and 9.

For each of our 27 resamplings, Table 13.12 shows the median, mean, S, and S^2 values, and Table 13.13 summarizes each of the four columns of Table 13.12 by

TABLE 13.11
Illustrative bootstrapping from a sample of $N = 3$

	Sample
	1
	2
	9
Median	2
Mean	4
S	4.36
S^2	19.00
$\sqrt{\dfrac{S^2}{N}}$	2.52[a]

[a]Standard error of the mean, where the 90% *CI* around the mean extends from
-3.35 to 11.35, computed from $M \pm t_{(.05)}\sqrt{\dfrac{S^2}{N}} = 4 \pm (2.92)(2.52) = 4 \pm 7.35.$

providing that column's median, mean, S, S^2, 95th percentile score, and 5th percentile score. The bootstrap estimate of the standard error is the standard deviation of the bootstrap samples. Thus, the standard errors of the median, mean, and S are 3.31, 2.09, and 1.92, respectively.

Bootstrap procedures have many more applications than those illustrated here. We can form confidence intervals for various measures of central tendency, variability, correlation, and linear and nonlinear regression. Indeed, we can use bootstrap procedures to help us estimate any kind of statistic, its variability, and its degree of bias.

TABLE 13.12
Median, mean, S, and S^2 for 27 resampled sets of three scores

	Resampled scores			*Mdn*	*M*	*S*	S^2
1.	1,	1,	1	1	1.0	0	0
2.	1,	1,	2	1	1.33	0.58	0.33
3.	1,	1,	9	1	3.67	4.62	21.33
4.	1,	2,	1	1	1.33	0.58	0.33
5.	1,	2,	2	2	1.67	0.58	0.33
6.	1,	2,	9	2	4.0	4.36	19.00
7.	1,	9,	1	1	3.67	4.62	21.33
8.	1,	9,	2	2	4.0	4.36	19.00
9.	1,	9,	9	9	6.33	4.62	21.33
10.	2,	1,	1	1	1.33	0.58	0.33
11.	2,	1,	2	2	1.67	0.58	0.33
12.	2,	1,	9	2	4.0	4.36	19.00
13.	2,	2,	1	2	1.67	0.58	0.33
14.	2,	2,	2	2	2.0	0	0
15.	2,	2,	9	2	4.33	4.04	16.33
16.	2,	9,	1	2	4.00	4.36	19.00
17.	2,	9,	2	2	4.33	4.04	16.33
18.	2,	9,	9	9	6.67	4.04	16.33
19.	9,	1,	1	1	3.67	4.62	21.33
20.	9,	1,	2	2	4.0	4.36	19.00
21.	9,	1,	9	9	6.33	4.62	21.33
22.	9,	2,	1	2	4.0	4.36	19.00
23.	9,	2,	2	2	4.33	4.04	16.33
24.	9,	2,	9	9	6.67	4.04	16.33
25.	9,	9,	1	9	6.33	4.62	21.33
26.	9,	9,	2	9	6.67	4.04	16.33
27.	9,	9,	9	9	9.00	0	0

TABLE 13.13
Summary statistics for the four columns of data in Table 13.12

	Mdn	*M*	*S*	*S²*
Median (*Mdn*)	2.00	4.00	4.04	16.33
Mean (*M*)	3.56	4.00	3.02	12.66
S	3.31	2.09	1.92	9.13
S²	10.95	4.38	3.67	83.31
95th percentile*	9.00	8.07	4.62	21.33
5th percentile**	1.00	1.13	0.00	0.00

* Found at the location of the $.95(N + 1)^{th}$ score.
** Found at the location of the $.05(N + 1)^{th}$ score.

Permutation Tests

In addition to the jackknife and the bootstrap, there is a third set of procedures that has benefited greatly from the availability of high-capacity personal computers. These are the so-called *permutation tests,* which are also referred to as *randomization tests, rerandomization tests,* and *exact tests* (Good, 1994). Although these tests were described as early as 1935 by R. A. Fisher and were incorporated into the basic statistical procedures used by behavioral researchers (Siegel, 1956), they could be used in practice only with small data sets.

The basic idea of permutation tests is simply to count the total number of permutations or rearrangements of the data obtained and determine from the list of all possible permutations the "rareness" of the obtained result. For example, if we have control group scores of 1, 3, 4, and treatment group scores of 5, 9, 76, we can find 20 possible rearrangements of these six scores. Because our obtained data show the arrangement or permutation most favorable to our hypothesis (that treatment scores would be higher than control group scores), our obtained $p = 1/20 = .05$ one-tailed. When sample sizes grow very large, it is no longer practical to list all the permutations possible even with high-capacity personal computers, and it is necessary to draw repeated samples of permutations from our obtained sample much as we would when using bootstrapping.

The jackknife, the bootstrap, and the permutation tests are all considered relatively robust when compared to the more traditional distribution-based statistics (e.g., t, F, Z, and χ^2). None of the resampling techniques described, however, are assumption-free. Although the assumption of an underlying normal distribution need not be met, failure to meet the assumptions of independence and identical distributions can be troublesome in various conditions for all three of our resampling approaches to estimating various statistics (Hayes, 1996; Shao & Tu, 1995).

Computer Programs

All of the resampling procedures were described as computer-intensive, and several of the sources cited in this section provide listings of appropriate computer programs (e.g., Davison & Hinkley, 1999; Efron & Tibshirani, 1993; Good, 1994; Mooney & Duval, 1993; Wilkinson & Engelman, 1999).

CHAPTER
14

ANALYSIS OF VARIANCE AND THE *F* TEST

THE *F* TEST AND THE *t* TEST

Along with William Sealy Gosset's *t* test, Ronald A. Fisher's *F* test is at the top of the list of popular statistical procedures in behavioral research. In chapters 16–18 we shift our attention to more complex designs, but we focus here on single-dimensional (or "one-way") designs in which there are two or more groups. The *F* test can be used to test the hypothesis that there is, in the population from which we have drawn two or more samples, (a) no difference between the two or more group means or, equivalently, (b) no relationship between membership in a group and the score on the dependent measure. The *F* test, like the *t* test, is another test of significance and, as is true of all such procedures, comprises two components, the size of the effect and the size of the study. When there are just two means to be compared, we can rewrite the general relationship Significance test = Size of effect × Size of study more specifically as

$$F = \frac{r^2}{1 - r^2} \times df. \tag{14.1}$$

We can therefore compute the point-biserial *r* between membership in one of the two groups (coded, for example, as 0, 1 or −1, +1) and the dependent variable and find *F* from Equation 14.1, which requires only that we also know the *df* for *r*. For this application, *df* = the number of pairs of scores less two, or $N-2$.

Taking the square root of both sides of Equation 14.1, we have

$$\sqrt{F} = \frac{r}{\sqrt{1 - r^2}} \times \sqrt{df}. \tag{14.2}$$

The right-hand side of Equation 14.2 equals not only $\sqrt{F}$, but t as well (see again Equation 2.2). For the special case of the comparison of two groups, then, $F = t^2$, or $\sqrt{F} = t$. Therefore, we can use either test to investigate the plausibility of the hypothesis that, in the population from which we have drawn two samples, there is no relationship between the independent variable and the dependent variable (i.e., H_0 is that $r = 0$). Just as is true of t, the distribution of F is readily available in tables for $r = 0$ (called the *central F distribution*). Thus, we can look up the probability that an F as large as or larger than the one we obtained could have occurred if r were, in fact zero. How, then, shall we decide whether to use t or F?

The advantage of t is that it is a signed statistic. That is, it can be positive or negative in value, so that we can tell whether r is positive or negative or, put another way, whether the mean of the first group is greater than or less than the mean of the second group. The F test operates on r^2, or on the squared difference between the means, so the F is the same whether the obtained r is positive or negative, or whether one group mean is smaller or larger by the obtained amount than the mean of the other group. The limitation of the standard independent t test (Equation 11.9) is that it is for use only when there are just two means to be compared, whereas F can operate just as well for three groups, or four, or *any* number of groups as it does for just two groups. However, as we show in the next chapter, we can adapt both t and F to use as focused significance tests when we want to investigate a specific prediction and there are more than just two means to be compared.

When the F test is used to make a diffuse (unfocused) comparison among three or more groups, we describe it as an omnibus F. We can easily recognize omnibus F tests from the fact that their numerator degrees of freedom ($df_{numerator}$) exceed 1, whereas focused F tests have $df_{numerator} = 1$ even when they focus on more than two means. When the F test is used to make a diffuse comparison of three or more groups, the relationship between that omnibus F test and the size of effect and size of study is generalized to

$$F = \frac{\eta^2}{1 - \eta^2} \times \frac{df_{error}}{df_{means}}, \tag{14.3}$$

where η^2 is a correlation index (eta^2) defined as the proportion of variance in the dependent variable attributable to group membership, df_{error} is analogous to the term df when we were discussing the t test, and the df_{means} is the number (k) of means being compared less one, or $k - 1$. (Later in this chapter we are more precise about the definition of η and df_{error}.)

THE ANALYSIS OF "VARIANCES"

In our discussion of t in the previous chapter, we noted that the size of the effect could be indexed by r or by an index of standardized distance between the group means, such as Hedges's g (Equation 2.5) or Cohen's d (Equation 2.4). In the case of Hedges's g, the difference between means is divided by S, the sample estimate of the population standard deviation, or the square root of the unbiased estimate of the population variance (S^2) pooled from the two groups. How might we incorporate the idea of standardized distances among means when more than two means are to be compared? We might take all $k(k - 1)/2$ possible pairs of absolute distances between means and find their average. With three means (M_1, M_2, and M_3), the average absolute distance between all the means is $\left[|M_1 - M_2| + |M_2 - M_3| + |M_1 - M_3|\right]/3$, which we then divide by S to yield an index of heterogeneity in the spirit of Hedges's g. Such an index would be fairly informative, but it turns out to be less useful in subsequent statistical procedures than an index focused on the squared differences among means, defined as

$$S^2_{means} = \frac{\Sigma(M_i - \overline{M})^2}{k - 1}, \tag{14.4}$$

where k is the number of means being compared, and the other terms are defined as above.

A large S^2_{means} implies that the means are far apart in the sense of squared distances from the grand mean. However, the precise meaning of *far* depends on the particular metric used in the research, and thus, we want to standardize the distance index, S^2_{means}, by the unit of measurement used. We can do this by dividing S^2_{means} by S^2, the variance computed separately within each group and averaged from all groups. When we want to compare the means of any number of independent groups, we can also define F in terms of this new effect-size estimate and n, the number of sampling units in each of the groups when all the groups have the same n:

$$F = \frac{S^2_{means}}{S^2} \times n. \tag{14.5}$$

When the ns of the groups are not equal, n may be replaced (for a conservative estimate of F) by the harmonic mean of the sample sizes. The estimate of the F based on the harmonic mean of unequal sample sizes is always conservative in the sense that the harmonic mean of unequal sample sizes is always smaller than the arithmetic mean of the same sample sizes. The harmonic mean (n_h) of two sample sizes was defined in Equation 12.2. A general equation for two or more sample sizes is

$$n_h = 1 \bigg/ \frac{1}{k}\left(\frac{1}{n_1} + \frac{1}{n_2} + \cdots + \frac{1}{n_k}\right) = k \bigg/ \left(\frac{1}{n_1} + \frac{1}{n_2} + \cdots + \frac{1}{n_k}\right), \tag{14.6}$$

where n_1 to n_k are the sizes of the samples on which the various means are based, and k is again the number of means being compared.

Studying closely the definition of F in Equation 14.5 will solve a mystery that plagues students beginning their study of the analysis of variance (abbreviated ANOVA). The mystery is Why do we call it analysis of *variance* when what we are "really" doing is comparing *means?* Of course, we are doing both. We are comparing variances, in that the variance among means is compared with the variance within conditions (i.e., the basic level of variation or "noise" in the system) in order to find out how far apart the means are on average (the "signal"). For any given size of sample n, the F will be larger if the S^2_{means} grows larger relative to the S^2 (the denominator value). It should also be pointed out that ANOVA is used in situations other than the comparison of means (e.g., in regression analysis, discussed in a later chapter) and that F tests are sometimes actually used to compare variabilities of groups rather than their means (discussed later in this chapter).

ILLUSTRATION OF AN OMNIBUS F

Suppose we have 12 patients available for an experimental study in which we are comparing four treatment conditions, with three patients randomly assigned to each of the four conditions. The (hypothetical) improvement scores are shown in Table 14.1. On the basis of these scores, we find $\overline{M} = (8 + 4 + 4 + 2)/4 = 4.5$. Because in this illustration we are using Equation 14.5 to solve for F, we begin by computing Equation 14.4:

$$S^2_{\text{means}} = \frac{(8 - 4.5)^2 + (4 - 4.5)^2 + (4 - 4.5)^2 + (2 - 4.5)^2}{4 - 1}$$

$$= \frac{(3.5)^2 + (-0.5)^2 + (-0.5)^2 + (-2.5)^2}{3} = \frac{19}{3} = 6.33.$$

Next we want S^2, the pooled within-group variance collected over all groups, computed as

$$S^2 = \frac{\Sigma(n_i - 1)S_i^2}{\Sigma(n_i - 1)}, \tag{14.7}$$

where n_i is the number of observations in the ith condition and S_i^2 is the variance of the ith condition, so we find

$$S^2 = \frac{(2)(1.0) + (2)(4.0) + (2)(1.0) + (2)(4.0)}{2 + 2 + 2 + 2} = \frac{20}{8} = 2.50.$$

And finally, from Equation 14.5 we find

$$F = \frac{S^2_{\text{means}}}{S^2} \times n$$

$$= \frac{6.33}{2.50} \times 3 = 7.60.$$

We now refer this result to a table of the F distribution to find the p level associated with an F of this magnitude or greater. (We return shortly to the use of F tables.)

TABLE 14.1
Improvement scores in four conditions

	Psychotherapy plus drug treatment	Psychotherapy plus no-drug treatment	No psychotherapy plus drug treatment	No psychotherapy plus no-drug treatment
	9	6	5	4
	8	4	4	2
	7	2	3	0
Σ	24	12	12	6
M	8	4	4	2
S^2	1.0	4.0	1.0	4.0

DIVIDING UP THE TOTAL VARIANCE

Although Equation 14.5 is conceptually instructive for showing F to be a product of the size of the effect (S^2_{means}/S^2) and the size of the study (n), there is something more about the analysis of variance that is of greater interest than the computation of F. The major purpose of an ANOVA is to divide the total variance of the observations into a number of separate sources of variance that can be compared with one another for purposes of both effect size estimation and significance testing. In our illustration above comparing the means of four groups, the total variation among 12 scores was divided into two sources of variation: (a) that between groups or conditions and (b) that within groups or conditions.

It will be useful to look again at the basic idea of variance (Equation 10.6), defined here as

$$S^2 = \frac{\Sigma(X - M)^2}{N - 1},$$

where S^2 is the unbiased estimate of the population value of σ^2, and σ^2 for a sample differs from S^2 only in that the denominator $N - 1$ is replaced by N. Particularly in the context of analysis of variance, the quantity S^2 is referred to as a **mean square** because the sum of the squares of the deviations [i.e., the $\Sigma(X - M)^2$] is divided by $N - 1$ (or df), yielding the squared deviation per df, or a kind of average.

In the analysis of variance we are especially interested in the numerators of quantities of S^2, as in (a) the variation between conditions and (b) the variation within conditions. The reason has to do with the additive property of the numerators, or **sums of squares** of deviations about the mean. These sums of squares add up to the total sum of squares in that Total sum of squares = Between-conditions sum of squares + Within-conditions sum of squares. Because the standard abbreviation for the sum of squares is SS, a simpler way of expressing that relationship is

$$\text{Total } SS = \text{Between-conditions } SS + \text{Within-conditions } SS,$$

or more succinctly as

$$\text{Total } SS = \text{Between } SS + \text{Within } SS.$$

The analysis of variance generally begins with the computation of these three sums of squares, defined as follows:

$$\text{Total } SS = \Sigma(X - \overline{M})^2, \tag{14.8}$$

where X is each observation, and $\overline{M}$ is the mean of the condition means, and we add up as many squared deviations as there are scores altogether:

$$\text{Between-conditions } SS = \Sigma\left[n_i (M_i - \overline{M})^2\right] \tag{14.9}$$

where n_i is the number of observations in the ith condition, M_i is the mean of the ith condition, and $\overline{M}$ is the mean of the condition means. Here we add up as many quantities as there are conditions.

$$\text{Within-conditions } SS = \Sigma(X - M_i)^2, \tag{14.10}$$

where X is each observation, M_i is the mean of the condition to which X belongs, and we add up as many quantities as there are scores altogether.

For the data in Table 14.1, using Equation 14.8 we find

$$
\begin{aligned}
\text{Total } SS = {} & (9 - 4.5)^2 + (8 - 4.5)^2 + (7 - 4.5)^2 + (6 - 4.5)^2 + (4 - 4.5)^2 \\
& + (2 - 4.5)^2 + (5 - 4.5)^2 + (4 - 4.5)^2 + (3 - 4.5)^2 + (4 - 4.5)^2 \\
& + (2 - 4.5)^2 + (0 - 4.5)^2 \\
= {} & 77.
\end{aligned}
$$

Then, from Equation 14.9 we find

$$
\begin{aligned}
\text{Between-conditions } SS = {} & 3(8 - 4.5)^2 + 3(4 - 4.5)^2 \\
& + 3(4 - 4.5)^2 + 3(2 - 4.5)^2 \\
= {} & 57.
\end{aligned}
$$

And finally, using Equation 14.10 we find

$$
\begin{aligned}
\text{Within-conditions } SS = {} & (9 - 8)^2 + (8 - 8)^2 + (7 - 8)^2 + (6 - 4)^2 \\
& + (4 - 4)^2 + (2 - 4)^2 + (5 - 4)^2 + (4 - 4)^2 \\
& + (3 - 4)^2 + (4 - 2)^2 + (2 - 2)^2 + (0 - 2)^2 \\
= {} & 20.
\end{aligned}
$$

Because they are sums of *squared* deviations, the sums of squares can take on only values of zero or above. Sums of squares are never negative, and thus, F tests are also never negative. As a check on our arithmetic, we can total the results of Equations 14.9 and 14.10 to make sure they sum to the result of Equation 14.8, that is,

$$
\begin{aligned}
\text{Total } SS = {} & \text{Between-conditions } SS + \text{Within-conditions } SS \\
77 = {} & 57 + 20.
\end{aligned}
$$

ANOVA SUMMARY TABLES

The results of an analysis of variance are often reported in a summary table so as to avoid cramming too many statistics into the narrative text. Table 14.2 shows such an ANOVA table of summary results, in which the first column gives the source of variance, and the second shows the sum of squares (SS) for each source of variance. The third column is the degrees of freedom (df) for each source. As four conditions are being compared, or four means, three of those means are free to vary once the mean of the means is determined. If there are k conditions, the df for conditions is $k - 1$, or 3 in this

TABLE 14.2
Summary ANOVA table

Source	SS	df	MS	F	η	p
Between conditions	57	3	19.0	7.60	.86	.01
Within conditions	20	8	2.5			
Total	77	11	7.0			

case. We obtain the *df* within the conditions by determining the *df* within each condition and then adding those values. Within each condition we have $n_i - 1$ degrees of freedom, because within each condition of *n* scores there are only $n - 1$ that are free to vary once we determine the mean of the condition. Thus, the value of the *df* within conditions is $\Sigma(n_i-1)$, which in our present illustration is

$$\Sigma(n_i - 1) = (3 - 1) + (3 - 1) + (3 - 1) + (3 - 1) = 8.$$

When we compute the *df* for between and within conditions as shown, we can check our arithmetic by summing those *df* to make sure that they agree with the *df* for the total, computed directly as $N - 1$ (i.e., the total number of observations less 1). In the present case we have

$$df \text{ total} = df \text{ between} + df \text{ within}$$
$$11 = 3 + 8$$

The fourth column of Table 14.2 provides the mean squares (*MS*), which we obtained by dividing the sums of squares by the corresponding *df*. The mean squares can be seen as the amounts of the total variation (measured in *SS*) attributable per *df*. The larger the *MS* for the between-conditions source of variance relative to the within-conditions source of variance, the less likely it is that the null hypothesis of no difference between condition means is true. If the null hypothesis were true, then the variation per *df* should be roughly the same for the *df* between groups and the *df* within groups.

The fifth column of Table 14.2 shows *F,* obtained, in applications of this type, by division of the mean square between conditions by the mean square within conditions. Another name for an *F* test is *F ratio,* because we generally obtain *F* by forming a ratio of two mean squares. The denominator mean square, often referred to as the **mean square for error,** serves as a kind of base rate for "noise level," or typical variation, and the numerator mean square serves to inform us simultaneously about the size of the effect and about the size of the study. Thus, a numerator *MS* can be large relative to a denominator *MS* because the effect-size index (defined in Equation 14.3 as $\eta^2/(1 - \eta^2)$, and in Equation 14.5 as S^2_{means}/S^2) is large, or because the *n* per condition is large, or because both of these components have large values. It follows that we cannot simply interpret a large *F* as reflecting a large effect. Any conclusion about the size of the effect must be based on the direct calculation of an effect size estimator.

The American Psychological Association (2001), which is the arbiter of publication style for many journals, recommends that an index of effect size or strength of relationship routinely be reported. The APA publication manual also properly cautions that, "as a general rule, multiple degree-of-freedom effect indicators tend to be less useful than effect indicators that decompose multiple degree-of-freedom tests into meaningful one degree-of-freedom effects" (p. 26). We also are rarely interested in multiple degree-of-freedom effect-size indicators, and in the next chapter we will describe a family of effect size correlations for use with focused statistical tests to assess predicted trends in three or more group or condition means. Nonetheless, we see in Table 14.2 that the effect size measure (η) is for a multiple degree-of-freedom *F* (i.e., an omnibus *F* with numerator *df* = 3), and there is a similar example in the APA manual (p. 162). Although we can usually do better than this, the effect size eta (η) and its squared value (η^2) are frequently used for multiple degree-of-freedom F tests, and thus need some explanation.

Eta can be defined as

$$\eta = \sqrt{\frac{SS_{between}}{SS_{between} + SS_{within}}}, \qquad (14.11)$$

or the square root of the proportion of the sums of squares (between + within) associated with the between-conditions source of variation. An equivalent formula that is convenient when we have access to an F but not to the original sums of squares is

$$\eta = \sqrt{\frac{F(df_{between})}{F(df_{between}) + df_{within}}}. \qquad (14.12)$$

In the present illustration, Table 14.2 shows η computed from Equation 14.11 as

$$\eta = \sqrt{\frac{57}{57 + 20}} = \sqrt{.7403} = .86,$$

or from Equation 14.12 as

$$\eta = \sqrt{\frac{7.6(3)}{7.6(3) + 8}} = \sqrt{\frac{22.8}{22.8 + 8}} = .86.$$

The η^2 is interpreted as a "proportion of variance accounted for," and the range, therefore, is like that for r^2, which is 0 to 1. However, r represents an index of linear relationship, whereas η^2 can serve as an index of any type of relationship. When there is only 1 df between conditions (as when there are only two conditions being compared), η and r are identical, and both are regarded as indices of linear relationships. As noted above, we are only rarely interested in etas based on more than a single df or in squared indices of effect size. The reason we are rarely interested in etas based on more than a single df is that, like other omnibus measures, they are difficult, if not impossible, to interpret in a substantively meaningful way. Furthermore, they tend to be overestimates of population values of eta—sometimes gross overestimates. The overestimation is more severe when the numerator df of F is large relative to the denominator df (Guilford & Fruchter, 1978). One problem with squared effect-size indices (discussed in chapter 11) is that they lose their directionality and thus are of little use in scientific work for which information on directionality is essential. Another problem is that the implications of squared indices of effect size are likely to be misconstrued as being much less important than is often true, and in Table 11.8 (chapter 11) we illustrated how r^2 is susceptible to the expository problem that very small, but quite meaningful, biomedical effects may seem to essentially disappear.

The last column of Table 14.2 indicates the probability (p) that an F of the size obtained or larger could have been obtained if the null hypothesis were true and there actually were no differences in the population between the means of the conditions of our research investigation. An alternative interpretation is that the p expresses the probability that an eta of the size obtained or larger could have occurred if the relationship between the independent variable of condition membership and the dependent variable of score on the response variable were actually zero in the population.

DISTRIBUTIONS OF *F*

In our discussion of the interpretation of t in the previous chapter, we noted that there is a different distribution of t values for every possible value of $n_1 + n_2 - 2$ (i.e., df). The situation for F is similar but more complicated because for every F ratio there are *two* relevant df to take into account: the df between conditions ($df_{between}$) and the df within conditions (df_{within}). For every combination of $df_{between}$ and df_{within}, there is a different F distribution. Whereas t distributions are centered at zero, with negative values running to negative infinity and positive values running to positive infinity, F distributions begin at zero and range upward to positive infinity. Also, whereas the expected value of t is zero when the null hypothesis is true, the expected value of F when df_{within} is greater than 2 is $df_{within}/(df_{within} - 2)$. For most values of df_{within}, then, the expected value of F is a little more than 1.0. Just as is true of t, values of F closer to zero are likely when the null hypothesis of no difference between groups is true, whereas larger values are less likely and thus are used as evidence that the null hypothesis is probably false.

Inspection of a large number of F distributions reveals that the critical values of F required to reach the .05, .01, and .001 levels of p decrease as the df_{within} increases for any given $df_{between}$. Similarly, the critical values of F decrease as the $df_{between}$ increase for any given df_{within}, except for the special case of $df_{within} = 1$ or 2. For $df_{within} = 1$, a substantial increase in the value of F is required to reach various critical levels as the $df_{between}$ increases from 1 to infinity. For $df_{within} = 2$, only a very small increase in the value of F is required to reach various critical levels as the $df_{between}$ increase from 1 to infinity. In practice, there are very few studies with large $df_{between}$ and only 1 or 2 df_{within}. A sample F distribution is shown in Figure 14.1 with the $df_{between} = 3$ and the $df_{within} = 16$. Were we to hold the $df_{between}$ constant and simultaneously vary the df_{within}, we would see only slight changes in the shape of the F distribution. But a substantial increase in the $df_{between}$ results in the F distribution's becoming noticeably less asymmetrical, morphing into a kind of bell shape, but retaining its right-skewness and still ranging from zero to infinity.

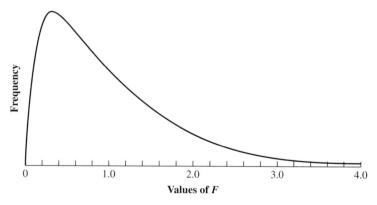

FIGURE 14.1
F distribution for $df_{between} = 3$ and $df_{within} = 16$.

Table 14.3 further illustrates the differences in various F distributions by giving the areas found in the upper tail of selected distributions. For each combination of $df_{between}$ and df_{within}, two values are given: the F values required to reach the .05 and the .01 levels, respectively. A much more detailed table of F values is found in Table B.4 of Appendix B. In the example of the ANOVA we have been discussing, we found $F = 7.60$, with 3 df in the numerator (between) and 8 df in the denominator (within or error), a result we write as $F(3, 8) = 7.60$. Referring this value to Table 14.3, we find at the intersection of 3 df for between conditions and 8 df for within conditions the values 4.07 and 7.59. Our obtained F, therefore, is substantially larger than an F required to be significant at $p = .05$ and almost exactly the size required to be significant at $p = .01$. The p value of .01 implies that we would obtain an F of this size or larger (for numerator $df = 3$, and denominator $df = 8$) only once in 100 times if (a) we repeatedly conducted a study of four groups of $n = 3$ each, and (b) in the population there were no differences among the four means or no relationship between group membership and the response or dependent variable.

Before leaving our discussion of the distributions of F, we should note that the F values computed in actual research situations are usually distributed only approximately as F. The assumptions to be met before we can regard the computed F to be actually distributed as F were abbreviated as *IID normal* in our discussion of the t test in the previous chapter. That is to say, (a) the units (or errors) are assumed to be independent of one another, (b) the population variance is the same in each group, and (c) the unit values are normally distributed in each group. Of these three assumptions, the independence of the sampling units is considered most important, because if it is badly violated, our interpretation of F can be very wrong. Violations of the homogeneity of variance and normality assumptions are less serious, in that F tends to be robust in the face of even some fairly serious violations of these assumptions.

One final point is simply a reminder that, in both the previous chapter and this chapter, we assumed that the t or F is being used to test the null hypothesis of no difference between the means or, equivalently, no relationship between group membership and score on a dependent measure. The null hypothesis in this case is sometimes described as the "nil" hypothesis. But what if a nonzero difference or nonzero relationship is specified in the null hypothesis? In that case, the usual t or F is referred not to the *central* distribution we have been discussing, but to a *noncentral t* or *noncentral F distribution* or to a *doubly noncentral distribution* (see, e.g., Bulgren & Amos, 1968; Bulgren, 1971; Scheffé, 1959). The noncentral F, for example, is more complex, with a family of distributions for the different values that treatment effects can take, and in general it is shifted to the right of the usual (central) F distribution (Keppel, 1991; cf. Thompson, 2002).

AFTER THE OMNIBUS F

Now we know that for the data of our example the group means are not likely to be so far apart if the null hypothesis is true. What does that tell us about the results of our experiment? By itself, not much. After all, we conducted our study to learn about the effects of psychotherapy and drug therapy separately and together. Knowing that

TABLE 14.3

F values required for significance at .05 (upper entry) and .01 α level

Degrees of freedom within conditions (denominator)	Degrees of freedom between conditions (numerator)						Expected value of F when H_0 true
	1	**2**	**3**	**4**	**6**	**∞**	
1	161	200	216	225	234	254	—
	4052	4999	5403	5625	5859	6366	
2	18.5	19.0	19.2	19.2	19.3	19.5	—
	98.5	99.0	99.2	99.2	99.3	99.5	
3	10.1	9.55	9.28	9.12	8.94	8.53	3.00
	34.1	30.8	29.5	28.7	27.9	26.1	
4	7.71	6.94	6.59	6.39	6.16	5.63	2.00
	21.2	18.0	16.7	16.0	15.2	13.5	
5	6.61	5.79	5.41	5.19	4.95	4.36	1.67
	16.3	13.3	12.1	11.4	10.7	9.02	
6	5.99	5.14	4.76	4.53	4.28	3.67	1.50
	13.7	10.9	9.78	9.15	8.47	6.88	
8	5.32	4.46	4.07	3.84	3.58	2.93	1.33
	11.3	8.65	7.59	7.01	6.37	4.86	
10	4.96	4.10	3.71	3.48	3.22	2.54	1.25
	10.0	7.56	6.55	5.99	5.39	3.91	
15	4.54	3.68	3.29	3.06	2.79	2.07	1.15
	8.68	6.36	5.42	4.89	4.32	2.87	
20	4.35	3.49	3.10	2.87	2.60	1.84	1.11
	8.10	5.85	4.94	4.43	3.87	2.42	
25	4.24	3.38	2.99	2.76	2.49	1.71	1.09
	7.77	5.57	4.68	4.18	3.63	2.17	
30	4.17	3.32	2.92	2.69	2.42	1.62	1.07
	7.56	5.39	4.51	4.02	3.47	2.01	
40	4.08	3.23	2.84	2.61	2.34	1.51	1.05
	7.31	5.18	4.31	3.83	3.29	1.81	
60	4.00	3.15	2.76	2.52	2.25	1.39	1.03
	7.08	4.98	4.13	3.65	3.12	1.60	
120	3.92	3.07	2.68	2.45	2.17	1.25	1.02
	6.85	4.79	3.95	3.48	2.96	1.38	
∞	3.84	2.99	2.60	2.37	2.09	1.00	1.00
	6.63	4.60	3.78	3.32	2.80	1.00	

the four groups probably differ does not tell us whether psychotherapy helps, whether drugs help, whether both together help, whether one helps more than the other, and so on. At the very least, we need now to examine the means of the four groups in Table 14.1, as follows:

Psychotherapy		No psychotherapy	
Drug	No drug	Drug	No drug
(PD)	(P)	(D)	(O)
8	4	4	2

Clearly, the greatest difference between means is that between the group receiving both psychotherapy and drug therapy ($M_{PD} = 8$) versus the group receiving neither psychotherapy nor drug therapy ($M_O = 2$). To find the statistical significance of this difference we can compute t using Equation 11.9:

$$t = \frac{M_1 - M_2}{\sqrt{\left(\frac{1}{n_1} + \frac{1}{n_2}\right)S^2}}.$$

In this application of t as a follow-up to an analysis of variance, we compute S^2 based on all the groups of the experiment, not just those directly involved in the t test. If we return to the definition of our mean square within (SS_{within}/df_{within}), then

$$MS_{within} = \frac{\Sigma(X - M_i)^2}{N - k}, \tag{14.13}$$

where N is the total number of sampling units in the study, and k is the number of conditions. We see that MS_{within} is the S^2 pooled over, or collected from, all the conditions of the analysis. Then, for the means of interest

$$t = \frac{M_1 - M_2}{\sqrt{\left(\frac{1}{n_1} + \frac{1}{n_2}\right)S^2}} = \frac{8 - 2}{\sqrt{\left(\frac{1}{3} + \frac{1}{3}\right)2.5}} = \frac{6}{1.29} = 4.65,$$

which is significant at $p < .001$ one-tailed or .002 two-tailed, when we refer to a table of the t distribution with $df = 8$. Because we have based our computation of S^2 (i.e., MS_{within}, or MS_{error}) on all the data of the experiment, not just on the data of the two groups being compared, our t test is made on the t distribution with df equal to that of the S^2, *not* in this case on $n_1 + n_2 - 2$. For many applications of the analysis of variance we assume homogeneity or similarity of variance from condition to condition, so that an S^2 (or MS_{within}) based on more groups is more likely to be a better estimate of the population value of σ^2. Therefore, the df available to estimate σ^2 defines the t distribution to which we refer our obtained t. The n_1 and n_2 of the denominator of the t test still reflect the actual number of cases per group on which the t is based. Thus, it is not the sample sizes that are increased by our using a more stable estimate of σ^2, but the df used for referring to t tables.

We might also want to compare the benefits of receiving both psychotherapy *and* drug ($M_{PD} = 8$) with the benefits of receiving either psychotherapy alone ($M_P = 4$) or the drug alone ($M_D = 4$). In both cases

$$t = \frac{8 - 4}{\sqrt{\left(\frac{1}{3} + \frac{1}{3}\right)2.5}} = \frac{4}{1.29} = 3.10,$$

which is significant at $p < .01$ one-tailed when we refer to the *t* distribution with 8 *df*.

We might want to compare the benefits of receiving either psychotherapy alone ($M_P = 4$) or the drug alone ($M_D = 4$) with the no-treatment control condition ($M_O = 2$). Both comparisons yield

$$t = \frac{4 - 2}{\sqrt{\left(\frac{1}{3} + \frac{1}{3}\right)2.5}} = \frac{2}{1.29} = 1.55,$$

which is significant at about the .08 level, one-tailed.

We have now compared each group with every other, except for psychotherapy alone ($M_P = 4$) versus the drug alone ($M_D = 4$), which must yield a *t* of 0. Other comparisons are possible, taking more than one group at a time. Identifying the four groups as PD, P, D, and O, so far we have made the following comparisons:

(PD)	versus	(O)
(PD)	versus	(P)
(PD)	versus	(D)
(P)	versus	(O)
(D)	versus	(O)
(P)	versus	(D)

But other comparisons are also possible:

(PD + P)	versus	(D + O)
(PD + D)	versus	(P + O)
(PD + O)	versus	(P + D)
(PD + P + D)	versus	(O)
(PD + P + O)	versus	(D)
(PD + D + O)	versus	(P)
(P + D + O)	versus	(PD)

PROTECTING AGAINST "TOO MANY *t* TESTS"

So far, then, 13 fairly obvious comparisons are possible. If we make them all, we expect some of those *t* tests to yield significant results even if the null hypothesis is true. For example, for six independent comparisons, each with alpha set at .05, the probability of one or more significant results is something like $6 \times .05 = .3$, or almost one chance in three. For 13 comparisons, with alpha at .05, the chances are something like $13 \times .05 = .65$, or about two chances in three (Dawson & Trapp, 2004). In general, as more tests of significance are computed on data for which the null hypothesis is true, more significant results will be obtained (i.e., more Type I errors will be made). We deal with this issue again in the next chapter, where we show that it is not always necessary to do so many a posteriori t tests, or even to do a preliminary omnibus F test. There are circumstances nonetheless in which we might wish to compute an overall F, particularly when lots of t tests are calculated.

Suppose we have actually planned a number of t tests before collecting or seeing the raw or summary data. A rule of thumb in this case is to perform all those planned t tests whether or not an overall (omnibus) F test is significant. Our reason for computing the omnibus ANOVA is simply to reap the benefit of a more stable estimate of the σ^2 required in the denominator of our t tests. Each t test will still be based on the n_1 and n_2 of the two groups being compared. But because we have an omnibus F with a pooled error term, the t distribution to which we refer when looking up the p values will be the one with the df of our pooled error term (i.e., the MS_{within}), usually $N - k$.

Alternatively, suppose we have unexpected but interesting results, and we want to run a number of a posteriori t tests just to explore some comparisons. It is customary to compute an overall (omnibus) F as insurance against the problem of "capitalizing on chance." If the overall F is significant, the idea is that some of the exploratory t tests *must* be "legitimately" significant, because the significant F tells us there are some nonchance variations among the means somewhere in the batch of means that we compared. For most practical purposes, the use of these "protected t tests" is considered at least an adequate solution and, quite possibly, an optimal one (Balaam, 1963; Carmer & Swanson, 1973; Snedecor & Cochran, 1989).

In both situations above, or even if many t tests are computed and the overall (omnibus) F is not significant and we are worried about the risk of capitalizing on chance, we can use another simple and conservative procedure to adjust the interpretation of the p values obtained. The basic idea of this approach, called the **Bonferroni procedure,** is simply to divide the alpha level we selected by the number of tests performed explicitly or implicitly (Harris, 1975, 1985; Hays, 1981, 1994; D. F. Morrison, 1976, 2005; Myers, 1979; Rosenthal & Rubin, 1983, 1984; Snedecor & Cochran, 1989). It makes no difference whether the tests performed are independent or not.

BONFERRONI PROCEDURES

Suppose, for example, that we plan to perform four t tests but want to keep the overall alpha at the .05 level. Dividing .05 by the number of tests planned (four), we find .0125 to be the adjusted level we want to obtain to declare any of the four t tests significant. If we have no planned t tests and include only the largest obtained t tests, then we divide the preferred alpha level (usually $p = .05$) by the number of *implicit* t tests. For example, if we have five groups to compare and decide to test the three largest differences, we divide the .05 level not by 3, but by $(5 \times 4)/2 = 10$, which indicates the number of possible pairwise comparisons of five means. In this instance we would require a p of $.05/10 = .005$ before declaring a t test significant at an "adjusted" .05 level.

The Bonferroni approach does not require us to set the same alpha level for each *t* test, so we can allocate the total alpha (say, .05) unequally. For example, suppose we plan to do eight *t* tests but want greater power for four of them because they address the questions of our major interest. We can set the alphas for these four *t* tests at .01 and set the alphas for the remaining four *t* tests at $[.05 - 4(.01)]/4 = .0025$. The eight *t* tests are now tested at .01, .01, .01, .01, .0025, .0025, .0025, .0025, respectively, which sum to $p = .05$, the overall preferred alpha level (Harris, 1975; Myers, 1979; Rosenthal & Rubin, 1983, 1984). Or suppose we plan 11 *t* tests but have an overwhelming interest in only one of them. Setting the alpha level at .04 for that *t*, and dividing the remaining .01 by 10, means that the alphas will become .04 for the prime *t* test and .001 for each of the remaining 10 *t* tests.

Basically, then, we have been adjusting the obtained *p* values associated with each *t* test for the number of *t* tests carried out, with the option of weighting the *t* tests unequally. We can assign a weight to each *t* test reflecting the importance of that test. Then the general procedure for adjusting alpha for the various weighted-for-importance *t* tests is

$$\alpha_j = \frac{\alpha W_j}{\Sigma W},$$ (14.14)

where α_j is the adjusted alpha level for the *j*th *t* test (i.e., the one in question), α is the overall probability of Type I error (usually .05), W_j is the weight reflecting the importance of the *j*th *t* test, and ΣW is the sum of the weights of all the *t* tests (Rosenthal & Rubin, 1983). Suppose we plan to examine six *t* tests, weighted in importance as follows: 12, 6, 3, 2, 1, 1. The adjusted α levels for each are shown in Table 14.4, and we see that they sum to .05, the overall alpha level.

TABLE 14.4
Adjusted alpha levels for *t* tests with different weights

t test	W_j	Adjusted α
1	12	$\frac{.05(12)}{25} = .024$
2	6	$\frac{.05(6)}{25} = .012$
3	3	$\frac{.05(3)}{25} = .006$
4	2	$\frac{.05(2)}{25} = .004$
5	1	$\frac{.05(1)}{25} = .002$
6	1	$\frac{.05(1)}{25} = .002$
Total	$\Sigma W = 25$	$\Sigma \alpha_j = .050$

TABLE 14.5
Ensemble-adjusted p values

t test	Ensemble-adjusted p value	t test	Ensemble-adjusted p value
1	$\dfrac{.005(25)}{12} = .010$	4	$\dfrac{.11(25)}{2} = 1.00^{a}$
2	$\dfrac{.07(25)}{6} = .292$	5	$\dfrac{.001(25)}{1} = .025$
3	$\dfrac{.08(25)}{3} = .667$	6	$\dfrac{.004(25)}{1} = .100$

[a]Values exceeding 1.00 are interpreted as 1.00.

Although we know how to adjust our alpha levels, it is usually much more informative to report the actual p level of each t test (adjusted for the number of t tests and their weights) rather than to report only whether a t test comparison did or did not reach the adjusted alpha level. The adjusted p value achieved (the *ensemble-adjusted p value*) is readily obtained from the following (Rosenthal & Rubin, 1983):

$$p \text{ adjusted} = \frac{p_j \Sigma W}{W_j}, \tag{14.15}$$

where p_j is the actual (i.e., unadjusted) p obtained for the jth t test (the one in question), ΣW is the sum of all the weights, and W_j is the weight of the specific t test in question. Suppose that we obtain the following unadjusted p values for six t tests: .005, .07, .08, .11, .001, .004. The corresponding ensemble-adjusted p values, which are listed in Table 14.5, reflect the conservative nature of the Bonferroni adjustment. Where three of the original six t tests showed $p \leq .005$, none of the adjusted p values are that low, and only two remain at $p < .05$.

Although it is often useful to weight t tests by their importance, it is not necessary to do so. If we prefer no weighting, which is equivalent to equal weighting, all our W_j values become 1, and ΣW becomes the sum of the k weights of 1 each, where k is the number of t tests. Therefore, in the unweighted case, we find

$$p \text{ adjusted} = \frac{p_j \Sigma W}{W_j} = \frac{p_j k(1)}{1} = p_j k. \tag{14.16}$$

For the six t tests we have been discussing, the unweighted ensemble-adjusted p values would simply be the unadjusted p multiplied by 6, or .03, .42, .48, .66, .006, .024, respectively. Note again that the particular weighting chosen to reflect the importance of each t of a set of t tests must be decided *before* the results of the t tests are known so that we cannot inadvertently assign importance weightings as a function of the results obtained. When using any of the Bonferroni procedures we have described, researchers should routinely report both the adjusted and the original p values.

BONFERRONI TOLERANCE VALUE

We have assumed all along that either we have planned all the *t* tests or, if not, we can calculate the number of implicit *t* tests computed. In large and complex data sets, it is sometimes difficult to calculate the number of implicit *t* tests. In such cases it is useful to compute an accurate *p* value for the most significant result of any interest in the data set (*p* max) and then to divide this *p* into α (usually .05) to yield a tolerance value (k_t) for the number of *t* tests computed, that is,

$$k_t = \frac{\alpha}{p \text{ max}}, \tag{14.17}$$

where the quantity k_t gives the number of *t* tests that could have been computed to keep the most significant result still properly adjusted within the α level chosen (usually .05).

For example, suppose a very complex study in which perhaps dozens, or even scores, of sensible *t* tests are possible. The most statistically significant result is significant at .00015. From Equation 14.17, we find $k_t = .05/.00015 = 333.3$. This tells us that we would have to carry out more than 333 implicit *t* tests to decide that the *p* max of .00015 is perhaps not significant after all. Whether such a number seems too high to be plausible depends on the research design used. In this application of the Bonferroni, as in all others, it makes no difference whether the tests being considered are independent of one another or not.

COMPARING TWO INDEPENDENT VARIABILITIES

There are both methodological and substantive reasons to compare the variabilities or dispersions of two groups we are comparing. Methodologically, we may be concerned about the homogeneity of the variance assumption underlying the use of *t* and *F* tests. We discussed this issue earlier but did not describe a procedure for comparing two independent variances to determine the degree to which the homogeneity assumption has been met. We now describe such a procedure, but first, we want to emphasize that there are often strong substantive grounds for comparing variances as well (Bryk & Raudenbush, 1988).

Suppose we theorize that a particular treatment will lead to greater variance than a control condition, that is, regardless of whether we have also predicted a difference in the group means. For example, suppose our hypothesis is that a moderate degree of stress will increase the variability of performance of an experimental group relative to a zero control group, on the assumption that moderate stress will energize some subjects to perform better but will upset and demoralize others. The predicted net effect will be to increase the variability of the experimental group. Or suppose that we want to know the variability of some new psychological treatment procedure to make sure that it is not simply helping a few patients a lot while also harming a few patients a lot. We cannot address this issue simply by comparing the mean performance of the two conditions.

Whatever our reason for wanting to compare the variabilities of two groups or conditions, the procedure is the same. We divide the larger of the two variances

(S^2_{larger}) by the smaller of the two variances $(S^2_{smaller})$ and refer the quotient to an F table, that is,

$$F = \frac{S^2_{larger}}{S^2_{smaller}} \tag{14.18}$$

There are some subtleties in the use of the standard F tables (e.g., Table B.4 in Appendix B) for this purpose of comparing variabilities. First, we determine the df associated with S^2_{larger} and find the column of our F table corresponding to that value of df. Next, we determine the df associated with $S^2_{smaller}$ and find the row of our F table corresponding to that value of df. Now we use the F table in the usual way *except that we must first double the p levels shown.* Thus, a p of .001 becomes .002, and a p of .005 becomes .01, and so forth, so that .01, .025, .05, .10, and .20 become ps of .02, .05, .10, .20, .40, respectively. The reason is that standard F tables are set up on the assumption that we will always have a particular S^2 in the numerator, for example, $S^2_{between}$ (or $MS_{between}$), and a particular S^2 in the denominator, for example, S^2_{within} (or MS_{within}). However, when using the F table for the purpose of comparing variabilities, the researcher does not usually decide beforehand which S^2 (or MS) will be the numerator but puts the larger S^2 over the smaller one. Doubling the p values shown in the standard F tables merely takes into account this unspecified direction of difference, or "two-tailed" feature of the F test when used in this way. Of course, if we have specifically predicted which particular variability will be larger, we need not double the p values shown, as we are now making a one-tailed test.

ILLUSTRATION USING TRANSFORMATIONS

By way of a detailed example, we turn to the experimental results shown in Table 14.6, where the question was whether the experimental group would show greater or less variability than the control group. The variability is noticeably greater in the experimental group ($S^2 = 83$) than in the control group ($S^2 = 3$), and using Equation 14.18 we find $F = 83/3 = 27.67$. Given four subjects in each group, the df are $4 - 1 = 3$ for both

TABLE 14.6
Illustrative results

	Experimental	Control
	4	1
	16	4
	9	1
	25	4
Σ	54	10
n	4	4
M	13.5	2.5
S^2	83	3

the larger and smaller S^2. Consulting Table B.4, we find at the intersection of $df_1 = 3$ and $df_2 = 3$ that an F of 29.46 is required for statistical significance at the .01 level, and an F of 15.44 is required for significance at the .025 level. For the present application, however, in which we did not specifically test the one-tailed hypothesis that the experimental group would be more variable, we need to *double* the tabled values of p. Therefore, our F is significant between the .02 and .05 levels, two-tailed.

Suppose we are also interested in comparing the means of our two groups and, in doing so, find

$$ t = \frac{M_1 - M_2}{\sqrt{\left(\frac{1}{n_1} + \frac{1}{n_2}\right)S^2}} = \frac{11}{\sqrt{\left(\frac{1}{4} + \frac{1}{4}\right)43}} = 2.37, $$

with 6 df, $p = .03$ one-tailed, and this t is associated with an effect size $r = .70$ or a Cohen's $d = 1.94$. Now we have learned that our experimental group scored significantly higher (from t) and more variably (from F) than our controls. But we may have a problem here.

Our F test comparing variabilities was quite large and, even with a very small sample size, statistically significant. We computed a t to compare means, a t that depends for its proper use on the assumption of equal variances for our two groups. Yet we know the variances to be unequal. It seems prudent here to transform our data in hopes that our transformation will make our variances more nearly equal. For data of this kind, a square root transformation often helps because it tends to pull the large outlying values close to the bulk of the scores, and we will try it here. The square roots of the original scores are shown in Table 14.7. Using Equation 14.18 to test the difference between the larger variance ($S^2 = 1.6667$) and the smaller variance ($S^2 = .3333$), we find $F = 1.6667/.3333 = 5.00$, with 3 df for both the numerator and the denominator. Table B.4 shows that F values of 5.39 and 2.94 are required to reach the .10 and .20 levels, respectively, which are equivalent to ps of .20 and .40 in our present application.

TABLE 14.7
Square root transformation of scores in Table 14.6

	Experimental	Control
	$2 (= \sqrt{4})$	$1 (= \sqrt{1})$
	$4 (= \sqrt{16})$	$2 (= \sqrt{4})$
	$3 (= \sqrt{9})$	$1 (= \sqrt{1})$
	$5 (= \sqrt{25})$	$2 (= \sqrt{4})$
Σ	14	6
n	4	4
M	3.5	1.5
S^2	1.6667	0.3333

Our p value now is not very small, and we may be satisfied that our transformation has worked quite well. Computing our t test to compare means using these transformed scores, we find

$$t = \frac{M_1 - M_2}{\sqrt{\left(\frac{1}{n_1} + \frac{1}{n_2}\right)S^2}} = \frac{2}{\sqrt{\left(\frac{1}{4} + \frac{1}{4}\right)1.00}} = 2.83,$$

and with 6 df, $p = .02$ two-tailed, the effect size $r = .76$, and Cohen's $d = 2.31$. This t test based on the square roots of the original scores is somewhat larger and more significant than was the t test based on our original scores ($t = 2.37$), and we see that the effect size is somewhat larger as well. These results are probably more accurate than those based on the original (i.e., untransformed) scores, because we have better met the assumption of homogeneity of variance on which the use of t distributions depends to some extent.

When our original scores were transformed to their square roots, the F for comparing the two variabilities (Equation 14.18) was not statistically significant. But the F was 5.00, perhaps a bit larger than we might like. Perhaps a different transformation would shrink that F even closer to the value of 1.00 we would obtain if the variabilities were the same. Thus, we will try a $\log_{10}$ transformation, which we can make as easily as a square root transformation by pushing a single key of an inexpensive handheld calculator. This particular transformation tends to pull large outlying values in more sharply than does the square root transformation. The $\log_{10}$ values of the original scores are shown in Table 14.8, and we observe that the variances are now identical in the two groups ($S^2 = .12$), so using Equation 14.18 gives us $F = .12/.12 = 1.00$, with 3 df for both the numerator and the denominator. Table B.4 shows that an F of 2.94 is required to reach the $p = .20$ level, which is equivalent to $p = .40$ in the present application, in which we are comparing variabilities without having made a specific prediction about which variability will be larger. Our $\log_{10}$ transformation has worked very well indeed in achieving homogeneity of variabilities. We now compute t in order to compare the two means

TABLE 14.8
Log transformation of scores in Table 14.6

	Experimental	Control
	.60 (= log 4)	.00 (= log 1)
	1.20 (= log 16)	.60 (= log 4)
	.95 (= log 9)	.00 (= log 1)
	1.40 (= log 25)	.60 (= log 4)
Σ	4.15	1.20
n	4	4
M	1.04	.30
S^2	.12	.12

TABLE 14.9
Comparison of Tables 14.6, 14.7, and 14.8

Data	$F(3, 3)$	$t(6)$	p	r	d
X	27.67	2.37	.03	.70	1.94
$\sqrt{X}$	5.00	2.83	.02	.76	2.31
$\log X$	1.00	3.02	.015	.78	2.47

based on the transformed scores:

$$t = \frac{M_1 + M_2}{\sqrt{\left(\frac{1}{n_1} + \frac{1}{n_2}\right)S^2}} = \frac{.74}{\sqrt{\left(\frac{1}{4} + \frac{1}{4}\right).12}} = 3.02,$$

and with 6 *df*, $p = .015$ one-tailed, the effect size $r = .78$, and Cohen's $d = 2.47$. This *t* test, based on the logs of the original scores, is somewhat larger and more significant than was the *t* test based on the square-root-transformed scores, and the effect size is somewhat larger as well.

Of these three sets of results—based on the original scores (X), the square roots of scores ($\sqrt{X}$), and the logs of scores ($X_{\log 10}$)—the log-transformed results are probably most accurate, as they best meet the assumption of homogeneity of variance. In the present example, however, all three expressions of the data yield quite comparable results (summarized in Table 14.9). The table illustrates the general finding that *t* tests and *F* tests used to compare means are not very badly affected by even substantial heterogeneities of variance, a finding that holds especially when sample sizes are equal (Hays, 1981, 1994; Scheffé, 1959).

COMPARING TWO CORRELATED VARIABILITIES

Our reasons for wanting to compare correlated variabilities are the same as for wanting to compare uncorrelated, or independent, variabilities. That is, we want to check the reasonableness of our assumption of homogeneity of variance, and we want to learn whether variabilities of the same sampling units differ under different conditions. For example, we may measure subjects before and after a treatment condition to learn whether the variability of their responses increased over time. (Of course, we cannot confidently ascribe such a change to the treatment unless we also have a randomized control.) We may want to learn whether two raters of children's behavior differ with respect to the variability of the scale points used. Or we may want to compare the variability of boys and girls in a sample of pairs of fraternal twins.

In all these cases, we would use the same procedure. We compute S^2 for each of the two variabilities to be compared. We also compute the correlation between the pairs of measurements made for our sample of N persons or other sampling units measured twice. If our sampling units are N subjects measured twice, we correlate the first and second measurements. If our sampling units are N children or N patients, each measured (rated) by two raters, we correlate the N pairs of ratings generated by the first and second raters. If our sampling units are N pairs of twins, we correlate the scores obtained by the girl and the boy members of the N pairs.

The statistical test we use for the comparison of correlated variabilities is t, computed as follows:

$$t = \frac{(S_1^2 - S_2^2)\sqrt{N-2}}{2(S_1)(S_2)\sqrt{1-r^2}}, \tag{14.19}$$

where S_1 and S_2 are the two variabilities to be compared (S_1 referring to the larger value), N is the number of pairs of scores, and r is the correlation between the N pairs of scores as described in the preceding paragraph (McNemar, 1969; Walker & Lev, 1953). The value of t obtained from Equation 14.19 is entered into a t table with $df = N - 2$.

As an illustration, suppose we have measured the same 18 sampling units twice (e.g., the same 18 persons pre and post, or the brothers and sisters of 18 pairs of siblings) and found the values of S^2 to be 64 and 36 for the two sets of scores, with a correlation of .90 between the 18 pairs of scores. Then, using Equation 14.19, we find

$$t = \frac{(64 - 36)\sqrt{18-2}}{2(8)(6)\sqrt{1-(.90)^2}} = \frac{112}{96\sqrt{.19}} = 2.68,$$

which, with 16 df, is significant at $p = .02$ two-tailed. Inspection of Equation 14.19 suggests that for any two different, nonzero values of S^2 and for $N > 2$, the larger the r, the larger also the t (i.e., r is an index of the sensitivity to differences between values of S^2). For the present example, Table 14.10 shows that rs from zero to .95 yield t values from 1.17 to 3.74, with associated p levels from .26 to .002.

TABLE 14.10
Associated t and p of r values from .00 to .95

r	t	p (two-tailed)
.00	1.17	.26
.20	1.19	.25
.40	1.27	.22
.60	1.46	.16
.80	1.94	.07
.90	2.68	.02
.95	3.74	.002

COMPARING THREE OR MORE INDEPENDENT VARIABILITIES

Just as for the comparison of two variabilities, there are methodological and substantive reasons for comparing three or more variabilities. The methodological reason again has to do with checking on the reasonableness of the assumption of homogeneity of variance. The substantive reason again has to do with the conditions that may increase or decrease the variabilities of some groups relative to others. The procedures described in this section (Hartley's F_{max}, Cochran's g, Bartlett's test, and Levene's test) permit us to evaluate the homogeneity of variance by procedures that take into account the number of implicit comparisons among the variabilities.

For example, suppose we have two variabilities, with values of S^2 of 64 and 4, each based on $n = 5$ (thus, $df = 4$). Using the procedure of comparing two independent variabilities, we find $F = 64/4 = 16$. Reference to Table B.4 for $df = 4$ for both the numerator and the denominator S^2 shows F to be significant at $p = .02$ two-tailed. (We doubled the p from the tabled value of .01 to .02, as explained earlier.) However, if the S^2 values 64 and 4 are the largest and smallest of several, or k, conditions, there is a total of $k(k - 1)/2$ possible comparisons of variabilities. The larger the k for any given sample size n (or $df = n - 1$), the larger we expect the largest obtained F to be, even if the null hypothesis of no differences among variances is true. The procedures we describe next are designed to adjust for this problem (Snedecor & Cochran, 1989; Walker & Lev, 1953; Winer, 1971).

Hartley's F_{max}

This procedure is elegantly simple, in that we again divide the largest by the smallest variability. Similar to Equation 14.18, but with terms redefined as follows, Hartley's procedure is

$$F_{max} = \frac{S^2_{max}}{S^2_{min}}, \tag{14.20}$$

where S^2_{max} is the largest variability, and S^2_{min} is the smallest variability. The resulting F is then looked up in a special table that takes into account the number of groups being compared and the df of each group. (If the ns are unequal, but not very unequal, the harmonic mean of the df can be used as a reasonable approximation.) Suppose we have six conditions to compare, each with the n, df, and S^2 listed in Table 14.11. From Equation 14.20, $F_{max} = 64/4 = 16$. We refer this value to Table B.11 of Appendix B, where the columns list the number of conditions being compared (6 in this case), and the rows list the df for each condition (4 in this case). The two entries at the intersection of the column headed 6 and the row headed 4 are 29.5 and 69, respectively. Thus, had F_{max} reached 29.5, it would have been significant at $p = .05$, and had it reached 69, it would have been significant at $p = .01$. Our F_{max} of 16 is not even close to being significant at the $p = .05$ level. Looking again at the row headed 4, we see that if the number of conditions (k) were only two or three, an F_{max} of 16 would be significant at the $p = .05$ level.

TABLE 14.11
Illustrative results of six conditions

Condition	n	df	S^2
1	5	4	25
2	5	4	36
3	5	4	9
4	5	4	49
5	5	4	4
6	5	4	64
Total	30	24	187

Cochran's g

Cochran's g is a useful alternative to Hartley's F_{max} especially when we do not have access to the individual S^2 values of each group, but we do have the pooled S^2 for all the groups in the form of the MS_{within}. If we know the largest of the S^2 values, we can test for its size relative to the sum of all the S^2 values. The sum is equivalent to MS_{within} multiplied by k (i.e., the number of conditions). Thus,

$$\text{Cochran's } g = \frac{S^2_{max}}{\Sigma S^2} = \frac{S^2_{max}}{k(MS_{within})}, \qquad (14.21)$$

Once again, tables are available that allow us to determine the significance of the obtained Cochran's g (Eisenhart, Hastay, & Wallis, 1947; Winer, 1971). For the example of six groups in Table 14.11, using Equation 14.21 we find

$$\text{Cochran's } g = \frac{S^2_{max}}{\Sigma S^2} = \frac{64}{187} = .3422,$$

which Table B.12 of Appendix B shows is not large enough to reach the $p = .05$ level. With $k = 6$ groups, $df = 4$ per group, we need Cochran's $g = .4803$ to reach the $p = .05$ level.

Bartlett's Test

Bartlett's test can be used even when the sample sizes of the various groups are very unequal. However, it is not recommended for checking the reasonableness of the assumption of homogeneity of variance. The reason for this cautionary note is that Bartlett's test is likely to yield more significant results than it should, relative to the substantial robustness of the F test that relies on the assumption of homogeneity of variance (Snedecor & Cochran, 1989). Therefore, we omit the computational details, which are available in Snedecor and Cochran (1989), McNemar (1969), Walker and Lev (1953), Winer (1971), Winer et al., (1991), and elsewhere.

Levene's Test

When we have access to the raw data, Levene's test can be very useful no matter how unequal the group sizes. For each observation in each group, we simply compute the *absolute* difference between the obtained score and the mean score of the condition. The absolute differences will be large when variabilities are large. But because no squaring is used, this procedure is robust if the observations come from distributions with long tails (extreme values). Levene's test is simply the *F* test of the analysis of variance of the absolute deviation scores. If *F* is statistically significant, the variances are judged as significantly heterogeneous (Snedecor & Cochran, 1989).

COMPARING THREE OR MORE CORRELATED VARIABILITIES

There is little discussion in textbooks of the comparison of three or more variabilities that are not independent, for example, a sample that is measured under three or more conditions. If such a test is needed, we recommend a natural extension of Levene's test, in which, for each sampling unit, we create a new score. This new score is the absolute difference between the original score and the mean of the condition. We then compute an analysis of variance on the new scores, which provides an *F* test of the null hypothesis of the homogeneity of variances of the original scores. Computational procedures for the required repeated-measures analysis of variance are described in chapter 18.

SUMMARY OF PROCEDURES FOR COMPARING VARIABILITIES

Table 14.12 provides an overview of these various procedures for comparing two or more independent or correlated variabilities.

TABLE 14.12
Tests for comparing variabilities

Number of variabilities	Independence of variabilities	
	Independent	Correlated
Two	*F* test	*t* test
Three or more	Hartley's F_{max}[a]	Extension of Levene's test
	Cochran's g[a]	
	Bartlett's test	
	Levene's test	

[a]Sample sizes of the groups should not be very different.

CHAPTER 15

ONE-WAY
CONTRAST
ANALYSES

FOCUSING OUR QUESTIONS
AND STATISTICAL TESTS

This chapter describes basic computations for focused F tests (i.e., F with numerator $df = 1$) and t tests for one-dimensional (one-way) between-subjects designs in which we want to ask a specific question of more than two groups. These focused statistical tests, called **contrasts,** use weights to represent the hypothesized effect. If the effect truly exists, we are much more likely to detect it and to believe it to be real if we use contrast F or t tests rather than unfocused tests, such as omnibus F tests (i.e., F with $df_{numerator} > 1$) that address only vague or diffuse questions. We also describe a family of effect size correlations (designated as $r_{alerting}$, $r_{contrast}$, $r_{effect\ size}$, and r_{BESD}) for use with contrasts, and we illustrate procedures for comparing and combining contrasts when appropriate. The chapter concludes with a brief discussion of optimal design and the differential allocation of sample sizes. In later chapters we discuss the use of contrasts in higher order designs, in designs with repeated measures, and in tables of counts. (For more detailed discussions of the issues that are raised in this chapter, as well as related issues in the use of contrasts and effect size indices in these and other designs, see Rosenthal, Rosnow, & Rubin, 2000.)

We begin with the hypothetical example of a one-way analysis of variance based on the research results in Table 15.1. In this study, children were administered a cognitive task and the dependent variable was a performance measure. The table shows the mean (M) performance score for each of five age groups (8, 9, 10, 11, 12), given equal sample sizes of $n = 10$ per age group. Table 15.2 shows the overall ANOVA, where we see that the omnibus F for age levels

TABLE 15.1
Performance scores at five age levels

Age level	8	9	10	11	12
M	2.0	3.0	5.0	7.0	8.0
n	10	10	10	10	10

TABLE 15.2
Summary ANOVA of study in Table 15.1

Source	SS	df	MS	F	p
Age levels	260	4	65	1.03	.40
Within error	2835	45	63		

equals 1.03, and the p of .40 for the differences among the five means is far from significant. Based on that omnibus F, should we conclude that age was not an effective variable? If we did so, we would be making a grave error, although, unfortunately, a fairly common one.

Figure 15.1 plots the performance means of the five age levels. We see quite clearly that the pattern of group means is not at all consistent with the conclusion that age and performance are unrelated. Furthermore, if we correlate the levels of age and the levels of performance, we find $r = .992$, and with $df = 3$, $p < .001$ two-tailed. How can we reconcile the clear and obvious results of the plot, the r with 3 df, and the p associated with the r with the omnibus F telling us that age did not matter? The answer, of course, is that the omnibus F in Table 15.2 addressed a question that was of little interest. The question was diffuse and unfocused, asking simply whether there were *any* differences among the five groups, and disregarding entirely the arrangement of the ages that constituted the levels of the independent variable. Rearranging those ages in any other order (e.g., as 12, 11, 10, 9, 8, or as 10, 9, 11, 12, 8), we would still find the same omnibus F of 1.03.

Suppose, however, the researcher who designed and conducted the study was very much interested in whether the children's performance scores were associated with the variable of age. The researcher might have predicted that the scores would increase linearly with age, or perhaps that the scores would be associated with age in some other way. The correlation we computed addressed the question of whether performance increased linearly with age, and that r worked pretty well even though we had only 3 df for testing its significance. What we would like is a way of asking more than one focused question of the data, a way that is more general, flexible, and powerful. These are precisely the characteristics of contrast analyses, and with such a procedure there should be relatively few circumstances in which we would prefer an unfocused, diffuse, omnibus test. Contrasts, as we will illustrate, give us not only greater statistical power, but also greater clarity of substantive interpretation of the research results.

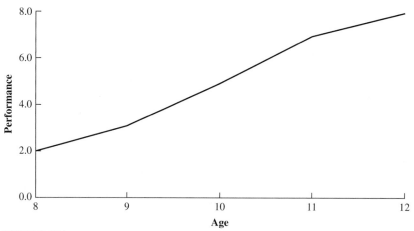

FIGURE 15.1
Mean performance score at five age levels.

CONTRAST *F* TESTS ON ORIGINAL DATA

Contrasts are comparisons, using two or more groups, set up in such a way that the results obtained from the several conditions involved in the research are compared ("contrasted") with the predictions based on theory, hypothesis, or hunch. The predictions are expressed in the form of lambda (λ) weights, also referred to as *lambda coefficients* or *contrast weights*. They can take on any convenient numerical value, as long as the sum of the weights is zero for any given contrast (i.e., $\Sigma\lambda = 0$). To illustrate, we will assume that the study results in Table 15.1 are based on our own original data, and that we predicted a linear increase in performance as the age of the children increased. Instead of relying on the omnibus F of Table 15.2, we compute a focused F that will directly evaluate the specific linear question we put to our data.

To compute the mean square (*MS*) or the sum of squares (*SS*) attributable to our contrast, we use a basic formula for equal sample size (*n*) per condition:

$$MS_{\text{contrast}} = SS_{\text{contrast}} = \frac{nL^2}{\Sigma\lambda_i^2} \tag{15.1}$$

where L equals the weighted sum of all condition means (M_i), and the weights are the corresponding lambda weights (λ_i), or

$$L = \Sigma[M_i\lambda_i] = M_1\lambda_1 + M_2\lambda_2 + M_3\lambda_3 + \cdots + M_k\lambda_k, \tag{15.2}$$

where k equals number of conditions (or groups), and $\Sigma\lambda = 0$. Notice in Equation 15.1 that $MS_{\text{contrast}} = SS_{\text{contrast}}$, the reason being that all contrasts are based on only 1 *df*. Thus, dividing the MS_{contrast} or SS_{contrast} by the appropriate MS_{error} yields an F test of the contrast.

To illustrate with the results of Table 15.1, our prediction is a linear trend, that is, a regular increment of performance for every regular increment of age. We might think of using age levels as our λ weights, and they would be 8, 9, 10, 11, 12. However, the sum of these values is not zero, as required, but 50. Fortunately, that is easy to correct. We simply subtract the mean age level of 10 (i.e., $50/5 = 10$), which gives us $(8 - 10)$, $(9 - 10)$, $(10 - 10)$, $(11 - 10)$, $(12 - 10)$, or $-2, -1, 0, +1, +2$, a set of weights that does sum to zero. To save ourselves the effort of having to calculate these weights, Table 15.3 (after Snedecor & Cochran, 1967, p. 572) provides them for linear, quadratic, and cubic orthogonal (i.e., independent) trends, curves, or polynomials (algebraic expressions of two or more terms). (Later in this chapter, we describe these orthogonal polynomials in more detail.)

The basic data for computing our linear contrast F are shown in Table 15.4. The first row repeats the group means from Table 15.1. The second row shows our linear contrast weights, and the row total shows that they sum to zero. The third row displays the products of multiplying the means and their corresponding lambda weights, where the row total is symbolized as $L = 16$. The fourth row shows the squared lambdas, and the row total shows that $\Sigma\lambda^2 = 10$. The bottom row shows the equal n per condition,

TABLE 15.3
Weights for orthogonal polynomial-based contrasts

k^a	Polynomial[b]					Ordered conditions					
		1	2	3	4	5	6	7	8	9	10
2	Linear	−1	+1								
3	Linear	−1	0	+1							
	Quadratic	+1	−2	+1							
4	Linear	−3	−1	+1	+3						
	Quadratic	+1	−1	−1	+1						
	Cubic	−1	+3	−3	+1						
5	Linear	−2	−1	0	+1	+2					
	Quadratic	+2	−1	−2	−1	+2					
	Cubic	−1	+2	0	−2	+1					
6	Linear	−5	−3	−1	+1	+3	+5				
	Quadratic	+5	−1	−4	−4	−1	+5				
	Cubic	−5	+7	+4	−4	−7	+5				
7	Linear	−3	−2	−1	0	+1	+2	+3			
	Quadratic	+5	0	−3	−4	−3	0	+5			
	Cubic	−1	+1	+1	0	−1	−1	+1			
8	Linear	−7	−5	−3	−1	+1	+3	+5	+7		
	Quadratic	+7	+1	−3	−5	−5	−3	+1	+7		
	Cubic	−7	+5	+7	+3	−3	−7	−5	+7		
9	Linear	−4	−3	−2	−1	0	+1	+2	+3	+4	
	Quadratic	+28	+7	−8	−17	−20	−17	−8	+7	+28	
	Cubic	−14	+7	+13	+9	0	−9	−13	−7	+14	
10	Linear	−9	−7	−5	−3	−1	+1	+3	+5	+7	+9
	Quadratic	+6	+2	−1	−3	−4	−4	−3	−1	+2	+6
	Cubic	−42	+14	+35	+31	+12	−12	−31	−35	−14	+42

[a]Number of conditions.

[b]Shape of trend.

TABLE 15.4
Basic data for linear contrast F

Age level	8	9	10	11	12	Row totals
M_i	2.0	3.0	5.0	7.0	8.0	
λ_i	-2	-1	0	$+1$	$+2$	$\Sigma\lambda = 0$
$M_i\lambda_i$	-4.0	-3.0	0	7.0	16.0	$L = 16.0$
λ_i^2	4	1	0	1	4	$\Sigma\lambda^2 = 10$
n_i	10	10	10	10	10	$N = 50$

TABLE 15.5
Summary ANOVA showing linear contrast

Source	SS	df	MS	F	p
Age levels	260	4	65	1.03	.40
Contrast	256	1	256	4.06	.05
Noncontrast	4	3	1.33	0.02	—
Within error	2835	45	63		
Total	3095	49			

which total $N = 50$. Substituting in Equation 15.1, we find

$$MS_{contrast} = \frac{nL^2}{\Sigma\lambda_i^2} = \frac{10 \times (16)^2}{10} = 256,$$

or working directly with the individual group values in Table 15.4, we find

$$MS_{contrast} = \frac{10[(2.0)(-2) + (3.0)(-1) + (5.0)(0) + (7.0)(+1) + (8.0)(+2)]^2}{(-2)^2 + (-1)^2 + (0)^2 + (+1)^2 + (+2)^2}$$

$$= \frac{10(16.0)^2}{10} = \frac{2560}{10} = 256.$$

To compute the F test for our contrast, we need only divide $MS_{contrast} = 256$ by the MS_{within} of 63 shown in Table 15.2, that is,

$$F_{contrast} = \frac{MS_{constrast}}{MS_{within}}, \tag{15.3}$$

which yields $F_{contrast} = 256/63 = 4.06$. This value of $F_{contrast}$, with $df_{numerator} = 1$ and $df_{denominator} = 45$, has $p = .05$. Table 15.5 provides a summary of what we have found so far, showing the sum of squares of our linear contrast carved out of the overall between-conditions sum of squares. As all Fs used to test contrasts have only 1 df in the numerator, we can take the square root of our $F_{contrast}$ to obtain the t test for our linear contrast, should we want to make a one-tailed t test. In this instance, a one-tailed t test would be quite sensible, and we find $t(45) = 2.02$, $p = .025$ one-tailed.

It is characteristic of contrast sums of squares that they are identical whether we use a given set of weights or their opposite (i.e., the weights multiplied by -1). Thus, had we used the weights $+2, +1, 0, -1, -2$ instead of the weights $-2, -1, 0, +1, +2$, we would still have obtained the same results from Equation 15.1, namely, $SS_{\text{contrast}} = 256$, and $F(1.45) = 4.06, p = .05$. This p value, though one-tailed in the F distribution (in that it refers only to the right-hand portion of the F distribution) is two-tailed with respect to the hypothesis that performance increases with age. If we take $\sqrt{F_{\text{contrast}}} = t$, as we did above, we must be very careful in making one-tailed t tests to be sure that the results do in fact bear out our prediction and not its opposite. A convenient device is to give t (and any associated effect-size estimates) a positive sign when the result is in the predicted direction and a negative sign when the result is in the opposite direction of what was predicted.

Of course, we are not limited to testing a linear trend, though it is certainly a natural procedure for developmental researchers. However, other contrasts may be preferred in other circumstances. Suppose, for example, we predicted only that 12-year-olds would exhibit superior performance to 8-year-olds. In that case we would have chosen weights of $-1, 0, 0, 0, +1$ for our five age levels. Multiplying the five group means by these five corresponding λ weights would give us $M_i\lambda_i$ scores of $-2, 0, 0, 0, 8$, which sum to $L = 6$. Squaring our five λ weights would give us $1, 0, 0, 0, 1$, which sum to $\Sigma\lambda^2 = 2$. Substituting the values into Equation 15.1, again with $n = 10$, we find

$$MS_{\text{contrast}} = \frac{nL^2}{\Sigma\lambda_i^2} = \frac{10 \times (6)^2}{2} = 180,$$

which, when divided by the mean square for error of our earlier ANOVA, yields

$$F_{\text{contrast}} = \frac{MS_{\text{contrast}}}{MS_{\text{within}}} = \frac{180}{63} = 2.86,$$

and with $df_{\text{numerator}} = 1$ and $df_{\text{denominator}} = 45, p = .098$. Alternatively, because $\sqrt{F_{\text{contrast}}} = t_{\text{contrast}}$, and $\sqrt{2.86} = 1.69$, we have the option of reporting $t_{\text{contrast}} = 1.69$, and with $df = 45$, one-tailed $p = .049$.

Or suppose our prediction was that both the 8- and 9-year-old children would score lower than the 12-year-olds. We could then have chosen lambda weights of $-1, -1, 0, 0, +2$ (recall that our lambdas must sum to zero, so the $+2$ of the 12-year-olds is needed to balance the -1 and -1 of the 8- and 9-year olds). Multiplying the group means by these five corresponding λ weights would give us $M_i\lambda_i$ scores of $-2, -3, 0, 0, 16$, which sum to $L = 11$. Squaring our five λ weights would give us $1, 1, 0, 0, 4$, which sum to $\Sigma\lambda^2 = 6$. Substituting these values in Equation 15.1, again with equal $n = 10$, we find

$$MS_{\text{contrast}} = \frac{nL^2}{\Sigma\lambda_i^2} = \frac{10 \times (11)^2}{6} = 201.67,$$

which, when divided by the mean square for error of 63, yields

$$F_{\text{contrast}} = \frac{MS_{\text{contrast}}}{MS_{\text{within}}} = \frac{201.67}{63} = 3.20,$$

and $p = .08$. Alternatively, as $\sqrt{3.20} = 1.79$, we have the option in this case as well of reporting $t(45) = 1.79, p = .04$ one-tailed.

CONTRAST t TESTS ON ORIGINAL DATA

We can also compute t directly, where the advantage of the procedure we now describe is that it can be used whether the ns are equal or unequal. The general expression for a contrast t is

$$t_{contrast} = \frac{\Sigma(M_i\lambda_i)}{\sqrt{MS_{within}\left(\Sigma\frac{\lambda_i^2}{n_i}\right)}} = \frac{L}{\sqrt{MS_{within}\left(\Sigma\frac{\lambda_i^2}{n_i}\right)}}, \tag{15.4}$$

where $L = \Sigma[M_i\lambda_i]$ as defined in Equation 15.2, and the degrees of freedom for $t_{contrast}$ are the degrees of freedom in MS_{within}.

Using Equation 15.4 with the data in Table 15.4, and given the prediction of a linear increment in performance scores, we find

$$t_{contrast} = \frac{(2.0)(-2) + (3.0)(-1) + (5.0)(0) + (7.0)(+1) + (8.0)(+2)}{\sqrt{63\left[\frac{(-2)^2}{10} + \frac{(-1)^2}{10} + \frac{(0)^2}{10} + \frac{(+1)^2}{10} + \frac{(+2)^2}{10}\right]}}$$

$$= \frac{16.0}{\sqrt{63}} = 2.02,$$

which, not unexpectedly, is the identical value of t we obtained previously by taking the square root of $F_{contrast}$. The appealing feature of Equation 15.4 is that we can use it even when we have different sample sizes in the various conditions and have only the mean and standard deviation for each condition. We can estimate the error term (MS_{within}) by weighting each squared standard deviation by its df ($n_i - 1$) and dividing the quantity $\Sigma[(n_i - 1)(SD)^2]$ by the sum of the df. Furthermore, we can always square $t_{contrast}$ to find $F_{contrast}$, a fact that is useful to remember when we discuss the calculation of effect sizes for contrasts.

CARVING CONTRASTS OUT OF PUBLISHED DATA

So far, we have concentrated on the computation of contrasts when we have the original data. Often, however, we want to compute a contrast based on other people's published data. As useful as Equation 15.4 is, not every study reports the within error, whereas many researchers report omnibus F tests quite routinely. Even if all we know are the results of the omnibus F, the df with which the F is associated, and the group means, we can easily compute a contrast. Suppose that all we know is that the overall $F(4,45) = 1.03$, and the group means on which that F was based are 2.0, 3.0, 5.0, 7.0, 8.0. The number of possible five-group sequences of the five group means is 120 (i.e., $5! = 5 \times 4 \times 3 \times 2 \times 1 = 120$), and any of these 120 permutations will yield the same omnibus F. Because we are specifically interested in whether there was any evidence of a linear progression as a function of age levels, we decide to compute a linear contrast, which we can do in three easy steps:

First, we determine the size of the maximum possible contrast F (symbolized as F_{MPC}) by multiplying the reported overall F by its numerator df. This F_{MPC} represents the largest value of F that any contrast carved out of the sum of squares of the numerator of the reported overall F can possibly achieve. It can achieve this value only if all of the variation among the means tested by the overall F is associated with the contrast computed, with nothing left over.

Second, we identify the proportion of variation among the means that is accounted for by our linear contrast as defined by its lambda weights. To do this, we simply correlate the means (M_i) and their respective lambda (λ_i) weights by punching a few keys of a good handheld calculator. This correlation is an alerting r (designated as either r_{alerting} or $r_{M\lambda}$). Squaring this value (r^2_{alerting}, or $r^2_{M\lambda}$) immediately gives the proportion of variation among means that is accounted for by our contrast weights.

Third, we multiply the results of the first and second steps to obtain our contrast F, that is,

$$F_{\text{contrast}} = F_{\text{MPC}} \times r^2_{\text{alerting}}. \tag{15.5}$$

To illustrate with our continuing example, first, we compute $F_{\text{MPC}} = 1.03 \times 4 = 4.12$. Next, we correlate the means of 2.0, 3.0, 5.0, 7.0, 8.0 with the lambdas of -2, -1, 0, $+1$, $+2$ and find that $r_{\text{alerting}} = .992$ and $r^2_{\text{alerting}} = .984$. The final step, described in Equation 15.5, is to multiply those results ($4.12 \times .984$), yielding $F_{\text{contrast}} = 4.05$ (which, within rounding error, is the value of F_{contrast} that we computed from the original data). And, of course, $\sqrt{F_{\text{contrast}}} = t_{\text{contrast}}$.

If we have an omnibus F and enough information to solve for the sum of squares between conditions, it is easy enough to estimate the sum of squares within conditions. That is, we simply rearrange the F ratio of $MS_{\text{between}}/MS_{\text{within}}$, so that we solve for MS_{within} by dividing the value of MS_{between} by F. But suppose we do not have a reported omnibus F, but we know the group means and the n per group and can estimate MS_{within} from the reported standard deviations (as we described in the preceding section). An alternative formula for F_{contrast} is

$$F_{\text{contrast}} = \frac{r^2_{\text{alerting}} \times SS_{\text{between}}}{MS_{\text{within}}}. \tag{15.6}$$

We compute r^2_{alerting} as before, and we can obtain the between-sum-of-squares from

$$SS_{\text{between}} = \Sigma[n_i (M_i - \overline{M})^2], \tag{15.7}$$

where $\overline{M}$ is the mean of the group means, and M_i is any group mean. With the results in Table 15.1, in this approach the first step is to obtain r_{alerting}, the correlation between the five group means and their corresponding lambda weights ($r_{\text{alerting}} = .992$), and then to square this value, which gives us $r^2_{\text{alerting}} = .984$. Step 2 is to compute the between-conditions sum of squares. Substituting in Equation 15.7, with $\overline{M} = (2.0 + 3.0 + 5.0 + 7.0 + 8.0)/5 = 5.0$, we find

$$\begin{aligned}
SS_{\text{between}} &= 10(2.0 - 5.0)^2 + 10(3.0 - 5.0)^2 + 10(5.0 - 5.0)^2 \\
&\quad + 10(7.0 - 5.0)^2 + 10(8.0 - 5.0)^2 \\
&= 90 + 40 + 0 + 40 + 90 = 260.
\end{aligned}$$

The final step is to substitute in Equation 15.6:

$$F_{\text{contrast}} = \frac{.984 \times 260}{63} = 4.06.$$

ORTHOGONAL CONTRASTS

When we consider a set of results based on k conditions, it is possible to compute up to $k - 1$ contrasts, each of which is uncorrelated with, or *orthogonal to,* every other contrast. Contrasts are orthogonal to each other when the correlation between them is zero. The correlation between them is zero when the sum of the products of the corresponding lambda weights is zero. For example, Table 15.6 shows two sets of contrast weights (λ_1 set and λ_2 set) as orthogonal. The λ_1 set can be seen to represent four points on a straight line. The λ_2 set can be seen to represent a concave, or U-shaped, function, also called a *quadratic trend.* Shown in the bottom row are the products of those linear and quadratic weights, which sum to zero and thus are orthogonal.

A particularly useful set of orthogonal contrasts based on the coefficients of orthogonal polynomials (curves or trends) should be considered whenever the k conditions of a study can be arranged from the smallest to the largest levels of the independent variable, usually when age levels, dosage levels, learning trials, or some other ordered levels constitute the independent variable. Returning to Table 15.3, we see that, when there are three levels or conditions (represented as $k = 3$), the weights defining a linear trend are $-1, 0, +1$. We also see that orthogonal weights defining a quadratic trend for $k = 3$ ordered conditions are $+1, -2, +1$. No matter how many levels of k there are in Table 15.3, the linear trend lambdas always show a consistent gain (or loss), and the orthogonal weights defining a quadratic trend always show a change in direction from down to up in a U-shaped curve (or up to down in a ∩-shaped curve). Cubic trends, which can be assessed when there are four or more conditions, show two changes of direction, from up to down to up (or down to up to down).

Figure 15.2 shows the results of three hypothetical studies that were (a) perfectly linear, (b) perfectly quadratic, and (c) perfectly cubic. The three plots show idealized results. In most real-world applications we find combinations of linear and nonlinear results. For example, the results in Figure 15.3 show a curve that has both strong linear and strong quadratic components.

We have noted that it is possible to compute up to $k - 1$ orthogonal contrasts among a set of k means or totals. For example, if we have four conditions, we can compute three orthogonal contrasts, each based on a different polynomial or trend: the linear, the quadratic, and the cubic. The sums of squares of these three contrasts would add up to the total sum of squares among the four conditions. Although there are only $k - 1$ orthogonal contrasts in a given set, such as those based on orthogonal polynomials, an infinite number of *sets* of contrasts can be computed, each comprising $k - 1$ orthogonal

TABLE 15.6

Illustration of orthogonal contrast weights

Contrast	Condition				
	A	**B**	**C**	**D**	**Σ**
λ_1 set	-3	-1	$+1$	$+3$	0
λ_2 set	$+1$	-1	-1	$+1$	0
$\lambda_1 \times \lambda_2$	-3	$+1$	-1	$+3$	0

contrasts. The *sets* of contrasts, however, are not orthogonal to one another. This point is illustrated in Table 15.7, in which both sets consist of three mutually orthogonal contrasts. However, none of the three contrasts in Set I is orthogonal to any of the contrasts of Set II.

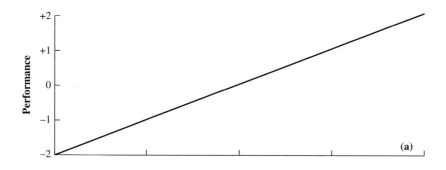

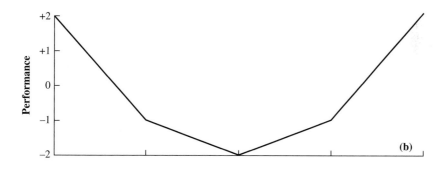

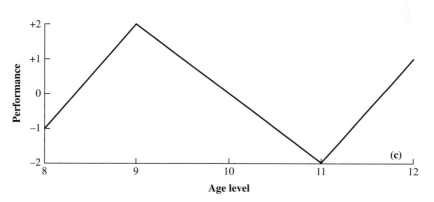

FIGURE 15.2
Illustrations of (a) linear, (b) quadratic, and (c) cubic trends.

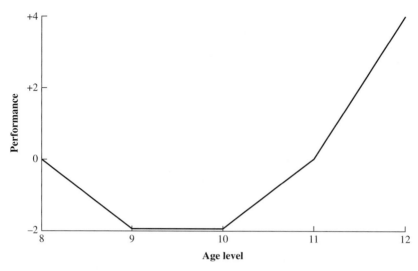

FIGURE 15-3
Curve showing linear and quadratic components.

TABLE 15.7
Further illustrations of sets of contrasts

	Contrast Set I					Contrast Set II			
	A	B	C	D		A	B	C	D
λ_1	−3	−1	+1	+3	λ_1	−1	−1	−1	+3
λ_2	+1	−1	−1	+1	λ_2	−1	−1	+2	0
λ_3	−1	+3	−3	+1	λ_3	−1	+1	0	0

NONORTHOGONAL CONTRASTS

The advantage of using orthogonal contrasts is that each contrast addresses a fresh and nonoverlapping question. Nonetheless, there is no a priori reason not to use correlated (or nonorthogonal) contrasts. An especially valuable use of these contrasts is in the comparison of competing hypotheses. Suppose a researcher is interested in evaluating two theories and a pair of hypotheses based on those theories. Each theory—and each hypothesis, in turn—implies a different pattern of psychological benefits as the number of counseling sessions is varied from one to four. Hypothesis I predicts there will be gradual improvement continuing over the four levels of session frequency. Hypothesis II predicts no difference in benefits except that people given four sessions will show greater benefits than those given fewer sessions. To assess the competing predictions, the researcher designs a fully randomized experiment consisting of four groups, corresponding to one, two, three, or four sessions of counseling, with three people in each group. Table 15.8 shows the hypothetical

TABLE 15.8

Hypothetical study of the effects of number of counseling sessions on psychological functioning[a]

	Number of counseling sessions				
	1	2	3	4	Σ
Means	2.0	3.0	4.0	7.0	16
Hypothesis I (λs)	−3	−1	+1	+3	0
Hypothesis II (λs)	−1	−1	−1	+3	0

$$SS_I = \frac{nL^2}{\Sigma\lambda_i^2} = \frac{n[\Sigma M_i\lambda_i]^2}{\Sigma\lambda_i^2} = \frac{3[(2.0)(-3) + (3.0)(-1) + (4.0)(+1) + (7.0)(+3)]^2}{(-3)^2 + (-1)^2 + (+1)^2 + (+3)^2} = 38.4$$

$$SS_{II} = \frac{nL^2}{\Sigma\lambda_i^2} = \frac{n[\Sigma M_i\lambda_i]^2}{\Sigma\lambda_i^2} = \frac{3[(2.0)(-1) + (3.0)(-1) + (4.0)(-1) + (7.0)(+3)]^2}{(-1)^2 + (-1)^2 + (-1)^2 + (+3)^2} = 36.0$$

$$SS_{between} = \Sigma[n(M_i - \overline{M})^2] = 3(2.0 - 4.0)^2 + 3(3.0 - 4.0)^2 + 3(4.0 - 4.0)^2 + 3(7.0 - 4.0)^2 = 42.0$$

[a]$n = 3$ in each group

results, the contrast weights used to test each hypothesis, the sums of squares associated with each contrast (Equation 15.1, with L defined in Equation 15.2), and the sums of squares between all conditions (Equation 15.7) with $df = k - 1 = 3$.

Both contrasts do an impressive job of fitting the data. The sum of squares of Hypothesis I (SS_I) accounts for $100(38.4/42.0) = 91.4\%$ of the $SS_{between}$, and the sum of squares of Hypothesis II (SS_{II}) accounts for $100(36.0/42.0) = 85.7\%$ of the $SS_{between}$. Hypothesis I did a little better than Hypothesis II, but Hypothesis II did well enough that the researcher is reluctant simply to abandon the underlying theory. That both hypotheses did well should not surprise us much, as the correlation between the weights representing the two hypotheses was quite substantial ($r = .77$). We will have more to say about comparing contrasts (as well as combining them when it appears useful to do so), but first, we turn to the issue of effect size indices for contrasts.

EFFECT SIZE INDICES FOR CONTRASTS

So far in our discussion of contrasts, we have mentioned only one effect-size indicator, the **alerting** r (i.e., $r_{alerting}$ or $r_{M\lambda}$), or the correlation between the group or condition means and their associated lambda weights. In previous chapters we described the **effect size correlation** between group (or condition) membership and individual scores on the dependent measure in two-group (or two-condition) designs. Besides those two effect-size indices, two others that are informative in the interpretation of contrasts are the **contrast** r and the **binomial effect-size** r. We begin in this section by discussing three members of this correlational family ($r_{alerting}$, $r_{contrast}$, and $r_{effect\ size}$), and in the following section we discuss the binomial effect-size r. In these and subsequent discussions, we will draw on some of our earlier writing (Rosenthal, Rosnow, & Rubin, 2000; Rosnow & Rosenthal, 1996a, 2002; Rosnow, Rosenthal, & Rubin, 2000).

The Alerting Correlation

As we have already seen, the alerting r is a convenient way of evaluating the "success" of any contrast, because the squared alerting correlation (i.e., r^2_{alerting} or $r^2_{\text{M}\lambda}$) immediately tells us the proportion of the between-conditions sum of squares (SS_{between}) that is accounted for by the particular contrast. That is,

$$r^2_{\text{alerting}} = \frac{SS_{\text{contrast}}}{SS_{\text{between}}}. \tag{15.8}$$

Suppose we have $k = 5$ groups, and therefore $df_{\text{between}} = k - 1 = 4$. Any r^2_{alerting} that is substantially greater than .25 will catch our eye, because we might have expected .25 (i.e., the reciprocal of the df) if each of our four df were associated with just its "fair share" of the SS_{between}.

The squared alerting r can also be computed from

$$r^2_{\text{alerting}} = \frac{F_{\text{contrast}}}{F_{\text{contrast}} + F_{\text{noncontrast}}(df_{\text{noncontrast}})}, \tag{15.9}$$

where $F_{\text{noncontrast}}$ is the noncontrast F for all sources of variation other than the contrast, and the $df_{\text{noncontrast}}$ is the df_{between} less 1. We can find $F_{\text{noncontrast}}$ from

$$F_{\text{noncontrast}} = \frac{(SS_{\text{between}} - MS_{\text{contrast}})/df_{\text{noncontrast}}}{MS_{\text{within}}}, \tag{15.10}$$

or

$$F_{\text{noncontrast}} = \frac{F_{\text{between}}(df_{\text{between}}) - F_{\text{contrast}}}{df_{\text{noncontrast}}}. \tag{15.11}$$

Equation 15.10 is more convenient when we have access to all the sums of squares, and Equation 15.11 is useful when we have access only to various Fs, a situation we frequently encounter when analyzing other investigators' results (e.g., in meta-analytic applications).

We can illustrate these calculations using the hypothetical study presented at the start of this chapter. The alerting r directly obtained by correlating the five means of 2.0, 3.0, 5.0, 7.0, 8.0 (Table 15.1) with their respective linear contrast weights of $-2, -1, 0, +1, +2$ was $r_{\text{M}\lambda} = .992$ and squaring this value gave $r^2_{\text{alerting}} = .984$. Similarly, substitution in Equation 15.8 with $SS_{\text{contrast}} = 256$ and $SS_{\text{between}} = 260$ (Table 15.5) gives us (within rounding error) $r^2_{\text{alerting}} = 256/260 = .9846$. Alternatively, using Equation 15.9 (along with the results in Table 15.5), we find

$$r^2_{\text{alerting}} = \frac{4.06}{4.06 + 0.02(3)} = .985.$$

Continuing with this example and the results in Table 15.5, substituting in Equation 15.10 gives

$$F_{\text{noncontrast}} = \frac{(260 - 256)/3}{63} = 0.02,$$

or substituting in Equation 15.11 gives

$$F_{\text{noncontrast}} = \frac{1.03(4) - 4.06}{3} = 0.02.$$

The Contrast Correlation

When we compute a t or F on two means, we are computing a "wired-in" contrast, where the implicit contrast weights are $+1$, -1 or -1, $+1$. In chapter 12, we described the effect size r in this situation as the point-biserial correlation between each subject's group membership (coded as 0 or 1) and the score on a continuous variable. A standard formula for computing $r_{\text{effect size}}$ from t with two groups was given in Equation 12.1 as

$$r = \sqrt{\frac{t^2}{t^2 + df}},$$

with $df = N - 2$. However, when the contrast is computed on more than two independent groups, $r_{\text{effect size}}$ is no longer a point-biserial correlation. Thus, when $k > 2$, we regard Equation 12.1 as the **contrast correlation** (r_{contrast}) rather than the $r_{\text{effect size}}$. The reason is that Equation 12.1 now gives the partial correlation between scores on the outcome variable and the lambdas associated with the group after the elimination of all between-group noncontrast variation. (For a more detailed description of this partial correlation, see Rosenthal, Rosnow, & Rubin, 2000.)

Therefore, on the understanding that all sources of between-group variation other than the contrast have been removed, we obtain r_{contrast} from

$$r_{\text{contrast}} = \sqrt{\frac{t_{\text{contrast}}^2}{t_{\text{contrast}}^2 + df_{\text{within}}}} = \frac{t_{\text{contrast}}}{\sqrt{t_{\text{contrast}}^2 + df_{\text{within}}}}. \tag{15.12}$$

We also refer to r_{contrast} as $r_{Y\lambda \cdot \text{NC}}$, denoting that it is the partial correlation between the individual scores on the dependent variable (Y) and a set of lambda weights (λ), with noncontrast (NC) sources of variation removed (Rosnow & Rosenthal, 1996a). Because any contrast F equals t^2, using the summary ANOVA results of Table 15.5 where the contrast $F = 4.06$, Equation 15.12 yields

$$r_{\text{contrast}} = \sqrt{\frac{4.06}{4.06 + 45}} = \frac{2.015}{\sqrt{4.06 + 45}} = .29.$$

The Effect Size Correlation

With $k = 2$, there are no sources of noncontrast variation to be eliminated, so that $r_{\text{contrast}} = r_{\text{effect size}}$ in two-group designs. Similarly, if r_{alerting}^2 revealed that a contrast had accounted for virtually all the between-group variation in a design with three or more groups, then r_{contrast} would be virtually equivalent to $r_{\text{effect size}}$. However, r_{contrast} can be quite large, yet not be a reflection of a similarly large $r_{\text{effect size}}$. The reason is that $r_{\text{effect size}}$ is the simple, unpartialed correlation between subjects' individual scores (Y_i) and the lambda weights associated with those scores (λ_i), and thus we can also symbolize $r_{\text{effect size}}$ as $r_{Y\lambda}$. When we think that r_{contrast} is probably a good approximation of $r_{\text{effect size}}$ in designs with more than two groups, then Equation 15.12 is a convenient way of estimating $r_{\text{effect size}}$.

To reiterate, $r_{\text{effect size}}$ (or $r_{Y\lambda}$) should be understood as the simple correlation (unpartialed) between the contrast weight (λ) associated with membership in a particular group or condition and scores on the dependent variable. To compute this simple correlation, we treat the noncontrast between-group variability as additional error variance, then

$$r_{\text{effect size}} = \sqrt{\frac{F_{\text{contrast}}}{F_{\text{contrast}} + F_{\text{noncontrast}}\left(df_{\text{noncontrast}}\right) + df_{\text{within}}}}, \tag{15.13}$$

which from the data in Table 15.5 gives

$$r_{\text{effect size}} = \sqrt{\frac{4.06}{4.06 + 0.02\,(3) + 45}} = .29.$$

Alternatively, we can use the omnibus F (i.e., F_{between}) and calculate

$$r_{\text{effect size}} = \sqrt{\frac{F_{\text{contrast}}}{F_{\text{between}}\left(df_{\text{between}}\right) + df_{\text{within}}}}, \tag{15.14}$$

which, in our example of the data in Table 15.5, gives

$$r_{\text{effect size}} = \sqrt{\frac{4.06}{1.03\,(4) + 45}} = .29.$$

The r_{contrast} and the $r_{\text{effect size}}$ are identical after rounding in this example because the r^2_{alerting} nearly equals 1.0. Thus, we use the squared alerting correlation as evidence to help us decide when we can conveniently use Equation 15.12 to estimate $r_{\text{effect size}}$ in contrast analyses based on $k > 2$ independent groups.

THE BESD AND THE BINOMIAL EFFECT-SIZE CORRELATION

In chapter 11 we described the binomial effect-size display (BESD) as a way of visually displaying the real-world implications of effect sizes in two-group designs with continuous or categorical data. It will be recalled that the purpose of the BESD is to represent the $r_{\text{effect size}}$ so that both the independent and dependent variables are cast as dichotomous and each is split at its median, with row and column margins set at 100 observations. The question we turn to now is how to generalize the use of the BESD to the situation of three or more groups.

As a review of our earlier description of the BESD, let us suppose that $r_{\text{effect size}} = .10$ in a clinical trial comparing the level of improvement in subjects who were randomly administered either a newly developed drug or a standard drug in a between-groups design. Table 15.9 shows the corresponding BESD, in which cell values can be interpreted as percentages. In the upper-left and lower-right cells, we calculated 55% by adding one half the value of $r_{\text{effect size}}$ to .50 and then multiplying by 100. In the upper-right and lower-left cells, we calculated 45% by subtracting one half the value of $r_{\text{effect size}}$ from .50 and then multiplying by 100. The difference between 45% and 55%, when divided

TABLE 15.9
Binomial effect-size display of $r_{\text{effect size}} = .10$

Condition	Level of improvement		Total
	Above median outcome	Below median outcome	
New drug	55	45	100
Old drug	45	55	100
Total	100	100	200

by 100, gives the original value of the effect size correlation, and it tells us that $r_{\text{effect size}}$ is equivalent to a difference in the rate of improvement of 10% in a population in which half the subjects received the new drug and half did not, with the outcome variable cast as split at the median.

When there are three or more groups involved in a contrast, it is not immediately obvious how to exhibit $r_{\text{effect size}}$ as a BESD or what might be gained from such a display. Under the assumption that the noncontrast sum of squares can be considered "noise," we have described a way of recasting the $r_{\text{effect size}}$ as a BESD (Rosenthal, Rosnow, & Rubin, 2000). For this method we assume that the contrast of interest does, in fact, capture the full predictable relation between the outcome variable (Y) and the treatment groups. In that case, we conceptualize the BESD as reflecting the $r_{\text{effect size}}$ that we would expect to see in a two-group replication of the current study with the same total N. In this conceptualization, the lower level is set at $-1\sigma_\lambda$, and the higher level is set at $+1\sigma_\lambda$, where

$$\sigma_\lambda = \sqrt{\frac{\Sigma\lambda^2}{k}}, \tag{15.15}$$

and, as before, k equals the number of conditions in the contrast.

For example, in a two-group design (with wired-in, or implicit, lambdas of $+1$ and -1), we find

$$\sigma_\lambda = \sqrt{\frac{(+1)^2 + (-1)^2}{2}} = 1,$$

which tells us that the BESD will compare the success rate of the upper level of the treatment (at the $+1\sigma_\lambda$ level) with the success rate of the lower level of the treatment (at the $-1\sigma_\lambda$ level). In designs with more than two groups, the BESD will capture only the levels found at $-1\sigma_\lambda$ and $+1\sigma_\lambda$.

To illustrate, we return to the five-group study of Table 15.1, where the predicted linear increment in performance for ages 8, 9, 10, 11, 12 was represented by lambdas of $-2, -1, 0, +1, +2$, respectively. Substituting those lambdas in Equation 15.15, we find

$$\sigma_\lambda = \sqrt{\frac{(-2)^2 + (-1)^2 + (0)^2 + (+1)^2 + (+2)^2}{5}} = 1.41,$$

and then we use this value to find the lower and upper levels for groups or treatment conditions of the BESD. The mean of the five age levels is $(8 + 9 + 10 + 11 + 12)/5 = 10$. Thus, we find the lower age level by subtracting $\sigma_\lambda = 1.41$ from the mean age level

TABLE 15.10
Linear contrast weights and σ_λ for $k = 2$ to 10 ordinal comparisons

	Ordinal conditions										
k	1	2	3	4	5	6	7	8	9	10	σ_λ
2	-1	$+1$									1.00
3	-1	0	$+1$								0.82
4	-3	-1	$+1$	$+3$							2.24
5	-2	-1	0	$+1$	$+2$						1.41
6	-5	-3	-1	$+1$	$+3$	$+5$					3.42
7	-3	-2	-1	0	$+1$	$+2$	$+3$				2.00
8	-7	-5	-3	-1	$+1$	$+3$	$+5$	$+7$			4.58
9	-4	-3	-2	-1	0	$+1$	$+2$	$+3$	$+4$		2.58
10	-9	-7	-5	-3	-1	$+1$	$+3$	$+5$	$+7$	$+9$	5.74

of 10, and we find the upper age level by adding 1.41 to the mean age level of 10. (To assist in estimating σ_λ, Table 15.10 shows values of σ_λ for linear predictions in designs consisting of 2–10 ordinal conditions.)

We now need to find the value of the $r_{\text{effect size}}$ to be represented in our BESD. If this is a two-group design with equal sample sizes, we can estimate $r_{\text{effect size}}$ from t by Equation 15.12 (i.e., the contrast r equation, or the effect size r in the case of two groups). If the sample sizes of our two-group design are unequal, we can calculate r_{BESD} by

$$r_{\text{BESD}} = \sqrt{\frac{t^2}{t^2 + df_{\text{within}}\left(\frac{n_h}{\bar{n}}\right)}}, \tag{15.16}$$

where n_h is the harmonic mean sample size (defined in Equation 12.2 for a two-group design), and $\bar{n}$ is the arithmetic mean sample size. (It may be recalled from our discussion in chapter 13 that the ratio of these two, subtracted from 1, was described as an indicator of efficiency loss in the unequal-n design relative to the equal-n design; see Equation 13.8.)

When $k > 2$, r_{BESD} is defined as the $r_{\text{effect size}}$ that we would expect to see in a $\pm 1\sigma_\lambda$ two-group replication (with the stipulations noted earlier), which can be calculated by

$$r_{\text{BESD}} = \sqrt{\frac{F_{\text{contrast}}}{F_{\text{contrast}} + F_{\text{noncontrast}}\left(df_{\text{noncontrast}} + df_{\text{within}}\right)}}. \tag{15.17}$$

If $F_{\text{noncontrast}}$ is less than 1.00, it is entered into Equation 15.17 as equal to 1.00. This restriction on $F_{\text{noncontrast}}$ requires the noise level underlying MS_{within} to be at least as large as the noise level of $MS_{\text{noncontrast}}$, and it arises because we are viewing noncontrast variability as the appropriate index of the noise level, which must be at least as large as the within variability.

TABLE 15.11
Binomial effect-size display of $r_{BESD} = .28$ for the study in Table 15.1

Age level	Level of performance		Total
	Above median	Below median	
High age ($M = 11.4$) ($+1\sigma_\lambda$)	64	36	100
Low age ($M = 8.6$) ($-1\sigma_\lambda$)	36	64	100
Total	100	100	200

In our example based on the original results in Table 15.1 and the summary ANOVA in Table 15.5 showing the linear contrast, we enter $F_{noncontrast} = 1.00$ in Equation 15.17 (as Table 15.5 shows it to be less than 1) and find that

$$r_{BESD} = \sqrt{\frac{4.06}{4.06 + [1.00(3 + 45)]}} = .28,$$

which we can interpret as the $r_{effect\ size}$ we would expect to find in a replication that compares the performance of children at the ($10 + 1.4\lambda$ units $=$) age level of 11.4 years with children at the ($10 - 1.4\lambda$ units $=$) age level of 8.6 years, assuming the same total N in the study for which we computed the r_{BESD} and equal sample sizes in these age levels. Table 15.11, interpreted in the usual way, is the BESD corresponding to this result.

OVERVIEW OF THE FOUR EFFECT-SIZE INDICES

It may be useful here to summarize the defining characteristics of the four correlational effect-size indices discussed in this chapter. For this purpose we refer to Table 15.12, which shows that the only differences among these indices occur in the second (or third) term of the denominator.

The $r_{alerting}$ equation in Table 15.12 is simply the square root of Equation 15.9. We recall that $r_{alerting}$ is the correlation between the group means and their associated lambda weights. The equation in the table ignores within-group noise, and its second denominator term incorporates information only about noncontrast between-group variation.

The $r_{contrast}$ equation in the table is a variant of Equation 15.12, which showed the $r_{contrast}$ obtained from $t_{contrast}$. Because $F_{contrast}$ equals t^2, we substituted one term for the other in Equation 15.12. It should also be recalled that $r_{contrast}$ refers to the partial correlation between the lambdas and the individual scores on the dependent measure after removal of the noncontrast sources of between-group variation. The equation for $r_{contrast}$ shown in Table 15.12 ignores noncontrast between-group variation, and its second denominator term incorporates information only about within-group variation.

The $r_{effect\ size}$ equation in the table is Equation 15.13 and refers to the correlation between the lambdas and the individual scores on the dependent measure, or the unpartialed correlation. The equation incorporates information about both the noncontrast

TABLE 15.12
Overview of four effect size indices

$$r_{\text{alerting}} = \sqrt{\frac{F_{\text{contrast}}}{F_{\text{contrast}} + F_{\text{noncontrast}}\left(df_{\text{noncontrast}}\right)}}$$

$$r_{\text{contrast}} = \sqrt{\frac{F_{\text{contrast}}}{F_{\text{contrast}} + df_{\text{within}}}}$$

$$r_{\text{effect size}} = \sqrt{\frac{F_{\text{contrast}}}{F_{\text{contrast}} + F_{\text{noncontrast}}\left(df_{\text{noncontrast}}\right) + df_{\text{within}}}}$$

$$r_{\text{BESD}} = \sqrt{\frac{F_{\text{contrast}}}{F_{\text{contrast}} + F_{\text{noncontrast}}\left(df_{\text{noncontrast}} + df_{\text{within}}\right)}}$$

between-group variation and the within-group variation. The second and third terms of the denominator are simply the second denominator terms imported from r_{alerting} and r_{contrast}.

The r_{BESD} equation in the table is Equation 15.17 and refers to the value of $r_{\text{effect size}}$ that we would expect to see in a two-group replication with the same total N and the two treatment levels chosen from σ_λ (defined in Equation 15.15). Like the $r_{\text{effect size}}$ equation, the r_{BESD} equation in the table incorporates information about the noncontrast between-group variation and the within-group variation, but with the restriction that the noise level of the within-group variation must be set at least as high as the noise level of the noncontrast variation. Thus, when $F_{\text{noncontrast}}$ is less than 1.00, it is entered into the r_{BESD} equation as equal to 1.00. It is the noise level of the noncontrast variation that we regard as the appropriate index of the noise level for doing interpolation to levels of the independent variable not in the study.

It is possible for r_{contrast}, $r_{\text{effect size}}$, and r_{BESD} to show identical values in a particular case, but in general we will find $r_{\text{effect size}}$ to be larger than r_{BESD}, and r_{contrast} to be larger than $r_{\text{effect size}}$, and these differences are sometimes quite substantial. The r_{alerting} tends to be larger than the other three effect-size correlations, but not necessarily. Figure 15.4 explains this idea with another example showing the results of two studies with identical values of $r_{\text{contrast}} = .80$.

The plot of the means shows Study 1 to have a clearly linear trend in the five means. That is, the correlation between the means and lambdas for linear trend is $r_{\text{alerting}} = 1.00$. But Study 2 does not imply a clearly linear trend because r_{alerting} is only .45. Indeed the five means of Study 2 show a greater quadratic trend, with $r_{\text{alerting}} = .76$ using lambdas of $-2, 1, 2, 1, -2$. The reason that both studies have the same r_{contrast} for linear trend despite their displaying different patterns is that Study 2, though it has a smaller alerting r, possesses far greater noncontrast variability among the means than does Study 1. Consequently, we have a smaller proportion of a larger variability in Study 2, yielding the same partial r (i.e., r_{contrast}) as in Study 1. Were we to compute an unpartialed r (i.e., $r_{\text{effect size}}$), putting all the nonlinear sources of between-groups variation into the error term, we would find Study 1 still to have an unpartialed r of .80, but Study 2 would have an unpartialed r of only .42. These unpartialed rs, not controlled for other between-groups sources of variability, are what we intuitively think of as $r_{\text{effect size}}$. When the leftover,

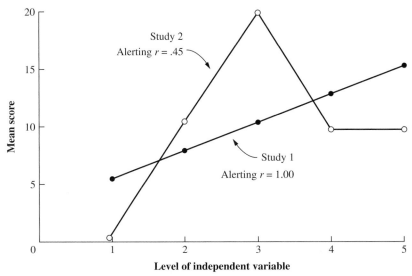

FIGURE 15.4
Results of two studies with identical values of linear contrast (partial) correlations, but
with very different patterns of means and alerting correlations for linear trends, thereby
implying different effect-size (unpartialed) correlations.

noncontrast between-groups variability is small in relation to the contrast variability,
$r_{\text{effect size}}$ tends to be very similar to r_{contrast}.

COMPARING COMPETING CONTRASTS

Earlier in this chapter we described two nonorthogonal contrasts to test two hypotheses
concerning the patterning of psychological benefits when the number of counseling
sessions was varied from one to four. Returning to Table 15.8, we are reminded that
both hypotheses did well, but that Hypothesis I accounted for a somewhat (6%) larger
proportion of the SS_{between} than did Hypothesis II. A more direct way of evaluating
competing contrasts is by means of a contrast on the difference between the corresponding λ weights of the two competing contrasts.

When contrast weights are added or subtracted, their sums and differences are
influenced more by the contrast weights with larger variance than by the weights with
smaller variance. To be sure that the comparison is fair (i.e., not simply reflecting the
contrast with greater variance), we standardize the lambda weights: We divide the
weights of each contrast by the standard deviation (σ) of the weights, which we
defined in Equation 15.15 as

$$\sigma_\lambda = \sqrt{\frac{\Sigma\lambda^2}{k}},$$

where the numerator ($\Sigma\lambda^2$) is the sum of the squared lambda weights, and the
denominator (k) is again the number of groups. In Table 15.8, the linear contrast
used to evaluate Hypothesis I had weights of -3, -1, $+1$, $+3$, and we find in

Table 15.10 that $\sigma_\lambda = 2.24$ corresponds to $k = 4$ and those same linear weights. Alternatively, we can calculate σ_λ directly from Equation 15.15 as

$$\sigma_\lambda = \sqrt{\frac{(-3)^2 + (-1)^2 + (+1)^2 + (+3)^2}{4}} = 2.236.$$

Dividing the original lambdas of -3, -1, $+1$, $+3$ by $\sigma_\lambda = 2.236$ gives standardized (i.e., Z-scored) lambda weights for Hypothesis I of -1.342, -0.447, $+0.447$, $+1.342$.

We now must do the same thing for Hypothesis II, where we recall that the prediction was that people would show greater benefits when given four sessions than when given only one, two, or three sessions, a prediction for which the contrast weights were -1, -1, -1, $+3$. Computing σ_λ from Equation 15.15, we find

$$\sigma_\lambda = \sqrt{\frac{(-1)^2 + (-1)^2 + (-1)^2 + (+3)^2}{4}} = 1.732,$$

and dividing the original weights of -1, -1, -1, $+3$ by $\sigma_\lambda = 1.732$ gives us the Z-scored weights of -0.577, -0.577, -0.577, $+1.732$ for Hypothesis II.

Subtracting the Z-scored lambda weights of Hypothesis II from the corresponding Z-scored weights of Hypothesis I gives us the precise weights we need for our difference contrast: -0.765, $+0.130$, $+1.024$, -0.390. Given group means to be 2.0, 3.0, 4.0, 7.0, $n = 3$ in each group, and assuming $S^2_{pooled} = 2.5$, we substitute in Equation 15.4 to find

$$t_{contrast} = \frac{\Sigma(M_i \lambda_i)}{\sqrt{MS_{within}\left(\Sigma \frac{\lambda_i^2}{n_i}\right)}}$$

$$= \frac{2(-0.765) + 3(0.130) + 4(1.024) + 7(-0.390)}{\sqrt{2.5\left[\frac{(-0.765)^2}{3} + \frac{(0.130)^2}{3} + \frac{(1.024)^2}{3} + \frac{(-0.390)^2}{3}\right]}}$$

$$= \frac{0.2260}{\sqrt{(2.5)(0.6009)}} = 0.1844,$$

which, with $df = 8$, has an associated one-tailed $p = .43$. The expected value of $t_{contrast}$ is zero when the null is true, and this t is not much larger than zero. Moreover, the alerting correlation is .0458, and thus $r^2_{alerting}$ is .0021, implying that one prediction has little superiority over the other.

We have a choice of procedures to calculate the contrast and effect size correlations. For example, we can use Equation 15.12 to estimate the contrast r, which yields

$$r_{contrast} = \sqrt{\frac{t^2_{contrast}}{t^2_{contrast} + df_{within}}} = \sqrt{\frac{(0.1844)^2}{(0.1844)^2 + 8}} = .065.$$

Alternatively, because we know from Table 15.8 that $SS_{between} = 42$, we can calculate the contrast sum of squares from

$$SS_{contrast} = r^2_{alerting} \times SS_{between}, \tag{15.18}$$

which yields $SS_{contrast} = .0021 \times 42 = .088$. The MS_{within} was 2.5, and we lost 1 df in each group, so we multiply 2.5 by 8 to find $SS_{within} = 20$. Then, we simply substitute in the following:

$$r_{\text{contrast}} = \sqrt{\frac{SS_{\text{contrast}}}{SS_{\text{contrast}} + SS_{\text{within}}}}, \tag{15.19}$$

which (with rounding differences) gives us

$$r_{\text{contrast}} = \sqrt{\frac{.088}{.088 + 20}} = .0662.$$

We could calculate the effect size r from Equations 15.13 or 15.14, but in this case we will use the following:

$$r_{\text{effect size}} = \sqrt{\frac{SS_{\text{contrast}}}{SS_{\text{total}}}}, \tag{15.20}$$

which yields

$$r_{\text{effect size}} = \sqrt{\frac{.088}{62}} = .038$$

and, like the contrast r, is (not surprisingly) small. We can conclude that neither hypothesis is noticeably superior to the other, whereas both fare well on their own. In some cases, the results from r_{contrast} may differ more from the results of $r_{\text{effect size}}$ than they do in this example. Thus, whenever it is possible to use both r_{contrast} and $r_{\text{effect size}}$, it seems wise to compute both.

COMBINING COMPETING CONTRASTS

Both hypotheses in the example above did so well individually that we wonder how they will do together. Assuming it makes sense to think of two processes operating simultaneously, we can find out how well they do together. We begin by summing the standardized weights of Hypothesis I (which yielded Z-scored weights of -1.342, -0.447, $+0.447$, $+1.342$) and Hypothesis II (which yielded Z-scored weights of -0.577, -0.577, -0.577, $+1.732$). Summing the values gives us combined lambdas of -1.919, -1.024, -0.130, $+3.074$. As both hypotheses contributed equally to the combined weights, the combined lambdas should correlate equally with the weights of each hypothesis, and indeed we find that the combined weights correlate .942 with the lambda weights for Hypothesis I and Hypothesis II. We now use the combined weights and Equation 15.4 to find

$$t_{\text{contrast}} = \frac{\Sigma(M_i \lambda_i)}{\sqrt{MS_{\text{within}}\left(\Sigma \frac{\lambda_i^2}{n_i}\right)}}$$

$$= \frac{2(-1.919) + 3(-1.024) + 4(-0.130) + 7(3.074)}{\sqrt{2.5\left[\frac{(-1.919)^2}{3} + \frac{(-1.024)^2}{3} + \frac{(-0.130)^2}{3} + \frac{(3.074)^2}{3}\right]}}$$

$$= \frac{14.088}{3.4397} = 4.096,$$

which, with $df = 8$, has an associated one-tailed $p = .0017$.

Routinely repeating all the other calculations we did previously, we start with the alerting correlation, which is now $r_{alerting} = .999$. The large size of the squared alerting correlation ($r^2_{alerting} = .998$) assures us that the combined predictions did exceedingly well in accounting for between-group variation. Using Equation 15.18, we find $SS_{contrast} = .998 \times 42 = 41.9$, which we substitute in Equation 15.19 to find $r_{contrast} = .8228$. Given the size of $r^2_{alerting}$, it is safe to assume that $r_{contrast}$ is similar to $r_{effect\ size}$, as there is hardly any noncontrast variability to worry about. Equation 15.20 confirms our expectation, yielding $r_{effect\ size} = .8221$. In sum, Hypothesis I and Hypothesis II are about equally good, and each fared well. Combining them gave the most accurate prediction, even though the increase over the two individual predictions was not spectacular. If combining the hypotheses makes sense intuitively, the researcher's next task is to make a compelling case that connects the two underlying processes formally on theoretical grounds.

OPTIMAL DESIGN AND THE ALLOCATION OF SAMPLE SIZES

In chapter 12 we discussed the power loss associated with an unequal-n study relative to an equal-n study, and we mentioned that some studies may be specifically designed in a way that allocates the subjects to conditions unequally. The statistical name for this strategy is **optimal design,** as the goal is to optimize the statistical precision of the study by emphasizing some conditions more than others. As Jacob Cohen (1962) brought "power to the people," G. H. McClelland (1997) brought optimal design to psychologists, on the assumption that "appropriate allocations can substantially increase statistical precision" when we are comparing groups or conditions in a planned contrast (p. 6). For example, if we have a linear prediction with contrast weights of $-2, -1, 0, +1, +2$, our optimal allocation is to assign half the subjects to the condition associated with the lambda weight of -2 and the remaining half to the condition associated with the lambda weight of $+2$. If our prediction of a linear trend is quite accurate, we expect the optimum allocation of sample size to result in a larger effect size estimate ($r_{contrast}$) and a more significant p value, compared to the more traditional allocation of equal sample sizes to all groups or conditions.

Suppose we wanted to compare the effectiveness of five dosage levels of a psychological, educational, or medical intervention: (a) very low, (b) low, (c) medium, (d) high, and (e) very high. Given a total sample size of $N = 50$, we could allocate the subjects equally or optimally as shown in Table 15.13. With $n = 10$ in each of the five dosage conditions, the contrast weights to test our linear trend prediction are $-2, -1, 0, +1, +2$. In the optimal allocation, with $n = 25$ assigned to the "very low" condition and the remaining $n = 25$ to the "very high" condition, the contrast weights would be -1 and $+1$ (because our optimal allocation assigns no units at all to the "low," "medium," and "high" conditions).

Suppose that we use all five conditions and find the corresponding five mean outcome scores to be 1, 3, 5, 7, 9, with pooled within-group variance (S^2) = 16. These results are clearly linear, and, indeed, the correlation between these five means and their corresponding linear contrast weights (Table 15.13) is $r_{alerting} = 1.00$. In Equation 15.4,

TABLE 15.13
Equal and optimal allocation of subjects in a hypothetical study with $N = 50$

Allocation		Very low	Low	Medium	High	Very high	Σ
				Dosage level			
Equal	Sample size	10	10	10	10	10	50
	λ weight	-2	-1	0	$+1$	$+2$	0
Optimal	Sample size	25	0	0	0	25	50
	λ weight	-1				$+1$	0

the contrast t for this result is

$$t_{\text{contrast}} = \frac{\Sigma(M_i\lambda_i)}{\sqrt{MS_{\text{within}}\left(\Sigma\frac{\lambda_i^2}{n_i}\right)}}$$

$$= \frac{1(-2) + 3(-1) + 5(0) + 7(+1) + 9(+2)}{\sqrt{16\left[\frac{(-2)^2}{10} + \frac{(-1)^2}{10} + \frac{(0)^2}{10} + \frac{(+1)^2}{10} + \frac{(+2)^2}{10}\right]}}$$

$$= \frac{20}{4} = 5.00,$$

with $df = 45$, one-tailed $p = 4.6^{-6}$, and $r_{\text{contrast}} = .60$. Now suppose that we use the optimal design, assigning half of our total N to the very lowest dosage level and the other half to the very highest dosage level. Using Equation 15.4, we now find

$$t_{\text{contrast}} = \frac{1(-1) + 9(+1)}{\sqrt{16\left[\frac{(-1)^2}{25} + \frac{(+1)^2}{25}\right]}} = \frac{8}{1.1314} = 7.07,$$

with $df = 48$, one-tailed $p = 3.0^{-9}$, and $r_{\text{contrast}} = .71$. As we might expect, the t_{contrast} for the (two-group) optimal design is larger, as is the effect size estimate (r_{contrast}), than those we found for the (five-group) equal-n design.

However, let us now imagine that we conduct the same experiment, with the very same linear prediction, and that we again compare the equal-n with the optimal design analysis. This time, we will imagine that the five means we find for our five dosage levels are 1, 5, 7, 9, 3, respectively, from the very lowest to the very highest dosages. We still observe a linear trend in those five means, with $r_{\text{alerting}} = .40$ between the condition means and respective linear contrast weights, but this r_{alerting} is very much lower than the r_{alerting} of 1.00 in the previous example. And using Equation 15.4, we find

$$t_{\text{contrast}} = \frac{1(-2) + 5(-1) + 7(0) + 9(+1) + 3(+2)}{\sqrt{16\left[\frac{(-2)^2}{10} + \frac{(-1)^2}{10} + \frac{(0)^2}{10} + \frac{(+1)^2}{10} + \frac{(+2)^2}{10}\right]}} = \frac{8}{4} = 2.00,$$

with $df = 45$, one-tailed $p = .026$, and $r_{\text{contrast}} = .29$. Both the t_{contrast} and the r_{contrast} are substantially lower than they were in the previous example, but that is what we might expect, knowing that $r_{alerting}$ dropped from 1.00 to .40. For comparison with the (five-group) equal-n design and analysis, we compute the contrast t for the (two-group) optimal n case and find

$$t_{contrast} = \frac{1(-1) + 3(+1)}{\sqrt{16\left[\frac{(-1)^2}{25} + \frac{(+1)^2}{25}\right]}} = \frac{2}{1.1314} = 1.77,$$

with $df = 48$, one-tailed $p = .042$, and $r_{contrast} = .25$. Thus, we see in this example (in which our hypothesis of linear increase is not supported by the data as strongly as it was in the preceding example) that our (five-group) equal-n design produced a larger effect size as well as a more significant $t_{contrast}$. The lesson? Had we used only our optimal design allocating $N/2$ to each of the extreme conditions, we would have missed the opportunity to learn that the actual trend showed linearity only over the first four dosage levels, with a noticeable drop for the highest dosage level.

There may indeed be occasions when we will want to consider using the principles of optimal design. When we do, however, it seems prudent to consider the possibility that, in so doing, we may be missing out on something new and interesting that would be apparent only if we used a nonoptimal design.

PART
VI

FACTORIAL DESIGNS

FACTORIAL ANALYSIS OF VARIANCE

CONFRONTING PERSISTENT MISUNDERSTANDINGS

In previous chapters we have addressed a number of lingering misconceptions having to do with the interpretation of data. One problem that we discussed is that many researchers have for too long operated as if the only proper significance testing decision is a dichotomous one in which the evidence is interpreted as "anti-null" if p is not greater than .05 and "pro-null" if p is greater than .05. We have also underscored the wasteful conclusions that can result when, in doing dichotomous significance testing, researchers ignore statistical power considerations and inadvertently stack the odds against reaching a given p level for some particular size of effect. We also emphasized the importance of not confusing the size of effect with its statistical significance, as even highly significant p values do not automatically imply large effects. In the case of F ratios, a numerator mean square (MS) may be large relative to a denominator MS because the effect size is large, the n per condition is large, or both values are large. On the other hand, even if an effect is considered "small" by a particular standard, small effect sizes sometimes have profound practical implications. There is a growing awareness that just about everything under the sun is context-dependent in one way or another, and effect size indices are no exception. Thus, it is essential to heed how study characteristics may influence the size as well as the implications of a magnitude-of-effect estimate.

We have also discussed the importance of replications, that is, as opposed to the monomaniacal preoccupation with the results of a single study. Replication of results suggests the robustness of the relationships observed, and in the final chapter of this book we describe the basic ideas of meta-analytic procedures to summarize a body of related studies. We have also discussed (and illustrated) the problem of overreliance on omnibus statistical tests that do not usually tell us anything we really want to know, although they provide protection for some researchers from "data mining" with multiple tests performed as if each were the only one to be considered. In the previous chapter, for example, we showed in one example that, while a predicted pattern among the means was evident to the naked eye, the omnibus F was not up to the task of addressing the question of greatest interest. We have demonstrated not only the value of focused t and F tests (i.e., contrasts) but also their easy performance with a calculator and computation on data in published reports as well as on original data.

Both in this chapter and in the following one, we turn to lingering problems involving the use of factorial analysis of variance (ANOVA). One core problem involves the most universally misinterpreted empirical results in behavioral research, namely, the results called *interaction effects*. As we will explain, the mathematical meaning of interaction effects in ANOVA is unambiguous. Nevertheless, there is palpable confusion in many research reports and psychological textbooks regarding the meaning and interpretation of obtained interactions. The nature of the problem is quite consistent. Once investigators find statistically significant interactions, they confuse the overall pattern of the cell means with the interaction (e.g., N. H. Anderson, 2001, pp. 210–211). As we will show, the cell means are made up only partially of interaction effects. One perceptive author suggested that the problem may be a consequence of "the lack of perfect correspondence between the meaning of 'interaction' in the analysis of variance model and its meaning in other discourse" (Dawes, 1969, p. 57). But whatever the etiology of the problem, looking only at the "uncorrected" cell means for the pattern of the statistical interaction is an error that has persisted for far too long in our field. We do not feel there is any great merit in computing interaction at all, but if it is computed and reported, it should be accurately interpreted. This chapter should not be read as an argument against comparing cell means, however, as we are very much in favor of comparing cell means, especially by the use of planned contrasts.

Simply stated, our position is that if one claims to speak of an *interaction*, the exercise of actually looking at the "corrected" group or condition (i.e., the cell) means is absolutely essential. The reason, as we illustrate in this chapter, is that "interaction" in ANOVA is defined basically in terms of the "leftover effects" (or *residuals*) after lower order effects have been removed from the original cell means. This is true even though the mean square for interaction in ANOVA can be seen as variability of the difference between the "uncorrected" cell means for the various rows of the table of overall effects. In the simplest case, that of a 2 × 2 ANOVA, the mean square for interaction has a nonzero value if the difference between any two cell means in any row differs from the corresponding difference in any other row. Focusing attention only on the original cell means, however, ignores the form and degree of relationship of the interaction itself. Just as when the skins of an onion are peeled away, if we are interested in seeing the interaction, we need to peel away the various constituent effects in order to separate the effects of the interaction from the other effects. But the important question is always "Am I sure I really want to look at the interaction rather than compute a contrast on the cell means?"

Other common misconceptions are that main effects are "meaningless" or "uninterpretable" in the presence of significant interaction and that only two-way or (perhaps at most) three-way interactions can be meaningfully interpreted. We address both of those mistaken beliefs in more detail in the next chapter. However, suppose we have a 2 × 2 design, with the four cells labeled A, B, C, D as follows:

A	B
C	D

In the context of an ANOVA, this design is basically a set of three orthogonal contrasts. Because they are independent, we can (and should) interpret each contrast separately—assuming we are interested in what they may have to tell us. However, no information would be lost by treating the 2 × 2 design as though it were a 1 × 4 design. Focusing on the four condition means, suppose we predicted A > B = C = D, which we can denote by contrast weights of +3, −1, −1, −1, respectively. Those lambdas are the sums of three orthogonal (i.e., uncorrelated) contrasts, with cell weights for A, B, C, and D, respectively, of (a) +1, +1, −1, −1, for rows; (b) +1, −1, +1, −1 for columns; and (c) +1, −1, −1, +1 for the interaction. If a 1 × 4 contrast addresses the major question of interest, then it provides the right answer to the right question. If the "wired-in" orthogonal contrasts of the 2 × 2 ANOVA miss questions of interest, they provide correct answers to the wrong questions. Just because we may think of an experimental design as 2 × 2 is not a good reason to subject the results to a 2 × 2 ANOVA. The 2 × 2 design is not some Mt. Everest that must be scaled by a 2 × 2 ANOVA just because "it is there."

In the remainder of this chapter we explore the logic, and also illustrate the computation, of the factorial ANOVA. As a consequence, it should become clear when we are predicting interaction and not something else that can be more precisely addressed by a planned contrast. We will also illustrate how to transcend the factorial structure by planned contrasts. In addition, we will discuss the stratification or subdivision of the subjects or other sampling units to increase statistical power, known as *blocking,* and we will compare blocking with the analysis of covariance. Finally, we will return to the use of transformations, not only as a way of meeting statistical assumptions underlying the use of the *F* test, but sometimes as a way of simplifying the nature of the relationship between independent and dependent variables. We will show how some transformations can be used to remove an interaction and thereby possibly simplify a more complex relationship to a linear relationship. In the next chapter we will deal in far more detail with the interpretation of interaction in between-groups designs arranged as factorial designs, and in chapter 18 we will concentrate on factorial designs with repeated measures.

AN ECONOMY OF DESIGN

To help us explore the logic of the factorial ANOVA, let us return to the example of a one-way design. In chapter 14 we described such a one-way between-groups design; the hypothetical results are repeated in Table 16.1. There were four treatment conditions (designated as PD, P, D, O), with three patients randomly assigned to each condition. We also identified 13 fairly obvious comparisons of those different conditions, made by t tests. One t test compared the psychotherapy-only group (P) and the zero (no-treatment) control (O) and found $t(8) = 1.55$, with $p = .08$ one-tailed, and effect size $r = .48$ (from Equation 12.1). Inspection of the four means in Table 16.1 suggests another possible comparison to test the effect of psychotherapy: PD versus D. That comparison, which we did earlier and found $t(8) = 3.10$, $p < .01$, and the effect size $r = .74$, is analogous to the comparison of P and O, except that now both the psychotherapy and the no-psychotherapy conditions are receiving drug therapy.

      Rather than conduct two t tests, on P and O and on PD and D, we can conduct one simultaneous t test of (PD + P)/2 versus (D + O)/2, so that the conditions including psychotherapy can be compared with those not including psychotherapy. The advantage of thus combining our tests is that it increases the n_1 and n_2 of the denominator of the t test, rendering t with greater power to reject the null hypothesis (H_0) if H_0 is false. An equally sensible (and quite analogous) test might ask whether drug therapy is beneficial, that is, (PD + D)/2 versus (P + O)/2. The t test for psychotherapy, based on Equation 11.8, is computed as

$$t = \frac{M_1 - M_2}{\sqrt{\left(\dfrac{1}{n_1} + \dfrac{1}{n_2}\right)S^2_{\text{pooled}}}}$$

$$= \frac{\left(\dfrac{8+4}{2}\right) - \left(\dfrac{4+2}{2}\right)}{\sqrt{\left(\dfrac{1}{6} + \dfrac{1}{6}\right)2.5}} = \frac{6-3}{0.913} = 3.29,$$

TABLE 16.1
Improvement scores in four groups

	Psychotherapy plus drug (PD)	Psychotherapy alone (P)	Drug treatment alone (D)	Zero control group (O)
	9	6	5	4
	8	4	4	2
	7	2	3	0
M	8	4	4	2
S^2	1.0	4.0	1.0	4.0

TABLE 16.2
Factorial design rearrayed from one-way design in Table 16.1

Drug therapy	Psychotherapy		Mean
	Present	**Absent**	
Present	$8^{|3}$	$4^{|3}$	$6^{|6}$
Absent	$4^{|3}$	$2^{|3}$	$3^{|6}$
Mean	$6^{|6}$	$3^{|6}$	$4.5^{|12}$

Note: Numbers within the ⌊ symbol indicate the number of units on which each mean is based.

which is significant at $p = .006$ one-tailed, when referred to the $t(8)$ distribution, and effect size $r = .76$. The results for the drug effect turn out in this example to be identical.

Ronald A. Fisher, for whom the F test is named, and who was largely responsible for so much of the development of the analysis of variance, noticed that in many situations a one-way ANOVA could be rearranged (or *rearrayed*) to form a two-dimensional (or higher order) design of much greater power to reject the null hypothesis. As we know from chapter 7, such experimental designs are called **factorial designs,** and they require that the two or more levels of each factor (variable) be administered in combination with the two or more levels of every other factor. For example, Table 16.2 shows how we would rearray the four means of the one-way design in Table 16.1 into a 2×2 factorial design. Now the comparison of the two column means is the test of the effect of psychotherapy, and the comparison of the two row means is the test of the effect of drug therapy. The number of observations on which each mean is based is doubled, from 3 to 6, as we move from a comparison of one group with another group to a comparison of a column (or row) comprising two groups with another column (or row) also comprising two groups.

This example clearly illustrates the great economy of the factorial design. That is, each condition or group contributes data to more than one comparison. In Table 16.2 we see, for example, that the upper-left condition (the cell previously denoted as A) contributes its $n = 3$ simultaneously to the comparison between columns and the comparison between rows.

EFFECTS AND THE STRUCTURE OF ANOVA

We can better understand our particular data, and we can better understand the nature of analysis of variance, by thinking of our obtained scores or means as comprising two or more components that can be summed to construct the obtained scores or means. Let us consider only the four group means of the one-way design in Table 16.1. We can decompose those four group means into two components, one due to the grand mean (4.5) and the other due to the *effect* of being in a particular group. Subtracting the grand mean from each of the four group means gives the "corrected" means shown

TABLE 16.3
Group means of one-way design of Table 16.1 "corrected" for grand mean

A. Residual (condition) effects

| | Psychotherapy | |
Drug therapy	Present	Absent
Present	3.5	−0.5
Absent	−0.5	−2.5

B. Residual effects = Group means − Grand mean

Residual (condition) effects	=	Group means	−	Grand mean
3.5	=	8	−	4.5
−0.5	=	4	−	4.5
−0.5	=	4	−	4.5
−2.5	=	2	−	4.5
Σ 0.0	=	18	−	18.0

C. Group means = Grand mean + Residual effects

Group means	=	Grand mean	+	Residual (condition) effects
8	=	4.5	+	3.5
4	=	4.5	+	(−0.5)
4	=	4.5	+	(−0.5)
2	=	4.5	+	(−2.5)
Σ 18	=	18.0	+	0.0

in Part A of Table 16.3. In subtables B and C, we see two alternative ways of visualizing that decomposition of group means, where the leftover amounts (after we "correct" the group means by subtracting the grand mean) are called either *residuals* (leftovers) or *effects* of group (or condition) membership. As those subtables illustrate, the sum of the condition effects (i.e., the residuals) is always equal to zero. Thus, examining the residuals for each group will quickly tell us which group scored the most above average (the positively signed group effect with the largest value) and which scored the most below average (the negatively signed group effect with the largest value). Here we see that the highest positive residual value is 3.5, and the highest negative residual value is −2.5. Subtable C also highlights the fact that the grand mean plus the condition residual (or effect) for each group mean is equal to the group mean.

Although Subtable A in Table 16.3 is depicted as two-dimensional, we have been thinking only of a one-way design so far. When we move from a one-way to a two-way ANOVA, as in the case of a two-way factorial design, the condition effects (or residuals) are subdivided into **row effects, column effects,** and **interaction effects,** where the interaction effects now constitute the **residual** (leftover) **effects.** That is to say, whereas in a one-way ANOVA design, we have

Group mean = Grand mean + Residual (condition) effect,

in a two-way ANOVA design, we have

Group mean = Grand mean + Row effect + Column effect + Interaction effect.

In order to decompose the group means into their four components, we must first calculate the grand mean, the row effects, the column effects, and the interaction effects. The grand mean is the mean of all group (or condition) means. The row effect for each row is the mean of that row minus the grand mean. The column effect for each column is the mean of that column minus the grand mean. Part A of Table 16.4 shows the results of those calculations. The row effects are $6 - 4.5$ and $3 - 4.5$ for drug present and absent, respectively. The column effects are $6 - 4.5$ and $3 - 4.5$ for psychotherapy present and absent, respectively. We obtain the interaction effect (or residual) for each group by subtracting the grand mean, the relevant row effect, and the relevant column effect from the particular group mean. Those calculations are indicated in Part B of Table 16.4, which shows for each group that

Interaction effect = Group mean − Grand mean − Row effect − Column effect

TABLE 16.4
Decomposition of two-way factorial design in Table 16.2

A. Row effects and column effects

	Psychotherapy		Row means	Row effects
	Present	**Absent**		
Drug therapy				
Present	8	4	6	1.5
Absent	4	2	3	−1.5
Column means	6	3	4.5 (grand mean)	
Column effects	1.5	−1.5		

B. Interaction effects defined

Group mean	−	Grand mean	−	Row effect	−	Column effect	=	Interaction effect
PD 8	−	4.5	−	1.5	−	1.5	=	0.5
D 4	−	4.5	−	1.5	−	(−1.5)	=	(−0.5)
P 4	−	4.5	−	(−1.5)	−	1.5	=	(−0.5)
O 2	−	4.5	−	(−1.5)	−	(−1.5)	=	0.5
Σ 18	−	18.0	−	0	−	0	=	0

TABLE 16.5
Summary table of effects

Group mean		=	Grand mean	+	Row effect	+	Column effect	+	Interaction effect
PD	8	=	4.5	+	1.5	+	1.5	+	0.5
D	4	=	4.5	+	1.5	+	(−1.5)	+	(−0.5)
P	4	=	4.5	+	(−1.5)	+	1.5	+	(−0.5)
O	2	=	4.5	+	(−1.5)	+	(−1.5)	+	0.5
Σ	18	=	18.0	+	0	+	0	+	0

or alternatively that

Interaction effect = Group mean − (Grand mean + Row effect + Column effect).

For the time being, we continue to think of interaction effects simply as the "leftover effects," but we will have a great deal more to say about them in the next chapter. To show that the group means are composed of additive pieces, we can rewrite the relationship above as follows:

Group mean = Grand mean + Row effect + Column effect + Interaction effect.

This expression notes that all effects (row, column, and interaction) sum to zero when added over all four conditions (PD, D, P, O), a characteristic of all residuals from a mean, as shown in Table 16.5. What can be learned from studying this table of effects? First, the grand mean tells us about the general "level" of our measurements and is usually not of great intrinsic interest. Second, the row effects indicate that the groups receiving drugs (PD and D) did better than those not receiving drugs (P and O). Third, the column effects indicate that the groups receiving psychotherapy (PD and P) did better than the groups that did not receive psychotherapy (D and O). Fourth, the interaction effects tell us that it was better overall to receive neither psychotherapy nor the drug than to receive either psychotherapy or the drug. The table of effects also tells us that, although it is slightly better from the point of view of the *interaction effect alone* to have received neither treatment, this advantage in the interaction effects (i.e., 0.5) was more than offset by the disadvantage in the row effects (i.e., −1.5) and the column effects (i.e., −1.5) to be receiving neither treatment.

INDIVIDUAL DIFFERENCES AS ERROR

We have seen how the mean of each group or condition can be decomposed into elements made up of the grand mean, the row effect, the column effect, and the interaction effect in a two-dimensional design, such as a two-way factorial design. That does not quite tell the whole story, however, because it does not take into account that the various *scores* found in each condition show variability from the *mean* of that condition. That is, each score can be rewritten as a deviation or residual from the mean of that condition. The magnitude of the deviations reflects how poorly we have done in predicting individual scores from a knowledge of condition or group membership. From our earlier discussion (in chapter 4) of random fluctuations, we recognize that those deviations or residuals are accordingly called *error.* Thus, a particular score shows a "large" error if it falls far from the mean of its condition, but only a "small" error if it falls close to the mean of its condition. We can write error as

$$\text{Error} = \text{Score} - \text{Group mean,}$$

so that

$$\text{Score} = \text{Group mean} + \text{Error,}$$

but

$$\text{Group mean} = \text{Grand mean} + \text{Row effect} + \text{Column effect}$$
$$+ \text{Interaction effect,}$$

so

$$\text{Score} = \text{Grand mean} + \text{Row effect} + \text{Column effect}$$
$$+ \text{Interaction effect} + \text{Error.}$$

From this process we can show the makeup of each of the original 12 scores of the study we have been using as our illustration (see Table 16.6). We can use the

TABLE 16.6
Table of effects for individual scores

Condition	Patient	Score	=	Grand mean	+	Row effect	+	Column effect	+	Interaction effect	+	Error
PD	1	9	=	4.5	+	1.5	+	1.5	+	0.5	+	1
PD	2	8	=	4.5	+	1.5	+	1.5	+	0.5	+	0
PD	3	7	=	4.5	+	1.5	+	1.5	+	0.5	+	(−1)
D	4	5	=	4.5	+	1.5	+	(−1.5)	+	(−0.5)	+	1
D	5	4	=	4.5	+	1.5	+	(−1.5)	+	(−0.5)	+	0
D	6	3	=	4.5	+	1.5	+	(−1.5)	+	(−0.5)	+	(−1)
P	7	6	=	4.5	+	(−1.5)	+	1.5	+	(−0.5)	+	2
P	8	4	=	4.5	+	(−1.5)	+	1.5	+	(−0.5)	+	0
P	9	2	=	4.5	+	(−1.5)	+	1.5	+	(−0.5)	+	(−2)
O	10	4	=	4.5	+	(−1.5)	+	(−1.5)	+	0.5	+	2
O	11	2	=	4.5	+	(−1.5)	+	(−1.5)	+	0.5	+	0
O	12	0	=	4.5	+	(−1.5)	+	(−1.5)	+	0.5	+	(−2)
	ΣX	54	=	54	+	0	+	0	+	0	+	0
	ΣX^2	320	=	243	+	27	+	27	+	3	+	20

decomposition of the individual scores to understand better the computation of the various terms of the analysis of variance. Beneath each column in Table 16.6 we have the sum of the 12 values (ΣX) and the sum of the squares of the values (ΣX^2). In analyzing the results of this hypothetical study as a one-way ANOVA in chapter 14, we computed the three sources of variance (defined in Equations 14.8, 14.9, and 14.10) with results as follows:

$$\text{Total } SS = \Sigma(X - \overline{M})^2 = 77$$
$$\text{Between-conditions } SS = \Sigma[n_i(M_i - \overline{M})^2] = 57$$
$$\text{Within-conditions } SS = \Sigma(X - M_i)^2 = 20.$$

The total SS is defined as the sum of the squared differences between every single score and the grand mean, that is, $(9 - 4.5)^2 + \cdots + (0 - 4.5)^2 = 77$. Alternatively, we can subtract the sum of the squared means, shown in Table 16.6 as 243 (expressed symbolically as $N\overline{M}^2$ or as $(\Sigma X)^2/N$), from the sum of the squared scores, shown as 320 (expressed symbolically as ΣX^2), to obtain the same value of 77. In the one-way analysis of variance, this total SS is allocated to two sources of variance, a between-conditions and a within-conditions source. When we move from a one-way to a two-way analysis of variance, the *within-conditions* source of variance, or the source attributable to error, remains unchanged. Table 16.6, indicating the contributions of various sources to each score, shows that the sum of the squared effects due to error is 20, as before. However, the *between-conditions* source of variance has now been further broken down into three components as follows:

Between-conditions SS = Row-effect SS + Column effect SS + Interaction effect SS,

| 57 | = | 27 | + | 27 | + | 3 |

where 57 is the between-conditions SS computed earlier showing the overall variation among the four treatment conditions, and the row, column, and interaction effects of 27, 27, and 3, respectively, are as shown in the bottom row of Table 16.6.

THE TABLE OF VARIANCE

The table of variance for the two-way ANOVA differs from the table of variance for the one-way ANOVA in reflecting the further subdivision of the between-conditions SS. This difference is illustrated in Table 16.7, where we see a large eta (.76) and significant ($p = .012$) effect of the drug and also a large eta (.76) and significant ($p = .012$) effect of psychotherapy. Tables 16.5 and 16.6 imply that it was more beneficial to have the drug than not to have it, and more beneficial to have the psychotherapy than not to have it. Table 16.7 shows that the interaction effect (the residual between-conditions variation after the row and column effects were removed) was not close to statistical significance, though the effect size eta of .36 is not trivial. Because of the importance of interaction effects in two-way and higher order analyses of variance, and because of the frequency with which they are misinterpreted by even very experienced investigators, we discuss them in more detail in the next chapter.

TABLE 16.7
Summary ANOVA showing row, column, and interaction SS carved out of $SS_{between}$

Source	SS	df	MS	F	η	p
Between conditions	57	3	19.0	7.60	.86	.01
Drug (row)	27	1	27.0	10.80	.76	.012
Psychotherapy (column)	27	1	27.0	10.80	.76	.012
Interaction	3	1	3.0	1.20	.36	.30
Within conditions	20	8	2.5			
Total	77	11	7.0			

In chapter 14 we discussed eta, or η (defined in Equations 14.11 and 14.12), and noted that we usually can do better than a multiple degree-of-freedom effect size indicator (as illustrated in chapter 15). It may be recalled that eta is a nonspecific index of effect size when it is based on a source of variance with $df > 1$ and is therefore much less informative than r, which tells us about linear relationship. For example, in Table 16.7, the eta of .86 based on 3 df for the between-conditions effect is large, but we cannot say much about what makes it large. The three etas based on just a single df are (as we noted in chapter 14) identical to r and may be interpreted as r. That helps quite a bit, as we can now say that the size of the effect of drug only is $r = .76$ with all the different ways we have of interpreting this effect size index, including the BESD. The size of the effect of psychotherapy-only is also $r = .76$, and the size of the effect of interaction is $r = .36$, which, although not significant in such a small-sized study, is not trivial. Our use of eta or r as an effect size estimate in the context of the factorial analysis of variance regards each effect (e.g., row, column, and interaction effects) as though it were the only one investigated in that study. We mention this fact so that it will not seem strange that the sum of the values of r^2 or of η^2 may exceed 1.00. Table 16.8 illustrates this point.

Inspecting the column for proportion of total SS in Table 16.8, we see what proportion of all the SS of the study is associated with each source of variation

TABLE 16.8
Summing the values of η^2

Source	SS	Proportion of total SS	r^2 or η^2
Drug	27	.35	.574
Psychotherapy	27	.35	.574
Interaction	3	.04	.130
Within conditions	20	.26	
Total	77	1.00	1.278

including the error term. Thus, we define each proportion as

$$\text{Proportion of total } SS = \frac{SS_{\text{effect of interest}}}{SS_{\text{effect of interest}} + SS_{\text{all other between effects}} + SS_{\text{within}}}. \quad (16.1)$$

When using Equation 16.1, we simply keep increasing the size of the denominator as we keep increasing the number of variables investigated. Ordinarily, however, when we define the proportion of variance as r^2 or η^2 we disregard all between-groups effects except for the one whose magnitude we are estimating. Therefore, in our more usual usage we define r^2 or η^2 as

$$r^2 \text{ or } \eta^2 = \frac{SS_{\text{effect of interest}}}{SS_{\text{effect of interest}} + SS_{\text{within}}} \quad (16.2)$$

TESTING THE GRAND MEAN BY t AND F

Earlier in our discussion of the grand mean we noted that we are ordinarily not interested in any intrinsic way in its magnitude. Our lack of interest is due in part to the arbitrary units of measurement that are often used in behavioral research. Scores on ability tests, for example, are equally well expressed as IQ scores with $M = 100$ and $\sigma = 20$, or as T scores with $M = 50$ and $\sigma = 10$, or as Z scores with $M = 0$ and $\sigma = 1$. The constant of measurement, then (e.g., 100, 50, 0), is of little interest. That is not always the case, however.

One reason we might be interested in the grand mean would be if we want to compare our own sample of subjects with an earlier sample to see whether the overall means are similar. Suppose we failed to replicate a relationship reported in an earlier study. We might start to wonder whether our sample differed so much from the earlier one on the dependent variable that some difference in the sample characteristics might account for our failure to replicate the earlier finding.

A second reason we might be interested in the grand mean is that our dependent variable might estimate some skill that is or is not better than chance. For example, in various measures of sensitivity to nonverbal communication, we might be interested in whether, on average, a particular skill, such as understanding tone of voice, surpassed a chance level of accuracy (Rosenthal, 1979b; Rosenthal, Hall, DiMatteo, Rogers, & Archer, 1979).

A third reason for being interested in the grand mean would be if our dependent variable is a difference score, such as the difference between a pre- and a posttest measurement. In that case a test of the grand mean is equivalent to a paired t test (chapter 13) and tells us whether the two measurements (pre- and posttest) differ systematically. Related closely to the assessment of change is the assessment of experimental difference, as when a sample of teachers or of experimenters is led to expect superior performance from some of their students or subjects. Then the dependent variable per teacher or experimenter sometimes is defined operationally as the difference between (a) the performance of students (or subjects) for whom higher expectations had been created and (b) the performance of those in the control condition. In that case, testing the grand mean would tell us whether, overall, teachers (or experimenters) had obtained the results they had been led to expect (Rosenthal, 1966, 1976; Rosenthal & Jacobson, 1968; Rosenthal & Rubin, 1978).

Computational Procedures Using t Tests

The general formula for the t test on the grand mean is

$$t = \frac{\overline{M} - C}{\sqrt{\left(\frac{1}{N}\right) MS_{error}}}, \tag{16.3}$$

where $\overline{M}$ is the grand mean, C is the comparison score established on theoretical grounds, N is the total number of subjects or other sampling units, and MS_{error} (also symbolized as MSE) is the estimate of the variation of the scores of the sampling units within their experimental conditions (i.e., the MS_{within}). For the illustration that we have been considering, if we want to know whether $\overline{M} = 4.5$ is significantly greater than zero, we find

$$t = \frac{4.5 - 0}{\sqrt{\left(\frac{1}{12}\right) 2.5}} = 9.86,$$

which, with 8 df (the df for the MS_{error} or MS_{within}), is significant at $p < 5.0^{-6}$ one-tailed, and $r_{effect\ size} = .96$.

Suppose we are also interested in comparing that grand mean with the comparison score based on the grand mean of a large norm group of patients. The comparison score (denoted as C) would not be zero, but the grand mean of the norm group. For the sake of illustration, let us say that we hypothesized $\overline{M} > C$, but in fact we found $C = 5.0$, which is the opposite of our prediction. Using a convention that we also mentioned in an earlier chapter, in which we label t as negative and use a two-tailed (rather than a one-tailed) test when the result is opposite what was predicted, we calculate

$$t = \frac{4.5 - 5.0}{\sqrt{\left(\frac{1}{12}\right) 2.5}} = -1.10,$$

which, with 8 df, has an associated p value of .303 two-tailed, and $r_{effect\ size} = .36$. Although the t test is not statistically significant, it is not surprising because we had so few subjects. Unless the true effect is quite large, it is difficult to reject the null hypothesis with a sample of only 12 patients, and we thereby invite Type II error.

In these two examples, we have been assuming that the comparison score is a theoretical score that is known exactly rather than a score that was only an estimate of a population value. Suppose, for example, that we want to compare the grand mean of 4.5 to a grand mean of 3.0 that we obtained in an earlier study using six patients. From Equation 16.3 again, we find

$$t = \frac{4.5 - 3.0}{\sqrt{\left(\frac{1}{12}\right) 2.5}} = 3.29,$$

which, with 8 df, is significant at about the .011 level, two-tailed, and $r_{effect\ size} = .76$. This p level is accurate if we assume the comparison score of 3.0 to be a theoretical value, but it is inaccurate if we want to take into account the comparison level's being only an estimate based on six patients. Assuming similar mean square error for both studies, we need a different formula to compute this type of t by using both sample sizes in the denominator:

$$t = \frac{\overline{M} - C}{\sqrt{\left(\frac{1}{N_{\overline{M}}} + \frac{1}{N_C}\right) MS_{\text{error}}}}. \tag{16.4}$$

For our data, then,

$$t = \frac{4.5 - 3.0}{\sqrt{\left(\frac{1}{12} + \frac{1}{6}\right) 2.5}} = 1.90,$$

which, with 8 df, is significant at the .094 level, two-tailed, and $r_{\text{effect size}} = .56$. Using the actual sample size on which the comparison score is based generally decreases the obtained t from what it would be with the use of a theoretical comparison score, and this decrease is greater when the actual sample size is smaller.

In this example we assumed that the mean square error (MS_{error} or MSE) for the two studies was equivalent but that we did not actually know the MSE of the comparison score. Hence, we used as the MSE for our t test only the MSE from our new study. The df for our t test was, therefore, only 8, because that was the number of df on which our MSE was based. Had we known the MSE of the earlier study, we could have pooled the mean square error values for the two studies as follows:

$$MSE_{\text{pooled}} = \frac{(df_1)(MS_{\text{error}_1}) + (df_2)(MS_{\text{error}_2})}{df_1 + df_2}, \tag{16.5}$$

and then we compute t from

$$t = \frac{\overline{M} - C}{\sqrt{\left(\frac{1}{N_{\overline{M}}} + \frac{1}{N_C}\right) MSE_{\text{pooled}}}}, \tag{16.6}$$

where the df for this t is the sum of the df of the two pooled MSE values, that is, df_1 plus df_2.

Computational Procedures for *F*

Recalling the special relationship between t and F when there is only a single degree of freedom in the numerator of the F ratio, we can use procedures similar to those described above to compute F instead of t. Whenever F addresses a focused question, such as when it is used to compare two group means (chapter 14) or when we compute a contrast F to compare an observed pattern of condition means with a set of lambda weights (chapter 15), then $\sqrt{F} = t$. Of course, we know that squaring t always gives F, because all t tests are focused whether they are comparing two group means (chapter 13) or comparing a pattern of means with a set of contrast weights (chapter 15). Thus, simply by squaring Equation 16.3, 16.4, or 16.6, we find that we can use those formulas to obtain F instead of t.

If we happen to be working with totals rather than means, the direct F test of the hypothesis that the grand mean differs from zero is obtained by

$$F = \frac{(\Sigma X)^2/N}{MS_{\text{error}}}, \tag{16.7}$$

where $(\Sigma X)^2$ is the square of the sum of all scores, and N is the total number of all such scores. For the example we have been discussing, the grand sum was 54 (i.e., the grand mean of 4.5 multiplied by the N of 12), so that

$$F = \frac{(54)^2/12}{2.5} = \frac{243}{2.5} = 97.20,$$

which, with $df_{\text{numerator}} = 1$ and $df_{\text{denominator}} = 8$, is significant at $p = 9.4^{-6}$, and $r_{\text{effect size}} = .96$. The square root of the obtained F is 9.86, precisely the value of t we obtained earlier when we tested the difference between the grand mean of 4.5 and zero using Equation 16.3.

We can relate the result of the preceding F test to our earlier discussion of individual differences as error (see Table 16.6). There we showed the decomposition of each of the 12 individual scores and the sum of the squared entries for each source of variance as follows:

	Score	=	Grand mean	+	Row effect	+	Column effect	+	Interaction effect	+	Error
ΣX^2	320	=	243	+	27	+	27	+	3	+	20

The grand mean is the sum of the 12 values of 4.5, each of which had been squared [i.e., $12(4.5)^2$]. Notice that this value is identical to the numerator of the F test computed from Equation 16.7, which addressed the hypothesis that the grand mean differs from zero. Subtracting the grand mean from the sum of the raw scores squared, we find $320 - 243 = 77$, the total sum of squares of deviations about the grand mean.

UNWEIGHTED MEANS ANALYSIS FOR EQUAL OR UNEQUAL SAMPLE SIZES

We assume that the reader is using a computer program to do the calculations of the factorial ANOVA. However, understanding those calculations will foster a deeper understanding of issues of sample size as well as the mechanics of the particular computational procedure that we describe, called an **unweighted means analysis.** In the case of a one-way overall or omnibus ANOVA, it did not matter for the computational procedure whether we had the same number of units per condition or not. In a two-way or higher order ANOVA, however, special care needs to be taken when the number of sampling units varies from condition to condition. Several procedures are available for dealing with this situation, of which the most wasteful is simply discarding a random subset of the units of each condition until the sample sizes of all conditions are equal. That procedure is almost never justified.

Several multiple-regression procedures are also available for handling the computations of a two-way ANOVA with unequal sample sizes per condition (Overall & Spiegel, 1969; Overall, Spiegel, & Cohen, 1975). All those procedures yield identical results when sample sizes are equal, but they can differ substantially as the sample sizes become increasingly unequal. The unweighted means procedure can be used when sample sizes are equal *or* unequal. Furthermore, it yields results that are closer to the *fully simultaneous multiple-regression method* (FSMR) recommended by Overall, Spiegel, and Cohen (1975) than do competing methods described by Overall and Spiegel (1969). Indeed, for factorial designs of any size, having always two levels per factor (i.e., 2^k factorial), the unweighted means procedure yields results that are identical to those obtained by FSMR (Horst & Edwards, 1982). In general, multiple-regression approaches to the analysis of variance proceed by converting the independent variables to dummy variables, all of which can then be used as predictors of the dependent variable.

Computational Procedures

The unweighted means analysis is especially useful in studies where we would have preferred equal sample sizes had they been possible. It can be used with equal or unequal sample sizes, and it requires only three simple steps (Walker & Lev, 1953; Winer, 1971; Winer, Brown, & Michels, 1991):

1. Compute a *one-way* analysis of variance on the k groups or conditions.
2. Compute a two-way (or higher) analysis of variance on the *means* of all conditions just as though each condition has yielded only a single score (i.e., the mean).
3. Compute the error term required for the analysis in Step 2 by multiplying the MS_{error} from Step 1 by the reciprocal of the harmonic mean of the sample sizes of the different conditions $(1/n_h)$, where the harmonic mean sample size (n_h) was previously defined in Equation 14.6, and the reciprocal of n_h is obtained by

$$\frac{1}{n_h} = \frac{1}{k}\left(\frac{1}{n_1} + \frac{1}{n_2} + \cdots + \frac{1}{n_k}\right), \tag{16.8}$$

where k = number of conditions, and n_1 to n_k are the number of sampling units per condition. The quantity $1/n_h$ is the factor by which we scale down the MS_{error} from Step 1 to make it the "appropriate size" for the analysis of Step 2.

We now apply these three steps to the set of data that have been serving as our illustration. As it happens, this set does have equal sample sizes, but the computational procedures are identical whether the sample sizes are equal or unequal.

Step 1: One-Way Analysis of Variance

The one-way ANOVA of the data in Table 16.1 is seen in the portion of Table 16.7 that is repeated below:

Source	SS	df	MS	F	η	p
Between conditions	57	3	19.0	7.60	.86	.01
Within conditions	20	8	2.5			

Recall from chapter 14 that equal sample sizes are *not* required for a one-way ANOVA.

Step 2: Two-Way Analysis of Variance

The two-way ANOVA on the *means* of all the conditions in Table 16.1 is computed as follows, beginning with the total sum of squares:

$$\text{Total } SS = \Sigma (M_i - \overline{M})^2 \tag{16.9}$$

where M_i is the mean of each condition, and $\overline{M}$ is the grand mean. Equation 16.9 instructs us to add up as many squared deviations as there are conditions altogether. For the row sum of squares, we compute as follows:

$$\text{Row } SS = \Sigma \left[c(M_r - \overline{M})^2 \right], \tag{16.10}$$

where c is the number of columns contributing to the computation of M_r, the mean of each row, and $\overline{M}$ is again the grand mean. Equation 16.10 instructs us to add up as many quantities as there are rows. For the column sum of squares, we compute

$$\text{Column } SS = \Sigma \left[r(M_c - \overline{M})^2 \right], \tag{16.11}$$

where r is the number of rows contributing to the computation of M_c, the mean of each column. Equation 16.11 instructs us to add up as many quantities as there are columns. And finally, for the interaction sum of squares, we compute

$$\text{Interaction } SS = \text{Total } SS - \text{Row } SS - \text{Column } SS \tag{16.12}$$

Applying Equations 16.9–16.12 to the data in Table 16.2, we have

$$\text{Total } SS = (8 - 4.5)^2 + (4 - 4.5)^2 + (4 - 4.5)^2 + (2 - 4.5)^2 = 19$$
$$\text{Row } SS = 2(6 - 4.5)^2 + 2(3 - 4.5)^2 = 9$$
$$\text{Column } SS = 2(6 - 4.5)^2 + 2(3 - 4.5)^2 = 9$$
$$\text{Interaction } SS = 19 - 9 - 9 = 1.$$

Note that in working only with condition means we have set all our "sample sizes" equal. That is, they all equal 1, the single mean of the condition.

Step 3: Error Term

The error term (MS_{error}) required for the sources of variance (computed in Step 2 from the means of conditions) we obtain by multiplying the MS_{error} of 2.5 from Step 1 by

TABLE 16.9
Unweighted means ANOVA

Source	SS	df	MS	F	η	p
Drug (row)	9	1	9	10.80	.76	.012
Psychotherapy (column)	9	1	9	10.80	.76	.012
Interaction	1	1	1	1.20	.36	.30
Error term ($MS_{error} \times 1/n_h$)	—	8	0.833			

the reciprocal of the harmonic mean of the sample sizes (Equation 16.8), where

$$\frac{1}{n_h} = \frac{1}{k}\left(\frac{1}{n_1} + \frac{1}{n_2} + \cdots + \frac{1}{n_k}\right)$$

$$= \frac{1}{4}\left(\frac{1}{3} + \frac{1}{3} + \frac{1}{3} + \frac{1}{3}\right) = 0.333.$$

Therefore, our new error term, appropriately scaled down, is found to be $2.5 \times 0.333 = 0.833$, and Table 16.9 summarizes our ANOVA.

Earlier, we showed the ANOVA table for the same study but with the computations based on the original 12 scores rather than on the means of the four different conditions (see Table 16.7). Notice that the results of our F tests and the magnitudes of eta and of p in Table 16.7 are identical with those obtained by the method of unweighted means shown in Table 16.9. What are different are the magnitudes of all the sums of squares (SS) and mean squares (MS), which in Table 16.9 are simply smaller by a factor of $1/n_h$. Thus, the effect of using the unweighted means analysis is to shrink the SS and MS in a uniform way that has no effect whatever on either significance tests or effect size estimates. This illustration also shows that when the sample sizes are equal, the unweighted means analysis yields results identical to those obtained from an ordinary analysis using all the original scores.

EFFECTS ON *F* OF UNEQUAL SAMPLE SIZES

In our discussion of the t test in chapter 13, we saw that, compared with a study with equal n, unequal sample sizes result in a loss of relative efficiency (see again Table 13.1). The implication is that, for any given total N, and assuming the effect size is not zero, t increases as the sample sizes become more nearly equal. The same holds for F tests. For any given total N, the value of the F test increases as the sizes of the two or more samples or conditions become more nearly equal. We can demonstrate this fact for the data we have been using for our illustration. The four groups were of equal size ($n = 3$ per group) with a total N of 12 patients. Table 16.10 shows the effects on F, eta (as computed from either Equation 14.11 or 14.12), and p as the sample sizes become increasingly heterogeneous. For our example we show the F, eta, and p only for the drug (row) effect, but that effect is sufficient to illustrate the point.

TABLE 16.10
Effects on F, eta, and p of heterogeneity of sample sizes

Sample sizes	σ of four sample sizes	n_h	$1/n_h$	MS_{error} $(2.5 \times 1/n_h)$	$F(1, 8)$	eta (η)	p
3, 3, 3, 3	0.00	3.00	.333	0.833	10.80	.76	.012
2, 2, 4, 4	1.00	2.67	.375	0.938	9.59	.74	.015
1, 1, 5, 5	2.00	1.67	.600	1.500	6.00	.65	.040
1, 1, 1, 9	3.46	1.29	.778	1.944	4.63	.61	.064

Table 16.10 shows that as the sample sizes become more heterogeneous, where *heterogeneity* is defined by the relative magnitude of the σ of the sample sizes, both F and eta decrease and p becomes larger (i.e., less significant). The F decreases by as much as 57%, the eta decreases by as much as 20%, and the significant p of .012 goes to "nonsignificance" ($p = .064$), a result that would cause great pain to researchers endorsing dichotomous decisions about whether or not to believe the null hypothesis— a view we do not encourage. The results shown in this table are by no means extreme. When the total N increases, much more extreme effects are possible. For example, in the four conditions of the experiment that has been serving as our example, if the N had been 100, equal-sized samples of 25 each would have yielded an $F(1, 96)$ of 131.58, keeping the effect size of $\eta = .76$ constant. However, if the N of 100 had been allocated as heterogeneously as possible (1, 1, 1, 97), then $F(1, 96)$ would have been 7.00 and η would have been .26, a reduction in F of 95% and a reduction in η of 66%!

When factorial designs have unequal sample sizes, it is often useful to have a quick estimate of what the F tests and effect size estimates might have been (i.e., had our total N been allocated equally to all conditions of the experiment). In the following equation, $F_{(equal\ n)}$ is the estimated F value that we would have obtained had our unequal-n factorial design been based instead on equal sample sizes, assuming the same total sample size of N for the entire study:

$$F_{(equal\ n)} = \frac{\bar{n}}{n_h} \times F_{(unequal\ n)}, \qquad (16.13)$$

where $\bar{n}$ is the arithmetic mean of the k sample sizes of the factorial design, n_h is the harmonic mean of the k sample sizes, and $F_{(unequal\ n)}$ is the value of F obtained for any main effect or interaction using the unweighted means procedure for the analysis of variance of factorial designs with unequal sample sizes.

For example, the bottom row of Table 16.10 shows the value of 1.29 for the harmonic mean of the four sample sizes of 1, 1, 1, 9 for a 2×2 factorial design for which an unequal-n-based F test yielded a value of 4.63. Using Equation 16.13, we find

$$F_{(equal\ n)} = \frac{3}{1.29} \times 4.63 = 10.77,$$

a result that is within rounding error of the equal-n-based F test of 10.80 in the top row of Table 16.9. Our estimate of the effect size eta (η) associated with the equal-n-based F uses Equation 14.12, which can also be expressed as

$$\eta = \sqrt{\frac{F(df_{\text{numerator}})}{F(df_{\text{numerator}}) + df_{\text{denominator}}}}.$$

There may be times when we have F tests and effect size estimates based on equal sample sizes in all the cells of a factorial design, but we still want to know how those F tests and effect size estimates will be affected if the sample sizes are found to be unequal (e.g., in a proposed replication with limits placed on treatment availability). In such situations we can simply rewrite Equation 16.13 to produce the predicted F based on unequal sample sizes, as follows:

$$F_{(\text{unequal n})} = \frac{n_h}{\bar{n}} \times F_{(\text{equal n})}. \tag{16.14}$$

For example, Table 16.10 shows $F(1, 8) = 10.80$ for a study with four conditions and $n = 3$ in each of the four conditions. If we knew that a replication study was forced to have four sample sizes of 1, 1, 5, 5, for which $n_h = 1.67$ and the mean sample size $(\bar{n})$ is 3, we predict

$$F_{(\text{unequal n})} = \frac{1.67}{3} \times 10.80 = 6.01,$$

which is within rounding error of the more precisely computed $F(1, 8) = 6.00$ of Table 16.10. Estimation of eta is computed in the usual way, as described above.

UNEQUAL SAMPLE SIZES AND CONTRASTS

Often, we have available data that can be arrayed in a factorial design comprising conditions or cells that have unequal sample sizes. In many of these situations we do better by analyzing the data with contrasts instead of the factorial design and analysis. Table 16.11 shows the results of a study arrayed as a 2×3 factorial in which two levels of severity of prior psychopathology are crossed with three levels of treatment intensity, with sample sizes ranging from 1 to 5 per cell (total $N = 18$). Part A of Table 16.12 shows the means of those six conditions, and Part B gives the factorial ANOVA.

Suppose we are interested in the magnitude of the severity-of-psychopathology effect. We can directly examine that effect by means of a contrast t test using Equation 15.4, where we find

$$
\begin{aligned}
t_{\text{contrast}} &= \frac{\sum(M_i \lambda_i)}{\sqrt{MS_{\text{within}}\left(\sum \frac{\lambda_i^2}{n_i}\right)}} \\
&= \frac{(5)(-1) + (6)(-1) + (7)(-1) + (7)(+1) + (10)(+1) + (13)(+1)}{\sqrt{2.50\left[\frac{(-1)^2}{5} + \frac{(-1)^2}{3} + \frac{(-1)^2}{1} + \frac{(+1)^2}{1} + \frac{(+1)^2}{5} + \frac{(+1)^2}{3}\right]}} \\
&= \frac{12}{\sqrt{2.50(3.0667)}} = 4.334,
\end{aligned}
$$

TABLE 16.11

Adjustment scores for 18 patients as a function of preexisting psychopathology and level of treatment intensity

		Treatment intensity		
		Low	Medium	High
Severe psychopathology		5	5	7
		6	7	
		7	6	
		4		
		3		
	Mean	5	6	7
	S^2	2.50	1.00	0
Mild psychopathology		7	10	13
			11	15
			12	11
			8	
			9	
	Mean	7	10	13
	S^2	0	2.50	4.00

TABLE 16.12

Means and 2 × 3 ANOVA of results in Table 16.11

A. Table of means

Psychopathology	Treatment intensity			Mean
	Low	Medium	High	
Severe	5	6	7	6
Mild	7	10	13	10
Mean	6	8	10	8

B. Summary ANOVA

Source	SS	df	MS	F	eta	p
Intensity (I)	16	2	8	6.26	.71	.014
Psychopathology (P)	24	1	24	18.78	.78	9.7^{-4}
I × P	4	2	2	1.57	.45	.25
Error ($MSE \times 1/n_h$)	—	12	1.2778			

Note: The error term of 1.2778 is the product of the mean square error (MSE) of the one-way ANOVA of all 18 scores in six conditions ($MSE = 2.50$) multiplied by the reciprocal of the harmonic mean sample size, which is $\frac{1}{n_h} = \frac{1}{6}\left(\frac{1}{5} + \frac{1}{3} + \frac{1}{1} + \frac{1}{1} + \frac{1}{5} + \frac{1}{3}\right) = 0.5111$, so Within error $= 2.50 \times 0.5111 = 1.2778$.

with $df = 12$ and $p = 4.9^{-4}$ one-tailed. Computing the contrast r by Equation 15.12, we find

$$r_{contrast} = \sqrt{\frac{t^2_{contrast}}{t^2_{contrast} + df_{within}}} = \sqrt{\frac{(4.334)^2}{(4.334)^2 + 12}} = .78.$$

Squaring the $t_{contrast}$ of 4.334 gives us $F_{contrast} = 18.78$, which is the F for severity of psychopathology in the unweighted means analysis of variance of Table 16.12. In other words, the F test for severity of psychopathology was simply a contrast (i.e., an F with only a single df for the numerator). However, the F for treatment intensity is *not* a contrast, as there are 2 df rather than only 1 df in the numerator. As we explained in chapter 15, when there is more than 1 df in the numerator of an F, that F is addressing a vague, diffuse, or omnibus question about any difference, of any kind, among the means.

Suppose we want to know whether regular increases in treatment intensity are associated with regular increases in patient adjustment scores. Our specific prediction might be that, of the six means, the two means of low intensity can each be represented by contrast weights (lambdas) of -1; the two means of high intensity can each be represented by contrast weights of $+1$; and the two means of medium intensity can each be given weights halfway between (i.e., lambdas of 0). The $t_{contrast}$ for those six conditions can be found from

$$t_{contrast} = \frac{\Sigma(M_i\lambda_i)}{\sqrt{MS_{within}\left(\Sigma\frac{\lambda_i^2}{n_i}\right)}}$$

$$= \frac{(7)(-1) + (5)(-1) + (10)(0) + (6)(0) + (13)(+1) + (7)(+1)}{\sqrt{2.50\left[\frac{(-1)^2}{1} + \frac{(-1)^2}{5} + \frac{(0)^2}{5} + \frac{(0)^2}{3} + \frac{(+1)^2}{3} + \frac{(+1)^2}{1}\right]}}$$

$$= \frac{8}{\sqrt{2.50(2.5333)}} = 3.18,$$

with $df = 12$, $p = .004$ one-tailed, and our effect size estimate is

$$r_{contrast} = \sqrt{\frac{t^2_{contrast}}{t^2_{contrast} + df_{within}}} = \sqrt{\frac{(3.18)^2}{(3.18)^2 + 12}} = .68.$$

This effect size estimate ($r_{contrast}$) directly addresses the specific, focused question of the degree to which changes in the independent variable of treatment intensity are linearly related to changes in the dependent variable of adjustment scores.

TRANSCENDING FACTORIAL STRUCTURE USING CONTRASTS

The development of factorial designs represented an advance over having to address all of the various comparisons among conditions in a one-way ANOVA. However, the ability to array the conditions of an experiment as a factorial ANOVA does not

TABLE 16.13
Contrast on 2 × 3 factorial

A. Predicted means

	Low	Medium	High
Severe	7	9	11
Mild	7	11	15
Difference	0	2	4

B. Contrast weights

	Low	Medium	High
Severe	−3	−1	+1
Mild	−3	+1	+5

make it *necessary,* or even desirable, to use such an analysis. For example, in considering the 2 × 3 factorial that we have been discussing, we might have brought everything we knew about likely row effects (i.e., severity of psychopathology) and about likely column effects (i.e., treatment intensity) and about likely interaction effects into a single overall contrast. Part A of Table 16.13 shows the cell means that we might have predicted based on the theory that (a) adjustment scores would be higher on average for patients with less severe psychopathology, (b) adjustment scores would also be higher for patients as the treatments became more intense, and (c) as treatments became more intense, the advantage in adjustment benefits to the less versus the more severely afflicted patients would also increase.

In order to convert the predicted cell means into proper contrast weights (λ weights), we need only subtract the mean of the six cell values from each prediction so that our contrast weights will sum to zero. The mean of the predicted cell values in Part A of Table 16.13 is 10, and subtracting that mean from each prediction leads to our meeting the two essential conditions for a set of contrast weights. First, they must accurately reflect our prediction, and second, they must sum to zero. Part B of Table 16.13 contains the resulting contrast weights, and we find

$$t_{\text{contrast}} = \frac{\sum(M_i \lambda_i)}{\sqrt{MS_{\text{within}}\left(\sum \frac{\lambda_i^2}{n_i}\right)}}$$

$$= \frac{(7)(-3) + (5)(-3) + (10)(+1) + (6)(-1) + (13)(+5) + (7)(+1)}{\sqrt{2.50\left[\frac{(-3)^2}{1} + \frac{(-3)^2}{5} + \frac{(+1)^2}{5} + \frac{(-1)^2}{3} + \frac{(+5)^2}{3} + \frac{(+1)^2}{1}\right]}}$$

$$= \frac{40}{\sqrt{2.50(20.6667)}} = 5.5649,$$

TABLE 16.14
Analysis of variance of λ weights in part B of Table 16.13

Source	SS	df	MS	Proportion of SS[a]
Intensity (I)	36	2	18	.78
Psychopathology (P)	6	1	6	.13
I × P	4	2	2	.09
Total	46	5		1.00

[a] The analogous proportions of the *SS* associated with the ANOVA of the means actually obtained (Table 16.12) were .36, .55, and .09 for (I), (P), and (I × P), respectively.

with $df = 12$, and $p = 6.1^{-5}$ one-tailed, and also

$$r_{contrast} = \sqrt{\frac{t^2_{contrast}}{t^2_{contrast} + df_{within}}} = \sqrt{\frac{(5.565)^2}{(5.565)^2 + 12}} = .849.$$

In addition to our overall theory assessment, we might also want to look at "subtheories." In that case we could also compute contrasts examining predictions derived from portions of our overall theory. We might, for example, have a prediction about the magnitude of the effect of severity of pathology, or a prediction of a linear trend in the effect of treatment intensity. If, after we have made our predictions for each condition of a factorial design, we would also like to see how our overall theory postulation will translate into the factors of a factorial design, we need only perform a factorial ANOVA on the contrast weights. For the contrast weights in Part B of Table 16.13, the summary ANOVA appears in Table 16.14. This ANOVA shows how much of the total variation (*SS*) of our overall theory is associated with each of the traditional sources of variance, and in the footnote to that table, we see the corresponding proportions of the total variation of the *SS* of the ANOVA of the means actually obtained and shown in Table 16.12. Comparing the proportions predicted by our theory of .78, .13, .09 with the proportions actually obtained of .36, .55, 09 suggests that, in this particular (fictitious) example, our theory overestimated the effect of the intensity factor and underestimated the effect of the psychopathology factor. Although comparisons of proportions of *SS* predicted versus obtained may help tweak our theory somewhat, we should not lose sight of the important finding that our theory, overall, was remarkably accurate, that is, associated with an $r_{contrast}$ of .85 (and an $r_{alerting}$ of .89).

HIGHER ORDER FACTORIAL DESIGNS

So far in our discussion of factorial designs we have dealt only with two-way (two-dimensional) designs, but there are many occasions to use higher order designs. Suppose the experiment described early in this chapter had been carried out twice, once with female patients and once with male patients. Had we decided to reap the general benefit of factorial designs, the implication is that we would be using subjects for more comparisons and building up the sample sizes per comparison by analyzing the two

TABLE 16.15
Improvement means in eight conditions

	Female patients		Male patients	
	Psychotherapy	No psychotherapy	Psychotherapy	No psychotherapy
Drug	10	5	6	3
No drug	4	1	4	3

experiments as a single, higher order factorial experiment. Table 16.15, illustrates this design, which we would describe as a 2 × 2 × 2 factorial or as a 2^3 factorial. That is, there are three factors, and each comprises two levels: (a) drug factor (drug present vs. drug absent), (b) psychotherapy factor (psychotherapy present vs. psychotherapy absent), and (c) sex of patient factor (female vs. male). Assume that there are three patients in each condition, so that $N = 3(2 \times 2 \times 2) = 24$. Assume further that our preliminary one-way analysis of variance (Step 1 of the unweighted means procedure) happens to yield a mean square error (MSE) of 2.5, or exactly what we found in our earlier one-way analysis of the original 12 scores. Step 3 of the unweighted means procedure requires us to multiply this MS error of 2.5 by $1/n_h$, which for this study is

$$\frac{1}{n_h} = \frac{1}{8}\left(\frac{1}{3} + \frac{1}{3} + \frac{1}{3} + \frac{1}{3} + \frac{1}{3} + \frac{1}{3} + \frac{1}{3} + \frac{1}{3}\right) = 0.333,$$

so that our error term is $2.5 \times 0.333 = 0.8333$, the same error term we found before. It remains now only to compute the three-way analysis of variance on the eight means shown in Table 16.15. Though we assume that the busy researcher will routinely use a computer program to perform this analysis, as a way of providing insight into the logic of that analysis, and also further insight into why interactions are called *residuals,* we illustrate the steps were it to be done by hand.

Computations via Subtables

In a three-way ANOVA we will compute three main effects (one for each factor), three two-way interactions of all factors taken two at a time, and one three-way interaction. We begin by constructing three two-way tables. We do this by averaging the two means (in this example) that contribute to the mean of each of the 2 × 2 tables. Those results are shown in Table 16.16. In Subtable 1, for example, we find the mean for the females given drugs (the upper-left cell) by averaging the two conditions in Table 16.15 in which there are females who were given drugs, namely, females given drugs who were also given psychotherapy ($M = 10$) and females given drugs who were not given psychotherapy ($M = 5$). Row and column means in Table 16.16 can be checked readily because each factor produces row or column means in two different 2 × 2 tables. Thus, the female and male mean improvement scores can be compared in Subtables 1 and 2 of Table 16.16. Similarly, we can compare drug and no-drug mean scores in Subtables 1 and 3, and the psychotherapy and no-psychotherapy mean scores in Subtables 2 and 3.

TABLE 16.16
Two-way tables of a three-way design

	Subtable 1: Sex of patient × Drug		
	Female	Male	Mean
Drug	7.5$\llcorner$2	4.5$\llcorner$2	6.0$\llcorner$4
No drug	2.5$\llcorner$2	3.5$\llcorner$2	3.0$\llcorner$4
Mean	5.0$\llcorner$4	4.0$\llcorner$4	4.5$\llcorner$8

	Subtable 2: Sex of patient × Psychotherapy		
	Female	Male	Mean
Psychotherapy	7.0$\llcorner$2	5.0$\llcorner$2	6.0$\llcorner$4
No psychotherapy	3.0$\llcorner$2	3.0$\llcorner$2	3.0$\llcorner$4
Mean	5.0$\llcorner$4	4.0$\llcorner$4	4.5$\llcorner$8

	Subtable 3: Drug × Psychotherapy		
	Psychotherapy	No psychotherapy	Mean
Drug	8.0$\llcorner$2	4.0$\llcorner$2	6.0$\llcorner$4
No drug	4.0$\llcorner$2	2.0$\llcorner$2	3.0$\llcorner$4
Mean	6.0$\llcorner$4	3.0$\llcorner$4	4.5$\llcorner$8

Note: Numbers within the $\llcorner$ symbol indicate the number of units on which each mean is based.

Our strategy is to begin by computing the main effects. Next, we compute two-way interactions, which are leftover effects (i.e., residuals) when the two contributing main effects are subtracted from the variation in the two-way tables. Then we compute the three-way interaction, which is a residual when the three main effects and the three two-way interactions are subtracted from the total variation among the eight condition means. The computational formulas follow, beginning with the "Total" sum of squares (SS), or ($SS_{\text{"Total"}}$):

$$SS_{\text{"Total"}} = \Sigma(M_i - \overline{M})^2,$$

where M_i is the mean of each condition, and $\overline{M}$ is the grand mean of all conditions. Here we simply add up as many squared deviations as there are conditions altogether. (The quotation marks around "Total" are a reminder that this is a "total" SS only when we view the data of the analysis as consisting only of the condition means.)

Next is the sex of patient sum of squares, or SS_{Sex} computed as

$$SS_{\text{Sex}} = \Sigma\left[dp(M_s - \overline{M})^2\right],$$

where d is the number of levels of the drug (D) factor, p is the number of levels of the psychotherapy (P) factor, M_s is the mean of all conditions of a given sex (S), and

$\overline{M}$ is the grand mean. Here we add up as many quantities as there are levels of the factor "sex of patient." Note that we have given up the row and column designations because in higher order designs we run out of things to call factors (e.g., in a five-way design). Accordingly, in higher order designs we use the names of the factors as the names of the dimensions.

For the drug sum of squares, or SS_{Drug}, we compute

$$SS_{Drug} = \Sigma\left[sp(M_D - \overline{M})^2\right],$$

where s is the number of levels of the sex of patient factor (S), p and $\overline{M}$ are as defined before, and M_D is the mean of all the conditions contributing observations to each level of the drug factor. Here we add up as many quantities as there are levels of the drug factor.

For the psychotherapy sum of squares, or $SS_{Psychotherapy}$, we compute

$$SS_{Psychotherapy} = \Sigma\left[sd(M_P - \overline{M})^2\right],$$

where s, d, and $\overline{M}$ are as defined above, and M_P is the mean of all the conditions contributing observations to each level of the psychotherapy factor (P). Here we add up as many quantities as there are levels of the psychotherapy factor.

For the two-way interaction of sex and drug, or $SS_{S\times D}$, we compute

$$SS_{S\times D} = \Sigma\left[p(M_{S\times D} - \overline{M})^2\right] - SS_{Sex} - SS_{Drug},$$

where $M_{S\times D}$ is the mean of all of the conditions contributing observations to each mean of Subtable 1 of Table 16.16, and the other terms are as defined above. Here we add up as many quantities as there are basic entries in that subtable (i.e., four entries).

For the two-way interaction of sex and psychotherapy, or $SS_{S\times P}$, we compute

$$SS_{S\times P} = \Sigma\left[d(M_{S\times P} - \overline{M})^2\right] - SS_{Sex} - SS_{Psychotherapy},$$

where $M_{S\times P}$ is the mean of all conditions contributing observations to each mean of Subtable 2, and the other terms are as defined above. Here we add up as many quantities as there are basic entries in that subtable (i.e., four entries).

For the two-way interaction of drug and psychotherapy, or $SS_{D\times P}$, we compute

$$SS_{D\times P} = \Sigma\left[s(M_{D\times P} - \overline{M})^2\right] - SS_{Drug} - SS_{Psychotherapy},$$

where $M_{D\times P}$ is the mean of all conditions contributing observations to each mean of Subtable 3, and the other terms are as defined above. Here we add up as many quantities as there are basic entries in that subtable (i.e., four entries).

And finally, for the three-way interaction of sex-by-drug-by-psychotherapy, or $SS_{S\times D\times P}$ we find

$$SS_{S\times D\times P} = SS_{\text{"Total"}} - SS_{Sex} - SS_{Drug} - SS_{Psychotherapy} - SS_{S\times D} - SS_{S\times P} - SS_{D\times P}.$$

For the data of our $2 \times 2 \times 2$ factorial, using the various procedures described above will yield the following:

$$
\begin{aligned}
SS_{\text{"Total"}} &= (10 - 4.5)^2 + (5 - 4.5)^2 + (6 - 4.5)^2 + (3 - 4.5)^2 \\
&\quad + (4 - 4.5)^2 + (1 - 4.5)^2 + (4 - 4.5)^2 + (3 - 4.5)^2 \\
&= 50
\end{aligned}
$$

$$SS_{Sex} = [2 \times 2(5 - 4.5)^2] + [2 \times 2(4 - 4.5)^2]$$
$$= 2$$

$$SS_{Drug} = [2 \times 2(6 - 4.5)^2] + [2 \times 2(3 - 4.5)^2]$$
$$= 18$$

$$SS_{Psychotherapy} = [2 \times 2(6 - 4.5)^2] + [2 \times 2(3 - 4.5)^2]$$
$$= 18$$

$$SS_{S \times D} = 2(7.5 - 4.5)^2 + 2(4.5 - 4.5)^2 + 2(2.5 - 4.5)^2$$
$$+ 2(3.5 - 4.5)^2 - SS_{Sex} - SS_{Drug}$$
$$= 8$$

$$SS_{S \times P} = 2(7 - 4.5)^2 + 2(5 - 4.5)^2 + 2(3 - 4.5)^2$$
$$+ 2(3 - 4.5)^2 - SS_{Sex} - SS_{Psychotherapy}$$
$$= 2$$

$$SS_{D \times P} = 2(8 - 4.5)^2 + 2(4 - 4.5)^2 + 2(4 - 4.5)^2$$
$$+ 2(2 - 4.5)^2 - SS_{Drug} - SS_{Psychotherapy}$$
$$= 2$$

$$SS_{S \times D \times P} = 50 - 2 - 18 - 18 - 8 - 2 - 2$$
$$= 0$$

Table of Variance

These computations are summarized in Table 16.17. As all of our F tests have numerator $df = 1$, they are all focused tests and, consequently, lend themselves to further interpretation by the effect size r. When we have focused F tests, $F = t^2$. Consequently, we can most conveniently estimate the effect size r from Equation 12.1,

TABLE 16.17
Unweighted means ANOVA

Source	SS	df	MS	F(1, 16)	$r_{effect\ size}$	p
Sex of patient (S)	2	1	2	2.40	.36	.14
Drug (D)	18	1	18	21.61	.76	.0003
Psychotherapy (P)	18	1	18	21.61	.76	.0003
S × D	8	1	8	9.60	.61	.007
S × P	2	1	2	2.40	.36	.14
D × P	2	1	2	2.40	.36	.14
S × D × P	0	1	0	0.00	.00	1.00
Error term ($MSE \times 1/n_h$)		16	0.833			

Note: The error term of 0.833, with $df_{error} = 16$, is based on the finding that the mean square error (*MSE*) equals 2.5, which we multiply by $1/n_h$. With numerator $df = 1$, the value of eta is equivalent to r, so the effect size r can be computed from Equation 14.12 as eta or from Equation 12.1 as r, where we substitute F for t^2, that is, $r = \sqrt{F/(F + df_{error})}$.

where we simply substitute as follows:

$$r = \sqrt{\frac{t^2}{t^2 + df}} = \sqrt{\frac{F}{F + df_{error}}},$$

and $df_{error} = 16$ in Table 16.17. Similarly, we can also estimate r from eta using Equation 14.12, as $\eta = r$ when we have a focused F with numerator $df = 1$. Examining the effect size correlations of the drug, psychotherapy, and the two-way interaction of drug and psychotherapy, we find that the values of .76, .76, and .36, respectively, are identical to those in our earlier two-way ANOVA in Table 16.9. That is as it should be, of course, because the subtable of the Drug $\times$ Psychotherapy combination (Table 16.16, Subtable 3) shows the same four means as were shown by the two-way table of our earlier 2×2 factorial analysis of variance (see Table 16.2). Notice also that our error term has remained the same. Though our effect sizes have not changed, all of our F values have increased, and the p values are noticeably smaller in Table 16.17 than in our earlier two-way analysis in Table 16.9. That outcome, too, is what we would expect, as the *size* of our study has increased. Consistent with Equation 14.1, which showed that

$$F = \frac{r^2}{1 - r^2} \times df,$$

our F tests have doubled because the size of our study (df_{error}) has doubled.

Inspection of the effect size r for sex of patient in Table 16.17 suggests at least a tendency ($r = .36$) for the sex of the patient to make some difference, and Subtables 1 and 2 of Table 16.16 do indeed show that, on average, females earned higher improvement scores than did males. We will postpone our discussion of the remaining interaction effects of Table 16.16 to the next chapter. The interpretation of interaction is so widely misunderstood, not perhaps in theory but in practice, that we want to highlight the topic in a chapter of its own. As it is not unusual for behavioral researchers to use factorial designs of more than three dimensions, we will show that there is no limit to the complexity of interactions that can be interpreted. For example, it is easy to imagine repeating the three-way factorial just described for two or more levels of age (e.g., patients between ages 20 and 40 and patients between ages 40 and 60). The computations for this 2^4 factorial design ($2 \times 2 \times 2 \times 2$) are quite analogous to those described for the 2^3 design. We proceed by constructing all possible two-way tables (AB, AC, AD, BC, BD, CD) as well as all possible three-way tables (ABC, ABD, ACD, BCD), and then compute the required four main effects, six two-way interactions, four three-way interactions, and one four-way interaction.

BLOCKING AND THE INCREASE OF POWER

We know that one way to increase power is to increase the size of the effect under investigation. One way to increase the size of the effect is to decrease the size of the within-group (or error) variation, which brings us to the strategy of blocking. **Blocking** means the stratification or subdivision of subjects (or other sampling units) in such a way that persons (or other units) within a common block (or level of stratification) are more similar to each other on the dependent variable than they are to persons (or other units) within a different block. As we show next, blocking helps us to achieve increased precision and serves other ends as well.

Suppose we are studying 10 patients who are suffering from different levels of chronic anxiety, and we are interested in a new type of treatment. Half the patients are to receive the new treatment, and half are to receive the placebo control. The dependent variable is the patients' subsequent anxiety level. Because the patients' anxiety levels (after the treatment condition or placebo control condition has been implemented) are likely to correlate substantially with the patients' anxiety levels before the experiment, the preexperimental level of anxiety is a natural candidate for the role of blocking variable. In order to employ a blocking procedure in our experiment while still maintaining the random assignment of subjects to conditions, we find the two patients highest in preexperimental anxiety and assign one of them at random to each of our two conditions. We then find the two patients with the next highest levels of anxiety and assign them at random to treatment and control conditions. We continue in this way until all the patients have been assigned. Table 16.18 shows the results in Part A, and the table of variance is provided in Part B. The treatment effect, which can be described as η or r (because the F for treatments is a focused test with numerator $df = 1$), is found to be large (.85) and significant at $p = .04$. For the

TABLE 16.18
Illustration of blocking

A. Results of blocking

Anxiety blocking levels		Treatment	Control	Σ
Highest		8	9	17
High		6	7	13
Medium		3	5	8
Low		1	3	4
Lowest		1	1	2
	Σ	19	25	44
	M	3.8	5.0	4.4

B. Summary ANOVA

Source	SS	df	MS	F^{a}	η	p
Treatments	3.60	1	3.60	10.29	.85	.04
Anxiety blocks	77.40[b]	4	19.35	55.29	.99	.002
Residual	1.40	4	0.35			

[a] Distributed as F assuming treatments and blocks to be fixed factors and assuming no true interaction. If there *is* a true interaction, F will be too small.

[b] Using contrasts, we can decompose this effect into a 1-df contrast for linear trend ($SS = 76.05$) and a 3-df leftover component ($SS = 1.35$). This leftover component can be aggregated with the residual error term to yield a more stable estimate of error based on 7 df instead of only 4 df.

TABLE 16.19
Results from Table 16.18, omitting blocking

A. Unblocked results

		Treatment	Control
		8	9
		6	7
		3	5
		1	3
		1	1
	Σ	19	25
	M	3.8	5.0

B. Summary ANOVA

Source	SS	df	MS	F	r	p
Treatments	3.60	1	3.60	0.37	.21[a]	.56
Residual	78.80	8	9.85			

[a] Notice that when blocking is omitted, there is a drop in the effect size (indicated as η or r, since $\eta = r$ when numerator $df = 1$). In Table 16.18, the effect size η (or r) was .85, but here it is only .21.

blocking variable the F is an omnibus test with $p = .002$, and we are limited because of the nature of the omnibus F to reporting η (which is even higher at .99).

What would have been the results of our experiment had we not bothered to block? Table 16.19 shows the unblocked results and the summary analysis of variance. Not using blocking resulted in a statistically nonsignificant effect of treatment. Comparison of the ANOVA results in Tables 16.18 and 16.19 reveals no difference between the mean square values for treatment. However, the residual (error) variance of the unblocked analysis has been decomposed into a large between-blocks component and a small residual variance in the blocked analysis. That decomposition illustrates the essence of blocking, which is that it removes from the unblocked error variance large sources of variation associated with systematic preexperimental differences among subjects (or other sampling units). The same difference between means can therefore be interpreted as not statistically significant in the unblocked case, whereas it can be interpreted as clearly significant in the case using blocking. The data of Tables 16.18 and 16.19 could also have been analyzed by t tests (i.e., a matched-pair t test and a t test for independent samples, respectively).

Assessing the Benefits of Blocking

The advantage of blocking can also be expressed in terms of the size of the sample required to achieve the same F value for blocked and unblocked analyses (Snedecor & Cochran, 1989, p. 263). To estimate the number of "pairs" of subjects needed in an

TABLE 16.20
Comparing a treatment with a control group

A. Basic data

	Treatment	Control	M
M	3.8	5.0	4.4
N	140.7	140.7	140.7

B. Summary ANOVA

Source	SS	df	MS	F	r	p
Treatments	101.30	1	101.30	10.28	.76	.01
Residual	78.80	8	9.85			

unblocked study to achieve the same value of F obtained in our blocked study, we use the following formula:

$$\text{reps} = \frac{MSE_{\text{unblocked}} \times \text{blocks}}{MSE_{\text{blocked}}}, \qquad (16.15)$$

where *reps* is shorthand for replications (defined more precisely below), MSE is the mean square error, and *blocks* refers to the number of blocking levels used. For our example, we find

$$\text{reps} = \frac{(9.85)(5)}{0.35} = 140.7.$$

This unusually large value tells us that we will need a small fraction over 140 "pairs" of subjects in an unblocked experiment in order to achieve the same F value that we obtained with only 5 pairs of subjects in our blocked experiment.

Table 16.20, based on the data that we have been examining, compares the treatment and control groups in Part A; the summary ANOVA appears in Part B. We computed the sum of squares (SS) between conditions by

$$SS_{\text{between}} = \sum \left[n_i (M_i - \overline{M})^2 \right] = 140.7(3.8 - 4.4)^2 + 140.7(5.0 - 4.4)^2 = 101.30,$$

and we obtained the SS_{residual} from the unblocked table of variance (Table 16.19). The F of 10.28 in Table 16.20 agrees (within rounding error) with the F of 10.29 in Table 16.18 (the ANOVA based on blocking). In Equation 16.15, we interpret *reps* as denoting the number of replications, subjects, or blocks needed for the F of an unblocked design to match the F of a blocked design, but it makes no allowance for the change in df brought about by increasing N and eliminating the blocking variable. In this example, the df for the blocked error term is 4 (the df for the original unblocked error term was 8). The df for the unblocked error term, based on the new N required to match the blocked design F, is $2(140.7) - 2 = 279.4$. Thus, whereas the old F of 10.29 with 4 df for the error term is significant at .04, the same F with 279.4 df for the error term is significant at $p < .002$, a noticeable difference in level of significance.

If we want to match the p level of the unblocked to that of the blocked design (rather than to match the F values), we can get an approximate value with the help of some algebra. In this example with only two treatments, the number of cases required in *each* unblocked condition to match the p level of the blocked conditions is given by

$$\text{reps} = \frac{2(F_\alpha)(MSE_{\text{unblocked}})}{(M_1 - M_2)^2}, \qquad (16.16)$$

where F_α is the approximate F required for the alpha (α) we are trying to match, and M_1 and M_2 are the condition means. In our example,

$$\text{reps} = \frac{2(4.41)(9.85)}{(1.2)^2} = 60.33.$$

Thus, when we were trying to match F values, the ratio of unblocked to blocked sampling units was 140.7/5 (or about 28:1). When we tried to match p levels, the ratio of unblocked to blocked sampling units was 60.3/5 (or about 12:1). In general, it is only when the blocked experiment is very small that we find such a large difference between the matching of F values and the matching of p values.

This example was designed to illustrate a dramatic effect of blocking. We ensured this effect by choosing our results to reflect a very large correlation between the blocking variable and the dependent variable. The larger this correlation, the greater the benefits of blocking in increasing the precision of the experiment. In our example of just two conditions, the intraclass correlation ($r_{\text{intraclass}}$) can be calculated as

$$r_{\text{intraclass}} = \frac{MS_{\text{blocks}} - MSE}{MS_{\text{blocks}} + MSE}, \qquad (16.17)$$

which, based on the ANOVA results in Table 16.18, gives

$$r_{\text{intraclass}} = \frac{19.35 - 0.35}{19.35 + 0.35} = .96.$$

Similarly, the correlation of the five treatment scores with their associated control scores is also .96. We will have more to say about intraclass correlations in chapter 18, where we discuss repeated measures in factorial designs. In that chapter we will also have a little more to say about blocking, because repeated measures is a kind of ultimate blocking.

BLOCKING AND THE ANALYSIS OF COVARIANCE

When students who are familiar with analysis of covariance are introduced to blocking, they often ask whether it might not be more profitable to use analysis of covariance rather than blocking as a way of increasing precision. Sometimes, in fact, analysis of covariance turns out to be even better than blocking in increasing precision. The **analysis of covariance** (ANCOVA) may be viewed roughly as a special case of ANOVA, in which the observed scores have been adjusted for individual differences within conditions on some predictor variable or covariate known to correlate with the dependent variable. One typical covariate is the pretest administration of the same (or a similar) "test" that is to be used as the dependent variable. When pretest and posttest scores are perfectly correlated and have equal variances, ANCOVA becomes the special case of the analysis of variance of the pre-post change scores.

With respect to the magnitude of the correlation between the pretest and posttest variables, D. R. Cox (1957) developed useful rules of thumb suggesting that:

1. Blocking may be superior to ANCOVA in increasing precision when the correlation between the blocking variable and the dependent variable is .6 or less.
2. ANCOVA may be superior to blocking when the correlation reaches or exceeds .8.
3. In the region between .6 and .8, neither blocking nor ANCOVA seems clearly superior.

A special advantage of blocking over ANCOVA must be noted, however. Blocking is equally efficient for curvilinear and for linear relationships between independent and dependent variables. ANCOVA, at least as it is typically applied, yields benefits only to the extent that the relationship between independent and dependent variables is linear. It can also be noted, however, that modern multiple regression approaches to ANCOVA would permit us to control for quadratic, cubic, etc., relationships as well as linear relationships between the independent and dependent variables (Cohen & Cohen, 1983; Cohen, Cohen, West, & Aiken, 2003).

To illustrate an advantage of blocking over ANCOVA, as ANCOVA is typically applied, we return to Part A of Table 16.18. Suppose we interchange the labels on the rows indicating the patients' level of anxiety. Leaving the scores in their present locations, we bring toward zero the linear correlation between the independent variable of anxiety level and the dependent variable of subsequent anxiety level, thus rendering ANCOVA useless as it is typically applied. However, interchanging labels without moving the obtained scores has no effect on the intraclass correlation (Equation 16.17), which remains unchanged as does the advantage of blocking. To put it another way, when ANCOVA would work well, blocking, especially if enough levels are used, would also work well. When blocking would work well, however, ANCOVA might or might not work well as it is typically applied.

Another advantage of blocking is that it can be used even when blocks differ in qualitative rather than quantitative ways. The blocks can be pairs of twins on whom no pretests are available; groups of countries, states, businesses, adjacent plots of land; or any other partitioning of the sampling units that stratifies them so that units within blocks are thought to be more similar to one another than to units in different blocks. Blocking always imposes some cost in loss of the *df* for error, but that cost is usually small in relation to decreased *MSE*. At any rate, if little reduction in *MSE* is associated with blocking, we can always unblock the blocking to regain our lost *df*.

Most of our discussion of blocking has dealt with its relative benefits in increasing precision. Another benefit of blocking is the detection of interactions between the experimental and the blocking variable. We most often examine such interactions in designs in which each block has a number of replications for each treatment condition. Table 16.21 gives an example of replications in a study of treatment effects on the anxiety level of people of three age groups. The table of variance for these data would

TABLE 16.21
Means and interaction residuals

Age	Means		Residuals	
	Treatment	Control	Treatment	Control
Above 60	6	7	.33	−.33
40–59	3	6	−.67	.67
Below 40	6	7	.33	−.33

show the mean squares for (a) treatments, (b) blocks, (c) Treatments × Blocks inter-action, and (d) a residual (within-cell) term to serve as the denominator for F tests on the preceding terms. The pattern of the interaction, of course, is revealed not by the means, but by the residuals. The direction of the residuals in Table 16.21 is such that middle-aged persons appeared to benefit more (i.e., had lower anxiety) from the treatment than did either older or younger persons.

TRANSFORMING DATA TO REMOVE INTERACTIONS

In chapter 14 we discussed the use of transformations to better meet certain statistical assumptions underlying the use of F tests. Transformations can also be of value in removing complexities in relationships. For example, interaction in a factorial ANOVA can sometimes be removed by transformations, and complex relationships between variables can sometimes be simplified to linear relationships by transformations. Tukey (1977) described one set of transformations as a "ladder of powers" to which to raise raw scores (X), ranging in power from −3 to +3. Thus, we can take the square roots (1/2 powers), or the reciprocals (−1 powers), or the reciprocals of the square roots (−1/2 powers). What about zero power? As Tukey noted, we were all taught that any value raised to the zero power is 1, and this is not wrong, but it does not mean that there can be nothing to fill the gap between −1/2 and +1/2 powers. Tukey suggested the logarithm of X (i.e., X^0), resulting in the following ladder of powers from −3 to +3:

X^3

X^2

X (no transformation)

$X^{1/2}$ (or $\sqrt{X}$)

X^0 (or log X)

$-1/\sqrt{X}$

$-1/X$

$-1/X^2$

$-1/X^3$

TABLE 16.22
Basic data in the form of raw scores

A. Raw scores

	Control A	Treatment A
Control B	1, 4, 9	16, 25, 36
Treatment B	49, 64, 81	100, 121, 144

B. Means (M) and variability (S)

	Control A	Treatment A
Control B	$M = 4.67$	$M = 25.67$
	$S = 4.04$	$S = 10.02$
Treatment B	$M = 64.67$	$M = 121.67$
	$S = 16.01$	$S = 22.01$

C. Residuals

	Control A	Treatment A
Control B	+9.00	−9.00
Treatment B	−9.00	+9.00

Starting at any point and moving up the ladder would emphasize the differences among larger X values in comparison with smaller X values, and moving down the ladder would have the opposite effect. Usually, of course, the range of powers used for transformations is relatively narrow, generally from −1 to +1.

One index of a need for transformation is F_{max}, which we discussed in chapter 14 and defined in Equation 14.20 as the ratio of the maximum to the minimum S^2, that is,

$$F_{max} = \frac{S^2_{max}}{S^2_{min}}.$$

Another such index is the correlation (r_{MS}) between the means and standard deviations of all the various conditions of a study. In Table 16.22, Part A shows the raw scores of three subjects in each of four conditions of a 2×2 factorial design, with total $N = 12$. Part B shows the condition means (M) and standard deviations (S), and we find $F_{max} = (22.01)^2/(4.04)^2 = 29.68$ and $r_{MS} = .98$, both of which are noticeably large values. What we would really like are an F_{max} value very close to 1.00 and an r_{MS} value close to zero. Part C shows the residuals (i.e., the leftover effects after subtraction of the grand mean and the row and column effects from the condition means), which define the interaction (or *nonadditivity*) of the row and column factors.

Now suppose we try a log transformation on the raw scores in Table 16.22. The transformed raw scores are shown in Part A of Table 16.23, with their means and standard deviations shown in Part B and the new table of residuals shown in Part C.

TABLE 16.23

Log_{10} transformation of raw scores in Table 16.22

A. Log_{10} transformed scores

	Control A	Treatment A
Control B	.00, .60, .95	1.20, 1.40, 1.56
Treatment B	1.69, 1.81, 1.91	2.00, 2.08, 2.16

B. Means (M) and variability (S)

	Control A	Treatment A
Control B	$M = 0.52$	$M = 1.39$
	$S = 0.48$	$S = 0.18$
Treatment B	$M = 1.80$	$M = 2.08$
	$S = 0.11$	$S = 0.08$

C. Residuals

	Control A	Treatment A
Control B	-0.15	$+0.15$
Treatment B	$+0.15$	-0.15

In this case we find $F_{max} = (0.48)^2/(0.08)^2 = 36.00$ and $r_{MS} = -.98$. The F_{max} is even larger than before, and the only change in the r_{MS} is that it went from a positive to a negative correlation. The residuals in Part C are, however, noticeably smaller than before, and we also see that the signs are reversed from those in Table 16.22. Thus, the log transformation did not remove the nonadditivity but simply changed its direction.

Table 16.24 shows what happens when we try a square root transformation on the raw scores in Table 16.22. Part B shows that the variability is now equivalent in all four cells ($S = 1.00$), and we will also find that $F_{max} = (1.00)^2/(1.00)^2 = 1.00$ and $r_{MS} = .00$. The square root transformation produced homogeneity of variance and the greatest symmetry, which is an aspect of normality. In this example, the raw scores were already fairly symmetrical, so no great violation of normality had occurred. Particularly interesting is that the table of residuals shows that the square root transformation has completely removed the nonadditivity, thereby greatly simplifying the interpretation of the 2 × 2 table of means in Part B. The plot of the four condition means against the equally spaced predicted benefits of control, Treatment A, Treatment B, and both treatments would show a straight line. The analogous plots for the raw data (Table 16.22) and for the log transformation (Table 16.23) would show a curvilinear relationship, although both would have strong linear components. Further details on the use of transformations can be found in Mosteller & Tukey (1977) and in Tukey (1977).

TABLE 16.24

Square root transformation of raw scores in Table 16.22

A. Square-root-transformed scores

	Control A	Treatment A
Control B	1, 2, 3	4, 5, 6
Treatment B	7, 8, 9	10, 11, 12

B. Means (M) and variability (S)

	Control A	Treatment A
Control B	$M = 2.00$	$M = 5.00$
	$S = 1.00$	$S = 1.00$
Treatment B	$M = 8.00$	$M = 11.00$
	$S = 1.00$	$S = 1.00$

C. Residuals

	Control A	Treatment A
Control B	0.00	0.00
Treatment B	0.00	0.00

INTERACTION EFFECTS IN ANALYSIS OF VARIANCE

THE INTERPRETATION OF INTERACTION

In the last chapter we illustrated a basic principle of the factorial analysis of variance (ANOVA), which is that when we add a second factor to cross the first, we generate sources of variation associated with the first factor, the second factor, and a third source of variation called the *interaction*. From surveys of published research studies and of researchers themselves (Rosnow & Rosenthal, 1989; Zuckerman, Hodgins, Zuckerman, & Rosenthal, 1993), as well as from arguments and rejoinders in journal articles and books, we know that interaction effects are a source of confusion to many psychological researchers. As we demonstrated in the previous chapter, the mathematical meaning of interaction effects as leftover effects (or *residuals*) after the removal of constituent effects (row and column effects in two-factor analyses) is unambiguous. A number of leading mathematical statisticians and a smaller number of psychological statisticians have explained the procedure of stripping away the constituent lower order variation from possible interactions obscured in the cell means (e.g., Guilford, 1956; Guilford & Fruchter, 1978; Keppel, 1991; Lindquist, 1953; Mosteller, Fienberg, & Rourke, 1983; Mosteller & Tukey, 1977; Snedecor & Cochran, 1980). Nonetheless, many behavioral and social researchers confuse the pattern of the condition means with the interaction. Certainly it is true in the case of a 2 × 2 design that the most frugal definition of interaction is the difference between orthogonal simple effects. We discussed that procedure in chapter 7 (in the context of R. L. Solomon's 2 × 2 design for identifying Pretest × Treatment interaction effects) and think it should be encouraged

TABLE 17.1
Interaction contrast in a 2 × 2 table

	Column 1	Column 2
Row 1	-1	$+1$
Row 2	$+1$	-1

because bizarre interpretations of such interactions are less likely to result. However, when all factors have more than two levels, that "differences-between-differences" procedure cannot be used.

Of course, simply because two or more factors can be crossed is no reason actually to cross them. We believe that the most useful data-analytic method (i.e., after a variety of exploratory procedures) is the contrast. For example, in a 2 × 2 factorial design, the interaction contrast is defined by the lambda weights noted in Table 17.1, and the interaction sum of squares is the sum of squares for that contrast. As implied in that table, 2 × 2 interactions when plotted are *always* ×-shaped. That is not true of interactions larger than 2^2, which may be ×-shaped (called *crossed-line* or *crossed-linear interactions*) or may have another symmetrical shape (e.g., crossed-quadratic interactions). The point is that if we claim an observed interaction, it should be described and interpreted accurately. Computing the residuals that define the interaction effects is not difficult, but it does take time. Computing the residuals for higher order interactions is also not difficult, but it takes increasingly more time if it must be done by hand (not every statistics program routinely provides the residuals defining the interactions). Of course, if the interaction is of no interest, it need not be computed. If all that we predicted is a certain ranking of cell means, our prediction should be tested by a planned contrast. Mistaking the pattern of the cell means for the interaction effects, however, is unacceptable.

We address these topics in some detail in this chapter, starting with two-way interactions. Before proceeding, we want to mention another erroneous belief—that F tests for main effects are "meaningless" and the results "not interpretable" in the presence of interaction (cf. Meyer, 1991; Rosnow & Rosenthal, 1991). However, consider Table 17.2, in which Part A shows the cell means for a hypothetical study of the sex of psychotherapist and the sex of patient, and Part B contains the corresponding table of effects. The interaction residuals show that same-sex dyads score higher than opposite-sex dyads; the column effects show that female therapists, in general, score higher than male therapists, and there are no row effects. The corresponding ANOVA would show $SS_{\text{interaction}} = 16$, $SS_{\text{columns}} = 4$, and $SS_{\text{rows}} = 0$. Clearly, even in the presence of interaction, the main effect of therapist sex is both meaningful and readily interpretable. We turn now to a more detailed discussion of how residuals, such as those displayed in Part B, are identified and interpreted. Perhaps the reader will recall the diner scene in the movie *Five Easy Pieces*. In that scene, Jack Nicholson asked for a side order of toast and the waitress told him, "We don't serve side orders of toast." He replied, "You make sandwiches, don't you?" and ordered a sandwich, telling her to remove all the ingredients until all that was

TABLE 17.2
Illustration of meaningful main and interaction effects

A. Table of means

Patient sex	Therapist sex	
	Female	Male
Female	6	0
Male	2	4

B. Row, column, interaction effects, and grand mean

Patient sex	Therapist sex		Row effect
	Female	Male	
Female	2	-2	0
Male	-2	2	0
Column effect	1	-1	$M_G = 3$

Note: M_G denotes the grand mean; the mean of the four means.

left was what he wanted: toast. It is the same with interaction in ANOVA. Interaction is always and exclusively defined by leftover effects (residuals). Therefore, anyone claiming an interaction should be prepared to display and interpret those particular residuals.

CROSSED AND UNCROSSED COMBINATIONS OF GROUP MEANS

Suppose a researcher is comparing a new method of teaching reading with an old method and has both female and male pupils as subjects. The resulting means and the corresponding two-way ANOVA appear in Table 17.3. In the published report, the researcher accurately states that there was a significant effect of method: Pupils taught by the new method performed better than those taught by the old method, and the effect size was $r = .25$. The researcher also correctly states that there was no significant effect of sex of pupil on performance, and indeed the corresponding F is similar in magnitude to the expected value when the null hypothesis is true (see again Table 14.3). Finally, the report also contains a display resembling Figure 17.1, but the researcher incorrectly states that "the interaction shown in the figure demonstrates that males, but not females, benefited from the new teaching method."

In what way did the researcher err in referring the reader to the display in Figure 17.1? The figure is a perfectly accurate display of the *overall* results of the study, including the two main effects *and* the interaction. However, it is not an accurate display of the interaction that the researcher believed was being plotted. In fact, displays of crossed and uncrossed combinations of group means are not at all uncommon. It is often pointed out, quite correctly, that when the lines cross, the implication is that an interaction is present; if the lines do not cross, but remain parallel to one another, the implication

TABLE 17.3
Hypothetical study comparing a new and an old method of teaching

A. Table of means

Method	Females	Males	Mean
Experimental (new method)	4	10	7
Control (old method)	4	2	3
Mean	4	6	5

B. Unweighted means ANOVA

Source	SS	df	MS	F	r	p
Method (row)	16	1	16	4.00	.25	.05
Sex of pupil (column)	4	1	4	1.00	.13	.32
Interaction	16	1	16	4.00	.25	.05
Error term ($MS_{error} \times 1/16$)	—	60	4			

is that there is no interaction. There is nothing wrong with that claim. The problem arises when the pattern of the obtained interaction is interpreted only on the basis of the configuration of group means. Furthermore, labeling this pattern the "interaction" in effect creates a non sequitur by ignoring the premise of the additive model underlying the factorial ANOVA (as described in the previous chapter).

Figure 17.2 provides an *accurate* picture of the interaction. It shows that males benefited from the new method precisely to the same degree that females were harmed by it. As is true *in general* of nonzero 2 × 2 interactions, the figure is ×-shaped. Why that is so should become clear as we explain the procedure also described as *mean polishing,* in which we "polish down" the cell means to the interaction residuals.

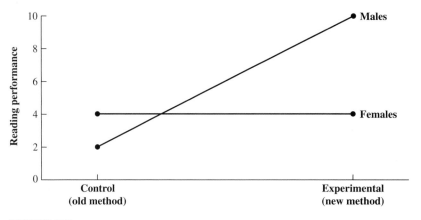

FIGURE 17.1
Display of two main effects as well as interaction.

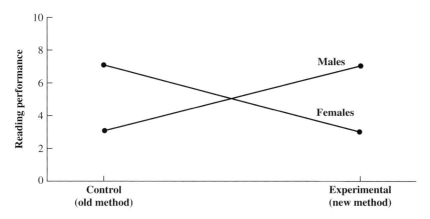

FIGURE 17.2
Display of interaction effect.

However, we should note that the term *residual* is also used in a more general way to refer to any leftover effect after the subtraction of a summary value from a given value (Tukey, 1977, p. 113). For example, when we subtract the median of a batch of scores from each score (a process called *median polishing*), we turn the raw scores into residuals. Tukey (1977, p. 125) thought that kind of polishing could be likened to what "powerful magnifying glasses, sensitive chemical tests for bloodstains, and delicate listening devices" are to a detective, in that "polishing down" batches of residual values enables us to detect hidden patterns.

In the previous chapter we explained that interaction effects are the effects still remaining in any analysis after certain "lower order" constituent effects have been removed. We can also remove the grand mean and thus polish down the cell values to their barest essential component. The *pattern* of the interaction will remain the same, however, whether or not the grand mean is present. In sum, ignoring for the moment the removal of the grand mean, the interaction effects in a two-way ANOVA design (A × B) are the residuals after the row and column effects (the effects of A and B) are removed. In a three-way ANOVA design (A × B × C), and in higher order designs, there are four or more different interactions. For example, in an A × B × C design, there are three two-way interactions: (a) A × B; (b) A × C; and (c) B × C (where each of the three is the residual set of effects remaining after the removal of the two main effects denoted by the letters naming the interaction). There is also, of course, the three-way interaction (A × B × C), or the residual set of effects remaining after the removal of the three constituent main effects and the three two-way interactions. In a four-way ANOVA design (A × B × C × D), there are six two-way interactions: (a) A × B; (b) A × C; (c) A × D; (d) B × C; (e) B × D; and (f) C × D, and also four three-way interactions: (a) A × B × C; (b) A × B × D; (c) A × C × D; and (d) B × C × D (as well as the single four-way interaction). In general, a *higher order interaction* is defined as the residual set of effects remaining after the main effects and all lower order interactions relevant to the higher order interaction have been removed. Thus, the A × B × C × D interaction is defined as the set of effects remaining after the four main effects, six two-way interactions, and four three-way interactions have been subtracted from the total of all between-conditions effects.

ILLUSTRATION OF MEAN POLISHING

As is true of any obtained interaction in analysis of variance, before it can be understood it must be identified and examined. That is, we need to display the residuals defining the obtained interaction. The logic of this process of mean polishing is straightforward, but in a very high-order interaction the computation becomes burdensome if we must do the arithmetic by hand. In a 2×2 design, however, the computations are simple. Consider again the results of the experiment on the effects of a new method of teaching reading on reading performance scores. In Table 17.4, the subtable in Part A is a repetition of the results in Table 17.3 with the addition of row and column effects. *Row effects* are defined for each row as the mean of that row minus the grand mean. The row effects are $7 - 5 = 2$ for the new (experimental) teaching method and $3 - 5 = -2$ for the old (control) teaching method. The column effects are defined for each column as the mean of that column minus the grand mean. Thus, the column effects are $4 - 5 = -1$ for the females and $6 - 5 = 1$ for the males.

The next step is to remove the row and column effects from the cell means. Part B of Table 17.4 shows the results after we removed (or "corrected" for) the row effects, which we did by subtracting the row effect from every condition within that row. Subtracting the row effect of 2 from the condition means of 4 and 10 yielded new cell values of 2 and 8, with a new row mean of 5. Subtracting the row effect of -2 from the condition means of 4 and 2 yielded new cell values of 6 and 4 (recall that subtracting a negative value is equivalent to adding a positive value), with another new row mean of 5. With the row effects removed from the condition means, the new row effects are shown as zero.

Next, we do the same thing for the column effects. Subtracting -1 from the first column of the row-corrected table in Part B yields new cell values of 3 and 7 in Part C. Subtracting 1 from the second column of the row-corrected table in Part B yields new cell values of 7 and 3 in Part C. The table of means we started with in Part A, now with both row and column effects removed, has been amended as shown in Part C. We also see that the row and column effects are all shown as zero. Once the row and column effects are all zero, we can be sure that what is left is only the set of residuals defining the interaction, although in this case with the grand mean added. Figure 17.2 displays the interaction residuals of Part C, and we see that the 2×2 interaction is, not surprisingly, $\times$-shaped.

If we want to compare the interaction with the condition means, then it is useful to display the results as shown in Figure 17.2. In most situations, however, we prefer to display the interaction effects freed of the effect of the grand mean, because it is then easier to compare them with row and column effects. We have more to say about this topic shortly, but to remove the grand mean from the four condition means in Part C of Table 17.4, all we need do is subtract 5 (the grand mean) from each condition mean. The resulting residuals, shown in Part D, are not inflated by the grand mean. Notice also that all four conditions show the same absolute value of the interaction effects; only the signs differ. That is always the case in a 2×2 ANOVA, and

TABLE 17.4
Polishing down cell means to expose the interaction

A. Cell means, row and column effects

	Sex of pupils		Mean	Row effects
	Females	**Males**	**Mean**	**Row effects**
Teaching method				
New (experimental)	4	10	7	2
Old (control)	4	2	3	−2
Mean	4	6	5	
Column effects	−1	1		

B. Cell means "corrected" for row effects

	Sex of pupils		Mean	Row effects
	Females	**Males**	**Mean**	**Row effects**
Teaching method				
New (experimental)	2	8	5	0
Old (control)	6	4	5	0
Mean	4	6	5	
Column effects	−1	1		

C. Cell means "corrected" for row and column effects

	Sex of pupils		Mean	Row effects
	Females	**Males**	**Mean**	**Row effects**
Teaching method				
New (experimental)	3	7	5	0
Old (control)	7	3	5	0
Mean	5	5	5	
Column effects	0	0		

D. Cell means "corrected" for row and column effects and for the grand mean

	Sex of pupils		Mean	Row effects
	Females	**Males**	**Mean**	**Row effects**
Teaching method				
New (experimental)	−2	2	0	0
Old (control)	2	−2	0	0
Mean	0	0	0	
Column effects	0	0		

the signs on one of the diagonals are always different from the signs on the other diagonal unless the interaction is precisely zero. Thus, it is convenient to think of interaction in a 2×2 table as the difference between the means of the two diagonals, just as it is convenient to think of the row or column effects as the differences between the row means or the column means.

Returning again to Figure 17.1, we can clearly see that it is an accurate display of the results of the experiment. It does show that females did not benefit from the new teaching method but that males did. That declaration, however, is not a statement about the obtained interaction effect by itself; rather, it is a statement about the four condition means. What that declaration presumes, in other words, is in part (a) a method effect (the new method is better); (b) a sex effect (males score higher, though not significantly so); and (c) an interaction effect (which we interpret as showing that females are hurt by the new method as much as males are helped by it).

CONSTRUCTING TABLES OF PREDICTED MEANS

As a check on one's understanding of interaction effects and the additive nature of the analysis of variance, it is useful to construct a table of means to particular specifications. To illustrate, we begin with the simplest case, the 2×2 table, and then proceed to a more complex two-way table.

Assembling a 2 × 2 Table

For this simplest case, suppose we hypothesized row, column, and interaction effects, with the row effect predicted as largest of those three effects and the column effect predicted as smallest. To get started, we need an empty 2×2 table, such as the following one, where the two levels of the row variable are labeled A1 and A2 and the two levels of the column variable are labeled B1 and B2:

	B1	B2	Row mean	Row effect
A1				
A2				

Column mean
Column effect

Beginning with the grand mean, we might choose any value (positive, zero, or negative), but we want to keep to a single-digit integer for simplicity. Suppose we choose a grand mean of 2, in which case we have:

	B1	B2	Row mean	Row effect
A1	2	2	2	0
A2	2	2	2	0
Column mean	2	2	2	
Column effect	0	0		

As we want the column effect to be smallest, we start with the column variable. Let us assume that we hypothesized B1 > B2. To keep the hypothesized column effect small, we choose the smallest possible integers (+1 and −1) to add to each condition within each of the two columns:

	B1	B2	Row mean	Row effect
A1	3	1	2	0
A2	3	1	2	0
Column mean	3	1	2	
Column effect	+1	−1		

So that the interaction effect will be larger than the column effect, we might choose the values of +2 and −2. Suppose we predicted the diagonal from upper-left to lower-right to be positive and the other diagonal to be negative. We simply add 2 to the cells representing conditions A1B1 and A2B2, and we subtract 2 from the cells representing conditions A2B1 and A1B2:

	B1	B2	Row mean	Row effect
A1	5	−1	2	0
A2	1	3	2	0
Column mean	3	1	2	
Column effect	+1	−1		

Finally, suppose our prediction for the row variable was that A1 > A2. So that the row effect will be larger than the interaction, we can choose the values of +3 and −3 to add to each condition within each of the two rows:

	B1	B2	Row mean	Row effect
A1	8	2	5	+3
A2	−2	0	−1	−3
Column mean	3	1	2	
Column effect	+1	−1		

As a check on the accuracy of our construction of this table, we can decompose it into its various components, as we did in the previous chapter. These results are shown in Table 17.5, where examination of the four group means and their additive components shows that row effects are larger than interaction effects, as required by our specifications. In a 2 × 2 table the absolute values of the two row effects are identical, with one of the signs positive and the other negative. Exactly the same situation holds for the column effects. For the interaction, all four effects are identical in their absolute value, but the two effects on one diagonal are opposite in sign to the two effects on the other diagonal. In this case, therefore, we can rank the sizes of effects by simply rank-ordering the absolute values of the three effects contributing to any one of the four means.

TABLE 17.5
2 × 2 table decomposed into its various components

	Group mean	=	Grand mean	+	Row effect	+	Column effect	+	Interaction effect
A1B1	8	=	2	+	3	+	1	+	2
A1B2	2	=	2	+	3	+	(−1)	+	(−2)
A2B1	−2	=	2	+	(−3)	+	1	+	(−2)
A2B2	0	=	2	+	(−3)	+	(−1)	+	2
ΣX	8	=	8	+	0	+	0	+	0
ΣX^2	72	=	16	+	36	+	4	+	16

Assembling a 3 × 4 Table

Constructing a 2 × 2 table of predicted effects was not very challenging, so let us try a more complex two-way table. For this example, we will assemble a 3 × 4 table in four steps, as illustrated in Table 17.6. First, we will select an average value. Then we will select a row effect. Next, we will select a column effect. And finally, we will select an interaction effect.

1. This time for the average value, we will begin by assigning a mean value to each cell that we believe reflects the typical value of the metric we have chosen. Suppose for this example we believe that the value 5 is representative, as shown in Part A of Table 17.6.

2. Next, we need to select a row effect to represent what we have hypothesized. Let us assume that we hypothesized a ∩-shaped quadratic trend in the row means, in which case we might choose weights of −1, +2, −1 for A1, A2, and A3, respectively. We now subtract 1 from each entry of A1, add 2 to each entry of A2, and subtract 1 from each entry of A3. The results are shown in Part B of Table 17.6. Notice that the column means, column effects, and grand mean are unchanged from Part A, because we have done nothing to the column variable or anything more to the average value.

3. For the column variable, assume we predicted column effects so that B1 and B2 are equal to each other and 3 units greater than B4, which, in turn, is 2 units greater than B3. A set of weights that will satisfy these requirements is +2, +2, −3, −1 for B1, B2, B3, and B4, respectively. Therefore, we simply add 2 to each entry of B1 and B2, subtract 3 from each entry of B3, and subtract 1 from each entry of B4. This step is reflected in Part C of Table 17.6. Notice that the row means, row effects, and grand mean are the same as in Part B.

4. Suppose we also predicted the interaction effects that conditions B1 and B3 will show linear trends in the row effects that are in opposite directions to each other, whereas conditions B2 and B4 will show quadratic trends in the row effects that are in opposite directions to each other. The weights we may choose to represent our predictions are shown in Part D, and adding them to the effects built up in Part C produces the final table of predicted means in Part E.

TABLE 17.6
Constructing a 3 × 4 table of means

A. Same mean for each cell

	B1	B2	B3	B4	Row Mean	Row effect
A1	5	5	5	5	5	0
A2	5	5	5	5	5	0
A3	5	5	5	5	5	0
Column mean	5	5	5	5	5	
Column effect	0	0	0	0		

B. Data of Part A after introduction of a quadratic row effect

	B1	B2	B3	B4	Row Mean	Row effect
A1	4	4	4	4	4	−1
A2	7	7	7	7	7	+2
A3	4	4	4	4	4	−1
Column mean	5	5	5	5	5	
Column effect	0	0	0	0		

C. Data of Part B after introducing a column effect such that B1 = B2 > B4 > B3

	B1	B2	B3	B4	Row Mean	Row effect
A1	6	6	1	3	4	−1
A2	9	9	4	6	7	+2
A3	6	6	1	3	4	−1
Column mean	7	7	2	4	5	
Column effect	+2	+2	−3	−1		

D. Weights for linear and quadratic interaction residuals

	B1	B2	B3	B4	Total
A1	−1	+1	+1	−1	0
A2	0	−2	0	+2	0
A3	+1	+1	−1	−1	0
Total	0	0	0	0	0

E. Data of Part C after introducing the interaction residuals of Part D

	B1	B2	B3	B4	Row Mean	Row effect
A1	5	7	2	2	4	−1
A2	9	7	4	8	7	+2
A3	7	7	0	2	4	−1
Column mean	7	7	2	4	5	
Column effect	+2	+2	−3	−1		

STUDYING INTERACTIONS
IN TWO-WAY TABLES

Once we have assembled such a complex two-way table, it should not be difficult to study the effects in any other two-way table. However, as this is a chapter on interaction, our focus in the following example is on the study of the interaction, which is emphazed here not because we regard interaction effects as in any way more important than main effects, but because interaction effects are so much more often misinterpreted than main effects. For our example we consider another 3×4 experimental design, a classic type of psychiatric study, in which four different treatment procedures are administered to three different types of patients, with the hypothetical results shown in Table 17.7. Patients of each of the three types were randomly assigned to either a course of 10 electroconvulsive treatments (ECT), or a course of 3 electroconvulsive treatments, or a combination of supportive psychotherapy and medication, or supportive psychotherapy alone.

1. *Remove the grand mean.* In order to reveal the pattern of the interaction of Treatment $\times$ Patient type, we must remove the row and column effects from the cell means. Usually it is desirable to subtract the grand mean as well, so we begin by doing that. Because the grand mean is 6, we subtract 6 from each of the 12 means and get the subtable shown in Part A of Table 17.8. When the grand mean is removed, the new row means are synonymous with the row effects, and the new column means are synonymous with the column effects. The reason, of course, is that the row and column effects are the row and column means from which we have subtracted the grand mean.

2. *Remove the row effects.* To remove the row effects from the "de-meaned" cell values in Part A of Table 17.8, we subtract the effect of each row from every condition within that row. Doing that for the results in Part A yields the cell values shown in Part B.

TABLE 17.7
Means of improvement scores in a 3 × 4 design

	Treatment conditions				
Patient type	**B1** **ECT(10)**	**B2** **ECT(3)**	**B3** **Support + drug**	**B4** **Support only**	**Mean**
A1 Psychotic depression	8	6	4	2	5
A2 Neurotic depression	11	8	5	8	8
A3 Paranoid reaction	2	4	6	8	5
Mean	7	6	5	6	6

Note: ECT denotes electroconvulsive treatments, consisting of a series of 10 such treatments in condition B1 and 3 such treatments in condition B2. In the remaining conditions, the patients received either supportive therapy *and* medication (B3) or supportive therapy alone (B4).

TABLE 17.8
Mean polishing of results in Table 17.7

A. Cell means of Table 17.7 "corrected" for grand mean

	B1	B2	B3	B4	Mean
A1	2	0	−2	−4	−1
A2	5	2	−1	2	2
A3	−4	−2	0	2	−1
Mean	1	0	−1	0	0

B. Data of part A "corrected" for row effects

	B1	B2	B3	B4	Mean
A1	3	1	−1	−3	0
A2	3	0	−3	0	0
A3	−3	−1	1	3	0
Mean	1	0	−1	0	0

C. Data of part B "corrected" for column effects

	B1	B2	B3	B4	Mean
A1	2	1	0	−3	0
A2	2	0	−2	0	0
A3	−4	−1	2	3	0
Mean	0	0	0	0	0

3. *Remove the column effects.* Using a similar procedure to remove the column effects, we have the results shown in Part C of Table 17.8. Those data are a picture of the interaction, that is, the leftover (residual) effects after removal of the grand mean, row effects, and column effects from the 12 cell means of Table 17.7.

The residual effects contributing most to the interaction are those furthest from zero, and one way to approach the interpretation of the interaction is one residual at a time, starting with the largest absolute value. In this case, the residual value of −4 for condition A3B1 is the largest absolute effect, implying that the least improvement was shown by paranoid patients given a course of 10 ECT treatments, when we disregard the row and column effects. The next two largest residuals are −3 for A1B4 and +3 for A3B4. The former suggests that support alone offered to psychotic depressive patients was relatively damaging (−3), and the latter suggests that support alone offered to paranoid patients was *relatively* quite beneficial (+3). When we say *relatively,* all we mean is that the effects shown by certain combinations of treatments and patients were large or small in relation to other effects that are also shown here *after the removal of the main effects of treatments and patients.*

We can be more systematic in our examination of these interaction residuals by listing them in their order of magnitude, as shown in Table 17.9. Examining first the positive residuals suggests that paranoid patients may do better given supportive

TABLE 17.9
Systematic ordering of residuals

Residual	Patient	Treatment
3	Paranoid	Support only
2	Psychotic depression	ECT 10
2	Neurotic depression	ECT 10
2	Paranoid	Support + drug
1	Psychotic depression	ECT 3
0	Psychotic depression	Support + drug
0	Neurotic depression	ECT 3
0	Neurotic depression	Support only
−1	Paranoid	ECT 3
−2	Neurotic depression	Support + drug
−3	Psychotic depression	Support only
−4	Paranoid	ECT 10

psychotherapy, whereas depressive patients may do better given ECT. Examining the negative residuals suggests that paranoid patients may do worse given ECT, and that depressive patients may do worse given supportive psychotherapy. It may also be useful to simplify the design from four treatments to two, which we do by combining the two conditions receiving ECT and the two conditions receiving supportive psychotherapy. We can also further simplify the design from three patient types to two by combining the two depressed groups. That simplifying procedure gives us Table 17.10, in each quarter of which we have recorded the sum of the residuals of Table 17.8 (Part C) contributing to that cell.

The complexity of an interaction depends in part on the *df* associated with it, with *df* computed as the product of the degrees of freedom associated with each of the constituent elements. In the study that we have just been discussing, there were four treatment conditions, so *df* = 3 for treatments. There were three types of patients, so *df* = 2 for patient type. Therefore, *df* for the Treatment × Patient-type interaction is simply 3 × 2 = 6. Finding a pattern in those 6 *df*, such as the one shown in Table 17.10,

TABLE 17.10
Sum of residuals of 3 × 4 Table 17.8 (part C) reduced to a 2 × 2 design

Patients	ECT (B1 + B2)	Support (B3 + B4)	Mean
Depressives (A1 + A2)	5	−5	0
Paranoids (A3)	−5	5	0
Mean	0	0	0

TABLE 17.11
Alternative simplification of 6-*df* interaction

Patients	(B1) High ECT (10)	(B2) Low ECT (3)	(B3 + B4) No ECT (0)	Mean
Depressives (A1 + A2)	4	1	−5	0
Paranoids (A3)	−4	−1	5	0
Mean	0	0	0	0

represents the simplifying of the 6-*df* interaction to a 1-*df* portion of that interaction. Elsewhere (Rosenthal & Rosnow, 1985) we provide procedures for assessing how well we have done in simplifying the interpretation of an interaction with multiple *df* in the numerator of its *F* test. In the previous chapter we illustrated how it may be possible to transcend the factorial structure by a planned contrast, or to simplify a complex relationship by using a transformation that causes the interaction to disappear.

Assuming that we really are interested in the structure of the interaction, an accurate description of the simplified structure of our interaction in Table 17.10 might be that depressed patients are benefited by ECT to the same degree that they are harmed by support, whereas paranoid patients benefit from support to the same degree that they are harmed by ECT. Note, however, that we are describing the interaction residuals in Table 17.10, not the original condition means of Table 17.7. As shown in Table 17.8, those original means are a reflection *not* merely of the interaction but of the row and column effects as well as the grand mean.

Still another alternative simplification of the 6-*df* interaction involves keeping in mind the number of electroconvulsive treatments administered as well as whether an ECT was administered at all. Thus, we might have three levels of ECT, as shown in Table 17.11. Interpretation of that simplification might be that in proceeding from none to some to more electroconvulsive treatments, depressed patients are increasingly benefited, whereas paranoid patients are decreasingly benefited.

THREE-WAY FACTORIAL DESIGNS

We turn now to three-way designs. Just as it is instructive to construct tables of means to our specifications in the case of two-way designs, it is instructive to do so for three-way designs. We illustrate this procedure by returning to the 2 × 2 × 2 factorial design that we discussed in the previous chapter, with means for those eight conditions shown in Table 16.15, its simplification into two-way tables shown in Table 16.16, and the summary ANOVA shown in Table 16.17. In that study there were three two-way interactions, and for the purpose of computation of the three-way ANOVA, we constructed subtables of means, one for each two-way combination of the three factors of the study. The three factors were sex of patient (S), drug (D), and psychotherapy (P). As we have already given several illustrations of how to go from a table of means to a table of effects, we will here simply show the table of effects corresponding to each table of means.

TABLE 17.12
Three-way design

A. Sex of patient × Drug combination

	Table of means			Table of effects		
	Female	Male	Mean	Female	Male	Mean
Drug	7.5	4.5	6.0	1.0	−1.0	1.5
No drug	2.5	3.5	3.0	−1.0	1.0	−1.5
Mean	5.0	4.0	4.5	0.5	−0.5	0

B. Sex of patient × Psychotherapy combination

	Table of means			Table of effects		
	Female	Male	Mean	Female	Male	Mean
Psychotherapy	7.0	5.0	6.0	0.5	−0.5	1.5
No psychotherapy	3.0	3.0	3.0	−0.5	0.5	−1.5
Mean	5.0	4.0	4.5	0.5	−0.5	0

C. Drug × Psychotherapy combination

	Table of means			Table of effects		
	Psychotherapy	No psychotherapy	Mean	Psychotherapy	No psychotherapy	Mean
Drug	8.0	4.0	6.0	0.5	−0.5	1.5
No drug	4.0	2.0	3.0	−0.5	0.5	−1.5
Mean	6.0	3.0	4.5	1.5	−1.5	0

Table 17.12 shows the table of means and the table of effects for each two-way combination of the three factors of the design in Table 16.15. In the tables of effects shown in Parts A, B, and C, the row and column "means" are row and column effects, respectively, and the four cell entries are the residuals defining the interaction. As previously reported in Table 16.17, the interaction of sex of patient and drug (S × D in Table 16.17) was found to be significant at $p = .007$, and the effect size r was .61. Examination of the residuals in Part A of Table 17.12 tells us that females did as much better with the drug as they did worse without it, whereas males did as much better without the drug as they did worse with it. Does this finding mean that males are better off without the drug? The answer is no, because in this study there was a large main effect of the drug, and it was better to have the drug than not have it for males as well as females. The S × D interaction implies only that the benefits of the drug are less for males than they are for females, not that the drug is disadvantageous to males in any *absolute* sense.

The interaction of Sex of patient $\times$ Psychotherapy (S $\times$ P in Table 16.17) had an associated p value of .14, though the effect size correlation was not trivial ($r = .36$). Examination of the residuals in Part B of Table 17.12 reveals that the female patients did better with psychotherapy, but the male patients did better without psychotherapy relative, respectively, to females receiving no psychotherapy and males receiving psychotherapy. Phrased another way, we could say that psychotherapy benefited females $[(0.5) - (-0.5) = 1.0\ ]$ more than it benefited males $[(-0.5) - (0.5) = -1.0]$.

The interaction of Drug $\times$ Psychotherapy (D $\times$ P in Table 16.17) also had an associated p value of .14 and an effect size r of .36. The residuals defining this interaction are shown in Part C of Table 17.12, where we see that psychotherapy was more beneficial to those receiving the drug, and that the absence of psychotherapy was more beneficial to those not receiving the drug, that is, relative to the remaining two combinations (disregarding the main effects, as interactions always do). Phrased another way, we could say that the D $\times$ P interaction shows that receiving *both* drug and psychotherapy and receiving *neither* drug nor psychotherapy were more beneficial than receiving *either* treatment alone. Again, we must emphasize that this result does not mean that patients are better off receiving no treatment than receiving either treatment alone. On the contrary, the table of means in Part C of Table 17.12 shows that either the drug or psychotherapy alone is more beneficial than neither treatment.

DEFINING THREE-WAY INTERACTIONS

Interactions are defined by the leftover effects after the removal of certain lower order effects, and we have now had some experience in computing those residuals for two-way interactions. When we have a three-way factorial design, we subtract all three main effects and all three two-way interactions in order to reveal the residuals defining the three-way interaction. From the results that we have been examining in Table 17.12, we can find all the effects needed to calculate the residuals for the three-way interaction. The original table of means is repeated in Table 17.13. For illustration we concentrate on the top-left condition in Table 17.13, which shows a mean of 10 for females who received both the drug and the psychotherapy. In Table 17.12 all three subtables showed the grand mean to be 4.5, so we begin by subtracting the grand mean from the condition mean of 10 and find that $10 - 4.5 = 5.5$. For this particular condition effect, we will, in turn, subtract the three main effects and the three two-way interactions.

The table of effects in Part A of Table 17.12 shows at the bottom of column 1 the effect of being female at 0.5 and at the end of the top row the effect of receiving

TABLE 17.13

Overall means corresponding to the three subtables in Table 17.12

	Female patients		Male patients	
	Psychotherapy	No psychotherapy	Psychotherapy	No psychotherapy
Drug	10	5	6	3
No drug	4	1	4	3

the drug at 1.5. The table of effects in Part B of Table 17.12 shows at the end of the top row the effect of receiving psychotherapy at 1.5. Each of those effects could also have been found in an alternative location (e.g., the effect of being female is also found at the bottom of column 1 of the table of effects in Part B, and the effect of receiving the drug is also found at the end of the top row of the table of effects in Part C). Simple subtraction of each of those three main effects from the residual defining the condition effect of 5.5 yields:

Condition effect	−	Sex effect	−	Drug effect	−	Psychotherapy effect	=	Combined interaction effect
5.5	−	0.5	−	1.5	−	1.5	=	2.0

The value of 2.0 above is now made up of all the contributions to the condition effect comprising all three of the two-way interactions plus the three-way interaction. To identify the three-way interaction residual, therefore, we need only subtract the three two-way interaction residuals from 2.0. The two-way interaction residuals are again found in Table 17.12. In Part A, the upper-left condition of the table of effects shows the Sex of patient × Drug interaction effect to be 1.0 for females receiving drugs. In Part B, the upper-left condition of the table of effects shows the Sex of patient × Psychotherapy interaction effect to be 0.5 for females receiving psychotherapy. In Part C, the upper-left condition of the table of effects shows the Drug × Psychotherapy interaction to be 0.5 for those patients receiving both drug and psychotherapy.

In identifying the interaction effect relevant to the condition mean or residual that we are trying to decompose into its elements, we must take great care to select the particular residual that actually applies to the condition mean we are working with. In a three-way design, when we are working with the mean of condition A1B1C1, the AB residual we need is A1B1, the AC residual is A1C1, and the BC residual is B1C1. In the present case of the mean of the A1B1C1 condition, the combined interaction effect had a residual value of 2.0, from which we subtract the residuals of the three two-way interactions and find the residual defining the three-way interaction:

Combined interaction effect	−	Sex × Drug interaction	−	Sex × Psychotherapy interaction	−	Drug × Psychotherapy interaction	=	Three-way interaction
2.0	−	1.0	−	0.5	−	0.5	=	0

Repeating this procedure for each of the eight condition means of Table 17.13, we find the three-way interaction effects to be zero in every case (i.e., there is no three-way interaction). Table 17.14 summarizes the main effects of sex (S), drug treatment (D), psychotherapy treatment (P), the three two-way interaction effects (S × D; S × P; D × P), and the three-way interaction effects (S × D × P) that, along with the grand mean (M_G), constitutes the eight condition means in Table 17.13. Table 17.14 is analogous to, and an extension of, our example in the previous chapter of the table of effects of a 2×2 design (Table 16.5), showing that condition means may be viewed as made up of additive pieces.

TABLE 17.14
Table of effects for 2 × 2 × 2 study in Table 17.13

M	=	M_G	+	S	+	D	+	P	+	SD	+	SP	+	DP	+	SDP
10	=	4.5	+	0.5	+	1.5	+	1.5	+	1.0	+	0.5	+	0.5	+	0
5	=	4.5	+	0.5	+	1.5	+	(−1.5)	+	1.0	+	(−0.5)	+	(−0.5)	+	0
4	=	4.5	+	0.5	+	(−1.5)	+	1.5	+	(−1.0)	+	0.5	+	(−0.5)	+	0
1	=	4.5	+	0.5	+	(−1.5)	+	(−1.5)	+	(−1.0)	+	(−0.5)	+	0.5	+	0
6	=	4.5	+	(−0.5)	+	1.5	+	1.5	+	(−1.0)	+	(−0.5)	+	0.5	+	0
3	=	4.5	+	(−0.5)	+	1.5	+	(−1.5)	+	(−1.0)	+	0.5	+	(−0.5)	+	0
4	=	4.5	+	(−0.5)	+	(−1.5)	+	1.5	+	1.0	+	(−0.5)	+	(−0.5)	+	0
3	=	4.5	+	(−0.5)	+	(−1.5)	+	(−1.5)	+	1.0	+	0.5	+	0.5	+	0
ΣX 36	=	36.0	+	0	+	0	+	0	+	0	+	0	+	0	+	0
ΣX^2 212	=	162	+	2	+	18	+	18	+	8	+	2	+	2	+	0

Note: The symbol M equals the particular condition mean in Table 17.13, M_G = the grand mean, S = the factor of sex (female vs. male), D = the drug factor (drug administered vs. absent), and P = the psychotherapy factor (psychotherapy administered vs. absent). Column headings with two or three letters denote, respectively, a two-way or a three-way interaction (e.g., SDP = the interaction of Sex × Drug × Psychotherapy).

As described in the previous chapter for a two-way design, we can use the decomposition of the condition means in Table 17.14 to understand better the computation of the terms of an ANOVA of a three-way design. Beneath each column of the display in the table are shown the sum of the eight values (ΣX) and the sum of the squares of those eight values (ΣX^2). For all three main effects, for all three two-way interactions, and for the three-way interaction, the sums of squared residuals are identical to the *SS* shown in the previous chapter in Table 16.17. Computing by hand the residuals defining the three-way interaction is not especially difficult, nor is it difficult to compute the residuals defining a four-way, five-way, or higher order interaction. However, it should be apparent why we said that it takes more and more time to do the arithmetic required, unless, of course, we have a computer program that will give us the residuals defining all the interactions tested. We have more to say shortly about interpreting residuals of higher order interactions, but first, we want to underscore again the difference between the cell means and the interaction residuals and to suggest some intuitive ways of interpreting both in two-way tables.

FURTHER NOTES ON INTERPRETATION

Organismic Interactions

Although interactions are defined by, and therefore described by, a table of residuals, such a table is not usually of interest to the researcher without some additional interpretation. In an abstract discussion of interaction we might view a table of interaction residuals without labeling the rows and columns and without feeling the necessity to

TABLE 17.15
Illustration of organismic interaction

Subjects	Drug A	Drug B
Male	+1	−1
Female	−1	+1

think very deeply about the theoretical implications of the interaction. However, if we claim an interaction in an investigation of a substantive question, we are obliged to make sense of the reported interaction. Suppose we obtain the interaction represented in Table 17.15, where the $+1$ and -1 cell entries denote the "effectiveness" of Drugs A and B for males and females. As is true of every nonzero 2×2 interaction, this one is ×-shaped. Interpreting the residuals in Table 17.15, we would conclude that the interaction implies that Drug A is relatively better for males, whereas Drug B is relatively better for females. Once again, the term *relatively* is used here to emphasize that the effects shown by certain combinations of drug and gender are viewed as large or small in relation to other effects shown *after the removal of the main effects of drug and gender* (and, in this case, after removal of the grand mean as well). In fact, it often happens in behavioral research that certain treatment techniques are differentially effective for different subject samples. Interactions like these, called **organismic interactions,** reflect the special effectiveness for some but not for other types of persons.

Positive Synergistic Effects

When we see other than an ×-shape in a 2×2 table of means (or in a figure), it is generally safe to assume that we are looking at more than just the interaction. Suppose that two treatments have been applied simultaneously, and the table of means indicates that people receiving both treatments had better results than we might have predicted from a knowledge of the likely results of administering each treatment. For example, the subtable shown in Part A of Table 17.16 implies that Treatment A alone or Treatment B alone has no beneficial value, and indeed the effects are no different from receiving neither treatment, but the joint administration of Treatments A and B is very beneficial. We can describe that pattern of the condition means as a **positive synergistic effect,** in that both treatments are required for any benefits to result.

Clearly, we are describing not the interaction residuals but the condition means. If we subtract the grand mean, row effects, and column effects, we find interaction effects that tell quite a different story: Row, column, and interaction effects for the four cell means in Part A are of equal magnitude. The obtained interaction, taken by itself, tells us that both treatments or neither treatment is superior to either one treatment or the other. Of course, if all that we are really interested in evaluating is an overall prediction stating that both treatments combined lead to beneficial effects, but that either treatment alone is no better than receiving neither treatment, then we can compute a 1×4 contrast with weights of $+3, -1, -1, -1$, respectively, for AB-present, A-only, B-only, and AB-absent.

TABLE 17.16
Illustrations of synergistic effects of condition means

A. Positive synergistic effect

		Treatment A	
		Present	Absent
Treatment B	Present	4	0
	Absent	0	0

B. Negative synergistic effect

		Treatment A	
		Present	Absent
Treatment B	Present	0	4
	Absent	4	4

C. Negative synergistic effect implying a ceiling effect

		Treatment A	
		Present	Absent
Treatment B	Present	4	4
	Absent	4	0

Negative Synergistic Effects

Suppose that the table of results showed that Treatments A and B had the same result as a placebo control, whereas receiving both Treatments A and B together was harmful. In this case we have a *negative synergistic effect,* as shown in Part B of Table 17.16. We again recognize the results to be cell means, not the interaction alone, as nonzero interactions in 2 × 2 tables are always ×-shaped. For the results in Part B, once we have done the mean polishing, we find that the row, column, and interaction effects are identical in size. Residuals defining the interaction suggest that receiving either treatment in isolation is better than receiving both treatments or neither treatment. Had we predicted the pattern of means shown in Part B, the contrast weights for evaluating that pattern would be $-3, +1, +1, +1$, respectively, for AB-present, A-only, B-only, and AB-absent.

Before leaving the topic of negative synergism, we should note that a possible basis for that kind of result is a ceiling effect, as when the measuring instrument is simply unable to record benefits above a certain level (e.g., 4 in this case). The subtable in Part C of Table 17.16 shows how a set of results might appear if the synergistic effect were due to a ceiling effect.

Crossed-Linear Interactions

We know that 2 × 2 interactions are invariably ×-shaped. Suppose, however, we have a factorial design other than 2 × 2 and want to interpret an obtained interaction. When the residuals for one group of subjects or sampling units show a relatively linear increase and the residuals for another group show a relatively linear decrease, we describe the pattern as a **crossed-linear interaction.** Although the ×-shaped pattern of the residuals in a 2 × 2 interaction are also crossed lines, we reserve the term *crossed-linear interaction* to describe factorial designs in which there are three or more levels for each of the groups being compared.

As an illustration, consider three measures of sensitivity to nonverbal communication that have been administered to female and male subjects. The three measures are designed to measure sensitivity to the face, to the body, and to the tone of voice. Of those three channels, the face is thought to be the most easily controlled, and tone is thought to be the least easily controlled (Rosenthal & DePaulo, 1979a, 1979b). A fairly typical result in research of this kind might yield the table of means for accuracy scores in Part A of Table 17.17, with the corresponding table of effects shown in Part B. The row effects show that females are better decoders of nonverbal cues than are males, a well-known result (Hall, 1979, 1984b). The column effects show that face cues are easiest to decode, and tone-of-voice cues are hardest to decode of the three types of cues, also a well-known result (Rosenthal, Hall, DiMatteo, Rogers, &

TABLE 17.17
Illustration of crossed-linear interaction

A. Table of means

Subjects	Channel			Mean
	Face	Body	Tone	
Female	6	4	2	4.0
Male	3	2	1	2.0
Mean	4.5	3.0	1.5	3.0

B. Table of effects

Subjects	Channel			Mean
	Face	Body	Tone	
Female	0.5	0.00	−0.5	1.0
Male	−0.5	0.00	0.5	−1.0
Mean	1.5	0.00	−1.5	0.0

C. Differences between row residuals in Part B

Subjects	Channel		
	Face	Body	Tone
Female	0.5	0.00	−0.5
Male	−0.5	0.00	0.5
Difference (female advantage)	1.0	0.00	−1.0

Archer, 1979). The interaction residuals show that, as the type of cue becomes more controllable by the encoder, the females' advantage over the males increases, which is also a frequently obtained result (Rosenthal & DePaulo, 1979a, 1979b). A plot of these residuals would show a crossed-linear interaction, with one group increasing as the other group is decreasing (reminiscent of the interaction shown in Figure 17.2, near the beginning of this chapter). Another convenient way to think about crossed-linear interactions is shown in the bottom row of Part C of Table 17.17, where we see the differences between the residuals for the two groups. Were we to plot the differences, our figure would show a linear increase in the superiority of women over men as the channels became more controllable.

Crossed-Quadratic Interactions

Sometimes the residuals of one group are ∪-shaped whereas the residuals of the other group are ∩-shaped (i.e., inverted ∪-shaped). That is, the quadratic relationships are symmetrically reversed in the two groups. We described those kinds of relationships in chapter 15, where a line changes direction once (going down and then up, or vice versa). Curves changing direction twice (i.e., down, up, and down, or vice versa) are called *cubic curves.* With each additional change in direction, a cubic curve becomes a *quartic curve,* a quartic curve becomes a *quintic curve,* and so on. As an example of a crossed-quadratic interaction, suppose that two groups of children have been tested under three conditions of arousal. Inspecting the cell means in Part A of Table 17.18, we infer that the younger group of children ($S^2 = 3.0$) were apparently less affected by arousal level than the older group ($S^2 = 12.0$). Part B shows the table of effects corresponding to the table of means. The row effects show that the older children performed better than the younger children, and the column effects show that medium

TABLE 17.18
Illustration of crossed-quadratic interaction

A. Table of means

Age	Arousal level			Mean
	Low	Medium	High	
Younger	3	6	3	4
Older	5	11	5	7
Mean	4.0	8.5	4.0	5.5

B. Table of effects

Age	Arousal level			Mean
	Low	Medium	High	
Younger	0.5	−1.0	0.5	−1.5
Older	−0.5	1.0	−0.5	1.5
Mean	−1.5	3.0	−1.5	0.0

arousal level was associated with better performance than was either low or high arousal level. The interaction residuals clearly show crossed-quadratic curves, with younger children showing a ∪-shaped performance curve relative to the older children, who show a ∩-shaped (inverted-∪) performance curve. Once again we must emphasize that those residuals refer exclusively to the interaction component of the factorial ANOVA. Inspection of the condition means reveals that each group produced a ∩-shaped (inverted-∪) function, but that the inverted ∪ of the older children was more dramatic ($S^2 = 12$) than was the inverted ∪ of the younger children ($S^2 = 3$).

SIMPLIFYING COMPLEX TABLES OF RESIDUALS

A general principle for the simplification of tables of interaction residuals is to subtract one level of a factor from the other level of that factor for any two-level factor for which the difference between the two levels can be regarded as substantively meaningful. In this procedure, a two-way interaction may be viewed as a change in a main effect due to the introduction of a second independent variable. And a three-way interaction may be viewed as a change in a main effect due to the introduction of a two-way interaction or as a change in a two-way interaction due to the introduction of a third independent variable. Another general principle for the simplification of tables of interaction residuals involves a process of concept formation for the diagonals of the table of residuals, usually a 2 × 2 table. If a suitable concept can be found to describe each diagonal of such a table, the interpretation of the interaction residuals is simplified to the interpretation of a main effect of the diagonals. We will illustrate each of these two principles using what we call (a) the method of meaningful differences and (b) the method of meaningful diagonals, and we will also discuss the possibility of combining these two methods.

Method of Meaningful Differences

We alluded to the method of meaningful differences in our discussion of crossed-linear interactions. In Part C of Table 17.17, we subtracted the residuals for males from the residuals for females to create difference scores that represented the advantage of being female over being male when a task calls for decoding nonverbal cues. Comparing those female advantage scores for three types of measures of sensitivity to nonverbal cues, we were able to interpret an interaction of Channel × Sex of subject simply as a main effect of channel on the differences between the sexes.

Table 17.19 provides an even simpler example, in which two treatment conditions, A and B, are both administered to two types of people, X and Y. By taking the difference

TABLE 17.19
Illustration of the method of meaningful differences

Subjects	A	B	(A − B)
Type X	+1	−1	2
Type Y	−1	+1	−2

TABLE 17.20
Illustration of the method of meaningful diagonals

A. Display of interaction residuals

Sex of patient	Sex of therapist	
	Female	Male
Female	+1	−1
Male	−1	+1

B. Reduction to one-dimensional display

	Same-sex dyad	Opposite-sex dyad
	+1	−1
	+1	−1
Mean	+1	−1

between Treatments A and B we form a new measure, namely, the advantage of A over B. These advantage scores (A − B) can then be compared for persons of Types X and Y. In this example the advantage of Treatment A over B is greater for Type X than for Type Y persons because 2 is greater than −2. By subtracting B from A, we reduce a two-dimensional display of residuals to a one-dimensional display.

Method of Meaningful Diagonals

The method of meaningful diagonals, calls for simplifying the table of residuals by imposing substantive meaning on the residuals located on the diagonals, again usually a 2 × 2 table. For example, we might be studying the outcome of psychotherapy as a function of the sex of the therapists and the sex of the patients, with interaction residuals as shown in Part A of Table 17.20. The upper-left and lower-right cells together constitute what we conceptualize as the *same-sex dyad* diagonal, and the lower-left and upper-right cells constitute what we conceptualize as the *opposite-sex dyad* diagonal. We can state that the mean residual for same-sex dyads is greater (+1) than that for opposite-sex dyads (−1). Thus, by using a construct to describe the diagonals, we have reduced the two-dimensional display of interaction residuals in Part A of Table 17.20 to the one-dimensional display in Part B.

Combining Methods

Table 17.21 illustrates how it may be possible to use both the methods just explained to achieve even greater simplification of a fairly complex interaction. In Part A, we see the residuals corresponding to an obtained three-way interaction in a study in which male and female experimenters administered a task to male and female subjects. Half the experimenters were led to expect high achievement from their subjects, and the other experimenters were led to expect low achievement from their subjects.

TABLE 17.21
Illustration of combining methods

A. Display of three-way interaction

	Experimenters' expectations and genders			
	Low expectations		High expectations	
Subjects	Female	Male	Female	Male
Females	−1	+1	+1	−1
Males	+1	−1	−1	+1

B. Method of meaningful differences applied to results in Part A

	High − low expectancy differences	
Subjects	Female experimenters	Male experimenters
Females	+2	−2
Males	−2	+2

C. Method of meaningful diagonals applied to results in Part B

	Same-sex dyads	Opposite-sex dyads
	+2	−2
	+2	−2
Mean	+2	−2

We begin the simplification process by applying the method of meaningful differences to the data in Part A of Table 17.21. In this case it makes the most substantive sense to subtract the residuals for low expectations from the residuals for high expectations. These differences then represent expectancy effects, which are positive in sign when they are in the predicted direction (high > low) and negative in sign when they are in the opposite direction (high < low). The results of this first step are shown in Part B, where the three-way interaction of sex of experimenter, sex of subject, and expectancy has been simplified to a two-way interaction of sex of experimenter and sex of subject, with the dependent variable of difference scores or expectancy effect scores. Applying the method of meaningful diagonals to that two-way table, we obtain the results shown in Part C. Thus, we can interpret the originally complex three-way interaction as indicating that same-sex dyads show greater expectancy effects than do opposite-sex dyads.

ILLUSTRATION OF A FIVE-WAY INTERACTION

The same general procedures can often be applied to an even more complicated situation, such as a five-way interaction, as shown in Table 17.22. This time we have female and male experimenters who are either black or white, administering a task to

TABLE 17.22
Residuals defining a five-way interaction

| | Black experimenter | | | | White experimenter | | | |
| | Male experimenter | | Female experimenter | | Male experimenter | | Female experimenter | |
Subjects	High expectancy	Low expectancy	High expectancy	Low expectancy	High expectancy	Low expectancy	High expectancy	Low expectancy
Black								
Male	+1	−1	−1	+1	−1	+1	+1	−1
Female	−1	+1	+1	−1	+1	−1	−1	+1
White								
Male	−1	+1	+1	−1	+1	−1	−1	+1
Female	+1	−1	−1	+1	−1	+1	+1	−1

male and female subjects who are either black or white, sometimes having been led to expect high, and sometimes low, performance. Thus, the 2^5 factorial design consists of Race of experimenter × Sex of experimenter × Race of subject × Sex of subject × Expectancy of experimenter.

Our first step again is to eliminate one dimension of the design by subtracting the low-expectancy residuals from the high-expectancy residuals; the results appear in Table 17.23. Notice that there are four sections, each section containing four cells in a 2 × 2 arrangement. The cell entries in the overall table, which are difference scores, can be viewed as a 2 × 2 interaction of race of experimenter by race of subject. Notice that the four cell entries in the upper-left section are identical to the four cell entries in the lower-right section of the overall table, and the signs are opposite those of the four cells in the upper-right and lower-left sections of the table. The diagonal consisting of upper-left and lower-right sections comprises the same-race dyads; the diagonal consisting of lower-left and upper-right sections contains the opposite-race dyads.

TABLE 17.23
High-minus-low expectancy effects

| | Black experimenters | | White experimenters | |
Subjects	Male	Female	Male	Female
Black				
Male	+2	−2	−2	+2
Female	−2	+2	+2	−2
White				
Male	−2	+2	+2	−2
Female	+2	−2	−2	+2

TABLE 17.24

Mean expectancy effects

Sex of dyad	Race of dyad	
	Same	**Different**
Same	$+2$	-2
Different	-2	$+2$

Our interpretation of the five-way interaction is that expectancy effects are greater for same-sex dyads that are also same-race dyads or different-sex dyads that are also different-race dyads than for dyads differing only on sex or only on race. We can redisplay this five-way interaction (or the four-way interaction of difference scores) as a two-way interaction of two-way interactions of difference scores, as shown in Table 17.24.

Applying the general principles illustrated in our earlier example, we made a single factor (same versus different) of the Race of experimenter $\times$ Race of subject interaction, and a single factor (same versus different) of the Sex of experimenter $\times$ Sex of subject interaction. That kind of simplification of a complex interaction is not always possible, but it is more likely when there is some implicit conceptual meaning in the diagonal cells of any 2×2 factorial contained within a 2^k factorial design, where $k > 2$. In general, such simplification is more likely when there are fewer levels in the factors of the experiment, hence, fewer degrees of freedom associated with the higher order interaction that we are trying to understand. Some higher order interactions prove more intractable than others. However, by carefully examining the residuals, by applying the methods of meaningful differences and meaningful diagonals, and by using the contrast procedures discussed in chapters 15 and 16 (and also described in more detail in Rosenthal, Rosnow, & Rubin, 2000), we can often make some progress.

A NOTE ON COMPLEXITY

Sometimes the research questions are complex, and it is quite possible that complex designs and analyses may be required. However, just because we know how to deal with complexity is no reason to value it for its own sake. If our questions are simple and precise, then simpler and highly focused designs and analyses are possible. Especially for the beginning researcher, considerable practical benefit can be derived from keeping the designs and analyses as simple and precise as possible.

CHAPTER 18

REPEATED MEASURES IN ANALYSIS OF VARIANCE

USE OF REPEATED OBSERVATIONS

Up to now in our discussion of analysis of variance, each of the sampling units was observed only once. Thus, for example, each subject, patient, school, city, or other unit contributed only one observation to the total number of observations. Earlier we mentioned that such arrangements are known as *between-subjects designs* because all of the variation among the obtained scores is based on individual differences between subjects (or other units). As we stated in chapter 7, the units in between-subjects designs are said to be *nested* within their treatment conditions, which simply means that subjects (or other sampling units) are observed under only a single condition of the study.

Often, however, it is more efficient to administer two or more treatment conditions to the same subjects, thereby permitting them to serve as their "own control." Also noted earlier was that subjects (or other sampling units) in these designs are described as *crossed* by treatment conditions rather than nested within them. The term *crossed* simply means that subjects (or other units) are observed under two or more conditions of the study. The more the scores of the sampling units under one condition are correlated with the scores of the sampling units under another condition of the study, the more advantageous it may be to have the units under more than one condition, that is, to use a repeated-measures design (also known as a *within-subjects design*).

Sometimes, too, the very nature of the research question seems to call for some type of repeated-measures design. For example, if we are interested in examining the effects of practice on the performance of a learning task, or the effects of age in a longitudinal study of development, it seems natural to observe the same subjects repeatedly. Another common natural and advantageous use of a repeated-measures design is in the administration of tests or subscales in a series. For example, we might want to administer the 11 subtests of a standardized measure of intelligence, or the 5 subscales of a standardized inventory of personality, or we might want to administer several tests quite different from each other (e.g., an intelligence test, a personality inventory, and a measure of sensitivity to nonverbal cues).

The simplest repeated-measures (or within-subjects) design measures or observes subjects twice. In that case we have a choice of statistical procedures for comparing the scores obtained under each of the two conditions of measurement or observation. We can, for example, use the analysis of variance procedures to be detailed in the pages that lie ahead, or we can compute the specialized t test for nonindependent samples described in chapter 13 (Equation 13.22). That matched-pairs t test is also an example of blocking (discussed in chapter 16), because each pair of observations comes from a single block of sampling units.

Matched-pair t tests are the simplest type of repeated measures, but all repeated-measures designs use some form of blocking. The more that the successive observations on the same sampling units are positively correlated with each other, the more we generally benefit in increased precision from choosing a repeated-measures design as opposed to a between-subjects design. But assuming we have one or more specific questions or predictions to put to the data, we can further enhance our repeated-measures analysis by the use of contrasts (discussed later in this chapter).

BASIC COMPUTATIONS

Suppose we want to study the effects on performance scores of repeated practice sessions. We administer the same task to four subjects on three occasions (i.e., in a 4 × 3 layout), with the results shown in Table 18.1. Our analysis begins just like that of any two-way ANOVA, yielding a row effect (subjects in this example), a column effect (sessions in this example), and a Row × Column interaction (i.e., Subjects × Sessions in this case). Our analysis will differ from those in other two-way designs discussed earlier in that there is now only a single observation in each combination of row and column.

TABLE 18.1
Performance scores on three occasions

	Session 1	Session 2	Session 3	Mean
Subject 1	0	7	3	3.33
Subject 2	1	7	4	4.00
Subject 3	3	8	5	5.33
Subject 4	4	8	6	6.00
Mean	2.0	7.5	4.5	4.67

The computational procedures were generally described in chapter 16 (Equations 16.9, 16.10, 16.11, and 16.12). However, the total sum of squares is now defined as the sum of the squared deviations of *each individual score* (X) from the grand mean $(\overline{M})$ of all the scores:

$$\text{Total } SS = \Sigma(X - \overline{M})^2. \qquad (18.1)$$

The other formulas are as noted earlier: Equation 16.10 for the row sum of squares instructed us to add up as many quantities as there are rows:

$$\text{Row } SS = \Sigma[c(M_r - \overline{M})]^2,$$

where c is the number of columns contributing to the computation of M_r, the mean of each row, and $\overline{M}$ is again the grand mean. For the column sum of squares, Equation 16.11 had us add up as many quantities as there are columns:

$$\text{Column } SS = \Sigma[r(M_c - \overline{M})^2],$$

where r is the number of rows contributing to the computation of M_c, the mean of each column. Finally, for the interaction sum of squares, Equation 16.12 stated as follows:

$$\text{Interaction } SS = \text{Total } SS - \text{Row } SS - \text{Column } SS.$$

For the data of our illustration in Table 18.1, we have

$$
\begin{aligned}
\text{Total } SS &= (0 - 4.67)^2 + (7 - 4.67)^2 + (3 - 4.67)^2 \\
&\quad + (1 - 4.67)^2 + (7 - 4.64)^2 + (4 - 4.67)^2 \\
&\quad + (3 - 4.67)^2 + (8 - 4.67)^2 + (5 - 4.67)^2 \\
&\quad + (4 - 4.67)^2 + (8 - 4.67)^2 + (6 - 4.67)^2 \\
&= 76.67
\end{aligned}
$$

$$
\begin{aligned}
\text{Row } SS &= 3(3.33 - 4.67)^2 + 3(4.00 - 4.67)^2 \\
&\quad + 3(5.33 - 4.67)^2 + 3(6.00 - 4.67)^2 \\
&= 13.35
\end{aligned}
$$

$$
\begin{aligned}
\text{Column } SS &= 4(2.0 - 4.67)^2 + 4(7.5 - 4.67)^2 \\
&\quad + 4(4.5 - 4.67)^2 \\
&= 60.67
\end{aligned}
$$

$$
\begin{aligned}
\text{Interaction } SS &= 76.67 - 13.35 - 60.67 \\
&= 2.65.
\end{aligned}
$$

The table of variance is best set up so that the distinction between the within-subjects and the between-subjects sources of variance is highlighted. Earlier we saw that between-subjects sources of variance are those associated with individual differences between subjects. The within-subjects sources of variance are those associated with differences in individual subjects' scores from condition to condition. In Table 18.2 we distinguish sharply between sources of variance that are due to within- and between-subject variation. Sharp distinctions like these are useful when there are several sources of variation due to between-subject sources and several due to within-subject sources. The distinctions simplify our bookkeeping and, as we shall see, help us decide on the appropriate error terms for tests of significance.

TABLE 18.2
Summary ANOVA of results in Table 18.1

Source	SS	df	MS	F	η	p
Between subjects[a]	13.35	3	4.45			
Within subjects[b]						
Sessions	60.67	2	30.33	68.93	.98	7.3^{-5}
Sessions × Subjects	2.65	6	0.44[c]			

[a] This term, the subjects effect, would not normally be tested for significance (as discussed in the following pages).

[b] Note that when we referred to *within* sources of variance in earlier chapters, we were referring to variation that was within *conditions* but *between* subjects.

[c] Error term for sessions effect is the mean square for Sessions × Subjects.

FIXED AND RANDOM EFFECTS

Another distinction that will help us choose the appropriate error terms is that between fixed and random factors. **Fixed factors** are variables for which we have selected specific levels not randomly but because of our interest in those particular effects. As these levels have not been selected by random sampling, we are not entitled to view them as representative of any other levels of the variable in question (i.e., we cannot generalize to other levels of the fixed factor). Most factors involving experimental manipulations—or such organismic variables as gender, race, and social class, and such repeated-measures factors as time, sessions, subtests, and so on—are usually viewed as fixed factors.

Random factors are those for which we view the levels of the variables as having been randomly sampled from a larger population or a theoretical pool of such levels. The most common random factor in behavioral and social research is sampling units, especially of persons or other organisms. In Table 18.2, if we regard the between-subjects variable as a random factor, we can test its statistical significance only very conservatively. If we regard it as a fixed factor (so that we restrict any inferences only to those four subjects), we can test the statistical significance of the subjects factor against the Sessions × Subjects interaction. However, that F test will be conservative if we also regard sessions as fixed effects. To clarify these issues, let us consider all combinations of fixed and random effects for between- and within-subject factors in the simplest factorial design, the two-way ANOVA.

Imagine we want to study four countries as our between-sampling-units factor. Suppose we are interested only in those four countries and do not choose to view them as a sample from a larger pool. In this case we define countries as a fixed factor. Alternatively, if we conceptualize the four countries as a sample from which we want to generalize to a larger pool, we instead define countries as a random factor. So far, all we have is a between-subjects factor, but now suppose we have a longitudinal design in which we have a summary score for each country for each of three decades. Those three scores constitute our repeated-measures (or within-sampling-units) factor. Had we chosen the scores specifically as critical

TABLE 18.3
Four combinations of fixed and random factors in two-way designs

		Within sampling units	
		Fixed	Random
Between sampling units	Fixed	Type A	Type B
	Random	Type C	Type D

decades of the century of interest, then we would regard the scores as fixed and the factor of decades as a fixed factor. Alternatively, we would define the scores as random if we regarded them as a sample of the pool of decades to which we want to generalize.

In our hypothetical two-way design, in which one factor is countries and the other is decades, we see that we can have four combinations of between- (e.g., countries) and within- (e.g., decades) sampling-units factors and fixed and random effects. The four combinations are shown in Table 18.3, and we turn next to the appropriate error terms required in each of the four combinations. The discussion that follows is intended to serve as a reference guide rather than as a detailed exposition of the underlying mathematical models that would be required for a theoretically based discussion (see, e.g., Green & Tukey, 1960; Snedecor & Cochran, 1989; Winer, 1971; Winer, Brown, & Michels, 1991).

ERROR TERMS IN THE FOUR BASIC COMBINATIONS

A general principle for determining the appropriate error term is that *the specific effect of interest (i.e., fixed or random) is properly tested by division of the mean square (MS) for that effect by the MS for a random source of variation.* The random source may be nested within the various levels of the factor of interest, or it may be crossed with the various levels of the factor of interest. Thus, the source of variance that would be a proper error term for "Factor A" might be the independent observations made under each level of that factor. Those nested observations always serve as the proper error term in the analyses of variance we discussed in earlier chapters. They remain the proper error terms for the between-subjects factors in analyses that include repeated-measures factors as well. When we want to test most repeated-measures factors, however, we typically use as our error term the interaction of a random factor (e.g., subjects nested within levels of a between-subjects factor) and the factor that we want to test. When there is no random factor available (either for nesting within or crossing with the factor that we want to test), there is no proper test of statistical significance available. Sometimes, however, a useful but conservative test *is* possible, as illustrated in three out of four of the following cases based on the four design combinations of Table 18.3.

Type A (Between Fixed, Within Fixed)

In the Type A case the interaction *MS* can be used as the error term for the *MS* between and the *MS* within subjects, although it is likely to lead to *F* values that are too conservative. Only if there is in *nature* a zero interaction will the *F* be accurate. The only way to test whether the interaction really is likely to be zero is to make multiple observations for each combination of the row and column effects. In our example of countries and decades, we might make those multiple observations by randomly sampling several years from each decade. This within-combination *MS*, computed as any other within-condition source of variance, is the appropriate error term for the between-conditions variable, the repeated-measures variable, and the interaction of these two variables. When the interaction *MS* is used as the error term for the row or column variable, an obtained large *F* can be trusted to be at least that large, but a small *F* may or may not reflect the absence of a row or column effect. The table of variance for the Type A situation is outlined in Table 18.4, where the symbols noted in that table (and in the following three tables) are defined as follows:

B = Between-subjects *MS*

W = Within-subjects *MS*

BW = Between $\times$ Within subjects interaction *MS*

O = Ordinary error (i.e., *MS* for replications within combinations of B $\times$ W)

Type B (Between Fixed, Within Random)

In this second case, Type B, as noted in Table 18.5, the interaction *MS* is the appropriate error term for the between-sampling-units effect. It is the appropriate error term for the within or repeated-measures effect only if the interaction effect is truly zero. The appropriate error term for the within-subjects effect (and for the interaction) is the variation of the multiple observations made for each combination of row and column.

TABLE 18.4
Illustration of Type A design (both factors fixed)

Source	Abbreviations	Error term, "proper"	Error term, "conservative"[a]
Between countries[b]	B	O	BW
Within countries			
Decades[c]	W	O	BW
Decades $\times$ Countries[d]	BW	O	
Years within decade $\times$ Country combinations[e]	O		

[a] Used when O is not available, as when only a single observation has been made for every B $\times$ W combination.
[b] Computed as is the row effect of any two-way factorial design.
[c] Computed as is the column effect of any two-way factorial design.
[d] Computed as is the interaction effect of any two-way factorial design.
[e] Computed as is the within-cell error of any two-way factorial design.

TABLE 18.5
Illustration of Type B design (between factor fixed, within factor random)

Source	Abbreviations	Error term, "proper"	Error term, "conservative"[a]
Between countries	B	BW[b]	
Within countries			
Decades	W	O	BW
Decades × Countries	BW	O	
Years within BW	O		

[a] Used when O is not available.

[b] Use of O as error term can lead to F values that are seriously inflated.

Type C (Between Random, Within Fixed)

In this third case, Type C, Table 18.6 notes that the interaction *MS* is the appropriate error term for the within-sampling-units effect. It is also the appropriate error term for the between-sampling-units effect only if the interaction effect is truly zero. The appropriate error term for the between-subjects effect (and for the interaction) is the variation of the multiple observations made for each combination of row and column.

Type D (Between Random, Within Random)

In this fourth case, Type D, Table 18.7 shows that the interaction *MS* is the appropriate error term for both the between- and within-subjects effects. The interaction effect can be tested against the variation of the multiple observations made for each combination of row and column (as noted in the table). More detailed information about the consequences for significance testing of various combinations of fixed and random factors can be found in Green and Tukey (1960), Snedecor and Cochran (1989), and Winer, Brown, and Michels (1991).

TABLE 18.6
Illustration of Type C design (between factor random, within factor fixed)

Source	Abbreviations	Error term, "proper"	Error term, "conservative"[a]
Between countries	B	O	BW
Within countries			
Decades	W	BW[b]	
Decades × Countries	BW	O	
Years within BW	O		

[a] Used when O is not available.

[b] Use of O as error term can lead to F values that are seriously inflated.

TABLE 18.7
Illustration of Type D design (both factors random)

Source	Abbreviations	Error term, "proper"	Error term, "conservative"[a]
Between countries	B	BW[b]	
Within countries			
Decades	W	BW[b]	
Decades × Countries	BW	O	
Years within BW	O		

[a] Not applicable to this design.

[b] Use of O as error term can lead to F values that are seriously inflated.

LATIN SQUARES AND COUNTERBALANCING

In the example we gave of four subjects, each measured three times (in Table 18.1), there is no alternative to administering the three sessions of testing in the sequence 1, 2, 3, because we want to find out how performance changes over time. We have suggested the term **intrinsically repeated measures** to describe situations like these, in which we *must* measure or observe the subjects more than once to address the question of interest (Rosenthal, Rosnow, & Rubin, 2000). We turn now to another common use of repeated measures in which, in principle, repeated measures are *not required,* but efficiency, precision, and statistical power may be increased if several treatments are administered to each of the subjects or other sampling units. We have used the term **nonintrinsically repeated measures** to describe such a situation, and we discuss intrinsically and nonintrinsically repeated measures in considerable detail in our book on contrasts and effect size indices (Rosenthal et al., 2000). As an illustration of nonintrinsically repeated measures, suppose we want to compare three medications in treating a rare disorder, but we have only three patients with that rare disorder. Indeed, we have so few eligible patients that we can randomly assign only a single patient to each medication. We cannot learn much from that approach, as we will never know whether any differences in treatment outcome were due to differences in the three medications or to ordinary individual differences among the patients.

As an alternative, though, we can administer all three treatments to all three patients. The basic design is shown in Part A of Table 18.8, which shows that we have decided to administer all three drugs (A, B, and C) to each of our three patients. Each patient will receive the three drugs in the same sequence: A, then B, then C (or ABC). The problem in using this design, however, is that we entangle, or confound, two different variables: the drug variable (A vs. B vs. C) and the order of administration of the drugs (first drug vs. second drug vs. third drug). Suppose we hypothesized that Drug A would be most beneficial, and in our study we find that Drug A is best. It would not be appropriate to conclude that Drug A truly is better than Drugs B and C, because a plausible rival hypothesis is that the first-administered drug is best. To avoid this type of confounding, we instead use a technique called *counterbalancing*

TABLE 18.8
Repeated-measures design with and without confounding

A. Confounding of drug variable and order of administration

Subjects	Drug A	Drug B	Drug C
Subject 1			
Subject 2			
Subject 3			

B. Latin-square with counterbalancing to prevent confounding

	Order of administration		
Sequence	1	2	3
Sequence 1 (ABC)	A	B	C
Sequence 2 (BCA)	B	C	A
Sequence 3 (CAB)	C	A	B

(first mentioned in chapter 7) as shown in Part B of Table 18.8, in which the sequence of administration of the treatments is balanced (or varied systematically) so that, on the average, there is no longer a relationship between, or confounding of, the variables that would have been entangled in our first proposed design.

Counterbalancing is essential whenever we want to study matters of organization and sequencing in the presentation of repeated stimuli. As another illustration, a classic question often investigated by social psychologists concerns when it may be advantageous to present a message before the opposition has a chance to reach the same audience, and when it is better to present the message afterward, in order to have the last word (e.g., Hovland, Mandell, Campbell, Brock, Luchins, Cohen, McGuire, Janis, Feierabend, & Anderson, 1957). Researchers who study this question use the term *primacy* to describe cases where opinions or actions are influenced more by arguments presented first, and *recency* where they are influenced more by arguments presented last. To test for primacy and recency, researchers use a counterbalanced design. Half the subjects, at random, receive one message first, and the remaining subjects receive the other message first. Using this approach should prevent the problem of confounding primacy and recency effects with the particular effects of the competing messages themselves (e.g., Corrozi & Rosnow, 1968; Miller & Campbell, 1959; Rosnow, 1966, 1968).

In our earlier discussion of counterbalancing, we mentioned that one design with built-in counterbalancing is the *Latin square*. Table 7.2 illustrates such a design, in which the number of rows equals the number of columns. A Latin square requires a square array of letters (or numbers) in which each letter (or number) appears once and only once in each row and each column. Frequently the rows represent sequences of administration of treatments, the columns represent the order of administration of the treatments, and the letters represent individual treatments administered in specific orders as part of specific sequences, as illustrated in Part B of Table 18.8. In Sequence 1, treatments are administered in the sequence A, then B, then C. In Sequences 2 and 3, the treatments are administered in different sequences, BCA and CAB, respectively.

The requirement of a Latin square is satisfied as long as each row and each column contains each treatment condition once and only once. If sequences are found to differ, the difference must be due to the differences in the sequence of treatments, not to differences in the treatments administered, because all treatments are administered in each sequence. The difference also cannot be due to differences in order or position (i.e., first, second, third), as all sequences are composed of the same set of orders or positions. If orders differ, the variability must be due to differences in the order, not to differences in the treatments administered, as all treatments are administered in each order. Difference also cannot be due to differences in the sequence (e.g., ABC, BCA, CAB), because all orders comprise equal parts of each sequence. If treatments (e.g., A vs. B vs. C) are found to be different, those differences must be due to differences in treatment not to differences in sequence, because all sequences contain all treatments. Difference also cannot be due to differences in order, because all treatments occur equally often in each order. It is in these senses, then, that the systematic counterbalancing in Latin squares prevents confounding.

ANALYSIS OF LATIN SQUARES

In a Latin square design the sequence effect tells us how the sequences differ, and the order effect tells us how orders differ. Neither of these effects is usually the reason for the research, however. Usually, what we want to know is how the treatments differ. But where is the treatment in a Latin square? Table 18.9 shows (in Part A) the smallest possible Latin square, a 2 × 2 design. In this smallest possible Latin square, it turns out that the treatment effect is identical to (or an "alias" of) the Sequence × Order interaction. In this design the interaction compares the diagonal comprising the A treatment (the upper-left and lower-right cells) with the diagonal comprising the B treatment (the lower-left and upper-right cells); this interaction is equivalent to the test of the treatment effect. The sources of variance are shown in Part B of Table 18.9, where we also see that there are no degrees of

TABLE 18.9
Smallest possible Latin square

A. The 2 × 2 Latin square			B. Sources of variance for 2 × 2 Latin square	
	Order		Source	df
Sequence	1	2	Sequences	1
Sequence 1 (AB)	A	B	Orders	1
Sequence 2 (BA)	B	A	Treatments (Sequences × Orders)	1

freedom (df) available for error terms for the three sources of variance shown. Very conservative F tests can be computed, however, if the mean of the MS values of the remaining two is used as the error term for each effect.

As the size of the Latin square increases, the df available for a suitable error term increase, and F tests become less conservative. The Sequences $\times$ Order interaction continues to provide the treatment effect, but the remainder of that interaction not associated with the treatment effect becomes the error term for all other effects. Though larger Latin squares yield more accurate F values (i.e., in the sense of fewer Type II errors), it remains a characteristic of Latin squares that, on the average, F values will be too small. The reason is that the denominator of those F tests is always some type of effect (i.e., row, column, or interaction) that could be nonzero. When nonzero effects are used as denominators of F tests, the resulting F values are too small. When the effects are zero, the F tests tend to be more accurate and less conservative. Some larger Latin square designs with their sources of variance and associated df are shown in Table 18.10.

In general, if the Latin square has a sequences, a orders, and a treatments, then the df for each source of variance are as shown in Table 18.11. With a sequences, orders, and treatments, and with M_S, M_O, M_T, and $\overline{M}$ denoting the means of sequences, orders, treatments, and the grand mean, respectively, we obtain the total sum of squares by using Equation 18.1:

$$\text{Total } SS = \Sigma(X - \overline{M})^2.$$

We obtain the other needed sums of squares as follows:

$$\text{Sequences } SS = \Sigma[a(M_s - \overline{M})^2] \tag{18.2}$$

$$\text{Orders } SS = \Sigma[a(M_o - \overline{M})^2] \tag{18.3}$$

$$\text{Sequences} \times \text{Orders } SS = \text{Total } SS - \text{Sequences } SS - \text{Orders } SS \tag{18.4}$$

$$\text{Treatment } SS = \Sigma[a(M_T - \overline{M})^2] \tag{18.5}$$

$$\text{Residual } SS = \text{Sequences} \times \text{Orders } SS - \text{Treatment } SS. \tag{18.6}$$

For example, assume that four patients were administered four treatments in counterbalanced order with the results shown in Part A of Table 18.12. Note that the sequences are completely confounded with the patients (i.e., we could label the sequences as subjects if we preferred). Substituting in the first four equations above, we find

$$
\begin{aligned}
\text{Total } SS ={}& (4 - 6)^2 + (3 - 6)^2 + (8 - 6)^2 + (5 - 6)^2 \\
&+ (0 - 6)^2 + (6 - 6)^2 + (7 - 6)^2 + (7 - 6)^2 \\
&+ (2 - 6)^2 + (2 - 6)^2 + (10 - 6)^2 + (10 - 6)^2 \\
&+ (6 - 6)^2 + (5 - 6)^2 + (7 - 6)^2 + (14 - 6)^2 \\
={}& 186
\end{aligned}
$$

$$
\begin{aligned}
\text{Sequences } SS ={}& 4(5 - 6)^2 + 4(5 - 6)^2 + 4(6 - 6)^2 + 4(8 - 6)^2 \\
={}& 24
\end{aligned}
$$

$$
\begin{aligned}
\text{Orders } SS ={}& 4(3 - 6)^2 + 4(4 - 6)^2 + 4(8 - 6)^2 + 4(9 - 6)^2 \\
={}& 104
\end{aligned}
$$

$$
\begin{aligned}
\text{Sequences} \times \text{Orders } SS ={}& 186 - 24 - 104 \\
={}& 58.
\end{aligned}
$$

TABLE 18.10
Three Latin squares and their sources of variance

3 × 3 Latin square

	Order				Source	df
	1	2	3		Sequences	2
Sequence 1	A	B	C		Orders	2
Sequence 2	B	C	A		(Sequences × Orders)	(4)
Sequence 3	C	A	B		Treatments	2
					Residual sequences × Orders	2

4 × 4 Latin square

	Order					Source	df
	1	2	3	4		Sequences	3
Sequence 1	A	B	C	D		Orders	3
Sequence 2	B	C	D	A		(Sequences × Orders)	(9)
Sequence 3	C	D	A	B		Treatments	3
Sequence 4	D	A	B	C		Residual sequences × Orders	6

5 × 5 Latin square

	Order						Source	df
	1	2	3	4	5		Sequences	4
Sequence 1	A	B	C	D	E		Orders	4
Sequence 2	B	C	D	E	A		(Sequences × Orders)	(16)
Sequence 3	C	D	E	A	B		Treatments	4
Sequence 4	D	E	A	B	C		Residual sequences × Orders	12
Sequence 5	E	A	B	C	D			

Note: In any of these Latin squares we can also think of the sequences effect as part of the Treatment × Order interaction, and we can think of the orders effect as part of the Treatment × Sequences interaction. These are only conceptual alternatives and do not yield different statistical results.

TABLE 18.11
Sources of variance in Latin squares

Source	df
Sequences	$a-1$
Orders	$a-1$
[Sequences × Orders]	$[(a-1)^2]$
Treatments	$a-1$
Residual sequences × Orders	$(a-1)(a-2)$

To compute the Treatment *SS* using Equation 18.5, we have to collect the scores associated with each of the four treatments (A, B, C, D). As we are doing the calculations by hand, in order to minimize clerical errors we can rearrange the display of the data from the Sequence × Order combination in Part A of Table 18.12 to the Sequence × Treatment combination in Part B. Then,

$$\text{Treatment } SS = 4(6.5 - 6)^2 + 4(5.0 - 6)^2 + 4(7.5 - 6)^2 + 4(5.0 - 6)^2$$
$$= 18.$$

Finally, using Equation 18.6, we find

$$\text{Residual } SS = 58 - 18 = 40.$$

The summary ANOVA appears in Part C of Table 18.12.

TABLE 18.12
Computation of ANOVA for 4 × 4 Latin square

A. Basic data for effects of four treatments

	Order				
	1	**2**	**3**	**4**	**Mean**
Sequence 1 (ABCD)	4	3	8	5	5
Sequence 2 (BCDA)	0	6	7	7	5
Sequence 3 (CDAB)	2	2	10	10	6
Sequence 4 (DABC)	6	5	7	14	8
Mean	3	4	8	9	6

B. Rearrangement of basic data of Part A

	Treatments				
	A	**B**	**C**	**D**	**Mean**
Sequence 1	4	3	8	5	5
Sequence 2	7	0	6	7	5
Sequence 3	10	10	2	2	6
Sequence 4	5	7	14	6	8
Mean	6.5	5.0	7.5	5.0	6

C. Summary ANOVA

Source	*SS*	*df*	*MS*	*F*	η	*p*
Sequences	24	3	8.00	1.20	.61	.39
Orders	104	3	34.67	5.20	.85	.042
(Sequences × Orders)	(58)	(9)				
Treatments	18	3	6.00	0.90	.56	.49
Residual sequences × Orders	40	6	6.67			

SOME LATIN SQUARES MAY BE BETTER THAN OTHERS

When Latin square designs are used, it is recommended that, given a particular square from 3 × 3 to 12 × 12, the rows, columns, and treatments all be randomized to prevent bias in the selection of some specific square (Cochran & G. M. Cox, 1957, p. 121; D. R. Cox, 1958, p. 207). However, even when using randomization, we may want to exclude certain squares. For example, in the 4 × 4 square in Part A of Table 18.13, we see that Treatment A always occurs just before or just after C, and B always occurs just before or just after D. Our concern is that data obtained for the four treatments may be affected by the consistent adjacency of these pairs of treatments. The only way we can be sure that the adjacencies will not be troublesome is to compare the treatment effects obtained from that particular square with the treatment effects obtained from another square without such consistent adjacencies.

Another 4 × 4 arrangement that we may not want to use is shown in Part B of Table 18.13. The problem in this case is that any treatment not the first in its sequence always follows the same treatment. That is, Treatment B follows only Treatment A (three times), Treatment C follows only Treatment B (three times), D follows only C (three times), and A follows only D (three times). We are concerned that results of the analysis of treatment effects for this 4 × 4 Latin square may therefore be partially confounded with the immediately preceding treatment. That is, any differences (or lack of differences) that we observe may not occur with different immediately preceding

TABLE 18.13
Illustrative 4 × 4 Latin squares

A. Design with consistent adjacencies

A	C	D	B
B	D	C	A
C	A	B	D
D	B	A	C

B. Problematic modification

A	B	C	D
B	C	D	A
C	D	A	B
D	A	B	C

C. Improved modification

A	B	C	D
B	D	A	C
C	A	D	B
D	C	B	A

TABLE 18.14
Improved 5 × 5 Latin square

A	B	C	D	E
B	D	A	E	C
C	E	B	A	D
D	C	E	B	A
E	A	D	C	B

treatments. An arrangement that does not present the possible problems of the two squares in Parts A and B is shown in Part C of Table 18.13.

We leave it as an exercise for the reader to reexamine the 5 × 5 Latin square of Table 18.10 and to check for any possible problem in the particular sequences. Table 18.14 shows an improved 5 × 5 Latin square that seems to us less problematic than the typical arrangement of Table 18.10. However, whenever selecting a particular Latin square arrangement because it seems less problematic than perhaps some other arrangement might be, it is always advisable to randomly assign sampling units (subjects, organizations, teams, etc.) to the sequences. In addition, each particular treatment needs to be assigned to its letter at random. Because it is often difficult to decide whether, in a given study, a specific Latin square arrangement may be problematic, we prefer to use more sequences than would fit neatly into a single Latin square, or perhaps to use some other counterbalancing design, as we describe next.

OTHER COUNTERBALANCING DESIGNS

Latin squares are used when the number of subjects or other sampling units equals the number of treatments we wish to administer to each subject. But suppose that we have more sampling units than we have treatments. What is to be done? Two general strategies that are quite useful are *rectangular arrays* and *multiple squares.*

Rectangular Arrays

If we have three treatments to administer to six subjects, we can randomly assign half the subjects to each of two squares of size 3 × 3 and treat each square as a different experiment or as a replication of the same experiment. Alternatively, we can assign each of the six subjects to a unique sequence of the three treatments. Because the number of unique sequences of treatments is $t!$ (i.e., t-factorial, where t is the number of treatments), and in this case $t! = 3! = (3)(2)(1) = 6$, we have just the right number of subjects for this study. If we have four treatments to administer to each subject and we want each subject to have a unique sequence, we need $4! = (4)(3)(2)(1) = 24$ subjects, and so on. Such arrangements may be described as $t \times t!$ **designs,** and their statistical analysis is analogous to that of the Latin square. Examples of two such designs are given in Tables 18.15 and 18.16. For the $t \times t!$ design in Table 18.15, $t = 3$, whereas $t = 4$ in Table 18.16. When $t = 2$, we have the familiar 2 × 2 Latin square once again.

TABLE 18.15
Example of $t \times t!$ design with $t = 3$

	Order				Source	df
	1	**2**	**3**		Sequences	5
Sequence 1	A	B	C		Orders	2
Sequence 2	A	C	B		(Sequences × Orders)	(10)
Sequence 3	B	A	C		Treatments	2
Sequence 4	B	C	A		Residual sequences × Orders	8
Sequence 5	C	A	B			
Sequence 6	C	B	A			

TABLE 18.16
Example of $t \times t!$ design with $t = 4$

	Order					Source	df
	1	**2**	**3**	**4**		Sequences	23
Sequence 1	A	B	C	D		Orders	3
Sequence 2	A	B	D	C		(Sequences × Orders)	(69)
Sequence 3	A	C	B	D		Treatments	3
Sequence 4	A	C	D	B		Residual sequences × Orders	66
Sequence 5	A	D	B	C			
Sequence 6	A	D	C	B			
Sequence 7	B	A	C	D			
Sequence 8	B	A	D	C			
Sequence 9	B	C	A	D			
Sequence 10	B	C	D	A			
Sequence 11	B	D	A	C			
Sequence 12	B	D	C	A			
Sequence 13	C	A	B	D			
Sequence 14	C	A	D	B			
Sequence 15	C	B	A	D			
Sequence 16	C	B	D	A			
Sequence 17	C	D	A	B			
Sequence 18	C	D	B	A			
Sequence 19	D	A	B	C			
Sequence 20	D	A	C	B			
Sequence 21	D	B	A	C			
Sequence 22	D	B	C	A			
Sequence 23	D	C	A	B			
Sequence 24	D	C	B	A			

If we have fewer sampling units available than the $t!$ required by our $t \times t!$ design, we can instead form a series of Latin squares. An alternative is to sample randomly from the $t!$ sequences, though with the constraint that each treatment must occur in each order as nearly equally often as possible. This constraint tends to maximize the degree of counterbalancing that *is* possible even though complete counterbalancing may *not* be possible. If we have more sampling units available than the $t!$ required by a $t \times t!$ design, two useful general arrangements are *subjects-within-sequences* and *multiple rectangular arrays*.

Subjects-Within-Sequences Designs

If we have $2 \times t!$ subjects available, we can randomly assign half the subjects to each of two rectangular arrays of size $t \times t!$ We then treat each array as a different experiment or as a replication of the same experiment. The same type of procedure can be used for any multiple of $t!$ subjects. Alternatively, we can assign several subjects at random to each of the $t!$ sequences in a way that will keep the number of subjects per sequence as nearly equal as possible. For example, what if we have 18 subjects available for a study of three treatments? The six possible sequences of three treatments ($3! = 6$) are as displayed in Table 18.15, and we assign three subjects at random to each of those six sequences. In this design, subjects are *not* confounded with sequences as they are in Latin squares or rectangular arrays lacking replications for each sequence. Instead, subjects are *nested* within sequences so that differences between sequences can be tested. The sources of variance for this example are shown in Table 18.17.

This design and analysis have a number of noteworthy features. First, there is more than a single error term in the design. In the preceding chapters on analysis of

TABLE 18.17
Sources of variance for subjects-within-sequences example

Source	df	Comments
Between subjects	(17)	
Sequences	5	Tested against subjects
Subjects within sequences	12	
Within subjects	$(36)^a$	
Orders	2	Tested against Orders $\times$ Subjects
Orders $\times$ Sequences[b]	10	Usually not tested
Treatments	2	Tested against Orders $\times$ Subjects
Residual orders $\times$ Sequences	8	Tested against Orders $\times$ Subjects
Orders $\times$ Subjects within sequences	24	

[a] Computed as (N of subjects) $\times$ (df for levels of repeated measures). In this study there are $N = 18$ subjects and three levels of the repeated-measures factor ($df = 3 - 1 = 2$), so there are $N \times df$ (levels) $= 18 \times 2 = 36$ df for within subjects. Put another way, the df for within subjects is 1 less than the number of observations per subject, multiplied by the number of subjects.

[b] This term is subdivided into the two listed below it, that is, "Treatments" and "Residual orders $\times$ Sequences."

variance, there was always only a single error term, and it was always associated with the individual differences among subjects (or other sampling units) collected from within each of the conditions of the study. In the present case there is also such an error term (subjects within sequences), and it is used to test whether the sequences of the study differ from one another. We want to note especially that this error term is within *conditions* but *between* subjects. The other error term in this design is the Orders × Subjects within-sequences interaction. This error term is used to test all the within-subjects sources of variation, and it is itself a *within-subjects* source of variation. It is typical for error terms used to test within-subjects sources of variation that they are formed by a crossing of the repeated-measures factors by the random factor of sampling units, usually either subjects or subjects-within-conditions. Another feature of this design (which happens to be common to both Latin square and rectangular repeated-measures designs) is that in order to test for treatments, we must reach into the Order × Sequence interaction and extract the variation of the treatment means around the grand mean. That procedure represents only a minor complication in the analysis, however.

The analysis is simply an extension of the computational procedures we have described so far in this chapter. Although we assume that the analysis will be done by computer, we can best explain it by starting with a 3 × 18 display consisting of 3 levels of order and 18 levels of subjects. The between-subjects *SS* is broken down into a sequences *SS* and a subjects-within-sequences *SS*. The latter can be obtained as the difference between the between-subjects *SS* and the sequences *SS*. The order *SS* is found in the usual manner, and the Order × Subjects interaction is broken down into an Order × Sequences *SS* and an Order × Subjects-within-sequences *SS*. The latter can be obtained as the difference between the Order × Subjects *SS* and the Order × Sequences *SS*.

THREE OR MORE FACTORS

Up to this point in our discussion of repeated-measures ANOVA, we have examined two-factor designs consisting of a between-subjects factor and a within-subjects (or repeated-measures) factor. But repeated-measures designs may, of course, be more complex in having two or more between-subjects factors, two or more within-subjects factors, or both.

Two or More Between-Subjects Factors

Increasing the number of between-subjects factors does not increase the complexity of the design as much as increasing the number of within-subjects factors. Suppose we want to analyze the scores of women and men at three age levels, and to administer to each subject four subtests of a personality inventory. Our design might appear as in Part A of Table 18.18. If we assume two subjects for each of the 3 × 2 = 6 between-subjects conditions, then the sources of variance and *df* are as shown in Part B.

The computation of the *SS* involves nothing new. It is easiest to think of this design as a 12-subject × 4-measurements array. Were we to calculate the overall ANOVA by hand, we would begin by computing all the between-subjects *SS*, starting with the total between-subjects *SS*. We then compute the age *SS*, the sex *SS*, and

TABLE 18.18
Design comprising two between factors and one within factor

A. The 3 × 2 × 4 design

Between factors		Repeated measures			
		Subtests			
Age	Sex	1	2	3	4
12	Female				
	Male				
14	Female				
	Male				
16	Female				
	Male				

B. Sources of variance and *df*

Source	df	
Between subjects	(11)	
Age	2	
Sex	1	
Age × Sex	2	
Subjects (within conditions)	6	
Within subjects	(36)[a]	
Subtests	3	
Subtests × Age	6	⎫
Subtests × Sex	3	Subtests × Between subjects
Subtests × Age × Sex	6	
Subtests × Subjects (within conditions)	18	⎭

[a] Computed as (*N* of subjects) × (*df* for levels of repeated measures). In this study there are *N* = 12 subjects and four levels of the repeated-measures factor (*df* = 4 − 1 = 3), so there are *N* × *df* (levels) = 12 × 3 = 36 *df* for within subjects.

the Age × Sex *SS* and subtract these three *SS* from the total between-subjects *SS*. That would give us the subjects-within-conditions *SS*. As designs become more complicated, being able to compute the *df* for each source of variance becomes increasingly useful as a check on whether we have omitted any sources of variance. For example, because there are 12 subjects in this design, we know there are 12 − 1 = 11 *df* available between subjects. We also know the *df* for age (3 − 1 = 2), sex (2 − 1 = 1), Age × Sex [(3 − 1 = 2) × (2 − 1 = 1) = 2], and subjects-within conditions [(2 − 1) × 6 = 6]. These four sources of variance are a decomposition of the total between-subjects source of variance; notice that the sum of their *df* equals the *df* for the total between-subjects variance.

The within-subjects sources of variation are made up of the main effect of subtests ($df = 3$) and the Subtests $\times$ Between-subjects interaction ($df = 3 \times 11 = 33$). The latter interaction is further decomposed into a series of interactions: Subtests $\times$ Age; Subtests $\times$ Sex; Subtests $\times$ Age $\times$ Sex; and Subtests $\times$ Subjects (within conditions). The df of these four interactions adds up ($6 + 3 + 6 + 18$) to 33, which is the total df for the Subtests $\times$ Between-subjects interaction.

Illustration of Computations

To show the calculations, we use the basic data given in Table 18.19 for a 2 (between) $\times$ 3 (between) $\times$ 4 (within) design. We begin by regarding the design as a simple 12-subject $\times$ 4-subtests array, for which we will first compute the row (subjects) and column (subtests) and the Row $\times$ Column interaction sums of squares as described at the beginning of this chapter. Thus, we find

$$\text{Total } SS = \sum(X - \overline{M})^2 = (2 - 5)^2 + (3 - 5)^2 + (7 - 5)^2$$
$$+ \cdots + (5 - 5)^2 + (7 - 5)^2 + (8 - 5)^2$$
$$= 340$$

TABLE 18.19
Results of a repeated-measures study with two between-subjects factors and one within-subjects factor

Age	Sex	Subject	1	2	3	4	Mean
12	Female	1	2	3	7	8	5.0
12	Female	2	1	2	3	6	3.0
12	Male	3	1	1	3	3	2.0
12	Male	4	1	2	1	4	2.0
14	Female	5	5	4	7	8	6.0
14	Female	6	4	5	8	7	6.0
14	Male	7	1	2	4	5	3.0
14	Male	8	1	4	6	9	5.0
16	Female	9	5	9	9	9	8.0
16	Female	10	6	5	8	9	7.0
16	Male	11	5	6	9	8	7.0
16	Male	12	4	5	7	8	6.0
	Mean		3.0	4.0	6.0	7.0	5.0

$$
\begin{aligned}
\text{Row (subject) } SS = \sum \left[c(M_r - \overline{M})^2 \right] &= 4(5.0 - 5)^2 + 4(3.0 - 5)^2 \\
&\quad + 4(2.0 - 5)^2 + \cdots + 4(7.0 - 5)^2 \\
&\quad + 4(7.0 - 5)^2 + 4(6.0 - 5)^2 \\
&= 184
\end{aligned}
$$

$$
\begin{aligned}
\text{Column (repeated measures) } SS = \sum \left[r(M_c - \overline{M})^2 \right] &= 12(3.0 - 5)^2 \\
&\quad + 12(4.0 - 5)^2 + 12(6.0 - 5)^2 \\
&\quad + 12(7.0 - 5)^2 \\
&= 120
\end{aligned}
$$

$$
\begin{aligned}
\text{Row} \times \text{Column (interaction) } SS &= \text{Total } SS - \text{Row } SS - \text{Column } SS \\
&= 340 - 184 - 120 \\
&= 36.
\end{aligned}
$$

Of the sums of squares computed above, we use only the column SS (or subtest SS) directly in our final table of variance. The remaining sums of squares above will be used in the computation of other sums of squares required for that final table.

Our next step is to decompose the row (or subjects) SS into its components of subject-age SS, subject-sex SS, Subject-age $\times$ Sex SS, and subjects-within conditions SS. We achieve this decomposition using the following formulas, beginning with the sum of squares for subject age:

$$
\text{Subject-age } SS = \sum \left[nst(M_A - \overline{M})^2 \right], \tag{18.7}
$$

where n is the number of subjects in each of the conditions formed by the crossing of the two between-subjects factors (or the harmonic mean of the numbers of subjects in each of those conditions when the ns are not equal), s is the number of levels of the sex factor, t is the number of levels of the subtests (column) factor, M_A is the mean of all conditions of a given age, and $\overline{M}$ is the grand mean (i.e., the mean of all condition means). We do the computations as follows:

$$
\text{Subject-sex } SS = \sum \left[nat(M_S - \overline{M})^2 \right], \tag{18.8}
$$

where a is the number of levels of the age factor; n, t, and $\overline{M}$ are as above; and M_S is the mean of all conditions of a given sex. Next,

$$
\text{Subject-age} \times \text{Sex } SS = \sum \left[nt(M_{AS} - \overline{M})^2 \right] \\
- \text{Subject-age } SS - \text{Subject-sex } SS, \tag{18.9}
$$

where M_{AS} is the mean of all observations contributing to each of the combinations of the two between-subjects factors, and n, t, and $\overline{M}$ are as above. And finally,

$$
\begin{aligned}
\text{Subjects-within-conditions } SS = \text{Row (subjects) } SS \\
- \text{Subject-age } SS - \text{Subject-sex } SS \\
- \text{Subject-age} \times \text{Sex } SS, \tag{18.10}
\end{aligned}
$$

where the row (subjects) SS was computed from our initial 12-subjects $\times$ 4-subtests array in Table 18.19.

Our arithmetic is simplified if we construct the table of means formed by the crossing of the two between-subjects factors of Table 18.19, as shown in Part A of Table 18.20. Using Equations 18.7–18.10, we find

$$\text{Subject-age } SS = [2 \times 2 \times 4(3.0 - 5)^2] + [2 \times 2 \times 4(5.0 - 5)^2]$$
$$+ [2 \times 2 \times 4(7.0 - 5)^2]$$
$$= 128$$

$$\text{Subject-sex } SS = [2 \times 3 \times 4(5.83 - 5)^2]$$
$$+ [2 \times 3 \times 4(4.17 - 5)^2]$$
$$= 33$$

$$\text{Subject-age} \times \text{Sex } SS = [2 \times 4(4.0 - 5)^2] + [2 \times 4(2.0 - 5)^2]$$
$$+ [2 \times 4(6.0 - 5)^2] + [2 \times 4(4.0 - 5)^2]$$
$$+ [2 \times 4(7.5 - 5)^2] + [2 \times 4(6.5 - 5)^2]$$
$$- \text{Age } SS - \text{Sex } SS$$
$$= 164 - 128 - 33$$
$$= 3$$

$$\text{Subjects-within-conditions } SS = 184 - 128 - 33 - 3$$
$$= 20.$$

Now that we have computed all the needed between-subjects sources of variance, we turn to the within-subjects sources of variance that are made up of the main effect of subtests (the already computed column effect) and the crossing of that main effect with Age, Sex, Age × Sex, and Subjects (within conditions) to form four interactions The various interaction sums of squares are computed as follows:

$$\text{Subtests} \times \text{Age } SS = \sum \left[ns(M_{TA} - \overline{M})^2 \right] - \text{Subtests } SS - \text{Age } SS, \quad (18.11)$$

where M_{TA} is the mean of all observations contributing to each combination of subtest (T) and age (A), and all other terms are as above.

$$\text{Subtests} \times \text{Sex } SS = \sum \left[na(M_{TS} - \overline{M})^2 \right] - \text{Subtests } SS - \text{Sex } SS, \quad (18.12)$$

where M_{TS} is the mean of all observations contributing to each combination of subtest and sex, and all other terms are as above.

$$\text{Subtests} \times \text{Age} \times \text{Sex } SS = \sum \left[n(M_{TAS} - \overline{M})^2 \right]$$
$$- \text{Subtests } SS$$
$$- \text{Age } SS$$
$$- \text{Sex } SS$$
$$- \text{Subtests} \times \text{Age } SS$$
$$- \text{Subtests} \times \text{Sex } SS$$
$$- \text{Age} \times \text{Sex } SS, \quad (18.13)$$

TABLE 18.20

Subtables of means for combinations of results in Table 18.19

A. Age × Sex of subject

	Sex of subject		
Age	Female	Male	Mean
12	$4.0^{\underline{8}}$	$2.0^{\underline{8}}$	$3.0^{\underline{16}}$
14	$6.0^{\underline{8}}$	$4.0^{\underline{8}}$	$5.0^{\underline{16}}$
16	$7.5^{\underline{8}}$	$6.5^{\underline{8}}$	$7.0^{\underline{16}}$
Mean	$5.83^{\underline{24}}$	$4.17^{\underline{24}}$	$5.0^{\underline{48}}$

B. Subtests × Age

	Subtests				
Age	1	2	3	4	Mean
12	$1.25^{\underline{4}}$	2.00	3.50	5.25	$3.00^{\underline{16}}$
14	2.75	3.75	6.25	7.25	5.00
16	5.00	6.25	8.25	8.50	7.00
Mean	$3.00^{\underline{12}}$	4.00	6.00	7.00	$5.00^{\underline{48}}$

C. Subtests × Sex

	Subtests				
Sex	1	2	3	4	Mean
Female	$3.83^{\underline{6}}$	4.67	7.00	7.83	$5.83^{\underline{24}}$
Male	2.17	3.33	5.00	6.17	4.17
Mean	$3.00^{\underline{12}}$	4.00	6.00	7.00	$5.00^{\underline{48}}$

D. Subtests × Sex × Age

		Subtests				
Age	Sex	1	2	3	4	Mean
12	Female	$1.5^{\underline{2}}$	2.5	5.0	7.0	$4.0^{\underline{8}}$
12	Male	1.0	1.5	2.0	3.5	2.0
14	Female	4.5	4.5	7.5	7.5	6.0
14	Male	1.0	3.0	5.0	7.0	4.0
16	Female	5.5	7.0	8.5	9.0	7.5
16	Male	4.5	5.5	8.0	8.0	6.5
Mean		$3.0^{\underline{12}}$	4.0	6.0	7.0	$5.0^{\underline{48}}$

Note: Numbers shown within the └ symbol indicate the number of observations on which each type of mean is based.

where M_{TAS} is the mean of all observations contributing to each combination of subtest, age, and sex, and all other terms are as above.

$$
\begin{aligned}
\text{Subtests} \times \text{Subjects-within-conditions } SS = \text{Row} \times \text{Column interaction } SS \\
- \text{Subtests} \times \text{Age } SS \\
- \text{Subtests} \times \text{Sex } SS \\
- \text{Subtests} \times \text{Age} \times \text{Sex } SS, \qquad (18.14)
\end{aligned}
$$

where the Row $\times$ Column interaction SS was computed earlier from our initial 12-subjects $\times$ 4-subtests array in Table 18.19. Again, our arithmetic will be simplified if, for each of the next three interactions to be computed, we construct the appropriate subtables of means. From the results in Part B of Table 18.20, we compute

$$
\begin{aligned}
\text{Subtest} \times \text{Age } SS &= [2 \times 2(1.25 - 5)^2] + [2 \times 2(2.00 - 5)^2] \\
&+ [2 \times 2(3.50 - 5)^2] + \cdots + [2 \times 2(6.25 - 5)^2] \\
&+ [2 \times 2(8.25 - 5)^2] + [2 \times 2(8.50 - 5)^2] \\
&- \text{Subtests } SS - \text{Age } SS = 252 - 120 - 128 \\
&= 4.
\end{aligned}
$$

From the results in Part C of Table 18.20, we compute

$$
\begin{aligned}
\text{Subtests} \times \text{Sex } SS &= [2 \times 3(3.83 - 5)^2] + [2 \times 3(4.67 - 5)^2] + \cdots \\
&+ [2 \times 3(5.00 - 5)^2] + [2 \times 3(6.17 - 5)^2] \\
&- \text{Subtests } SS - \text{Sex } SS = 154 - 120 - 33 \\
&= 1.
\end{aligned}
$$

From the results in Part D of Table 18.20, we compute

$$
\begin{aligned}
\text{Subtests} \times \text{Age} \times \text{Sex } SS &= 2(1.5 - 5)^2 + 2(2.5 - 5)^2 + \cdots \\
&+ 2(8.0 - 5)^2 + 2(8.0 - 5)^2 - \text{Subtests } SS \\
&- \text{Age } SS - \text{Sex } SS - \text{Subtests} \times \text{Age } SS \\
&- \text{Subtests} \times \text{Sex } SS - \text{Age} \times \text{Sex } SS \\
&= 300 - 120 - 128 - 33 - 4 - 1 - 3 \\
&= 11
\end{aligned}
$$

$$
\begin{aligned}
\text{Subtests} \times \text{Subjects-within-conditions } SS &= 36 - 4 - 1 - 11 \\
&= 20.
\end{aligned}
$$

We have now computed all the ingredients required to complete our table of variance, as shown in Table 18.21. The analysis of variance of these data shows that all three main effects were statistically significant. Although none of the interactions were significant, we note that the etas were quite substantial for several of those interactions, suggesting that replications with larger sample sizes might well reach statistical significance. The example that we have been following used an equal number of subjects ($n = 2$) within each combination of the between-subjects factor. Had the number of subjects not been equal within those conditions, we could still have used the same computational procedures with only one small modification. We would have replaced n, wherever it occurred, by n_h, the harmonic mean of the sample sizes (defined in Equation 14.6).

TABLE 18.21
Summary ANOVA for results in Table 18.19

Source	SS	df	MS	F	η^a	p
Between subjects	(184)	(11)				
Age	128	2	64.00	19.22	.93	.003
Sex	33	1	33.00	9.91	.79	.02
Age × Sex	3	2	1.50	0.45	.36	.66
Subjects (within conditions)	20	6	3.33			
Within Subjects	(156)	(36)				
Subtests	120	3	40.00	36.04	.93	.0001
Subtests × Age	4	6	.67	0.60	.41	.73
Subtests × Sex	1	3	.33	0.30	.22	.82
Subtests × Age × Sex	11	6	1.83	1.65	.60	.19
Subtests × Subjects (within conditions)	20	18	1.11			

$$^a\eta = \sqrt{\frac{F(df_{\text{numerator}})}{F(df_{\text{numerator}}) + (df_{\text{denominator}})}}$$

The four interactions involving subtests in Table 18.21 are formed by the crossing of the subtests factor with each of the between-subjects effects in turn. This procedure can be illustrated by the incorporation of an additional between-subjects factor into the present design, say, diagnosis. We assume that half the children in each of the six conditions are hyperactive and half are not, as shown in Part A of Table 18.22. The diagnosis factor is listed as hyperactive versus normal. Suppose we have five children in each of our 12 between-subjects conditions, in which case the new listing of sources of variance are as shown in Part B of Table 18.22. We again form all interactions involving the within-subjects factor (i.e., subtests in this case) by prefixing the within-subjects factor to each of the between-subjects factors in turn. Even with this four-factor design (three between and one within), the computations are not difficult to understand. Once again, it is easiest to conceptualize the design as a Subjects × Subtests array, with all between-subjects main effect and interaction sums of squares subtracted from the total between-subjects SS to yield the subjects-within-conditions SS.

No matter how many between-subjects sources of variance there are, all of them are tested against the MS for subjects within conditions. This assumes that all between-subjects sources of variance are seen as fixed effects, the most frequent situation (but shortly we discuss the situation in which these effects are not all regarded as fixed). It is essential to keep in mind, however, that the various between-subjects sources of variance have meaning only if the *sum* of the repeated-measures scores is meaningful. For example, if the four subtests of the personality inventory we have been using as our illustration are all scored so that a high number reflects "good adjustment" (or "poor adjustment"), the sum of those scores is meaningful,

TABLE 18.22

Illustrative design with three between factors and one within (repeated-measures) factor

A. Basic design

Between factors			Repeated measures			
				Subtests		
Age	Sex	Diagnosis	1	2	3	4
12	Female	Hyperactive				
		Normal				
	Male	Hyperactive				
		Normal				
14	Female	Hyperactive				
		Normal				
	Male	Hyperactive				
		Normal				
16	Female	Hyperactive				
		Normal				
	Male	Hyperactive				
		Normal				

B. Sources of variance

Source	df
Between subjects	(59)
Age	2
Sex	1
Diagnosis	1
Age × Sex	2
Age × Diagnosis	2
Sex × Diagnosis	1
Age × Sex × Diagnosis	2
Subjects (within conditions)	48
Within subjects	(180)[a]
Subtests	3
Subtests × Age	6
Subtests × Sex	3
Subtests × Diagnosis	3
Subtests × Age × Sex	6
Subtests × Age × Diagnosis	6
Subtests × Sex × Diagnosis	3
Subtests × Age × Sex × Diagnosis	6
Subtests × Subjects	144

[a] Computed as (N of subjects) × (df for levels of repeated measures). In this study there are $N = 60$ subjects and four levels of the repeated-measures factor ($df = 4 - 1 = 3$), so there are $N \times df$ (levels) = $60 \times 3 = 180$ df for within subjects.

and all the between-subjects effects are interpretable. However, if some of the subtests reflect good adjustment and some reflect poor adjustment, the sum (and the mean) of the four scores are meaningless, and all between-subjects effects are essentially meaningless. (In situations of this sort we can readily transform the one or two scores coded in the opposite direction so that their direction of scoring is consistent with that of the other scores.)

It should also be noted that when we have decided that the sum of the repeated-measures scores is meaningful, the components have not necessarily contributed equally to the sum. Those components that are more variable (in the sense of S^2) contribute more to the variation in the sum of the components. Thus, if the values of S^2 differ appreciably from each other, and if we want all components to contribute equally to the variation in the sum, we should first transform each component to its standard scores with mean $= 0$ and $\sigma^2 = 1$. But even if the between-subjects sources of variance are meaningless because the sum of the repeated measures is not a meaningful variable, it is still possible for the within-subjects sources of variance to be quite informative. The interactions of the within-subjects factor and the between-subjects factors indicate the extent to which the main effect of the repeated measure (i.e., the subtest in this example) is affected by the various between-subjects sources of variance.

Where there is only a single within-subjects factor, as in the present illustrations, there is only a single error term for all the within-subjects sources of variation, the Repeated-measures factor $\times$ Subjects-within-conditions interaction, or (in this example) the Subtests $\times$ Subjects-within-conditions interaction. However, as we add within-subjects factors, the number of error terms grows very quickly, so that every main effect within subjects has its own error term, as does every interaction between two or more within-subjects factors. These error terms are generally formed by the crossing of each source of variance by the subjects-within-conditions source of variance. Table 18.23 shows how quickly the number of error terms for the within-subjects sources of variance grows as the number of within-subjects factors grows. We see that for each additional within-subjects factor, the number of error terms more than doubles. We will illustrate only for three and for seven error terms.

TABLE 18.23
Number of within-subjects error terms required as a function of number of within-subjects factors

Number of factors	Number of error terms	Number of factors	Number of error terms
1	1	6	63
2	3	7	127
3	7	8	255
4	15	9	511
5	31	10	1023

TWO WITHIN-SUBJECTS FACTORS

Suppose our subjects are five female and five male teachers, each assigned a different set of four pupils to teach in a brief instructional situation. Of each of these 10 sets of four pupils, two are female and two are male. Furthermore, one female and one male pupil are designated (at random) to the particular teacher as showing special intellectual promise (high expectancy), but nothing is said of the remaining pupils (low expectancy). The main conditions of this design are displayed in Part A of Table 18.24.

Special note should be taken that the four *different* pupils can still be regarded as providing repeated measures. The reason is that we decided we would use teachers as our sampling units (a random factor) and each pupil's score is viewed as a repeated measurement of the teacher who instructed that pupil. Further note should be taken that

TABLE 18.24
Design with two within-subjects factors

A. Basic design

	Repeated measures			
	Female		Male	
Sex of teacher[a]	Low	High	Low	High
Female				
Male				

B. Error terms for two within-subjects factors

Source	df	Error terms
Between subjects	(9)	
Sex of teacher	1	
Teachers (within sex)	8	Error term for preceding line
Within subjects	(30)[b]	
Expectancy	1	
Expectancy × Sex of teacher	1	
Expectancy × Teachers (within sex)	8	Error term for preceding two lines
Pupil sex	1	
Pupil sex × Sex of teacher	1	
Pupil sex × Teachers (within sex)	8	Error term for preceding two lines
Expectancy × Pupil sex	1	
Expectancy × Pupil sex × Sex of teacher	1	
Expectancy × Pupil sex × Teachers (within sex)	8	Error term for preceding two lines

[a] Teachers are serving as subjects, and sex of teachers is the between-subjects factor.

[b] Computed as (N of subjects) × (df for levels of repeated measures). This study has four levels of repeated measures (i.e., two levels of expectancy for each of two genders). Therefore, the df (levels) = 4 − 1 = 3, and as N = 10 subjects, the df for within subjects = 10 × 3 = 30.

TABLE 18.25

Results of repeated-measures study with one between-subjects factor and two within-subjects factors

| | Teacher | Repeated measures | | | | Mean |
| | | Female pupil | | Male pupil | | |
		Low	High	Low	High	
	1	3	7	2	8	5.0
Female	2	3	9	3	5	5.0
teachers	3	5	8	5	6	6.0
	4	7	10	4	7	7.0
	5	7	11	6	4	7.0
	6	2	6	0	4	3.0
	7	1	5	1	5	3.0
Male	8	3	7	3	3	4.0
teachers	9	4	9	2	5	5.0
	10	5	8	4	3	5.0
	Mean	4.0	8.0	3.0	5.0	5.0

the four repeated measurements can, in this study, be viewed as a 2×2 design, that is, two levels of expectancy by two levels of pupil sex. Sources of variance, *df*, and error terms are as shown in Part B of Table 18.24. It should be noted that each of the three repeated-measures error terms was formed by crossing the relevant repeated-measures factor by the random factor of sampling units, or in this case, teachers (within sex).

To illustrate the computations for the 2 (between) $\times$ 2 (within) $\times$ 2 (within) table of results in Table 18.25, we begin by regarding the design as a simple 10-teacher $\times$ 4-levels of repeated measurement array. We will compute first the row (teachers) and the column (repeated-measures) sums of squares, using the equations described previously:

$$\text{Total } SS = \sum (X - \overline{M})^2 = (3 - 5)^2 + (7 - 5)^2 (2 - 5)^2 + \cdots$$
$$+ (8 - 5)^2 + (4 + 5)^2 + (3 - 5)^2$$
$$= 260$$

$$\text{Row (teacher) } SS = \sum [c(M_R - \overline{M})^2] = 4(5.0 - 5)^2 + 4(5.0 - 5)^2$$
$$+ 4(6.0 - 5)^2 + \cdots + 4(4.0 - 5)^2$$
$$+ 4(5.0 - 5)^2 + 4(5.0 - 5)^2$$
$$= 72$$

$$\text{Column (repeated measures) } SS = \sum [r(M_C - \overline{M})^2] = 10(4.0 - 5)^2 + 10(8.0 - 5)^2$$
$$+ 10(3.0 - 5)^2 + 10(5.0 - 5)^2$$
$$= 140$$

Row × Column (interaction) SS = Total SS − Row SS − Column SS

$$= 260 - 72 - 140$$
$$= 48.$$

Our next step is to decompose the row (or teacher) SS into its components of sex-of-teacher SS and teachers-within-sex SS by means of the following definitional equations, beginning with the sum of squares for sex of teachers, where

$$\text{Sex-of-teacher } SS = \sum[npe(M_S - \overline{M})^2],$$

and n is the number of teachers nested within each sex of teacher (or n_h if those ns are not equal), p is the number of levels of the pupil sex factor, e is the number of levels of the expectancy factor, M_S is the mean of all conditions of a given teacher sex, and $\overline{M}$ is the grand mean, (i.e., the mean of all condition means). Given that the mean scores obtained by female teachers and male teachers are 6.0 and 4.0, respectively, we find

$$\text{Sex-of-teacher } SS = [5 \times 2 \times 2(6.0 - 5)^2] + [5 \times 2 \times 2(4.0 - 5)^2] = 40.$$

Next we compute

$$\text{Teachers-within-sex } SS = \text{Row(teachers) } SS - \text{Sex-of-teacher } SS$$
$$= 72 - 40 = 32.$$

We now turn our attention to the various within-teachers sources of variance. We consider first the SS for expectancy, Expectancy × Sex of teacher, and Expectancy × Teachers (within sex):

$$\text{Expectancy } SS = \sum[nsp(M_E - \overline{M})^2],$$

where s is the number of levels of the sex-of-teacher factor, M_E is the mean of all conditions of a given level of expectancy, and the other terms are as above.

$$\text{Expectancy} \times \text{Sex-of-teacher } SS = \sum[np(M_{ES} - \overline{M})^2]$$
$$- \text{Expectancy } SS - \text{Sex-of-teacher } SS,$$

where M_{ES} is the mean of all observations contributing to each combination of expectancy and teacher sex, and the other terms are as above.

$$\text{Expectancy} \times \text{Teachers-within-sex } SS = \sum[p(M_{ET} - \overline{M})^2]$$
$$- \text{Expectancy } SS$$
$$- \text{Row (teacher) } SS$$
$$- \text{Expectancy} \times \text{Sex-of-teacher } SS,$$

where M_{ET} is the mean of all observations contributing to each combination of expectancy and individual teacher, and the other terms are as above. Note that the row SS term is identical to the sex-of-teacher SS plus the teachers-within-sex SS.

To help us in our arithmetic, we construct a table of the appropriate means, as shown in Part A of Table 18.26. From this table we find

$$\text{Expectancy } SS = [5 \times 2 \times 2(3.5 - 5)^2] + [5 \times 2 \times 2(6.5 - 5)^2] = 90.$$

Condensing the data in Part A in order to obtain the means of the Expectancy × Sex-of-teacher combinations (M_{ES}) gives the 2 × 2 table in Part B of Table 18.26. We find

TABLE 18.26

Expectancy × teachers' means for results shown in Table 18.25

A. Two-way table of means

	Teacher	Expectancy Low	Expectancy High	Mean
	1	2.5[2]	7.5	5.0[4]
Female	2	3.0	7.0	5.0
teachers	3	5.0	7.0	6.0
	4	5.5	8.5	7.0
	5	6.5	7.5	7.0
	6	1.0	5.0	3.0
	7	1.0	5.0	3.0
Male	8	3.0	5.0	4.0
teachers	9	3.0	7.0	5.0
	10	4.5	5.5	5.0
	Mean	3.5[20]	6.5	5.0[40]

B. Condensing of data in Part A

Teacher sex	Expectancy Low	High
Female	4.5[10]	7.5
Male	2.5	5.5

Note: Numbers shown within the ∟ symbol indicate the number of observations on which each type of mean is based.

$$\text{Expectancy} \times \text{Sex-of-teacher } SS = [5 \times 2(4.5 - 5)^2] + [5 \times 2(7.5 - 5)^2]$$
$$+ [5 \times 2(2.5 - 5)^2] + [5 \times 2(5.5 - 5)^2]$$
$$- \text{Expectancy } SS - \text{Sex-of-teacher } SS$$
$$= 130 - 90 - 40 = 0,$$

and we also find

$$\text{Expectancy} \times \text{Teachers-within-sex } SS = 2(2.5 - 5)^2 + 2(7.5 - 5)^2$$
$$+ \cdots + 2(4.5 - 5)^2 + 2(5.5 - 5)^2$$
$$- \text{Expectancy } SS$$
$$- \text{Row (teacher) } SS$$
$$- \text{Expectancy} \times \text{Sex-of-teacher } SS$$
$$= 180 - 90 - 72 - 0 = 18.$$

Note again that the row (teacher) SS is identical with the sex-of-teacher SS plus the teachers-within-sex SS.

We consider next the SS for Pupil-sex, Pupil-sex $\times$ Sex-of-teacher, and Pupil-sex $\times$ teachers (within sex):

$$\text{Pupil-sex } SS = \sum [nse(M_P - \overline{M})^2],$$

where M_P is the mean of all conditions of a given level of pupil sex, and the other terms are as above.

$$\text{Pupil-sex} \times \text{Sex-of-teacher } SS = \sum [ne(M_{PS} - \overline{M})^2] - \text{Pupil-sex } SS \\ - \text{Sex-of-teacher } SS,$$

where M_{PS} is the mean of all observations contributing to each combination of pupil sex and teacher sex, and the other terms are as above.

$$\text{Pupil-sex} \times \text{Teachers-within-sex } SS = \sum [e(M_{PT} - \overline{M})^2] \\ - \text{Pupil-sex } SS - \text{Row (teacher) } SS \\ - \text{Pupil-sex} \times \text{Sex-of-teacher } SS,$$

where M_{PT} is the mean of all observations contributing to each combination of pupil sex and individual teacher, and the other terms are as above. The row SS is identical with sex-of-teacher SS plus the teachers-within sex SS.

Again we construct a table of the appropriate means, as shown in Part A of Table 18.27. From that table we find

$$\text{Pupil-sex } SS = [5 \times 2 \times 2(6.0 - 5)^2] + [5 \times 2 \times 2(4.0 - 5)^2] = 40.$$

Condensing the table in Part A to obtain the means of the Pupil-sex $\times$ Sex-of-teacher combinations (M_{PS}) gives us the 2×2 table in Part B of Table 18.27, on the basis of which we find

$$\text{Pupil-sex} \times \text{Sex-of teacher } SS = [5 \times 2(7.0 - 5)^2] + [5 \times 2(5.0 - 5)^2] \\ + [5 \times 2(5.0 - 5)^2] + [5 \times 2(3.0 - 5)^2] \\ - \text{Pupil-sex } SS - \text{Sex-of-teacher } SS \\ = 80 - 40 - 40 = 0$$

and

$$\text{Pupil-sex} \times \text{Teachers-within-sex } SS = 2(5.0 - 5)^2 + 2(5.0 - 5)^2 + \cdots \\ + 2(6.5 - 5)^2 + 2(3.5 - 5)^2 \\ - \text{Pupil-sex } SS - \text{Row (teacher) } SS \\ - \text{Pupil-sex} \times \text{Sex-of-teacher } SS \\ = 128 - 40 - 72 - 0 \\ = 16.$$

The row SS is identical to the sex-of-teacher SS plus the teachers-within-sex SS.

Finally, we consider the SS for the two-way interaction of Expectancy $\times$ Pupil-sex, the three-way interaction of Expectancy $\times$ Pupil-sex $\times$ Sex-of-teacher, and the three-way interaction of Expectancy $\times$ Pupil-sex $\times$ Teachers (within sex):

$$\text{Expectancy} \times \text{Pupil-sex } SS = \sum [ns(M_{EP} - \overline{M})^2] - \text{Expectancy } SS - \text{Pupil-sex } SS$$

TABLE 18.27
Pupil sex × teachers' means for results shown in Table 18.25

A. Two-way table of means

	Teacher	Pupil sex Female	Male	Mean
	1	5.0[2]	5.0	5.0[4]
Female	2	6.0	4.0	5.0
teachers	3	6.5	5.5	6.0
	4	8.5	5.5	7.0
	5	9.0	5.0	7.0
	6	4.0	2.0	3.0
	7	3.0	3.0	3.0
Male	8	5.0	3.0	4.0
teachers	9	6.5	3.5	5.0
	10	6.5	3.5	5.0
	Mean	6.0[20]	4.0	5.0[40]

B. Condensing of data in Part A

Teacher sex	Pupil sex Female	Male
Female	7.0[10]	5.0
Male	5.0	3.0

Note: Numbers shown within the └ symbol indicate the number of observations on which each type of mean is based.

where M_{EP} is the mean of all observations contributing to each combination of expectancy and pupil sex, and the other terms are as above.

Expectancy × Pupil-sex × Sex-of-teacher $SS = \sum[n(M_{\text{EPS}} - \overline{M})^2]$
 − Expectancy SS
 − Pupil-sex SS
 − Sex-of-teacher SS
 − Expectancy × Pupil-sex SS
 − Expectancy × Sex-of-teacher SS
 − Pupil-sex × Sex-of-teacher SS,

where M_{EPS} is the mean of all observations contributing to each combination of expectancy, pupil sex, and sex of teacher, and the other terms are as above.

Expectancy × Pupil-sex × Teachers-within-sex $SS = \sum[(M_{\text{EPT}} - \overline{M})^2]$
 − Expectancy SS
 − Pupil-sex SS

— Row (teacher) SS
— Expectancy $\times$ Pupil-sex SS
— Expectancy $\times$ Sex-of-teacher SS
— Pupil-sex $\times$ Sex-of-teacher SS
— Expectancy $\times$ Pupil sex $\times$ Sex-of-teacher SS
— Expectancy $\times$ Teachers-within-sex SS
— Pupil-sex $\times$ Teachers-within-sex SS

(or more compactly, Total SS minus all other sums of squares),

where M_{EPT} is the mean of all observations contributing to each combination of expectancy, pupil sex, and individual teacher. In this example, there is only one such observation for each combination of these three factors, and Table 18.25 (the original 10 teachers $\times$ 4 repeated-measures table) shows these combinations (M_{EPT}). Note also that, in this example, $\Sigma(M_{EPT} - \overline{M})^2$ is identical to $\Sigma(X - \overline{M})^2 =$ Total SS.

To show the calculations, we begin again with another condensed table, as shown in Part A of Table 18.28. Then,

$$
\begin{aligned}
\text{Expectancy} \times \text{Pupil-sex } SS = &\ [5 \times 2(4.0 - 5)^2] + [5 \times 2(3.0 - 5)^2] \\
&+ [5 \times 2(8.0 - 5)^2] + [5 \times 2(5.0 - 5)^2] \\
&- \text{Expectancy } SS - \text{Pupil-sex } SS \\
= &\ 140 - 90 - 40 = 10.
\end{aligned}
$$

Next we turn to Part B of Table 18.28, which contains the table of eight means (M_{EPS}) required for the three-way interaction of Expectancy $\times$ Pupil-sex $\times$ Sex of teacher.

TABLE 18.28
Expectancy $\times$ pupil sex and three-way interaction means of Table 18.25

A. Expectancy $\times$ Pupil sex combination

	Pupil sex	
Expectancy	**Female**	**Male**
Low	4.0[10]	3.0
High	8.0	5.0

B. Expectancy $\times$ pupil sex $\times$ sex of teacher combination

	Female		Male	
Teacher sex	**Low**	**High**	**Low**	**High**
Female	5.0[5]	9.0	4.0	6.0
Male	3.0	7.0	2.0	4.0

We find

Expectancy $\times$ Pupil-sex $\times$ Sex of teacher $SS = 5(5.0 - 5)^2 + 5(9.0 - 5)^2$
$$+ \cdots + 5(2.0 - 5)^2$$
$$+ 5(4.0 - 5)^2 - 90 - 40 - 40$$
$$- 10 - 0 - 0 = 180 - 180$$
$$= 0$$

and

Expectancy $\times$ Pupil-sex $\times$ Teachers-within-sex $SS = 260$ (total SS)
$$- 90 - 40 - 72 - 10 - 0 - 0 - 0 - 18 - 16 = 14.$$

We have now computed all the SS required to complete our table of variance, and the results are shown in Table 18.29. The analysis of variance shows all three main effects and one two-way interaction to be significant. In this example we used an equal number of teachers ($n = 5$) in each condition of teacher sex. Had these numbers not been equal, we could have used the same computational procedures with only one modification: We would have replaced the quantity n by n_h wherever n was required, with n_h defined as the harmonic mean of the sample sizes found in each between-subjects condition of the study (see Equation 14.6).

AGGREGATING ERROR TERMS

When the df per error term is small, as it is in Table 18.29, we may want to consider aggregating the within-subjects error terms in order to obtain a more stable single estimate (in this example, based on 24 df). This averaging together of error terms

TABLE 18.29
Summary ANOVA for results shown in Table 18.25 (one between-subjects and two within-subjects factors)

Source	SS	df	MS	F	η	p
Between subjects	(72)	(9)				
Sex of teacher	40	1	40.00	10.00	.75	.013
Teachers (within sex)	32	8	4.00			
Within subjects	(188)	(30)				
Expectancy	90	1	90.00	40.00	.91	.0002
Expectancy $\times$ Sex of teacher	0	1	0.00	0.00	.00	1.00
Expectancy $\times$ Teachers (within sex)	18	8	2.25			
Pupil sex	40	1	40.00	20.00	.85	.002
Pupil sex $\times$ Sex of teacher	0	1	0.00	0.00	.00	1.00
Pupil sex $\times$ Teachers (within sex)	16	8	2.00			
Expectancy $\times$ Pupil sex	10	1	10.00	5.71	.65	.044
Expectancy $\times$ Pupil sex $\times$ Sex of teacher	0	1	0.00	0.00	.00	1.00
Expectancy $\times$ Pupil sex $\times$ Teachers (within sex)	14	8	1.75			

(each weighted by its *df*) is generally recommended only if the ratio of the largest to the smallest error term is roughly 2.0 or less (Green & Tukey, 1960). *Aggregation* is often referred to as *pooling,* especially when the decision to aggregate is based on tests of significance of differences among error variances. In Table 18.29, the three within-subjects error terms range from 1.75 to 2.25, with the ratio of the largest mean square to the smallest mean square only $2.25/1.75 = 1.29$. Therefore, those three error terms are good candidates for aggregation.

The general formula for the aggregation of k terms is

$$MS_{\text{aggregated}} = \frac{MS_1(df_1) + MS_2(df_2) + \cdots + MS_k(df_k)}{df_1 + df_2 + \cdots + df_k}, \tag{18.15}$$

where MS_1 to MS_k are the k error terms to be aggregated, and df_1 to df_k are the k degrees of freedom that are associated with the k mean squares for error. For the ANOVA in Table 18.29, we have

$$MS_{\text{aggregated}} = \frac{2.25(8) + 2.00(8) + 1.75(8)}{8 + 8 + 8} = 2.00.$$

When it is more convenient to work with sums of squares, the general formula can be written as

$$MS_{\text{aggregated}} = \frac{SS_1 + SS_2 + \cdots + SS_k}{df_1 + df_2 + \cdots + df_k}, \tag{18.16}$$

where SS_1 to SS_k are the k sums of squares of the k error sources of variance, and df_1 to df_k are their associated degrees of freedom. For the data of Table 18.29, we have

$$MS_{\text{aggregated}} = \frac{18 + 16 + 14}{8 + 8 + 8} = 2.00.$$

Once we have computed an aggregated error term, it replaces all the individual error terms that contributed to its computation. Some of the F tests computed with the new error term will be larger (those in which the original MS_{error} was larger) and some will be smaller (those in which the original MS_{error} was smaller).

THREE WITHIN-SUBJECTS FACTORS

In our example of three within-subjects factors, we retain the basic plan of the preceding example but assume that each teacher teaches eight pupils instead of four. In addition, we assume that for each combination of expectancy and pupil sex, there is one hyperactive child and one normal child. The basic design is shown in Table 18.30, and the sources of variance, *df,* and error terms of that design are shown in Table 18.31. Note how easily we generate all new sources of variance simply by adding the new within-subjects factor of diagnosis and then crossing that term systematically with all preceding sources of variance.

Just as in the previous example, we want to consider aggregating the various error terms to form a more stable overall error term. In this example we have one error term that is a four-way interaction, three error terms that are three-way interactions, and

TABLE 18.30

Design with three within-subjects factors

	Repeated measures							
	Female				Male			
	Hyperactive		Normal		Hyperactive		Normal	
Sex of teacher[a]	Low[b]	High	Low	High	Low	High	Low	High
Female								
Male								

[a] Between-subjects factor.

[b] Level of expectancy.

TABLE 18.31

Error terms for three within-subjects factors

Source	df	Error terms
Between subjects	(9)	
Sex of teacher	1	
Teachers (within sex)	8	Error term for preceding line
Within subjects	(70)[a]	
Expectancy	1	
Expectancy × Sex of teacher	1	
Expectancy × Teachers (within sex)	8	Error term for preceding two lines
Pupil sex	1	
Pupil sex × Sex of teacher	1	
Pupil sex × Teachers (within sex)	8	Error term for preceding two lines
Expectancy × Pupil sex	1	
Expectancy × Pupil sex × Sex of teacher	1	
Expectancy × Pupil sex × Teachers (within sex)	8	Error term for preceding two lines
Diagnosis	1	
Diagnosis × Sex of teacher	1	
Diagnosis × Teachers (within sex)	8	Error term for preceding two lines
Diagnosis × Expectancy	1	
Diagnosis × Expectancy × Sex of teacher	1	
Diagnosis × Expectancy × Teachers (within sex)	8	Error term for preceding two lines
Diagnosis × Pupil sex	1	
Diagnosis × Pupil sex × Sex of teacher	1	
Diagnosis × Pupil sex × Teachers (within sex)	8	Error term for preceding two lines
Diagnosis × Expectancy × Pupil sex	1	
Diagnosis × Expectancy × Sex (P) × Sex (T)	1	
Diagnosis × Expectancy × Sex (P) × Teachers (within sex)	8	Error term for preceding two lines

[a] Computed as (N of subjects) × (df for levels of repeated measures). This study has eight levels arranged as a $2 \times 2 \times 2$ format, so df for levels of repeated measures = $8 - 1 = 7$, the N of subjects = 10, and df for within subjects = $10 \times 7 = 70$.

three error terms that are two-way interactions. In this situation it is useful to begin with the higher order interactions and aggregate them first. For example, we might begin by aggregating ($F < 2$) the three-way interactions (along with the four-way, because there is just one) to form the new error term for all terms tested by any of these error terms. We then aggregate the two-way interaction error terms ($F < 2$) to form the new error term for all terms tested by any of these error terms. Finally, if the two new error terms can be aggregated ($F < 2$), we can use this new super-error term to test all within-subjects sources of variation. In any of the aggregations described, the error terms should be weighted by their *df*.

FIXED OR RANDOM FACTORS

So far in our discussion of three or more factors in designs using repeated measures, we have assumed that all factors other than subjects-within-conditions have been fixed rather than random. That is, in fact, the most common situation. We should, however, note the consequences for significance testing of having other factors in the design that are random rather than fixed. In our illustration, assume we have randomly assigned five female and five male teachers to each of four schools to instruct two pupils briefly. One of each of the two pupils has been designated at random as a student of high intellectual potential. The design is shown in Table 18.32, and the sources of variance, *df*, and error terms are shown in Table 18.33.

If all our variables, including school, had been fixed factors, there would have been only two error terms. Teachers (within conditions) would have served as the error term for all three between-subjects effects, and Expectancy × Teachers would have served as the error term for all four within-subjects effects. However, when schools are considered a random factor, we find five error terms rather than two. Now the sex-of-teacher effect is tested against the Sex-of-teacher × School interaction, an error term that has only 3 *df*. These 3 *df* contrast to the 32 *df* associated with the error term that we would use if schools were a fixed factor rather than a random factor.

TABLE 18.32
Fixed versus random factors?

Between subjects		Repeated measures	
School	Sex	Control	High expectancy
1	Female		
	Male		
2	Female		
	Male		
3	Female		
	Male		
4	Female		
	Male		

TABLE 18.33

Error terms for two between- and one within-subjects ANOVA with one between factor random, not fixed

Source	df	Error terms[a]
Between subjects	(39)	
Sex of teacher	1	
School	3	
Sex of teacher × School	3	Error term for sex of teacher
Teachers (within conditions)	32	Error term for preceding two lines
Within subjects	(40)[b]	
Expectancy	1	
Expectancy × Sex of teacher	1	
Expectancy × School	3	Error term for expectancy
Expectancy × Sex of teacher × School	3	Error term for expectancy × Sex of teacher
Expectancy × Teachers	32	Error term for preceding two lines

[a] Assuming school to be a random rather than a fixed factor.

[b] Computed as (N of subjects) × (df for levels of repeated measures). In this study there are $N = 40$ subjects and two levels of the repeated measures factor ($df = 2 - 1 = 1$), so there are $N \times df$ (levels) $= 40 \times 1 = 40$ df for within subjects.

The advantage of considering schools a random factor is that we can generalize to the population of schools represented by those four schools. The disadvantage of considering schools a random factor is the low power to reject the null hypothesis associated with our having only four schools in the study.

In practice, it sometimes happens that we have the best of both worlds, when the MS_{error} considering the effect random is similar in size to the MS_{error} considering the effect fixed. In our example, that would occur if the mean square for Sex-of-teacher × School were similar in size to the mean square for teachers-within-conditions. If that *were* the case, we could aggregate the two error terms. We would weight each by its *df* and use the new pooled error term instead of either of the two components.

Turning to the within-subjects factors, we find that expectancy is tested against the Expectancy × School interaction, and the Expectancy × Sex-of-teacher interaction is tested against the Expectancy × Sex-of-teacher × School interaction. The comments made above in the discussion of the sex-of-teacher effect apply here as well. Note that both of the fixed effects (sex-of-teacher and expectancy) and their interaction (Sex-of-teacher × Expectancy) are tested against error terms that we form by crossing the effect to be tested by the random effect (schools, in this example). More detailed discussions of forming error terms in repeated measures are available in Winer, Brown, and Michels (1991).

When we have three or more factors, two or more of which are random effects, we cannot properly test one or more of the effects by any error term. Nevertheless, useful approximate procedures employing "quasi *F*s" are available and have been discussed by Maxwell and Delaney (2000), Myers and Well (2003), Snedecor and

Cochran (1989), Wickens and Keppel (1983), and Winer, Brown, and Michels (1991).

DID REPEATED MEASURES HELP?

Perhaps the primary reason for using repeated-measures designs (i.e., in which the effects of greatest interest are the main effects of the repeated-measures factors or the interactions involving the repeated-measures factors) is to use subjects as their "own control" in hopes of increasing the precision of the experiment. As we said at the beginning of this chapter, the more the scores of the subjects (or other sampling units) under one condition are correlated with the scores of the subjects under another condition of the same experiment, the more advantage we find in repeated-measures designs. Very low correlations between scores earned under one condition and scores earned under other conditions of the experiment suggest using a repeated-measures design has little statistical advantage. There may still be a logistical advantage, however, because it is usually more efficient to measure n subjects k times each than to measure $n \times k$ subjects once each.

To understand whether using repeated measures does indeed help, consider the simple repeated-measures design in Part A of Table 18.34, in which five subjects are each measured on three subtests. For these five subjects we can compute the correlation (r) between their performance on Subtests 1 and 2, 1 and 3, and 2 and 3. The resulting correlations are .64, .80, and .58, respectively, with a mean r of .67. This very substantial average correlation suggests that a repeated-measures design would be much more efficient than a between-subjects design. Computing the mean of three rs

TABLE 18.34
Five subjects tested three times each

A. Scores on three subtests

	Subtests		
	1	**2**	**3**
Subject 1	5	6	7
Subject 2	3	6	4
Subject 3	3	4	6
Subject 4	2	2	3
Subject 5	1	4	4

B. Summary ANOVA

Source	**SS**	**df**	**MS**
Between subjects	24.0	4	6.00
Within subjects			
Subtests	11.2	2	5.60
Subtests $\times$ Subjects	6.8	8	0.85

was not arduous. Suppose, however, there were 10 subtests instead of 3. We would need to compute $(10 \times 9)/2 = 45$ correlations. A more convenient approach is simply using the analysis of variance summary table. This approach involves the computation of the intraclass r, an index that was described briefly in chapter 4 (notice that the subjects' scores in Part A of Table 18.34 are identical to those in Table 4.4, and the only difference is the substitution of the column heading "Subtests" in Table 18.34 for "Judges" in Table 4.4).

THE INTRACLASS r REVISITED

In chapter 4 we used the intraclass r to obtain an estimate of judge-to-judge reliability. Stated more generally, the intraclass r is an index of the degree of similarity of all observations made on a given sampling unit, such as a subject. If all the pairs of observations made on the subjects (e.g., Subtest 1 and Subtest 2), show a high correlation, the intraclass r tends to be high. In fact, the intraclass r is a good estimate of the mean correlation obtained from the correlation of all possible pairs of observations made on subjects (e.g., Subtest 1 with 2, 1 with 3, 2 with 3, etc.). To compute the intraclass r we begin with the mean squares of the analysis of variance, as shown in Part B of Table 18.34 (a repeat of Table 4.5, except for the new label of the repeated-measures variable). The intraclass r is computed from

$$r_{intraclass} = \frac{MS_S - MS_{S \times k}}{MS_S + (k-1)MS_{S \times k}}, \tag{18.17}$$

where MS_S = mean square for subjects, $MS_{S \times k}$ = mean square for Subjects $\times$ Repeated-measures factor, and k = number of levels of the repeated-measures factor. For our example,

$$r_{intraclass} = \frac{6.00 - 0.85}{6.00 + (3-1)0.85} = .67,$$

a value that agrees with the mean r of .67 reported earlier.

As an illustration of the use of the intraclass r in a more complex design, consider an experiment in which the effects of two treatments are measured over three successive weeks. Our aim is to assess the typical correlation among the three occasions of measurement, but with the correlation computed separately within each treatment condition. Note that if we computed the correlation among the occasions for all subjects, our correlations would be inflated by the magnitude of the treatment effect. The data are shown in Part A of Table 18.35, and the summary ANOVA is shown in Part B. The intraclass r, computed from Equation 18.17, is

$$r_{intraclass} = \frac{.89 - .56}{.89 + (3-1).56} = .16.$$

Had we computed the correlations among the three occasions separately within each treatment condition, our rs would have been .00, $-.50$, $+.50$, $+.50$, .00, $+.50$, with a mean r of .17, a value agreeing well with the intraclass r of .16 computed from the mean squares.

TABLE 18.35
Design with two treatments measured on three occasions

A. Scores on three occasions

	Occasions 1	2	3
Treatment A			
Subject 1	2	2	4
Subject 2	2	0	3
Subject 3	1	1	3
Subject 4	3	1	2
Treatment B			
Subject 5	3	3	5
Subject 6	3	2	3
Subject 7	4	2	4
Subject 8	2	1	4

B. Summary ANOVA

Source	SS	df	MS
Between subjects			
1. Treatments	6.00	1	6.00
2. Subjects within treatments	5.33	6	0.89
Within subjects		(16)	
3. Occasions	16.00	2	8.00
4. Occasions × Treatments	0.00	2	0.00
5. Occasions × Subjects	6.66	12	0.56
6. Aggregated terms 2 and 5	11.99	18	0.67
7. Aggregated terms 2, 4, and 5	11.99	20	0.60

Lines 6 and 7 of the summary ANOVA in Table 18.35 suggest two ways of aggregating sources of variance. Had we used the aggregated terms, our intraclass rs would have been .10 and .14 for aggregated terms 6 and 7, respectively. These values are not dramatically different from the original (not aggregated) value of .16. In the present example the use of any of the three error terms would have been quite reasonable. In general, the fewer the df for the original error term, and the less dramatic the difference between the terms considered for aggregation, the better it is in the long run to aggregate terms.

One thing that we usually should *not* do to find out the correlations among the three occasions of measurement is to correlate the scores for all subjects, disregarding their treatment conditions. In the present example, such a correlation would yield rs of .50, .17, .67, with a mean r of .44. The difference between this mean r of .44 and the mean r of .17 (when rs are computed within the two treatment conditions) is due entirely to the effects of the treatment. The equivalent intraclass r is one in which the treatment effect is aggregated with the subjects-within-treatment effect and is then regarded as the MS_S, for example, $(SS_{\text{treatments}} + SS_{\text{subjects}})/(df_{\text{treatments}} + df_{\text{subjects}}) = (6 + 5.33)/(1 + 6) = 1.62$. Hence,

$$r_{\text{intraclass}} = \frac{1.62 - .56}{1.62 + (3 - 1).56} = .39,$$

a value greatly inflated by the addition of the treatment variation to the subject variation.

COMPOSITE VARIABLES AND ADDITIONAL ASSUMPTIONS

Formation of Composite Variables

In chapter 5 we discussed the strategy of forming composites and other redescriptions of variables. In many repeated-measures designs each of the repeated measures can be viewed as a replication of the measurement of some underlying construct. For example, if the repeated measurements are the 11 subtests of a standard measure of intelligence, or the 4 subtests of a social adjustment inventory, or the 3 psychophysiological indices of stress reaction, then the sum of the 11, or 4, or 3 subtests constitutes a meaningful composite index of intelligence, social adjustment, or stress reaction. The between-subjects sources of variance are essentially analyses of the repeated measures viewed as a composite variable. Where the sum of the repeated measures is sensibly interpretable as an index of some construct, repeated-measures analyses have special advantages in terms of statistical power and in terms of testing for homogeneity of effects.

The advantages of statistical power accrue because, as we add more measurements of an underlying construct, we are better able to observe the effects of experimental conditions on the composite measure of the construct than on randomly chosen subsets of the composite. The principle at work here is that we have a better chance to show effects with better measured constructs, and all else being equal, more repeatedly measured constructs *are* better measured (Guilford, 1954; Rosenthal & Rubin, 1986). The advantages of the repeated-measures analysis of the components over an analysis of the results only for the sum of the measures (i.e., the composite) are that we can learn whether the experimental treatments, or other factors of the design, are affecting different components or subtests differentially. That is exactly what the Treatment × Subtests interaction will tell us.

In applications of this kind, the repeated measurements tend to be positively correlated, often between .20 and .80. It turns out that the advantages of repeated-measures designs, in the sense of using more rather than fewer repeated measures of a construct, tend to increase when the intercorrelations among the repeated measurements are *lower*. This effect can be seen to be reasonable when we note that each measure contributes more that is unique to the composite when that measure is not too highly correlated with other measures. If the correlations among the measures are 1.00, after all, any one measure would be as good as the total.

Assumptions of *F* Tests on Repeated Measures

When we discussed the IID-normal assumptions underlying the use of *t* and *F* tests in chapters 13 and 14, we mentioned the implications of heterogeneity of variance. Here we want to note a special implication of heterogeneity of variance of repeated-measures variables for the interpretation of the sum of the repeated measures (i.e., the composite index of the construct). This implication is that individual variables contribute to the composite in proportion to their variance. Those measures with large variances may contribute much more to the formation of the composite than the investigator may intend. One way of dealing with this problem and ensuring that all variables will contribute equally to the composite is to transform each variable to Z scores (with a mean of zero and a standard deviation of 1.00). We have more to say about composite variables in chapter 20 (see also Rosenthal, 1987), but we should also note that *F* tests computed in actual research situations are usually distributed only approximately as *F*.

It will be recalled that the IID-normal assumptions have to do with the independence of errors (or sampling units), homogeneity of variance, and normality. In the case of repeated-measures analyses, there is a further assumption having to do with the relative magnitudes of the intercorrelations among the various levels of the repeated-measures factors. For practical purposes, we regard this assumption as met to the degree that we have homogeneity of correlation coefficients among the levels of the repeated-measures factors (Hays, 1981; Snedecor & Cochran, 1989; Winer, Brown, & Michels, 1991). In those repeated-measures designs in which there are two or more levels of between-subjects factors (such as treatments, sex, age, ability), there is still another assumption, which is that the pattern of intercorrelations among levels of the repeated-measures factors is consistent from level to level of the between-subjects factors (Winer, 1971). Both assumptions apply only to *F* tests on repeated measures with more than a single *df* in the numerator (i.e., omnibus *F* tests). Thus, any *F* test in which there are only two levels of the repeated-measures factor does not need to meet these assumptions. Indeed, when there are only two levels, only one correlation is possible! Even when there are more than two levels of the repeated-measures factor, however, these assumptions are not needed when we have tested some focused hypothesis by means of a contrast, because contrasts also have only a single *df* for the numerator of the *F* used to test them.

CONTRASTS IN REPEATED MEASURES

In chapter 15 we described the advantages of computing planned contrasts rather than using diffuse, unfocused omnibus *F* tests in the analysis of variance. Contrasts allow researchers to ask crisp, focused, specific questions of the data, and in return, the researchers receive crisp, focused, specific answers in terms of effect size estimates and tests of significance. Similar benefits accrue in the realm of repeated-measures analysis of variance when we use contrasts rather than diffuse, unfocused, omnibus tests. But in the case of repeated-measures analyses, contrasts can provide an enormous additional advantage. Contrasts often allow us to greatly simplify our analysis by completely removing the repeated-measures factor altogether. This great simplification is made possible by the use of individual contrast scores for each subject or other sampling unit (Rosenthal & Rosnow, 1985; Rosenthal, Rosnow, & Rubin, 2000).

Contrast (*L*) Scores

Contrast scores, more commonly called L (for lambda) scores, are metrics that define, for each sampling unit, the degree to which that particular unit's repeated measures are consistent with the prediction made in terms of the λ weights defining it. Suppose we predicted that, over the course of three measurements, the subjects measured would exhibit a linear increase in performance scores, which we represent by contrast weights of -1, 0, $+1$. If some given subject had three consecutive scores of 3, 5, and 7, that subject would provide better support for our prediction than would a subject who had scores of 5, 7, 3, or 5, 5, 5. We quantify the degree of support, by which we mean the L scores for each sampling unit, as follows:

$$L = \Sigma(Y_i\lambda_i) = Y_1\lambda_1 + Y_2\lambda_2 + \cdots + Y_k\lambda_k, \tag{18.18}$$

which may be recognized as a variation on Equation 15.2; in Equation 18.18 we have substituted the individual (Y) scores for the group means of Equation 15.2.

To illustrate the use of Equation 18.18, we return to Table 18.1. That table displays the scores of four subjects who were each measured on three occasions. Subject 1 earned scores of 0, 7, and 3 on the three occasions of measurement. Had our prediction been that subjects' performance would increase linearly, our smallest integer contrast (λ) weights would be -1, 0, $+1$. Thus, we find the L score of Subject 1 to be

$$L = \Sigma(Y_i\lambda_i) = 0(-1) + 7(0) + 3(+1) = 3.$$

For the remaining three subjects of Table 18.1, the L scores are

$$\text{Subject 2 } L = 1(-1) + 7(0) + 4(+1) = 3$$
$$\text{Subject 3 } L = 3(-1) + 8(0) + 5(+1) = 2$$
$$\text{Subject 4 } L = 4(-1) + 8(0) + 6(+1) = 2$$

To address the question of the degree to which the scores of this sample of subjects support our linear prediction (defined by λ weights of $-1, 0, +1$), we compute a one-sample t test as follows:

$$t_{\text{contrast}} = \frac{\bar{L}}{\sqrt{\left(\frac{1}{n}\right)S_L^2}} \tag{18.19}$$

where $\bar{L}$ is the mean of the L scores, and S_L^2 is the variance (S^2) of the L scores. Substituting in Equation 18.19, we find

$$t_{\text{contrast}} = \frac{2.5}{\sqrt{\left(\frac{1}{4}\right).3333}} = 8.66,$$

which, with df $= n - 1 = 3$, is significant at $p = .0016$ one-tailed, and (from Equation 15.12) $r_{\text{contrast}} = .98$.

TABLE 18.36
Performance scores on three occasions for two conditions of tutoring

		Session 1	Session 2	Session 3	Mean	L
Tutored	S_1	0	7	3	3.33	3
	S_2	1	7	4	4.00	3
	S_3	3	8	5	5.33	2
	S_4	4	8	6	6.00	2
	M	2.0	7.5	4.5	4.67	2.5
Control	S_5	1	5	1	2.33	0
	S_6	3	6	4	4.33	1
	S_7	4	5	3	4.00	−1
	S_8	0	6	2	2.67	2
	M	2.0	5.5	2.5	3.33	0.5
Mean of means		2.0	6.5	3.5	4.00	1.5

Compare the directness and simplicity of this single t test with the analysis of variance of the data of Table 18.1 as shown in Table 18.2. Not only is the analysis of variance of Table 18.2 more complicated than our one-sample t test on the L scores, but Table 18.2 never does address our prediction that performance will increase linearly. The sessions effect of Table 18.2 tells us only that there is some greater-than-chance hetero-geneity of session means; it tells us nothing about the nature of that heterogeneity.

We now consider a slightly more complex research question. Suppose we want to know whether one particular group will show a greater linear increase in performance over time than will another group. Table 18.36 displays the results of an experiment in which four children were randomly assigned to tutoring for the improvement of reading skills and four other children were randomly assigned to a control (untutored) group. All children were tested for their reading skills on three occasions: one, two, and three months after the treatment conditions were implemented. Although there would, of course, be considerable interest in the overall effectiveness of the tutoring, the primary reason for this particular small-scale study was to compare the degree to which the tutored and untutored children showed a linear increment in their performance skills over the three occasions of testing.

Table 18.37 shows the analysis of variance of the data of Table 18.36. The between-subjects effect of treatment was quite large in magnitude, but given the size of this study, the p value is .14, or .07 if a one-tailed t test is employed. The within-subjects terms showed an enormous effect of sessions, with a very low p value reflecting the great differences among scores earned on the three occasions of testing. There was also a substantial interaction of Sessions × Treatment, reflecting the fact that the treatment effect varied over the three sessions.

Our mean polish of the data of Table 18.36 gives the results shown in Table 18.38. Table 18.38 contains not only (a) the residuals defining the interaction in the six cells of the 2 × 3 design, but also (b) the row effects, (c) the column effects, and (d) the

TABLE 18.37
Analysis of variance of the data of Table 18.36

Source	SS	df	MS	F	η	p
Between subjects	(32.67)	(7)				
Treatment	10.67	1	10.67	2.91	.57	.14
Subjects nested	22.00	6	3.67			
Within subjects	(99.33)	(16)				
Sessions	84.00	2	42.00	50.40	.95	1.4^{-6}
Sessions × Treatment	5.33	2	2.67	3.20	.59	.077
Sessions × Subjects	10.00	12	0.83			

grand mean. The mean polish provides a useful summary of the results of the study, but it does nothing to address our primary question about the difference between the treatment group and the control group in the degree of linearity of improvement. However, the question is easy enough to address simply by the use of L scores.

Because the L scores define the degree to which any individual subject reflected, showed, or bore out the prediction, we need only compare the L scores associated with each of the two conditions (i.e., tutored vs. untutored control). That comparison is easily made from the following formula for a two-sample t test:

$$t = \frac{\bar{L}_1 - \bar{L}_2}{\sqrt{\left(\frac{1}{n_1} + \frac{1}{n_2}\right)S_L^2}},\tag{18.20}$$

and we find

$$t = \frac{2.5 - 0.5}{\sqrt{\left(\frac{1}{4} + \frac{1}{4}\right)1.00}} = 2.83,$$

which, with $df = N - 2 = 6$, is significant at $p = .015$ one-tailed and (from Equation 15.12) $r_{\text{contrast}} = .76$. The results show directly and clearly that, as predicted, the children assigned to the tutoring condition reflected a greater upward linearity of performance over occasions than did the children of the control group.

TABLE 18.38
Mean polish of the data of Table 18.36

	Sessions			
	1	2	3	Row effects
Tutored	−.67	+.33	+.33	+.67
Control	+.67	−.33	−.33	−.67
Column effects	−2.00	+2.50	−.50	(4.00)

Had the experiment used more than two groups (e.g., several treatment and/or control groups), and had we wanted to examine a specific hypothesis stating that our treatment and control groups would show a particular pattern of L scores, we could have extended the two-group comparison of Equation 18.20 to the more general t test of Equation 15.4, which we rewrite here as

$$t_{contrast} = \frac{\sum(M_i\lambda_i)}{\sqrt{\left(\sum\frac{\lambda_i^2}{n_i}\right)S_{aggregated}^2}} = \frac{\sum(\overline{L}_i\lambda_i)}{\sqrt{\left(\sum\frac{\lambda_i^2}{n_i}\right)S_{L\,aggregated}^2}} \tag{18.21}$$

HIERARCHICALLY NESTED DESIGNS

In the analyses of variance we have considered so far, only a single factor was usually nested within other factors, and that single factor was usually subjects (or other sampling units) nested within conditions. There are many data-analytic situations, however, in which we have a hierarchy of nested sampling units. For example, we may have a sample of states, within each of which there is a sample of counties, within each of which there is a sample of towns or cities, within each of which there is a sample of precincts, within each of which there is a sample of voters. In hierarchically nested designs of this sort, the analysis depends a great deal on whether each of the hierarchical levels is regarded as a fixed factor or a random factor. Data structures of this sort give us rich opportunities to maximize the power and precision of our investigations of treatment effects of many kinds. Consider the hierarchically nested data structure in which we have

> 6 school systems sampled from the state,
> 4 schools sampled from each system,
> 2 classes sampled from each school, and
> 20 children sampled from each classroom

Schematically, we can represent the data structure as shown in Table 18.39.

In the remainder of this chapter we review five schematic designs in the order of their increasing power and precision. The five designs are shown in Table 18.40, where we see that they differ in the level at which we introduce the treatment condition, that is, (1) between systems; (2) within systems; (3) within schools; (4) within classrooms; and (5) within children. Designs 2–5 are repeated-measures designs in

TABLE 18.39
Illustration of hierarchically nested design

Systems	1		2 3 4 5		6
Schools	/ / \ \ 1 2 3 4......	....			/ / \ \ 21 22 23 24
Classes	/ \ 1 2....................	....			/ \ 47 48
Children	/ \ 1 20.........................	....			/ \ 941...960

TABLE 18.40
Five schematic designs

Design 1: Between systems

	Treatment	Control
Systems	1, 2, 3	4, 5, 6

Design 2: Within systems

	Treatment	Control
System 1		
System 2		
System 3		
System 4		
System 5		
System 6		

Design 3: Within schools

	Treatment	Control
School 1		
School 2		
:		
:		
:		
School 24		

Design 4: Within classrooms

	Treatment	Control
Classroom 1		
Classroom 2		
:		
:		
:		
Classroom 48		

Design 5: Within children

	Treatment	Control
Child 1		
Child 2		
:		
:		
:		
Child 960		

which the sampling units are measured twice, once under the treatment condition and once again under the control condition. The following is a preview of each design shown in Table 18.40 and the most obvious *t* or *F* test; alternative tests of significance are described after we give this preview:

Design 1: Between Systems. Six systems are nested within conditions (i.e., treatment vs. control), not crossed by conditions, so it is not a repeated-measures design. Most simply, we can compare the three treated systems with the three control systems using a two-sample *t* test on 4 *df* or an *F* test on 1 and 4 *df*.

Design 2: Within Systems. The six systems are crossed by conditions (treatment vs. control), so this can be viewed as a repeated-measures design. Most simply, we can compare the treated subunits of each of the six systems with their corresponding control subunits using a one-sample *t* test on 5 *df* or an *F* test on 1 and 5 *df*.

Design 3: Within Schools. The 24 schools are crossed by conditions, and the simplest significance test uses a one-sample *t* test on 23 *df* or an *F* test on 1 and 23 *df*.

Design 4: Within Classrooms. The 48 classrooms are crossed by conditions, and the simplest test of significance uses a one-sample *t* test on 47 *df* or an *F* on 1 and 47 *df*.

Design 5: Within Children. The 960 children are crossed by conditions, and the simplest test of significance uses a one-sample *t* test on 959 *df* or an *F* on 1 and 959 *df*.

THE CHOICE OF ERROR TERMS

For each of the five designs proposed, our preview has described the simplest, most obvious *t* test or *F* test. Actually, for each of those designs there are 3 or 4 proper error terms for the *F* tests (or *t* tests). Which error term we select depends on whether we regard each potential source of variation as a random factor or a fixed factor. Recall that factors are random when we view their levels as having been sampled at random from a larger population of levels of those factors to which we want to generalize, and factors are fixed when we view their levels as exhaustive (i.e., as constituting the entire population of levels, so that we do not have the goal of generalizing the results to other levels of the factors than the ones specifically used in the study). In the present instance, we can view systems, schools, and classrooms as fixed or random.

In hierarchically nested designs where classes are nested in schools, which are nested in systems, the four possible arrangements of fixed versus random factors are as shown in Part A of Table 18.41. Four arrangements of fixed versus random factors that would *not* be possible are shown in Part B of Table 18.41. The four impossible arrangements are characterized by having a fixed factor nested within a random factor. Such nesting is impossible because we cannot generalize to new systems while, for example, restricting ourselves to the particular schools nested within the sampled districts. If we generalize to other systems, we are forced also to generalize to other schools in those systems.

To illustrate the error terms in the five schematic designs of Table 18.40, we again review each in turn. For these illustrations there is another factor lower in the

TABLE 18.41
Fixed versus random factors

A. Arrangements that are possible

	Arrangements			
Level	1	2	3	4
Systems	Fixed	Random	Fixed	Fixed
Schools	Fixed	Random	Fixed	Random
Classes	Fixed	Random	Random	Random

B. Arrangements that are *not* possible

	Arrangements			
Level	5	6	7	8
Systems	Fixed	Random	Random	Random
Schools	Random	Fixed	Fixed	Random
Classes	Fixed	Fixed	Random	Fixed

hierarchy than classes, and that is children nested within classrooms. It is regarded as a random factor and can therefore be added as the lowest level of our hierarchy of factors in Arrangements 1 to 4. In discussing the sources of variation, we use the term *treatments* to refer to the conditions (treatment vs. control) factor.

Design 1

Design 1 is the between-systems design in which all factors are nested within a treatment or a control condition, and no factors are crossed. Three of the systems are randomly assigned to the treatment condition and three to the control condition. In the analysis of the data we have the sources of variation as shown in Table 18.42. The error term for treatments (i.e., the denominator of the F test for treatments) is the lowest numbered Roman numeral error term that we regard as a random factor. If we regard systems nested in treatments (I) as a random factor, then systems (I) is the error term for treatments. If we regard Term I as fixed but II as random, then II is the proper error term. If we regard both I and II as fixed and III as random, then III is the proper error term, and so on. If we could aggregate (e.g., by Paull's rule of $F < 2.00$) the fixed terms above the first random term (the lower Roman numeral error terms) with that first random term, then the fixed terms can be regarded as random effects. Thus, if Terms I, II, and III can be aggregated, we can generalize not only to other classes in the 24 schools (III), but also to other schools in the systems (II), *and* to other systems (I) as well. If we cannot aggregate the three error terms, and we had regarded Terms I and II as fixed and III as random, we could generalize only to other classrooms in the specific 24 schools that are part of the specific 6 systems.

TABLE 18.42
Sources of variation in Design 1 (Table 18.40)

	Sources	df	
	Between units (systems)	(5)	
	Treatments	1	
I	Systems nested in treatments	4	
	Within units	(954)	
II	Schools nested in systems	18	
III	Classes nested in schools	24	
IV	Children nested in classes	912	(48×19)
	Total	959	

Design 2

In Design 2 the treatments are applied within each of the six systems, with two schools randomly assigned to the treatment condition and two schools randomly assigned to the control condition. Therefore, there is a partial "de-nestification" so that treatments are now crossed by systems. That is to say, each condition (treatment and control) now co-occurs with every level of the systems factor of six levels. Within each combination of treatment and system, the remaining two schools are nested, the classes are still nested in their schools, and the children are still nested in their classrooms. The sources of variation for this design are shown in Table 18.43. Just as in Design I, the error term for treatments (i.e., the conditions of treatment vs. control) is the lowest numbered Roman numeral error term that we regard as a random effect. The rest of the discussion of Design 1 (e.g., aggregation of error terms) applies also to Design 2.

TABLE 18.43
Sources of variation in Design 2 (Table 18.40)

	Sources	df	
	Between units (systems)	5	
	Within units	(954)	
	Treatments	1	
I	Treatments $\times$ Systems	5	
II	Schools nested in treatments $\times$ Systems	12	
III	Classes nested in schools	24	
IV	Children nested in classes	912	(48×19)
	Total	959	

TABLE 18.44
Sources of variation in Design 3 (Table 18.40)

	Sources	df	
	Between units (schools)	(23)	
	Systems	5	
	Schools nested in systems	18	
	Within units	(936)	
	Treatments	1	
I	Treatments × Systems	5	
II	Treatments × Schools nested in systems	18	
III	Children nested in classes	912	(48 × 19)
	Total	959	

Design 3

The conditions (treatment and control) are implemented within each of the 24 schools in Design 3. Of the two classrooms in each of the 24 schools, one is randomly assigned to the treatment condition and the other is randomly assigned to the control condition. The "classrooms" term disappears because classrooms are intentionally confounded with treatments. The 24 schools are still nested within systems, but they are now crossed by the condition factor, and the children are still nested in their classrooms. The sources of variation for this design are shown in Table 18.44. Just as in Designs 1 and 2, the error term for treatments (i.e., treatment condition vs. control condition) is the lowest numbered Roman numeral error term that we regard as a random factor. The rest of the discussion of Design 1 applies also to Design 3.

Design 4

The conditions (treatment and control) in Design 4 are implemented in each of the 48 classrooms, with 10 children randomly assigned to the treatment condition and 10 children randomly assigned to the control condition. Classrooms are now the units of analysis, and they are crossed by the treatment factor. Children are still nested, but now within their Treatment × Classroom combination (i.e., within one of the 96 semi-classrooms of 10 children each). The sources of variation for this design are shown in Table 18.45. The selection of error terms for treatments is just as for the preceding designs (i.e., the lowest numbered Roman numeral error term that we regard as a random factor). The rest of the discussion of Design 1 applies also to Design 4.

Design 5

The conditions (treatment and control), in Design 5 are implemented within each of the 960 sampling units (i.e., children). Thus, each child is administered both the treatment and the control condition, with half the children randomly assigned to the treatment condition first, and the remainder to the control condition first. (For simplicity, we do not build the sequence of treatment first versus control first

TABLE 18.45
Sources of variation in Design 4 (Table 18.40)

	Sources	df
	Between units (classrooms)	(47)
	Systems	5
	Schools nested in systems	18
	Classes nested in schools	24
	Within units	(912)
	Treatments	1
I	Treatments × Systems	5
II	Treatments × Schools nested in systems	18
III	Treatments × Classes nested in schools	24
IV	Children nested in semiclasses	864 (96 semiclasses × 9)
	Total	959

into the analysis in Design 5, but we do so next in Design 5A). Children are now the units of analysis and they are crossed by the treatment factor. The sources of variation for Design 5 are shown in Table 18.46. The selection of error terms for the treatments factor is just as for the preceding designs (i.e., the lowest numbered Roman numeral error term that we regard as a random factor). The rest of the discussion of Design 1 applies also to Design 5.

TABLE 18.46
Sources of variation in Design 5 (Table 18.40)

	Sources	df
	Between units (children)	(959)
	Systems	5
	Schools nested in systems	18
	Classes nested in schools	24
	Children nested in classes	912 (48 × 19)
	Within Units	(960)
	Treatments	1
I	Treatments × Systems	5
II	Treatments × Schools nested in systems	18
III	Treatments × Classes nested in schools	24
IV	Treatments × Children nested in classes	912
	Total	1,919

Design 5A

The variant of Design 5 designated Design 5A builds the sequence of administration of treatments to children into the design as an additional factor. Design 5A
allows us to investigate the overall effect of the sequence (treatment, then control
vs. control, then treatment) and the effect of the Treatment × Sequence interaction,
which is actually an "alias" of the order effect comparing the first-administered to
the second-administered condition. A major improvement of the analysis shown in
Table 18.47 for Design 5A over that of Design 5 (in Table 18.46) is the systematic
decomposition of the 912 df error terms of Design 5 into five separate sources of
variation based on sequences ($df = 1$), systems ($df = 5$), schools ($df = 18$), classes
($df = 24$), and children ($df = 864$), which gives greater flexibility in the selection
of error terms. Selection of error terms for treatments is just as in the preceding
designs. Selection of error terms for the Treatments × Sequences interaction
(i.e., the effect of order) is the lowest lettered (A, then B, etc.) error term that we
regard as a random factor.

TABLE 18.47
Sources of variation in Design 5A

	Sources	df
	Between units (children)	(959)
	Systems	5
	Schools nested in systems	18
	Classes nested in schools	24
	Sequences	1
	Sequences × Systems	5
	Sequences × Schools nested in systems	18
	Sequences × Classes nested in schools	24
	Children nested in sequences × Classes	864 (96 × 9)
	Within units	(960)
	Treatments	1
I	Treatments × Systems	5
II	Treatments × Schools nested	18
III	Treatments × Classes nested	24
	Treatments × Sequences (order)	1
A	Treatments × Sequences × Systems	5
B	Treatments × Sequences × Schools	18
C	Treatments × Sequences × Classes	24
D IV	Treatments × Children nested	864
	Total	1,919

PART
VII

ADDITIONAL
TOPICS
IN DATA
ANALYSIS

CHAPTER
19

SIGNIFICANCE TESTING AND ASSOCIATION IN TABLES OF COUNTS

TABLE ANALYSIS AND CHI-SQUARE

In this chapter we present some material on the analysis of frequency counts that are cast into tabular form. Such *tables of counts* are also commonly known as *contingency tables,* and by far the most popular data-analytic procedure used with them is the chi-square (χ^2) test. Indeed, in an authoritative tutorial on "association and estimation in contingency tables," the statistician and social scientist Frederick Mosteller (1968) remarked that "the first act of most social scientists upon seeing a contingency table is to compute chi-square for it" (p. 1). He added, "Sometimes this process is enlightening, sometimes wasteful, but sometimes it does not go quite far enough" (p. 1). The chi-square test was introduced by Karl Pearson in 1900. Stigler (1986), in his book on the history of statistics, noted that Pearson had been preoccupied with the randomness of Monte Carlo roulette and, while in correspondence with another statistician (Francis Edgeworth), had described preliminary ideas for a goodness-of-fit statistical significance test. In 1894, Pearson published a polemic in which he urged colleagues to implore the French government to close the gaming salons and "hand over the remaining resources of the Casino to the Académie des Sciences for the endowment of a laboratory of orthodox probability" (quoted in Stigler, pp. 328–329). The chi-square test apparently evolved in Pearson's thinking in this pragmatic context.

Perhaps the most famous application of Pearson's significance test, however, was published in 1936 by R. A. Fisher to evaluate the great Austrian biologist Gregor Mendel's own reported data. In their history of the concept of probability, Gigerenzer et al. (1989) noted that the chi-square test had in fact been applied to the assessment of Mendelian hypotheses as early as 1912 by the American statistician J. A. Harris. It was Fisher, however, who in 1925 was inspired to use the test to decide whether deviations from expected Mendelian ratios were statistically significant enough to allow rejection of the hypothesis in question (Gigerenzer et al., 1989, p. 150). In 1936, Fisher wrote a paper in which he argued that Mendel's results were so close to what he had theoretically predicted as to raise a suspicion that the data had been "cooked." Among Mendel's predictions, for example, was a 3:1 ratio for round versus wrinkled peas, and his results were 5,474 round and 1,850 wrinkled peas. Similarly, a 3:1 ratio had been predicted for yellow to green peas, and the reported data were almost perfectly correct: 6,022 yellow and 2,001 green peas. Fisher surmised that it was not Mendel but an overzealous research assistant who had "adjusted" the results to the Mendelian ratio (Gigerenzer et al., 1989, pp. 151–152).

We have much to say about chi-square in this chapter, but because it is an approximate method, we also discuss an exact probability test developed by Fisher for 2×2 contingency tables when expected frequencies are quite small. When working with tables of counts larger than 2×2, there are several possible strategies, which we discuss in this chapter, including again the use of contrasts. We also describe an inspection procedure developed by Mosteller, which is particularly useful for larger tables of counts. In the case of 2×2 tables in biomedical trials, the Mosteller procedure frequently preserves a relationship known as the *odds ratio*. We illustrate the limitations of the odds ratio (and two other popular effect-size indicators in biomedical trials) and describe an adjusted approach based on the binomial effect-size display (Rosenthal, Rosnow, & Rubin, 2000). The 2×2 is not the smallest imaginable table of counts, nor are we limited only to two-dimensional tables of counts, and the chapter concludes with a discussion of one-sample tables in which there are two or more levels of just a single variable ($1 \times k$ tables of counts).

We are often asked *which procedure* or *which strategy* we recommend when researchers feel they must narrow their choices to one particular data-analytic approach. As we have said before, we almost always prefer statistical procedures that address specific, focused questions rather than diffuse, unfocused ones. But even within this framework, more than one approach is usually possible. That being the case, our habit is to recommend perhaps analyzing the data more than once, that is, by more than one focused test or by an approach from more than one exploratory perspective. The tenor of the conclusions reached should be unchanged, in which case we ought to have more confidence in the robustness of our inferences. Different strategies leading to different conclusions is a not-very-subtle hint to think deeply about *why* those conclusions are so tenuous. Continuing in the spirit of methodological pluralism, we again make a point in this chapter of demonstrating the utility (and the limitations) of different strategies for analyzing tables of counts. And as in previous discussions, we concentrate not just on the *p* values, but also on *r*-type indices of effect sizes for 1-*df* chi-square and other focused procedures.

THE 1-*df* CHI-SQUARE TEST

As is true of all statistical significance tests, the chi-square test can be understood in terms of a conceptual relationship (Equation 11.10) that we have referred to repeatedly in previous chapters, namely,

$$\text{Significance test} = \text{Size of effect} \times \text{Size of study.}$$

For 2×2 tables of independent frequencies, one specific form of this relationship was stated as follows in chapter 2 in the very first equation in this book (Equation 2.1):

$$\chi^2_{(1)} = \phi^2 \times N,$$

where $\chi^2_{(1)}$ is the chi-square test statistic on $df = 1$, and we determine df in any two-dimensional table of counts by multiplying the number of rows minus 1 by the number of columns minus 1. Thus, for a 2×2 table of counts we have $(2 - 1)(2 - 1) = 1$ df. We also referred to the term ϕ^2 (phi-square) in our discussion of correlation in chapter 11, where ϕ^2 was defined as the squared product-moment correlation between the variable represented by the two rows and the variable represented by the two columns in a 2×2 table of counts. As usual, N refers to the total number of sampling units, or in this case to the total number of independent frequencies in all four cells of the 2×2 table of counts.

Thus, $\chi^2_{(1)}$ can also be understood as a test of significance of the effect size estimate ϕ^2. To be consistent with our preference for product-moment correlation coefficients (rather than their squares) as effect size estimates, we might prefer to say that Z (the standard normal deviate and the square root of $\chi^2_{(1)}$) is a test of significance of ϕ because, as previously expressed in Equation 11.15,

$$Z = \phi \times \sqrt{N}.$$

When computing χ^2 from tables of counts, it is essential to keep the independence assumption in mind. Thus, in a 2×2 table, there must be N independent sampling units, each having contributed to only one of the four cells of the 2×2 table. It would not do, for example, to have $N/2$ sampling units, each having contributed two observations to the total number of observations (N).

We would also like the frequencies that are *expected* in each cell, if the null hypothesis of no relationship is true, not to be too small. At one time it was thought that an expected frequency should not fall below 5 for any cell. Evidence now indicates, however, that very usable χ^2 values can be obtained even with expected frequencies as low as 1, that is, as long as the total number of independent observations (N) is not too small. We know from the work of Gregory Camilli and Kenneth Hopkins (1978) that an N of 20 is large enough, but that small expected frequencies may work quite well in even smaller studies. The same authors also showed that corrections for continuity may do more harm than good. One adjustment for continuity, the *Yates correction,* involves reducing each occurrence of the term $O - E$ by 0.5 before using the computational formula for $\chi^2_{(1)}$, expressed in Equation 11.14 as

$$\chi^2_{(1)} = \Sigma \frac{(O - E)^2}{E},$$

where O is the observed frequency in each cell, and E is the expected frequency in that cell (see our earlier discussion in chapter 11). (We have more to say about the Yates correction later in this chapter.)

LARGER TABLES OF COUNTS

There is a growing literature on the analysis of tables of counts of any size, much of it emphasizing the *log-linear model*. A definitive text using that model was coauthored by Yvonne Bishop, Stephen Fienberg, and Paul Holland (1975). An excellent brief introduction can be found in Hays (1994), and discussions of varying intermediate lengths are available in texts by Agresti (2002), Everitt (1977, 1992), Fienberg (1977), Fleiss, Levin, and Paik (2003), Kennedy (1983, 1992), and Upton (1978). The log-linear model approaches tables of counts in a manner analogous to analysis of variance. Though we do not describe the log-linear model in this book, our approach to contingency tables larger than 2×2 is consistent with the use of log-linear contrasts as developed by John Kennedy and Andy Bush (1988) and with our preference for testing focused rather than omnibus hypotheses. Just as in our approach to the F statistic, in which we want the numerator df to be no greater than unity, we also want the df for any χ^2 tests to be no greater than unity. (The denominator df for F is roughly analogous to N in tables of counts, and given a choice, we like *those* quantities to be large rather than small.)

Dummy-Coding Qualitative Data

In chapter 11 we saw how we could quantify qualitative data in the specific case of the 2×2 table of counts reproduced in Table 19.1. As noted earlier, the small group sizes are for pedagogical convenience, as we assume that the sample sizes in an investigation of this nature would be substantially larger. The qualitative difference shown between the two groups can be quantified simply by assigning the value of 0 to one group and the value of 1 to the other. Thus, if we gave "being a Republican" a 1 and "being a Democrat" a 0, we would have a scale of "Republican-ness," and if we assigned a 1 to "being a Democrat," we would have a scale of "Democrat-ness." Similarly, we can assign a 0 or a 1 to the dependent variable of item response. If we assigned a 1 to "yes" and a 0 to "no," we would have a scale of agreement with the item, or "yes-ness," and reversing the numbers would give us a scale of disagreement, or "no-ness." Using the procedure described in chapter 11 (and Equation 11.12), we find that $\phi = .60$ when being a Republican is coded 1 and responding "yes" is coded 1, whereas "Democrat" and "no" are coded 0.

TABLE 19.1
Illustration of 2 × 2 table of counts

	Democrats	Republicans	Σ
Yes	1	4	5
No	4	1	5
Σ	5	5	10

Imagine, however, that we have instead the 2 × 3 contingency table shown in Part A of Table 19.2. We could still dummy-code the yes-versus-no dependent variable as before. But what should we do with the three levels of the independent variable? Suppose we know nothing at all about the composition of the "Others"

TABLE 19.2
Illustration of 2 × 3 table of counts

A. The 2 × 3 table

		Independent variable			
		Democrats	Republicans	Others	Σ
Dependent variable	Yes	1	4	2	7
	No	4	1	2	7
	Σ	5	5	4	14

B. Individual respondents and dummy-coded variables

	Dependent variable	Independent variable		
	Agreement	"Democrat-ness"	"Republican-ness"	"Other-ness"
Respondent 1	1	1	0	0
Respondent 2	1	0	1	0
Respondent 3	1	0	1	0
Respondent 4	1	0	1	0
Respondent 5	1	0	1	0
Respondent 6	1	0	0	1
Respondent 7	1	0	0	1
Respondent 8	0	1	0	0
Respondent 9	0	1	0	0
Respondent 10	0	1	0	0
Respondent 11	0	1	0	0
Respondent 12	0	0	1	0
Respondent 13	0	0	0	1
Respondent 14	0	0	0	1

C. Intercorrelations among the four variables

	Agreement	"Democrat-ness"	"Republican-ness"	"Other-ness"
Agreement	—	−.45	+.45	.00
"Democrat-ness"		—	−.56	−.47
"Republican-ness"			—	−.47
"Other-ness"				—

group; then it would make no sense to assign that group a value of .5. The reason is that doing so would mean creating a scale in which that group is assumed to belong halfway between the anchoring ends of our Democrat-Republican scale. That might be a reasonable numerical assignment for some political group, but not for one whose composition is a mystery to us. Instead, we would create a series of dummy variables as follows:

"Democrat-ness"	Democrats = 1;	Republicans = 0;	Others = 0
"Republican-ness"	Republicans = 1;	Democrats = 0;	Others = 0
"Other-ness"	Others = 1;	Democrats = 0;	Republicans = 0

Given the three dummy-coded groups and the single dummy-coded dependent variable of "Yes-ness" (or agreement with the item presented), we might rewrite the data as shown in Part B of Table 19.2. The table of intercorrelations (phi coefficients) among the four variables is shown in Part C. Inspecting that correlation matrix informs us that the Republicans, compared with the non-Republicans (Democrats-plus-Others), were more likely to agree with the particular item (i.e., answer it "yes"). The Democrats, compared with the non-Democrats (Republicans-plus-Others), were less likely to agree with the item, and being in the category Other rather than non-Other (Democrats-plus-Republicans) was unrelated to agreement. Notice as well that the three correlations among the independent variables are all negative and comparatively strong, as we might expect. That is, we might expect this result on the assumption that the more one belongs to Group A, the "less" one can belong to Group B or Group C. In the extreme case of just two variables (e.g., Democrat vs. Republican), the intercorrelation would be -1.00, so no information would be gained by the use of both variables.

Ordering the Levels of a Dimension

Sometimes we can do better than dummy-coding the variables. Instead, if we can order the levels of a dimension on some underlying conceptual continuum, we can create a score that is based on the position of each row or each column on the continuum. Suppose we obtain the observational data shown in Part A of Table 19.3. Rather than form a series of dummy variables, we might choose to conceptualize "severity of depression" as a predictor variable (i.e., an independent variable), so that

$$\begin{array}{lll} \text{Mildly depressed} = 1 & \left(\text{or } 0\right) & \left(\text{or } -1\right) \\ \text{Moderately depressed} = 2 & \left|\text{or } 1\right| & \left|\text{or } 0\right| \\ \text{Severely depressed} = 3 & \left(\text{or } 2\right) & \left(\text{or } +1\right) \end{array}$$

Similarly, we can create a scaled dependent variable of "degree of improvement after therapy," so that

$$\begin{array}{lll} \text{No improvement} = 1 & \left(\text{or } 0\right) & \left(\text{or } -1\right) \\ \text{Slight improvement} = 2 & \left|\text{or } 1\right| & \left|\text{or } 0\right| \\ \text{Moderate improvement} = 3 & \left(\text{or } 2\right) & \left(\text{or } +1\right) \end{array}$$

TABLE 19.3
Counts with ordered levels

A. Observed frequencies

	Level of improvement			
Level of depression	**None**	**Slight**	**Moderate**	**Σ**
Mildly depressed	1	2	5	8
Moderately depressed	2	5	1	8
Severely depressed	5	2	1	8
Σ	8	9	7	24

B. Scaled scores for independent variable (IV) and dependent variable (DV)

Level of depression (IV)					
Mild (n = 8)		**Moderate (n = 8)**		**Severe (n = 8)**	
IV	**DV**	**IV**	**DV**	**IV**	**DV**
1	1	2	1	3	1
1	2	2	1	3	1
1	2	2	2	3	1
1	3	2	2	3	1
1	3	2	2	3	1
1	3	2	2	3	2
1	3	2	2	3	2
1	3	2	3	3	3

We then simply compute the correlation (r) between the level of depression and the level of improvement. Part B of Table 19.3 shows, for each of the 24 scores, the independent variable (IV) score of 1, 2, or 3 and the dependent variable (DV) score of 1, 2, or 3. Correlating those paired scores gives us $r = -.52$, implying that increasing levels of depression had a tendency to be associated with decreasing levels of improvement. As described in chapter 11, we can test the significance of that r by means of t (using Equation 2.2). It would *not* do simply to test significance by means of the $\chi^2_{(4)}$ test on the results in Part A, that is, the chi-square test with $df = (3 - 1)(3 - 1) = 4$. The reason is not just that the expected frequencies might be somewhat low for our taste. Rather, it is that the overall $\chi^2_{(4)}$ addresses a different, more diffuse hypothesis, namely, that there is "some type of relationship" between rows and columns in Part A, instead of the more focused hypothesis of a linear relationship addressed by Equation 2.2 (the t test for r). In reporting these results we would want to make clear that this was a relational-type study, and thus, no conclusion of a *causal* relationship is implied.

DISTRIBUTIONS OF CHI-SQUARE

The chi-square for a contingency table of any size is most easily computed from the general expression of the formula reiterated earlier (Equation 11.14) as

$$\chi^2 = \Sigma \frac{(O - E)^2}{E}.$$

This quantity, when based on independent observations and expected frequencies not too small, tends to be distributed as chi-square on $df =$ (number of rows $-$ 1) $\times$ (number of columns -1).

As is the case for t (chapter 13) and for F (chapter 14), there is a different chi-square distribution for every value of df. However, recall that F distributions begin at zero and range to positive infinity, whereas the symmetrical bell shape of t distributions is always centered at 0. Hence, we noted that the expected value of t is zero when the null hypothesis (H_0) is true, and the expected value of F is $df/(df - 2)$, where these df are for the denominator mean square. All chi-square distributions also begin at zero and range upward to positive infinity. The expected value of a chi-square distribution when the H_0 of no relationship between row and column frequencies is true is equal to the degrees of freedom defining the particular chi-square distribution. Thus, for χ^2 tests based on 1, 4, and 10 df, the average values of the χ^2 obtained if the H_0 is true are 1, 4, and 10, respectively. The median value of a given chi-square

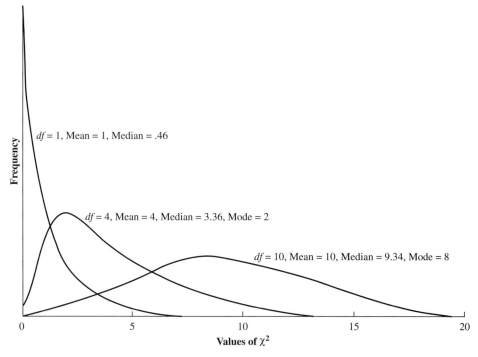

FIGURE 19.1
Three chi-square distributions, with $df = 1$, 4, and 10, respectively.

TABLE 19.4

Chi-square values required for significance at various p levels

					p level				
df	.80	.50	.30	.20	.10	.05	.02	.01	.001
1	.06	.46	1.07	1.64	2.71	3.84	5.41	6.64	10.83
2	.45	1.39	2.41	3.22	4.60	5.99	7.82	9.21	13.82
3	1.00	2.37	3.66	4.64	6.25	7.82	9.84	11.34	16.27
4	1.65	3.36	4.88	5.99	7.78	9.49	11.67	13.28	18.46
5	2.34	4.35	6.06	7.29	9.24	11.07	13.39	15.09	20.52
6	3.07	5.35	7.23	8.56	10.64	12.59	15.03	16.81	22.46
8	4.59	7.34	9.52	11.03	13.36	15.51	18.17	20.09	26.12
10	6.18	9.34	11.78	13.44	15.99	18.31	21.16	23.21	29.59
15	10.31	14.34	17.32	19.31	22.31	25.00	28.26	30.58	37.70
20	14.58	19.34	22.78	25.04	28.41	31.41	35.02	37.57	45.32
25	18.94	24.34	28.17	30.68	34.38	37.65	41.57	44.31	52.62
30	23.36	29.34	33.53	36.25	40.26	43.77	47.96	50.89	59.70

Note: For $df > 30$, we can estimate the p value for any χ^2 by first finding the standard normal deviate Z associated with that p (e.g., $Z = 1.96$ is associated with $p = .05$ two-tailed). We find Z from $Z = \sqrt{2\chi^2} - \sqrt{2df - 1}$.

distribution tends to be just less than the mean (df), and the mode for χ^2 distributions of $df = 2$ or more is $df - 2$.

As is also characteristic of F, values of χ^2 further and further into the right-hand tail are less and less likely if the null hypothesis is true and are used to suggest that the null hypothesis is probably false. Although in data-analytic work we use tables of chi-square and computer output rather than pictured distributions, it is instructive to see some examples of χ^2 distributions. Figure 19.1 (after Lindquist, 1953) displays three such distributions. Notice that they move to the right with an increase in df, and they tend to show greater symmetry as well. Table 19.4 shows the differences in various χ^2 distributions by giving the area found to the right of the tabled values. Thus, for a single degree of freedom, the table shows that a χ^2 value of 3.84 would be found only 5% (i.e., .05) of the time if the null hypothesis of no relationship were true. A value of 10.83 or greater would be found only 0.1% (i.e., .001) of the time.

PROCEDURES FOR LARGER CONTINGENCY TABLES

For our illustration of the analysis of a table larger than 2×2, we present the results of a 3×3 study that will serve as a continuing illustration through much of our discussion (Gilbert, McPeek, & Mosteller, 1977). The units in this study consist of 53 medical investigations that can be categorized along two dimensions, each comprising three levels. One dimension is the degree of experimental control achieved by the investigators; the second dimension is the degree of enthusiasm shown by the

TABLE 19.5
Study by Gilbert, McPeek, and Mosteller (1977)

A. The 3 × 3 table of counts

	Degree of enthusiasm			
Degree of control	High	Medium	Low	Σ
High	0	3	3	6
Medium	10	3	2	15
Low	24	7	1	32
Σ	34	13	6	53

B. Expected frequencies for results in Part A

	Degree of enthusiasm			
Degree of control	High	Medium	Low	Σ
High	3.85	1.47	0.68	6.00
Medium	9.62	3.68	1.70	15.00
Low	20.53	7.85	3.62	32.00
Σ	34.00	13.00	6.00	53.00

C. Table of $(O - E)^2/E$ values (or "partial" chi-square values)

	Degree of enthusiasm			
Degree of control	High	Medium	Low	Σ
High	3.85	1.59	7.92	13.36
Medium	0.02	0.13	0.05	0.20
Low	0.59	0.09	1.90	2.58
Σ	4.46	1.81	9.87	16.14

investigators for their newly tested medical treatments. The categorizing of those 53 investigations is shown in Part A of Table 19.5. We begin by describing the computation of an omnibus chi-square (i.e., χ^2 with $df > 1$) on those data. As we have stated repeatedly, omnibus statistical tests are generally deficient in that they are diffuse and unfocused, seldom telling us precisely what we want to know. Thus, we will also illustrate some alternative or follow-up analyses for the same data.

Omnibus Chi-Square Analysis

For each of the observed (O) frequencies in Part A of Table 19.5, we need also to compute the expected (E) values around which those observed frequencies fluctuate only moderately if the null hypothesis of no relationship between the rows and columns is true. We find the expected (E) value for each cell by multiplying the row total of the row to which the cell belongs by the column total to which the cell belongs, then dividing the product by the total number (N) of observations. That is,

$$E = \frac{\text{Row total} \times \text{Column total}}{N}. \qquad (19.1)$$

To illustrate for the upper-left cell value of zero in the table of counts, substituting in Equation 19.1 gives us an expected frequency of $(6 \times 34)/53 = 3.85$. When we do these calculations for each cell of observed frequencies, we obtain the expected frequencies shown in Part B of Table 19.5. Notice that the row and column totals (i.e., the marginal values) are identical in A and B, as they should be if our calculations are correct.

We now simply substitute in the general equation for the chi-square test, which was given as

$$\chi^2 = \Sigma \frac{(O - E)^2}{E},$$

and we find

$$\chi^2_{(4)} = \frac{(0 - 3.85)^2}{3.85} + \frac{(3 - 1.47)^2}{1.47} + \frac{(3 - 0.68)^2}{0.68}$$
$$+ \frac{(10 - 9.62)^2}{9.62} + \frac{(3 - 3.68)^2}{3.68} + \frac{(2 - 1.70)^2}{1.70}$$
$$+ \frac{(24 - 20.53)^2}{20.53} + \frac{(7 - 7.85)^2}{7.85} + \frac{(1 - 3.62)^2}{3.62}$$
$$= 16.13.$$

Another way of visualizing these calculations is shown in Part C of Table 19.5, where the sum of the $(O - E)^2/E$ cell entries is the value of $\chi^2_{(4)}$. (The final table value of 16.14 differs slightly from the result above, 16.13, because the "partial" chi-square values and marginal values are rounded off to two decimal places.) The degrees of freedom are denoted by the subscript in $\chi^2_{(4)}$. Another reporting standard notes the degrees of freedom and total sample size in parentheses, followed by the significance level, which in this example would be reported as $\chi^2(4, N = 53) = 16.13, p = .0028$. No effect size estimate is indicated because this is an omnibus chi-square (i.e., $df > 1$).

A chi-square value this large or larger (i.e., occurring only .0028 of the time in repeated sampling if the null hypothesis of no relationship between the row and column variables of experimental control and enthusiasm of the investigator is true) unfortunately tells us only that there is likely to be some sort of relationship. However, the significant χ^2 tells us nothing at all about the type of relationship there might be. The situation is analogous to that of an omnibus F test (i.e., F with more than 1 df in the numerator) in which we must also examine the condition means to see what the results actually show. In the present case we might inspect the individual $(O - E)^2/E$ cell entries (or "partial" chi-square values) to see which contributed most and least to the omnibus χ^2. Then again, as we show next, more satisfactory approaches to tables larger than 2 × 2 are available than settling for an omnibus χ^2 test of $df > 1$.

Analysis of Variance on Qualitative Data

One alternative to the χ^2 test on qualitative data involves the application of analysis of variance. In this approach, suggested by William Cochran (1950), we begin by quantifying the qualitative data as we described earlier in this chapter. If the rows or columns representing the dependent variable can be scaled or ordered, as in our earlier case of three levels of improvement (scored 1, 2, or 3), then each sampling unit can be assigned one of several numbers to serve as the dependent variable score. Even if scaling is not possible, we can still create a number of dependent variables, each one dummy-coded (0 or 1). Once we have scaled or dummy-coded (a special case of scaling) a score for each unit (e.g., for each subject), we compute the analysis of variance in the usual way. However, now the unit's scores will be only 0 or 1; or 1, 2, or 3; or some other (usually small) set of possible values.

Except for very small studies (say, $df < 20$), and for very extreme splits of dichotomous (i.e., 0 vs. 1) data, the F tests obtained from the analysis of variance generally give quite accurate results (Edwards, 1972; Hsu & Feldt, 1969; Lunney, 1970; Snedecor & Cochran, 1989; Winer, Brown, & Michels, 1991). Commonly regarded as an extreme dichotomous split would be one in which 90% of the observations were of one type (0 or 1) and 10% were of the other type. When neither especially small sample sizes nor extreme splits pose a problem, Cochran (1950) suggested that results based on F might, under some conditions, be more accurate than those based on chi-square. Ralph D'Agostino (1971; following Snedecor & Cochran, 1967) showed that, even for fairly extreme splits, transformations (e.g., arcsin, logit) can usually be used to make the analysis of variance still work well.

We will illustrate the use of analysis of variance by using the data of our continuing example, but we can do better than dichotomize the dependent variable of degree of enthusiasm. We can assign the scale scores of 1, 2, and 3 to the categories low, medium, and high levels of enthusiasm, respectively. We then write the scores for each of the three levels of the independent variable of degree of experimental control as shown in Table 19.6

TABLE 19.6
Analysis of variance of χ^2 results reported by Gilbert, McPeek, and Mosteller (1977)

A. Listing of scores in Part A of Table 19.5

Degree of control	Listing of scores	Mean
High (6 observations)	2 2 2 1 1 1	1.50
Medium (15 observations)	3 3 3 3 3 3 3 3 3 3 2 2 2 1 1	2.53
Low (32 observations)	3 3 3 3 3 3 3 3 3 3 3 3 3 3 3 3 3 3 3 3 3 3 3 2 2 2 2 2 2 2 2 1	2.72

B. Summary ANOVA

Source	SS	df	MS	F	η	p
Between conditions	7.505	2	3.753	10.60	.55	1.5^{-4}
Within conditions	17.702	50	0.354			

(Part A). The results of the overall ANOVA are shown in Part B, and we note that the p value of the omnibus F test ($p = .00015$) is smaller than the p value of the omnibus chi-square ($p = .0028$). We might have expected this outcome if we felt that degree of enthusiasm would be affected by degree of control, because the scores used in the analysis of variance were able to use the information that $3 > 2 > 1$. The omnibus χ^2 would not have been any different even if levels of enthusiasm (columns) had been interchanged.

Focused Contrasts on Qualitative Data

Although our omnibus F used more information than did the omnibus χ^2, the omnibus F still addressed only a diffuse question. For the conditions of high, medium, and low degree of control in Part A of Table 19.6, we see that the row means are 1.50, 2.53, and 2.72, respectively. The pattern of these means implies that studies reflecting a higher degree of control elicited, on average, less enthusiasm from the investigators than did studies reflecting a lower degree of control. Of course, the p value for that statement has not yet been determined. The omnibus F implies only that the three row means differ somehow. As we saw in chapter 15, most omnibus tests of significance are best replaced by planned contrasts. In the present case, let us assume that we predicted a negative linear relationship between degree of experimental control and level of enthusiasm for the results. We compute a planned contrast with λ weights of -1, 0, $+1$ for the mean levels of enthusiasm found for studies categorized as reflecting high, medium, and low degrees of control, respectively. The formula for t_{contrast} in Equation 15.4 was

$$t_{\text{contrast}} = \frac{\Sigma(M_i \lambda_i)}{\sqrt{MS_{\text{within}} \left(\Sigma \frac{\lambda_i^2}{n_i} \right)}},$$

and substituting in this equation we find

$$t_{\text{contrast}} = \frac{(1.50)(-1) + (2.53)(0) + (2.72)(+1)}{\sqrt{.354 \left[\frac{(-1)^2}{6} + \frac{(0)^2}{15} + \frac{(+1)^2}{32} \right]}}$$

$$= \frac{1.22}{\sqrt{.0701}} = 4.61,$$

which, with $df = 50$, has an associated one-tailed $p = 1.4^{-5}$ or two-tailed $p = 2.8^{-5}$. Using Equation 15.12, we find $r_{\text{contrast}} = .55$.

How do we report these results? In an earlier discussion we mentioned our preference for reporting the effect size indicator as positive when the pattern of observed results is in the predicted direction and negative when the observed relationship is in the opposite direction of what was predicted. This convention is particularly useful in meta-analytic work (to be discussed in chapter 21). On the other hand, some researchers might prefer to report the r_{contrast} as negative in this case just to remind readers (and themselves) that *high* degrees of control were associated with *low* degrees of enthusiasm. Because of these two practices, it is recommended that the researcher explain in a sentence or two which practice is being followed in the research report. In this discussion we will think of r_{contrast} as $-.55$ simply as a reminder to ourselves that high degrees of control are associated with low degrees of enthusiasm.

In our discussion of contrasts (in chapter 15) we mentioned that we often want to compute focused statistical tests on other people's data. In such situations we may lack the information required to compute Equation 15.4 because, for example, we are not given MS_{within} (i.e., S^2_{pooled}) or the sample sizes for each of the groups. In that earlier discussion we described a procedure for computing $F_{contrast}$ (Equation 15.5) when all we have are the minimal ingredients of an omnibus F test and the condition means. We mentioned that it is easy enough to compute the alerting r between those condition means and our lambda weights (also symbolized as $r_{M\lambda}$). Given this basic information, we can also usually get a very useful approximate $t_{contrast}$ from the following equation (Rosenthal & Rosnow, 1985):

$$t_{contrast} = \sqrt{(r^2_{alerting})(F_{omnibus})(df_{numerator})}, \tag{19.2}$$

where $r^2_{alerting}$ is the square of the correlation between the condition means and their associated contrast (λ) weights; $F_{omnibus}$ is the overall, diffuse F test comparing the condition means; and $df_{numerator}$ is the number of degrees of freedom in the numerator of the $F_{omnibus}$. It will be recalled from our discussion in chapter 15 that multiplying $F_{omnibus}$ by $df_{numerator}$ gives us the maximum possible contrast F that can be carved out of the sum of squares of the numerator of the overall F test.

For our example, we return to the omnibus $F(2, 50) = 10.60$ as shown in the ANOVA of Table 19.6. We obtained that F by comparing the three degrees of experimental control. Now all we require to apply Equation 19.2 is the correlation between the condition means of 1.50, 2.53, and 2.72 and their associated contrast weights of -1, 0, and $+1$, respectively, which we square to obtain $r^2_{M\lambda}$ (i.e., $r^2_{alerting}$). Using a calculator we find that $r^2_{alerting} = .8635$, and therefore $t_{contrast} = \sqrt{(.8635)(10.60)(2)} = 4.28$, $p = 8.4^{-5}$ two-tailed, and $r_{contrast} = -.52$, a result not so very different from the $r_{contrast}$ of $-.55$ obtained from the $t_{contrast}$ value of 4.61 reported a few paragraphs earlier. (We again think of our obtained $r_{contrast}$ as a negative value simply to remind ourselves that degree of control was inversely related to level of enthusiasm.)

Correlational Approach

A fourth and quite direct estimate of the size of the relationship between the categorized variables is illustrated in Table 19.7. Because the independent variable of degree of experimental control can be scaled (i.e., high = 3, medium = 2, low = 1), we can correlate it with the dependent variable of enthusiasm (also scored 1, 2, 3). Those scaled scores are shown in Table 19.7, and correlating the 53 paired scores results in $r(51) = -.49$, $t(51) = 3.97$, $p = 2.3^{-4}$ two-tailed, a value that is in fairly good agreement with those obtained by our two previous methods (yielding values of $-.52$ and $-.55$).

SUBDIVIDING TABLES TO TEST SPECIFIC HYPOTHESES

By using an analysis of variance approach to tables of counts, we were able to apply familiar methods (t tests, contrasts, and correlations) to the investigation of specific hypotheses rather than having to settle for an overall, unfocused, diffuse χ^2. Methods are also available for computing contrasts in the log-linear models, but we will not

SIGNIFICANCE TESTING AND ASSOCIATION IN TABLES OF COUNTS **599**

TABLE 19.7

Scaled scores for independent variable (IV) of degree of control and dependent variable (DV) of degree of enthusiasm

Degree of control (IV)					
High ($n = 6$)		Medium ($n = 15$)		Low ($n = 32$)	
IV	DV	IV	DV	IV	DV
3	1	2	1	1	1
3	1	2	1	1	2
3	1	2	2	1	2
3	2	2	2	1	2
3	2	2	2	1	2
3	2	2	3	1	2
		2	3	1	2
		2	3	1	2
		2	3	1	3
		2	3	1	3
		2	3	1	3
		2	3	1	3
		2	3	1	3
		2	3	1	3
		2	3	1	3
				1	3
				1	3
				1	3
				1	3
				1	3
				1	3
				1	3
				1	3
				1	3
				1	3
				1	3
				1	3
				1	3
				1	3
				1	3
				1	3
				1	3

cover them here. For a detailed discussion, see Bishop, Fienberg, and Holland (1975). Here we describe only some simple, useful methods for subdividing tables of counts into one or more 2×2 tables, each based on only a single *df*. That is, each table addresses only a single question. Although these are not contrasts in the usual sense, they are very much in the spirit of contrasts.

Chi-Square Corner-Cells Test

When data in both the rows and the columns can be arranged in a meaningful order from more to less of that variable, a simple $\chi^2_{(1)}$ test can be performed on the four corner cells of the contingency table. Because this test does not use as much information as the analysis of variance with contrasts, we recommend it only as a quick preliminary test. The chi-square corner-cells test examines the effects of the most extreme levels of the independent variable on the distribution of cases between the most extreme possible outcomes. The example of degree of experimental control and degree of enthusiasm is a good case in point. Because both the rows and the columns in the original 3×3 table (Part A of Table 19.5) were arranged in an order of magnitude (high, medium, low), the corner-cells test is applicable.

The four corners of the original 3×3 table of counts are shown again in Part A of Table 19.8, and the expected frequencies are shown in Part B. For example, to obtain the expected frequency in the upper-left corner, we substituted in Equation 19.1 to find $(3 \times 24)/28 = 2.57$. The resulting $\chi^2_{(1)}$ is the sum of the $(O - E)^2/E$ values in Part C or, more precisely calculated, 20.16, $p = 7.1^{-6}$, and $\phi = -.85$. The size of the effect

TABLE 19.8
Illustration for chi-square corner-cells test

A. Corners of table of counts in Table 19.5

	High	Low	Σ
High	0	3	3
Low	24	1	25
Σ	24	4	28

B. Expected frequencies computed from marginals

	High	Low	Σ
High	2.57	0.43	3.00
Low	21.43	3.57	25.00
Σ	24.00	4.00	28.00

C. Table of $(O - E)^2/E$ values

	High	Low	Σ
High	2.57	15.36	17.93
Low	0.31	1.85	2.16
Σ	2.88	17.21	20.09

is, of course, "inflated" by our having compared extreme groups rather than using all, or nearly all, the scores. There is nothing wrong with this approach, as good research design frequently involves choosing extreme groups. However, it is important to keep in mind that the large χ^2 and phi are due in part to our having chosen extreme groups on both the independent and the dependent variables. Another issue to be addressed, though, is that the expected frequency of 0.43 is too small for comfort. One way to get an "independent opinion" about the correct significance level is to use the Fisher exact test, which we consider in some detail in a moment. Another way to get a second opinion is to use the combined-category chi-square test.

Combined-Category Chi-Square Test

This test combines adjacent rows or columns that have been meaningfully arranged from higher to lower levels of the variables that are defined by the rows and columns. Our corner-cells test involved the four corners of the 3×3 table of counts in Table 19.5, as shown in Part A of Table 19.8. Expected frequencies for the four corners were given in Part B of Table 19.8, where the upper-right corner cell shows the very low expected frequency (0.43). Hence, that cell is most in need of having its expected frequency increased. There are two ways of increasing the expected frequency by combining categories: We can recruit (a) the row or (b) the column adjacent to the cell (or any other cell that is in need of augmented expected frequency). Recruiting the adjacent row, we get the obtained and expected frequencies in Part A of Table 19.9, yielding $\chi^2_{(1)} = 6.32$, $p = .012$, $\phi = -.40$. And recruiting the adjacent column, we get the obtained and expected frequencies in Part B of Table 19.9, yielding $\chi^2_{(1)} = 12.21$, $p = .0005$, $\phi = -.57$.

TABLE 19.9
Illustration for combined-category chi-square test

A. Recruiting the adjacent row of Table 19.5

	Obtained frequencies				Expected frequencies		
	High	Low	Σ		High	Low	Σ
High	10	5	15	High	12.75	2.25	15.00
Low	24	1	25	Low	21.25	3.75	25.00
Σ	34	6	40	Σ	34.00	6.00	40.00

B. Recruiting the adjacent column of Table 19.5

	Obtained frequencies				Expected frequencies		
	High	Low	Σ		High	Low	Σ
High	0	6	6	High	3.79	2.21	6.00
Low	24	8	32	Low	20.21	11.79	32.00
Σ	24	14	38	Σ	24.00	14.00	38.00

It is not appropriate to compute both of those chi-squares and present only the results of the more "favorable" test. We either report both sets of results or adopt a set of rules beforehand telling us which chi-square to compute. For example, Rule 1 might be that we choose the table of which the smallest expected frequency is 5 or more. Were both tables (or neither table) to give an expected frequency of 5 or more, we would go to Rule 2, which might be that we choose the table with the more nearly equal (in percentage of total N) column totals, on the grounds that binomial data are better behaved when the splits are closer to 50:50. A third rule, if it is needed, might be to choose the table with the more nearly equal row totals (i.e., in the percentage of total N), on the grounds that groups more nearly equal in size generally yield more powerful tests of significance. Note that in our terminology we have used *columns* to refer to the dependent variable and *rows* to refer to the independent variable. If we choose to set up our table differently, the rows and columns of Rules 2 and 3 above become the columns and rows, respectively. Of course, whatever rationale we adopt, we need to report it as well as the relevant results.

In the present situation, Rule 1 would not help, because neither the recruitment of rows nor the recruitment of columns would lead to the smallest expected frequency reaching or exceeding 5. Rule 2, however, would lead us to choose the column recruitment method, because it yields a column split of 63% versus 37% of the total N, whereas the row recruitment method yields a column split of 85% versus 15% of the total N. In this example the column recruitment method results in $\phi = -.57$, a value that agrees fairly well with the correlations obtained by the various other procedures described earlier ($-.55$, $-.52$, $-.49$). Sometimes neither the recruitment of rows nor the recruitment of columns helps much to increase the expected frequency of the cell with the smallest expected frequency. In that case we can continue to recruit columns or rows until we have achieved a satisfactory expected frequency.

FISHER EXACT PROBABILITY TEST

The Fisher exact test is another way to get a second opinion about the data in a 2 × 2 table of counts. A detailed discussion is available in Siegel (1956) and in Siegel and Castellan (1988), and a shorter discussion can be found in Hays (1994) and various other texts. We find the Fisher exact test especially useful when we have a 2 × 2 table of independent observations, as in the 2 × 2 chi-square situation, but when the expected frequencies are very low. The Fisher exact test gives us the one-tailed p that could have occurred for a particular table of counts, or one reflecting a still stronger relationship between the two variables, if the null hypothesis of no relationship between the row and column variables were true and if the row and column totals were regarded as fixed. With cells and marginal values labeled as illustrated below:

Group	Dependent variable		
	High	**Low**	
High	A	B	$(A + B)$
Low	C	D	$(C + D)$
	$(A + C)$	$(B + D)$	$N = (A + B + C + D)$

we find p for any one outcome (i.e., the obtained outcome, or one more extremely disconfirming of the null hypothesis of no relationship between row and column variables) from the following equation:

$$p = \frac{(A+B)!(C+D)!(A+C)!(B+D)!}{N!A!B!C!D!}. \tag{19.3}$$

In using the Fisher exact test we compute p for our obtained table *and for each possible table showing a more extreme outcome than the one we obtained.* The p that we use to test our hypothesis of no relationship is the sum of those p values.

Fisher Exact Test on the Most Extreme Cell Entries

The data for which we are seeking a second opinion are those in Part A of Table 19.8. In this case the table of counts is the most extreme one (i.e., the result most inconsistent with the null hypothesis of no relationship between the variables) that we could possibly obtain given the fixed row and column marginal totals. We know that these are the most extreme results because when one of the four cell entries is zero, we cannot have a more extreme result (i.e., given the fact that the marginals are fixed). Therefore, we need only obtain a single p value, and applying Equation 19.3 to those extreme cell entries gives us

$$p = \frac{(3!)(25!)(24!)(4!)}{(28!)(0!)(3!)(24!)(1!)} = .0012,$$

which we interpret to mean that there is only a 12-in-10,000 chance of obtaining cell entries as extreme as those shown in Part A of Table 19.8 if there is no relationship between the independent and dependent variables (given the fixed row and column totals for those data). Using Equation 19.3 would be burdensome without a computer or a programmable scientific calculator with sufficient memory. (Recall that, e.g., $12! = 1 \times 2 \times 3 \times 4 \times 5 \times 6 \times 7 \times 8 \times 9 \times 10 \times 11 \times 12 = 479,001,600$; also recall that $0! = 1! = 1$.) There are tables available for the Fisher exact test (e.g., Siegel, 1956; Siegel & Castellan, 1988; Zar, 1984), but it is preferable to compute the actual p rather than to use only critical values of p.

Our Fisher exact probability result of .0012 (or 1.2^{-3}), although significant, is not nearly as impressive as the p of 7.1^{-6} (or .0000071) based on our chi-square corner-cells test. The difference appears to be due primarily to the unusually small expected frequency (0.43) in Cell B of Table 19.8 (Part B). That expected frequency is small enough to make us apprehensive about the accuracy of the chi-square corner-cells test.

What about an effect size estimate? A serviceable approximation is obtained from the standard normal deviate (Z) that corresponds to our obtained p. Squaring Z and dividing by N gives us an estimate of the effect size analogous to that obtained by $\chi^2_{(1)}/N = \phi^2$. As described in chapter 11, we generally prefer the "nonsquared" effect-size estimate, and thus, we use a variant of Equation 11.16, namely,

$$\phi_{\text{estimated}} = \sqrt{\frac{Z^2}{N}}, \tag{19.4}$$

because, as previously expressed in Equation 4.15,

$$\phi = \sqrt{\frac{\chi^2_{(1)}}{N}}$$

and

$$\chi^2_{(1)} = Z^2. \tag{19.5}$$

The Fisher exact test p value for our data was .0012, so $Z = 3.04$, and substituting in Equation 19.4 we find

$$\phi_{\text{estimated}} = \sqrt{\frac{(3.04)^2}{28}} = -.57,$$

a value that is considerably more accurate than the ϕ of $-.85$ we found when we computed $\chi^2_{(1)}$ based in part on the very small expected frequency of 0.43 (in Table 19.8). We have obtained a more accurate estimate of the effect size correlation because the p value from which we found Z and our Z^2 (i.e., $\chi^2_{(1)}$) was more accurately estimated from the Fisher exact test than it had been from the suspect $\chi^2_{(1)}$ with its very small expected frequency (of 0.43).

Especially when sample sizes are small, we can often obtain somewhat more accurate effect-size estimates from Fisher's exact test by going from the exact one-tailed p value to t instead of to Z, that is, by using Equation 12.1:

$$r = \sqrt{\frac{t^2}{t^2 + df}},$$

rather than by using

$$r = \phi = \sqrt{\frac{Z^2}{N}} = \sqrt{\frac{\chi^2_{(1)}}{N}}.$$

The t values and Z values associated with particular p values can be approximated from tables but are more accurately determined by computer programs (some available online at reliable Web sites) and certain scientific calculators. For the data in Table 19.8 (Part A) we find that the one-tailed p of .0012 is associated with a t value of 3.36, with $df = N - 2 = 28 - 2 = 26$. Consequently, we obtain the effect size r from Equation 12.1:

$$r = \sqrt{\frac{t^2}{t^2 + df}} = \sqrt{\frac{(3.36)^2}{(3.36)^2 + 26}} = -.55,$$

a value only slightly different from the $-.57$ obtained when we used $\sqrt{\chi^2_{(1)}/N}$ (Equation 4.15) to compute the effect size correlation.

Fisher Exact Test on Less Extreme Cell Entries

For the 2 × 2 table of corners in Part A of Table 19.8, the four cell entries were the most extreme that could have occurred as evidence against the hypothesis of no relationship between the row and column variables, given the fixed marginal

TABLE 19.10
Illustration of "relatively" extreme cell entries,
not as extreme as in Table 19.8 (Part A)

	High	Low	Σ
High	1	2	3
Low	23	2	25
Σ	24	4	28

totals. Earlier we stated that, if the outcome obtained is not the most extreme possible, we must compute p values for the observed result *and for every outcome more extreme*. The p value we then need is the sum of the p values obtained from all those tables (i.e., our own data-outcome p plus the p values of all outcomes more extreme). As an illustration, suppose we obtained the results in Table 19.10, results not as extreme as those in Part A of Table 19.8. Applying Equation 19.3 to the data in Table 19.10, we find

$$p = \frac{(3!)(25!)(24!)(4!)}{(28!)(1!)(2!)(23!)(2!)} = .044$$

The p of .044 is the Fisher exact probability of the particular data in Table 19.10, but the p value we need is for those data and any result more extreme. One approach to finding all of the outcomes more extreme than a given outcome is to reduce by 1 the smallest cell frequency, a procedure that increases by 1 the two adjacent frequencies and decreases by 1 the diagonally opposite frequency, while the marginal totals remain unchanged. We then continue this procedure until one of our cell frequencies is zero. In this case the only more extreme result possible is that shown in Table 19.8, for which we found that the Fisher exact p was .0012. Thus, we simply sum these two p values to obtain:

$$p = .044 + .0021 = .045.$$

Notice that the margin totals in Table 19.10 remain the same as those in Part A of Table 19.8; only the cell counts change.

Before we leave this section of the Fisher exact test as a procedure for getting a second opinion on a 1-*df* chi-square, we want to comment briefly on both those tests (Fisher exact and $\chi^2_{(1)}$) as examples of *nonparametric* statistical procedures. As we stated in chapter 13, we know that t tests and F tests depend on the assumption of normal distributions, though both are fairly effective even when that assumption is not rigorously met. It is widely believed that chi-square tests are nonparametric in the sense that no assumption about the population distribution is made. Long ago, Cochran (1950) pointed out that chi-square tests may depend as much as do F tests on the assumption of normality. Nonparametric tests are tests in which it is less important to know the shape of the population distribution from which the sampling units were drawn (Snedecor & Cochran, 1989), but it appears that chi-square tests are not so "nonparametric" after all. The Fisher exact test is far more truly nonparametric. One of the reasons we have not tried to cover nonparametric tests in this book is that data transformations often make the more flexible and powerful "parametric" procedures work about as well as the nonparametric procedures.

STRENGTHENING THE FISHER EXACT TEST

We have seen that we are most likely to want to use the Fisher exact test when the sample sizes are small (i.e., when some of the expected frequencies are very small). However, it is just in such cases that the Fisher test is quite conservative (because counts increase not gradually but only in discontinuous jumps, such as 2 to 3 rather than 2 to 2.1 or 2.2), leading us too often to conclude that there is no significant effect. Fortunately, Overall (1980) and Overall, Rhoades, and Starbuck (1987) described a procedure that appreciably strengthens the Fisher exact test. To use that procedure we need only augment by 1 the frequencies of those cells of the 2 × 2 table in which the observed frequency is greater than the expected frequency, and then we proceed with the usual computation of the Fisher exact test.

Suppose a small study in which 5 of 11 patients are randomly assigned to a new treatment procedure and the remaining 6 are assigned to the control group. If the null hypothesis of no difference between treatment and control were true, what would be the probability of obtaining the results shown in Part A of Table 19.11? We could begin to answer that question by using the Fisher test, knowing that if we obtain a significant result (say, .05 or less), the true probability is lower still. Substituting in Equation 19.3, the Fisher exact test probability is

$$p = \frac{(5!)(6!)(8!)(3!)}{(11!)(5!)(0!)(3!)(3!)} = .12.$$

Because one of the cell entries is zero, there is no more extreme outcome possible than shown in Part A of Table 19.11, and so the one-tailed p of .12 is the only p value required for the Fisher test of these data.

To use the adjustment suggested by Overall, we begin by computing the expected frequency for each cell in Table 19.11. Thus, the expected frequency for Cell A is computed as $[(A + B)(A + C)]/N$, and all the resulting expected frequencies are shown in Part B of the table. Because in Part A the cells in the upper-left to lower-right diagonal show larger obtained frequencies (5 and 3) than the corresponding expected frequencies in Part B (3.64 and 1.64), we augment those cells in Part A by 1 each and recompute the Fisher exact test. This augmentation gives us the table of "obtained" frequencies in Part C of Table 19.11, and applying Equation 19.3 to those results yields

$$p = \frac{(6!)(7!)(9!)(4!)}{(13!)(6!)(0!)(3!)(4!)} = .049.$$

Thus, with the use of Overall's correction, the one-tailed p of .12 of the uncorrected Fisher exact test has been reduced to a one-tailed $p < .05$.

TABLE 19.11

Strengthening the Fisher exact test

A. Frequencies obtained in a small study

	Outcome		
Condition	**Improved**	**Not improved**	**Σ**
Experimental	5	0	5
Control	3	3	6
Σ	8	3	11

B. Expected frequencies for results in Part A

	Outcome		
Condition	**Improved**	**Not improved**	**Σ**
Experimental	3.64	1.36	5
Control	4.36	1.64	6
Σ	8	3	11

C. "Obtained" frequencies after augmentation

	Outcome		
Condition	**Improved**	**Not improved**	**Σ**
Experimental	6	0	6
Control	3	4	7
Σ	9	4	13

ADJUSTMENTS FOR $\chi^2_{(1)}$ IN 2 × 2 TABLES

Suppose that for the data in Part A of Table 19.11 we had used not the Fisher exact test but the more common χ^2 test. We could use the general formula for chi-square (Equation 11.14) or, as illustrated in chapter 11, the raw score formula in Equation 11.13. Substituting in Equation 11.13 in this case would give us

$$\chi^2_{(1)} = \frac{N(BC - AD)^2}{(A + B)(C + D)(A + C)(B + D)}$$

$$= \frac{11[(0)(3) - (5)(3)]^2}{(5 + 0)(3 + 3)(5 + 3)(0 + 3)}$$

$$= 3.44.$$

To obtain the significance level, we find the Z from $\sqrt{\chi^2_{(1)}}$ to be 1.85, and $p = .032$ one-tailed. Notice that this value is quite close to the adjusted Fisher test result of .049 even though all four cells in Part B of Table 19.11 have expected frequencies less than 5, and two cells have expected frequencies between 1 and 2. Suppose that we had not computed

TABLE 19.12
**Expected frequencies of augmented cell entries in
Part C of Table 19.10**

Condition	Outcome		Σ
	Improved	**Not improved**	
Experimental	4.15	1.85	6
Control	4.85	2.15	7
Σ	9	4	13

the strengthened Fisher test and were concerned about the small expected frequencies. A traditional adjustment of χ^2 is the Yates correction for continuity (referred to earlier in this chapter). When applied to the data in Table 19.11, the Yates correction yields a $\chi^2_{(1)}$ of 1.37 and a Z of 1.17, with a one-tailed p of .12, just as we found with the overly conservative, unadjusted Fisher exact test.

Fortunately, more accurate procedures than the Yates correction are available to help us guard against the increase in Type I errors that may occur when some cells of the $\chi^2_{(1)}$ have very small expected frequencies. One of these procedures, also attributable to Overall (1980), first uses the same augmentation procedure we used to strengthen the Fisher exact test and *then* employs the Yates correction. To illustrate, the original cell frequencies of 5, 0, 3, 3 (in Part A of Table 19.11) were augmented to 6, 0, 3, 4 (in Part C of Table 19.11), yielding a Fisher exact $p = .049$. The expected frequencies for the four augmented cell entries are shown in Table 19.12. The second step is to compute chi-square with the Yates correction, as follows:

$$\chi^2_{(1)} = \frac{N\left(|BC - AD| - \frac{N}{2}\right)^2}{(A+B)(C+D)(A+C)(B+D)},\qquad(19.6)$$

which gives us

$$\chi^2_{(1)} = \frac{13\left(|(0)(3) - (6)(4)| - \frac{13}{2}\right)^2}{(6+0)(3+4)(6+3)(0+4)} = 2.63.$$

For the significance level, we again find Z from $\sqrt{\chi^2_{(1)}}$, yielding 1.62, and the one-tailed $p = .053$.

TABLE 19.13
Summary of p values with and without Overall (1980) adjustment

	Fisher exact	$\sqrt{\chi^2_{(1)}}$
No adjustment	.12[a]	.032
Overall (1980) adjustments	.049	.053

[a] The Yates-corrected $\sqrt{\chi^2_{(1)}}$ yielded the same p of .12.

Table 19.13 provides a recap of the various results. The table shows the p values obtained by the $\sqrt{\chi^2_{(1)}}$ test and the Fisher exact test with and without the Overall (1980) adjustments. The p value of the Fisher exact test is noticeably different from the other three p values, which differ relatively little among themselves. When the unadjusted $\chi^2_{(1)}$ seems risky, either of the Overall (1980) adjustments can be recommended. For other procedures, see Haber (1986) and Overall, Rhoades, and Starbuck (1987).

COMPLETE PARTITIONING OF LARGER TABLES

In chapter 15 we showed that for any diffuse, overall F test with numerator $df = k$ we can compute a set of k orthogonal contrasts, each of which addresses a focused, precise question. In an analogous way we can take a table of counts larger than 2×2, with $df = $ (number of rows -1) $\times$ (number of columns $- 1$) $= k$ and subdivide or partition the table into a set of k tables of 2×2 size that address focused, precise questions. A summary of procedures for partitioning, as well as a general method for computing $\chi^2_{(1)}$ for any of the resulting 2×2 tables, was presented by Jean Bresnahan and Martin Shapiro (1966).

Illustration of Partitioning

One procedure for the complete partitioning of a table of counts begins, for example, with the upper-left corner cell, so that for the top row the two new cells will contain the frequency of the upper-left cell and the remainder of the frequencies in that row, respectively. For the bottom row, the two new cells will contain the frequency of the first column minus the frequency of the top-left cell and the balance of all frequencies not in either the top row or the leftmost column, respectively. We illustrate with our continuing example of degree of enthusiasm as a function of degree of experimental control.

Because there are $(3 - 1)(3 - 1) = 4$ df, we can partition the 3×3 overall table (in Part A of Table 19.5) into four 1-df (i.e., 2×2) subtables. The following four steps in constructing our four subtables are all illustrated in Table 19.14.

First, as shown in Part A of Table 19.14, we make the partition of the overall table that is indicated by the vertical and horizontal lines within the table. That is, we separate the first column from the remaining two columns and also separate the first row from the remaining two rows. Summary values resulting from this partition, indicated as Subtable 1, are shown in Part B.

Second, we subdivide the overall table in Part A by omitting the first column completely and then repeating the procedure shown for the remainder of the overall table. In Part C of Table 19.14, the vertical and horizontal lines within the table show this partitioning of the overall table, and in Part D, we see the resulting Subtable 2.

Third, as we have now run out of columns to drop, we begin to drop rows. We return to the overall table in Part A and drop the top row, leaving as our remainder the partitioned table in Part E. The vertical and horizontal lines within the table indicate where we make the partitions of the remainder table to yield Subtable 3 in Part F.

TABLE 19.14

Partitioning of table of counts in Part A of Table 19.5

A. Partitions producing Subtable 1

Control	Enthusiasm			Σ
	High	Medium	Low	
High	0	3	3	6
Medium	10	3	2	15
Low	24	7	1	32
Σ	34	13	6	53

B. Subtable 1

	High	Lower	Σ
High	0	6	6
Lower	34	13	47
Σ	34	19	53

C. Partitions producing Subtable 2

	Medium	Low	Σ
High	3	3	6
Medium	3	2	5
Low	7	1	8
Σ	13	6	19

D. Subtable 2

	Medium	Low	Σ
High	3	3	6
Lower	10	3	13
Σ	13	6	19

E. Partitions producing Subtable 3

	High	Medium	Low	Σ
Medium	10	3	2	15
Low	24	7	1	32
Σ	34	10	3	47

F. Subtable 3

	High	Lower	Σ
Medium	10	5	15
Lower	24	8	32
Σ	34	13	47

G. Subtable 4

	Medium	Low	Σ
Medium	3	2	5
Low	7	1	8
Σ	10	3	13

610

Finally, as we have now run out of rows to drop, we can return to dropping columns. We drop the first column of the remainder table in Part E to produce Subtable 4 in Part G.

Computing $\chi^2_{(1)}$ Tests on Subtables

The general formula for computing a 1-df chi-square test for each subtable is

$$\chi^2_{(1)} \text{ partitioned} = \text{``}\chi^2\text{''} \text{ cells} - \text{``}\chi^2\text{''} \text{ rows} - \text{``}\chi^2\text{''} \text{ columns} + \text{``}\chi^2\text{''} \text{ total.} \quad (19.7)$$

The first component is defined as

$$\text{``}\chi^2\text{''} \text{ cells} = \sum^{4} \frac{(O_c - E_c)^2}{E_c}, \quad (19.8)$$

which denotes the sum (over the four cells of the subtable) of the standard chi-square quantity $(O - E)^2/E$, but where the expected frequencies have been computed not from the subtable but from the full table. The second component is

$$\text{``}\chi^2\text{''} \text{ rows} = \sum^{2} \frac{(O_r - E_r)^2}{E_r}, \quad (19.9)$$

denoting the sum (over the two row totals of the subtable) of the standard chi-square quantity $(O - E)^2/E$, but where the observed row total is based on the subtable and the expected row total is obtained from the full table-derived expected frequencies found in the subtable. The third component of the general formula is

$$\text{``}\chi^2\text{''} \text{ columns} = \sum^{2} \frac{(O_k - E_k)^2}{E_k}, \quad (19.10)$$

which is defined as for the rows in Equation 19.9. And finally,

$$\text{``}\chi^2\text{''} \text{ total} = \frac{(O_t - E_t)^2}{E_t}, \quad (19.11)$$

denotes the squared difference between the observed and expected total (N) for the subtable.

To illustrate the computations, we begin with the expected frequencies of the original 3 × 3 table, shown again in Table 19.15. Next we display in Table 19.16

TABLE 19.15
Expected frequencies of original 3 × 3 Table 19.5

Degree of control	Degree of enthusiasm			
	High	Medium	Low	Σ
High	3.85	1.47	0.68	6.00
Medium	9.62	3.68	1.70	15.00
Low	20.53	7.85	3.62	32.00
Σ	34.00	13.00	6.00	53.00

TABLE 19.16
Subtables of observed and expected frequencies

	Observed frequencies			Expected frequencies		
Subtable 1	0	6	6	3.85	2.15	6.00
	34	13	47	30.15	16.85	47.00
	34	19	53	34.00	19.00	53.00
Subtable 2	3	3	6	1.47	0.68	2.15
	10	3	13	11.53	5.32	16.85
	13	6	19	13.00	6.00	19.00
Subtable 3	10	5	15	9.62	5.38	15.00
	24	8	32	20.53	11.47	32.00
	34	13	47	30.15	16.85	47.00
Subtable 4	3	2	5	3.68	1.70	5.38
	7	1	8	7.85	3.62	11.47
	10	3	13	11.53	5.32	16.85

the four subtables of observed frequencies, each accompanied by its own table of expected frequencies. The expected frequencies are based *not* on the adjacent subtables of observed frequencies, but on the expected frequencies in Table 19.15. This is most clearly seen in the expected frequencies for Subtable 4 in Table 19.16, which are identical to the corresponding expected frequencies in Table 19.15. As another illustration, for the observed frequency of 34 in Subtable 1 of Table 19.16, the expected frequency is based on the sum of the relevant expected frequencies in Table 19.15. The expected frequency of 30.15 (Table 19.16) is simply the sum of the expected frequencies of 9.62 (medium control) and 20.53 (low control) in Table 19.15.

Finally, we display the results of each step of our calculations in Table 19.17, designed to provide computational checks. However, we illustrate the computational

TABLE 19.17
Partitioned $\chi^2_{(1)}$ tests of results in Table 19.16

	Partitioned $\chi^2_{(1)}$	=	"χ^2" cells	−	"χ^2" rows	−	"χ^2" columns	+	"χ^2" total
Subtable 1	12.12	=	12.12	−	0	−	0	+	0
Subtable 2	2.95	=	10.72	−	7.77	−	0	+	0
Subtable 3	0.31	=	1.68	−	0	−	1.37	+	0
Subtable 4	0.76	=	2.17	−	1.08	−	1.21	+	0.88
Σ	16.14	=	26.69	−	8.85	−	2.58	+	0.88

TABLE 19.18
Summary of chi-square, *p*-level, and phi coefficients

Subtable	$\chi^2_{(1)}$	p	ϕ
1	12.12	.0005	.48
2	2.95	.09	.39
3	0.31	.58	.08
4	0.76	.38	.24

details only for Subtable 4. Substituting in Equations 19.8–19.11, we find

$$\text{``}\chi^2\text{'' cells} = \frac{(3-3.68)^2}{3.68} + \frac{(2-1.70)^2}{1.70} + \frac{(7-7.85)^2}{7.85} + \frac{(1-3.62)^2}{3.62} = 2.17$$

$$\text{``}\chi^2\text{'' rows} = \frac{(5-5.38)^2}{5.38} + \frac{(8-11.47)^2}{11.47} = 1.08$$

$$\text{``}\chi^2\text{'' columns} = \frac{(10-11.53)^2}{11.53} + \frac{(3-5.32)^2}{5.32} = 1.21$$

$$\text{``}\chi^2\text{'' total} = \frac{(13-16.85)^2}{16.85} = 0.88.$$

As a check on our calculations, we see that the sum of the four partitioned $\chi^2_{(1)}$ values in Table 19.17 is equivalent (within rounding error) to the overall $\chi^2_{(4)}$ based on the original 3 × 3 table of counts. Now we can see which of the components of the overall chi-square has made the greatest contribution to that overall test. That contribution is based in part on the strength of the correlation (ϕ) found in each subtable and partly on the N for each subtable. Therefore, as usual, we want to compare phi coefficients as much as we want to compare $\chi^2_{(1)}$ values, as summarized in Table 19.18.

Notice that Subtable 1 showed the largest and the most significant result. That subtable presented data indicating that higher levels of enthusiasm were associated with lower levels of experimental control. Subtable 2, although not significant at the .05 level, showed nearly as large an effect as Subtable 1. But we need to be cautious in interpreting this result. The expected frequencies for Subtable 2 inform us that most of the "χ^2" cells' value is due to the upper-right cell with expected frequency of only 0.68. Consequently, we may not want to place too much confidence in the result of Subtable 2. Regarding the remaining data, Subtables 3 and 4 appear to require little comment. A further word of caution is required, however: When interpreting individual 2 × 2 chi-square results, there is a tendency to look only at the observed frequencies. Accurate interpretation of the computed χ^2 results requires that we examine the observed frequencies *in relation to the expected frequencies.*

The particular partitioning of our overall 3 × 3 table is not unique. Just as many sets of orthogonal contrasts can be computed for omnibus F tests, alternative sets of 2 × 2 tables can be computed for omnibus χ^2 tests. For example, instead of beginning with the upper-left cell of the full table, we could have followed the exactly analogous procedure beginning with some other corner. When we begin with the lower-left cell,

TABLE 19.19

Subtables formed by alternative partitioning of Table 19.5, starting with lower-left cell

	Observed frequencies		Expected frequencies		χ^2	p	ϕ
Subtable 1	10	11	13.47	7.53	4.13	.042	.28
	24	8	20.53	11.47			
Subtable 2	6	5	5.15	2.38	2.36	.12	.35
	7	1	7.85	3.62			
Subtable 3	0	6	3.85	2.15	8.29	.004	.63
	10	5	9.62	5.38			
Subtable 4	3	3	1.47	0.68	1.34	.25	.35
	3	2	3.68	1.70			

we obtain the four sets of observed and expected frequencies, $\chi^2_{(1)}$ results, p levels, and phi coefficients shown in Table 19.19. Each of the four subtables supports the same hypothesis that decreasing degrees of experimental control are associated with increasing levels of enthusiasm about the results, but the size of the effect and its level of significance vary.

A further point about partitioning, however, is that just because it is *possible* to partition a table of frequencies completely is no reason to do so. It is a useful exploratory procedure and may be quite valuable as a source of hypotheses for further investigation. Typically, however, we would approach the 2×2 $\chi^2_{(1)}$ tests in the same spirit that we approach contrasts following an analysis of variance. We compute the $df = 1$ tests that we planned to make, that is, those that address the specific questions of interest.

THE CORNER-CELLS TEST SUBTABLE

When the data are ordered from more to less in both the rows and the columns (as in the case of our continuing example), it is natural to use the corner-cells test we described earlier. The modification we make here is based on the idea of partitioning a table completely. It involves using the expected frequencies computed from the full table, not just from the corner cells alone. Our computations are the same as for any of the subtables of a partitioned table, stated in Equation 19.7 as

$$\chi^2_{(1)} \text{ partitioned} = \text{``}\chi^2\text{'' cells} - \text{``}\chi^2\text{'' rows} - \text{``}\chi^2\text{'' columns} + \text{``}\chi^2\text{'' total.}$$

For the corner-cells test of our continuing example, as shown in Table 19.20, we find

$$\chi^2_{(1)} = 14.25 - 0.55 - 0.03 + 0.02 = 13.69.$$

For a one-tailed test of significance, we find Z from $\sqrt{\chi^2_{(1)}}$ yielding 3.70, so $p = .00011$, and $\phi = .70$.

TABLE 19.20

Corner cells of 3 × 3 tables of observed and expected frequencies in Table 19.5

	Observed frequency				Expected frequency		
	High	**Low**	**Σ**		**High**	**Low**	**Σ**
High	0	3	3	High	3.85	0.68	4.53
Low	24	1	25	Low	20.53	3.62	24.15
Σ	24	4	28	Σ	24.38	4.30	28.68

This corner-cells test with expected frequencies based on the entire table yields a somewhat more conservative value of χ^2 and ϕ than the original corner-cells test with expected frequencies based only on the data from the four corner cells. That $\chi^2_{(1)}$ was 20.16, $\phi = .85$, which was probably inflated by an unusually low expected frequency of 0.43 in one of the cells.

CONTRASTS IN PROPORTIONS

Throughout our discussion of subdividing contingency tables larger than 2 × 2, we emphasized the conceptual relationship between the utility of contrasts following the analysis of variance and the utility of 2 × 2 contingency tables following the analysis of larger tables of counts. It sometimes happens in larger tables that one dimension can be ordered from more to less and information from the other dimension can be expressed as a proportion of the total frequency found in each level of the ordered dimension. In such situations, contrasts can be computed directly from a formula suggested by Donald B. Rubin (personal communication, January 4, 1981). We illustrate this procedure first for a study with a large total sample, as Rubin's originally suggested formula works best with large total samples. With smaller samples it can become more problematic, which we demonstrate in the next section, in which we also suggest a simple adjustment of the standard error estimate.

In this example we imagine a large clinical study ($N = 1,976$) in which it was predicted that one treatment per week would be half as beneficial as two treatments per week, and that the benefits (the dependent variable) are defined in terms of two levels of self-rated personal satisfaction: not very satisfied (A) and very satisfied (B). The independent variable of the number of weekly treatments is defined by three levels: no treatments, one treatment, and two treatments. Table 19.21 shows the results in a 2 × 3 table of counts, with rows indicating the two levels of satisfaction and columns indicating the three levels of number of weekly treatments. Suppose we predicted a linear increase in treatment benefits as the number of treatments increased from zero to one to two. For each of our three treatment levels, we compute the proportion of subjects that were very satisfied as shown in Table 19.21, in the row labeled $p = B/n$.

The linear contrast weights we will use are shown in the bottom row of Table 19.21 $(-1, 0, +1)$, and Rubin's suggested formula for testing the linear contrast in proportions is

$$Z_{\text{contrast}} = \frac{\Sigma(p_i \lambda_i)}{\sqrt{\Sigma(S_i^2 \lambda_i^2)}}, \qquad (19.12)$$

TABLE 19.21

Observed frequencies for effects of number of treatments on satisfaction in between-subjects design

	Number of weekly treatments		
Level of satisfaction	None	One	Two
Not very satisfied (A)	189	164	653
Very satisfied (B)	145	174	651
Sample size (n)	334	338	1,304
$p = B/n$	.434	.515	.499
$S_i^2 = p_i(1 - p_i)/n_i$	.000736	.000739	.000192
Linear contrast (λ)	-1	0	$+1$

where the numerator is the sum of the proportions (p_i) after each proportion has been multiplied by its corresponding contrast weight (λ_i). The denominator in the equation is the square root of the sum of the squared standard errors (S_i^2) of each proportion after they have been multiplied by their corresponding squared contrast weight, where S_i^2 (the squared standard error of each proportion) is defined as

$$S_i^2 = \frac{p_i(1 - p_i)}{n_i}. \tag{19.13}$$

In the case of a large total N, the contrast r can be estimated from

$$r_{contrast} = \frac{Z_{contrast}}{\sqrt{N}}, \tag{19.14}$$

where N = total number of observations.

We illustrate the application of Equation 19.13 for the proportion indicated as .434, and we calculate

$$S_i^2 = \frac{.434(1 - .434)}{334} = .000736.$$

For the remaining two proportions, indicated as .515 and .499, we find that $S_i^2 = .000739$ and .000192, respectively. Substituting in Equation 19.12 yields

$$Z_{contrast} = \frac{.434(-1) + .515(0) + .499(+1)}{\sqrt{.000736(1) + .000739(0) + .000192(1)}} = 2.13,$$

with one-tailed $p = .017$, and from Equation 19.14, we find

$$r_{contrast} = \frac{2.13}{\sqrt{1976}} = .048,$$

indicating that there is not a large linear relationship.

Suppose we had an alternative theory that predicted a quadratic, ∩-shaped relationship between the number of weekly treatments and satisfaction (i.e., No treatment $<$ 1 treatment $>$ 2 treatments). Substituting in Equation 19.12, with lambda weights of -1, $+2$, and -1, our planned contrast for this hypothesized relationship becomes

$$Z_{contrast} = \frac{.434(-1) + .515(+2) + .499(-1)}{\sqrt{.000736(1) + .000739(4) + .000192(1)}} = 1.56,$$

with one-tailed $p = .060$, and the associated contrast r (from Equation 19.14) is

$$r_{contrast} = \frac{1.56}{\sqrt{1,976}} = .035,$$

a value not very different from the $r_{contrast}$ based on our earlier linear prediction ($r = .048$).

   As we stated in an earlier chapter, it is no great trick to fit a contrast to data we have already seen, but that contrast should be differentiated from a planned contrast. In this example, a very simple and sensible unplanned contrast is the theoretically parsimonious one that treated research participants (i.e., one treatment or two treatments) were more satisfied than untreated participants, with $Z_{contrast} = 2.35$, two-tailed $p = .019$, and $r_{contrast} = .053$. We report the two-tailed p because that result was not predicted. In addition, we may want to multiply the two-tailed p of .019 by 3 to yield .057, on the assumption that there are three two-tailed ways to compare any one group with the other two (see the section on Bonferroni procedures in chapter 14). When there are only three treatment conditions, unplanned pairwise comparisons are not a major problem because only three such comparisons are possible. In our example comparing three treatment conditions, one treatment is better than no treatment ($\chi^2_{(1)} = 4.38$, $Z = 2.09$, $p = .018$ one-tailed, and $\phi = .081$); two treatments are better than no treatment ($\chi^2_{(1)} = 4.51$, $Z = 2.12$, $p = .017$ one-tailed, and $\phi = .052$), but two treatments are not any better than one treatment with $\chi^2_{(1)} = 0.260$, $Z = -.51$, $p = .61$ two-tailed, and $\phi = -.013$. Note that the effect size ϕ's absolute value of .013 is given a negative sign to indicate that the results are in the unpredicted direction.

ALTERNATIVE ANALYSES FOR SMALLER SAMPLE STUDIES

We stated that Equation 19.12 is a large sample test, and we now illustrate its limitations (and a useful adjustment) with samples considerably smaller than the total N in Table 19.21. We also describe some alternative analyses. For our illustrations we turn to the data in Table 19.22, where the dependent variable comprises two levels (A and B) and there are three levels of the independent variable (Conditions 1, 2, 3). Our attention is focused on the observed frequencies in Level B, as we predicted a quadratic trend, so that the results in Conditions 1 and 3 would be better than in Condition 2, with no predicted difference between Conditions 1 and 3. Thus, the quadratic contrast is $\cup$-shaped, with lambda weights of $+1$, -2, $+1$. Summary values are computed as before, where we form the proportions of interest by dividing the counts in Level B by the appropriate sample n, and the squared standard error of each proportion is obtained by Equation 19.13.

TABLE 19.22
Observed frequencies for effects of three treatments on outcome in between-subjects design

Dependent variable	Condition 1	Condition 2	Condition 3
	Independent variable		
Level A	8	16	8
Level B	12	4	12
Sample size (n)	20	20	20
p = Level B/n	.60	.20	.60
$S_i^2 = p_i(1 - p_i)/n_i$	.012	.008	.012
Quadratic contrast (λ)	+1	−2	+1

Contrast Z on Proportions

For our first analysis, we again substitute in Equation 19.12 to compute the contrast Z on proportions:

$$Z_{contrast} = \frac{\Sigma(p_i \lambda_i)}{\sqrt{\Sigma(S_i^2 \lambda_i^2)}}$$

$$= \frac{.60(+1) + .20(-2) + .60(+1)}{\sqrt{.012(1) + .008(4) + .012(1)}} = 3.381,$$

with $p = 3.6^{-4}$ one-tailed and, using Equation 19.14, $r_{contrast} = 3.381/\sqrt{60} = .436$. When the total sample N is small, however, we obtain a more accurate estimate of $r_{contrast}$ from t using Equation 12.1:

$$r = \sqrt{\frac{t^2}{t^2 + df}},$$

where we get the value of t from the p value of Z using t tables, calculators, or computers. The p value for Z of 3.381 is 3.6^{-4} (i.e., .00036), and the corresponding $t_{(57)} = 3.575$, so from Equation 12.1 we find

$$r = \sqrt{\frac{(3.575)^2}{(3.575)^2 + 57}} = .428,$$

in this case, a value close to $r = .436$ from Z using Equation 19.14.

Contrast Z from $r_{p\lambda}$

An alternative would be to estimate the contrast Z by carving it out of the omnibus chi-square with the help of an analog of the alerting r previously given as $r_{M\lambda}$. Table 19.23 illustrates the steps in computing the omnibus chi-square, where we go from the table of observed frequencies, to expected frequencies, to $(O - E)^2/E$ values. The omnibus $\chi_{(2)}^2$ is the sum of those "partial" chi-square values, shown as 8.573 in Part C. An analog

TABLE 19.23

Counts, expected frequencies, and "partial" chi-square values for observed frequencies in Table 19.22

A. Observed frequencies

Dependent variable	Condition 1	Condition 2	Condition 3	Σ
Level A	8	16	8	32
Level B	12	4	12	28
Σ	20	20	20	60

B. Expected frequencies

Dependent variable	Condition 1	Condition 2	Condition 3	Σ
Level A	10.667	10.667	10.667	32.000
Level B	9.333	9.333	9.333	28.000
Σ	20.000	20.000	20.000	60.000

C. $(O - E)^2/E$ values

Dependent variable	Condition 1	Condition 2	Condition 3	Σ
Level A	.667	2.667	.667	4.001
Level B	.762	3.048	.762	4.572
Σ	1.429	5.715	1.429	8.573

of the alerting r given earlier is the r we get by correlating proportions and lambdas ($r_{p\lambda}$). For the data in Table 19.22, by correlating the $p = B/n$ proportions of .60, .20, .60 with their respective lambdas of $+1$, -2, $+1$, we find $r_{p\lambda} = 1.00$ and thus $r_{p\lambda}^2 = 1.00$. Because $Z_{contrast} = \sqrt{\chi_{(1)}^2} = \sqrt{r_{p\lambda}^2 \times \chi_{k>1}^2}$, we take the square root of the product of $r_{p\lambda}^2$ times the omnibus chi-square and get $Z_{contrast} = \sqrt{1.00 \times 8.573} = 2.928$, and $p = .0017$. Getting the contrast r from Equation 19.14 gives $r = Z/\sqrt{N} = 2.928/\sqrt{60} = .378$. In view of the smaller total sample, however, we prefer to get the contrast r from t using Equation 12.1:

$$r = \sqrt{t^2/(t^2 + df)} = \sqrt{(3.056)^2/[(3.056)^2 + 57]} = .375.$$

Contrast F from $r_{M\lambda}$

Another alternative is the contrast F test, which we can carve out of the omnibus F on the dummy-coded scores. Part A of Table 19.24 shows those dummy-coded scores, where Level A is coded 0 and Level B is coded 1. The summary ANOVA is shown in Part B, where the omnibus $F(2, 57) = 4.75$. Correlating the condition means (.60, .20, .60) with their respective lambda weights ($+1$, -2, $+1$) gives $r_{M\lambda} = 1.00$. Multiplying $r_{M\lambda}^2$ by the overall between-conditions sum of squares tells us the proportion of the between-conditions sum of squares that is associated with a particular contrast. In this case, as $r_{M\lambda}^2 = 1.00$, we know that the quadratic contrast accounts for all of the overall between-conditions

TABLE 19.24
Dummy-coded scores and summary ANOVA for results in Table 19.22

A. Dummy-coded scores (A = 0; B = 1)

	Condition 1	Condition 2	Condition 3
	0, 0, 0, 0, 0	0, 0, 0, 0, 0	0, 0, 0, 0, 0
	0, 0, 0, 1, 1	0, 0, 0, 0, 0	0, 0, 0, 1, 1
	1, 1, 1, 1, 1	0, 0, 0, 0, 0	1, 1, 1, 1, 1
	1, 1, 1, 1, 1	0, 1, 1, 1, 1	1, 1, 1, 1, 1
Σ	12	4	12
N	20	20	20
M	0.60	0.20	0.60
S^2	.2526	.1684	.2526
λ	+1	−2	+1

B. Overall ANOVA

Source	SS	df	MS	F	p
Between	2.1333	2	1.0667	4.75	.012
Within	12.8000	57	0.2246		
Total	14.9333	59			

sum of squares. Substituting in Equation 15.6 gives us

$$F_{contrast} = \frac{r_{M\lambda}^2 \times SS_{between}}{MS_{within}} = \frac{1.00 \times 2.1333}{0.2246} = 9.50,$$

which, with numerator $df = 1$ and denominator $df = 57$, has an associated p of 3.2^{-3}. The contrast r can be found directly from $\sqrt{F/(F + df_{denominator})} = \sqrt{9.50/(9.50 + 57)} = .378$, a value very close to those obtained from the $r_{alerting}^2 \times \chi_{omnibus}^2$ procedures (.378 and .375).

Contrast t from Dummy-Coded Scores

We can in this case, of course, quickly calculate the contrast t simply by taking the square root of the contrast F. Hence, $t_{contrast} = \sqrt{9.50} = 3.082$ and, with $df = 57$, the associated one-tailed $p = 1.6^{-3}$, and $r = .378$. Another alternative would be to compute $t_{contrast}$ from Equation 19.2, in which the basic ingredients are the same as those above, or we can compute it from the information in Part A of Table 19.24. That is, we estimate the pooled variance from the S^2 values, and given the condition means and sample sizes shown in Part A, we substitute in Equation 15.4:

$$t_{contrast} = \frac{\Sigma(M_i \lambda_i)}{\sqrt{MS_{within}\left(\Sigma \frac{\lambda_i^2}{n_i}\right)}},$$

TABLE 19.25
**Summary of four "$r_{contrast}$ from t"
results**

Method	$r_{contrast}$
Contrast z on proportions	.428
Contrast z from $r_{p\lambda}$	.375
Contrast F from $r_{M\lambda}$	.378
Contrast t obtained directly	.378

to find

$$t_{contrast} = \frac{(.60)(+1) + (.20)(-2) + (.60)(+1)}{\sqrt{.2246\left[\frac{(+1)^2}{20} + \frac{(-2)^2}{20} + \frac{(+1)^2}{20}\right]}},$$

$$= \frac{0.80}{\sqrt{.2246(0.30)}} = 3.082,$$

and $p = .0016$ one-tailed, and $r_{contrast} = .378$ from Equation 15.12.

Adjustment for Computing $Z_{contrast}$ by Equation 19.12

Table 19.25 summarizes the $r_{contrast}$ values that we obtained from t by the four methods described in this section. Notice that the first method (contrast z on proportions) yielded a noticeably higher r than did the other methods. As we said earlier, Equation 19.12 is a large-sample formula, and when used with small samples it often yields estimates of r that are too high (and estimates of p that are too low). A convenient procedure for making Equation 19.12 more usefully conservative with small samples is to define S_i^2 as $.25/n$. This adjustment makes the standard error of the proportion the maximum possible value for any given n. For our data of Table 19.22, substituting in Equation 19.12 gives us

$$Z_{contrast} = \frac{\Sigma(p_i\lambda_i)}{\sqrt{\Sigma(S_i^2\lambda_i^2)}}$$

$$= \frac{.60(+1) + .20(-2) + .60(+1)}{\sqrt{\left[\left(\frac{.25}{20}\right)(1)\right] + \left[\left(\frac{.25}{20}\right)(4)\right] + \left[\left(\frac{.25}{20}\right)(1)\right]}} = 2.921,$$

with $p = .0017$ and, from Equation 15.12, $r_{contrast} = .374$, a value more consistent with the results of the other three methods described in this section.

STANDARDIZING ROW AND COLUMN TOTALS

As the number of rows and columns of tables of counts grows larger, it becomes more and more difficult to determine by inspection just what is going on in the data. A major problem is that our attention is likely to be drawn to very large cell frequencies. For

TABLE 19.26
Table of counts

24	10	6
36	15	9
48	20	12
132	55	33

example, in Table 19.26, what stands out? We are most likely to see the 132 as a standout cell. Actually, though, that cell frequency is exactly what we would expect if the null hypothesis of no relationship between the row and column variables were true. As mentioned earlier, we can do better than inspecting the raw counts by making a table of partial chi-square values, that is, the $(O - E)^2/E$ cell values. That would at least tell us where the bulk of the omnibus χ^2 value comes from. However, what should we do about very small expected frequencies that yield perhaps exaggeratedly large $(O - E)^2/E$ values? Mosteller (1968) described a method of *standardizing the margins* of tables of counts in order to get a clearer look at what is actually going on. The method sets all row totals equal to each other and all column totals equal to each other.

An Example

We first illustrate the Mosteller method of standardizing the margins with the earlier example of 53 medical investigations that were categorized by Gilbert, McPeek, and Mosteller (1977) according to the degree of experimental control and the degree of the experimenter's enthusiasm about the results. Part A of Table 19.27 shows again the original 3×3 table of counts that we have seen before in this chapter. The first step is to divide each cell count by the sum of the column in which we find the count. For example, we divide the cell count of 24 in the lower-left corner of Part A by 34 (the sum at the bottom of the first column). The results of these computations are shown in Part B, where we see that the first step has equalized to 1.00 the column totals, but the row totals are far from equal. Thus, the next step is to set those row totals as equal, which we do by dividing each cell entry in Part B by its row total. For example, we divide the cell entry of .71 in the lower-left corner of Part B by 1.42 (the row total in Part B). The results of these computations are shown in Part C, where we see that the second step has equalized to 1.00 the row totals, but the column totals are now unequal again.

For simplicity we present only two decimal places, but it is usually prudent to work with three or four decimal places when calculating the results by hand. We now continue the process begun in Table 19.27 by dividing the new cell entries in Part C by the column totals, and then the cell entries in the resulting table by their new row totals, and so on, until the row totals are equal and the column totals are equal. The individual row totals will not equal the individual column totals except in cases where the number of rows and columns is equal, as in the present illustration. The steps in these repetitions (called *iterations*) following the standardization of Part C of Table 19.27 are summarized in Table 19.28. In this summary table the subtables on the right always follow the

TABLE 19.27

Illustration of first two steps in standardizing the margins

A. Results reported by Gilbert, McPeek, and Mosteller (1977)

Degree of control	Degree of enthusiasm			
	High	Medium	Low	Σ
High	0	3	3	6
Medium	10	3	2	15
Low	24	7	1	32
Σ	34	13	6	53

B. Results after dividing each entry in Part A by its column total

	High	Medium	Low	Σ
High	.00	.23	.50	.73
Medium	.29	.23	.33	.85
Low	.71	.54	.17	1.42
Σ	1.00	1.00	1.00	3.00

C. Results after dividing each entry in Part B by its row total

	High	Medium	Low	Σ
High	.00	.32	.68	1.00
Medium	.34	.27	.39	1.00
Low	.50	.38	.12	1.00
Σ	.84	.97	1.19	3.00

subtables immediately to their left; the results of the division in a subtable on the right are displayed in the subtable below on the left, so that progress through the whole of Table 19.28 is like reading sentences down a page.

The final subtable is at the bottom right of Table 19.28, where we see that the row totals are equal and the column totals are equal. We can take one more step to throw the final results into bolder relief: We can subtract from each cell entry of the final subtable the grand mean of all cells. Table 19.29 shows again (in Part A) the cell values from the final subtable, and the grand mean is $3.00/9 = .33$. After subtracting the grand mean from the individual cell values, we have the subtable shown in Part B of Table 19.29. The interpretation of this adjusted subtable is quite direct and, of course, quite consistent with the results in our continuing analysis of the original data. The greatest overrepresentation is in the upper-right and lower-left corners, and the greatest underrepresentation is in the upper-left and lower-right corners. Thus, the higher the degree of control the lower the level of enthusiasm. Cell entries from the middle row and the middle column are all fairly small. It is the corners where the action is, and the crossed-linear contrast weights in Part C of Table 19.29 fit these results very well.

TABLE 19.28
Steps in standardizing the margins of the bottom subtable (C) in Table 19.27

	Dividing by column totals				Dividing by row totals			
	High	**Medium**	**Low**	**Σ**	**High**	**Medium**	**Low**	**Σ**
High	.00	.33	.58	0.91	.00	.36	.64	1.00
Medium	.41	.28	.32	1.01	.40	.28	.32	1.00
Low	.59	.39	.10	1.08	.55	.36	.09	1.00
Σ	1.00	1.00	1.00	3.00	.95	1.00	1.05	3.00
High	.00	.36	.61	0.97	.00	.37	.63	1.00
Medium	.42	.28	.30	1.00	.42	.27	.31	1.00
Low	.58	.36	.09	1.03	.56	.35	.09	1.00
Σ	1.00	1.00	1.00	3.00	.98	.99	1.03	3.00
High	.00	.37	.62	0.99	.00	.38	.62	1.00
Medium	.43	.27	.30	1.00	.43	.27	.30	1.00
Low	.57	.36	.08	1.01	.57	.35	.08	1.00
Σ	1.00	1.00	1.00	3.00	1.00	1.00	1.00	3.00

TABLE 19.29
Throwing the standardized results into bolder relief

A. Final subtable (lower-right corner) of Table 19.28

	Enthusiasm		
Control	**High**	**Medium**	**Low**
High	.00	.38	.62
Medium	.43	.27	.30
Low	.57	.35	.08

B. After subtracting the grand mean (.33) from each entry

	Enthusiasm		
Control	**High**	**Medium**	**Low**
High	−.33	.05	.29
Medium	.10	−.06	−.03
Low	.24	.02	−.25

C. Crossed-linear contrast weights to represent the results

	Enthusiasm		
Control	**High**	**Medium**	**Low**
High	−1	0	+1
Medium	0	0	0
Low	+1	0	−1

The correlation over the nine cells of the relative frequencies in Part B of Table 19.29 and the weights in Part C is $r = .966$, which tells us how good the fit of the data is to the crossed-linear contrast weights. We can regard this correlation as a kind of "alerting r" and use it to get an estimate of $\chi^2_{contrast}$ as long as we have an omnibus chi-square for the original raw data of counts (where $\chi^2_{(4)} = 16.13$ in this example). That is, with $r_{alerting}$ defined as above, we calculate

$$\chi^2_{contrast} = r^2_{alerting} \times \chi^2_{omnibus}, \tag{19.15}$$

and for the data just above, we find

$$\chi^2_{contrast} = (.966)^2 \times 16.13 = 15.05,$$

with $p = 1.0^{-4}$. Alternatively, $Z_{contrast} = \sqrt{\chi^2_{contrast}} = 3.88$, with one-tailed $p = 5.2^{-5}$.

Recalling that $r_{alerting}$ in this case is the correlation between k predicted values or contrast weights (i.e., the λ weights in Part C of Table 19.29) and the data for each of the k conditions (in Part B of Table 19.29), we see that, although a useful effect-size estimate, it is based only on k conditions (9 cell values in this case). To estimate the $r_{contrast}$ for our $\chi^2_{contrast}$, we will instead want to use the information from the original 53 sampling units. One formula that we can use is Equation 4.15, $\left(\phi = \sqrt{\chi^2_{(1)}/N}\right)$, so, since $\chi^2_{(1)} = \chi^2_{contrast}$, we find

$$r_{contrast} = \sqrt{\frac{\chi^2_{contrast}}{N}} = \sqrt{\frac{15.05}{53}} = -.53,$$

and we have described the contrast r as negative to reflect the inverse relationship between the row and column variables. Usually a more accurate procedure, especially with smaller sample sizes, is to estimate the contrast r from t, as we did earlier. In this case we go from our obtained one-tailed p value of 5.2^{-5} (i.e., .000052 to the associated critical t value on $df = N - 2 = 51$, which is $t_{(51)} = 4.21$), and then from Equation 12.1 we find

$$r_{contrast} = \sqrt{\frac{t^2}{t^2 + df}} = \sqrt{\frac{(4.21)^2}{(4.21)^2 + 51}} = -.51.$$

Both estimates of $r_{contrast}$ fall well within the range of values reported earlier ($-.55$, $-.52$, and $-.49$).

A More Complex Example

As a further illustration of standardizing the margins, as well as another example of exploratory data analysis, Table 19.30 shows in Part A the results of a cross-classification of 1,264 college students. The row variable is the field of study in which students said they had intended to concentrate, and the column variable is the field of study in which they actually took their degree. After the first step in standardizing the column margin, we obtain the results in Part B. We omit the next 10 row and column iterations and show the final table in Part C. To throw those results into bolder relief, we subtract from each cell entry the grand mean of all the cells (i.e., $4.00/16 = .25$) and get the residuals in Part D.

TABLE 19.30

More complex example of standardizing the margins

A. Observed frequencies in a 4 × 4 table of counts

Intended field of study	Field in which degree was awarded				
	Humanities	Social science	Biological science	Physical science	Σ
Humanities	133	158	14	4	309
Social science	57	312	17	5	391
Biological science	16	72	94	10	192
Physical science	34	102	56	180	372
Σ	240	644	181	199	1,264

B. After dividing each entry in Part A by its column total

	Humanities	Social science	Biological science	Physical science	Σ
Humanities	.55	.25	.08	.02	.90
Social science	.24	.48	.09	.03	.84
Biological science	.07	.11	.52	.05	.75
Physical science	.14	.16	.31	.90	1.51
Σ	1.00	1.00	1.00	1.00	4.00

C. Final table after 10 more iterations

	Humanities	Social science	Biological science	Physical science	Σ
Humanities	.60	.26	.09	.05	1.00
Social science	.27	.55	.12	.06	1.00
Biological science	.08	.13	.66	.13	1.00
Physical science	.05	.06	.13	.76	1.00
Σ	1.00	1.00	1.00	1.00	4.00

D. After subtracting the grand mean (.25) from each entry in Part C

	Humanities	Social science	Biological science	Physical science
Humanities	.35	.01	−.16	−.20
Social science	.02	.30	−.13	−.19
Biological science	−.17	−.12	.41	−.12
Physical science	−.20	−.19	−.12	.51

The overwhelming result, of course, is that students are much more likely to graduate in their intended field than in any other. Contrast weights will help us evaluate the extent to which that is the case. Such weights are shown in Part A of Table 19.31. Correlating those weights with the relative frequencies shown in Part D of Table 19.30 gives us $r = .951$, indicating a very good fit between the data and the contrast weights.

TABLE 19.31

Contrast weights for two ad hoc hypotheses to account for the final results in Table 19.30

A. Students are much more likely to graduate in their intended field than in any other field

	H	SS	BS	PS
H	3	−1	−1	−1
SS	−1	3	−1	−1
BS	−1	−1	3	−1
PS	−1	−1	−1	3

B. When students do not graduate in their intended field, they are more likely to graduate in a field more adjacent (rather than not adjacent) on a theoretical scale of "soft" to "hard" sciences

	H	SS	BS	PS
H	0	2	−1	−1
SS	1	0	1	−2
BS	−2	1	0	1
PS	−1	−1	2	0

Naturally, we also remind readers that our comparison is based on an ad hoc observation, not on a specific prediction or a contrast planned before our exploration of the results.

That qualification notwithstanding, we can go a little further in understanding the data if we assume that the four fields of study can be arrayed along a dimension of "soft" to "hard." That is, humanities are "softer" than the social sciences, which in turn are "softer" than the biological sciences, and these in turn are "softer" than the physical sciences. If that ordering is acceptable as a theoretical assumption, we may suggest (as another ad hoc hypothesis) that when people do not graduate in their intended field, they are more likely to graduate in a field more adjacent (rather than not adjacent) on the soft-versus-hard dimension. The weights indicated in Part B of Table 19.31 are appropriate to this hypothesis and are orthogonal to the weights shown in Part A. The correlation of the weights in Part B of Table 19.31 with the relative frequencies in Part D of Table 19.30 is $r = .193$, which supports the idea of at least a moderate relationship between second choices of field for graduation and adjacency to the original choice.

ODDS RATIO, RELATIVE RISK, RISK DIFFERENCE, AND PHI

Earlier in this chapter we noted that the Mosteller procedure often preserves a particular effect-size indicator for 2×2 tables, where that effect size indicator is known as the *odds ratio*. We turn now to the odds ratio and to two other common

TABLE 19.32
The 1954 Salk poliomyelitis vaccine trial

Condition	Paralytic polio present	Paralytic polio absent
A. Coding of cells		
Control	A	B
Treatment	C	D
B. Raw counts in four conditions		
Placebo	115	201,114
Vaccination	33	200,712
C. Binomial effect-size display of $r = .011$		
Placebo	50.5	49.5
Vaccination	49.5	50.5
Total	100.0	100.0

effect-size indicators, *relative risk* and *risk difference;* these three indicators are frequently used in biomedical research. As a case in point we use the 1954 Salk vaccine study, which was mentioned briefly in chapter 11 (and the results were shown in Table 11.9). What was so striking about those results was the minuscule value of phi ($r = .011$), and we noted that effect size correlations smaller than .10 are not at all unusual in influential biomedical trials (see again Table 11.8). In this section we describe some limitations of the odds ratio, relative risk, and risk difference, and we suggest an adjustment by means of BESD (binomial effect-size display) standardized tables.

To set the stage for this discussion, we refer to Table 19.32. The part labeled A shows the coding of the four cells, and B shows the Salk vaccine study results discussed in chapter 11, but with the cells rearranged to fit the model in Part A. Part C shows the binomial effect-size display of an effect size of $r = .011$. Recall that the results in Part B were those judged by Brownlee (1955) to be "convincing evidence for the effectiveness of the vaccine" (p. 1010), that is, despite particular deficiencies he found in the investigation as a whole. It will also be recalled that the binomial effect-size display is applicable to any r-type effect size. We compute the "success rate" for the BESD as $100(.50 \pm r/2)$. Therefore, an r of .011 (rounded to .01) in the Salk trial yields a vaccination success rate (i.e., paralytic polio absent) of $100(.50 + .005) = 50.5$ and a placebo success rate of $100(.50 - .005) = 49.5$. The difference between these rates divided by 100 is .01, the effect size indexed by r rounded to two decimal places. Recall that the BESD procedure is specifically designed to display the effect size r in a standard 2×2 table of $n = 100$ for each row and each column total.

Relative Risk

With reference to the cells labeled A, B, C, D in Table 19.32, relative risk (RR) is defined as

$$RR = \left(\frac{A}{A + B}\right) \Big/ \left(\frac{C}{C + D}\right), \qquad (19.16)$$

that is, the ratio of the proportion of the control patients at risk to the proportion of the treated patients at risk. Applied to the Salk vaccine trial, the relative risk is

$$RR = \left(\frac{115}{115 + 201,114}\right) \Big/ \left(\frac{33}{33 + 200,712}\right) = 3.48.$$

A limitation of relative risk as an effect size estimate is illustrated in Table 19.33, where the extreme "success rate" variable (the column variable) is survival (i.e., live vs. die). We ask readers to examine the three outcomes closely and to ask themselves the following question: "If I *had* to be in the *control group,* would it matter to me whether I was in Study 1, Study 2, or Study 3?" We think most people would have preferred Study 1 to Study 2. We also think that virtually no one would prefer membership in the

TABLE 19.33

Three hypothetical examples of four effect-size estimates in 2 × 2 contingency tables

	Die	Live	Relative risk	Odds ratio	Risk difference	Phi (ϕ)
Control	A	B	(Eq. 19.16)	(Eq. 19.17)	(Eq. 19.18)	(Eq. 11.12)
Treatment	C	D				
Study 1						
	Die	**Live**				
Control	10	990	10.00	10.09	.01	.06
Treatment	1	999				
Study 2						
	Die	**Live**				
Control	10	10	10.00	19.00	.45	.50
Treatment	1	19				
Study 3						
	Die	**Live**				
Control	10	0	10.00	∞	.90	.90
Treatment	1	9				

control group in Study 3. Yet, despite the obviously important phenomenological differences among the three studies, Table 19.33 shows that all three relative risks are identical (RR = 10.00). That feature may be a serious limitation on the value and informativeness of the relative risk index.

Odds Ratio

With Cells A, B, C, D again as shown in Table 19.32, the odds ratio (OR) is defined as

$$OR = \left(\frac{A}{B}\right) \Big/ \left(\frac{C}{D}\right), \qquad (19.17)$$

that is, in the context of Table 19.33, the ratio of the not-surviving control patients to the surviving control patients divided by the ratio of the not-surviving treated patients to the surviving treated patients. Applied to the Salk vaccine trial (Table 19.32), where the dependent variable was the presence or absence of paralytic polio, the odds ratio is

$$OR = \left(\frac{115}{201,114}\right) \Big/ \left(\frac{33}{200,712}\right) = 3.48.$$

Incidentally, were we to use Mosteller's procedure to standardize the margins of the raw counts in Part B of Table 19.32, and then to substitute in Equation 19.17 the new cell values (.651, .349, .349, .651 for Cells A, B, C, D, respectively), we would obtain the same odds ratio (3.48).

Notice that the odds ratio in Table 19.33 behaves more as expected than does the relative risk. That is, the OR increases with our phenomenological discomfort as we go from the results of Study 1 to those of Study 2 to those of Study 3. But the high odds ratio for Study 1 seems alarmist. Suppose the data were as shown in Results A of Table 19.34, which indicates an even smaller proportion of patients at risk; the odds ratio is still 10, which is an even more alarmist result. The odds ratio for Study 3 in Table 19.33 is also unattractive; but because all the controls die, perhaps we can forgive the infinite odds ratio. However, very different phenomenological results yield an identical odds ratio. If the data resembled Results B of Table 19.34, we would again have an infinite odds ratio, definitely an

TABLE 19.34
Further illustrations of extreme outcomes

Results A					Results B			
	Die	Live	Totals			Die	Live	Totals
Control	10	999,990	10^6		Control	1,000,000	0	10^6
Treated	1	999,999	10^6		Treated	999,999	1	10^6
Totals	11	1,999,989	$2(10^6)$		Totals	1,999,999	1	$2(10^6)$

Note: In Results A, the relative risk (RR) = 10.00, the odds ratio (OR) = 10.00, the risk difference (RD) = .000009, $\chi^2_{(1)}$ = 7.36, and ϕ = .0019. In Results B, the RR = 1.00, OR = ∞, RD = .000001, $\chi^2_{(1)}$ = 1.00, and ϕ = .00071.

alarmist result. In this case, even the problematic relative risk index would yield a phenomenologically more realistic result of 1.00.

Risk Difference

With cells again labeled as shown in Table 19.32, the risk difference (RD) is defined as

$$RD = \left(\frac{A}{A+B}\right) - \left(\frac{C}{C+D}\right), \tag{19.18}$$

that is, the difference between the proportion of the control patients at risk and the proportion of the treated patients at risk. Applied to the Salk vaccine results in Table 19.32, the risk difference is

$$RD = \left(\frac{115}{115 + 201,114}\right) - \left(\frac{33}{33 + 200,712}\right) = .0004,$$

a value somewhat smaller than the effect size index ϕ calculated to be .011.

The last column of Table 19.33 shows the ϕ between the independent variable of control-versus-treatment (scored 0, 1) and the dependent variable of die-versus-live (also scored 0, 1). Comparing risk differences with ϕ in that table shows that RD is never unreasonably far from the value of ϕ. For that reason, the RD index may be the one least likely to be quite misleading under special circumstances. Thus, if we had to choose among RR, OR, and RD, we would select RD as our all-purpose index among these three. But even here we feel we can do better.

Standardizing the Three Risk Indices

We have proposed an adjustment that standardizes the RR, OR, and RD indices (Rosenthal, 2000; Rosenthal, Rosnow, & Rubin, 2000). We compute the r between the independent and dependent variables and then display that r in a BESD as described earlier. Table 19.35 shows these BESD-based results for the three studies of Table 19.33. Total sample sizes in the tables of counts of Table 19.33 vary considerably (2,000, to 40, to 20). However, the corresponding BESD-based indices of Table 19.35 all show the standard margins of 100 (which, of course, is a design feature of the BESD). The calculation of our new effect-size indices is straightforward. We simply compute the relative risks, odds ratios, and risk differences on our BESD tables to obtain standardized (BESD-based) relative risks, odds ratios, and risk differences. The computation of these three indices is simplified because the A and D cells of a BESD always have the same value (as do the B and C cells).

With cells of the 2 × 2 table now labeled A, C, C, A from upper left to lower right (as shown at the top of Table 19.35), the calculation is simple and direct. The BESD-standardized relative risk is calculated as

$$RR_{BESD-based} = \frac{A}{C}. \tag{19.19}$$

To apply Equation 19.19 to the Salk vaccine BESD (in Part C of Table 19.32), where the values of Cells A and C are 50.5 and 49.5, respectively, the BESD-based

TABLE 19.35
BESD-standardized outcomes of Table 19.33

	Die	Live	Relative risk	Odds ratio	Risk difference	Phi (ϕ)
Control	A	C	(Eq. 19.19)	(Eq. 19.20)	(Eq. 19.21)	(Eq. 11.12)
Treatment	C	A				

Study 1

	Die	Live				
Control	53	47	1.13	1.27	.06	.06
Treatment	47	53				

Study 2

	Die	Live				
Control	75	25	3.00	9.00	.50	.50
Treatment	25	75				

Study 3

	Die	Live				
Control	95	5	19.00	361.00	.90	.90
Treatment	5	95				

$RR = 50.5/49.5 = 1.02$. The odds ratio standardized is calculated as

$$OR_{BESD-based} = \left(\frac{A}{C}\right)^2, \tag{19.20}$$

which, applied to the Salk vaccine BESD yields BESD-based $OR = (50.5/49.5)^2 = 1.04$. Finally, the risk difference standardized, which is now actually equivalent to ϕ, is calculated as

$$RD_{BESD-based} = \frac{A - C}{100} \tag{19.21}$$

and applied to the Salk vaccine BESD (Table 19.32) yields BESD-based $RD = (50.5 - 49.5)/100 = .01$.

Table 19.35 compares these BESD-standardized indices using the outcomes of Table 19.33. We see the BESD-based RR in Table 19.35 increasing, as it should, in going from Study 1 to Study 3. The BESD-based OR in Table 19.35 also increases from Study 1 to Study 3, but without the alarmist value in Study 1 and the infinite value in Study 3. (A standardized odds ratio could go to infinity only if ϕ were exactly 1.00, an unlikely event in behavioral, social, or biomedical research.) The BESD-based RD is shown in Table 19.35 to be identical to the effect size index ϕ, an attractive feature emphasizing the interpretability of r-type effect-size indices when exhibited in a BESD.

ONE-SAMPLE TABLES OF COUNTS

Up to this point in our discussion of tables of independent counts, all of the tables have been two-dimensional. That is, two or more levels of one variable were represented in the rows and also two or more levels of another variable were represented in the columns of the table. In this section we note that there are also tables of counts in which there are two or more columns but only a single row, that is, $1 \times k$ tables. For example, we began by mentioning Fisher's reanalysis of Mendel's reported data where the observed ratio of yellow to green peas was remarkably close to the expected Mendelian 3:1 ratio—suspiciously close, Fisher argued.

As another illustration, suppose that, in a small survey of voters in an election in which there were only two candidates, A and B, we observe that 60 voted for A and 40 voted for B. What is the probability that these values were obtained by random sampling from a population in which exactly half the voters preferred each of the two candidates? In this illustration we must supply the expected value of voters for A versus voters for B. The null hypothesis is that half the voters are expected to vote for each candidate, and therefore the expected frequency for A is equal to the expected frequency for B. Thus, the expected frequency in this case is the total number of sampling units ($N = 100$ voters) divided by 2, or 50 expected voters for each of the candidates.

We now simply substitute in the general equation for chi-square, where

$$\chi^2 = \sum \frac{(O - E)^2}{E}$$
$$= \frac{(60 - 50)^2}{50} + \frac{(40 - 50)^2}{50} = 4.0,$$

which, with $df = 1$, is significant at $p = .046$, a not very likely outcome if in the population there were no preference for either candidate. The degrees of freedom for one-sample chi-square tests are simply the number of columns (k) minus 1.

Using racetrack data made famous by Siegel (1956), we illustrate another one-sample chi-square, computed on eight starting-gate positions, in which the working hypothesis was that horses closer to the "inside" of the track (at lower numbered gates) would win more races than horses that were closer to the "outside" of the track (at higher numbered gates). Part A of Table 19.36 shows both the number of races won from each of eight starting gates and the number of races expected to be won ($144/8 = 18$ wins in each starting position) if the null hypothesis of no relationship between starting position and number of wins were true. Part B shows the partial chi-square values, which sum to $\chi^2_{(7)} = 16.333$, $p = .022$.

That omnibus chi-square might be of some interest, but it does not directly address the working hypothesis that lower numbered starting gates would be associated with more than their fair share of wins. We use Equation 19.15 to address this specific prediction, that is,

$$\chi^2_{contrast} = r^2_{alerting} \times \chi^2_{omnibus},$$

where the "alerting r" in this example is the correlation between post position and

TABLE 19.36
The racetrack study (Siegel, 1956)

A. Observed (*O*) and expected (*E*) wins

| | Starting positions | | | | | | | | |
	1	2	3	4	5	6	7	8	Σ
Wins	29	19	18	25	17	10	15	11	144
Expected	18	18	18	18	18	18	18	18	144

B. Table of $(O - E)^2/E$ values (or "partial" chi-square values)

| Starting positions | | | | | | | | |
1	2	3	4	5	6	7	8	Σ
6.722	0.056	0.000	2.722	0.056	3.556	0.500	2.722	16.333

the number of wins, and we find $r_{alerting} = -.80$, so $r^2_{alerting} = .64$. Substituting in Equation 19.15, we find $\chi^2_{contrast} = .64 \times 16.33 = 10.48$, with $p = .0012$. Our effect-size estimate can be obtained from Equation 4.15 or Equation 11.16:

$$r_{contrast} = \sqrt{\frac{\chi^2_{(1)}}{N}} = \frac{Z}{\sqrt{N}} = \frac{3.24}{\sqrt{144}} = .27,$$

which we think of as $-.27$ because of the inverse relationship between post position and number of wins. However, because the meta-analytic convention is to report the effect size as negative only when the observed effect is opposite what was predicted (whereas in this situation the working hypothesis actually predicted an inverse relationship), we need to specify the reporting practice that we are using if we report the effect size as $-.27$.

A final point is that, in this example, our alerting r was based on a large enough sample of conditions (eight starting-gate positions) that it seems natural to examine the $r_{alerting}$ more closely. Although our $r_{contrast}$ was $-.27$ (based on a sample of 144 races), our $r_{alerting}$ was $-.80$ (based on a "sample" of eight post positions) and is associated with $t_{(6)} = 3.27$, $p = .0086$. This example reflects the common (but not inevitable) occurrence that $r_{alerting}$ is substantially greater than $r_{contrast}$, an occurrence discussed in some detail in chapter 15.

MULTIPLE-CHOICE-TYPE DATA AND THE PROPORTION INDEX

Much of the research on human abilities, skills, learning, and judgment uses multiple-choice-type measuring instruments. For example, in the area of sensitivity to nonverbal cues, participants may be given a multiple-choice test in which they guess one of four affects that the stimulus person has experienced. The proportion of correct answers given by each participant can then be compared to the proportion expected under the null hypothesis that participants can perform no better than chance (Ekman,

1973; Rosenthal, 1979b). In the area of parapsychological inquiry known as *ganzfeld experiments,* participants are asked to guess which of four (or, in other experiments, five or six) stimuli has been transmitted by a "sender"; the guesses are made under conditions of sensory restriction. In the area of survey research, opinion polling, or voting behavior, the investigator may want to know whether a certain position on the ballot draws more endorsements or votes than would be expected under the null hypothesis. In a classroom, the teacher may want to know whether a particular student has performed better than chance on a multiple-choice test or on a true-false test. In all of these cases the investigator may be interested in a test of significance and almost surely will benefit from a standard, easy-to-interpret effect-size estimate. In the past the primary effect-size indicator has been h, the difference between the obtained proportion and the proportion expected under the null hypothesis after both proportions have been arcsin-transformed (Cohen, 1988). Although such an effect size indicator is very valuable in power calculations, it has no intuitive interpretation that helps us to evaluate the practical significance of the effect. Accordingly, the following index, Π, was proposed (Rosenthal & Rubin, 1989, 1991; Shaffer, 1991) and discussed briefly in chapter 12.

The Proportion Index

It may be recalled that the proportion index shows the hit rate, or proportion correct, on a scale on which .50 is always the null value. Thus, when only two choices are equally likely under the null hypothesis (e.g., as in a true-false test), Pi, or Π, is simply the proportion of correct responses. When there are more than two equally likely choices, the index Π converts the proportion of hits to the proportion of hits that would have been made if there had been only two equally likely choices. Thus, if there were three choices, choosing the correct alternative .60 of the time would be equivalent to choosing the correct alternative .75 of the time, given only two choices. The value of Π, the proportion correct transformed to a two-choice standard, depends simply on k, the number of alternative choices available, and P, the raw proportion of hits:

$$\Pi = \frac{P(k-1)}{P(k-1)+(1-P)} = \frac{P(k-1)}{1+P(k-2)}, \tag{19.22}$$

where we recognize that the right side of the equation was previously given in chapter 12 as Equation 12.10. Table 19.37 shows Π as a function of selected levels of P and of k (from 2 to 10). For any given level of k, a larger P yields a larger Π, and for any given level of P, Π increases as k increases. Table 19.38 has been prepared to show more readily how the proportion of correct choices or hits required to reach any given level of Π decreases as k increases.

Design of One-Sample Research

As noted in chapter 12, the primary purpose of Π is to provide an effect size estimate adjusted for the number of alternatives in a multiple-choice context. However, Π can also play a valuable role in the design of one-sample research. In studies of this type, the

TABLE 19.37
Values of Π for selected values of P and k

		Number of choices, k			
P	2	3	4	5	10
.10	.10	.18	.25	.31	.50
.20	.20	.33	.43	.50	.69
.30	.30	.46	.56	.63	.79
.40	.40	.57	.67	.73	.86
.50	.50	.67	.75	.80	.90
.60	.60	.75	.82	.86	.93
.70	.70	.82	.88	.90	.95
.80	.80	.89	.92	.94	.97
.90	.90	.95	.96	.97	.99

TABLE 19.38
Values of P for selected values of Π and k

		Number of levels, k			
Π	2	3	4	5	10
.10	.10	.05	.04	.03	.01
.20	.20	.11	.08	.06	.03
.30	.30	.18	.12	.10	.05
.40	.40	.25	.18	.14	.07
.50	.50	.33	.25	.20	.10
.60	.60	.43	.33	.27	.14
.70	.70	.54	.44	.37	.21
.80	.80	.67	.57	.50	.31
.90	.90	.82	.75	.69	.50

TABLE 19.39
Best[a] choice of k for varying levels of Π

Π	Best choice of k	Π	Best choice of k
.50	2	.88	8
.67	3	.89	9
.75	4	.90	10
.80	5	.95	20
.83	6	.98	50
.86	7	.99	100

[a] In the sense of a smallest confidence interval for Π.

investigator often has a choice of k, for example, the number of categories, the number of alternatives in a multiple-choice test, and the number of alternative affects from which the correct one is to be selected. The best choice of k (in the sense of the most precisely estimated effect-size Π) can be obtained from the following equation:

$$k_{best} = \frac{1}{1 - \Pi} \qquad (19.23)$$

for any value of Π greater than .5 and less than 1.00. Values of Π less than .5 are less likely to be of interest, but we can use them in Equation 19.23 by substituting $(1 - \Pi)$ for Π.

Table 19.39 shows that for most levels of Π likely to be encountered in psychological and educational research, the best choice of k tends to be small. In general, the smaller the effect size is expected to be, the smaller should be the value of k that is selected. Another simple way to decide on the optimal k is to ask the following question: For the anticipated effect, how large a k can be chosen and still be expected to yield a 50% hit rate? The answer to this question is the same as the answer in Table 19.39.

CHAPTER
20

MULTIVARIATE
DATA
ANALYSIS

BACKGROUND

The purpose of this chapter is to provide an overview of the statistical procedures generally called *multivariate,* though several of the procedures described in detail in earlier parts of this book were in some sense also multivariate. Before the advent of the computer and the availability of packaged statistical programs, the procedures described here were not as widely used as they are currently. This chapter is by no means an exhaustive introduction to this topic; it is instead a survey of major procedures within the framework of a system of classification that should make it easier to conceptualize and think about them.

Whereas in preceding chapters we provided computational details for all of the methods presented, we shall not do so here for several reasons. First, it would take more space than just a single chapter to cover this topic. Second, the computations are often complex and wearying even with the help of a programmable calculator. Third, the computations can be easily done by a computer. Fourth, there are authoritative books currently available, including general sources such as Cohen, Cohen, West, and Aiken (2003); Cooley and Lohnes (1985); Hair, Anderson, Tatham, and Black (1998); Harris (2001); Judd and McClelland (1989); Morrison (2005); Stevens (2002); and Tabachnick and Fidell (2001). There are also more specialized sources such as Marcoulides and Schumacker (1996).

Though we cannot describe, even briefly, all the various multivariate procedures covered in detail in other sources, the classification and overview provided here should be sufficient that most omitted procedures may be perceived as close relatives, special cases, or combinations of those described. It simplifies our thinking about multivariate procedures if we conceive of one or more sets of independent or predictor variables and one or more sets of dependent or criterion variables. Then our first classificatory principle is whether the procedure is concerned with *either* the independent (predictor) *or* the dependent (criterion) variable(s), or whether it is concerned with *both* the independent (predictor) *and* the dependent (criterion) variables.

REDESCRIBING RELATIONSHIPS WITHIN SETS OF VARIABLES

The first class of procedures has in common that a set of variables—either independent (predictor) variables or dependent (criterion) variables—is to be "redescribed" in such a way as to meet one or more of the following goals:

1. *Reduce the number of variables* required to describe, predict, or explain the phenomenon (or phenomena) of interest.
2. *Assess the psychometric properties* of standardized measures or measures under construction.
3. *Improve the psychometric properties* of measures under construction by suggesting (a) how test and subtest reliability might be improved by the addition of relatively homogeneous items or variables, (b) how subtests are related to each other, and (c) what new subtests might be usefully constructed.
4. *Test hypotheses* derived from theories implying certain types of patterns of descriptors emerging from the analyses.
5. *Generate hypotheses* in the spirit of exploratory data analysis on the basis of unexpected descriptors emerging from the analyses.

Of the many specific procedures falling into this class, we focus on one (called *principal components analysis*) to give a flavor of redescriptors. Afterward, we describe, though more briefly, some other procedures also falling into this general class. However, we begin by giving an example of a related procedure that conveys the spirit of forming composites. The procedure we describe, known as *cluster analysis,* is used to reduce a set of variables to a smaller number of *composites* (or *components,* or *clusters*) that can be meaningfully defined in some way. This procedure is useful when there are only a few variables and we can eyeball the similarities and differences that seem to comprise and differentiate clusters. When there are many variables, we might prefer a more formal procedure (such as principal components analysis) as an aid to the naked eye. In either case the variables may be individuals, ratings on particular dimensions, objects, or any other entities.

CLUSTER ANALYSIS FOR REDESCRIPTION

The term *cluster analysis* actually describes not a single method but a family of methods (whose names may vary from one discipline to another) for identifying and classifying variables. We have more to say about clustering later in this chapter, but the nature of

TABLE 20.1
Forming clusters (or composites) by simple grouping

A. The correlation matrix

Variables	A	B	C	D	E
A (Warm)	1.00				
B (Friendly)	.85	1.00			
C (Likable)	.65	.90	1.00		
D (Professional)	.15	.20	.10	1.00	
E (Competent)	.15	.10	.20	.85	1.00

B. Decomposition of 10 intercorrelations among five variables

Intra-Cluster I		Intercluster			Intra-Cluster II

```
      Intra-Cluster I                          Intercluster              Intra-Cluster II

        A      B
                                          A      B      C
   B │ .85                          D │  .15    .20    .10                    D
                                                                    
   C │ .65    .90                   E │  .15    .10    .20          E │  .85
```

C. Average (median) intercorrelations

Intra-Cluster I	Intercluster	Intra-Cluster II

.85-- .15 -------------------------------.85

cluster analysis is illustrated by the hypothetical case in Table 20.1. Cluster analysis, like principal components analysis (and related procedures), begins with a matrix of intercorrelations, such as that shown in Part A. The variables might, for example, refer to five rating scales on which a sample of patients rate the demeanor of their family physicians, or graduate students rate their mentors, or judges rate the videotaped behavior of experimenters running research subjects, or any other situation of interest. The variables that correlate most highly with one another are listed closest to one another in the table (i.e., A, B, and C, and then D and E).

We simply decompose the large triangle of Part A (made up of the 10 correlations beneath the diagonal of five correlations of 1.00) into three smaller geometric shapes: a triangle of three correlations, a rectangle of six correlations, and a tiny "square" of a single correlation (in this example), as shown in Part B. The first geometric shape, the smaller triangle on the left, consisting of three correlations (.85, .65, .90), represents all of the intercorrelations of Variables A, B, and C, where the median intercorrelation is .85. The small "square" rectangle on the right contains only the correlation of .85 between Variables D and E. The larger rectangle in the middle contains the correlations of Variables A, B, and C with Variables D and E, where the median intercorrelation is .15.

We think of the triangle in Part B as constituting a cluster or composite, which we might decide to call the *warmth cluster* or *composite* because it consists of the variables labeled "warm," "friendly," and "likable." We think of the small "square" consisting of only one correlation—that between the variables labeled "professional" and "competent"—as representing a second cluster or composite cluster that we might decide to call the *competence cluster*. The six correlations in the middle rectangle, the intercluster correlations, represent the variable-by-variable similarity of Cluster I with Cluster II.

The diagram in Part C of Table 20.1 gives the average intercorrelation *within* a group of variables constituting a cluster and also the average intercorrelation *between* the variables constituting a cluster. The differences between the median of all within and the median of all between correlations (.85 vs. .15) provides information on the clarity, strength, and "purity" of the clusters. In this example the two clusters are relatively independent of each other and highly consistent internally. (See the section "Quantifying the Clarity of Composites" in chapter 5.)

PRINCIPAL COMPONENTS ANALYSIS
FOR REDESCRIPTION

Instead of working with just 5 variables, suppose we have 11 variables and the subjects or judges of our study comprise a large total sample. Our variables might, for example, be 11 personality characteristics, or 11 different commodities in a market research study, or 11 stimuli in a perception experiment, and so forth. We could be gathering the data in a questionnaire study, a field observation study, or a laboratory experiment or using some combination of these or other procedures. Suppose further that what we want to know is whether we can do an adequate job of describing the total variation in the data on all 11 variables using a much smaller number of supervariables or components.

Principal components analysis would "rewrite" the original set of 11 variables into a new set of 11 components (usually) that have several recognizable properties. One of those properties is that the first principal component rewrites the original variables into the linear combination of variables that does the best job of discriminating among the subjects of the sample. (In a linear combination, each of the original values is multiplied by a mathematically determined weight, and the products of those original values and their weights are summed for each subject to form that person's new score on the component.) This first principal component is the single supervariable that accounts for the maximum possible variance in all the original variables.

Another typical property of principal components analysis is that the second principal component is essentially the same *type* of supervariable as the first component, except that the second operates on the variation in the data remaining after removal of the variation attributable to the first component. The first and second components are orthogonal, because there is no overlap between them (i.e., the second principal component operates only on the leftovers of the first component). After the second principal component has been extracted, the third component is computed, and so on, until as many components have been extracted as there are variables. (If one or more of the original variables is completely predictable from the other original variables, the total number of components computed is reduced accordingly.)

How might it help us in our search for supervariables to rewrite the 11 variables as 11 components? The logic of this method is that the first few components computed tend to account for much more of the total variation among the subjects on the full set of variables than would be the case for an equal number of the original variables chosen at random. For example, the first principal component alone might account for 30%, 40%, or 50% of the total variation among the subjects on the 11 variables. In contrast, only 9.1% would be expected if the early components were no more supervariables than any variable chosen randomly from the original set of 11.

IMPROVING INTERPRETATION BY ROTATION

To illustrate with a more concrete (but smaller) example, suppose we have six variables and want to rewrite them into their principal components. The process of principal components analysis begins with the intercorrelations of our six variables. Then we compute the components and the *loading* (also called a *component loading* or *factor loading*) of each variable on each component. These loadings are the correlations between each variable (usually the rows) and the newly computed components (usually the columns). Each component is then understood or interpreted in terms of the pattern of its loadings. Typically, the components as first extracted from the correlations among the variables are not very interpretable (except perhaps for the first component), but usually they are made more interpretable by a process called *rotation*.

Part A of Table 20.2 shows the correlations of our six variables with the first two components before rotation. Notice that all the variables load highly on Component I,

TABLE 20.2
Loadings of six variables on two principal components before and after rotation

A. Loadings before rotation

Variables	Component I	Component II
Variable 1	.60	.55
Variable 2	.50	.50
Variable 3	.70	.60
Variable 4	.50	−.50
Variable 5	.60	−.55
Variable 6	.70	−.60

B. Loadings after rotation

Variables	Component I	Component II
Variable 1	.04	.82
Variable 2	.00	.70
Variable 3	.06	.92
Variable 4	.70	.00
Variable 5	.82	.04
Variable 6	.92	.06

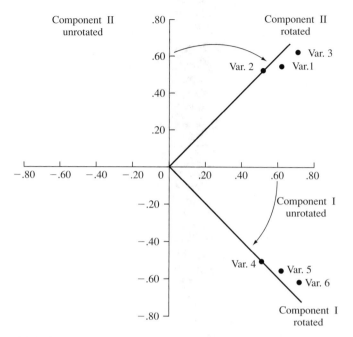

FIGURE 20.1
Loadings of the six variables of Table 20.2 on two rotated and unrotated components (or factors).

and half the variables show a strong positive and half show a strong negative loading on Component II. Shown in Part B of the table are the loadings after the axes are rotated 45 degrees clockwise in this particular case. We see that three of the variables load highly only on one rotated component, and the other three load highly only on the other rotated component. Figure 20.1 provides a visual plot of the loadings in Table 20.2 both before and after rotation.

Let us suppose we are now told that Variables 1, 2, and 3 are alternative measures of sociability, and Variables 4, 5, and 6 are alternative measures of intellectual ability. Clearly the rotated components will be far more useful than the unrotated. The unrotated would be very difficult to interpret, but the rotated suggest that our six variables can be reduced to two supervariables, or composite variables (sociability and intellectual ability), that are independent of each other (orthogonal). That is, when we rotate the axes of Components I and II, we keep them orthogonal (at right angles to one another).

The most commonly used method of orthogonal rotation is called **varimax rotation.** This method tries to maximize the variation of the squared loadings for each component by making the loadings go to 0 or to 1.00 to the extent possible. Using varimax rotation usually helps to make the components easier to interpret. Sometimes, however, it is useful to allow the rotations to be nonorthogonal, such as when the hypothesized underlying supervariables are thought to be somewhat correlated in the real world. Such nonorthogonal rotations are described as *oblique.*

PSYCHOMETRIC APPLICATIONS OF PRINCIPAL COMPONENTS ANALYSIS

As a further illustration of the utility of principal components analysis, we turn next to three particular applications that were part of a program of research to develop a measure of sensitivity to nonverbal cues (Rosenthal, Hall, DiMatteo, Rogers, & Archer, 1979), called the PONS test (for Profile of Nonverbal Sensitivity). The three applications we describe involved its construct validation, subtest construction, and reliability analysis.

Construct Validation

As part of the construct validation of the PONS, it was important to assess its independence from measures of intellectual functioning. Scores on the PONS on items reflecting sensitivity to nonverbal cues that were positive and submissive in content, positive and dominant, negative and submissive, and negative and dominant were available for a convenience sample of 110 high school students. Also available were the students' scores on the verbal SAT, the math SAT, and the Otis IQ test. The researchers hypothesized that the PONS was independent of intellectual ability and expected that, after varimax rotation, two orthogonal principal components would be found reflecting (a) intelligence and (b) nonverbal sensitivity.

The actual loadings after rotation are shown in Table 20.3, and we see that those results are in good agreement with the researchers' hypothesis. That is, the first rotated component is essentially a PONS component; the second is an intellectual component. Before varimax rotation, the first principal component showed positive loadings by all the variables, and the second principal component showed positive loadings by the three intellectual variables and negative loadings by the four variables of sensitivity to nonverbal cues. By making the loadings within each component as close to 0 or to 1.0 as possible, the varimax rotation improved the clarity and specificity of the loadings.

TABLE 20.3
Illustration of principal components in construct validation

	Loadings after rotation	
	Component I	**Component II**
Otis IQ	.19	.64
Verbal SAT	−.02	.89
Math SAT	−.07	.84
PONS		
Positive-submissive	.66	.02
Positive-dominant	.82	−.00
Negative-submissive	.77	.06
Negative-dominant	.78	.06

TABLE 20.4

Visual and auditory channels of PONS test of sensitivity to nonverbal cues

	Visual channels			
Auditory channels	None	Face	Body	Face + body
None		1	2	3
Content-filtered	4	5	6	7
Random-spliced	8	9	10	11

Subtest Construction

Another psychometric application in this investigation involved the formation of subtests, as the PONS consisted of 220 items, 20 in each of 11 nonverbal channels. Those channels were constructed in either the visual or the auditory domain or in both, as denoted more specifically by the cells numbered from 1 to 11 in Table 20.4. The face channel items in Cells 1, 5, and 9 showed only facial cues. The body channel items in Cells 2, 6, and 10 showed only body cues. The face-plus-body-channel items in Cells 3, 7, and 11 showed both types of cues. The content-filtered items in Cells 4–7 preserved tone, but not content, by removing high frequencies. The random-spliced items in Cells 8–11 preserved different aspects of tone, but not content, by random scrambling of speech.

The analytic process started with intercorrelating the 11 channels and channel combinations shown in Table 20.4. Table 20.5 shows the four orthogonal principal components obtained after varimax rotation. Interpretation of those results is that the first component is characterized by face presence, reflecting ability to decode nonverbal cues from any combination of channels as long as the face is included as a source of information. The second and third principal components are interpreted as reflecting a specific skill, namely, the decoding of random-spliced and content-filtered cues, respectively, in the absence of visual cues. The fourth principal component is interpreted as reflecting the ability to decode body cues in the absence of facial cues.

The first row of summary data at the bottom of Table 20.5 gives the sums of the squared loadings—the amount of variance accounted for by that factor. Alternative terms for the sum of the squared loadings, before rotation, are *eigenvalue, latent root, characteristic root,* and just *root* (Armor, 1974). The next row of summary data gives the percentage of variance accounted for by each component. It is computed by division of the sum of the squared loadings for that component by the total number of variables, or 11 in this illustration. For the present analysis these first two rows show that the first and fourth components are more important in the sense of accounting for more variance than the second and third components. Note that this result can occur only after rotation. Before rotation, no succeeding component can be larger than a preceding component. The reason is that each succeeding component is extracted only from the residuals of the preceding one. The third row of summary data lists the number of variables serving to define each component. The last row lists the number of raw test items contributing to the variables defining each component.

A variety of techniques are available for forming subscales from principal components analyses. Many of these techniques generate scores for each subject for

TABLE 20.5
Loadings of 11 PONS subtests on four components

Variables	Loadings on components			
	1	2	3	4
Face	.62	.12	.10	.15
Face + body	.68	.07	.11	.24
Face + random-spliced	.70	.02	.06	.22
Face + content-filtered	.65	−.03	.09	.20
Face + body + random-spliced	.67	.30	.09	.05
Face + body + content-filtered	.70	.06	.10	.32
Random-spliced	.14	.95	.03	.12
Content-filtered	.20	.04	.96	.14
Body	.47	−.04	.02	.59
Body + random-spliced	.33	.07	.12	.57
Body + content-filtered	.11	.13	.08	.82
Sum of squared loadings	3.11	1.04	1.01	1.66
Percentage of variance	28	9	9	15
Number of variables defining components	6	1	1	3
Number of items defining components	120	20	20	60

each component in such a way as to keep the scores on the various components uncorrelated with one another. In our own research, however, we have used a simple procedure that often leads to psychologically more interpretable scales, subtests, or composite variables, although the composite variables may no longer be entirely uncorrelated with each other. We simply combine the variables serving to define each component, giving equal weight to each variable, a method that is recommended for both theoretical and statistical reasons (Dawes & Corrigan, 1974). How we actually combine variables depends on their form, however. If all the variables were measured on similar scales and have similar standard deviations, then we simply add or average the variables. This method also assumes that all the variables have loadings of the same sign or are positively correlated with each other. A variable negatively correlated with the others can be used only after its scale is changed into the proper direction (e.g., by multiplying each observation by −1).

In the study shown in Table 20.5, scores of each variable could range from 0 to 20, and the standard deviations were similar, so the researchers summed the subjects' scores on the variables serving to define each component. Thus, each subject could have a score of 0 to 120 on the composite variable based on the first rotated component, then a score of 0 to 20 on the second and third rotated components, and finally scores of 0 to 60 on the fourth rotated component. Had the variables not been on the same scale or metric, the researchers would have transformed all variables to standard scores before adding or averaging. When there are no missing data, it may not matter whether one adds or averages the scores on the variables defining each component. But when data may be missing, it is safer to use the mean of the variables rather than their sum as the new composite or supervariable.

Rarely are we interested in seeing the loadings of as many principal components (either unrotated or rotated) as there are variables. A number of quantitative criteria are available to help researchers decide how many components they may need to examine. In the case of subtest or composite variable construction, we recommend a step-up approach, examining in turn the rotated first two components, then the first three, then the first four, and so on. The solution we choose should be the one that makes the most substantive sense. Experience has taught us that looking only at the rotated end result (i.e., the loadings of all variables on all the components extracted based on any of several quantitative rules for stopping the extraction process) typically yields more components than are needed to construct useful, meaningful subtests or composite variables, as well as fewer components that are interpretable. It should be noted that at each step-up, the definition of each component changes. Thus, the first component after the rotation of two components will not be the same as the first component after the rotation of three or four or more components.

Reliability Analysis

Earlier in this book we discussed the internal-consistency reliability of a test, which tells us the degree of relatedness of the individual items when we want to use those items to obtain a single score (chapter 4). We described three approaches: the Spearman-Brown equation, Kuder and Richardson's Formula 20, and Cronbach's alpha. Another approach, suggested by David Armor (1974), is particularly useful in the context of principal components analysis. Because the first unrotated principal component is the best single summarizer of the linear relationships among all the variables; it can be used as the basis for an estimate of the internal-consistency reliability of a test. We would probably use such an estimate only where it made substantive sense to envision an overall construct that had been tapped to some degree by all of the variables; this might be the case for many measures of ability, adjustment, achievement, and the like.

In the case of the PONS, the researchers theorized that there might be a general ability to decode nonverbal cues. Therefore, they reasoned, it should be possible to estimate the internal consistency of the PONS from the first principal component *before rotation*. After rotation, the first principal component would no longer be the best single summarizer, but it would probably give a far better structure to the data working in concert with other rotated components. Armor's index of reliability, theta (θ), computes a maximum possible reliability as follows:

$$\theta = \frac{V}{V-1}\left(\frac{L-1}{L}\right), \tag{20.1}$$

where V is the number of variables, and L is the latent root (eigenvalue, or the sum of the squared loadings). For the 220 items of the PONS, with each item regarded as a variable, the researchers computed

$$\theta = \frac{220}{219}\left(\frac{13.217 - 1}{13.217}\right) = .929.$$

The analogous reliability based on the 11 channels in Table 20.4, rather than the 220 items, was

$$\theta = \frac{11}{10}\left(\frac{4.266 - 1}{4.266}\right) = .842.$$

It should be noted that the latent root of 4.266 for the 11-variable analysis is substantially (37%) larger than the latent root of 3.11 (shown in Table 20.5) for the first principal component after rotation.

Armor's theta is a very convenient index of internal-consistency reliability that can be used routinely as long as there are also reasons to use principal components analysis. However, because θ is an index of maximum possible reliability, we generally recommend using it along with the more conservative reliability procedures discussed in chapter 4 (e.g., those based on analysis of variance or intercorrelations adjusted by the Spearman-Brown equation).

Before we leave this illustration of reliability analysis, it may be useful to think about how it is possible to make up a test of several orthogonal principal components that still has high internal-consistency reliability. By their very definition, we know that orthogonal components cannot make any contribution of correlation to each other. However, given the way that internal-consistency reliability for a total test score is defined, this reliability increases as the mean of the intercorrelations increases and as the number of items increases. Thus, a mean intercorrelation lowered by the presence of orthogonal components can be compensated for by an increase in the number of items that correlate positively with some other items. Longer tests, therefore, can have high internal-consistency reliability even when they comprise orthogonal components or factors.

ALTERNATIVES FOR THE REDESCRIPTION OF VARIABLES

Factor Analysis

The most commonly used alternative method to principal components analysis for the redescription of variables is actually an entire family of alternatives known as *factor analysis*. Sometimes principal components analysis is viewed as a special type of factor analysis, but there are subtle, yet sometimes important, differences between principal components and factor analysis.

Principal components analysis and factor analysis both operate on a matrix of correlations similar to that for the cluster analysis example in Part A of Table 20.1. The two methods differ, however, in their entries on the diagonal of the correlation matrix. In principal components analysis, the value of 1.00 is entered on the diagonal that shows the correlation between a variable and itself. In factor analysis, the value entered on that diagonal is usually less than 1.00 and is an estimate of the shared or common variance that sets aside error variance and variance unique to a particular variable. Principal components analysis is a mathematically simpler procedure that can be exactly duplicated by other researchers from the same correlation matrix. Factor analyses are more complex mathematically and yield different results for the various methods of extracting factors, so that different investigators exercising different options will obtain different factor structures from the same data. More detailed discussions of factor analysis can be found in Comrey and Lee (1992); Hair, Anderson, and Tatham (1987); Harman (1976, 2003); J.-O. Kim and Mueller (1978); Loehlin (2004); Mulaik (1972); Rummel (1970); Stevens (2002); Tabachnick and Fidell (2001); and Thompson (2004). Beginners would do well to use principal components with varimax rotation as their standard redescriptor.

Cluster Analysis

Earlier we mentioned that cluster analysis is a family of methods for identifying and grouping variables. These methods range from some very simple to some very complicated procedures. In our initial example (Table 20.1), we illustrated a simple form of cluster analysis in which we used as the criterion of cluster tightness the difference between the average within-cluster intercorrelations and the average between-cluster correlations. Overviews and discussions of cluster analysis can be found in Bailey (1974), K. H. Kim and Roush (1980), and Hair, Anderson, and Tatham (1987).

In clustering, it is not necessary that it be variables that are grouped together. We can instead cluster the subjects or other sampling units for whom measurements have been obtained. Then, instead of grouping variables together that correlate highly over a list of persons, we can group persons together that correlate highly over a list of variables. A typology of persons or other sampling units can thereby be constructed. We should note, however, that factor analysis and principal components analysis can also be used to the same end. We illustrate with a small example. These procedures involve what amounts to an exchange of rows with columns, assuming that we always intercorrelate columns with an eye to their redescription.

Part A of Table 20.6 shows two data matrices: The one on the left (IA) has each person's scores on all variables in one row, and the one on the right (IIA) has each variable's scores for each person in one row. From these data matrices we compute the correlation matrices shown in Part B by correlating each column's scores with every other column's scores. Clustering or factoring the correlation matrices in Part B results in a redescription of the five variables in terms of some (usually smaller) number of groupings of the variables in the case of the matrix on the left (IB). For the matrix on the right (IIB), that clustering or factoring leads to a redescription of the six persons in terms of some (usually smaller) number of groupings. This example of six persons measured on five variables is convenient as an illustration, but we should note that, in general, factors are more reliable when the N on which each correlation is based is much larger than the number of variables or persons being intercorrelated and factor-analyzed.

TABLE 20.6
Redescribing data and correlation matrices

A. Data matrices

IA. Redescribing variables[a]

	Variable				
	1	2	3	4	5
Person 1					
Person 2					
Person 3					
Person 4					
Person 5					
Person 6					

IIA. Redescribing persons[b]

	Person					
	1	2	3	4	5	6
Variable 1						
Variable 2						
Variable 3						
Variable 4						
Variable 5						

[a] Redescribing the variables as clusters, factors, or types.
[b] Redescribing the persons as clusters, factors, or types.

B. Correlation matrices

IB[a]

	Variable				
	1	2	3	4	5
Variable 1					
Variable 2					
Variable 3					
Variable 4					
Variable 5					

IIB[b]

	Person					
	1	2	3	4	5	6
Person 1						
Person 2						
Person 3						
Person 4						
Person 5						
Person 6						

[a] In Matrix IB, each correlation is based on six pairs of observations (i.e., from the six persons).
[b] In Matrix IIB, each correlation is based on five pairs of observations (i.e., from the five variables).

Other Alternatives

Many other procedures and techniques have been developed to serve as redescriptors. They have in common that they examine the relationships among the objects, stimuli, or other entities in terms of some measure of similarity-dissimilarity. On the basis of the results we then try to infer some number of dimensions that will meaningfully account for the obtained pattern of similarities and/or dissimilarities among the objects, stimuli, or other entities. The methods have been called *dimensional analysis* (a term referring to distance analysis), *multidimensional scaling, multidimensional unfolding, proximity analysis, similarity analysis, smallest space analysis,* and some other procedures summarized by various authors (e.g., Coombs, Dawes, & Tversky, 1970;

Rummel, 1970; and the more detailed discussions by Guttman, 1966; Lazarsfeld & Henry, 1968; Torgerson, 1958; Young & Hamer, 1987; and especially by Shepard, Romney, & Nerlove, 1972). To give a flavor of similarity-dissimilarity judgments and a concrete example of multidimensional scaling, we turn next to an application in the social psychology of psychological research.

MULTIDIMENSIONAL SCALING ILLUSTRATION

In chapter 7 we discussed the notion of the "good subject" as put forward by Orne (1962, 1969) in his research on demand characteristics and quasi controls. Orne's idea was that typical subjects in psychological experiments were *altruistically* motivated to "further the cause of science," and he demonstrated empirically the remarkable lengths to which volunteer subjects would frequently go to comply with demand characteristics. Thus, we noted that the volunteer subject frequently serves as a proxy for the "good subject" (Rosenthal & Rosnow, 1975). We also discussed an alternative role enactment that was proposed by Rosenberg (1965, 1969), who argued that typical subjects in psychological experiments more often worry about how they will be evaluated (*evaluation apprehension,* he called it) than about whether the experiment will turn out to be beneficial to science. A third type of role enactment, not discussed previously, is attributed to Stanley Milgram's work on *obedience,* the idea being that typical subjects are simply obedient to authority (e.g., the authority of the experimenter). A question that has been frequently debated in the literature concerns which of these three interpretations best defines the predominant role expectation of typical research subjects in psychology: the altruism hypothesis, the evaluation hypothesis, or the obedience hypothesis. Another question of interest has been whether there are differences in the salient role expectations of volunteers and nonvolunteers for psychological research. Both questions were explored in a study using similarity-dissimilarity judgments and a multidimensional scaling (MDS) procedure (L. S. Aiken & Rosnow, 1973).

The subjects were drawn from sections of an introductory psychology class and identified as "verbal volunteers" or "verbal nonvolunteers" by a procedure in which all of the students had previously been given an opportunity by another experimenter to volunteer for another psychological study. The names of those who had signed up were compared with the current class roster to identify verbal volunteers and nonvolunteers. All of the subjects in the class were given questionnaires during a regular class meeting and asked to judge each of 55 unique pairs of $k = 11$ different stimuli that were presented in a complete paired-comparison schedule. One stimulus, the "target situation," was simply "being a subject in a psychology experiment." The other 10 stimuli were designed either to represent proxy experiences related to the three role expectations or to serve as control items for tapping positive or negative affect. The 10 comparison stimuli are shown in Table 20.7, and the subjects were instructed to rate each paired set of stimuli on how similar the experiences were in the expectations they had about them. A 15-point scale was provided, ranging from "very similar expectations" (15) to "very dissimilar expectations" (1). After the subjects had practiced on some sample pairs, they rated the similarity of their personal expectations for the 55 unique pair members.

TABLE 20.7
**Ten comparison stimuli and the five conditions
they represented**

Altruism hypothesis

    1. Giving anonymously to charity
    2. Working free as a laboratory assistant

Evaluation hypothesis

    3. Taking a final exam
    4. Being interviewed for a job

Obedience-to-authority hypothesis

    5. Obeying a no-smoking sign
    6. Not arguing with the professor

Positive control

    7. Spending the evening with a good friend
    8. Taking a walk in the woods

Negative control

    9. Going to school on the subway
    10. Having to work on a weekend or holiday

     For the assessment of the consistency or test-retest reliability of the judgments, the subjects were given a second questionnaire containing 15 pairs that had been chosen from across the pair sequence and were asked once again to make similarity-dissimilarity judgments. For each subject, a correlation was computed on the original versus the second set of judgments of the 15 reliability pairs. The median reliability among verbal volunteers was .68, and among verbal nonvolunteers it was .48. Reasoning that the inclusion of unreliable protocols would tend to obscure or confound differences between groups, the researchers used an arbitrary cutoff of $r = .51$, thereby upping the median reliability coefficients of the remaining 40 verbal volunteers and 48 verbal nonvolunteers to .77 and .79, respectively. In passing, we should note that the original difference in reliabilities was consistent with some previous results, for which one interpretation was that volunteers may have a tendency to show greater care in responding or in answering questions (i.e., consistent with the good subject hypothesis).

     Of the 55 total judgments that each subject made, 10 were direct assessments of the target stimulus ("being a subject in a psychology experiment") with the comparison stimuli. From these judgments five scores were computed for each subject, the scores representing the similarity of each of the five comparison categories (i.e., altruism, evaluation, obedience, positive control, and negative control) to the target stimulus. Within each of those categories this score was the sum of the judged similarities of the paired situations in that category to the target stimulus. The results, which are shown in Table 20.8, revealed that the category with the highest similarity to the target stimulus among both the verbal volunteers and nonvolunteers was that corresponding to Orne's altruism hypothesis. Notice also that the positive control stimuli were judged to be closer to the target stimulus by

TABLE 20.8

Judged similarity of the target stimulus ("being a subject in a psychology experiment") to five categories of paired experiences

Status of subjects	Experiential categories				
	Altruism hypothesis	Evaluation hypothesis	Obedience hypothesis	Positive control	Negative control
Volunteers	20.3	14.5	12.8	15.1	12.7
	(7.1)	(6.8)	(7.2)	(8.8)	(5.8)
Nonvolunteers	16.9	14.5	9.4	10.0	9.4
	(7.4)	(6.5)	(6.9)	(6.9)	(6.1)

Note: The maximum possible similarity score was 30; the higher the score, the greater was the judged similarity in role expectations between the target stimulus and the combined category stimuli (numbers in parentheses are standard deviations).

the verbal volunteers than by the nonvolunteers, and evidently there are a few other differences as well between those two groups that invite further exploration.

Next, a multidimensional scaling procedure (MDS) was used to explore the structure underlying the subjective similarity judgments between all situations. MDS is similar in spirit to both factor analysis and principal components analysis in that the purpose of MDS is to extract dimensions (analogous to factors or components) underlying sets of interstimulus similarities (analogous to intervariable correlations). MDS gives for each stimulus its projections on the dimensions of the underlying configuration (analogous to factor or component loadings). How many dimensions are chosen to represent the structure of a set of judgments traditionally depends on the goodness-of-fit of a solution to the original judgments as well as on the interpretability of the dimensions of the solution. In this particular study, the mean judged similarity to each category pair was computed separately for verbal volunteers and nonvolunteers. These mean judgments were then analyzed by a method called TORSCA (Young, 1968). Four-, three-, two-, and one-dimensional solutions were derived for verbal volunteers and nonvolunteers separately so that goodness-of-fit could be examined as a function of solution dimensionality. The results indicated that two dimensions were appropriate for representing the original judgments of both groups.

The raw judgments of the 88 individual subjects were next rescaled by a procedure called INDSCAL (Carroll & Chang, 1970), which treats subjects and stimuli simultaneously. In this procedure, a single stimulus configuration is recovered. The configuration is that unique solution that best represents the judgments of all individual subjects. The two-dimensional stimulus configuration derived for the INDSCAL procedure can be seen in Figure 20.2. The researchers interpreted the first dimension as "work orientation," with the nonwork experiences of "taking a walk in the woods" and "spending the evening with a good friend" located at one extreme and with the highly work-oriented experiences at the other extreme. The second dimension was interpreted as affective, with "giving anonymously to charity" at one extreme and "taking a final

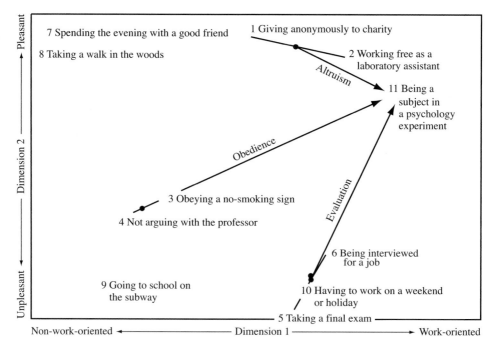

FIGURE 20.2
Two-dimensional INDSCAL solution based on individual judgments of 88 subjects. Lines labeled "Altruism," "Evaluation," and "Obedience" reflect the relative distances between these three categories and the target stimulus ("Being a subject in a psychology experiment"). The proximity between any pair of situations reflects the perceived similarity in role expectations for the pair members.

exam" at the other extreme. In the scaling solution the ordering of distances of the altruism, evaluation, and obedience categories from the target stimulus is plotted, as shown in the figure. Altruism stimuli were closest to the target stimulus, followed by the evaluation and obedience stimuli. Among the verbal volunteers, the median correlation of the individual subjects' original judgments and weighted distances was .67 with a semi-interquartile range of .10. Among the verbal nonvolunteers, the median correlation was .65 with a .06 semi-interquartile range. On the basis of these results, the researchers concluded that the judgments of all individual subjects could be properly represented in the common stimulus configuration given in Figure 20.2.

Last, the researchers turned to the question of whether the verbal volunteers and verbal nonvolunteers could be differentiated on the basis of the weight placed on each dimension in making their judgments. For this purpose the dimension weights of individual subjects derived from the INDSCAL procedure were examined for a differentiation of the groups on the basis of dimension salience. That analysis revealed that the nonvolunteers placed more weight on the work orientation dimension than did the volunteers (mean weights of .36 and .28, respectively), with $F(1, 86) = 9.3$, $p = .003$, $r = .31$. Volunteers placed somewhat more weight on the pleasant-unpleasant dimension than did the nonvolunteers (mean weights of .55 and .49, respectively), with $F(1, 86) = 3.3$, $p = .073$, $r = .19$. Further analysis showed that the work orientation dimension contributed to the distinction between groups more than the affective dimension.

The researchers interpreted these collective results as being consistent with the idea that all three conceptions (altruism, evaluation, and obedience) operate in the role expectations that subjects associate with research participation. No single hypothesis was exclusively valid or invalid, but there was an indication that Orne's altruistic situations bore the closest resemblance to the target stimulus. Regarding differences between verbal volunteers and nonvolunteers, the results were viewed as suggesting that nonvolunteers put heavier emphasis on a work-oriented dimension than do verbal volunteers, whereas volunteers place more weight on an affective dimension. That verbal nonvolunteers tended to amplify the distinction between situations involving work and nonwork activities and judged participation in research more as a work-oriented experience seemed consistent with some other findings (Straits & Wuebben, 1973) suggesting that the negative aspects of experimental participation are likely to be more salient for captive (or coerced) subjects. The collective findings were also interpreted as possibly helping to explain why nonvolunteers can be very unenthusiastic about being research subjects, as well as why their behavior is generally sluggish when they are unpaid, captive subjects; that is, being compelled to work when there is no personal monetary gain attached to the effort could be seen as promoting uncooperative behavior in subjects who are perhaps already attuned to the negative aspects of the "work" situation.

As we noted earlier, this particular study is meant to give only a flavor of MDS and the related techniques described, where the subjective similarity judgments were used as a kind of projective measure. That is, the judgments the subjects made were presumably projections of their underlying states of mind, experiences, expectations, and so on. Various MDS procedures are quite commonly used in marketing research to provide a visual perceptual map of the key dimensions underlying customer evaluations of products, services, and companies (see, e.g., discussion and further illustration in Hair, Anderson, & Tatham, 1987). However, we have seen that it is also a complex method and, as Hair et al. noted, one that is often misused in marketing research. Thus, they wisely recommended that, before deciding to use a packaged program to run MDS, researchers familiarize themselves with the nuances of the procedure and "view the output as only the first step in the determination of perceptual information" (p. 369).

RELATIONSHIPS AMONG SETS OF VARIABLES

The remaining multivariate procedures summarized here only briefly pertain to the relationship between two or more sets of variables heuristically classified as independent (predictor) and dependent (criterion) variables. Table 20.9 provides a structure for the survey of these procedures. The left half of the table lists the procedures in which a set of independent or predictor variables is assessed for its relationship to a single dependent or criterion variable. The right half of the table lists the analogous procedure, but for more than one dependent or criterion value. Thus, in each of the six method pairs of the

TABLE 20.9
Multivariate procedures for examining relationships among sets of variables

Traditionally labeled	Method pair	Dependent-variable status	
		Single	Multiple[a]
Correlational	Method pair 1	Multiple correlation	Canonical correlation
	Method pair 2	Discriminant function	Multiple discriminant function
	Method pair 3	Path analysis	Multiple path analysis
	Method pair 4	Multiple partial correlation	Complex multiple partial correlation
Analysis of variance	Method pair 5	Multilevel analysis of variance	Multivariate multilevel analysis of variance
	Method pair 6	Analysis of covariance	Multivariate analysis of covariance

[a] Interpretation of the results of these procedures is almost always ambiguous, and special caution should be exercised before any of these procedures are used in anything but the most exploratory spirit.

table, one member of the pair is based on a single dependent variable and one is based on multiple dependent variables.

The first four method pairs are labeled "correlational," and the last two method pairs are labeled "analysis of variance." Although this traditional distinction is useful in helping us find our way to the various packaged computer programs, it is also useful for conceptual purposes to view the ANOVA procedures as special cases of the correlational. That is, both are subsumed under the same fundamental model for the analysis of data, the general linear model (Cohen, Cohen, West, & Aiken, 2003). In what follows we describe briefly each of the method pairs in turn.

Method Pair 1: Multiple (Canonical) Correlation

Multiple correlation (briefly discussed in chapter 11) is the correlation between two or more predictor variables and a single dependent variable. The multiple correlation coefficient, R, is a product-moment r between the dependent variable and a composite independent variable. That composite variable is made up, to varying degrees, of the individual independent variables in proportion to their importance in helping to maximize the value of R. Thus, we can learn from the procedures of multiple correlation and regression both (a) the absolute value as a predictor of the entire set of predictors and (b) the relative value as a predictor of each independent variable compared with the others. By dummy-coding the various factors of an ANOVA and using those dummy-coded factors as independent variables, we can readily approach many (but not all, i.e., fixed but not random factor designs) models of the ANOVA by way of multiple correlation or regression. (It should be noted that we are using the terms *correlation* and *regression* interchangeably, whereas a more technical usage would have us refer to *regression* in contexts where we want to relate changes in the level of

X to changes in the level of Y, whereas we would refer to *correlation* as a more global index of closeness of relationship.)

Because multiple correlation or multiple regression can be viewed as having a structure that is basic to all the multivariate procedures shown in Table 20.9, we will spend a little more time describing its virtues (well known) and its problems (too infrequently recognized). Our discussion draws heavily on the authoritative work of Lincoln E. Moses (1986).

In multiple regression the value of the predicted or outcome variable, Y, is viewed as depending on α, the intercept on the Y axis, and the values of the predictor variables, $X_1, X_2, X_3, \ldots, X_k$, each multiplied by a coefficient β chosen in practice so as to minimize the sum of the squared discrepancies between the predicted and obtained values of Y. A term, ε, is added to describe the discrepancy between a particular value of Y and the predicted value of that Y. Thus, for two predictor variables, X_1 and X_2, the equation, formula, or model is

$$Y = \alpha + \beta_1 X_1 + \beta_2 X_2 + \varepsilon \qquad (20.2)$$

As the number of predictor variables increases, we become increasingly grateful for the availability of computers to help us calculate the changing values of α and β. As the computer brings any new predictor variable into the equation, all the betas (and the alpha) change so that the magnitude, sign, and statistical significance of each regression coefficient *depend entirely on exactly which other predictor variables are in the regression equation.* Thus, in describing the results of a regression analysis, statements about which predictors are most important, least important, second-most important, and so on will depend not only on the peculiarities of the particular sample being studied, but also on the precise battery of predictors that has been used.

A word of caution is also required about the interpretation of significance levels provided by multiple-regression statistical packages. The standard output of p values provided by programs for the overall R and for the regression coefficients of each predictor variable are the same whether the particular battery of predictors was planned as the only battery of predictors to be used (almost never the case) or whether some algorithm was used to pick out the best set of k predictors from a larger set of possible predictors (almost always the case). The p values will be accurate only in the former (unlikely) case; they are not accurate in the latter (common) case. Indeed, it is not a trivial matter how one would even go about obtaining an accurate p value (Moses, 1986).

There are special problems of replicability in multiple regression. Particularly when the k predictors of the first study were selected from a larger set of possible predictors, it is very likely that the multiple-R^2 will decrease substantially in a replication study. Such predictable decreases in the cross-validation of a battery of predictors are called *shrinkage* in the context of multiple regression.

A special problem of multiple regression is *collinearity,* or high correlations, among predictor variables. Collinearity makes it hard to interpret the substantive meaning of regression coefficients. For example, how should we think of the regression coefficient for the variable of having made Phi Beta Kappa in the context of a regression equation with college grades and SAT scores as fellow predictor variables? One consequence of collinearity is that we may have a large R^2 and yet find none of the regressors to be significant (Moses, 1986). Because of collinearity, the work of any one predictor is not very important to the overall prediction enterprise. The analogy given by Moses (1986) was 10 people carrying a load that could be carried by 8. The group is doing its job, but any 1 or 2 people could be omitted and never be missed.

In the preceding paragraphs we have tried to create a cautious attitude toward the use of multiple regression in its generic application as a procedure for predicting an outcome variable from a battery of predictor variables. When using multiple-regression procedures to draw causal inferences in the absence of the randomized assignment of subjects, we want to create an attitude of caution greater still! Some years ago, Donald Campbell and Robert Boruch (1975), Thomas Cook and Campbell (1979), and others (e.g., Director, 1979) argued quite convincingly that multiple-regression approaches to inferring causality can yield very misleading results (for a recent update and discussion, see also Shadish, Cook, & Campbell, 2002). In particular, evidence from multiple-regression analyses of the effects of societal intervention programs frequently underestimates the benefits of those programs. Their effects are likely to be seen (erroneously) as ostensibly harmful when the pretest differences favor the control group over the intervention group.

Canonical correlation is the correlation between two or more predictor variables and two or more dependent variables. The canonical correlation coefficient, *CR*, is a product-moment *r* between a composite independent variable and a composite dependent variable. We construct these composite variables by weighting each constituent variable in proportion to the importance of its contribution to maximizing the value of *CR*. Multiple-*R* can be seen as a special case of *CR* when there is only one dependent variable. When there are multiple dependent variables, we can compute more *CR* values—in fact, as many as there are dependent variables (or independent variables if there are fewer of them than of dependent variables). Each successively computed *CR* is again a correlation between a composite independent variable and a composite dependent variable, but with each computed so as to be independent of the preceding composites computed. Because each *CR* operates on the residuals from the preceding *CR*, successive *CR* values will diminish just as successive principal components do.

From a practical point of view, we would not often recommend the canonical correlation, as the results obtained are usually difficult to interpret. In particular, the statistical significance level associated with a canonical correlation is likely to have little substantive meaning. When canonical correlations do apply, we have found it more useful to generate several reasonably uncorrelated independent composite variables (with the help of principal components or cluster analysis) and several reasonably uncorrelated dependent composite variables (again with the help of principal components or cluster analysis). We would then use ordinary correlation, and sometimes multiple correlation, separately for each of the relatively orthogonal dependent variables. Although we do not recommend canonical correlation for hypothesis testing or for confirmatory analysis, we have found the procedure useful from time to time as a hypothesis-generating method in the spirit of exploratory data analysis (see, e.g., Rosenthal, Blanck, & Vannicelli, 1984).

Method Pair 2: (Multiple) Discriminant Function

The *discriminant function* is the set of optimal weights (given the predictor variables) that does the best job of discriminating whether subjects or other sampling units are members of one or another group. Because we can dummy-code group membership as 0 and 1, we can regard discriminant function analysis as a special case of multiple correlation or regression in which we have a dichotomous (0 vs. 1) dependent variable.

The *multiple discriminant function* is the set of optimal weights given each predictor variable that does the best job of discriminating among subjects' memberships in three or more groups. Inasmuch as multiple groups can be turned into multiple dependent variables by dummy coding (so that we have one less variable than we had groups), we can regard multiple discriminant function analysis as a special case of canonical correlation in which each dependent variable is dichotomous. (It should be noted that we obtain the same result whether we regard the dummy-coded group membership variables as the dependent variables or as the independent variables.)

The same note of caution on practical usage that we offered in the case of multiple and canonical correlation applies to these special cases.

Method Pair 3: (Multiple) Path Analysis

Path analysis is a special case of multiple regression in which the goal is usually the drawing of causal inference, and in which there is presumably a strong basis for ordering causal priorities. For example, if our predictor variables include gender, social class, and education, we can order these three variables on a dimension of time, with gender being determined first, then social class (defined, say, as parental income and occupation when the subject began formal education), and finally education of subject (defined as number of years). Multiple regression is then used in a repeated way, each variable contributing to the prediction of every other variable coming later in time. If the dependent variable is income, then all three predictors are relevant to income, with gender contributing directly to income and also by way of influencing social class and education, which in turn also affect the dependent variable. Social class, being partially affected by gender, can then affect income directly and also by way of education. Education, being affected by gender and social class, can then also affect income directly. The diagram in Figure 20.3 summarizes the lines of influence. In chapter 9 we discussed the problem of missing data; James L. Arbuckle (1996), who created the structural equation modeling program called AMOS, has written an informative article dealing with missing data in the context of path analysis.

Multiple path analysis is a logically implied special case of canonical correlation again involving the repeated application of multiple correlational methods to time-ordered variables, but with two or more ultimate dependent variables. A composite dependent variable is created with weights maximizing the predictive relationships between the time-ordered predictor variables and the composite dependent variable. As many sets of predictive relationships can be computed as there are dependent variables. Figure 20.4 illustrates the procedure.

All of the cautions we have raised in connection with multiple regression and canonical correlation apply as well to path-analytic procedures (some others are

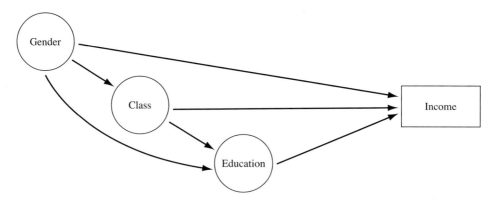

FIGURE 20.3
Path analysis showing the prediction of income from three time-ordered variables.

also raised in chapter 8 on nonrandomized research and functional relationships). As path-analytic procedures are so often employed in the service of drawing causal inference, we urge special caution in their use. The short version of this caution is that no statistical procedures are guaranteed to permit drawing strong causal inference from nonexperimental research—not path analysis, not structural equation modeling, not anything. The longer version of this caution can be found in part in D. A. Freedman's cautionary work (1987a, 1987b, 1997) and in that of his respondents (e.g., Bentler, 1987; Rogosa, 1987, and others who contributed to a special issue of the *Journal of Educational Statistics*, 1987, Vol. 12, No. 2), as well as in McKim and Turner (1997). Other useful discussions can be found in Kenny's (1979) book and in Shadish, Cook, and Campbell's (2002) thorough update of classic works by Campbell and Stanley (1963, 1966) and T. D. Cook and Campbell (1979).

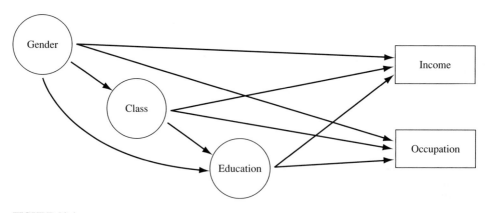

FIGURE 20.4
Multiple path analysis showing the prediction of income and occupation from three time-ordered variables.

Method Pair 4: (Complex) Multiple Partial Correlation

Multiple partial correlation is ordinary multiple correlation or regression performed on a set of variables from which the effects of one or more other variables have been removed. The effects of those *third-party variables* (also called *covariates* or *control variables*) can be removed from either the independent or the dependent variable set (*multiple part correlations*) or from both (*multiple partial correlations*); for details see, for example, Cooley and Lohnes (1971).

    Complex multiple partial correlation is ordinary canonical correlation performed on a set of variables from which the effects of one or more other variables have been removed. Effects of the third-party variables can be removed from either the independent or the dependent variable set (*complex multiple part correlation*) or from both (*complex multiple partial correlation*). For details see Jacob Cohen's paper on *set correlation* (1982), and the book by Cohen, Cohen, West, and Aiken (2003).

Method Pair 5: (Multivariate) Multilevel Analysis of Variance

The *multilevel analysis of variance* has been discussed in detail in earlier chapters. We list it here only to be consistent, as the procedure does involve more than one independent variable. Even a one-way ANOVA, if there are more than two levels, can be viewed as made up of a series of (dummy-coded) independent variables. Given a series of independent variables and a single dependent variable, we can readily approach many types of analysis by means of multiple correlation or regression. Fixed-effects analyses can be handled very easily, for example, but random-effects analyses can be handled only with considerably greater difficulty.

    Multivariate multilevel analysis of variance is the generalization of ANOVA to more than a single dependent variable. As such, it can be seen as closely akin to canonical correlation, especially the type of canonical correlation in which one set of variables is dichotomous (*multiple discriminant function*). Many types of multivariate analysis-of-variance problems can be approached readily through canonical correlation if the independent variables are fixed rather than random. (For a discussion of fixed and random factors, see chapter 18.)

Method Pair 6: (Multivariate) Analysis of Covariance

The *analysis of covariance* can be understood as an analysis of variance performed on a dependent variable that has been corrected or adjusted for a subject's score on some other variable (a covariate) that correlates (usually substantially) with the dependent variable. Analysis of covariance (ANCOVA) procedures are used successfully to increase the precision of the analysis and, with far more dubious success, to reduce bias in nonexperimental studies (Judd & Kenny, 1981). These procedures are closely related to those of the multiple partial correlation and other multiple-regression procedures. Covariates are usually chosen for their high degree of correlation with the dependent variable within the various conditions of the design of the study. In a before-after (i.e., pretest-posttest) design, for example, one can perform a repeated-measures analysis, or use several levels of blocking, or do an analysis only on the posttest but with the pretest used as a covariate. Some comparisons among these procedures were given in chapter 16 in our discussion of the use of blocking and the analysis of covariance. When ANCOVA is used to reduce bias in nonexperimental studies, the same cautions apply as were offered in our discussion of the use of multiple regression to draw causal inferences.

Multivariate analysis of covariance is ANCOVA used with multiple dependent variables. It is closely related to complex multiple partial correlation. As a practical matter we would only rarely recommend the use of either the multivariate analysis of variance or covariance. With correlated dependent variables we have found it more useful to generate several fairly orthogonal composite variables (usually by means of principal components analysis or clustering methods) to serve as our dependent variables and then to use ANOVA or ANCOVA separately for each dependent variable.

A final word about multivariate procedures: It is just about as easy to have the computer produce a multiple discriminant function analysis as a *t* test, and we have seen eager researchers call for them by the dozen. But as we have argued against the diffuse, unfocused *F* test (or effect size estimators) based on more than a single *df* in the numerator, we want to argue against the diffuse, unfocused tests of significance and effect size estimates that typically emerge from many of the multivariate procedures. We encourage their use, however, in exploratory contexts and as preliminary tests analogous to the omnibus *F* of the analysis of variance when they are to be followed up by focused, precise tests of significance and effect size estimates.

CHAPTER

21

META-ANALYSIS: COMPARING AND COMBINING RESEARCH RESULTS

STATISTICAL ANALYSIS OF STATISTICAL ANALYSES

It has become almost obligatory to end research reports with the clarion call for further research. Yet it seems fair to say that, traditionally, behavioral and social scientists have been better at issuing such calls than at knowing what to do with the answers. In many areas we do have the results of numerous studies all addressing essentially the same question. Summaries of those collective sets of studies, however, have not been nearly so informative as one would like them to be. The most insightful narrative reviews of research by the most sophisticated workers have rarely told us more about each study of a set of studies than (a) that it did or did not reach a given significance level and (b) what was the direction of the observed relationship between the variables investigated. Fortunately, this state of affairs has begun to change very noticeably. An increasing number of literature reviews have moved from the more literary, narrative format to more quantitative summaries of research domains. Such reviews, using procedures known collectively as *meta-analytic,* usually describe (a) the typical magnitude of the effects or phenomena, (b) their variability, (c) their level of statistical significance (or *p* value), and (d) the nature of the moderator variables from which one can predict the relative magnitude of observed effects.

The term *meta-analysis* was coined by Gene Glass in 1976 to refer to the "statistical analysis of a large collection of analysis results from individual studies for the purpose of integrating the findings" (p. 3). Morton Hunt's *How Science Takes Stock* (1997) tells the story of the development of meta-analysis and its use in various research areas. However, although many are inclined to think of meta-analysis as a recent development, it is actually older than the *t* test, which (as we mentioned in chapter 13) dates back to Gosset (1908). Four years earlier, Karl Pearson (1904) had collected six correlation coefficients (.58, .58, .60, .63, .66, .77) because he wanted to know the degree to which inoculation against smallpox saved lives. The weighted mean of the correlations was .64, the unweighted mean was .63, and the median correlation was .61. Pearson's prescient meta-analytic summary was that there was a .6 correlation between inoculation and survival. From our discussion in chapter 11 of effect sizes in biomedical research, particularly Table 11.8, it would appear that Pearson's median *r* was extraordinarily huge for a biomedical effect.

In Pearson's day, approaching studies from a meta-analytic orientation was unusual. A few decades later, there were other prophetic examples in other research areas. For instance, in the area of agricultural science, Lush (1931) investigated the relationship between the initial weight of steers and their subsequent gain in weight. Lush had six samples of steers available, and he was interested in computing the average of the six correlations he had available (*Mdn* = .39). What made those six samples famous, however, was not Lush's averaging of correlations, but the statistician George Snedecor's (1946) using the six correlations in his classic statistics text as an example of how to combine correlation coefficients. Subsequent editions have retained that famous example (e.g., Snedecor & Cochran, 1967, 1980, 1989). Snedecor's longtime coauthor, William G. Cochran, had himself been a pioneer in the development of meta-analytic thinking. He had addressed himself early to the statistical issues involved in comparing and combining the results of series of studies (Cochran, 1937, 1943).

Recently, there has been an explosion of meta-analytic reviews. However, like any increasingly popular innovation or technology, meta-analysis is not emerging without controversy and criticism. We examine those criticisms in the next section; but here we can point out several fairly obvious advantages of meta-analysis. For example, our quantitative summaries of research domains using meta-analytic procedures are likely to be more complete, more explicit, and more powerful (in the sense of decreasing Type II errors) than typical narrative reviews and, for all these reasons, conducive to a more cumulative view of behavioral and social science. Moderator variables are more easily spotted and evaluated in the context of quantitative syntheses and thereby are advantageous to theory development and increased empirical richness. Meta-analysis also, of course, has less obvious benefits, such as the idea of thinking about science not simply as an individual enterprise but more as a collective effort in which we build on one another's discoveries and insights. It also focuses our attention more on the implications of ranges of effect sizes and their contextual moderators rather than on dichotomous decision making based on some arbitrary significance level.

In chapter 12 we described effect size estimators in the correlational family (*r* and *r*-type indices) and in the difference family (Cohen's *d*, Hedges's *g*, etc.), and in chapter 19 we discussed indices in the ratio family (such as relative risk, the BESD-based relative risk, etc.). As we first discussed in chapter 2, when we need to make a decision about how to convert effect sizes to one particular index (as in meta-analytic work), we generally prefer r-type indices because of their utility, flexibility, and interpretability in a wide range of circumstances. That preference, however, certainly does not preclude the use of difference-type indices, and in fact they are commonly and usefully employed in many meta-analytic reviews of clinical trials in biomedical research in which a single treatment condition is compared with a single control group (e.g., discussions in Dawson & Trapp, 2004; Hasselblad & McCrory, 1995). For behavioral and social scientists, a detailed examination of meta-analytic procedures can be found in a handbook edited by Harris Cooper and Larry V. Hedges (1994). As is the case in the analysis of data of any individual study, the analysis of a set of studies can vary greatly in complexity and completeness. Among the various texts that are currently available on meta-analysis, those by G. Glass, McGaw, and Smith (1981), Hedges and Olkin (1985), and Hunter and Schmidt (2004) tend to be more detailed and more quantitatively demanding than the books by Cooper (1989, 1998), Light and Pillemer (1984), Lipsey and Wilson (2001), and Rosenthal (1991a).

An overall emphasis in this chapter is the observation that the level of quantitative skill and training needed to use basic meta-analytic procedures is so modest that any researchers capable of analyzing the results of their own research can perform the small number of calculations required to address standard meta-analytic questions. Later in this chapter we give some examples based on comparing and combining the results of just two studies, and then we expand our discussion to three or more studies. Meta-analytic reviews of the literature often involve many studies, but the simple procedures we describe for comparing and summarizing the results of just a pair of studies can be directly applied by researchers who are reporting a study and its replication in the same journal article.

The most important aspect of a meta-analysis is the descriptive part in which the effect sizes are reported or displayed and their distribution and central tendency are summarized. Guidelines are available in the textbooks cited above and in other sources (e.g., Rosenthal, 1995c; Rosenthal & DiMatteo, 2001, 2002). Good meta-analytic practice, like good data-analytic practice more generally, typically adopts an exploratory orientation toward these displays and summaries (Tukey, 1977). The computations required for the most basic meta-analytic work are so trivial that, in much of our own meta-analytic work, going back many years, we have never felt the need to use a software package that "does meta-analysis." Good software can be a timesaver when the data set is quite large, but a drawback is that some researchers who feel less expert than they might like believe the software will "do the analysis." Alas, that is not the case. The software will do the calculations, and it will do them quickly. But for any given application, those calculations may be wise or they may be foolish. Keeping it simple, staying close to the data, and emphasizing description prevents most serious errors.

CRITICISMS OF META-ANALYSIS

Does the increase in the number of meta-analytic reviews of the literature represent a giant stride forward in the development of the behavioral and social sciences generally, or does it instead signal a lemming-like flight to disaster? Some three dozen scholars were invited to respond to a meta-analysis of studies of interpersonal expectancy effects (Rosenthal & Rubin, 1978). Though much of the commentary dealt with the substantive topic at hand, a good deal of it was directed at methodological issues having to do with the use of meta-analysis. The criticisms can be grouped into a half-dozen conceptual categories, some of which were accurately anticipated by Glass (1978), who had earlier received commentary on his own meta-analytic work (Glass, 1976) and that of his colleagues (Glass et al., 1981; M. L. Smith & Glass, 1977).

1. *Sampling bias and the file drawer problem.* This criticism holds that there is a retrievability bias because studies retrieved do not reflect the population of studies conducted. One version of this criticism is that the probability of publication is increased by the statistical significance of the results, so published studies are not representative of the studies conducted. This criticism is well taken, but it applies equally to traditional narrative reviews of the literature. Procedures that can be used to address this problem are described in the texts cited earlier, including ways of retrieving hard-to-find studies (M. C. Rosenthal, 1994; 2006). Later in this chapter we discuss a particular procedure that addresses the concern that researchers file away their statistically nonsignificant studies, making them unavailable for meta-analysis. The procedure we describe involves estimating the number of such studies it would take to nudge an obtained overall p level down to a "barely significant" level.

2. *Loss of information.* One version of this criticism holds that summarizing a research domain by a single value (such as a mean effect size) loses valuable information. However, comparing a set of studies, which means trying to understand differences in their results, is as much a part of meta-analytic procedures as summarizing the overall results of the set. Even *within* a single study, experimenters have historically found it quite helpful to compute the means of the experimental and control groups, even though computing a mean always involves a "loss of information." Furthermore, there is nothing to prevent the meta-analyst from reading each study as carefully and assessing it as creatively as might be done by a more traditional reviewer of the literature. We have something of an operational check on reading articles carefully in the case of meta-analysis: If we do not read the results carefully, we cannot compute accurate effect sizes. In traditional reviews, results may have been read carefully, or not read at all, or with only the abstract or the discussion section providing "the results" to the reviewer.

   Another version of this criticism is that, by emphasizing average values, meta-analysts overlook negative instances. There are several ways that "negative" instances might be defined by researchers, for example, $p > .05$, or $r = 0$, or r negative, or r significantly negative, and so on. However negative instances are defined, when we divide the sample of studies into negative and positive cases, we have dichotomized an underlying continuum of effect sizes (or significance levels). Accounting for the "negative" instances is, therefore, simply a special case of finding moderator variables.

3. *Heterogeneity of method and quality.* One version of this criticism is that meta-analysts summarize studies with quite different operationalizations of independent and dependent variables, as well as different types of sampling units, and therefore, the results are muddied because the data are not uniform. This was called the "apples and oranges issue" by Glass (1978). They are good things to mix, he wrote, when we are trying to generalize to fruit. Indeed, if we are willing to generalize over subjects *within* studies (as most experimenters routinely do), why should we not be willing to generalize *across* studies? If subjects behave very differently within studies, we can simply block on subject characteristics to help us understand why. If studies yield very different results from each other, we can block on study characteristics to help us figure out why. It is very useful to be able to make general statements about fruit. If, in addition, it is also useful to make general statements about apples, about oranges, and about the differences between them, there is nothing in meta-analytic procedures to prevent us from doing so.

   Another version of the heterogeneity criticism is that bad studies are thrown in with good studies. This criticism might be broken down into two questions: What is a bad study? and What shall we do about bad studies? Regarding the first question, too often it seems that deciding what is a bad study is a procedure unusually susceptible to bias or to claims of bias (Fiske, 1978). Bad studies are too often those whose "results" the critic finds uncongenial or, as Glass et al. (1981) put it, the studies of our "enemies." Therefore, when reviewers of research tell us they have omitted the bad studies, we should satisfy ourselves that the elimination has been by criteria we find acceptable. Regarding the second question, the distribution of studies on a dimension of quality is, of course, not really dichotomous (good vs. bad) but continuous, with all possible degrees of quality. The fundamental method of coping with bad studies or, more accurately, variations in the quality of research is by differential weighting of studies (described in this chapter). Dropping studies is merely the special case of zero weighting. However, the most important question to ask about the quality of studies was that raised by Glass (1976), who wondered whether there is a relationship between quality of research and effect size obtained. If there is not, the inclusion of poorer quality studies will have no effect on the estimate of the average effect size, though it will help to decrease the size of the confidence interval around that mean. If there *is* a relationship between the quality of research and the effect size obtained, we can use whatever weighting system that we find reasonable (and that we can persuade our colleagues and critics also to find reasonable).

4. *Problems of independence.* There are also two parts of this criticism. One is that several effect-size estimates and several tests of significance may be generated by the same subjects within each study. This can be a very apt criticism under some conditions, and technical procedures are available for adjusting for nonindependence (Rosenthal, 1991a; Rosenthal & Rubin, 1986). Another part of the criticism is perhaps more subtle, however. It is that possible nonindependence arises when different studies conducted in one lab yield results that are more correlated with each other than with the results of different studies in another lab.

In other words, there may be "laboratory effects" (Jung, 1978; Rosenthal, 1966, 1969, 1976). We can handle such effects by treating them as moderator variables and then by analyzing domains by laboratory as well as by study (Rosenthal, 1969, 1991a).

5. *Exaggeration of significance levels.* This is perhaps the only criticism of meta-analysis that is based entirely on a misunderstanding of the fundamental equation of data analysis (Equation 11.10): Significance test = Size of effect × Size of study. The criticism is that as further studies are added to a meta-analysis, the results are more and more significant. That is certainly true, but difficult to perceive as a "negative feature" or as anything other than a mathematical fact. When the null hypothesis is false and therefore ought to be rejected, it is indeed true that adding observations (either sampling units within studies or new studies) will increase statistical power. However, it is hard to accept, as a legitimate criticism of a procedure, a characteristic that increases its accuracy and decreases its error rate. If the null hypothesis of zero effect were really true, adding studies could not lead to an increased probability of rejecting the null hypothesis. Interestingly, a related feature of meta-analysis is that it may, in general, lead to decreases in Type II errors even when the number of studies is modest. Procedures requiring the research reviewer to be more systematic and to use more of the information in the data seem to be associated with increases in power, and therefore with decreases in the Type II error rate (H. Cooper & Rosenthal, 1980).

6. *Small effects.* This final criticism is that the results of substantively important meta-analyses show only "small effects" because the r^2 values obtained are small. This criticism was addressed in chapter 11, where we showed that r^2 values of nearly zero sometimes have profound substantive implications in biomedical and other types of research. The problem with squaring the effect size r is that it may make small, but conceivably quite meaningful, effects seem virtually to disappear. That was given as one reason we prefer to work with the raw product-moment r and then to view its implications within the framework of the binomial effect-size display.

INTERPRETING TWO
OR MORE STUDIES

We turn now to some examples of meta-analytic procedures. Our goal is not to enumerate the many quantitative procedures used in meta-analytic reviews, because they are discussed in detail in the various texts cited at the beginning of this chapter. Many were also illustrated in our earlier chapters, such as stem-and-leaf plots, box plots (if several types of studies are to be compared), measures of central tendency and variability, and, of course, contrasts. For example, in chapter 15 we illustrated a procedure for making meta-analytic comparisons and combinations of competing contrasts (see also Rosenthal, Rosnow, & Rubin, 2000). In the remainder of this chapter we describe a few additional procedures that may be of interest not only to those contemplating a meta-analytic review, but also to researchers who are interested in summarizing the results of only a pair of studies in reports of original research. Regardless of how complex the particular procedures become in a given report, providing certain basic information will make it easier for research consumers to independently assess the tenability of specific conclusions. Without implying that all good meta-analyses will look alike, suggestions for the kind of basic information that might be reported, as well as criteria for the inclusion of studies, for the recording of variables, and other tips and suggested guidelines for preparing different sections of a meta-analytic review can be found elsewhere (Rosenthal, 1995c).

Even when researchers have been rigorous and sophisticated in their interpretation of the results of a single study, they are often apt to err in the interpretation of two or more studies. In chapter 2 we gave an example of such error involving a report by a researcher (Jones) who expressed skepticism after having failed to replicate an experiment by another researcher (Smith) that had shown one type of leadership style to be better than another. The results of both Jones's and Smith's experiments were clearly in the same direction, but Jones reported a "failure to replicate" because his t test was not statistically significant. We noted, however, that Jones's effect size (which he neglected to report) was exactly the size of the effect in Smith's study (which Smith also neglected to report, but we could easily calculate). In other words, Jones had replicated the same relationship that Smith had found but had not replicated Smith's p value. Upon closer inspection of the results of those two studies, we concluded that the power of Jones's t test was less than a third the power of Smith's t test because Jones's total sample size (N) was so much smaller than Smith's sample size. Furthermore, a comparison of their respective significance levels (by procedures described in the next section) would have revealed to Jones the futility of his argument, as the p levels of the two studies were not significantly different. As a guide to the various cases that follow, Table 21.1 lists each example number and the meta-analytic procedure it illustrates.

TABLE 21.1
Guide to 20 examples of meta-analytic procedures

	Example numbers	
	Significance testing	**Effect size estimation**
Comparing:		
Two studies	1, 2, 3	4, 5, 6
Three or more studies		
Diffuse tests	13	14
Focused tests	15	16
Combining:		
Two studies	7, 8, 9	10, 11, 12
Three or more studies	17, 18	19, 20

COMPARING TWO SIGNIFICANCE LEVELS

Ordinarily, when we compare the results of two studies, we are more interested in comparing their effect sizes than their test statistics or p values. In fact, it is hard to imagine why anyone would realistically be interested in comparing two p values. Nonetheless, the question of how to do so does occasionally arise in research methods classes, and it would seem to be relevant to the Jones-versus-Smith controversy noted above. Of course, even when all we have is a p value and the sample size, we can do better by estimating $r_{equivalent}$ (described in chapter 12) and then concentrating on effect sizes rather than on p levels (Rosenthal & Rubin, 2003). Nonetheless, if we feel we really must compare the p values of two reported test statistics, it is simple enough to do.

For each of the two test statistics we obtain an accurate p level—accurate, say, to two meaningful digits (i.e., not counting zeros before the first nonzero value), such as $p = .43$ or $.024$, or $.0012$. That is, if $t(30) = 3.03$, we give p as $.0025$, not as "$<.05$." Extended tables of the t distribution are helpful here (e.g., Federighi, 1959, which is reproduced in Table B.3, Appendix B), as are scientific calculators with built-in distributions of Z, t, F, and χ^2, and there are also reliable Web sites with links to this information. For each p we find Z, the standard normal deviate corresponding to the p value. The last row of Table B.3 and the table of Z values of Appendix B are both useful in finding the accurate Z. Both p values should be one-tailed, and the corresponding Z values will have the same sign if both studies show effects in the same direction, but different signs if the results are in the opposite direction. It is customary to assign positive signs to Z values falling in the predicted direction, and negative signs to Z values falling in the unpredicted direction. The difference between the two Z values when divided by $\sqrt{2}$ yields a new Z that corresponds to the p value that the difference between the Z values could be so large, or larger, if the two Z values did not really differ.

Recapping, to compare the p values of two independent tests, we compare the corresponding Z values by

$$Z \text{ of difference} = \frac{Z_1 - Z_2}{\sqrt{2}}, \tag{21.1}$$

where the result is distributed as the standard normal deviate, Z, so we can enter this newly calculated Z in Table B.1 (Appendix B) to identify the p value associated with finding a Z of the size obtained or larger.

Example 1

Studies A and B yield results in opposite directions, and neither is "significant." One p is $.06$ one-tailed; the other is $.12$ one-tailed, but in the opposite tail. The Z values corresponding to the two p values are found in a table of the normal curve to be $+1.56$ and -1.18 (note the opposite signs to indicate results in opposite directions). Then, from Equation 21.1 we have

$$Z = \frac{(1.56) - (-1.18)}{1.41} = 1.94$$

as the Z of the difference between the two p values of their corresponding Z values. The p value associated with $Z = 1.94$ is .026 one-tailed, or .052 two-tailed. The two p values of Studies A and B may be seen to differ significantly, or nearly so, a finding suggesting that the "results" of the two studies are not consistent with respect to significance levels even allowing for normal sampling fluctuation.

Example 2

Studies C and D yield results in the same direction, and both are significant. One p is .04, and the other is 2.5^{-5} (i.e., $p = .000025$). The Z values corresponding to these p values are 1.75 and 4.06, respectively (both have the same sign because they are in the same tail). From Equation 21.1 we have

$$Z = \frac{(4.06) - (1.75)}{1.41} = 1.64$$

as our obtained Z of the difference. The p associated with this Z is .05 one-tailed, or .10 two-tailed, so we may want to conclude that the two p values of Studies C and D differ significantly, or nearly so. It should be emphasized, however, that finding one Z greater than another does not tell us whether the Z is greater because the size of the effect is greater, the size of the study is greater, or both.

Example 3

Studies E and F yield results in the same direction, but one is "significant" ($p = .05$) and the other is $p = .06$. This example illustrates the worst case scenario for inferential errors, where investigators might conclude that the two results are "inconsistent" merely because one is "significant" and the other is not. Regrettably, this example is not merely theoretical. Just such errors have been made and documented (Nelson, Rosenthal, & Rosnow, 1986; Rosenthal & Gaito, 1963, 1964). The Z values corresponding to the p values are 1.64 and 1.55. Therefore,

$$Z = \frac{(1.64) - (1.55)}{1.41} = .06$$

is our obtained Z of the difference between p values of .05 and .06. The p associated with this difference is .476 one-tailed, or .952 two-tailed. This example illustrates clearly just how trivial the difference between "significant" and "nonsignificant" results can be.

COMPARING TWO EFFECT-SIZE CORRELATIONS

When we ask whether two studies are telling the same story, what we *should* mean is whether the independent (and dependent) variables are fairly similar, and whether the estimated effect sizes are reasonably consistent with each other. Our discussion is restricted to r as the effect-size indicator, but analogous procedures are available for comparing other effect-size indicators (see, e.g., Cooper & Hedges, 1994). For these calculations we work with the Fisher z_r transformation of r (defined in Equation 11.2). (In this chapter, as in earlier discussions, we use the lowercase z for the Fisher transformation and the capital Z for the standard normal deviate.) As mentioned earlier, the advantage of the z_r transformation is that equal differences between any pair of Fisher z_r values are equally detectable, a situation that does not hold for untransformed r values. For raw r values, the difference between .00 and .86, for example (a difference of .86 units of r but a difference of about 1.3 units of z_r), is no more detectable than the difference between .86 and .99 (a difference of .13 units of r but a difference of about 1.3 units of z_r). In addition, significance tests of differences between r values are more accurate when this transformation is used (R. A. Alexander, Scozzaro, & Borodkin, 1989).

For each of the two studies to be compared, we compute the effect size r and find for each of those r values the associated Fisher z_r. A table that converts our obtained r values to Fisher z_r values is available in Appendix B (Table B.7). Then, when N_1 and N_2 represent the number of sampling units (e.g., subjects) in each of our two studies, the quantity

$$Z \text{ of difference} = \frac{z_{r1} - z_{r2}}{\sqrt{\dfrac{1}{N_1 - 3} + \dfrac{1}{N_2 - 3}}} \tag{21.2}$$

is distributed as the standard normal deviate Z, and the quantity $N - 3$ corresponds to the df for each of the Fisher z_r values (Snedecor & Cochran, 1989).

Example 4

Studies G and H yield results in opposite directions with effect sizes of $r = .60$ ($N = 15$) and $r = -.20$ ($N = 100$), respectively. The Fisher z_r values corresponding to these r values are $z_{r1} = .69$ and $z_{r2} = -.20$, respectively (the opposite signs correspond to the opposite signs of the raw r values). Then, from Equation 21.2 we have

$$Z = \frac{(.69) - (-.20)}{\sqrt{\dfrac{1}{12} + \dfrac{1}{97}}} = 2.91$$

as the Z of the difference between the two effect sizes. The p value associated with $Z = 2.91$ is .002 one-tailed, or .004 two-tailed. The two effect sizes of Studies G and H, then, differ significantly.

Example 5

Studies I and J yield results in the same direction with effect sizes of $r = .70$ ($N = 20$) and $r = .25$ ($N = 95$), respectively. The Fisher z_r values corresponding to these raw r values are $z_{r1} = .87$ and $z_{r2} = .26$, respectively. From Equation 21.2 we have

$$Z = \frac{(.87) - (.26)}{\sqrt{\dfrac{1}{17} + \dfrac{1}{92}}} = 2.31$$

as our obtained Z of the difference. The p associated with this Z is .01 one-tailed, or .02 two-tailed. Here is an example of two studies that agree on a significant positive relationship between variables X and Y, but disagree significantly in their estimates of the magnitude of the relationship.

Example 6

Studies K and L yield effect size estimates of $r = .00$ ($N = 17$) and $r = .30$ ($N = 45$), respectively. The Fisher z_r values corresponding to the r values are $z_{r1} = .00$ and $z_{r2} = .31$, respectively. Therefore,

$$Z = \frac{(.00) - (.31)}{\sqrt{\dfrac{1}{14} + \dfrac{1}{42}}} = -1.00$$

is our obtained Z of the difference between the two effect-size estimates of Studies K and L. The p value associated with the Z is .16 one-tailed, or .32 two-tailed. Here we have an example of two effect sizes, one zero ($r = .00$), the other ($r = .30$), significantly different from zero ($t_{(43)} = 2.06$, $p < .025$ one-tailed), that do not differ significantly from one another. This example illustrates how careful we must be in concluding that the results of two studies are heterogeneous just because one is significant and the other is not, or because one has a zero estimated effect size and the other does not.

COMBINING TWO SIGNIFICANCE LEVELS

After we compare the results of any two independent studies, it is an easy matter also to combine the p levels of the two studies. In this way we obtain an overall estimate of the probability that the two p levels might have been obtained if the null hypothesis of no relationship between X and Y were true. Many methods for combining the results of two or more studies are available and have been described elsewhere (Rosenthal, 1978a, 1983, 1991a). Here it is necessary to give only the simplest and most versatile of the procedures, the method of adding Z values called the *Stouffer method* by Mosteller and Bush (1954). We begin by illustrating the unweighted method of adding Z values and then illustrate the weighted method of adding Z values.

The unweighted method of adding Z values, just like the method of comparing p values, asks us first to obtain accurate p levels for each of our two studies and then to find the Z corresponding to each of those p values. Both p values must be given in one-tailed form, and the corresponding Z values will have the same sign if both studies show effects in the same direction. They will have different signs if the results are in the opposite direction. The sum of the two Z values when divided by $\sqrt{2}$ yields a new Z. This new Z value corresponds to the p value that the results of the two studies combined, or results even further out in the same tail, could have occurred if the null hypothesis of no relationship between X and Y were true.

Recapping,

$$Z_{\text{unweighted}} = \frac{Z_1 + Z_2}{\sqrt{2}} \qquad (21.3)$$

is distributed as the standard normal deviate Z.

Example 7

Studies M and N yield results in opposite directions, and both are significant. One p is .05 one-tailed; the other is 1.0^{-7} one-tailed, but in the opposite tail. Z values corresponding to these p values are found in a table of normal deviates (such as Table B.1 in Appendix B) to be $Z_1 = -1.64$ and $Z_2 = 5.20$, respectively (note the opposite signs to indicate results in opposite directions). Then, from Equation 21.3 we have

$$Z = \frac{(-1.64) + (5.20)}{1.41} = 2.52$$

as the Z of the combined results of Studies M and N. The p value associated with $Z = 2.52$ is .006 one-tailed, or .012 two-tailed. Thus, the combined p supports the more significant of the two research results. If these were actual studies, we would want to be very cautious in interpreting our combined p because the two p values we combined were so significantly different from each other. We would try to discover what differences between Studies M and N might have led to results so significantly different.

Example 8

Studies O and P yield results in the same direction, but neither is significant. One p is .11, the other is .09, and their associated Z values are 1.23 and 1.34, respectively. From Equation 21.3 we have

$$Z = \frac{(1.23) + (1.34)}{1.41} = 1.82$$

as our combined Z. The p associated with this Z is .034 one-tailed, or .068 two-tailed.

Should we want to do so, we could weight each Z by its df, its estimated quality, or any other desired weights (Mosteller & Bush, 1954; Rosenthal, 1978a, 1980, 1991a). The general procedure for weighting Z values is to (a) multiply each Z by any desired weight (symbolized by omega, ω, and assigned before inspection of the data), (b) add the weighted Z values, and (c) divide the sum of the weighted Z values by the square root of the sum of the squared weights as follows:

$$Z_{\text{weighted}} = \frac{\omega_1 Z_1 + \omega_2 Z_2}{\sqrt{\omega_1^2 + \omega_2^2}}, \qquad (21.4)$$

which is illustrated in the following example.

Example 9

Studies M and N are those of Example 7, but suppose now we have found from a panel of experts that Study M earns a quality weight (ω_1) of 3.4 on assessed internal validity, whereas Study N earns only a weight of .09. The Z values for Studies M and N were -1.64 and 5.20, respectively. Therefore, using Equation 21.4 we have

$$Z = \frac{[(3.4)(-1.64)] + [(0.9)(5.20)]}{\sqrt{(3.4)^2 + (0.9)^2}} = \frac{-0.896}{3.517} = -0.25$$

as the Z of the weighted combined results of Studies M and N. The p value associated with this Z is .40 one-tailed, or .80 two-tailed. The weighting has led to a nonsignificant result in this example. In Example 7, where there was no weighting (or, more accurately, equal weighting with $\omega_1 = \omega_2 = 1$), the p value was significant at .012 two-tailed.

As a further illustration of weighting the combined Z, suppose we had wanted to weight not by quality of study but by df. If the df for Studies M and N had been 36 and 144, respectively, the weighted Z using Equation 21.4 would have been

$$Z = \frac{[(36)(-1.64)] + [(144)(5.20)]}{\sqrt{(36)^2 + (144)^2}} = \frac{689.76}{148.43} = 4.65.$$

This result shows the combined Z ($p < .000002$ one-tailed) to have moved strongly in the direction of the Z with the larger df because of the substantial difference in df between the two studies. Note that when weighting Z values by df, we have decided to have the size of the study play a large role in determining the combined p. The role is particularly large in this case because the size of the study has already entered into the determination of each Z and is therefore entering a second time into the weighting process.

COMBINING TWO EFFECT-SIZE CORRELATIONS

When we want to combine the results of two studies, we are as interested in the combined estimate of the effect size as we are in the combined probability. Just as when we compared two effect-size estimates, we consider r as our effect-size estimate in the combining of effect sizes. However, as described earlier (in chapters 12, 15, and 19), we know that many other effect-size indicators are possible. Here we begin by computing r and the associated Fisher z_r for each of the two studies. Then we compute the mean Fisher z_r (denoted as $\bar{z}_r$) as

$$\bar{z}_r = \frac{z_{r1} + z_{r2}}{2}. \tag{21.5}$$

We use an r to Fisher z_r table or a Fisher z_r to r table (see Appendix B, Tables B.7 and B.8) to look up the r that is associated with $\bar{z}_r$. Tables are preferable to finding r from z_r from the following:

$$r = \frac{e^{2z} - 1}{e^{2z} + 1}, \tag{21.6}$$

where $e \cong 2.71828$, the base of the system of natural logarithms. Should we want to do so, we could weight each z_r by its df, its rated quality, or any other desired weights assigned before inspection of the data. Example 12 will illustrate this procedure, in which the weighted mean Fisher z_r is obtained from

$$\text{Weighted } \bar{z}_r = \frac{\omega_1 z_{r1} + \omega_2 z_{r2}}{\omega_1 + \omega_2} \qquad (21.7)$$

Example 10

Studies Q and R yield results in opposite directions, with one $r = .80$ and the second $r = -.30$, respectively. The Fisher z_r values corresponding to these r values are $z_{r1} = 1.10$ and $z_{r2} = -0.31$, respectively. Therefore, the unweighted mean Fisher z_r from Equation 21.5 is

$$\bar{z}_r = \frac{(1.10) + (-0.31)}{2} = .395.$$

From our z_r to r table we find that the Fisher $\bar{z}_r$ of .395 is associated with $r = .38$.

Example 11

Studies S and T yield results in the same direction, with one $r = .95$ and the second $r = .25$. The Fisher z_r values corresponding to these r values are $z_{r1} = 1.83$ and $z_{r2} = 0.26$, respectively. Using Equation 21.5 we have

$$\bar{z}_r = \frac{1.83 + 0.26}{2} = 1.045.$$

From our z_r to r table we find the Fisher $\bar{z}_r$ of 1.045 is associated with $r = .78$. Note that if we had averaged the two r values without first transforming them to Fisher z_r values, we would have found the mean r to be $(.95 + .25)/2 = .60$, substantially smaller than .78. This difference illustrates that the use of Fisher's z_r gives heavier weight to r values that are further from zero in either direction.

Example 12

Studies K and L are again those of Example 6, but now we have decided to weight the studies by their df (i.e., $N - 3$ in this application; Snedecor & Cochran, 1989). Therefore, we replace the general weight indicators ω_1 and ω_2 in Equation 21.7 by df_1 and df_2 to find the weighted mean z_r from

$$\text{Weighted } \bar{z}_r = \frac{df_1 z_{r1} + df_2 z_{r2}}{df_1 + df_2}. \qquad (21.8)$$

In Example 6 we had r values of .00 and .30, based on $N = 17$ and 45, respectively. The Fisher z_r values corresponding to these two r values are $z_{r1} = .00$ and $z_{r2} = .31$. Therefore, from Equation 21.8 we find our weighted average z_r to be

$$\bar{z}_r = \frac{[(17 - 3).00] + [(45 - 3).31]}{(17 - 3) + (45 - 3)} = \frac{13.02}{56} = .232,$$

which corresponds to an r of .23.

Finally, it should be noted that before combining effect size estimates, it can be useful first to test the significance of the difference between the two effect sizes. If the results of the studies *do* differ, it is a signal that we need to be cautious about combining the effect sizes without giving further thought to the matter, especially when the results are in opposite directions.

OVERALL COMPARISONS OF THREE OR MORE STUDIES

Although we can do quite a lot in comparing and combining the results of sets of studies with just the procedures given so far, we often have three or more studies of the same relationship that we want to compare, combine, or both. In this section we present generalizations of the procedures given in the preceding sections so that we can compare and combine the results of any number of studies. We begin with an overall comparison of three or more p levels, not because we can imagine often wanting to make such a comparison, but to follow the line of illustrations in our previous discussion. First, we find the standard normal deviate, Z, corresponding to each p level. All p levels must be one-tailed, and the corresponding Z values will be given the same sign if all studies show effects in the same direction and will have different signs if the results are not in the same direction. The statistical significance of the heterogeneity of the Z values can be obtained from a chi-square test (Rosenthal & Rubin, 1979a), where

$$\chi^2_{(K-1)} = \Sigma(Z_j - \overline{Z})^2, \tag{21.9}$$

and K equals the number of independent p values being tested for heterogeneity as a set, and $df = K - 1$. In this equation Z_j is the standard normal deviate value for any one study, and $\overline{Z}$ is the mean of all the Z values. A significant $\chi^2_{(K-1)}$ tells us that the set of Z values tested for heterogeneity (or the set of p values associated with that set of Z values) shows significant differences.

Example 13

Suppose we have four studies, which we have numbered 1 through 4, and their one-tailed p levels are .15, .05, .01, .001, respectively. Study 3, however, shows results opposite in direction from those of Studies 1, 2, and 4. From our normal deviate table we find the Z values corresponding to the four p levels to be 1.04, 1.64, -2.33, 3.09. (Note the negative sign for the Z associated with the result in the opposite direction.) Then, from Equation 21.9 we have

$$\chi^2_{(3)} = [(1.04) - (0.86)]^2 + [(1.64) - (0.86)]^2 + [(-2.33) - (0.86)]^2 + [(3.09) - (0.86)]^2$$
$$= 15.79,$$

which, with $df = K - 1 = 3$, is significant at $p = .0013$. Clearly the four p levels compared are significantly heterogeneous. Beyond the question of whether a set of p levels differ significantly among themselves, we sometimes want to test a specific hypothesis about which studies will show the more significant p levels (Rosenthal & Rubin, 1979a). These computations are presented in the next section, dealing with contrasts.

Presumably of more interest than whether a bunch of p levels differ is whether a set of effect sizes is heterogeneous. We again restrict our discussion to r as the effect size index, but analogous procedures are available for comparing other effect-size estimators (Rosenthal & Rubin, 1982b). For each of the three or more studies to be compared, we compute the effect size r, its associated Fisher z_r, and $N - 3$, where N is the number of sampling units on which each r is based. The statistical significance of the heterogeneity of the r values can be obtained from chi-square (Snedecor & Cochran, 1989), computed as

$$\chi^2_{(K-1)} = \Sigma\left[(N_j - 3)(z_{r_j} - \bar{z}_r)^2\right], \tag{21.10}$$

where $df = K - 1$, and K is the number of independent effect sizes that we are testing for heterogeneity as a set. In this equation the z_r with subscript j is the Fisher z_r corresponding to any r, and $\bar{z}_r$ is the weighted mean Fisher z_r, that is,

$$\text{Weighted } \bar{z}_r = \frac{\Sigma\left[(N_j - 3)z_{r_j}\right]}{\Sigma(N_j - 3)}. \tag{21.11}$$

Example 14

We have four studies, numbered 1 through 4. For study 1 the effect size $r = .70$, and the sample size is $N = 30$. For Study 2 we have $r = .45$, and $N = 45$. For Study 3 we have $r = .10$, and $N = 20$. For Study 4 we have $r = -.15$, and $N = 25$. The Fisher z_r values corresponding to these r values are found from our table of Fisher z_r to be .87, .48, .10, and $-.15$, respectively. The weighted mean z_r is found from Equation 21.11 to be

$$\bar{z}_r = \frac{[27(.87)] + [42(.48)] + [17(.10)] + [22(-.15)]}{27 + 42 + 17 + 22}$$

$$= \frac{42.05}{108} = .39.$$

Then, from Equation 21.10 we have

$$\chi^2_{(3)} = [27(.87 - .39)^2] + [42(.48 - .39)^2] + [17(.10 - .39)^2] + [22(-.15 - .39)^2]$$
$$= 14.41,$$

which, with $df = K - 1 = 3$, is significant at $p = .0024$. The four effect sizes we compared are significantly heterogeneous. Just as for a set of p values, procedures are available for computing contrasts among the obtained effect-size estimates (Rosenthal & Rubin, 1982b), as described in the next section.

FOCUSED COMPARISONS OF THREE OR MORE STUDIES

Suppose we want to know whether, given a set of p values for younger and older subjects, the results from the younger subjects are more statistically significant than the results from the older subjects. Normally, our curiosity would not be aroused by questions like these about a set of p values, but we would be very interested in the relationship between weights derived from theory and the obtained effect sizes. However, let us assume that we want to make a focused comparison of significance levels. We begin just as we did for the diffuse tests. That is, first we find the standard normal deviate, Z, corresponding to each p level. All p levels must be one-tailed, and the corresponding Z values will have the same sign if all studies have effects in the same direction but different signs if the results are not in the same direction. Statistical significance of the contrast testing any specific hypothesis about the set of p levels can be obtained from a Z computed as follows (Rosenthal & Rubin, 1979a):

$$Z = \frac{\Sigma \lambda_j Z_j}{\sqrt{\Sigma \lambda_j^2}}. \tag{21.12}$$

In this equation λ_j is the theoretically derived prediction or contrast weight for any one study, chosen so that the sum of the λ_j values will be zero, and Z_j is the Z for any one study.

Example 15

Our four studies yield one-tailed p values of $1/10^7$, .0001, .21, and .007, all with results in the same direction. From a standard normal deviate table we find Z values corresponding to the four p levels to be 5.20, 3.72, 0.81, and 2.45. Suppose the studies used differing amounts of peer tutor contact of 8, 6, 4, and 2 hours per month, respectively, and we are interested in whether there is a significant linear relationship between the number of hours of contact and the statistical significance of the result favoring peer tutoring. The λ_j weights of a linear contrast involving four studies are $+3, +1, -1, -3$. From Equation 21.12 we have

$$Z = \frac{[(3)5.20] + [(1)3.72] + [(-1)0.81] + [(-3)2.45]}{\sqrt{(3)^2 + (1)^2 + (-1)^2 + (-3)^2}}$$

$$= \frac{11.16}{\sqrt{20}} = 2.50,$$

which is significant at $p = .006$ one-tailed. The four p values, then, tend to grow linearly more significant as the number of hours of contact time increases.

Of greater interest would be a focused question on a set of effect sizes. Given a set of effect sizes for independent studies of peer tutoring, we might ask whether the effects increased or decreased linearly with the number of hours of contact per month. We again emphasize r as the effect size estimator, but analogous procedures are available for comparing other effect-size estimators (Rosenthal & Rubin, 1982a). We begin by computing the effect size r, its associated Fisher z_r, and $N - 3$, where N is the number of sampling units on which each r is based. The statistical significance of the contrast, testing any specific hypothesis about the set of effect sizes, can be obtained from a Z computed as follows (Rosenthal & Rubin, 1982b):

$$Z = \frac{\Sigma \lambda_j z_{r_j}}{\sqrt{\Sigma \dfrac{\lambda_j^2}{\omega_j}}} \tag{21.13}$$

In this equation, λ_j is the contrast weight determined from some theory for any one study, chosen so that the sum of the lambda weights will be zero. The Fisher z_r with the subscript j refers to any one study, and ω_j is the inverse of the variance of the effect size for each study. For Fisher z_r transformations of the effect size r, the variance is $1/(N_j - 3)$, so $\omega_j = N_j - 3$.

Example 16

Studies 1 through 4 yield effect sizes of $r = .89$, .76, .23, and .59, respectively, all with $N = 12$. The Fisher z_r values corresponding to these r values are found from tables of Fisher z_r to be 1.42, 1.00, 0.23, and 0.68, respectively. Assuming again that the four studies used differing amounts of peer tutor contact of 8, 6, 4, and 2 hours per month, respectively, we might be interested in whether there is a significant linear relationship between the number of hours of contact and the size of the effect favoring peer tutoring. As in Example 15, the linear weights are $+3$, $+1$, -1, and -3. Therefore, from Equation 21.13 we have

$$Z = \frac{[(3)1.42] + [(1)1.00] + [(-1)0.23] + [(-3)0.68]}{\sqrt{\dfrac{(3)^2}{9} + \dfrac{(1)^2}{9} + \dfrac{(-1)^2}{9} + \dfrac{(-3)^2}{9}}}$$

$$= \frac{2.99}{\sqrt{2.222}} = 2.01,$$

which is significant at $p = .022$ one-tailed. In sum, the four effect sizes tend to grow linearly larger as the number of hours of contact time increases. Interpretation of this relationship must be very cautious. After all, the studies were not assigned at random to the four conditions of contact hours. Generally, variables moderating the magnitude of effects found should not be interpreted as giving strong evidence for any causal relationships. Moderator variables can, however, be very valuable in raising the possibility of causal relationships, which might then be studied experimentally (or as nearly so as ethically and practically feasible).

COMBINING THREE OR MORE p LEVELS

After comparing the results of any set of three or more studies, it is easy to combine the p values of the set of studies to obtain an overall estimate of the probability that the set of p levels might have been obtained if the null hypothesis of no relationship between X and Y were true. Of the various methods available, we discuss here only the generalized version of the method presented earlier in our discussion of combining the results of two groups. This method requires only that we obtain Z for each of our p levels, all of which should be given as one-tailed. The Z values disagreeing in direction from the bulk of the findings are given negative signs. Then the sum of the Z values, divided by the square root of the number (K) of studies, yields a new statistic distributed as Z:

$$Z = \frac{\Sigma Z_j}{\sqrt{K}} \tag{21.14}$$

Example 17

Four independent studies have associated one-tailed p values of .15, .05, .01, and .001. Study 3 shows results opposite in direction from the results of the other three studies.

The Z values associated with the four p values are 1.04, 1.64, −2.33, and 3.09, respectively. From Equation 21.14 we have

$$Z = \frac{(1.04) + (1.64) + (-2.33) + (3.09)}{\sqrt{4}}$$

$$= 1.72,$$

which has an associated p value of .043 one-tailed, or .086 two-tailed. We would normally use the one-tailed p value if we correctly predicted the net direction of the findings, but we would use the two-tailed p value if we did not. The combined p that we obtain in this example supports the results of the majority of the individual studies. However, even if those p values (.043 and .086) were more significant, we would want to be very cautious about drawing any simple overall conclusion because of the very great heterogeneity of the four p values being combined. Example 13, using the same p values, showed that the heterogeneity was significant at $p = .0013$. It should be emphasized again, however, that this great heterogeneity of p values could be due to heterogeneity of effect sizes, heterogeneity of sample sizes, or both. To find out about the sources of heterogeneity, we need to look very carefully at the effect sizes and sample sizes of each of the studies involved.

Should we want to do so, we could weight each of the Z values by its df, its judged quality, or any other desired weights, as long as they are assigned before inspection of the results (Mosteller & Bush, 1954; Rosenthal, 1978a, 1991a). The general procedure for weighting Z values is to (a) multiply each Z by the desired weight, (b) sum the weighted Z values, and (c) divide that sum by the square root of the sum of the squared weights:

$$Z_{\text{weighted}} = \frac{\Sigma \omega_j Z_j}{\sqrt{\Sigma \omega_j^2}} \tag{21.15}$$

Example 18

Our studies are the same as those of Example 17, but now we have decided to weight each study by the mean rating of internal validity assigned it by a panel of methodologists. These weights (ω) are 2.4, 2.2, 3.1, and 3.8 for Studies 1 through 4, respectively. From Equation 21.15 we have

$$Z = \frac{[(2.4)(1.04)] + [(2.2)(1.64)] + [(3.1)(-2.33)] + [(3.8)(3.09)]}{\sqrt{(2.4)^2 + (2.2)^2 + (3.1)^2 + (3.8)^2}}$$

$$= \frac{10.623}{\sqrt{34.65}} = 1.80,$$

which is significant at $p = .036$ one-tailed, or .072 two-tailed. In this example, weighting by quality of study did not lead to a very different result from that obtained without weighting (Example 17). In both cases the p value was approximately .04 one-tailed. Actually, it might be more accurate to say for Example 17 that weighting was equal, with all values of $\omega = 1$, than to say that no weighting was used.

COMBINING THREE OR MORE
EFFECT-SIZE CORRELATIONS

When we combine the results of three or more studies, we are at least as interested in the combined estimate of the effect size as we are in the combined probability. In fact, in most cases, we are even more interested in this estimate than in the probability. We follow here our earlier procedure of considering r our primary effect size estimator, while knowing that many other estimates are possible. For each of the three or more independent effect-size r values to be combined, we compute the associated Fisher z_r and have

$$\bar{z}_r = \frac{\Sigma z_r}{K} \tag{21.16}$$

as the Fisher z_r corresponding to our mean r, where $K =$ the number of studies combined. We use a table of Fisher z_r to find the r associated with our $\bar{z}_r$

Example 19

Four studies yield effect sizes of $r = .70, .45, .10,$ and $-.15$. The Fisher z_r values corresponding to these r values are $.87, .48, .10,$ and $-.15$, respectively. Therefore, from Equation 21.16 we find

$$\bar{z}_r = \frac{(.87) + (.48) + (.10) + (-.15)}{4} = .32$$

as our mean Fisher z_r. From our table of Fisher z_r values, we find that $\bar{z}_r = .32$ corresponds to an r of .31. As in our earlier example of combined p levels, however, we want to be cautious in interpreting this combined effect size. If the r values we have just averaged were based on substantial sample sizes, as in Example 14, they would be significantly heterogeneous. Therefore, averaging without special thought and comment would be inappropriate.

   Should we want to give greater weight to larger studies or to better studies, we could weight each z_r by $df = N - 3$ (Snedecor & Cochran, 1989), by its estimated research quality, or by any other weights that we assigned before inspection of the data. The weighted mean z_r is obtained as follows:

$$\text{Weighted } \bar{z}_r = \frac{\Sigma \omega_j z_{r_j}}{\Sigma \omega_j}, \tag{21.17}$$

with terms defined as before.

Example 20

Our four studies are those of Example 19, but we have decided to weight each study by a mean rating of ecological validity assigned to it by several experts. The weights are 1.7, 1.6, 3.1, and 2.5, respectively. Therefore, from Equation 21.17 we find

$$\bar{z}_r = \frac{[(1.7)(0.87)] + [(1.6)(0.48)] + [(3.1)(0.10)] + [(2.5)(-0.15)]}{1.7 + 1.6 + 3.1 + 2.5}$$

$$= \frac{2.182}{8.90} = .24$$

as our mean Fisher z_r, which corresponds to an r of .24. In this example, weighting by quality of research led to a somewhat smaller estimate of combined effect size than did equal weighting (.24 vs. .31).

RESULTS THAT ARE NOT INDEPENDENT

In all the meta-analytic procedures we have described so far, it has been assumed that the results being compared or combined are from separate, independent studies. That is, we have assumed that different subjects (or other sampling units) were found in the studies being compared or summarized. Sometimes, however, the same subjects (or other sampling units) contribute data to two or more studies or to two or more dependent variables within the same study. In such cases the results of the two or more studies or the results based on two or more dependent variables are not independent, and the meta-analytic procedures we have described so far cannot be applied without adjustment. General procedures have been suggested for comparing and combining nonindependent significance levels (Strube, 1985) and nonindependent effect sizes (Rosenthal & Rubin, 1986). We cannot give the details of all those procedures here. However, because comparing nonindependent effect sizes is frequently of interest, we will describe two such procedures: (a) Hotelling's t test (and a modification of it, the Williams t) and (b) another procedure more recently proposed by Meng, Rosenthal, and Rubin (1992).

Hotelling's Test

In the situation described, a sample of persons is measured on three variables that are denoted as A, B, and C. Variables A and B are conceptualized as predictor variables, and Variable C is conceptualized as an outcome variable. Three correlations are possible among the three variables, that is, r_{AC}, r_{BC}, and r_{AB}. We want to compare the magnitude of two of those correlations, namely, r_{AC} and r_{BC}. The standard procedure for this comparison is Hotelling's t test, which is distributed as t with $df = N - 3$ (Walker & Lev, 1953):

$$t_{\text{Hotelling}} = (r_{AC} - r_{BC})\sqrt{\frac{(N-3)(1 + r_{AB})}{2(1 - r_{AB}^2 - r_{AC}^2 - r_{BC}^2 + 2r_{AB}r_{AC}r_{BC})}}. \qquad (21.18)$$

As an illustration using Equation 21.18, suppose that, in a study of the classroom behavior of children, teachers' ratings of 347 children were available on three variables. Variable A is the degree of curiosity of the child (a predictor variable). Variable B is the degree to which the child is affectionate (another predictor variable). Variable C is the teacher's estimate of the likelihood that the child will be successful in the future (the projected outcome variable). The three correlations among these variables are $r_{AC} = .63$, $r_{BC} = .23$, and $r_{AB} = .28$. We want to know whether ratings of curiosity predict ratings of projected future success ($r_{AC} = .63$) significantly better than ratings of affectionateness predict ratings of projected future success ($r_{BC} = .23$). Substituting in Equation 21.18, we have

$$t_{\text{Hotelling}} = (.63 - .23)\sqrt{\frac{344(1 + .28)}{2[1 - (.28)^2 - (.63)^2 - (.23)^2 + 2(.28)(.63)(.23)]}}$$

$$= (.40)\sqrt{\frac{440.32}{2(.552944)}} = 7.98$$

and, with $df = 344$, $p = 2.2^{-14}$ two-tailed. Therefore, there is little question that the variable of "curiosity" correlates more highly with the variable of "projected future success" than does the variable of "affectionateness." Of course, we knew this simply from eyeballing the two correlations (.63 vs. .23), though without information about the probability that such a difference, or one even larger, would be found if the null hypothesis of zero difference were true.

Williams's Modification of the Hotelling t Test

The Hotelling t test for comparing nonindependent correlation coefficients works well under most circumstances. However, in special (and probably rare) circumstances, it will yield t values that are substantially too large. Steiger (1980) recommended that a modification of Hotelling's test proposed by E. J. Williams (1959) be used instead of Equation 21.18:

$$t_{\text{Williams}} = (r_{AC} - r_{BC})\sqrt{\frac{(N-1)(1 + r_{AB})}{2X\left(\frac{N-1}{N-3}\right) + Y}} \tag{21.19}$$

where

$$X = \left(1 - r_{AB}^2 - r_{AC}^2 - r_{BC}^2 + 2r_{AB}r_{AC}r_{BC}\right)$$

and

$$Y = \left(\frac{r_{AC} + r_{BC}}{2}\right)^2 (1 - r_{AB})^3.$$

In the example above, $X = .552944$, and $Y = .069014$. Therefore, substituting in Equation 21.19, we find

$$t_{\text{Williams}} = (.63 - .23)\sqrt{\frac{346(1.28)}{2(.552944)\left(\frac{346}{344}\right) + .069014}}$$

$$= (.40)\sqrt{\frac{442.88}{1.181332}} = 7.74$$

and, with $df = 344$, $p < 1.1^{-13}$. In this example, then, the conservative Equation 21.19 yielded a value of t only 3% smaller than that from Equation 21.18.

Z-Test Procedure

A still more accurate procedure, using a Z test, has been proposed by Meng, Rosenthal, and Rubin (1992), in which

$$Z = (z_{r1} - z_{r2})\sqrt{\frac{N - 3}{2(1 - r_{AB})h}}, \tag{21.20}$$

where z_{r1} and z_{r2} are Fisher transformations of the r values being compared (r_{AC} and r_{BC}), N is the number of sampling units, r_{AB} is the correlation between the two predictor variables, and

$$h = \frac{1 - f\bar{r}^2}{1 - \bar{r}^2}$$

where

$$f = \frac{1 - r_{AB}}{2(1 - \bar{r}^2)}$$

which must be ≤ 1, and $\bar{r}^2$ is the mean of r_{AC}^2 and r_{BC}^2.

For the data we have been using as our illustration, then,

$$\bar{r}^2 = \frac{(.63)^2 + (.23)^2}{2} = .2249,$$

and

$$f = \frac{1 - .28}{2(1 - .2249)} = .4645,$$

and

$$h = \frac{1 - (.4645)(.2249)}{1 - .2249} = 1.1554.$$

Finally, substituting in Equation 21.20, we find

$$Z = (.741 - .234)\sqrt{\frac{347 - 3}{2(1 - .28)1.1554}}$$

$$= (.507)\sqrt{\frac{344}{2(.72)1.1554}} = 7.29,$$

and $p = 1.55^{-13}$ one-tailed, or 3.1^{-13} two-tailed. Based on the following relationship (D. L. Wallace, 1959):

$$Z = \left[df \log_e\left(1 + \frac{t^2}{df}\right)\right]^{1/2}\left[1 - \frac{1}{2df}\right]^{1/2}, \tag{21.21}$$

we find that a Z value of 7.29 is equivalent to a t of 7.59. Thus, we can compare the results of the present t test to those obtained from Equations 21.18 and 21.19 (7.98 and 7.74). The present result, then, is about 5% smaller than the Hotelling t (Equation 21.18) and about 2% smaller than the Williams t (Equation 21.19). In most cases these three tests yield similar results, but it seems best generally to use Equation 21.20.

THE FILE DRAWER PROBLEM

Behavioral researchers and statisticians have long suspected that studies published in behavioral and social science journals are a biased sample of the studies that are actually carried out (Bakan, 1967; McNemar, 1960; Smart, 1966; Sterling, 1959). The extreme view of the **file drawer problem** is that the journals are filled with the 5% of the studies that show Type I errors, whereas the file drawers back at the lab are filled with the 95% of the studies that show nonsignificant (e.g., $p > .05$) results (Rosenthal, 1979a; Rosenthal & Rubin, 1988; Wachter, 1988). Although no definitive solution is available, we can establish reasonable boundaries on the problem and estimate the possible damage to any research conclusion when researchers tuck away studies that did not make the magic .05 level. The fundamental idea in coping with the file drawer problem is simply to calculate the number of studies averaging null results ($Z = 0.00$) that must be "filed away" before the overall probability of a Type I error can be just brought to any desired level of significance (say, $p = .05$). This number of filed studies, or the *tolerance for future null results,* is then evaluated for whether such a tolerance level is small enough to jeopardize the overall conclusion drawn by the reviewer. If the overall level of significance of the research review will be brought down to the level of "just significant" by the addition of only a few more null results, the finding is not resistant to the file drawer threat.

Alternative Computational Procedures

To find the number (X) of new, filed, or unretrieved studies averaging null results required to bring the new overall p for all the studies (i.e., studies already published plus those filed away in obscurity) to any desired level (say, significance at $p = .05$, or $Z = 1.645$), we write

$$1.645 = \frac{K(\overline{Z}_K)}{\sqrt{K + X}}, \tag{21.22}$$

where K is the number of studies already included in the meta-analysis, and $\overline{Z}_K$ is the arithmetic mean Z obtained for the K studies. Rearrangement of Equation 21.22 shows that

$$X = \left(\frac{K}{2.706}\right)[K(\overline{Z}_K)^2 - 2.706]. \tag{21.23}$$

An alternative formula that may be more convenient when the sum of the Z values is given (rather than the mean Z) is

$$X = \left[\frac{(\Sigma Z)^2}{2.706}\right] - K. \tag{21.24}$$

One method, based on counting rather than summing Z values, may be easier to compute and can be used when exact p levels are not available. However, this method is probably less powerful than Equations 21.23 and 21.24. If X is the number of new studies required to bring the overall p to .50 (not to .05), then,

$$X = 19n_s - n_{ns}, \tag{21.25}$$

where n_s is the number of summarized studies significant at $p \leq .05$, and n_{ns} is the number of summarized studies not significant at .05. Another conservative alternative (used when exact p levels are not available) sets Z at 0.00 for *any* nonsignificant result and sets Z at 1.645 for any result significant at $p < .05$.

The equations above all assume that each of the K studies is independent of all other $K - 1$ studies, at least in the sense of having different sampling units. *Independence* is used in other senses, however. We can, for example, think of two or more studies conducted in a given laboratory as less independent than two or more studies conducted in different laboratories. That kind of nonindependence can be assessed by such procedures as intraclass correlations. Whether nonindependence of that type serves to increase Type I or Type II errors appears to depend in part on the relative magnitude of the Z values obtained from the studies that are "correlated" or "too similar." If the correlated Z values are, on average, as high as (or higher than) the grand mean Z corrected for nonindependence, the combined Z we compute treating all studies as independent will be too large. If the correlated Z values are, on average, clearly low relative to the grand mean Z corrected for nonindependence, then the combined Z we compute treating all studies as independent will tend to be too small.

An Illustration

In 1969, 94 separate experiments examining the effects of interpersonal self-fulfilling prophecies (such as those discussed in chapter 7) were summarized (Rosenthal, 1969). The mean Z of those 94 independent studies $(\overline{Z}_{K=94})$ was 1.014, and the Z for the studies combined was $94(1.014)/(94)^{1/2} = 9.83$. How many new, filed, or unretrieved studies (X) would it take to bring that very large combined Z down to a barely significant $Z = 1.645$? From Equation 21.23 we have

$$X = (94/2.706)[94(1.014)^2 - 2.706] = 3,263.$$

That is, we find that 3,263 studies averaging null results $(\overline{Z} = .00)$ must be squirreled away in obscurity before we can safely conclude that the overall results (from published plus filed-away studies) were due to sampling bias in the studies summarized by the reviewer. In a subsequent summary of the same area of research (Rosenthal & Rubin, 1978), the mean Z of 345 studies was estimated to be 1.22; the number of filed-away studies (averaging a null result) that would be required to move the combined Z to a barely significant Z was $X = 65,123$. In a follow-up summary of the same area of research, the mean Z was 1.30, K was 443, and X was 122,778. Thus, over 120,000 unreported studies averaging a null result would have to exist somewhere before the overall results could reasonably be ascribed to sampling bias.

The Tolerance Table

Table 21.2 is a table of tolerance values with five convenient levels of $\overline{Z}$ (the mean Z) heading the columns and various numbers of available studies (K) indexing the rows. The intersection of any row and column tells us the number of new studies averaging a null result (X) that would be required to bring the combined p for all studies

Table 21.2

Tolerances for future null results as a function of the mean Z ($\overline{Z}$) and the number (K) of studies summarized

K	$\overline{Z}$				
	+0.50	+1.00	+1.50	+2.00	+2.50
1	—	—	—	—	1
2	—	—	1	3	7
3	—	—	4	10	17
4	—	1	9	19	32
5	—	4	15	31	52
6	—	7	23	47	77
7	—	11	33	65	106
8	—	15	45	86	139
9	—	20	58	110	178
10	—	26	73	137	220
15	5	68	172	317	504
20	16	127	312	571	903
25	32	205	494	898	1,418
30	53	302	718	1,300	2,048
40	107	551	1,290	2,325	3,655
50	180	873	2,028	3,645	5,724
60	272	1,270	2,933	5,261	8,254
80	511	2,285	5,241	9,380	14,701
100	823	3,595	8,214	14,681	22,996
150	1,928	8,164	18,558	33,109	51,817
200	3,495	14,581	33,059	58,927	92,187
300	8,014	32,959	74,533	132,737	207,571
500	22,596	91,887	207,371	369,049	576,920

Note: The one-tailed p values corresponding to $\overline{Z}$ (the mean Z) are .309, .159, .067, .023, and .006, respectively. Dashes in the table indicate that $X < 1$ (where X is the number of new studies required to bring the combined p for all studies to the level of being "just significant" at $p = .05$).

combined (i.e., old and new together) down to the level of being just significant at $p = .05$ ($Z = 1.645$).

There is both a sobering and a cheering lesson to be learned from this table and from the equations given earlier in this section on the file drawer problem. The sobering lesson is that small numbers of studies, even when the combined p is significant, may well be misleading if the combined p is not *highly* significant. The reason is that only a few studies filed away could change the combined significant results to statistically nonsignificant. Suppose we have 15 studies averaging $\overline{Z} = +0.50$, with a combined p of .026. If there were only 6 studies tucked away showing a mean Z of 0.00, the tolerance level for null results (the table indicates 5) would be exceeded, and the significant result would become nonsignificant. Or if there were 2 studies with a $\overline{Z}$ of +2.00, the combined p would be about .002. But uncovering 4 new studies that averaged a Z of 0.00 would bring p into the "not significant" region, because 4 exceeds the tabled tolerance level (indicated as 3 in the table).

The cheering lesson is that, when the number of studies available is large, or the mean directional $\overline{Z}$ grows large, or both situations are present, the file drawer as a plausible rival hypothesis can be safely ruled out. If 300 studies are found averaging a $\overline{Z}$ of 1.00, it would take 32,959 + 1 studies, averaging $Z = .00$, to bring the combined p of the old and new studies pooled together to a nonsignificant level. That many file drawers full are simply too improbable.

In some areas of research, 100 or even 500 unpublished and unretrieved studies may be plausible, whereas in other areas even 10 or 20 would seem most unlikely. Although we can give no firm guidelines on what constitutes an unlikely number of unretrieved or unpublished studies, we can suggest a general guide based partly on K. As more studies are known, it becomes more plausible that other studies with null results may be in file drawers. Perhaps we could regard as robust to the file drawer problem any combined results for which the tolerance level (X) reaches $5K + 10$. That seems a conservative but reasonable tolerance level. The $5K$ portion suggests that it is unlikely that the file drawers have more than five times as many studies as the reviewer, and the +10 portion sets the minimum number of studies that could be filed away at 15 (when $K = 1$).

AN EYE TO VARIABILITY

In this chapter we have primarily emphasized summary measures, including simple χ^2 tests of the heterogeneity of significance levels and effect sizes. One problem in the use of such tests is the widespread belief that a test of heterogeneity must be found to be significant before contrasts can be computed among the obtained effect sizes. That is not the case. Contrasts, particularly planned contrasts, can and should be computed among the obtained effect sizes whether the overall test of heterogeneity is significant or not. The situation is identical to that in a one-way ANOVA, where many investigators believe it is improper to compute contrasts unless the overall F is significant. Actually, planned contrasts should be computed without reference to the overall F, and even unplanned contrasts can be computed with appropriate adjustments of their levels of significance. If overall tests of heterogeneity are not to serve as licenses to pursue contrast analysis, why compute them at all? They do provide some useful information. If very significant, they alert us to the likelihood that all our effect sizes are not cut from the same cloth and that we should try to find the moderator variables accounting for the significant heterogeneity of our effect sizes. Thus, were Equation 21.10 to yield a statistically significant χ^2, we should feel obligated to search for moderator variables. However, a nonsignificant χ^2 for heterogeneity does not preclude our search for moderators.

The second common problem in the use of heterogeneity tests is treating them as though they are estimates of the *magnitude* of heterogeneity. They are not. They are tests of significance, and like all tests of significance they are a function of the magnitude of the effect and the sample sizes (i.e., Equation 11.10). The widely varying ($S = .40$) effect sizes of $r = .80$, $.40$, and $.00$ may be found not to differ significantly if they are based on small sample sizes (e.g., $n = 10$), whereas the homogeneous ($S = .05$) effect sizes of $r = .45$, $.40$, and $.35$ may be found to differ significantly if they are based on large sample sizes (e.g., $n = 800$). The *magnitude* of the effect size heterogeneity can be assessed by various indices of variability, in particular by S, the standard deviation of the effect sizes (see also H. Cooper & Hedges, 1994; Rosenthal & DiMatteo, 2002).

We also recommend that confidence intervals be computed around mean effect sizes, preferably by means of a random effects approach. The standard error of the mean effect-size estimate (e.g., $\bar{z}_r$) should be computed as $S/\sqrt{K}$, with K being the number of independent effects. At least the 95% confidence interval should be recorded, though it may be useful to give the 90%, the 99%, or other intervals as well. To illustrate, suppose we have $K = 25$ independent studies available with an unweighted average Cohen's d of $.50$ and a standard deviation (S) of 1.00 for those 25 d values. Then the standard error (SE) of the 25 d values is $1.00/\sqrt{25} = .20$. Because the 95% confidence interval is approximately given by $\bar{d} \pm 2(SE)$, we have $.50 \pm 2(.20) =$ an interval from $d = .10$ to $.90$. We obtain a more accurate interval by replacing the 2 with the critical $.025$ one-tailed value *of t for* the appropriate df (i.e., $K - 1$). The critical value *of t for* $K = 25$ (i.e., $df = 24$) is 2.064. Therefore, the confidence interval in this example is $.50 \pm (2.064)(.20)$, which stretches from $d = .09$ to $.91$ (Rosenthal & Rubin, 1978). Our interpretation of this confidence interval is that if we claim that the effect size for the population (from which the 25 studies must be viewable as a random sample) falls within the 95% confidence interval, our claim will be correct 95% of the time.

There are other useful indices of variability, such as the null-counternull interval (first mentioned in chapter 2 and described in more detail in chapter 11). Many different visual displays can be useful under particular conditions, such as those described by H. Cooper (1989); Glass, McGaw, and Smith (1981); Greenhouse and Iyengar (1994); Hedges and Olkin (1985); Hoaglin, Mosteller, and Tukey (1983); Light and Pillemer (1984); Light, Singer, and Willett (1994); and Tukey (1977). Sometimes we may need a specially created graphic not found in any of these references. It would be instructive in that case to consult some of the excellent general texts available on visual displays (e.g., Cleveland, 1985, 1993, 1994; Kosslyn, 1994; Tufte, 1990, 1997, 2001, 2006; Wainer, 2000). By exploiting the variability, and comparing results across many studies, we can frequently achieve deeper insights into the contextual moderators of the observed effects. In Wachter and Straf's book on *The Future of Meta-Analysis* (1990), there is a wonderfully perceptive statement by Ingram Olkin (1990) where he likens the meta-analytic process to a ride in a helicopter: "On the ground individual trees are visible with high resolution. This resolution diminishes as the helicopter rises, and in its place we begin to see patterns not visible from the ground" (pp. 6–7). It might seem a lofty vision of meta-analysis, but it is one that has already begun to be fulfilled.

PART
VIII

APPENDIXES

APPENDIX

A

LIST OF NUMBERED EQUATIONS

CHAPTER 2

$$\chi^2_{(1)} = \phi^2 \times N \tag{2.1}$$

$$t = \frac{r}{\sqrt{1 - r^2}} \times \sqrt{df} \tag{2.2}$$

$$t = \frac{M_1 - M_2}{\sigma_{\text{pooled}}} \times \frac{\sqrt{df}}{2} \tag{2.3}$$

$$\text{Cohen's } d = \frac{M_1 - M_2}{\sigma_{\text{pooled}}} \tag{2.4}$$

$$\text{Hedges's } g = \frac{M_1 - M_2}{S_{\text{pooled}}} \tag{2.5}$$

$$\text{Glass's } \Delta = \frac{M_1 - M_2}{S_{\text{control}}} \tag{2.6}$$

$$p_{\text{rep}} = \frac{1}{1 + \left(\dfrac{p}{1 - p}\right)^{2/3}} \tag{2.7}$$

CHAPTER 4

$$R^{\text{SB}} = \frac{n r_{\text{ii}}}{1 + (n - 1) r_{\text{ii}}} \tag{4.1}$$

$$n = \frac{R^{\text{SB}} (1 - r_{\text{ii}})}{r_{\text{ii}} (1 - R^{\text{SB}})} \tag{4.2}$$

$$R^{\text{KR20}} = \left(\frac{n}{n - 1}\right)\left(\frac{\sigma_t^2 - \Sigma PQ}{\sigma_t^2}\right) \tag{4.3}$$

$$\sigma_t^2 = \frac{\Sigma (t_p - \bar{t}_p)^2}{p} \tag{4.4}$$

693

$$S_t^2 = \frac{\Sigma(t_p - \bar{t}_p)^2}{p - 1} \tag{4.5}$$

$$R^{\text{Cronbach}} = \left(\frac{n}{n-1}\right)\left(\frac{S_t^2 - \Sigma(S_i^2)}{S_t^2}\right) \tag{4.6}$$

$$R^{\text{Cronbach}} = \left(\frac{n}{n-1}\right)\left(1 - \frac{\Sigma(S_i^2)}{S_t^2}\right) \tag{4.7}$$

$$R^{\text{Cronbach}} = \left(\frac{n}{n-1}\right)\left(1 - \frac{MS_{\text{persons}} + (n-1)MS_{\text{residual}}}{(n)MS_{\text{persons}}}\right) \tag{4.8}$$

$$R^{\text{SB}} = \frac{nr_{jj}}{1 + (n-1)r_{jj}} \tag{4.9}$$

$$R^{\text{Hoyt}} = \frac{MS_{\text{persons}} - MS_{\text{residual}}}{MS_{\text{persons}}} \tag{4.10}$$

$$r_{\text{intraclass}} = r_{jj} = \frac{MS_{\text{persons}} - MS_{\text{residual}}}{MS_{\text{persons}} + (n-1)MS_{\text{residual}}} \tag{4.11}$$

$$EC_j = C_j\left(\frac{1 - r_{jj}}{r_{jj}}\right) \tag{4.12}$$

$$\text{Percentage agreement} = \left(\frac{A}{A+D}\right)100 \tag{4.13}$$

$$\text{Net agreement} = \left(\frac{A-D}{A+D}\right)100 \tag{4.14}$$

$$\phi = \sqrt{\frac{\chi_{(1)}^2}{N}} \tag{4.15}$$

$$\kappa = \frac{O - E}{N - E} \tag{4.16}$$

$$r_{nx.y} = \frac{r_{xy}}{\sqrt{\left(\frac{1 - r_{xx}}{n}\right) + r_{xx}}} \tag{4.17}$$

$$r_{nx.y} = r_{xy} \times \sqrt{n} \times \frac{1}{\sqrt{1 + (n-1)r_{xx}}} \tag{4.18}$$

CHAPTER 5

$$R\text{-adjusted} = R - \frac{W}{A - 1} \tag{5.1}$$

$$R\text{-adjusted} = \frac{K}{A} \tag{5.2}$$

$$m = \sqrt{\frac{n}{1 + r_{yy}(n-1)}} \tag{5.3}$$

$$r_{composite} = r_{individual} \times m \tag{5.4}$$

$$r_{individual} = \frac{r_{composite}}{m} \tag{5.5}$$

$$g = \frac{r_{intra} - r_{inter}}{S_{aggregated}} \tag{5.6}$$

$$rmr = \frac{r_{intra} - r_{inter}}{\left[\dfrac{r_{intra} + r_{inter}}{2}\right]} \tag{5.7}$$

CHAPTER 9

$$95\% \ CI = M \pm \frac{(t_{(.05)})(S)}{\sqrt{N}} \tag{9.1}$$

$$95\% \ CI = P \pm \left(1.96\sqrt{PQ/N}\right) \tag{9.2}$$

CHAPTER 10

$$M = \frac{\Sigma X}{N} \tag{10.1}$$

$$CR = H - L \tag{10.2}$$

$$ER = (H - L) + 1 \text{ unit} \tag{10.3}$$

$$\overline{D} = \frac{\Sigma|X - M|}{N} = \frac{\Sigma|D|}{N} \tag{10.4}$$

$$\sigma^2 = \frac{\Sigma(X - M)^2}{N} \tag{10.5}$$

$$S^2 = \frac{\Sigma(X - M)^2}{N - 1} \tag{10.6}$$

$$Z \text{ score} = \frac{X - M}{\sigma} \tag{10.7}$$

$$S = \sqrt{\frac{\Sigma(X - M)^2}{N - 1}} \tag{10.8}$$

$$Z_{modified} = \frac{0.6745(X - Mdn)}{Mdn_{AD}} \tag{10.9}$$

CHAPTER 11

$$r_{xy} = \frac{\Sigma Z_x Z_y}{N} \tag{11.1}$$

$$\text{Fisher } z_r = \frac{1}{2}\log_e\left(\frac{1+r}{1-r}\right) \tag{11.2}$$

$$95\% \; CI = z_r \pm 1.96/\sqrt{N-3} \tag{11.3}$$

$$r = \frac{e^{2z_r} - 1}{e^{2z_r} + 1} \tag{11.4}$$

$$ES_{\text{counternull}} = 2ES_{\text{obtained}} - ES_{\text{null}} \tag{11.5}$$

$$r_{\text{counternull}} = \sqrt{\frac{4r^2}{1 + 3r^2}} \tag{11.6}$$

$$NC\% = 100[1.00 - 2(p \text{ one-tailed})] \tag{11.7}$$

$$\rho = 1 - \frac{6\Sigma D^2}{N^3 - N} \tag{11.8}$$

$$t = \frac{M_1 - M_2}{\sqrt{\left(\dfrac{1}{n_1} + \dfrac{1}{n_2}\right)S^2_{\text{pooled}}}} \tag{11.9}$$

$$\text{Significance test} = \text{Size of effect} \times \text{Size of study} \tag{11.10}$$

$$r = \sqrt{\frac{t^2}{t^2 + (n_1 + n_2 - 2)}} \tag{11.11}$$

$$\phi = \frac{BC - AD}{\sqrt{(A+B)(C+D)(A+C)(B+D)}} \tag{11.12}$$

$$\chi^2_{(1)} = \frac{N(BC - AD)^2}{(A+B)(C+D)(A+C)(B+D)} \tag{11.13}$$

$$\chi^2_{(1)} = \Sigma \frac{(O - E)^2}{E} \tag{11.14}$$

$$Z = \phi \times \sqrt{N} \tag{11.15}$$

$$\phi = \frac{Z}{\sqrt{N}} \tag{11.16}$$

$$r_{12.3} = \frac{r_{12} - r_{13}r_{23}}{\sqrt{(1 - r_{13}^2)(1 - r_{23}^2)}} \tag{11.17}$$

$$r_{1.23} = \sqrt{\frac{r_{12}^2 + r_{13}^2 - 2r_{12}r_{13}r_{23}}{1 - r_{23}^2}} \tag{11.18}$$

$$r_{1.23} = \sqrt{r_{12}^2 + r_{13}^2} \tag{11.19}$$

$$R_{12\ full} = \frac{r_{12\ restricted}\left(\dfrac{S_{full}}{S_{restricted}}\right)}{\sqrt{1 - r_{12\ restricted}^2 + r_{12\ restricted}^2\left(\dfrac{S_{full}}{S_{restricted}}\right)^2}} \tag{11.20}$$

$$r_{12\ restricted} = \frac{R_{12\ full}\left(\dfrac{S_{restricted}}{S_{full}}\right)}{\sqrt{1 - R_{12\ full}^2 + R_{12\ full}^2\left(\dfrac{S_{restricted}}{S_{full}}\right)^2}} \tag{11.21}$$

$$r_{12\ full} = \frac{R_{12\ extreme}\left(\dfrac{S_{full}}{S_{extreme}}\right)}{\sqrt{1 - R_{12\ extreme}^2 + R_{12\ extreme}^2\left(\dfrac{S_{full}}{S_{extreme}}\right)^2}} \tag{11.22}$$

CHAPTER 12

$$r = \sqrt{\frac{t^2}{t^2 + df}} \tag{12.1}$$

$$n_h = \frac{2n_1 n_2}{n_1 + n_2} \tag{12.2}$$

$$d = \frac{M_1 - M_2}{\sqrt{\dfrac{\sigma_1^2 + \sigma_2^2}{2}}} \tag{12.3}$$

$$r = \sqrt{\frac{d^2}{d^2 + 4}} \tag{12.4}$$

$$r = \sqrt{\frac{d^2}{d^2 + \left(\dfrac{1}{PQ}\right)}} \tag{12.5}$$

Cohen's $q = z_{r1} - z_{r2}$ \hfill (12.6)

$$Z = \frac{z_{r1} - z_{r2}}{\sqrt{\dfrac{1}{n_1 - 3} + \dfrac{1}{n_2 - 3}}} \tag{12.7}$$

Cohen's $g = P - .50$, or $.50 - P$ *(if directional)* \hfill (12.8)
$$= |P - .50|\ (if\ nondirectional)$$

Cohen's $h = (\arcsin P_1) - (\arcsin P_2)$ \hfill (12.9)

APPENDIX A

$$\Pi = \frac{P(k-1)}{1+P(k-2)} \tag{12.10}$$

$$\text{Cohen's } w = \sqrt{\sum \frac{(P_{\text{expected}} - P_{\text{obtained}})^2}{P_{\text{expected}}}} \tag{12.11}$$

$$\phi = w = \sqrt{\frac{\chi^2_{(1)}}{N}} \tag{12.12}$$

$$\text{Cohen's } f = \frac{\sigma_{\text{means}}}{\sigma_{\text{within}}} \tag{12.13}$$

$$n^1 = \frac{df_{\text{error}} + df_{\text{effect}} + 1}{df_{\text{effect}} + 1} \tag{12.14}$$

CHAPTER 13

$$t = \frac{M_1 - M_2}{S} \times \frac{1}{\sqrt{\frac{1}{n_1} + \frac{1}{n_2}}} \tag{13.1}$$

$$t = \frac{M_1 - M_2}{S} \times \sqrt{\frac{n_1 n_2}{n_1 + n_2}} \tag{13.2}$$

$$t = \frac{M_1 - M_2}{\sigma} \times \left[\frac{\sqrt{n_1 n_2}}{(n_1 + n_2)} \times \sqrt{df} \right] \tag{13.3}$$

$$t = d \times \frac{\sqrt{df}}{2} \tag{13.4}$$

$$d = \frac{t(n_1 + n_2)}{\sqrt{df} \sqrt{n_1 n_2}} \tag{13.5}$$

$$d = \frac{2t}{\sqrt{df}} \tag{13.6}$$

$$\text{Hedges's } g = \frac{2t}{\sqrt{N}} \tag{13.7}$$

$$\text{Efficiency loss} = 1 - \left(\frac{n_{\text{h}}}{\bar{n}} \right) \tag{13.8}$$

$$\text{Effective loss of } N = N \left[1 - \left(\frac{n_{\text{h}}}{\bar{n}} \right) \right] \tag{13.9}$$

$$\text{Cohen's } d = g \sqrt{\frac{N}{df_{\text{within}}}} \tag{13.10}$$

$$\text{Hedges's } g = d \sqrt{\frac{df_{\text{within}}}{N}} \tag{13.11}$$

$$\sigma_{\text{within}} = S_{\text{within}} \sqrt{\frac{df_{\text{within}}}{N}}$$ (13.12)

$$\text{Hedges's } g = \left(\frac{2t}{\sqrt{N}}\right)\sqrt{\frac{\bar{n}}{n_h}}$$ (13.13)

$$\text{Cohen's } d = \left(\frac{2t}{\sqrt{df_{\text{within}}}}\right)\sqrt{\frac{\bar{n}}{n_h}}$$ (13.14)

$$r_{\text{pb}} = \frac{g}{\sqrt{g^2 + 4\left(\frac{\bar{n}}{n_h}\right)\left(\frac{df_{\text{within}}}{N}\right)}}$$ (13.15)

$$r_{\text{pb}} = \frac{d}{\sqrt{d^2 + 4\left(\frac{\bar{n}}{n_h}\right)}}$$ (13.16)

$$S^2 = \frac{\Sigma(X_1 - M_1)^2 + \Sigma(X_2 - M_2)^2}{n_1 + n_2 - 2}$$ (13.17)

$$S^2 = \frac{\left(\Sigma X_1^2 - \frac{(\Sigma X_1)^2}{n_1}\right) + \left(\Sigma X_2^2 - \frac{(\Sigma X_2)^2}{n_2}\right)}{n_1 + n_2 - 2}$$ (13.18)

$$95\% \, CI = d \pm t_{(.05)}\left(S_{\text{Cohen's }d}\right)$$ (13.19)

$$S^2_{\text{Cohen's }d} = \left(\frac{n_1 + n_2}{n_1 n_2} + \frac{d^2}{2df}\right)\frac{n_1 + n_2}{df}$$ (13.20)

$$S^2_{\text{Hedges's }g} = \frac{n_1 + n_2}{n_1 n_2} + \frac{g^2}{2df}$$ (13.21)

$$t = \frac{M_D}{\sqrt{\left(\frac{1}{N}\right)S^2_D}}$$ (13.22)

$$S^2_D = \frac{\Sigma(D - M_D)^2}{N - 1}$$ (13.23)

$$95\% \, CI = M_D \pm t_{(.05)}\left(S_D\right)/\sqrt{N}$$ (13.24)

$$t = \frac{M_D}{S_D} \times \sqrt{N}$$ (13.25)

$$t = d \times \sqrt{df}$$ (13.26)

$$\text{Cohen's } d = \frac{M_D}{\sigma_D}$$ (13.27)

$$r = \sqrt{\frac{SS_{\text{groups}}}{SS_{\text{groups}} + SS_{\text{error}}}}$$ (13.28)

$$t = \frac{M_1 - M_2}{\sqrt{\frac{S_1^2}{n_1} + \frac{S_2^2}{n_2}}} \tag{13.29}$$

$$df_{\text{Satterthwaite}} = \frac{\left[\frac{S_1^2}{n_1} + \frac{S_2^2}{n_2}\right]^2}{\left[\frac{\left(S_1^2/n_1\right)^2}{n_1 - 1} + \frac{\left(S_2^2/n_2\right)^2}{n_2 - 1}\right]} \tag{13.30}$$

CHAPTER 14

$$F = \frac{r^2}{1 - r^2} \times df \tag{14.1}$$

$$\sqrt{F} = \frac{r}{\sqrt{1 - r^2}} \times \sqrt{df} \tag{14.2}$$

$$F = \frac{\eta^2}{1 - \eta^2} \times \frac{df_{\text{error}}}{df_{\text{means}}} \tag{14.3}$$

$$S_{\text{means}}^2 = \frac{\Sigma(M_i - \overline{M})^2}{k - 1} \tag{14.4}$$

$$F = \frac{S_{\text{means}}^2}{S^2} \times n \tag{14.5}$$

$$n_h = 1 \left/ \frac{1}{k}\left(\frac{1}{n_1} + \frac{1}{n_2} + \cdots + \frac{1}{n_k}\right)\right. = k \left/ \left(\frac{1}{n_1} + \frac{1}{n_2} + \cdots + \frac{1}{n_k}\right)\right. \tag{14.6}$$

$$S^2 = \frac{\Sigma(n_i - 1)S_i^2}{\Sigma(n_i - 1)} \tag{14.7}$$

Total $SS = \Sigma(X - \overline{M})^2$ \hfill (14.8)

Between-conditions $SS = \Sigma\left[n_i(M_i - \overline{M})^2\right]$ \hfill (14.9)

Within-conditions $SS = \Sigma(X - M_i)^2$ \hfill (14.10)

$$\eta = \sqrt{\frac{SS_{\text{between}}}{SS_{\text{between}} + SS_{\text{within}}}} \tag{14.11}$$

$$\eta = \sqrt{\frac{F(df_{\text{between}})}{F(df_{\text{between}}) + df_{\text{within}}}} \tag{14.12}$$

$$MS_{\text{within}} = \frac{\Sigma(X - M_i)^2}{N - k} \tag{14.13}$$

$$\alpha_j = \frac{\alpha W_j}{\Sigma W} \tag{14.14}$$

$$p \text{ adjusted} = \frac{p_j \Sigma W}{W_j} \tag{14.15}$$

$$p \text{ adjusted} = \frac{p_j \Sigma W}{W_j} = \frac{p_j k(1)}{1} = p_j k \tag{14.16}$$

$$k_t = \frac{\alpha}{p \text{ max}} \tag{14.17}$$

$$F = \frac{S_{larger}^2}{S_{smaller}^2} \tag{14.18}$$

$$t = \frac{(S_1^2 - S_2^2)\sqrt{N-2}}{2(S_1)(S_2)\sqrt{1 - r^2}} \tag{14.19}$$

$$F_{max} = \frac{S_{max}^2}{S_{min}^2} \tag{14.20}$$

$$\text{Cochran's } g = \frac{S_{max}^2}{\Sigma S^2} = \frac{S_{max}^2}{k(MS_{within})} \tag{14.21}$$

CHAPTER 15

$$MS_{contrast} = SS_{contrast} = \frac{nL^2}{\Sigma \lambda_i^2} \tag{15.1}$$

$$L = \Sigma[M_i \lambda_i] = M_1 \lambda_1 + M_2 \lambda_2 + M_3 \lambda_3 + \cdots + M_k \lambda_k \tag{15.2}$$

$$F_{contrast} = \frac{MS_{contrast}}{MS_{within}} \tag{15.3}$$

$$t_{contrast} = \frac{\Sigma(M_i \lambda_i)}{\sqrt{MS_{within}\left(\Sigma \frac{\lambda_i^2}{n_i}\right)}} = \frac{L}{\sqrt{MS_{within}\left(\Sigma \frac{\lambda_i^2}{n_i}\right)}} \tag{15.4}$$

$$F_{contrast} = F_{MPC} \times r_{alerting}^2 \tag{15.5}$$

$$F_{contrast} = \frac{r_{alerting}^2 \times SS_{between}}{MS_{within}} \tag{15.6}$$

$$SS_{between} = \Sigma\left[n_i (M_i - \overline{M})^2\right] \tag{15.7}$$

$$r_{alerting}^2 = \frac{SS_{contrast}}{SS_{between}} \tag{15.8}$$

$$r_{alerting}^2 = \frac{F_{contrast}}{F_{contrast} + F_{noncontrast}(df_{noncontrast})} \tag{15.9}$$

$$F_{noncontrast} = \frac{(SS_{between} - MS_{contrast})/df_{noncontrast}}{MS_{within}} \tag{15.10}$$

$$F_{\text{noncontrast}} = \frac{F_{\text{between}} \left(df_{\text{between}} \right) - F_{\text{contrast}}}{df_{\text{noncontrast}}} \tag{15.11}$$

$$r_{\text{contrast}} = \sqrt{\frac{t^2_{\text{contrast}}}{t^2_{\text{contrast}} + df_{\text{within}}}} = \frac{t_{\text{contrast}}}{\sqrt{t^2_{\text{contrast}} + df_{\text{within}}}} \tag{15.12}$$

$$r_{\text{effect size}} = \sqrt{\frac{F_{\text{contrast}}}{F_{\text{contrast}} + F_{\text{noncontrast}} \left(df_{\text{noncontrast}} \right) + df_{\text{within}}}} \tag{15.13}$$

$$r_{\text{effect size}} = \sqrt{\frac{F_{\text{contrast}}}{F_{\text{between}} \left(df_{\text{between}} \right) + df_{\text{within}}}} \tag{15.14}$$

$$\sigma_\lambda = \sqrt{\frac{\Sigma \lambda^2}{k}} \tag{15.15}$$

$$r_{\text{BESD}} = \sqrt{\frac{t^2}{t^2 + df_{\text{within}} \left(\frac{n_{\text{h}}}{n} \right)}} \tag{15.16}$$

$$r_{\text{BESD}} = \sqrt{\frac{F_{\text{contrast}}}{F_{\text{contrast}} + F_{\text{noncontrast}} \left(df_{\text{noncontrast}} + df_{\text{within}} \right)}} \tag{15.17}$$

$$SS_{\text{contrast}} = r^2_{\text{alerting}} \times SS_{\text{between}} \tag{15.18}$$

$$r_{\text{contrast}} = \sqrt{\frac{SS_{\text{contrast}}}{SS_{\text{contrast}} + SS_{\text{within}}}} \tag{15.19}$$

$$r_{\text{effect size}} = \sqrt{\frac{SS_{\text{contrast}}}{SS_{\text{total}}}} \tag{15.20}$$

CHAPTER 16

$$\text{Proportion of total } SS = \frac{SS_{\text{effect of interest}}}{SS_{\text{effect of interest}} + SS_{\text{all other between effects}} + SS_{\text{within}}} \tag{16.1}$$

$$r^2 \text{ or } \eta^2 = \frac{SS_{\text{effect of interest}}}{SS_{\text{effect of interest}} + SS_{\text{within}}} \tag{16.2}$$

$$t = \frac{\overline{M} - C}{\sqrt{\left(\frac{1}{N} \right) MS_{\text{error}}}} \tag{16.3}$$

$$t = \frac{\overline{M} - C}{\sqrt{\left(\frac{1}{N_{\overline{M}}} + \frac{1}{N_C} \right) MS_{\text{error}}}} \tag{16.4}$$

$$MSE_{\text{pooled}} = \frac{(df_1)(MS_{\text{error}_1}) + (df_2)(MS_{\text{error}_2})}{df_1 + df_2} \tag{16.5}$$

$$t = \frac{\overline{M} - C}{\sqrt{\left(\dfrac{1}{N_{\overline{M}}} + \dfrac{1}{N_C}\right) MSE_{pooled}}} \tag{16.6}$$

$$F = \frac{(\Sigma X)^2 / N}{MS_{error}} \tag{16.7}$$

$$\frac{1}{n_h} = \frac{1}{k}\left(\frac{1}{n_1} + \frac{1}{n_2} + \cdots + \frac{1}{n_k}\right) \tag{16.8}$$

Total $SS = \Sigma(M_i - \overline{M})^2$ (16.9)

Row $SS = \Sigma\left[c(M_r - \overline{M})^2\right]$ (16.10)

Column $SS = \Sigma\left[r(M_c - \overline{M})^2\right]$ (16.11)

Interaction $SS =$ Total $SS -$ Row $SS -$ Column SS (16.12)

$$F_{(equal\ n)} = \frac{\overline{n}}{n_h} \times F_{(unequal\ n)} \tag{16.13}$$

$$F_{(unequal\ n)} = \frac{n_h}{\overline{n}} \times F_{(equal\ n)} \tag{16.14}$$

$$reps = \frac{MSE_{unblocked} \times blocks}{MSE_{blocked}} \tag{16.15}$$

$$reps = \frac{2(F_\alpha)(MSE_{unblocked})}{(M_1 - M_2)^2} \tag{16.16}$$

$$r_{intraclass} = \frac{MS_{blocks} - MSE}{MS_{blocks} + MSE} \tag{16.17}$$

CHAPTER 18

Total $SS = \Sigma(X - \overline{M})^2$ (18.1)

Sequences $SS = \Sigma\left[a(M_s - \overline{M})^2\right]$ (18.2)

Orders $SS = \Sigma\left[a(M_o - \overline{M})^2\right]$ (18.3)

Sequences $\times$ Orders $SS =$ Total $SS -$ Sequences $SS -$ Orders SS (18.4)

Treatment $SS = \Sigma\left[a(M_T - \overline{M})^2\right]$ (18.5)

Residual $SS =$ Sequences $\times$ Orders $SS -$ Treatment SS (18.6)

Subject-age $SS = \Sigma\left[nst(M_A - \overline{M})^2\right]$ (18.7)

Subject-sex $SS = \Sigma\left[nat(M_S - \overline{M})^2\right]$ (18.8)

$$\text{Subject-age} \times \text{Sex } SS = \sum \left[nt(M_{AS} - \overline{M})^2 \right] - \text{Subject-age } SS \\ - \text{Subject-sex } SS \tag{18.9}$$

$$\text{Subjects-within-conditions } SS = \text{Row (subjects) } SS \\ - \text{Subject-age } SS \\ - \text{Subject-sex } SS \\ - \text{Subject-age} \times \text{Sex } SS \tag{18.10}$$

$$\text{Subtests} \times \text{Age } SS = \sum \left[ns(M_{TA} - \overline{M})^2 \right] - \text{Subtests } SS - \text{Age } SS \tag{18.11}$$

$$\text{Subtests} \times \text{Sex } SS = \sum \left[na(M_{TS} - \overline{M})^2 \right] - \text{Subtests } SS - \text{Sex } SS \tag{18.12}$$

$$\text{Subtests} \times \text{Age} \times \text{Sex } SS = \sum \left[n(M_{TAS} - \overline{M})^2 \right] \\ - \text{Subtests } SS \\ - \text{Age } SS \\ - \text{Sex } SS \\ - \text{Subtests} \times \text{Age } SS \\ - \text{Subtests} \times \text{Sex } SS \\ - \text{Age} \times \text{Sex } SS \tag{18.13}$$

$$\text{Subtests} \times \text{Subjects-within-conditions } SS \\ = \text{Row} \times \text{Column interaction } SS \\ - \text{Subtests} \times \text{Age } SS \\ - \text{Subtests} \times \text{Sex } SS \\ - \text{Subtests} \times \text{Age} \times \text{Sex } SS \tag{18.14}$$

$$MS_{\text{aggregated}} = \frac{MS_1(df_1) + MS_2(df_2) + \cdots + MS_k(df_k)}{df_1 + df_2 + \cdots + df_k} \tag{18.15}$$

$$MS_{\text{aggregated}} = \frac{SS_1 + SS_2 + \cdots + SS_k}{df_1 + df_2 + \cdots + df_k} \tag{18.16}$$

$$r_{\text{intraclass}} = \frac{MS_S - MS_{S \times k}}{MS_S + (k-1)MS_{S \times k}} \tag{18.17}$$

$$L = \Sigma(Y_i \lambda_i) = Y_1 \lambda_1 + Y_2 \lambda_2 + \cdots + Y_k \lambda_k \tag{18.18}$$

$$t_{\text{contrast}} = \frac{\overline{L}}{\sqrt{\left(\frac{1}{n}\right) S_L^2}} \tag{18.19}$$

$$t = \frac{\overline{L}_1 - \overline{L}_2}{\sqrt{\left(\frac{1}{n_1} + \frac{1}{n_2}\right) S_L^2}} \tag{18.20}$$

$$t_{\text{contrast}} = \frac{\Sigma(M_i \lambda_i)}{\sqrt{\left(\Sigma \frac{\lambda_i^2}{n_i}\right) S_{\text{aggregated}}^2}} = \frac{\Sigma(\overline{L}_i \lambda_i)}{\sqrt{\left(\Sigma \frac{\lambda_i^2}{n_i}\right) S_{L \text{ aggregated}}^2}} \tag{18.21}$$

CHAPTER 19

$$E = \frac{\text{Row total} \times \text{Column total}}{N} \tag{19.1}$$

$$t_{\text{contrast}} = \sqrt{\left(r^2_{\text{alerting}}\right)\left(F_{\text{omnibus}}\right)\left(df_{\text{numerator}}\right)} \tag{19.2}$$

$$p = \frac{(A+B)!(C+D)!(A+C)!(B+D)!}{N!\,A!\,B!\,C!\,D!} \tag{19.3}$$

$$\phi_{\text{estimated}} = \sqrt{\frac{Z^2}{N}} \tag{19.4}$$

$$\chi^2_{(1)} = Z^2 \tag{19.5}$$

$$\chi^2_{(1)} = \frac{N\left(|BC - AD| - \frac{N}{2}\right)^2}{(A+B)(C+D)(A+C)(B+D)} \tag{19.6}$$

$$\chi^2_{(1)}\,\text{partitioned} = \text{"}\chi^2\text{" cells} - \text{"}\chi^2\text{" rows} - \text{"}\chi^2\text{" columns} + \text{"}\chi^2\text{" total} \tag{19.7}$$

$$\text{"}\chi^2\text{" cells} = \sum^{4}\frac{(O_c - E_c)^2}{E_c} \tag{19.8}$$

$$\text{"}\chi^2\text{" rows} = \sum^{2}\frac{(O_r - E_r)^2}{E_r} \tag{19.9}$$

$$\text{"}\chi^2\text{" columns} = \sum^{2}\frac{(O_k - E_k)^2}{E_k} \tag{19.10}$$

$$\text{"}\chi^2\text{" total} = \frac{(O_t - E_t)^2}{E_t} \tag{19.11}$$

$$Z_{\text{contrast}} = \frac{\Sigma(p_i \lambda_i)}{\sqrt{\Sigma(S_i^2 \lambda_i^2)}} \tag{19.12}$$

$$S_i^2 = \frac{p_i(1 - p_i)}{n_i} \tag{19.13}$$

$$r_{\text{contrast}} = \frac{Z_{\text{contrast}}}{\sqrt{N}} \tag{19.14}$$

$$\chi^2_{\text{contrast}} = r^2_{\text{alerting}} \times \chi^2_{\text{omnibus}} \tag{19.15}$$

$$RR = \left(\frac{A}{A+B}\right)\Big/\left(\frac{C}{C+D}\right) \tag{19.16}$$

$$OR = \left(\frac{A}{B}\right)\Big/\left(\frac{C}{D}\right) \tag{19.17}$$

$$RD = \left(\frac{A}{A+B}\right) - \left(\frac{C}{C+D}\right) \tag{19.18}$$

$$RR_{BESD-based} = \frac{A}{C} \tag{19.19}$$

$$OR_{BESD-based} = \left(\frac{A}{C}\right)^2 \tag{19.20}$$

$$RD_{BESD-based} = \frac{A - C}{100} \tag{19.21}$$

$$\Pi = \frac{P(k-1)}{P(k-1) + (1-P)} = \frac{P(k-1)}{1 + P(k-2)} \tag{19.22}$$

$$k_{best} = \frac{1}{1 - \Pi} \tag{19.23}$$

CHAPTER 20

$$\theta = \frac{V}{V-1}\left(\frac{L-1}{L}\right) \tag{20.1}$$

$$Y = \alpha + \beta_1 X_1 + \beta_2 X_2 + \varepsilon \tag{20.2}$$

CHAPTER 21

$$Z \text{ of difference} = \frac{Z_1 - Z_2}{\sqrt{2}} \tag{21.1}$$

$$Z \text{ of difference} = \frac{z_{r1} - z_{r2}}{\sqrt{\dfrac{1}{N_1 - 3} + \dfrac{1}{N_2 - 3}}} \tag{21.2}$$

$$Z_{unweighted} = \frac{Z_1 + Z_2}{\sqrt{2}} \tag{21.3}$$

$$Z_{weighted} = \frac{\omega_1 Z_1 + \omega_2 Z_2}{\sqrt{\omega_1^2 + \omega_2^2}} \tag{21.4}$$

$$\bar{z}_r = \frac{z_{r1} + z_{r2}}{2} \tag{21.5}$$

$$r = \frac{e^{2z} - 1}{e^{2z} + 1} \tag{21.6}$$

$$\text{Weighted } \bar{z}_r = \frac{\omega_1 z_{r1} + \omega_2 z_{r2}}{\omega_1 + \omega_2} \tag{21.7}$$

$$\text{Weighted } \bar{z}_r = \frac{df_1 z_{r1} + df_2 z_{r2}}{df_1 + df_2} \tag{21.8}$$

$$\chi^2_{(K-1)} = \Sigma(Z_j - \bar{Z})^2 \tag{21.9}$$

$$\chi^2_{(K-1)} = \Sigma\left[(N_j - 3)(z_{r_j} - \bar{z}_r)^2\right] \tag{21.10}$$

$$\text{Weighted } \bar{z}_r = \frac{\Sigma\left[(N_j - 3)z_{r_j}\right]}{\Sigma(N_j - 3)} \tag{21.11}$$

$$Z = \frac{\Sigma\lambda_j Z_j}{\sqrt{\Sigma\lambda_j^2}} \tag{21.12}$$

$$Z = \frac{\Sigma\lambda_j z_{rj}}{\sqrt{\Sigma\dfrac{\lambda_j^2}{\omega_j}}} \tag{21.13}$$

$$Z = \frac{\Sigma Z_j}{\sqrt{K}} \tag{21.14}$$

$$Z_{\text{weighted}} = \frac{\Sigma\omega_j Z_j}{\sqrt{\Sigma\omega_j^2}} \tag{21.15}$$

$$\bar{z}_r = \frac{\Sigma z_r}{K} \tag{21.16}$$

$$\text{Weighted } \bar{z}_r = \frac{\Sigma\omega_j z_{r_j}}{\Sigma\omega_j} \tag{21.17}$$

$$t_{\text{Hotelling}} = (r_{AC} - r_{BC})\sqrt{\frac{(N-3)(1+r_{AB})}{2\left(1 - r_{AB}^2 - r_{AC}^2 - r_{BC}^2 + 2r_{AB}r_{AC}r_{BC}\right)}} \tag{21.18}$$

$$t_{\text{Williams}} = (r_{AC} - r_{BC})\sqrt{\frac{(N-1)(1+r_{AB})}{2X\left(\dfrac{N-1}{N-3}\right) + Y}} \tag{21.19}$$

$$Z = (z_{r1} - z_{r2})\sqrt{\frac{N-3}{2(1-r_{AB})h}} \tag{21.20}$$

$$Z = \left[df \, \log_e\left(1 + \frac{t^2}{df}\right)\right]^{1/2}\left[1 - \frac{1}{2df}\right]^{1/2} \tag{21.21}$$

$$1.645 = \frac{K(\bar{Z}_K)}{\sqrt{K+X}} \tag{21.22}$$

$$X = \left(\frac{K}{2.706}\right)\left[K(\bar{Z}_K)^2 - 2.706\right] \tag{21.23}$$

$$X = \left[\frac{(\Sigma Z)^2}{2.706}\right] - K \tag{21.24}$$

$$X = 19n_s - n_{ns} \tag{21.25}$$

APPENDIX
B

STATISTICAL
TABLES

TABLE B.1

Table of standard normal deviates (Z)

Z	.00	.01	.02	.03	.04	.05	.06	.07	.08	.09
					Second digit of Z					
.0	.5000	.4960	.4920	.4880	.4840	.4801	.4761	.4721	.4681	.4641
.1	.4602	.4562	.4522	.4483	.4443	.4404	.4364	.4325	.4286	.4247
.2	.4207	.4168	.4129	.4090	.4052	.4013	.3974	.3936	.3897	.3859
.3	.3821	.3783	.3745	.3707	.3669	.3632	.3594	.3557	.3520	.3483
.4	.3446	.3409	.3372	.3336	.3300	.3264	.3228	.3192	.3156	.3121
.5	.3085	.3050	.3015	.2981	.2946	.2912	.2877	.2843	.2810	.2776
.6	.2743	.2709	.2676	.2643	.2611	.2578	.2546	.2514	.2483	.2451
.7	.2420	.2389	.2358	.2327	.2296	.2266	.2236	.2206	.2177	.2148
.8	.2119	.2090	.2061	.2033	.2005	.1977	.1949	.1922	.1894	.1867
.9	.1841	.1814	.1788	.1762	.1736	.1711	.1685	.1660	.1635	.1611
1.0	.1587	.1562	.1539	.1515	.1492	.1469	.1446	.1423	.1401	.1379
1.1	.1357	.1335	.1314	.1292	.1271	.1251	.1230	.1210	.1190	.1170
1.2	.1151	.1131	.1112	.1093	.1075	.1056	.1038	.1020	.1003	.0985
1.3	.0968	.0951	.0934	.0918	.0901	.0885	.0869	.0853	.0838	.0823
1.4	.0808	.0793	.0778	.0764	.0749	.0735	.0721	.0708	.0694	.0681
1.5	.0668	.0655	.0643	.0630	.0618	.0606	.0594	.0582	.0571	.0559
1.6	.0548	.0537	.0526	.0516	.0505	.0495	.0485	.0475	.0465	.0455
1.7	.0446	.0436	.0427	.0418	.0409	.0401	.0392	.0384	.0375	.0367
1.8	.0359	.0351	.0344	.0336	.0329	.0322	.0314	.0307	.0301	.0294
1.9	.0287	.0281	.0274	.0268	.0262	.0256	.0250	.0244	.0239	.0233
2.0	.0228	.0222	.0217	.0212	.0207	.0202	.0197	.0192	.0188	.0183
2.1	.0179	.0174	.0170	.0166	.0162	.0158	.0154	.0150	.0146	.0143
2.2	.0139	.0136	.0132	.0129	.0125	.0122	.0119	.0116	.0113	.0110
2.3	.0107	.0104	.0102	.0099	.0096	.0094	.0091	.0089	.0087	.0084
2.4	.0082	.0080	.0078	.0075	.0073	.0071	.0069	.0068	.0066	.0064
2.5	.0062	.0060	.0059	.0057	.0055	.0054	.0052	.0051	.0049	.0048
2.6	.0047	.0045	.0044	.0043	.0041	.0040	.0039	.0038	.0037	.0036
2.7	.0035	.0034	.0033	.0032	.0031	.0030	.0029	.0028	.0027	.0026
2.8	.0026	.0025	.0024	.0023	.0023	.0022	.0021	.0021	.0020	.0019
2.9	.0019	.0018	.0018	.0017	.0016	.0016	.0015	.0015	.0014	.0014
3.0	.0013	.0013	.0013	.0012	.0012	.0011	.0011	.0011	.0010	.0010
3.1	.0010	.0009	.0009	.0009	.0008	.0008	.0008	.0008	.0007	.0007
3.2	.0007									
3.3	.0005									
3.4	.0003									
3.5	.00023									
3.6	.00016									
3.7	.00011									
3.8	.00007									
3.9	.00005									
4.0*	.00003									

Note: All p values are one-tailed in this table.

*Additional values of Z are found in the bottom row of Table B.3, as t values for $df = \infty$ are also Z values.

(Reproduced from *Nonparametric Statistics* (p. 247), by S. Siegel, 1956, New York: McGraw-Hill, with the permission of the publisher.)

TABLE B.2

Summary table of *t*

df	p = .9	.8	.7	.6	.5	.4	.3	.2	.1	.05	.02	.01
1	.158	.325	.510	.727	1.000	1.376	1.963	3.078	6.314	12.706	31.821	63.657
2	.142	.289	.445	.617	.816	1.061	1.386	1.886	2.920	4.303	6.965	9.925
3	.137	.277	.424	.584	.765	.978	1.250	1.638	2.353	3.182	4.541	5.841
4	.134	.271	.414	.569	.741	.941	1.190	1.533	2.132	2.776	3.747	4.604
5	.132	.267	.408	.559`	.727	.920	1.156	1.476	2.015	2.571	3.365	4.032
6	.131	.265	.404	.553	.718	.906	1.134	1.440	1.943	2.447	3.143	3.707
7	.130	.263	.402	.549	.711	.896	1.119	1.415	1.895	2.365	2.998	3.499
8	.130	.262	.399	.546	.706	.889	1.108	1.397	1.860	2.306	2.896	3.355
9	.129	.261	.398	.543	.703	.883	1.100	1.383	1.833	2.262	2.821	3.250
10	.129	.260	.397	.542	.700	.879	1.093	1.372	1.812	2.228	2.764	3.169
11	.129	.260	.396	.540	.697	.876	1.088	1.363	1.796	2.201	2.718	3.106
12	.128	.259	.395	.539	.695	.873	1.083	1.356	1.782	2.179	2.681	3.055
13	.128	.259	.394	.538	.694	.870	1.079	1.350	1.771	2.160	2.650	3.012
14	.128	.258	.393	.537	.692	.868	1.076	1.345	1.761	2.145	2.624	2.977
15	.128	.258	.393	.536	.691	.866	1.074	1.341	1.753	2.131	2.602	2.947
16	.128	.258	.392	.535	.690	.865	1.071	1.337	1.746	2.120	2.583	2.921
17	.128	.257	.392	.534	.689	.863	1.069	1.333	1.740	2.110	2.567	2.898
18	.127	.257	.392	.534	.688	.862	1.067	1.330	1.734	2.101	2.552	2.878
19	.127	.257	.391	.533	.688	.861	1.066	1.328	1.729	2.093	2.539	2.861
20	.127	.257	.391	.533	.687	.860	1.064	1.325	1.725	2.086	2.528	2.845
21	.127	.257	.391	.532	.686	.859	1.063	1.323	1.721	2.080	2.518	2.831
22	.127	.256	.390	.532	.686	.858	1.061	1.321	1.717	2.074	2.508	2.819
23	.127	.256	.390	.532	.685	.858	1.060	1.319	1.714	2.069	2.500	2.807
24	.127	.256	.390	.531	.685	.857	1.059	1.318	1.711	2.064	2.492	2.797
25	.127	.256	.390	.531	.684	.856	1.058	1.316	1.708	2.060	2.485	2.787
26	.127	.256	.390	.531	.684	.856	1.058	1.315	1.706	2.056	2.479	2.779
27	.127	.256	.389	.531	.684	.855	1.057	1.314	1.703	2.052	2.473	2.771
28	.127	.256	.389	.530	.683	.855	1.056	1.313	1.701	2.048	2.467	2.763
29	.127	.256	.389	.530	.683	.854	1.055	1.311	1.699	2.045	2.462	2.756
30	.127	.256	.389	.530	.683	.854	1.055	1.310	1.697	2.042	2.457	2.750
∞	.12566	.25335	.38532	.52440	.67449	.84162	1.03643	1.28155	1.64485	1.95996	2.32634	2.57582

Note: All *p* values are *two-tailed* in this table. Table B.3 presents a more detailed table of *t* values for *one-tailed p* ≤ .25. (Reproduced from *Design and Analysis of Experiments in Psychology and Education* (p. 38), by E. F. Lindquist, Boston: Houghton Mifflin, with the permission of the publisher.)

TABLE B.3
Extended table of *t*

df \ p	.25	.01	.05	.025	.01	.005	.0025	.001
1	1.000	3.078	6.314	12.706	31.821	63.657	127.321	318.309
2	.816	1.886	2.920	4.303	6.965	9.925	14.089	22.327
3	.765	1.638	2.353	3.182	4.541	5.841	7.453	10.214
4	.741	1.533	2.132	2.776	3.747	4.604	5.598	7.173
5	.727	1.476	2.015	2.571	3.365	4.032	4.773	5.893
6	.718	1.440	1.943	2.447	3.143	3.707	4.317	5.208
7	.711	1.415	1.895	2.365	2.998	3.499	4.029	4.785
8	.706	1.397	1.860	2.306	2.896	3.355	3.833	4.501
9	.703	1.383	1.833	2.262	2.821	3.250	3.690	4.297
10	.700	1.372	1.812	2.228	2.764	3.169	3.581	4.144
11	.697	1.363	1.796	2.201	2.718	3.106	3.497	4.025
12	.695	1.356	1.782	2.179	2.681	3.055	3.428	3.930
13	.694	1.350	1.771	2.160	2.650	3.012	3.372	3.852
14	.692	1.345	1.761	2.145	2.624	2.977	3.326	3.787
15	.691	1.341	1.753	2.131	2.602	2.947	3.286	3.733
16	.690	1.337	1.746	2.120	2.583	2.921	3.252	3.686
17	.689	1.333	1.740	2.110	2.567	2.898	3.223	3.646
18	.688	1.330	1.734	2.101	2.552	2.878	3.197	3.610
19	.688	1.328	1.729	2.093	2.539	2.861	3.174	3.579
20	.687	1.325	1.725	2.086	2.528	2.845	3.153	3.552
21	.686	1.323	1.721	2.080	2.518	2.831	3.135	3.527
22	.686	1.321	1.717	2.074	2.508	2.819	3.119	3.505
23	.685	1.319	1.714	2.069	2.500	2.807	3.104	3.485
24	.685	1.318	1.711	2.064	2.492	2.797	3.090	3.467
25	.684	1.316	1.708	2.060	2.485	2.787	3.078	3.450
26	.684	1.315	1.706	2.056	2.479	2.779	3.067	3.435
27	.684	1.314	1.703	2.052	2.473	2.771	3.057	3.421
28	.683	1.313	1.701	2.048	2.467	2.763	3.047	3.408
29	.683	1.311	1.699	2.045	2.462	2.756	3.038	3.396
30	.683	1.310	1.697	2.042	2.457	2.750	3.030	3.385
35	.682	1.306	1.690	2.030	2.438	2.724	2.996	3.340
40	.681	1.303	1.684	2.021	2.423	2.704	2.971	3.307
45	.680	1.301	1.679	2.014	2.412	2.690	2.952	3.281
50	.679	1.299	1.676	2.009	2.403	2.678	2.937	3.261
55	.679	1.297	1.673	2.004	2.396	2.668	2.925	3.245
60	.679	1.296	1.671	2.000	2.390	2.660	2.915	3.232
70	.678	1.294	1.667	1.994	2.381	2.648	2.899	3.211
80	.678	1.292	1.664	1.990	2.374	2.639	2.887	3.195
90	.677	1.291	1.662	1.987	2.368	2.632	2.878	3.183
100	.677	1.290	1.660	1.984	2.364	2.626	2.871	3.174
200	.676	1.286	1.652	1.972	2.345	2.601	2.838	3.131
500	.675	1.283	1.648	1.965	2.334	2.586	2.820	3.107
1,000	.675	1.282	1.646	1.962	2.330	2.581	2.813	3.098
2,000	.675	1.282	1.645	1.961	2.328	2.578	2.810	3.094
10,000	.675	1.282	1.645	1.960	2.327	2.576	2.808	3.091
∞	.674	1.282	1.645	1.960	2.326	2.576	2.807	3.090

Note: All *p* values are one-tailed in this table. For *p* values > .25 see Table B.2.

TABLE B.3 (*continued*)

df \ p	.0005	.00025	.0001	.00005	.000025	.00001
1	636.619	1,273.239	3,183.099	6,366.198	12,732.395	31,830.989
2	31.598	44.705	70.700	99.992	141.416	223.603
3	12.924	16.326	22.204	28.000	35.298	47.928
4	8.610	10.306	13.034	15.544	18.522	23.332
5	6.869	7.976	9.678	11.178	12.893	15.547
6	5.959	6.788	8.025	9.082	10.261	12.032
7	5.408	6.082	7.063	7.885	8.782	10.103
8	5.041	5.618	6.442	7.120	7.851	8.907
9	4.781	5.291	6.010	6.594	7.215	8.102
10	4.587	5.049	5.694	6.211	6.757	7.527
11	4.437	4.863	5.453	5.921	6.412	7.098
12	4.318	4.716	5.263	5.694	6.143	6.756
13	4.221	4.597	5.111	5.513	5.928	6.501
14	4.140	4.499	4.985	5.363	5.753	6.287
15	4.073	4.417	4.880	5.239	5.607	6.109
16	4.015	4.346	4.791	5.134	5.484	5.960
17	3.965	4.286	4.714	5.044	5.379	5.832
18	3.922	4.233	4.648	4.966	5.288	5.722
19	3.883	4.187	4.590	4.897	5.209	5.627
20	3.850	4.146	4.539	4.837	5.139	5.543
21	3.819	4.110	4.493	4.784	5.077	5.469
22	3.792	4.077	4.452	4.736	5.022	5.402
23	3.768	4.048	4.415	4.693	4.972	5.343
24	3.745	4.021	4.382	4.654	4.927	5.290
25	3.725	3.997	4.352	4.619	4.887	5.241
26	3.707	3.974	4.324	4.587	4.850	5.197
27	3.690	3.954	4.299	4.558	4.816	5.157
28	3.674	3.935	4.275	4.530	4.784	5.120
29	3.659	3.918	4.254	4.506	4.756	5.086
30	3.646	3.902	4.234	4.482	4.729	5.054
35	3.591	3.836	4.153	4.389	4.622	4.927
40	3.551	3.788	4.094	4.321	4.544	4.835
45	3.520	3.752	4.049	4.269	4.485	4.766
50	3.496	3.723	4.014	4.228	4.438	4.711
55	3.476	3.700	3.986	4.196	4.401	4.667
60	3.460	3.681	3.962	4.169	4.370	4.631
70	3.435	3.651	3.926	4.127	4.323	4.576
80	3.416	3.629	3.899	4.096	4.288	4.535
90	3.402	3.612	3.878	4.072	4.261	4.503
100	3.390	3.598	3.862	4.053	4.240	4.478
200	3.340	3.539	3.789	3.970	4.146	4.369
500	3.310	3.504	3.747	3.922	4.091	4.306
1,000	3.300	3.492	3.733	3.906	4.073	4.285
2,000	3.295	3.486	3.726	3.898	4.064	4.275
10,000	3.292	3.482	3.720	3.892	4.058	4.267
∞	3.291	3.481	3.719	3.891	4.056	4.265

Note: All *p* values are one-tailed in this table.

TABLE B.3 (*continued*)

df	.000005	.0000025	.000001	.0000005	.00000025	.0000001
1	63,661.977	127,323.954	318,309.886	636,619.772	1,273,239.545	3,183,098.862
2	316.225	447.212	707.106	999.999	1,414.213	2,236.068
3	60.397	76.104	103.299	130.155	163.989	222.572
4	27.771	33.047	41.578	49.459	58.829	73.986
5	17.807	20.591	24.771	28.477	32.734	39.340
6	13.555	15.260	17.830	20.047	22.532	26.286
7	11.215	12.437	14.241	15.764	17.447	19.932
8	9.782	10.731	12.110	13.257	14.504	16.320
9	8.827	9.605	10.720	11.637	12.623	14.041
10	8.150	8.812	9.752	10.516	11.328	12.492
11	7.648	8.227	9.043	9.702	10.397	11.381
12	7.261	7.780	8.504	9.085	9.695	10.551
13	6.955	7.427	8.082	8.604	9.149	9.909
14	6.706	7.142	7.743	8.218	8.713	9.400
15	6.502	6.907	7.465	7.903	8.358	8.986
16	6.330	6.711	7.233	7.642	8.064	8.645
17	6.184	6.545	7.037	7.421	7.817	8.358
18	6.059	6.402	6.869	7.232	7.605	8.115
19	5.949	6.278	6.723	7.069	7.423	7.905
20	5.854	6.170	6.597	6.927	7.265	7.723
21	5.769	6.074	6.485	6.802	7.126	7.564
22	5.694	5.989	6.386	6.692	7.003	7.423
23	5.627	5.913	6.297	6.593	6.893	7.298
24	5.566	5.845	6.218	6.504	6.795	7.185
25	5.511	5.783	6.146	6.424	6.706	7.085
26	5.461	5.726	6.081	6.352	6.626	6.993
27	5.415	5.675	6.021	6.286	6.553	6.910
28	5.373	5.628	5.967	6.225	6.486	6.835
29	5.335	5.585	5.917	6.170	6.426	6.765
30	5.299	5.545	5.871	6.119	6.369	6.701
35	5.156	5.385	5.687	5.915	6.143	6.447
40	5.053	5.269	5.554	5.768	5.983	6.266
45	4.975	5.182	5.454	5.659	5.862	6.130
50	4.914	5.115	5.377	5.573	5.769	6.025
55	4.865	5.060	5.315	5.505	5.694	5.942
60	4.825	5.015	5.264	5.449	5.633	5.873
70	4.763	4.946	5.185	5.363	5.539	5.768
80	4.717	4.896	5.128	5.300	5.470	5.691
90	4.682	4.857	5.084	5.252	5.417	5.633
100	4.654	4.826	5.049	5.214	5.376	5.587
200	4.533	4.692	4.897	5.048	5.196	5.387
500	4.463	4.615	4.810	4.953	5.094	5.273
1,000	4.440	4.590	4.781	4.922	5.060	5.236
2,000	4.428	4.578	4.767	4.907	5.043	5.218
10,000	4.419	4.567	4.756	4.895	5.029	5.203
∞	4.417	4.565	4.753	4.892	5.026	5.199

Note: All p values are one-tailed in this table. Standard normal deviates (Z) corresponding to t can be estimated quite accurately from

$$Z = \left[df \ \log_e \left(1 + \frac{t^2}{df} \right) \right]^{1/2} \left[1 - \frac{1}{2df} \right]^{1/2}.$$

(Reproduced from "Extended tables of the percentage points of Student's t-distribution," by E. T. Federighi, 1959, *Journal of the American Statistical Association, 54,* 683–688, with the permission of the publisher.)

TABLE B.4
Table of F

df₂	p	1	2	3	4	5	6	8	12	24	∞
1	.001	405284	500000	540379	562500	576405	585937	598144	610667	623497	636619
	.005	16211	20000	21615	22500	23056	23437	23925	24426	24940	25465
	.01	4052	4999	5403	5625	5764	5859	5981	6106	6234	6366
	.025	647.79	799.50	864.16	899.58	921.85	937.11	956.66	976.71	997.25	1018.30
	.05	161.45	199.50	215.71	224.58	230.16	233.99	238.88	243.91	249.05	254.32
	.10	39.86	49.50	53.59	55.83	57.24	58.20	59.44	60.70	62.00	63.33
	.20	9.47	12.00	13.06	13.73	14.01	14.26	14.59	14.90	15.24	15.58
2	.001	998.5	999.0	999.2	999.2	999.3	999.3	999.4	999.4	999.5	999.5
	.005	198.50	199.00	199.17	199.25	199.30	199.33	199.37	199.42	199.46	199.51
	.01	98.49	99.00	99.17	99.25	99.30	99.33	99.36	99.42	99.46	99.50
	.025	38.51	39.00	39.17	39.25	39.30	39.33	39.37	39.42	39.46	39.50
	.05	18.51	19.00	19.16	19.25	19.30	19.33	19.37	19.41	19.45	19.50
	.10	8.53	9.00	9.16	9.24	9.29	9.33	9.37	9.41	9.45	9.49
	.20	3.56	4.00	4.16	4.24	4.28	4.32	4.36	4.40	4.44	4.48
3	.001	167.5	148.5	141.1	137.1	134.6	132.8	130.6	128.3	125.9	123.5
	.005	55.55	49.80	47.47	46.20	45.39	44.84	44.13	43.39	42.62	41.83
	.01	34.12	30.81	29.46	28.71	28.24	27.91	27.49	27.05	26.60	26.12
	.025	17.44	16.04	15.44	15.10	14.89	14.74	14.54	14.34	14.12	13.90
	.05	10.13	9.55	9.28	9.12	9.01	8.94	8.84	8.74	8.64	8.53
	.10	5.54	5.46	5.39	5.34	5.31	5.28	5.25	5.22	5.18	5.13
	.20	2.68	2.89	2.94	2.96	2.97	2.97	2.98	2.98	2.98	2.98
4	.001	74.14	61.25	56.18	53.44	51.71	50.53	49.00	47.41	45.77	44.05
	.005	31.33	26.28	24.26	23.16	22.46	21.98	21.35	20.71	20.03	19.33
	.01	21.20	18.00	16.69	15.98	15.52	15.21	14.80	14.37	13.93	13.46
	.025	12.22	10.65	9.98	9.60	9.36	9.20	8.98	8.75	8.51	8.26
	.05	7.71	6.94	6.59	6.39	6.26	6.16	6.04	5.91	5.77	5.63
	.10	4.54	4.32	4.19	4.11	4.05	4.01	3.95	3.90	3.83	3.76
	.20	2.35	2.47	2.48	2.48	2.48	2.47	2.47	2.46	2.44	2.43

TABLE B.4 (continued)

df_2	p	1	2	3	4	5	6	8	12	24	∞
5	.001	47.04	36.61	33.20	31.09	29.75	28.84	27.64	26.42	25.14	23.78
	.005	22.79	18.31	16.53	15.56	14.94	14.51	13.96	13.38	12.78	12.14
	.01	16.26	13.27	12.06	11.39	10.97	10.67	10.29	9.89	9.47	9.02
	.025	10.01	8.43	7.76	7.39	7.15	6.98	6.76	6.52	6.28	6.02
	.05	6.61	5.79	5.41	5.19	5.05	4.95	4.82	4.68	4.53	4.36
	.10	4.06	3.78	3.62	3.52	3.45	3.40	3.34	3.27	3.19	3.10
	.20	2.18	2.26	2.25	2.24	2.23	2.22	2.20	2.18	2.16	2.13
6	.001	35.51	27.00	23.70	21.90	20.81	20.03	19.03	17.99	16.89	15.75
	.005	18.64	14.54	12.92	12.03	11.46	11.07	10.57	10.03	9.47	8.88
	.01	13.74	10.92	9.78	9.15	8.75	8.47	8.10	7.72	7.31	6.88
	.025	8.81	7.26	6.60	6.23	5.99	5.82	5.60	5.37	5.12	4.85
	.05	5.99	5.14	4.76	4.53	4.39	4.28	4.15	4.00	3.84	3.67
	.10	3.78	3.46	3.29	3.18	3.11	3.05	2.98	2.90	2.82	2.72
	.20	2.07	2.13	2.11	2.09	2.08	2.06	2.04	2.02	1.99	1.95
7	.001	29.22	21.69	18.77	17.19	16.21	15.52	14.63	13.71	12.73	11.69
	.005	16.24	12.40	10.88	10.05	9.52	9.16	8.68	8.18	7.65	7.08
	.01	12.25	9.55	8.45	7.85	7.46	7.19	6.84	6.47	6.07	5.65
	.025	8.07	6.54	5.89	5.52	5.29	5.12	4.90	4.67	4.42	4.14
	.05	5.59	4.74	4.35	4.12	3.97	3.87	3.73	3.57	3.41	3.23
	.10	3.59	3.26	3.07	2.96	2.88	2.83	2.75	2.67	2.58	2.47
	.20	2.00	2.04	2.02	1.99	1.97	1.96	1.93	1.91	1.87	1.83
8	.001	25.42	18.49	15.83	14.39	13.49	12.86	12.04	11.19	10.30	9.34
	.005	14.69	11.04	9.60	8.81	8.30	7.95	7.50	7.01	6.50	5.95
	.01	11.26	8.65	7.59	7.01	6.63	6.37	6.03	5.67	5.28	4.86
	.025	7.57	6.06	5.42	5.05	4.82	4.65	4.43	4.20	3.95	3.67
	.05	5.32	4.46	4.07	3.84	3.69	3.58	3.44	3.28	3.12	2.93
	.10	3.46	3.11	2.92	2.81	2.73	2.67	2.59	2.50	2.40	2.29
	.20	1.95	1.98	1.95	1.92	1.90	1.88	1.86	1.83	1.79	1.74

TABLE B.4 (*continued*)

df_2	p	1	2	3	4	5	6	8	12	24	∞
9	.001	22.86	16.39	13.90	12.56	11.71	11.13	10.37	9.57	8.72	7.81
	.005	13.61	10.11	8.72	7.96	7.47	7.13	6.69	6.23	5.73	5.19
	.01	10.56	8.02	6.99	6.42	6.06	5.80	5.47	5.11	4.73	4.31
	.025	7.21	5.71	5.08	4.72	4.48	4.32	4.10	3.87	3.61	3.33
	.05	5.12	4.26	3.86	3.63	3.48	3.37	3.23	3.07	2.90	2.71
	.10	3.36	3.01	2.81	2.69	2.61	2.55	2.47	2.38	2.28	2.16
	.20	1.91	1.94	1.90	1.87	1.85	1.83	1.80	1.76	1.72	1.67
10	.001	21.04	14.91	12.55	11.28	10.48	9.92	9.20	8.45	7.64	6.76
	.005	12.83	9.43	8.08	7.34	6.87	6.54	6.12	5.66	5.17	4.64
	.01	10.04	7.56	6.55	5.99	5.64	5.39	5.06	4.71	4.33	3.91
	.025	6.94	5.46	4.83	4.47	4.24	4.07	3.85	3.62	3.37	3.08
	.05	4.96	4.10	3.71	3.48	3.33	3.22	3.07	2.91	2.74	2.54
	.10	3.28	2.92	2.73	2.61	2.52	2.46	2.38	2.28	2.18	2.06
	.20	1.88	1.90	1.86	1.83	1.80	1.78	1.75	1.72	1.67	1.62
11	.001	19.69	13.81	11.56	10.35	9.58	9.05	8.35	7.63	6.85	6.00
	.005	12.23	8.91	7.60	6.88	6.42	6.10	5.68	5.24	4.76	4.23
	.01	9.65	7.20	6.22	5.67	5.32	5.07	4.74	4.40	4.02	3.60
	.025	6.72	5.26	4.63	4.28	4.04	3.88	3.66	3.43	3.17	2.88
	.05	4.84	3.98	3.59	3.36	3.20	3.09	2.95	2.79	2.61	2.40
	.10	3.23	2.86	2.66	2.54	2.45	2.39	2.30	2.21	2.10	1.97
	.20	1.86	1.87	1.83	1.80	1.77	1.75	1.72	1.68	1.63	1.57
12	.001	18.64	12.97	10.80	9.63	8.89	8.38	7.71	7.00	6.25	5.42
	.005	11.75	8.51	7.23	6.52	6.07	5.76	5.35	4.91	4.43	3.90
	.01	9.33	6.93	5.95	5.41	5.06	4.82	4.50	4.16	3.78	3.36
	.025	6.55	5.10	4.47	4.12	3.89	3.73	3.51	3.28	3.02	2.72
	.05	4.75	3.88	3.49	3.26	3.11	3.00	2.85	2.69	2.50	2.30
	.10	3.18	2.81	2.61	2.48	2.39	2.33	2.24	2.15	2.04	1.90
	.20	1.84	1.85	1.80	1.77	1.74	1.72	1.69	1.65	1.60	1.54

TABLE B.4 (*continued*)

df_2	p	1	2	3	4	5	6	8	12	24	∞
13	.001	17.81	12.31	10.21	9.07	8.35	7.86	7.21	6.52	5.78	4.97
	.005	11.37	8.19	6.93	6.23	5.79	5.48	5.08	4.64	4.17	3.65
	.01	9.07	6.70	5.74	5.20	4.86	4.62	4.30	3.96	3.59	3.16
	.025	6.41	4.97	4.35	4.00	3.77	3.60	3.39	3.15	2.89	2.60
	.05	4.67	3.80	3.41	3.18	3.02	2.92	2.77	2.60	2.42	2.21
	.10	3.14	2.76	2.56	2.43	2.35	2.28	2.20	2.10	1.98	1.85
	.20	1.82	1.83	1.78	1.75	1.72	1.69	1.66	1.62	1.57	1.51
14	.001	17.14	11.78	9.73	8.62	7.92	7.43	6.80	6.13	5.41	4.60
	.005	11.06	7.92	6.68	6.00	5.56	5.26	4.86	4.43	3.96	3.44
	.01	8.86	6.51	5.56	5.03	4.69	4.46	4.14	3.80	3.43	3.00
	.025	6.30	4.86	4.24	3.89	3.66	3.50	3.29	3.05	2.79	2.49
	.05	4.60	3.74	3.34	3.11	2.96	2.85	2.70	2.53	2.35	2.13
	.10	3.10	2.73	2.52	2.39	2.31	2.24	2.15	2.05	1.94	1.80
	.20	1.81	1.81	1.76	1.73	1.70	1.67	1.64	1.60	1.55	1.48
15	.001	16.59	11.34	9.34	8.25	7.57	7.09	6.47	5.81	5.10	4.31
	.005	10.80	7.70	6.48	5.80	5.37	5.07	4.67	4.25	3.79	3.26
	.01	8.68	6.36	5.42	4.89	4.56	4.32	4.00	3.67	3.29	2.87
	.025	6.20	4.77	4.15	3.80	3.58	3.41	3.20	2.96	2.70	2.40
	.05	4.54	3.68	3.29	3.06	2.90	2.79	2.64	2.48	2.29	2.07
	.10	3.07	2.70	2.49	2.36	2.27	2.21	2.12	2.02	1.90	1.76
	.20	1.80	1.79	1.75	1.71	1.68	1.66	1.62	1.58	1.53	1.46
16	.001	16.12	10.97	9.00	7.94	7.27	6.81	6.19	5.55	4.85	4.06
	.005	10.58	7.51	6.30	5.64	5.21	4.91	4.52	4.10	3.64	3.11
	.01	8.53	6.23	5.29	4.77	4.44	4.20	3.89	3.55	3.18	2.75
	.025	6.12	4.69	4.08	3.73	3.50	3.34	3.12	2.89	2.63	2.32
	.05	4.49	3.63	3.24	3.01	2.85	2.74	2.59	2.42	2.24	2.01
	.10	3.05	2.67	2.46	2.33	2.24	2.18	2.09	1.99	1.87	1.72
	.20	1.79	1.78	1.74	1.70	1.67	1.64	1.61	1.56	1.51	1.43

df_1

TABLE B.4 (*continued*)

df_2	p	1	2	3	4	5	6	8	12	24	∞
17	.001	15.72	10.66	8.73	7.68	7.02	6.56	5.96	5.32	4.63	3.85
	.005	10.38	7.35	6.16	5.50	5.07	4.78	4.39	3.97	3.51	2.98
	.01	8.40	6.11	5.18	4.67	4.34	4.10	3.79	3.45	3.08	2.65
	.025	6.04	4.62	4.01	3.66	3.44	3.28	3.06	2.82	2.56	2.25
	.05	4.45	3.59	3.20	2.96	2.81	2.70	2.55	2.38	2.19	1.96
	.10	3.03	2.64	2.44	2.31	2.22	2.15	2.06	1.96	1.84	1.69
	.20	1.78	1.77	1.72	1.68	1.65	1.63	1.59	1.55	1.49	1.42
18	.001	15.38	10.39	8.49	7.46	6.81	6.35	5.76	5.13	4.45	3.67
	.005	10.22	7.21	6.03	5.37	4.96	4.66	4.28	3.86	3.40	2.87
	.01	8.28	6.01	5.09	4.58	4.25	4.01	3.71	3.37	3.00	2.57
	.025	5.98	4.56	3.95	3.61	3.38	3.22	3.01	2.77	2.50	2.19
	.05	4.41	3.55	3.16	2.93	2.77	2.66	2.51	2.34	2.15	1.92
	.10	3.01	2.62	2.42	2.29	2.20	2.13	2.04	1.93	1.81	1.66
	.20	1.77	1.76	1.71	1.67	1.64	1.62	1.58	1.53	1.48	1.40
19	.001	15.08	10.16	8.28	7.26	6.61	6.18	5.59	4.97	4.29	3.52
	.005	10.07	7.09	5.92	5.27	4.85	4.56	4.18	3.76	3.31	2.78
	.01	8.18	5.93	5.01	4.50	4.17	3.94	3.63	3.30	2.92	2.49
	.025	5.92	4.51	3.90	3.56	3.33	3.17	2.96	2.72	2.45	2.13
	.05	4.38	3.52	3.13	2.90	2.74	2.63	2.48	2.31	2.11	1.88
	.10	2.99	2.61	2.40	2.27	2.18	2.11	2.02	1.91	1.79	1.63
	.20	1.76	1.75	1.70	1.66	1.63	1.61	1.57	1.52	1.46	1.39
20	.001	14.82	9.95	8.10	7.10	6.46	6.02	5.44	4.82	4.15	3.38
	.005	9.94	6.99	5.82	5.17	4.76	4.47	4.09	3.68	3.22	2.69
	.01	8.10	5.85	4.94	4.43	4.10	3.87	3.56	3.23	2.86	2.42
	.025	5.87	4.46	3.86	3.51	3.29	3.13	2.91	2.68	2.41	2.09
	.05	4.35	3.49	3.10	2.87	2.71	2.60	2.45	2.28	2.08	1.84
	.10	2.97	2.59	2.38	2.25	2.16	2.09	2.00	1.89	1.77	1.61
	.20	1.76	1.75	1.70	1.65	1.62	1.60	1.56	1.51	1.45	1.37

TABLE B.4 *(continued)*

df_2	p	1	2	3	4	5	6	8	12	24	∞
21	.001	14.59	9.77	7.94	6.95	6.32	5.88	5.31	4.70	4.03	3.26
	.005	9.83	6.89	5.73	5.09	4.68	4.39	4.01	4.60	3.15	2.61
	.01	8.02	5.78	4.87	4.37	4.04	3.81	3.51	3.17	2.80	2.36
	.025	5.83	4.42	3.82	3.48	3.25	3.09	2.87	2.64	2.37	2.04
	.05	4.32	3.47	3.07	2.84	2.68	2.57	2.42	2.25	2.05	1.81
	.10	2.96	2.57	2.36	2.23	2.14	2.08	1.98	1.88	1.75	1.59
	.20	1.75	1.74	1.69	1.65	1.61	1.59	1.55	1.50	1.44	1.36
22	.001	14.38	9.61	7.80	6.81	6.19	5.76	5.19	4.58	3.92	3.15
	.005	9.73	6.81	5.65	5.02	4.61	4.32	3.94	3.54	3.08	2.55
	.01	7.94	5.72	4.82	4.31	3.99	3.76	3.45	3.12	2.75	2.31
	.025	5.79	4.38	3.78	3.44	3.22	3.05	2.84	2.60	2.33	2.00
	.05	4.30	3.44	3.05	2.82	2.66	2.55	2.40	2.23	2.03	1.78
	.10	2.95	2.56	2.35	2.22	2.13	2.06	1.97	1.86	1.73	1.57
	.20	1.75	1.73	1.68	1.64	1.61	1.58	1.54	1.49	1.43	1.35
23	.001	14.19	9.47	7.67	6.69	6.08	5.65	5.09	4.48	3.82	3.05
	.005	9.63	6.73	5.58	4.95	4.54	4.26	3.88	3.47	3.02	2.48
	.01	7.88	5.66	4.76	4.26	3.94	3.71	3.41	3.07	2.70	2.26
	.025	5.75	4.35	3.75	3.41	3.18	3.02	2.81	2.57	2.30	1.97
	.05	4.28	3.42	3.03	2.80	2.64	2.53	2.38	2.20	2.00	1.76
	.10	2.94	2.55	2.34	2.21	2.11	2.05	1.95	1.84	1.72	1.55
	.20	1.74	1.73	1.68	1.63	1.60	1.57	1.53	1.49	1.42	1.34
24	.001	14.03	9.34	7.55	6.59	5.98	5.55	4.99	4.39	3.74	2.97
	.005	9.55	6.66	5.52	4.89	4.49	4.20	3.83	3.42	2.97	2.43
	.01	7.82	5.61	4.72	4.22	3.90	3.67	3.36	3.03	2.66	2.21
	.025	5.72	4.32	3.72	3.38	3.15	2.99	2.78	2.54	2.27	1.94
	.05	4.26	3.40	3.01	2.78	2.62	2.51	2.36	2.18	1.98	1.73
	.10	2.93	2.54	2.33	2.19	2.10	2.04	1.94	1.83	1.70	1.53
	.20	1.74	1.72	1.67	1.63	1.59	1.57	1.53	1.48	1.42	1.33

TABLE B.4 *(continued)*

df_2 \ df_1	p	1	2	3	4	5	6	8	12	24	∞
25	.001	13.88	9.22	7.45	6.49	5.88	5.46	4.91	4.31	3.66	2.89
	.005	9.48	6.60	5.46	4.84	4.43	4.15	3.78	3.37	2.92	2.38
	.01	7.77	5.57	4.68	4.18	3.86	3.63	3.32	2.99	2.62	2.17
	.025	5.69	4.29	3.69	3.35	3.13	2.97	2.75	2.51	2.24	1.91
	.05	4.24	3.38	2.99	2.76	2.60	2.49	2.34	2.16	1.96	1.71
	.10	2.92	2.53	2.32	2.18	2.09	2.02	1.93	1.82	1.69	1.52
	.20	1.73	1.72	1.66	1.62	1.59	1.56	1.52	1.47	1.41	1.32
26	.001	13.74	9.12	7.36	6.41	5.80	5.38	4.83	4.24	3.59	2.82
	.005	9.41	6.54	5.41	4.79	4.38	4.10	3.73	3.33	2.87	2.33
	.01	7.72	5.53	4.64	4.14	3.82	3.59	3.29	2.96	2.58	2.13
	.025	5.66	4.27	3.67	3.33	3.10	2.94	2.73	2.49	2.22	1.88
	.05	4.22	3.37	2.98	2.74	2.59	2.47	2.32	2.15	1.95	1.69
	.10	2.91	2.52	2.31	2.17	2.08	2.01	1.92	1.81	1.68	1.50
	.20	1.73	1.71	1.66	1.62	1.58	1.56	1.52	1.47	1.40	1.31
27	.001	13.61	9.02	7.27	6.33	5.73	5.31	4.76	4.17	3.52	2.75
	.005	9.34	6.49	5.36	4.74	4.34	4.06	3.69	3.28	2.83	2.29
	.01	7.68	5.49	4.60	4.11	3.78	3.56	3.26	2.93	2.55	2.10
	.025	5.63	4.24	3.65	3.31	3.08	2.92	2.71	2.47	2.19	1.85
	.05	4.21	3.35	2.96	2.73	2.57	2.46	2.30	2.13	1.93	1.67
	.10	2.90	2.51	2.30	2.17	2.07	2.00	1.91	1.80	1.67	1.49
	.20	1.73	1.71	1.66	1.61	1.58	1.55	1.51	1.46	1.40	1.30
28	.001	13.50	8.93	7.19	6.25	5.66	5.24	4.69	4.11	3.46	2.70
	.005	9.28	6.44	5.32	4.70	4.30	4.02	3.65	3.25	2.79	2.25
	.01	7.64	5.45	4.57	4.07	3.75	3.53	3.23	2.90	2.52	2.06
	.025	5.61	4.22	3.63	3.29	3.06	2.90	2.69	2.45	2.17	1.83
	.05	4.20	3.34	2.95	2.71	2.56	2.44	2.29	2.12	1.91	1.65
	.10	2.89	2.50	2.29	2.16	2.06	2.00	1.90	1.79	1.66	1.48
	.20	1.72	1.71	1.65	1.61	1.57	1.55	1.51	1.46	1.39	1.30

TABLE B.4 (*continued*)

df_2	p	df_1 1	2	3	4	5	6	8	12	24	∞
29	.001	13.39	8.85	7.12	6.19	5.59	5.18	4.64	4.05	3.41	2.64
	.005	9.23	6.40	5.28	4.66	4.26	3.98	3.61	3.21	2.76	2.21
	.01	7.60	5.42	4.54	4.04	3.73	3.50	3.20	2.87	2.49	2.03
	.025	5.59	4.20	3.61	3.27	3.04	2.88	2.67	2.43	2.15	1.81
	.05	4.18	3.33	2.93	2.70	2.54	2.43	2.28	2.10	1.90	1.64
	.10	2.89	2.50	2.28	2.15	2.06	1.99	1.89	1.78	1.65	1.47
	.20	1.72	1.70	1.65	1.60	1.57	1.54	1.50	1.45	1.39	1.29
30	.001	13.29	8.77	7.05	6.12	5.53	5.12	4.58	4.00	3.36	2.59
	.005	9.18	6.35	5.24	4.62	4.23	3.95	3.58	3.18	2.73	2.18
	.01	7.56	5.39	4.51	4.02	3.70	3.47	3.17	2.84	2.47	2.01
	.025	5.57	4.18	3.59	3.25	3.03	2.87	2.65	2.41	2.14	1.79
	.05	4.17	3.32	2.92	2.69	2.53	2.42	2.27	2.09	1.89	1.62
	.10	2.88	2.49	2.28	2.14	2.05	1.98	1.88	1.77	1.64	1.46
	.20	1.72	1.70	1.64	1.60	1.57	1.54	1.50	1.45	1.38	1.28
40	.001	12.61	8.25	6.60	5.70	5.13	4.73	4.21	3.64	3.01	2.23
	.005	8.83	6.07	4.98	4.37	3.99	3.71	3.35	2.95	2.50	1.93
	.01	7.31	5.18	4.31	3.83	3.51	3.29	2.99	2.66	2.29	1.80
	.025	5.42	4.05	3.46	3.13	2.90	2.74	2.53	2.29	2.01	1.64
	.05	4.08	3.23	2.84	2.61	2.45	2.34	2.18	2.00	1.79	1.51
	.10	2.84	2.44	2.23	2.09	2.00	1.93	1.83	1.71	1.57	1.38
	.20	1.70	1.68	1.62	1.57	1.54	1.51	1.47	1.41	1.34	1.24
60	.001	11.97	7.76	6.17	5.31	4.76	4.37	3.87	3.31	2.69	1.90
	.005	8.49	5.80	4.73	4.14	3.76	3.49	3.13	2.74	2.29	1.69
	.01	7.08	4.98	4.13	3.65	3.34	3.12	2.82	2.50	2.12	1.60
	.025	5.29	3.93	3.34	3.01	2.79	2.63	2.41	2.17	1.88	1.48
	.05	4.00	3.15	2.76	2.52	2.37	2.25	2.10	1.92	1.70	1.39
	.10	2.79	2.39	2.18	2.04	1.95	1.87	1.77	1.66	1.51	1.29
	.20	1.68	1.65	1.59	1.55	1.51	1.48	1.44	1.38	1.31	1.18

TABLE B.4 (*continued*)

df_2	p	df_1 1	2	3	4	5	6	8	12	24	∞
120	.001	11.38	7.31	5.79	4.95	4.42	4.04	3.55	3.02	2.40	1.56
	.005	8.18	5.54	4.50	3.92	3.55	3.28	2.93	2.54	2.09	1.43
	.01	6.85	4.79	3.95	3.48	3.17	2.96	2.66	2.34	1.95	1.38
	.025	5.15	3.80	3.23	2.89	2.67	2.52	2.30	2.05	1.76	1.31
	.05	3.92	3.07	2.68	2.45	2.29	2.17	2.02	1.83	1.61	1.25
	.10	2.75	2.35	2.13	1.99	1.90	1.82	1.72	1.60	1.45	1.19
	.20	1.66	1.63	1.57	1.52	1.48	1.45	1.41	1.35	1.27	1.12
∞	.001	10.83	6.91	5.42	4.62	4.10	3.74	3.27	2.74	2.13	1.00
	.005	7.88	5.30	4.28	3.72	3.35	3.09	2.74	2.36	1.90	1.00
	.01	6.64	4.60	3.78	3.32	3.02	2.80	2.51	2.18	1.79	1.00
	.025	5.02	3.69	3.12	2.79	2.57	2.41	2.19	1.94	1.64	1.00
	.05	3.84	2.99	2.60	2.37	2.21	2.09	1.94	1.75	1.52	1.00
	.10	2.71	2.30	2.08	1.94	1.85	1.77	1.67	1.55	1.38	1.00
	.20	1.64	1.61	1.55	1.50	1.46	1.43	1.38	1.32	1.23	1.00

Note: Reproduced from *Design and Analysis of Experiments in Psychology and Education* (pp. 41–44), by E. F. Lindquist, 1953, Boston: Houghton Mifflin, with the permission of the publisher.

TABLE B.5
Table of χ^2

df	Probability													
	.99	.98	.95	.90	.80	.70	.50	.30	.20	.10	.05	.02	.01	.001
1	.00016	.00063	.00393	.0158	.0642	.148	.455	1.074	1.642	2.706	3.841	5.412	6.635	10.827
2	.0201	.0404	.103	.211	.446	.713	1.386	2.408	3.219	4.605	5.991	7.824	9.210	13.815
3	.115	.185	.352	.584	1.005	1.424	2.366	3.665	4.642	6.251	7.815	9.837	11.345	16.268
4	.297	.429	.711	1.064	1.649	2.195	3.357	4.878	5.989	7.779	9.488	11.668	13.277	18.465
5	.554	.752	1.145	1.610	2.343	3.000	4.351	6.064	7.289	9.236	11.070	13.388	15.086	20.517
6	.872	1.134	1.635	2.204	3.070	3.828	5.348	7.231	8.558	10.645	12.592	15.033	16.812	22.457
7	1.239	1.564	2.167	2.833	3.822	4.671	6.346	8.383	9.803	12.017	14.067	16.622	18.475	24.322
8	1.646	2.032	2.733	3.490	4.594	5.527	7.344	9.524	11.030	13.362	15.507	18.168	20.090	26.125
9	2.088	2.532	3.325	4.168	5.380	6.393	8.343	10.656	12.242	14.684	16.919	19.679	21.666	27.877
10	2.558	3.059	3.940	4.865	6.179	7.267	9.342	11.781	13.442	15.987	18.307	21.161	23.209	29.588
11	3.053	3.609	4.575	5.578	6.989	8.148	10.341	12.899	14.631	17.275	19.675	22.618	24.725	31.264
12	3.571	4.178	5.226	6.304	7.807	9.034	11.340	14.011	15.812	18.549	21.026	24.054	26.217	32.909
13	4.107	4.765	5.892	7.042	8.634	9.926	12.340	15.119	16.985	19.812	22.362	25.472	27.688	34.528
14	4.660	5.368	6.571	7.790	9.467	10.821	13.339	16.222	18.151	21.064	23.685	26.873	29.141	36.123
15	5.229	5.985	7.261	8.547	10.307	11.721	14.339	17.322	19.311	22.307	24.996	28.259	30.578	37.697
16	5.812	6.614	7.962	9.312	11.152	12.624	15.338	18.418	20.465	23.542	26.296	29.633	32.000	39.252
17	6.408	7.255	8.672	10.085	12.002	13.531	16.338	19.511	21.615	24.769	27.587	30.995	33.409	40.790
18	7.015	7.906	9.390	10.865	12.857	14.440	17.338	20.601	22.760	25.989	28.869	32.346	34.805	42.315
19	7.633	8.567	10.117	11.651	13.716	15.352	18.338	21.689	23.900	27.204	30.144	33.687	36.191	43.820
20	8.260	9.237	10.851	12.443	14.578	16.266	19.337	22.775	25.038	28.412	31.410	35.020	37.566	45.315
21	8.897	9.915	11.591	13.240	15.445	17.182	20.337	23.858	26.171	29.615	32.671	36.343	38.932	46.797
22	9.542	10.600	12.338	14.041	16.314	18.101	21.337	24.939	27.301	30.813	33.924	37.659	40.289	48.268
23	10.196	11.293	13.091	14.848	17.187	19.021	22.337	26.018	28.429	32.007	35.172	38.968	41.638	49.728
24	10.856	11.992	13.848	15.659	18.062	19.943	23.337	27.096	29.553	33.196	36.415	40.270	42.980	51.179
25	11.524	12.697	14.611	16.473	18.940	20.867	24.337	28.172	30.675	34.382	37.652	41.566	44.314	52.620
26	12.198	13.409	15.379	17.292	19.820	21.792	25.336	29.246	31.795	35.563	38.885	42.856	45.642	54.052
27	12.879	14.125	16.151	18.114	20.703	22.719	26.336	30.319	32.912	36.741	40.113	44.140	46.963	55.476
28	13.565	14.847	16.928	18.939	21.588	23.647	27.336	31.391	34.027	37.916	41.337	45.419	48.278	56.893
29	14.256	15.574	17.708	19.768	22.475	24.577	28.336	32.461	35.139	39.087	42.557	46.693	49.588	58.308
30	14.953	16.306	18.493	20.599	23.364	25.508	29.336	33.530	36.250	40.256	43.773	47.962	50.892	59.703

Note: For larger values of *df*, the expression $\sqrt{2\chi^2} - \sqrt{2df - 1}$ may be used as a normal deviate with unit variance, remembering that the probability for χ^2 corresponds with that of a single tail of the normal curve.

(Reproduced from *Design and Analysis of Experiments in Psychology and Education* (p. 29), by E. F. Lindquist, 1953, Boston: Houghton Mifflin, with the permission of the publisher.)

TABLE B.6

Significance levels of r $\left[\,from\ t = r\sqrt{(N-2)/(1-r^2)}\,\right]$

$(N-2)$	Probability level						
	.20	.10	.05	.02	.01	.001	.0001
1	.951	.988	.997	.9995	.9999	1.000	1.0000
2	.800	.900	.950	.980	.990	.999	.9999
3	.687	.805	.878	.934	.959	.991	.998
4	.608	.729	.811	.882	.917	.974	.992
5	.551	.669	.754	.833	.874	.951	.981
6	.507	.622	.707	.789	.834	.925	.966
7	.472	.582	.666	.750	.798	.898	.948
8	.443	.550	.632	.716	.765	.872	.929
9	.419	.521	.602	.685	.735	.847	.910
10	.398	.497	.576	.658	.708	.823	.891
11	.380	.476	.553	.634	.684	.801	.873
12	.365	.458	.532	.612	.661	.780	.854
13	.351	.441	.514	.592	.641	.760	.837
14	.338	.426	.497	.574	.623	.742	.820
15	.327	.412	.482	.558	.606	.725	.804
16	.317	.400	.468	.542	.590	.708	.789
17	.308	.389	.456	.528	.575	.693	.774
18	.299	.378	.444	.516	.561	.679	.760
19	.291	.369	.433	.503	.549	.665	.747
20	.284	.360	.423	.492	.537	.652	.734
22	.271	.344	.404	.472	.515	.629	.711
24	.260	.330	.388	.453	.496	.607	.689
25	.255	.323	.381	.445	.487	.597	.679
30	.233	.296	.349	.409	.449	.554	.633
35	.216	.275	.325	.381	.418	.519	.596
40	.202	.257	.304	.358	.393	.490	.564
45	.190	.243	.288	.338	.372	.465	.537
50	.181	.231	.273	.322	.354	.443	.513
55	.172	.220	.261	.307	.338	.424	.492
60	.165	.211	.250	.295	.325	.408	.474
65	.159	.203	.240	.284	.312	.393	.457
70	.153	.195	.232	.274	.302	.380	.442
75	.148	.189	.224	.264	.292	.368	.429
80	.143	.183	.217	.256	.283	.357	.416
85	.139	.178	.211	.249	.275	.347	.405
90	.135	.173	.205	.242	.267	.338	.395
95	.131	.168	.200	.236	.260	.329	.385
100	.128	.164	.195	.230	.254	.321	.376
125	.115	.147	.174	.206	.228	.228	.338
150	.105	.134	.159	.189	.208	.264	.310
175	.097	.124	.148	.174	.194	.248	.288
200	.091	.116	.138	.164	.181	.235	.270
300	.074	.095	.113	.134	.148	.188	.222
500	.057	.074	.088	.104	.115	.148	.173
1000	.041	.052	.062	.073	.081	.104	.123
2000	.029	.037	.044	.052	.058	.074	.087
5000	.018	.023	.028	.033	.037	.047	.055

Note: All p values are two-tailed in this table. (Reproduced, in part, from *Statistical Inference* (p. 470), by H. M. Walker and J. Lev, 1953, New York: Holt, with the permission of the author and publisher; and from *Some Extension of Student's t and Pearson's r Central Distributions,* by A. L. Sockloff and J. N. Edney, May 1972, Temple University Measurement and Research Center, Technical Report 72-5, with the permission of the first author.)

TABLE B.7
Table of Fisher's z transformation of r

r	.00	.01	.02	.03	.04	.05	.06	.07	.08	.09
.0	.000	.010	.020	.030	.040	.050	.060	.070	.080	.090
.1	.100	.110	.121	.131	.141	.151	.161	.172	.182	.192
.2	.203	.213	.224	.234	.245	.255	.266	.277	.288	.299
.3	.310	.321	.332	.343	.354	.365	.377	.388	.400	.412
.4	.424	.436	.448	.460	.472	.485	.497	.510	.523	.536
.5	.549	.563	.576	.590	.604	.618	.633	.648	.662	.678
.6	.693	.709	.725	.741	.758	.775	.793	.811	.829	.848
.7	.867	.887	.908	.929	.950	.973	.996	1.020	1.045	1.071
.8	1.099	1.127	1.157	1.188	1.221	1.256	1.293	1.333	1.376	1.422

Second digit of r

r	.000	.001	.002	.003	.004	.005	.006	.007	.008	.009
.90	1.472	1.478	1.483	1.488	1.494	1.499	1.505	1.510	1.516	1.522
.91	1.528	1.533	1.539	1.545	1.551	1.557	1.564	1.570	1.576	1.583
.92	1.589	1.596	1.602	1.609	1.616	1.623	1.630	1.637	1.644	1.651
.93	1.658	1.666	1.673	1.681	1.689	1.697	1.705	1.713	1.721	1.730
.94	1.738	1.747	1.756	1.764	1.774	1.783	1.792	1.802	1.812	1.822
.95	1.832	1.842	1.853	1.863	1.874	1.886	1.897	1.909	1.921	1.933
.96	1.946	1.959	1.972	1.986	2.000	2.014	2.029	2.044	2.060	2.076
.97	2.092	2.109	2.127	2.146	2.165	2.185	2.205	2.227	2.249	2.273
.98	2.298	2.323	2.351	2.380	2.410	2.443	2.477	2.515	2.555	2.599
.99	2.646	2.700	2.759	2.826	2.903	2.994	3.106	3.250	3.453	3.800

Third digit of r

Note: z is obtained as $\frac{1}{2}\log_e\frac{(1+r)}{(1-r)}$.

(Reprinted by permission from *Statistical Methods* (7th ed.), by George W. Snedecor and William G. Cochran, © 1980, by the Iowa State University Press, Ames, Iowa 50010.)

TABLE B.8

Table of *r* equivalents of Fisher's *z*

z	.00	.01	.02	.03	.04	.05	.06	.07	.08	.09
.0	.000	.010	.020	.030	.040	.050	.060	.070	.080	.090
.1	.100	.110	.119	.129	.139	.149	.159	.168	.178	.187
.2	.197	.207	.216	.226	.236	.245	.254	.264	.273	.282
.3	.291	.300	.310	.319	.327	.336	.345	.354	.363	.371
.4	.380	.389	.397	.405	.414	.422	.430	.438	.446	.454
.5	.462	.470	.478	.485	.493	.500	.508	.515	.523	.530
.6	.537	.544	.551	.558	.565	.572	.578	.585	.592	.598
.7	.604	.611	.617	.623	.629	.635	.641	.647	.653	.658
.8	.664	.670	.685	.680	.686	.691	.696	.701	.706	.711
.9	.716	.721	.726	.731	.735	.740	.744	.749	.753	.757
1.0	.762	.766	.770	.774	.778	.782	.786	.790	.793	.797
1.1	.800	.804	.808	.811	.814	.818	.821	.824	.828	.831
1.2	.834	.837	.840	.843	.846	.848	.851	.854	.856	.859
1.3	.862	.864	.867	.869	.872	.874	.876	.879	.881	.883
1.4	.885	.888	.890	.892	.894	.896	.898	.900	.902	.903
1.5	.905	.907	.909	.910	.912	.914	.915	.917	.919	.920
1.6	.922	.923	.925	.926	.928	.929	.930	.932	.933	.934
1.7	.935	.937	.938	.939	.940	.941	.942	.944	.945	.946
1.8	.947	.948	.949	.950	.951	.952	.953	.954	.954	.955
1.9	.956	.957	.958	.959	.960	.960	.961	.962	.963	.963
2.0	.964	.965	.965	.966	.967	.967	.968	.969	.969	.970
2.1	.970	.971	.972	.972	.973	.973	.974	.974	.975	.975
2.2	.976	.976	.977	.977	.978	.978	.978	.979	.979	.980
2.3	.980	.980	.981	.981	.982	.982	.982	.983	.983	.983
2.4	.984	.984	.984	.985	.985	.985	.986	.986	.986	.986
2.5	.987	.987	.987	.987	.988	.988	.988	.988	.989	.989
2.6	.989	.989	.989	.990	.990	.990	.990	.990	.991	.991
2.7	.991	.991	.991	.992	.992	.992	.992	.992	.992	.992
2.8	.993	.993	.993	.993	.993	.993	.993	.994	.994	.994
2.9	.994	.994	.994	.994	.994	.995	.995	.995	.995	.995

Note: *r* is obtained as $\dfrac{e^{2z}-1}{e^{2z}+1}$.

(Reprinted by permission from *Statistical Methods* (7th ed.), by George W. Snedecor and William G. Cochran, © 1980, by the Iowa State University Press, Ames, Iowa 50010.)

TABLE B.9
Table of random digits

000	10097	32533	76520	13586	34673	54876	80959	09117	39292	74945
001	37542	04805	64894	74296	24805	24037	20636	10402	00822	91665
002	08422	68953	19645	09303	23209	02560	15953	34764	35080	33605
003	99019	02529	09376	70715	38311	31165	88676	74397	04436	27659
004	12807	99970	80157	36147	64032	36653	98951	16877	12171	76833
005	66065	74717	34072	76850	36697	36170	65813	39885	11199	29170
006	31060	10805	45571	82406	35303	42614	86799	07439	23403	09732
007	85269	77602	02051	65692	68665	74818	73053	85247	18623	88579
008	63573	32135	05325	47048	90553	57548	28468	28709	83491	25624
009	73796	45753	03529	64778	35808	34282	60935	20344	35273	88435
010	98520	17767	14905	68607	22109	40558	60970	93433	50500	73998
011	11805	05431	39808	27732	50725	68248	29405	24201	52775	67851
012	83452	99634	06288	98083	13746	70078	18475	40610	68711	77817
013	88685	40200	86507	58401	36766	67951	90364	76493	29609	11062
014	99594	67348	87517	64969	91826	08928	93785	61368	23478	34113
015	65481	17674	17468	50950	58047	76974	73039	57186	40218	16544
016	80124	35635	17727	08015	45318	22374	21115	78253	14385	53763
017	74350	99817	77402	77214	43236	00210	45521	64237	96286	02655
018	69916	26803	66252	29148	36936	87203	76621	13990	74400	56418
019	09893	20505	14225	68514	46427	56788	96297	78822	54382	14598
020	91499	14523	68479	27686	46162	83554	94750	89923	37089	20048
021	80336	94598	26940	36858	70297	34135	53140	33340	42050	82341
022	44104	81949	85157	47954	32979	26575	57600	40881	22222	06413
023	12550	73742	11100	02040	12860	74697	96644	89439	28707	25815
024	63606	49329	16505	34484	40219	52563	43651	77082	07207	31790
025	61196	90446	26457	47774	51924	33729	65394	59593	42582	60527
026	15474	45266	95270	79953	59367	83848	82396	10118	33211	59466
027	94557	28573	67897	54387	54622	44431	91190	42592	92927	45973
028	42481	16213	97344	08721	16868	48767	03071	12059	25701	46670
029	23523	78317	73208	89837	68935	91416	26252	29663	05522	82562
030	04493	52494	75246	33824	45862	51025	61962	79335	65337	12472
031	00549	97654	64051	88159	96119	63896	54692	82391	23287	29529
032	35963	15307	26898	09354	33351	35462	77974	50024	90103	39333
033	59808	08391	45427	26842	83609	49700	13021	24892	78565	20106
034	46058	85236	01390	92286	77281	44077	93910	83647	70617	42941
035	32179	00597	87379	25241	05567	07007	86743	17157	85394	11838
036	69234	61406	20117	45204	15956	60000	18743	92423	97118	96338
037	19565	41430	01758	75379	40419	21585	66674	36806	84962	85207
038	45155	14938	19476	07246	43667	94543	59047	90033	20826	69541
039	94864	31994	36168	10851	34888	81553	01540	35456	05014	51176
040	98086	24826	45240	28404	44999	08896	39094	73407	35441	31880
041	33185	16232	41941	50949	89435	48581	88695	41994	37548	73043
042	80951	00406	96382	70774	20151	23387	25016	25298	94624	61171
043	79752	49140	71961	28296	69861	02591	74852	20539	00387	59579
044	18633	32537	98145	06571	31010	24674	05455	61427	77938	91936

TABLE B.9 (*continued*)

045	74029	43902	77557	32270	97790	17119	52527	58021	80814	51748
046	54178	45611	80993	37143	05335	12969	56127	19255	36040	90324
047	11664	49883	52079	84827	59381	71539	09973	33440	88461	23356
048	48324	77928	31249	64710	02295	36870	32307	57546	15020	09994
049	69074	94138	87637	91976	35584	04401	10518	21615	01848	76938
050	09188	20097	32825	39527	04220	86304	83389	87374	64278	58044
051	90045	85497	51981	50654	94938	81997	91870	76150	68476	64659
052	73189	50207	47677	26269	62290	64464	27124	67018	41361	82760
053	75768	76490	20971	87749	90429	12272	95375	05871	93823	43178
054	54016	44056	66281	31003	00682	27398	20714	53295	07706	17813
055	08358	69910	78542	42785	13661	58873	04618	97553	31223	08420
056	28306	03264	81333	10591	40510	07893	32604	60475	94119	01840
057	53840	86233	81594	13628	51215	90290	28466	68795	77762	20791
058	91757	53741	61613	62269	50263	90212	55781	76514	83483	47055
059	89415	92684	00397	58391	12607	17646	48949	72306	94541	37408
060	77513	03820	86864	29901	68414	82774	51908	13980	72893	55507
061	19502	37174	69979	20288	55210	29773	74287	75251	65344	67415
062	21818	59313	93278	81757	05686	73156	07082	85046	31853	38452
063	51474	66499	68107	23621	94049	91345	42836	09191	08007	45449
064	99559	68331	62535	24170	69777	12830	74819	78142	43860	72834
065	33713	48007	93584	72869	51926	64721	58303	29822	93174	93972
066	85274	86893	11303	22970	28834	34137	73515	90400	71148	43643
067	84133	89640	44035	52166	73852	70091	61222	60561	62327	18423
068	56732	16234	17395	96131	10123	91622	85496	57560	81604	18880
069	65138	56806	87648	85261	34313	65861	45875	21069	85644	47277
070	38001	02176	81719	11711	71602	92937	74219	64049	65584	49698
071	37402	96397	01304	77586	56271	10086	47324	62605	40030	37438
072	97125	40348	87083	31417	21815	39250	75237	62047	15501	29578
073	21826	41134	47143	34072	64638	85902	49139	06441	03856	54552
074	73135	42742	95719	09035	85794	74296	08789	88156	64691	19202
075	07638	77929	03061	18072	96207	44156	23821	99538	04713	66994
076	60528	83441	07954	19814	59175	20695	05533	52139	61212	06455
077	83596	35655	06958	92983	05128	09719	77433	53783	92301	50498
078	10850	62746	99599	10507	13499	06319	53075	71839	06410	19362
079	39820	98952	43622	63147	64421	80814	43800	09351	31024	73167
080	59580	06478	75569	78800	88835	54486	23768	06156	04111	08408
081	38508	07341	23793	48763	90822	97022	17719	04207	95954	49953
082	30692	70668	94688	16127	56196	80091	82067	63400	05462	69200
083	65443	95659	18288	27437	49632	24041	08337	65676	96299	90836
084	27267	50264	13192	72294	07477	44606	17985	48911	97341	30358
085	91307	06991	19072	24210	36699	53728	28825	35793	28976	66252
086	68434	94688	84473	13622	62126	98408	12843	82590	09815	93146
087	48908	15877	54745	24591	35700	04754	83824	52692	54130	55160
088	06913	45197	42672	78601	11883	09528	63011	98901	14974	40344
089	10455	16019	14210	33712	91342	37821	88325	80851	43667	70883
090	12883	97343	65027	61184	04285	01392	17974	15077	90712	26769
091	21778	30976	38807	36961	31649	42096	63281	02023	08816	47449
092	19523	59515	65122	59659	86283	68258	69572	13798	16435	91529
093	67245	52670	35583	16563	79246	86686	76463	34222	26655	90802
094	60584	47377	07500	37992	45134	26529	26760	83637	41326	44344

TABLE B.9 (*continued*)

095	53853	41377	36066	94850	58838	73859	49364	73331	96240	43642
096	24637	38736	74384	89342	52623	07992	12369	18601	03742	83873
097	83080	12451	38992	22815	07759	51777	97377	27585	51972	37867
098	16444	24334	36151	99073	27493	70939	85130	32552	54846	54759
099	60790	18157	57178	65762	11161	78576	45819	52979	65130	04860
100	03991	10461	93716	16894	66083	24653	84609	58232	88618	19161
101	38555	95554	32886	59780	08355	60860	29735	47762	71299	23853
102	17546	73704	92052	46215	55121	29281	59076	07936	27954	58909
103	32643	52861	95819	06831	00911	98936	76355	93779	80863	00514
104	69572	68777	39510	35905	14060	40619	29549	69616	33564	60780
105	24122	66591	27699	06494	14845	46672	61958	77100	90899	75754
106	61196	30231	92962	61773	41839	55382	17267	70943	78038	70267
107	30532	21704	10274	12202	39685	23309	10061	68829	55986	66485
108	03788	97599	75867	20717	74416	53166	35208	33374	87539	08823
109	48228	63379	85783	47619	53152	67433	35663	52972	16818	60311
110	60365	94653	35075	33949	42614	29297	01918	28316	98953	73231
111	83799	42402	56623	34442	34994	41374	70071	14736	09958	18065
112	32960	07405	36409	83232	99385	41600	11133	07586	15917	06253
113	19322	53845	57620	52606	66497	68646	78138	66559	19640	99413
114	11220	94747	07399	37408	48509	23929	27482	45476	85244	35159
115	31751	57260	68980	05339	15470	48355	88651	22596	03152	19121
116	88492	99382	14454	04504	20094	98977	74843	93413	22109	78508
117	30934	47744	07481	83828	73788	06533	28597	20405	94205	20380
118	22888	48893	27499	98748	60530	45128	74022	84617	82037	10268
119	78212	16993	35902	91386	44372	15486	65741	14014	87481	37220
120	41849	84547	46850	52326	34677	58300	74910	64345	19325	81549
121	46352	33049	69248	93460	45305	07521	61318	31855	14413	70951
122	11087	96294	14013	31792	59747	67277	76503	34513	39663	77544
123	52701	08337	56303	87315	16520	69676	11654	99893	02181	68161
124	57275	36898	81304	48585	68652	27376	92852	55866	88448	03584
125	20857	73156	70284	24326	79375	95220	01159	63267	10622	48391
126	15633	84924	90415	93614	33521	26665	55823	47641	86225	31704
127	92694	48297	39904	02115	59589	49067	66821	41575	49767	04037
128	77613	19019	88152	00080	20554	91409	96277	48257	50816	97616
129	38688	32486	45134	63545	59404	72059	43947	51680	43852	59693
130	25163	01889	70014	15021	41290	67312	71857	15957	68971	11403
131	65251	07629	37239	33295	05870	01119	92784	26340	18477	65622
132	36815	43625	18637	37509	82444	99005	04921	73701	14707	93997
133	64397	11692	05327	82162	20247	81759	45197	25332	83745	22567
134	04515	25624	95096	67946	48460	85558	15191	18782	16930	33361
135	83761	60873	43253	84145	60833	25983	01291	41349	20368	07126
136	14387	06345	80854	09279	43529	06318	38384	74761	41196	37480
137	51321	92246	80088	77074	88722	56736	66164	49431	66919	31678
138	72472	00008	80890	18002	94813	31900	54155	83436	35352	54131
139	05466	55306	93128	18464	74457	90561	72848	11834	79982	68416
140	39528	72484	82474	25593	48545	35247	18619	13674	18611	19241
141	81616	18711	53342	44276	75122	11724	74627	73707	58319	15997
142	07586	16120	82641	22820	92904	13141	32392	19763	61199	67940
143	90767	04235	13574	17200	69902	63742	78464	22501	18627	90872
144	40188	28193	29593	88627	94972	11598	62095	36787	00441	58997

TABLE B.9 (*continued*)

145	34414	82157	86887	55087	19152	00023	12302	80783	32624	68691
146	63439	75363	44989	16822	36024	00867	76378	41605	65961	73488
147	67049	09070	93399	45547	94458	74284	05041	49807	20288	34060
148	79495	04146	52162	90286	54158	34243	46978	35482	59362	95938
149	91704	30552	04737	21031	75051	93029	47665	64382	99782	93478
150	94015	46874	32444	48277	59820	96163	64654	25843	41145	42820
151	74108	88222	88570	74015	25704	91035	01755	14750	48968	38603
152	62880	87873	95160	59221	22304	90314	72877	17334	39283	04149
153	11748	12102	80580	41867	17710	59621	06554	07850	73950	79552
154	17944	05600	60478	03343	25852	58905	57216	39618	49856	99326
155	66067	42792	95043	52680	46780	56487	09971	59481	37006	22186
156	54244	91030	45547	70818	59849	96169	61459	21647	87417	17198
157	30945	57589	31732	57260	47670	07654	46376	25366	94746	49580
158	69170	37403	86995	90307	94304	71803	26825	05511	12459	91314
159	08345	88975	35841	85771	08105	59987	87112	21476	14713	71181
160	27767	43584	85301	88977	29490	69714	73035	41207	74699	09310
161	13025	14338	54066	15243	47724	66733	47431	43905	31048	56699
162	80217	36292	98525	24335	24432	24896	43277	58874	11466	16082
163	10875	62004	90391	61105	57411	06368	53856	30743	08670	84741
164	54127	57326	26629	19087	24472	88779	30540	27886	61732	75454
165	60311	42824	37301	42678	45990	43242	17374	52003	70707	70214
166	49739	71484	92003	98086	76668	73209	59202	11973	02902	33250
167	78626	51594	16453	94614	39014	97066	83012	09832	25571	77628
168	66692	13986	99837	00582	81232	44987	09504	96412	90193	79568
169	44071	28091	07362	97703	76447	42537	98524	97831	65704	09514
170	41468	85149	49554	17994	14924	39650	95294	00566	70481	06905
171	94559	37559	49678	53119	70312	05682	66986	34099	74474	20740
172	41615	70360	64114	58660	90850	64618	80620	51790	11436	38072
173	50273	93113	41794	86861	24781	89683	55411	85667	77535	99892
174	41396	80504	90670	08289	40902	05069	95083	06783	28102	57816
175	25807	24260	71529	78920	72682	07385	90726	57166	98884	08583
176	06170	97965	88302	98041	21443	41808	68984	83620	89747	98882
177	60808	54444	74412	81105	01176	28838	36421	16489	18059	51061
178	80940	44893	10408	36222	80582	71944	92638	40333	67054	16067
179	19516	90120	46759	71643	13177	55292	21036	82808	77501	97427
180	49386	54480	23604	23554	21785	41101	91178	10174	29420	90438
181	06312	88940	15995	69321	47458	64809	98189	81851	29651	84215
182	60942	00307	11897	92674	40405	68032	96717	54244	10701	41393
183	92329	98932	78284	46347	71209	92061	39448	93136	25722	08564
184	77936	63574	31384	51924	85561	29671	58137	17820	22751	36518
185	38101	77756	11657	13897	95889	57067	47648	13885	70669	93406
186	39641	69457	91339	22502	92613	89719	11947	56203	19324	20504
187	84054	40455	99396	63680	67667	60631	69181	96845	38525	11600
188	47468	03577	57649	63266	24700	71594	14004	23153	69249	05747
189	43321	31370	28977	29896	76479	68562	62342	07589	08899	05985
190	64281	61826	18555	64937	13173	33365	78851	16499	87064	13075
191	66847	70495	32350	02985	86716	38746	26313	77463	55387	72681
192	72461	33230	21529	53424	92581	02262	78438	66276	18396	73538
193	21032	91050	13058	16218	12470	56500	15292	76139	59526	52113
194	95362	67011	06651	16136	01016	00857	55018	56374	35824	71708

TABLE B.9 (*continued*)

195	49712	97380	10404	55452	34030	60726	75211	10271	36633	68424
196	58275	61764	97586	54716	50259	46345	87195	46092	26787	60939
197	89514	11788	68224	23417	73959	76145	30342	42077	11049	72049
198	15472	50669	48139	36732	46874	37088	73465	09819	58869	35220
199	12120	86124	51247	44302	60883	52109	21437	36786	49226	77837
200	19612	78430	11661	94770	77603	65669	86868	12665	30012	75989
201	39141	77400	28000	64238	73258	71794	31340	26256	66453	37016
202	64756	80457	08747	12836	03469	50678	03274	43423	66677	82556
203	92901	51878	56441	22998	29718	38447	06453	25311	07565	53771
204	03551	90070	09483	94050	45938	18135	36908	43321	11073	51803
205	98884	66209	06830	53656	14663	56346	71430	04909	19818	05707
206	27369	86882	53473	07541	53633	70863	03748	12822	19360	49088
207	59066	75974	63335	20483	43514	37481	58278	26967	49325	43951
208	91647	93783	64169	49022	98588	09495	49829	59068	38831	04838
209	83605	92419	39542	07772	71568	75673	35185	89759	44901	74291
210	24895	88530	70774	35439	46758	70472	70207	92675	91623	61245
211	35720	26556	95596	20094	73750	85788	34264	01703	46833	65248
212	14141	53410	38649	06343	57256	61342	72709	75318	90379	37562
213	27416	75670	92176	72535	93119	56077	06886	18244	92344	31374
214	85071	07429	81007	47749	40744	54974	23336	88821	53841	10536
215	21445	82793	24831	93241	14199	76268	70883	68002	03829	17443
216	72513	76400	52225	92348	62308	98481	29744	33165	33141	61020
217	71479	45027	76160	57411	13780	13632	52308	77762	88874	33697
218	83210	51466	09088	50395	26743	05306	21706	70001	99439	80767
219	68749	95148	94897	78636	96750	09024	94538	91143	96693	61886
220	05184	75763	47075	88158	05313	53439	14908	08830	60096	21551
221	13651	62546	96892	25240	47511	58483	87342	78818	07855	39269
222	00566	21220	00292	24069	25072	29519	52548	54091	21282	21296
223	50958	17695	58072	68990	60329	95955	71586	63417	35947	67807
224	57621	64547	46850	37981	38527	09037	64756	03324	04986	83666
225	09282	25844	79139	78435	35428	43561	69799	63314	12991	93516
226	23394	94206	93432	37836	94919	26846	02555	74410	94915	48199
227	05280	37470	93622	04345	15092	19510	18094	16613	78234	50001
228	95491	97976	38306	32192	82639	54624	72434	92606	23191	74693
229	78521	00104	18248	75583	90326	50785	54034	66251	35774	14692
230	96345	44579	85932	44053	75704	20840	86583	83944	52456	73766
231	77963	31151	32364	91691	47357	40338	23435	24065	08458	95366
232	07520	11294	23238	01748	41690	67328	54814	37777	10057	42332
233	38423	02309	70703	85736	46148	14258	29236	12152	05088	65825
234	02463	65533	21199	60555	33928	01817	07396	89215	30722	22102
235	15880	92261	17292	88190	61781	48898	92525	21283	88581	60098
236	71926	00819	59144	00224	30570	90194	18329	06999	26857	19238
237	64425	28108	16554	16016	00042	83229	10333	36168	65617	94834
238	79782	23924	49440	30432	81077	31543	95216	64865	13658	51081
239	35337	74538	44553	64672	90960	41849	93865	44608	93176	34851
240	05249	29329	19715	94082	14738	86667	43708	66354	93692	25527
241	56463	99380	38793	85774	19056	13939	46062	27647	66146	63210
242	96296	33121	54196	34108	75814	85986	71171	15102	28992	63165
243	98380	36269	60014	07201	62448	46385	42175	88350	46182	49126
244	52567	64350	16315	53969	80395	81114	54358	64578	47269	15747

TABLE B.9 (*continued*)

245	78498	90830	25955	99236	43286	91064	99969	95144	64424	77377
246	49553	24241	08150	89535	08703	91041	77323	81079	45127	93686
247	32151	07075	83155	10252	73100	88618	23891	87418	45417	20268
248	11314	50363	26860	27799	49416	83534	19187	08059	76677	02110
249	12364	71210	87052	50241	90785	97889	81399	58130	64439	05614
250	59467	58309	87834	57213	37510	33689	01259	62486	56320	46265
251	73452	17619	56421	40725	23439	41701	93223	41682	45026	47505
252	27635	56293	91700	04391	67317	89604	73020	69853	61517	51207
253	86040	02596	01655	09918	45161	00222	54577	74821	47335	08582
254	52403	94255	26351	46527	68224	91083	85057	72310	34963	83462
255	49465	46581	61499	04844	94626	02963	41482	83879	44942	61915
256	94365	92560	12363	30246	02086	75036	88620	91088	67691	67762
257	34261	08769	91830	23313	18256	28850	37639	92748	57791	71328
258	37110	66538	39318	15626	44324	82827	08782	65960	58167	01305
259	83950	45424	72453	19444	68219	64733	94088	62006	89985	36936
260	61630	97966	76537	46467	30942	07479	67971	14558	22458	35148
261	01929	17165	12037	74558	16250	71750	55546	29693	94984	37782
262	41659	39098	23982	29899	71594	77979	54477	13764	17315	72893
263	32031	39608	75992	73445	01317	50525	87313	45191	30214	19769
264	90043	93478	58044	06949	31176	88370	50274	83987	45316	38551
265	79418	14322	91065	07841	36130	86602	10659	40859	00964	71577
266	85447	61079	96910	72906	07361	84338	34114	52096	66715	51091
267	86219	81115	49625	48799	89485	24855	13684	68433	70595	70102
268	71712	88559	92476	32903	68009	58417	87962	11787	16644	72964
269	29776	63075	13270	84758	49560	10317	28778	23006	31036	84906
270	81488	17340	74154	42801	27917	89792	62604	62234	13124	76471
271	51667	37589	87147	24743	48023	06325	79794	35889	13255	04925
272	99004	70322	60832	76636	56907	56534	72615	46288	36788	93196
273	68656	66492	35933	52293	47953	95495	95304	50009	83464	28608
274	38074	74083	09337	07965	65047	36871	59015	21769	30398	44855
275	01020	80680	59328	08712	48190	45332	27284	31287	66011	09376
276	86379	74508	33579	77114	92955	23085	92824	03054	25242	16322
277	48498	09938	44420	13484	52319	58875	02012	88591	52500	95795
278	41800	95363	54142	17482	32705	60564	12505	40954	46174	64130
279	63026	96712	79883	39225	52653	69549	36693	59822	22684	31661
280	88298	15489	16030	42480	15372	38781	71995	77438	91161	10192
281	07839	62735	99218	25624	02547	27445	69187	55749	32322	15504
282	73298	51108	48717	92926	75705	89787	96114	99902	37749	96305
283	12829	70474	00838	50385	91711	80370	56504	56857	80906	09018
284	76569	61072	48568	36491	22587	44363	39592	61546	90181	37348
285	41665	41339	62106	44203	06732	76111	79840	67999	32231	76869
286	58652	49983	01669	27464	79553	52855	25988	18087	38052	17529
287	13607	00657	76173	43357	77334	24140	53860	02906	89863	44651
288	55715	26203	65933	51087	98234	40625	45545	63563	89148	82581
289	04110	66683	99001	09796	47349	65003	66524	81970	71262	14479
290	31300	08681	58068	44115	40064	77879	23965	69019	73985	19453
291	26225	97543	37044	07494	85778	35345	61115	92498	49737	64599
292	07158	82763	25072	38478	57782	75291	62155	52056	04786	11585
293	71251	25572	79771	93328	66927	54069	58752	26624	50463	77361
294	29991	96526	02820	91659	12818	96356	49499	01507	40223	09171

TABLE B.9 (*continued*)

295	83642	21057	02677	09367	38097	16100	19355	06120	15378	56559
296	69167	30235	06767	66323	78294	14916	19124	88044	16673	66102
297	86018	29406	75415	22038	27056	26906	25867	14751	92380	30434
298	44114	06026	97553	55091	95385	41212	37882	46864	54717	97038
299	53805	64150	70915	63127	63695	41288	38192	72437	75075	18570

Note: Reprinted from *A Million Random Digits with 100,000 Normal Deviates*, by the Rand Corporation, 1955, New York: Free Press, with the permission of the Rand Corporation and the publisher.

TABLE B.10
Significance levels of ρ, the Spearman Rank-Correlation Coefficient

N	.10	.05	.02	.01	.001
4	1.000				
5	.900	1.000	1.000		
6	.829	.886	.943	1.000	
7	.714	.786	.893	.929	1.000
8	.643	.738	.833	.881	.976
9	.600	.700	.783	.833	.933
10	.564	.648	.745	.794	.903
11	.536	.618	.709	.755	.873
12	.503	.587	.678	.727	.846
13	.484	.560	.648	.703	.824
14	.464	.538	.626	.679	.802
15	.446	.521	.604	.654	.779
16	.429	.503	.582	.635	.762

Note: All *p* values are two-tailed in this table. For *N* greater than 16 see Table B.6.
(Reproduced from *Biostatistical Analysis* (2d ed., p. 577), by J. H. Zar, 1984, Englewood Cliffs, NJ: Prentice-Hall, with the permission of the author and publisher.)

TABLE B.11

Significance levels of $F_{max} = S^2_{max}/S^2_{min}$ in a set of k independent variances, each based on $n-1$ degrees of freedom

$n-1$	k = 2	3	4	5	6	7	8	9	10	11	12
2	39.0 / 199.	87.5 / 448.	142. / 729.	202. / 1036.	266. / 1362.	333. / 1705.	403. / 2063.	475. / 2432.	550. / 2813.	626. / 3204.	704. / 3605.
3	15.4 / 47.5	27.8 / 85.	39.2 / 120.	50.7 / 151.	62.0 / 184.	72.9 / 216.	83.5 / 249.	93.9 / 281.	104. / 310.	114. / 337.	124. / 361.
4	9.60 / 23.2	15.5 / 37.	20.6 / 49.	25.2 / 59.	29.5 / 69.	33.6 / 79.	37.5 / 89.	41.1 / 97.	44.6 / 106.	48.0 / 113.	51.4 / 120.
5	7.15 / 14.9	10.8 / 22.	13.7 / 28.	16.3 / 33.	18.7 / 38.	20.8 / 42.	22.9 / 46.	24.7 / 50.	26.5 / 54.	28.2 / 57.	29.9 / 60.
6	5.82 / 11.1	8.38 / 15.5	10.4 / 19.1	12.1 / 22.	13.7 / 25.	15.0 / 27.	16.3 / 30.	17.5 / 32.	18.6 / 34.	19.7 / 36.	20.7 / 37.
7	4.99 / 8.89	6.94 / 12.1	8.44 / 14.5	9.70 / 16.5	10.8 / 18.4	11.8 / 20.	12.7 / 22.	13.5 / 23.	14.3 / 24.	15.1 / 26.	15.8 / 27.
8	4.43 / 7.50	6.00 / 9.9	7.18 / 11.7	8.12 / 13.2	9.03 / 14.5	9.78 / 15.8	10.5 / 16.9	11.1 / 17.9	11.7 / 18.9	12.2 / 19.8	12.7 / 21.
9	4.03 / 6.54	5.34 / 8.5	6.31 / 9.9	7.11 / 11.1	7.80 / 12.1	8.41 / 13.1	8.95 / 13.9	9.45 / 14.7	9.91 / 15.3	10.3 / 16.0	10.7 / 16.6
10	3.72 / 5.85	4.85 / 7.4	5.67 / 8.6	6.34 / 9.6	6.92 / 10.4	7.42 / 11.1	7.87 / 11.8	8.28 / 12.4	8.66 / 12.9	9.01 / 13.4	9.34 / 13.9
12	3.28 / 4.91	4.16 / 6.1	4.79 / 6.9	5.30 / 7.6	5.72 / 8.2	6.09 / 8.7	6.42 / 9.1	6.72 / 9.5	7.00 / 9.9	7.25 / 10.2	7.48 / 10.6
15	2.86 / 4.07	3.54 / 4.9	4.01 / 5.5	4.37 / 6.0	4.68 / 6.4	4.95 / 6.7	5.19 / 7.1	5.40 / 7.3	5.59 / 7.5	5.77 / 7.8	5.93 / 8.0
20	2.46 / 3.32	2.95 / 3.8	3.29 / 4.3	3.54 / 4.6	3.76 / 4.9	3.94 / 5.1	4.10 / 5.3	4.24 / 5.5	4.37 / 5.6	4.49 / 5.8	4.59 / 5.9
30	2.07 / 2.63	2.40 / 3.0	2.61 / 3.3	2.78 / 3.4	2.91 / 3.6	3.02 / 3.7	3.12 / 3.8	3.21 / 3.9	3.29 / 4.0	3.36 / 4.1	3.39 / 4.2
60	1.67 / 1.96	1.85 / 2.2	1.96 / 2.3	2.04 / 2.4	2.11 / 2.4	2.17 / 2.5	2.22 / 2.5	2.26 / 2.6	2.30 / 2.6	2.33 / 2.7	2.36 / 2.7
∞	1.00 / 1.00	1.00 / 1.00	1.00 / 1.00	1.00 / 1.00	1.00 / 1.00	1.00 / 1.00	1.00 / 1.00	1.00 / 1.00	1.00 / 1.00	1.00 / 1.00	1.00 / 1.00

Note: The upper value in each cell is the .05 level; the lower value is the .01 level.

TABLE B.12
Significance levels of Cochran's $g = S^2_{max}/\Sigma S^2$ in a set of k independent variances, each based on $n-1$ degrees of freedom

$n-1$ \ k	2	3	4	5	6	7	8	9	10	15	20
1	.9985	.9669	.9065	.8412	.7808	.7271	.6798	.6385	.6020	.4709	.3894
	.9999	.9933	.9676	.9279	.8828	.8376	.7945	.7544	.7175	.5747	.4799
2	.9750	.8709	.7679	.6838	.6161	.5612	.5157	.4775	.4450	.3346	.2705
	.9950	.9423	.8643	.7885	.7218	.6644	.6152	.5727	.5358	.4069	.3297
3	.9392	.7977	.6841	.5981	.5321	.4800	.4377	.4027	.3733	.2758	.2205
	.9794	.8831	.7814	.6957	.6258	.5685	.5209	.4810	.4469	.3317	.2654
4	.9057	.7457	.6287	.5441	.4803	.4307	.3910	.3584	.3311	.2419	.1921
	.9586	.8335	.7212	.6329	.5635	.5080	.4627	.4251	.3934	.2882	.2288
5	.8772	.7071	.5895	.5065	.4447	.3974	.3595	.3286	.3029	.2195	.1735
	.9373	.7933	.6761	.5875	.5195	.4659	.4226	.3870	.3572	.2593	.2048
6	.8534	.6771	.5598	.4783	.4184	.3726	.3362	.3067	.2823	.2034	.1602
	.9172	.7606	.6410	.5531	.4866	.4347	.3932	.3592	.3308	.2386	.1877
7	.8332	.6530	.5365	.4564	.3980	.3535	.3185	.2901	.2666	.1911	.1501
	.8988	.7335	.6129	.5259	.4608	.4105	.3704	.3378	.3106	.2228	.1748
8	.8159	.6333	.5175	.4387	.3817	.3384	.3043	.2768	.2541	.1815	.1422
	.8823	.7107	.5897	.5037	.4401	.3911	.3522	.3207	.2945	.2104	.1646
9	.8010	.6167	.5017	.4241	.3682	.3259	.2926	.2659	.2439	.1736	.1357
	.8674	.6912	.5702	.4854	.4229	.3751	.3373	.3067	.2813	.2002	.1567
16	.7341	.5466	.4366	.3645	.3135	.2756	.2462	.2226	.2032	.1429	.1108
	.7949	.6059	.4884	.4094	.3529	.3105	.2779	.2514	.2297	.1612	.1248
36	.6602	.4748	.3720	.3066	.2612	.2278	.2022	.1820	.1655	.1144	.0879
	.7067	.5153	.4057	.3351	.2858	.2494	.2217	.1992	.1811	.1251	.0960
144	.5813	.4031	.3093	.2513	.2119	.1833	.1616	.1446	.1308	.0889	.0675
	.6062	.4230	.3251	.2644	.2229	.1929	.1700	.1521	.1376	.0934	.0709

Note: The upper value in each cell is the .05 level; the lower value is the .01 level.
(Reproduced from *Statistical Principles in Experimental Design* (2d ed) (p. 876), by B. J. Winer, 1971, New York: McGraw-Hill, with the permission of the author and publisher.)

APPENDIX B

TABLE B.13
Arcsin transformation ($a = 2$ arcsin $\sqrt{X}$)

X	a	X	a	X	a	X	a	X	a
.001	.0633	.041	.4078	.36	1.2870	.76	2.1177	.971	2.7993
.002	.0895	.042	.4128	.37	1.3078	.77	2.1412	.972	2.8053
.003	.1096	.043	.4178	.38	1.3284	.78	2.1652	.973	2.8115
.004	.1266	.044	.4227	.39	1.3490	.79	2.1895	.974	2.8177
.005	.1415	.045	.4275	.40	1.3694	.80	2.2143	.975	2.8240
.006	.1551	.046	.4323	.41	1.3898	.81	2.2395	.976	2.8305
.007	.1675	.047	.4371	.42	1.4101	.82	2.2653	.977	2.8371
.008	.1791	.048	.4418	.43	1.4303	.83	2.2916	.978	2.8438
.009	.1900	.049	.4464	.44	1.4505	.84	2.3186	.979	2.8507
.010	.2003	.050	.4510	.45	1.4706	.85	2.3462	.980	2.8578
.011	.2101	.06	.4949	.46	1.4907	.86	2.3746	.981	2.8650
.012	.2195	.07	.5355	.47	1.5108	.87	2.4039	.982	2.8725
.013	.2285	.08	.5735	.48	1.5308	.88	2.4341	.983	2.8801
.014	.2372	.09	.6094	.49	1.5508	.89	2.4655	.984	2.8879
.015	.2456	.10	.6435	.50	1.5708	.90	2.4981	.985	2.8960
.016	.2537	.11	.6761	.51	1.5908	.91	2.5322	.986	2.9044
.017	.2615	.12	.7075	.52	1.6108	.92	2.5681	.987	2.9131
.018	.2691	.13	.7377	.53	1.6308	.93	2.6062	.988	2.9221
.019	.2766	.14	.7670	.54	1.6509	.94	2.6467	.989	2.9315
.020	.2838	.15	.7954	.55	1.6710	.95	2.6906	.990	2.9413
.021	.2909	.16	.8230	.56	1.6911	.951	2.6952	.991	2.9516
.022	.2978	.17	.8500	.57	1.7113	.952	2.6998	.992	2.9625
.023	.3045	.18	.8763	.58	1.7315	.953	2.7045	.993	2.9741
.024	.3111	.19	.9021	.59	1.7518	.954	2.7093	.994	2.9865
.025	.3176	.20	.9273	.60	1.7722	.955	2.7141	.995	3.0001
.026	.3239	.21	.9521	.61	1.7926	.956	2.7189	.996	3.0150
.027	.3301	.22	.9764	.62	1.8132	.957	2.7238	.997	3.0320
.028	.3363	.23	1.0004	.63	1.8338	.958	2.7288	.998	3.0521
.029	.3423	.24	1.0239	.64	1.8546	.959	2.7338	.999	3.0783
.030	.3482	.25	1.0472	.65	1.8755	.960	2.7389		
.031	.3540	.26	1.0701	.66	1.8965	.961	2.7440		
.032	.3597	.27	1.0928	.67	1.9177	.962	2.7492		
.033	.3654	.28	1.1152	.68	1.9391	.963	2.7545		
.034	.3709	.29	1.1374	.69	1.9606	.964	2.7598		
.035	.3764	.30	1.1593	.70	1.9823	.965	2.7652		
.036	.3818	.31	1.1810	.71	2.0042	.966	2.7707		
.037	.3871	.32	1.2025	.72	2.0264	.967	2.7762		
.038	.3924	.33	1.2239	.73	2.0488	.968	2.7819		
.039	.3976	.34	1.2451	.74	2.0715	.969	2.7876		
.040	.4027	.35	1.2661	.75	2.0944	.970	2.7934		

Note: Reproduced from *Statistical Principles in Experimental Design* (2d ed.) (p. 872), by B. J. Winer, 1971, New York: McGraw-Hill, with the permission of the author and publisher.

GLOSSARY OF CONCEPTS AND TERMS

A-B design Simplest single-case design, in which the dependent variable is measured throughout the pretreatment or baseline period (the A phase) and the treatment period (the B phase).

A-B-A design Single-case design in which there are repeated measures before the treatment (the A phase), during the treatment (the B phase), and then with the treatment withdrawn (the final A phase).

A-B-A-B design Single-case design in which two types of occasions (B to A and A to B) are used to demonstrate the effects of the treatment variable, where A is the no-treatment baseline and B is the treatment phase.

A-B-A-B-A design Single-case design in which there are repeated measures before, during, and after treatment (the B phase).

A-B-BC-B design Single-case design in which there are repeated measures before the introduction of the treatments (the A phase), then during Treatment B, during the combination of Treatments B and C, and, finally, during Treatment B alone; the purpose of the design is to tease out the effect of B both in combination with C and apart from C.

a priori method Reasoning from cause to effect, or from a general to a particular instance, independent of any scientific observation (one of Charles Sanders Peirce's "methods for the fixation of belief").

abscissa The horizontal axis of a distribution.

absolute values Values not taking their signs (+ or −) into account.

accidental plagiarism Unwittingly falling into plagiarism.

acquiescent response set The tendency of individuals to go along with any request or attitudinal statement.

action research Research with the objective of promoting social change.

active deception (deception by commission) The active misleading of the research participants, such as giving them false information about the purpose of the study, or having them unwittingly interact with confederates.

ad hoc hypothesis A conjecture or speculation developed on the spot to explain a particular result.

additive model The components sum to the group means in ANOVA.

aesthetics A sense of the beautiful; just as art is grounded in beauty, scientists are conscious of the aesthetics of their theoretical and mathematical propositions.

after-only design A standard experimental design in which subjects' reactions are measured only after the treatment has been administered.

aggregating sources of variance Combining terms that are sufficiently similar, with the similarity defined as, for example, $F < 2$.

alerting correlation ($r_{alerting}$) The correlation between group means and contrast (λ) weights.

algebraic values Values taking their signs (+ or −) into account.

alias A source of variation completely confounded with another.

737

alpha (α) Probability of a Type I error, this term is typically used when the p value is stated in advance in null hypothesis significance testing.

alpha coefficient A measure of internal-consistency reliability, also termed **Cronbach's alpha** (after Lee J. Cronbach).

alternate-form reliability The correlation between two forms of a test with different items that are measuring the same attribute; also termed **equivalent-forms reliability.**

alternative hypothesis (H_1) The working hypothesis or the experimental hypothesis (that is, as opposed to the null hypothesis).

analogical rhetoric or thinking Visualizing one thing in terms of another.

analysis of covariance (ANCOVA) Analysis of variance with the dependent variable adjusted for one or more covariates or predictor variables.

analysis of variance (ANOVA) Subdivision of the total variance of a set of scores into its components. **ANOVA** Analysis of variance.

antirealism The doctrine that scientific theories do not give a literally true account of the world, a view associated with Pierre Duhem, Thomas Kuhn, and Imre Lakatos. See also *realism.*

"anything-goes" view of science Paul Feyerabend's radical philosophical view that successful empirical science relies on more than one "trick," and that these tricks cannot always be articulated by the researchers themselves.

APA code A popular expression referring to the ethical guidelines codified by the American Psychological Association.

APA publication manual *Publication Manual of the American Psychological Association.*

archives Relatively permanent repositories of data or material, including running records, personal documents, and episodic records.

arcsin transformation Transformation for proportions making equal differences equally detectable.

area probability sampling A type of survey sampling in which the subclasses are geographic areas.

ARIMA See *Box-Jenkins procedure.*

arithmetic mean (M) Arithmetic average.

Armor's theta David J. Armor's index of test reliability based on the eigenvalue of the first (unrotated) principal component.

artifact A specific threat to validity, or a confounded aspect of the scientist's observations.

asymmetrical distribution A distribution of scores in which there is not an exact correspondence in arrangement on the opposite sides of the middle line.

attenuation Reduction.

Aufforderungscharakter Demand value. See also *demand characteristics.*

authority method See *method of authority.*

autocorrelation The relation of observations or measures to one another. See also *regular autocorrelation* and *seasonal autocorrelation.*

autoethnography The ethnographic investigation of one's own culture.

autonomy The person's "independence," in the context of research ethics; also refers to a prospective participant's right as well as ability "to choose" whether to participate in the study or to continue in the study.

average deviation The average distance from the mean of all scores.

average error An index of the variability of a set of data around the most typical value.

back-to-back box plots Box plots summarizing back-to-back stem-and-leaf displays.

back-to-back stem-and-leaf chart The back-to-back plots of distributions in which the original data are preserved with any desired precision.

back-translation See *translation and back-translation.*

bar chart A histogram; a graphic display of the distribution of data.

baseline A comparison base, also called a **behavioral baseline** in single-case experimental research.

Bayesian estimation A nonimputational procedure for dealing with missing data.

before-after design A design in which the subjects' reactions are measured both before and after the experimental treatment, or both at the beginning and at the end of the experiment.

behavior Comportment, or what someone does or how someone acts.

behavior control The shaping of learned behavior based on a particular schedule of reinforcement designed to elicit the behavior in question.

behavioral baseline A comparison base, usually operationally defined as the continuous, and continuing, behavior or performance of a single unit in single-case experimental research.
behavioral diaries Data collection method in which the research participant keeps an account of events at the time they occur.
behavioral research The empirical investigation of motivation, cognition, emotion, and behavior.
behavioral sampling Periodic observation of the behavior of interest.
behavioral science A general term that encompasses scientific disciplines in which empirical inquiry is used to study motivation, cognition, emotion, and behavior (including social science, such as social and developmental psychology).
behaviorism A movement in which the idea was that the behavioral sciences should focus on the study of the relations among observable stimuli and responses; also called **methodological behaviorism** and **pure empiricism** when cognitive functioning is disallowed as a legitimate area of scientific analysis.
Belmont Report A report developed by a national commission in 1974 to protect the rights and welfare of participants in biomedical and behavioral research, named after the Smithsonian Institution's Belmont Conference Center in Washington, DC (where these discussions were held).
beneficence The "doing of good," which is one of the guidelines of the *APA code.*
BESD See *binomial effect-size display.*
BESD-based OR The BESD standardized odds ratio.
BESD-based RD The BESD standardized risk difference.
BESD-based RR The BESD standardized risk ratio for relative risk.
beta (β) Probability of a Type II error.
between-subjects designs Design in which the sampling units are exposed to one treatment each.
bias Net systematic error.
bimodal A distribution showing two modes.
binomial effect-size display (BESD) A standardized procedure for the display of an effect size correlation of any magnitude, where row and column totals are set at 100.
binomial effect-size r Effect size index for interpreting contrasts.
biosocial experimenter effects Experimenter-related artifacts that are a function of biosocial attributes of the researcher.
bipolar rating scales Rating scales in which the ends of the scales are extreme opposites.
Birge's ratio A reliability coefficient that gives an estimate of the degree to which the measurement estimates differ from one another by more than random errors.
blind controls Control group participants who are not made aware of their status as members of the control condition.
blind experimenters Researchers who are kept unaware of which participants will be assigned to the experimental and control conditions.
blocking Subdividing sampling units into meaningful classes.
Bonferroni procedure Redefining the alpha level of significance to protect against post hoc selection of the largest effects.
bootstrap Computer-generated resampling procedure more versatile than the jackknife, but usually more computer-intensive.
Box-Jenkins procedure Statistical method used to assess an underlying model of serial effects in an interrupted time-series design; called **ARIMA,** for autoregressive integrated moving average.
box plots or box graph Graphic displays of five or more numbers summarizing characteristics of a distribution.
"bucket theory" of science Karl Popper's characterization of the verifiability principle of logical positivism, or the idea that the wine of knowledge is presumed to flow pure and simple from patiently and industriously gathered facts.
built-in contrasts Contrasts that are obtained as a natural consequence of an experimental design, such as any source of variance in a 2^k factorial design (not including error terms), or any other effect with a single *df.*
canonical correlation Correlation between two or more predictor variables and two or more dependent variables.
categorical responses Judgments or ratings using categories of responses.
causal inference The act or process of inferring that *X* causes *Y.*

causal relations A relation implied between a cause and an effect.

causation The relation of cause to effect.

causism Implying a causal relationship where none has been established on the basis of the available data.

ceiling The maximum score attainable on a test or scale.

ceiling effect The limitation of the amount of change that can be produced; this limit is dictated by the upper boundary of the measure.

central tendency The location of the bulk of a distribution; measured by means, medians, modes, and trimmed means.

central tendency bias A type of response set in which the respondent is reluctant to give extreme ratings and instead rates in the direction of the mean of the total group.

certificate of confidentiality A formal agreement between the investigator and the government agency sponsoring the research that requires the investigator to keep the data confidential.

characteristic root Sum of squared factor loadings.

checklists Method of counting the frequency of occurrence.

chi-square (χ^2) A statistic used to test the degree of agreement between the frequency data actually obtained and the frequencies expected under a particular hypothesis (e.g., the null hypothesis).

chi-square corner-cells test Chi-square test performed on the four corners of a table of counts.

closed items Questions with fixed options; also described as **structured** or **fixed-response items.**

cluster analysis Formal procedure for grouping variables or sampling units.

clusters See *strata.*

coefficient of correlation Index of association, typically Pearson r or a related product-moment correlation.

coefficient of determination (r^2) Proportion of variance shared by two variables.

coefficient of equivalence The correlation between scores on different (alternate) forms of a measuring instrument that was administered to the same people at approximately the same time.

coefficient of nondetermination Proportion of variance "not accounted for" (k^2, or $1 - r^2$).

Cogito ergo sum "I think, therefore I am," the philosophical principle of René Descartes.

Cohen's d An index of effect size in z-score-like terms, defined as a ratio of the difference between two means divided by the pooled population standard deviation.

Cohen's f Effect size index for use in Jacob Cohen's power tables for F tests of significance.

Cohen's g The raw difference between an observed proportion and .50.

Cohen's h The difference between two arcsin-transformed population proportions.

Cohen's kappa (κ) See *kappa.*

Cohen's q The difference between two Fisher z_r transformed r values.

Cohen's w Effect size index for use in Jacob Cohen's power tables for chi-square tests of significance.

coherence The extent to which things (e.g., components of a theory or hypothesis) "stick together" logically.

cohort A collection of individuals who were born in the same period.

cohort-sequential design A design in which several cohorts are studied, with the initial measurements taken in successive years.

cohort table The basic data of a cohort-sequential study.

column effects Column means minus grand mean.

combined category chi-square test Chi-square test performed on redefined tables of counts in which adjacent rows, columns, or both have been meaningfully combined.

complex multiple partial correlation Canonical correlation performed on variables from which the effects of third-party variables have been removed.

component loading See *factor loadings.*

composite reliability The aggregate reliability of two or more items or judges' ratings.

concealed measurement The use of hidden measurements, such as a hidden recording device that eavesdrops on conversations.

conceptual definitions See *theoretical definition.*

concurrent validity The extent to which test results are correlated with some criterion in the present.

confidence The probability of not making a Type I error.

confidence interval Region in which a population parameter is likely to be found.

confidentiality Protection of research participants' or survey respondents' disclosures against unwarranted access.

confirmatory data analysis Analysis of data for the purpose of testing hypotheses.

confounded Mixed or confused.

confounded hypotheses (in panel designs) The inability to separate the effect attributed to one hypothesis from the effect attributed to another hypothesis in cross-lagged panel designs.

confounded variables Variables that are correlated with one another.

consensus tests Checks for consensus among F tests formed from the largest and smallest relevant error terms.

consequentialist view The argument that whether an action is right or wrong depends on its consequences. Contrast with *deontological view.*

constant conjunction The third in David Hume's list of "rules by which to judge of causes and effects," which is that "there must be a constant union betwixt the cause and effect. 'Tis chiefly this quality, that constitutes the relation." Also reflected in his fourth rule, that "the same cause always produces the same effect, and the same effect never arises but from the same cause." See also *contiguity* and *priority.*

construct An abstract or conjectural variable that serves as an explanatory concept, or as a link to explain the observed relations between independent and dependent variables.

construct validation The procedure by which a means for the measurement of a construct is devised and then related to subjects' performance in a variety of other spheres as the construct would predict or imply.

construct validity A type of test or research validity that addresses the psychological qualities contributing to the relation between variables, or the degree to which a test or questionnaire is a measure of the psychological characteristic of interest.

constructivism See *social constructionism.*

content analysis A strategy for decomposing written messages and pictorial documents in which basic information is categorized and counted.

content validity A type of test validity that addresses whether the test adequately samples the relevant material.

context of discovery Hans Reichenbach's term for the origin, creation, or invention of ideas and hypotheses for scientific justification.

context of justification Hans Reichenbach's term for the logical and empirical defense or adjudication of scientific hypotheses or theories.

contextualism A worldview (given prominence in the writings of the philosopher Stephen C. Pepper) that human understanding occurs against an experiential and sociocultural background of beliefs. See also *psychological contextualism.*

contiguity The first in David Hume's list of "rules of which to judge of causes and effects," which is that "the cause and effect must be contiguous in space and time." See also *priority* and *constant conjunction.*

contingency table A table of frequencies (or **counts**) coded by row and column variables.

continuous variable A variable for which we can imagine another value falling between any two adjacent scores.

contrast correlation ($r_{contrast}$) The pure correlation between scores on the dependent variable and the lambda coefficients after removal of any other patterns in the data.

contrast weights See *lambda coefficients.*

contrasts Statistical procedures that address specific questions or predictions in the data, such as testing for a particular trend in the results.

contrived unobtrusive observation Observation in which one or more variables are manipulated, but the research observations are inconspicuous.

control A term originally meaning a "check" on something, but also meaning a restraint of some kind; now used in several different ways, for example, to refer to the "constancy of conditions," the use of a "control series" in psychophysical research, "behavior control," or a "control group."

control group A group or condition with which the effects of the experimental procedure or test condition are to be compared.

control series The presentation of stimuli in a particular sequence in psychophysical research.

conventionalism The philosophical view that scientific theories can never be logically refuted by any body of evidence but instead undergo a linguistic tinkering process and evolve on the basis of certain linguistic conventions (like "simplicity"); also referred to as the **Duhem-Quine thesis,** after W. V. Quine's development of insights anticipated to an extent in the earlier work of Pierre Duhem.

convergent validity Validity supported by a substantial correlation of conceptually similar measures.

corner-cells test See *chi-square corner-cells test.*

corrected range Crude range plus one unit (also termed the **extended range**).

correction for continuity A procedure for decreasing the absolute difference between obtained and expected frequencies to adjust for the difference between discrete and continuous distributions.

correlated data Observations that are not independent of one another.

correlated replicators The nonindependence of the researchers who replicate one another's results.

correlated sample *t* See *paired t.*

correlation An index of the closeness of a relationship between variables.

correlation coefficient An index of the degree of association between two variables, typically Pearson *r* or a related product-moment correlation.

correlation family of effect sizes A group of effect sizes that includes the Pearson product-moment correlation in any of its customary incarnations, as well as the Fisher *z* transformation of *r*, and squared indices of *r* and *r*-like quantities; also called the **r-type family of effect sizes.**

correlational designs A broad class of quasi-experimental designs.

correlational research Another common name for relational research, that is, research in which two or more variables or conditions are measured and related to one another.

correspondence with reality The extent to which a hypothesis agrees with accepted truths based on reliable empirical findings.

counterbalancing Presenting treatment conditions in a sequence that controls for confounding.

counternull The non-null magnitude of the effect size that is supported by the same amount of evidence as the null value of the effect size.

counts Frequencies.

covariance Average of the products of deviations from the mean, or $(X - M_X)(Y - M_Y)$.

covariation rule The principle in the rhetoric of causal inference that, in order to demonstrate causation, what is labeled as the "cause" must be positively correlated with what is labeled as the "effect."

covary To have variations (in one variable) that are correlated with variations in another variable.

criterion validity The extent to which a measurement, test, or scale correlates with one or more outcome criteria.

criterion variable The outcome variable.

critical incident technique Open-ended method that instructs the respondent to describe an observable action the purpose of which is fairly clear to the respondent and the consequences of which are sufficiently definite to leave little doubt about its effects.

Cronbach's alpha A measure of internal consistency reliability, proposed by L. J. Cronbach.

cross-lagged correlations Correlations of the degree of association between two sets of variables, of which one is treated as a lagged value of the outcome variable.

cross-lagged panel designs Relational research designs using cross-lagged correlations, cross-sectional correlations repeated over time, and test-retest correlations.

cross-sectional design Research that takes a slice of time and compares subjects on one or more variables simultaneously.

cross-sequential design A design in which several different cohorts, all initially measured in the same period, are then observed over successive periods.

crossed contrasts Contrasts formed from the crossing of contrasts in two or more main effects.

crossed design Another name for the basic within-subjects design, because the subjects can be said to be "crossed" by treatment conditions.

crossed-linear interaction Interaction residuals showing an ascending linear trend for one subgroup and a descending linear trend for another subgroup.

crude range The highest score minus the lowest score.

cubic trend Curvilinear relation between two variables in which the line changes direction twice.

curvilinear (quadratic) correlation The correlation between scores on one variable and extremeness of scores on the other variable.

cue words Guiding labels that define particular points or categories of response.

d See *Cohen's d.*

D The difference between scores or ranks.

$\overline{D}$ The mean of a set of *D* values.

debriefing Disclosing to participants the nature of the research in which they have participated, also referred to as "dehoaxing" when a deception was used in the research and the purpose of the debriefing is to remove any misconceptions the subjects may have about the true purpose of the research.

deception by commission See *active deception.*

deception by omission See *passive deception.*

deception research Any method of research in which the subjects are misled (active deception) or not informed (passive deception) about the nature of the investigation.

deductive-statistical explanation A form of syllogistic argument in which the conclusion is presumed to be unequivocally true if the premises are true, for example, the syllogism "All A is B; all B is C; therefore all A is C."

degrees of freedom (*df***)** The number of observations minus the number of restrictions limiting the observations' freedom to vary.

demand characteristics Martin Orne's term for the mixture of various hints and cues that govern the research participant's perception of his or her role and of the experimenter's hypothesis or expectations regarding the outcome of the study; derived from Kurt Lewin's concept of *Aufforderungscharakter.*

deontological view The doctrine that some actions can be presumed to be categorically wrong no matter what their consequences. Contrast with *consequentialist view.*

dependent variable A variable whose changes are viewed as dependent on changes in one or more other (independent) variables.

descriptive inquiry A method of research that seeks to map out what happens behaviorally, that is, to tell "how things are."

descriptive measures Measures such as σ and σ^2 that are used to calculate population values.

descriptive research orientation An empirical approach in which the observational focus or objective is to map out a situation or set of events.

df See *degrees of freedom.*

df **between conditions** Degrees of freedom for the means of conditions.

df **error** Degrees of freedom for the denominator of the *F* ratio.

df **means** Degrees of freedom for the numerator of the *F* ratio.

df **within conditions** Degrees of freedom for observations within conditions.

diachronic research Research in which an event or behavior is scientifically observed so as to reveal changes that occur over a period of time.

diary method Having subjects keep diaries of their experiences (also called **self-recorded diaries**).

dichotomous variable A variable that is divided into two classes.

difference family of effect sizes A group of effect sizes that includes certain difference-type indices, such as Cohen's *d*, Hedges's *g*, Glass's Δ, and the risk difference (RD) and BESD-based RD.

difference in success rates See *binomial effect-size display.*

differencing Subtracting the first observation from the second, the second from the third, and so forth.

diffuse tests of significance Significance tests addressing unfocused (diffuse) questions, as in chi-square with $df > 1$ or *F* with numerator $df > 1$.

dimensional analysis Set of redescriptions (termed **redescriptors**) of relations among objects in terms of measures of similarity or dissimilarity.

dimensional judgments Responses by judges on some form of more-or-less continuous rating scale.

direct replication Murray Sidman's expression for the repetition of the same single-case study. See also *systematic replication.*

discovery See *context of discovery.*

discrete variable A variable taking on two or more distinct values.

discriminant function Special case of multiple correlation with a dichotomous dependent variable.

discriminant validity Validity supported by a lack of correlation between conceptually unrelated measures.

disguised measures Measuring tools used to study behavior indirectly (see, e.g., *projective test*) or unobtrusively (see *nonreactive observation*).

dispersion Spread or variability.

distance analysis Set of redescriptions (termed **redescriptors**) of relations among objects in terms of measures of similarity or dissimilarity.

distribution The relative frequencies as we move over varying values of the independent variable.

double-blind study Study in which neither the experimenter nor the participants know who has been assigned to the experimental and control groups. Contrast with *single-blind study.*

double deception A deception embedded in what the research participant thinks is the official debriefing.

drunkard's search A search for something in a place that is convenient but not where the thing is actually located.

Duhem-Quine thesis See *conventionalism.*

dummy-coding Giving arbitrary numerical values (often 0 and 1) to the two levels of a dichotomous variable.

ecologically valid Egon Brunswik's description of representative research designs.

Edgington method of adding probabilities Procedure for combining the *p* values of a set of studies.

effect size The magnitude of the research findings, such as the size of the relationship between an independent variable and a dependent variable.

effect size correlation ($r_{effect\ size}$) The magnitude of an experimental effect defined on the basis of the correlation between X and Y.

effective cost The effective reliability cost of a single judge (EC_j), or a single item (EC_i) or a single clinician ($EC_{clinician}$) of a particular type.

effective power The actual power (i.e., $1 - \beta$) of the statistical test used.

effective reliability The composite, or aggregate, reliability of two or more judges' ratings as a group.

effective sample size The net equivalent sample size that the researcher ends up with.

effects See *residuals.*

efficient cause The propelling or instigating condition (i.e., the X that sets in motion or alters Y).

eigenvalue Sum of squared factor loadings.

empirical Characterized by controlled observation and measurement.

empirical method Any procedure using controlled experience, observation, or experiment to map out the nature of reality.

empirical principles Empirically based generalizations.

empirical reasoning A use of logic and evidence in empirical science (not to be confused with logical positivism's verifiability principle, however).

epistemology Philosophy having to do with the origin, nature, methods, and limits of human knowledge or human understanding of the world.

equal-appearing intervals method L. L. Thurstone's attitude-scale construction procedure in which values are obtained for statements or items on the assumption that the underlying intervals are psychologically equidistant (also called a **Thurstone scale,** although Thurstone developed other scaling procedures as well).

equitable trimming Dropping the same number of scores from both ends of a distribution.

equivalent-forms reliability The correlation between alternate forms of a test or some other measuring instrument (e.g., an attitude scale); also termed **alternate-form reliability.**

error Fluctuation in measurements; also deviation of a score from the mean of the group or condition.

error of central tendency See *central tendency bias.*

error of estimate Closeness of estimate to actual value.

error of leniency See *leniency bias.*

error term The denominator of an F ratio in the analysis of variance.

eta (η) Index of correlation not limited to linear relationships.

eta-squared (η^2) Proportion of variance accounted for.

ethical guidelines A set of principles (such as those discussed in chapter 3) that helps researchers decide what aspects of a study might pose an ethical problem.

ethics The system of moral values by which behavior is judged, derived from the Greek *ethos,* meaning "character" or "disposition."

ethnographers Scientists who study cultural settings and the people who live in them.

ethnography The study of cultural settings and the people who live in them.

evaluation apprehension Milton Rosenberg's expression for the experience of feeling anxious about being negatively evaluated or not positively evaluated.

evaluation, potency, and activity Three primary dimensions of connotative meaning, which are typically measured by a semantic differential.

events Relatively brief occurrences that are observed at their onset or at some single defining moment.

evolutionary epistemology A philosophical view of the development of genuine knowledge in scientific psychology, emphasizing that theories evolve in a constant struggle for survival of the fittest.

expectancy control design An experimental design in which the expectancy variable operates separately from the independent variable of interest.

expectancy control groups Control conditions used to compare the effects of experimenter expectancies with the effects of some other behavioral variable.

expected frequency (f_e) Counts expected under specified row and column conditions if certain hypotheses (e.g., the null hypothesis) are true.

expedited review The evaluation of proposed research without undue delay.

experimental group A group or condition in which the subjects are assigned the experimental treatment (e.g., they undergo a manipulation or an intervention).

experimental hypothesis The experimenter's working hypothesis; also an alternative to the null hypothesis.

experimental inquiry Any method of research that seeks to describe what happens behaviorally when something of interest to the experimenter is introduced into the situation, that is, to tell "how things are and how they got to be that way."

experimental realism Elliot Aronson and J. Merrill Carlsmith's term describing the idea that the experimental manipulation was engaging, or that participants were "drawn into" the experimental treatment.

experimental research orientation An empirical approach in which the observational focus or objective is a causal explanation.

experimenter expectancy bias Another name for the **experimenter expectancy effect.**

experimenter expectancy effect An experimenter-related artifact that results when the hypothesis held by the experimenter leads unintentionally to behavior toward the subjects that, in turn, increases the likelihood that the hypothesis will be confirmed.

Experimentum Crucis Isaac Newton's expression for his crucial empirical observations on the nature of white light, an expression he apparently borrowed from Robert Hooke, based on an earlier idea of Francis Bacon's (who referred to *instantia crucis,* or "crucial instances").

exploratory data analysis A detective-like searching in the data for clues, leads, and insights.

extended range (corrected range) Crude range plus one unit.

external validity The degree of generalizability.

f See *Cohen's f.*

F The symbol for an *F* test in the analysis of variance or the analysis of covariance.

F **distributions** Family of distributions centered at $(df)/(df - 2)$, where both *df* refer to the denominator of the *F* ratio, and ranging from zero to positive infinity.

F **ratios** Ratios of mean squares that are distributed as *F* when the null hypothesis is true, where *F* is a test of significance used to judge the tenability of the null hypothesis of no relation between two or more variables (or of no difference between two or more variabilities).

F **test** See *F ratios.*

face-to-face interview Direct interaction of the interviewer and the respondent.

face validity The extent to which a test or other measuring instrument seems on its surface to be appraising what it purports to measure.

facet analysis Uriel Foa's logical technique for creating a classification system (a typology) based on assumed structural patterns, where the dimensions are called *facets.*

factor analysis The rewriting of a set of variables into a new set of orthogonal factors.

factorial design Research design with more than one factor and two or more levels of each factor.

factor loadings Correlations between variables and factors serving as their redescriptors.

fair-mindedness Impartiality.

fallacy of period centrism See *period centrism fallacy.*

false-negative conclusions Conclusions in which real differences or real effects go undetected.

false precision The outcome when something relatively vague is reported as if the measuring instrument was sensitive to very slight differences.

falsifiable hypotheses Plausible suppositions that can be tested.

falsifiability (refutability) The principle (advanced by Karl Popper) that a theoretical assertion is scientific only if it can be stated in a way that, if incorrect, can be refuted by some empirical means (characterized as the "searchlight theory" by Popper).

falsificationism The name for Karl Popper's antipositivist movement; those who embraced it were called **fallibilists.**

$F_{contrast}$ The symbol used in this book to denote an F test (with numerator $df = 1$) that is used to address a focused question or hypothesis, for example, comparing two groups or conditions.

field experiments Experimental research that is done in a naturalistic setting.

fieldwork journal The ethnographer's written diary of personal experiences, ideas, fears, mistakes, confusions, and problems.

file drawer problem The concern that a substantial number of studies with nonsignificant results are tucked away in file drawers, thus complicating the quantitative summary of research domains.

final (teleological) cause The end goal toward which a person or thing naturally tends to strive or to be directed (Aristotle).

finite A term that applies when all the units or events can, at least in theory, be completely counted.

Fisher exact probability test Test of significance for a 2×2 table of counts based on exact probability rather than reference to a distribution.

Fisher method of adding logs Procedure for combining p values of a set of studies.

Fisher z_r The log transformation of r, that is, $\frac{1}{2} \log_e[(1 + r)/(1 - r)]$.

fixed-choice measures See *structured items.*

fixed factors (effects) Levels of a factor chosen because of the researcher's specific interest rather than their representativeness of a population of levels of a factor.

fixed-response items Questions with fixed options; also described as **structured items** or **closed items.**

floor effects The limitation of the amount of change that can be produced; this limit is dictated by the lower boundary of the measure.

$F_{noncontrast}$ The result of dividing the mean square noncontrast by the mean square within, which can be used to compute an effect size r for $F_{contrast}$.

focus group A group whose discussion is led by an interviewer who focuses the group on particular issues or a basic question or problem.

focused chi-square χ^2 with 1 df.

focused statistical procedures Any t test, 1-df χ^2, or F with numerator $df = 1$.

focused tests of significance Another name for **focused statistical procedures.**

forced-choice scales Measures requiring the respondent to select a single item (or a specified number of items) from a presented set of choices, even when the respondent finds no choice or more than one of the choices acceptable.

formal cause The implicit form or meaning of something (Aristotle).

fortuitous sampling The haphazard (as opposed to random or systematic) selection of sampling units.

fractional factorial design A design in which only some combination of factor levels is used, and higher-order interactions are intentionally confounded with lower-order effects.

free association method A method in which the subjects express whatever thoughts pass through their minds.

frequency distribution A set of data scores arranged according to incidence of occurrence, or a chart that shows the number of times each score or other unit of observation occurs in a set of scores.

frequency polygon A line-graph distribution of frequencies of occurrence.

fugitive literature Hard-to-find literature.

full factorials Statistical designs in which all combinations of all factors' levels are available.

funnel sequence of questions Items begin with very general questions and then narrow down to more specific ones.

g See *Cohen's g* and *Hedges's g.*

g method A strategy for quantifying the degree of success in constructing clear composite variables, based on Hedges's *g.*

generative Describing theories that allow us to generate new hypotheses and observations.

geometric mean The antilog of the mean of log-transformed values.

Glass's Δ An index of effect size in z-score-like terms, defined as a ratio of the difference between two means divided by the estimate of the standard deviation of the control group.

good subject Research participant who seeks to provide responses that will validate the experimenter's hypothesis.

good subject effect A subject's cooperative behavior that complies with demand characteristics.

grand mean The mean of means, or the mean of all observations.

graphic scale A rating scale in the form of a straight line with cue words attached.

_h_ See *Cohen's h*.

H_0 Null hypothesis.

H_1 Alternative hypothesis, that is, the experimental or working hypothesis.

halo effect A response set in which the bias results from the judge's overextending a favorable impression of someone, based on some central trait, to the person's other characteristics.

haphazard sampling The fortuitous (as opposed to random or systematic) selection of sampling units.

harmonic mean The reciprocal of the arithmetic mean of values that have been transformed to their reciprocals.

Hawthorne effect The general principle that scientific observations of behavior may influence the behavior itself; the concept takes its name from research performed at the Hawthorne plant of the Western Electric Company between 1924 and 1932. Although the claims resulting from that research have been disputed, the general principle of subject reactivity has received support in other research and is not in doubt.

HCT Historical control trial. See also *historical controls*.

Hedges's _g_ An index of effect size in *z*-score-like terms, defined as a ratio of the difference between two means divided by the estimate of the standard deviation.

heterogeneity Dissimilarity among the elements of a set.

hidden nesting The concealed nonindependence of observations brought about by sampling without regard to sources of similarity in the persons sampled.

hierarchical structure A system in which one thing is ranked above another.

higher order interaction Residuals remaining after all main effects and all lower order interactions relevant to the higher order interaction have been subtracted.

historical controls Recently treated patients all of whom suffered from the same disorder as those in the experimental treatment group.

history Donald Campbell and Julian Stanley's term for a plausible threat to internal validity when an event or incident that takes place between the premeasurement and the postmeasurement contaminates the results of research not using randomization.

homogeneity Similarity among the elements of a set.

homogeneity of covariances Degree of similarity of covariances found between any two levels of a repeated-measures factor.

homogeneity of variance Equality of the population variance of the groups to be compared.

hot deck imputation A single imputation procedure for dealing with missing data in which we find cases without the missing data that are similar to those with the missing data, and then one case is chosen at random as that whose corresponding value will be imputed for the missing observation.

how-questions In philosophy of science, questions about "how" things work, that is, "what-is-happening" questions.

hyperclaim A claim implying that the research is likely to achieve goals that it is, in fact, unlikely to achieve (also called *hyperclaiming*).

hypotheses Research ideas that serve as a premise or supposition that organizes facts and guides observations.

idealism A classical philosophical doctrine that human understanding of "reality" is a construct of cognitive and perceptual minds or mental operations. See also *social constructionism*.

IID normal Assumptions underlying the use of *t* and *F* tests, that error is "independently and identically distributed" in a normal distribution.

imputation procedures Statistical procedures that yield estimates of parameters after the missing data are filled in, including single imputation (e.g., mean substitution, regression substitution, stochastic regression imputation, or hot deck imputation) and multiple imputation.

incomplete factorial design A design in which the higher order interactions are intentionally confounded with the lower order effects.

independent sample _t_ The *t* test used to compare samples that are independent.

independent variable A variable on which the dependent variable depends; in experiments, a variable that the experimenter manipulates to determine whether there are effects on another variable, the dependent variable.

indirect measures Observations or measurements of behavior in which subjects are aware of being observed or measured but are unaware of the particular implications of their responses.

inductive-statistical explanation A form of syllogistic argument in which the conclusion is "likely to be true" if the premises are true (i.e., a probabilistic assertion).

inferential measure Measures such as S and S^2 that are used to estimate population values based on a sample of values.

inferential validity Validity in which the implication is that causal inferences made in a laboratory setting are applicable to the real-life experiences they are meant to represent.

infinite Boundless, or without limits.

informants The indigenous members of a culture who provide ethnographic researchers with information.

informed consent The procedure in which prospective subjects, who have been told what they will be getting into, give their formal consent to participate in the research.

institutional review board (IRB) A group set up by research organizations to make risk-benefit analyses of proposed studies.

instrumentation Donald Campbell and Julian Stanley's term for a plausible threat to internal validity that occurs when changes in the measuring instrument (e.g., deterioration of the instrument) bias the results of research not using randomization.

intensive case study An analysis that is characterized by meticulous records and sharp discriminations rather than by the usual casual discriminations and inferences that are associated with our daily encounters with "cases."

intentional experimenter effects Noninteractional experimenter-related artifacts that result in systematic errors owing to dishonesty in reporting data.

interaction effects (residuals) In a factorial design, the condition means minus the grand mean, row effects, and column effects.

interaction of independent variables The mutually moderating effects of two or more independent variables.

interactional experimenter effects Artifacts resulting from the interaction between experimenters and their subjects.

interactions See *interaction of independent variables.*

intercoder reliability The extent to which raters or judges who code data are in agreement.

interitem correlation (r_{ii}) The relation of responses to one item with the responses to another item.

internal-consistency reliability Reliability based on the intercorrelation among the components of a test, such as subtests or all the individual test items; it tells us the degree of relatedness of the individual components when we want to use them to obtain a single score.

internal validity The degree of validity of statements made about whether changes in one variable result in changes in another variable.

interpreter biases Systematic errors that result when the researcher's interpretation of the observational record is slanted.

interquartile range The difference between the 75th and 25th percentile.

interrupted time-series designs Designs in which the effects of a treatment or intervention are inferred from a comparison of outcome measures obtained at different time intervals before and after the treatment or intervention is introduced.

interval estimates The extent to which point estimates are likely to be in error.

intervention An experimental treatment.

interview schedule A script that contains the questions the interviewer will ask.

intraclass correlation The average intercorrelation among the repeated observations obtained from a set of sampling units, for example, the average item-to-item (r_{ii}) or judge-to-judge (r_{jj}) reliability.

intrinsically repeated measures Measurements that *must* be repeated to address the question of interest.

item analysis A procedure used for selecting items (e.g., for a Likert attitude scale).

item-to-item reliability (r_{ii}) The relation of responses to one item with those to another item.

iterations Repetitions.

jackknife Computer-generated resampling procedure designed for estimating such statistics as bias, standard errors, and confidence intervals.

joint method of agreement and difference J. S. Mill's method that tells us that X is both necessary and sufficient for the occurrence of $Y.$

judges Coders, raters, decoders, or others who assist in describing and categorizing ongoing events or existing records of events.

judge-to-judge reliability (r_{ij}) The relation of one judge's responses to those of another judge.

judgment studies Studies in which raters, coders, decoders, or others evaluate or categorize the variables of interest.

justice A synonym for *fairness,* and one of the guidelines of the APA code.

justification A term used by philosophers of science to refer to the evaluation, defense, truth, or confirmation of a hypothesis.

k Coefficient of alienation or "noncorrelation"; also used to denote the number of conditions or classifications.

***k*^{2}** Coefficient of nondetermination.

kappa (κ) A statistic (proposed by Jacob Cohen) used to indicate the proportion of agreements between raters after chance agreement has been removed.

KR20 A measure of internal-consistency reliability, developed by G. F. Kuder and M. W. Richardson, symbolized here as R^{KR20}.

Kuder-Richardson Formula 20 See *KR20.*

kurtosis A term that describes the flatness or peakedness of a distribution.

***L* scores** Contrast scores that index for each sampling unit the degree to which it reflects the accuracy of the particular prediction.

lambda coefficients (λ weights) Values that sum to zero and are used to state a prediction.

latent root Sum of squared factor loadings.

Latin square A square of letters or numbers in which each letter or number appears once and only once in each row and in each column; used as a specific repeated-measures design with built-in counterbalancing.

leading questions Questions that can constrain responses and produce biased answers.

leaves The trailing digits of a stem-and-leaf display.

leftover effects See *residual effects.*

leniency bias A type of rating error in which the ratings are consistently more positive than they should be. See also *severity error.*

leptokurtic distribution A term used to describe a very peaked curve.

Lie (L) Scale A set of items in the MMPI that were designed to identify respondents who are deliberately trying to appear "better" than they believe they are.

Likert scales Attitude scales constructed by Rensis Likert's method of summated ratings.

line graph See *frequency polygon.*

linear trend Straight-line relationship between two variables.

linearity The mutual relation between two variables that resembles a straight line.

listwise deletion Deletion of all subjects who have any missing data.

literature controls Historical controls formulated on the basis of archival data.

loading See *factor loadings.*

location measures Measurements of central tendency, such as the mean, median, and mode.

logical error in rating A type of response set in which the judge gives similar ratings for variables or traits that are only intuitively related.

logical positivism A philosophical movement that dominated philosophy during the 1920s and 1930s, based on the idea that, just as there is a sound, verifiable basis of ideas and propositions in natural science (i.e., the verifiability principle), there might be a similar objective foundation for problems in philosophy.

log-linear model An approach to the analysis of tables analogous to the analysis of variance.

logit *d'* A measure of effect size defined as the difference between logit-transformed population proportions.

longitudinal study Research in which the same subjects are studied over a period of time.

M The mean of a set of scores.

magnitude scale A scaling procedure, pioneered by S. S. Stevens, in which the number of total points is decided by the individual judge or rater rather than preset by the researcher.

main effect The effect of an independent variable apart from its interaction with other independent variables.

manipulation check A separate confirmation of the effectiveness of experimental treatments.

margin of error Interval within which an anticipated value is expected to occur.

margins Row and column marginal values.

Marlowe-Crowne Social Desirability Scale (MCSD) A standardized scale, created by David Marlowe and Douglas P. Crowne, that measures social desirability responding and the need for social approval.

matched pairs Pairs of observations made on the same sampling units.

matched pair *t* See *paired t.*

matching The pairing of sampling units on certain relevant variables.

material cause The substance out of which something is made (Aristotle).

maturation Donald Campbell and Julian Stanley's term for a plausible threat to internal validity that occurs when the results of nonrandomized studies are confounded by the participants' having grown older, wiser, stronger, or more experienced between the pretest and the posttest.

maximum likelihood estimation A nonimputation procedure for dealing with missing data.

MCSD See *Marlowe-Crowne Social Desirability Scale.*

mean (*M*) The arithmetic average of a set of scores.

mean polishing Removing grand mean, row, and column effects to expose residuals defining the interaction.

mean square (S^2), or *MS* Variance.

mean square for error Variance used as the denominator of F ratios.

mean substitution procedure The replacement of all missing values for any given variable by the mean value of that variable; one of several single imputation procedures for dealing with missing data.

median (*Mdn*) The midmost score of a distribution.

mediator variables Conditions, states, or other factors that are presumed to intervene between the independent variable and the outcome variable.

mental images Thinking in which perceptible ideas or visual images have a hand; presumed to be an aspect of the scientific method and explanatory reasoning.

meta-analysis The use of quantitative and graphic methods to summarize a group of similar studies.

metaphor A word or phrase applied to a concept or phenomenon that it does not literally denote.

metaphorical themes Thematic analogies that represent a particular view of the world, or of a phenomenon or experience.

metaphysics Assumptions or questions about universal truths, existence, and causality.

method of adding logs Procedure for combining independent probabilities.

method of adding probabilities Procedure for combining independent probabilities.

method of adding *t*s Procedure for combining independent probabilities.

method of adding weighted *z*s Procedure for combining independent probabilities.

method of adding *z*s Procedure for combining independent probabilities.

method of agreement If *X,* then *Y*—which implies that *X* is a sufficient condition of *Y* (J. S. Mill).

method of authority The acceptance of an idea as valid because it is stated by someone in a position of power or authority (one of Charles Sanders Peirce's "methods for the fixation of belief").

method of concomitant variation Method relating changes in amount or degree between two variables; stated as $Y = f(X)$, which means that variations in Y are functionally related to variations in X.

method of difference If not-*X,* then not-*Y*—which implies that *X* is a necessary condition of *Y* (J. S. Mill).

method of equal-appearing intervals See *equal-appearing intervals method.*

method of meaningful diagonals Forming a concept to summarize the data found on the diagonals of a two-way table of means or of residuals.

method of meaningful differences Method reducing a two-dimensional display of residuals or means to a one-dimensional display.

method of self-report The procedure of having the research participants describe their own behavior or state of mind (e.g., used in interviews, questionnaires, and behavioral diaries).

method of successive intervals A scaling procedure developed by Allen L. Edwards, similar to the equal-appearing intervals method, but providing a check on the assumption of equal intervals.

method of tenacity Clinging stubbornly to an idea or belief because it seems obvious or is "common sense" or brings peace of mind (one of Charles Sanders Peirce's "methods for the fixation of belief").

method of testing mean *p* Procedure for combining independent probabilities.

method of testing mean *z* Procedure for combining independent probabilities.

methodological behaviorism See *behaviorism.*

methodological pluralism The idea that more than one method and operation are needed to develop a holistic picture, because each method or operation is limited in some way.

methodological triangulation The approach of "zeroing in" on a pattern by using multiple but imperfect methodological perspectives.

microworld simulations The use of computer-generated environments to simulate real-world settings.

Milgram experiments Stanley Milgram's program of research on the willingness of participants to give "electric shocks" to another subject, who was (unbeknownst to the participants) actually a confederate of the experimenter.

Mill's methods Logical "methods" (or propositions) popularized by J. S. Mill, exemplified by the method of agreement and the method of difference.

minimal risk (research) Studies in which the likelihood and extent of harm to subjects are no greater than those typically experienced in everyday life.

Minnesota Multiphasic Personality Inventory (MMPI) A structured personality test containing hundreds of statements that reflect general health, sexual attitude, religious attitude, emotional state, and so on.

missing data Information missing because one or more responses that were to be collected by the investigator are unavailable, including data "missing completely at random" (MCAR), "missing at random" (MAR), or "missing not at random" (MNAR). See also *imputation procedures* and *nonimputation procedures.*

mixed factorial designs Statistical designs consisting of both between- and within-subjects factors.

mixed longitudinal designs Designs in which several cohorts are followed, and age effects, time effects, and cohort effects are examined periodically.

MMPI See *Minnesota Multiphasic Personality Inventory.*

mode The score occurring with the greatest frequency.

modeling effects Experimenter-related artifacts that are a function of the example set by the experimenter or interviewer.

moderator variables Conditions that alter the relationship between X and Y.

moments The distances from the mean.

MS **(mean square)** Variance.

$MS_{between}$ Mean square between conditions.

$MS_{contrast}$ The contrast mean square, which is equivalent to the contrast sum of squares.

MS_{error} Mean square used as denominator of F ratios.

MS_{within} Mean square within conditions.

multidimensional scaling (unfolding) Set of redescriptors of relations among objects in terms of measures of similarity or dissimilarity.

multilevel analysis of variance Analysis of variance with two or more independent variables and one dependent variable.

multiple correlation Correlation between two or more predictor variables and a single dependent variable.

multiple discriminant function Special case of canonical correlation with dichotomous dependent variables.

multiple imputation Process in which each missing observation is replaced by a set of m reasonable estimates that will yield m pseudocomplete data sets; one of several imputation procedures for dealing with missing data.

multiple operationalism Donald Campbell and Donald Fiske's term for the idea that different methodological operations are needed to "triangulate" on phenomena of interest.

multiple partial correlation Multiple correlation performed on variables from which the effects of third-party variables have been removed.

multiple path analysis Canonical correlation with time-ordered predictor variables.

multiple R^2 Proportion of variance in the dependent variable predictable from two or more predictor variables.

multistage cluster sampling Sampling in which, by stages, the population is divided and subdivided into segments in which the units selected have the same probability of being chosen as the unselected units in the population.

multitrait-multimethod matrix A table of intercorrelations, the purpose of which is to triangulate on the convergent and discriminant validity of a construct.

multivariate analysis of covariance Analysis of covariance for the case of multiple dependent variables.

multivariate multilevel analysis of variance Analysis of variance with two or more independent and two or more dependent variables.

multivariate procedures Statistical procedures involving two or more independent (predictor) variables, two or more dependent (criterion) variables, or both.

mundane realism Elliot Aronson and J. Merrill Carlsmith's term for a condition in which the various dimensions of an experiment appear similar to those in the real world.

mutually exclusive A term describing the condition "If A is true, then *not-A* is false."

n The number of scores in one condition or one subgroup of a study.

N The total number of scores in a study.

N-of-1 experimental research Another name for **single-case experimental studies.**

naturalistic observation The observation of behavior in its usual natural environment.

necessary condition A requisite or essential condition.

need for social approval The desire to be positively evaluated or approved of.

negative synergistic effects Synergistic effects that lower scores.

negatively skewed distribution An asymmetrical distribution in which the pointed end is toward the left (i.e., toward the negative tail).

negativistic subject The research participant who approaches the investigation with an uncooperative attitude.

nested design Another name for the basic between-subjects design, because the subjects are "nested" within their own treatment conditions.

nested sampling units Sampling units observed under only one condition of a study.

n_h The harmonic-mean n.

NHST See *null hypothesis significance testing.*

no-shows People who fail to show up for their scheduled research appointments.

noise The variability within the samples.

nonequivalent-groups designs Nonrandomized research in which the responses of a treatment group and a control group are compared (usually on measures collected at the beginning and end of the research).

nonimputation procedures Statistical procedures that yield estimates of parameters without "filling in" the missing data (such as listwise deletion, pairwise deletion, maximum likelihood estimation, and Bayesian estimation).

noninteractional artifacts (e.g., interpreter and observer biases) Experimenter-related artifacts that occur without affecting the actual responses of the subjects.

noninteractional experimenter effects Experimenter-related artifacts that occur without affecting the actual responses of the subjects.

nonintrinsically repeated measures Repeated-measures research in which it is not actually essential to use repeated measures, but their use increases the efficiency, precision, and power of the study.

nonlinearity A relation between two variables that does not resemble a straight line.

nonmaleficence Not doing harm, which is one of the guidelines of the APA code.

nonorthogonal contrasts Correlated contrasts.

nonparametric statistical tests Statistical procedures that are less dependent on the shape of the population distribution from which the observations are drawn.

nonreactive observation (measure) Any observation or measurement that does not affect what is being observed.

nonresponse bias Systematic error due to nonresponse or nonparticipation.

nonskewed distribution A symmetrical distribution.

normal distribution Bell-shaped curve that is completely described by its mean and standard deviation.

norm-referenced Term applied to a standardized test that has norms (i.e., typical values), so that a person's score can be compared with the scores of a reference group.

norms Tables of values representing the typical performance of a given group.

null-counternull interval An interval estimate anchored at one end by the null value of the observed effect size and at the other end by its counternull value.

null hypothesis (H_0) The hypothesis to be nullified; usually states that there is no relation between two or more variables.

null hypothesis significance testing (NHST) The use of statistics and probabilities to evaluate the null hypothesis.

numerical scales Rating scales in which the respondent works with a sequence of defined numbers.

oblique rotations Factor-analytic rotations that are nonorthogonal.

observation of disproportionate influence (*OODI*) Observation that radically changes a correlation's magnitude.

observed frequency (f_o) Counts obtained in specific rows and columns.

observer effects Experimenter-related artifacts that result in overstatements or understatements of some criterion value during the observation and recording phase of the research process.

Occam's razor The principle that explanations should be as parsimonious as possible (William of Occam, or Ockham).

odds ratio (OR) The ratio of the not-surviving control subjects to the surviving control subjects divided by the ratio of the not-surviving treated subjects to the surviving treated subjects.

omnibus chi-square χ^2 with $df > 1$.

omnibus statistical procedures Statistical procedures with $df > 1$, such as F with numerator $df > 1$ or χ^2 with $df > 1$.

omnibus tests Another name for **omnibus statistical procedures.**

one-group pre-post design (O-X-O) A preexperimental design in which the reactions of only one group of subjects are measured before and after exposure to the treatment.

one-sample *t* See *paired t*

one-shot case study (X-O) A preexperimental design in which the reactions of only one group of subjects are measured after the event or treatment has occurred.

one-tailed *p* value The *p* value associated with a result supporting a prediction of a specific direction of a research result, for example, $M_A > M_B$ or the sign of *r* is positive.

one-tailed test Test of significance in which the null hypothesis is rejected only if the results are significant in one of the two possible directions.

one-way design A statistical design in which two or more groups comprise a single dimension.

ontological realism The idea that reality is a "given" or a priori assumption.

open-ended measures Items that offer the respondent an opportunity to express feelings, motives, or behaviors spontaneously.

operational definition An empirically based definition, that is, the meaning of a variable in terms of the operations that are used to measure it or the experimental method involved in its determination.

operationalism Percy W. Bridgman's term for the assumption that scientific concepts can be defined on empirical grounds by specifiable observational procedures.

operationally Term describing the measurement of a variable in an empirical way.

opportunistic sampling The selection of units merely because they are conveniently available.

opportunity samples See *opportunistic sampling*.

optimal design A design that optimizes the statistical power of a study by allocating more sampling units to some conditions than to others.

OR See *odds ratio*.

ordinal data Information on objects or events that can be ranked from high to low on some characteristic.

ordinate The vertical axis of a distribution.

organismic interactions Results showing that different treatments have different effects for different subgroups.

orthogonal contrasts Uncorrelated contrasts.

orthogonal polynomial contrasts Sets of orthogonal contrasts in which linear, quadratic, and higher order trends can be evaluated.

orthogonal relationship Relationship in which correlation equals zero.

orthogonal rotations Factor-analytic rotations in which the axes are kept at right angles to one another.

outliers Extreme scores, that is, those lying far outside the normal range.

overall *F* test An *F* test with $df > 1$ in the numerator; serves as appropriate protection for subsequent unplanned contrasts.

***p* value** Probability value or level obtained in a test of statistical significance.

paired *t* (correlated sample *t* or matched pair *t*) The *t* test computed on nonindependent samples.

pairwise deletion A nonimputational procedure for dealing with missing data in which the parameters of interest are computed on all the data that are available for that computation.

panel study A longitudinal study.

paradigm shifts Thomas Kuhn's idea that the history of science is punctuated by revolutionary insights that forever change the way we perceive the world.

paradox of sampling A term meaning that the appropriateness of a sample is validated by the method used to arrive at its appropriateness.

paradoxical incident An occurrence characterized by seemingly self-contradictory aspects.

parameters Population values.

parsimony The degree to which the propositions of a theory are "sparing" or "frugal"; see also *Occam's razor.*

partial aggregation Aggregation of only a subset of all relevant sources of variance.

partial concealment A researcher's concealment of only who or what is being observed.

partial correlation The correlation between two variables when the influence of other variables on their relationship has been eliminated statistically.

participant observation The study of a group or a community from within by a researcher who records behavior as its occurs. For example, ethnographers usually interact with members of a culture even as they observe those members.

partitioning of tables Subdivision of larger chi-square tables into smaller tables (e.g., into 2 $\times$ 2 tables).

passive deception (deception by omission) The withholding of certain information from the subjects, such as not informing them of the meaning of their responses when they are given a projective test or not fully disclosing the purpose of an experiment.

path analysis Multiple regression with time-ordered predictor variables.

payoff potential Subjective assessment of the likelihood that an idea will be corroborated.

Pearson *r* Standard index of linear relationship.

percentile A point in a distribution of scores below and above which a specified percentage of scores falls.

perceptibility The ability to apprehend a particular idea in the mind's eye as a perceptible image. See also *visualizations.*

period centrism fallacy The mistake of assuming that the results of an analysis of one particular period are generalizable to other periods.

permutation tests Procedure for determining statistical significance based on counts of rearrangements of the data.

perspectivism See *contextualism.*

phi coefficient (ϕ) Pearson *r* where both variables are scored dichotomously.

physical traces Material evidence of behavior.

Pi The effect size Π, or proportion of correct guesses if there were only two choices from which to select.

pilot test A way of selecting judges or raters by comparing all recruits in the pool of potential judges for their accuracy of judgments on some relevant criterion.

pilot testing The evaluation of some aspect of the research before the study is implemented.

placebo A substance without any pharmacological benefit given as a pseudomedicine to a control group.

placebo control group A control group that receives a placebo.

placebo effects The "healing" effects of inert substances or nonspecific treatments.

plagiarism Representing someone else's work as one's own; from the Latin word meaning "kidnapper."

planned contrasts Contrasts intended before the data were examined.

platykurtic distribution Charateristic of a relatively flattened curve.

plausible rival hypotheses Propositions, or sets of propositions, that provide a reasonable alternative to the working hypothesis.

point-biserial correlation (r_{pb}) Pearson *r* where one of the variables is scored dichotomously and the other variable is continuous.

point estimates Estimates of particular characteristics of the population (e.g., the number of times an event occurs).

PONS Profile of Nonverbal Sensitivity; a test for measuring sensitivity to nonverbal cues.

pooling sources of variance Combining terms that are not markedly different.

population The aggregate of elements from which sampling units are drawn, or the aggregate of elements to which we want to generalize.

positive synergistic effects Synergistic effects serving to raise scores.

positively skewed distribution An asymmetrical distribution in which the pointed end is toward the right (i.e., the positive tail).

positivism After Auguste Comte's term *positivisme,* the idea that sociology (another term coined by Comte) could, by embracing a "positive observational" approach, develop into an empirical natural science like chemistry and physics (i.e., a kind of "social physics"). See also *logical positivism.*

post hoc contrasts Contrasts computed only after the data have been examined.

postdictive validity The extent to which the results of a test correlate with some criterion in the past.

posttest-only control-group design An after-only experimental design containing an experimental and a control group.

power (1 − β) In significance testing, the probability of not making a Type II error.

power analysis Estimation of the effective power of a statistical test, or of the sample size needed to detect an obtained effect given a specified level of power.

power of a test The probability, when a particular test statistic (e.g., t, F, χ^2) is used, of not making a Type II error (i.e., the sensitivity of the significance test in providing an adequate opportunity to reject H_0 when it warrants rejection).

practical validity The real-life importance of the magnitude of a particular effect-size estimate.

pragmatism The idea that the meaning of conceptions is to be found in their applications (associated with Charles S. Peirce, William James, John Dewey, and George Herbert Mead).

pre-post control-group design Before-after experimental design.

preanalysis of an experiment The statistical analysis of the data predicted by a theory to clarify how the predictions will be tested in the data-analytic model.

precision Sharpness or exactness of observations or measures.

predictive validity The extent to which scores on a test, scale, or other instrument can predict future outcomes.

predictor variable The variable that is used to predict a particular outcome, as measured by the criterion variable.

preexperimental designs Research designs in which there is such a total absence of control that they are of minimal value in establishing causality.

pretest The measurement made before an experimental manipulation or intervention.

pretest sensitization The confounding of pretesting and X, the independent variable of interest.

principal components analysis The rewriting of a set of variables into a new set of orthogonal components.

principle of the drunkard's search The search for data in a convenient place but not a truly relevant one.

priority The second in David Hume's list of "rules by which to judge of causes and effects," which is that "the cause must be prior to the effect." See also *contiguity* and *constant conjunction.*

probabilistic assertion Our term for an empirically based statement, claim, or inference that is presumed to be "likely to be true," that is, given particular assumptions or a specific context of explanation. See also *inductive-statistical explanation.*

probability The mathematical chance of an event's occurring.

probability sampling The random selection of sampling units so that the laws of mathematical probability apply.

probit d' A measure of effect size defined as the difference between standard-normal-deviate-transformed proportions of two populations.

product-moment correlation coefficient Standard index of linear relationship, or Pearson r.

product The number resulting from the multiplication of one value by another.

projective test A psychological measure that operates on the principle that the subject will project some unconscious aspect of his or her life experience and emotions onto ambiguous stimuli in the spontaneous responses that come to mind (e.g, the Rorschach test and the Thematic Apperception Test).

propensity scores Donald B. Rubin's term for composite scores that effectively summarize all the differences on all the variables (the covariates) on which "treated" and "untreated" subjects differ.

proportion of variation explained See *coefficient of determination.*

prospectivism See *contextualism.*

protected t test The t test computed under the umbrella of an overall F to minimize capitalizing on the post hoc selection of the largest effects.

proximity analysis Set of redescriptors of relations among objects in terms of measures of similarity or dissimilarity.

pseudoscience Bogus claims masquerading as scientific facts.

GLOSSARY

pseudosubject A confederate of the experimenter who plays the role of a research subject.

psychological contextualism A philosophical view in modern behavioral and social science, in which the emphasis is on the process-like nature of behavior (i.e., it is constantly changing), the dynamical contexts of all human knowledge, and the doctrine of methodological pluralism and theoretical ecumenism.

psychophysics The study of the relationship between physical stimuli and our experience of them.

PsycINFO The American Psychological Association's abstract database.

psychosocial experimenter effects Experimenter-related artifacts that are a function of psychosocial attributes of the researcher (e.g., the experimenter's personality).

pulse function An abrupt change lasting only a short time.

pure empiricism See *behaviorism*.

pure longitudinal designs Research in which a cohort is followed over time.

q See *Cohen's q.*

Q-sort A rating procedure in which the subjects sort stimuli into piles to resemble a bell-shaped distribution; developed by William Stephenson.

quadratic trend Curvilinear relation between two variables in which the line changes direction once.

qualitative data Information in a nonnumeric form, such as recorded conversations, narrative responses in interviews, or observable behavior in ethnographic research.

quantitative data The raw data existing in a numerical form, such as ratings of behavior, scores on a test, or instrument readings.

quartile range The range of scores found between the 75th and 25th percentiles.

quasi control strategy Martin Orne's expression for the procedure in which some subjects are invited to step out of their "subject roles" and to act as "coinvestigators" in the identification of demand characteristics.

quasi control subjects Research participants who are asked to reflect on the context in which an experiment is conducted and to speculate on how the context may influence their own and other subjects' behaviors.

quasi-experimental A term describing study designs that are "something like" an experimental design (in that there are treatments, outcome measures, and experimental units), but random assignment is not used to create the comparisons from which treatment-caused changes are inferred in randomized designs.

quota sampling An antiquated data collection procedure in opinion polling that assigned a quota of people to be interviewed and let the questioner build up a sample that was roughly representative of the population.

r Pearson's product-moment correlation.

r **method** A strategy for quantifying the degree of success in constructing clear composite variables; based on the point-biserial correlation.

r^2 See *coefficient of determination.*

r-**type family of effect sizes** See *correlation family of effect sizes.*

r_{alerting} The Pearson product-moment correlation between group (or condition) means (*M*) and contrast weights (λs)—also symbolized as $r_{M\lambda}$.

random assignment A synonym for randomization, that is, the assignment to conditions at random.

random-digit dialing A process in which the researcher selects the first three digits of telephone numbers and then uses a computer program to select the last digits at random.

random effects Levels of a factor chosen as representative of a population of levels of a factor.

random errors Chance fluctuations that are self-canceling, in that the average of the errors is presumed to equal zero over a large number of random observations. See also *systematic error.*

random factors Levels of a factor viewed as having been randomly sampled.

random response set Responses that are made without regard to item content.

random sample A sample chosen by chance procedures and with known probabilities of selection so that every unit in a set or population has the same likelihood of being chosen at each draw.

random sampling with replacement A process in which the randomly selected units are placed in the sampling pool again and may be reselected on subsequent draws.

random sampling without replacement A process in which the randomly selected units cannot be reselected and must be disregarded on any later draw.

random selection Another name for **random sampling.**

randomization (random assignment) Random allocation of sampling units to conditions.

randomized experiments Experimental designs that use randomization.

randomized response technique Method for eliminating evasive answers by using a randomizing instrument to select how the subject will respond concerning sensitive questions while still providing the investigator usable data for the entire sample.

randomized trials A popular term for controlled medical or pharmaceutical experiments that use randomized experimental designs.

range Distance between the highest and lowest score.

range-to-midrange-ratio method A strategy for quantifying the degree of success in constructing clear composite variables.

rater biases Systematic errors that can be attributed to particular judges' ratings.

rating errors (response biases) Systematic errors in responses on rating scales.

rating scales The common name for a variety of measuring instruments on which the observer or subject gives a numerical value (either explicitly or implicitly) to certain judgments or assessments.

ratio family of effect sizes Includes relative risk (RR) and the odds ratio (OR), as well as the BESD-based RR and BESD-based OR.

$r_{contrast}$ The partial correlation between individual sampling unit scores on the dependent variable (Y) and the predicted mean score (represented by λ, the contrast weight) of the group to which they belong, with other between-group variation (i.e., noncontrast variation, NC) removed—also symbolized as $r_{Y\lambda \cdot NC}$.

$r_{counternull}$ The counternull value of the obtained r.

$R^{Cronbach}$ Cronbach's alpha coefficient for internal-consistency reliability.

RCT Randomized control trial. See *randomized trials*.

RD See *risk difference*.

reactive measures Measurements that affect the behavior that is being measured; also known as **reactive observation** (i.e., an observation that affects what is being observed).

realism Position that things and events are literally real and knowable; also the philosophical doctrine that established ("mature") scientific theories describe literal reality (called **scientific realism**). See also *antirealism*.

rectangular arrays Generalizations of Latin squares to $t \times t!$ dimensions, where $t =$ number of treatments.

redescriptors Multivariate procedures serving to redescribe a set of variables, often in a smaller set of variables.

$r_{effect\ size}$ The simple (unpartialed) correlation between the contrast weights (λs) associated with membership in a group or condition and scores on the dependent variable (Y); also symbolized as $r_{Y\lambda}$.

regression Changes in level of the outcome variable predicted from changes in a predictor variable.

regression analysis Loosely equivalent to correlational analysis; more technically refers to relations of changes in level of Y to changes in level of X.

regression substitution procedure The replacement of all missing values by the predicted value of that variable from a regression analysis using only cases with no missing data; one of several single imputation procedures for dealing with missing data.

regression toward the mean A mathematical concept that refers to the relation between two paired variables, X and Y, for which cases at one extreme on X (the independent variable) will, on the average over time, be less extreme on the other variable.

regular autocorrelation The dependence of adjacent observations on one another in time series analysis.

relational inquiry Any method of research that seeks to tell "how things are in relation to other things."

relational research orientation An empirical approach to investigation in which the observational focus or objective is to identify relations or associations among variables.

relative risk (RR) The ratio of the proportion of control subjects at risk to the proportion of treated subjects at risk.

reliable A synonym for *consistent* or *dependable*.

reliability The degree to which observations or measures are consistent or stable.

reliability coefficient A quantitative measure of consistency or stability, for example, test-retest, alternate form, and internal-consistency reliability.

reliability of components Another name for **internal-consistency reliability.**

repeated-measures design Statistical design in which the sampling units generate two or more measurements.

replicate To repeat or duplicate a scientific observation.

replication The duplication or repetition of a scientific observation or research study, usually an experimental result or experimental study.

representative Typical, such as when a segment is representative (or typical) of the larger aggregate.

representative research design Egon Brunswik's term for any design that involves the sampling of both subjects and stimuli.

$r_{equivalent}$ The effect size correlation that is equivalent to the sample point-biserial correlation (r_{pb}) between the condition indicator and an exactly normally distributed outcome in a two-condition experiment with $N/2$ units in each group and the obtained p value.

resampling procedures Procedures for creating replications of a data set by repeatedly setting aside a fraction of the data to compute various statistics, replacing the set-aside data, and then drawing another sample.

residual effects Effects left over when appropriate components are subtracted from scores or means.

residuals See *interaction effects, row effects,* and *column effects.*

response The consequence of, or reaction to, a stimulus.

response biases See *rating errors.*

response set An attitudinal disposition determining a person's answers to questions or other responses.

response variable The dependent variable.

retest reliability Another name for **test-retest reliability.**

reversal design Single-case design in which the conditions end on a positive note, such as an A-B-A-B design.

rhetoric The persuasive language of a given field, which in science encompasses the proper use of technical terms and arguments to warrant, defend, or excuse certain beliefs (called the **rhetoric of justification** in this book).

rho (ρ) Spearman rank correlation.

R^{Hoyt} Hoyt internal-consistency reliability.

risk-benefit analysis An evaluation of the ethical risks and benefits of proposed studies.

risk difference (RD) The difference between the proportion of the control subjects at risk and the proportion of the treated subjects at risk.

rival hypotheses Competing hypotheses.

rival interpretations Plausible explanations that provide reasonable alternatives to working hypotheses.

R^{KR20} Kuder-Richardson internal-consistency reliability.

role play A type of simulation in which subjects act out a given scenario; also known as *emotional role play* when the researcher achieves a high degree of experimental realism by increasing the subjects' involvement.

root mean square See *standard deviation.*

Rorschach test A projective test that consists of a set of inkblots on pieces of cardboard.

rotation of factors or components Rotation of the axes on which the variables have been located, with the aim of making the factors or components more interpretable.

row effects Row means minus grand mean.

r_{pb} See *point-biserial correlation.*

RR See *relative risk.*

R^{SB} Spearman-Brown internal-consistency reliability.

running records A subcategory of archival material that includes actuarial data, political and judicial data, mass media information, and other continuing information.

Rushton study A field experiment, conducted in a mining company, that raised the ethical issue of fair-mindedness.

S Square root of the unbiased estimator of the population value of σ^2.

S^2 Unbiased estimator of the population value of σ^2.

S^2 **means** The variance of means around the grand mean.

S^2 **pooled** Variance collected from two or more samples.

sample A subset of the population.

sample selection bias Systematic error resulting from the nature of the sampling units.

sampling plan A design, scheme of action, or procedure that specifies how the participants are to be selected in a survey study.

sampling stability The concept that all samples produced by the same sampling plan will yield essentially the same results.

sampling units The elements that make up the sample (e.g., people, schools, or cities).

sampling with replacement A type of random sampling in which the selected names are placed in the selection pool again and may be reselected in subsequent draws.

sampling without replacement A type of random sampling in which a previously selected name cannot be chosen again and must be disregarded in any later draw.

SAT Scholastic Assessment Test.

scatter diagram See *scatter plot.*

scatter plot (scatter diagram) A visual display of the correlation between two variables that looks like a cloud of scattered dots.

Scheffé test Significance test appropriate for use when the contrast has been formulated after examination of the data.

scientific method A general approach or outlook (rather than a single method) emphasizing the use of empirical reasoning; also one of Charles Sanders Peirce's "methods for the fixation of belief."

scientific notation A compact way of reporting numbers with many decimal places.

scientific realism See *realism.*

SE See *standard error.*

"searchlight theory" Karl Popper's characterization of falsifiability as an essential criterion of scientific conjectures.

seasonal autocorrelation The dependence of observations separated by one period or cycle in time series analysis.

secondary analysis The reanalysis of an existing database.

secondary observation An observation that is twice removed from the source.

secular trend Systematic increase or systematic decrease.

segmented graphic scale A rating scale in the form of a line that is broken into segments.

selection Donald Campbell and Julian Stanley's term for a plausible threat to the internal validity of research not using randomization when the kinds of research subjects selected for one treatment group are different from those selected for another group.

self-fulfilling prophecy Robert Merton's term for a prediction that leads to its own fulfillment.

self-recorded diaries See *diary method.*

self-report data Information reported by the subjects themselves, usually self-descriptions of feelings, attitudes, thinking, or behavior.

self-report measures See *method of self-report.*

self-selection The subject's choosing for himself or herself whether to enter a treatment condition.

semantic differential method A type of rating procedure in which connotative (or subjective) meaning is judged in terms of several dimensions, usually evaluation, potency, and activity; developed by Charles E. Osgood and his coworkers.

sense-making In ethnographic research, the objective of imposing meaning on the observed or recorded behaviors, that is, of making sense of them.

sensitive Term pertaining to the degree to which an instrument is able to detect changes in behavior.

sentence completion test A type of projective test in which the subject responds by completing an incomplete sentence.

serendipity A lucky or accidental finding, insight, or discovery.

severity error A type of rating error in which the ratings are consistently more negative than they should be. See also *leniency bias.*

σ The standard deviation of a set of scores.

σ^2 The variance of a set of scores.

Σ Symbol telling us to sum a set of scores.

sign test Test of significance of the preponderance of positive versus negative difference scores for matched-pair data.

signal Information.

signal-to-noise ratio A ratio of information to lack of information, for example, the ratio of the variability between samples (the signal) to the variability within the samples (the noise).

significance level The probability of a Type I error.

significance testing The use of statistical procedures (e.g., t, F, chi-square) to estimate the p value, or statistical probability of a Type I error.

simple cross-sectional design A design in which subjects at different ages are observed at the same time.

simple effects Differences between group or condition means.

simple longitudinal design A design in which several cohorts are studied, the initial measurements being taken in successive years.

simple observation Unobtrusive observation of events without any attempt to affect them.

simple random sampling A sampling plan in which the participants are selected individually on the basis of a randomized procedure (e.g, a table of random digits).

simple unobtrusive observation A procedure in which no variables are manipulated, and the research observations are inconspicuous. See also *contrived unobtrusive observation.*

Simpson's paradox The paradox that bivariate statistical relationships may be reversed by the inclusion of other factors in the analysis.

simulation experiment An experiment based on a model in order to reveal what will happen under conditions that mimic the environment in a definite way.

single-blind study Study in which the participants do not know the group or condition to which they have been randomly assigned. Contrast with *double-blind study.*

single-case experimental studies Within-subjects designs on a single unit or a few units.

single-imputation procedures The general term for any imputation procedure that deals with missing data in which each missing value is replaced by a reasonable estimate of what that value might have been had it been observed (e.g., mean substitution, regression substitution, stochastic regression imputation, or hot deck imputation).

situational experimenter effects Experimenter-related artifacts that are a function of situationally determined experimenter attributes.

size of the study The number of sampling units.

skewness A characteristic of distributions in which extreme scores are concentrated on one side of the mean.

small-N experimental research Studies using repeated-measures designs in which the treatment effect is evaluated within the same subject or a small number of subjects.

smallest space analysis The use of a set of redescriptors of relations among objects in terms of measures of similarity or dissimilarity.

social constructionism A social-philosophical view in psychology (primarily associated with the writings of Kenneth Gergen), with roots in classical philosophical idealism and the modern philosophical view in sociology known as **constructivism,** in which the primary emphasis is on narrative analysis and an interpretive model of social understanding.

social experimentation The application of experimental or quasi-experimental methods to the analysis of community problems and to the development, testing, and assessment of workable interventions meant to reduce the problems.

social psychology of the experiment The ways in which subject-related and experimenter-related artifacts operate.

social research See *behavioral research.*

social science See *behavioral science.*

socially desirable responding The tendency to respond in ways that seem to elicit a favorable evaluation.

Solomon design An extended control-group experimental design proposed by R. L. Solomon as a means of assessing pretest sensitization effects.

Spearman-Brown equation The *Spearman-Brown prophecy formula.*

Spearman-Brown prophecy formula A traditional equation for measuring the overall internal-consistency reliability of a test from a knowledge of the reliability of its components.

Spearman rho (r_s) Pearson r computed on scores in ranked form.

split-half reliability Realiability obtained by splitting a test in half and correlating the scores on the halves with one another (e.g., correlating the odd- and even-numbered items).

spread Dispersion or variability.

SS Sum of squares.

SS$_{between}$ Sum of squares between conditions.

SS$_{total}$ Total sum of squares.

SS$_{within}$ Sum of squares within conditions.

stability The extent to which a set of measurements does not vary.

stability coefficients Correlations between scores on the same instrument administered to the same people at different times.

standard deviation (root mean square) An index of the variability of a set of data around the mean value in a distribution.

standard error (*SE*) The degree of imprecision with which we have estimated, for example, the mean or median of a population.

standard normal curve (distribution) Normal curve (distribution) with Mean $= 0$ and $\sigma = 1$.

standard normal deviate z-score location on a standard normal curve.

standard score (*z* score) Score converted to a standard deviation unit.

standardized measure A measurement (e.g., of ability, personality, judgment, or attitude) that requires that certain rules be followed in the development, administration, and scoring of the measuring instrument.

standardizing the margins Setting all row totals equal to each other and all column totals equal to each other.

states Occurrences or characteristics of relatively appreciable duration.

stationary Reflecting an absence of secular trend in time series data.

statistical conclusion validity The relative accuracy of drawing statistical conclusions.

statistical power See *power of a test.*

stem The leading digits of a stem-and-leaf chart.

stem-and-leaf chart The plot of a distribution in which the original data are preserved with any desired precision.

stochastic regression imputation The addition of a random residual term to the estimates based on regression substitution; one of several single-imputation procedures for dealing with missing data.

Stouffer method of adding *zs* Procedure for combining the *p* values of a set of studies.

strata (clusters) Subpopulations (or layers) in survey sampling.

stratified random sampling Probability sampling plan in which a separate sample is randomly selected within each homogeneous stratum (or layer) of the population.

strong inference A type of research approach or design in which one hypothesis or fact vies with another.

structured items Questions with fixed options; also described as **fixed-response items** or **closed items.**

Student's *t* The pen name used by the inventor of the *t* test, William Sealy Gosset, was "Student."

study size An indicator of the number of observations or sampling units in a study, as in the expression "Significance test = Effect size $\times$ Study size."

subject and experimenter artifacts Systematic errors that are attributed to uncontrolled subject- and experimenter-related variables.

sufficient condition A condition that is adequate to bring about some effect or result.

sum of squares (*SS*) The sum of the squared deviations from the mean in a set of scores.

summated ratings method A method of attitude scaling, developed by Rensis Likert, that uses item analysis to select the best items.

symmetrical distribution A distribution of scores in which there is an exact correspondence in arrangement on the opposite sides of the middle line.

synchronic research Any study in which an event is observed as it occurs at one period in time, not using information about the event's development or long-term consequences or changes.

synchronous correlations In panel designs, correlations representing the degree of relationship of variables at a moment in time.

synergistic effects Nonadditive effects of several treatments.

systematic error Fluctuations that push measurements in the same direction and thus cause the mean value to be either too big or too small; systematic errors are not self-canceling in the way that random errors are presumed to be.

systematic observation Observation that is guided or influenced by preexisting questions or hypotheses.

systematic replication Murray Sidman's term for the repetition of a single-case experiment with a slight variation from the original study (an example of what we more generally refer to as **varied replication**). Contrast with *direct replication.*

systematic sampling The methodical selection of the sampling units in sequence separated on lists by the interval of selection.

systematic selection plans Method of selection of sampling units in which particular intervals determine the units to be selected after a random start.

t **distributions** Family of distributions centered at zero and ranging from negative to positive infinity.

t **test** A test of significance used to judge the tenability of the null hypothesis of no relation between two variables.

table analysis Statistical analysis of frequency counts cast into tabular form.

tacit knowledge Michael Polanyi's term for unvoiceable wisdom, or the idea that humans know more than they can precisely communicate in everyday language.

tally sheets Recording materials for counting frequencies.

Taylor-Russell tables H. C. Taylor and J. T. Russell's tables demonstrating that the practical utility of tests used in personnel selection increases as the validity coefficient increases and as the selection ratio decreases (i.e., as selectivity increases).

t_{contrast} The symbol used in this book to denote a *t* test that is used to address a focused question or hypothesis in a comparison of more than two groups or conditions.

teleological cause See *final cause.*

telephone interview An interview that is conducted by phone.

temporal erosion Decay in the strength of a relationship over lapses of time.

temporal precedence The principle that what is labeled as the "cause" must be shown to have occurred before the "effect."

tenacity method See *method of tenacity.*

test of significance Statistical test giving information on the tenability of the null hypothesis of, for example, no relation between two or more variables.

test-retest correlations Correlations that represent the stability of a variable over time.

test-retest reliability The degree of consistency of a test or measurement, or of the characteristic it is designed to measure, from one administration to another.

testing error Error whereby familiarity with a test or scale artificially enhances performance.

testing the grand mean Evaluating whether the grand mean differs from zero or some other value of theoretical interest.

tests of simple effects Statistical tests of differences between group or condition means.

Thematic Apperception Test (TAT) A projective test consisting of a set of pictures, usually of people in various life contexts.

theoretical (conceptual) definition The meaning of a variable in abstract or conceptual terms.

theoretical ecumenism The need for more than one relevant perspective to foster a holistic picture, because each theory focuses on a particular level of understanding.

theory A set of proposed explanatory statements connected by logical arguments and by explicit and implicit assumptions.

theta David Armor's index of internal-consistency reliability.

third-variable problem A condition in which a variable correlated with X and Y is the cause of both.

three Rs of humane animal experimentation The argument that scientists should (a) *reduce* the number of animals used in research, (b) *refine* the experiments so that there is less suffering, and (c) *replace* animals with other procedures whenever possible.

Thurstone scale See *equal-appearing intervals method.*

time sampling The sampling of specified periods and the recording of everything of interest during each period.

time-sequential design A design in which subjects of different ages are observed at different times.

time series designs Studies in which the effects of an intervention are inferred from a comparison of the outcome measures obtained at different time intervals before and after the intervention.

tolerance for future null results Number of "filed" (unavailable) studies with mean effect size of zero required to bring the combined probability of the available and unavailable studies to a nonsignificant level (or to any particular *p* level of interest).

total aggregation Aggregation of all relevant sources of variance.

transformation Conversion of data to another mathematical form.

translation and back-translation Method used in cross-cultural research, in which the researcher has one bilingual person translate the questionnaire items from the source to the target language and then has another bilingual person independently translate the items back into the source language (called **back-translation**). The researcher then compares the original with the twice-translated version to see whether anything important was lost in the translation.

treatments The procedures or conditions of an experiment.

trials See *randomized trials.*

trimmed mean The mean of a distribution from which a specified highest and lowest percentage of scores has been dropped.

trimmed range Range of a distribution remaining after a specified highest and lowest percentage of scores has been dropped.

true experimental designs Donald Campbell and Julian Stanley's term for randomized experimental designs.

true population value The actual population value, that is, the point value we would obtain by analyzing all the scores in the population.

two-by-two factorial design A two-way statistical design with two rows and two columns.

two-tailed p value The p value associated with a result supporting a prediction of a nonspecific direction of a research result (e.g., either $M_A > M_B$ or $M_B > M_A$, or the sign of r is either positive or negative).

two-tailed test Test of significance in which the null hypothesis is rejected if the results are significant in either of the two possible directions.

two-way design (two-way factorial) A statistical design in which each entry in the table is associated with a row variable and a column variable.

two-way factorial See *two-way design.*

Type I error The error of rejecting the null hypothesis when it is true.

Type II error The error of failing to reject the null hypothesis when it is false.

unbiased A term describing a case in which the values produced by the sample coincide with the true values of the population.

unbiased estimator of the population value of σ^2 A specific statistic usually written as S^2.

unbiased sampling plan Survey design in which the average of the values produced by the samples coincides in the long run with the true value in the population.

unipolar rating scales Scales that run from a low amount to a high amount on a particular dimension.

unobtrusive measures Measurements or observations used to study behavior when the subjects are unaware of being measured or observed.

unplanned contrasts Contrasts computed only after the data have been examined.

unstructured measures See *open-ended measures.*

unweighted means analysis Analysis weighting all means equally even if sample sizes differ.

validity The degree to which the measures or observations are appropriate or meaningful in the way they claim to be.

variability See *spread.*

variables Attributes of sampling units that can take on two or more values.

variance (mean square) The mean of the squared deviations of scores from their means in a population or the unbiased estimate of that mean.

varied replication The repetition of a study with a slight variation from the original design. See also *systematic replication.*

varimax rotation Common method of orthogonal factor rotation that tries to make loadings within each factor as close to 0 or to 1.0 as possible.

verifiability principle The logical positivist notion that "truth" can be revealed by the amassing of factual observations (called the "bucket theory of the mind" by Popper).

visualizations Mental imagery, or the ideas that reverberate in the mind's eye.

volunteer bias Systematic error resulting when participants who volunteer respond differently from how individuals in the general population would respond.

w See *Cohen's w.*

WAIS See *Wechsler Adult Intelligence Scale.*

wait-list control group A control group in which the subjects wait to receive the experimental treatment until after it has been administered to and found effective in the experimental group.

Wechsler Adult Intelligence Scale (WAIS) The most widely used of the individual intelligence tests; divided into verbal and performance scores.

why-questions An expression, in philosophy of science, for questions about "why" things work the way they do.

wild scores Extreme scores that result from computational or recording mistakes.

Winer method of adding ts Procedure for combining the p values of a set of studies.

within-subjects designs Statistical designs in which the sampling units (e.g., the research participants) generate two or more measurements.

word association test A type of projective test in which the participant, who is read a list of words, responds with the first word that comes to mind immediately after hearing each stimulus word.

working hypothesis An empirically testable conjecture or supposition.

x **axis (abscissa)** The horizontal axis of a distribution.

X Any score; also a symbol for the cause or independent variable in the expression $Y = f(X)$, read as "*Y* is a function of *X*."

$\overline{X}$ The mean of a set of scores.

$\overline{\overline{X}}$ Grand mean.

y **axis (ordinate)** The vertical axis of a distribution.

Yates correction for continuity Specific correction for continuity in which the absolute difference between the obtained and the expected frequencies is decreased by .5.

yea-sayers Respondents who answer questions consistently in the affirmative.

z **score** See *standard score.*

Zeitgeist The general temper or ambience characteristic of a particular period of history.

zero control group A group that receives no treatment of any kind.

z_r See Fisher z_r.

REFERENCES

Adair, J. G. (1984). The Hawthorne effect: A reconsideration of the methodological artifact. *Journal of Applied Psychology, 69,* 334–345.

Adair, J. G., & Vohra, N. (2003). The explosion of knowledge, references, and citations: Psychology's unique response to a crisis. *American Psychologist, 58,* 15–23.

Aditya, R. N. (1996). *The not-so-good subject: Extent and correlates of pseudovolunteering in research.* Unpublished M.A. thesis, Temple University Department of Psychology, Philadelphia.

Aditya, R. N. (1997). *Toward the better understanding of managerial success: An exploration of interpersonal acumen.* Unpublished doctoral dissertation, Temple University, Philadelphia.

Aditya, R. N., Darkangelo, D., & Morris, M. L. (1999, June). The structure of interpersonal acumen in adult interaction. Poster presented at American Psychological Society meeting, Denver.

Aditya, R., & House, R. J. (2002). Interpersonal acumen and leadership across cultures: Pointers from the GLOBE study. In R. E. Riggio, S. E. Murphy, & F. J. Pirozzolo (Eds.), *Multiple intelligences and leadership* (pp. 215–240). Mahwah, NJ: Erlbaum.

Aditya, R., & Rosnow, R. L. (2002). Executive intelligence and interpersonal acumen: A conceptual framework. In B. Pattanayak & V. Gupta, with P. Niranjana (Eds.), *Creating performing organizations: International perspectives for Indian management* (pp. 225–246). New Delhi, India: Response Book/Sage Publications.

Adorno, T. W., Frenkel-Brunwik, E., Levinson, D. J., & Sanford, R. N. (1950). *The authoritarian personality.* New York: Harper & Row.

Agresti, A. (2002). *Categorical data analysis* (2nd ed.). New York: Wiley.

Aiken, L. S., & Rosnow, R. L. (1973). Role expectations for psychological research participation. Unpublished study, Temple University, Philadelphia. [Study results reported in R. Rosenthal & R. L. Rosnow (1975). *The volunteer subject* (pp. 163–169). New York: Wiley.]

Albright, L., & Malloy, T. E. (2000). Experimental validity: Brunswik, Campbell, Cronbach, and enduring issues. *Review of General Psychology, 4,* 337–353.

Aleksander, I. (1977). *The human machine: A view of intelligent mechanisms.* St. Saphorin, Switzerland: Georgi.

Alexander, C. N., Jr., & Knight, G. W. (1971). Situated identities and social psychological experimentation. *Sociometry, 34,* 65–82.

Alexander, R. A., Scozzaro, M. J., & Borodkin, L. J. (1989). Statistical and empirical examination of the chi-square test for homogeneity of correlations in meta-analysis. *Psychological Bulletin, 106,* 329–331.

Allen, C. T. (2004). A theory-based approach for improving demand artifact assessment in advertising experiments. *Journal of Advertising, 33,* 63–73.

Allen, J. J. B., Schnyer, R. N.. & Hitt, S. K. (1998). The efficacy of acupuncture in the treatment of major depression in women. *Psychological Science, 9,* 397–401.

Allport, F. H., & Lepkin, M. (1945). Wartime rumors of waste and special privilege: Why some believe them. *Journal of Abnormal and Social Psychology, 40,* 3–36.

Allport, G. W. (1937). *Personality: A psychological interpretation.* New York: Holt, Rinehart & Winston.

Allport, G. W. (1942). *The use of personal documents in psychological science.* New York: Social Science Research Council.

Allport, G. W., & Postman, L. (1947). *The psychology of rumor.* New York: Holt, Rinehart & Winston.

Alpha-Tocopherol, Beta Carotene Cancer Prevention Study Group. (1994). The effect of vitamin E and beta carotene on the incidence of lung cancer and other cancers in male smokers. *New England Journal of Medicine, 330,* 1029–1035.

Altman, L. K. (1994, February 21). In major finding, drug limits H.I.V. infection in newborns. *New York Times,* pp. A1, A13.

Altman, L. K. (1998, April 7). Researchers find the first drug known to prevent breast cancer. *New York Times,* pp. A1, A21.

Altman, L. K. (1999, June 16). Breast cancer risk slashed by drug, study says. *Press Enterprise,* pp. A1, A11.

Altmann, J. (1974). Observational study of behavior: Sampling methods. *Behaviour, 49,* 227–267.

Alwin, D. (1974). An analytic comparison of four approaches to the interpretation of relationships in the multitrait-multimethod matrix. In H. Costner (Ed.), *Sociological Methodology 1973–74.* San Francisco: Jossey-Bass.

American Association for the Advancement of Science. (1988). *Project on scientific fraud and misconduct.* Washington, DC: Author.

American Psychiatric Association. (1994). *Diagnostic and statistical manual of mental disorders* (4th ed.). Washington, DC: Author.

American Psychological Association. (1973). *Ethical principles in the conduct of research with human participants.* Washington, DC: Author.

American Psychological Association. (1982). *Ethical principles in the conduct of research with human participants.* Washington, DC: Author.

American Psychological Association. (1985). *Standards for psychological and educational testing.* Washington, DC: Author.

American Psychological Association. (1994). *Publication manual of the American Psychological Association* (4th ed.). Washington, DC: Author.

American Psychological Association. (1996). *Guidelines for ethical conduct in the care and use of animals.* Washington, DC: Author.

American Psychological Association. (1998). *The ethics of research with human participants* (draft report). Washington, DC: Author.

American Psychological Association. (2001). *Publication manual of the American Psychological Association* (5th ed.). Washington, DC: Author.

Anastasi, A. (1988). *Psychological testing* (6th ed.). New York: Macmillan.

Anastasi, A., & Urbina, S. (1997). *Psychological testing* (7th ed.). Upper Saddle River, NJ: Prentice Hall.

Anderson, C. A., Berkowitz, L., Donnerstein, E., Huesmann, L. R., Johnson, J. D., Linz, D., Malamuth, N. M., & Wartella, L. R. (2003). The influence of media violence on youth. *Psychological Science in the Public Interest, 4,* 81–110.

Anderson, C. A., & Bushman, B. J. (1997). External validity of "trivial" experiments: The case of laboratory aggression. *Review of General Psychology, 1,* 19–41.

Anderson, C. A., Lindsay, J. L., & Bushman, B. J. (1999). Research in the psychological laboratory: Truth or triviality? *Current Directions in Psychological Science, 8,* 3–9.

Anderson, N. H. (1968). Likeableness ratings of 555 personality-trait words. *Journal of Personality and Social Psychology, 9,* 272–279.

Anderson, N. H. (2001). *Empirical direction in design and analysis.* Mahwah, NJ: Erlbaum.

Andreski, S. (Ed.). (1974). *The essential Comte: Selected from Cours de Philosophie Positive.* London: Croom Helm.

Arbuckle, J. L. (1996). Full information estimation in the presence of incomplete data. In G. A. Marcoulides & R. E. Schumacker (Eds.), *Advanced structural equation modeling: Issues and techniques* (pp. 242–277). Mahwah, NJ: Erlbaum.

Arbuckle, J. W., & Wothke, W. (1999). *Amos 4.0 user's guide.* Chicago: SPSS.

Arellano-Galdames, F. J. (1972). *Some ethical problems in research on human subjects.* Unpublished doctoral dissertation, University of New Mexico, Albuquerque.

Armor, D. J. (1974). Theta reliability and factor scaling. In H. L. Costner (Ed.), *Sociological methodology 1973–1974.* San Francisco: Jossey-Bass.

Aronson, E., & Carlsmith, J. M. (1968). Experimentation in social psychology. In G. Lindzey & E. Aronson (Eds.), *The handbook of social psychology* (2nd ed., Vol. 2, pp. 1–79). Reading, MA: Addison-Wesley.

Asch, S. E. (1946). Forming impressions of personality. *Journal of Abnormal and Social Psychology, 41,* 258–290.

Asch, S. E. (1951). Effects of group pressure upon the modification and distortion of judgments. In H. Guetzkow (Ed.), *Groups, leadership and men.* Pittsburgh: Carnegie Press.

Associated Press. (1995, November 1). NIH: Thalidomide heals AIDS ulcers. *Boston Globe,* Section: National/Foreign, p. 4

Associated Press. (1996, February 21). Study links Alzheimer's, early linguistic ability. *Boston Globe,* Section: National/Foreign, p. 9.

Associated Press. (1996, May 7). Contraceptive trials set for a link to AIDS research. *Boston Globe,* p. B1.

Atkinson, L. (1986). The comparative validities of the Rorschach and MMPI: A meta-analysis. *Canadian Psychology, 27,* 238–247.

Atwell, J. E. (1981). Human rights in human subjects research. In A. J. Kimmel (Ed.), *Ethics of human subject research* (pp. 81–90). San Francisco: Jossey-Bass.

Averill, J. R. (1982). *Anger and aggression.* New York: Springer-Verlag.

Averill, J. R., Stanat, P., & More, T. A. (1998). Aesthetics and the environment. *Review of General Psychology, 2,* 153–174.

Axinn, S. (1966). Fallacy of the single risk. *Philosophy of Science, 33,* 154–162.

Ayer, A. J. (1936). *Language, truth, and logic.* London: V. Gollancz.

Babad, E. (1993). Pygmalion—25 years after interpersonal expectations in the classroom. In P. D. Blanck (Ed.), *Interpersonal expectations: Theory, research, and applications* (pp. 125–153). New York: Cambridge University Press.

Bacon, F. (1994). *Novum organum* (P. Urbach & J. Gibson, Trans. and Eds.). Chicago: Open Court.

Baenninger, R. (1980). Comparative social perspectives on aggression. *Contemporary Psychology, 25,* 978–979.

Baenninger, R. (1987). Some comparative aspects of yawning in *Betta splendens, Homo sapiens, Panthera leo,* and *Papio sphinx. Journal of Comparative Psychology, 101,* 349–354.

Baenninger, R. (1988, February 16). Personal communication to R. L. Rosnow.

Baenninger, R., Estes, R. D., & Baldwin, S. (1977). Anti-predator behavior of baboons and impalas toward a cheetah. *Journal of East African Wildlife, 15,* 327–329.

Bailar, J. C., & Mosteller, F. (1988). Guidelines for statistical reporting in articles for medical journals: Amplifications and explanations. *Annals of Internal Medicine, 108,* 266–273.

Bailey, K. D. (1974). Cluster analysis. In D. R. Heise (Ed.), *Sociological methodology 1975* (pp. 59–128). San Francisco: Jossey-Bass.

Bakan, D. (1967). *On method: Toward a reconstruction of psychological investigation.* San Francisco: Jossey-Bass.

Balaam, L. N. (1963). Multiple comparisons—A sampling experiment. *Australian Journal of Statistics, 5,* 62–84.

Baldwin, W. (2000). Information no one else knows: The value of self-report. In A. A. Stone, J. S. Turkkan, C. A. Bachrach, J. B. Jobe, H. S. Kurtzman, & V. S. Cain (Eds.), *The science of self-report* (pp. 3–7). Mahwah, NJ: Erlbaum.

Bales, R. F. (1950a). A set of categories for analysis of small group interaction. *American Sociological Review, 15,* 257–263.

Bales, R. F. (1950b). *Interaction process analysis: A method for the study of small groups.* Cambridge, MA: Addison-Wesley.

Bales, R. F., & Cohen, S. P. (1979). *Symlog: A system for the multiple-level observation of groups.* New York: Free Press.

Barbe, P., & Bertail, P. (1995). *The weighted bootstrap.* New York: Springer-Verlag.

Barber, B. (1961). Resistance by scientists to scientific discovery. *Science, 134,* 596–602.

Barefoot, J. C. (1969). Anxiety and volunteering. *Psychonomic Science, 16,* 283–284.

Baring-Gould, W. S. (Ed.). (1967). *The annotated Sherlock Holmes* (Vol. 1). New York: Clarkson N. Potter.

Barlow, D. H. (1984). *Single-case experimental designs* (2nd ed.). New York: Allyn & Bacon.

Barnes, D. M. (1986). Promising results halt trial of anti-AIDS drug. *Science, 234,* 15–16.

Barnes, M. L., & Rosenthal, R. (1985). Interpersonal effects of experimenter attractiveness, attire, and gender. *Journal of Personality and Social Psychology, 48,* 435–446.

Barnett, R. C., & Rivers, C. (1996). *She works/he works: How two-income families are happier, healthier, and better-off.* New York: HarperCollins.

Barnett, V., & Lewis, T. (1978). *Outliers in statistical data.* Chichester, England: Wiley.

Baron, R. A. (1977). *Human aggression.* New York: Plenum.

Baron, R. M., & Kenny, D. A. (1986). The moderator-mediator variable distinction in social psychological research: Conceptual, strategic, and statistical considerations. *Journal of Personality and Social Psychology, 51,* 1173–1182.

Barrass, R. (1978). *Scientists must write.* London: Chapman & Hall.

Bartoshuk, L. (2000, August). *Do you hear what I hear? Or taste?* Paper presented at annual meeting of the American Psychological Association, Washington, DC.

Bartoshuk, L. (2002). Self-reports and across-group comparisons: A way out of the box. *APS Observer, 15:*3, 7, 26–28.

Bartoshuk, L. M., Duffy, V. B., Fast, K., Green, B. G., & Prutkin, J. M. (2001). Invalid sensory comparisons across groups: Examples from PROP research. *Chemical Sciences, 26,* 761–762.

Basford, K. E., & Tukey, J. W. (1999). *Graphical analysis of multiresponse data.* New York: Chapman & Hall.

Battig, W. F. (1962). Parsimony in science. *Psychological Reports, 11,* 555–572.

Bauer, M. I., & Johnson-Laird, P. N. (1993). How diagrams can improve reasoning. *Psychological Science, 4,* 372–378.

Baughman, E. E., & Dahlstrom, W. G. (1968). *Negro and white children: A psychological study in the rural South.* New York: Academic Press.

Baumrind, D. (1964). Some thoughts on ethics of research: After reading Milgram's "Behavioral Study of Obedience." *American Psychologist, 19,* 421–423.

Becker, H. S., & Geer, B. (1960). Participant observation: The analysis of qualitative field data. In R. N. Adams & J. J. Preiss (Eds.), *Human organization research.* Homewood, IL: Dorsey.

Beecher, H. K. (1966, July 2). Documenting the abuses. *Saturday Review,* pp. 45–46.

Beecher, H. K. (1970). *Research and the individual: Human studies.* Boston: Little, Brown.

Bem, D. J. (1965). An experimental analysis of self-persuasion. *Journal of Experimental Social Psychology, 1,* 199–218.

Bem, D. J. (1972). Self-perception theory. In L. Berkowitz (Ed.), *Advances in experimental social psychology* (Vol. 6, pp. 1–62). New York: Academic Press.

Bem, D. J., & Funder, D. C. (1978). Predicting more of the people more of the time: Assessing the personality of situations. *Psychological Review, 85,* 485–501.

Bem, S. L. (1974). The measurement of psychological androgyny. *Journal of Consulting and Clinical Psychology, 42,* 155–162.

Bentler, P. M. (1987). Structural modeling and the scientific method: Comments on Freedman's critique. *Journal of Educational Statistics, 12,* 151–157.

Berelson, B. (1952). *Content analysis in communication research.* Glencoe, IL: Free Press.

Berelson, B. (1954). Content analysis. In G. Lindzey (Ed.), *Handbook of social psychology* (Vol. 1, pp. 488–522). Reading, MA: Addison-Wesley.

Berg, B. L. (1998). *Qualitative methods for the social sciences* (3rd ed.). Boston: Allyn & Bacon.

Berk, R. A. (1983). An introduction to sample selection bias in sociological data. *American Sociological Review, 48,* 386–398.

Berk, R. A., & Ray, S. C. (1982). Selection biases in sociological data. *Social Science Research, 11,* 352–398.

Berlin, I. (1953). *The hedgehog and the fox: An essay on Tolstoy's view of history.* New York: Simon & Schuster.

Bernard, C. (1957). *An introduction to the study of experimental medicine.* New York: Dover. (Original work published 1865)

Bernard, H. B., & Killworth, P. D. (1970). Informant accuracy in social network data, Part 2. *Human Communication Research, 4,* 3–18.

Bernard, H. B., & Killworth, P. D. (1980). Informant accuracy in social network data: 4. A comparison of clique-level structure in behavioral and cognitive network data. *Social Networks, 2,* 191–218.

Bersoff, D. (1995). *Ethical conflict in psychology.* Washington, DC: American Psychological Association.

Bersoff, D. M., & Bersoff, D. N. (2000). Ethical issues in the collection of self-report data. In A. A. Stone, J. S. Turkkan, C. A. Bachrach, J. B. Jobe, H. S. Kurtzman, & V. S. Cain (Eds.), *The science of self-report: Implications for research and practice* (pp. 9–24). Mahwah, NJ: Erlbaum.

Beveridge, W. I. B. (1957). *The art of scientific investigation.* New York: Vintage.

Bhaskar, R. (1983). Beef, structure, and place: Notes from a critical naturalist perspective. *Journal for the Theory of Social Behaviour, 13,* 81–97.

Biddle, B. J., & Thomas, E. J. (Eds.). (1966). *Role theory: Concepts and research.* New York: Wiley.

Biocca, F., & Levy, M. R. (Eds.). (1995). *Communication in the age of virtual reality.* Hillsdale, NJ: Erlbaum.

Birnbaum, M. H. (1999). How to show that $9 > 221$: Collect judgments in a between-subjects design. *Psychological Methods, 4,* 243–249.

Bishop, G. F., Oldendick, R. W., & Tuchfarber, A. J. (1982). Political information processing: Question order and context effects. *Political Behavior, 4,* 177–200.

Bishop, Y. M. M., Fienberg, S. E., & Holland, P. W. (1975). *Discrete multivariate analysis: Theory and practice.* Cambridge, MA: MIT Press.

Black, R. W., Jr., Schumpert, J., & Welch, F. A. (1972). A "partial reinforcement extinction effect" in perceptual-motor performance: Coerced versus volunteer subject populations. *Journal of Experimental Psychology, 92,* 143–145.

Blair, J. (2000). Assessing protocols for child interviews. In A. A. Stone, J. S. Turkkan, C. A. Bachrach, J. B. Jobe, H. S. Kurtzman, & V. S. Cain (Eds.), *The science of self-report: Implications for research and practice* (pp. 161–174). Mahwah, NJ: Erlbaum.

Blanck, P. D. (Ed.). (1993). *Interpersonal expectations: Theory, research, and applications.* Cambridge, UK: Cambridge University Press.

Blanck, P. D., Bellack, A. S., Rosnow, R. L., Rotheram-Borus, M. J., & Schooler, N. R. (1992). Scientific rewards and conflicts of ethical choices in human subjects research. *American Psychologist, 47,* 959–965.

Block, J. (1978). *The Q-sort method in personality assessment and psychiatric research.* Palo Alto, CA: Consulting Psychologists Press.

Block, J. B., Schneiderman, M., Chalmers, T. C., & Lee, S. (1975). Nonevaluable patients in clinical cancer research. *Cancer, 36,* 1169–1173.

Bloom, D. E. (1998). Technology, experimentation, and the quality of survey data. *Science, 280,* 847–848.

Blumberg, M. (1980). Job switching in autonomous work groups: An exploratory study in a Pennsylvania coal mine. *Academy of Management Journal, 23,* 287–306.

Blumberg, M., & Pringle, C. D. (1983). How control groups can cause loss of control in action research: The case of Rushton coal mine. *Journal of Applied Behavioral Science, 19,* 409–425.

Bogdan, R. C., & Biklen, S. K. (1998). *Qualitative research in education: An introduction to theory and methods* (3rd ed.). Boston: Allyn & Bacon.

Bok, S. (1978). *Lying: Moral choice in public and private life.* New York: Pantheon.

Bok, S. (1984). *Secrets: On the ethics of concealment and revelation.* New York: Vintage Books.

Bollen, K. A. (1989). *Structural equations with latent variables.* New York: Wiley.

Bonate, P. L. (2000). *Analysis of pretest-posttest designs.* Boca Raton, FL: Chapman & Hall/CRC.

Bond, C. F., Jr., Wiitala, W. L., & Richard, F. D. (2003). Meta-analysis of raw mean differences. *Psychological Methods, 8,* 406–418.

Bordia, P. (1996). Studying verbal interaction on the Internet: The case of rumor transmission research. *Behavior Research Methods, Instruments, & Computers, 28,* 149–151.

Bordia, P., & DiFonzo, N. (2002). When social psychology became less social: Prasad and the history of rumor research. *Asian Journal of Social Psychology, 5,* 49–61.

Bordia, P., & Rosnow, R. L. (1995). Rumor rest stops on the information highway: A naturalistic study of transmission patterns in a computer-mediated rumor chain. *Human Communication Research, 25,* 163–179.

Boring, E. G. (1942). *Sensation and perception in the history of experimental psychology.* New York: Appleton-Century-Crofts.

Boring, E. G. (1954). The nature and history of experimental controls. *American Journal of Psychology, 67,* 573–589.

Boring, E. G. (1957). *A history of experimental psychology* (2nd ed.). New York: Appleton-Century-Crofts.

Boring, E. G. (1969). Perspective: Artifact and control. In R. Rosenthal & R. L. Rosnow (Eds.), *Artifact in behavioral research* (pp. 1–11). New York: Academic Press.

Boruch, R. F. (1997). *Randomized experiments for planning and evaluation: A practical guide.* Thousand Oaks, CA: Sage.

Boruch, R. F., & Cecil, J. S. (1979). *Assuring the confidentiality of social research data.* Philadelphia: University of Pennsylvania Press.

Box, G. E. P., Hunter, W. G., & Hunter, J. S. (1978). *Statistics for experimenters.* New York: Wiley.

Box, G. E. P., & Jenkins, G. M. (1970). *Time-series analysis: Forecasting control.* San Francisco: Holden-Day.

Boyatzis, R. E. (1998). *Transforming qualitative information: Thematic analysis and code development.* Thousand Oaks, CA: Sage.

Bradburn, N. M. (1982). Question-wording effects in surveys. In R. Hogarth (Ed.), *New directions for methodology of social and behavioral science: Question framing and response consistency* (pp. 65–76). San Francisco: Jossey-Bass.

Bradburn, N. M. (1983). Response effects. In P. H. Rossi, J. D. Wright, & A. B. Anderson (Eds.), *Handbook of survey research* (pp. 289–328). New York: Academic Press.

Bradburn, N. M. (2000). Temporal representation and event dating. In A. A. Stone, J. S. Turkkan, C. A. Bachrach, J. B. Jobe, H. S. Kurtzman, & V. S. Cain (Eds.), *The science of self-report: Implications for research and practice* (pp. 49–61). Mahwah, NJ: Erlbaum.

Bradburn, N. M., Rips, L. J., & Shevell, S. K. (1987). Answering autobiographical questions: The impact of memory and inference on surveys. *Science, 236,* 157–161.

Bradley, J. V. (1968). *Distribution-free statistical tests.* Englewood Cliffs, NJ: Prentice Hall.

Brady, J. V. (1958). Ulcers in "executive" monkeys. *Scientific American, 199,* 95–100.

Brady, J. V., Porter, R. W., Conrad, D. G., & Mason, J. W. (1958). Avoidance behavior and the development of gastroduodenal ulcers. *Journal for the Experimental Analysis of Behavior, 1,* 69–72.

Bramel, D., & Friend, R. (1981). Hawthorne, the myth of the docile worker, and class bias in psychology. *American Psychologist, 36,* 867–878.

Braun, H. I., & Wainer, H. (1989). Making essay test scores fairer with statistics. In J. M. Tanur, F. Mosteller, W. H. Kruskal, E. L. Lehmann, R. F. Link, R. S. Pieters, & G. S. Rising (Eds.), *Statistics: A guide to the unknown* (3rd ed., pp. 178–187). Pacific Grove, CA: Wadsworth & Brooks/Cole.

Braver, M. C. W., & Braver, S. L. (1988). Statistical treatment of the Solomon four-group design: A meta-analytic approach. *Psychological Bulletin, 104,* 150–154.

Brehmer, B., & Dörner, D. (1993). Experiments with computer-simulated microworlds: Escaping both the narrow straits of the laboratory and the deep blue sea of the field study. *Computers in Human Behavior, 9,* 171–184.

Bresnahan, J. L., & Shapiro, M. M. (1966). A general equation and technique for the exact partitioning of chi-square contingency tables. *Psychological Bulletin, 66,* 252–262.

Brewer, J. K. (1972). On the power of statistical tests in the *American Educational Research Journal. American Educational Research Journal, 9,* 391–401.

Brewer, M. B., & Collins, B. E. (Eds.). (1981). *Scientific inquiry and the social sciences: A volume in honor of Donald T. Campbell.* San Francisco: Jossey-Bass.

Bridgman, P. W. (1927). *The logic of modern physics.* New York: Macmillan.

Bridgman, P. W. (1945). Some general principles of operational analysis. *Psychological Review, 52,* 246–249.

Bridgstock, M. (1982). A sociological approach to fraud in science. *Australian and New Zealand Journal of Sociology, 18,* 364–383.

Brinberg, D., Lynch, J. G., Jr., & Sawyer, A. G. (1992). Hypothesized and confounded explanations in theory tests: A Bayesian analysis. *Journal of Consumer Research, 19,* 139–154.

Brinton, J. E. (1961). Deriving an attitude scale from semantic differential data. *Public Opinion Quarterly, 25,* 289–295.

Broad, W., & Wade, N. (1982). *Betrayers of the truth.* New York: Simon & Schuster.

Brooks-Gunn, J., & Rotheram-Borus, M. J. (1994). Rights to privacy in research: Adolescents versus parents. *Ethics and Behavior, 4,* 109–121.

Broome, J. (1984). Selecting people randomly. *Ethics, 95,* 38–55.

Brown, R. & Kulik, J. (1977). Flashbulb memories. *Cognition, 5,* 73–99.

Brown, W. (1910). Some experimental results in the correlation of mental abilities. *British Journal of Psychology, 3,* 296–322.

Browne, M. W. (1984). The decomposition of multitrait-multimethod matrices. *British Journal of Mathematical and Statistical Psychology, 37,* 1–21.

Brownlee, K. A. (1955). Statistics of the 1954 Polio vaccine trials. *Journal of the American Statistical Association, 50*(No. 272), 1005–1013.

Brunswik, E. (1947). *Systematic and representative design of psychological experiments.* Berkeley: University of California Press.

Bryk, A. S., & Raudenbush, S. W. (1988). Heterogeneity of variance in experimental studies: A challenge to conventional interpretations. *Psychological Bulletin, 104,* 396–404.

Buckner, H. T. (1965). A theory of rumor transmission. *Public Opinion Quarterly, 29,* 54–70.

Bulgren, W. G. (1971). On representations of the doubly non-central *F* distribution. *Journal of the American Statistical Association, 66,* 184–171.

Bulgren, W. G., & Amos, D. E. (1968). A note on representations of the doubly non-central *t* distribution. *Journal of the American Statistical Association, 63,* 1013–1019.

Bunge, M. (1982). Demarcating science from pseudoscience. *Fundamenta Scientiae, 3,* 369–388.

Bunzl, M. (1993). *The context of explanation.* Dordrecht, Netherlands: Kluwer.

Burnham, J. R. (1966). *Experimenter bias and lesion labeling.* Unpublished manuscript, Purdue University.

Bushman, B. J., & Anderson, C. A. (2001). Media violence and the American public: Scientific facts versus media misinformation. *American Psychologist, 56,* 477–489.

Bushman, B. J., & Cooper, H. M. (1990). Effect of alcohol on human aggression: An integrative research review. *Psychological Bulletin, 107,* 341–354.

Bushman, B. J., & Huesmann, L. R. (2001). Effects of televised violence on aggression. In D. G. Singer & J. L. Singer (Eds.), *Handbook of children and the media* (pp. 223–254). London: Sage.

Buss, A. H. (1971). Aggression pays. In J. L. Singer (Ed.), *The control of aggression and violence.* New York: Academic Press.

Buss, D. M., Haselton, M. G., Shackelford, T. K., Bleske, A. L., & Wakefield, J. C. (1998). Adaptations, exaptations, and spandrels. *American Psychologist, 53,* 533–548.

Cameron, N. W. (1950). Role concepts in behavior pathology. *American Journal of Sociology, 55,* 450–463.

Camilli, G., & Hopkins, K. D. (1978). Applicability of chi-square to 2×2 contingency tables with small expected cell frequencies. *Psychological Bulletin, 85,* 163–167.

Campbell, D. T. (1950). The indirect assessment of attitudes. *Psychological Bulletin, 47,* 15–38.

Campbell, D. T. (1959). Methodological suggestions from a comparative psychology of knowledge process. *Inquiry, 2,* 152–182.

Campbell, D. T. (1963). From description to experimentation: Interpreting trends as quasi-experiments. In C. W. Harris (Ed.), *Problems in measuring change.* Madison: University of Wisconsin Press.

Campbell, D. T. (1988a). The author responds: Popper and selection theory. *Social Epistemology, 2,* 371–377.

Campbell, D. T. (1988b). *Methodology and epistemology of social science: Selected papers.* Chicago: University of Chicago Press.

Campbell, D. T., & Boruch, R. F. (1975). Making the case for randomized assignment to treatments by considering the alternatives: Six ways in which quasi-experimental evaluations in compensatory education tend to underestimate effects. In C. A. Bennett & A. A. Lumsdaine (Eds.), *Evaluation and experiment*. New York: Academic Press.

Campbell, D. T., & Fiske, D. W. (1959). Convergent and discriminant validation by the multitrait-multimethod matrix. *Psychological Bulletin, 56,* 81–105.

Campbell, D. T., & Kenny, D. A. (1999). *A primer on regression artifacts*. New York: Guilford.

Campbell, D. T., & O'Connell, E. J. (1967). Methods factors in multitrait-multimethod matrices: Multiplicative rather than additive? *Multivariate Behavioral Research, 2,* 409–426.

Campbell, D. T., & O'Connell, E. J. (1982). Methods as diluting trait relationships rather than adding irrelevant systematic variance. In D. Brinberg & L. H. Kidder (Eds.), *Forms of validity in research* (pp. 93–111). San Francisco: Jossey-Bass.

Campbell, D. T., & Stanley, J. C. (1963). Experimental and quasi-experimental designs for research on teaching. In N. L. Gage (Ed.), *Handbook of research on teaching* (pp. 171–246). Chicago: Rand McNally.

Campbell, D. T., & Stanley, J. C. (1966). *Experimental and quasi-experimental designs for research*. Chicago: Rand McNally. (Reissued by Houghton Mifflin, Boston.)

Canadian Multicentre Transplant Study Group. (1983). A randomized clinical trial of cyclosporine in cadaveric renal transplantation. *New England Journal of Medicine, 309,* 809–815.

Cannell, C. F., Miller, P. V., & Oksenberg, L. (1981). Research on interviewing techniques. In S. Leinhardt (Ed.), *Sociological methodology* (pp. 389–437). San Francisco, CA: Jossey-Bass.

Cantril, H., & Research Associates. (1944). *Gauging public opinion*. Princeton, NJ: Princeton University Press.

Capaldi, N. (1969). *Human knowledge: A philosophical analysis of its meaning and scope*. New York: Pegasus.

Carmer, S. G., & Swanson, M. R. (1973). An evaluation of ten pairwise multiple comparison procedures by Monte Carlo methods. *Journal of the American Statistical Association, 68,* 66–74.

Carr, K., & England, R. (Eds.). (1995). *Simulated and virtual realities: Elements of perception*. London: Taylor & Francis.

Carroll, J. D., & Chang, J. (1970). Analysis of individual differences in multidimensional scaling via an n-way generalization of Eckhart-Young decomposition. *Psychometrika, 35,* 282–319.

Cassell, J. (1982). Harms, benefits, wrongs, and rights of fieldwork. In J. E. Sieber (Ed.), *The ethics of social research: Fieldwork, regulation, and publication* (Vol. 1, pp. 7–31). New York: Springer-Verlag.

Catania, J. A., Gibson, D. R., Chitwood, D. D., & Coates, T. J. (1990). Methodological problems in AIDS behavioral research: Influences on measurement error and participation bias in studies of sexual behavior. *Psychological Bulletin, 108,* 339–362.

Caws, P. (1969). The structure of discovery. *Science, 166,* 1375–1380.

Ceci, S. J., & Bruck, M. (1995). *Jeopardy in the courtroom: A scientific study of children's testimony*. Washington, DC: American Psychological Association.

Ceci, S. J., & Peters, D. (1984). Letters of reference: A naturalistic study of the effects of confidentiality. *American Psychologist, 39,* 29–31.

Ceci, S. J., Peters, D., & Plotkin, J. (1985). Human subjects review, personal values, and the regulation of social science research. *American Psychologist, 40,* 994–1002.

Centers for Disease Control Vietnam Experience Study. (1988). Health status of Vietnam veterans: 1. Psychosocial characteristics. *Journal of the American Medical Association, 259,* 2701–2707.

Chambers, J. M., Cleveland, W. S., Kleiner, B., & Tukey, P. A. (1983). *Graphical methods for data analysis*. Belmont, CA: Wadsworth.

Chandler, D. L. (1993, February 15). Study finds evidence of ESP phenomenon. *Boston Globe*, pp. 1, 8.

Chandrasekhar, S. (1987). *Truth and beauty: Aesthetics and motivations in science*. Chicago: University of Chicago Press.

Chase, L. J., & Chase, R. B. (1976). A statistical power analysis of applied psychological research. *Journal of Applied Psychology, 61,* 234–237.

Child Abuse Prevention and Treatment and Adoption Reform Act, 42 U.S.C.A. 5101 *et seq.*, Pub. L. No. 102–295 (West 1992).

Church, A. H. (1993). Estimating the effect of incentives on mail survey response rates: A meta-analysis. *Public Opinion Quarterly, 51,* 233–248.

Cichetti, D. V., Showalter, D., & Tyrer, P. J. (1985). The effect of number of rating scales categories on levels of interrater reliability: A Monte Carlo investigation. *Applied Psychological Measurement, 9,* 31–36.

Cicourel, A. V. (1982). Interviews, surveys, and the problem of ecological validity. *American Sociologist, 17,* 11–20.

Clark, R. W. (1971). *Einstein: The life and times.* New York: World.

Cleveland, W. S. (1985). *The elements of graphing data.* Monterey, CA: Wadsworth.

Cleveland, W. S. (1993). *Visualizing data.* Summit, NJ: Hobart.

Cleveland, W. S. (1994). *The elements of graphing data* (Rev. ed.). Summit, NJ: Hobart.

Cleveland, W. S., & McGill, R. (1985). Graphical perception and graphical methods for analyzing scientific data. *Science, 229,* 828–833.

Cochran, W. G. (1937). Problems arising in the analysis of a series of similar experiments. *Journal of the Royal Statistical Society,* Supplement 4(1), 102–118.

Cochran, W. G. (1943). The comparison of different scales of measurement for experimental results. *Annals of Mathematical Statistics, 14,* 205–216.

Cochran, W. G. (1950). The comparison of percentages in matched samples. *Biometrika, 37,* 256–266.

Cochran, W. G. (1963). *Sampling techniques* (2nd ed.). New York: Wiley.

Cochran, W. G. (1968). The effectiveness of adjustment by subclassification in removing bias in observational studies. *Biometrics, 24,* 295–313.

Cochran, W. G., & Cox, G. M. (1957). *Experimental designs* (2nd ed.). New York: Wiley.

Cochran, W. G., Mosteller, F., & Tukey, J. W. (1953). Statistical problems of the Kinsey report. *Journal of the American Statistical Association, 48,* 673–716.

Cohen, J. (1960). A coefficient of agreement for nominal scales. *Educational and Psychological Measurement, 20,* 37–46.

Cohen, J. (1962). The statistical power of abnormal-social psychological research: A review. *Journal of Abnormal and Social Psychology, 65,* 145–153.

Cohen, J. (1965). Some statistical issues in psychological research. In B. B. Wolman (Ed.), *Handbook of clinical psychology* (pp. 95–121). New York; McGraw-Hill.

Cohen, J. (1969). *Statistical power analysis for the behavioral sciences.* New York: Academic Press.

Cohen, J. (1973). Statistical power analysis and research results. *American Educational Research Journal, 10,* 225–229.

Cohen, J. (1982). Set correlation as a general multivariate data-analytic method. *Multivariate Behavioral Research, 17,* 301–341.

Cohen, J. (1988). *Statistical power analysis for the behavioral sciences* (2nd ed.). Hillsdale, NJ: Erlbaum.

Cohen, J. (1990). Things I have learned (so far). *American Psychologist, 45,* 1304–1312.

Cohen, J. (1994). The earth is round ($p < .05$). *American Psychologist, 49,* 997–1003.

Cohen, J., & Cohen, P. (1983). *Applied multiple regression/correlation analysis for the behavioral sciences* (2nd ed.). Hillsdale, NJ: Erlbaum.

Cohen, J., Cohen, P., West, S. G., & Aiken, L. S. (2003). *Applied multiple regression/correlation analysis for the behavioral sciences* (3rd ed.). Mahwah, NJ: Erlbaum.

Cohen, Jon. (1993). A new goal: Preventing disease, not infection. *Science, 262,* 1820–1821.

Cohen, Jon. (1996). Results on new AIDS drugs bring cautious optimism. *Science, 271,* 755–756.

Cohen, M. R. (1978). *Reason and nature: An essay on the meaning of scientific method.* New York: Dover. (Original work published 1931)

Cole, S. (1992). *Making science: Between nature and society.* Cambridge, MA: Harvard University Press.

Collins, L. M., Schafer, J. L., & Kam, C.-M. (2001). A comparison of inclusive and restrictive strategies in modern missing data procedures. *Psychological Methods, 6,* 330–351.

Comrey, A. L., & Lee, H. B. (1992). *A first course in factor analysis* (2nd ed.). Hillsdale, NJ: Erlbaum.

Conant, J. B. (1957). Introduction. In J. B. Conant and L. K. Nash (Eds.), *Harvard case studies in experimental science* (Vol. 1, pp. xx–xvi). Cambridge, MA: Harvard University Press.

Conover, W. J. (1974). Some reasons for not using the Yates continuity correction on 2×2 contingency tables. *Journal of the American Statistical Association, 69,* 374–376.

Conover, W. J. (1980). *Practical nonparametric statistics* (2nd ed.). New York: Wiley.

Conover, W. J. (1999). *Practical nonparametric statistics* (3rd ed.). New York: Wiley.

Conrad, F. G., & Schober, M. F. (2000). Clarifying question meaning in a household telephone survey. *Public Opinion Quarterly, 64,* 1–28.

Conrath, D. W. (1973). Communications environment and its relationship to organizational structure. *Management Science, 20,* 586–603.

Conrath, D. W., Higgins, C. A., & McClean, R. J. (1983). A comparison of the reliability of questionnaire versus diary data. *Social Networks, 5,* 315–322.

Converse, J. M., & Presser, S. (1986). *Survey questions: Handcrafting the standardized questionnaire.* Beverly Hills, CA: Sage.

Conway, III, L. G., & Schaller, M. (2002). On the verifiability of evolutionary psychological theories: An analysis of the psychology of scientific persuasion. *Personality and Social Psychology Review, 6,* 152–166.

Cook, N. R., & Ware, J. H. (1983). Design and analysis methods for longitudinal research. *Annual Review of Public Health, 4,* 1–23.

Cook, S. W., Hicks, L. H., Kimble, G. A., McGuire, W. J., Schoggen, P. H., & Smith, M. B. (1972, May). Ethical standards for research with human subjects. *APA Monitor,* I–XIX.

Cook, S. W., Kimble, G. A., Hicks, L. H., McGuire, W. J., Schoggen, P. H., & Smith, M. B. (1971, July). Ethical standards for psychological research: Proposed ethical principles submitted to the APA membership for criticism and modification (by the) ad hoc Committee on Ethical Standards in Psychological Research. *APA Monitor,* 9–28.

Cook, T. D., & Campbell, D. T. (1979). *Quasi-experimentation: Design and analysis issues for field settings.* Chicago: Rand McNally.

Cooley, W. W., & Lohnes, P. R. (1985). *Multivariate data analysis.* Malabar, FL: Krieger.

Coombs, C. H., Dawes, R. M., & Tversky, A. (1970). *Mathematical psychology: An elementary introduction.* Englewood Cliffs, NJ: Prentice Hall.

Cooper, H. (1989). *Integrating research: A guide for literature reviews* (2nd ed.). Newbury Park, CA: Sage.

Cooper, H. (1998). *Synthesizing research* (3rd ed.). Thousand Oaks, CA: Sage.

Cooper, H., & Hedges, L. V. (Eds.). (1994). *The handbook of research synthesis.* New York: Russell Sage Foundation.

Cooper, H., & Rosenthal, R. (1980). Statistical versus traditional procedures for summarizing research findings. *Psychological Bulletin, 87,* 442–449.

Cooper, W. H. (1981). Ubiquitous halo. *Psychological Bulletin, 90,* 218–244.

Corrozi, J. F., & Rosnow, R. L. (1968). Consonant and dissonant communications as positive and negative reinforcements in opinion change. *Journal of Personality and Social Psychology, 8,* 27–30.

Cotter, P. R., Cohen, J., & Coulter, P. B. (1982). Race-of-interviewer effects in telephone interviews. *Public Opinion Quarterly, 46,* 278–284.

Couch, A., & Keniston, K. (1960). Yeasayers and naysayers: Agreeing response set as a personality variable. *Journal of Abnormal and Social Psychology, 60,* 151–174.

Cox, D. R. (1957). The use of a concomitant variable in selecting an experimental design. *Biometrika, 44,* 150–158.

Crabb, P. B., & Bielawski, D. (1994). The social representation of maternal culture and gender in children's books. *Sex Roles, 30,* 69–79.

Crabb, P. B., & Rosnow, R. L. (1988). What is aggressive? Some contextual factors in judging international behavior. *Aggressive Behavior, 14,* 105–112.

Cromie, W. J. (1990, October 5). Report: Drugs affect lung cancer survival. *Harvard Gazette,* pp. 1, 10.

Cromie, W. J. (1991, September 13). Study: Hospitalization recommended for problem drinkers. *Harvard Gazette,* pp. 3–4.

Cromie, W. J. (1996, February 29). No major hazard found for breast implants. *Harvard Gazette,* pp. 1, 6.

Cronbach, L. J. (1951). Coefficient alpha and the internal consistency of tests. *Psychometrika, 16,* 297–334.

Cronbach, L. J. (1960). *Essentials of psychological testing* (2nd ed.). New York: Harper.

Cronbach, L. J., & Meehl, P. E. (1955). Construct validity in psychological tests. *Psychological Bulletin, 52,* 281–302.

Cronbach, L. J., & Quirk, T. J. (1971). Test validity. In L. C. Deighton (Ed.), *Encyclopedia of education* (Vol. 9, pp. 165–175). New York: Macmillan and Free Press.

Crosby, F., Bromley, S., & Saxe, L. (1980). Recent unobtrusive studies of black and white discrimination and prejudice: A literature review. *Psychological Bulletin, 87,* 546–563.

Crowne, D. P. (1979). *The experimental study of personality.* Hillsdale, NJ: Erlbaum.

Crowne, D. P. (2000). Social desirability. In A. E. Kazdin (Ed.), *Encyclopedia of psychology.* New York: American Psychological Association and Oxford University Press.

Crowne, D. P., & Marlowe, D. (1964). *The approval motive: Studies in evaluative dependence.* New York: Wiley.

Csikszentmihalyi, M., & Larson, R. (1984). *Being adolescent: Conflict and growth in the teenage years.* New York: Basic Books.

Czarniawska, B. (1997). *Narrating the organization: Dramas of institutional identity.* Chicago: University of Chicago Press.

Czarniawska, B. (1998). *A narrative approach to organization studies.* Thousand Oaks, CA: Sage.

Czarniawska, B. (1999). *Writing management: Organization theory as a literary genre.* Oxford, UK: Oxford University Press.

Dabbs, J. M., Jr., & Morris, R. (1990). Testosterone, social class, and antisocial behavior in a sample of 4,462 men. *Psychological Science, 1,* 209–211.

D'Agostino, R. B. (1971). A second look at analysis of variance on dichotomous data. *Journal of Educational Measurement, 8,* 327–333.

Danziger, K. (1985). The methodological imperative in psychology. *Philosophy of the Social Sciences, 15,* 1–13.

Danziger, K. (1988). A question of identity: Who participated in psychological experiments? In J. Morawski (Ed.), *The rise of experimentation in American psychology* (pp. 35–52). New Haven, CT: Yale University Press.

Davison, A. C., & Hinkley, D. V. (1999). *Bootstrap methods and their application.* Cambridge, UK: Cambridge University Press.

Davison, G. C. (2000). Case study. In A. E. Kazdin (Ed.), *Encyclopedia of psychology.* New York: American Psychological Association and Oxford University Press.

Davison, G. C., & Lazarus, A. A. (1995). The dialectics of science and practice. In S. C. Hayes, V. M. Follette, T. Risley, R. D. Dawes, & K. Grady (Eds.), *Scientific standards of psychological practice: Issues and recommendations* (pp. 95–120). Reno, NV: Context Press.

Dawes, R. M. (1969). "Interaction effects" in the presence of asymmetrical transfer. *Psychological Bulletin, 71,* 55–57.

Dawes, R. M., & Corrigan, B. (1974). Linear models in decision making. *Psychological Bulletin, 81,* 95–106.

Dawson, B., & Trapp, R. G. (2004). *Basic and clinical biostatistics* (4th ed.). New York: Lange/McGraw-Hill.

Dean, C. (1977). Are serendipitous discoveries a part of normal science? The case of the pulsars. *Sociological Review, 25,* 73–86.

Dehue, T. (2000). From deception trials to control reagents: The introduction of the control group about a century ago. *American Psychologist, 55,* 264–268.

de Jong-Gierveld, J., & Kamphuis, F. (1985). The development of a Rasch-type loneliness scale. *Applied Psychological Measurement, 9,* 289–299.

Delgado, J. M. R. (1963). Cerebral heterostimulation in a monkey colony. *Science, 141,* 161–163.

Delgado, R., & Leskovac, H. (1986). Informed consent in human experimentation: Bridging the gap between ethical thought and current practice. *UCLA Law Review, 34,* 67–130.

Dempster, A. P., Laird, N. M., & Rubin, D. B. (1977). Maximum likelihood from incomplete data via the EM algorithm. *Journal of the Royal Statistical Society, Series B, 39,* 1–38.

Dennenberg, V. H. (2002, May). Placebo effect? *APA Monitor on Psychology,* p. 8.

Denzin, N. K., & Lincoln, Y. S. (Eds.). (1994). *Handbook of qualitative research.* Beverly Hills, CA: Sage.

Department of Health and Human Services. (1983). Protection of human subjects. *Code of Federal Regulations, 45,* Section 46–115.

Department of Health, Education, and Welfare. (1978). Protection of human subjects; institutional review board; report and recommendations of National Commission for the Protection of

Human Subjects of Biomedical and Behavioral Research. *Federal Register, 43,* 56174–56198.

DePaulo, B. M., & Kashy, D. A. (1998). Everyday lies in close and casual relationships. *Journal of Personality and Social Psychology, 74,* 63–79.

DePaulo, B. M., Kashy, D. A., Kirkendol, S. E., Wyer, M. M., & Epstein, J. A. (1996). Lying in everyday life. *Journal of Personality and Social Psychology, 70,* 979–995.

DePaulo, B. M., & Rosenthal, R. (1979a). Age changes in nonverbal decoding skills: Evidence for increasing differentiation. *Merrill-Palmer Quarterly, 25,* 145–150.

DePaulo, B. M., & Rosenthal, R. (1979b). Ambivalence, discrepancy, and deception in nonverbal communication. In R. Rosenthal (Ed.), *Skill in nonverbal communication* (pp. 204–248). Cambridge, MA: Oelgeschlager, Gunn & Hain.

DePaulo, B. M., & Rosenthal, R. (1979c). Telling lies. *Journal of Personality and Social Psychology, 37,* 1713–1722.

DePaulo, B. M., & Rosenthal, R. (1982). Measuring the development of sensitivity to nonverbal communication. In C. E. Izard (Ed.), *Measuring emotions in infants and children* (pp. 208–247). New York: Cambridge University Press.

DeVault, M. L. (1999). *Liberating method: Feminism and social research.* Philadelphia: Temple University Press.

DeVore, I., & Hall, K. R. L. (1965). Baboon ecology. In I. DeVore (Ed.), *Primate behavior* (pp. 20–52). New York: Holt.

Devore, I., & Washburn, S. L. (1963). Baboon ecology and human evolution. In F. C. Howell & F. Bourliere (Eds.), *African ecology and human evolution* (pp. 335–367). New York: Viking Fund.

de Waal, F. B. M. (2002). Evolutionary psychology: The wheat and the chaff. *General Directions in Psychological Science, 11,* 187–191.

Dickersin, K. (1994). Research registers. In H. Cooper & L. V. Hedges (Eds.), *The handbook of research synthesis* (pp. 71–83). New York: Russell Sage Foundation.

Diener, E., & Crandall, R. (1978). *Ethics in social and behavioral research.* Chicago: University of Chicago Press.

DiFonzo, N., Bordia, P., & Rosnow, R. L. (1994). Reining in rumors. *Organizational Dynamics, 23,* 47–62.

DiFonzo, N., Hantula, D. A., & Bordia, P. (1998). Microworlds for experimental research: Having your (control and collection) cake, and realism too. *Behavior Research Methods, Instruments, & Computers, 30,* 278–286.

Diggle, P. J. (1990). *Time series: A biostatistical introduction.* Oxford, UK: Oxford University Press.

Dillman, D. A., Singer, E., Clark, J. R., & Treat, J. B. (1996). Effects of benefits appeals, mandatory appeals, and variations in statements of confidentiality on completion rates for census questionnaires. *Public Opinion Quarterly, 60,* 376–389.

DiNitto, D. (1983). Time-series analysis: An application to social welfare policy. *Journal of Applied Behavioral Science, 19,* 507–518.

Director, S. M. (1979). Underadjustment bias in the evaluation of manpower training. *Evaluation Quarterly, 3,* 190–218.

Dissanayake, E. (1995). *Homo aestheticus: Where art comes from and why.* Seattle: University of Washington Press.

Doan, R. K. (1968, March 28). WFIL telephone poll spreads nation-wide. *Philadelphia Inquirer,* p. 22.

Dohrenwend, B. S. (1965). Some effects of open and closed questions on respondents' answers. *Human Organization, 24,* 175–184.

Dohrenwend, B. S., & Dohrenwend, B. P. (1968). Sources of refusals in surveys. *Public Opinion Quarterly, 32,* 74–83.

Dollard, J. (1953, September 13). The Kinsey report on women: "A strangely flawed masterpiece." *New York Herald Tribune,* Section 6, p. 3.

Domjan, M., & Purdy, J. E. (1995). Animal research in psychology: More than meets the eye of the general psychology student. *American Psychologist, 50,* 496–503.

Dorn, L. D., Susman, E. J., & Fletcher, J. C. (1995). Informed consent in children and adolescents: Age, maturation, and psychological state. *Journal of Adolescent Health, 16,* 185–190.

Downs, C. W., Smeyak, G. P., & Martin, E. (1980). *Professional interviewing.* New York: Harper & Row.

Doyle, A. C. (1967). *The annotated Sherlock Holmes: Vol. 1. The four novels and the fifty-six short stories complete* (W. S. Baring-Gould, Ed.). NY: Clarkson N. Potter.

Dudewicz, E. J. (1992). The generalized bootstrap. In K. H. Jöckel, G. Rothe, & W. Sendler (Eds.), *Bootstrapping and related techniques* (pp. 31–37). Berlin: Springer-Verlag.

Duhem, P. (1954). *The aim and structure of physical theory*. Princeton, NJ: Princeton University Press.

Dunning, D., Heath, C., & Suls, J. M. (2004). Flawed self-assessment: Implications for health, education, and the workplace. *Psychological Science in the Public Interest, 5(3),* 69–106.

Eagly, A. H. (1978). Sex differences in influenceability. *Psychological Bulletin, 85,* 86–116.

Eagly, A. H., & Chaiken, S. (1993). *The psychology of attitudes*. Fort Worth, TX: Harcourt Brace Jovanovich.

Eagly, A. H., & Chaiken, S. (1998). Attitude structure and function. In D. T. Gilbert, S. T. Fiske, & G. Lindzey (Eds.), *The handbook of social psychology* (4th ed., Vol. I, pp. 269–322). Boston: McGraw-Hill.

Easley, J. A. (1971). Scientific method as an educational objective. In L. C. Deighton (Ed.), *The encyclopedia of education* (Vol. 8, pp. 150–157). New York: Free Press and Macmillan.

Easley, J. A., & Tatsuoka, M. M. (1968). *Scientific thought: Cases from classical physics*. Boston: Allyn & Bacon.

Ebbinghaus, H. (1885). *Über das Gedächtnis: Untersuchungen zur experimentellen Psychologie*. Leipzig, Germany: Duncker & Humblot.

Ebbinghaus, H. (1913). *Memory: A contribution to experimental psychology* (H. A. Ruger & C. E. Bussenius, trans.). New York: Columbia University Teachers College.

Eckler, A. R., & Hurwitz, W. N. (1958). Response variance and biases in censuses and surveys. *Bulletin de L'Institut International de Statistique, 36,* 12–35.

Edmonds, D., & Eidinow, J. (2001). *Wittgenstein's poker: The story of a ten-minute argument between two great philosophers*. New York: HarperCollins.

Edwards, A. L. (1952). The scaling of stimuli by the method of successive intervals. *Journal of Applied Psychology, 36,* 118–122.

Edwards, A. L. (1957a). *The social desirability variable in personality assessment and research*. New York: Dryden.

Edwards, A. L. (1957b). *Techniques of attitude scale construction*. New York: Appleton-Century-Crofts.

Edwards, A. L. (1964). *Statistical methods for the behavioral sciences*. New York: Holt, Rinehart & Winston.

Edwards, A. L. (1972). *Experimental design in psychological research* (4th ed.). New York: Holt.

Edwards, A. L. (1985). *Experimental design in psychological research* (5th ed.). New York: Harper & Row.

Efron, B. (1979). Bootstrap methods: Another look at the jackknife. *Annals of Statistics, 7,* 1–26.

Efron, B. (1982). *The jackknife, the bootstrap and other resampling plans*. Philadelphia: Society for Industrial and Applied Mathematics.

Efron, B., & Tibshirani, R. J. (1993). *An introduction to the bootstrap*. New York: Chapman & Hall.

Einstein, A. (1934). *Essays in science*. New York: Philosophical Library.

Einstein, A., & Infeld, L. (1938). *The evolution of physics: The growth of ideas from early concepts to relativity and quanta*. New York: Simon & Schuster.

Eisenhart, C. Hastay, M. W., & Wallis, W. A. (Eds.). (1947). *Techniques of statistical analysis*. New York: McGraw-Hill.

Ekman, P. (1973). Cross-cultural studies of facial expression. In P. Ekman (Ed.), *Darwin and facial expression: A century of research in review*. New York: Academic Press.

Elder, G. H., Jr., Pavalko, E. K., & Clipp, E. C. (1993). *Working with archival data: Studying lives*. Newbury Park, CA: Sage.

Elgie, D. M., Hollander, E. P., & Rice, R. W. (1988). Appointed and elected leader responses to favorableness of feedback and level of task activity from followers. *Journal of Applied Social Psychology, 18,* 1361–1370.

Elms, A. C. (1994). *Uncovering lives: The uneasy alliance of biography and psychology*. New York: Oxford University Press.

Emerson, J. D., & Hoaglin, D. C. (1983). Stem-and-leaf displays. In D. C. Hoaglin, F. Mosteller, & J. W. Tukey (Eds.), *Understanding robust and exploratory data analysis* (pp. 7–32). New York: Wiley.

Enders, C. K. (2001). The impact of nonnormality on full information maximum-likelihood estimation for structural equation models with missing data. *Psychological Methods, 6,* 352–370.

Entwisle, D. R. (1961). Interactive effects of pretesting. *Educational and Psychological Measurement, 21,* 607–620.

Eron, L. D. (1963). Relationship of television viewing habits and aggressive behavior in children. *Journal of Abnormal and Social Psychology, 67,* 193–196.

Eron, L. D., & Huesmann, L. R. (1980). Sohn should let sleeping dogs lie. *American Psychologist, 36,* 231–233.

Eron, L. D., Huesmann, L. R., Lefkowitz, M. M., & Walder, L. O. (1972). Does television violence cause aggression? *American Psychologist, 27,* 253–263.

Eron, L. D., Walder, L. O., & Lefkowitz, M. M. (1971). *Learning of aggression in children.* Boston: Little, Brown.

Esposito, J. L., Agard, E., & Rosnow, R. L. (1984). Can confidentiality of data pay off? *Personality and Individual Differences, 5,* 477–480.

Esposito, J. L., Rothgeb, J., Polivka, A. E., Hess, J., & Campanelli, P. C. (1992, June). *Methodologies for evaluating survey questions: Some lessons from the redesign of the current population survey.* Paper presented at the International Conference on Social Science Methodology, Trento, Italy.

Estes, W. K. (1991). *Statistical models in behavioral research.* Hillsdale, NJ: Erlbaum.

Estes, W. K. (1997). On the communication of information by displays of standard errors and confidence intervals. *Psychonomic Bulletin and Review, 4,* 330–341.

Evans, I. H. (Ed.). (1993). *The Wordsworth dictionary of phrase and fable.* London: Wordsworth Editions.

Everitt, B. S. (1977). *The analysis of contingency tables.* New York: Wiley.

Everitt, B. S. (1992). *The analysis of contingency tables* (2nd ed.). New York: Chapman & Hall.

Ewart, C. K., Jorgensen, R. S., Suchday, S., Chen, E., & Matthews, K. A. (2002). Measuring stress resilience and coping in vulnerable youth: The social competence interview. *Psychological Assessment, 14,* 339–352.

Ewart, C. K., & Kolodner, K. B. (1991). Social competence interview for assessing physiological reactivity in adolescents. *Psychosomatic Medicine, 53,* 289–304.

Fairchild, A. L., & Bayer, R. (1999). Uses and abuses of Tuskegee. *Science, 284,* 919–921.

Falbo, T. (1977). Multidimensional scaling of power strategies. *Journal of Personality and Social Psychology, 35,* 537–547.

Farr, R. M. (1978). On the social significance of artifacts in experimenting. *British Journal of Social and Clinical Psychology, 17,* 299–306.

Feingold, A. (1994). Gender differences in personality: A meta-analysis. *Psychological Bulletin, 116,* 429–456.

Feldman, R. E. (1968). Response to compatriot and foreigner who seek assistance. *Journal of Personality and Social Psychology, 10,* 202–214.

Festinger, L. (1957). *A theory of cognitive dissonance.* Evanston, IL: Row, Peterson.

Festinger, L., Pepitone, A., & Newcomb, T. (1952). Some consequences of de-individuation in a group. *Journal of Personality and Social Psychology, 4,* 382–389.

Feyerabend, P. (1988). *Against method* (Rev. ed.). London: Verso.

Feynman, R. P. (1989). *"What do you care what other people think?" Further adventures of a curious character.* New York: Bantam Books.

Feynman, R. P. (1999). *The pleasure of finding things out.* Cambridge, MA: Perseus.

Fidler, D. S., & Kleinknecht, R. E. (1977). Randomized response versus direct questioning: Two data-collection methods for sensitive information. *Psychological Bulletin, 84,* 1045–1049.

Fidler, F., Thomason, N., Cumming, G., Finch, S., & Leeman, J. (2004). Editors can lead researchers to confidence intervals, but can't make them think: Statistical reform lessons from medicine. *Psychological Science, 15,* 119–126.

Fiedler, K. (2000). Illusory correlations: A simple associative algorithm provides a convergent account of seemingly divergent paradigms. *Review of General Psychology, 4,* 25–58.

Fielding, N. G., & Lee, R. M. (1998). *Computer analysis and qualitative research.* Thousand Oaks, CA: Sage.

Fienberg, S. E. (1977). *The analysis of cross-classified categorical data.* Cambridge, MA: MIT Press.

Figlio, R. M. (1978). *The national survey of crime severity: Result of the pretest.* Monograph, Department of Criminology, University of Pennsylvania.

Fine, G. A., & Deegan, J. G. (1996). Three principles of Serendip: Insight, chance, and discovery in qualitative research. *Qualitative Studies in Education, 9,* 434–447.

Fine, G. A., & Elsbach, K. D. (2000). Ethnography and experiment in social psychological theory building: Tactics for integrating qualitative field data with quantitative lab data. *Journal of Experimental Social Psychology, 36,* 51–76.

Fine, G. A., & Turner, P. A. (2001). *Whispers on the color line: Rumor and race in America.* Berkeley: University of California Press.

Fishbein, M. (1963). An investigation of the relationship between beliefs about an object and the attitude toward that object. *Human Relations, 16,* 233–240.

Fishbein, M., & Azjen, I. (1974). Attitudes toward objects as predictors of single and multiple behavioral criteria. *Psychological Review, 81,* 59–74.

Fishbein, M., & Azjen, I. (1975). *Belief, attitude, intention and behavior: An introduction to theory and research.* Reading, MA: Addison-Wesley.

Fisher, C. B. (1994). Reporting and referring research participants: Ethical challenges for investigators studying children and youths. *Ethics and Behavior, 4,* 87–95.

Fisher, C. B., & Fyrberg, D. (1994). Participant partners: College students weigh the costs and benefits of deceptive research. *American Psychologist, 49,* 417–427.

Fisher, C. B., & Tryon, W. W. (Eds.). (1990). *Ethics in applied developmental psychology: Emerging issues in an emerging field.* Norwood, NJ: Ablex.

Fisher, R. A. (1925). *Statistical methods for research workers.* Edinburgh: Oliver & Boyd.

Fisher, R. A. (1935). *The design of experiments.* Reprinted in J. H. Bennett (Ed.), *Fisher's statistical methods, experimental design, and statistical inference.* (1991). Oxford, UK: Oxford University Press.

Fisher, R. A. (1936). Has Mendel's work been rediscovered? *Annals of Science, 1,* 115–137.

Fisher, R. A. (1971). *The design of experiments* (8th ed.). Oxford: Oxford University Press.

Fisher, R. A. (1973a). *Statistical methods and scientific inference* (3rd. ed.). New York: Hafner.

Fisher, R. A. (1973b). *Statistical methods for research workers* (14th ed.). New York: Hafner.

Fisher, R. A. (1979). *The design of experiments* (7th ed.). New York: Hafner.

Fisher, R. A. (1990). *Statistical methods, experimental design, and scientific inference* (Reissue of *Statistical methods for research workers, The design of experiments,* and *Statistical methods and scientific inference*). Oxford, UK: Oxford University Press.

Fiske, D. W. (1978). The several kinds of generalization. *Behavioral and Brain Sciences, 3,* 393–394.

Fiske, D. W. (1982). Convergent-discriminant validation in measurements and research strategies. In D. Brinberg & L. H. Kidder (Eds.), *Forms of validity in research* (pp. 77–92). San Francisco: Jossey-Bass.

Fiske, D. W. (2000). Research methods: Concepts and practices. In A. E. Kazdin (Ed.), *Encyclopedia of psychology.* New York: American Psychological Association and Oxford University Press.

Flacks, R. (1967). The liberated generation: An exploration of the roots of social protest. *Journal of Social Issues, 23,* 52–75.

Flanagan, J. C. (1954). The critical incident technique. *Psychological Bulletin, 51,* 327–358.

Fleiss, J. L., Levin, B., & Paik, M. C. (2003). *Statistical methods for rates and proportions* (3rd ed.). Hoboken, NJ: Wiley.

Foa, U. G. (1963). A facet approach to the prediction of communalities. *Behavioral Science, 8,* 220–226.

Foa, U. G. (1965). New developments in facet design and analysis. *Psychological Review, 72,* 262–274.

Foa, U. G. (1968). Three kinds of behavioral changes. *Psychological Bulletin, 70,* 460–473.

Foa, U. G. (1971). Interpersonal and economic resources. *Science, 171,* 345–351.

Foreman, J. (1995, July 27). Medical notebook: A new confirmation for a pregnancy drug. *Boston Globe,* Section: National/Foreign, p. 3.

Forsyth, D. R. (1980). A taxonomy of ethical ideologies. *Journal of Personality and Social Psychology, 39,* 175–184.

Forsyth, D. R., & Pope, W. R. (1984). Ethical ideology and judgments of social psychological research: Multidimensional analysis. *Journal of Personality and Social Psychology, 46,* 1365–1375.

Foster, E. K. (2003). METASTATS: Behavioral science statistics for Microsoft Windows and the HP49G programmable calculator. *Behavior Research Methods, Instruments, & Computers, 35,* 325–328.

Fowler, F. J., Jr. (1993). *Survey research methods* (2nd ed.). Newbury Park, CA: Sage.

Fowler, F. J., Jr. (2000). Survey methodology. In A. E. Kazdin (Ed.), *Encyclopedia of psychology.* New York: American Psychological Association and Oxford University Press.

Fowler, W. S. (1962). *The development of scientific method.* Oxford, UK: Pergamon.

Francis, T., Jr., Korns, R. F., Voight, R. B., Boisen, M., Hemphill, F., Napier, J., & Tolchinsky, E. (1955). An evaluation of the 1954 poliomyelitis vaccine trials—Summary report. *American Journal of Public Health, 45* (5), 1–63.

Franke, R. H., & Kaul, J. D. (1978). The Hawthorne experiments: First statistical interpretation. *American Sociological Review, 43,* 623–643.

Fraser, D. A. S. (1957). *Nonparametric methods in statistics.* New York: Wiley.

Frasure-Smith, N., Lesperance, F., Juneau, M., Talajic, M., & Bourassa, M. G. (1999). Gender, depression, and one-year prognosis after myocardial infarction. *Psychosomatic Medicine, 61*(1), 26–37.

Freedman, D., Pisani, R., Purves, R., & Adhikari, A. (1991). *Statistics* (2nd ed.). New York: W. W. Norton.

Freedman, D. A. (1987a). As others see us: A case study in path analysis. *Journal of Educational Statistics, 12,* 101–129.

Freedman, D. A. (1987b). A rejoinder on models, metaphors, and fables. *Journal of Educational Statistics, 12,* 206–223.

Freedman, D. A. (1997). From association to causation via regression. In V. R. McKim & S. P. Turner (Eds.), *Causality in crisis? Statistical methods and the search for causal knowledge in the social sciences* (pp. 113–161). Notre Dame, IN: University of Notre Dame Press.

French, J. R. P. (1953). Experiments in field settings. In L. Festinger and D. Katz (Eds.), *Research methods in the behavioral sciences* (pp. 98–135). New York: Holt.

Frey, J. H. (1986). An experiment with a confidentiality reminder in a telephone survey. *Public Opinion Quarterly, 50,* 267–269.

Friedman, C. J., & Gladden, J. W. (1964). Objective measurement of social role concept via the semantic differential. *Psychological Reports, 14,* 239–247.

Friedman, H. S., Tucker, J. S., Schwartz, J. E., Tomlinson-Keasey, C., Martin, L. R., Wingard, D. L., & Criqui, M. H. (1995). Psychosocial and behavioral predictors of longevity: The aging and death of the "Termites." *American Psychologist, 50,* 69–78.

Funder, D. C., & Dobroth, K. M. (1987). Differences between traits: Properties associated with interjudge agreement. *Journal of Personality and Social Psychology, 52,* 409–418.

Funder, D. C., Furr, R. M., & Colvin, C. R. (2000). The Riverside Behavioral Q-sort: A tool for the description of social behavior. *Journal of Personality, 68,* 451–489.

Fung, S. S. K., Kipnis, D., & Rosnow, R. L. (1987). Synthetic benevolence and malevolence as strategies of relational compliance-gaining. *Journal of Social and Personal Relationships, 4,* 129–141.

Funke, J. (1991). Dealing with dynamic systems: Research strategy, diagnostic approach and experimental results. *German Journal of Psychology, 16,* 24–43.

Furr, R. M., & Rosenthal, R. (2003a). Evaluating theories efficiently: The nuts and bolts of contrast analysis. *Understanding Statistics: Statistical Issues in Psychology, Education, and the Social Sciences, 2,* 45–67.

Furr, R. M., & Rosenthal, R. (2003b). Repeated measures for "multiple patterns" hypotheses. *Psychological Methods, 8,* 275–293.

Gahan, C., & Hannibal, M. (1998). *Doing qualitative research using QSR NUD.IST.* Thousand Oaks, CA: Sage.

Galton, F. (1869). *Hereditary genius: An inquiry into its laws and consequences.* London: Macmillan.

Galtung, J. (1972). A structural theory of aggression. In I. K. Feierabend, R. L. Feierabend, & T. R. Gurr (Eds.), *Anger, violence, and politics* (pp. 85–97). Englewood Cliffs, NJ: Prentice Hall.

Gardner, G. T. (1978). Effects of federal human subject regulations on data obtained in environmental stressor research. *Journal of Personality and Social Psychology, 36,* 628–634.

Gardner, H. (1983). *Frames of mind: The theory of multiple intelligences.* New York: Basic Books.

Gardner, H. (1985). *Frames of mind: The theory of multiple intelligences.* New York: Basic Books.

Gardner, M. (1957). *Fads and fallacies in the name of science.* New York: Dover.

Garfield, E. (1989a). Art and science: 1. The art-science connection. *Current Contents, 21*(8), 3–8.

Garfield, E. (1989b). Art and science: 2. Science for art's sake. *Current Contents, 21*(9), 3–8.

Garner, W. R., Hake, H. W., & Erikson, C. W. (1956). Operationism and the concept of perception. *Psychological Review, 63,* 149–159.

Gauld, A., & Shotter, J. (1977). *Human action and its psychological investigation.* London: Routledge & Kegan Paul.

Gazzaniga, M. S., & LeDoux, J. E. (1978). *The integrated mind.* New York: Plenum Press.

Geddes, D. P. (Ed.). (1954). *An analysis of the Kinsey reports.* New York: New American Library.

Gelman, A., Carlin, J. B., Stern, H. S., & Rubin, D. B. (1995). *Bayesian data analysis.* London: Chapman & Hall.

Gentner, D., Holyoak, K. J., & Kokinov, B. N. (Eds.). (2001). *The analogical mind: Perspectives from cognitive science.* Cambridge, MA: MIT Press.

Gentner, D., & Markman, A. B. (1997). Structure mapping in analogy and similarity. *American Psychologist, 52,* 45–56.

Georgoudi, M., & Rosnow, R. L. (1985a). Notes toward a contextualist understanding of social psychology. *Personality and Social Psychology Bulletin, 11,* 5–22.

Georgoudi, M. & Rosnow, R. L. (1985b). The emergence of contextualism. *Journal of Communication, 35,* 76–88.

Gergen, K. J. (1973a). Codification of research ethics: Views of a doubting Thomas. *American Psychologist, 28,* 907–912.

Gergen, K. J. (1973b). Social psychology as history. *Journal of Personality and Social Psychology, 26,* 309–320.

Gergen, K. J. (1977). Stability, change, and chance in understanding human development. In N. Datan & H. Reese (Eds.), *Advances in life-span development* (Vol. 4). New York: Academic Press.

Gergen, K. J. (1978). Experimentation in social psychology. *European Journal of Social Psychology, 8,* 507–527.

Gergen, K. J. (1982). *Toward transformation in social knowledge.* New York: Springer-Verlag.

Gergen, K. J. (1985). The social constructionist movement in modern psychology. *American Psychologist, 40,* 266–275.

Gergen, K. J. (1995). *Realities and relationships: Soundings in social construction.* Cambridge, MA: Harvard University Press.

Gersick, C. J. (1989). Marking time: Predictable transitions in task groups. *Academy of Management Journal, 32,* 274–309.

Gersick, C. J. (1991). Revolutionary change theories: A multilevel exploration of the punctuated equilibrium paradigm. *Academy of Management Review, 16,* 20–36.

Giannelli, M. A. (1986). Three blind mice, see how they run: A critique of behavioral research with animals. In M. W. Fox & L. D. Mickley (Eds.), *Advances in animal welfare science 1985* (pp. 109–163). Boston: Martinus Nijhoff.

Gibbons, J. D. (1985). *Nonparametric statistical inference* (2nd ed.). New York: Marcel Dekker.

Gibbons, J. D., & Chakraborti, S. (2003). *Nonparametric statistical inference* (4th ed.). New York: Marcel Dekker.

Gigerenzer, G. (1987). Probabilistic thinking and the fight against subjectivity. In L. Krüger, G. Gigerenzer, & M. S. Morgan (Eds.), *The probabilistic revolution* (Vol. 2, pp. 11–33). Cambridge, MA: Bradford/MIT Press.

Gigerenzer, G., & Murray, D. J. (1987). *Cognition as intuitive statistics.* Hillsdale, NJ: Erlbaum.

Gigerenzer, G., Swijtink, Z., Porter, T., Daston, L., Beatty, J., & Krüger, L. (1989). *The empire of chance: How probability changed science and everyday life.* Cambridge, UK: Cambridge University Press.

Gilbert, J. P., McPeek, B., & Mosteller, F. (1977). Statistics and ethics in surgery and anesthesia. *Science, 198,* 684–689.

Gillespie, R. (1988). The Hawthorne experiments and the politics of experimentation. In J. Morawski (Ed.), *The rise of experimentation in American psychology* (pp. 114–137). New Haven, CT: Yale University Press.

Gilovich, T. (1991). *How we know what isn't so: The fallibility of human reason in everyday life.* New York: Free Press.

GISSI [Gruppo Italiano per lo Studio della Streptochinasi Nell'Infarto Miocardico]. (1986, February 22). *Lancet, 397–402.*

Glaser, B. G., & Strauss, A. L. (1967). *The discovery of grounded theory: Strategies for qualitative research.* Hawthorne, NY: Aldine de Gruyter.

Glass, D. C., & Singer, J. F. (1972). *Urban stress: Experiments on noise and social stressors.* New York: Academic Press.

Glass, G. V (1976). Primary, secondary, and meta-analysis of research. *Educational Researcher, 6,* 3–8.

Glass, G. V (1978). In defense of generalization. *Behavioral and Brain Sciences, 3,* 394–395.

Glass, G. V, McGaw, B., & Smith, M. L. (1981). *Meta-analysis in social research.* Beverly Hills, CA: Sage.

Gleick, J. (2003). *Isaac Newton.* New York: Pantheon.

Gleitman, H., Rozin, P., & Sabini, J. (1997). Solomon E. Asch (1907–1996). *American Psychologist, 52,* 984–985.

Gniech, G. (1986). *Störeffekte in psychologischen Experimenten.* Stuttgart, Germany: W. Kohlhammer.

Goldberg, L. R. (1993). The structure of phenotypic personality traits. *American Psychologist, 48,* 26–34.

Goldfinger, S. E. (1991, August). Garlic: Good for what ails you. *Harvard Health Letter, 16*(10), 1–2.

Goldstein, J. H., Rosnow, R. L., Goodstadt, B. E., & Suls, J. M. (1972). The "good subject" in verbal operant conditioning research. *Journal of Experimental Research in Personality, 6,* 29–33.

Gombrich, E. H. (1963). *Meditations on a hobby horse and other essays on the theory of art.* London: Phaidon.

Good, P. (1994). *Permutation tests: A practical guide to resampling methods for testing hypotheses.* New York: Springer-Verlag.

Goode, E. (2001, January 2). Researcher challenges a host of psychological studies. *New York Times,* Science Times Section, pp. 1, 7.

Goodenough, W. H. (1980). Ethnographic field techniques. In H. C. Triandis & J. W. Berry (Eds.), *Handbook of cross-cultural psychology: Methodology* (Vol. 2, pp. 29–55). Boston: Allyn & Bacon.

Gorden, R. L. (1969). *Interviewing: Strategy, techniques, and tactics.* Homewood, IL: Dorsey.

Gordon, M. E., & Gross, R. H. (1978). A critique of methods for operationalizing the concept of fakeability. *Educational and Psychological Measurement, 38,* 771–782.

Gorsuch, R. L. (1983). *Factor analysis* (2nd ed.). Hillsdale, NJ: Erlbaum.

Gosling, S. D., Vazire, S., Srivastava, S., & John, O. P. (2004). Should we trust Web-based studies? A comparative analysis of six preconceptions about Internet questionnaires. *American Psychologist, 59,* 93–104.

Grady, D. (2003, February 25). Safe therapy is found for high blood-clot risk. *New York Times,* pp. A1, A22.

Graesser, A. C., & Franklin, S. P. (1990). QUEST: A cognitive model of question-answering. *Discourse Processes, 13,* 279–303.

Graham, J. R. (1993). *MMPI-2: Assessing personality and psychopathology* (2nd ed.). New York: Oxford University Press.

Graham, J. R., & Lilly, R. S. (1984). *Psychological testing.* Englewood Cliffs, NJ: Prentice Hall.

Graumann, C. F., & Gergen, K. J. (Eds.). (1996). *Historical dimensions of psychological discourse.* New York: Cambridge University Press.

Gray, B. H., & Cook, R. A. (1980). The impact of IRBs on research. *Hastings Center Report, 10,* 36–41.

Gray, H. L., & Schucany, W. R. (1972). *The generalized jackknife statistic.* New York: Marcel Dekker.

Green, B. F., Jr., & Tukey, J. W. (1960). Complex analysis of variance: General problems. *Psychometrika, 25,* 127–152.

Greene, J. D., Sommerville, R. B., Nystrom, L. E., Darley, J. M., & Cohen, J. D. (2001). An fMRI investigation of emotional engagement in moral judgment. *Science, 293,* 2105–2108.

Greenhouse, J. B., & Iyengar, S. (1994). Sensitivity analysis and diagnostics. In H. Cooper & L. V. Hedges (Eds.), *Handbook of research synthesis* (pp. 383–398). New York: Russell Sage Foundation.

Greenwald, A. G. (1976). Within-subjects designs: To use or not to use? *Psychological Bulletin, 83,* 314–320.

Greenwald, A. G., & Banaji, M. R. (1995). Implicit social cognition: Attitudes, self-esteem, and stereotypes. *Psychological Review, 102,* 4–27.

Greenwald, A. G., Banaji, M. R., Rudman, L. A., Farnham, S. D., Nosek, B. A., & Rosier, M. (2000). Prologue to a unified theory of attitudes, stereotypes, and self-concept. In J. P. Forgas (Ed.), *Feeling and thinking: The role of affect in social cognition* (pp. 308–330). New York: Cambridge University Press.

Greenwald, A. G., & Ronis, D. L. (1978). Twenty years of cognitive dissonance: Case study of the evolution of a theory. *Psychological Bulletin, 82,* 1–20.

Grice, G. R. (1966). Dependence of empirical laws upon the source of experimental variation. *Psychological Bulletin, 66,* 488–498.

Griffin, W. E. B. (2002). *Under fire.* New York: G. P. Putnam's Sons.

Gross, A. E., & Fleming, I. (1982). Twenty years of deception in social psychology. *Personality and Social Psychology Bulletin, 8,* 402–408.

Gross, A. G. (1983). A primer on tables and figures. *Journal of Technical Writing and Communication, 13,* 33–55.

Gross, A. G. (1996). *The rhetoric of science.* Cambridge, MA: Harvard University Press.

Groth-Marnat, G. (1984). *Handbook of psychological assessment.* New York: Van Nostrand.

Gruppo Italiano per lo Studio della Streptochinasi Nell'Infarto Miocardico (GISSI). (1986, February 22). Effectiveness of intravenous thrombolytic treatment in acute myocardial infarction. *Lancet,* 397–402.

Gubrium, J. F., & Holstein, J. A. (Eds.). (2002). *Handbook of interview research: Context and method.* Thousand Oaks, CA: Sage.

Guilford, J. P. (1950). *Fundamental statistics in psychology and education.* New York: McGraw-Hill.

Guilford, J. P. (1954). *Psychometric methods* (2nd ed.). New York: McGraw-Hill.

Guilford, J. P. (1956). *Fundamental statistics in psychology and education* (3rd ed.). New York: McGraw-Hill.

Guilford, J. P., & Fruchter, B. (1978). *Fundamental statistics in psychology and education* (6th ed.). New York: McGraw-Hill.

Gulliksen, H. (1950). *Theory of mental tests.* New York: Wiley.

Gumperz, J. J., & Levinson, S. C. (Eds.). (1996). *Rethinking linguistic relativity.* Cambridge, UK: Cambridge University Press.

Guttman, L. (1944). A basis for scaling qualitative data. *American Sociological Review, 9,* 139–150.

Guttman, L. (1966). Order analysis of correlation matrices. In R. B. Cattell (Ed.), *Handbook of multivariate experimental psychology* (pp. 438–458). Chicago: Rand McNally.

Haase, R. F., Waechter, D. M., & Solomon, G. S. (1982). How significant is a significant difference? Average effect size of research in counseling psychology. *Journal of Counseling Psychology, 29,* 58–65.

Haber, M. (1986). An exact unconditional test for the 2 × 2 comparative trial. *Psychological Bulletin, 99,* 129–132.

Hagan, R. L. (1997). In praise of the null hypothesis statistical test. *American Psychologist, 52,* 15–24.

Hagenaars, J. A., & Cobben, N. P. (1978). Age, cohort and period: A general model for the analysis of social change. *Netherlands Journal of Sociology, 14,* 58–91.

Hahn, L. E. (1942). *A contextualist theory of perception.* Berkeley: University of California Press.

Hair, J. F., Jr., Anderson, R. E., & Tatham, R. L. (1987). *Multivariate data analysis with readings* (2nd ed.). New York: Macmillan, 1987.

Hair, J. F., Jr., Anderson, R. E., Tatham, R. L., & Black, W. C. (1998). *Multivariate data analysis* (5th ed.). Upper Saddle River, NJ: Prentice Hall.

Hall, J. A. (1979). Gender, gender roles, and nonverbal communication skills. In R. Rosenthal (Ed.), *Skill in nonverbal communication: Individual differences* (pp. 32–67). Cambridge, MA: Oelgeschlager, Gunn & Hain.

Hall, J. A. (1984a). *Instructor's manual to accompany Rosenthal/Rosnow: Essentials of behavioral research.* New York: McGraw-Hill.

Hall, J. A. (1984b). *Nonverbal sex differences: Communication accuracy and expressive style.* Baltimore: Johns Hopkins University Press.

Hall, J. A., & Halberstadt, A. G. (1986). Smiling and gazing. In J. S. Hyde & M. C. Linn (Eds.), *The psychology of gender: Advances through meta-analysis* (pp. 136–158). Baltimore: Johns Hopkins University Press.

Hallett, T., & Fine, G. A. (2000). Ethnography 1900: Learning from the field research of an old century. *Journal of Contemporary Ethnography, 29,* 593–617.

Hammond, K. R. (1954). Representative vs. systematic design in clinical psychology. *Psychological Bulletin, 51,* 150–159.

Haney, D. Q. (2001, March 20). Drug called big step in heart treatment. *Press Enterprise,* pp. A1, A7.

Harlow, H. F. (1959). Love in infant monkeys. In S. Coopersmith (Ed.), *Frontiers of psychological research* (pp. 92–98). San Francisco: W. H. Freeman.

Harlow, H. F., & Harlow, M. K. (1965). The affectional systems. In A. M. Schrier, H. F. Harlow, & F. Stollnitz (Eds.), *Behavior of nonhuman primates: Modern research trends* (Vol. 2, pp. 287–334). New York: Academic Press.

Harlow, H. F., & Harlow, M. K. (1966). Learning to love. *American Scientist, 54,* 244–272.

Harlow, H. F., & Harlow, M. K. (1970). The young monkeys. In P. Cramer (Ed.), *Readings in developmental psychology today* (pp. 93–97). Del Mar, CA: CRM Books.

Harlow, L. L., Mulaik, S. A., & Steiger, J. H. (Eds.). (1997). *What if there were no significance tests?* Mahwah, NJ: Erlbaum.

Harman, H. H. (1976). *Modern factor analysis.* Chicago: University of Chicago Press.

Harman, H. H. (2003). *Modern factor analysis.* Temecula, CA: Textbook Publishers. (Reprint of 1976 edition)

Harris, J. A. (1912). A simple test of the goodness of fit of Mendelian ratios. *American Naturalist, 46,* 741–745.

Harris, M. J., & Rosenthal, R. (1985). Mediation of interpersonal expectancy effects: 31 meta-analyses. *Psychological Bulletin, 97,* 363–386.

Harris, R. J. (1975). *A primer of multivariate statistics.* New York: Academic Press.

Harris, R. J. (1985). *A primer of multivariate statistics* (2nd ed.). New York: Academic Press.

Harris, R. J. (2001). *A primer of multivariate statistics* (3rd ed.). Mahwah, NJ: Erlbaum.

Hasher, L., Goldstein, D., & Toppino, T. (1977). The frequency and the conference of referential validity. *Journal of Verbal Learning and Verbal Behavior, 16,* 107–112.

Hasselblad, V., & McCrory, D. C. (1995). Meta-analytic tools for medical decision making: A practical guide. *Medical Decision Making, 15,* 81–96.

Hayes, A. F. (1996). Permutation test is not distribution-free: Testing H_0 $\rho = 0$. *Psychological Methods, 1,* 184–198.

Hayes, S. C., Hayes, L. J., Reese, H. W., & Sarbin, T. R. (Eds.). (1993). *Varieties of scientific contextualism.* Reno, NV: Context Press.

Haynes, S. N., Richard, D. C. S., & Kubany, E. S. (1995). Content validity in psychological assessment: A functional approach to concepts and methods. *Psychological Assessment, 7,* 238–247.

Hays, W. L. (1963). *Statistics for psychologists.* New York: Holt, Rinehart & Winston.

Hays, W. L. (1981). *Statistics* (3rd ed.). New York: Holt.

Hays, W. L. (1994). *Statistics* (5th ed.). Fort Worth, TX: Harcourt Brace.

Haywood, H. C. (1976). The ethics of doing research . . . and of not doing it. *American Journal of Mental Deficiency, 81,* 311–317.

Heckman, J. J. (1980). Sample selection bias as a specification error. In J. P. Smith (Ed.), *Female labor supply: Theory and estimation* (pp. 206–248). Princeton, NJ: Princeton University Press.

Hedges, L. V. (1981). Distribution theory for Glass's estimator of effect size and related estimators. *Journal of Educational Statistics, 6,* 107–128.

Hedges, L. V. (1987). How hard is hard science, how soft is soft science? The empirical cumulativeness of research. *American Psychologist, 42,* 443–455.

Hedges, L. V., & Olkin, I. (1985). *Statistical methods for meta-analysis.* New York: Academic Press.

Heisenberg, W. (1971). *Physics and beyond: Encounters and conversations.* New York: Harper & Row.

Heisenberg, W. (1974). *Across the frontiers.* New York: Harper & Row.

Helson, H. (1959). Adaptation level theory. In S. Koch (Ed.), *Psychology: A study of a science* (Vol. 1, pp. 565–621). New York: McGraw-Hill.

Hempel, C. G., & Oppenheim, P. (1965). *Aspects of scientific explanation and other essays in the philosophy of science.* New York: Free Press.

Henning, H. J., & Rudinger, G. (1985). Analysis of qualitative data in developmental psychology. In J. R. Nesselroade & A. von Eye (Eds.), *Individual development and social change: Explanatory analysis* (pp. 295–341). Orlando, FL: Academic Press.

Heritage, J. (1984). *Garfinkel and ethnomethodology.* Cambridge, England: Polity Press.

Hersen, M. (1982). Single-case experimental designs. In A. Bellack, M. Hersen, & A Kazdin (Eds.), *International handbook of behavior modification and therapy* (pp. 167–203). New York: Plenum.

Hersen, M., & Barlow, D. H. (1976). *Single-case experimental designs: Strategies for studying behavior change.* Oxford: Pergamon Press.

Highland, R. W., & Berkshire, J. A. (1951). *A methodological study of forced-choice performance rating* (Research report 51-9). San Antonio, TX: Human Resources Research Center.

Hildebrand, D. K. (1986). *Statistical thinking for behavioral scientists.* Boston: Duxbury.

Hill, M. R. (1993). *Archival strategies and techniques.* Newbury Park, CA: Sage.

Hiller, J. B., Rosenthal, R., Bornstein, R. F., Berry, D. T. R., & Brunell-Neuleib, S. (1999). A comparative meta-analysis of Rorschach and MMPI validity. *Psychological Assessment, 11,* 278–296.

Hineline, P. N. (1980). The language of behavior analysis: Its community, its functions, and its limitations. *Behaviorism, 8,* 67–86.

Hineline, P. N. (1986). Re-tuning the operant-respondent distinction. In T. Thompson & M. D. Zeiler (Eds.), *Analysis and interpretation of behavioral units* (pp. 55–79). Hillsdale, NJ: Erlbaum.

Hineline, P. N., & Lattal, K. A. (2000). Single-case experimental design. In A. E. Kazdin (Ed.), *Encyclopedia of psychology* (Vol. 7, pp. 287–289). New York: Oxford University Press and American Psychological Association.

Hoaglin, D. C., Mosteller, F., & Tukey, J. W. (1983). *Understanding robust and exploratory data analysis.* New York: Wiley.

Hochschild, A. (1989). *The second shift: Working parents and the revolution at home.* New York: Viking Press.

Hodgkinson, H. (1970). Student protest: An institutional and national profile. *The Record (Columbia University Teachers' College), 71,* 537–555.

Hoffman, R. R., & Nead, J. M. (1983). General contextualism, ecological sciences, and cognitive research. *Journal of Mind and Behavior, 4,* 507–560.

Holden, C. (1995a). Random samples: Sex and fingerprints. *Science, 267,* 451.

Holden, C. (1995b). Random samples: Confirmation for combination AIDS therapy. *Science, 270,* 33.

Hollander, E. P. (1992). The essential independence of leadership and followership. *Current Directions in Psychological Science, 1,* 71–74.

Hollander, M., & Wolfe, D. A. (1973). *Nonparametric statistical methods.* New York: Wiley.

Hollander, M., & Wolfe, D. A. (1999). *Nonparametric statistical methods* (2nd ed.). New York: Wiley.

Holsti, O. R. (with the collaboration of J. K. Loomba & R. C. North). (1968). Content analysis. In G. Lindzey & E. Aronson (Ed.), *The handbook of social psychology* (2nd ed., Vol. 2, pp. 596–692). Reading, MA: Addison-Wesley.

Holton, G. (1973). *Thematic origins of scientific thought: Kepler to Einstein.* Cambridge, MA: Harvard University Press.

Holton, G. (1978). From the endless frontier to the ideology of limits. In G. Holton & R. S. Morison (Eds.), *Limits of scientific inquiry* (pp. 227–241). New York: Norton.

Holyoak. K. J., & Thagard, P. (1995). *Mental leaps: Analogy in creative thought.* Cambridge, MA: MIT Press.

Honeck, R. P. (1997). *A proverb in mind: The cognitive science of proverbial wit and wisdom.* Mahwah, NJ: Erlbaum.

Horowitz, I. A. (1969). Effects of volunteering, fear arousal, and number of communications on attitude change. *Journal of Personality and Social Psychology, 11,* 34–37.

Horst, P., & Edwards, A. L. (1982). Analysis of nonorthogonal designs: The 2^k factorial experiment. *Psychological Bulletin, 91,* 190–192.

Houts, A. C., Cook, T. D., & Shadish, W., Jr. (1986). The person-situation debate: A critical multiplist perspective. *Journal of Personality, 54,* 52–105.

Hovey, H. B. (1928). Effects of general distraction on the higher thought processes. *American Journal of Psychology, 40,* 585–591.

Hovland, C. I., Mandell, W., Campbell, E. H., Brock, T., Luchins, A. S., Cohen, A. R., McGuire, W. J., Janis, I. L., Feierabend, R. L., & Anderson, N. H. (1957). *The order of presentation in persuasion.* New Haven, CT: Yale University Press.

Howell, D. C. (1992). *Statistical methods for psychology* (3rd ed.). Boston: PWS-Kent.

Hoyt, C. (1941). Test reliability estimated by analysis of variance. *Psychometrika, 6,* 153–160.

Hoyt, W. T. (2000). Rater bias in psychological research: When is it a problem and what can we do about it? *Psychological Methods, 5,* 64–86.

Hsu, T. C., & Feldt, L. S. (1969). The effect of limitations on the number of criterion score values on the significance level of the *F*-test. *American Educational Research Journal, 6,* 515–527.

Huber, P. J. (1981). *Robust statistics.* New York: Wiley.

Huesmann, L. R., Moise-Titus, J., Podolski, C.-L., & Eron, L. D. (2003). Longitudinal relations between children's exposure to TV violence and their aggressive and violent behavior in young adulthood: 1977–1992. *Developmental Psychology, 39,* 201–221.

Hume, D. (1955). *Inquiry concerning human understanding.* New York: Liberal Arts Press. (Original work published 1748)

Hume, D. (1978). *A treatise of human nature: Being an attempt to introduce the experimental method of reasoning into moral subjects* (2nd ed.). Oxford, UK: Oxford University Press. (Original work published 1739–1740)

Hunt, M. (1997). *How science takes stock: The story of meta-analysis.* New York: Russell Sage Foundation.

Hunter, J. E., & Schmidt, F. L. (2004). *Methods of meta-analysis: Correcting error and bias in research findings* (2nd ed.). Thousand Oaks, CA: Sage.

Hurvich, L. W. (1969). Hering and the scientific establishment. *American Psychologist, 24,* 497–514.

Hutchinson, J. W., Kamakura, W. A., & Lynch, J. G., Jr. (2000). Unobserved heterogeneity as an alternative explanation for "reversal" effects in behavioral research. *Journal of Consumer Research, 27,* 324–344.

Hyman, H. H. (1954). *Interviewing in social research.* Chicago: University of Chicago Press.

Hyman, H. H., Cobb, W. J., Feldman, J. J., Hart, C. W., & Stember, C. H. (1954). *Interviewing in social research.* Chicago: University of Chicago Press.

Iglewicz, B., & Hoaglin, D. C. (1993). *How to detect and handle outliers.* Milwaukee: ASQC Quality Press.

Imber, S. D., Glanz, L. M., Elkin, I., Sotsky, S. M., Boyer, J. L., & Leber, W. R. (1986). Ethical issues in psychotherapy research: Problems in a collaborative clinical trials study. *American Psychologist, 41,* 137–146.

Jackson, D. N. (1969). Multimethod factor analysis in the evaluation of convergent and discriminant validity. *Psychological Bulletin, 72,* 30–49.

Jackson, J. A. (Ed.). (1972). *Role.* Cambridge: Cambridge University Press.

Jackson, L. A., Hunter, J. E., & Hodge, C. N. (1995). Physical attractiveness and intellectual competence: A meta-analytic review. *Social Psychology Quarterly, 58,* 108–122.

Jaeger, M. E., & Rosnow, R. L. (1988). Contextualism and its implications for psychological inquiry. *British Journal of Psychology, 79,* 63–75.

Jaeger, M. E., Skleder, A. A., Rind, B., & Rosnow, R. L. (1994). Gossip, gossipers, gossipees. In R. F. Goodman & A. Ben-Ze'ev (Eds.), *Good gossip* (pp. 154–168). Lawrence: University Press of Kansas.

Jaeger, M. E., Skleder, A. A., & Rosnow, R. L. (1998). Who's up on the low down: Gossip in interpersonal relations. In B. H. Spitzberg & W. R. Cupach (Eds.), *The dark side of close relationships* (pp. 103–117). Mahwah, NJ: Erlbaum.

Jammer, M. (1966). *The conceptual development of quantum mechanics.* New York: McGraw-Hill.

Jenkins, J. J. (1974). Remember that old theory of learning? Well, forget it! *American Psychologist, 11,* 785–795.

Johnson, C. G. (1982). Risks in the publication of fieldwork. In J. E. Sieber (Ed.), *The ethics of social research: Fieldwork, regulation, and publication* (Vol. 1, pp. 71–91). New York: Springer-Verlag.

Johnson, D. M. (1945). The "phantom anesthetist" of Mattoon: A field study of mass hysteria. *Journal of Abnormal and Social Psychology, 40,* 175–186.

Johnson, G. (2002, September 24). Here they are, science's 10 most beautiful experiments. *New York Times,* p. F3.

Johnson, M. L. (1953). Seeing's believing. *New Biology, 15,* 60–80.

Johnson-Laird, P. N. (1983). *Mental models: Towards a cognitive science of language, inference, and consciousness.* Cambridge, MA: Harvard University Press.

Johnson-Laird, P. N., & Byrne, R. N. J. (1991). *Deduction.* Hillsdale, NJ: Erlbaum.

Johnston, J. M., & Pennypacker, H. S. (1993). *Strategies and tactics of behavioral research* (2nd ed.). Hillsdale, NJ: Erlbaum.

Jones, E. E., & Gerard, H. B. (1967). *Foundations of social psychology.* New York: Wiley.

Jones, F. P. (1964). Experimental method in antiquity. *American Psychologist, 19,* 419.

Jones, H. H. (1993). *Bad blood: The Tuskegee syphilis experiment* (Rev. ed.). New York: Free Press.

Jones, M. B., & Fennell, R. S. (1965). Runway performance in two strains of rats. *Quarterly Journal of the Florida Academy of Sciences, 28,* 289–296.

Jöreskog, K. G., & Sörbom, D. (2001). *LISREL 8.5: User's reference guide.* Chicago: Scientific Software International.

Jourard, S. M. (1967). Experimenter-subject dialogue: A paradigm for a humanistic science of psychology. In J. F. T. Bugental (Ed.), *Challenges of humanistic psychology* (pp. 109–133). New York: McGraw-Hill.

Jourard, S. M. (1968). *Disclosing man to himself.* New York: Van Nostrand Reinhold.

Judd, C. M., & Kenny, D. A. (1981). *Estimating the effects of social interventions.* Cambridge, UK: Cambridge University Press.

Judd, C. M., & McClelland, G. H. (1989). *Data analysis: A model-comparison approach.* New York: Harcourt Brace Jovanovich.

Jung, J. (1978). Self-negating functions of self-fulfilling prophecies. *Behavioral and Brain Sciences, 3,* 397–398.

Kahane, H. (1989). *Logic and philosophy: A modern introduction* (6th ed.). Belmont, CA: Wadsworth.

Kahn, R. L., & Cannell, C. F. (1965). *The dynamics of interviewing.* New York: Wiley.

Kalleberg, A. L., & Kluegel, J. R. (1975). Analysis of the multitrait-multimethod matrix: Some limitations and an alternative. *Journal of Applied Psychology, 60,* 1–9.

Kalton, G. (1983). *Introduction to survey sampling.* Beverly Hills, CA: Sage.

Kanner, L. (1943). Autistic disturbances of affect contact. *Nervous Child, 2,* 217–250.

Kaplan, A. (1964). *The conduct of inquiry: Methodology for behavioral science.* Scranton, PA: Chandler.

Karpinski, A., & Hilton, J. L. (2001). Attitudes and the implicit association test. *Journal of Personality and Social Psychology, 81,* 774–788.

Kashy, D. A., & DePaulo, B. M. (1996). Who lies? *Journal of Personality and Social Psychology, 70,* 1037–1051.

Katz, D., & Cantril, H. (1937). Public opinion polls. *Sociometry, 1,* 155–179.

Katz, E., & Lazarsfeld, P. F. (1955). *Personal influence: The part played by people in the flow of mass communications.* New York: Free Press.

Katz, J. (1972). *Experimentation with human beings.* New York: Russell Sage.

Kazdin, A. E. (1992). *Research design in clinical psychology* (2nd ed.). Boston: Allyn & Bacon.

Kazdin, A. E. (1998). Faltering fate. *Contemporary Psychology, 43,* 533–534.

Kazdin, A. E., & Kagan, J. (1994). Models of dysfunction in developmental psychopathology. *Clinical Psychology: Science and Practice, 1,* 35–52.

Kazdin, A. E., & Tuma, A. H. (Eds.). (1982). *Single-case research design.* San Francisco: Jossey-Bass.

Kelly, D., Julian, T., & Hollander, E. P. (1992, April). *Further effects of good and bad leadership as revealed by critical incidents and rating scales.* Paper presented at Eastern Psychological Association meeting, Boston.

Kelly, J. A. (1986). Psychological research and the rights of animals: Disagreement with Miller. *American Psychologist, 41,* 839–841.

Kelman, H. C. (1967). Human use of human subjects: The problem of deception in social psychological experiments. *Psychological Bulletin, 67,* 1–11.

Kelman, H. C. (1968). *A time to speak: On human values and social research.* San Francisco: Jossey-Bass.

Keniston, K. (1967). The sources of student dissent. *Journal of Social Issues, 23,* 108–137.

Keniston, K. (1969, April 27). You have to grow up in Scarsdale to know how bad things really are. *New York Times Magazine, SM* 27 (9 pages).

Kennedy, J. J. (1983). *Analyzing qualitative data: Introductory log-linear analysis for behavioral research.* New York: Praeger.

Kennedy, J. J. (1992). *Analyzing qualitative data: Introductory log-linear analysis for behavioral research* (2nd ed.). New York: Praeger.

Kennedy, J. J., & Bush, A. J. (1988, April). Focused comparisons in logit-model contingency table analysis. Paper presented at the meeting of the American Educational Research Association, New Orleans.

Kenny, D. A. (1973). Cross-lagged and synchronous common factors in panel data. In A. S. Goldenberger & O. D. Duncan (Eds.), *Structural equation models in the social sciences.* New York: Seminar Press.

Kenny, D. A. (1979). *Correlation and causality.* New York: Wiley.

Kenny, D. A., & Judd, C. M. (1986). Consequences of violating the independence assumption in analysis of variance. *Psychological Bulletin, 99,* 422–431.

Kenrick, D. T., & Keefe, R. C. (1992). Age preferences in mates reflect sex differences in human reproductive strategies. *Behavioral and Brain Sciences, 15,* 75–133.

Keppel, G. (1991). *Design and analysis: A researcher's handbook* (3rd ed.). Englewood Cliffs, NJ: Prentice Hall.

Kerin, R. A., & Peterson, R. A. (1983). Scheduling telephone interviews. *Journal of Advertising Research, 23,* 41–47.

Killeen, P. R. (2005). An alternative to null-hypothesis significance tests. *Psychological Science, 16,* 345–353.

Kim, J.-O., & Mueller, C. W. (1978). *Introduction to factor analysis: What it is and how to do it.* Beverly Hills, CA: Sage.

Kim, K. H., & Roush, F. W. (1980). *Mathematics for social scientists.* New York: Elsevier.

Kimble, G. (1989). Psychology from the standpoint of a generalist. *American Psychologist, 34,* 633–635.

Kimmel, A. J. (1988). *Ethics and values in applied social research.* San Francisco: Jossey-Bass.

Kimmel, A. J. (1991). Predictable biases in the ethical decision making of American psychologists. *American Psychologist, 46,* 786–788.

Kimmel, A. J. (1996). *Ethical issues in behavioral research: A survey.* Cambridge, MA: Blackwell.

Kimmel, A. J. (1998). In defense of deception. *American Psychologist, 53,* 803–805.

Kimmel, A. J. (2004). Ethical issues in social psychology research. In C. Sansone, C. C. Morf, & A. T. Panter (Eds.), *The Sage handbook of methods in social psychology* (pp. 45–70). Thousand Oaks, CA: Sage.

King, D. W., & King, L. A. (1991). Validity issues in research on Vietnam veteran adjustment. *Psychological Bulletin, 109,* 107–124.

King, L. A., & King, D. W. (1990). Role conflict and role ambiguity: A critical assessment of construct validity. *Psychological Bulletin, 107,* 48–64.

Kinsey, A. C., Pomeroy, W. B., & Martin, C. E. (1948). *Sexual behavior in the human male.* Philadelphia: Saunders.

Kinsey, A. C., Pomeroy, W. B., Martin, C. E., & Gebhard, P. H. (1953). *Sexual behavior in the human female.* Philadelphia: Saunders.

Kipnis, D. (1976). *The powerholders.* Chicago: University of Chicago Press.

Kipnis, D. (1984). The uses of power in organizations and in interpersonal settings. In S. Oskamp (Ed.), *Applied social psychology annual* (Vol. 5, pp. 179–210). Beverly Hills, CA: Sage.

Kirk, R. E. (1996). Practical significance: A concept whose time has come. *Educational and Psychological Measurement, 5,* 746–759.

Kish, L. (1965). *Survey sampling.* New York: Wiley.

Klahr, D., & Simon, H. A. (2001). What have psychologists (and others) discovered about the process of scientific discovery? *Current Directions in Psychological Science, 10,* 75–79.

Kneeland, N. (1929). That lenient tendency in rating. *Personnel Journal, 7,* 356–366.

Knorr-Cetina, K. D. (1981). *The manufacture of knowledge: An essay on the constructivist and contextual nature of science.* Oxford, UK: Pergamon.

Knox, R. A. (1995, November 16). Research boosts the case for cholesterol-cutting drugs. *Boston Globe,* Section: National/Foreign, pp. 1, 22.

Knox, R. A. (1997, February 25). AIDS trial terminated: 3-drug therapy hailed. *Boston Globe,* pp. A1, A16.

Koch, S. (1959). General introduction to the series. In S. Koch (Ed.), *Psychology: A study of a science* (Vol. 1, pp. 1–18). New York: McGraw-Hill.

Kolata, G. B. (1981). Drug found to help heart attack survivors. *Science, 214,* 774–775.

Kolata, G. B. (1986). What does it mean to be random? *Science, 231,* 1068–1070.

Kolodner, J. (1993). *Case-based reasoning.* San Mateo, CA: Morgan Kaufmann.

Kong, D. (1996, February 28). Breast implant study finds some risk. *Boston Globe,* Section: National/Foreign, p. 13.

Koocher, G. P., & Keith-Spiegel, P. C. (1990). *Children, ethics, and the law.* Lincoln: University of Nebraska Press.

Koocher, G. P., & Keith-Spiegel, P. C. (1998). *Ethics in psychology* (2nd ed.). Washington, DC: American Psychological Assn.

Kordig, D. R. (1978). Discovery and justification. *Philosophy of Science, 45,* 110–117.

Koshland, D. E., Jr. (1988). Science, journalism, and whistle-blowing. *Science, 240,* 585.

Kosslyn, S. M. (1994). *Elements of graph design.* New York: Freeman.

Kotses, H., Glaus, K. D., & L. E. Fisher (1974). Effects of subject recruitment procedure on heart rate and skin conductance measures. *Biological Psychology, 2,* 59–66.

Kourany, J. A. (Ed.). (1987). *Scientific knowledge.* Belmont, CA: Wadsworth.

Kramer, M. S., & Shapiro, S. (1984). Scientific challenges in the application of randomized trials. *Journal of the American Medical Association, 252,* 2739–2745.

Krippendorff, K. (1980). *Content analysis: An introduction to its methodology.* Beverly Hills, CA: Sage.

Krueger, R. A. (1988). *Focus groups: A practical guide for applied research* (2nd ed.). Thousand Oaks, CA: Sage.

Kruglanski, A. W. (1973). Much ado about the "volunteer artifacts." *Journal of Personality and Social Psychology, 28,* 348–354.

Kruskal, J. B. (1964). Multidimensional scaling by optimizing goodness of fit to a nonmetric hypothesis. *Psychometrika, 29,* 1–27.

Kuder, G. F., & Richardson, M. W. (1937). The theory of the estimation of test reliability. *Psychometrika, 2,* 151–160.

Kuhfield, W. F., Tobias, R. D., & Garratt, M. (1994). Efficient experimental design with marketing applications. *Journal of Marketing Research, 31,* 545–557.

Kuhn, T. S. (1962). *The structure of scientific revolutions.* Chicago: University of Chicago Press.

Kuhn, T. S. (1977). *The essential tension.* Chicago: University of Chicago Press.

Labaw, P. (1980). *Advanced questionnaire design.* Cambridge, MA: ABT Books.

LaFollette, M. C. (1992). *Stealing into print: Fraud, plagiarism, and misconduct in scientific publishing.* Berkeley: University of California Press.

Lakatos, I. (1978). *The methodology of scientific research programs.* Cambridge, UK: Cambridge University Press.

Lakoff, G., & Johnson, M. (1980). *Metaphors we live by.* Chicago: University of Chicago Press.

Laming, D. R. J. (1967). On procuring human subjects. *Quarterly Journal of Experimental Psychology, 19,* 64–69.

Lana, R. E. (1959a). A further investigation of the pretest-treatment interaction effect. *Journal of Applied Psychology, 43,* 421–422.

Lana, R. E. (1959b). Pretest-treatment interaction effects in attitudinal studies. *Psychological Bulletin, 56,* 293–300.

Lana, R. E. (1964). The influence of the pretest on order effects in persuasive communications. *Journal of Abnormal and Social Psychology, 69,* 337–341.

Lana, R. E. (1966). Inhibitory effects of a pretest on opinion change. *Educational and Psychological Measurement, 26,* 139–150.

Lana, R. E. (1969). Pretest sensitization. In R. Rosenthal & R. L. Rosnow (Eds.), *Artifact in behavioral research* (pp. 119–141). New York: Academic Press.

Lana, R. E. (1986). Descartes, Vico, contextualism and psychology. In R. L. Rosnow & M. Georgoudi (Eds.), *Contextualism and understanding in behavioral science: Implications for research and theory* (pp. 67–85). New York: Praeger.

Lana, R. E. (1991). *Assumptions of social psychology: A reexamination.* Hillsdale, NJ: Erlbaum.

Lana, R. E. (2002). Choice and chance in the formation of society: Behavior and cognition in social theory. *Journal of Mind and Behavior, 23,* 1–192.

Lana, R. E., & Rosnow, R. L. (1972). *Introduction to contemporary psychology.* New York: Holt, Rinehart & Winston.

Lance, C. E., & Woehr, D. J. (1986). Statistical control of halo: Clarification from two cognitive models of the performance appraisal process. *Journal of Applied Psychology, 71,* 679–685.

Landesman, C. (1971). *The problem of universals.* New York: Basic Books.

Lane, F. W. (1960). *Kingdom of the octopus.* New York: Sheridan House.

Latané, B., & Darley, J. M. (1970). *The unresponsive bystander: Why doesn't he help?* New York: Appleton-Century-Crofts.

Laudan, L. (1977). *Progress and its problems: Towards a theory of scientific growth.* Berkeley: University of California Press.

Laudan, L. (1982). Two puzzles about science: Reflections about some crises in the philosophy and sociology of science. *Minerva, 20,* 253–268.

Lautenschlager, G. J. (1986). Within-subject measures for the assessment of individual differences in faking. *Educational and Psychological Measurement, 46,* 309–316.

Lavrakas, P. J. (1987). *Telephone survey methods: Sampling, selection, and supervision.* Beverly Hills, CA: Sage.

Lazarsfeld, P. F. (1948). The use of panels in social research. *Proceedings of the American Philosophical Society, 92,* 405–410.

Lazarsfeld, P. F. (1978). Some episodes in the history of panel analysis. In D. B. Kandel (Ed.), *Longitudinal research for drug abuse.* New York: Hemisphere Press.

Lazarsfeld, P. F., Berelson, B., & Gaudet, H. (1944). *The people's choice.* New York: Duell, Sloan, & Pearce.

Lazarsfeld, P. F., & Henry, N. W. (1968). *Latent structure analysis.* Boston: Houghton Mifflin.

Lazarus, A. A., & Davison, G. C. (1971). Clinical innovation in research and practice. In A. E. Bergin & S. L. Garfield (Eds.), *Handbook of psychotherapy and behavior change: An empirical analysis* (pp. 196–213). New York: Wiley.

Lee, R. M. (1993). *Doing research on sensitive topics.* London: Sage.

Lehmann, E. L. (1975). *Nonparametrics: Statistical methods based on ranks.* San Francisco: Holden-Day.

Lehmann, E. L., & D'Abrera, H. J. M. (1998). *Nonparametrics: Statistical methods based on ranks* (Rev. 1st ed.). Upper Saddle River, NJ: Prentice Hall.

Lerner, R. M., Hultsch, D. F., & Dixon, R. A. (1983). Contextualism and the characteristics of developmental psychology in the 1970s. *Annals of the New York Academy of Sciences, 412,* 101–128.

Lessac, M. S., & Solomon, R. L. (1969). Effects of early isolation on the later adaptive behavior of beagles: A methodological demonstration. *Developmental Psychology, 1,* 14–25.

Levi, P. (1984). *The periodic table.* New York: Schocken Books.

Levine, M. (1980). Investigative reporting as a research method: An analysis of Bernstein and Woodward's *All the President's Men. American Psychologist, 35,* 626–638.

LeVine, R. A., & Campbell, D. T. (1972). *Ethnocentrism: Theories of conflict, ethnic attitudes, and group behavior.* New York: Wiley.

Levine, R. J., Carpenter, W. T., & Appelbaum, P. S. (2003, June 13). Clarifying standards for using placebos. *Science, 300,* 1659, 1661

Lewin, K. (1935). *A dynamic theory of personality: Selected papers.* New York: McGraw-Hill.

Lewis, C. (1993). Bayesian methods for the analysis of variance. In G. Keren & C. Lewis (Eds.), *Handbook for data analysis in the behavioral sciences: Statistical issues* (pp. 233–258). Hillsdale, NJ: Erlbaum.

Lewis, M. (1997). *Altering fate: Why the past does not predict the future.* New York: Guilford.

Li, H. (1994). A note on the maximal reliability of a linear composite (Tech. Rep. 94–176). Cambridge, MA: Harvard University, Department of Statistics.

Li, H., Rosenthal, R., & Rubin, D. B. (1996). Reliability of measurement in psychology: From Spearman-Brown to maximal reliability. *Psychological Methods, 1,* 98–107.

Li, H., & Wainer, H. (1998). Toward a coherent view of reliability in test theory. *Journal of Educational and Behavioral Statistics, 23,* 478–484.

Lieberman, L. R., & Dunlap, J. T. (1979). O'Leary and Borkovec's conceptualization of placebo: The placebo paradox. *American Psychologist, 34,* 553–554.

Light, R. J., & Pillemer, D. B. (1984). *Summing up: The science of reviewing research.* Cambridge, MA: Harvard University Press.

Light, R. J., Singer, J. D., & Willett, J. B. (1994). The visual presentation and interpretation of meta-analyses. In H. Cooper & L. V. Hedges (Eds.), *Handbook of research synthesis* (pp. 439–453). New York: Russell Sage Foundation.

Likert, R. A. (1932). A technique for the measurement of attitudes. *Archives of Psychology, 140,* 1–55.

Lincoln, Y. S., & Guba, E. G. (1985). *Naturalistic inquiry.* Beverly Hills, CA: Sage.

Lindquist, E. F. (1953). *Design and analysis of experiments in psychology and education.* Boston: Houghton Mifflin.

Lindzey, G., & Borgatta, E. F. (1954). Sociometric measurement. In G. Lindzey (Ed.), *Handbook of social psychology* (pp. 405–448). Cambridge, MA: Addison-Wesley.

Linsky, A. S. (1975). Stimulating responses to mailed questionnaires: A review. *Public Opinion Quarterly, 39,* 83–101.

Lipsey, M. W., & Wilson, D. B. (2001). *Practical meta-analysis.* Thousand Oaks, CA: Sage.

Liss, M. T. (1994). Child abuse: Is there a mandate for researchers to report? *Ethics and Behavior, 4,* 133–146.

Little, R. J. A., & Rubin, D. B. (1987). *Statistical analysis with missing data.* New York: Wiley.

Lodge, M. (1981). *Magnitude scaling: Quantitative measurement of opinions.* Newbury Park, CA: Sage.

Loeber, R., & Stouthamer-Loeber, M. (1998). Development of juvenile aggression and violence. *American Psychologist, 53,* 242–259.

Loehlin, J. C. (2004). *Latent variable models: An introduction to factor, path, and structural equation analysis* (4th ed). Mahwah, NJ: Erlbaum.

Loftus, E. F. (2004). Memories of things unseen. *Current Directions in Psychological Science, 13,* 145–147.

Loftus, G. R. (1996). Psychology will be a much better science when we change the way we analyze data. *Current Directions in Psychological Science, 5,* 161–171.

Long, P. O. (Ed.). (1985). *Science and technology in medieval society.* New York: New York Academy of Sciences.

Lorenz, K. (1971). *On aggression.* New York: Bantam Books.

Lott, A. J., & Lott, B. E. (1968). A learning theory approach to interpersonal attitudes. In A. G. Greenwald, T. C. Brock, & T. M. Ostrom (Eds.), *Psychological foundations of attitudes* (pp. 67–88). New York: Academic Press.

Lott, B. E., & Lott, A. J. (1960). The formation of positive attitudes toward group members. *Journal of Abnormal and Social Psychology, 61,* 297–300.

Lotz, J. (1968). Social science research and northern development. *Arctic, 21,* 291–294.

Lowry, R. (1969). Galilean and Newtonian influences on psychological thought. *American Journal of Psychology, 82,* 391–400.

Lowry, R. (1971). *The evolution of psychological theory: 1650 to the present.* Chicago: Aldine.

Luchins, A. S., & Luchins, E. H. (1965). *Logical foundations of mathematics for behavioral scientists.* New York: Holt.

Ludwig, A. M. (1995). *The price of greatness: Resolving the creativity and madness controversy.* New York: Guilford.

Lunney, G. H. (1970). Using analysis of variance with a dichotomous dependent variable: An empirical study. *Journal of Educational Measurement, 7,* 263–269.

Lush, J. L. (1931). Predicting gains in feeder cattle and pigs. *Journal of Agricultural Research, 42,* 853–881.

Lynch, J. G., Jr. (1982). On the external validity of experiments in consumer research. *Journal of Consumer Research, 9,* 225–239.

MacCoun, R. J. (1998). Biases in the interpretation and use of research results. *Annual Review of Psychology, 49,* 259–287.

Maher, B. A. (1978). Stimulus sampling in clinical research: Representative design reviewed. *Journal of Consulting and Clinical Psychology, 46,* 643–647.

Mahler, I. (1953). Attitudes toward socialized medicine. *Journal of Social Psychology, 38,* 273–282.

Mahoney, M. J. (1976). *Scientist as subject: The psychological imperative.* Cambridge, MA: Ballinger.

Mallon, T. (1991). *Stolen words: Forays into the origins and ravages of plagiarism.* New York: Penguin.

Mann, R. D. (1959). A review of the relationships between personality and performance in small groups. *Psychological Bulletin, 56,* 241–270.

Mann, T. (1994). Informed consent for psychological research: Do subjects comprehend consent forms and understand their legal rights? *Psychological Science, 5,* 140–143.

Marascuilo, L. A., & McSweeney, M. (1977). *Nonparametric and distribution-free methods for the social sciences.* Monterey, CA: Brooks/Cole.

Marcoulides, G. A., & Schumacker, R. E. (Eds.). (1996). *Advanced structural equation modeling: Issues and techniques.* Mahwah, NJ: Erlbaum.

Margolis, H. (1993). *Paradigms and barriers: How habits of mind govern scientific beliefs.* Chicago: University of Chicago Press.

Martin, L. R., Friedman, H. S., Tucker, J. S., Tomlinson-Keasey, C., Criqui, M. H., & Schwartz, J. E. (2002). A life course perspective on childhood cheerfulness and its relation to mortality risk. *Personality and Social Psychology Bulletin, 28,* 1155–1165.

Martin, P., & Bateson, P. (1986). *Measuring behavior: An introductory guide.* Cambridge, UK: Cambridge University Press.

Martin, R. M., & Marcuse, F. L. (1958). Characteristics of volunteers and nonvolunteers in psychological experimentation. *Journal of Consulting Psychology, 22,* 475–479.

Martindale, C. (1978). The evolution of English poetry. *Poetics, 7,* 231–248.

Martindale, C. (Ed.). (1988). *Psychological approaches to the study of literary narratives.* Hamburg, Germany: Buske.

Martindale, C. (1990). *The clockwork muse: The predictability of artistic change.* New York: Basic Books.

Martindale, C. (1997). Lombroso was right. *Contemporary Psychology, 42,* 218–219.

Maslow, A. H. (1942). Self-esteem (dominance feelings) and sexuality in women. *Journal of Social Psychology, 16,* 259–293.

Maslow, A. H., & Sakoda, J. M. (1952). Volunteer-error in the Kinsey study. *Journal of Abnormal and Social Psychology, 47,* 259–262.

Massey, D. S. (2000). When surveys fail: An alternative for data collection. In A. A. Stone, J. S. Turkkan, C. A. Bachrach, J. B. Jobe, H. S. Kurtzman, & V. S. Cain (Eds.), *The science of self-report: Implications for research and practice* (pp. 145–160). Mahwah, NJ: Erlbaum.

Masson, M. E. J., & Loftus, G. R. (2003). Using confidence intervals for graphically based data interpretation. *Canadian Journal of Experimental Psychology, 57,* 203–220.

Matarazzo, J. D., Wiens, A. N., & Saslow, G. (1965). Studies in interview speech behavior. In L. Krasner & L. P. Ullman (Eds.), *Research in behavior modification* (pp. 179–210). New York: Holt.

Mausner, J. S., & Gezon, H. M. (1967). Report on a phantom epidemic of gonorrhea. *American Journal of Epidemiology, 85,* 320–331.

Maxwell, S. E. (2004). The persistence of underpowered studies in psychological research: Causes, consequences, and remedies. *Psychological Methods, 9,* 147–163.

Maxwell, S. E., & Delaney, H. D. (2000). *Designing experiments and analyzing data: A model comparison perspective.* Mahwah, NJ: Erlbaum.

Mayer, L. S., & Carroll, S. S. (1987). Testing for lagged, cotemporal, and total dependence in cross-lagged panel analysis. *Sociological Methods and Research, 16,* 187–217.

McCann, J. T. (1999). *Assessing adolescents with the MACI.* New York: Wiley.

McClelland, G. H. (1997). Optimal design in psychological research. *Psychological Methods, 2,* 3–19.

McCormack, T. (1982). Content analysis: The social history of a method. *Studies in Communication, 2,* 143–178.

McCrae, R. R., & Costa, P. T., Jr. (1997). Personality traits structure as a human universal. *American Psychologist, 52,* 509–516.

McGinniss, J. (1969). *The selling of the president 1968.* New York: Trident.

McGuire, W. J. (1964). Inducing resistance to propaganda: Some contemporary approaches. In L. Berkowitz (Ed.), *Advances in experimental social psychology* (Vol. 1, pp. 191–229). New York: Academic Press.

McGuire, W. J. (1969). Suspiciousness of experimenter's intent. In R. Rosenthal & R. L. Rosnow (Eds.), *Artifact in behavioral research* (pp. 13–57). New York: Academic Press.

McGuire, W. J. (1973). The yin and yang of progress in social psychology: Seven koan. *Journal of Personality and Social Psychology, 26,* 446–456.

McGuire, W. J. (1976). Historical comparisons: Testing psychological hypotheses with cross-era data. *International Journal of Psychology, 11,* 161–183.

McGuire, W. J. (1983). A contextualist theory of knowledge: Its implications for innovation and reform in psychological research. In L. Berkowitz (Ed.), *Advances in experimental social psychology* (Vol. 16, pp. 1–47). New York: Academic Press.

McGuire, W. J. (1985). Attitudes and attitude change. In G. Lindzey & E. Aronson (Eds.), *Handbook of social psychology: Vol. 2. Special fields and applications* (3rd ed., pp. 233–346). New York: Random House.

McGuire, W. J. (1986). A perspectivist looks at contextualism and the future of behavioral science. In R. L. Rosnow & M. Georgoudi (Eds.), *Contextualism and understanding in behavioral science: Implications for research and theory* (pp. 271–301). New York: Praeger.

McGuire, W. J. (1997). Creative hypothesis generating in psychology: Some useful heuristics. *Annual Review of Psychology, 48,* 1–30.

McGuire, W. J. (2004). A perspectivist approach to theory construction. *Personality and Social Psychology Review, 8,* 173–182.

McGuire, W. J., & McGuire, C. V. (1981). The spontaneous self-concept as affected by personal distinctiveness. In M. D. Lynch, A. A. Norem-Hebeisen, & K. Gergen (Eds.), *Self-concept: Advances in theory and research* (pp. 147–171). Cambridge, MA: Ballinger.

McGuire, W. J., & McGuire, C. V. (1982). Significant others in self-space: Sex differences and development trends in the social self. In J. Suls (Ed.), *Psychological perspectives on the self* (pp. 71–96). Hillsdale, NJ: Erlbaum.

McKim, V. R., & Turner, S. P. (1997). *Causality in crisis? Statistical methods and the search for causal knowledge in the social sciences.* Notre Dame, IN: University of Notre Dame Press.

McLoyd, V. C. (1998). Socioeconomic disadvantage and child development. *American Psychologist, 53,* 185–204.

McNemar, Q. (1946). Opinion-attitude methodology. *Psychological Bulletin, 43,* 289–374.

McNemar, Q. (1960). At random: Sense and nonsense. *American Psychologist, 15,* 295–300.

McNemar, Q. (1962). *Psychological statistics* (3rd ed.). New York: Wiley.

McNemar, Q. (1969). *Psychological statistics* (4th ed.). New York: Wiley.

Medawar, P. B. (1969). *Induction and intuition in scientific thought.* (Jayne Lectures for 1968). Philadelphia: American Philosophical Society.

Meehl, P. E. (1978). Theoretical risks and tabular asterisks: Sir Karl, Sir Ronald, and slow progress of soft psychology. *Journal of Consulting and Clinical Psychology, 46,* 806–834.

Meier, P. (1978). The biggest public health experiment ever: The 1954 field trial of the Salk poliomyelitis vaccine. In J. M. Tanur (Ed). *Statistics: A guide to the unknown* (2nd ed.; pp. 3–15). San Francisco: Holden-Day.

Meier, P. (1989). The biggest public health experiment ever: The 1954 field trial of the Salk poliomyelitis vaccine. In J. M. Tanur, F. Mosteller, W. H. Kruskal, E. L. Lehmann, R. F. Link, R. S. Pieters, & G. R. Rising (Eds.), *Statistics: A guide to the unknown* (3rd ed.). Pacific Grove, CA: Wadsworth.

Melton, G. B., Levine, R. J., Koocher, G. P., Rosenthal, R., & Thompson, W. C. (1988). Community consultation in social sensitive research: Lessons from clinical trials of treatments of AIDS. *American Psychologist, 43,* 573–581.

Melzack, R. (1975). The McGill pain questionnaire: Major properties and scoring methods. *Pain, 1,* 277–299.

Melzack, R., & Katz, J. (1992). The McGill pain questionnaire: Appraisal and current status. In D. C. Turk & R. Melzack (Eds.), *Handbook of pain assessment* (pp. 152–168). New York: Guilford.

Meng, X. L., Rosenthal, R., & Rubin, D. B. (1992). Comparing correlated correlation coefficients. *Psychological Bulletin, 111,* 172–175.

Merriam, S. B. (1991). *Case study research in education: A qualitative approach.* San Francisco: Jossey-Bass.

Merton, R. K. (1948). The self-fulfilling prophecy. *Antioch Review, 8,* 193–210.

Merton, R. K. (1968). *Social theory and social structure* (Enlarged ed.). New York: Free Press.

Merton, R. K. (1993). *On the shoulders of giants: A Shandean postscript.* Chicago: University of Chicago Press.

Meyer, D. L. (1991). Interpretation of interaction: A reply to Rosnow and Rosenthal. *Psychological Bulletin, 110,* 571–573.

Milgram, S. (1963). Behavioral study of obedience. *Journal of Abnormal and Social Psychology, 67,* 371–378.

Milgram, S. (1964). Issues in the study of obedience: A reply to Baumrind. *American Psychologist, 19,* 848–852.

Milgram, S. (1965). Some conditions of obedience and disobedience to authority. *Human Relations, 18,* 57–76.

Milgram, S. (1970). The experience of living in cities. *Science, 167,* 1461–1468.

Milgram, S. (1975). *Obedience to authority: An experimental view.* New York: Harper Colophon Books.

Milgram, S. (1977). *The individual in a social world: Essays and experiments.* Reading, MA: Addison-Wesley.

Miller, A. I. (1986). *Imagery in scientific thought: Creating 20th century physics.* Cambridge: MA: MIT Press.

Miller, A. I. (1996). *Insights of genius: Imagery and creativity in science and art.* New York: Springer-Verlag.

Miller, N., & Campbell, D. T. (1959). Recency and primacy in persuasion as a function of the timing of speeches and measurements. *Journal of Abnormal and Social Psychology, 59,* 1–9.

Miller, N. E. (1985). The value of behavioral research on animals. *American Psychologist, 40,* 423–440.

Mills, J. (1976). A procedure for explaining experiments involving deception. *Personality and Social Psychology Bulletin, 2,* 3–13.

Milmoe, S., Rosenthal, R., Blane, H. T., Chafetz, M. E., & Wolf, I. (1967). The doctor's voice: Postdictor of successful referral of alcoholic patients. *Journal of Abnormal Psychology, 72,* 78–84.

Mingay, D. J., Shevell, S. K., Bradburn, N. H., & Ramirez, C. (1994). Self and proxy reports of everyday events. In N. Schwarz & S. Sudman (Eds.), *Autobiographical memory and validity of retrospective reports* (pp. 225–250). New York: Springer-Verlag.

Minturn, E. B., Lansky, L. M., & Dember, W. N. (1972). *The interpretation of levels of significance by psychologists: A replication and extension.* Paper presented at the meeting of the Eastern Psychological Association, Boston.

Mischel, W. (1968). *Personality and assessment.* New York: Wiley.

Mishler, E. G. (1979). Meaning in context: Is there any other kind? *Harvard Educational Review, 49,* 1–19.

Mitroff, I. (1974). Norms and counter-norms in a select group of the Apollo moon scientists: A case study of the ambivalence of scientists. *American Sociological Review, 39,* 579–595.

Monk, R. (1990). *Ludwig Wittgenstein: The duty of genius.* New York: Free Press.

Mook, D. G. (1983). In defense of external invalidity. *American Psychologist, 38,* 379–387.

Mooney, C. Z., & Duval, R. D. (1993). *Bootstrapping: A nonparametric approach to statistical inference.* Newbury Park, CA: Sage.

Moreno, J. L. (1934). *Who shall survive?* Beacon, NY: Beacon House.

Morgan, D. L. (1996). Focus groups. *Annual Review of Sociology, 22,* 129–152.

Morgan, D. L. (1997). *Focus groups as qualitative research* (2nd ed.). Thousand Oaks, CA: Sage.

Morgan, D. L., & Morgan, R. K. (2001). Single-participant research design: Bringing science to managed care. *American Psychologist, 56,* 119–127.

Morrison, D. E., & Henkel, R. E. (Eds.). (1970). *The significance test controversy*. Chicago: Aldine.

Morrison, D. F. (1976). *Multivariate statistical methods* (2nd ed.). New York: McGraw-Hill.

Morrison, D. F. (2005). *Multivariate statistical methods* (4th ed.). Belmont, CA: Brooks/Cole Thomson Learning.

Morrison, E. W. (1993). Longitudinal study of the effects of information seeking on newcomer socialization. *Journal of Applied Psychology, 78,* 173–183.

Moses, L. (1986). *Think and explain with statistics.* Reading, MA: Addison-Wesley.

Mosteller, F. (1968). Association and estimation in contingency tables. *Journal of the American Statistical Association, 63,* 1–28.

Mosteller, F. (1995). The Tennessee study of class size in the early school grades. *Future of Children: Critical Issues for Children and Youths, 5,* 113–127.

Mosteller, F., & Bush, R. R. (1954). Selected quantitative techniques. In G. Lindzey & E. Aronson (Eds.), *Handbook of social psychology* (Vol. 1, pp. 328–331). Cambridge, MA: Addison-Wesley.

Mosteller, F., Fienberg, S. E., & Rourke, R. E. K. (1983). *Beginning statistics with data analysis.* Reading, MA: Addison-Wesley.

Mosteller, F., & Rourke, R. E. K. (1973). *Sturdy statistics: Nonparametrics and order statistics.* Reading, MA: Addison-Wesley.

Mosteller, F., Rourke, R. E. K., & Thomas, G. B., Jr. (1961). *Probability and statistics.* Reading, MA: Addison-Wesley.

Mosteller, F., & Tukey, J. W. (1977). *Data analysis and regression.* Reading, MA: Addison Wesley.

Mulaik, S. A. (1972). *The foundations of factor analysis.* New York: McGraw-Hill.

Mullen, B., & Copper, C. (1994). The relation between group cohesiveness and performance: An integration. *Psychological Bulletin, 115,* 210–227.

Murphy, K. R., Jako, R. A., & Anhalt, R L. (1993). Nature and consequences of halo effect: A critical analysis. *Journal of Applied Psychology, 78,* 218–225.

Myers, J. L. (1979). *Fundamentals of experimental design* (3rd ed.). Boston: Allyn & Bacon.

Myers, J. L., & Well, A. D. (2003). *Research design and statistical analysis* (2nd ed.). Mahwah, NJ: Erlbaum.

National Commission for the Protection of Human Subjects of Biomedical and Behavioral Research. (1979). *The Belmont Report: Ethical principles and guidelines for the protection of human subjects of research.* Washington, DC: U.S. Government Printing Office.

Nederhof, A. J. (1981). *Some sources of artifact in social science research: Nonresponse, volunteering and research experience of subjects.* Leiden, Netherlands: Pasmans.

Nelson, N., Rosenthal, R., & Rosnow, R. L. (1986). Interpretation of significance levels and effect sizes by psychological researchers. *American Psychologist, 44,* 1276–1284.

Neuringer, A. (1992). Choosing to vary and repeat. *Psychological Science, 3,* 246–250.

Neuringer, A. (1996). Can people behave "randomly?" The role of feedback. *Journal of Experimental Psychology: General, 115,* 62–75.

Neuringer, A., & Voss, C. (1993). Approximating chaotic behavior. *Psychological Science, 4,* 113–119.

Nicks, S. D., Korn, J. H., & Mainieri, T. (1997). The rise and fall of deception in social psychology and personality research, 1921 to 1994. *Ethics and Behavior, 7,* 69–77.

Nie, N. H., Hull, C. H., Jenkins, J. G., Steinbrenner, K., & Bent, D. H. (1975). *SPSS: Statistical package for the social sciences* (2nd ed.). New York: McGraw-Hill.

Nijsse, M. (1988). Testing the significance of Kendall's τ and Spearman's r_s. *Psychological Bulletin, 103,* 235–237.

Niles, H. E. (1922). Correlation, causation, and Wright's theory of "path coefficients." *Genetics, 7,* 258–273.

Niles, H. E. (1923). The method of path coefficients—An answer to Wright. *Genetics, 8,* 256–260.

Nisbet, R. (1976). *Sociology as an art form.* London: Oxford University Press.

Nisbett, R. E., & Wilson, T. D. (1977). Telling more than we can know: Verbal reports on mental processes. *Psychological Review, 84,* 231–259.

Noether, G. E. (1967). *Elements of nonparametric statistics.* New York: Wiley.

Norman, D. A. (1973). Memory, knowledge, and the answering of questions. In R. S. Solso (Ed.), *Contemporary issues in cognitive psychology: The Loyola symposium* (pp. 135–165). Washington, DC: Winston.

Norwick, R., Choi, Y. S., & Ben-Shachar, T. (2002). In defense of self reports. *APS Observer, 15*(3), 7, 24.

Nunnally, J. C. (1978). *Psychometric theory.* New York: McGraw-Hill.

Nunnally, J. C., & Bernstein, I. H. (1994). *Psychometric theory* (3rd ed.). New York: McGraw-Hill.

Nye, M. J. (1985). Pierre Duhem. *Science, 230,* 165–166.

Oakes, M. (1986). *Statistical inference: A commentary for the social and behavioral sciences.* New York: Wiley.

Olkin, I. (1990). History and goals. In K. W. Wachter & M. L. Straf (Eds.), *The future of meta-analysis* (pp. 3–10). New York: Russell Sage Foundation.

Omodei, M. M., & Wearing, A. J. (1995). The Fire Chief microworld generating program: An illustration of computer-simulated microworlds as an experimental paradigm for studying complex decision-making behavior. *Behavioral Research Methods, Instruments, & Computers, 27,* 303–316.

Oppenheim, A. N. (1966). *Questionnaire design and attitude measurement.* New York: Basic Books.

Oppenheimer, R. (1956). Analogy in science. *American Psychologist, 11,* 127–135.

Orne, M. T. (1959). The nature of hypnosis: Artifact and essence. *Journal of Abnormal and Social Psychology, 58,* 277–299.

Orne, M. T. (1962). On the social psychology of the psychological experiment: With particular reference to demand characteristics and their implications. *American Psychologist, 17,* 776–783.

Orne, M. T. (1969). Demand characteristics and the concept of quasi-control. In R. Rosenthal & R. L. Rosnow (Eds.), *Artifact in behavioral research* (pp.143–179). New York: Academic Press.

Orne, M. T. (1970). Hypnosis, motivation, and the ecological validity of the psychological experiment. In W. J. Arnold & M. M. Page (Eds.), *Nebraska Symposium on Motivation* (pp. 187–265). Lincoln: University of Nebraska Press.

Orne, M. T., & Bauer-Manley, N. K. (1991). Disorders of self: Myth, metaphors, and demand characteristics of treatment. In J. Strauss & G. R. Goethals (Eds.), *The self: Interdisciplinary approaches* (pp. 93–106). New York: Springer-Verlag.

Orne, M. T., & Whitehouse, W. G. (2000). Demand characteristics. In A. E. Kazdin (Ed.), *Encyclopedia of psychology.* New York: Oxford University Press and American Psychological Association.

Osgood, C. E., & Luria, Z. (1954). A blind analysis of a case of triple personality using the semantic differential. *Journal of Abnormal and Social Psychology, 49,* 579–591.

Osgood, C. E., Suci, G. J., & Tannenbaum, P. H. (1957). *The measurement of meaning.* Urbana: University of Illinois Press.

Oskamp, S. (1977). *Attitudes and opinions.* Englewood Cliffs, NJ: Prentice Hall.

OSS Assessment Staff. (1948). *Assessment of men: Selection of personnel for the Office of Strategic Services.* New York: Rinehart.

Overall, J. E. (1965). Reliability of composite ratings. *Educational and Psychological Measurement, 25,* 1011–1022.

Overall, J. E. (1980). Continuity correction for Fisher's exact probability test. *Journal of Educational Statistics, 5,* 177–190.

Overall, J. E., Rhoades, H. M., & Starbuck, R. R. (1987). Small sample tests for homogeneity of response probabilities in 2×2 contingency tables. *Psychological Bulletin, 102,* 307–314.

Overall, J. E., & Spiegel, D. K. (1969). Concerning least squares analysis of experimental data. *Psychological Bulletin, 72,* 311–322.

Overall, J. E., Spiegel, D. K., & Cohen, J. (1975). Equivalence of orthogonal and nonorthogonal analysis of variance. *Psychological Bulletin, 82,* 182–186.

Overton, W. F. (1998). Developmental psychology: Philosophy, concepts, and methodology. In W. Damon (Ed.), *Handbook of child psychology* (5th ed., Vol. 1, pp. 108–188). New York: Wiley.

Page, M. (1974). Demand characteristics and the classical conditioning of attitudes experiment. *Journal of Personality and Social Psychology, 30,* 468–476.

Paik, H., & Comstock, G. (1994). The effects of television violence on antisocial behavior: A meta-analysis. *Communication Research, 21,* 516–546.

Pareek, U., & Rao, T. V. (1980). Cross-cultural surveys and interviewing. In H. C. Triandis & J. W. Berry (Eds.), *Handbook of cross-cultural psychology: Methodology* (Vol. 2, pp. 127–179). Boston: Allyn & Bacon.

Parker, K. C. H., Hanson, R. K., & Hunsley, J. (1988). MMPI, Rorschach, and WAIS: A meta-analytic comparison of reliability, stability, and validity. *Psychological Bulletin, 103,* 367–373.

Parsons, H. M. (1978). What caused the Hawthorne effect? A scientific detective story. *Administration and Society, 10,* 259–283.

Parsons, H. M. (1992). Assembly ergonomics in the Hawthorne studies. In M. Helander & M. Nagamachi (Eds.), *Design for manufacturability: A systems approach to concurrent engineering and ergonomics* (pp. 244–253). London: Taylor & Francis.

Paulhus, D. L. (1991). Measurement and control of response bias. In J. P. Robinson, P. R. Shaver, & L. S. Wrightsman (Eds.), *Measures of personality and social psychological attitudes* (Vol. 1, pp. 17–59). San Diego: Academic Press.

Paulos, J. A. (1990). *Innumeracy: Mathematical illiteracy and its consequences.* New York: Vintage Books.

Paulos, J. A. (1991, April 24). Math moron myths. *New York Times,* Op-Ed, p. 25.

Payne, R. L. (1996). Contextualism in context. In C. L. Cooper & I. T. Robertson (Eds.), *International review of industrial and organizational psychology* (Vol. 11, pp. 181–217). New York: Wiley.

Pearl, J. (2000). *Causality: Models, reasoning, and inference.* Cambridge, UK: Cambridge University Press.

Pearson, E. S., & Wishart, J. (Eds.). (1958). *Student's collected papers.* Cambridge, UK: Cambridge University Press.

Pearson, K. (1894). Science and Monte Carlo. *Fortnightly Review, 50,* 183–193.

Pearson, K. (1902). On the mathematical theory of errors of judgment with special reference to the personal equation. *Philosophical Transactions of the Royal Society of London, 198,* 235–299.

Pearson, K. (1904, November 5). Report on certain enteric fever inoculation statistics. *British Medical Journal,* 1243–1246.

Peek, C. J. (1977). A critical look at the theory of placebo. *Biofeedback and Self-Regulation, 2,* 327–335.

Pelz, D. C., & Andrew, F. M. (1964). Detecting causal priorities in panel study data. *American Sociological Review, 29,* 836–848.

Pepper, S. C. (1942). *World hypotheses: A study of evidence.* Berkeley: University of California Press.

Pepper, S. C. (1966). *Concept and quality: A world hypothesis.* LaSalle, IL: Open Court.

Pepper, S. C. (1973). Metaphor in philosophy. In P. P. Wiener (Ed.), *Dictionary of the history of ideas: Studies of selected pivotal ideas* (Vol. 3, pp. 196–201). New York: Scribner.

Pera, M., & Shea, W. R. (Eds.). (1991). *Persuading science: The art of scientific rhetoric.* Canton, MA: Science History.

Peterson, R. E. (1968a). *The scope of organized student protest in 1967–68.* Princeton, NJ: Princeton University Press.

Peterson, R. E. (1968b). The student left in American higher education. *Daedalus, 97,* 293–317.

Pfungst, O. (1911). *Clever Hans (The horse of Mr. Von Osten).* New York: Henry Holt. (Reissued 1965 by Holt, New York, with introduction by R. Rosenthal.)

Phillips, D. P. (1980). The deterrent effect of capital punishment: New evidence on an old controversy. *American Journal of Sociology, 86,* 139–148.

Phillips, D. P. (2000). Field experiments. In A. E. Kazdin (Ed.), *Encyclopedia of psychology.* New York: American Psychological Association and Oxford University Press.

Phillips, D. P., & Hensley, J. (1984). When violence is rewarded or punished: The impact of mass media stories on homicide. *Journal of Communication, 34,* 101–116.

Pierce, C. A., & Aguinas, H. (1997). Using virtual reality technology in organizational behavior research. *Journal of Organizational Behavior, 18,* 407–410.

Pinsoneault, T. B. (1998). A variable response inconsistency scale and a true response inconsistency scale for the Jesness Inventory. *Psychological Assessment, 10,* 21–32.

Pinsoneault, T. B. (2002). A variable responses inconsistency scale and a true response inconsistency scale for the Millon Adolescent Clinical Inventory. *Psychological Assessment, 14,* 320–330.

Platt, J. (1981a). Evidence and proof in documentary research: 1. Some specific problems of documentary research. *Sociological Review, 29,* 31–52.

Platt, J. (1981b). Evidence and proof in documentary research: 2. Some shared problems in documentary research. *Sociological Review, 29,* 53–66.

Plous, S. (1996). Attitudes toward the use of animals in psychological research and education: Results from a national survey of psychologists. *American Psychologist, 51,* 1167–1180.

Polanyi, M. (1963). The potential theory of adsorption. *Science, 141,* 1010–1013.

Polanyi, M. (1966). *The tacit dimension.* New York: Doubleday Anchor.

Pollard, P., & Richardson, J. T. E. (1987). On the probability of making Type I errors. *Psychological Bulletin, 102,* 159–163.

Popper, K. R. (1934). *Logik der Forschung.* Vienna: Springer-Verlag.

Popper, K. R. (1957). *The poverty of historicism.* London: Routledge.

Popper, K. R. (1958). *The logic of scientific discovery.* London: Hutchinson.

Popper, K. R. (1959). *The logic of scientific inquiry.* New York: Basic Books.

Popper, K. R. (1962). *Conjectures and refutations: The growth of scientific knowledge.* New York: Basic Books.

Popper, K. R. (1963). *Conjectures and refutations: The growth of scientific knowledge* (Rev. ed.). London: Routledge.

Popper, K. R. (1972). *Objective knowledge: An evolutionary approach.* Oxford, UK: Oxford University Press.

Prasad, J. (1950). A comparative study of rumours and reports in earthquakes. *British Journal of Psychology, 41,* 129–144.

Pratt, J. W., & Gibbons, J. D. (1981). *Concepts of nonparametric theory.* New York: Springer-Verlag.

Quenouille, M. H. (1949). Approximate tests of correlation in time-series. *Journal of the Royal Statistical Society,* Series B (Methodological), *11*(1), 68–84.

Quenouille, M. H. (1956). Notes on bias in estimation. *Biometrika, 43,* 353–360.

Quine, W. V. (1987). *Quiddities: An intermittently philosophical dictionary.* Cambridge, MA: Harvard University Press.

Ragin, C. C., & Becker, H. S. (Eds.). (1992). *What is a case? Exploring the foundations of social inquiry.* Cambridge, UK: Cambridge University Press.

Ramsay, D. S., & Woods, S. C. (2001). The use and usefulness of placebo controls. *Science, 294,* 785.

Ramul, K. (1963). Some early measurements and ratings in psychology. *American Psychologist, 18,* 653–659.

RAND Corporation. (1955). *A million random digits with 100,000 normal deviates.* New York: Free Press.

Randhawa, B. S., & Coffman, W. E. (Eds.). (1978). *Visual learning, thinking, and communication.* New York: Academic Press.

Rasch, G. (1960). *Probabilistic models for some intelligence and attainment tests.* Copenhagen: Danish Institute for Educational Research. (Expanded edition 1980, University of Chicago Press.)

Rasch, G. (1966). An item analysis which takes individual differences into account. *British Journal of Mathematical and Statistical Psychology, 19,* 49–57.

Raudenbush, S. W. (1984). Magnitude of teacher expectancy effects on pupil IQ as a function of the credibility of expectancy induction: A synthesis of findings from 18 experiments. *Journal of Educational Psychology, 76,* 85–97.

Reed, J. G., & Baxter, P. M. (1994). Using reference databases. In H. Cooper & L. V. Hedges (Eds.), *The handbook of research synthesis* (pp. 57–70). New York: Russell Sage Foundation.

Reed, S. K. (1988). *Cognition: Theory and applications* (2nd ed.). Pacific Grove, CA: Brooks/Cole.

Regis, E. (1987). *Who got Einstein's office? Eccentricity and genius at the Institute for Advanced Study.* Reading, MA: Addison-Wesley.

Reichardt, C. S. (2002). The priority of just-identified, recursive models. *Psychological Methods, 7,* 307–315.

Reichenbach, H. (1938). *Experience and prediction: An analysis of the foundations and structure of knowledge.* Chicago: University of Illinois Press.

Reilly, F. E. (1970). *Charles Peirce's theory of scientific method.* New York: Fordham University Press.

Remmers, H. H. (1963). Rating methods in research on teaching. In N. L. Gage (Ed.), *Handbook of research on teaching* (pp. 329–378). Chicago: Rand McNally.

Resnick, J. H., & Schwartz, T. (1973). Ethical standards as an independent variable in psychological research. *American Psychologist, 28,* 134–139.

Richard, F. D., Bond, C. F., Jr. & Stokes-Zoota, J. J. (2003). One hundred years of social psychology quantitatively described. *Review of General Psychology, 7,* 331–363.

Riessman, C. K. (1993). *Narrative analysis.* Newbury Park, CA: Sage.

Robert, J. S. (2004). *Embryology, epigenesis, and evolution: Taking development seriously.* Cambridge, UK: Cambridge University Press.

Roberts, L. (1987). Study bolsters case against cholesterol. *Science, 237,* 28–29.

Roberts, L. (1988). Vietnam's psychological toll. *Science, 241,* 159–161.

Roberts, R. M. (1989). *Serendipity: Accidental discoveries in science.* New York: Wiley.

Robinson, J. P., Shaver, P. R., & Wrightsman, L. S. (Eds.). (1991). *Measures of personality and social psychological attitudes.* San Diego: Academic Press.

Robinson, W. S. (1957). The statistical measurement of agreement. *American Sociological Review, 22,* 17–25.

Roethlisberger, F. J., & Dickson, W. J. (1939). *Management and the worker.* Cambridge, MA: Harvard University Press.

Rogosa, D. (1987). Causal models do not support scientific conclusions: A comment in support of Freedman. *Journal of Educational Statistics, 12,* 185–195.

Rorty, R. (1979). *Philosophy and the mirror of nature.* Princeton, NJ: Princeton University Press.

Rose, T. L. (1978). The functional relationship between artificial food colors and hyperactivity. *Journal of Applied Behavior Analysis, 11,* 439–446.

Rosen, E. (1951). Differences between volunteers and nonvolunteers for psychological studies. *Journal of Applied Psychology, 35,* 185–193.

Rosenbaum, P. R., & Rubin, D. B. (1983a). The central role of the propensity score in observational studies for causal effects. *Biometrika, 70,* 41–55.

Rosenbaum, P. R., & Rubin, D. B. (1983b). Assessing sensitivity to an unobserved binary covariate in an observational study with binary outcome. *Journal of the Royal Statistical Society, Series B, 45,* 212–218.

Rosenbaum, P. R., & Rubin, D. B. (1984). Reducing bias in observational studies using subclassification on the propensity score. *Journal of the American Statistical Association, 79,* 516–524.

Rosenbaum, P. R., & Rubin, D. B. (1985a). Constructing a control group using multivariate matched sampling methods that incorporate the propensity score. *American Statistician, 39,* 33–38.

Rosenbaum, P. R., & Rubin, D. B. (1985b). The bias due to incomplete matching. *Biometrics, 41,* 103–116.

Rosenberg, M. J. (1965). When dissonance fails: On eliminating evaluation apprehension from attitude measurement. *Journal of Personality and Social Psychology, 1,* 28–42.

Rosenberg, M. J. (1969). The conditions and consequences of evaluation apprehension. In R. Rosenthal & R. L. Rosnow (Eds.), *Artifact in behavioral research* (pp. 279–349). New York: Academic Press.

Rosengren, K. E. (Ed.). (1981). *Advances in content analysis.* Beverly Hills, CA: Sage.

Rosenhan, D. L. (1973). On being sane in insane places. *Science, 179,* 250–258.

Rosenthal, M. C. (1994). The fugitive literature. In H. Cooper & L. V. Hedges (Eds.), *The handbook of research synthesis* (pp. 85–94). New York: Russell Sage Foundation.

Rosenthal, M. C. (2006). Retrieving literature for meta-analysis: Can we really find it all? In D. A. Hantula (Ed.), *Advances in social and organizational psychology* (pp. 75–92). Mahwah, NJ: Erlbaum.

Rosenthal, R. (1966). *Experimenter effects in behavioral research.* New York: Appleton-Century-Crofts.

Rosenthal, R. (1967). Covert communication in the psychological experiment. *Psychological Bulletin, 67,* 356–367.

Rosenthal, R. (1968). Experimenter expectancy and the reassuring nature of the null hypothesis decision procedure. *Psychological Bulletin Monograph Supplement, 70,* Part 2, 30–47.

Rosenthal, R. (1969). Interpersonal expectations. In R. Rosenthal & R. L. Rosnow (Eds.), *Artifact in behavioral research* (pp. 181–277). New York: Academic Press.

Rosenthal, R. (1976). *Experimenter effects in behavioral research* (Enlarged ed.). New York: Irvington.

Rosenthal, R. (1978a). Combining results of independent studies. *Psychological Bulletin, 85,* 195–193.

Rosenthal, R. (1978b). How often are our numbers wrong? *American Psychologist, 33,* 1005–1008.

Rosenthal, R. (1979a). The "file drawer problem" and tolerance for null results. *Psychological Bulletin, 86,* 638–641.

Rosenthal, R. (Ed.). (1979b). *Skill in nonverbal communication: Individual differences.* Cambridge, MA: Oelgeschlager, Gunn & Hain.

Rosenthal, R. (1980). Summarizing significance levels. In R. Rosenthal (Ed.), *New directions for methodology of social and behavioral science: Quantitative assessment of research domains* (pp. 33–46). San Francisco: Jossey-Bass.

Rosenthal, R. (1983). Meta-analysis: Toward a more cumulative social science. In L. Bickman (Ed.), *Applied social psychology annual* (Vol. 4, pp. 65–93). Beverly Hills, CA: Sage.

Rosenthal, R. (1985a). Designing, analyzing, interpreting, and summarizing placebo studies. In L. White, B. Tursky, & G. E. Schwartz (Eds.), *Placebo: Theory, research, and mechanisms* (pp. 110–136). New York: Guilford.

Rosenthal, R. (1985b). From unconscious experimenter bias to teacher expectancy effect. In J. B. Dusek (Ed.), *Teacher expectancies* (pp. 37–65). Hillsdale, NJ: Erlbaum.

Rosenthal, R. (1987). *Judgment studies: Design, analysis, and meta-analysis.* Cambridge UK: Cambridge University Press.

Rosenthal, R. (1990a). How are we doing in soft psychology? *American Psychologist, 45,* 775–777.

Rosenthal, R. (1990b). Replication in behavioral research. *Journal of Social Behavior and Personality, 5,* 1–30.

Rosenthal, R. (1991a). *Meta-analytic procedures for social research* (Rev. ed.). Newbury Park, CA: Sage.

Rosenthal, R. (1991b). Some indices of the reliability of peer review. *Behavioral and Brain Sciences, 14,* 160–161.

Rosenthal, R. (1994a). Interpersonal expectancy effects: A 30-year perspective. *Current Directions in Psychological Science, 3,* 176–179.

Rosenthal, R. (1994b), Parametric measures of effect size. In H. Cooper & L. V. Hedges (Eds.), *Handbook of research synthesis* (pp. 231–244). New York: Russell Sage Foundation.

Rosenthal, R. (1994c). Science and ethics in conducting, analyzing, and reporting psychological research. *Psychological Science, 5,* 127–134.

Rosenthal, R. (1995a). Ethical issues in psychological science: Risk, consent, and scientific quality. *Psychological Science, 6,* 322–323.

Rosenthal, R. (1995b). Progress in clinical psychology: Is there any? *Clinical Psychology: Science and Practice, 2,* 133–150.

Rosenthal, R. (1995c). Writing meta-analytic reviews. *Psychological Bulletin, 118,* 183–192.

Rosenthal, R. (2000). Effect sizes in behavioral and biomedical research: Estimation and interpretation. In L. Bickman (Ed.), *Validity and social experimentation: Donald Campbell's legacy* (pp. 121–139). Thousand Oaks, CA: Sage.

Rosenthal, R., & Blanck, P. D. (1993). Science and ethics in conducting, analyzing, and reporting social science research: Implications for social scientists, judges, and lawyers. *Indiana Law Journal, 68,* 1209–1228.

Rosenthal, R., Blanck, P. D., & Vannicelli, M. (1984). Speaking to and about patients: Predicting therapists' tone of voice. *Journal of Consulting and Clinical Psychology, 52,* 679–686.

Rosenthal, R., & DePaulo, B. M. (1979a). Sex differences in accommodation in nonverbal communication. In R. Rosenthal (Ed.), *Skill in nonverbal communication: Individual differences* (pp. 68–103). Cambridge, MA: Oelgeschlager, Gunn & Hain.

Rosenthal, R., & DePaulo, B. M. (1979b). Sex differences in eavesdropping on nonverbal cues. *Journal of Personality and Social Psychology, 37,* 273–285.

Rosenthal, R., & DiMatteo, M. R. (2001). Meta-analysis: Recent developments in quantitative methods for literature reviews. *Annual Review of Psychology, 52,* 59–82.

Rosenthal, R., & DiMatteo, M. R. (2002). Meta-analysis. In H. Pashler & J. Wixted (Eds.), *Stevens' handbook of experimental psychology: Vol. 4. Methodology in experimental psychology* (pp. 391–428). New York: Wiley.

Rosenthal, R., & Fode, K. L. (1963). The effect of experimenter bias on the performance of the albino rat. *Behavioral Science, 8,* 183–189.

Rosenthal, R., & Gaito, J. (1963). The interpretation of levels of significance by psychological researchers. *Journal of Psychology, 55,* 33–38.

Rosenthal, R., & Gaito, J. (1964). Further evidence for the cliff effect in the interpretation of levels of significance. *Psychological Reports, 15,* 570.

Rosenthal, R., Hall, J. A., DiMatteo, M. R., Rogers, P. L., & Archer, D. (1979). *Sensitivity to nonverbal communication: The PONS Test.* Baltimore: Johns Hopkins University Press.

Rosenthal, R., Hiller, J., Bornstein, R. F., Berry D. T. R., & Brunell-Neuleib, S. (2001). Meta-analytic methods, the Rorschach, and the MMPI. *Psychological Assessment, 13,* 449–451.

Rosenthal, R., & Jacobson, L. (1968). *Pygmalion in the classroom: Teacher expectation and pupils' intellectual development.* New York: Holt, Rinehart & Winston.

Rosenthal, R., & Lawson, R. (1964). A longitudinal study of the effects of experimenter bias on the operant learning of laboratory rats. *Journal of Psychiatric Research, 2,* 61–72.

Rosenthal, R., & Rosnow, R. L. (Eds.). (1969a). *Artifact in behavioral research.* New York: Academic Press.

Rosenthal, R., & Rosnow, R. L. (1969b). The volunteer subject. In R. Rosenthal & R. L. Rosnow (Eds.), *Artifact in behavioral research* (pp. 59–118). New York: Academic Press.

Rosenthal, R., & Rosnow, R. L. (1975). *The volunteer subject.* New York: Wiley.

Rosenthal, R., & Rosnow, R. L. (1984). Applying Hamlet's question to the ethical conduct of research: A conceptual addendum. *American Psychologist, 39,* 561–563.

Rosenthal, R., & Rosnow, R. L. (1985). *Contrast analysis: Focused comparisons in the analysis of variance.* Cambridge, UK: Cambridge University Press.

Rosenthal, R., Rosnow, R. L., & Rubin, D. B. (2000). *Contrasts and effect sizes in behavioral research: A correlational approach.* New York: Cambridge University Press.

Rosenthal, R., & Rubin, D. B. (1971). Pygmalion reaffirmed. In J. D. Elashoff & R. E. Snow, *Pygmalion reconsidered* (pp. 139–155). Worthington, OH: C. A. Jones.

Rosenthal, R., & Rubin, D. B. (1978). Interpersonal expectancy effects: The first 345 studies. *Behavioral and Brain Sciences, 3,* 377–386.

Rosenthal, R., & Rubin, D. B. (1979a). Comparing significance levels of independent studies. *Psychological Bulletin, 86,* 1165–1168.

Rosenthal, R., & Rubin, D. B. (1979b). A note on percent variance explained as a measure of the importance of effects. *Journal of Applied Social Psychology, 9,* 395–396.

Rosenthal, R., & Rubin, D. B. (1982a). A simple general purpose display of magnitude of experimental effect. *Journal of Educational Psychology, 74,* 166–169.

Rosenthal, R., & Rubin, D. B. (1982b). Comparing effect sizes of independent studies. *Psychological Bulletin, 92,* 500–504.

Rosenthal, R., & Rubin, D. B. (1983). Ensemble-adjusted p values. *Psychological Bulletin, 94,* 540–541.

Rosenthal, R., & Rubin, D. B. (1984). Multiple contrasts and ordered Bonferroni procedures. *Journal of Educational Psychology, 76,* 1028–1034.

Rosenthal, R., & Rubin, D. B. (1985). Statistical analysis: Summarizing evidence versus establishing facts. *Psychological Bulletin, 97,* 527–529.

Rosenthal, R., & Rubin, D. B. (1986). Meta-analytic procedures for combining studies with multiple effect sizes. *Psychological Bulletin, 99,* 400–406.

Rosenthal, R., & Rubin, D. B. (1988). Comment: Assumptions and procedures in the file drawer problem. *Statistical Science, 3,* 120–125.

Rosenthal, R., & Rubin, D. B. (1989). Effect size estimation for one-sample multiple-choice-type data: Design, analysis, and meta-analysis. *Psychological Bulletin, 106,* 332–337.

Rosenthal, R., & Rubin, D. B. (1991). Further issues in effect size estimation for one-sample multiple-choice-type data. *Psychological Bulletin, 109,* 351–352.

Rosenthal, R., Rubin, D. B. (1994). The counternull value of an effect size: A new statistic. *Psychological Science, 5,* 329–334.

Rosenthal, R., & Rubin, D. B. (2003). $r_{equivalent}$: A simple effect size estimator. *Psychological Methods, 8,* 492–496.

Rosenzweig, S. (1933). The experimental situation as a psychological problem. *Psychological Review, 40,* 337–354.

Rosenzweig, S. (1977). Outline of a denotative definition of aggression. *Aggressive Behavior, 3,* 379–383.

Rosenzweig, S. (1981). The current status of the Rosenzweig picture-frustration study as a measure of aggression in personality. In P. F. Brain & D. Benton (Eds.), *Multidisciplinary approaches to aggression research* (pp. 113–125). New York: Elsevier.

Rosnow, R. L. (1966). Whatever happened to the "law of primacy"? *Journal of Communication, 16,* 10–31.

Rosnow, R. L. (1968). A "spread of effect" in attitude formation. In A. G. Greenwald, T. C. Brock, & T. M. Ostrom (Eds.), *Psychological foundations of attitudes* (pp. 89–107). New York: Academic Press.

Rosnow, R. L. (1971). Experimental artifact. In L. C. Deighton (Ed.), *The encyclopedia of education* (Vol. 3, pp. 483–488). New York: Macmillan and Free Press.

Rosnow, R. L. (1972, March). Poultry and prejudice. *Psychology Today, 5*(10), 53–56.

Rosnow, R. L. (1978). The prophetic vision of Giambattista Vico: Implications for the state of social psychological theory. *Journal of Personality and Social Psychology, 36,* 1322–1331.

Rosnow, R. L. (1980). Psychology of rumor. *Psychological Bulletin, 87,* 578–591.

Rosnow, R. L. (1981). *Paradigms in transition: The methodology of social inquiry.* New York: Oxford University Press.

Rosnow, R. L. (1986). Shotter, Vico and fallibilistic indeterminacy. *British Journal of Social Psychology, 25,* 215–216.

Rosnow, R. L. (1990). Teaching research ethics through role-play and discussion. *Teaching of Psychology, 17,* 179–181.

Rosnow, R. L. (1991). Inside rumor: A personal journey. *American Psychologist, 46,* 484–496.

Rosnow, R. L. (1997). Hedgehogs, foxes, and the evolving social contract in psychological science: Ethical challenges and methodological opportunities. *Psychological Methods, 2,* 345–356.

Rosnow, R. L. (2000). Longitudinal research. In A. E. Kazdin (Ed.), *Encyclopedia of psychology* (Vol. 5, pp. 76–77). New York: Oxford University Press and American Psychological Association.

Rosnow, R. L. (2001). Rumor and gossip in interpersonal interaction and beyond: A social exchange perspective. In R. M. Kowalski (Ed.), *Behaving badly: Aversive behaviors in interpersonal relationships* (pp. 203–232). Washington, DC: American Psychological Association.

Rosnow, R. L. (2002). Experimenter and subject artifacts. In N. J. Smelser & P. B. Baltes (Eds.), *International encyclopedia of the social and behavioral sciences.* New York: Elsevier.

Rosnow, R. L., & Aiken, L. S. (1973). Mediation of artifacts in behavioral research. *Journal of Experimental Social Psychology, 9,* 181–201.

Rosnow, R. L., & Arms, R. L. (1968). Adding versus averaging as a stimulus-combination rule in forming impressions of groups. *Journal of Personality and Social Psychology, 10,* 363–369.

Rosnow, R. L., & Davis, D. J. (1977). Demand characteristics and the psychological experiment. *ETC: A Review of General Semantics, 34,* 301–313.

Rosnow, R. L., & Fine, G. A. (1974). Inside rumors. *Human Behavior, 3*(8), 64–68.

Rosnow, R. L., & Fine, G. A. (1976). *Rumor and gossip: The social psychology of hearsay.* New York: Elsevier.

Rosnow, R. L., & Georgoudi, M. (Eds.). (1986). *Contextualism and understanding in behavioral science: Implications for research and theory.* New York: Praeger.

Rosnow, R. L., Goodstadt, B. E., Suls, J. M., & Gitter, A. G. (1973). More on the social psychology of the experiment: When compliance turns to self-defense. *Journal of Personality and Social Psychology, 27,* 337–343.

Rosnow, R. L., & Rosenthal, R. (1970). Volunteer effects in behavioral research. In K. H. Craik, B. Kleinmuntz, R. L. Rosnow, R. Rosenthal, J. A. Cheyne, & R. H. Walters, *New directions in psychology* (No. 4, pp. 211–277). New York: Holt, Rinehart & Winston.

Rosnow, R. L., & Rosenthal, R. (1974). Taming of the volunteer problem: On coping with artifacts by benign neglect. *Journal of Personality and Social Psychology, 30,* 188–190.

Rosnow, R. L., & Rosenthal, R. (1976). The volunteer subject revisited. *Australian Journal of Psychology, 28,* 97–108.

Rosnow, R. L., & Rosenthal, R. (1989a). Definition and interpretation of interaction effects. *Psychological Bulletin, 105,* 143–146.

Rosnow, R. L., & Rosenthal, R. (1989b). Statistical procedures and the justification of knowledge in psychological science. *American Psychologist, 44,* 1276–1284.

Rosnow, R. L., & Rosenthal, R. (1991). If you're looking at the cell means, you're not looking at *only* the interaction (unless all main effects are zero). *Psychological Bulletin, 110,* 574–576.

Rosnow, R. L., & Rosenthal, R. (1995). "Some things you learn aren't so": Cohen's paradox, Asch's paradigm, and the interpretation of interaction. *Psychological Science, 6,* 3–9.

Rosnow, R. L., & Rosenthal, R. (1996a). Computing contrasts, effect sizes, and counternulls on other people's published data: General procedures for research consumers. *Psychological Methods, 1,* 331–340.

Rosnow, R. L., & Rosenthal, R. (1996b). Contrasts and interactions redux: Five easy pieces. *Psychological Science, 7,* 253–257.

Rosnow, R. L., & Rosenthal, R. (1997). *People studying people: Artifacts and ethics in behavioral research.* New York: W. H. Freeman.

Rosnow, R. L., & Rosenthal, R. (2002). Contrasts and correlations in theory assessment. *Journal of Pediatric Psychology, 27,* 59–66.

Rosnow, R. L., & Rosenthal, R. (2003). Effect sizes for experimenting psychologists. *Canadian Journal of Experimental Psychology, 57,* 221–237.

Rosnow, R. L., & Rosenthal, R. (2008). *Beginning behavioral research: A conceptual primer* (6th ed.). Upper Saddle River, NJ: Prentice Hall.

Rosnow, R. L., Rosenthal, R., & Rubin, D. B. (2000). Contrasts and correlations in effect size estimation. *Psychological Science, 11,* 446–453.

Rosnow, R. L., & Rosnow, M. (2006). *Writing papers in psychology* (7th ed.). Belmont, CA: Thomson/ Wadsworth.

Rosnow, R. L., Rotheram-Borus, M. J., Ceci, S. J., Blanck, P. D., & Koocher, G. P. (1993). The institutional review board as a mirror of scientific and ethical standards. *American Psychologist, 48,* 821–826.

Rosnow, R. L., Skleder, A. A., Jaeger, M. E., & Rind, B. (1994). Intelligence and the epistemics of interpersonal acumen: Testing some implications of Gardner's theory. *Intelligence, 19,* 93–116.

Rosnow, R. L., Strohmetz, D., & Aditya, R. (2000). Artifact in research. In A. E. Kazdin (Ed.), *Encyclopedia of psychology* (Vol. 1, pp. 242–245). New York: Oxford University Press and American Psychological Association.

Rosnow, R. L., & Suls, J. M. (1970). Reactive effects of pretesting in attitude research. *Journal of Personality and Social Psychology, 15,* 338–343.

Rosnow, R. L., Wainer, H., & Arms, R. L. (1969). Anderson's personality-trait words rated by men and women as a function of stimulus sex. *Psychological Reports, 24,* 787–790.

Rosnow, R. L., Wainer, H., & Arms, R. L. (1970). Personality and group impression formation as a function of the amount of overlap in evaluative meaning of the stimulus elements. *Sociometry, 33,* 472–484.

Ross, L., Greene, D., & House, P. (1977). The "false consensus effect": An egocentric bias in social perception and attribution processes. *Journal of Experimental Social Psychology, 13,* 279–301.

Ross, S., Krugman, A. D., Lyerly, S. B., & Clyde, D. J. (1962). Drugs and placebos: A model design. *Psychological Reports, 10,* 383–392.

Rossi, P. H., Wright, J. D., & Anderson, A. B. (1983). Sample surveys: History, current practice, and future prospects. In P. H. Rossi, J. D. Wright, & A. B. Anderson (Eds.), *Handbook of survey research* (pp. 1–20). New York: Academic Press.

Rothenberg, R. (1990, October 5). Surveys proliferate, but answers dwindle. *New York Times,* pp. A1, D4.

Rotheram-Borus, M., Koopman, C., & Bradley, J. (1989). Barriers to successful AIDS prevention programs with runaway youth. In J. O. Woodruff, D. Doherty, & J. G. Athey (Eds.), *Troubled adolescents and HIV infection: Issues in prevention and treatment* (pp. 37–55). Washington, DC: Janis Press.

Rozeboom, W. W. (1960). The fallacy of the null hypothesis significance test. *Psychological Bulletin, 57,* 416–428.

Rozelle, R. M., & Campbell, D. T. (1969). More plausible rival hypotheses in the cross-lagged panel correlation technique. *Psychological Bulletin, 71,* 74–80.

Rozynko, V. V. (1959). Social desirability in the sentence completion test. *Journal of Consulting Psychology, 23,* 280.

Rubin, D. B. (1973). The use of matched sampling and regression adjustment to control bias in observational studies. *Biometrics, 29,* 184–203.

Rubin, D. B. (1976). Inference and missing data. *Biometrika, 63,* 581–592.

Rubin, D. B. (1978). Multiple imputations in sample surveys: A phenomenological Bayesian approach to nonresponse. In *Proceedings of the Survey Research Methods Section* (pp. 20–34). Alexandria, VA: American Statistical Association.

Rubin, D. B. (1979). Using multivariate matched sampling and regression adjustment to control bias in observational studies. *Journal of the American Statistical Association, 74,* 366, 318–328.

Rubin, D. B. (1980). Bias reduction using Mahalanobis' metric matching. *Biometrics, 36,* 295–298.

Rubin, D. B. (1987). *Multiple imputation for nonresponse in surveys.* New York: Wiley.

Rubin, D. B. (1988). Estimation from nonrandomized treatment comparisons using subclassification on propensity scores. *Annals of Internal Medicine, 127,* 8(2), 757–763. (Expanded version)

Rubin, D. B. (1996). Multiple imputation after 18+ years. *Journal of the American Statistical Association, 90,* 822–828.

Rubin, D. B. (1998). Estimation from nonrandomized treatment comparisons using subclassification on propensity scores. Written version of invited presentation, April 10, 1997, at the German Cancer Research Center, Heidelberg, Germany.

Rubin, D. B., & Thomas, N. (1992a). Affinely invariant matching methods with ellipsoidal distributions. *Annals of Statistics, 20,* 1079–1093.

Rubin, D. B., & Thomas, N. (1992b). Characterizing the effect of matching using linear propensity score methods with normal covariates. *Biometrika, 79,* 797–809.

Rubin, D. B., & Thomas, N. (1996). Matching using estimated propensity scores: Relating theory to practice. *Biometrics, 52,* 249–264.

Rubin, D. B., & Thomas, N. (1997). Combining propensity score matching with additional adjustments for prognostic covariates. *Journal of the American Statistical Association, 95,* 573–585.

Ruch, F. L. (1942). A technique for detecting attempts to fake performance on a self-inventory type of personality test. In Q. McNemar & M. A. Merrill (Eds.), *Studies in personality.* New York: McGraw-Hill.

Ruehlmann, W. (1977). *Stalking the feature story.* Cincinnati, OH: Writer's Digest.

Rummell, R. J. (1970). *Applied factor analysis.* Evanston, IL: Northwestern University Press.

Ruse, M. (1995). Evolutionary epistemology. In R. Audi (Ed.), *The Cambridge dictionary of philosophy* (pp. 253–254). Cambridge, UK: Cambridge University Press.

Russell, B. (1945). *A history of western philosophy.* New York: Simon & Schuster.

Russell, B. (1957). *Understanding history.* New York: Philosophical Library.

Russell, B. (1992). *Human knowledge: Its scope and limits.* London: Routledge. (Original work published 1948)

Russell, W. M. S., & Burch, R. L. (1959). *The principles of human experimental technique.* London: Methuen.

Ryder, N. B. (1965). The cohort as a concept in the study of social change. *American Sociological Review, 30,* 843–861.

Sacks, H., Berrier, J., Reitman, D., Ancona-Berk, V. A., & Chalmers, T. C. (1987). Meta-analysis of randomized controlled trials. *New England Journal of Medicine, 316,* 450–455.

Sacks, H., Chalmers, T. C., & Smith, H., Jr. (1982). Randomized versus historical controls for clinical trials. *American Journal of Medicine, 72,* 233–240.

Sales, B. D., & Folkman, S. (Eds.). (2000). *Ethics in research with human participants.* Washington, DC: American Psychological Association.

Salsburg, D. (2001). *The lady tasting tea: How statistics revolutionized science in the twentieth century.* New York: W. H. Freeman.

Sambursky, S. (Ed.). (1975). *Physical thought: From the presocratics to the quantum physicists: An anthology.* New York: Pica Press.

Sands, B., & Gillyatt, P. (1996). Promising drugs of the future. *Harvard Health Letter, 21*(5), 7–8.

Sarbin, T. R. (1944). The logic of prediction in psychology. *Psychological Review, 51,* 210–228.

Sarbin, T. R. (1977). Contextualism: A world view for modern psychology. In J. K. Cole & A. W. Landfield (Eds.), *Nebraska Symposium on Motivation* (Vol. 24). Lincoln: University of Nebraska Press.

Sarbin, T. R. (Ed.). (1985). *Narrative psychology: The storied nature of human conduct.* New York: Praeger.

Sarbin, T. R., & Allen, V. L. (1968). Role theory. In G. Lindzey & E. Aronson (Eds.), *The handbook of social psychology* (Rev. ed., Vol. 1, pp. 488–567). Reading, MA: Addison-Wesley.

Sartre, J.-P. (1956). *Being and nothingness: A phenomenological essay on ontology.* New York: Washington Square Press.

Saxe, L. (1991). Lying: Thoughts of an applied social psychologist. *American Psychologist, 46,* 409–415.

Scarr, S. (1994). Ethical problems in research on risky behaviors and risky populations. *Ethics and Behavior, 4,* 147–155.

Scarr, S. (1998). American child care today. *American Psychologist, 53,* 95–108.

Schacter, D. L. (1996). *Searching for memory: The brain, the mind, and the past.* New York: Basic Books.

Schacter, D. L. (1999). The seven sins of memory: Insights from psychology and cognitive neuroscience. *American Psychologist, 54,* 182–203.

Schaeffer, N. C. (2002). Asking questions about threatening topics: A selective overview. In A. A. Stone, J. S. Turkkan, C. A. Bachrach, J. B. Jobe, H. S. Kurtzman, & V. S. Cain (Eds.), *The science of self-report: Implications for research and practice* (pp. 105–121). Mahwah, NJ: Erlbaum.

Schafer, J. L. (1997). *Analysis of incomplete multivariate data.* London: Chapman & Hall.

Schafer, J. L. (1999). NORM: Multiple Imputation of Incomplete Multivariate Data Under a Normal Model [Computer software]. Retrieved May 1, 2000, from http://methodology.psu.edu.

Schaie, K. W. (1965). A general model for the study of developmental problems. *Psychological Bulletin, 64,* 92–107.

Schaie, K. W. (1993). The Seattle longitudinal studies of adult intelligence. *Current Directions in Psychological Science, 2,* 171–175.

Schaie, K. W. (1994). The course of adult intellectual development. *American Psychologist, 49,* 304–313.

Schaie, K. W., & Willis, S. L. (1986). Can intellectual decline in the elderly be reversed? *Developmental Psychology, 22,* 223–232.

Scheffé, H. (1959). *The analysis of variance.* New York: Wiley.

Schlaifer, R. (1980). The relay assembly test room: An alternative statistical interpretation. *American Sociological Review, 45,* 995–1005.

Schlottmann, A. (2001). Perception versus knowledge of cause and effect in children: When seeing is believing. *Current Directions in Psychological Science, 10,* 111–115.

Schmidt, F. L. (1996). Statistical significance testing and cumulative knowledge in psychology: Implications for training of researchers. *Psychological Methods, 1,* 115–129.

Schneider, K. J. (1998). Toward a science of the heart: Romanticism and the revival of psychology. *American Psychologist, 53,* 277–289.

Schober, M. F. (1999). Making sense of questions: An interactional approach. In M. G. Sirken, D. J. Herrmann, S. Schechter, N. Schwartz, J. M. Tanur, & R. Tourangeau (Eds.), *Cognition and survey research* (pp. 77–93). New York: Wiley.

Schober, M. F., & Conrad, F. G. (2002). A collaborative view of standardized survey interviews. In D. Maynard, H. Houtkoop, N. C. Schaeffer, & J. van der Zouwen (Eds.), *Standardization and tacit knowledge: Interaction and practice in the survey interview.* New York: Wiley.

Schuler, H. (1981). Ethics in Europe. In A. J. Kimmel (Ed.), *Ethics of human subject research* (pp. 41–48). San Francisco: Jossey-Bass.

Schuler, H. (1982). *Ethical problems in psychological research* (M. S. Woodruff & R. A. Wicklund, Trans.). New York: Academic Press. (Original work published 1980)

Schulman, K. A., Berlin, J. A., Harless, W., Kerner, J. F., Sistrunk, S., Gersh, B. J., Dube, R., Taleghani, C. K., Burke, J. E., Williams, S., Eisenberg, J. M., & Escarce, J. J. (1999). The effect of race and sex on physicians' recommendations for cardiac catheterization. *New England Journal of Medicine, 340,* 618–626. Erratum in *New England Journal of Medicine, 340,* 1130.

Schuman, H., Kalton, G., & Ludwig, J. (1983). Context and contiguity. *Public Opinion Quarterly, 47,* 112–228.

Schuman, H., & Presser, S. (1996). *Questions and answers in attitude surveys: Experiments on question form, wording, and context.* Thousand Oaks, CA: Sage.

Schwandt, T. A. (1997). *Qualitative inquiry: A dictionary of terms.* Thousand Oaks, CA: Sage.

Scott-Jones, D. (1994). Ethical issues in reporting and referring in research with low-income minority children. *Ethics and Behavior, 42,* 97–108.

Scott-Jones, D., & Rosnow, R. L. (1998). Ethics and mental health research. In H. Friedman (Ed.), *Encyclopedia of mental health* (Vol. 2, pp. 149–160). San Diego: Academic Press.

Seale, C. F. (2002). Computer-assisted analysis of qualitative interview data. In J. F. Gubrium & J. A. Holstein (Eds.), *Handbook of interview research: Context and methods* (pp. 651–694). Thousand Oaks, CA: Sage.

Sedlmeier, P., & Gigerenzer, G. (1989). Do studies of statistical power have an effect on the power of studies? *Psychological Bulletin, 105,* 309–316.

Sellin, J. T., & Wolfgang, M. E. (1964). *The measurement of delinquency.* New York: Wiley.

Shadish, W. R. (1996). Meta-analysis and the exploration of causal mediating processes: A primer of examples, methods, and issues. *Psychological Methods, 1,* 47–65.

Shadish, W. R. (2000). Nonrandomized designs. In A. E. Kazdin (Ed.), *Encyclopedia of psychology.* New York: American Psychological Association and Oxford University Press.

Shadish, W. R., Cook, T. D., & Campbell, D. T. (2002). *Experimental and quasi-experimental designs for generalized causal inference.* Boston: Houghton Mifflin.

Shadish, W. R., Hu, X., Glaser, R. R., Kownacki, R., & Wong, S. (1998). A method for exploring the effects of attrition in randomized experiments with dichotomous outcomes. *Psychological Methods, 3,* 3–22.

Shaffer, J. P. (1991). Comment on "Effect size estimation for one-sample multiple-choice-type data: Design, analysis, and meta-analysis" by Rosenthal and Rubin (1989). *Psychological Bulletin, 109,* 348–350.

Shain, R. N., Piper, J. M., Newton, E. R., Perdue, S. T., Ramos, R., Champion, J. D., & Guerra, F. A. (1999). A randomized, controlled trial of a behavioral intervention to prevent sexually transmitted disease among minority women. *New England Journal of Medicine, 340,* 93–100.

Shao, J., & Tu, D. (1995). *The jackknife and bootstrap.* New York: Springer.

Shapiro, A. K., & Morris, L. A. (1978). The placebo effect in medical and psychological therapies. In J. L. Garfield & A. E. Bergin (Eds.), *Handbook of psychotherapy and behavioral change: An empirical analysis* (2nd ed., pp. 369–410). New York: Wiley.

Shaw, M. E., & Wright, J. M. (1967). *Scales for the measurement of attitudes.* New York: McGraw-Hill.

Shea, J. D. C., & Jones, J. (1982). A model for the use of attitude scales across cultures. *International Journal of Psychology, 17,* 331–343.

Shenker, I. (1971, December 9). Struggling with perennial and elusive problem: Defining aggression. *New York Times,* p. 14.

Shepard, R. N., Romney, A. K., & Nerlove, S. B. (Eds.). (1972). *Multidimensional scaling* (2 vols.). New York: Seminar Press.

Sherif, M. (1936). *The psychology of social norms.* New York: Harper & Row.

Shermer, M. (1997). *Why people believe weird things: Pseudoscience, superstition, and other confusions of our time.* New York: W. H. Freeman.

Sherwood, J. J., & Nataupsky, M. (1968). Predicting the conclusions of Negro-white intelligence research from biographical characteristics of the investigator. *Journal of Personality and Social Psychology, 8,* 53–58.

Shibutani, T. (1966). *Improvised news: A sociological study of rumor.* Indianapolis: Bobbs-Merrill.

Shotter, J. (1984). *Social accountability and selfhood.* Oxford, UK: Blackwell.

Shotter, J. (1986). A sense of place: Vico and the social production of social identities. *British Journal of Social Psychology, 25,* 199–211.

Shrout, P. E., & Bolger, N. (2002). Mediation in experimental and nonexperimental studies: New procedures and recommendations. *Psychological Methods, 7,* 422–445.

Shrout, P. E., & Fiske, S. T. (Eds.). (1995). *Personality research, methods, and theory: A Festschrift honoring Donald W. Fiske.* Hillsdale, NJ: Erlbaum.

Shumaker, S. A., Legault, C., Rapp, S. R., Thal, L., Wallace, R. B., Ocken, J. K., Hendrix, S. L., Jones, B. N., III, Assaf, A. R., Jackson, R, D., Kotchen, J. M., Wassertheil-Smoller, S., & Wactawski-Wende, J. (2003). Estrogen plus progestin and the incidence of dementia and mild cognitive impairment in postmenopausal women. The Women's Health Initiative Memory Study: A randomized controlled trial. *Journal of the American Medical Association, 289,* 2651–2662.

Shuy, R. W. (2002). In-person versus telephone interviewing. In J. F. Gubrium & J. A. Holstein (Eds.), *Handbook of interview research: Context and method* (pp. 537–555). Thousand Oaks, CA: Sage.

Sidman, M. (1960). *Tactics of scientific research: Evaluating experimental data in psychology.* New York: Basic Books.

Sieber, J. E. (Ed.). (1982a). *The ethics of social research: Fieldwork, regulation, and publication.* New York: Springer-Verlag.

Sieber, J. E. (Ed.). (1982b). *The ethics of social research: Surveys and experiments.* New York: Springer-Verlag.

Siegel, S. (1956). *Nonparametric statistics for the behavioral sciences.* New York: McGraw-Hill.

Siegel, S., & Castellan, N. J. Jr. (1988). *Nonparametric statistics for the behavioral sciences* (2nd ed.). New York: McGraw-Hill.

Sigall, H., Aronson, E., & Van Hoose, T. (1970). The cooperative subject: Myth or reality? *Journal of Experimental Social Psychology, 6,* 1–10.

Silverman, I. (1977). *The human subject in the psychological laboratory.* New York: Pergamon.

Simon, H. A. (1979). Fit, finite, and universal axiomatization of theories. *Philosophy of Science, 46,* 295–301.

Simon, H. A. (1983). Fitness requirements for scientific theories. *British Journal of the Philosophy of Science, 34,* 355–365.

Simon, H. A., & Groen, G. J. (1973). Ramsey eliminability and the testability of scientific theories. *British Journal of the Philosophy of the Science, 24,* 367–380.

Simon, W. M. (1972). *European positivism in the nineteenth century.* Ithaca, NY: Cornell University Press.

Singer, E., Groves, R. M., & Corning, A. D. (1999). Differential incentives: Beliefs about practices, perceptions of equity, and effects on survey participation. *Public Opinion Quarterly, 63,* 251–260.

Singer, E., Hippler, H.-J., & Schwarz, N. (1992). Confidentiality assurances in surveys: Reassurance or threat? *International Journal of Public Opinion, 4,* 256–268.

Singer, E., Van Hoewyk, J., Gebler, N., Raghunathan, T., & McGonagle, K. (1999). The effect of incentives on response rates in interviewer-mediated surveys. *Journal of Official Statistics, 15,* 217–230.

Singer, E., Van Hoewyk, J., & Maher, M. P. (1998). Does the payment of incentives create expectation effects? *Public Opinion Quarterly, 62,* 152–164.

Singer, E., Van Hoewyk, J., & Maher, M. P. (2000). Experiments with incentives in telephone surveys. *Public Opinion Quarterly, 64,* 171–188.

Singleton, R. A., Jr., & Straits, B. C. (2002). Survey interviewing. In J. F. Gubrium & J. A. Holstein (Eds.), *Handbook of interview research: Context and method* (pp. 59–82). Thousand Oaks, CA: Sage.

Sinharay, S., Stern, H. S., & Russell, D. (2001). The use of multiple imputation for the analysis of missing data. *Psychological Methods, 6,* 317–329.

Skagestad, P. (1981). Hypothetical realism. In M. B. Brewer & B. E. Collins (Eds.), *Scientific inquiry and the social sciences* (pp. 77–97). San Francisco: Jossey-Bass.

Skinner, B. F. (1938). *The behavior of organisms.* New York: Appleton-Century-Crofts.

Skinner, B. F. (1953). Some contributions of an experimental analysis of behavior to psychology as a whole. *American Psychologist, 8,* 69–73.

Skinner, B. F. (1957). The experimental analysis of behavior. *American Scientist, 45,* 343–371.

Smart, R. G. (1966). Subject selection bias in psychological research. *Canadian Psychologist, 7a,* 115–121.

Smith, A. F. (1991). *Cognitive processes in long-term dietary recall.* Vital and Health Statistics, Series 6, No. 4. Hyattsville, MD: National Center for Health Statistics.

Smith, A. F., Jobe, J. B., & Mingay, D. (1991). Retrieval from memory of dietary information. *Applied Cognitive Psychology, 5,* 269–296.

Smith, C. (1980). *Selecting a source of local television news in the Salt Lake City SMSA: A multivariate analysis of cognitive and affective factors for 384 randomly-selected news viewers.* Unpublished doctoral dissertation, Temple University School of Communication, Philadelphia.

Smith, C. E., Fernengel, K., Holcroft, C., Gerald, K., & Marien, L. (1994.). Meta-analysis of the associations between social support and health outcomes. *Annals of Behavioral Medicine, 16,* 352–362.

Smith, C. P. (1983). Ethical issues: Research on deception, informed consent, and debriefing. In L. Wheeler & P. Shaver (Eds.), *Review of personality and social psychology* (Vol. 4, pp. 297–328). Beverly Hills, CA: Sage.

Smith, M. B. (1967). Conflicting values affecting behavioral research. *Children, 14*, 53–58.

Smith, M. B. (1969). *Social psychology and human values*. Chicago: Aldine.

Smith, M. L., & Glass, G. V (1977). Meta-analysis of psychotherapy outcome studies. *American Psychologist, 32*, 752–760.

Smith, M. L., Glass, G. V, & Miller, T. I. (1980). *The benefits of psychotherapy*. Baltimore: Johns Hopkins University Press.

Smith, T. W. (1995). Trends in nonresponse rates. *International Journal of Public Opinion Research, 7*, 157–171.

Snedecor, G. W. (1946). *Statistical methods* (4th ed.). Ames: Iowa State University Press.

Snedecor, G. W., Cochran, W. G. (1967). *Statistical methods* (6th ed.). Ames: Iowa State University Press.

Snedecor, G. W., & Cochran, W. G. (1980). *Statistical methods* (7th ed.). Ames: Iowa State University Press.

Snedecor, G. W., & Cochran, W. G. (1989). *Statistical methods* (8th ed.). Ames: Iowa State University Press.

Snider, J. G., & Osgood, C. E. (Eds.). (1969). *Semantic differential technique: A sourcebook*. Chicago: Aldine.

Sobal, J. (1982). Disclosing information in interview introductions: Methodological consequences of informed consent. *Sociology and Social Research, 66*, 348–361.

Society for Research in Child Development. (1993). Ethical standards for research with children. In *Directory of members* (pp. 337–339). Ann Arbor, MI: Author.

Solomon, R. L. (1949). An extension of control group design. *Psychological Bulletin, 46*, 137–150.

Solomon, R. L., & Lessac, M. S. (1968). A control group design for experimental studies of developmental processes. *Psychological Bulletin, 70*, 145–150.

Sommer, R. (1968). Hawthorne dogma. *Psychological Bulletin, 70*, 145–150.

Spearman, C. (1910). Correlation calculated from faulty data. *British Journal of Psychology, 3*, 271–295.

Spence, J. T., & Helmreich, R. (1978). *Masculinity and femininity: Their psychological dimensions, correlates, and antecedents*. Austin: University of Texas Press.

Sperry, R. W. (1968). Hemisphere disconnection and unity in conscious awareness. *American Psychologist, 23*, 723–733.

Spradley, J. P. (1980). *Participant observation*. New York: Holt.

Squire, P. (1988). Why the 1936 *Literary Digest* poll failed. *Public Opinion Quarterly, 52*, 125–133.

Stanley, B., & Sieber, J. (Eds.). (1992). *Social research on children and adolescents: Ethical issues*. Newbury Park, CA: Sage.

Stanley, J. (1971). Test reliability. In L. C. Deighton (Ed.), *Encyclopedia of education* (Vol. 9, pp. 143–153). New York: Macmillan and Free Press.

Starobin, P. (1997, January 28). Why those hidden cameras hurt journalism. *New York Times*, p. A21.

Steeh, C. G. (1981). Trends in nonresponse rates, 1952–1979. *Public Opinion Quarterly, 45*, 40–57.

Steering Committee of the Physicians' Health Study Research Group. (1988). Preliminary report: Findings from the aspirin component of the ongoing physicians' health study. *New England Journal of Medicine, 318*, 262–264.

Steiger, J. H. (1980). Tests for comparing elements of a correlation matrix. *Psychological Bulletin, 87*, 245–251.

Steiger, J. H. (2004). Beyond the *F* test: Effect size confidence intervals and tests of close fit in the analysis of variance and contrast analysis. *Psychological Methods, 9*, 164–182.

Stephens, N. G., Parsons, A., Schofield, P. M., Kelly, F., Cheeseman, K., Mitchinson, M. J., & Brown, M. J. (1996). Randomised controlled trial of vitamin E in patients with coronary disease: Cambridge Heart Antioxidant Study (CHAOS). *Lancet, 347*, 781–786.

Stephenson, W. (1953). *The study of behavior: Q-technique and its methodology*. Chicago: University of Illinois Press.

Stephenson, W. (1980). Newton's fifth rule and Q methodology: Application to educational psychology. *American Psychologist, 35*, 882–889.

Sterling, T. D. (1959). Publication decisions and their possible effects on inferences drawn from tests of significance—or vice versa. *Journal of the American Statistical Association, 54*, 30–34.

Sternberg, M. L. A. (Ed.). (1981). *American Sign Language: A comprehensive dictionary*. New York: Harper & Row.

Steuer, J. (1992). Defining virtual reality: Dimensions determining telepresence. *Journal of Communication, 42,* 73–93.

Stevens, J. (2002). *Applied multivariate statistics for the social sciences* (4th ed.). Mahwah, NJ: Erlbaum.

Stevens, S. S. (1936). A scale for the measurement of a psychological magnitude: Loudness. *Psychological Review, 43,* 405–416.

Stevens, S. S. (1966). A metric for the social consensus. *Science, 151,* 530–541.

Stevens, S. S., & Galanter, E. H. (1957). Ratio scales and category scales for a dozen perceptual continua. *Journal of Experimental Psychology, 54,* 377–411.

Stigler, S. M. (1986). *The history of statistics: The measurement of uncertainty before 1900*. Cambridge, MA: Belknap Press.

Stockman, N. (1983). *Antipositivist theories of the sciences*. Dordrecht, Netherlands: D. Reidel.

Stone, P. (1997). Thematic text analysis: New agendas for analyzing text content. In C. W. Roberts (Ed.), *Text analysis for the social sciences: Methods for drawing statistical inferences from texts and transcripts*. Mahwah, NJ: Erlbaum.

Stone, P. (2000). Content analysis. In A. E. Kazdin (Ed.), *Encyclopedia of psychology*. New York: American Psychological Association and Oxford University Press.

Stone, P., Dunphy, D., Smith, M., & Ogilvie, D. (1966). *The General Inquirer: A complete approach to content analysis*. Cambridge, MA: MIT Press.

Straits, B. C., & Wuebben, P. L. (1973). College students' reactions to social scientific experimentation. *Sociological Methods and Research, 1,* 355–386.

Strauss, A., & Corbin, J. (Eds.). (1997). *Grounded theory in practice*. Thousand Oaks, CA: Sage.

Strauss, A., & Corbin, J. (Eds.). (1998). *Basics of qualitative research: Techniques and procedures for developing grounded theory* (2nd ed.). Thousand Oaks, CA: Sage.

Stricker, L. J. (1967). The true deceiver. *Psychological Bulletin, 68,* 13–20.

Strohmetz, D. B., Alterman, A. I., & Walter, D. (1990). Subject selection bias in alcoholics volunteering for a treatment study. *Alcoholism: Clinical and Experimental Research, 14,* 736–738.

Strohmetz, D. B., & Rosnow, R. L. (1994). A mediational model of research artifacts. In J. Brzezinski (Ed.), *Probability in theory-building: Experimental and non-experimental approaches to scientific research in psychology* (pp. 177–196). Amsterdam: Editions Rodopi.

Strube, M. J. (1985). Combining and comparing significance levels from nonindependent hypothesis tests. *Psychological Bulletin, 97,* 334–341.

Stryker, J. (1997, April 13). Tuskegee's long arm still touches a nerve. *New York Times*, p. 4.

Student. (1908). The probable error of a mean. *Biometrika, 6,* 1–25.

Sudman, S. (1983). Applied sampling. In P. H. Rossi, J. D. Wright, & A. B. Anderson (Eds.), *Handbook of survey research* (pp. 145–194). New York: Academic Press.

Sudman, S., & Bradburn, N. M. (1974). *Response effects in surveys: A review and synthesis*. Chicago: Aldine.

Sudman, S., Sirken, M. G., & Cowan, C. D. (1988). Sampling rare and elusive populations. *Science, 240,* 991–996.

Sullivan, D. S., & Deiker, T. E. (1973). Subject-experimenter perceptions of ethical issues: A validation study. *Teaching of Psychology, 19,* 106–108.

Suls, J. M., & Rosnow, R. L. (1981). The delicate balance between ethics and artifacts in behavioral research. In A. J. Kimmel (Ed.), *Ethics of human subject research* (pp. 55–67). San Francisco: Jossey-Bass.

Suls, J. M., & Rosnow, R. L. (1988). Concerns about artifacts in psychological experiments. In J. G. Morawski (Ed.), *The rise of experimentation in American psychology* (pp. 163–187). New Haven, CT: Yale University Press.

Susman, E. J., Dorn, L. D., & Fletcher, J. C. (1992). Participation in biomedical research: The consent process as viewed by children, adolescents, young adults, and physicians. *Journal of Pediatrics, 121,* 547–552.

Susman, G. I. (1976). *Autonomy at work: A sociotechnical analysis of participative management*. New York: Praeger.

Symonds, P. M. (1925). Notes on rating. *Journal of Applied Psychology, 9,* 188–195.

Tabachnick, B. G., & Fidell, L. S. (2001). *Using multivariate statistics* (4th ed.). Boston: Allyn & Bacon.

Tannenbaum, P. H., & Noah, J. E. (1959). Sportugese: A study of sports page communication. *Journalism Quarterly, 36,* 163–170.

Taylor, H. C., & Russell, J. T. (1939). The relationship of validity coefficients to the practical effectiveness of tests in selection: Discussion and tables. *Journal of Applied Psychology, 23,* 565–578.

Taylor, S. E., Pham, L. B., Rivkin, I. D., & Armor, D. A. (1998). Harnessing the imagination: Mental stimulation, self-regulation, and coping. *American Psychologist, 53,* 429–439.

Taylor, S. J., & Bogdan, R. (1998). *Introduction to qualitative research methods: A guidebook and resource* (3rd ed.). New York: Wiley.

Taylor, S. J., Bogdan, R., & Walker, P. (2000). Qualitative research. In A. E. Kazdin (Ed.), *Encyclopedia of psychology.* New York: American Psychological Association and Oxford University Press.

Tedlock, B. (2000). Ethnography and ethnographic representation. In N. K. Denzin & Y. S. Lincoln (Eds.), *Handbook of qualitative research* (2nd ed., pp. 455–486). Thousand Oaks, CA: Sage.

Terman, L. M., assisted by Baldwin, B. T., Bronson, E., DeVoss, J. C., Fuller, F., Goodenough, F. L., Kelley, T. L., Lima, M., Marshall, H., Moore, A. H., Raubenheimer, A. S., Ruch, G. M., Wiloughby, R. L., Wyman, J. B., & Yates, D. H.. (1925). *Genetic studies of genius: Vol. 1. Mental and physical traits of a thousand gifted children.* Stanford, CA: Stanford University Press.

Terman, L. M., & Oden, M. H. (1947). *Genetic studies of genius: Vol. 4. The gifted child grows up.* Stanford, CA: Stanford University Press.

Thayer, H. S. (Ed.). (1982). *Pragmatism: The classic writings.* Indianapolis: Hackett.

Thigpen, C. H., & Cleckley, H. (1954). A case of multiple personality. *Journal of Abnormal and Social Psychology, 49,* 135–151.

Thomas, W. I., & Znaniecki, F. (1918). *The Polish peasant in Europe and America.* Boston: Badger.

Thompson, B. (Ed.). (1993). Statistical significance testing in contemporary practice: Some proposed alternatives with comments from journal editors [Whole issue]. *Journal of Experimental Education, 61,* 285–393.

Thompson, B. (1996). AERA editorial policies regarding statistical significance testing: Three suggested reforms. *Educational Researcher, 25*(2), 26–30.

Thompson, B. (1999). Why "encouraging" effect size reporting is not working: The etiology of researcher resistance to changing practices. *Journal of Psychology, 133,* 133–140.

Thompson, B. (2002). What future quantitative social science research could look like: Confidence intervals for effect sizes. *Educational Researcher, 31*(2), 25–32.

Thompson, B. (2004). *Exploratory and confirmatory factor analysis: Understanding concepts and applications.* Washington, DC: American Psychological Association.

Thompson, G. E. (1960). Children's group. In P. H. Mussen (Ed.), *Handbook of research methods in child development* (pp. 821–853). New York: Wiley.

Thorndike, E. L. (1920). A constant error in psychological ratings. *Journal of Applied Psychology, 4,* 25–29.

Thorndike, R. L. (1933). The effect of the interval between test and retest on the constancy of the IQ. *Journal of Educational Psychology, 24,* 543–549.

Thurstone, L. L. (1929). Theory of attitude measurement. *Psychological Bulletin, 36,* 222–241.

Thurstone, L. L. (1929–1934). *The measurement of social attitudes.* Chicago: University of Chicago Press.

Tinsley, H. E. A., & Weiss, D. J. (1975). Interrater reliability and agreement of subjective judgments. *Journal of Counseling Psychology, 22,* 358–376.

Tolman, E. C. (1959). Principles of purposive behavior. In S. Koch (Ed.), *Psychology: A study of a science* (Vol. 2, pp. 92–157). New York: McGraw-Hill.

Torgerson, W. S. (1958). *Theory and methods of scaling.* New York: Wiley.

Toulman, S., & Leary, D. E. (1985). The cult of empiricism in psychology, and beyond. In S. Koch & D. E. Leary (Eds.), *A century of psychology as a science: Retrospections and assessment* (pp. 594–617). New York: McGraw-Hill.

Tourangeau, R. (1984). Cognitive sciences and survey methods. In T. B. Jabine, M. L. Straf, J. M. Tanur, & R. Tourangeau (Eds.), *Cognitive aspects of survey methodology: Building a bridge between disciplines* (pp. 73–101). Washington, DC: National Academy Press.

Tourangeau, R. (2000). Remembering what happened: Memory errors and survey reports. In A. A. Stone, J. S. Turkkan, C. A. Bachrach, J. B. Jobe, H. S. Kurtzman, & V. S. Cain (Eds.), *The science of self-report: Implications for research and practice* (pp. 29–47). Mahwah, NJ: Erlbaum.

Tourangeau, R., Rips, L. J., & Rasinski, K. (2000). *The psychology of survey responses.* Cambridge, UK: Cambridge University Press.

Tourangeau, R., & Smith, T. W. (1998). Collecting sensitive information with different modes of data collection. In M. Couper, R. Baker, Jr., J. Bethlehem, C. Clark, J. Martin, W. Nicholls, & J. O'Reilly (Eds.), *Computer-assisted survey information collection* (pp. 431–454). New York: Wiley.

Triandis, H. C. (1964). Exploratory factor analyses of the behavioral component of social attitudes. *Journal of Abnormal and Social Psychology, 68,* 420–430.

Triandis, H. C. (1971). *Attitude and attitude change.* New York: Wiley.

Triandis, H. C. (2000). Data collection: Field research. In A. E. Kazdin (Ed.), *Encyclopedia of psychology.* New York: American Psychological Association and Oxford University Press.

Trist, E. L., & Bamforth, K. W. (1951). Some social and psychological consequences of the long wall method of goal-getting. *Human Relations, 4,* 3–38.

Trist, E. L., Higgin, G. W., Murray, H., & Pollock, A. B. (1963). *Organizational choice: Capabilities of groups at the coal face under changing technologies.* London: Tavistock.

Tsai, C. C., Follis, K. E., Sabo, A, Beck, T. W., Grant, R. F., Bischofberger, N., Benveniste, R. E., & Black, R. (1995). Prevention of SIV infection in macaques by (R)-9-(2-phosphonylmethoxypropyl). *Science, 270,* 1197–1199.

Tufte, E. R. (1983). *The visual display of quantitative information.* Cheshire, CT: Graphics Press.

Tufte, E. R. (1990). *Envisioning information.* Cheshire, CT: Graphics Press.

Tufte, E. R. (1997). *Visual explanations: Images and quantities, evidence and narrative.* Cheshire, CT: Graphics Press.

Tufte, E. R. (2001). *The visual display of quantitative information* (2nd ed.). Cheshire, CT: Graphics Press.

Tufte, E. R. (2006). *Beautiful evidence.* Cheshire, CT: Graphics Press.

Tukey, J. W. (1958). Bias and confidence in not-quite large samples [Abstract]. *Annals of Mathematical Statistics, 29*(2), 614.

Tukey, J. W. (1977). *Exploratory data analysis.* Reading, MA: Addison-Wesley.

Turner, C. F., Ku, L., Rogers, S. M., Lindberg, J. H., Pleck, & Sonenstein, F. L. (1998). Adolescent sexual behavior, drug use, and violence: Increased reporting with computer survey technology. *Science, 280,* 867–873.

Turner, S. (1997). "Net effects": A short history. In V. R. McKim & S. P. Turner (Eds.), *Causality in crisis? Statistical methods and the search for causal knowledge in the social sciences* (pp. 23–45). Notre Dame, IN: University of Notre Dame Press.

Uppenbrink, J. (2000). Organizing the elements. *Science, 289,* 1696.

Upton, G. J. G. (1978). *The analysis of cross-tabulated data.* New York: Wiley.

Van Rompay, K., & Marthas, M. L. (1995). "The Duesberg Phenomenon": What does it mean? *Science, 267,* 157.

Vaught, R. S. (1977). What if subjects can't be randomly assigned? *Human Factors, 19,* 227–234.

Vico, G. (1970). *The new science of Giambattista Vico* (T. G. Bergin & M. H. Fisch, Trans.). Ithaca, NY: Cornell University Press. (Abridged translation of the third edition, 1744)

Vico, G. (1988). *On the most ancient wisdom of the Italians* (L. M. Parker, Trans.). Ithaca, NY: Cornell University Press. (Original work published 1710)

Vico, G. (1990). *On the study methods of our time* (E. Gianturco, Trans.). Ithaca, NY: Cornell University Press. (Original work published 1709)

Vogt, D. S., King, D. W., & King, L. A. (2004). Focus groups in psychological assessment: Enhancing content validity by consulting members of the target population. *Psychological Assessment, 16,* 231–243.

von Sternberg, J. (1965). *Fun in a Chinese laundry.* San Francisco: Mercury House.

Wachter, K. W. (1988). Disturbed by meta-analysis? *Science, 241,* 1407–1408.

Wachter, K. W., & Straf, M. (Eds.). (1990). *The future of meta-analysis*. New York: Russell Sage Foundation.

Wagner, G. P. (2004). The embryo of a dialogue. *Science, 305*, 1405–1406.

Wainer, H. (1972). Draft of Appendix for R. E. Lana & R. L. Rosnow's *Introduction to contemporary psychology*. New York: Holt, Rinehart & Winston.

Wainer, H. (1984). How to display data badly. *American Statistician, 38*, 137–147.

Wainer, H. (1999). The most dangerous profession: A note on nonsampling error. *Psychological Methods, 4*, 250–256.

Wainer, H. (2000). *Visual revelations: Graphical tales of fate and deception from Napoleon Bonaparte to Ross Perot*. Mahwah, NJ: Erlbaum.

Wainer, H., & Thissen, D. (1981). Graphical data analysis. *Annual Review of Psychology, 32*, 191–241.

Wainer, H., & Thissen, D. (1993). Graphical data analysis. In G. Keren & C. Lewis (Eds.), *A handbook for data analysis in the behavioral sciences: Statistical issues* (pp. 391–457). Hillsdale, NJ: Erlbaum.

Wainer, H., & Velleman, P. F. (2001). Statistical graphics: Mapping the pathways of science. *Annual Review of Psychology, 52*, 305–335.

Walker, H. M., & Lev, J. (1953). *Statistical inference*. New York: Henry Holt.

Wallace, D. A. (1954). A case for- and against-mail questionnaires. *Public Opinion Quarterly, 18*, 40–52.

Wallace, D. L. (1959). Bounds on normal approximations to Student's and the chi-square distributions. *Annals of Mathematical Statistics, 30*, 1121–1130.

Wallace, W. A. (1972). *Causality and scientific explanation: Medieval and early classical science*. Ann Arbor: University of Michigan Press.

Wallis, W. A., & Roberts, H. V. (1956). *Statistics: A new approach*. New York: Free Press.

Warner, S. L. (1965). Randomized response: A survey response for eliminating evasive answers. *Journal of the American Statistical Association, 60*, 63–69.

Warwick, D. P., & Lininger, C. A. (1975). *The sample survey: Theory and practice*. New York: McGraw-Hill.

Waterman, A. S. (1988). On the use of psychological theory and research in the process of ethical inquiry. *Psychological Bulletin, 103*, 283–298.

Watson, J. D. (1969). *The double helix*. New York: Mentor.

Watson, J. D. (1993). Succeeding in science: Some rules of thumb. *Science, 261*, 1812–1813.

Watzlawick, P. (Ed.). (1984). *The invented reality: How do we know what we believe we know? Contributions to constructivism*. New York: Norton.

Weaver, C. (1972). *Human listening*. Indianapolis: Bobbs-Merrill.

Webb, E. J., Campbell, D. T., Schwartz, R. F., & Sechrest, L. (1966). *Unobtrusive measures: Nonreactive research in the social sciences*. Chicago: Rand McNally.

Webb, E. J., Campbell, D. T., Schwartz, R. F., Sechrest, L., & Grove, J. B. (1981). *Nonreactive measures in the social sciences* (2nd ed.). Boston: Houghton Mifflin.

Webber, R. A. (1970). Perception of interactions between superiors and subordinates. *Human Relations, 23*, 235–248.

Weber, R. P. (1985). *Basic content analysis*. Beverly Hills, CA: Sage.

Wechler, J. (Ed.). (1978). *On aesthetics in science*. Cambridge, MA: MIT Press.

Wechsler, D. (1958). *The measurement and appraisal of adult intelligence* (4th ed.). Baltimore: Williams & Wilkins.

Weimann, G. (1982). The prophecy that never fails: On the uses and gratifications of horoscope reading. *Sociological Inquiry, 52*, 274–290.

Weiner, H. L., Mackin, G. A., Matsui, M., Orav, E. J., Khoury, S. J., Dawson, D. M., & Hafler, D. A. (1993). Double-blind pilot trial of oral tolerization with myelin antigens in multiple sclerosis. *Science, 259*, 1321–1324.

Weisberg, R. W. (1986). *Creativity: Genius and other myths*. New York: Freeman.

Weisberg, R. W. (1993). *Creativity: Beyond the myth of genius*. New York: Freeman.

Weisberg, R. W. (1994). Genius and madness? A quasi-experimental test of the hypothesis that manic-depression increases creativity. *Psychological Science, 5*, 361–367.

Weiss, J. M. (1968). Effects of coping responses on stress. *Journal of Comparative and Physiological Psychology, 65*, 251–260.

Welkowitz, J., Ewen, R. B., and Cohen, J. (1982). *Introductory statistics for the behavioral sciences* (3rd ed.). New York: Academic Press.

Welkowitz, J., Ewen, R. B., & Cohen, J. (2000). *Introductory statistics for the behavioral sciences* (5th ed.). New York: Harcourt Brace.

West, S. G. (2001). New approaches to missing data in psychological research: Introduction to the special section. *Psychological Methods, 6,* 315–316.

West, S. G., & Gunn, S. P. (1978). Some issues on ethics and social psychology. *American Psychologist, 33,* 30–38.

Westen, D., & Rosenthal, R. (2003). Quantifying construct validity: Two simple measures. *Journal of Personality and Social Psychology, 84,* 608–618.

Westen, D., & Rosenthal, R. (2005). Improving construct validity: Cronbach, Meehl, and Neurath's ship. *Psychological Assessment, 17,* 409–412.

Wheelan, S. A. (1994). *Group processes: A developmental perspective.* Boston: Allyn & Bacon.

Wheelwright, P. (Ed.). (1951). *Aristotle.* New York: Odyssey Press.

White, H. D. (1994). Scientific communication and literature retrieval. In H. Cooper & L. V. Hedges (Eds.), *The handbook of research synthesis* (pp. 41–55). New York: Russell Sage Foundation.

White, R. K. (1984). *Fearful warriors.* New York: Free Press.

Whiteley, J. M., Burkhart, M. Q., Harway-Herman, M., & Whiteley, R. M. (1975). Counseling and student development. *Annual Review of Psychology, 26,* 337–366.

Wickens, T. D., & Keppel, G. (1983). On the choice of design and of test statistic in the analysis of experiments with sampled materials. *Journal of Verbal Learning and Verbal Behavior, 22,* 296–309.

Wickesberg, A. K. (1968). Communication networks in a business organization structure. *Journal of the Academy of Management, 11,* 253–262.

Wiener, P. P. (Ed.). (1966). *Charles S. Peirce: Selected writings (Values in a universe of chance).* New York: Dover.

Wiggins, J. S. (Ed.). (1996). *The five-factor model of personality.* New York: Guilford.

Wilcox, B., & Gardner, D. (1993). Political intervention in scientific peer review: Research on adolescent sexual behavior. *American Psychologist, 48,* 972–983.

Wilcox, R. R. (1996). *Statistics for the social sciences.* New York: Academic Press.

Wilkes, K. V. (1978). *Physicalism: Studies in philosophical psychology.* Atlantic Highlands, NJ: Humanities Press.

Wilkins, W. (1984). Psychotherapy: The powerful placebo. *Journal of Consulting and Clinical Psychology, 52,* 570–573.

Wilkinson, L., & Engelman, L. (1996). Descriptive statistics. In L. Wilkinson (Ed.), *SYSTAT 9: Statistics I* (pp. 205–225). Chicago: SPSS.

Wilkinson, L., & Engelman, L. (1999). Bootstrapping and sampling. In SPSS Inc. Staff (Eds.), *SYSTAT 9: Statistics I.* Upper Saddle River, NJ: Prentice Hall PTR.

Wilkinson, L., & Task Force on Statistical Inference (1999). Statistical methods in psychology journals: Guidelines and explanations. *American Psychologist, 54,* 595–604.

Williams, C. D. (1959). The elimination of tantrum behavior by extinction procedures. *Journal of Abnormal and Social Psychology, 59,* 269.

Williams, E. J. (1959). The comparison of regression variables. *Journal of the Royal Statistical Society, Series B, 21,* 396–399.

Williams, P. C. (1984). Success in spite of failure: Why IRBs falter in reviewing risks and benefits. *IRB: A Review of Human Subjects Research, 6*(3), 1–4.

Willis, G., Brittingham, A., Lee, L., Tourangeau, R., & Ching, P (1999). *Response errors in surveys of children's immunizations.* Vital and Health Statistics, Series 6, No. 8. Hyattsville, MD: National Center for Health Statistics.

Willis, S. L., & Schaie, K. W. (1986). Training the elderly on the ability factors of spatial orientation and inductive reasoning. *Psychology and Aging, 1,* 239–247.

Willis, S. L., & Schaie, K. W. (1988). Gender differences in spatial ability in old age: Longitudinal and intervention findings. *Sex Roles, 18,* 189–203.

Winer, B. J. (1962). *Statistical principles in experimental design.* New York: McGraw-Hill.

Winer, B. J. (1971). *Statistical principles in experimental design* (2nd ed.). New York: McGraw-Hill.

Winer, B. J., Brown, D. R., & Michels, K. M. (1991). *Statistical principles in experimental design* (3rd ed.). New York: McGraw-Hill.

Wing, R. R., & Jeffery, R. W. (1999). Benefits of recruiting participants with friends and increasing social support for weight loss and maintenance. *Journal of Consulting and Clinical Psychology, 67,* 132–138.

Winkler, R. L. (1993). Bayesian statistics: An overview. In G. Keren & C. Lewis (Eds.), *Handbook for data analysis in the behavioral sciences: Statistical issues* (pp. 201–232). Hillsdale, NJ: Erlbaum.

Wittgenstein, L. (1978). *Tractatus logico-philosophicus.* London: Routledge & Kegan Paul.

Wohlwill, J. R. (1970). Methodology and research strategy in the study of developmental change. In L. Goulet & P. Baltes (Eds.), *Life-span developmental psychology* (pp. 92–191). New York: Academic Press.

Wolcott, H. F. (1994). *Transforming qualitative data: Description, analysis, and interpretation.* Thousand Oaks, CA: Sage.

Woodrum, E. (1984). "Mainstreaming" content analysis in social science: Methodological advantages, obstacles, and solutions. *Social Science Research, 13,* 1–19.

Wright, S. (1921). Correlation and causation. *Journal of Agricultural Research, 20,* 557–585.

Wright, S. (1923). The theory of path coefficients—A reply to Niles's criticisms. *Genetics, 8,* 239–255.

Young, F. W. (1968). A FORTRAN IV program for nonmetric multidimensional scaling. *L. L. Thurstone Psychometric Laboratory Monograph,* No. 56.

Young, F. W., & Hamer, R. M. (Eds.). (1987). *Multidimensional scaling: History, theory, and applications.* Hillsdale, NJ: Erlbaum.

Yule, G. U. (1903). Notes on the theory of association of attributes in statistics. *Biometrika, 2*(2), 121–134.

Zaitzow, B. H., & Fields, C. B. (1996). Using archival sets. In F. T. L. Leong & J. T. Austin (Eds.), *The psychology research handbook: A guide for graduate students and research assistants* (pp. 251–261). Thousand Oaks, CA: Sage.

Zajonc, R. F. (1968). Attitudinal effects of mere exposure. *Journal of Personality and Social Psychology, 9*(Part 2), 211–215.

Zar, J. H. (1984). *Biostatistical analysis* (2nd ed.). Englewood Cliffs, NJ: Prentice Hall.

Zechmeister, E. G., & Nyberg, S. E. (1982). *Human memory: An introduction to research and theory.* Monterey, CA: Brooks/Cole.

Zillman, D. (1979). *Hostility and aggression.* Hillsdale, NJ: Erlbaum.

Ziman, J. (1978). *Reliable knowledge: An exploration of the grounds for belief in science.* Cambridge, UK: Cambridge University Press.

Zuckerman, M., Hodgins, H. S., Zuckerman, A., & Rosenthal, R. (1993). Contemporary issues in the analysis of data: A survey of 551 psychologists. *Psychological Science, 4,* 49–53.

SUBJECT INDEX

(Additional terms are listed in the Glossary of this book.)

A

a priori method, 14–15, 737
A-B-A (and variant) designs, 241, 489, 737
Abscissa (*X* axis), 294–295, 737
Absolute values, 302, 309, 737
Accidental plagiarism, 79, 737
Acquiescent response set, 175–176, 737
Action research, 124, 737
Active deception (deception by commission), 64, 737
Activity (as dimension of meaning), 148, 178
Ad hoc hypothesis, 22, 737
Adlerian psychology (in quotation), 50–51
Aesthetics, 17–18, 737
Age effect, 254–255
Aggregating (pooling) error terms, 561–562, 568–569, 577–578
Aggression (in examples), 46–47, 246–247
Agreement, method of, 201–202
Aircraft armor (in example), 275–276
Alcohol problem (in example), 321–322
Alerting correlation ($r_{alerting}$), 445–447, 451–453, 737
Algebraic values, 302, 737
Alpha (α), 53, 422–423, 738
Alpha coefficient, 97, 738
Alternate hypothesis (H_1), 53–54, 738
Alternate-form reliability, 90–91, 738
Analogical rhetoric or thinking, 738
Analysis of variance (*See* ANOVA)
Ancestry search, 82–83
ANCOVA (analysis of covariance), 493–495, 738
  multivariate, 661–662
Animal subjects (in research), 82–83, 241–242
ANOVA (analysis of variance), 97, 99, 410–414, 434–435, 482–484, 593, 738
  and blocking, 490–492
  and interaction effects, 499–501

and lambda (λ) weights, 484
and Latin squares, 539
multivariate multilevel, 661
one-way, 464–466, 470, 476–477
and qualitative data, 596–597
and summary tables, 414–417
three-way, 485–486
2 × 2, 462–463
2 × 3, 480–481, 483
two-way, 467–468, 470, 476–477, 528–531
unweighted means, 475–478, 488
Antisemitism study (as example), 175–176
"Anything goes" view of science, 738
APA (American Psychological Association), 62–63
APA code, 64–67, 69, 738
APA publication manual, 393, 415, 738
Archival data, 131–132
Archives, 130–131, 737
Arcsin transformation, 736, 738
Area probability sampling, 271, 737
ARIMA (autoregressive integrated moving average), 238–239, 738
Arithmetic mean (*M*), 300, 363, 384, 738
Armor's theta, 647–648, 738
Artifacts, 738
  as threat to validity, 216–220, 231–232
  noninteractional, 128–129
Aspirin study (as example), 57–58, 327
Associative, 245
Astronomy (in example), 197
Asymmetrical distributions, 738
Attenuation, 245, 738
Attitude scales, 177–178
Aufforderungscharakter, 220, 738
Authority method, 14, 738
Autocorrelation (of observation), 239, 738
Autoethnography, 124, 738
Average deviation ($\overline{D}$), D302 , 738

815

NAME INDEX

828

H

Among the many equations listed in Appendix A are those that describe the definitions and interpretation of effect size indicators (see chapter 12). Shown below are equations illustrating three of the most popular indices: Pearson's r, Cohen's d, and Hedges's g. Each equation is understood within the context of the pertinent discussion corresponding to the location of the particular equation in the text.

	EQUATION NUMBER	EFFECT SIZE	=	COMPUTATION OF EFFECT SIZE
DEFINITION:	11.1	Pearson r	=	$\dfrac{\Sigma Z_x Z_y}{N}$
	12.12	r	=	$\sqrt{\dfrac{\chi^2_{(1)}}{N}}$
	11.16	r	=	$\dfrac{Z}{\sqrt{N}}$
	12.1	r	=	$\sqrt{\dfrac{t^2}{t^2 + df}}$
	12.4	r	=	$\sqrt{\dfrac{d^2}{d^2 + 4}}$
	12.5	r	=	$\sqrt{\dfrac{d^2}{d^2 + \left(\dfrac{1}{PQ}\right)}}$
	13.15	r	=	$\dfrac{g}{\sqrt{g^2 + 4\left(\dfrac{n}{n_h}\right)\left(\dfrac{df_{within}}{N}\right)}}$
	13.16	r	=	$\dfrac{d}{\sqrt{d^2 + 4\left(\dfrac{n}{n_h}\right)}}$
	15.8	$r_{alerting}$	=	$\sqrt{\dfrac{SS_{contrast}}{SS_{between}}}$
	15.19	$r_{contrast}$	=	$\sqrt{\dfrac{SS_{contrast}}{SS_{contrast} + SS_{within}}}$
	15.20	$r_{effect\ size}$	=	$\sqrt{\dfrac{SS_{contrast}}{SS_{total}}}$